VALENCIA AND MURCIA
Pages 242–263

ARAGÓN
Pages 226–241

CATALONIA
Pages 206–225

Donostia
(San Sebastián)

Iruña
(Pamplona)

0 kilometres   100

0 miles   100

Zaragoza

Lleida

Barcelona

EASTERN SPAIN

BARCELONA
Pages136–195

Cuenca

THE BALEARIC ISLANDS

Palma de
Mallorca

Valencia

Albacete

Alacant
(Alicante)

Murcia

THE BALEARIC ISLANDS
Pages 506–527

Almería

ANDALUSIA
Pages 458–501

THE CANARY ISLANDS

THE CANARY ISLANDS
Pages 528–551

Santa Cruz
de Tenerife

Las Palmas
de Gran Canaria

EYEWITNESS TRAVEL

SPAIN

EYEWITNESS TRAVEL

SPAIN

DK

LONDON, NEW YORK,
MELBOURNE, MUNICH AND DELHI
www.dk.com

PROJECT EDITOR Nick Inman
ART EDITORS Jaki Grosvenor, Janis Utton
EDITORS Catherine Day, Lesley McCave, Seán O'Connell
DESIGNERS Susan Blackburn, Dawn Davies-Cook,
Joy Fitzsimmons, Helen Westwood

MAIN CONTRIBUTORS
John Ardagh, David Baird, Mary-Ann Gallagher, Vicky Hayward,
Adam Hopkins, Lindsay Hunt, Nick Inman, Paul Richardson,
Martin Symington, Nigel Tisdall, Roger Williams

PHOTOGRAPHERS
Max Alexander, Joe Cornish, Neil Lukas, Neil Mersh,
John Miller, Kim Sayer, Linda Whitwam, Peter Wilson

ILLUSTRATORS
Stephen Conlin, Gary Cross, Richard Draper,
Isidoro González-Adalid Cabezas (Acanto Arquitectura y
Urbanismo S.L.), Claire Littlejohn, Maltings Partnership,
Chris Orr & Assocs, John Woodcock

Reproduced by Colourscan (Singapore)
Printed and bound by South China Printing Co. Ltd, China

First American Edition, 1996
06 07 08 09 10 9 8 7 6 5 4 3 2 1
Published in the United States by Dorling Kindersley
Publishing, Inc., 375 Hudson Street, New York 10014
**Reprinted with revisions 1997, 1999, 2000, 2001,
2002, 2003, 2004, 2005, 2006**

FLOORS ARE REFERRED TO THROUGHOUT IN ACCORDANCE WITH
EUROPEAN USAGE; IE THE "FIRST FLOOR" IS ONE FLOOR UP.

Front cover main image: Caseras village, Andalusia, Southern Spain

---

**The information in this
DK Eyewitness Travel Guide is checked annually.**

Every effort has been made to ensure that this book is as up-to-date
as possible at the time of going to press. Some details, however,
such as telephone numbers, prices, opening hours, gallery hanging
arrangements and travel information, are liable to change. The
publishers cannot accept responsibility for any consequences arising
from the use of this book, nor for any material on third-party
websites, and cannot guarantee that any website address in this
book will be a suitable source of travel information. We value the
views and suggestions of our readers very highly.
Please write to: Publisher, DK Eyewitness Travel Guides,
80 Strand, London WC2R 0RL, Great Britain.

CONTENTS

King Alfonso X the Learned

INTRODUCING
SPAIN

NORTHERN SPAIN

BARCELONA

Grapes growing in La Mancha, the world's largest expanse of vineyards

Statue of Alfonso XII, Madrid

Iglesia de Santa
María del
Naranco in
Asturias

HOW TO USE THIS GUIDE

This guide helps you to get the most from your visit to Spain. It provides detailed practical information and expert recommendations. *Introducing Spain* maps the country and sets it in its historical and cultural context. The five regional sections, plus Barcelona and Madrid, describe important sights, using maps, photographs and illustrations. Features cover topics from food and wine to fiestas and beaches. Restaurant and hotel recommendations can be found in *Travellers' Needs*. The *Survival Guide* has tips on everything from transport to using the telephone system.

BARCELONA, MADRID AND SEVILLE

These cities are divided into areas, each with its own chapter. A last chapter, *Further Afield*, covers peripheral sights. Madrid Province, surrounding the capital, has its own chapter. All sights are numbered and plotted on the chapter's area map. Information on each sight is easy to locate as it follows the numerical order on the map.

Sights at a Glance lists the chapter's sights by category: Churches and Cathedrals, Museums and Galleries, Streets and Squares, Historic Buildings, Parks and Gardens.

All pages relating to Madrid have green thumb tabs. Barcelona's are pink and Seville's are red.

A locator map shows where you are in relation to other areas of the city centre.

1 Area Map
For easy reference, sights are numbered and located on a map. City centre sights are also marked on Street Finders: Barcelona (pages 179–85); Madrid (pages 307–315); Seville (pages 447–51).

2 Street-by-Street Map
This gives a bird's-eye view of the key areas in each chapter.

Stars indicate the sights that no visitor should miss.

A suggested route for a walk is shown in red.

3 Detailed information
The sights in the three main cities are described individually. Addresses, telephone numbers, opening hours, admission charges, tours, photography and wheelchair access are also provided, as well as public transport links.

CASTILLA-LA MANCHA

GUADALAJARA · CUENCA · TOLEDO · ALBACETE · CIUDAD REAL

*L*a Mancha's empty beauty, its windmills and medieval castles silhouetted above the vast plains, was immortalized by Cervantes in Don Quixote's adventures. Its brilliantly sunlit, wide horizons are one of the classic images of Spain. This sparsely visited region has great scenic mountain ranges, dramatic gorges and the two monument-filled cities of Toledo and Cuenca.

1 Introduction
The landscape, history and character of each region is outlined here, showing how the area has developed over the centuries and what it has to offer to the visitor today.

SPAIN AREA BY AREA

Apart from Barcelona, Madrid and Seville, the country has been divided into 12 regions, each of which has a separate chapter. The most interesting cities, towns and villages, and other places to visit are numbered on a *Regional Map*.

2 Regional Map
This shows the road network and gives an illustrated overview of the whole region. All interesting places to visit are numbered and there are also useful tips on getting to, and around, the region by car and public transport.

Fiesta boxes highlight the best traditional fiestas in the region.

Each area of Spain can be quickly identified by its colour coding, shown on the inside front cover.

3 Detailed information
All the important towns and other places to visit are described individually. They are listed in order, following the numbering on the Regional Map. *Within each town or city, there is detailed information on important buildings and other sights.*

For all top sights, a Visitors' Checklist provides the practical information you will need to plan your visit.

4 Spain's top sights
These are given two or more full pages. Historic buildings are dissected to reveal their interiors. The most interesting towns or city centres are shown in a bird's-eye view, with sights picked out and described.

INTRODUCING SPAIN

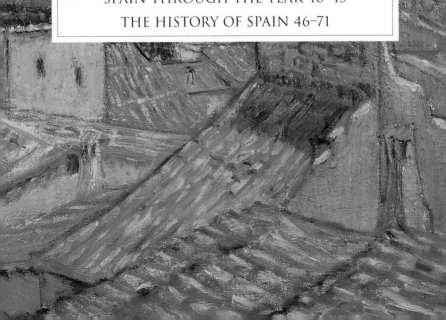

DISCOVERING SPAIN

Few countries offer more choice to the visitor than Spain, with its lush forests and wild mountain peaks, its busy cities crammed with great art and architecture and the endless stretch of laid-back beach resorts. To find out what you

A ceramic plate made in Seville

want from a trip to Spain amid all this variety, you need to know where to look. These pages offer an at-a-glance guide on where to go, with the different characteristics of each region, city or island group explained and the main sights highlighted.

Finisterre beach, Galicia

GALICIA

- **Verdant landscapes**
- **Santiago de Compostela**
- **Dramatic coastlines**
- **Rural idylls**

The northwest corner of Spain is the wettest and, because of this, also the greenest region of the country. The medieval city of **Santiago de Compostela** *(see pp90–93)* draws large numbers of visitors as it stands at the end of a legendary pilgrimage route and centres on an awe-inspiring cathedral. The other great attraction is the

long, heavily indented coastline. One stretch of this, the **Rias Baixas** *(see p95)*, has just the right blend of beaches, low-key holiday resorts and scenery. Inland, Galicia has hills, meadows, forests, monasteries and handsome old towns where time seems slowed down and you can be sure to get away from the crowds.

CANTABRIA AND ASTURIAS

- **Picos de Europa mountains**
- **Enigmatic cave art**
- **Ancient churches of Oviedo**
- **Medieval towns**

These two regions form the central part of the green north coast. Both are composed of inland uplands descending to a gentle coastline punctuated by pretty bays and good beaches. The two regions share Spain's most approachable mountain range, the **Picos de Europa** *(see pp108–109)*, whose canyons and summits are a draw for

hikers. Prehistory and history are other regional fortes. The most famous of many caves painted by early humanity are those of **Altamira** *(see p112)*. The exquisite, pre-Romanesque churches of **Oviedo** *(see pp106–7)* and the town of **Santillana del Mar** *(see p112)*, seemingly frozen in the Middle Ages, are also worth a visit.

The stunning titanium façade of Museo Guggenheim, Bilbao

THE BASQUE COUNTRY, NAVARRA AND LA RIOJA

- **Museo Guggenheim**
- **San Sebastián beaches**
- **Pamplona bullrunning**
- **Superb Riojan wines**

The futuristic **Museo Guggenheim** *(see pp120–21)* has put the city of Bilbao on the map and introduced the Basque Country to a wealth of new visitors, and its two neighbouring regions attract tourists in search of rural Spain. The pride of the Basque's short coast is **San Sebastián** *(see p122)*, a well-established resort on an

Parque Nacional de los Picos de Europa, Cantabria

almost perfectly rounded bay. Navarra is made up of picturesque green Pyrenean foothills and valleys in the north and charming little towns, castles and Romanesque churches in the south. Its capital, **Pamplona** *(see pp132–3)* – scene of the famous bullrunning festival in July – stands in the middle. For wine-lovers, La Rioja, the smallest region of Spain, is the place to visit.

BARCELONA

- **Gaudí and Modernisme**
- **Contemporary art**
- **Medieval streets**
- **Exhilerating nightlife**

For most people, Barcelona is synonymous with Modernisme, and in particular the enchanting buildings of Antoni Gaudí. It is also famed for its innovation and design, and leads Spain in contemporary art and architecture. At the heart of this city of cutting-edge creativity is the Gothic Quarter, with its well preserved medieval architecture. Barcelona's draw is also in its shops, bars, clubs and street life – any visit has to include a stroll down the **Las Ramblas** *(see pp150–51)*.

Barcelona can easily be combined with a beach holiday in one of the resorts a short way north or south of the city.

CATALONIA

- **Cava wine region**
- **Beautiful beaches**
- **Poblet and Monserrat**
- **Dalí masterpieces**

This self-assured region with its own language stretches from the Pyrenees in the north to the rice fields of the Ebro delta in the south, taking in vineyards which produce the famous *cava* sparkling wine. The **Costa Brava** *(see p217)*, a rugged mix of cliffs and bays, is its most attractive strip of coast but the Costa Daurada,

The sculptured rooftop chimneys of Casa Milà ("La Pedrera"), Barcelona

around the Roman city of **Tarragona** *(see pp224–5)*, also has popular resorts. Catalonia also has two of Spain's greatest monasteries: **Poblet** *(see pp222–3)* and **Montserrat** *(see pp218–9)*.

The city of **Figures** *(see p215)* is the birthplace of Surrealist artist Salvador Dalí, and many of his works can be viewed here.

ARAGÓN

- **Pyrenean grandeur**
- **Ordesa National Park**
- **San Juan de la Peña**
- **Mudéjar architecture**

Aragón is one of the least known regions of Spain, but rewarding to explore. Its sights are grouped to the north and south, with **Zaragoza** *(see pp236–7)*, the country's fifth largest city, in the centre. The Pyrenees and their foothills hold most appeal, particularly the awesome canyons and cliffs of the **Ordesa National Park** *(see pp232–3)*. Also worth seeking out is the secluded monastery of **San Juan de la Peña** *(see p234)*. The mountains are popular for walking, skiing and a range of other sports.

Teruel province in the south is known for its Mudéjar architecture, along with several historic towns, most notably **Albarracín** *(see p241)* and **Jaca** *(see p231)*.

Sculpture in Jaca cathedral, Aragón

VALENCIA AND MURCIA

- **City of Arts and Sciences**
- **Costa Blanca beaches**
- **Baroque architecture**
- **Spectacular fiestas**

These two regions take up the middle of Spain's Mediterranean coast and enjoy a pleasant climate. Valencia city is drawing increasing numbers of visitors to its gleaming white **City of Arts and Sciences** *(see p253)*. The Costa Blanca, a popular coastline, has a range of resorts, from the brash **Benidorm** *(see p260)* to quieter places like **Xàbia** *(see p255)*. The region of Murcia is distinguished by its Baroque architecture and the coastal lagoon of **Mar Menor** *(see p262)*. Both regions have spectacular fiestas, such as the lively Fallas festival in **Valencia** *(see p255)*.

A stretch of golden beach in Calp, Costa Blanca

The imposing San Lorenzo de El Escorial palace, Madrid province

MADRID

• **World famous art museums**
• **Royal residences**
• **Historic squares and streets**
• **Vibrant nightlife**

Spain's capital has three of the world's greatest art museums within an easy stroll of each other: the **Museo del Prado** *(see pp292–5)*, the **Thyssen-Bornemisza** *(see pp288–9)* and the **Centro Reina Sofía** *(see pp298–9)*. Art can also be seen in Madrid's three magnificent royal palaces, two of them – the **Escorial** *(see pp330–31)* and **Aranjuez** *(see p333)* – involving pleasurable day trips into nearby countryside.

The medieval part of the city, meanwhile, is a dense tangle of streets around two squares dotted with many attractive bars and cafés. Madrid is known for its buzzing nightlife, and is also a great place to come for the finest in Spanish cuisine.

CASTILLA Y LEÓN

• **Historic cities**
• **Gothic cathedral of Burgos**
• **Defiant castles**

Distances between sights can be daunting in the country's largest region, but five historic cities reward the intrepid visitor: the harmonious Renaissance university city of **Salamanca**

Detail, Salamanca University

(see pp358–61); **Segovia** *(see pp364–5)* with its towering Roman aqueduct and exquisite royal castle; **Burgos** *(see pp370–73)* built around a Gothic cathedral; **León** *(see pp353–5)*, its cathedral famous for its stained-glass windows; and **Avila** *(see pp362–3)*, ringed by medieval walls. En route between these cities there are vast empty tracts of land but you are rarely out of sight of a castle, a distinguishing feature of this part of Spain.

CASTILLA-LA MANCHA

• **Historic architecture**
• **Dramatically sited towns**
• **Don Quixote's windmills**

This region is not an obvious choice for many tourists but it does have one of Spain's most attractive cities – **Toledo** *(see pp388–91)*, crammed with interesting architecture from the Middle Ages. Two unusually sited towns also worth a visit are **Cuenca** *(see pp384–5)* perched on a ravine and **Alcalá del Júcar** *(see p395)*, where some of the houses have been extended into the soft rock of the chalky hills into which they are built.

Although daunting at first, the plains of **La Mancha** *(see pp379–99)*, well known for Spain's most famous fictional character, Don Quixote, has a certain charm in its quirky landscape of windmills and castles.

EXTREMADURA

• **Birds and wildflowers**
• **Roman theatre at Mérida**
• **Mansions of Cáceres**
• **Monastery of Guadalupe**

Although not a huge tourist destination, Extremadura has a lot to offer any visitor. With the lowest population density of any region, it has a corresponding richness in wildlife – in spring and summer the countryside is full of wildflowers and storks can be seen nesting on rooftops and church spires.

Extremadura also has a formidable collection of historic monuments, such as the Roman theatre at **Mérida** *(see pp410–11)*, which still hosts performances today, and the cluster of Renaissance mansions at **Cáceres** *(see pp408–9)*. The other place to see is **Guadalupe monastery** *(see pp406–7)*, though a long trek up winding mountain roads is required to get to it.

SEVILLE

• **Cathedral and La Giralda**
• **Moorish Real Alcázar**
• **Bars and bullfighting**
• **Semana Santa (Easter Week)**

This lively southern city on the Guadalquivir river combines the glories of Moorish and Christian Spain in its great cathedral and

The parade of the Virgin during Semana Santa, Seville

La Giralda, its bell tower *(see pp436–7)*, and in the lavishly decorated royal palace of the **Real Alcázar** *(see pp440–41)*.

Visitors also flock to Seville to relish the exciting atmosphere, particularly in the whitewashed streets of the Santa Cruz quarter and, when there's a fight on, in the **Plaza de Toros de la Maestranza** *(see p430)*, Spain's most famous bullring.

Seville is even more animated during the intense celebrations of *Semana Santa* (Holy Week) *(see p431)* and the passionate April Fair that follows, when the city hums to the sound of *Sevillanas*, its own brand of flamenco.

The Alhambra Palace, Granada

ANDALUSIA

- **Flamenco rhythms**
- **Sun and sea**
- **The Alhambra in Granada**
- **Doñana national park**

Stretching from the Atlantic to the Mediterranean across the south of the Iberian peninsula, this is Spain's second largest region and easily the most varied. It is the home to all things "typically Spanish": sherry *(see pp420–21)*, flamenco *(see pp424–5)*, guitars, tapas, gypsies, bullfighting, white towns and the Costa del Sol *(see pp472–3)*. Blazing Mediterranean sunshine makes it a good place for beach holidays, but it is not short of countryside or grandiose monuments either.

Coves d'Arta, Mallorca

The superb Moorish architecture of Granada's **Alhambra Palace** *(see pp490–91)* and the **Mezquita** in Cordoba *(see pp480–81)* continue to dazzle visitors. The region's landscapes vary enormously from the wildlife refuge of **Doñana** *(see pp464–5)* to Europe's only desert in **Almería** *(see p501)*.

THE BALEARIC ISLANDS

- **Beaches, cliffs and coves**
- **Pretty Ibizan villages**
- **Minorcan monuments**

This archipelago off the eastern Mediterranean coast has long been regarded as a holiday playground for Europe. However, as well as beaches, there is plenty of interest to discover. **Mallorca** *(see pp514–21)*, the largest island, has impressive mountains and caves as well as a splendid Gothic

cathedral in the capital, **Palma** *(see pp520–21)*.

Despite its reputation for a busy nightlife, **Ibiza** *(see pp510–12)* also has secluded coves, and quiet countryside dotted with pretty villlages. **Menorca** *(see pp522–3)* boasts prehistoric monuments, handsome small towns and a spectacular horse-riding fiesta *(see p523)*.

THE CANARY ISLANDS

- **Subtropical vegetation**
- **Volcanic landscapes**
- **Beaches and watersports**

Most visitors are drawn to the Canaries by their reliable subtropical warmth – despite many of the beaches being composed of black sand. The islands have a great contrast of scenery from luxuriant vegetation to spectacular volcanic formations.

La Gomera, **La Palma** and **El Hierro** *(see pp532–3)* are small but with wonderful scenery making for good hiking. **Lanzarote** *(see pp548–51)*, a choice place for beach holidays, is dry and still volcanically active. **Fuerteventura** *(see pp546–7)* also has beautiful beaches but with a windy climate. **Tenerife** *(see pp534–6)* and **Gran Canaria** *(see pp542–5)* offer the most variety, with northern coasts swathed in banana plantations and lively tourist spots in the hot and sunny south.

A cactus park in San Nicolás de Tolentino, Gran Canaria

Putting Spain on the Map

Spain, in southwestern Europe, covers the greater part of the Iberian Peninsula. The third largest country in Europe, it includes two island groups: the Canaries in the Atlantic and the Balearics in the Mediterranean, and two small territories in North Africa. Its southernmost point faces Morocco across a strait, making Spain a bridge between continents.

Satellite image showing the Iberian Peninsula

KEY

✈	International airport
⛴	Ferry service
▬	Motorway
▬	Major road
═	Minor road
—	Main railway line
✦—	AVE high-speed railway line

◁ *Rooftops, Fortna Lux, Mallorca* (1969) by Frederick Gore

Spain's Most Southerly Islands
This chain of seven islands in the Atlantic is 1,150 km (700 miles) southwest of Cádiz and 150 km (70 miles) off Morocco.

THE CANARY ISLANDS

Cádiz *Cádiz*

Arrecife

Santa Cruz de la Palma

Puerto de la Cruz

Santa Cruz de Tenerife

Las Palmas de Gran Canaria

Puerto del Rosario

San Sebastián de la Gomera

Valverde

Maspalomas

Biarritz

Bilbo (Bilbao)

Donostia (San Sebastián)

F R A N C E

Iruña (Pamplona)

N111

N240

ANDORRA

Perpignan

N111

A15

A68 AP68 (E804)

Ebro

A23 (E7)

Huesca

N230

N240

Girona

C17

Soria

N234

Zaragoza

Lleida

A2 AP2 (E90)

A2 AP2 (E90)

NII A2

Barcelona

Calatayud

NII A2 (E90)

N122

N234

N232

Tarragona

C32

M e d i t e r r a n e a n   S e a

Genoa

adalajara

N320

N330

Cuenca

N400 (E901)

A3 (E901)

N420 A31

N330

Albacete

A7 AP7 (E15)

Maó

Palma de Mallorca

N501

Júcar

Valencia

N430 A31

N322

N340

A30

A7

AP7 (E15)

Segura

Alacant (Alicante)

N332

N301

Murcia

N340 A7 E(15)

Eivissa (Ibiza)

0 kilometres   100

0 miles   50

Oran

(E15)

Almería

EUROPE AND NORTH AFRICA

NORWAY

FINLAND

SWEDEN

ESTONIA

RUSSIAN FED.

LATVIA

DENMARK

LITHUANIA

RUSSIAN FED.

BELORUSSIA

REPUBLIC OF IRELAND

UNITED KINGDOM

NETHERLANDS

POLAND

GERMANY

CZECH REPUBLIC

UKRAINE

BELGIUM

LUXEMBOURG

SLOVAKIA

FRANCE

AUSTRIA

HUNGARY

SWITZERLAND

SLOVENIA

CROATIA

ROMANIA

ITALY

BOSNIA AND HERZEGOVINA

SERBIA AND MONTENEGRO

BULGARIA

ALBANIA

GREECE

PORTUGAL

Madrid

SPAIN

MOROCCO

ALGERIA

TUNISIA

LIBYA

Spain's Frontiers
Spain has land borders with France, Portugal, Andorra and Gibraltar (a British territory on the south coast). The Strait of Gibraltar is only 13 km (8 miles) wide between Tarifa, the peninsula's southernmost point, and northern Morocco.

Melilla

Regional Spain

Spain has a population of 41 million and receives more than 57 million visitors a year. It covers an area of 504,780 sq km (194,900 sq miles). Madrid is the largest city, followed by Barcelona and Valencia. The country is dominated by a central plateau drained by the Duero, Tagus (Tajo) and Guadiana rivers. This book divides Spain into 15 areas, but officially it has 17 independent regions called *comunidades autónomas*.

GETTING AROUND

Spain's regional capitals and islands are linked by regular flights and there is a shuttle service between Madrid and Barcelona. The TALGO and AVE high-speed trains provide fast rail services and are backed up by regional and local rail networks. Some motorways have expensive tolls, but are fast. The Balearic and Canary islands are served by regular ferries. Be aware that Spain is in the process of changing its road number-ing system. Some of the roads featured here may differ from new road signs.

KEY

— Motorway

— Major road

═ Minor road

0 kilometres   100

0 miles   100

Eyewitness Spain Regions

Each of the chapters in this guide has a colour code. The chapters are grouped into five sections: Northern, Eastern, Central and Southern Spain and Spain's Islands; and two cities: Madrid and Barcelona.

KEY TO COLOUR CODING

Northern Spain

- Galicia
- Asturias and Cantabria
- The Basque Country, Navarra and La Rioja

Eastern Spain

- Barcelona
- Catalonia
- Aragón
- Valencia and Murcia

Central Spain

- Madrid
- Castilla y León
- Castilla-La Mancha
- Extremadura

Southern Spain

- Seville
- Andalusia

Spain's Islands

- The Balearic Islands
- The Canary Islands

nostia
(San Sebastián)

Iruña
(Pamplona)

N135

Huesca

N240

N260   N260

La Seu
d'Urgell   N152   N260   Figueres

Tudel

C14   C26   Vic   Girona

Zaragoza

Lleida   Manresa

Ebro   A2 AP2 (E90)   NII A2   A2 AP2 (E90)   A7 AP7 (E15)   Barcelona

N211   Reus

Teruel   Tortosa   Tarragona

CV15   CV130   CV15

Castelló de la Plana

THE BALEARIC ISLANDS

Ciutadella   Menorca

Mallorca   Maó

Palma de
Mallorca   Manacor

Sagunt

Valencia

Ibiza   Eivissa (Ibiza)   *Cabrera*

Almansa   *Formentera*

Alcoi

Alacant
(Alicante)   Benidorm

Elx

Murcia

Cartagena

THE CANARY ISLANDS

Lanzarote
Arrecife

La Palma   Santa Cruz
de la Palma

Puerto de
la Cruz   Santa Cruz
de Tenerife   *Fuerteventura*   Puerto del
Rosario

La Gomera   *Tenerife*   Las Palmas
de Gran Canaria

San Sebastián
de la Gomera   *Gran Canaria*

El Hierro   Valverde   Maspalomas

Spain's Atlantic Territories

The Canary Islands, in the Atlantic Ocean off the coast of Africa, are an integral part of Spain. They are one hour behind the rest of the country.

A PORTRAIT OF SPAIN

The familiar images of Spain – flamenco dancing, bullfigh[...] tapas bars and solemn Easter processions – do no mor[e...] hint at the diversity of the country. Spain has four [...] languages, two major cities of almost equal importance and [...] range of landscapes than any other European country. Thes[e...] able contrasts make Spain an endlessly fascinating coun[try...]

Separated from the rest of Europe by the Pyrenees, Spain reaches south to the coast of North Africa. It has both Atlantic and Mediterranean coastlines, and includes two archipelagos – the Balearics and the Canary Islands.

The climate and landscape vary from snow-capped peaks in the Pyrenees, through the green meadows of Galicia and the orange groves of Valencia, to the desert of Almería. Madrid is the highest capital in Europe, and Spain its most mountainous country after Switzerland and Austria. The innumerable sierras have always hindered communications. Until railways were

built it was easier t[...] from Barcelona to [...] than to Madrid.

In early times, S[pain...] prize for foreign[...] ing the Phoenic[...] During the M[...] was rule[d...] arrived [...] 8th cen[...] by Ch[...] at th[...] A succ[...] impose a co[...] but Spain remains as [...] ally diverse as ever. Several regions have maintained a strong sense of their own independent identities. Many Basques and Catalans, in particular, do not consider themselves to

Statue of Don Quixote and Sancho Panza, Madrid

Landscape with a solitary cork tree near Albacete in Castilla-La Mancha

◁ The outlandishly dressed *Peliqueiros* who take to the streets during Carnival in Laza, Galicia

Peñafiel castle in the Duero valley (Castilla y León), built between the 10th and 13th centuries

be Spanish. Madrid may be the nominal capital but it is closely rivalled in commerce, the arts and sport by Barcelona, the main city of Catalonia.

THE SPANISH WAY OF LIFE

The inhabitants of this very varied country have few things in common except for a natural sociability and a zest for living. Spaniards commonly put as much energy into enjoying life as they do into their work. The stereotypical *"mañana"* (leave everything until tomorrow) is a myth, but time is flexible in Spain and many people bend their work to fit the demands

"Vinegar Face" in Pamplona's Los Sanfermines fiesta

of their social life, rather than let themselves be ruled by the clock. The day is long in Spain and Spanish has a word, *madrugada*, for the time between midnight and dawn, when city streets are often still lively.

Spaniards are highly gregarious. In many places people still go out in the evening for the *paseo*, when the streets are crowded with strollers. Eating is invariably communal and big groups often meet up for tapas or dinner. Not surprisingly, Spain has more bars and restaurants per head than any other country.

Underpinning Spanish society is the extended family. Traditionally, the state in Spain has been very inefficient at providing public services – although this has improved in the last 20 years. The Spanish have therefore always relied on their families and personal connections, rather than institutions, to find work or seek assistance in a crisis. This attitude has sometimes led to a disregard for general interests – such as the environment – when they have conflicted with private ones.

Most Spaniards place their family at the centre of their lives. Three generations may live together under one roof, or at least see each other often. Even

Tables outside a café in Madrid's Plaza Mayor

lifelong city-dwellers refer fondly to their *pueblo* – the town or village where their family comes from and where they return whenever they can. Children are adored in Spain and, consequently, great importance is attached to education. The family in Spain, however, is under strain as couples increasingly opt for a higher income and better lifestyle

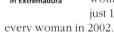

Virgin of Guadalupe in Extremadura

rather than a large family. One of the most striking transformations in modern Spain has been in the birth rate, from one of the highest in Europe, at 2.72 children for every woman in 1975, to just 1.24 children for every woman in 2002.

Catholicism is still a pervasive influence over Spanish society, although church attendance among those under 35 has declined in recent years to below 25 per cent. The images of saints watch over some shops, bars and lorry drivers' cabs. Church feast days are marked by countless traditional

The windmills and castle above Consuegra, La Mancha

fiestas which are enthusiastically maintained in modern Spain.

SPORT AND THE ARTS

Spanish cultural life has been reinvigorated in recent years. Spanish-made films – notably those of cult directors Pedro Almodóvar and Bigas Luna – have been able to compete effectively with Hollywood for audiences. The overall level of reading has risen (though only one in ten buy a daily newspaper), and contemporary literature has steadily gained a wider readership. The performing arts have been restricted by a lack of facilities, but recent major investments have provided new venues, regional arts centres and new symphony orchestras. The country has

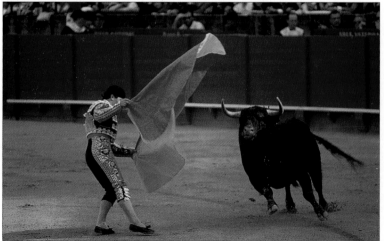

A matador plays a bull in the Plaza de Toros de la Maestranza, Seville

Poster for a Pedro Almodóvar film

the mainstays of TV programming. Spanish sportsmen and women have been very successful – for example, tennis players Conchita Martínez, Juan Carlos Ferrero, and Arantxa Sánchez Vicario, cyclists Miguel Induráin and Oscar Freire. Such role models have encouraged participation in sport and new facilities have been provided to meet this demand. Most popular are basketball and, above all, soccer.

Bullfighting has enjoyed renewed popularity since the late 1980s. For aficionados, a *corrida* is a unique occasion that provides a link to Spain's roots, and the noise, colour and argumentative attitude of the crowd are as much of an attraction as the bullfight itself.

produced many remarkable opera singers including Montserrat Caballé, Plácido Domingo and José Carreras. Spain has also excelled in design, particularly evident in the interior furnishings shops of Barcelona.

Spaniards are the most avid TV-watchers in Europe after the British. There are now 16 state-owned TV channels in Spain, as well as the various independent channels and many regional TV stations. Sports are one of

SPAIN TODAY

In the last 40 years Spain has undergone more social change than anywhere else in western Europe. Until the 1950s, Spain was predominantly a poor, rural country, in which only 37 per cent of the population lived in towns of over 10,000 people. By the 1990s, the figure was 65 per cent. As people flooded into towns and cities many rural areas became depopulated. The 1960s saw the beginning of spec-

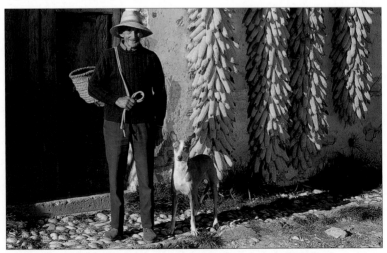
A farmer with his crop of maize hanging to dry on the outside of his house in the hills of Alicante

Beach near Tossa de Mar on the Costa Brava

Basque terrorist group ETA is a constant thorn in the side of Spanish democracy.

During the 1980s Spain enjoyed an economic boom as service industries and manufacturing expanded. Even so, GDP remains below the European Union average and growth has been very unevenly spread around the country. Agriculture is an important industry but while it is highly developed in some regions, it is inefficient in others. Tourism provides approximately ten per cent of the country's earnings. Most tourists still come for beaches. But increasingly, foreign visitors are drawn by Spain's rich cultural heritage and spectacular countryside. Anyone who knows this country, however, will tell you that it is the Spanish people's capacity to enjoy life to the full that is Spain's biggest attraction.

tacular economic growth, partly due to a burgeoning tourist industry. In that decade, car ownership increased from 1 in 100 to 1 in 10.

After the death of dictator General Franco in 1975 Spain became a constitutional monarchy under King Juan Carlos I. The post-Franco era, up until the mid-1990s, was dominated by the Socialist Prime Minister Felipe González. As well as presiding over major improvements in roads, education and health services, the Socialists increased Spain's international standing. The PSOE could not continue forever, however, and in 1996 revelations of a series of scandals lost the PSOE the election. Spain joined the European Community in 1986, triggering a spectacular increase in the country's prosperity. The country's fortunes seemed to peak in the extraordinary year of 1992, when Barcelona staged the Olympic Games and Seville hosted a world fair, Expo '92.

With the establishment of democracy, the 17 autonomous regions of Spain have acquired considerable powers. Several have their own languages which are officially given equal importance to Spanish (strictly called Castilian). A significant number of Basques favour independence for the Basque Country. The

King Juan Carlos I and Queen Sofía

Demonstration for Catalan independence

Architecture in Spain

Spain has always imported its styles of architecture: Moorish from North Africa, Romanesque and Gothic from France and Renaissance from Italy. Each style, however, was interpreted in a distinctively Spanish way, with sudden and strong contrasts between light and shady areas; façades alternating between austerity and extravagant decoration; and thick walls pierced by few windows to lessen the impact of heat and sunlight. Styles vary from region to region, reflecting the division of Spain before unification. The key design of a central patio surrounded by arcades has been a strong feature of civil buildings since Moorish times.

The 15th-century Casa de Conchas in Salamanca *(see p361)*

ROMANESQUE AND EARLIER (8TH–13TH CENTURIES)

Romanesque churches were mainly built in Catalonia and along the pilgrim route to Santiago *(see p83)*. Their distinctive features include round arches, massive walls and few windows. Earlier churches were built in Pre-Romanesque *(see p106)* or Mozarabic *(see p352)* style.

Round arch   Multiple apses

The Romanesque Sant Climent, Taüll *(p201)*

MOORISH (8TH–15TH CENTURIES)

The Moors *(see pp52–3)* reserved the most lavish decoration for the interior of buildings, where ornate designs based on geometry, calligraphy and plant motifs were created in *azulejos* (tiles) or stucco. They made extensive use of the horseshoe arch, a feature inherited from the Visigoths *(see pp50–1)*. The greatest surviving works of Moorish architecture *(see pp422–3)* are in Southern Spain.

The Salón de Embajadores *in the Alhambra (see p490) has exquisite Moorish decoration.*

GOTHIC (12TH–16TH CENTURIES)

Gothic was imported from France in the late 12th century. The round arch was replaced by the pointed arch which, because of its greater strength, allowed for higher vaults and taller windows. External buttresses were added to prevent the walls of the nave from leaning outwards. Carved decoration was at its most opulent in the Flamboyant Gothic style of the 15th century. After the fall of Granada, Isabelline, a late Gothic style, developed. Meanwhile, Moorish craftsmen working in reconquered areas created the highly decorative hybrid Christian-Islamic style Mudéjar *(see p55)*.

Gothic arched window

Rose window   Tracery
Pointed arch   Flying buttress

The nave *of León Cathedral (see pp354–5), built in the 13th century, is supported by rib vaulting and is illuminated by the finest display of stained glass in Spain.*

Sculptural decoration *above the doorways of León cathedral's south front depicted biblical stories for the benefit of the largely illiterate populace.*

RENAISSANCE (16TH CENTURY)

Around 1500 a new style was introduced to Spain by Italian craftsmen and Spanish artists who had studied in Italy. The Renaissance was a revival of the style of Ancient Rome. It is distinguished by its sense of symmetry and the use of the round arch, and Doric, Ionic and Corinthian columns. Early Spanish Renaissance architecture is known as Plateresque because its fine detail resembles ornate silverwork (*platero* means silversmith).

The Palacio de las Cadenas *in Úbeda (see p497) has a severely Classical façade.*

Medallions   Classical columns   Sculpted parapet   Round arch

The Hostal de San Marcos in León *(see p353),* **one of Spain's finest Plateresque buildings**

BAROQUE (17TH–18TH CENTURIES)

Baroque was driven by a desire for drama and movement. Decoration became extravagant, with exuberant sculpture and twisting columns. Although the excessive Baroque style of Churrigueresque is named after the Churriguera family of architects, it was their successors who were its main exponents.

The ornamentation *on the Baroque façade of Valladolid University (see p366) is concentrated above the doorway.*

Finials

Statues on parapet

The façade of the Museo Municipal in Madrid *(pp304–5)*

MODERN (LATE 19TH CENTURY ONWARDS)

Modernisme *(see pp140–1)*, a Catalan interpretation of Art Nouveau, is seen at its best in Barcelona. Its architects experimented with a highly original language of ornament. In recent decades, Spain has seen an explosion of bold, functionalist architecture in which the form of a building reflects its use and decoration is used sparingly.

Curving parapet   Spiral chimney   Decorative ironwork

Torre de Picasso in Madrid

Casa Milà, *in Barcelona (see p165), was built in 1910 by Modernisme's most famous and best-loved architect, Antoni Gaudí, who drew much of his inspiration from nature.*

Vernacular Architecture

Window in Navarra

As well as its cathedrals and palaces, Spain has a great variety of charming vernacular buildings. These have been constructed by local craftsmen to meet the practical needs of rural communities and to take account of local climate conditions, with little reference to formal architectural styles. Due to the high expense involved in transporting raw materials, builders used whatever stone or timber lay closest to hand. The three houses illustrated below incorporate the most common characteristics of village architecture seen in different parts of Spain.

A cave church in Artenara *(see p545)*, on Gran Canaria

STONE HOUSE

The climate is wet in the north and houses like this one in Carmona *(see p111)*, in Cantabria, are built with overhanging eaves to shed the rain. Wooden balconies catch the sun.

Supporting pillar   **Large doors** accommodate carts and animals.   **The walls** are built of irregularly shaped stones.

Detail of stonework

Family and farm *often share rural houses. The ground floor is used to stable animals, or store tools and firewood.*

TIMBER-FRAMED HOUSE

Spain, in general, has few large trees and wood is in short supply. Castilla y León is one of the few regions where timber-framed houses, such as this one in Covarrubias *(see p370)*, can be found. These houses are quick and cheap to build. The timber frame is filled in with a coarse plaster mixed from lime and sand, or adobe (bricks dried in the sun).

Portico   **Gently sloping roof**

The verandah runs the length of the building.

Balcony

In town squares, *upright struts of timber supporting horizontal beams were used to form porticoes. A shady space was created for people to meet, talk and trade.*

Half-timbered wall

The ends of the beams supporting the floorboards are visible.

Stone plinths below upright timbers provide protection from damp.

WHITEWASHED HOUSE

Houses in the south of Spain – often built of baked clay – are regularly whitewashed to deflect the sun's intense rays. Andalusia's famous white towns *(see p468)* exemplify this attractive form of architecture.

Irregularly shaped houses are joined together.   **Few, small windows**

Shallow-pitched roof

Windows *are small and few in number, and deeply recessed, in order to keep the interior cool.*

Clay-tiled roof

Whitewashed walls

THE PLAZA MAYOR

Almost every town in Spain centres on a main square, the plaza mayor, like this one in Pedraza de la Sierra *(see p365)*, near Segovia. More than a market square, it acts as a focus for local life. It is usually overlooked by the church, the town hall, shops and bars and the mansions of aristocratic families.

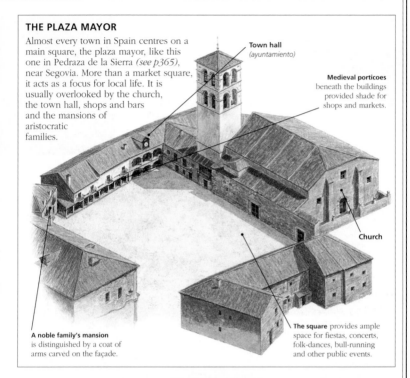

Town hall *(ayuntamiento)*

Medieval porticoes beneath the buildings provided shade for shops and markets.

Church

A noble family's mansion is distinguished by a coat of arms carved on the façade.

The square provides ample space for fiestas, concerts, folk-dances, bull-running and other public events.

RURAL ARCHITECTURE

A variety of distinctive buildings dots the countryside.

Where the rock is soft and the climate hot, subterranean dwellings have been excavated. Insulated from extremes of temperature, they provide a comfortable place to live.

Hórreos, granaries raised on stone stilts to prevent rats climbing up into the grain, are a common sight in Galicia (where they are stone-built) and Asturias (where they are made of wood). In fields you will often see shelters for livestock or for storing crops, such as the *teitos* of Asturias.

Windmills provided power in parts of Spain where there was little running water but plentiful wind, like La Mancha and the Balearic Islands.

Almost everywhere in the Spanish countryside you will come across *ermitas*, isolated chapels or shrines dedicated to a local saint. An *ermita* may be opened only on the patron saint's feast day.

Cave houses in Guadix near Granada *(see p493)*

Teito in Valle de Teverga in Asturias *(see p105)*

Hórreo, a granary, on the Rias Baixas *(see p95)* in Galicia

Windmill above Consuegra *(see p394)* in La Mancha

Farming in Spain

Spain's varied geography and climate have created a mosaic of farming patterns ranging from lush dairylands to stony hillsides where goats graze. Land can be broadly divided into *secano*, or dry cultivation (used for olives, wheat and vines), and much smaller areas of *regadío*, irrigated land (planted with citrus trees, rice and vegetables). Farming in many parts is a family affair relying on traditional, labour-intensive methods but it is becoming increasingly mechanized.

Donkey in Extremadura

Plains of cereals *make up much of the farmland of the central meseta of Spain. Wheat is grown in better-watered, more fertile western areas; barley is grown in the drier south.*

Cork oaks thrive in Extremadura and western Andalusia.

MADRID

SEVILLA

0 kilometres 200

0 miles 100

Sheep *grazed on the rough pastures of Central Spain are milked to make cheese, especially* manchego, *which is produced in La Mancha (see p339).*

THE AGRICULTURAL YEAR

	Summer	Autumn	Winter
	Jul–Aug Wheat harvested in Central Spain	**Sep** Rice harvest in Eastern Spain. Grape harvest at its height	**Oct** Maize harvested in Northern Spain **Oct–Nov** Table olives picked	**Dec–Mar** Olives for making oil picked

Spring	Summer	Autumn	Winter
Mar–Apr Orange trees in blossom on Mediterranean coast		**Nov–Dec** Oranges picked	**Feb** Almond trees in blossom
Jun–Aug Haymaking in Northern Spain	**Sep** Start of wild mushroom season	**Dec** Pigs are slaughtered when cold weather arrives	

The high rainfall *and mild summers of Northern Spain make it suitable for dairy farming. Farms are often small, especially in Galicia, one of the country's most underdeveloped regions. Crops such as maize and wheat are grown in small quantities.*

Wine is produced in many parts of Spain *(see pp606–7)*. The country's best sparkling wine grapes are grown in Catalonia.

Cork oaks are stripped of their bark every ten years

CROPS FROM TREES

The almond, orange and olive create the three most characteristic landscapes of rural Spain but several other trees provide important crops. Wine corks are made from the bark of the cork oak. Tropical species, such as avocado and cherimoya, a delicious creamy fruit little known outside Spain, have been introduced to the so-called Costa Tropical of Andalusia *(see p483)*; and bananas are a major crop of the Canary Islands. Elsewhere, peaches and loquats are also grown commercially. Figs and carobs – whose fruit is used for fodder and as a substitute for chocolate – grow semi-wild.

Rice is grown in the Ebro delta, in the Marismas del Guadalquivir, around L'Albufera near Valencia and also at Calasparra in Murcia.

Almonds *grow on dry hillsides in many parts of Spain. The spring blossom can be spectacular. The nut, enclosed by a fleshy green skin, is used in a variety of sweetmeats including the Christmas treat* turrón (see p201).

Oranges, *lemons and clementines are grown on the irrigated coastal plains beside the Mediterranean. The region of Valencia is the prime producer of oranges.*

Olive trees *grow slowly and often live to a great age. The fruit is harvested in winter and either pickled in brine for eating as a to extract the oil which is widely used in Spanish cuisine.*

Olive trees *are planted in long, straight lines across large swaths of Andalusia, especially in the province of Jaén. Spain is the world's leading producer of olive oil.*

Sweet oranges *are grown in dense, well-irrigated groves near the frost-free coasts. The sweet smell of orange blossom in springtime is unmistakeable. Trees of the bitter orange are often planted for shade and decoration in parks and gardens.*

BARCELONA

Spain's National Parks

Few other countries in western Europe have such unspoiled scenery as Spain, or can boast tracts of wilderness where brown bears live and wolves hunt. More than 200 nature reserves protect a broad range of ecosystems. The most important areas are the 12 national parks, the first of which was established in 1918. Natural parks *(parques naturales)*, regulated by regional governments, are also vital to the task of conservation.

Giant orchid

Clear mountain river, Ordesa

MOUNTAINS

Much of Spain's finest scenery is found in the mountains. Rivers have carved gorges between the peaks of the Picos de Europa. Ordesa and Aigüestortes share some of the most dramatic landscapes of the Pyrenees, while the Sierra Nevada has an impressive range of indigenous wildlife.

Rough terrain in the Picos de Europa

Eagle owls *are Europe's largest owl, easily identified by their large ear tufts. At night they hunt small mammals and birds.*

Chamois *are well adapted to climbing across slopes covered in scree. They live in small groups, always alert to predators, and feed on grass and flowers.*

WETLANDS

Wetlands, including coastal strips and freshwater marshes, are ever-changing environments. Seasonal floods rejuvenate the water providing nutrients for animal and plant growth. These areas are rich feeding grounds for birds. Spain's best-known wetland is Doñana. Tablas de Daimiel, in La Mancha, is much smaller.

Lynx, *endangered by hunting and habitat loss, can occasionally be spotted in Doñana (see pp464–5).*

Black-winged stilts, *with their long, straight legs, are adept at stalking tiny freshwater crustaceans.*

Laguna del Acebuche, Parque Nacional de Doñana

Cabrera archipelago, Balearic Islands

ISLANDS

Cabrera, off Mallorca, is home to rare plants, reptiles and seabirds, such as Eleonara's falcon. The surrounding waters are important for their marine life.

Lizards *are often found in rocky terrain and on cliff faces.*

NATIONAL PARKS

① Mountains

⑤ Wetlands

⑦ Islands

⑨ Woods and Forests

⑪ Volcanic Landscapes

MOUNTAINS

① Picos de Europa *pp108–9*
② Ordesa y Monte Perdido *pp232–3*
③ Aigüestortes y Estany de Sant Maurici *p211*
④ Sierra Nevada *p485*

WETLANDS

⑤ Tablas de Daimiel *p399*
⑥ Doñana *pp464–5*

ISLANDS

⑦ Archipiélago de Cabrera *p517*
⑧ Islas Atlánticas de Galicia *p95*

WOODS AND FORESTS

⑨ Cabañeros *p387*
⑩ Garajonay *p533*

VOLCANIC LANDSCAPES

⑪ Caldera de Taburiente *p532*
⑫ Teide *pp538–9*
⑬ Timanfaya *pp548–9*

VISITORS' CHECKLIST

All but one of the national parks are managed by the Ministerio de Medio Ambiente. **Tel** *915 96 46 00. Parque Nacional d'Aigüestortes y Estany de Sant Maurici is administered jointly with Catalonia's Department of Environment.* **Tel** *973 62 40 36. Most, but not all, of Spain's national parks have visitors' centres.*

WOODS AND FORESTS

Deciduous broad-leaved forests grow in the northwest of Spain, and stands of Aleppo and Scots pine cover many mountainous areas. On the central plateau there are stretches of open woodland of evergreen holm oak and cork oak in the Parque Nacional de Cabañeros. Dense, lush *laurasilva* woodland grows in the Parque Nacional de Garajonay, on La Gomera, one of the smaller Canary Islands.

Parque Nacional de Garajonay

Black vultures *are the largest birds of prey in Europe, with an enormous wingspan of over 2.5 m (8 ft).*

Hedgehogs, *common in woodlands, root among fallen leaves and grass to find worms and slugs.*

VOLCANIC LANDSCAPES

Three very different parks protect parts of the Canary Islands' amazing volcanic scenery. Caldera de Taburiente on La Palma is a volcanic crater surrounded by woods. Mount Teide in Tenerife has unique alpine flora, and Lanzarote's Timanfaya is composed of barren but atmospheric lava fields.

Rabbits *are highly opportunistic, quickly colonizing areas in which they can burrow. In the absence of predators, populations may increase, damaging fragile ecosystems.*

Canaries *belong to the finch family of songbirds. The popular canary has been bred from the wild serin, native to the Canaries.*

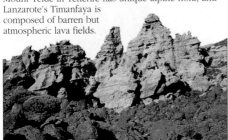

Colonizing plant species, Mount Teide (Tenerife)

Spanish Art

Three Spanish painters stand out as milestones in the history of Western art. Diego de Velázquez was a 17th-century court portrait painter and his *Las Meninas* is a seminal work. Francisco de Goya depicted Spanish life during one of its most violent periods. The prolific 20th-century master, Pablo Picasso, is recognized as the founder of modern art. To these names must be added that of El Greco – who was born in Crete but who lived in Spain, where he painted religious scenes in an individualistic style. The work of these and Spain's many other great artists can be seen in world-renowned galleries, especially the Prado *(see pp292–5)*.

In his series, *Las Meninas* *(1957), Picasso interprets the frozen gesture of the five-year-old Infanta Margarita. Altogether, Picasso produced 44 paintings based on Velzáquez's canvas. They can be seen in Barcelona's Museu de Picasso* (see p153).

RELIGIOUS ART IN SPAIN

The influence of the Catholic Church on Spanish art through the ages is reflected in the predominance of religious imagery. Many churches and museums have Romanesque altarpieces or earlier icons. El Greco *(see p391)* painted from a highly personal religious vision. Baroque religious art of the 17th century, when the Inquisition *(see p274)* was at its height, often graphically depicts physical suffering and spiritual torment.

The Burial of the Count of Orgaz by El Greco (see p390)

Self-portrait of Velázquez

The king and queen, reflected in a mirror behind the painter, may be posing for their portrait.

LAS MENINAS *(1656)*
In Velázquez's painting of the Infanta Margarita and her courtiers, in the Prado *(see pp292–5)*, the eye is drawn into the distance where the artist's patron, Felipe IV, is reflected in a mirror.

TIMELINE OF GREAT SPANISH ARTISTS

1285–1348 Ferrer Bassá	**1390–1410** Pere Nicolau	*The Saviour by José de Ribera*
		1598–1664 Francisco de Zurbarán
1363–95 Jaume Serra	**1428–1460** Luis Daimau	
		1591–1652 José de Ribera
1300	**1400**	**1500**
1388–1424 Luis Borrassa	**1474–95** Bartolomé Bermejo	**1565–1628** Francisco Ribalta
Virgin and Child by Ferrer Bassá	**1450–1504** Pedro Berruguete	**1599–1660** Diego de Velázquez
	1427–52 Bernat Martorell	**1541–1614** El Greco

José Nieto, the queen's chamberlain, stands in the doorway in the background of the painting.

Court jester

MODERN ART

The early 20th-century artists Joan Miró *(see p172)*, Salvador Dalí *(see p215)* and Pablo Picasso *(see p152)* all belonged to the Paris School. More recent artists of note include Antonio Saura and Antoni Tàpies *(see p164)*. Among many great Spanish art collections, the Centro de Reina Sofia in Madrid *(see pp298–9)* specializes in modern art. Contemporary artists are accorded great prestige in Spain. Their work is to be seen in town halls, banks and public squares, and many towns have a museum dedicated to a local painter.

Salvador Dalí's painting of the *Colossus of Rhodes* (1954)

***Collage* (1934) by Joan Miró**

The Family of King Charles IV
was painted in 1800 by Francisco de Goya (see p239), nearly 150 years after Las Meninas. *Its debt to Velázquez's painting is evident in its frontal composition, compact grouping of figures and in the inclusion of a self-portrait.*

The Holy Children
with the Shell
by Murillo

1893–1983 Joan Miró

1881–1973 Pablo Picasso

1904–89
Salvador Dalí

1746–1828
Francisco de Goya

1863–1923
Joaquín Sorolla

1923–
Antoni
Tàpies

1700	1800	1900

1642–93 Claudio Coello

1887–1927
Juan Gris

1618–82 Bartolomé
Esteban Murillo

Jug and Glass
(1916) by Juan Gris

1930–1998
Antonio Saura

Literary Spain

The best-known work of Spanish literature, *Don Quixote* is considered the first modern novel, but Spain has produced many major works over the last 2,000 years. The Roman writers Seneca, Lucan and Martial were born in Spain. Later, the Moors developed a flourishing, but now little-known, literary culture. Although Spanish

The 14th-century *El Libro de Buen Amor*

(Castilian) is the national tongue, many enduring works have been written in the Galician and Catalan regional languages. Basque literature, hitherto an oral culture, is a more recent development. Many foreign writers, such as Alexandre Dumas, Ernest Hemingway and Karel Capek, have written accounts of their travels in Spain.

MIDDLE AGES

As the Roman empire fell, Latin evolved into several Romance languages. The earliest non-Latin literature in Spain derives from an oral tradition that arose before the 10th century. It is in the form of *jarchas*, snatches of love poetry written in Mozarab, the Romance language that was spoken by Christians living under the Moors.

In the 12th century, the first poems appeared in Castilian. During the next 300 years, two separate schools of poetry developed. The best-known example of troubadour verse is the anonymous epic, *El Cantar del Mío Cid*, which tells of the heroic exploits of El Cid *(see p370)* during the Reconquest. Works of clerical poetry – for example, Gonzalo de Berceo's *Milagros de Nuestra Señora*, relating the life of the Virgin – convey a moral message.

Spanish literature evolved in the 13th century after Alfonso X the Learned *(see p55)* replaced Latin with Castilian

Alfonso X the Learned (1221–84)

Romance (later called Spanish) as the official language. Under his supervision a team of Jews, Christians and Arabs wrote scholarly treatises. The king himself was a poet, writing in Galician Romance.

The first great prose works in Spanish appeared in the 14th and 15th centuries. *El Libro de Buen Amor*, by an ecclesiastic, Juan Ruiz, is a tale of the love affairs of a priest, interleaved with other stories. Fernando de Rojas uses skilful characterization in *La Celestina* to tell a tragic love story about two nobles and a scheming go-between. This was an age in which tales of chivalry were also popular.

GOLDEN AGE

The prolific Golden Age dramatist, Félix Lope de Vega

The 16th century hailed the start of Spain's Golden Age of literature. But it was also a period of domestic strife. This found expression in the picaresque novel, a Spanish genre originating with the anonymous *El Lazarillo de Tormes*, a bitter reflection on the misfortunes of a blind man's guide.

Spiritual writers flourished under the austere climate of the Counter-Reformation. St John of the Cross's *Cántico Espiritual* was influenced by oriental erotic poetry and the Bible's *Song of Songs*.

The 17th century saw the emergence of more great talents. The life and work of Miguel de Cervantes *(see p333)* straddles the two centuries of the Golden Age. He published his masterpiece, *Don Quixote*, in 1615. Other important writers of the time include Francisco de Quevedo and Luis de Góngora.

Corrales (public theatres) appeared in the 17th century, opening the way for Lope de Vega *(see p290)*, Calderón de la Barca and other dramatists.

Don Quixote's adventures portrayed by José Moreno Carbonero

18TH AND 19TH CENTURIES

Influenced by the French Enlightenment, literature in the 18th century was seen as a way to educate the people. Such was the aim, for instance, of Leandro Fernández de Moratín's comedy *El Sí de las Niñas*. This period saw the development of journalism as well as the emergence of the essay as a literary form. Romanticism had a short and late life in Spain. *Don Juan Tenorio*, a tale of the legendary irrepressible Latin lover by José Zorrilla, is the best-known Romantic play.

The satirical essayist Larra stands out from his contemporaries at the beginning of the 19th century. Towards the end of the century, the novel became a vehicle for realistic portrayals of Spanish society. Benito Pérez Galdós, regarded by many to be Spain's greatest novelist after Cervantes,

José Zorrilla (1817–93)

studied the human condition in his *Episodios Nacionales*. The heroine in Clarín's *La Regenta* is undone by the reactionary prejudices of provincial town society.

20TH CENTURY

Writers at the turn of the century, including Pío Baroja (*see p64*), Miguel de Unamuno and Antonio Machado, described a Spain falling behind the rest of Europe. Exploring the grotesque, the only way he could describe society, led Ramón María del Valle-Inclán to lay the foundations for modern Spanish theatre. In poetry, the Nobel Prize winner, Juan Ramón Jiménez, strived for pureness of form.

The so-called "Generation of 27" combined European experimental art with Spain's traditional literary subjects and forms. The best-known of them is the poet and playwright Federico García Lorca

who was executed by a Fascist firing squad in 1936 (*see p67*). He drew on the legends and stereotypes of his native Andalusia to make universal statements in his poems and plays, such as *Yerma*.

In the aftermath of the Civil War, many intellectuals who had backed the Republic were forced into exile. The Franco regime tried to create its own propagandist culture. Yet the finest literature of the period was written in spite of the prevailing political climate. Camilo José Cela's *La Colmena*, a description of everyday life in the hungry, postwar city of Madrid, set a mood of social realism that inspired other writers.

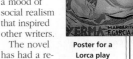

Poster for a Lorca play

The novel has had a rebirth in Spain since the 1960s, with the emergence of writers like Juan Goytisolo, Joan Benet, Julio Llamazares, Antonio Muñoz Molina, José Manuel Caballero Bonald and Juan Marsé.

The 20th century has also witnessed a surge of great Spanish literature from Latin America. Prominent authors include Jorge Luis Borges and Gabriel García Márquez.

Camilo José Cela, Nobel Prize-winning novelist, by Alvaro Delgado

The Art of Bullfighting

Poster for a bullfight

Bullfighting is a sacrificial ritual in which men (and also a few women) pit themselves against an animal bred for the ring. In this "authentic religious drama", as poet García Lorca described it, the spectator experiences vicariously the fear and exaltation felt by the matador. Although some Spaniards oppose it on grounds of its cruelty, nowadays it is as popular as ever. Many Spaniards see talk of banning bullfighting as striking at the essence of their being, for they regard the *toreo*, the art of bullfighting, as a noble part of their heritage. Bullfights today, however, are often debased by practices which weaken the bull, especially shaving its horns to reduce its aim.

Plaza de Toros de la Maestranza, *Seville. This ring is regarded, with Las Ventas in Madrid, as one of the top venues for bullfighting in Spain.*

Well treated at the ranch, *the* toro bravo *(fighting bull) is specially bred for qualities of aggressiveness and courage. As aficionados of bullfighting point out in its defence, the young bull enjoys a full life while it is being prepared for its 15 minutes in the ring. Bulls must be at least four years old before they fight.*

The matador wears a *traje de luces* (suit of lights), a colourful silk outfit embroidered with gold sequins.

The passes are made with a *muleta*, a scarlet cape stiffened along one side.

THE BULLFIGHT

The *corrida* (bullfight) has three stages, called *tercios*. In the first one, the *tercio de varas*, the matador and *picadores* (horsemen with lances) are aided by *peones* (assistants). In the *tercio de banderillas*, *banderilleros* stick pairs of darts in the bull's back. In the *tercio de muleta* the matador makes a series of passes at the bull with a *muleta* (cape). He then executes the kill, the *estocada*, with a sword.

The matador *plays the bull with a* capa *(red cape) in the* tercio de varas. Peones *will then draw the bull towards the* picadores.

Horses are now padded.

Picadores *goad the bull with steel-pointed lances, testing its bravery. The lances weaken the animal's shoulder muscles.*

THE BULLRING

The *corrida* audience is seated in the *tendidos* (stalls) or in the *palcos* (balcony), where the *presidencia* (president's box) is situated. Opposite are the *puerta de cuadrillas*, through which the matador and team arrive, and the *arrastre de toros* (exit for bulls). Before entering the ring, the matadors wait in a corridor *(callejón)* behind *barreras* and *burladeros* (barriers). Horses are kept in the *patio de caballos* and the bulls in the *corrales*.

Plan of a typical bullring

KEY

☐	Tendidos
☐	Palcos
☐	Presidencia
☐	Puerta de cuadrillas
☐	Arrastre de toros
☐	Callejón
☐	Barreras
☐	Burladeros
☐	Patio de caballos
☐	Corrales

Banderillas, barbed darts, are thrust into the bull's already weakened back muscles.

Manolete *is regarded by most followers of bullfighting as one of the greatest matadors ever. He was eventually gored to death by the bull Islero at Linares, Jaén, in 1947.*

The bull may go free if it shows courage – spectators wave white handkerchiefs, asking the *corrida* president to let it leave the ring alive.

Joselito *is one of Spain's leading matadors today. He is famous for his purist approach and for his flair and technical skill with both the* capa *and the* muleta.

The bull weighs about 500 kg (1,100 lbs).

Banderilleros *enter to provoke the wounded bull in the* tercio de banderillas, *sticking pairs of* banderillas *in its back.*

The matador *makes passes with the cape in the* tercio de muleta, *then lowers it and thrusts in the sword for the kill.*

The estocada recibiendo *is a difficult kill, rarely seen. The matador awaits the bull's charge rather than moving to meet it.*

The Fiestas of Spain

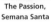

On any day of the year there is a fiesta happening somewhere in Spain – usually more than one. There isn't a village, town or city in the country which doesn't honour its patron saint, the Virgin or the changing seasons with processions, bull-running, fireworks, re-enacted battles, some ancestral rite or a *romería* – a mass pilgrimage to a rural shrine. Whatever the pretext, a fiesta is a chance for everyone to take a break from normal life (most shops and offices close) and let off steam, with celebrations sometimes going on around the clock.

The Passion, Semana Santa

Many *romerías* wind through the countryside during the year

SPRING FIESTAS

The end of winter and the start of spring are marked by Valencia's great fire festival, Las Fallas *(see p255)*, in which huge papier-mâché sculptures are set alight in a symbolic act of burning the old in order to make way for the new.

Alcoi's noisy mock battles between costumed armies of Moors and Christians in April *(see p255)* are the most spectacular of the countless fiestas which commemorate the battles of the Reconquest.

Seville's great April Fair *(see p431)*, is the biggest celebration held in Andalusia.

During Los Mayos, on 30 April and the following days, crosses are decorated with flowers in parts of Spain.

EASTER

Easter is Spain's main fiesta. Almost every community observes it in some form with pomp and solemnity.

It is heralded by the processions of Palm Sunday. The most impressive of these is in

Elx, where intricate sculptures are woven from blanched leaves cropped from the most extensive forest of palm trees in Europe *(see p261)*.

The best Semana Santa (Easter Week) processions are those held in Seville *(see p431)*, Málaga, Murcia and Valladolid. Brotherhoods of robed men carry *pasos*, huge sculptures depicting the Virgin, Christ or scenes of the Passion, through the streets. They are accompanied by people dressed as biblical characters or penitents, in tall conical hats. In some towns passion plays are acted out. In others, people carry heavy crosses. Sometimes the centuries-old ritual of self-flagellation can be witnessed.

SUMMER FIESTAS

The first major fiesta of the summer is Pentecost (also known as Whitsun), in May or June, and its most famous celebration is at El Rocío *(see p463)*, where many thousands of people gather in a frenzy of religious devotion.

At Corpus Christi (in May or June) the consecrated host is carried in procession through many cities in an ornate silver monstrance. The route of the procession is often covered with a carpet of flowers. The main Corpus Christi celebrations take place in Valencia, Toledo and Granada.

On Midsummer's Eve, bonfires are lit all over Spain, especially in the areas along the Mediterranean coast, to

The Brotherhood of Candlemas, Semana Santa (Easter Week) in Seville

herald the celebration of St
John the Baptist on 24 June.

During Los Sanfermines (see
p128) in Pamplona in July,
young people run through
the streets in front of six bulls.

The Virgin of Carmen,
who is revered as the patron
of fishermen, is honoured in
many ports on 16 July.

The important Catholic holiday of Assumption Day, 15
August, is marked by a huge
number and variety of fiestas.

AUTUMN FIESTAS

There are few fiestas in
autumn, but in most wine
regions the grape harvest is
fêted. The annual pig slaughter has become a jubilant
public event in some villages,
especially in Extremadura. In
Galicia it is traditional to roast
chestnuts on street bonfires.

On All Saints' Day, 1 November, people remember the
dead by visiting cemeteries
to lay flowers, especially
chrysanthemums, on graves.

CHRISTMAS AND
NEW YEAR

Nochebuena (Christmas Eve)
is the main Christmas
celebration, when families
gather for an evening meal
before attending Midnight
Mass, known as *misa del
gallo* (Mass of the rooster).
During the Christmas period,
belenes (crib scenes) of painted
figurines abound. You may
also see a "living crib", peo-
pled by costumed actors.

The losers end up in the harbour in Denia's July fiesta (see p255)

Spain's "April Fools' Day" is
28 December, the Day of the
Holy Innocents, when people
play practical jokes on each
other. Clown-like characters
may act out the role of mayor
and make fun of passers-by.

To celebrate New Year's Eve
(Noche Vieja), crowds gather
beneath the clock in Madrid's
central square, the Puerta del
Sol (see p272). Traditionally
people eat 12 grapes, one on
each chime of midnight, to
bring good luck for the year.

Spanish children do not receive their Christmas presents
until Epiphany, on 6 January.

WINTER FIESTAS

Animals hold centre stage
in a variety of fiestas on 17
January, the Day of St
Anthony, patron saint of animals, when pets and livestock
are blessed by priests.

St Agatha, the patron saint of
married women, is honoured
on 5 February when women,
for once, are the protagonists
of many fiestas. In Zamarramala (Segovia), for example,
women take over the mayor's
privileges and powers for
this particular day (see p368).

St Anthony's Day in Villanueva
de Alcolea (Castellón province)

CARNIVAL

Carnival, in February or
early March (depending on
the date of Easter), brings a
chance for a street party as
winter comes to an end and
before Lent begins. The biggest celebrations are held in
Santa Cruz de Tenerife (see
p536) – comparable with
those of Rio de Janeiro – and
in Cádiz (see p463). Carnival
was prohibited by the Franco
regime because of its licen-
tiousness and frivolity. It ends
on or after Ash Wednesday
with the Burial of the Sardine,
a "funeral" in which a mock
sardine, representing winter,
is ritually burned or buried.

A spectacularly costumed choir singing during Carnival in Cádiz

SPAIN THROUGH THE YEAR

Festivals, cultural events and sports competitions crowd the calendar in Spain. Even small villages have at least one traditional fiesta, lasting a week or more, when parades, bull-fights and fireworks displays replace work *(see pp38–9)*. Many rural and coastal towns celebrate the harvest or' fishing catch with a gastronomic fair at which you can sample local produce.

Music, dance, drama and film festivals are held in Spain's major cities throughout the year. Meanwhile, the country's favourite outdoor sports – football, basketball, cycling, sailing, golf and tennis – culminate in several national and international championships. It is a good idea to confirm specific dates of events with the local tourist board as some vary from year to year.

Matador with a cape playing a bull

SPRING

Life in Spain moves outdoors with the arrival of spring, and terrace-cafés begin to fill with people. The countryside is at its best as wild flowers bloom, and irrigation channels flow to bring water to the newly sown crops. The im-portant Easter holiday is a time of solemn processions throughout the country.

MARCH

Feria del Caballo (Festival of the Horses) in Jerez de la Frontera

International Vintage Car Rally *(first weekend)*, from Barcelona to Sitges.
Las Fallas *(15–19 Mar)*, Valencia *(see p255)*. A spec-tacular fiesta which also marks the start of the bullfighting *(see pp36– 7)* season. **Fiestas** Castellón de la Plana *(13–21 Mar)*. All in the honour of Mary Magdalene.

APRIL

Religious Music Week *(4–11 Apr)*, Cuenca.

Trofeo Conde de Godó *(mid-Apr)*, Barcelona. Spain's inter-national tennis championship.
Moors and Christians *(21–24 Apr)*, Alcoi *(see p258)*. Costumed celebration of the Christian victory over the Moors in 1276.
April Fair *(two weeks after Easter)*, Seville. Exuberant Andalusian fiesta*(see p431)*.
Feria Nacional del Queso *(late Apr/early May)*, Trujillo (Cáceres). A festival celebrat-ing Spanish cheese *(see p407)*.

MAY

Feria del Caballo *(first week)*, Jerez de la Frontera. Horse fair showing Andalusia at its most traditional, with fine horses, and beautiful women in flamenco dresses.
Spanish Motorcycle Grand Prix *(May)*, Jerez de la Frontera race track.
Fiestas de San Isidro *(8–15 May)*, Madrid *(see p290)*. Bullfights at Las Ventas bull-ring are the highlights of the taurine year.
National Flamenco Compe-tition *(mid-May, every third year: 2004, 2007)*, Córdoba.
Peugeot Open de España *(mid-May)*, Club de Campo, Madrid. Golf tournament.
Spanish Formula One Grand Prix *(May/Jun)*, Montmeló circuit, Barcelona. International motor race.
A Rapa das Bestas *(May and Jun)*, Pontevedra (Galicia). Wild horses are rounded up so that their manes and tails can be cut *(see p99)*.

Onlookers lining the street during the Vuelta Ciclista a España

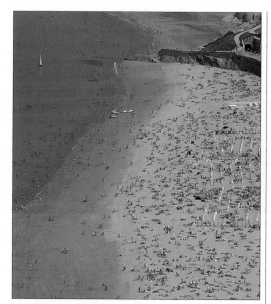

San Sebastián, one of the most popular resorts on the north coast

SUMMER

August is Spain's big holiday season. The cities empty as Spaniards flock to the coast or to their second homes in the hills. Their numbers are swelled by millions of foreign tourists, and beaches and camp sites are often full to bursting. As the heat starts in the centre and south, entertainment often takes place only in the evening, when the temperature has dropped. In late summer the harvest begins and there are gastronomic fiestas everywhere to celebrate food and drink, from the fishing catches of the north coast to the sausages of the Balearic Islands.

JUNE

International Festival of Music and Dance *(mid-Jun–early Jul)*, Granada. Classical music and ballet staged in the Alhambra and the Generalife.
Grec Arts Festival *(Jun–Aug)*, Barcelona. Both Spanish and international theatre, music and dance.
Copa del Rey *(Apr–Jun)* Football cup final.

JULY

Classical Theatre Festival *(Jul–Aug)*, Mérida. Staged in the Roman theatre and amphitheatre *(see p410)*.
Guitar Festival *(first two weeks)*, Córdoba. Performances range from classical to flamenco *(see pp424–5)*.
International Classical Theatre Festival of Almagro *(4–28 Jul)*. Spanish and classical repertoire performed in one of the oldest theatres in Europe *(see p399)*.

Cider Festival *(second Sat, even years only)*, Nava (Asturias). Includes traditional cider-pouring competitions.
International Festival of Santander *(Jul–Aug)*. Celebration of music, dance and theatre.
Pyrenean Folklore Festival *(late Jul/early Aug, odd years only)*, Jaca (Aragón). Display of folk costumes, music and dance.
International Jazz Festivals in San Sebastián *(third week)*, Getxo *(first week)* and Vitoria *(mid-Jul)*.

AUGUST

Certamen Internacional de Habaneras y Polifonía *(late Jul–early Aug)*, Torrevieja (Alicante). Musical competition of 19th-century seafarers' songs.
HM the King's International Cup *(first week)*, Palma de Mallorca. Sailing competition in which Juan Carlos I participates.
Descent of the Río Sella *(first Sat)*. Canoe race in Asturias from Arriondas to Ribadesella *(see p107)*.
Assumption Day *(15 Aug)* The Assumption is celebrated throughout the country.

Participants in the Descent of the Río Sella canoe race

Semanas Grandes *(early–mid-Aug)*, Bilbao and San Sebastián. "Great Weeks" of sporting and cultural events.
Misteri d'Elx *(11–15 Aug)*, Elx *(see p265)*. Unique liturgical drama performed in a church and featuring spectacular special effects.

The pouring and tasting of cider in Asturias's Cider Festival

Vines and the village of Larouco in the Valdeorras wine region of Galicia *(see p78)* in autumn

AUTUMN

Autumn usually brings rain after the heat of summer, and with the high tourist season over, a large number of resorts practically close down. Harvest festivities continue, however, and the most important celebrations are in honour of the grape. The first pressings are blessed and, in some places, wine is served for free.

Wild mushrooms

In woodland areas, freshly picked wild mushrooms start to appear in various dishes on local restaurant menus. The hunting season begins in the middle of October and runs until February. Autumn is also the start of the new drama and classical music seasons in the major cities of Spain.

SEPTEMBER

Vuelta Ciclista a España *(Sep)*. Annual bicycle race around Spain.
International Folklore Gala *(late Aug/early Sep)*, Ronda (Málaga). Music and dancing.
Grape Harvest *(first week)*, Jerez de la Frontera. Celebration of the new crop in the country's sherry capital.
Madrid Autumn Festival *(mid-Sep–mid-Nov)*. Drama, dance and music by national and foreign companies.
San Sebastián Film Festival *(last two weeks)*. Gathering of film-makers *(see p123)*.
Bienal de Arte Flamenco *(last two weeks, even years only)*, Seville. Top flamenco artists perform.

OCTOBER

Día de la Hispanidad *(12 Oct)*. Spain's national holiday marks Columbus's discovery of America in 1492. The biggest celebration in the country is the exuberant fiesta of Día del Pilar in Zaragoza *(see p239)*, which marks the end of the bullfighting year.

Driving down the fairway in the Volvo Masters Golf Championship

Moors and Christians *(mid-Oct)*, Callosa D'en Sarria (Alicante). Parades in honour of the local madonna.
Saffron Festival *(late Oct)*, Consuegra (Toledo).
Volvo Masters Golf Championship *(late Oct)*, Valderrama (Cádiz).

NOVEMBER

All Saints' Day *(1 Nov)*. The start of the *matanza* (pig slaughter) in rural Spain.
Os Magostos *(11 Nov)*. Chestnut-harvest fairs in Galicia.
Latin American Film Festival *(last two weeks)*, Huelva *(see p462)*.

Lana Turner on centre-stage at the San Sebastián Film Festival

Assumption Day in La Alberca (Salamanca)

PUBLIC HOLIDAYS

Besides marking the national holidays below, each region *(comunidad autónoma)* celebrates its own holiday and every town and village has at least one other fiesta each year. If a holiday falls on a Tuesday or a Thursday shops, offices and monuments may also be closed on the intervening Monday or Friday, making a long weekend called a *puente* ("bridge").

Año Nuevo *(New Year's Day)* (1 Jan)
Día de los Reyes *(Epiphany)* (6 Jan)
Jueves Santo *(Maundy Thursday)* (Mar/Apr)
Viernes Santo *(Good Friday)* (Mar/Apr)
Día de Pascua *(Easter Sunday)* (Mar/Apr)
Día del Trabajo *(Labour Day)* (1 May)
Asunción *(Assumption Day)* (15 Aug)
Día de la Hispanidad *(National Day)* (12 Oct)
Todos los Santos *(All Saints' Day)* (1 Nov)
Día de la Constitución *(Constitution Day)* (6 Dec)
Inmaculada Concepción *(Immaculate Conception)* (8 Dec)
Navidad *(Christmas Day)* (25 Dec)

WINTER

Winter varies greatly from region to region. In the mountains, snowfalls bring skiers to the slopes; while in lower areas, olive and orange picking are in full swing. The higher parts of Central Spain can become very cold. Andalusia, the east coast and the Balearic Islands have cool nights but often sunny days. The winter warmth of the Canary Islands brings the high tourist season. Christmas is a special time of celebration – an occasion for families to re-unite, share food and attend religious celebrations.

"El Gordo", the largest Spanish lottery prize, being drawn

Skiers in the Sierra de Guadarrama, north of Madrid *(see p329)*

DECEMBER

El Gordo *(22 Dec)*. Spain's largest lottery prize, "the Fat One", is drawn *(see p622)*.
Noche Buena *(24 Dec)* is a family Christmas Eve, followed by Midnight Mass for the devout *(see p35)*.
Santos Inocentes *(28 Dec)*, Spain's version of April Fools' Day, when people play tricks.
Noche Vieja *(31 Dec)*. New Year's Eve is most celebrated in Madrid's Puerta del Sol.

JANUARY

Canary Islands International Music Festival *(Jan–Feb)*. Classical concerts are held on La Palma and Tenerife.
Opera Season *(Jan–Apr)*, Palacio de la Música y Con-gresos Euskelduna, Bilbao.
Vigo Video Festival *(last week)*. Screenings and other events exploring all aspects of video film-making.

FEBRUARY

Festival of Ancient Music *(Feb–Mar)*, Seville. Played on period instruments.
ARCO *(mid-Feb)*, Madrid. International contemporary art fair attracting galleries from across the world.
Pasarela Cibeles (Fashion Week) *(mid-Feb)*, Madrid. Women's and men's fashion shows in the capital.
Carnival *(Feb/Mar)*. Final fiesta before Lent, with colourful costumes. Those in Santa Cruz de Tenerife and Cádiz are among the best.

The Climate of Spain

Spain's large landmass, with its extensive high plateaus and mountain ranges, and the influences of the Mediterranean and Atlantic produce a wide range of climatic variation, especially in winter. The north is wettest year round, the eastern and southern coasts and the islands have mild winters, while winter temperatures in the interior are often below freezing. Summers everywhere are hot, except in upland areas.

MADRID

- Average monthly maximum temperature
- Average monthly minimum temperature
- Freezing point
- Average daily hours of sunshine
- Average monthly rainfall

°C/F

	Apr	Jul	Oct	Jan
max	25/77	36/97	24/75	14/57
min	3/37	13/55	3/38	-5/23
☼ hrs	8 hrs	12 hrs	6.5 hrs	5 hrs
☂ mm	48 mm	11 mm	53 mm	39 mm
month	Apr	Jul	Oct	Jan

ASTURIAS AND CANTABRIA

°C/F

	Apr	Jul	Oct	Jan
max	24/75	29/84	25/77	18/64
min	6/43	13/55	8/46	2/36
☼ hrs	6 hrs	6.5 hrs	4.5 hrs	2.5 hrs
☂ mm	83 mm	54 mm	133 mm	119 mm
month	Apr	Jul	Oct	Jan

GALICIA

°C/F

	Apr	Jul	Oct	Jan
max	22/72	29/84	25/77	17/63
min	5/41	12/54	7/45	2/36
☼ hrs	6.5 hrs	8.5 hrs	5 hrs	3 hrs
☂ mm	67 mm	28 mm	87 mm	118 mm
month	Apr	Jul	Oct	Jan

CASTILLA Y LEÓN

°C/F

	Apr	Jul	Oct	Jan
max	25/77	36/97	26/79	14/57
min	0/32	9/48	1/34	-7/19
☼ hrs	8 hrs	12 hrs	6.5 hrs	3.5 hrs
☂ mm	37 mm	14 mm	36 mm	37 mm
month	Apr	Jul	Oct	Jan

EXTREMADURA

°C/F

	Apr	Jul	Oct	Jan
max	28/82	41/106	31/88	18/64
min	6/43	14/57	7/45	-2/28
☼ hrs	9 hrs	12.5 hrs	7 hrs	5 hrs
☂ mm	46 mm	3 mm	52 mm	61 mm
month	Apr	Jul	Oct	Jan

ANDALUSIA

°C/F

	Apr	Jul	Oct	Jan
max	27/81	38/100	28/82	22/72
min	10/50	18/64	12/54	4/39
☼ hrs	8 hrs	11.5 hrs	7 hrs	6 hrs
☂ mm	46 mm	1 mm	64 mm	61 mm
month	Apr	Jul	Oct	Jan

Santander
Oviedo
Bil(Bilba
Santiago de Compostela
León
Burgos
Vigo
Valladolid
Salamanca
MADRID
Toledo
Cáceres
Ciudad Real
Badajoz
Córdoba
Sevilla
Granada
Cádiz
Málaga
Alme

BASQUE COUNTRY, NAVARRA & RIOJA

°C/F

36/97			
25/77		26/79	
	10/50		15/59
1/34		2/36	
			-7/19

☀	6 hrs	9.5 hrs	5 hrs	2.5 hrs
☂	83 mm	46 mm	107 mm	120 mm
month	Apr	Jul	Oct	Jan

ARAGÓN

°C/F

	37/99		
26/79		27/81	
	14/57		18/64
4/39		5/41	
			-4/25

☀	8 hrs	11.5 hrs	6.5 hrs	5 hrs
☂	34 mm	15 mm	34 mm	17 mm
month	Apr	Jul	Oct	Jan

CATALONIA

°C/F

	38/100		
28/82		28/82	
	13/55		18/64
3/37		3/37	
			-5/23

☀	8.5 hrs	11.5 hrs	6.5 hrs	4 hrs
☂	46 mm	24 mm	30 mm	22 mm
month	Apr	Jul	Oct	Jan

THE BALEARIC ISLANDS

°C/F

	33/91		
24/75		27/81	
	17/63		18/64
6/43		9/48	
			2/36

☀	7.5 hrs	11.5 hrs	6 hrs	5 hrs
☂	32 mm	3 mm	77 mm	39 mm
month	Apr	Jul	Oct	Jan

Donostia (San Sebastián)

Iruña (Pamplona)

Zaragoza

Lleida

Barcelona

Palma de Mallorca

enca

Valencia

acete

Alacant (Alicante)

Murcia

Santa Cruz de Tenerife

Las Palmas de Gran Canaria

CASTILLA-LA MANCHA

°C/F

	36/97		
24/75		26/79	
	8/46		16/61
-2/28		-1/30	-10/14

☀	7.5 hrs	12 hrs	6 hrs	4.5 hrs
☂	48 mm	19 mm	52 mm	43 mm
month	Apr	Jul	Oct	Jan

VALENCIA AND MURCIA

°C/F

	36/97		
27/81		30/86	
	17/63		23/73
7/45		9/48	
			1/34

☀	8.5 hrs	11.5 hrs	7 hrs	6 hrs
☂	40 mm	4 mm	52 mm	30 mm
month	Apr	Jul	Oct	Jan

THE CANARY ISLANDS

°C/F

	32/90	30/86	
26/79			25/77
	17/63	16/61	
12/54			11/52

☀	7.5 hrs	9.5 hrs	7 hrs	6.5 hrs
☂	13 mm	0 mm	28 mm	36 mm
month	Apr	Jul	Oct	Jan

THE HISTORY OF SPAIN

The Iberian Peninsula, first inhabited around 800,000 BC, has long been subject to foreign influences. From the 11th century BC it was colonized by sophisticated eastern Mediterranean civilizations, starting with the Phoenicians, then the Greeks and Carthaginians.

The Romans arrived in 218 BC to fight the Carthaginians, thus sparking off the Second Punic War. They harvested the peninsula's agricultural and mineral wealth and established cities with aqueducts, temples and theatres.

Gold Aztec statue from America

With the fall of the Roman Empire in the early 5th century AD, Visigothic invaders from the north assumed power. Their poor political organization, however, made them easy prey to the Moors from North Africa. In the 8th century, the peninsula came almost entirely under Moorish rule. Europe's only major Muslim territory, the civilization of Al Andalus excelled in mathematics, geography, astronomy and poetry. In the 9th and 10th centuries Córdoba was Europe's leading city.

From the 11th century, northern Christian kingdoms initiated a military reconquest of Al Andalus. The marriage, in 1469, of Fernando of Aragón and Isabel of Castile, the so-called Catholic Monarchs, led to Spanish unity. They took Granada, the last Moorish kingdom, in 1492. Columbus discovered the Americas in the same year, opening the way for the Spanish conquistadors, who plundered the civilizations of the New World.

The succeeding Habsburg dynasty spent the riches from the New World in endless foreign wars. Spain's decline was exacerbated by high inflation and religious oppression. Although the Enlightenment in the late 18th century created a climate of learning, Spain's misfortunes continued into the next century with an invasion by Napoleon's troops and the loss of her American colonies. A new radicalism began to emerge, creating a strong Anarchist movement. The political instability of the late 19th and early 20th centuries led to dictatorship in the 1920s and a republic in the 1930s, which was destroyed by the Spanish Civil War. Victorious General Franco ruled by repression until his death in 1975. Since then Spain has been a democratic state.

Bullfighting in Madrid's Plaza Mayor in the 17th century

◁ **Moors paying homage to Fernando and Isabel, the 15th-century Catholic Monarchs**

Prehistoric Spain

Helmet of Celt-iberian warrior

The Iberian Peninsula was first inhabited by hunter-gatherers around 800,000 BC. They were eclipsed by a Neolithic farming population from 5000 BC. First in a wave of settlers from over the Mediterranean, the Phoenicians landed in 1100 BC, to be followed by the Greeks and Carthaginians. Invading Celts mixed with native Iberian tribes (forming the Celtiberians). They proved a formidable force against the Romans, the next conquerors of Spain.

SPAIN IN 5000 BC

☐ *Neolithic farming settlements*

Iron Dagger *(6th century BC)*
Weapons, like this dagger from Burgos, represent the later Iron Age, in contrast to earlier metal objects which were for domestic use.

Stone Age Man
This skull belongs to a Palaeolithic man, who hunted deer and bison with tools made of wood and stone.

The 28 bracelets have perforations and moulded decorations.

Small silver bottle

Incised geometric pattern

La Dama de Elche
Dating from the 4th century BC, this stone statue is a fine example of Iberian art. Her austere beauty reveals traces of Greek influence.

THE VILLENA TREASURE

Discovered in 1963 during works in Villena, near Alicante, this Bronze Age find consists of 66 dazzling objects mostly of gold, including bowls, bottles and jewellery *(see p260)*. The treasure dates from around 1000 BC.

TIMELINE

800,000 BC *Homo erectus* arrives in Iberian Peninsula		**2500 BC** Los Millares *(p501)* is inhabited by early metal-workers with belief in the afterlife
300,000 BC Tribes of *Homo erectus* live in hunting camps in Soria and Madrid	**35,000 BC** Cro-Magnon man evolves in Spain	**1800–1100 BC** Civilization of El Argar, an advanced agrarian society, flourishes in southeast Spain

800,000 BC	2500	2000

500,000 BC Stones used as tools by hominids (probably *Homo erectus*)	**100,000–40,000 BC** Neanderthal man in Gibraltar	**5000 BC** Farming begins in Iberian Peninsula
Bison cave drawing, Altamira		**18,000–14,000 BC** Drawings by cave dwellers at Altamira (Cantabria), near Ribadesella (Asturias) and at Nerja (Andalusia)

Greek Ceramic Vase
The Greek colonizers brought new technology, including the potter's wheel, as well as refined artistic ideals. Ceramics, such as this 6th-century BC vase depicting the Labours of Hercules, provided sophisticated models.

WHERE TO SEE PREHISTORIC SPAIN

The most famous cave paintings in Spain are at Altamira *(see p112)*. There are dolmens in many parts of the country; among the largest are those at Antequera *(see p475)*. The Guanches – the indigenous inhabitants of the Canary Islands – left behind more recent remains *(see p547)*.

La Naveta d'es Tudons *is one of the many prehistoric stone monuments scattered across the island of Menorca (see p527).*

An excavated Celtic village, *with its round huts, can be seen near A Guarda in Pontevedra (see p97).*

The largest of the treasure's five bottles, made of silver, stands 22.5 cm (9 in) high.

Bowls of beaten gold may have originated in southwest Spain.

Brooches with separate clasps

The smaller pieces are of unknown use.

Astarte *(8th century BC)*
Worship of Phoenician deities was incorporated into local religions. One of the most popular was the fertility goddess Astarte, shown on this bronze from the kingdom of Tartessus.

Phoenician gold ornament

1100 BC Phoenicians believed to have founded modern-day Cádiz	**600 BC** Greek colonists settle on northeast coast of Spain		**228 BC** Carthaginians occupy south-east Spain

1500	**1000**	**500**

| **1200 BC** The "talaiotic" people of Menorca erect three unique types of stone building: *taulas, talaiots* and *navetas* | **775 BC** Phoenicians establish colonies along the coast near Málaga | **300 BC** *La Dama de Elche* is carved *(p296)* | |
| *Taula in Menorca* | | **700 BC** Semi-mythical kingdom of Tartessus thought to be at its height | *Carthaginian glass necklace* |

Romans and Visigoths

The Romans came to Spain to fight the Carthaginians and take possession of the Iberian Peninsula's huge mineral wealth. Later, Hispania's wheat and olive oil became mainstays of the empire. It took 200 years to subdue the peninsula, which was divided in three provinces: Tarraconensis, Lusitania and Baetica. In time, cities with Roman infrastructure developed. The fall of the empire in the 5th century left Spain in the hands of the Visigoths, invaders from the north. Politically disorganized, they fell victim to the Moors in 711.

Roman vase

SPAIN (HISPANIA) IN 5 BC

☐ *Tarraconensis*

☐ *Lusitania*

☐ *Baetica*

Trajan *(AD 53–117)*
Trajan was the first Hispanic Roman emperor (AD 98–117). He improved public administration and expanded the empire.

Seneca *(4 BC– AD 65)*
Born in Córdoba, the Stoic philosopher Seneca lived in Rome as Nero's adviser.

Portico overlooking the gardens

Good acoustics at every level

A Classical façade served as a backdrop for tragedies. Additional scenery was used for comedies.

The *orchestra*, a semicircular open space for the choir

Visigothic Relief
This crude Visigothic stone carving, based on a Roman relief, is in the 7th-century church of Quintanilla de las Viñas, near Burgos (p370).

The auditorium seated over 5,000. The audience was placed according to social status.

TIMELINE

218 BC Scipio the Elder lands with a Roman army at Emporion (p216). The Second Punic War begins	**c.200 BC** Romans reach Gadir (modern Cádiz) after driving Carthaginians out of Hispania	**26 BC** Emerita Augusta (Mérida) is founded and soon becomes capital of Lusitania
	155 BC Lusitanian Wars begin. Romans invade Portugal	**19 BC** Augustus takes Cantabria and Asturias, ending 200 years of war

200 BC	100	AD 1	AD 100

219 BC Hannibal takes Saguntum (p249) for Carthaginians *Hannibal*	**133 BC** Celtiberian Wars culminate in destruction of Numantia, Soria (p377)	**61 BC** Julius Caesar, governor of Hispania Ulterior, begins final conquest of northern Portugal and Galicia **82–72 BC** Roman Civil War. Pompey founds Pompaelo (Pamplona) in 75 BC	**AD 74** Emperor Vespasian grants Latin status to all towns in Hispania, completing process of Romanization

Gladiator Mosaic
Mosaics were used as decoration both indoors and out. Themes range from mythical episodes to portrayals of daily life. This 4th-century AD mosaic shows gladiators in action and has helpful labels to name the fighters and show who is dead or alive.

WHERE TO SEE ROMAN SPAIN

Like Mérida, Tarragona *(see p224)* has extensive Roman ruins and Itálica *(see p476)* is an excavated town. A magnificent Roman wall rings Lugo in Galicia *(see p99)*. Built in Trajan's rule, the bridge over the Tagus at Alcántara *(see p410)* has a temple on it.

Emporion, *a Roman town, was built next to a former Greek colony in the 3rd century BC. The ruins include grand villas and a forum (see p216).*

Segovia's Roman aqueduct (see p365), *a huge monument with 163 arches, dates from the end of the 1st century AD.*

The gardens were used as a foyer during intervals by the Hispanic nobility, dressed in elegant togas.

Stage building in granite and marble

Scaena, the platform on which the actors performed

ROMAN THEATRE, MÉRIDA
Theatre was an extremely popular form of entertainment in Hispania. This reconstruction shows the theatre at Mérida *(see p410)*, built in 16–15 BC.

Visigothic Cross
Although Visigothic kings seldom ruled long enough to make an impact on society, the early Christian Church grew powerful. Fortunes were spent on churches and religious art.

Mosaic from Mérida

415 Visigoths establish their court at Barcelona

409 Vandals and their allies cross Pyrenees into Tarraconensis

446 Romans attempt to win back rest of Hispania

476 Overthrow of the last Roman emperor leads to end of Western Roman Empire

200	300	400	500

258 Franks cross Pyrenees into Tarraconensis and sack Tarragona

312 Christianity officially recognized as religion under rule of Constantine, the first Christian emperor

The Codex Vigilianus, *a Christian manuscript*

589 Visigothic King Reccared converts from Arianism to Catholicism at Third Council of Toledo

Al Andalus: Muslim Spain

Alhambra Vase
(see p467)

The arrival of Arab and Berber invaders from North Africa, and their defeat of the Visigoths, gave rise to the most brilliant civilization of early medieval Europe. These Muslim settlers, often known as the Moors, called Spain "Al Andalus". A rich and powerful caliphate was established in Córdoba and mathematics, science, architecture and the decorative arts flourished. The caliphate eventually broke up into small kingdoms or *taifas*. Meanwhile small Christian enclaves expanded in the north.

SPAIN IN 750

☐ *Extent of Moorish domination*

Water Wheel
Moorish irrigation techniques, such as the water wheel, revolutionized agriculture. New crops, including oranges and rice, were introduced.

The palace, dating from the 11th century, was surrounded by patios, pools and gardens.

Astrolabe
Perfected by the Moors around AD 800, the astrolabe was used by navigators and astronomers.

Remains of a Roman amphitheatre

Silver Casket of Hisham II
In the Caliphate of Córdoba, luxury objects of brilliant craftsmanship were worked in ivory, silver and bronze.

Fortified entrance gate

Curtain walls with watchtowers

TIMELINE

711 Moors, led by Tariq, invade Spain and defeat Visigoths at battle of Guadalete

732 Moors' advance into France is halted by Charles Martel at Poitiers

778 Charlemagne's rearguard defeated by Basques at Roncesvalles (p134)

785 Building of great mosque at Córdoba begins

Charlemagne (742–814)

750	800	850

722 Led by Pelayo, Christians defeat Moors at Covadonga (p109)

756 Abd al Rahman I proclaims independent emirate in Córdoba

744 Christians under Alfonso I of Asturias take León

Pelayo (718–37)

822 Abd al Rahman II begins 30-year rule marked by patronage of the arts and culture

c.800 Tomb of St James (Santiago) is supposedly discovered at Santiago de Compostela

Puerta de Sabbath in Córdoba's Mezquita
Wealth and artistic brilliance were lavished on mosques, especially in Córdoba (see pp480–1). Calligraphy was a major element in decoration.

WHERE TO SEE MOORISH SPAIN

The finest Moorish buildings are in Andalusia, mainly in the cities of Córdoba *(see pp478–9)* and Granada *(see pp486–92)*. Almería *(see p501)* has a large, ruined *alcazaba* (castle). In Jaén *(see p493)* there are Moorish baths. Further north, in Zaragoza, is the castle-palace of La Aljafería *(see p237)*.

Medina Azahara (see p477), *sacked in the 11th century but partly restored, was the final residence of Córdoba's caliphs.*

Torre del Homenaje, the keep, was built by Abd al Rahman I (756–88).

Baths

Patio with Moorish decoration

ALCAZABA AT MÁLAGA

An *alcazaba* was a castle built into the ramparts of a Moorish city, often protected by massive concentric walls. In Málaga *(see p474)* – the principal port of the Moorish kingdom of Granada – the vast Alcazaba was built in the 8–11th centuries on the site of a Roman fortress, and incorporated massive curtain walls and fortified gates.

Moorish Sword
A fine example of late Moorish craftsmanship, this sword has a golden pommel. The blade is inscribed with Arabic writing.

Warrior Helmet
Practical as well as ornate, this Islamic nobleman's helmet, made of iron, gold and silver, incorporates inscriptions, a coat of arms and chain mail.

---

905 Emergent Navarra becomes Christian kingdom under Sancho I

976 Al Mansur, military dictator, usurps caliphal powers and sacks Barcelona. Córdoba Mezquita finished

1010 Medina Azahara sacked by Berbers

900   **950**   **1000**

913 Christian capital is established at León

936 Building of Medina Azahara palace starts near Córdoba

Bronze stag from Medina Azahara

1013 Caliphate of Córdoba breaks up. Emergence of *taifas*: small, independent Moorish kingdoms

The Reconquest

The infant Christian kingdoms in the north – León, Castile, Navarra, Aragón and Catalonia – advanced south gradually in the 11th century, fighting in the name of Christianity to regain land from the Moors. After the fall of Toledo in 1085, the struggle became increasingly a holy war. Militant North African Muslims – Almoravids and Almohads – rallied to the Moorish cause and ultimately took over Al Andalus in the 12th century. As the Christians pushed further south, soon only Granada remained under Moorish control.

Cross of the Knights of St James

SPAIN IN 1173
☐ *Christian kingdoms*
▨ *Al Andalus*

Golden Goblet
The exquisite goblet (1063) of Doña Urraca, daughter of Alfonso VI, shows the quality of medieval Christian craftsmanship.

Fernando I
Fernando formed the first Christian power bloc in 1037 by uniting Léon with Castile, which was emerging as a major military force.

Armies of Castile, Aragón and Navarra

The Almohads fight until the bitter end, although many comrades lay slain.

LAS NAVAS DE TOLOSA
The Christian victory over the Almohads in the battle of Las Navas de Tolosa (1212) led to Moorish Spain's decline. The army of Muhammad II al Nasir was no match for the forces of Sancho VII of Navarra, Pedro II of Aragón and Alfonso VIII of Castile. A stained-glass window in Roncesvalles *(see p134)* depicts the battle.

Alhambra, Palace of the Nasrids
Moorish art and architecture of singular beauty continued to be produced in the Nasrid kingdom of Granada. Its apogee is the exquisite Alhambra (see pp490–1).

TIMELINE

1037 León and Castile united for first time under Fernando I

1065 Death of Fernando I precipitates fratricidal civil war between his sons

1086 Almoravids respond to pleas for help from Moorish emirs by taking over *taifas* (splinter states)

Uniforms of military orders

1158 Establishment of the Order of Calatrava, the first military order of knights in Spain

1050	1100	1150	1200

1085 Toledo falls to Christians under Alfonso VI of Castile

1094 The legendary El Cid *(see p370)* captures Valencia

El Cid

1137 Ramón Berenguer IV of Catalonia marries Petronila of Aragón, uniting the two kingdoms under their son, Alfonso II

1147 Almohads arrive in Al Andalus and make Seville their capital

1143 Portugal becomes separate kingdom

1212 Combined Christian forces defeat Almohads at battle of Las Navas de Tolosa

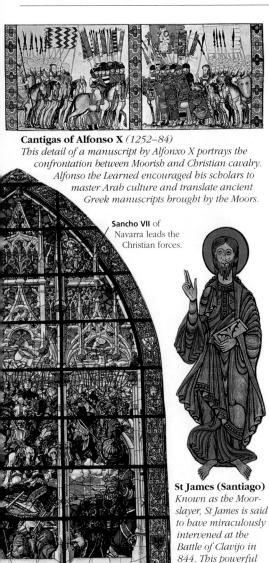

Cantigas of Alfonso X *(1252–84)*
This detail of a manuscript by Alfonxo X portrays the confrontation between Moorish and Christian cavalry. Alfonso the Learned encouraged his scholars to master Arab culture and translate ancient Greek manuscripts brought by the Moors.

Sancho VII of Navarra leads the Christian forces.

St James (Santiago)
Known as the Moor-slayer, St James is said to have miraculously intervened at the Battle of Clavijo in 844. This powerful figurehead is the patron saint of Spain.

WHERE TO SEE MUDÉJAR SPAIN

The Mudéjares – Muslims who remained in territories under Christian occupation – created a distinctive architectural style distinguished by its ornamental work in brick, plaster and ceramics. Aragón, particularly Zaragoza *(see pp236–7)* and Teruel *(see pp240–41)*, boasts some of the finest Mudéjar buildings. Seville's Reales Alcázares is an exquisitely harmonious collection of patios and halls built under Pedro I *(see pp440–1)*.

The Mudéjar tower *of Teruel cathedral combines both brick and colourful ceramics to highly decorative effect.*

Santa María la Blanca (see p393), *a former synagogue and church, shows the fusion of cultures in medieval Toledo.*

Crest of Castile and León

215 Foundation of Salamanca University

1230 Fernando III reunites Castile and León

1385 Portuguese defeat Castilians at Aljubarrota, crushing King Juan's aspirations to throne of Portugal

1388–9 Treaties end Spanish phase of Hundred Years War

1250	1300	1350	1400

1250 Toledo at its height as a centre of translation and learning, influenced by Alfonso X the Learned

1232 Granada becomes capital of future Nasrid kingdom. Building of the Alhambra begins

Alfonso X

1386 Invasion of Galicia by the English, ended by Bayonne Treaty

1401 Work starts in Seville on what was then the world's largest Gothic cathedral

The Catholic Monarchs

Fernando of
Aragón

The foundation of the Spanish nation-state
was laid by Isabel I of Castile and Fernando II
of Aragón *(see p70)*. Uniting their lands in
military, diplomatic and religious matters, the
"Catholic Monarchs", as they are known, won
back Granada, the last Moorish kingdom,
from Boabdil. The Inquisition gave Spain a
reputation for intolerance, yet in art and
architecture brilliant progress was made
and the voyages of Columbus
opened up the New World.

**SPAIN'S EXPLORATION OF
THE NEW WORLD**

— *Route of Columbus's first voyage*

Tomb of El Doncel *(15th century)*
*This effigy of a page who died in the
fight for Granada combines ideals
of military glory and
learning (see p383).*

Alhambra

Boabdil, the grief-
stricken king, moves
forward to hand over
the keys to Granada.

The Inquisition
*Active from 1478, the
Inquisition (see p274)
persecuted those suspected
of heresy with increasing
vigour. This member of the
Brotherhood of Death
took victims to the stake.*

Baptizing Jews
*After the Christian
reconquest of
Granada, Jews
were forced to
convert or leave
Spain. The con-
versos (converted
Jews) were often
treated badly.*

THE FALL OF GRANADA *(1492)*
This romantic interpretation by Francisco
Pradilla (1846–1921) reflects the chivalry of
Boabdil, ruler of Granada, as he surrenders
the keys of the last Moorish kingdom to the
Catholic Monarchs, Fernando and Isabel,
following ten long years of war.

TIMELINE

1454 Enrique IV,
Isabel's half-
brother, accedes to
throne of Castile

1465 Civil
war erupts
in Castile

1478 Papal bull authorizes
Castilian Inquisition with
Tomás de Torquemada
as Inquisitor General

Torquemada

1450	1460	1470	1480

1451 Birth
of Isabel of
Castile

*Fernando and
Isabel on 15th-
century gold coin*

1469 Marriage of Fernando
and Isabel in Valladolid
unites Castile and Aragón

1474 Death of Enrique IV leads to civil war;
Isabel triumphs over Juana la Beltraneja,
Enrique's supposed daughter, to become queen

1479
Fernando
becomes
Fernando II
of Aragón

Columbus Arriving in the Americas
The Catholic Monarchs financed Columbus's daring first voyage partly because they hoped for riches in return, but also because they expected him to convert infidels.

Fernando of Aragón

Isabel, queen of Castile, witnesses the surrender of Granada, surrounded by a glittering entourage.

Boabdil
As the forlorn king left Granada, his mother reputedly said, "Don't cry as a child over what you could not defend as a man".

WHERE TO SEE GOTHIC ARCHITECTURE IN SPAIN

Spain has many great Gothic cathedrals, especially in Seville *(pp436–37)*, Burgos *(pp372–3)*, Barcelona *(pp148–9)*, Toledo *(pp392–3)* and Palma de Mallorca *(pp520–1)*. Secular buildings from this era include commodity exchanges like La Lonja in Valencia *(p251)* and castles *(pp344–5)*.

León cathedral (pp354–5) *has a west front covered in statuary. Here Christ is seen presiding over the Last Judgment.*

Crown of Isabel
Worn at the surrender, Isabel's crown is now in her final resting place, the Capilla Real in Granada (see p486).

1494 Treaty of Tordesillas divides the New World territories between Portugal and Spain

1496 Foundation of Santo Domingo, on Hispaniola, first Spanish city in the Americas

1509 Cardinal Cisneros' troops attack Oran in Algeria and temporarily occupy it

Cardinal Cisneros

1490	1500	1510

1492 Fall of Granada after ten-year war. Columbus reaches America. Expulsion of Jews from Spain

Columbus's ship, the Santa María

1502 Unconverted Moors expelled from Spain

1504 Following death of Isabel, her daughter Juana la Loca becomes queen of Castile with Fernando as regent

1512 Annexation of Navarra, leading to full unification of Spain

1516 Death of Fernando

The Age of Discovery

Following Columbus's arrival in the Bahamas in 1492, the conquistadors went into Central and South America, conquering Mexico (1519), Peru (1532) and Chile (1541). In doing so, they destroyed Indian civilizations. In the 16th century, vast quantities of gold and silver flowed across the Atlantic to Spain. Carlos I and his son Felipe II spent some of it on battles to halt the spread of Protestantism in Europe, and in the Holy War against the Turks.

Aztec god (c.1540)

SPANISH EMPIRE IN 1580

☐ *Dominions of Felipe II*

Mapping the World
This 16th-century German map reflects a new world, largely unknown to Europe before the era of conquistadors.

Galleons were armed with cannons as a defence against pirates and rival conquerors.

Aztec Mask
In their great greed and ignorance, the Spanish destroyed the empires and civilizations of the Aztecs in Mexico and the Incas in Peru.

The lookout was essential for spotting enemies and making landfall.

Forecastle

Seville
Granted the trading monopoly with the Americas, Seville, on the banks of the Guadalquivir, was Europe's richest port in the early 16th century.

TIMELINE

1519 Magellan, Portuguese explorer, leaves Seville under Spanish patronage to circumnavigate the globe

1520-21 Revolt by Castilian towns when Carlos I appoints foreigner, Adrian of Utrecht, as regent

1532 Pizarro takes Peru with 180 men and destroys Inca empire

Pizarro

1554 International Catholic alliance created by marriage of future king Felipe II with Mary Tudor of England

1520	1530	1540	1550

1519 Conquest of Mexico by Cortés. Carlos I crowned Holy Roman Emperor Charles V

Conquistador Hernán Cortés

1540 Father Bartolomé de las Casas writes book denouncing the oppression of Indians

Bartolomé de las Casas

Defeat of the Spanish Armada
Spain's self-esteem suffered a hard blow when its "invincible" 133-ship fleet was destroyed in an attempt to invade Protestant England in 1588.

NEW WORLD CROPS

Cacao plant

Not only did Spain profit from the gold and silver brought across the ocean from the Americas, but also from an amazing range of new crops. Some, including potatoes and maize, were introduced for cultivation in Spain while others, such as tobacco and cacao, were mainly grown in native soil. Cocoa, from cacao beans, gained favour as a drink.

Peruvian with exotic New World fruit

Armour of Felipe II
Felipe II (1556–98) was a cunning administrator, who claimed to rule the world with paper rather than military might.

Flag of Spain (until 1785)

Storage space for New World treasures

SPANISH GALLEON

Although sturdily built to carry New World treasure back to Spain, these ships were hard to manoeuvre except with the wind behind. They were often no match for smaller, swifter pirate vessels.

Carlos I *(1516–56)*
During his tumultuous 40-year reign, Carlos I (Holy Roman Emperor Charles V) often led his troops on the battlefield.

1557 First of a series of partial bankruptcies of Spain

1561 Building of El Escorial, near Madrid, begins

El Escorial (see pp330–31)

1588 Spanish Armada fails in attack on Britain

1560	1570	1580	1590

1561 Madrid becomes capital of Spain

1571 Spanish victory over Turks in naval battle of Lepanto

1580 Portugal unites with Spain for the next 60 years

1568 Moriscos (converted Moors) in the Alpujarras (Granada) rebel against high taxes and persecution

1569 Bible published for first time in Castilian

The Golden Age

Spain's Golden Age was a time of great artistic and literary achievement led by the painters – El Greco and Velázquez *(see pp32–3)* – and writers *(see pp34–35)*, especially Cervantes and the prolific dramatists, Lope de Vega and Calderón de la Barca. This brilliance occurred, however, against a background of economic deterioration and ruinous wars with the Low Countries and France. Spain was gradually losing its influence in Europe and the reigning house of Habsburg entered irreversible decline.

THE SPANISH EMPIRE IN EUROPE IN 1647

☐ *Spanish territories*

Don Quixote and Sancho Panza
Cervantes' satire on chivalrous romance, Don Quixote, contrasts the fantasy of the main character with his servant's realism.

A clock is a reminder of the inevitable passage of time.

The knight is dressed in mid-17th-century fashion.

Money represents worldly wealth.

Duke of Lerma
This bronze statue depicts the Duke of Lerma (c.1550–1625), a favourite of King Felipe III.

THE KNIGHT'S DREAM *(1650)*
This painting, attributed to Antonio de Pereda, is on a familiar Golden Age theme: human vanity. A young gentleman sits asleep beside a table piled with objects symbolizing power, wealth and mortality. The pleasures of life, we are told, are no more real than a dream.

TIMELINE

Felipe III

1600 Capital temporarily moves to Valladolid

1605 Publication of first of two parts of Cervantes' Don Quixote

1609 Felipe III orders the expulsion of the Moriscos

1619 Construction of Plaza Mayor, Madrid

1609 Lope de Vega publishes poem on the art of comic drama

1621 Low Countries war resumes after 12-year truce

1625 Capture of Breda, Netherlands, after one-year siege

1622 Velázquez moves from Seville to Madrid to become court painter the following year

Lope de Vega (1562–1635)

1643 Fall of Count-Duke Olivares. Spain heavily defeated by France at battle of Rocroi

1640 Secession of Portugal, amalgamated with Spain since 1580

1600	1610	1620	1630	1640

Fiesta in the Plaza Mayor in Madrid
This famous square (see p273) became the scene for pageants, royal celebrations, bullfights and executions, all overlooked from the balconies.

SEVILLE SCHOOL OF ART

Seville's wealth, together with the patronage of the Church, made it a centre of the arts, second only to the royal court. Velázquez, who was born in Seville, trained under the painter Pacheco. Sculptor Juan Martínez Montañés and painters Zurbarán and Murillo created great works which are displayed in the Museo de Bellas Artes *(see p430).*

San Diego de Alcalá Giving Food to the Poor (c.1646) by Murillo

An angel warns that death is near.

The banner says, "It [death] pierces perpetually, flies quickly and kills".

A mask symbolizes the Arts.

Expulsion of the Moriscos
Although they had converted to Christianity, the last Moors were still expelled in 1609.

Weapons represent power.

The skull on the book shows death triumphant over learning.

Surrender of Breda
Spain took the Dutch city of Breda on 5 June 1625 after a year-long siege. The event was later painted by Velázquez.

1652 Spanish troops regain Catalonia, following 12-year war with France

Calderón de la Barca

1669 Calderón de la Barca's last work, La Estátua de Prometeo, is published

1683–4 Louis XIV attacks Catalonia and Spanish Netherlands

1650	1660	1670	1680	1690	1700

1648 Holland achieves independence from Spain by Treaty of Westphalia, ending the Thirty Years War

1659 Peace of the Pyrenees signed with France. Louis XIV marries Felipe IV's daughter María Teresa, leading to Bourbon succession in Spain

Coin from the reign of Felipe IV

1700 Death of Carlos II brings Habsburg line to an end. Felipe V, the first Bourbon king, ascends the throne

Bourbons to First Republic

Isabel II

The War of the Spanish Succession ended in triumph for the Bourbons, who made Spain a centralized nation. Their power was at its height during the reign of the enlightened despot, Carlos III. But the 19th century was a troubled time. An invasion by revolutionary France led to the War of Independence (Peninsular War). Later came the Carlist Wars – caused by another dispute over the succession – liberal revolts and the short-lived First Republic.

SPAIN IN 1714

☐ *Domain after Treaty of Utrecht*

The Enlightenment
The Enlightenment brought new learning and novel projects. On 5 July 1784 this Montgolfier balloon rose above Madrid.

Spanish rebel faces death in a gesture of crucifixion.

A Franciscan friar is among the innocent victims.

Queen María Luisa
The dominating María Luisa of Parma, portrayed by Goya, forced her husband Carlos IV to appoint her lover, Manuel Godoy, prime minister in 1792.

Battle of Trafalgar
The defeat of the Franco-Spanish fleet by the British admiral, Lord Nelson, off Cape Trafalgar in 1805 was the end of Spanish sea power.

Hundreds of lives were taken in the executions, which lasted several days.

TIMELINE

1702–14 War of the Spanish Succession. Spain loses Netherlands and Gibraltar by Treaty of Utrecht

1724 Luis I (son of Felipe V) gains throne when his father abdicates, but dies within a year; Felipe V reinstated

1767 Carlos III expels Jesuits from Spain and Spanish colonies

1700	1720	1740	1760	178

1714 Siege and reduction of Barcelona by Felipe V

Felipe V, the first Bourbon king (1700–24)

Count of Floridablanca (1728–1808)

1762–3 English government declares war on Spanish over colonies in America

1782 Count of Floridablanca helps to recover Menorca from England

Carlos III Leaving Naples
When Fernando VI died without an heir in 1759, his half-brother Carlos VII of Naples was put on the Spanish throne as Carlos III. His enlightened reign saw the foundation of academies of science and art and the beginning of free trade.

French soldiers, operating on orders from Marshal Murat, execute Spanish patriots.

General Prim *(1814–70)*
General Prim was one of 19th-century Spain's most influential figures. He forced the abdication of Isabel II, and pursued liberal policies until assassinated in Madrid.

French infantry helmet

THE 3RD OF MAY BY GOYA *(1814)*
On 2 May 1808, in reaction to Napoleon's occupation of Spain, the people of Madrid rose in vain against the occupying French forces. The next day the French army took its revenge by executing hundreds of people, both rebels and bystanders. These events sparked off the War of Independence.

Baroque Magnificence
The sacristy of the Monasterio de la Cartuja in Granada is typical of Spanish Baroque, more sumptuous than anywhere else in Europe.

1805 Battle of Trafalgar. Nelson defeats French and Spanish at sea

1809 Wellington's troops join with Spanish to triumph over French at Talavera

Duke of Wellington

1841–3 María Cristina, followed by General Espartero, acts as regent for Isabel II

1868 Revolution under General Prim forces Isabel II into exile. Amadeo I is king for three years from 1870

| 1800 | 1820 | 1840 | 1860 |

1808–14 Joseph Bonaparte on throne. War of Independence

1812 Promulgation of liberal constitution in Cádiz leads to military uprising

1824 Peru is the last South American country to gain independence

1833–9 First Carlist War

1836 Mendizábal seizes monastic property for the Spanish state

1847–9 Second Carlist War

Carlist soldiers

Republicans and Anarchists

Primo de Rivera

Spain's First Republic lasted only a year (1873) and consumed four presidents. The late 19th century was a time of national decline, with Anarchism developing in reaction to rampant political corruption. The loss of Cuba, in 1898, was a low point for Spain, although there was a flurry of literary and artistic activity in the following years. The country's increasing instability was briefly checked by the dictatorship of Primo de Rivera. Spanish politics, however, were becoming polarized. Alfonso XIII was forced to abdicate and the ill-fated Second Republic was declared in 1931.

THE LEGACY OF SPANISH COLONIZATION IN 1900

☐ *Spanish-speaking territories*

Anarchist Propaganda
Anarchism was idealistic, though often violent. This poster states, "Anarchist books are weapons against Fascism".

Workers unite, calling for radical social reform.

Pío Baroja
Baroja (1872–1956) was one of the most gifted novelists of his day. He was too original to be grouped with the writers of the Generation of 1898, who tried to create a national renaissance after the loss of Spain's colonies.

POWER TO THE PEOPLE
Political protest was rife under the Second Republic, as shown by this Communist demonstration in the Basque Country in 1932. Industrial workers banded together, forming trade unions to demand better pay and working conditions, and staging strikes. The Spanish Communist Party developed later than the Anarchists, but eventually gained more support.

TIMELINE

1873 Declaration of First Republic, lasting only one year

First Republic's last president, Emilio Castelar (1832–99)

1888 Universal Exhibition in Barcelona creates new buildings and parks, such as the Parc de la Ciutadella

1897 Prime Minister Cánovas del Castillo assassinated by an Italian Anarchist

1870	1880	1890	1900

1875 Second Bourbon restoration puts Alfonso XII on throne

Alfonso XII and Queen María

1893 Anarchists bomb opera-goers in the Barcelona Liceu

1898 Cuba and Philippines gain independence from Spain following the Spanish-American War

1870–75 Third Carlist War

Tragic Week
Led by Anarchists and Republicans, workers in Barcelona took to the streets in 1909 to resist a military call-up. The reprisals were brutal.

Universal Exhibitions
In 1929, Seville and Barcelona were transformed by exhibitions promoting art and industry. The fairs brought international recognition.

EXPOSICION
INTERNACIONAL
BARCELONA 1929

The banner appeals for working-class solidarity.

Picasso
Born in Málaga in 1881, the artist Pablo Picasso spent his formative years as a painter in the city of Barcelona (see p148) before moving to Paris in the 1930s.

Cuban War of Independence
Cuba began its fight for freedom in 1895, led by local patriots such as Antonio Maceo. In the disastrous campaign, Spain lost 50,000 soldiers and most of its navy.

The Garrotte
Convicted Anarchists were executed by the garrotte – an iron collar that brutally strangled the victim while crushing the neck.

1912 Prime Minister José Canalejas murdered by Anarchists in Madrid

Second Republic election poster

1921 Crushing defeat of Spanish army at Anual, Morocco

1931 Proclamation of Second Republic with a two-year coalition between Socialists and Republicans

1933 General election returns right-wing government

1910   **1920**   **1930**

1909 Semana Trágica (Tragic Week) in Barcelona. Workers' revolt against conscription for Moroccan Wars quashed by Government troops

1923 Primo de Rivera stages victorious coup to become military dictator under Alfonso XIII

1930 Primo de Rivera resigns after losing military support

1931 Republicans win local elections, causing Alfonso XIII to abdicate

1934 Revolution of Asturian miners suppressed by army under General Franco

Civil War and the Franco Era

Nationalist generals rose against the government in 1936, starting the Spanish Civil War. The Nationalists, under General Franco, were halted by the Republicans outside Madrid, but with support from Hitler and Mussolini they inched their way to victory in the north and east. Madrid finally fell in early 1939. After the war, thousands of Republicans were executed in reprisals. Spain was internationally isolated until the 1950s, when the United States brought her into the western military alliance.

Franco

SPAIN ON 31 JULY 1936

☐ *Republican-held areas*

▨ *Nationalist-held areas*

Franco's Ideal World
Under Franco, Church and state were united. This poster shows the strong influence of religion on education.

Anguished mother with dead child

Composition reflecting total chaos

Nationalist Poster
A Nationalist poster adorned with Fascist arrows reads "Fight for the Fatherland, Bread and Justice".

GUERNICA *(1937)*
On behalf of advancing Nationalists, the Nazi Condor Legion bombed the Basque town of Gernika *(see p118)* on 26 April 1937 – a busy market day. This was Europe's first air raid on civilians, and it inspired Picasso's shocking *Guernica (see p299)*. Painted for a Republican Government exhibition in Paris, it is full of symbols of disaster.

TIMELINE

1936 Republican Popular Front wins the general election on 16 January. On 17 July, Nationalist generals rise against Republicans

1938 On 8 January, Republicans lose battle for Teruel in bitter cold

1939 In March, Madrid, Valencia and Alicante fall in quick succession to Franco's troops

1945 By end of World War II, Spain is diplomatically and politically isolated

1947 Spain declared monarchy with Franco as regent

1935	1940	1945	1950

1936 Nationalists declare Franco head of state on 29 September

1937 On 26 April, Nazi planes bomb Basque town of Guernica (Gernika-Lumo)

1939 Franco declares end of war on 1 April and demands unconditional surrender from Republicans

1938 On 23 December, Nationalists bomb Barcelona

1953 Deal with US permits American bases on Spanish soil in exchange for aid

Soldiers surrendering to Nationalist troops

GARCIA LORCA

Federico García Lorca (1898–1936) was Spain's most brilliant dramatist and lyric poet of the 1920s and 1930s. His homosexuality and association with the left, however, made him a target for Nationalist assassins. He was shot by an ad hoc firing squad near his home town of Granada.

Scene from his play *Blood Wedding*

A wounded horse representing the Spanish people

Witnesses to the massacre stare in wonder and disbelief.

The flower is a symbol of hope in the midst of despair.

Anarchist Poster
Anarchists fought for the Republic, forming agricultural collectives behind the lines. Their influence waned when they were discredited by the Communist Party.

Crucifixion gesture

Spanish Refugees
As the Nationalists came closer to victory, thousands of artists, writers, intellectuals and other Republican supporters fled Spain into indefinite exile.

The Hungry Years
Ration cards illustrate the post-war period when Spain nearly starved. Shunned by other nations, she received aid from the US in 1953 in return for accepting military bases.

1962 Tourism on the Mediterranean coast is boosted by official go-ahead

Sunbathers

1969 Franco declares Prince Juan Carlos his successor

1973 ETA assassinates Admiral Carrero Blanco, Franco's hard-line prime minister

1955	1960	1965	1970	1975

1959 Founding of ETA, Basque separatist group

1955 Spain joins United Nations

Franco's funeral, 23 November 1975

1970 "Burgos trials" of the regime's opponents outrage world opinion

1975 Death of Franco results in third Bourbon restoration as Juan Carlos is proclaimed king

Modern Spain

Franco's death left Spain's political future hanging in the balance. But few people wanted to preserve the old regime and the transition from dictatorship to democracy proved surprisingly swift and painless. The previously outlawed Socialist Workers' Party, under Felipe González, won the general election in 1982 and set about modernizing Spain. Considerable power has since been devolved to the regions. A major threat facing central government has been the persistent violence of ETA, the Basque separatist organization. Spain's international relations have been strengthened by her membership of NATO and the European Union.

Contemporary Spanish fashion

SPAIN TODAY

☐ *Spain*

▨ *Other European Union states*

Coup d'Etat, 23 February 1981
Civil Guard colonel, Antonio Tejero, held parliament at gunpoint for several hours. Democracy survived because King Juan Carlos refused to support the rebels.

Anti-NATO Protest Rally
When Spain joined NATO in 1982, some saw it as a reversal of Socialist ideals. To others it represented an improvement in Spain's international standing.

Castilla and León's modern pavilion was one of EXPO's 150 pavilions built to innovative designs.

Hi-tech floodlight

EXPO '92
Over 100 countries were represented at the Universal Exposition which focused world attention on Seville in 1992. The many pavilions displayed scientific, technological and cultural exhibits.

TIMELINE

Spanish royal family

1977 First free elections return centrist government under Adolfo Suárez. Political parties, including Communists, are legalized

1981 Military officers stage attempted coup d'etat to overthrow democracy

1983 Semi-autonomous regional governments are established to appease Basque Country and Catalonia

1992 Spain celebrates quincentenary of Columbus's voyage to America

1980

1985

1990

1982 Landslide electoral victory brings Socialist Workers' Party (PSOE), under Felipe González, to power. Football World Cup held in Spain

1986 Spain joins EC (now EU) and NATO

1992 Barcelona Olympics and Seville Expo '92 place Spain firmly within community of modern European nations

Tourism
From 1959–73 the number of annual visitors to Spain grew from 3 million to 34 million, transforming the once-quiet coasts and islands.

Felipe González Elected
In 1982 the Spanish Socialist Workers' Party (PSOE) leader was elected prime minister. González transformed Spain during his 13 years in power.

Leaning blue tower rises above Andalusia's pavilion.

Ana Belén
Spanish women have enjoyed ever greater freedom and opportunity since the advent of democracy. In a 1980s opinion poll, they voted the singer and actress, Ana Belén, the woman they most admired.

El País
Founded in Madrid in 1976, the liberal daily El País is the best-selling newspaper in Spain. During the transition to democracy it had a great influence on public opinion.

A monorail carried visitors around the site.

Barcelona Olympic Games
The opening ceremony of the Barcelona Olympics included stunning displays of music, dance and colourful costumes.

1994/5 Corruption scandals rock the long-serving government	**1996** In the general election on 3 March, González loses to a coalition led by Aznar		
	1998 ETA, the Basque separatist terrorist group, announces a ceasefire that lasts a year	**2004** José Luis Rodríguez Zapatero of the Spanish Socialist Party comes into power on 14 March	
1995	**2000**	**2005**	**2010**
Cobi, Barcelona Olympic Mascot	**2000** Spain celebrates 25 years of democracy and reign of Juan Carlos I	**2004** Madrid is hit by the worst terrorist attacks in Spain's modern history in March. Bombs detonated on the city's trains killed 191 people	

Rulers of Spain

Spain became a nation-state under Isabel and Fernando, whose marriage eventually united Castile and Aragón. With their daughter Juana's marriage, the kingdom was delivered into Habsburg hands. Carlos I and Felipe II were both capable rulers, but in 1700 Carlos II died without leaving an heir. After the War of the Spanish Succession, Spain came under the French Bourbons, who have ruled ever since – apart from an interregnum, two republics and Franco's dictatorship. The current Bourbon king, Juan Carlos I, a constitutional monarch, is respected for his support of democracy.

1665–1700
Carlos II

1479–1516
Fernando, King
of Aragón

1474–1504 Isabel,
Queen of Castile

1516–56 Carlos I of Spain
(Holy Roman Emperor
Charles V)

1598–1621 Felipe III

1400	1450	1500	1550	1600	1650
INDEPENDENT KINGDOMS		HABSBURG DYNASTY			
1400	1450	1500	1550	1600	1650

1469 Marriage of
Isabel and Fernando
leads to unification
of Spain

1504–16 Juana la
Loca (with
Fernando as regent)

1621–65 Felipe IV

Fernando and Isabel, the Catholic Monarchs

UNIFICATION OF SPAIN

In the late 15th century the two largest kingdoms in developing Christian Spain – Castile, with its military might, and Aragón (including Barcelona and a Mediterranean empire) – were united. The marriage of Isabel of Castile and Fernando of Aragón in 1469 joined these powerful kingdoms. Together the so-called Catholic Monarchs defeated the Nasrid Kingdom of Granada, the last stronghold of the Moors (see pp56–7). With the addition of Navarra in 1512, Spain was finally unified.

1556–98
Felipe II

1843–68 Isabel II reigns following the regency of her mother María Cristina (1833–41) and General Espartero (1841–3)

1814–33 First Bourbon restoration, following French rule: Fernando VII

1871–3 Break in Bourbon rule: Amadeo I of Savoy

1939–75 General Franco Head of State

1724 Luis I reigns after Felipe V's abdication, but dies within a year

1759–88 Carlos III

1931–9 Second Republic

1875–85 Second Bourbon restoration: Alfonso XII

1700	1750	1800	1850	1900	1950

BOURBON DYNASTY | BOURBON | BOURBON

1700	1750	1800	1850	1900	1950

1808–13 Break in Bourbon rule: Napoleon's brother, Joseph Bonaparte, rules as José I

1746–59 Fernando VI

1724–46 Felipe V reinstated as king upon the death of his son, Luis I

1788–1808 Carlos IV

1902–31 Alfonso XIII

1886–1902 María Cristina of Habsburg-Lorraine as regent for Alfonso XIII

1700–24 Felipe V

1873–4 First Republic

1868–70 The Septembrina Revolution

1975 Third Bourbon restoration: Juan Carlos I

NORTHERN SPAIN

Introducing Northern Spain

Increasing numbers of visitors are discovering the quiet, sandy beaches and deep green landscapes of Northern Spain. The Atlantic coast, from the Pyrenees to the Portuguese border, is often scenic but at its most attractive in the cliffs and rias of Galicia. Inland, the mild, wet climate has created lush meadows and broad-leaved forests, making this area ideal for a peaceful, rural holiday. The famous medieval pilgrimage route to the city of Santiago de Compostela crosses Northern Spain, its way marked by magnificent examples of Romanesque architecture. Plentiful seafood and dairy produce, and the outstanding red wines of La Rioja, add to the pleasure of a tour through this part of Spain.

Oviedo (see p106) *has a number of Pre-Romanesque churches, most notably the graceful Santa María del Naranco, and a fine Gothic cathedral.*

Lugo

A Coruña

Asturias

GALICIA
(See pp84–85)

ASTURIAS AND CANTABRIA
(see pp100–13)

Pontevedra

Ourense

The Rías Baixas (see p95) *is one of Spain's prettiest coastlines. Scattered around its pretty towns and villages are many quaint hórreos, grain stores, raised on stone stilts.*

Santiago de Compostela (see pp90–3) *attracts thousands of pilgrims and tourists each year. Its majestic cathedral was one of the most important shrines in medieval Christendom.*

The Picos de Europa *mountain range (see pp108–9) dominates the landscape of Asturias and Cantabria. Rivers have carved deep gorges through the mountains and there are many footpaths through a variety of spectacular scenery.*

| 0 kilometres | 50 |
| 0 miles | 25 |

Santillana del Mar (see p112), *with its well-preserved medieval streets, is one of the most picturesque towns in Spain. The Convento de Regina Coeli houses a small museum containing a collection of painted wooden figures and other works of religious art.*

San Sebastián (see p122), *the most elegant holiday resort in the Basque Country, is sited around a beautiful horseshoe bay of golden sandy beaches. The city hosts international arts events, including Spain's premier film festival.*

Cantabria

Vizcaya

Guipúzcoa

Álava

Navarra

THE BASQUE COUNTRY, NAVARRA AND LA RIOJA *(see pp114–35)*

La Rioja

Pamplona (see pp132–3), *the capital of Navarra since the 9th century, is best known for its annual fiesta, Los Sanfermines. The highlight of each day of riotous celebration is the* Encierro, *in which bulls stampede through the streets of the city.*

The Monasterio de Leyre (see p135), *founded in the early 11th century, was built in a lonely but attractive landscape. The monastery was once the burial place of the kings of Navarra and its crypt is among the finest examples of early Romanesque art in Spain.*

The Flavours of Northern Spain

The wild, wet north of Spain is as famous for its rain as it is for its culinary excellence. The rain keeps the pastures lush and green – perfect dairy farming terrain – and the Atlantic provides an incredible variety of seafood. The Basques, in particular, are celebrated chefs, and the region boasts some of the finest restaurants in Europe, along with gastronomic societies (called *txokos*) in every village. Inland and in the remoter regions you'll find old-fashioned country cooking – roast lamb and tender young beef, slow-cooked stews – and traditionally made cheeses.

Idiazbel cheese

Goose-neck barnacles piled high for sale in a local market

GALICIA

The westernmost tip of Spain, battered by the Atlantic into a series of plunging *rías*, is famous for its extraordinary wealth of seafood – from staples like cod to unusual delicacies like barnacles (*percebes*), which look like tiny dinosaur feet. Every bar will serve up a plate of *pulpo a la gallega* or a dish of

pimientos del padrón (one in every dozen has a spicy kick). Inland, you'll find tender veal, free-range chicken and delicate soft cheeses such as such as delicious *tetilla*.

ASTURIAS AND CANTABRIA

The bay-pocked coastline provides delicious fresh fish, often served simply grilled (try the fabulous sardines offered in almost every port)

or slowly simmered in casseroles. Inland, the lush green pastures form Spain's dairy country – most Spanish milk, cream and some of its finest cheeses come from this region. Try Asturian Cabrales, a pungent blue cheese, best accompanied by a glass of local cider. The mountains provide succulent meat and game, often traditionally stewed with beans, as in the celebrated Asturian dish of *fabada*.

Clams   Red mullet   Mackerel   Oysters
Elvers   Squid

Fish and seafood from the waters of northern Spain

REGIONAL DISHES AND SPECIALITIES

Unsurprisingly, seafood rules supreme along the coastline, from the ubiquitous octopus in a piquant sauce served in Galicia, to the extraordinary spider crabs which are a sought-after delicacy in the Basque Lands. The verdant pastures and rich farmland provide a wealth of fresh vege-tables, including Navarra's justly famous asparagus, along with all kinds of wonderful cheeses. Slow-cooked stews, an Asturian speciality, are particularly good in the mount-ains, along with tender lamb and outstanding game in season. The renowned wines from La Rioja are excellent, but those of adjoining Navarra are less pricey and often equally interesting. The crisp whites of Galicia and the Basque Lands are the perfect accompani-ment to the fresh seafood, and throughout the North you'll find powerful liqueurs flavoured with local herbs.

Cherries

Bacalao al Pil Pil *Salted cod is slowly cooked with olive oil, chilli and garlic to create this classic Basque dish.*

Array of *pinxos* laid out in a bar in the Basque Country

BASQUE COUNTRY

The Basque Country is a paradise for gourmets, renowned throughout Spain for the excellence of its natural produce and the creative brilliance of its chefs. Basque cuisine leans towards seafood, of which there is a dazzling variety: humble salted cod and hake (made extraordinary with delicious sauces) are most common, but sought-after delicacies include elvers (baby eels) and spider crab. Basque wines, drunk young and tart, are the perfect counterpoint. Bar counters groan with platters of *pinxos* (crusty bread with gourmet toppings), each one of them a miniature work of art, and the Basques also make wonderful cheeses, including delicate, smoky Idiazábel.

NAVARRA AND LA RIOJA

The fertile farmland of land-locked Navarra produces a spectacular array of fruit and vegetables such as aspara-gus, artichokes, cherries, chestnuts and peppers

Red peppers strung up to dry in the sun outside a house

(often hung in pretty strings to dry and used to flavour *embutidos*, or cured meats). In the Navarrese mountains, lamb is the most popular meat and you will find *cordero al chilindrón* (lamb stew) featuring on almost every menu. In season, you'll also find richly flavoured game, including partridge, hare and pheasant.

Tiny La Rioja is Spain's most famous wine region, producing rich, oaky reds and whites *(see pp78–9)*. The cuisine of La Rioja borrows from the neighbouring Basque Country and Navarra, with lamb featuring heavily, along with seafood and top-quality local vegetables.

ON THE MENU

Angulas a la Bilbaína Baby eels cooked in olive oil with garlic – a Basque delicacy.

Cocido Montañés Cantabrian stew of pork, spicy sausage, vegetables – and a pig's ear.

Fabada Asturiana Asturian beans stewed with cured meats and pork.

Pimientos del padrón A Gal-lego dish of green peppers fried in olive oil with rock salt.

Pulpo a la Gallega Octopus, cooked until tender in a spicy paprika sauce.

Trucha a la Navarra Trout, stuffed with ham and quickly grilled or fried.

Empanada Gallega *The perfect picnic snack, these golden pastries are stuffed with all kinds of fillings.*

Chilindrón de Cordero *A rich, hearty stew from the mountains of Navarra, this is made with succulent lamb.*

Leche Frita *"Fried milk" is a scrumptious, custardy dessert from Cantabria. Simple but utterly delicious.*

Wines of Northern Spain

Spain's most prestigious wine region, Rioja, is best
known for its red wines, matured to a distinctive
vanilla mellowness. Some of the most prestigious
bodegas were founded by émigrés from Bordeaux, and
Rioja reds are similar to claret. Rioja also produces
good white and rosé wines. Navarra reds and some
whites have improved dramatically, thanks to a government research programme. The Basque region
produces a tiny amount of the prickly, tart *txacoli*
(*chacolí*). Larger quantities of a similar wine are made
further west in Galicia, whose best
wines are full-bodied whites.

Repairing barrels in Haro, Rioja

Ribeiro, *the popular everyday wine
of Galicia, is slightly fizzy. It is often
served in white porcelain cups* (tazas).

Lagar de Cervera
*is from Rías Baixas,
where Spain's most
fashionable whites
are made from the
Albariño grape.*

KEY

- Rías Baixas
- Ribeiro
- Valdeorras
- Txacoli de Guetaria
- Rioja
- Navarra

0 kilometres   50

0 miles   25

WINE REGIONS

The wine regions of Northern Spain are
widely dispersed. Cradled between the
Pyrenees and the Atlantic are the important
regions of Rioja and Navarra. Rioja is divided
into the sub-regions of Rioja Alavesa, Rioja
Alta and Rioja Baja, divided by the Río Ebro.
The river also cuts through the wine region
of Navarra. To the north are some of the
vineyards of the Basque country: the miniscule Txacoli de Guetaria region. In the far
west lie the four wine regions of rugged,
wet Galicia: Rías Baixas, Ribeiro, Valdeorras,
and the newly created Ribera Sacra.

Wine village of El Villar de Álava in Rioja Alta

Gathering the grape harvest in the traditional way in Navarra

Remelluri, *one of the new single-estate "Château" Riojas, from the vineyards of Rioja Alavesa, is soft and not too oaky.*

Chivite, *from a family bodega in Navarra, is made entirely from Tempranillo and aged in the barrel, resulting in a style similar to Rioja.*

Viña Ardanza *is blended, as are most red Riojas. The best, like this* reserva, *are aged for two or more years in American oak casks.*

SANTANDER

BILBO (BILBAO)
Zumaia
Getaria
DONOSTIA (SAN SEBASTIÁN)

GASTEIZ (VITORIA)

IRUÑA (PAMPLONA)

Lizarra (Estella)

Haro
Logroño
Tafalla
Olite

Nájera
Calahorra
Arnedo
Alfaro
Corella
Tudela

KEY FACTS ABOUT WINES OF NORTHERN SPAIN

Location and Climate

Rioja and Navarra are influenced by both Mediterranean and Atlantic weather systems. The hillier, northwestern parts receive some Atlantic rain while the hot Ebro plain has a Mediterranean climate. The Basque region and Galicia are both cool, Atlantic regions with high rainfall. Soils everywhere are stony and poor, except in the Ebro plain.

Grape Varieties

The great red grape of Rioja and Navarra is Tempranillo. In Rioja it is blended with smaller quantities of Garnacha, Graciano and Mazuelo, while in Navarra Cabernet Sauvignon is permitted and blends excitingly with Tempranillo. Garnacha, also important in Navarra, is used for the excellent *rosados* (rosés). Whites of Navarra and Rioja are made mainly from the Viura grape. Galicia has many local varieties, of which the most important are Albariño, Loureira and Treixadura, which is now taking over from the inferior Palomino.

Good Producers

Rías Baixas: Fillaboa, Lagar de Fornelos, Morgadío, Santiago Ruiz. *Ribeiro:* Cooperativa Vinícola del Ribeiro. *Rioja:* Bodegas Riojanas (Canchales, Monte Real), CVNE (Imperial, Viña Real Oro), Faustino Martínez, Federico Paternina, Marqués de Cáceres, Marqués de Murrieta, Martínez Bujanda, Remelluri, La Rioja Alta (Viña Ardanza). *Navarra:* Bodega de Sarría, Guelbenzu, Julián Chivite (Gran Feudo), Magaña, Ochoa, Príncipe de Viana.

Forests of the North

Purple emperor butterfly

Much of Spain was once blanketed by a mantle of trees. Today, just ten per cent of the original cover remains, mostly in the mountainous north, where rainfall is high and slopes too steep for cultivation. Large areas of mixed deciduous forest – mainly beech, Pyrenean oak and chestnut, with some ash and lime – dominate the landscape, particularly in Cantabria and the Basque Country. The undergrowth of shrubs and flowering plants provides habitats for many insects, mammals and birds. The forests are also the refuge of Spain's last brown bears *(see p104)*.

Forest in Northern Spain in autumn

REGENERATION OF THE FOREST

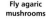

Fly agaric mushrooms

Dead materials – leaves, twigs and the excrement and bodies of animals – are broken down by various organisms on the forest floor, especially fungi, bacteria and ants. This process releases nutrients which are absorbed by trees and other plants, enabling them to grow.

Lichens *grow slowly and are sensitive to pollution. Their presence in a forest often indicates that it is in good health.*

The stag beetle *takes its name from the huge antler-like mandibles of the male. Despite their ferocious appearance, these beetles are harmless to humans.*

Millipede and fungus on a woodland floor

BEECH FOREST

Beech leaf and mast

Beech, the dominant species in the Cantabrian mountains and Pyrenees, grows on well-drained soils. Some trees retain their distinctive copper-red leaves through the winter. Beech mast (nuts) are collected to feed to pigs.

The thick crown shuts out light, inhibiting undergrowth.

Long, thin orange buds

Male golden orioles, *among the most colourful European birds, are hard to spot because they spend much of their time in the thick cover provided by old woodlands. Females and juveniles are a duller yellow-green with a brownish tail.*

Beech martens *are nocturnal. By day, they sleep in a hollow tree or another animal's abandoned nest. At night they feed on fruit, birds and small mammals.*

DISTRIBUTION OF BROAD-LEAVED FORESTS

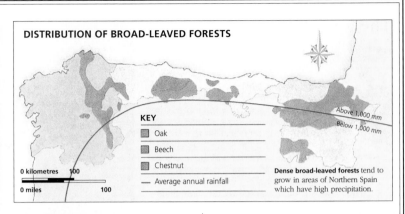

KEY

- Oak
- Beech
- Chestnut
- — Average annual rainfall

Above 1,000 mm

Below 1,000 mm

0 kilometres 100

0 miles 100

Dense broad-leaved forests tend to grow in areas of Northern Spain which have high precipitation.

CHESTNUT FOREST

Chestnut trees grow on well-drained acidic soils. They have slender yellow flowers and in summer produce their fruit, which is eaten by wild boar, dormice, squirrels and mice. The wood is hard and durable but splits easily.

Leaf and chestnut

Large leaves have sharp, serrated edges.

Few massive, spreading branches

Deep spiral ridges on trunk

OAK FOREST

Three main species of oak tree – pedunculate, Pyrenean and the evergreen holm oak – dominate the ancient woodlands of the north. Over 300 species of animal, such as wild boar, squirrels and nuthatches, feed off oaks.

Oak leaf and acorn

Grey twigs ending in numerous buds

The pipistrelle bat *is a nocturnal species common in woodlands. It catches and eats small insects in flight. Larger insects are taken to a perch. The bat hibernates in winter in a hollow tree or cave.*

The jay, *a member of the crow family, is a common but somewhat shy woodland bird with a distinctively raucous cry. It can be identified in flight by its white rump, black tail and above all by its bright blue wing patch.*

Blue tits *feed mainly in the tree canopy of broad-leaved woods and rarely come down to the ground. The male and female have similar, distinctive plumage. They may raise the back feathers of the crown if alarmed.*

Red squirrels *bury large numbers of acorns during autumn to last through winter, since these diurnal creatures do not hibernate. Many of the acorns are left to sprout into seedlings.*

The Road to Santiago

According to legend the body of Christ's apostle James was brought to Galicia. In 813 the relics were supposedly discovered at Santiago de Compostela, where a cathedral was built in his honour *(see pp92–3)*. In the Middle Ages half a million pilgrims a year flocked there from all over Europe, crossing the Pyrenees at Roncesvalles *(see p134)* or via the Somport Pass *(see p230)*. They often donned the traditional garb of cape, long staff and curling felt hat adorned with scallop shells, the symbol of the saint. The various routes, marked by the cathedrals, churches and hospitals built along them, are still used by travellers today.

St James on horseback

19th-century painting of the Pórtico da Gloria of Santiago cathedral

Astorga (see p352), *once a Roman city, was an important halt on the pilgrim route in the Middle Ages. The museum within its cathedral has a collection of gold and silver plate including a 13th-century gold filigree cross.*

A certificate *is given to pilgrims covering 100 km (62 miles) of the route on foot, or 200 km (125 miles) on horseback.*

O Cebreiro *(see p99)* has a 9th-century church and some of the ancient *pallozas* the pilgrims often used for shelter.

León *was one of the main pilgrim stops. Its cathedral (see pp354–5) contains one of Spain's finest collections of stained glass.*

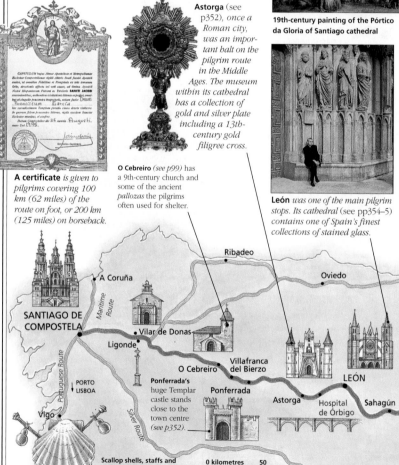

Ribadeo

A Coruña

Oviedo

SANTIAGO DE COMPOSTELA

Maritime Route

Vilar de Donas

Ligonde

Villafranca del Bierzo

O Cebreiro

LEÓN

Portuguese Route

PORTO LISBOA

Ponferrada's huge Templar castle stands close to the town centre *(see p352).*

Ponferrada

Astorga

Hospital de Órbigo

Sahagún

Vigo

Silver Route

Scallop shells, staffs and gourds to carry water are symbols of the pilgrimage.

| 0 kilometres | 50 |
| 0 miles | 50 |

SALAMANCA

ROMANESQUE CHURCH ARCHITECTURE

The Romanesque style of architecture *(see p24)* was brought to Spain from France during the 10th and 11th centuries. As the pilgrimage to Santiago became more popular, many glorious religious buildings were constructed along its main routes. Massive walls, few windows, round heavy arches and barrel vaulting are typical features of Romanesque architecture.

Carved capital

Octagonal lantern   **Twin round towers**   **Barrel vault**

Thick walls   **Round arch**

Façade   **Cross-section**

San Martín de Frómista (see p368), *built in the 11th century, is the only complete example of the "pilgrimage" style of Romanesque. The nave and aisles are almost the same height and there are three parallel apses.*

Parallel apses   **Aisle**   **Nave**

Floorplan

Pamplona's (see p132) *Gothic cathedral was one of the pilgrims' first stops after crossing the Pyrenees at Roncesvalles.*

Santo Domingo de la Calzada's *(see p128)* pilgrim hospital is now a parador.

Puente la Reina (see p131) *takes its name from the 11th-century humpbacked bridge (puente), built for pilgrims and still used by pedestrians.*

ROUTES TO SANTIAGO

Several traditional pilgrimage roads converge on Santiago de Compostela. The main road from the Pyrenees is known as the French Route, with the Aragonese Route as a variation.

Santander

Donostia (San Sebastián) ↗ PARIS

Bilbo (Bilbao)

Northern Route

Frómista preserves one of the finest Romanesque churches on the French route.

↗ LE PUY VEZELAY

Orreaga (Roncesvalles)   Valcarlos

↑ ARLES

Iruña (Pamplona)

Lizarra (Estella)

Santo Domingo de la Calzada   Puente la Reina   Sangüesa   Jaca

San Juan de Ortega   French Route   San Juan de la Peña

Frómista   Nájera   Logroño

BURGOS

Burgos has a magnificent Gothic cathedral *(see pp372–3).*

GALICIA

LUGO · A CORUNA · PONTEVEDRA · OURENSE

emote in the northwest corner of the peninsula, Galicia is the country's greenest region. In its hilly interior, smallholdings are farmed by traditional methods. Galicia is Spain's main seafaring region – three of its four provinces have an Atlantic coast-line, and its cuisine is based on superb seafood. The Galicians, whose origins are Celtic, are fiercely proud of their culture and language.

Much of Galicia still has a medieval quality. Some inland farms are divided into plots too tiny or steep for tractors to work, so oxen and horses are used for ploughing. Grain is stored in quaint, pillared granaries called *hórreos*. The misty, emerald countryside abounds with old granite villages and is dotted with *pazos* – traditional stone manor houses.

The discovery of the supposed tomb of St James the Apostle, in the 9th century, confirmed medieval Santiago de Compostela as Europe's most important religious shrine after St Peter's in Rome. Pilgrims and tourists still follow this ancient route of pilgrimage across Northern Spain. The Galician coast is incised by many fjord-like rias; the loveliest of these are the Rías Baixas in the west. Elsewhere it juts defiantly into the Atlantic in rocky headlands, such as Cabo Fisterra, Spain's most westerly point. Many people still make a living from the sea. Vigo in Pontevedra is the most important fishing port in Spain.

Galicia's official language, used on most signs, is *gallego*. It has similarities to the language of Portugal, which borders Galicia to the south. The Celtic character of this haunting land is still evident in the Galicians' favourite traditional instrument, the bagpipes.

Staple crops – maize, cabbages and potatoes – growing on the harsh land around Cabo Fisterra

◁ The west façade of Santiago de Compostela's cathedral, overlooking the Praza do Obradoiro

Exploring Galicia

Santiago de Compostela is Galicia's major tourist attraction. This beautiful city is the centrepiece of a region with many fine old towns, especially Betanzos, Mondoñedo, Lugo and Pontevedra. The resorts along the coastline of the wild Rías Altas, with their backdrop of forest-covered hills, offer good bathing. The Rías Baixas, the southern part of Galicia's west coast, has sheltered coves and sandy beaches, and excellent seafood in abundance. Travelling through the interior, where life seems to have changed little in centuries, is an ideal way to spend a peaceful, rural holiday.

Students in traditional dress playing music in Pontevedra

SIGHTS AT A GLANCE

The isolated monastery at Ribas de Sil

GETTING AROUND

The region's main airports are at A Coruña, Santiago de Compostela and Vigo. A network of motorways connects Verín, Vigo, A Coruña and O Cebreiro, but traffic along the coast can be heavy. Rail lines link Galicia's major cities and towns along the north coast are served by the FEVE line (*see p679*). There are coach services between the major cities. Be aware that as Spain is changing its road numbering system some of the roads featured here may differ from new road signs.

Calvary in Pontevedra's Praza de la Herreria

KEY

▬▬	Motorway
= =	Motorway under construction
▬	Major road
▬	Minor road
▬	Scenic route
▬	Main railway
—	Minor railway
▨▨	International border
▬	Regional border

Carved coat of arms on a house-front in Mondoñedo

Rías Altas ❶

Lugo & A Coruña. 🚶 10,000. 🚂 Ribadeo. 🚌 Viveiro. 🚏 Foz, 982 14 06 75. 🛒 Tue.

Deep rias are interspersed with coves and headlands along the beautiful north coast from Ribadeo to A Coruña. Inland are hills covered with forests of pine and eucalyptus. Many of the small resorts and fishing villages are charming.

The lovely, winding **Ría de Ribadeo** forms the border with Asturias. To the west of it is the small fishing port of **Foz**, which has two good beaches. Nearby, the 10th-century Iglesia de San Martín de Mondoñedo, standing alone on a hill, contains carvings of biblical scenes on its transept capitals – note the story of Lazarus. **Viveiro**, a summer holiday resort 35 km (22 miles) away, is a handsome old town surrounded by Renaissance walls and gateways, typically Galician glassed-in balconies or *galerías*, and a Romanesque church. Near the pretty fishing village of O Barqueiro is the headland of Estaca de Bares, with its lighthouse and wind turbines.

Westward along the coast, the lovely **Ría de Ortigueira** leads to the fishing port of the same name, characterized by neat white houses. Around this area there are also many wild and unspoiled beaches.

High cliffs rise out of the sea near the village of **San Andrés de Teixido**, whose church is the focal point for

pilgrims on 8 September. According to legend, those who fail to visit the church in their lifetime will come back to it as an animal in the afterlife. The village of **Cedeira**, which sits on a quiet bay, is a rich summer resort with neat lawns, modern houses with *galerías*, and a long, curving beach.

Mondoñedo ❷

Lugo. 🚶 4,900. 🚂 🚏 Plaza de la Catedral 34, 982 50 71 77. 🛒 Thu. 🎉 Nuestra Señora de los Remedios (1st Sun after 8 Sep), San Lucas (18 Oct), As Quendas (1st May).

This delightful town is set in a fertile inland valley. Stately houses with carved coats of arms and *galerías* are in the main square. This is dominated by the **cathedral**, a building of golden stone in a mix of styles. It has 18th-century Baroque towers, a Roman-esque portal with a 16th-century stained-glass rose window and 17th-century cloisters. A statue in the south ambulatory, Nuestra Señora la Inglesa, was rescued from St Paul's cathedral in London. The **Museo Dioces-ano**, which is entered through the cathedral, contains statues, altarpieces and works by Zurbarán and El Greco.

🏛 **Museo Diocesano**
Plaza de la Catedral. **Tel** 982 50 70 90. 🕐 Summer (otherwise call to visit). 🎫

Betanzos ❸

A Coruña. 🚶 13,000. 🚂 🚌 🚏 Calle Emilio Romay 1, 981 77 36 93. 🛒 Tue, Thu & Sat. 🎉 San Roque (14–25 Aug).

The handsome town of Betanzos lies in a fertile valley slightly inland. Its broad main square has a replica of the Fountain of Diana at Versailles. In its steep narrow streets are fine old houses and Gothic churches. The **Iglesia de Santiago**, built in the 15th century by the tailors' guild, has a statue of St James on horseback above the door. The **Iglesia de San Francisco**, dated 1387, has statues of wild boars and a heraldic emblem of Knight Fernán Pérez de Andrade, whose 15th-century tomb is inside the church. For centuries his family were the overlords of the region.

Environs: 20 km (12 miles) north is the large, though pretty, fishing village of **Pontedeume**, with its narrow, hilly streets. Its medieval bridge still carries the main road to the large industrial town of **Ferrol**, to the north.

Ornate tomb in the Iglesia de San Francisco in Betanzos

Originally a medieval port, Ferrol became an important naval base and dockyard town in the 18th century, and its Neo-Classical buildings survive from that time. General Franco (*see pp66–7*) was born in Ferrol in 1892.

Pavement cafés in Betanzos' Plaza de García Hermanos

Stone cross standing above the perilous waters of the Costa da Morte

A Coruña ④

A Coruña. 🏛 246,000. ✈ 🚂 🚌
🛈 Avda. de la Marina 18, 981 18
43 44. 🎉 Fiestas de María Pita (Aug).
www. turismocoruna.com

This proud city and busy port
has played a sizeable role in
Spanish maritime history.
Felipe II's doomed Armada
sailed from here to England
in 1588 *(see p59)*. Today, the
sprawling industrial suburbs
contrast with the elegant
town centre, which is laid out
on an isthmus leading to a
headland. The **Torre de
Hércules**, Europe's oldest
working lighthouse, is a
famous local landmark. Built
by the Romans and rebuilt in
the 18th century, it still flashes
across the deep. Climb its 242
steps for a wide ocean view.

On the large, arcaded Praza
María Pita, the city's main
square, is the handsome town
hall. The sea promenade of
La Marina is lined with tiers of
glass-enclosed balconies or
galerías. Built as protection
against the strong winds, they
explain why A Coruña is often
referred to as the City of Glass.
The peaceful, tiny Prazuela
da Bárbaras is enchanting.

A Coruña has several fine
Romanesque churches such as
the **Iglesia de Santiago**, with
a carving of its saint on horseback situated beneath the

tympanum, and the **Iglesia de
Santa María**. This church, featuring a tympanum carved with
the Adoration of the Magi, is
one of the best-preserved 12th-
century buildings in Galicia.

The quiet Jardín de San
Carlos contains the tomb of
the Scottish general Sir John
Moore who was killed in
1809 as the British army
evacuated the port during
Spain's War of Independance
from France *(see p62)*.

The lofty Torre de Hércules
lighthouse at A Coruña

Costa da Morte ⑤

A Coruña. 🚌 A Coruña, Malpica,
Santiago de Compostela. 🛈 A Coruña,
981 22 18 22.

From Malpica to Fisterra the
coast is wild and remote. It is
called the "Coast of Death"
because of the many ships
lost in storms or smashed on
the rocks by gales over the
centuries. But the headlands
are majestic and the sunsets
beautiful. Inland, the countryside is breezy and open. There
are no coastal towns, only simple villages, where fishermen
gather gastronomic *percebes*
(barnacles), destined for the
region's restaurants.

One of the most northerly
points of the Costa da Morte,
Malpica, has a seabird sanctuary. Laxe has good beaches
and safe bathing. **Camariñas**,
one of the most appealing
places on this coast, is a fishing
village where women make
bobbin-lace in the streets.
Beside the lighthouse on
nearby Cabo Vilán, a group
of futuristic wind turbines, tall
and slender, swirl in graceful
unison – a haunting sight.

To the south is Corcubión,
exuding a faded elegance,
and lastly, **Cabo Fisterra**
"where the land ends". This
cape, with its lighthouse, is a
good place to watch the sun
go down over the Atlantic.

Street-by-Street: Santiago de Compostela ❻

In the Middle Ages Santiago de Compostela was Christendom's third most important place of pilgrimage *(see pp82–3)*, after Jerusalem and Rome. Around the Praza do Obradoiro is an ensemble of historic buildings that has few equals in Europe. The local granite gives a harmonious unity to the mixture of architectural styles. With its narrow streets and old squares, the city centre is compact enough to explore on foot. Two other monuments worth seeing are the Convento de Santo Domingo de Bonaval, to the east of the centre and the Colegiata Santa Maria la Real del Sar, a 12th-century Romanesque church, located to the east of the city.

Vegetable stall in Santiago market

★ Convento de San Martiño Pinario
The Baroque church of this monastery has a huge double altar and an ornate Plateresque façade with carved figures of saints and bishops.

Pazo de Xelmírez

★ Hostal de los Reyes Católicos
Built by the Catholic Monarchs as an inn and hospital for sick pilgrims, and now a parador (see p562), this magnificent building has an elaborate Plateresque doorway.

Praza do Obradoiro
This majestic square is one of the world's finest and the focal point for pilgrims arriving in the city. The cathedral's Baroque façade dominates the square.

The Pazo de Raxoi, with its Classical façade, was built in 1772 and houses the town hall.

Convento de San Paio de Antealtares
This is one of the oldest monasteries in Santiago. It was founded in the 9th century to house the tomb of St James, now in the cathedral.

VISITORS' CHECKLIST

A Coruña. 🏘 97,000. ✈ 12 km (6 miles) north. 🚍 Calle Hórreo 75a, 902 24 02 02. 🚌 Avenida Rodriguez de Viguri, 981 54 24 16. 🛈 Calle Rúa do Villar 63, 981 55 51 29. 🛒 Wed (animal), Thu. 🎉 Semana Santa (Easter Week), Santiago Day (25 July).

Praza da Quintana, under the cathedral clock tower, is one of the city's most elegant squares.

Praza das Praterias
The Goldsmiths' Doorway of the cathedral opens on to this charming square with Fountain dos Cavalos in the centre.

KEY

─ ─ ─ Suggested route

─ ─ ─ Pilgrims' route

Rúa Nova is a handsome arcaded old street leading from the cathedral to the newer part of the city.

To tourist information

0 metres 100
0 yards 100

Colegio de San Jerónimo

STAR SIGHTS

★ Convento de San Martiño Pinario

★ Hotel de los Reyes Católicos

★ Cathedral

★ Cathedral
This grand towering spectacle has welcomed pilgrims to Santiago for centuries. Though the exterior has been remodelled over the years, the core of the building has remained virtually unchanged since the 11th century.

Santiago Cathedral

With its twin Baroque towers soaring high over the Praza do Obradoiro, this monument to St James is a majestic sight, as befits one of the great shrines of Christendom (*see pp82–3*). The present building dates from the 11th–13th centuries and stands on the site of the 9th-century basilica built by Alfonso II. Through the famous Pórtico da Gloria is the same interior that met pilgrims in medieval times. The choir, designed by Maestro Mateo, has been completely restored.

The gigantic botafumeiro

"Passport" – proof of a pilgrim's journey

The twin towers are the cathedral's highest structures at 74 m (243 ft).

Statue of St James

★ **West Façade**
The richly sculpted Baroque Obradoiro façade was added in the 18th century.

Pazo de Xelmírez

★ **Pórtico da Gloria**
The sculpted Doorway of Glory, with its statues of apostles and prophets, is 12th century.

The Santo dos Croques (Saint of Bumps) has greeted pilgrims since the 12th century. Touching this statue with the forehead is said to impart luck and wisdom.

Tapestry Museum
A new addition to this collection of antique tapestries is an exhibition of Oriental medieval cloths dating as far back as the 13th century.

STAR FEATURES

★ West Façade

★ Pórtico da Gloria

★ Porta das Praterias

The *botafumeiro*, a giant censer, is swung high above the altar by eight men during important services.

Mondragon Chapel (1521) contains fine wrought-iron grilles and vaulting.

VISITORS' CHECKLIST

Praza do Obradoiro. *Tel* 981 58 35 48. ☐ 7am–10pm daily. ✚ 9:30am, noon, 7:30pm Mon–Fri, 10am, noon, 1pm, 6pm & 7:30pm Sat & Sun. ☐ **Museum** *Tel* 981 56 05 27. ☐ daily. ● 1 & 6 Jan, 25 Jul, 15 Aug, 25 Dec. 🖺

Clock Tower

High Altar
Visitors can pass behind the ornate high altar to embrace the silver mantle of the 13th-century statue of St James.

Cloisters

★ **Porta das Praterias**
The 12th-century Gold-smiths' Doorway is rich in bas-relief sculptures of biblical scenes.

Crypt
The relics of St James and two disciples are said to lie in a tomb in the crypt, under the altar, in the original 9th-century foundations.

Chapterhouse

Padrón **❼**

A Coruña. 🏘 *9,500.* 🚉 🚌 🛈
Avenida Compostela, 627 21 07 77.
📅 *Sun.* 🎉 *San Isidro (15 May),
Santiago (24–5 Jul).*

This quiet town on the Río
Ulla, known for its piquant
green peppers, was a major
seaport until it silted up. Legend has it the boat carrying
the body of St James to Galicia
(see p82) arrived here. The
supposed mooring stone, or
padrón, lies below the altar
of the church by the bridge.
   The leafy avenue beside the
church features in the poems of
one of Galicia's greatest writers,
Rosalia de Castro (1837–85).
Her home, where she spent
her final years, has been
converted into a museum.

Environs
The estuary town of Noia
(Noya) lies on the coast 20 km
(12 miles) west. Its Gothic
church has a finely carved portal.
East of Padrón is Pazo de Oca, a
manor house, with a crenellated
tower, idyllic gardens and a lake.

🏛 **Museo Rosalia de Castro**
La Matanza. **Tel** *981 81 12 04.*
⬭ *Tue–Sun.* 🎟 ♿

The picturesque gardens and lake of Pazo de Oca

A Toxa **❽**

Near O Grove. 🚌 🛈 *Ayuntamiento,
O Grove, 986 73 14 15.* 📅 *Fri.*

A tiny pine-covered island
joined to the mainland by a
bridge, A Toxa (La Toja) is
one of the most stylish resorts
in Galicia. The *belle époque*
palace-hotel *(see p561)* and
luxury villas add to the island's
elegant atmosphere. A Toxa's
best-known landmark is the
small church covered with
scallop shells. Across the bridge
is O Grove (El Grove), a
thriving family resort and fishing port on a peninsula, with
holiday hotels and flats alongside glorious beaches.

Scallop-covered roof of the church on A Toxa island

Pontevedra **❾**

Pontevedra. 🏘 *80,000.* 🚉 🚌
🛈 *Calle General Gutierrez Mellado 1,
986 85 08 14.* 📅 *Sat.* 🎉 *Fiestas de
la Peregrina (second week in Aug).*

Pontevedra lies inland, at the
head of a long ria that is
backed by green hills. The
delightful old town is typically
Galician and has a network of
cobbled alleys and tiny graceful squares with granite calvaries, arcades, flower-filled balconies and excellent tapas bars.
On the south side of the old
town are the Gothic **Ruinas
de Santo Domingo**. It is now a
museum containing Roman
steles and Galician coats of
arms and tombs. To the west,
the 16th-century **Iglesia de
Santa María la Mayor** contains a magnificent Plateresque
(see p25) façade that includes
richly carved figures of oars-
men and fishermen at the top.
   On the **Praza de la Leña**,
two 18th-century mansions
form the **Museo de
Pontevedra**, one of the best
museums in Galicia. The
Bronze Age treasures found
locally are superb. Among the
paintings on display are 15th-
century Spanish primitives, and
canvases by Zurbarán and
Goya. The top floor holds a
collection of drawings and
paintings by Alfonso Castelao, a
Galician artist and nationalist,
who forcefully depicted the
misery endured by his people
during the Spanish Civil War.

🏛 **Museo de Pontevedra**
Calle Pasanteria 10–12. **Tel** *986 85
14 55.* ⬭ *Oct– May: 10am–1:30pm,
4:30–8pm Tue–Sat; Jun–Sep: 10am–
2:15pm, 5–8:45pm Tue–Sat, 11am–
2pm Sun.* 🎟 *for non-EU.*

Rías Baixas

This southern part of Galicia's west coast consists of four large rias or inlets between pine-covered hills. The beaches are good, the scenery is lovely, the bathing safe and the climate much milder than on the wilder coast to the north. Though areas such as Vilagarcía de Arousa and Panxón have become popular holiday resorts, much of the Rías Baixas (Rías Bajas) coastline is unspoiled, such as the quiet stretch from Muros to Noia. This part of the coastline provides some of Spain's most fertile fishing grounds. Mussel-breeding platforms are positioned in neat rows along the rias, looking like half-submerged submarines; and in November, the women harvest clams.

Muros, a pretty little fortified port, has well-preserved examples of typical Galician architecture.

Between Muros and Noia
the coast is less built-up than further south. This beautiful open coast, bare and rocky, is backed by hills.

Vilagarcía de Arousa is a popular resort with a pleasant waterfront promenade and good sailing and water sports facilities.

Cambados, known for its white wine, has a paved square, the Plaza de Fefiñanes, lined by fine old houses.

Pontevedra is the lively provincial capital and has a picturesque setting by a deep ria.

Hío, a small fishing village with a good beach, is noted for having one of the finest carved calvaries in Galicia.

Combarro *is a picturesque fishing village known for its* hórreos (see p27) *on the seafront.*

The Illas Cíes have white sand, clear water and a bird sanctuary.

Panxón, *across the broad bay from Baiona (see p96), is a popular holiday resort with excellent sandy beaches.*

0 kilometres   10

0 miles   5

Noia · Muros · Porto do Son · Mirador da Curota · Illa de Arousa · Ribeira · Vilagarcía de Arousa · Vilanova de Arousa · Cambados · Illa de Sálvora · Illa da Toxa · Combarro · Pontevedra · Illa de Ons · Sanxenxo · Marín · Mirador de Cotorredondo · Hío · Cangas · Mirador da Madroa · Illas Cíes · Vigo · Panxon · Baiona

Cannons on the battlements of Monterreal fortress, Baiona

Vigo **⑩**

Pontevedra. 🏠 *300,000.* ☒ 🚉
🚌 🛈 *Calle Teófilo Llorente 5, 986
22 47 57.* 🚢 *Wed, Sun.* 🎉 *Cristo
de los Afligidos (3rd Sun in Jul), Cristo
de la Victoria (1st Sun in Aug).*

Galicia's largest town is
also the biggest fishing port
in Spain. It is situated in an
attractive setting near the
mouth of a deep ría spanned
by a high suspension bridge,
and is surrounded by wooded
hills. Vigo isn't noted for its
old buildings but
does have striking
modern sculptures
such as Juan José
Oliveira's horses
statue in the Praza
de España. The
oldest part of the town,
Barrio del Berbes, is
near the port and
used to be the
sailors' quarter.
Its cobbled alleys
are full of bars,
and you can
find some
of the

Bronze sculpture by Oliveira in
Vigo's Praza de España

finest tapas, especially the
seafood. The Mercado de la
Piedra, near the port, sells
reasonably priced fish and
shellfish – particularly oysters.

Baiona **⑪**

Pontevedra. 🏠 *11,000.* 🚉 🛈
Calle Ventura Misa 17, 986 35 63 85.
🚢 *Mon in Sabaris (nearby).* 🎉 *Santa
Liberata (20 Jul), Virgen de la Anunciada
(1st Sun in Aug).* www.baiona.org

The Pinta, one of the caravels
from the fleet of Christopher
Columbus, arrived at this small
port on 1 March 1493,
bringing the first news of the
discovery of the New World.
Today Baiona (Bayona), which
is sited on a broad bay, is a
popular summer resort, its
harbour a mix of pleasure
and fishing boats. The 12th to
17th-century **Iglesia Antigua
Colegiata de Santa María** is
Romanesque with Cistercian
influences. Symbols on the
arches indicate the local guilds
that helped build the church.
A royal fortress once stood
on Monterreal promontory, to
the north of town. Sections of
its defensive walls remain, but
the interior has been converted
into a smart parador *(see
p560).* A walk around the
battlements offers superb
views of the coast.
On the coast a short dis-
tance to the south is a huge
granite and porcelain statue of
the **Virgen de la Roca** sculpted
by Antonio Palacios in 1930. It
is possible for visitors to climb
up inside the statue.

A Guarda **⑫**

Pontevedra. 🏠 *10,000.* 🚉 🛈 *Praza
do Reló, 986 61 00 00.* 🚢 *Sat.* 🎉
*Monte de Santa Tecla (second week of
Aug).* www.concellodaguarda.com

The little fishing port of A
Guarda (La Guardia) has a
reputation for good seafood
and is particularly well known
for the quality of its lobsters.
On the slopes of Monte de
Santa Tecla are the remains of
a Celtic settlement of some
100 round stone dwellings
which are dated around
600–200 BC. The **Museo de
Monte de Santa Tecla** is
situated on a nearby hilltop.

Environs
About 10 km (6 miles) north,
the tiny Baroque **Monasterio
de Santa María** stands by the
beach at Oia. Semi-wild horses
roam the surrounding hills and,
in May and June, are rounded
up for branding in a series of
day-long fiestas *(see p98).*

🏛 **Museo de Monte de
Santa Tecla**
A Guarda. *Tel 986 61 00 00.* ⭘
Mar– Dec: daily. 🎫 *for hilltop access.*

Circular foundations of Celtic
dwellings at A Guarda

Tui **⑬**

Pontevedra. 🏠 *17,500.* 🚉 🚌
🛈 *Calle Colon, 986 60 17 89.* 🚢 *Thu.*
🎉 *San Telmo (week after Easter);
Descent of the Río Miño (Aug).*

Spain's main frontier town
with Portugal, Tui (Tuy)
stands on a hillside above the
Río Miño. Its graceful old
streets curve up to an old quarter and the 12th-century hilltop
cathedral. The two countries
were often at war during the
Middle Ages, and as a result
the church is built in the style

Unloading the catch in Spain's largest fishing port, Vigo

FISHING IN SPAIN

The Spanish eat more seafood per head of population than any other European nation except Portugal. Half of this is caught by Galician fishing fleets. Some 90,000 fishermen and 20,000 boats land over a million tonnes of fish and shellfish a year, much of this caught offshore where sardines, tuna, lobster and clams are plentiful. In recent years, the stocks in the seas around Spain have become depleted by over-fishing, forcing deep-sea trawlers to travel as far as Canada and Iceland.

ornate altarpiece and Gothic choir stalls. In the garden is the 10th-century Mozarabic **Iglesia de San Miguel**.

Environs

At **Santa Comba de Bande**, 26 km (16 miles) to the south, is an even older little church. The features of this 7th century Visigothic *(see pp50–1)* church include a lantern turret and a horseshoe arch that has carved marble pillars.

Verín **❶**

Ourense. 🏠 *14,500.* 🚉 **ℹ**
Avenida San Lazaro 26–8, 988 41 16 14. 🚃 *3rd, 11th & 23rd of month.*
🎪 *Santa Maria la Mayor (15 Aug).*

Though it stands amid vineyards, Verín produces more than wine. Its mineral springs have given it a thriving bottled water industry. The town has many old houses with arcades and glass balconies *(galerías)*.

of a fortress, with towers and battlements. It has a cloister and choir stalls and a richly decorated west porch.

Nearby is the **Iglesia de San Telmo**, dedicated to the patron saint of fishermen, whose Baroque ornamentation shows a Portuguese influence. Near the cathedral is an iron bridge, the **Puente Internacional**, built by Gustave Eiffel in 1884 to stretch across the river to Valença do Minho in Portugal.

The Romanesque **Iglesia de Santo Domingo**, situated beside the Parque de la Alameda, contains ivy-covered cloisters and tombs with delicately carved effigies. The church overlooks the river, which is used in August for the Descent of the Río Miño, a canoe race and fiesta.

Celanova **❶**

Ourense. 🏠 *6,200.* 🚉 **ℹ** *Plaza Mayor 1, 988 43 22 01.* 🚃 *Thu.*
🎪 *San Roque (15 Aug).*

On the main square of this little town is the massive **Monasterio de San Salvador**, which was formerly one of the most important monasteries in Spain. Founded during the 10th century and later rebuilt, it is mainly Baroque, though one of its two lovely cloisters is Renaissance. The enormous church of this Benedictine monastery has an

Ceramic tiled floor of the Iglesia de San Miguel

The **Castillo de Monterrei**, built during the wars with Portugal, is 3 km (2 miles) to the west. Inside its three rings of walls are a 15th-century keep, an arcaded courtyard, and a 13th-century church with a delicately carved portal. The castle once housed a monastery and hospital (now a hostal for the pilgrims).

The Castillo de Monterrei, standing high above the town of Verín

GALICIA'S FIESTAS

Os Peliqueiros *(Carnival, Feb/Mar),* Laza (Ourense). Dressed up in grinning masks and outlandish costumes, with cowbells tied to their belts and brandishing sticks, Os Peliqueiros take to the streets on Carnival Sunday. They are licensed to lash out at onlookers, who are forbidden to retaliate. On Carnival Monday morning a battle takes place, with flour, water and live ants used as ammunition. Laza's carnival comes to an end on the Tuesday with a reading of the satirical "Donkey's Will" and the burning of an effigy.

The outrageous costumes of
Os Peliqueiros in Laza

A Rapa das Bestas *(May and Jun),* Oia (Pontevedra). Semi-wild horses are rounded up by local farmers for their manes and tails to be cut. What was once a chore is now a popular fiesta.
Flower pavements *(Corpus Christi, May/Jun),* Ponteareas (Pontevedra). The streets of the town along which the Corpus Christi procession passes are carpeted with intricate designs made from brightly coloured flower petals.
St James's Day *(25 Jul),* Santiago de Compostela. On the night before, there is a firework display in the Praza do Obradoiro. The celebrations are especially wild when 25 July falls on a Sunday.

Ourense   🔟

Ourense. 🏛 *110,000.* 🚉 🚌
ℹ *Calle as Burgas 12, 988 36 60 64.*
📅 *7th & 17th of each month.* 🎉
Os Maios (3 May); San Martin (11 Nov).

The old quarter of Ourense was built around the city's well-known thermal springs, Fonte as Burgas. Even today, these spout water at a temperature of 65°C (150°F) from three fountains.

This old part of the town is the most interesting, particularly the small area around the arcaded Plaza Mayor. Here the **cathedral**, founded in 572 and rebuilt in the 12th–13th centuries, has a vast gilded reredos by Cornelis de Holanda. On the triple-arched doorway are carved multicoloured figures reminiscent of the Pórtico da Gloria at Santiago *(see p92).* Nearby is the elegant 14th-century cloister, the **Claustro de San Francisco**.

One of the city's landmarks is the 13th-century **Puente Romano**, a seven-arched bridge which crosses the Río Miño, north of the town. It is built on Roman foundations and still used by traffic.

Environs
Allariz, 25 km (16 miles) south, and Ribadavia, to the west, have old Jewish quarters with narrow streets and Romanesque churches. Ribadavia is also noted for its Ribeiro wines – a dry white and a port-like red *(see p78)* – and has a wine museum.

Ornate Gothic reredos in the
cathedral at Ourense

Monasterio de Ribas de Sil   🔟

Ribas de Sil. 🚌 *San Esteban de Sil.*
🚌 *from Ourense.* **Tel** *988 01 01 01
(town hall).* ⭕ *Wed–Sun.*

Near its confluence with the Miño, the Río Sil carves a deep curving gorge in which dams form two reservoirs of dark green water. A hairpin road winds to the top of the gorge, where the Romanesque-Gothic Monasterio de Ribas de Sil is situated high on a crag above the chasm. Recently restored and undergoing conversion to a parador *(see p558),* it has an enormous glass wall in one of the three cloisters and fine views.

The Río Sil winding its way through the gorge

The grandiose Monasterio de Oseira surrounded by the forests of the Valle de Arenteiro

Monasterio de Oseira ⓲

Oseira. 🚉 🚌 *from Ourense.* **Tel** *988 28 20 04.* ◯ *10am–noon Mon–Sat, 5:30–6:30pm daily.* 🎥 🎫

This monastery stands on its own in a wooded valley near the hamlet of Oseira, named after the bears *(osos)* that once lived in this region. It is a grey building with a Baroque façade dating from 1709. On the doorway is a statue of the Virgin as nurse, with St Bernard kneeling at her feet. The interior of the 12th–13th-century church is typically Cistercian in its simplicity. The vaulted chapterhouse is particularly impressive.

Fresco of a *dona* in the monastery at Vilar de Donas

Vilar de Donas ⓳

Lugo. 🏘 *80.* 🛈 *Avda de Compostela 28, 982 38 00 01.* ◯ **Church** *11am–2pm, 3–6pm daily.* 🎥 *San Antonio (13 Jun), San Salvador (6 Aug).*

This hamlet on the Road to Santiago *(see pp82–3)* has a small church, just off the main road. Inside are tombs of some of the Knights of the Order of Santiago. Also

found inside are 15th-century frescoes of the nuns who lived here until the 15th-century.

The Cistercian **Monasterio Sobrado de los Monjes**, to the northwest, has a medieval kitchen and chapterhouse, and a church with unusual domes.

Lugo ⓴

Lugo. 🏘 *90,000.* 🚉 🚌 🛈 *Praza Maior, 982 29 71 87.* 🗓 *Tue & Fri.* 🎉 *San Froilán (4–12 Oct).* **www.**concellodelugo.org

Capital of Galicia's largest province, Lugo was also an important centre under the Romans. Attracted to the town by its thermal springs, they constructed what is now the finest surviving **Roman wall** in Spain. The wall, which encircles the city, is about 6 m (20 ft) thick and 10 m (33 ft) high with ten gateways. Six of these give access to the top of the wall, from where there is a good view of the city.

Inside the wall, the old town is lively though dignified, with pretty squares. In the **Praza de Santo Domingo** is a black statue of a Roman eagle, built to commemorate Augustus' capture of Lugo from the Celts in the 1st century BC. The Romanesque **cathedral** is large and rambling, and modelled on that of Santiago. It features an elegant Baroque cloister, and a chapel containing the alabaster statue of Nuestra Señora de los Ojos Grandes (Virgin of the Big Eyes). The **Museo Provincial** exhibits Celtic gold

torcs, local Roman finds, a life-size model of a farm kitchen, modern Galician paintings and a statue of a peasant woman holding a miniature priest.

Environs

The stone hamlet of **Santa Eulalia**, situated in lovely open country to the west, conceals a curious building, discovered in 1924: a tiny temple, with lively, bright frescoes of birds and leaves. Though its exact purpose is unknown, it is thought to be an early Christian church and has been dated at around the 3rd century AD.

🏛 **Museo Provincial**
Praza da Soidade. **Tel** *982 24 21 12.* ◯ *10:30am–2pm, 4:30–8:30pm* ⬤ *Sun in Aug.* 🔶

O Cebreiro ㉑

Lugo. 🏘 *16.* 🚌 🛈 *982 36 70 25.* 🎉 *Santo Milagro (8 Sep), Santa Maria Real (17 Sep).*

Up in the hills in the east of Galicia, close to the border with León, is one of the most unusual villages on the Road to Santiago. Its 9th-century church was supposedly the scene of a miracle in 1300 when the wine was turned into blood and the bread into flesh. Near the church there are several *pallozas*, round thatched stone huts of a Celtic design. Some have been restored, and one of them is now a folk museum.

🏛 **Museo Etnográfico**
O Cebreiro. ◯ *11am–2pm, 3–6pm (to 7pm in summer) Wed–Sun.*

Painted gourd in O Cebreiro's museum

ASTURIAS AND CANTABRIA

ASTURIAS · CANTABRIA

The spectacular Picos de Europa massif sits astride the border between Asturias and Cantabria. In this rural region cottage crafts are kept alive in villages in remote mountain valleys and forested foothills. There are many ancient towns and churches, and pretty fishing ports on the coasts. Cave paintings, such as those at Altamira, were made by people living here over 10,000 years ago.

Asturias is proud that it resisted invasion by the Moors. The Reconquest of Spain is held to have begun in 718 when a Moorish force was defeated by Christians at Covadonga in the Picos de Europa.

The Christian kingdom of Asturias was founded in the 8th century, and in the brilliant, brief artistic period that followed many churches were built around the capital, Oviedo. Some of these pre-Romanesque churches still stand. Today, Asturias is a province and a principality under the patronage of the heir to the Spanish throne. In the charming, unspoiled Asturian countryside cider is produced and a quaint dialect, *bable,* is spoken.

Cantabria centres on Santander, its capital, a port and an elegant resort. It is a mountainous province with a legacy of Romanesque churches in isolated spots. It also has well-preserved towns and villages such as Santillana del Mar, Carmona and Bárcena Mayor.

Mountains cover more than half of both provinces, so mountain sports are a major attraction. Expanses of deciduous forests remain in many parts, some sheltering Spain's last wild bears. Along the coasts are pretty fishing ports and resorts, such as Castro Urdiales, Ribadesella and Comillas, and sandy coves for bathing. Both the coastal plains and uplands are ideal for quiet rural holidays.

Peaceful meadow around Lago de la Ercina in the Picos de Europa massif

◁ One of the pretty cobbled streets of Santillana del Mar, Cantabria

Exploring Asturias and Cantabria

The most obvious attraction in this area is the group of mountains that straddles the two provinces – the Picos de Europa. These jagged peaks offer excellent rock climbing and rough hiking, and in certain parts can be explored by car or bicycle. These and several other nature reserves in the area are home to rare species of flora and fauna, including the capercaillie and brown bear. The coast offers many sandy coves for bathing. Santander and Oviedo are lively university cities with a rich cultural life. There are innumerable unspoiled villages to explore, especially the ancient town of Santillana del Mar. Some of the earliest examples of art exist in Cantabria, most notably at Altamira, where the cave drawings and engravings are among the oldest to be found in Europe.

Typical flower-covered balcony in the village of Bárcena Mayor

A view along the crowded beach of Playa del Camello, Santander

SIGHTS AT A GLANCE

Cantabrian dairy farmers loading hay on to their cart

GETTING AROUND

The main road through the region is the N634. Most other major roads follow the directions of the valleys and run north to south. Minor roads are generally good but can be slow and winding. The private FEVE railway, which follows the coast from Bilbao to Ferrol in Galicia, is both useful and extremely scenic. A twice-weekly Brittany Ferries service links Santander with Plymouth. Asturias has a small international airport near Avilés. Be aware that as Spain is changing its road numbering system some roads featured here may differ from new road signs.

Carved figure in the
Convento de Regina
Coeli, Santillana del Mar

KEY

▭▭	Motorway
≡ ≡	Motorway under construction
▬	Secondary road
═	Minor road
▬	Scenic route
▬	Main railway
▬	Minor railway
▬	Regional border
△	Summit

Craftsman making knife blades in a forge at Taramundi

Taramundi ❶

Asturias. 🏘 850. 🚉 Plaza del Poyo 1, 985 64 68 77, 985 64 67 02 (Mon). 🎉 San José (19 Mar). **www**.taramundi.net

Situated in the remote Los Oscos region, this small village houses a rural tourism centre which organizes forest tours in four-wheel drive vehicles and has several hotels and holiday cottages to rent. Taramundi has a tradition of wrought-iron craftsmanship. Iron ore was first mined in the area by the Romans. There are approximately 13 forges in and around the village, where craftsmen can still be seen making traditional knives with decorated wooden handles.

Environs
About 20 km (12 miles) to the east, at **San Martín de Oscos**, there is an 18th-century palace. At **Grandas de Salime**, 10 km (6 miles) further southeast, the Museo Etnográfico has displays showing local crafts, traditional life and farming.

🏛 **Museo Etnográfico**
Avenida el Ferreiro 17. **Tel** 98 562 72 43. ⭘ Tue–Sun. 🖼 ♿

Castro de Coaña ❷

Asturias. 🚉 5km from Navia. **Tel** 985 97 84 01. ⭘ Tue–Sun.

One of the most important Celtic settlements in Spain, Castro de Coaña was established by the Romans. Set on a hillside in the Navia valley are the well-preserved remains of its fortifications

and the stone foundations of oval and rectangular dwellings, some of which stand head high. Inside can be found hollowed-out stones which are thought to have been used for crushing corn.

The museum on the site displays many of the finds that have been unearthed at Castro de Coaña. Among the interesting remains on display are pottery, tools and Roman coins.

Circular stone foundations of dwellings at Castro de Coaña

Costa Verde ❸

Asturias. 🚉 Avilés. 🚉 Oviedo, Gijón. 🚉 Plaza del Ayuntamiento, Aviles, Calle Ruiz Gomez 21, 985 54 43 25.

The aptly named "green coast" is a succession of attractive sandy coves and dramatic cliffs, punctuated by deep estuaries and numerous fishing villages. Inland, there are lush meadows, and pine and eucalyptus forests, backed by mountains. This stretch of coastline has been less spoiled than most in Spain; the resorts tend to be modest in size, like the hotels.

Two pretty fishing ports, **Castropol** and **Figueras**, stand by the eastern shore of the Ría de Ribadeo, forming the border with Galicia. To the east are other picturesque villages such as Tapia de Casariego and Ortiguera, in a small rocky cove. Following the coast, **Luarca** lies beside a church and a quiet cemetery on a headland, and has a neat little harbour packed with red, blue and white boats. The village of **Cudillero** is even more delightful – outdoor cafés and excellent seafood restaurants crowd the tiny plaza beside the port, all of which are squeezed into a narrow cove. Behind, white cottages are scattered over the steep hillsides.

Further along the coast is the rocky headland of Cabo de Peñas where, in the fishing village of **Candas**, bullfights are sometimes held on the sand at low tide. East of Gijón, **Lastres** is impressively located below a cliff, and **Isla** has a broad open beach. Beyond Ribadesella is the lively town

---

THE BROWN BEAR
The population of Spain's brown bears (*Ursus arctos*) has dwindled from about 1,000 at the beginning of the 20th century to about 100. Hunting by man and the destruction of the bear's natural forest habitat have caused the decline. But now, protected by nature reserves such as Somiedo, where most of the bears in Asturias are found, together with new conservation laws, it is hoped this magnificent omnivore will thrive again.

One of the few remaining bears in the forests of Asturias

Church and cemetery overlooking the sea from the headland at Luarca

of **Llanes**. Among the attractions of this old fortified seaport, with its dramatic mountain backdrop, are ruined ramparts and good beaches.

Teverga ❹

Asturias. 🏘 *2,100*. 🚌 *La Plaza*. 🛈 *Dr Garcia Miranda, s/n, San Martin de Teverga, 985 76 42 93*.

This area, southwest of Oviedo, is rich in scenery, wildlife and ancient churches. Near the southern end of the Teverga gorge is **La Plaza**. Its church, Iglesia de San Pedro de Teverga, is a fine example of Romanesque architecture.

Just to the west of La Plaza is **Villanueva**, with its Romanesque Iglesia de Santa María. The area's 20 km (12 mile) Senda del Oso path skirts the edge of a bear enclosure.

Environs
The large **Parque Natural de Somiedo** straddles the mountains bordering León. Its high meadows and forests are a sanctuary for wolves, brown bears and capercaillies, as well as a number of rare species of wild flowers.

The park has 4 glacial lakes, and is peppered with herdsmen's traditional thatched huts, known as *teitos (see p27)*.

Avilés ❺

Asturias. 🏘 *84,000*. ✈ 🚌 🚃 🛈 *Calle Ruiz Gomez 21, 985 54 43 25*. 🛥 *Mon*. 🎉 *San Agustin (28 Aug)*.

Aviles became the capital of Asturias' steel industry during the 19th century, and is still ringed by big factories. Even though it is sometimes criticized for having little to offer

the visitor, the town hides a medieval heart of some character, especially around the Plaza de España. The **Iglesia de San Nicolás Bari** is decorated with ancient frescoes and has a Renaissance cloister. The **Iglesia de Padres Franciscanos** contains a fine 14th-century chapel and holds the tomb of the first Governor of the US state of Florida. All around are arcaded streets. The international airport outside Avilés serves all Asturias.

Gijón ❻

Asturias. 🏘 *270,000*. 🚃 🚌 🛈 *Calle Rodríquez San Pedro, s/n, 985 34 17 71*. 🛥 *Sun*. 🎉 *San Antonio (13 Jun); La Virgen de Begoña (15 Aug)*.

The province's largest city, this industrial port has been much rebuilt since the Civil War when it was bombarded by the Nationalist navy. The city's most famous son is Gaspar Melchor de Jovellanos, an eminent 18th-century author, reformer and diplomat.

Gijon's old town is on a small isthmus and headland. It centres on the arcaded Plaza Mayor and the 18th-century **Palacio de Revillagigedo**, a Neo-Renaissance folly with towers and battlements. The long sandy beach, near the city centre, is popular in summer.

🏛 **Palacio de Revillagigedo**
Plaza del Marqués 2. **Tel** *985 34 69 21*.
⬜ *10:30am–1:30pm, 4–8pm; noon–2:30pm Sun*. ⬛

The pretty 12th-century Iglesia de San Pedro at La Plaza

Oviedo ⑦

🏛 200,000. 🚉 ✈ ℹ Marqués de Santa Cruz 1, 985 22 75 86. 🚌 Thu, Sat & Sun. 🎭 San Mateo (14–21 Sep).

Oviedo, a university city and the cultural and commercial capital of Asturias, stands on a raised site on a fertile plain. The nearby coal mines have made it an important industrial centre since the 19th century. It retains some of the atmosphere of that time, as described by Leopoldo Alas ("Clarín") in his great novel *La Regenta (see p35)*.

In and around Oviedo are many Pre-Romanesque buildings. This style flourished in the 8th–10th centuries and was confined to a small area of the kingdom of Asturias, one of the few enclaves of Spain not invaded by the Moors.

The nucleus of the medieval city is the stately Plaza Alfonso II, bordered by a number of handsome old palaces. On this square is situated the Flamboyant Gothic **cathedral** *(see p24)* with its high tower and asymmetrical west façade. Inside are tombs of Asturian kings and a majestic 16th-century gilded reredos. The cathedral's supreme treasure is the Cámara Santa, a restored 9th-century chapel containing statues of Christ and the apostles. The chapel also houses many

Cross of Angels in the treasury of Oviedo cathedral

works of 9th-century Asturian art including two crosses and a reliquary – all made of gold, silver and precious stones.

Also situated in the Plaza Alfonso II is the **Iglesia de San Tirso**. This church was originally constructed in the 9th century, but subsequent restorations have left the east window as the only surviving Pre-Romanesque feature.

Sited immediately behind the cathedral is the **Museo Arqueológico**, housed in the old Benedictine monastery of San Vicente, with its fine cloisters. It contains local prehistoric, Romanesque and Pre-Romanesque treasures.

The **Museo de Bellas Artes**, in the handsome 18th-century Velarde Palace, has a good range of Asturian and Spanish paintings, such as Carreño's portrait of Carlos II *(see p70)*.

Two of the most magnificent Pre-Romanesque churches are on Mount Naranco, to the north.

SANTA MARIA DEL NARANCO

This church, on Mount Naranco, was originally built as a summer palace for Ramiro I in the 9th century. It is one of the finest examples of Pre-Romanesque or Asturian architecture, a style characterized by the slender proportions of its buildings and their original and graceful ornamentation.

The Hall has an unusually high ceiling.

Arcaded galleries at both ends of the building were designed to let in an enormous amount of light and were an architectural innovation.

Columns carved with *soqueado* or rope effect, were typical of the Pre-Romanesque style.

Vaultings of this size were a technical achievement and not adopted throughout Europe until the 11th century.

Church overlooking the sea at Ribadesella

Santa María del Naranco has a large barrel-vaulted hall on the main floor and arcaded galleries at either end. Some of the intricate reliefs on the door jambs of the nearby San Miguel de Lillo show acrobats and animal tamers in a circus.

The early 9th-century church of San Julián de los Prados stands on the road leading northeast out of Oviedo. The largest of Spain's surviving Pre-Romanesque churches, it is noted for the frescoes which cover all of its interior.

🏛 **Museo Arqueológico**
Calle San Vicente 5. *Tel* 985 21 54 05. ☐ *Tue–Sun (Renovations until 2006).* ✍

🏛 **Museo de Bellas Artes**
Calle Santa Ana 1. *Tel* 985 21 30 61. ☐ *Tue–Sun.* ♿

Valdediós ❽

Asturias. 🚶 *150.* ❱ *Villaviciosa, 985 89 23 24.*

Set alone in a field near this hamlet, the tiny 9th-century **Iglesia de San Salvador** is a jewel of Pre-Romanesque art. Its ceiling has vivid Asturian frescoes, and by the portal are stone recesses where pilgrims slept. The church in the monastery next door is 13th-century Cistercian, with cloisters dating from the 16th century.

Environs
To the north, the graceful little resort town of **Villaviciosa** lies amid apple orchards and glorious hilly scenery, and has glass-fronted mansions in its narrow streets. In nearby **Amandi**, the hilltop Iglesia de San Juan has a 13th-century portal and delicate carvings and friezes.

Iglesia de San Salvador de Valdediós in its idyllic setting

Ribadesella ❾

Asturias. 🚶 *6,400.* 🚌 🚉 ❱ *Calle Marqueses de Argüelles, 985 86 00 38.* ⊙ *Wed.* 🎉 *Descent of the Río Sella (first Sat of Aug).*

This enchanting little seaside town bestrides a broad estuary. On one side is the lively old seaport full of tapas bars below a clifftop church. Across the estuary is a holiday resort. A multicoloured flotilla of kayaks arrives here from Arriondas (upstream) in an international regatta that is held every year on the first Saturday in August.

On the edge of town is the **Cueva de Tito Bustillo**. This cave is rich in stalactites but is best known for its many prehistoric drawings, which were discovered in 1968, some dating from around 18,000 BC. These include red and black pictures of stags and horses. To protect the paintings, only 360 visitors are allowed in per day; numbered tickets are given out from 10am every day. A museum on the site includes an artist's impressions of prehistoric living conditions.

🏮 **Cueva de Tito Bustillo**
Ribadesella. *Tel 985 86 11 20.* ☐ *Wed–Sun.* ◉ *caves: Oct–Apr.* ✍

Cangas de Onís ❿

Asturias. 🚶 *6,000.* 🚉 ❱ *Plaza del Ayuntamiento 1, 985 84 80 05.* ⊙ *Sun.* 🎉 *San Antonio (13 Jun), Santina (8 Sep).*

Cangas de Onís, one of the gateways to the Picos de Europa *(see pp108–9),* is where Pelayo, the 8th-century Visigothic nobleman and hero of the Reconquest, set up his court. The town has a Romanesque bridge and the 8th-century chapel of Santa Cruz.

Environs
About 3 km (2 miles) east in Cardes is the **Cueva del Buxu**, which has engravings and rock-drawings over 10,000 years old. Only 25 visitors, in groups of five, are allowed in each day.

🏮 **Cueva del Buxu**
Tel 608 17 54 67 (mobile). ☐ *10am–3pm Wed–Sun.* 🎫 ✍ *Free on Wed.*

Parque Nacional de los Picos de Europa ⓫

Lefebvre's Ringlet

These beautiful mountains were reputedly christened the "Peaks of Europe" by returning sailors for whom this was often the first sight of their homeland. The range straddles three regions – Asturias, Cantabria and Castilla y León – and has diverse terrain. In some parts, deep winding gorges cut through craggy rocks while elsewhere verdant valleys support orchards and dairy farming. The celebrated creamy blue cheese, Cabrales (see p77), is made here. The Picos offer rock climbing and upland hiking as well as a profusion of flora and fauna. Tourism in the park is well organized.

Covadonga
The Neo-Romanesque basilica, built between 1886 and 1901, stands on the site of Pelayo's historic victory.

Lago de la Ercina
Together with the nearby Lago Enol, this lake lies on a wild limestone plateau above Covadonga and below the peak of Peña Santa.

Desfiladero de los Beyos
This deep, narrow gorge with its high limestone cliffs winds spectacularly for 10 km (6 miles) through the mountains. Tracing the route of the Río Sella below, it carries the main road from Cangas de Onís to Riaño.

KEY

▬▬	Major road
═══	Minor road
– –	Footpath
──	National park boundary
🚡	Cable car
🛈	Tourist information
🅿	Parador
⚶	Viewpoint

Desfiladero del Río Cares
The River Cares forms a deep gorge in the heart of the Picos. A dramatic footpath follows the gorge, passing through tunnels and across high bridges up to 1,000 m (3,280 ft) above the river.

A dramatic view of the mountains of the Picos de Europa

Bulnes, one of the remotest villages in Spain, enjoys fine views of Naranjo de Bulnes and can now be accessed by an underground funicular railway from Puente Poncebos as well as by foot.

(see pp53–5)

VISITORS' CHECKLIST

🛈 Casa Dago, Cangas de Onís.
🚌 Oviedo to Cangas de Onís.
Fuente Dé cable car Tel 942 73 66 10. ☐ Jul–Sep: 9am–8pm daily, Oct–Jun: 10am–6pm daily. ● 6 Jan–1 Mar.

PELAYO THE WARRIOR

A statue of this Visigothic nobleman who became king of Asturias guards the basilica at Covadonga. It was close to this site, in 722, that Pelayo and a band of men – though vastly out-numbered – are said to have defeated a Moorish army. The victory inspired Christians in the north of Spain to reconquer the peninsula (see pp53–5). The tomb of the warrior is in a cave which has become a shrine, also containing a painted image of the Virgin.

Pelayo's statue

Naranjo de Bulnes, with its tooth-like crest, is in the heart of the massif. At 2,519 m (8,264 ft) it is one of the highest summits in the Picos de Europa.

Fuente Dé Cable Car
The 900-m (2950-ft) ascent from Fuente Dé takes visitors up to a wild rocky plateau pitted with craters. From here there is a spectacular panorama of the Picos' peaks and valleys.

0 kilometres   5
0 miles   5

**Statue of the Virgin, San
Vicente de la Barquera**

ASTURIAS AND CANTABRIA'S FIESTAS

La Folía *(Apr)*, San Vicente
de la Barquera (Cantabria).
The statue of the Virgen de
la Barquera is said to have
arrived at San Vicente in a
boat with no sails, oars or
crew. Once a year, it is put
in a fishing boat decorated
with flags and flowers,
which sails at the head of
a procession to bless the
sea. Groups of young girls,
called *picayos,* stand on the
shore singing traditional
songs of the region in honour of the Virgin. La Folía
usually falls at the end of
April, but its date is de-
pendent on the local tides.
**Fiesta de los Pastos y los
Lagos** *(25 Jul),* near
Cangas de Onís (Asturias).
Regional songs and dances
are performed at this
festival beside the shores
of Lake Enol in the Picos
de Europa National Park.
Battle of the Flowers *(last
Fri of Aug)*, Laredo
(Cantabria). Floats adorned
with flowers are paraded
through this small resort. A
flower-throwing free-for-all
follows the procession.
**Nuestra Señora de
Covadonga** *(8 Sep)*, Picos
de Europa (Asturias). Huge
crowds converge on the
shrine of Covadonga *(see
p108)* to pay homage to the
patron saint of Asturias.

Potes ⓬

Cantabria. 🏠 *1,600.* 🚹 *Plaza de la
Serna, s/n, 942 73 07 87.* 🚌 *Mon.*
🎉 *Ntra. Sra. de Valmayor (15 Aug),
Santisima Cruz (14 Sep).*

A small ancient town, with
old balconied houses lining
the river, Potes is the main
centre of the eastern Picos de
Europa. It is situated in the
broad Valle de Liébana, whose
fertile soil yields prime crops of
walnuts, cherries and grapes.
A potent spirit called *orujo* is
made in the town. The **Torre
del Infantado**, in the main
square, is a defensive tower
built in the 15th century.

Environs
Between Potes and the coast
runs a gorge, the **Desfiladero
de la Hermida**. Halfway up it
is **Santa María de Lebeña**, a
10th-century Mozarabic *(see
p335)* church.
West of Potes is the monastery church of **Santo Toribio
de Liébana**, one of the most
revered spots in the Picos de

Europa. Founded in the 7th
century, it became known
throughout Spain a century
later when it received reputedly the largest fragment of
the True Cross. An 8th century monk, St Beatus of Liébana, wrote the *Commentary
on the Apocalypse*, later much
copied and illuminated. The
restored Romanesque mon-
astic buildings were rebuilt in
the 1200s, and are now occupied by Franciscan monks.

Comillas ⓭

Cantabria. 🏠 *2,500.* 🚹 *Calle la
Aldea 6, 942 72 07 68.* 🚌 *Fri.*
🎉 *El Cristo (16 Jul).* **Palacio** ⬜ *Jul–
9 Sep: 10am–9pm daily; 10 Sep–Jun:
10:30am–2pm, 4–7pm Wed–Sun.*

This pretty resort is known
for its unusual buildings by
Catalan Modernista architects
(see pp140–1). Antonio López
y López, the first Marquis of
Comillas, hired Joan Martorell
to design the **Palacio Sobrellano** (1881), a huge Neo-

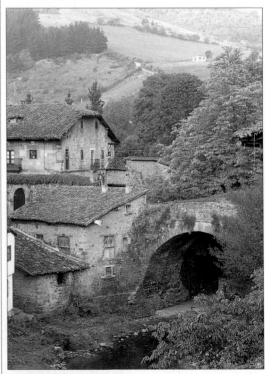

Stone bridge and houses in the ancient town of Potes

Surviving Classical columns among the ruins of the Roman town of Juliobriga, near Reinosa

Gothic edifice. Comillas's best-known monument is Gaudí's *(see p164)* **El Capricho**, now a restaurant *(see p611)*. It was designed for a rich business-man from 1883–9 and is a Mudéjar-inspired fantasy with a minaret-like tower covered in green and yellow tiles. Another of the town's Mod-ernista buildings is the **Universidad Pontificia**, which overlooks the sea from a hilltop. It was designed by Joan Martorell to plans by Domènech i Montaner *(see p140)*.

Wall tile on the façade of El Capricho

Environs
The fishing port of **San Vicente de la Barquera** has arcaded streets, ramparts and the Gothic Romanesque church of Nuestra Señora de los Ángeles.

Valle de Cabuérniga ⓮

Cantabria. 🚌 *Bárcena Mayor.*
ℹ️ *Ayuntamiento, 942 70 60 87, 942 70 60 01.*

Two exceptionally pictur-esque towns, notable for their superb examples of rural architecture, draw visitors to the Cabuérniga Valley. A good road takes you to the once-remote **Bárcena Mayor**. Its cobbled streets are furnished with old lamps and filled with boutiques, and restaurants ser-ving a range of regional dishes. The pretty houses have flower-covered balconies, and cattle byres on the ground floor.

Carmona is an old, unspoil-ed village approximately 20 km (12 miles) to the northwest of Bárcena Mayor. Its solid stone houses, with pantiled roofs and wooden balcon-ies, are typically Cantabrian *(see p26)*. Woodcarv-ing, the traditional craft of the region, is still practised in this village, where men work outside their houses on a variety of artifacts including bowls, fiddles, *albarcas* (clogs) and chairs. The 13th-century Palacio de los Mier, a manor house in the centre of the village, has been restored and is now a hotel.

The extensive, wild beech woods near **Saja** have been designated a nature reserve.

Traditional balconied houses in Bárcena Mayor

Alto Campoo ⓯

Cantabria. 🚠 *1,900.* 🚪 🚪
ℹ️ *Estación de Montaña, 942 77 92 22 (am only).* 🎉 *Nuestra Señora de las Nieves (5 Aug), San Roque (16 Aug).*

Sited high in the Cantabrian mountains, this winter resort lies below the Pico de Tres Mares (2,175 m/7,000 ft), the "Peak of the Three Seas", so called because the rivers rising near it flow into the Mediterr-anean, the Atlantic and the Bay of Biscay. The Río Ebro, one of Spain's longest rivers, rises in this area and its source, at Fontibre, is a beauty spot. A road and a chair lift reach the summit of Tres Mares for a breathtaking panorama of the Picos de Europa and other mountain chains. The resort is small, with 19 pistes totalling 17 km (10 miles) in length, and has few facilities for après-ski.

Environs
Reinosa, some 26 km (16 miles) to the east of Alto Campoo, is a handsome market town with old stone houses. Further southeast is Retortillo, a hamlet where the remains of **Juliobriga**, a town built by the Romans as a bastion against the wild tribes of Cantabria, can be seen.

The main road south out of Reinosa leads to **Cervatos**, where the former collegiate church has erotic carvings on its façade. This novel device was meant to deter the villagers from pleasures of the flesh.

At **Arroyuelo** and **Cadalso**, to the southeast, are two churches built into rock faces in the 9th and 10th centuries.

One of the many paintings of bison at Altamira

Cuevas de Altamira ⑯

Cantabria. **Tel** 942 81 80 05 📞
Santillana del Mar. **Caves** 🚃
Museum 🕐 Oct–May: 9:30am–5pm
Tue–Sat; Jun–Sep: 9:30am–7:30pm
Tue–Sat; 9:30am–3pm Sun. 📷 24,
25, 31 Dec, 1 & 6 Jan, 1 May. 📷 ♿
🌐 www.museodealtamiramcu.es

These caves contain some of the world's finest examples of prehistoric art. The earliest engravings and drawings, discovered in 1879, date back to around 18,000 BC (see p48). Public entry to the caves is no longer permitted, but the on-site museum contains

Carved figure of Christ in the Convento de Regina Coeli

a replica of the caves. Similar sites that remain open to the public can be found at nearby Puente Viesgo, Ribadesella (see p107) in Asturias and at Nerja (see p483) in Andalusia.

Santillana del Mar ⑰

Cantabria. 👥 4,000. 📞 ℹ️ Calle Jesus Otero 20, 942 81 88 12. 🎉 Santa Juliana (28 Jun), San Rogue (16 Aug).

Set just inland, belying its name, this town is one the prettiest in Spain. Its ensemble of 15th- to 17th-century golden stone houses survives largely intact despite the many tourists and souvenir shops.

The town grew up around a monastery, which was an important pilgrimage centre, the Romanesque **La Colegiata**. The church houses the tomb of the local early-medieval martyr St Juliana, and contains a 17th-century painted reredos and a carved south door. In its lovely cloisters, vivid biblical scenes have been sculpted on the capitals.

On the town's two main cobbled streets there are houses built by local noblemen. These have either fine wooden galleries or iron balconies, and coats of arms inlaid into their stone façades. In the past, farmers used the open ground floors as byres for stabling their cattle.

In the enchanting **Plaza Mayor**, in the centre of town, is a mansion-turned-parador

(see p564). The **Museo Diocesano** is housed in the restored Convento de Regina Coeli, east of the town centre, and has a collection of painted carvings of religious figures.

🏛️ **Museo Diocesano**
El Cruce. **Tel** 942 84 03 17. 🕐
Tue–Sun. 📷

Puente Viesgo ⑱

Cantabria. 👥 2,500. 🚉 ℹ️ Calle Manuel Pérez Mazo 2, 942 59 81 05 (town hall). 🎉 San Miguel (28–9 Sep).

The spa of Puente Viesgo is best known for **El Monte Castillo**; a complex of caves that are dotted around the limestone hills above the town. Decorated by prehistoric man, it is thought the late Palaeolithic cave dwellers used the deep interior as a kind of sanctuary. They left drawings of horses, bison and other animals there, and some 50 hand prints – almost always the left hand. The ochre and other colours used to create the images were extracted from minerals in the cave.

Environs
The lush Pas valley, to the southeast, is home to transhumant dairy farmers, the Pasiegos. In the main town of **Vega de Pas**, you can buy two Pasiego specialities – sobaos, or sponge cakes (see p77), and quesadas, a sweet which is made from milk, butter and eggs. In **Villacarriedo** there is a handsome 18th-century mansion, with two Baroque façades of carved stone hiding a medieval tower.

🏠 **El Monte Castillo**
Puente Viesgo. **Tel** 942 59 84 25.
⚫ Mon. 📷 📷

Main façade of La Colegiata in Santillana del Mar

The Palacio de la Magdalena in El Sardinero

Santander ⓳

Cantabria. 🏠 180,000. ✈ 🚆 🚌 🚢
🛈 Hernán Cortés 4, 942 31 07 08. 🚌
Mon–Thu. 🎭 Santiago (25 Jul).

Cantabria's capital, a busy port, enjoys a splendid site near the mouth of a deep bay. The town centre is modern – after being ravaged by fire in 1941 it was reconstructed. The **cathedral** was rebuilt in Gothic style, but retains its 12th-century crypt. The **Museo de Bellas Artes** houses work by Goya as well as other artists of the 19th and 20th centuries. The town's **Museo de Prehistoria y Arqueología** displays finds from caves at Altamira and Puente Viesgo (see p112), such as Neolithic axe heads, and Roman coins, pottery and figurines. The **Museo Marítimo** has rare whale skeletons and 350 species of local fish. Call to check opening times.

The town extends along the coast around the Península de la Magdalena, a headland on which there is a park, a small zoo and the **Palacio de la Magdalena** – a summer palace built for Alfonso XIII in 1912, reflecting the resort's popularity at the time with the Royal Family.

The seaside suburb of **El Sardinero**, north of the headland, is a smart resort with a long graceful beach, backed by gardens, elegant cafés and a majestic white casino. In July and August El Sardinero plays host to a major theatre and music festival.

🏛 **Museo de Bellas Artes**
Calle Rubio 6. **Tel** 942 20 31 20.
⬜ Mon–Sat. 🎟

🏛 **Museo de Prehistoria y Arqueología**
Calle Casimiro Saenz 4. **Tel** 942 20 71 09. ⬜ Tue–Sun. 🚌 🎟

🏛 **Museo Marítimo**
C/ San Martin de Bajamar. **Tel** 942 27 49 62. 🎟 🖼

Laredo ⓴

Cantabria. 🏠 13,500. 🚆 🛈 Calle Lopez Seña, 942 61 10 96. 🎭 Batalla de Flores (last Fri of Aug), Carlos V's last landing (3rd week in Sep)

The excellent long, sandy beach of this small town has made it one of Cantabria's most popular bathing resorts. The attractive old town has narrow streets with balconied houses leading up to the 13th-century **Iglesia de Santa María de la Asunción**, with its Flemish altar and bronze lecterns. One of the highlights of the year in Laredo is the colourful fiesta of the Battle of the Flowers (see p110).

Castro Urdiales ㉑

Cantabria. 🏠 25,000. 🚆 🛈 Avenida de la Constitución 1, 942 87 15 12. 🚌 Thu. 🎭 Coso Blanco (1st Fri of Jun), Semana Grande (Jun), San Andrés (last Fri of Nov). **Iglesia** ⬜ 4–6pm daily.

Castro Urdiales, a busy fishing town and popular holiday resort, is built around a picturesque harbour. Above the port, on a high promontory, stands the pinkish Gothic **Iglesia de Santa María**, as big as a cathedral. Beside it the recently restored castle, said to have been built by the Knights Templar, has been converted into a lighthouse. Handsome glass-fronted houses, or *galerías*, line the promenade. The small town beach often becomes crowded but there are bigger ones to the west, such as the Playa de Ostende.

Environs
Near the village of **Ramales de la Victoria**, 40 km (25 miles) south, are prehistoric caves containing etchings and engravings, reached by a very steep mountain road.

Small boats moored in the harbour at Castro Urdiales

NORTHERN SPAIN

THE BASQUE COUNTRY, NAVARRA AND LA RIOJA

VIZCAYA · GUIPUZCOA · ÁLAVA · LA RIOJA · NAVARRA

*G*reen hills meet Atlantic beaches in the Basque Country, land of an ancient people of mysterious origin. Navarra, also partly Basque, was a powerful medieval kingdom. The beautiful western Pyrenees form part of its charming countryside. The vineyards of La Rioja, to the south, produce many of Spain's finest wines.

The Basques are a race apart – they will not let you forget that theirs is a culture different from any in Spain. Although the Basque regional government enjoys considerable autonomy, there is a strong separatist movement seeking to sever links with the government in Madrid.

The Basque Country (Euskadi is the Basque name) is an important industrial region. The Basques are great deep-sea fishermen and fish has a major role in their imaginative cuisine, regarded by many as the best in Spain.

Unrelated to any other tongue, the Basque language, *Euskera,* is widely used on signs and most towns have two names; the fashionable resort of San Sebastián, for example, is known to locals as Donostia. *Euskera* is also spoken in parts of Navarra, which is counted as part of the wider (unofficial) Basque Country. Many of its finest sights – the towns of Olite and Estella, and the monastery of Leyre – date from the Middle Ages when Navarra was a kingdom straddling the Pyrenees. Pamplona, its capital, is best known for its daredevil bull-running fiesta, which is held in July.

As well as its vineyards and bodegas, La Rioja is a region of market gardens. Among its many historic sights are the cathedral of Santo Domingo de la Calzada and the monasteries of San Millán de la Cogolla and Yuso.

Basque farmhouse near Gernika-Lumo in the Basque Country

◁ A street in the village of Roncal, in the foothills of the Navarrese Pyrenees

Exploring the Basque Country, Navarra and La Rioja

These green, hilly regions have diverse attractions. The Pyrenees in Navarra offer skiing in winter and climbing, caving and canoeing the rest of the year. The cliffs of the Basque Country are broken by rocky coves, rias, and wide bays with beaches of fine yellow sand, interspersed with fishing villages. Inland, minor roads wind through wooded hills, valleys and gorges past lonely castles and isolated homesteads. In La Rioja, to the south, they cross vineyards, passing villages and towns clustered round venerable churches and monasteries.

COSTA VASCA

Plentzia
Bakio
Bermeo
Lekeitio
Mungia
GERNIKA-LUMO ❷
Cuevas de Santimamiñe
Ondá
Markina-Xemein
Algorta
Areeta
Santander
Portugalete
BILBAO (BILBO) ❶
Elgoit
Eibar
Carranza
Sodupe
SANTUARIC DE LOIOLA
Balmaseda
Llodio
Castillo-Elejabeitia
Bergara
Artziniega
Amurrio
AP68
A68
PAÍS
VASCO
Orduña
N240
ON
Berberana
Aranta
CASTILLO DE MENDOZA ❾
Salvatierra
Salinas de Añana
VITORIA (GASTEIZ) ❽
Puerto de Aza 890m
La Puebla de Arganzón
Treviño
Miranda de Ebro
N1
Burgos
A68
Ace
Casalarreina
HARO ❶❶
LAGUARDIA ❿
SANTO DOMINGO DE LA CALZADA ❶❷
N232
Fuenmayor
LOGRC ❶❺
N120
NÁJERA ❶❹
Navarrete
SAN MILLÁN DE LA COGOLLA ❶❸
LA RIOJA
Torrecilla en Cameros
Sierra de la Demanda
N111
Sierra de Cameros
ENCISC
Puerto de Piqueras 1710m
Soria

The scenic Río Cárdenas valley below the village of San Millán de la Cogolla in La Rioja

KEY

===	Motorway
—	Major road
===	Minor road
—	Scenic route
---	Main railway
—	Minor railway
	International border
	Regional border

SEE ALSO

- **Where to Stay** pp565–8
- **What to Eat** pp613–17

0 kilometres   25
0 miles   15

SIGHTS AT A GLANCE

GETTING AROUND

The main road in the north is the A8 (E5). The A68 AP68 (E804) runs southwards from Bilbao via Haro and follows the Ebro Valley. Motorway spurs extend to Vitoria and Pamplona. The rail net-work connects the cities and the larger towns, and most towns are served by coach. Bilbao has an international airport. As Spain is in the process of changing its road numbering system some roads featured here may differ from new road signs.

The fashionable Playa de Ondarreta, one of San Sebastián's three beaches

Buildings overlooking the Río Nervión in Bilbao

Bilbao ❶

Vizcaya. 🏙 *360,000.* ✈ 🚌 🚗 ⛴
ℹ *Pl. Ensanche 11, 944 79 57 60.*
🎉 *Santiago (25 Jul), La Asunción (15 Aug), Semana Grande (late-Aug).*
www.bilbao.net

Bilbao (Bilbo) is the centre of Basque industry, Spain's leading commercial port and the largest Basque city. It is surrounded by high, bare hills. Its suburbs spread 16 km (10 miles) along the Río Nervión (Nerbioi) to its estuary. The river between Las Arenas and the fishing port of Portugalete is crossed via the **Puente Colgante**. This iron transporter bridge, built in 1888, has a suspended cabin for cars and passengers. On the east bank of the estuary is Santurtzi (Santurce), from where ferries sail to the UK *(see p676).*

Bilbao has flourished as an industrial city since the mid-19th century, when iron ore began to be extracted from deposits northwest of the city. Soon, steelworks and chemical factories became a major part of the local landscape.

The city is not beautiful, but it is prosperous and its once heavy pollution is now much reduced. An urban development scheme has introduced pieces of fascinating modernist architecture to break up the monotone industrial sprawl.

By the river, however, is the city's medieval heart, the *casco viejo*, built in the 14th century. Here, amid alleys lively with tapas bars, is the arcaded Plazuela de Santiago and the **Catedral Basílica de Santiago**. The **Museo Arqueológico, Etnográfico e Histórico Vasco** displays Basque art, folk artifacts and photographs of Basque life. In the cloister is the Idol of Mikeldi, an animal-like carving dating from the 3rd–2nd century BC.

In the newer town is the large **Museo de Bellas Artes** (Museum of Fine Art), one of Spain's best art museums. It displays art ranging from 12th-century Catalan masterpieces to works by modern artists of international fame, including Vasarely, Kokoschka, Bacon, Delaunay and Léger. There are also several rooms of paintings by Basque artists.

The jewel in the area's cultural crown is the **Museo Guggenheim Bilbao** *(see pp120–1),* which opened in 1997. The museum is part of a redevelopment of the city which includes the expansion of the capacity of its port and the new metro system, designed in a futuristic style by Norman Foster. Another striking new building is the **Palacio de la Música y Congresos Euskalduna**. Designed to resemble a ship, it has a number of auditoriums, one seating 2,200 people and is the home of the Bilbao Symphony Orchestra.

West of the city, a funicular railway ascends to the village of La Reineta and a panorama across the dockyards.

🏛 **Museo Arqueológico, Etnográfico e Histórico Vasco**
Plaza Miguel Unamuno 4. *Tel 94 415 54 23.* 🕐 *Tue–Sun.* ⚫ *public hols.* 🎫 ♿

🏛 **Museo de Bellas Artes**
Plaza del Museo 2. *Tel 94 439 60 60.* 🕐 *Tue–Sun.* 🎫 📷 ♿

🎭 **Palacio de la Música y Congresos Euskalduna**
Avenida Abandoibarra 4. *Tel 94 403 50 00.* 🕐 *for concerts.* 🎫 📷 ♿

Gernika-Lumo ❷

Vizcaya. 🏙 *15,400.* 🚌 🚗 ℹ *Artekalea 8, 94 625 58 92.* ⚫ *Mon.* 🎉 *Aniversario del Bombardeo de Guernica (26 Apr), San Roke (15 & 16 Aug).*

This little town is of great symbolic significance to the Basques. For centuries, Basque leaders met in democratic assembly under an oak on a hillside here. On 26 April 1937 Gernika-Lumo (Guernica) was the target of the world's first saturation bombing raid, carried out by Nazi aircraft at the request of General Franco. Picasso's powerful painting *(see pp66–7)* of this outrage can be seen in Madrid *(see p299).*

The town has since been rebuilt and is rather dull. But in a garden, inside a pavilion and closely guarded, is the 300-year-old petrified trunk of the oak tree, the *Gernikako Arbola*, or Oak of Gernika, symbol of the ancient roots of the Basque people. Younger oaks, nurtured from its acorns, have been planted beside it. The Basque people make visits to this ancient tree as if

Zuloaga's *Condesa Mathieu de Noailles* **(1913), Bilbao Museum of Fine Art**

Basque fishermen depicted in the stained-glass ceiling of the Casa de Juntas in Gernika-Lumo

on a pilgrimage. The **Casa de Juntas**, nearby, is a former chapel where the parliament of the province of Vizcaya re-convened in 1979, when the Basque provinces regained their autonomy. In one room a stained-glass ceiling depicts the Oak of Gernika with Basque citizens debating their rights.

The Europa Park, next door, has peace sculptures by Henry Moore and Eduardo Chillida.

Environs

Five km (3 miles) northeast of Gernika, near Kortézubi (Cortézubi), are the **Cuevas de Santimamiñe**. On the walls of a small chamber are drawings in charcoal of bison and other animals made by Cro-Magnon cave dwellers around 11,000 BC. They were discovered in 1917. A guide shows visitors around, and leads them down the Long Gallery, an under-ground passage full of oddly shaped stalagmites and stalactites, some of them shot through with brilliant colours. This is one of several huge cave complexes in this area – most are closed to the public.

🏛 **Casa de Juntas**
C/ Allende Salazar. **Tel** 94 625 11 38. ⬜ daily. ● 1 & 6 Jan, 24, 25, 31 Dec. ♿

♠ **Cuevas de Santimamiñe**
Barrio Basondo, Kortézubi. **Tel** 94 625 58 92. ⬜ Mon–Fri. ● public hols.

Costa Vasca ❸

Vizcaya & Guipúzcoa. 🚉 Bilbao.
🚌 Bilbao. ℹ Getxo, 94 491 08 00.

The Basque country's 176 km (110 miles) of coastline is heavily indented: rugged cliffs alternate with inlets and coves, the whole backed by wooded hills. Some of the fishing villages are over-developed, but the scenery inland is attractive.

There are good beaches north of Algorta (near Bilbao). **Plentzia** is a pleasant estuary town with a marina. Eastwards on the coast is **Bakio**, a large fishing village also known for its beaches. Beyond it the BI3101, a dramatic corniche road, winds high above the sea past the tiny island hermitage,

Anglers on the quayside at Lekeitio, a port on the Costa Vasca

San Juan de Gaztelugatxe, and Matxitxaco, a headland light-house. It passes Bermeo, a port with a fishery museum, the **Museo del Pescador**, and Mundaka, a small surfing re-sort. On the serene Ría de Guernica there are two sandy beaches, **Laida** and **Laga**.

Lekeitio, a fishing port to the east, has a pretty shore-line. Old Basque houses line the seafront below the 15th-century church of Santa María. One long beach, good for swimming, sweeps round the village of **Saturrarán** and the old port of **Ondarroa**. The Lekeitio–Ondarroa road is pleasantly planted with pines.

Zumaia is a beach resort with an old quarter. In the **Museo de Ignacio Zuloaga**, the former home of the well-known Basque painter who lived from 1870–1945, colour-ful studies of Basque rural and maritime life are on display. **Getaria**, along the coast, is a trawler port with lively cafés. and the 14th-century Iglesia de San Salvador. **Zarautz**, once a fashionable resort, has sizeable beaches and elegant mansions.

🏛 **Museo del Pescador**
Plaza Torrontero 1. **Tel** 94 688 11 71.
⬜ Tue–Sun. ● public hols. ♿

🏛 **Museo de Ignacio Zuloaga**
Santiago Auzoa 50, Zumaia. **Tel** 943 86 23 41. ⬜ Easter–15 Sept: Wed–Sun. 📷

Bilbao: Museo Guggenheim

The Museo Guggenheim is the jewel in Bilbao's
cultural crown. The building itself is a star attraction:
a mind-boggling array of silvery curves by the
American architect Frank Gehry, which are alleged
to resemble a ship or a flower. The Guggenheim's
collection represents an intruigingly broad spectrum
of modern and contemporary art, and includes works
by Abstract Impressionists such as Willem de Kooning
and Mark Rothko. Most of the art shown here is displayed as part of an ongoing series of temporary
exhibitions and major retrospectives. Some of these
are also staged at the
Guggenheim museums
in New York, Venice
and Berlin.

Roofscape
*The Guggenheim's prow-like
points and metallic material
make it comparable to a ship.*

The tower, on the far side of the
bridge, was designed to resemble a
sail. It is not an exhibition space.

**The
Puente de la
Salve** was incorpo-
rated into the design
of the building, which
extends underneath it.

★ **Titanium
façade**
*Rarely used in build-
ings, titanium is more
usually used for air-
craft parts. In total
60 tons were used, but
the layer is only 3 mm
(0.1 inches) thick.*

The Snake, by
Richard Serra, was
created in hot-rolled steel.
It is over 30 m (100 ft) long.

Fish Gallery
*Dominated by Richard Serra's Snake, this
gallery is the museum's largest. The fish
motif, seen in the flowing shape, is one of
architect Frank Gehry's favourites.*

★ Atrium
The space in which visitors to the museum first find themselves is the extraordinary 60-m (165-ft) high atrium. It serves as an orientation point and its height makes it a dramatic setting for exhibiting large pieces.

VISITORS' CHECKLIST

Avenida Abandoibarra 2. *Tel* 944 35 90 80. Ⓜ *Moyua*. 🚌 1, 10, 11, 13, 18, 27, 38, 46, 48, 71. ⬜ 10am–8pm daily. ⬤ Mon (Sep–Jun), 25 Dec, 1 Jan.
🎫 📷 ♿ 📷 🏛 🍴 🏪
www.guggenheim-bilbao.es

Puppy, by American artist Jeff Koons, has a coat of flowers irrigated by an internal system. Originally a temporary feature, the sculpture's popularity with Bilbao's residents earned it a permanent spot.

Second-floor balcony

Main entrance

The museum's restaurant, under rising star Basque chef Martín Berasategui, serves local specialities.

Water garden beside the River Nervión

STAR FEATURES

★ Titanium façade
───────────
★ Atrium

View from the City
Approaching along the Calle de Iparraguirre, the "Guggen", as the museum has been nicknamed by locals, stands out amid traditional buildings.

For hotels and restaurants in this region see pp565–8 and pp613–17

San Sebastián's Playa de Ondarreta, with its view across the bay

San Sebastián ❹

Guipúzcoa. 🏙 180,000. ✈ 🚉 ℹ
Reina Regente 3, 943 48 11 66. ⛴
Sun. 🎭 *San Sebastián (20 Jan);
Semana Grande (late-Aug).*
www.sansebastianturismo.com

Gloriously situated on a
neat, shell-shaped bay, San
Sebastián (Donostia) is the
most elegant and fashionable
Spanish seaside resort. At
either end of the bay is a
tower-topped hill – Monte
Urgull in the east and Monte
Igueldo in the west. Between
the two, in the mouth of the
bay, lies a small island, the
Isla de Santa Clara.

San Sebastián became a
smart resort in the late 19th
century, and has remained
popular with the aristocracy. It
still has many smart shops and
one of Spain's grandest luxury
hotels, the María Cristina *(see
p567)*, but San Sebastián is
now primarily a family resort.

The city is renowned for its
great summer arts festivals.
Jazz and theatre festivals are
held in July, a classical music
festival in August, and the San
Sebastián International Film
Festival in September. The
Semana Grande in August is
the city's principle fiesta.

Cuisine also plays a huge
part in local life: many
Basque men in San Sebastián
belong to gastronomic clubs
where they gather to cook, eat,
drink and talk. Even these
days, women are seldom
invited to such gatherings.

The Old Town

San Sebastián's fascinating
old town, called the Parte
Vieja, is wedged between the
bay and the Río Urumea. The
alleys of the old town,
packed with restaurants and
tapas bars, are intensely
animated at night. In the large
local fish market, stalls piled
high with delicacies testify to
the key role of fish in the life
of the town.

The heart of the old town is
the **Plaza de la Constitución**, a
handsome, arcaded square
with coloured shutters. The
numbers on the balconies
date from when the square
was used as a bullring –
organizers sold a ticket for
each numbered place. Nearby
is the 16th-century church of
Iglesia de San Vicente.

Monte Urgull rises behind
the old town. On the summit
are a statue of Christ and the

ruined **Castillo de Santa Cruz
de la Mota**, with old cannons.

Beaches

San Sebastián's two principal
beaches follow the bay round
to **Monte Igueldo**. The **Playa
de Ondarreta** is the more
fashionable of the two while
the **Playa de la Concha** is the
larger. Between them is the
Palacio Miramar, built in 1889
by the Basque architect, José
Goicoa, to designs by Selden
Wornum, a British architect.
The palace, built for Queen
María Cristina as a summer
residence, established San
Sebastián as an aristocratic
resort. The gardens are open
to the public, and the palace
often plays host to local events.

At the water's edge near the
Playa de Ondarreta is a striking
group of modern iron sculptures, *The Comb of the Winds*
by Eduardo Chillida. A road
and a funicular railway, built
in 1912, lead to the top of
Monte Igueldo, where there is
a small amusement park.

To the east of the Playa de
la Concha is the surfer's
favourite beach, **Playa de la
Zurriola**, which is overlooked
by the hill, **Monte Ulía**.

🐠 Aquarium

Plaza Carlos Blasco de Imaz 1.
Tel *943 44 00 99.* ⭕ *Sep–Jun:
10am–8pm; Jul–Aug: 10am–9pm
daily.* ⭕ *25 Dec & 1 Jan.* ♿ 📷
This remodeled aquarium
boasts a 360° underwater
tunnel, where visitors can view
over 5,000 fish, including two
small sharks. Tickets allow entry
to a Naval Museum, containing
exhibits of Basque naval history.

The Comb of the Winds by Eduardo Chillida

Josep Maria Sert's murals of Basque life in the Museo de San Telmo

by Vicente López and master-pieces by El Greco. The chapel holds 11 murals by the Catalan artist Josep Maria Sert, depicting Basque legends, culture and the region's seafaring life.

🏛 Chillida-Leku

Caserío Zabalaga, B° Jáuregui 66, Hernani. *Tel* 943 33 60 06. ⬤ Tue. 🖼 ♿ www.museochillidaleku.com

Set in a 16th-century farm-house surrounded by pleasant gardens, this new museum displays a permanent collection of 40 sculptures by the acclaimed Basque artist Eduardo Chillida.

Kursaal

Avenida de la Zurriola 1. *Tel* 943 00 30 00. 🖼 💼 🍴 ♿

These giant cubes stand out as the most prominent feature on Zurriola beach, especially when lit up at night. Designed by Rafael Moneo, the cubes contain large auditoriums, for most of the year home to conferences and concerts.

🏛 Museo de San Telmo

Plaza Zuloaga. *Tel* 943 48 15 80. ⬤ Tue–Sun.

This is a large museum in a 16th-century monastery below Monte Urgull. In the cloister is a collection of Basque funerary columns dating from the 15th–17th centuries.

The museum also contains displays of furniture, tools and other artifacts, and paintings by local Basque artists: 19th-century works by Antonio Ortiz Echagüe, modern paintings by Ignacio Zuloaga, portraits

Environs

5 km (3 miles) east of San Sebastián is **Pasaia Donibane**, a picturesque fishing village consisting of a jumble of houses with a cobbled main street which has some good fish restaurants.

The waterfront of the tiny fishing village of Pasaia Donibane

Old balconied houses in the upper town, Hondarribia

Hondarribia ⑤

Guipúzcoa. 🏘 16,000. 🚌 Calle Javier Ugarte 6, 943 64 54 58. 🎉 La Kutxa Entrega (25 Jul), Alarde (6–8 Sep).

Hondarribia (Fuenterrabía), the historic town at the mouth of the Río Bidasoa, was attacked by the French over many centuries. The upper town is protected by 15th-century walls and entered via their original gateway, the handsome **Puerta de Santa María**. They enclose alleys of old houses with carved eaves, balconies and coats of arms.

The streets cluster round the church of **Nuestra Señora de la Asunción y del Manzano**, with its massive buttresses, tall Baroque tower, and, inside, a gold reredos. At the town's highest point is the 10th century **castle**, now a parador *(see p566)*.

Hondarribia has seafront cafés in La Marina, its lively fishermen's quarter. It is also a seaside resort, with beaches stretching to the north.

Environs

A hill road climbs westwards to the shrine of the Virgin of Guadalupe. Further along this road are panoramic views of the coast and the mountains. From the **Ermita de San Marcial**, which stands on a hill 9 km (6 miles) to the south, there are views of the Bidasoa plain straddling the border – the French towns are neatly white, the Spanish ones are greyer.

SAN SEBASTIÁN FILM FESTIVAL

This festival, founded in 1953, is one of the five leading European annual film festivals. It is held in late September, drawing more than 100,000 spectators. The special Donostia Prize is awarded as a tribute to the career of a star or director: recent winners include Susan Sarandon, Jeanne Moreau and Jeremy Irons. Visiting celebrities have included Quentin Tarantino, Greta Scacchi and William Hurt. Prizes also go to individual new films. An early winner was Hitchcock's *Vertigo*. The festival's website is www.sansebastianfestival.ya.com

Lauren Bacall receiving an award

The Renaissance façade of the former Basque university in Oñati

Santuario de Loiola ❻

Loiola (Guipúzcoa). **Tel** 943 02 50 00. 🚻 ⏺ 10am–1pm, 3–7pm daily. **www**.santuariodeloyola.org

Saint Ignatius of Loiola (San Ignacio de Loyola), founder of the Jesuits, was born in the 1490s in the Santa Casa (holy house), a stone manor near Azpeitia. In the 17th century it was enclosed by the Basílica de San Ignacio, and the rooms in which the aristocratic Loiola family lived were converted into chapels. The Chapel of the Conversion is the room in which Ignatius, as a young soldier, recovered from a war injury, and had a profound religious experience.

A diorama depicts episodes in the saint's life: dedicating his life to Christ at the Monastery of Montserrat (see pp218–9);

writing his *Spiritual Exercises* in a cave at Manresa; his imprisonment by the Inquisition; and his pilgrimage to the Holy Land. The basilica, built from 1681–1738, has a Churrigueresque dome and a circular nave with rich carvings.

Oñati ❼

Guipúzcoa. 🏠 10,600. 🚻 🛈 Calle San Juan 14, 943 78 34 53. 🚌 Sat. 🎉 Corpus Christi (May/Jun), San Miguel (29 Sep).

This historic town in the Udana Valley has a distinguished past. In the First Carlist War, 1833–9 (see p63), it was a seat of the court of Don Carlos, brother of King Fernando VII and pretender to the throne. Its former **university**, built in about 1540, was for centuries the only one in the Basque Country. It has a Renaissance façade,

decorated with statues of saints, and an elegant patio.

In the Plaza de los Fueros is the **Iglesia de San Miguel**, a Gothic church with a stone cloister in Gothic-Flemish style. It contains the tomb of Bishop Zuázola of Ávila, the founder of the university. Opposite is the Baroque **town hall** (ayuntamiento).

Environs

A mountain road ascends 9 km (6 miles) to the **Santuario de Arantzazu**, below the peak of Aitzgorri. In 1469 it is believed a shepherd visualized the Virgin here. Over the door of the church, built in the 1950s, are sculptures of the apostles by Jorge Oteiza

🏛 **Universidad de Sancti Spiritus** Avenida de la Universidad Vasca. **Tel** 943 78 34 53. ⏺ Mon–Sun for guided tours (phone in advance). 📷 Only afternoons in Aug.

The imposing Santuario de Loiola, with its Churrigueresque cupola

THE FOUNDING OF THE JESUIT ORDER

The Society of Jesus was founded in Rome in 1539 by Saint Ignatius and a group of priests who were dedicated to helping the poor. Pope Paul III soon approved the order's establishment, with Ignatius as Superior General. The order, which grew wealthy, vowed military obedience to the Pope and became his most powerful weapon against the Reformation. Today, there are approximately 20,000 Jesuits working, mainly in education, in 112 countries.

Saint Ignatius of Loiola

Basque Culture

The Basques may be Europe's oldest race. Anthropologists think they could be descended from Cro-Magnon people, who lived in the Pyrenees 40,000 years ago. The dolmens and carved stones of their ancestors are evidence of the Basques' pagan roots.

Long isolated in their mountain valleys, the Basques preserved their unique language, myths and art for millennia, almost untouched by other influences.

Basque policeman

Many families still live in the isolated, chalet-style stone *caseríos*, or farmhouses, built by their forebears. Their music and high-bounding dances are unlike those of any other culture, and their cuisine is varied and imaginative.

The *fueros* or ancient Basque laws and rights were suppressed under General Franco, but since the arrival of democracy in 1975 the Basques have had their own parliament and police force, having won great autonomy over their own affairs.

THE BASQUE REGION

☐ *Areas of Basque culture*

The national identity *is symbolized by the region's flag:* La Ikurriña. *The white cross symbolizes Christianity. The green St Andrew's Cross commemorates a battle won on his feast day.*

Bertsolaris *are bards. They improvise witty, sometimes humorous songs, whose verses relate current events or legends.* Bertsolaris *sing, unaccompanied, to gatherings in public places, such as bars and squares, often in competition. This oral tradition has preserved Basque folklore, legends and history. No texts were written in* Euskera *(Basque) until the 16th century.*

The Basque economy *has always relied on fishing and associated industries, such as shipbuilding and agriculture. In recent history, heavy industries have made this region prosperous.*

Traditional sports *are highly respected in Basque culture. In pelota (frontón), teams hit a ball at a wall then catch it with a wicker scoop or their hands. Sports involving strength, such as log-splitting and weightlifting, are the most popular.*

VITORIA CITY CENTRE

Catedral de Santa María ③
Iglesia de San Miguel ⑥
Museo de Arqueología ②
Museo de Naipes ⑤
Palacio de Escoriaza-Esquibel ④
Plaza de la Virgen Blanca ⑦
El Portalón ①

0 metres   250
0 yards   250

Key to Symbols *see back flap*

Vitoria ❽

Álava. 👥 *222,000.* ✈ 🚌 🚆 ℹ
Plaza General Loma, 945 16 15 98.
🏛 *Thu.* 🎭 *Romería de San Prudencio
(28 Apr), Fiestas de la Virgen Blanca
(4–9 Aug).* www.vitoria-gasteiz.org

Vitoria (Gasteiz), the seat of
the Basque government,
was founded on a hill – the
province's highest point and
the site of an ancient Basque
town, Gasteiz. Vitoria's oldest
part, El Campillo, was rebuilt
in 1200 after a fire. The city
later grew rich on the iron
and wool trades.

The old town focuses on the
Plaza de la Virgen Blanca,
with its monument to a battle
fought nearby in 1813, when

the British Duke of Wellington
defeated the French. Around
the plaza are old houses with
miradores (glazed balconies).

On the hillside above the
plaza is the Gothic **Iglesia de
San Miguel.** An outside niche
contains a statue of the Virgen
Blanca (White Virgin), Vitoria's
patron saint. A big festival *(see
p132)* starts before her feast
day, which is on 5 August.
On the wall of San Miguel
facing the **Plaza del Machete**
there is a recess with a replica
of the machete on which the
city's rulers swore to uphold
the laws or be slain.

The old town has several
Renaissance palaces, including
the 16th-century **Palacio de
Escoriaza-Esquibel**, which

has a Plateresque *(see p25)*
patio. Around it is a charming
area of old alleys linked by
steep steps.

The city has two cathedrals.
The oldest, currently under
restoration, is the Gothic
Catedral de Santa María, with
a sculpted west porch. Close
by, in Calle Correría, a street
of old houses, is the
enchanting **El Portalón**, a
merchant's house and hostel
from the 15th century. The
building, which is full of
Basque country furniture and
art, is now a restaurant.

Among the city's later architectural gems are an arcaded
street, **Los Arquillos**, and the
adjoining **Plaza de España**,
also arcaded. They were built
in the late 18th century to link
the old town with the new
quarter then being built. South
of the old town is the Neo-
Gothic **Catedral Nueva de
María Inmaculada**, begun in
1907 and finished in 1973.

🏛 Museo de Arqueología
Calle Correria 116. **Tel** *945 18
19 22.* 🕐 *Tue–Sun.*
The exhibits in this museum,
in a 16th-century half-timbered
house, include dolmens erected more than 4,000 years ago,
Roman sculptures found in
Álava, and medieval artifacts.

The quiet Plaza de España in the centre of Vitoria

The Gothic west door of Vitoria's Catedral de Santa María

🏛 Museo de Naipes

Palacio de Bendaña, C/ Cuchillería 54. **Tel** *945 18 19 20.* ⬜ *Tue–Sun.* ♿

The grandson of Heraclio Fournier, who founded a playing cards factory in Vitoria in 1868, displays his collection of more than 6,000 items in this museum. The oldest exhibits are late 14th-century Italian cards. Among the many sets of tarot cards are some designed by Salvador Dalí in the 1980s.

🏛 Museo de Armería

Paseo Fray Francisco 3. **Tel** *945 18 19 25.* ⬜ *Tue–Sun.*

The weapons exhibited in this museum range in age from prehistoric axes to 20th-century pistols. There are also displays of medieval armour and an exhibit tracing the events of the 1813 Battle of Vitoria.

🏛 Museo Diocesano de Arte Sacro

Catedral Nueva de María Inmaculada, Calle Cadena y Elta 2. **Tel** *945 15 06 31.* ⬜ *10am–2pm, 4–6:30pm Tue–Fri, 10am–2pm Sat, 11am–2pm Sun & public hols.*

The design of this museum is considerate to the surrounding cathedral. Exhibits of religious art are displayed in sections which relate to their medium, such as stone, wood or silver.

Castillo de Mendoza 🔟

Mendoza (Álava). **Tel** *945 18 16 17.* ⬜ *Tue–Sun.*

In the centre of Mendoza village, 10 km (6 miles) west of Vitoria, stands this small, square, much restored fortress dating from the 13th century. There are marvellous views from the tops of the four towers. Once a ducal residence, the thick-walled castle now houses the **Museo Heráldica**. In it are displayed the coats of arms of noble Basque families and items relating to them.

Environs

On the A2622 Pobes–Tuesta road are the **Salinas de Añana**, a group of tiered saltpans that are fed by mineral springs. The nearby village of **Tuesta** boasts a Romanesque church with a decorated portal. Inside are capitals carved with historical scenes, and a medieval wood sculpture of St Sebastian.

Laguardia 🔟

Álava. 🏘 *1,500.* 🚏 *Plaza San Juan 1, 945 60 08 45.* 🚌 *Tue.* 🎉 *San Juan and San Pedro (24 Jun).*

This little wine town is the capital of La Rioja Alavesa, a part of southern Álava province where Rioja wines (*see pp78–9*) have been produced for centuries. It is a fertile, vine-clad plain, sheltered by high hills to the north. There are fine panoramic views from the road that climbs up to the Herrera pass. Laguardia is a medieval hill town, its encircling ramparts, towers and fortified gateways visible from afar. Along its steep, narrow cobbled streets there are many **bodegas** (wine cellars), offering wine tastings and tours throughout the year. It is usually necessary to make a booking in advance.

The Gothic **Iglesia de Santa María de los Reyes** has an austere façade and an unusual portal. The Virgin and Child are delicately sculptured on a door inside.

Virgin and child statue in Laguardia

Vineyards near Laguardia, capital of La Rioja Alavesa, a wine-producing region since the Middle Ages

Haro ⓫

La Rioja. 🏠 *10,300*. 🚉 🚌 🛈
*Plaza Monseñor Florentino Rodriguez,
941 30 33 66.* 🚌 *Tue & Sat.* 📷
*Wine Battle (29 Jun), San Pedro (29
Jun), Virgen de la Vega (8 Sep).*

A graceful town on the Río
Ebro, Haro has a lively old
quarter with wine taverns and
mansions. It is crowned by
the hilltop **Iglesia de Santo
Tomás**, a Gothic church with
a Plateresque *(see p25)* portal.
   Haro is the centre for the
vineyards and bodegas of the
Rioja Alta wine region, which
is higher and cooler than the
Rioja Baja *(see pp78–9)*. The
clay soil and the climate –
Haro is sheltered by a sierra
to the north – create the conditions in which the famous
regional wines are produced.
Many bodegas run tours and
tastings. To join one, you may
need to book ahead at the
bodega. There may be a small
charge. The cafés in the old
town offer local wines and
tapas at low prices and a
convivial atmosphere,
especially in the evenings.
   A wine-throwing orgy is the
climax of the area's fiesta *(see
p132)* held every June.

Tomb of St Dominic in the cathedral of Santo Domingo de la Calzada

**Rows of Rioja vines on the rolling
hills near Haro**

Santo Domingo de
la Calzada ⓬

La Rioja. 🏠 *6,600*. 🚉 🛈 *Calle
Mayor 70, 941 34 12 30.* 🚌 *Sat.*
📷 *Día del Patron (12 May), San
Jerónimo Hermosilla (19 Sep),
Immaculada Concepción (8 Dec).*

This town on the Road to
Santiago de Compostela *(see
pp82–3)* is named after the
11th-century saint who built
bridges and roads *(calzadas)*
to help pilgrims. He also built
a hospital, which now serves
as a parador *(see p567)*.

Miracles performed by the
saint are recorded in carvings
on his tomb in the town's
part-Romanesque, part-Gothic
cathedral, and in paintings on
the wall of the choir. The
most obvious and bizarre
record is a sumptuously decorated cage set in a wall in
which, for centuries, a live
cock and hen are kept. The
cathedral has a carved walnut
reredos at the high altar, the
last work, in 1541,
of the artist Damià Forment.
The restored 14th-century
ramparts of the town are also
worth seeing.

THE COCK AND HEN OF ST DOMINIC

A live cock and hen are kept in the cathedral of
Santo Domingo de la Calzada as a tribute to the
saint's miraculous life-giving powers. Centuries ago,
it is said, a German pilgrim refused the advances of
a local girl, who denounced him as a thief. He was
hanged as a consequence, but later his parents found
him alive on the gallows. They rushed to a judge, who
said, dismissively, "Nonsense, he's no more alive
than this roast chicken on my plate". Whereupon,
the chicken stood up on the plate and crowed.

The cock and hen in their decorated cage

San Millán de la Cogolla ⓭

La Rioja. 🏠 *300.* ℹ️ *Monasterio de Yuso, Edificio Aula de la Lengua, 941 37 32 59.* 🎪 *Traslación de las Reliquias (26 Sep), San Millán (12 Nov).* **www.**fsanmillan.com

This village grew up around two monasteries. On a hillside above the village is the **Monasterio de San Millán de Suso**. It was built in the 10th century on the site of a community founded by St Emilian, a shepherd hermit, in 537. The church, hollowed out of pink sandstone, has Romanesque and Mozarabic features. It contains the carved alabaster tomb of St Emiliano.

The **Monasterio de San Millán de Yuso** is below it, in the Cárdenas Valley. It was built between the 16th and 18th centuries on the site of an earlier monastery. The part-Renaissance church has Baroque golden doors and a rococo sacristy, where 17th-century paintings are hung.

In the treasury there is a collection of ivory plaques. They were once part of two 11th-century jewelled reliquaries, which were plundered by French troops in 1813.

Medieval manuscripts are also displayed in the treasury. Among them is a facsimile of one of the earliest known texts in Castilian Romance *(see p34)*. It is a commentary by a 10th-century Suso monk on a work by San Cesáreo de Arles, the *Glosas Emilianenses.*

The Monasterio de San Millán de Yuso in the Cárdenas valley

Cloister of the Monasterio de Santa María la Real, Nájera

Nájera ⓮

La Rioja. 🏠 *7,200.* 🚌 ℹ️ *Plaza de San Miguel, s/n, 941 36 00 41.* 🅿️ *Thu.* 🎪 *San Prudencio (28 Apr), Santa María la Real (16, 19 Sep).*

The old town of Nájera, west of Logroño, was the capital of La Rioja and Navarra until 1076, when La Rioja was incorporated into Castile. The royal families of Navarra, León and Castile are buried in the **Monasterio de Santa María la Real**. It was founded in the 11th century beside a sandstone cliff where a statue of the Virgin was found in a cave. A 13th-century Madonna can be seen in the cave, beneath the carved choir stalls of the 15th-century church.

The 12th-century carved tomb of Blanca of Navarra, the wife of Sancho III, is the finest of many royal sarcophagi.

🏛️ **Monasterio de Santa María la Real**
Nájera. **Tel** *941 36 36 50.* ⬜ *Tue–Sun.* 🎫

Logroño ⓯

La Rioja. 🏠 *140,000.* 🚌 🚉 ℹ️ *Paseo del Espolón, Príncipe de Vergara 1, 941 29 12 60.* 🎪 *San Bernabé (11 Jun), San Mateo (21 Sep).*

The capital of La Rioja is a tidy, modern city of wide boulevards and smart shops. It is the commercial centre of a fertile plain where quality vegetables are produced, in addition to Rioja wines.

In Logroño's pleasant old quarter on the Río Ebro is the Gothic **cathedral**, with twin towers. Above the south portal of the nearby **Iglesia de Santiago el Real**, which houses an image of the patron saint Our Lady of Hope, is an equestrian statue of St James as Moorslayer *(see p55).*

Environs
About 50 km (30 miles) south of Logroño, the N111 winds through the dramatic **Iregua Valley**, through tunnels and gorges, to the Sierra de Cameros.

The ornate Baroque west door of Logroño cathedral

Enciso ⓰

La Rioja. 🏠 *175.* 🚌 *from Logroño.* ℹ️ *Plaza Mayor, 941 39 60 05.* 🎪 *San Roque (16 Aug).*

Near this remote hill village west of Calahorra is Spain's "Jurassic Park". Signposts point to the *huellas de dinosaurios* (dinosaur footprints). Embedded in rocks overhanging a stream are the prints of many giant, three-toed feet, up to 30 cm (1 ft) long. They were made around 150 million years ago, when dinosaurs moved between the marshes of the Ebro valley, at that time a sea, and these hills. Prints can also be seen at other locations in the area.

Environs
Arnedillo, 10 km (6 miles) to the north, is a spa with thermal baths once used by Fernando VI. In **Autol**, to the east, there are two unusual limestone peaks.

The intricately carved portal of Tudela cathedral

Tudela

Navarra. ⚡ *32,000.* 🚉 ✈
🛈 *Calle de Juicio 4, 948 84 80 58.*
📅 *Sat.* ⚐ *Santa Ana (26–30 Jul).*

Navarra's second city is the great commercial centre of the vast agricultural lands of the Ebro valley in Navarra, the Ribera. Although much of Tudela consists of modern developments, its origins are ancient. Spanning the Ebro is a 13th-century bridge with 17 irregular arches. The old town has well-preserved Mudéjar and two Jewish districts.

The **Plaza de los Fueros** is old Tudela's main square. It is surrounded by houses with wrought-iron balconies. On some of their façades are paintings of bullfights, a reminder that the plaza was formerly used as a bullring.

The **cathedral**, begun in 1194, exemplifies the religious toleration under which Tudela was governed after the Reconquest. It is Early Gothic, with a carved portal depicting the Last Judgement. The Romanesque cloister encloses the ruins of a 9th-century mosque, and a Mudéjar chapel, the first synagogue in the city.

Environs
To the north is the **Bárdenas Reales**, an arid area of limestone cliffs and crags. About 20 km (12 miles) west of Tudela is the spa town of **Fitero**, with the 12th-century Monasterio de Santa María.

Monasterio de La Oliva

Carcastillo (Navarra). **Tel** *948 72 50 06.* 🚌 *from Pamplona.* ⭕ *daily.* 🏛

French Cistercian monks built this small monastery on a remote plain in the 12th century. The church is simple, in typical Cistercian style, but adorned with rose windows.

One of the cloisters in the Monasterio de La Oliva

The serene cloister, dating from the 14th and 15th centuries, adjoins a 12th-century chapterhouse. The church also has a 17th century tower. Today, the monks survive by selling local honey and cheese, their own wine, and by accepting paying guests *(see p556).*

Ujué

Navarra. ⚡ *240.* 🛈 *Plaza Municipal, 948 73 90 46.* ⚐ *Virgen de Ujué (8 Sep).*

One of Spain's least spoiled hill villages, Ujué commands a high spur at the end of a winding road. It has quaint façades, cobbled alleys and steep steps. The **Iglesia de Santa María** is in Gothic style with a Romanesque chancel and an exterior lookout gallery. The ruined fortifications around the church offer views of the Pyrenees.

On the Sunday after 25 April, pilgrims in black capes visit the Virgin of Ujué, whose Romanesque image is displayed in the church.

Olite

Navarra. ⚡ *3,000.* 🚉 🛈 *Pl. de Teobaldos 10, 948 74 17 03.* 📅 *Wed.* ⚐ *Medieval Markets (late Aug), Exaltación de la Santa Cruz (14–20 Sep).*

The historic town of Olite was founded by the Romans and later chosen as a royal residence by the kings of Navarra. Part of the town's old walls can be seen. They enclose a

Prince Carlos de Viana, Carlos III's grandson

THE KINGDOM OF NAVARRA

Navarra emerged as an independent Christian kingdom in the 10th century, after Sancho I Garcés became king of Pamplona. Sancho III the Great expanded the kingdom, and at his death, in 1035, Navarra stretched all the way from Ribagorza in Aragón to Valladolid. Sancho VI the Wise, who reigned 1150–94, recognized the independent rights *(fueros)* of many towns. In 1234, Navarra passed by marriage to a line of French rulers. One, Carlos III the Noble, built Olite castle. His grandson, Carlos de Viana, wrote the *Chronicle of the Kings of Navarra* in 1455. In 1512 Navarra was annexed by Fernando II of Castile, as part of united Spain, but it kept its own laws and currency until the 1800s.

delightful jumble of steep, narrow streets and little squares, churches and the **Monasterio de Santa Clara**, begun in the 13th century. The houses along the Rúa Cerco de Fuera and the Rúa Mayor were built between the 16th and 18th centuries.

The castle, the **Palacio Real de Olite**, was built about 1406 by Carlos III, and has earned Olite its nickname "the Gothic town". It was heavily fortified, but was brilliantly decorated inside by Mudéjar artists with *azulejos* (ceramic tiles) and marquetry ceilings. The walkways were planted with vines and orange trees, and there was an aviary and a lions' den.

During the War of Independence *(see pp62–3)* the castle was burned to prevent it falling into French hands. Since 1937, however, it has been restored to a semblance of its former glory. Part of it houses a parador *(see p567)*.

Today, the castle is a complex of courtyards, passages, steep stairs, large halls, royal chambers, battlements, towers and turrets. From the "windy tower" monarchs were able to watch tournaments.

Adjoining the castle is a 13th-century former royal chapel, the **Iglesia de Santa María**, which features a richly carved Gothic portal.

Olite is in the Navarra wine region *(see pp78–9)* and the town has several bodegas.

♣ **Palacio Real de Olite**
Plaza de Carlos III. **Tel** 948 74 00 35. ◯ *daily.* 🚫

The five-arched, medieval pilgrims' bridge at Puente la Reina

Puente la Reina ㉑

Navarra. 🏠 *2,500.* ℹ *c/ Mayor 105, 948 34 08 45 / 948 34 00 07 (in winter).* 🚌 *Sat.* 🎉 *Santiago (25 Jul).*

Few towns along the Road to Santiago de Compostela *(see pp82–3)* evoke the past as vividly as Puente la Reina. The town takes its name from the graceful, humpbacked pedestrian bridge over the Río Arga. The bridge was built for pilgrims during the 11th century by royal command.

On Puente la Reina's narrow main street is the **Iglesia de Santiago**, which has a gilded statue by the west door showing the saint as a pilgrim. On the edge of town is the **Iglesia del Crucifijo**, another pilgrim church which was built in the 12th century by the Knights Templar. Contained within the church is a

Distinctive crucifix
in Puente la Reina

Y-shaped wooden crucifix of a sorrowful Christ with arms upraised, which is said to have been a gift from a German pilgrim in the 14th century.

Environs
Isolated in the fields about 5 km (3 miles) to the east is the 12th-century **Iglesia de Santa María de Eunate**. This octagonal Romanesque church may once have been a cemetery church for pilgrims, as human bones have been unearthed here. Pilgrims would shelter beneath the church's external arcade. West of Puente la Reina is the showpiece hill village of **Cirauqui**. It is also charming, if rather over-restored. Chic little balconied houses line tortuously twisting alleys linked by steps. The Iglesia de San Román, built in the 13th century on top of the hill, has a sculpted west door.

The battlements and towers of the Palacio Real de Olite

BASQUE COUNTRY, NAVARRA AND LA RIOJA'S FIESTAS

Los Sanfermines *(6–14 Jul)*, Pamplona (Navarra). In the famous *encierro* (bull running) six bulls are released at 8am each morning to run from their corral through the narrow, cobbled streets of the old town. On the last night of this week-long, non-stop party, crowds with candles sing Basque songs in the main square. The event gained worldwide fame after Ernest Hemingway described it in his novel, published in 1926, *The Sun Also Rises*.

Bulls scattering the runners in Pamplona

Wine Battle *(29 Jun)*, Haro (La Rioja). People dressed in white clothes squirt each other with wine from leather drinking bottles in the capital of the Rioja Alta wine region. **Danza de los Zancos** *(22 Jul and last Sat of Sep)*, Anguiano (La Rioja). Dancers on stilts, wearing ornate waistcoats and yellow skirts, hurtle down the stepped alley from the church to the main square. **La Virgen Blanca** *(4 Aug)*, Vitoria (Álava). A dummy holding an umbrella (the *celedón*) is lowered from San Miguel church to a house below – from which a man in similar dress emerges. The mayor fires a rocket and the crowds in the square light cigars.

Pilgrims drinking from the wine tap near the monastery at Irache

Estella ②②

Navarra. 🏘 *13,000.* 🚌 🛈 *Calle de San Nicolás 3, 948 55 63 01.* 🚍 *Thu.* 🎉 *San Andrés (early Aug).*

In the Middle Ages Estella (Lizarra) was the centre of the royal court of Navarra and a major stopping point on the pilgrims' Road to Santiago de Compostela *(see pp82–3)*. The town was a stronghold of the Carlists *(see p63)* in the 19th century. A memorial rally is held here on the first Sunday of May every year.

The most important monuments in Estella are sited on the edge of town, across the bridge over the Río Ega. Steps climb steeply from the arcaded Plaza de San Martín to the remarkable 12th-century **Iglesia de San Pedro de la Rúa**, built on top of a cliff. It features a a Mudéjar-influenced, sculpted doorway. The carved capitals are all that now remain of the Romanesque cloister, which was destroyed when a castle overlooking the church was blown up in 1592. The **Palacio de los Reyes de Navarra**, on the other side of the Plaza de San Martín, is a rare example of civil Romanesque architecture. It also houses a gallery of Navarrese art.

In the town centre, on the arcaded Plaza de los Fueros, the **Iglesia de San Juan Bautista** has a Romanesque porch. The north portal of the **Iglesia de San Miguel** has Romanesque carvings of St Michael slaying a dragon.

Environs

The **Monasterio de Nuestra Señora de Irache**, 3 km (2 miles) southwest of Estella, was a Benedict monastery which sheltered pilgrims on their way to Santiago. The church is mainly Transitional Gothic in style, but it has Romanesque apses and a cloister in Plateresque style. It is capped by a remarkable dome.

A bodega next to the monastery provides pilgrims with wine from a tap in a wall.

A small road branches off the NA120 north of Estella and winds through a wooded gorge to reach the **Monasterio de Iranzu**, built in the 12th century. The graceful austerity of its church and cloisters are typically Cistercian features.

The Lizarraga Pass, further up the NA120, offers views of attractive beech woods.

Pamplona ②③

Navarra. 🏘 *200,000.* ✈ 🚆 🚌 🛈 *C/ Eslava 1, 848 420 420.* 🎉 *Sanfermines (6–14 Jul), San Saturnino (29 Nov).* **www**.pamplona.net

The old fortress city of Pamplona (Iruña) is said to have been founded by the Roman general, Pompey. In the 9th century it became the capital of Navarra. This fairly busy city explodes into even more life in July during the fiesta of Los Sanfermines, with its daredevil bull running.

From the old **city walls** *(murallas)* you can get a good overview of Pamplona. The nearby **cathedral**, which

Sumptuous interior of the Palacio de Navarra, Pamplona

Stone tracery in the elegant cloister of Pamplona cathedral

is built in ochre-coloured stone, looks down on a loop in the Río Arga. It was built on the foundations of its 12th-century predecessor, and is mainly Gothic in style, with twin towers and an 18th-century façade. Inside there are lovely choir stalls and the alabaster tomb of Carlos III and Queen Leonor.

The southern entrance to the cloister is the beautifully carved, medieval Puerta de la Preciosa. The cathedral priests would gather here to sing an antiphon (hymn) to La Preciosa (Precious Virgin) before the night service.

The Museo Diocesano in the cathedral's 14th-century kitchen and refectory displays Gothic altarpieces, polychrome wood statues from all over Navarra, and a French 13th-century reliquary of the Holy Sepulchre.

West of the cathedral is the old town, cut through with many alleys. The neo-classical **Palacio del Gobierno de Navarra** lies in the Plaza del Castillo and is the seat of the Navarrese government. Outside, a statue of 1903 shows a symbolic woman upholding the *fueros* (historic laws) of Navarra (see p130). North of the

Sculpture in Pamplona depicting the *encierro*

palace is the medieval **Iglesia de San Saturnino**, built on the site where St Saturninus is said to have baptized some 40,000 pagan townspeople, and the Baroque **town hall** *(ayuntamiento)*.

Beneath the old town wall, in a 16th-century hospital with a Plateresque doorway, is the **Museo de Navarra**. This is a museum of regional archaeology, history and art. Exhibits include Roman mosaics and an 11th-century, Islam-inspired ivory casket. There are murals painted during the 14th–16th centuries, a portrait by Goya, and a collection of paintings by Basque artists.

To the southeast is the city's massive 16th-century **citadel**, erected in Felipe II's reign. It is designed with five bastions in a star shape. Beyond it are the spacious boulevards of the new town, and also the university's green campus.

🏛 **Museo de Navarra**
Calle Santo Domingo 47. *Tel 848 42 64 92.* ◯ *Tue–Sun.* 🖼 &

🏛 **Palacio de Navarra**
Avenida Carlos III 2. *Tel 848 42 70 00.* ◯ *by appointment.* &

PAMPLONA CITY CENTRE

Cathedral ③
City walls ②
Iglesia de San Saturnino ⑤
Museo de Navarra ①
Palacio de Navarra ⑥
Town Hall ④

0 metres 250
0 yards 250

KEY

Bull-running route

Key to Symbols *see back flap*

Basque houses in the picturesque
town of Etxalar, Valle de Bidasoa

Las Cinco Villas Del Valle de Bidasoa 24

Navarra. ⏚ *Pamplona, San
Sebastián.* ℹ *Bera, 948 63 12 22 /
948 63 00 05.* **www**.navarra.es

Five attractive Basque towns
lie in or near this valley, the
most northerly being **Bera**
(Vera). The houses in **Lesaka**

have wooden balconies under
deep eaves. The road south
passes hills dotted with white
farmsteads to reach **Igantzi**,
(Yanci), with its red-and-white
houses. **Arantza** is the most remote town. Since the 12th
century, pigeons have been
caught in huge nets strung
across a pass above **Etxalar**
(Echalar). From the summit of
La Rhune, on the French border above the valley, there is
a great view of the Pyrenees.

Elizondo 25

Navarra. 🏛 *3,000.* 🚌 ℹ *Casa
Cultura, 948 58 12 79.* 🚂 *Thu.* 🎉
Santiago (25 Jul), Feria (late Oct).

This is the biggest of a string
of typical Basque villages in
the very beautiful valley of
Baztán. By the river are noble
houses bearing coats of arms.
Arizkun, further up the valley, has old fortified houses
and a 17th-century convent.
The **Cueva de Brujas**, in
Zugarramurdi, was once a
meeting place for witches.

Canopy over the Virgin and Child in
the Colegiata Real

Roncesvalles 26

Navarra. 🏛 *27.* ℹ *Roncesvalles,
Antiguo Molino, s/n, 948 76 03 01.* 🎉
Día de la Virgen de Roncesvalles (8 Sep).

Roncesvalles (Orreaga), on
the Spanish side of a pass
through the Pyrenees, is a major halt on the Road to Santiago
(see pp82–3). Before it became associated with the pilgrim's way, Roncesvalles was
the site of a major battle in
778, in which the Basques of
Navarra slaughtered the rearguard of Charlemagne's army
as it marched homeward. This
event is described in the 12th-
century French epic poem, *The
Song of Roland*.
    The 13th-century **Colegiata
Real**, which has served travellers down the centuries, has a
silver-plated Virgin and Child
below a high canopy. In the
graceful chapterhouse, off the
cloister, is the white tomb of
Sancho VII the Strong (1154–
1234), looked down upon by
a stained-glass window of his
great victory, the Battle of Las
Navas de Tolosa *(see pp54–5)*.
Exhibits in the church museum
include "Charlemagne's chess-
board", an enamelled reliquary
which is so-called because of
its chequered design.

Valle de Roncal 27

Navarra. 🚌 *from Pamplona.* ℹ
*Roncal, Paseo Julian Gayarre, s/n, 948
47 52 56.*

Running perpendicular to
the Pyrenees, this valley is still
largely reliant on sheep, and
the village of **Roncal** is known
for its cheeses. Because of the
relative isolation of the valley,
the inhabitants have preserved their own identity and

The forested countryside around Roncesvalles

local costumes are worn during fiestas. The ski resort of **Isaba**, further up the valley, has a museum of local life and history. A spectacular road winds from Isaba to the tree-lined village of Ochagavia in the parallel **Valle de Salazar**. To the north, the **Selva de Irati**, one of Europe's largest woodlands, spread over the Pyrenees into France, below the snowy summit of Monte Ori at 2,017 m (6,617 ft).

Colourful balconies of houses in the village of Roncal

Monasterio de Leyre ㉘

Yesa (Navarra). **Tel** 948 88 41 50. Yesa. daily.

The Monastery of San Salvador de Leyre is situated high above a reservoir, alone amid grand scenery, backed by limestone cliffs. The abbey has been here since the 9th century when it was a great spiritual and political centre. Sancho III and his successors made it the royal pantheon of Navarra. The monastery began to decline in the 12th century. It was abandoned from 1836 until 1954, when it was restored by Benedictines. They turned part of it into a modestly priced hotel (see p568). To see the monastery you must join one of the tours run every morning and afternoon.

The big 11th century church has a Gothic vault and three lofty apses. On its west portal are weatherworn carvings of strange beasts, as well as biblical figures. The Romanesque crypt has unusually short columns with chunky capitals. The monks' Gregorian chant (see p376) during services is wonderful to hear.

Castillo de Javier ㉙

Javier (Navarra). **Tel** 948 88 40 00. from Pamplona. daily (the basilica only until 2005).

St Francis Xavier, the patron saint of Navarra, a missionary and a co-founder of the Jesuit order (see p124), was born in this 13th-century castle in 1506. It has since been restored and is now a Jesuit spiritual centre. Of interest are the saint's bedroom and a museum in the keep devoted to his life. In the oratory is a 13th-century polychrome Christ and a macabre 15th-century mural of grinning skeletons entitled *The Dance of Death*.

Crucifix in the oratory of the Castillo de Javier

Sangüesa ㉚

Navarra. 4,500. Calle Mayor 2, 948 87 14 11. Fri. San Sebastián (11 Sep).

Since medieval times this small town beside a bridge over the Río Aragón has been a stop on the Aragonese pilgrimage route to Santiago (see pp82–3).

The richly sculpted south portal of the **Iglesia de Santa María la Real** is a 13th-century treasure of Romanesque art (see p24). It is crammed with figures and details depicting the Last Judgement and society in the 13th century.

The Gothic **Iglesia de Santiago** and the 13th-century Gothic **Iglesia de San Francisco** are also worth seeing. On the main street the 16th-century **town hall** (ayuntamiento) and the square beside it, stand on sites that were once part of the medieval palace of the Prince of Viana and a residence of the kings of Navarra. The library beside the square is housed in what remains of the palace and is open to the public.

Environs

To the north of Sangüesa there are two deep, narrow gorges. The most impressive of them is the **Hoz de Arbayún**, whose limestone cliffs are inhabited by colonies of vultures. It is best seen from the NA178 north of Domeño. The **Hoz de Lumbier** can be seen from a point on the N240.

The roughly carved columns in the crypt of the Monasterio de Leyre

BARCELONA

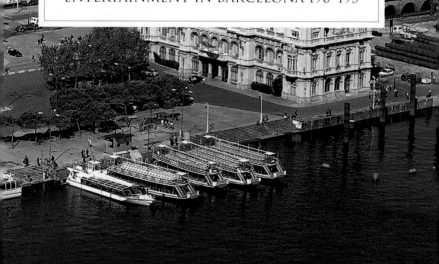

Introducing Barcelona

Barcelona, one of the Mediterranean's busiest ports, is more than the capital of Catalonia. In culture, commerce and sport it not only rivals Madrid, but also considers itself on a par with the greatest European cities. The success of the 1992 Olympic Games, staged in the Parc de Montjuïc, confirmed this to the world. Although there are plenty of historical monuments in the Old Town (Ciutat Vella), Barcelona is best known for the scores of buildings in the Eixample left by the artistic explosion of Modernisme *(see pp140–41)* in the decades around 1900. Always open to outside influences because of its location on the coast, not too far from the French border, Barcelona continues to sizzle with creativity: its bars and the public parks speak more of bold contemporary design than of tradition.

Casa Milà (see p165) *is the most avant-garde of all the works of Antoni Gaudí (see p164). Barcelona has more Art Nouveau buildings than any other city in the world.*

Palau Nacional (see p172), *on the hill of Montjuïc, dominates the monumental halls and fountain-filled avenue built for the 1929 International Exhibition. It now houses the Museu Nacional d'Art de Catalunya with an exceptional collection of medieval art, rich in Romanesque frescoes.*

MONTJUIC
(see pp168–73)

Montjuïc Castle (see p173) *is a massive fortification dating from the 17th century. Sited on the crest of the hill of Montjuïc, it offers panoramic views of the city and port, and forms a sharp contrast to the ultra-modern sports halls built nearby for the 1992 Olympic Games.*

Christopher Columbus *surveys the waterfront from the top of a 60-m (200-ft) column (see p156) in the heart of the Port Vell (Old Port). From the top, visitors can look out over the new promenades and quays that have revitalized the area.*

0 kilometres   1

0 miles   0.5

◁ The Ramblas and the Old Town stretching out behind Barcelona's monument to Columbus

The Sagrada Família (see pp166–7), *Gaudí's unfinished masterpiece, begun in 1882, rises above the streets of the Eixample. Its polychromatic ceramic mosaics and sculptural forms inspired by nature are typical of his work.*

EIXAMPLE (see pp158–67)

Barcelona cathedral (see pp148–9) *is a magnificent 14th-century building in the heart of the Barri Gòtic (Gothic Quarter). It has 28 side chapels which encircle the nave and contain some splendid Baroque altarpieces. The keeping of white geese in the cloisters is a centuries-old tradition.*

OLD TOWN (see pp142–57)

Parc de la Ciutadella (see p154), *between the Old Town and the Vila Olímpica, has something for everyone. The gardens full of statuary offer relaxation, the boating lake and the zoo are fun, while the two museums within its gates cover geology and zoology.*

Las Ramblas (see pp150–51) *is the most famous street in Spain, alive at all hours of the day and night. A stroll down its length to the seafront, taking in its palatial buildings, shops, cafés and street vendors, makes a perfect introduction to Barcelona life.*

Gaudí and Modernisme

Chimney,
Casa Vicens

Towards the end of the 19th century a new style of art and architecture, Modernisme, a variant of Art Nouveau, was born in Barcelona. It became a means of expression for Catalan nationalism and counted Josep Puig i Cadafalch, Lluís Domènech i Montaner and, above all, Antoni Gaudí i Cornet *(see p164)* among its major exponents. Barcelona's Eixample district *(see pp158–67)* is full of the highly original buildings that they created for their wealthy clients.

All aspects of decoration *in a Modernista building even interior design were planned by the architect. This door and its tiled surround are in Gaudí's 1906 Casa Batlló (see p164).*

A dramatic cupola *covers the central salon, which rises through three floors. It is pierced by small round holes, inspired by Islamic architecture, giving the illusion of stars.*

Upper galleries are richly decorated with carved wood and cofferwork.

The spiral carriage ramp *is an early sign of Gaudí's predilection for curved lines. He would later exploit this to the full in the wavy façade of his masterpiece, the Casa Milà (see p165).*

THE EVOLUTION OF MODERNISME

1859 Civil engineer Ildefons Cerdà i Sunyer submits proposals for expansion of Barcelona

1878 Gaudí graduates as an architect

1900 Josep Puig i Cadafalch builds Casa Amatller *(see p164)*

1903 Lluís Domènech i Montaner builds Hospital de la Santa Creu i de Sant Pau *(see p165)*

Hospital detail

1850	1865	1880	1895	1910	1925

1883 Gaudí takes over design of Neo-Gothic Sagrada Família *(see pp166–7)*

Detail of Sagrada Família

1888 Barcelona Universal Exhibition gives impetus to Modernisme

1912 Casa Milà completed

1905 Domènech i Montaner builds Casa Lleó Morera *(see p164)*. Puig i Cadafalch builds Casa Terrades *(see p165)*

1926 Gaudí dies

Bizarrely decorated chimneys *became one of the trademarks of Gaudí's later work. They reach a fantastic extreme on the gleaming, hump-backed roof of the Casa Batlló.*

Elaborate wrought iron lamps light the grand hall.

Ceramic tiles decorate the chimneys.

Escutcheon alludes to the Catalan coat of arms.

GAUDÍ'S MATERIALS

Gaudí designed, or collaborated on designs, for almost every known media. He combined bare, undecorated materials – wood, rough-hewn stone, rubble and brickwork – with meticulous craftwork in wrought iron and stained glass. Mosaics of ceramic tiles were used to cover his fluid, uneven forms.

Stained-glass window in the Sagrada Família

Mosaic of ceramic tiles, Parc Güell *(see p178)*

Detail of iron gate, Casa Vicens *(see p164)*

Ceramic tiles on El Capricho *(see p111)*

Parabolic arches, *used extensively by Gaudí, beginning in the Palau Güell, show his interest in Gothic architecture* (see p24). *These arches form a corridor in his 1890 Col·legio Teresiano, a convent school in the west of Barcelona.*

PALAU GÜELL *(1889)*

Gaudí's first major building in the centre of the city *(see p151)* established his international reputation for outstandingly original architecture. Built for his life-long patron, the industrialist Eusebi Güell, the mansion stands on a small plot of land in a narrow street, making the façade difficult to view. Inside, Gaudí creates a sense of space by using carved screens, galleries and recesses. His unique furniture is also on display.

Organic forms *inspired the wrought iron around the gates to the palace. Gaudí's later work teems with wildlife, such as this dragon, covered with brightly coloured tiles, which guards the steps in the Parc Güell.*

OLD TOWN

The Old Town, traversed by the city's most famous avenue, Las Ramblas, is one of the most extensive medieval city centres in Europe. The Barri Gòtic contains the cathedral and a maze of streets and squares. Across from the Via Laietana, the El Born neighbourhood is dominated by the Santa Maria del Mar church and is replete with 14th-century mansions. This area is bounded by the leafy Parc de la Ciutadella, home to the city's zoo. The revitalized seafront is a stimulating mix of old and new. Trendy shops and restaurants make up the fashionable marina, contrasted with the old maritime neighbourhood of Barceloneta and the new Olympic port.

SIGHTS AT A GLANCE

Museums and Galleries
Museu d'Art Contemporani **8**
Museu Frederic Marès **2**
Museu de Geologia **21**
Museu Marítim and
  Drassanes **28**
Museu Picasso **13**
Museu de la Xocolata **17**
Museu de Zoologia **20**

Streets and Districts
Barceloneta **24**
El Born **12**
Carrer Montcada **15**
Las Ramblas **9**
El Raval **7**

Harbour Sights
Golondrinas **27**
Port Olímpic **23**
Port Vell **25**

Churches
Basílica de Santa Maria
  del Mar **14**
Cathedral (pp148–9) **6**

Historic Buildings
Casa de l'Ardiaca **1**
Casa de la Ciutat **4**
La Llotja **11**
Mercat del Born **16**
Palau de la Generalitat **5**
Palau de la Música Catalana **10**
Palau Reial and Museu
  d'Història de la Ciutat **3**

Monuments
Arc del Triomf **18**
Monument a Colom **26**

Parks and Gardens
Parc de la Ciutadella **19**
Parc Zoològic **22**

GETTING THERE
The area is well served by metro lines 1, 3 and 4; Jaume I station is in the heart of the Barri Gòtic. Many buses pass the Plaça de Catalunya, the centre of the modern city.

KEY

Street-by-Street map pp144–5

Ⓜ Metro station

🚉 Railway station

🚌 Main bus stop

🚋 Tram

ℹ️ Tourist information

0 metres 500
0 yards 500

◁ Stunning floral mosaic pillars in the Palau de la Música Catalana

Street-by-Street: Barri Gòtic

The Barri Gotic (Gothic Quarter) is the true heart
of Barcelona. The oldest part of the city, it was
the site chosen by the Romans in the reign of
Augustus (27 BC–AD 14) on which to found a
new *colonia* (town), and has been the location
of the city's administrative buildings ever since.
The Roman forum was on the Plaça de Sant
Jaume, where now stand the medieval Palau
de la Generalitat, Catalonia's parliament, and the Casa de la Ciutat,
Barcelona's town hall. Close
by are the Gothic cathedral
and royal palace, where
Columbus was received by Fernando
and Isabel on his return from his voyage
to the New World in 1492 *(see p57)*.

**Wax candle,
Cereria
Subirà**

Casa de l'Ardiaca
*Built on the Roman city wall,
the Gothic-Renaissance
archdeacon's residence
now houses Barcelona's
historical archives* ❶

To Plaça de Catalunya

SANT SEVER

CARRER DEL BISBE

PIE

SANT DOMÈNEC DEL CALL

SANT HONORAT

PLAÇA DE
SANT JAUME

CARRER DE FERRAN

CARRER DE LA CIUTAT

★ **Cathedral**
*The façade and
spire are 19th-
century additions
to the original
Gothic building.
Among the artistic
treasures inside are
medieval Catalan
paintings* ❻

**Palau de la
Generalitat**
*The seat of Catalonia's
governor has superb
Gothic features, which
include the chapel
and a stone staircase
rising to an open-air,
arcaded gallery* ❺

To Las Ramblas

Casa de la Ciutat
*Barcelona's town hall was built in
the 14th and 15th centuries. The
façade is a Neo-Classical addition.
In the entrance hall stands* Three
Gypsy Boys *by Joan Rebull (1899–
1981), a 1976 copy of a sculpture
he originally created in 1946* ❹

KEY
– – – Suggested route

Museu Frederic Marès
This medieval doorway is from an extensive display of Spanish sculpture – the mainstay of this museum's extraordinarily eclectic and high-quality collections ❷

LOCATOR MAP
See Street Finder map 5

EIXAMPLE

OLD TOWN

MONTJUÏC

Roman city wall

Saló del Tinell

TAPINERIA

CARRER DELS COMTES DE BARCELONA

★ **Palau Reial**
The 14th-century Capella Reial de Santa Àgata, with a 1466 altarpiece, is one of the best surviving sections of the palace ❸

Capella Reial de Santa Àgata

Plaça del Rei

Palau del Lloctinent

Cereria Subirà candle shop

VIA LAIETANA

CARRER DE JAUME I

Jaume I
Metro

The Museu d'Història de la Ciutat features the most extensive subterranean Roman ruins in the world. Accessed through this 14th-century mansion, visitors can view the streets and squares of Roman Barcelona. The ruins extend underground, through to the exit at the Palau Reial.

CARRER DAGUERIA

SOTS-TINENT NAVARRA

The Centre Excursionista de Catalunya, housed in a medieval mansion, displays Roman columns from the Temple of Augustus, whose site is marked by a millstone in the street outside.

STAR SIGHTS

★ Cathedral

★ Palau Reial

| 0 metres | 100 |
| 0 yards | 100 |

Decorated marble letterbox, Casa de l'Ardiaca

Casa de l'Ardiaca ❶

Carrer de Santa Llúcia 1. **Map** 5 B2.
Tel 93 318 11 95. 🚇 Jaume I.
🕐 9am–8pm Mon–Fri, 9am–1pm
Sat. 🔲 public hols.
www.bcn.es/arxiu/arxiuhistoric

Standing beside what was
originally the Bishop's
Gate in the Roman wall is
the Archdeacon's House.
It was built in the 12th
century, but its present
appearance dates from
around 1500 when it was
remodelled and a colon-
nade added. In 1870 this
was extended to form
the Flamboyant Gothic
(see p24) patio around a
fountain. The Modernista
architect Domènech i Montaner
(1850–1923) added the fanciful
marble letterbox, carved with
three swallows and a tortoise,
beside the Renaissance portal.
Upstairs is the Arxiu Històric
de la Ciutat (City Archives).

Museu Frederic Marès ❷

Plaça de Sant Iu 5. **Map** 5 B2.
Tel 933 10 58 00. 🚇 Jaume I.
🕐 10am–7pm Tue –Sat, 10am–3pm
Sun. 🔲 1 Jan, Good Fri, 1 May, 25 &
26 Dec. 🎟️ (free first Sun of each
month & Wed pm). 🔲 🎟️ by appt.
www.museumares.bcn.es

The sculptor Frederic Marès i
Deulovol (1893–1991) was also
a traveller and collector, and
this extraordinary museum is a
monument to his eclectic
taste. The building is part of
the Royal Palace complex and
was occupied by 13th-century
bishops, 14th-century counts

**Virgin, Museu
Frederic Marès**

of Barcelona, 15th-century
judges, and 18th-century nuns,
who lived here until they
were expelled in 1936.
Marès, who had a
small apartment in the
building, opened this
museum in 1948. It
is one of the most
fascinating in the
city and has an out-
standing collection
of Romanesque and
Gothic religious art.
In the crypt there
are stone sculptures
and two complete
Romanesque por-
tals. Exhibits on
the three floors
above range
through clocks,
crucifixes, costumes, antique
cameras, pipes, tobacco jars
and postcards to an amusement room full of toys.

Palau Reial & Museu d'Història de la Ciutat ❸

Plaça del Rei. **Map** 5 B2. **Tel** 93 315
11 11. 🚇 Jaume I. 🕐 Jun–Sep:
10am–8pm Tue–Sat, 10am–3pm Sun;
Oct–May: 10am–2pm, 4–8pm Tue–
Sat, 10am–3pm Sun. 🔲 1 Jan, 1
May, 24 Jun, 25 & 26 Dec. 🎟️ free for
under 16s on 1st Sat of each month,
after 3pm. 🎟️ by appointment.

The Royal Palace was the
residence of the count-kings
of Barcelona from its
foundation in the 13th century. The complex includes
the 14th-century Gothic Saló
del Tinell, a vast room with
arches spanning 17 m (56 ft).
This is where Isabel and
Fernando (see p70) received
Columbus after his triumphal
return from America. It is also

**Gothic nave of the Capella de Santa
Àgata, Palau Reial**

BARCELONA'S EARLY JEWISH COMMUNITY

Hebrew tablet

From the 11th to the 13th centuries Jews
dominated Barcelona's commerce and
culture, providing doctors and founding
the first seat of learning. But in 1243, 354
years after they were first documented in
the city, violent anti-Semitism led to the
Jews being consigned to a ghetto, El Call.
Ostensibly to provide protection, the
ghetto had only one entrance, which led
into the Plaça de Sant Jaume. Jews were
heavily taxed by the monarch, who
viewed them as "royal serfs"; but in return they also received
privileges, as they handled most of Catalonia's lucrative trade
with North Africa. However, official and popular persecution
finally led to the disappearance of the ghetto in 1401, 91
years before Judaism was fully outlawed in Spain (see p57).
Originally there were three synagogues. The main one,
Sinagoga Mayor at No. 5 Carrer de Marlet, is said to be the
oldest in Europe. A 14th-century Hebrew tablet is embedded
in the wall which reads: "Holy Foundation of Rabbi Samuel
Hassardi, for whom life never ends".

where the Holy Inquisition sat, believing the walls would move if lies were told.

On the right, built into the Roman city wall, is the royal chapel, the Capella de Santa Àgata, with a painted wood ceiling and an altarpiece (1466) by Jaume Huguet. Its bell tower is formed by part of a watchtower on the Roman wall. Stairs on the right of the altar lead to the 16th-century tower of Martí the Humanist (who reigned from 1396– 1410), the last ruler of the 500-year dynasty of the count-kings of Barcelona. From the top of the tower there are fine views.

The main attraction of the Museu d'Història lies underground. Entire streets and squares of old Barcino are accessible via a lift and walkways suspended over the ruins of Roman Barcelona. The site was discovered when the Casa Clariana-Padellàs, the Gothic building from which you enter, was moved here stone by stone in 1931, as demonstrated by an extraordinary photo of the original dig towards the end of the exhibit. The water and drainage systems, baths, homes with mosaic floors, dye works, laundries and even the old forum now make up the most extensive and complete subterranean Roman ruins in the world.

Casa de la Ciutat ❹

Plaça de Sant Jaume 1. **Map** 5 A2.
Tel 934 02 73 00. 🚇 Jaume I, Liceu.
🕐 10am–1:30pm Sun & public hols;
10am–8pm 12 Feb & 23 Apr, or by
appointment (93 402 73 64). 🎫 ♿

The magnificent 14th-century city hall *(ajuntament)* faces the Palau de la Generalitat. Flanking the entrance of the Casa de la Ciutat are statues of Jaime (Jaume) I, who granted the city rights to elect councillors in 1249, and Joan Fiveller, who levied taxes on court members in the 1500s.

Inside is the huge council chamber, the 14th-century Saló de Cent, built for the city's 100 councillors. The Saló de les Cròniques, on the first floor, was commissioned for the 1929 International Exhibition and decorated by Josep-Marià Sert with murals of momentous events in Catalan history.

Palau de la Generalitat ❺

Plaça de Sant Jaume 4. **Map** 5 A2.
Tel 93 402 46 00. 🚇 Jaume I.
🕐 23 Apr (St Jordi's Day), 2nd & 4th
Sat & Sun of every month: 10:30am–
1:30pm. ♿ 🎫 www.gencat.es

Since 1403, the Generalitat has been the seat of the Catalonian Governor. Above

The Italianate façade of the Palau de la Generalitat

the entrance, in its Renaissance façade, is a statue of Sant Jordi (St George) – the patron saint of Catalonia – and the Dragon. The late Catalan-Gothic courtyard is by Marc Safont (1416).

Among the fine interiors are the Gothic chapel of Sant Jordi, also by Safont, and Pere Blai's Italianate Saló de Sant Jordi. At the back, one floor above street level, lies the *Pati dels Tarongers*, the Orange Tree Patio, by Pau Mateu, which has a bell tower built by Pere Ferrer in 1568.

The Catalan president has offices here as well as in the Casa dels Canonges. The two buildings are connected by a bridge across Carrer del Bisbe, built in 1928 and modelled on the famous Bridge of Sighs in Venice.

The magnificent council chamber, the Saló de Cent, in Casa de la Ciutat

Barcelona Cathedral ⑥

This compact Gothic cathedral, with a Romanesque chapel (Capella de Santa Llúcia) and beautiful cloister, was begun in 1298 under Jaime (Jaume) II, on the foundations of a site dating back to Visigothic times. It was not finished until the late 19th century, when the main façade was completed. A white marble choir screen, sculpted in the 16th century, depicts the martyrdom of St Eulàlia, the city's patron. Next to the font, a plaque records the baptism of six Caribbean Indians, whom Columbus brought back from the Americas in 1493.

Statue of St Eulalia

The twin octagonal bell towers date from 1386–93. The bells were installed in this tower in 1545.

The main façade was not completed until 1889, and the central spire until 1913. It was based on the original 1408 plans of the French architect Charles Galters.

Nave Interior
The Catalan-style Gothic interior has a single wide nave with 28 side chapels. These are set between the columns supporting the vaulted ceiling, which rises to 26 m (85 ft).

★ Choir Stalls
The top tier of the beautifully carved 15th-century stalls contains the coats of arms (1518) of the 12 knights of the Order of Toisón del Oro.

Capella del Santíssim Sagrament
This small chapel houses the 16th-century Christ of Lepanto crucifix.

Capella de Sant Benet
*This chapel, dedicated to the
founder of the Benedictine
Order and patron saint
of Europe, houses a
magnificent altarpiece
showing* The Trans-
figuration *by Bernat
Martorell (1452).*

VISITORS' CHECKLIST

Plaça de la Seu. **Map** 5 A2.
Tel 93 315 15 54. Ⓜ *Jaume I.*
🚌 17, 19, 45. ⬜ 8am–7:30pm
daily. 📷 free 8am–12:45pm,
5:15–7:30pm 📷 1–5pm ♿

Sacristy Museum
⬜ 9am–1pm, 4–7pm daily. 📷
✝ *numerous services daily.*

★ **Crypt**
*In the crypt, beneath
the main altar, is the
alabaster sarcophagus
(1339) of St Eulàlia,
martyred for her beliefs
by the Romans during
the 4th century AD.*

★ **Cloisters**
*The fountain, set in a corner
of the Gothic cloisters and
decorated with a statue
of St George,
provided
fresh
water.*

**Porta de Santa Eulàlia,
entrance to Cloisters**

STAR FEATURES

★ Choir Stalls
━━━━━━━━━━━━
★ Crypt
━━━━━━━━━━━━
★ Cloisters

The Sacristy Museum has a
small treasury. Pieces include
an 11th-century font, tapestries
and liturgical artifacts.

**Capella de
Santa Llúcia**

TIMELINE

	559 Basilica dedicated to St Eulàlia and Holy Cross	**1339** St Eulàlia's relics transferred to alabaster sarcophagus		**1913** Central spire completed	
	877 St Eulàlia's remains brought here from Santa Maria del Mar	**1046–58** Romanesque cathedral built under Ramon Berenguer I		**1889** Main façade completed, based on plans dating from 1408 by architect Charles Galters	
400	**700**	**1000**	**1300**	**1600**	**1900**
4th century Original Roman (paleo-Christian) basilica built	**985** Building destroyed by the Moors	**1257–68** Romanesque Capella de Santa Llúcia built	**1493** Indians brought back from the Americas are baptized		
		1298 Gothic cathedral begun under Jaime II		*Plaque of the Indians' baptism*	

El Raval ❼

Map 2 F3. Catalunya, Liceu.

The district of El Raval lies to the west of La Rambla and includes the old red-light area near the port, which was once known as the Barri Xinès (Chinese quarter).

From the 14th century, the city hospital was in Carrer de l'Hospital, which still has several herbal and medicinal shops. Gaudí (see p160) was brought here after being fatally hit by a tram in 1926. The buildings now house the Biblioteca de Catalunya (Catalonian Library), but the elegant former dissecting room has been fully restored.

Towards the port in Carrer Nou de la Rambla is Gaudí's Palau Güell (see p141). At the end of Sant Pau is the city's most complete Romanesque church, the 12th-century Sant Pau del Camp, where resident Franciscan monks still sing a plainsong mass.

Museu d'Art Contemporani ❽

Plaça dels Angels 1. **Map** 2 F2. *Tel 93 412 08 10.* Universitat, Catalunya. 11am–7:30pm Mon & Wed–Fri, 10am–8pm Sat, 10am–3pm Sun & public hols. 1 Jan, 25 Dec. 6pm Wed & Sat, noon Sun. **www**.macba.es **Centre de Cultura Contemporània** Montalegre 5. *Tel 93 306 41 00.* **www**.cccb.org

This dramatic, glass-fronted building was designed by the American architect Richard Meier. Its light, airy galleries act as the city's contemporary art mecca. The permanent collection of predominantly Spanish painting, sculpture and installation from the 1950s onwards is complemented by temporary exhibitions from foreign artists such as the US painter Susana Solano and South African photojournalist David Goldblatt.

Next to the MACBA, a remodelled 18th-century hospice houses the **Centre de Cultura Contemporània**, a lively arts centre that hosts major arts festivals and puts on regular shows of cutting edge contemporary culture.

Las Ramblas ❾

The historic avenue of Las Ramblas (Les Rambles in Catalan) is busy around the clock, especially in the evenings and at weekends. Newsstands, caged bird and flower stalls, tarot readers, musicians and mime artists throng the wide, tree-shaded central walkway. Among its famous buildings are the Liceu Opera House, the huge Boqueria food market and some grand mansions.

Exploring Las Ramblas

The name of this long avenue, also known as Les Rambles, comes from the Arabic *ramla*, meaning the dried-up bed of a seasonal river. The 13th-century city wall followed the left bank of such a river that flowed from the Collserola hills to the sea. Convents, monasteries and the university were built on the other bank in the 16th century. As time passed, the riverbed was filled in and those buildings demolished, but they are remembered in the names of the five consecutive Rambles that make up the great avenue between the Port Vell and Plaça de Catalunya.

Palau Güell C/ Nou de la Rambla 3–5. **Map** 2 F3. *Tel 93 317 39 74.* Liceu. mid-Mar–Sep: 10am–6:15pm Mon–Sat; Oct–mid-Mar: 10am–4:30pm Mon–Fri. until end 2006. **Museu de Cera** Pg de la Banca 7. **Map** 2 F4. *Tel 93 317 26 49.* Drassanes. Jul–Sep: 10am–10pm daily; Oct–Jun: 10am–1:30pm & 4–7:30pm Mon–Fri, 11am–2pm & 4:30–8:30pm Sat, Sun & public hols.

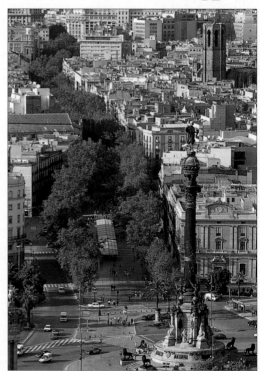

The monument to Columbus at the bottom of the tree-lined Ramblas

Font de Canaletes ①
Saying that someone "drinks the waters of Canaletes" – from this 19th-century fountain – indicates he or she is from Barcelona.

Reial Acadèmia de Ciències i Arts ②
Converted to a theatre in 1910, this building has Barcelona's first official public clock.

Palau de la Virreina ④
The first occupant of this great palace, in 1777, was the *virreina* (viceroy's wife) of Spain in Peru.

Mercat de Sant Josep ⑤
Popularly known as "La Boqueria", this is Barcelona's most colourful food market.

Gran Teatre del Liceu ⑦
The opera house has had to be restored twice after fires – in 1861 and 1994.

Palau Güell ⑨
This Neo-Gothic palace is considered to be one of Gaudí's most important works *(see p141)*.

KEY

🚆	FGC train station
Ⓜ	Metro station
🅿	Parking
✝	Church

0 metres	100
0 yards	100

Palau Moja ③
The Baroque first-floor salon of this Classical building of 1790 is used for exhibitions.

Plaça de la Boqueria ⑥
This square features a mosaic pavement by Miró (1976) and an Art Deco dragon designed for a former umbrella shop.

Plaça Reial ⑧
Barcelona's most lively square was built in the 1850s. The Neo-Classical lampposts were designed by Gaudí.

Museu de Cera ⑩
This waxwork museum, in an atmospheric, 19th-century building, contains about 300 exhibits.

Monument a Colom
Plaça del Portal de la Pau

Glorious stained-glass dome, Palau de la Música Catalana

Although the Orfeó is now based at the more state-of-the-art L'Auditori in Plaça de les Glòries *(see p191)*, there is a concert at the Palau nearly every night; it is the main venue for the city's jazz and guitar festivals and national and international symphony orchestras regularly grace its flamboyant stage.

The Palau's new era is beginning with the completion of the work carried out by the top local architect Oscar Tusquets. An underground concert hall and an outdoor square for summer concerts are being added, consolidating the Palau's reputation as Barcelona's most loved music venue.

La Llotja ⓫

Carrer del Consolat de Mar 2. **Map** 5 B3. **Tel** *93 319 24 12.* ⓜ *Barceloneta, Jaume I.* 🗓 *10am–2pm Mon–Fri.* ⬜ *call for opening times.*

La Llotja (meaning commodity exchange) was built in the 1380s as the headquarters of the Consolat de Mar. It was remodelled in Neo-Classical style in 1771 and housed the city's stock exchange until 1994, the original Gothic hall acting as the main trading room. It can still be seen through the windows.

The upper floors housed the Barcelona School of Fine Arts from 1849 to 1970, attended by the young Picasso and Joan Miró. It is now occupied by a public library and local government offices.

Statue of Poseidon in the courtyard of La Llotja

Palau de la Música Catalana ⓾

Carrer de Sant Francesc de Paula 2. **Map** 5 B1. **Tel** *90 244 28 82.* ⓜ *Urquinaona.* ⬜ *Sep–Jun: 10am–3:30pm daily; Jul–Aug: 10am–6pm daily; and for concerts.* 📷 ♿ *limited* 🎫 *on the hour (book ahead).* **www**.palaumusica.org

This is a real palace of music, a Modernista celebration of tilework, sculpture and glorious stained glass. It is the only concert hall in Europe lit by natural light. Designed by Lluís Domènech i Montaner, it was completed in 1908. Although a few extensions have been added, the building still retains its original appearance. The elaborate red-brick façade is hard to appreciate fully in the confines of the narrow street. It is lined with mosaic-covered pillars topped by busts of the great composers Palestrina, Bach and Beethoven. The large stone sculpture of St George and other figures at the corner of the building portrays an allegory from Catalan folksong by Miquel Blay.

But it is the interior of the building that is truly inspiring. The auditorium is lit by a huge inverted dome of stained glass depicting angelic choristers. The sculptures of composers Wagner and Clavé on the proscenium arch that frames the stage area were designed by Domènech but finished by Pau Gargallo. The stunning "Muses of the Palau", the group of 18 highly stylized, instrument-playing maidens are the stage's backdrop. Made of terracotta and trencadís (broken pieces of ceramic) they have become the buildings most admired feature.

The work of Josep Anselm Clavé (1824–74) in promoting Catalan song led to the creation of the Orfeó Català choral society in 1891, a focus of Catalan nationalism and the inspiration behind the Palau.

El Born @

Map 5 B3. @ Jaume I.

Named after the jousting sessions that once took place in its central boulevard, El Born is a tiny pocket of the La Ribera district. The village-like atmosphere of the neighbourhood makes it popular with local residents and young urbanites. Trendy bars, fashion and design shops are juxtaposed with medieval architecture. The 14th century mansions of Carrer Montcada have remained intact and now house high-calibre galleries and museums, whilst the tiny, pedestrianised streets and squares fanning out from the Mercat del Born are the centre of the city's café culture. The numerous bars and restaurants are a magnet for revellers, much to the annoyance of the full time residents who voice their complaints visually through the banners hanging from El Born's balconies.

Museu Picasso @

Carrer Montcada 15–23. **Map** 5 B2.
Tel 93 319 63 10. @ Jaume I.
◯ 10am–7:30pm Tue–Sat & public hols, 10am–2:30pm Sun. ● 1 Jan, Good Fri, 1 May, 24 Jun, 25 & 26 Dec. ▨ free 1st Sun of each month
🏛 www.museupicasso.bcn.es

One of Barcelona's most popular attractions, the Picasso Museum is housed in five adjoining medieval palaces on Carrer Montcada: Berenguer d'Aguilar, Baró de Castellet, Meca, Mauri and Finestres.

The museum opened in 1963 showing works donated by Jaime Sabartes, a friend of Picasso. Following Sabartes' death in 1968, Picasso himself donated paintings, including early examples. These were complemented by graphic works, left in his will, and 141 ceramic pieces given by his widow, Jacqueline.

The strength of the 3,000-piece collection are Picasso's early works. These show how, even at the ages of 15 and 16, he was painting major works such as *The First Communion* (1896) and *Science and Charity* (1897). There are only a few pictures from his Blue and Rose periods. The most famous work is his series of 44 paintings, *Las Meninas*, inspired by Velázquez's masterpiece.

Basílica de Santa Maria del Mar @

Plaza Sta Maria 1. **Map** 5 B3.
Tel 93 310 23 90. @ Jaume I.
◯ 9am–1:30pm, 4:30–8pm daily (Sun from 10am).

The city's favourite church with superb acoustics for concerts, is the only example of a church entirely in the Catalan Gothic style. It took just 55 years to build, with money donated by merchants and shipbuilders. The speed – unrivalled in the Middle Ages – gave it a unity of style both inside and out. The west front has a 15th-century rose window of the Coronation of the Virgin. More stained glass, from the 15th–18th centuries, lights the nave and aisles.

The choir and furnishings were burned in the Civil War *(see p67)*, adding to the sense of space and simplicity.

A wedding service in the Gothic interior of Santa Maria del Mar

Pablo Picasso, *Self-Portrait* in charcoal (1899–1900)

PABLO PICASSO IN BARCELONA

Picasso (1881–1973) was born in Málaga and was almost 14 when he came to Barcelona, where his father had found a job in the city's art academy. Picasso enrolled, and was a precocious talent among his contemporaries. He was a regular visitor to Els Quatre Gats, an artists' café still in existence in Carrer Montsió, where he held his first exhibition. He also exhibited in Sala Parks, a gallery still functioning in Carrer Petritxol. The family lived in Carrer Mercé and Picasso had a studio in Carrer Nou de la Rambla. It was among the prostitutes of Carrer d'Avinyò that he found inspiration for the work that many art historians see as the wellspring of modern art, *Les Demoiselles d'Avignon* (1906–7). Picasso left Barcelona for Paris in his early twenties and initially returned several times. After the Civil War his opposition to Franco kept him in France, but he designed a frieze for Barcelona's College of Architects in 1962 and was persuaded to allow the city to open a museum of his work, which it did the following year.

Renaissance-style 17th-century façades lining Carrer Montcada

Carrer Montcada ⑮

Map 5 B3. ⓜ *Jaume I.* **Museu Tèxtil i d'Indumentària** *at No. 12.* ***Tel*** *93 310 45 16.* ⏰ *10am–6pm Tue–Sat, 10am–3pm Sun & public hols.* ⬤ *1 & 5 Jan, Good Fri, 1 May, 24 Jun, 25 & 26 Dec.* 📷 ♿

The most authentic medieval street in the city is a narrow lane, overshadowed by gargoyles and roofs that almost touch overhead. The Gothic palaces that line it date back to Catalonia's expansion in the 13th century. Almost all of the buildings were modified over the years, particularly during the 17th century. The only building that retains its original façade is the Casa Cervelló-Guidice at No. 25.

The **Museu Tèxtil i d'Indumentària** in Palau Mora displays textiles and clothing from the 4th century onwards. At No. 22 is the city's best-known champagne and *cava* bar, El Xampanyet.

Display of gowns at the Museu Tèxtil i d'Indumentària

Mercat del Born ⑯

Map 5 C3. ⓜ *Jaume I, Barceloneta.*

This covered market, with its ornate iron work and crystal roof, was inspired by the original Les Halles in Paris and it was Barcelona's principal wholesale market until the early 70s when it outgrew its location. The street names in the vicinity reflect what went on in Barcelona's former mercantile hub: L'Argentaria was lined with silversmiths, Flassaders was where you went for a weaved blanket and Vidrieria was once lit up with glass blowers' torches. A few of these establishments remain, but they are rapidly being replaced by tourist-friendly boutiques.

The market itself has been the focus of a fierce debate. When work started in 2002 to convert the space into a library, extensive remains dating from the 1700s were discovered. The architectural importance of the subterranean streets and homes were questioned, but the historical significance of the dig sealed the market's fate as a future museum. In 1714 Barcelona fell to French-Spanish forces in the War of Succession (*see p62*), with particularly heavy losses in El Born, and became an occupied city. This key event in Catalonia's history is remembered each year on September 11th in flag-waving celebrations centred near the market.

Museu de la Xocolata ⑰

Comerç 36. **Map** 5 C2. ⓜ *Jaume I, Arc de Triomf.* ***Tel*** *93 268 78 78.* ⏰ *10am–7pm Mon, Wed–Sat, 10am–3pm Sun & pub hols.* ⬤ *1 Jan, 1 May, 25 & 26 Dec.* 📷 ♿ 🅿 **www**.museudelaxocolata.com

Founded by Barcelona's chocolate and pastry-makers union, this museum takes you through the history of one of the most universally-loved foodstuffs: from the discovery of cocoa in South America to the invention of the first chocolate machine in

Barcelona. This is ingeniously executed through old posters, photographs and footage. The real thing is displayed in a homage to the art of the *mona*. A Catalan invention, this was a traditional easter cake that over the centuries evolved into an edible sculpture. Every year, pastissers compete for the most imaginative piece, decorating their chocolate versions of well-known buildings or folk figures with jewels, feathers and a cornucopia of other materials. The museum café serves some of best chocolate temptations in the city.

The pink brick façade of the late 19th-century Arc del Triomf

Arc del Triomf ⑱

Passeig Lluís Companys. **Map** 5 C1. ⓜ *Arc de Triomf.*

The main gateway to the 1888 Universal Exhibition, which filled the Parc de la Ciutadella, was designed by Josep Vilaseca i Casanovas. It is built of brick in Mudéjar (*see p55*) style, with sculpted allegories of crafts, industry and business. The frieze by Josep Reynés on the main façade represents the city welcoming foreign visitors.

Parc de la Ciutadella ⑲

Avda del Marquès de l'Argentera. **Map** 6 D2. ⓜ *Barceloneta, Ciutadella-Vila Olímpica.* ⏰ *8am–10:30pm daily.* ♿

This popular park has a boating lake, orange groves and parrots living in the palm trees. It was once the site of a massive star-shaped citadel, built for Felipe V between 1715 and 1720 following a 13-month siege of the city. The fortress was intended to house soldiers to keep law and order, but was never used for this purpose. Converted into a prison, the citadel became notorious during the Napoleonic occupation *(see p63)*, and, during the 19th-century liberal repressions, it was hated as a symbol of centralized power. In 1878, under General Prim, whose statue stands in the middle of the park, the citadel was pulled down and the park given to the city, to become, in 1888, the venue of the Universal Exhibition *(see p64)*. Three buildings survived: the Governor's Palace, now a school; the chapel; and the arsenal, occupied by the Catalan parliament.

The park offers more cultural and leisure activities than any other in the city and is particularly popular on Sunday afternoons when people gather to play instruments, dance and relax, or visit the museums and zoo. A variety of works by Catalan sculptors such as Marès, Arnau, Carbonell, Clarà, Llimona, Gargallo, Dunyac and Fuxà, can be seen in the park, alongside work by modern artists such as Tapies and Botero.

The gardens in the Plaça de Armes were laid out by the French landscape gardener Jean Forestier and centre on a cascade based around a triumphal arch. It was designed by architect Josep Fontseré, with the help of Antoni Gaudí, then still a young student.

One of the galleries inside the spacious Museu de Zoologia

Museu de Zoologia ⓴

Passeig de Picasso. **Map** 5 C2.
Tel 93 319 69 12. Arc de Triomf or Jaume I. 10am–3pm Tue–Sun & public hols (Thu till 6:30pm). free 1st Sun each month. www.museuzoologia.bcn.es

At the entrance to the Parc de la Ciutadella is the fortress-like Castell dels Tres Dragons (Castle of the Three Dragons), named after a play by Frederic Soler that was popular at the time it was built.

This crenellated brick edifice was built by Lluís Domènech i Montaner for the 1888 Universal Exhibition. His inspiration was Valencia's Gothic commodities exchange. He later used it as a workshop for Modernista design, and it became a focus of the movement. It has housed the Zoological Museum since 1937.

Museu de Geologia ㉑

Parc de la Ciutadella. **Map** 5 C3.
Tel 93 319 68 95. Arc de Triomf, Jaume I. 10am–3pm Tue–Sun & public hols (Thu till 6:30pm). 1 Jan, Good Fri, 1 May, 25 & 26 Dec. free 1st Sun each month.

Barcelona's oldest museum opened in 1882, the same year the Parc de la Ciutadella became a public space. It has a large collection of fossils and minerals, including specimens from Catalonia. Beside it is the Hivernacle, a glasshouse by Josep Amargós now used for concerts, and the Umbracle, a brick and wood conservatory by the park's architect, Josep Fontseré. Both date from 1884.

Parc Zoològic ㉒

Parc de la Ciutadella. **Map** 6 D3.
Tel 93 225 67 80. Ciutadella-Vila Olimpica. Oct–Feb: 10am–5pm, Mar: 10am–6pm, Apr & Sep: 10am–7pm, May–Aug: 9:30am–7:30pm. www.zoobarcelona.com

This zoo was laid out in the 1940s to a relatively enlightened design – the animals are separated by moats instead of bars. Dolphin and whale shows are held in one of the aquariums. The zoo is very child-friendly with pony rides, electric cars and a train. Roig i Soler's 1885 sculpture by the entrance, *The Lady with the Umbrella* has become a symbol of Barcelona.

Ornamental cascade in the Parc de la Ciutadella designed by Josep Fontseré and Antoni Gaudí

Smart boats and the twin skyscrapers at the Port Olímpic

Port Olímpic ㉓

Map 6 F4. ⓜ *Ciutadella-Vila Olímpica.*

The most dramatic rebuilding for the 1992 Olympics was the demolition of the old industrial waterfront and the laying out of 4 km (2 miles) of promenade and pristine sandy beaches. Suddenly Barcelona seemed like a seaside resort. At the heart of the project was a 65-ha (160-acre) new estate of 2,000 apartments and parks called Nova Icària. The area is still popularly known as the Vila Olímpica because the buildings originally housed the Olympic athletes.

On the sea front there are twin 44-floor blocks, Spain's tallest skyscrapers, one occupied by offices and the other by the Arts hotel *(see p569)*. They stand beside the Port Olímpic, which was also built for 1992. The main reason for visiting are the two levels of restaurants in a wonderful setting around the marina.

Barceloneta ㉔

Map 5 B5. ⓜ *Barceloneta.*

Barcelona's fishing "village", which lies on a triangular tongue of land jutting into the sea just below the city centre, is renowned for its fish restaurants and port-side cafés.

Barceloneta was built by the architect and military engineer Juan Martín de Cermeño in 1753 to rehouse people made homeless by the construction,

just inland, of a large fortress, La Ciutadella *(see p154)*. Since then it has housed largely workers and fishermen. Laid out on a grid system with narrow houses of two or three floors, in which each room has a window on the street, the area has a friendly air.

In the small Plaça de la Barceloneta, at the centre of the district, is the Baroque church of Sant Miquel del Port, also by Cermeño. A market is often held in the square here.

Today, Barceloneta's fishing fleet is still based in the nearby industrial docks by a small clock tower. On the opposite side of this harbour is the Torre de Sant Sebastià, terminus of the cable car that runs right across the port, via the World Trade Centre, to Montjuïc.

Port Vell ㉕

Map 5 A4. ⓜ *Barceloneta, Drassanes.* **Aquàrium** *Tel* 93 221 74 74. ☐ *Oct–May: 9:30am–9pm Mon–Fri, 9:30am– 9:30pm Sat, Sun & public hols; Jun & Sep: 9:30am–9:30pm daily; Jul–Aug: 9:30am–11pm daily.* 🔲 🔥 **www**.aquariumbcn.com

The city's new leisure port is at the foot of Las Ramblas, just beyond the old customs house. This was built in 1902 at the Portal de la Pau, the former maritime entrance to the city, where steps lead into the water. To the south, the Moll de Barcelona, with a new World Trade Centre, serves as the passenger pier for visiting liners. In front of the customs house, Las Ramblas is linked to the yacht clubs on the Moll

d'Espanya by a swing bridge and pedestrian jetty. The Moll d'Espanya (*moll* meaning quay, wharf or pier) has a shopping and restaurant complex, the Maremàgnum, plus an IMAX cinema and the largest aquarium in Europe.

The Moll de la Fusta (Timber Wharf), with terrace cafés, has red structures inspired by Van Gogh's bridge at Arles. At the end of the wharf stands *El Cap de Barcelona (Barcelona Head)*, a 20-m (66-ft) sculpture by Pop artist Roy Lichtenstein.

Monument a Colom ㉖

Plaça del Portal de la Pau. **Map** 2 F4. *Tel* 93 302 52 24. ⓜ *Drassanes.* ☐ *Oct–Mar: 10am–1:30pm, 3:30–6:30pm Mon–Fri, 10am–6:30pm Sat, Sun & public hols; Apr–May: 10am–7:30pm daily; Jun–Sep: 9am–8:30pm daily.* 🔲

The Columbus Monument in the Portal de la Pau (the "Gate of Peace") was designed by Gaietà Buigas for the 1888 Universal Exhibition.

The 60-m (200-ft) cast iron monument marks the spot where Columbus stepped ashore in 1493 after discovering America, bringing with him six Caribbean Indians. He was accorded a state welcome by the Catholic Monarchs in the Saló del Tinell *(see p146)*. The Indians' conversion to Christianity is commemorated in the cathedral *(see pp148–9)*.

A lift gives access to a viewing platform at the top of the monument, where a bronze statue, points out to sea.

Fishing boat moored at the quayside of Barceloneta

A *golondrina* departing from the Plaça del Portal de la Pau

Golondrinas ㉗

Plaça del Portal de la Pau. **Map** 2 F5.
Tel *93 442 31 06.* Drassanes.
☐ *times variable – phone ahead for
information.*

Sightseeing trips around
Barcelona's harbour can be
made on small double-decker
boats called *golondrinas* (literally "swallows"). They moor
beside the steps of the Plaça
del Portal de la Pau in front
of the Columbus Monument.

Tours last around half an
hour. The boats go out beneath the steep, castle-topped
hill of Montjuïc towards the
industrial port. They usually
stop off at the breakwater,
which reaches out to sea from
Barceloneta, to allow passengers to disembark for a stroll.

An alternative one-and-a-
half-hour trip takes in
Barcelona Harbour, the commercial port and beaches and
stops off at the Port Olímpic.

Museu Marítim and Drassanes ㉘

Avinguda de les Drassanes.
Map 2 F4. ***Tel*** *93 342 99 20.*
Drassanes. ☐ *10am–7pm daily.*
● *1 & 6 Jan, 25 & 26 Dec.*
by appointment.

The great galleys that made
Barcelona a major seafaring
power were built in the sheds
of the Drassanes (shipyards),
which now house the maritime
museum. These royal dry
docks are the largest and most
complete surviving medieval
complex of their kind in the

world. They were founded in
the mid-13th century, when
dynastic marriages uniting the
kingdoms of Sicily and Aragón
meant that better maritime
communications between the
two became a priority. Three
of the yards' four original
corner towers survive.

Among the vessels to slip
from the Drassanes' vaulted
halls was the *Real*, flagship of
Don Juan of Austria, Charles
V's illegitimate son, who led
the Christian fleet to victory
against the Turks at Lepanto
in 1571 *(see p59).* The
museum's showpiece is a
full-scale replica decorated in
red and gold.

The *Llibre del Consulat de
Mar*, a book of nautical codes
and practice, is a reminder
that Catalonia was once the
arbiter of Mediterranean
maritime law. The expertise
of its sailors is also evident in
the collection of pre-Colum-
bian charts and maps, including one of 1439 which was
used by Amerigo Vespucci.

**Stained-glass window in the
Museu Marítim**

EIXAMPLE

Barcelona claims to have the greatest collection of Art Nouveau buildings of any city in Europe. The style, known in Catalonia as Modernisme, flourished after 1854, when it was decided to pull down the medieval walls to allow the city to develop into what had previously been a construction-free military zone.

The designs of the civil engineer Ildefons Cerdà i Sunyer (1815–76) were chosen for the new expansion *(eixample)* inland. These plans called for a rigid grid system of streets, but at each intersection the corners were chamfered to allow the buildings there to overlook the junctions or squares. The few exceptions

Jesus of the Column, Sagrada Família

to this grid system include the Diagonal, a main avenue running from the wealthy area of Pedralbes down to the sea, and the Hospital de la Santa Creu i de Sant Pau by Modernista architect Domènech i Montaner (1850–1923). He hated the grid system and deliberately angled the hospital to look down the diagonal Avinguda de Gaudí towards Antoni Gaudí's church of the Sagrada Família, the city's most spectacular Modernista building *(see pp166–7)*. The wealth of Barcelona's commercial elite, and their passion for all things new, allowed them to give free rein to the age's most innovative architects in designing their residences as well as public buildings.

SIGHTS AT A GLANCE

Museums and Galleries
Fundació Antoni Tàpies ❷

Churches
Sagrada Família pp166–7 ❻

Modernista Buildings
Casa Milà, "La Pedrera" ❸
Casa Terrades, "Casa de les Punxes" ❹
Hospital de la Santa Creu i de Sant Pau ❺
Illa de la Discòrdia ❶

KEY

Street-by-Street map *pp182–3*

Ⓜ Metro station

🚉 Railway station

🚌 Main bus stop

ℹ Tourist information

GETTING THERE

Metro line 3 has stations at either end of the Passeig de Gràcia (Catalunya and Diagonal), and one in the middle, at the Illa de la Discòrdia (Passeig de Gràcia). Metro line 5 takes you straight to the Sagrada Família and Hospital de Sant Pau (a long walk from other sights).

| 0 metres | 500 |
| 0 yards | 500 |

◁ Nativity façade of the Sagrada Família – the only façade to be more or less completed in Gaudí's lifetime

Street-by-Street: Quadrat d'O

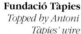

Perfume bottle, Museu del Perfum

The hundred or so city blocks centring on the Passeig de Gràcia are known as the Quadrat d'Or, "Golden Square", because they contain so many of Barcelona's best Modernista buildings *(see pp140–41)*. This was the area within the Eixample favoured by the wealthy bourgeoisie, who embraced the new artistic and architectural style with enthusiasm, not only for their residences, but also for commercial buildings. Most remarkable is the Illa de la Discòrdia, a single block containing houses by Modernisme's most illustrious exponents. Many interiors can be visited by the public, revealing a feast of stained glass, ceramics and ornamental ironwork.

Diagonal Metro

Vinçon home decor store *(see p187)*

Passeig de Gràcia, the Eixample's main avenue, is a showcase of highly original buildings and smart shops. The graceful street lamps are by Pere Falqués (1850–1916).

RAMBLA DE CATALUNYA

PASSEIG DE GRÀCIA

Fundació Tàpies
Topped by Antoni Tàpies' wire sculpture Cloud and Chair, this 1879 building by Domènech i Montaner houses a wide variety of Tàpies' paintings, graphics and sculptures ❷

Casa Amatller

Museu del Perfum

Casa Ramon Mulleras

★ Illa de la Discòrdia
In this city block, four of Barcelona's most famous Modernista houses vie for attention. All were created between 1900 and 1910. This ornate tower graces the Casa Lleó Morera by Domènech i Montaner ❶

To Plaça de Catalunya

Casa Batlló

Casa Lleó Morera

Passeig de Gràcia Metro

The Palau Baro de Quadras was designed by Puig i Cadafalch in 1904. The facade, in neo-Gothic style, is highly ornate and covered with distinctive sculptures. This carving adorns the doorway.

LOCATOR MAP
See Street Finder map 3

AVINGUDA DIAGONAL

CARRER DE PAU CLARIS

CARRER DE PROVENÇA

CARRER DE MALLORCA

CARRER DE LLÚRIA

CARRER DE ROGER DE LLÚRIA

CARRER DE VALÈNCIA

CARRER DEL BRUC

CARRER D'ARAGÓ

Casa Thomas

To Sagrada Família

Palau Ramon de Montaner

Casa Terrades
Built in red brick with carved stone ornamentation, this 1905 house by Puig i Cadafalch echoes the Gothic buildings of northern Europe **❹**

★ Casa Milà "La Pedrera"
Gaudí put all his architectural daring into this, his most famous house. The result is a remarkable wave-like façade and a roofscape of chimneys and vents resembling abstract sculptures **❸**

0 metres 100
0 yards 100

KEY

– – – Suggested route

STAR SIGHTS

★ Illa de la Discòrdia

★ Casa Milà "La Pedrera"

Sumptuous interior of the Casa Lleó Morera, Illa de la Discòrdia

Illa de la Discòrdia ❶

Passeig de Gràcia, between Carrer d'Aragó and Carrer del Consell de Cent. **Map** 3 A4. ⓦ *Passeig de Gràcia.* **Casa Amatller Tel** *93 488 01 39.* ☐ *10am–7pm Mon–Sat, 10am–2pm Sun & public hols.* ▣

The most famous group of Modernista *(see pp140–1)* buildings in Barcelona amply illustrates the range of styles involved in the movement. The city block in which they stand has been dubbed the Illa de la Discòrdia, "Block of Discord", owing to the startling visual argument between them.

The three most famous houses, on Passeig de Gràcia, were remodelled in Modernista style from existing houses early in the 20th century, but named after their original owners.

No. 35 is **Casa Lleó Morera** (1902–6), the first residential work of Lluís Domènech i Montaner. The ground floor was gutted to create a shop in 1943, but the Modernista interiors upstairs still exist.

Beyond the next two houses, one of which is a beauty shop

containing a perfume museum, is **Casa Amatller**, designed by Puig i Cadafalch in 1898. Its façade is a harmonious blend of styles, featuring Moorish and Gothic windows encased in iron grilles. The stepped gable roof is dotted with tiles. Inside the wrought-iron main doors is a fine stone staircase beneath a stained-glass roof. The building is now used by the Institut

Amatller d'Art Hispànic and the Centre del Modernisme. Free tours of the house façades are available here.

Next door is Antoni Gaudí's **Casa Batlló** (1904–6). Its façade has heavily tiled walls and curving iron balconies pierced with holes to look like masks or skulls. The hump-backed, scaly-looking roof is thought to represent a dragon, with St George (the patron saint of Catalonia) as a chimney.

Fundació Antoni Tàpies ❷

Carrer d'Aragó 255. **Map** 3 A4. **Tel** *93 487 03 15.* ⓦ *Passeig de Gràcia.* ☐ *10am–8pm Tue–Sun & public hols.* ⬤ *1 & 6 Jan, 25 & 26 Dec.* ▣ ♿

Antoni Tapies, born in 1923, is Barcelona's best-known living artist. Inspired by Surrealism, his abstract work is executed in a variety of materials, including concrete and metal *(see p160)*. It is not easy to appreciate at first, but the exhibits should help those interested obtain a clearer perspective, even if there are not enough here to gain a full understanding of the artist's work. They are housed in the first domestic building in Barcelona to be built with iron (1880), designed by Domènech i Montaner for his brother's publishing firm.

ANTONI GAUDÍ (1852–1926)

Born in Reus (Tarragona) into a family of artisans, Gaudí was the leading exponent of Catalan Modernisme. Following a stint as a blacksmith's apprentice, he studied at Barcelona's School of Architecture. Inspired by a nationalistic search for a romantic medieval past, his work was supremely original. His first major achievement was the Casa Vicens (1888) at No. 24 Carrer de les Carolines. But his most celebrated building is the extravagant church of the Sagrada Família *(see pp166–7)*, to which he devoted his life from 1914. He gave all his money to the project and often went from house to house begging for more, until his death a few days after being run over by a tram.

Decorated chimney pot, Casa Vicens

◁ **Extraordinary sculptured and ceramic-encrusted chimneys of Gaudí's Casa Milà**

The rippled façade of Gaudí's apartment building, Casa Milà

Renaissance styles. The towers and gables are influenced in particular by north European Gothic architecture. However, the deeply carved, floral stone ornament of the exterior, in combination with red brick as the principal building material, are typically Modernista.

Hospital de la Santa Creu i de Sant Pau ❺

Carrer de Sant Antoni Maria Claret 167. **Map** 4 F1. **Tel** 93 291 91 99. Hospital de Sant Pau. **Grounds** daily; write in advance for permission. www.hspau.com

Lluís Domènech i Montaner began designing a new city hospital in 1902. Totally innovative in concept, his scheme consisted of 26 attractive Mudéjar-style pavilions set in large gardens, as he strongly disliked huge wards and believed that patients would recover better amid fresh air and trees. All the connecting corridors and service areas were hidden underground.

Also believing art and colour to be therapeutic, he decorated the pavilions profusely. The turreted roofs were tiled with ceramics, and the reception pavilion embellished with sculptures by Pau Gargallo and mosaic murals. The vast project was completed after Domènech's death, in 1930, by his son Pere.

Casa Milà ❸

Passeig de Gràcia 92. **Map** 3 B3. **Tel** 90 240 09 73. Diagonal. 10am–8pm daily. public hols. 4pm http://obrasocial.caixacatalunya.es.

Usually called "La Pedrera" ("the stone quarry"), the Casa Milà is Gaudí's greatest contribution to Barcelona's civic architecture, and his last work before he devoted himself entirely to the Sagrada Família (see pp166–7).

Built between 1906 and 1910, "La Pedrera" completely departed from the established construction principles of the time and, as a result, was ridiculed and strongly attacked by Barcelona's intellectuals.

Gaudí designed this corner apartment block, eight storeys high, around two circular courtyards. The intricate ironwork balconies, by Josep Maria Jujol, are like seaweed against the wave-like walls of white undressed stone. There are no straight walls anywhere in the building.

The Milà family had an apartment on the first floor. The top floor now houses the Gaudí Museum. Regular guided tours from an office on the ground floor take in the extraordinary roof, where the multitude of sculpted air ducts and chimneys look so threatening they have been dubbed the *espantabruixes*, the witch-scarers.

Casa Terrades ❹

Avinguda Diagonal 416. **Map** 3 B3. Diagonal. to public.

This free-standing, six-sided apartment block by Modernista architect Puig i Cadafalch gets its nickname, "Casa de les Punxes" (House of the Points), from the spires on its six corner turrets, which are shaped like witches' hats. It was built between 1903 and 1905 by converting three existing houses on the site and was Puig's largest work. It is an eclectic mixture of medieval and

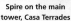

Spire on the main tower, Casa Terrades

Statue of the Virgin, Hospital de la Santa Creu i de Sant Pau

For hotels and restaurants in this region see pp568–70 and pp617–20

Sagrada Família ⑥

A carved whelk

Europe's most unconventional church, the Temple Expiatori de la Sagrada Família, is an emblem of a city that likes to think of itself as individualistic. Crammed with symbolism inspired by nature and striving for originality, it is Gaudí's *(see pp140–1)* greatest work. In 1883, a year after work had begun on a Neo-Gothic church on the site, the task of completing it was given to Gaudí who changed everything, extemporizing as he went along. It became his life's work and he lived like a recluse on the site for 16 years. He is buried in the crypt. At his death only one tower on the Nativity façade had been completed, but work resumed after the Civil War and several more have since been finished to his original plans. Work continues today, financed by public subscription.

Bell Towers
Eight of the 12 spires, one for each apostle, have been built. Each is topped by Venetian mosaics.

THE FINISHED CHURCH

Gaudí's initial ambitions have been scaled down over the years, but the design for the completion of the building remains impressive. Still to come is the central tower, which is to be encircled by four large towers representing the Evangelists. Four towers on the Glory (south) façade will match the existing four on the Passion (west) and Nativity (east) façades. An ambulatory – like an inside-out cloister – will run round the outside of the building.

Tower with lift

The apse was the first part of the church Gaudí completed. Stairs lead down from here to the crypt below.

The altar canopy, designed by Gaudí, is still waiting for the altar.

★ **Passion Façade**
This bleak façade was completed in the late 1980s by artist Josep Maria Subirachs. A controversial work, its sculpted figures are angular and often sinister.

Main entrance

Spiral Staircases
*Steep stone steps –
400 in each – allow
access to the towers
and upper galleries.
Majestic views
reward those who
climb or take the lift.*

**Tower
with lift**

★ **Nativity Façade**
*The most complete part of Gaudí's
church, finished in 1904, has
doorways which represent Faith,
Hope and Charity. Scenes of the
Nativity and Christ's childhood are
embellished with symbolism, such as
doves representing the congregation.*

★ **Crypt**
*The crypt, where Gaudí is buried,
was built by the original architect,
Francesc de Paula Villar i Lozano,
in 1882. This is where services are
held. On the lower floor a museum
traces the careers of both architects
and the church's history.*

Nave
*In the nave, which is still under
construction, a forest of fluted
pillars will support four galleries
above the side aisles, while
skylights let in natural light.*

**Entrance to
Crypt Museum**

STAR FEATURES

★ Passion Façade

★ Nativity Façade

★ Crypt

MONTJUIC

The hill of Montjuic, rising to 213 m (699 ft) above the commercial port on the south side of the city, is Barcelona's biggest recreation area. Its museums, art galleries, gardens and nightclubs make it a popular place in the evenings as well as during the day.

There was probably a Celtiberian settlement here before the Romans built a temple to Jupiter on their Mons Jovis, which may have given Montjuïc its name – though another theory suggests that a Jewish cemetery on the hill inspired the name Mount of the Jews.

The absence of a water supply meant that there were few buildings on Montjuïc until the castle was erected on the top in 1640.

Statue, gardens of the Palau Nacional

The hill finally came into its own as the site of the 1929 International Fair. With great energy and flair, buildings were erected all over the north side, with the grand Avinguda de la Reina Maria Cristina, lined with huge exhibition halls, leading into it from the Plaça d'Espanya. In the middle of the avenue is the Font Màgica (Magic Fountain), which is regularly illuminated in colour. Above it is the Palau Nacional, home of the city's historic art collections. The Poble Espanyol is a crafts centre housed in copies of buildings from all over Spain. The last great surge of building on Montjuïc was for the 1992 Olympic Games, which left Barcelona with international-class sports facilities.

SIGHTS AT A GLANCE

Historic Buildings
Castell de Montjuïc **7**

Modern Architecture
Estadi Olímpic de Montjuïc **8**
Pavelló Mies van der Rohe **4**

Museums and Galleries
Fundació Joan Miró **1**
Museu Arqueològic **2**
Museu Nacional d'Art de Catalunya **3**

Squares
Plaça d'Espanya **6**

Theme Parks
Poble Espanyol **5**

GETTING THERE

Apart from the exhibition halls near Espanya Metro station, reaching most of Montjuïc's attractions on foot involves a steep climb. However, buses 13 and 50 will take you up the hill from Plaça d'Espanya. For the castle, take the funicular from Metro Paral·lel, then the cable car. These run daily from 9am–8pm in winter, and daily in summer to 10pm.

KEY

	Street-by-Street map pp170–71
Ⓜ	Metro station
	Cable car station
	Funicular railway station
	Main bus stop

0 metres   500
0 yards   500

◁ Changing colours of the Font Màgica (Magic Fountain) on the grand avenue leading up to Montjuïc

Street-by-Street: Montjuïc

Montjuïc is a spectacular vantage point
from which to view the city. It has a wealth
of art galleries and museums, an amusement
park and an open-air theatre. The most
interesting buildings lie around
the Palau Nacional, where Europe's greatest
Romanesque art collection is housed.
Montjuïc is approached from the Plaça
d'Espanya between brick pillars based on the
campanile of St Mark's in Venice, which give
a foretaste of the eclecticism
of building styles. The
Poble Espanyol illustrates
the traditional architecture
of Spain's regions, while
the Fundació Joan Miró
is boldly modern.

**Pavelló Mies van
der Rohe**
*This statue by Georg
Kolbe (see p173)
stands serenely in
the steel, glass, stone
and onyx pavilion
built in the Bauhaus
style as the German
contribution to the
1929 International
Exhibition* ❹

AVINGUDA DEL MARQUES DE COMILLAS

AVINGUDA DELS MONTANYANS

PASSEIG DE LES CAS

★ **Poble
Espanyol**
*Containing
replicas of build-
ings from many
regions, this "village" provides a fascinating glimpse
of vernacular styles* ❺

AVINGUDA DE L'ESTADI

★ **Museu Nacional
d'Art de Catalunya**
*Displayed in the
National Palace, the
main building of the
1929 International
Exhibition, is Europe's
finest collection of
early medieval
frescoes. These were
a great source of
inspiration for Joan
Miró (see p172)* ❸

To Montjuïc castle and
Olympic stadium

STAR SIGHTS

★ Poble Espanyol

★ Museu Nacional d'Art
de Catalunya

★ Fundació Joan Miró

For hotels and restaurants in this region see pp568–70 and pp617–20

Fountains and cascades descend in terraces from the Palau Nacional. Below them is the Font Màgica (Magic Fountain). On summer evenings, from Thursday to Sunday, its jets are programmed to a multi-coloured music and light show. This marvel of water-and-electrical engineering was originally built by Carles Buigas (1898–1979) for the 1929 International Exhibition.

LOCATOR MAP
See Street Finder map 1

Plaça d'Espanya

Museu Etnològic
displays artifacts from Oceania, Africa, Asia and Latin America.

Museu Arqueològic
The museum displays important finds from prehistoric cultures in Catalonia and the Balearic Islands. The Dama de Ibiza, *a 4th-century sculpture, was found in Ibiza's Carthaginian necropolis (see p511)* ❷

Mercat de les Flors theatre *(see p191)*

Teatre Grec is an open-air theatre set among gardens.

★ Fundació Joan Miró
This tapestry by Joan Miró hangs in the centre he created for the study of modern art. In addition to Miró's works in various media, the modern building by Josep Lluís Sert is of architectural interest ❶

To funfair, Montjuïc castle and cable car

KEY

– – – Suggested route

0 metres   100
0 yards   100

Flame in Space and Naked Woman (1932) by Joan Miró

Fundació Joan Miró ❶

Parc de Montjuïc. **Map** 1 B3. **Tel** 93 443 94 70. Ⓜ *Espanya, then bus 50, 55 or Paral.lel, the Montjuïc funicular.* ☐ *Jul–Sep: 10am–8pm Tue–Sat; Oct–Jun: 10am–7pm Tue–Sat; all year: 10am–9:30pm Thu, 10am–2:30pm Sun & public hols.* ● *1 Jan, 25, 26 Dec.* 🎫 ♿ www.bcn.fjmiro.es

Joan Miró (1893–1983) studied at the fine art school at La Llotja (*see p152*). From 1919, he spent much of his time in Paris. Though opposed to Franco, he returned to Spain in 1940 and from then on lived mainly in Mallorca, where he died.

An admirer of primitive Catalan art and Gaudí's Modernisme (*see p140*), Miró always remained a Catalan painter but developed a Surrealistic style, with vivid colours and fantastical forms suggesting dream-like situations.

In 1975, after the return of democracy to Spain (*see p68*), his friend, the architect Josep Lluís Sert, designed the stark,

white building to house a permanent collection of paintings, sculptures and tapestries lit by natural light. Miró himself donated the works and some of the best pieces on display include his *Barcelona Series* (1939–44), a set of 50 black-and-white lithographs. Periodic exhibitions of other artists' work are also held.

Museu Arqueològic ❷

Passeig Santa Madrona 39–41. **Map** 1 B3. **Tel** 93 424 65 77. Ⓜ *Espanya, Poble Sec.* ☐ *9:30am–7pm Tue–Sat, 10am–2:30pm Sun & public hols.* ● *1 Jan, 25, 26 Dec.* 🎫 *(free 11 Feb, 23 Apr, 18 May, 11 & 24 Sep).* ♿

Housed in the Renaissance-inspired 1929 Palace of Graphic Arts, the museum shows artifacts from prehistory to the Visigothic period (AD 415–711). Highlights are finds from the Greco-Roman town of Empúries (*see p216*) and Iberian silver treasure. There is also a splendid collection of Visigothic jewellery.

Museu Nacional d'Art de Catalunya ❸

Parc de Montjuïc, Palau Nacional. **Map** 1 A2. **Tel** 93 622 03 60. Ⓜ *Espanya.* ☐ *10am–7pm Tue–Sat, 10am–2:30pm Sun & public hols.* ● *1 Jan, 1 May, 25 & 26 Dec.* 🎫 ♿ *noon by appt (93 622 03 75), free 1st Thu each month.*

The austere Palau Nacional was built for the 1929 International Exhibition, but in 1934 it was used to house an art collection that has since become the most important in the city.

The museum has probably the world's greatest display of Romanesque (*see pp24–25*) items, centred around a series of magnificent 12th-century frescoes taken from Catalan Pyrenean churches. The most remarkable are the wall paintings from Sant Climent de Taüll (*see p24*) and from Santa Maria de Taüll (*see p211*).

There is also an expanding Gothic collection, covering the whole of Spain but particularly good on Catalonia and a collection of notable Baroque and Renaissance works from all over Europe.

The museum has made way for an entire body of 20th century art, furniture and sculpture, previously on show at the Museu d' Art Modern in the Ciutadella park. These new additions offer a rare opportunity to view more than a millennium of Catalan artistic activity in a single location.

12th-century *Christ in Majesty*, Museu Nacional d'Art de Catalunya

Morning by Georg Kolbe (1877–1945), Pavelló Mies van der Rohe

Pavelló Mies van der Rohe ❹

Avinguda del Marqués de Comillas. **Map** 1 B2. *Tel* 93 423 40 16. Espanya. 50. 10am–8pm daily. 1 Jan, 25 Dec. under 18s free.

If the simple lines of the glass and polished stone German Pavilion look modern today, they must have shocked visitors to the International Exhibition in 1929. Designed by Ludwig Mies van der Rohe (1886–1969), director of the Avant-Garde Bauhaus school, it includes his famous *Barcelona Chair*. The building was demolished after the exhibition, but a replica was built on the centenary of his birth.

Poble Espanyol ❺

Avinguda del Marqués de Comillas. **Map** 1 A2. *Tel* 93 508 63 00. Espanya. 9am–8pm Mon, 9am–2am Tue–Thu, 9am–4am Fri & Sat, 9am–midnight Sun. www.poble-espanyol.com

The idea behind the Poble Espanyol (Spanish Village) was to display Spanish architectural styles and crafts. It was laid out for the 1929 International Exhibition, but has proved enduringly popular.

Building styles from all over Spain are illustrated by 116 houses. These are arranged on streets radiating from a main square and were created by many well-known architects and artists of the time. The village was refurbished at the end of the 1980s and is now a favourite place to visit for both tourists and native *Barcelonins*.

Resident artisans produce a wide range of crafts including hand-blown glass, ceramics, sculpture, Toledo damascene (*see p390*) and Catalan canvas sandals. The Torres de Avila (*see p191*), which form the huge main entrance, have been converted into one of the city's most popular nightspots, with an interior by designers Alfredo Arribas and Javier Mariscal. There are also shops, cafés, bars and a children's theatre.

View from Palau Nacional downhill towards the Plaça d'Espanya

Plaça d'Espanya ❻

Avinguda de la Gran Via de les Corts Catalanes. **Map** 1 B1. Espanya.

The fountain in the middle of this road junction, the site of public gallows until they were transferred to Ciutadella in 1715, is by Josep Maria Jujol, one of Gaudí's followers. The sculptures are by Miquel Blay. The 1899 bullring to one side is by Font i Carreras, but Catalans have never taken to bullfighting and the arena is now used as a music venue.

On the Montjuïc side of the roundabout is the Avinguda de la Reina Maria Cristina. This is flanked by two 47-m (154-ft) high brick campaniles by Ramon Raventós, modelled on the bell towers of St Mark's in Venice and built as the entrance way to the 1929 International Exhibition. The avenue, lined with exhibition buildings, leads up to Carles Buigas's illuminated *Font Màgica* (Magic Fountain) in front of the Palau Nacional.

Castell de Montjuïc ❼

Parc de Montjuïc. **Map** 1 B5. *Tel* 93 329 86 13. Paral·lel, then funicular & cable car. **Museum** Nov–15 Mar: 9:30am–5pm Tue–Sun; 16 Mar– Oct: 9:30am–8pm. 1 Jan, Good Fri, 1 May, 25–26 Dec.

The whole of the summit of Montjuïc is occupied by an 18th-century castle with views over the port. The first castle was built in 1640, but was destroyed by Felipe V in 1705. The present fortress was built for the Bourbon family. During the War of Independence it was captured by French troops. After the Civil War it became a prison, where the Catalan leader Lluís Companys was executed in 1940.

The castle is now a military museum with a display of ancient weaponry.

Estadi Olímpic de Montjuïc ❽

Passeig Olímpic 17–19. **Map** 1 A3. *Tel* 93 426 20 89. Espanya, Poble Sec. 50, 51. Oct–May: 10am–6pm daily; Jun–Sep: 10am–8pm daily. 1 Jan, 25 Dec.

The Neo-Classical façade has been preserved from the original stadium, built by Pere Domènech i Roura for the 1936 "Alternative" Olympics, cancelled at the outbreak of the Civil War. The arena was refitted to a capacity of 70,000 for the 1992 Olympics.

Nearby are the steel-and-glass **Palau Sant Jordi** indoor stadium, by Japanese architect Arata Isozaki, and swimming pools by Ricardo Bofill.

Entrance to the refurbished 1992 Olympic Stadium

FURTHER AFIELD

The radical redevelopment of Barcelona's outskirts in the late 1980s and early 1990s gave it a wealth of new buildings, parks and squares. The city's main station, Sants, was rebuilt and the neighbouring Parc de l'Espanya Industrial and Parc de Joan Miró were created, containing lakes, modern sculpture and futuristic architecture. The Parc de Clot, beyond the new national theatre (see p190), is also of striking modern design. In the west of the city, where

Parc Güell gateway signs

the streets start to climb steeply, are the historic royal palace and monastery of Pedralbes, and Gaudí's famous Parc Güell, dating from 1910. Beyond is the Serra de Collserola, the city's closest rural area. Two funiculars provide an exciting way of reaching its heights, which offer superb views of the city. Tibidabo, the highest point, with a funfair, the Neo-Gothic church of the Sagrat Cor and a modern steel-and-glass communications tower, is a favourite place among Barcelonins for a day out.

SIGHTS AT A GLANCE

Museums and Galleries
Museu de la Ciència ❽
Museu del Futbol Club Barcelona ❸

Historic Buildings
Monestir de Pedralbes ❺
Palau Reial de Pedralbes ❹

Modern Buildings
Torre de Collserola ❻

Parks and Gardens
Parc de l'Espanya Industrial ❷
Parc Güell ❾
Parc de Joan Miró ❶

Theme Parks
Tibidabo ❼

0 metres   500
0 yards   500

KEY

	Barcelona City Centre
	Built-up area
🚇	Railway station
🚟	Funicular railway station
═	Motorway
━	Major road
─	Minor road

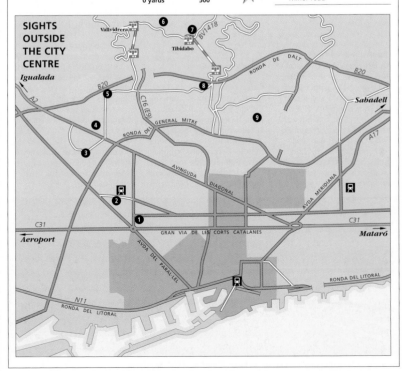

SIGHTS OUTSIDE THE CITY CENTRE

Igualada
Vallvidrera
Tibidabo
BV1418
RONDA DE DALT
B20
Sabadell
A2
B20
C16 (E9)
RONDA DEL GENERAL MITRE
A17
AVINGUDA DIAGONAL
AVDA MERIDIANA
Aeroport
C31
GRAN VIA DE LES CORTS CATALANES
C31
Mataró
AVDA DEL PARAL·LEL
N11
RONDA DEL LITORAL
RONDA DEL LITORAL

◁ The Neo-Gothic Temple Expiatori del Sagrat Cor, dominating Barcelona from the summit of Tibidabo

Dona i Ocell (1983) by Joan Miró in the Parc de Joan Miró

Parc de Joan Miró ❶

Carrer d'Aragó 1. ⊕ *Tarragona.*

Barcelona's 19th-century slaughterhouse *(escorxador)* was transformed in the 1980s into this unusual park, hence its alternative name, Parc de l'Escorxador.

It is constructed on two levels, the lower of which is devoted to football pitches interspersed with landscaped sections of palms, pines, eucalyptus trees and flowers. The upper level is completely paved and is dominated by a magnificent 1983 sculpture by the Catalan artist Joan Miró *(see p172)* entitled *Dona i Ocell* (Woman and Bird). Standing 22 m (72 ft) high in the middle of a pool, its surface is coated with colourful pieces of glazed tile.

Parc de l'Espanya Industrial ❷

Plaça de Joan Peiró. ⊕ *Sants-Estació.*

This modern park, designed by the Basque architect Luis Peña Ganchegui, owes its name to the textile mill that used to stand on the 5-hectare (12-acre) site.

Laid out in 1986 as part of Barcelona's policy to provide more open spaces within the city, the park has canals and a rowing lake – with a Classical statue of Neptune at its centre. Tiers of steps rise around the lake like an amphitheatre and on one side a row of ten futuristic watchtowers dominates the entire area. Their only function is to serve as public viewing platforms and lamp standards.

Six contemporary sculptors are represented in the park, among them Andrés Nagel, whose huge metal dragon incorporates a children's slide.

Museu del Futbol Club Barcelona ❸

Avda de Aristides Maillol. *Tel* 93 496 36 08. ⊕ *Maria Cristina, Collblanc.* ☐ 10am–6:30pm Mon–Sat, 10am–2pm Sun & public hols. ☐ 1 & 6 Jan, 24 Sep, 25 & 26 Dec. ☑ ☐ **www**.fcbarcelona.com

Camp Nou, Europe's largest football stadium, is home to the city's famous football club, Barcelona FC (Barça, as it is known locally). Founded in 1899, it is one of the world's richest soccer clubs, and has more than 100,000 members.

The stadium is a magnificent, sweeping structure, built in 1957

Line of watchtowers in the Parc de l'Espanya Industrial

to a design by Francesc Mitjans. An extension was added in 1982 and it can now comfortably seat 100,000 fans.

The club's museum, which displays club memorabilia and trophies on two floors, and has a souvenir shop, is one of the most popular in Barcelona. There are also paintings and sculptures of famous club footballers commissioned for the Blau-grana Biennial, an exhibition held in celebration of the club in 1985 and 1987. *Blau-grana* (blue-burgundy) are the colours of Barça's strip. The club's flags were used as an expression of local nationalist feelings during the Franco dictatorship, when the Catalan flag was banned.

As well as hosting its own high-profile matches (mainly at weekends), Camp Nou also accommodates affiliated local soccer clubs and promotes a number of other sports in its sports centre, ice rink and mini-stadium.

View across Camp Nou stadium, prestigious home of the Futbol Club Barcelona

For hotels and restaurants in this region see pp568–70 and pp617–20

Palau Reial de Pedralbes **❹**

Avinguda Diagonal 686. Ⓜ *Palau Reial.* Ⓟ *to the public.* **Museu de Ceràmica & Museu de Arts Decoratives** *Tel* 93 280 50 24. ☐ *10am–6pm Tue–Sat, 10am–3pm Sun & public hols.* ☐ *1 Jan, 1 May, 24 Jun, 25 & 26 Dec.* 🎫 ♿ 📷 *by appt*

The Palace of Pedralbes was once the main house on the estate of Count Eusebi Güell. In 1919 he offered it to the Spanish royal family. The first visit was from Alfonso XIII in 1926, before which the interior was refurbished and a new throne, supported by golden lions, was created for him.

Two fascinating museums and the gardens are open to the public. The Museu de Arts Decoratives, opened in 1937, displays period furniture from other great houses in the city and fine household items from the Middle Ages to the present. A genealogical tree traces the 500-year dynasty of the count-kings of Barcelona.

The palace also houses the Museu de Ceràmica, which has displays of historic Catalan and Moorish pottery and modern ceramics, including works by Miró and Picasso (*see p152*).

The palace gardens are well laid out with small ponds and paths. Just behind the gardens, in Avinguda de Pedralbes, is the entrance to the original Güell estate. It is guarded by a black wrought-iron gate, its top forged into a great, open-jawed dragon, and two gate houses, all by Gaudí (*see pp140–1*).

Madonna of Humility, Monestir de Santa Maria de Pedralbes

Monestir de Santa Maria de Pedralbes **❺**

Monastery ☐ *10am–2pm Tue–Sun.* 📷 *by appointment (93 315 11 11). Baixada del Monestir 9. Tel* 93 203 92 82. 🚇 *Reina Elisenda.* ☐ *10am–2pm Tue–Sun.* ⬤ *public hols.* 🎫 ♿ *ground floor only.*

Approached through an arch in its walls, the monastery of Pedralbes still has the air of a living enclosed community. This is heightened by its furnished cells, kitchens, infirmary and refectory. But the nuns of the Order of St Clare

moved to an adjoining building in 1983. The monastery was founded in 1326 by Elisenda de Montcada de Piños, fourth wife of Jaime II of Catalonia and Aragón. Her tomb lies between the church and the cloister. On the church side her effigy is dressed in royal robes; on the other as a nun.

The monastery is built around a spacious, three-storey cloister. The main rooms encircling the cloister include a dormitory, a refectory, a chapterhouse, an abbey and day cells. Numerous works of art, as well as liturgical ornaments, pottery, furniture, altar cloths and gold and silver work, are on display here.

The most important room in the monastery is the Capella (chapel) de Sant Miquel, with murals of the *Passion* and the *Life of the Virgin*, both painted by Ferrer Bassa in 1346, when Elisenda's niece, Francesca Saportella, was abbess.

Torre de Collserola **❻**

Carretera de Vallvidrera al Tibidabo. *Tel* 93 406 93 54. 🚠 *Peu de Funicular, then Funicular de Vallvidrera & bus 211.* ☐ *11am–2:30 & 3:30–7pm Wed–Sun.* ⬤ *25 Dec, 1 Jan & 6 Jan.* 🎫 ♿ **www**.torredecollserola.com

In a city that enjoys thrills, the ultimate ride is offered by the communications tower near Tibidabo mountain (*see p178*). A glass-sided lift takes less than two minutes to reach the top of this 288-m (944-ft) tall structure standing on the summit of a 445-m (1,460-ft) hill – not a pleasant experience for those who fear heights.

The tower was designed by English architect Norman Foster for the 1992 Olympic Games. Needle-like in form, it is a tubular steel mast on a concrete pillar. There are 13 levels. The top one has an observatory with a powerful telescope, and a public viewing platform with a 360° view encompassing Barcelona, the sea and the mountain chain on which Tibidabo sits.

BARCELONA V REAL MADRID

FC Barcelona

Més que un club is the motto of Barcelona FC: "More than a club". More than anything else it has been a symbol of the struggle of Catalan nationalism against the central government in Madrid. To fail to win the league is one thing. To come in behind Real Madrid is a complete disaster. Each season the big question is which of the two teams will win the title. Under the Franco regime in a memorable episode in 1941, Barça won 3–0 at home. At the return match in Madrid, the crowd was so hostile that the police and referee "advised" Barça to prevent trouble. Demoralized by the intimidation, they lost 11–1. Loyalty is paramount: one Barça player who left to join Real Madrid received death threats.

Real Madrid

Merry-go-round, Tibidabo

Tibidabo ❼

Plaça del Tibidabo 3–4. **Tel** 93 211 79 42. 🚃 Avda Tibidabo, then Tramvia Blau & Funicular. **Amusement Park** ◻ variable – phone ahead for times. 🌐 Oct–Apr: Mon–Fri. ♿ **Temple del Sagrat Cor. Tel** 93 417 56 86. ◻ 10am–8pm, Mon–Fri. ♿

The heights of Tibidabo are reached by the Tramvia Blau (Blue Tram), Barcelona's one last surviving tram, and a funicular railway. The name, inspired by Tibidabo's views of the city, comes from the Latin *tibi dabo* (I shall give you) – a reference to the Temptation of Christ when Satan took him up a mountain and offered him the world spread at his feet.

The hugely popular Parc d'Atraccions first opened in 1908. The rides were completely renovated in the 1980s. While the old ones retain their charm, the newer ones provide the latest in vertiginous experiences. Their hilltop location at 517 m (1,696 ft) adds to the thrill. Also in the park is the Museu d'Automates, displaying automated toys, juke boxes and gaming machines.

Tibidabo is crowned by the Temple Expiatori del Sagrat Cor (Church of the Sacred Heart), built with religious zeal but little taste by Enric Sagnier between 1902 and 1911. A lift takes you up to the feet of an enormous figure of Christ.

Just a short bus ride away is another viewpoint worth visiting – the Torre de Collserola (see p177).

Museu de la Ciència ❽

Carrer Teodor Roviralta 55. **Tel** 93 212 60 50. 🚃 Avinguda del Tibidabo, then Tramvia Blau. ◻ 10am–8pm Tue–Sun. 🌐 (free first Sun of every month). ♿

The new science museum offers the hands-on experiences that are popular with children. One of the most modern of its kind, all forms of matter from Inert to Living and Intelligent are questioned and explored over its five subterranean galleries. Above ground, an extensive garden and play area completes this family-friendly museum.

Parc Güell ❾

Carrer d'Olot. **Tel** 93 413 24 00. 🚇 Lesseps. ◻ summer 10am–9pm daily, winter 10am–6pm daily. ♿ 🚌 **Casa-Museu Gaudí. Tel** 93 219 38 11. ◻ Apr–Sep: 10am–8pm daily; Oct–Mar: 10am–6pm daily. 🌐 1 Jan, 25 Dec. 🌐

Designated a World Heritage Site by UNESCO, the Parc Güell is Antoni Gaudí's *(see*

pp140–1) most colourful creation. He was commissioned in the 1890s by Count Eusebi Güell to design a garden city on 20 hectares (50 acres) of the family estate. Little of the grand design for decorative public buildings and 60 houses among landscaped gardens became reality. What we see today was completed between 1910 and 1914, and the park opened in 1922.

Most atmospheric is the Room of a Hundred Columns, a cavernous covered hall of 84 crooked pillars, which is brightened by glass and ceramic mosaics. Above it, reached by a flight of steps flanked by ceramic animals, is the Gran Plaça Circular, an open space with a snaking balcony of coloured mosaics, said to have the longest bench in the world. It was executed by Josep Jujol, one of Gaudí's collaborators.

Two pavilions at the entry are by Gaudí, but the Casa-Museu Gaudí, a gingerbread-style house where Gaudí lived from 1906–26, was built by Francesc Berenguer. It contains drawings and furniture by Gaudí.

Mosaic-encrusted chimney by Gaudí at the entrance of the Parc Güell

BARCELONA STREET FINDER

The map references given with the sights, shops and entertainment venues described in the Barcelona section of the guide refer to the street maps on the following pages. Map references are also given for Barcelona hotels *(see*

pp568–70), and for bars and restaurants *(see pp617–20)*. The schematic map below shows the area of Barcelona covered by the *Street Finder*. The symbols used for sights and other features and services are listed in the key at the foot of the page.

KEY TO STREET FINDER

◼ Major sight	🚢 Golondrina boarding point	🏛 Police station
◼ Place of interest	🚡 Cable car	✝ Church
◻ Other building	🚞 Funicular railway station	⊠ Post office
➘ Main railway station	🚋 Tram	═ Railway line
Ⓕ Local (FF CC) railway station	🚕 Taxi rank	▭ Pedestrianized street
Ⓜ Metro station	P Parking	
🚌 Main bus stop	ℹ Tourist information	**SCALE OF MAP PAGES**
🚍 Coach station	✚ Hospital with casualty unit	0 metres 250
		0 yards 250

0 kilometres   2

0 miles   1

SHOPPING IN BARCELONA

Barcelona is known for its style and sophistication, and can be neatly divided into distinctive shopping districts – Passeig de Gràcia for designer stores and old shops with beautiful Modernista frontages, Barri Gòtic for eclectic antiques and boutiques, El Born for serious fashion divas, and El Raval for markets and museum shops. Though these categories are not fixed, they do provide a useful rule of

Wall tile outside La Manual Alpargatera

thumb, and help define the city when time is limited. There are numerous food markets as well – 44 in all – and a scattering of flea markets such as the Parisian-style Els Encants and the charming Sant Cugat antiques fair. There is something for everyone in Barcelona – from high-street fashion and unique boutiques to local shops selling traditional crafts such as carnival masks and handmade espadrilles.

Some of the beautifully displayed confectionery at Escribà

MARKETS

Barcelona has an impressive range of markets selling a wide variety of things. Everyone should explore **La Boqueria** on Las Ramblas, one of the the most spectacular food markets in Europe. The small and lively Plaça del Pi is also home to a food market selling cheese, honey and sweets. It is held on the 1st and 3rd Friday, Saturday and Sunday of each month.

On Sunday mornings, coin and stamp stalls are set up in the Plaça Reial, while antiques are sold in Plaça Nova on Thursdays. The city's main flea market, **Encants Vells**, takes place on Monday, Wednesday, Friday and Saturday. It offers a variety of goods including jewellery and clothing.

In December, a Christmas street market is held near the cathedral, where Christmas trees, figurines and other decorative items are sold.

FOOD AND DRINK

Barcelonans are proud of their culinary heritage, and rightly so. The land produces superlative vegetables and fruits, flavourful meats and a huge array of cheeses. The bountiful sea offers fresh fish and other seafood, and the wine-growing regions of the Penedès and the Priorat make some of the best vintages in the world. As if all this wasn't enough, chocolate shops, candy makers and patisseries also do their best to complete the feast.

La Boqueria food market, is the obvious place to start a gastronomical journey, but Barcelona's numerous specialist food shops are not to be ignored either.

Origins 99.9% in El Born specializes in strictly Catalan products – jars of small, dusky Arbequina olives, truffle-scented salt, vinegars, oils and home-made preserves. Around the corner,

La Botifarrería de Santa María stocks wonderful artisan charcuterie and a lip-smacking selection of home-made sausages. These include inventive combinations such as pork and cuttlefish, beef and beetroot and lamb and wild mushroom. **Casa Gispert** is the stop for top-grade dried fruit and nuts, as well as coffee toasted in-house. The fabulous **Formatgeria La Seu** is a walk-in dairy where you can choose from a great seasonal collection of cheeses made by small producers.

Xocoa is the trendiest of the many chocolate-makers in the city, with its retro packaging and fun shapes, including chocolate CDs and giant keys. **Escribà Pastisseries** is more extravagant, with magnificently sculpted cakes and life-size chocolate models of famous personalities. **Cacao Sampaka**, an innovative sweet shop, is owned by chef Albert Adrià, and offers amazing off-the-

Mouthwatering fruit stalls in La Boqueria market

wall fillings such as anchovy, black olive and blue cheese, as well as more familiar herb, spice and floral flavours.

Antiga Casa Mauri is ideal for those who want to sample traditional Spanish sweets such as *turrón* (nougat made with almonds). **Caelum**, where all the sweetmeats are made by nuns, sells lovely *yemas* (a sweet made with egg yolks) and *mazapans* (marzipan treats) and other tasty confections. **Papabubble**, a gorgeous wood-panelled shop, adds modern touches to old-fashioned sweets. You can watch the sweet chefs preparing these handmade concoctions.

For the best breads in town, visit **Bopan** near Rambla de Catalunya. This smart café has its own versions of many different types of bread, ranging from Continental favourites to African specialities.

For sheer scope, you can't beat **Lavinia**, the biggest wine shop in Spain, which stocks thousands of labels from all over the world. In El Born, **Vila Viniteca** sells a formidable range of Spanish and Catalan wines. You can find cheap and cheerful table wines here, as well as decadently expensive Priorats and Riojas. Also remember that leaving Barcelona without a bottle of the nation's beloved Catalan champagne, *cava*, would be verging on the sacrilegious. You can buy it everywhere, but for something truly special, head for **Xampany**, which specializes in wonderful artisan *cavas* from the Penedés wine producing region.

DEPARTMENT STORES AND GALERÍAS

The Plaça Catalunya branch of **El Corte Inglés**, the largest department store chain in Spain, is a Barcelona landmark. It is a handy place with everything under one roof, including plug adaptors and services such as photographic development. There are other branches around the city.

The *galerías* (fashion malls), built mostly during the 1980s,

Menswear department in Adolfo Domínguez

are hugely popular. **Bulevard Rosa** on the Passeig de Gràcia has hundreds of stores selling clothes and accessories. On the Avingunda Diagonal is **L'Illa**, a large, lively shopping mall containing chain stores as well as specialist retailers.

HIGH STREET AND SPORTS FASHION

Ubiquitous Spanish fashion houses, Zara and Mango, have stores all over the city, with both flagships on the Passeig de Gràcia. They are great for good value basics, work-wear and fashionable party dresses. Both also offer a decent menswear range.

Those looking for more upmarket buys can rely on **Massimo Dutti** and **Adolfo Domínguez**. Both labels offer classically styled, elegant and fairly affordable clothing for men and women.

For more individualized fashion, try one of the smaller, independent shops in El Born and the Barri Gòtic. Carrer d'Avinyó, a lively street in the Old Town, is particularly good for such clothing and droves of hipsters flock to it.

Custo Barcelona is one of the city's most famous design labels. Both branches of this store are in the Old Town, and are piled high with their trademark bright prints and daringly mismatched coats and skirts.

Finally, football fans can head for FC Barcelona's official store, the **Botiga del Barca**. It stocks every conceivable item of merchandise related to the team, including stripes, scarves, boots, balls and keychains.

SPANISH AND INTERNATIONAL DESIGNER LABELS

Independent design house **Giménez & Zuazo** offers truly unique clothing for women, and is well worth seeking out if reasonably priced couture is what you are looking for.

El Born has several stores that stock a range of top designer labels. **Black Jazz** is excellent for menswear, with seasonal collections from Vivienne Westwood, Dolce & Gabbana and many others.

Host to big designer labels such as Gucci, Chanel and Caroline Herrera, Avenida Diagonal and the Passeig de Gràcia are where fashionistas like to go shopping. **Loewe** stocks sleek luxury luggage, and is also a reputed name in fashion.

The stylishly sparse display of furniture at Vinçon *(see p188)*

SECOND-HAND AND VINTAGE FASHION

The diminutive Carrer Riera Baixa in El Raval is home to many interesting second-hand stores. Once a theatre, the vintage shop **Lailo** sells whimsical collectibles such as costumes from the Liceu opera house and 1950s bathing suits. Across the road is **Mies & Felj**, which specializes in fashions from the 1960s and 70s, vintage sportswear, Chinese dresses and brightly patterned curtains.

JEWELLERY, BAGS AND ACCESSORIES

Barcelona has plenty of tiny, Aladdin's Cave-type shops to help put together the perfect outfit. **New Born** may be small, but it sells gorgeous handmade jewellery fashioned from enamel butterflies and flowers in luscious colours. Visit **Rafa Teja Atelier** for embroidered jackets, patchwork scarves, appliqué handbags and hand-painted silk kerchiefs in sumptuous textures and colours.

Take a bit of the city's street-life home – literally – with a Demano handbag. Recycled polyester PVC from banners and placards is transformed into bags in this endeavor by three designers and the city hall. The innovative and eco-friendly range is available from stockists all over town.

With around 650 designers on its books, **Hipótesis** stores many unique pieces. It stocks jewellery as well as scarves and bags. Materials as diverse as white gold, wood, platinum, buttons and beads have been used to create a number of interesting designs.

HATS AND SHOES

Patterned leather shoes and decorative soles from the cult Mallorcan shoemaker, **Camper**, can be purchased cheaper in Barcelona than anywhere else outside of Spain. **La Manual Alpargatera** is another cult classic, beloved by Sardana dancers (see p225) and celebrities alike for its exquisite, individually fitted espadrilles

and straw hats. **Le Shoe** is the place for the discerning buyer willing to spend lavishly for superbly classy stilettos. The store has a collection of gorgeous Miu Mius, Jimmy Choos and Manolo Blahniks.

Bargain hunters can head for **I12** nearby, where last season's Marc Jacobs, Emma Hoes and Sonia Rykiels are sold at rock-bottom prices.

For trendily old-fashioned hats, go to **Sombrereria Obach** where you will find classics ranging from Basque berets to stetsons and hand-woven Montechristi Panamas.

BOOKS AND MUSIC

Arguably the finest specialist travel bookshop in Spain, **Altaïr** stocks a stupendous range of maps, travel guides and coffee-table books for anyone who loves to live on the move. If you are simply looking for some holiday reading, try **Casa del Llibre**, the city's biggest bookstore for English language books and magazines.

Barcelona has become a hot spot for music collectors, largely due to Sonár, the city's annual electronica festival. **Cable Records** and **El Raval** are good for stocking up on the latest club tunes and old vinyl, while **FNAC** has a wide variety of books, CDs and DVDs.

UNUSUAL GIFTS AND KNICK-KNACKS

Barcelona is a wonderful city for unearthing intriguing knick-knacks and one-of-a-kind gifts. **Brasil Style** stocks a wide and unusual range of things for the home, including charming hand-made dinner sets. The more risqué **La Condoneria** (the condom emporium) stocks condoms in every shape, size, colour and flavour possible.

Cereria Subirà is the city's oldest shop, and sells a phenomenal array of decorative and votive candles in a variety of beautiful designs.

Arlequí Màscares specializes in hand-painted, papier-

mâché folk masks such as Italian Commedia dell'Arte masks, glossy French party masks, Japanese Noh masks and many others.

ARTS AND ANTIQUES

Antiques aficionados will be delighted by what Barcelona has to offer. Equivalent to an antiques shopping mall, the Bulevard dels Antiquaris, in Passeig de Gràcia, is home to over 70 shops filled with vintage relics and every sort of antique imaginable. These range from ancient coins to tin drums and 19th-century candelabras.

Carrer del Call in the Barri Gòtic is another such hub with plush shops, including **L'Arca de l'Àvia**, which sells antique lace, dolls and fine furniture. **Heritage** is a purveyor of semi-precious stone jewellery and antique silks. Also check out the several **Artur Ramon** shops on Carrer de la Palla for 18th- and 19th-century ceramics, and 14th-century paintings.

Sala Parés, the city's oldest and most prestigious gallery, exhibits Catalan artists, both past and present. For pictures that won't break the bank, try the **Boutique Galería Picasso** for prints, lithographs and posters of works by the great Spanish masters, Picasso, Dalí and Miró.

INTERIORS

Pilé 43 seems more like a café than a shop, but it sells everything from the ashtrays to the battered leather armchairs. **Ici et Là** is good for one-off pieces for the home and also for design classics at unbeatable prices.

Dom, on the other hand, is more trendy and quirky, with its metallic bead curtains and inflatable sofas in shocking neon shades.

Vinçon is the star among Barcelona's design stores, and a favourite with fans of gizmos and gadgets. Housed in a 1900s apartment, it is filled with everything from French Creuset cookware to straight-edged tumblers and silk bean bags and futons.

DIRECTORY

MARKETS

La Boqueria
Las Ramblas 101.
Map 5 A2.

Encants Vells
Plaça de les Glóries.
Map 4 F5.

FOOD AND DRINK

Antiga Casa Mauri
C/ Flassanders 32.
Map 5 C2.
Tel 933 10 04 58.

Bopan
Rambla de Catalunya 119.
Map 3 A3.
Tel 932 37 35 23.

Cacao Sampaka
C/ Consell de Cent 292.
Map 3 A4.
Tel 932 72 08 33.

Caelum
C/ Palla 8. **Map** 5 A2.
Tel 933 01 69 93.

Casa Gispert
C/ Sombrerers 23.
Map 5 B3.
Tel 933 19 75 35.

Escribà Pastisseries
Las Ramblas 83.
Map 5 A1.
Tel 933 01 60 27.

Formatgeria La Seu
C/ Dagueria 16.
Map 5 B3.
Tel 934 12 65 48.

**La Botifarrería de
Santa María**
Carrer Santa María 4.
Map 5 B3.
Tel 933 19 97 84.

Lavinia
Av Diagonal 605.
Map 3 A2.
Tel 933 63 44 45.

Origins 99.9%
C/Vidrería 6.
Tel 933 10 75 31.

Papabubble
C/ Ample 28.
Map 5 A3.
Tel 932 68 86 25.

Vila Viniteca
C/ Agullers 7.
Map 5 B3.
Tel 933 10 19 56.

Xampany
C/Valencia 200. **Map** 3 A4
Tel 934 53 93 38 .

Xocoa
C/ Vidrería 4.
Map 5 B2.
Tel 933 19 63 71.

DEPARTMENT STORES AND GALERÍAS

Bulevard Rosa
Passeig de Gràcia 55. **Map**
3 A4. *Tel 933 78 91 91.*

El Corte Inglés
Plaça de Catalunya 14.
Map 5 B1.
Tel 933 06 38 00.

La Illa
Avinguda Diagonal 545.
Tel 934 44 00 0.

HIGH STREET AND SPORTS FASHION

Adolfo Domínguez
Passeg de Gràcia 89.
Map 3 A2–A5.
Tel 932 15 13 39.

Botiga del Barca
Maremàgnum (Moll
d'Espanya). **Map** 5 A4.
Tel 932 25 80 45.

Custo Barcelona
Plaça de les Olles 7.
Map 5 B3.
Tel 932 68 78 93.

Massimo Dutti
C/ Argenteria 65.
Map 5 B2.
Tel 933 10 30 15.

SPANISH AND INTERNATIONAL DESIGNER LABELS

Black Jazz
C/ Rec 28. **Map** 5 C3.
Tel 933 10 42 36.

Giménez & Zuazo
C/ Elisabets 20.
Map 2 F2.
Tel 934 12 33 81.

Loewe
Passeig de Gràcia 35.
Map 3 A2–A5.
Tel 932 16 04 00.

SECOND-HAND AND VINTAGE FASHION

Lailo
C/ Riera Baixa 20.
Map 2 F2.
Tel 934 41 37 49.

Mies & Felj
C/ Riera Baixa 4.
Map 2 F2.
Tel 934 42 07 55.

JEWELLERY, BAGS AND ACCESSORIES

Hipótesis
Rambla de Catalunya 105.
Map 3 A3.
Tel 932 15 02 98.

New Born
C/ Princesa 24.
Map 5 B2.
Tel 935 11 31 25.

Rafa Teja Atelier
C/ Sta. Maria 18.
Map 5 B3.
Tel 933 10 27 85.

HATS AND SHOES

Camper
C/ Elizabets 9.
Map 2 F2.
Tel 933 42 41 41.

I12
C/ Laforja 105.
Map 3 A1.
Tel 934 14 55 13.

**La Manual
Alpargatera**
C/ D'Avinyó 7.
Map 5 A3.
Tel 933 01 01 72.

Le Shoe
C/ Viñas 6.
Map 3 A2–A5.
Tel 932 41 10 12.

Sombrerería Obach
Carrer del Call 2.
Map 5 A2.
Tel 933 18 40 94.

BOOKS AND MUSIC

Altaïr
Gran Via 616.
Map 3 A4.
Tel 933 42 71 71.

Cable Records
C/ Joaquín Costa 46.
Map 2 F2.
Tel 933 17 20 59.

Casa del Llibre
Passeig de Gràcia 62.
Map 3 A2–A5.
Tel 932 72 34 80.

El Raval
Gran Via 616.
Map 3 A2–A5.
Tel 933 42 71 71.

FNAC
Plaça de Catalunya 4.
Map 3 A4.
Tel 933 44 18 00.

UNUSUAL GIFTS AND KNICK KNACKS

Arlequí Màscares
C/ Princesa 7.
Map 5 B2.
Tel 932 68 27 52.

Brasil Style
Plaça Comercial 3.
Map 5 C3.
Tel 932 68 86 30.

Cereria Subirà
Baixada Llibreteria 7.
Map 5 A2.
Tel 933 15 26 06.

La Condonería
Plaça Sant Josep Oriol 7.
Map 2 F2.
Tel 933 02 77 21.

ARTS AND ANTIQUES

Artur Ramon
C/ Palla 23.
Map 5 A2.
Tel 933 02 59 70.

**Boutique Galería
Picasso**
C/ Barra de Ferro 7.
Map 5 A3.
Tel 932 68 44 50.

Heritage
C/ Banys Nous 14.
Map 5 A2.
Tel 933 17 85 15.

L'Arca de l'Àvia
C/ Banys Nous 20.
Map 5 A2.
Tel 933 02 15 98.

Sala Parés
C/ Petritxol 5.
Map 5 A2.
Tel 933 18 70 08.

INTERIORS

Dom
C/Provença, 249.
Map 3 A3.
Tel 934 87 11 81.

Ici et Là
Plaça de Santa María del
Mar 2. **Map** 5 B3.
Tel 932 68 11 67.

Pilé 43
C/ Agla 43.
Map 5 A3.
Tel 933 01 30 54.

Vinçon
Passeig de Gràcia 96.
Map 3 A2–A5.
Tel 932 15 60 50.

ENTERTAINMENT IN BARCELONA

Barcelona has one of the most colourful and alternative live arts scenes in Europe, offering a variety of entertainment, from the spectacular Modernista masterpiece the Palau de la Música and the gilded Liceu opera house, to small independent theatres hosting obscure Catalan comedies and dark Spanish dramas. But there's also much to see

Busker in the Barri Gòtic

simply by walking around the city. Street peformances you may stumble upon range from the human statues on Las Ramblas to excellent classical, ragtime and jazz buskers in the squares. In addition, there are a series of weekend-long musical and arts fiestas that run throughout the year, many of which now attract international performers from all over Europe and beyond.

The magnificent interior of the Palau de la Música Catalana

ENTERTAINMENT GUIDES

The most complete guide to what's going on each week in Barcelona is the *Guía del Ocio*, out every Thursday. This guide also includes cinema listings. The Friday *El País* and *La Vanguardia* feature entertainment supplements. Barcelona's free English-language magazine, *Metropolitan*, also offers extensive details of cultural events going on in town.

SEASONS AND TICKETS

Theatre and concert seasons for the main venues run from September to June, with limited programmes at other times. The city's varied menu of entertainment reflects its rich, multi-cultural artistic heritage. In summer, the city hosts the **Festival del Grec**, a showcase of international music, theatre and dance, held at open-air venues.

There is also a wide variety of concerts to choose from during the **Festa de la Mercè**, held in September. The **Festival del Sónar**, which takes place in June, has become Europe's biggest electronic music festival, drawing musicians from around the world. The **Clàssics als Parcs**, held in June and July, presents classical music in serene surroundings.

The simplest way to get theatre and concert tickets is to buy them at the box office, although tickets for many theatres can also be bought from branches of Caixa de Catalunya and the Caixa savings banks, or from ServiCaixa machines. Tickets for the Grec festival are sold at tourist offices and at the Palau de la Virreina.

THEATRE AND DANCE

Most theatre in Barcelona is performed in Catalan and English-language productions are still in short supply. However, many Catalan and

Spanish shows are well worth seeing, regardless of language constraints. There are some good independent theatre groups, such as Els Comediants and La Cubana, that perform at the **Llantiol Teatre** in El Raval. They offer a thrilling mélange of theatre, music, mime and elements from traditional Mediterranean fiestas. Also staged at the tiny Llantiol is a weekly repertoire of alternative shows, comedy, magic and other off-the-cuff performances designed to attract a mixed crowd, from the city's growing expatriate community to local arts lovers. Similarly, the **L'Antic Teatre** in La Ribera is a cultural centre and bar with a scruffy, but pleasant, summer roof-terrace and small vegetarian restaurant. It hosts a number of alternative production companies, such as the Argentinean company 4D Òptic.

Las Ramblas and Paral.lel are the main hubs of the city's bigger and more mainstream

Outrageous stage show at one of Barcelona's many clubs

The façade of the modern Teatre Nacional de Catalunya

theatres. The **Teatre Tívoli** is a gargantuan theatre where high-quality productions, dance and musical recitals by Catalan, Spanish and international stars are held. The **Teatre Poliorama** on Las Ramblas, meanwhile, is known more for musicals, occasional operas and contemporary flamenco performances. The **Teatre Apolo** is good for big-bang musicals such as Queen's "We Will Rock You" and ABBA's "Mamma Mia!"

For serious theatre-lovers, the **Teatre Nacional de Catalunya (TNC)** is an imposing, columned affair designed by the Catalan architect Ricard Bofill, with state-of-the-art facilities and a weighty line-up of Spanish and Catalan directors. Good for avant-garde performances and music is the **Mercat de les Flors**, a converted flower market in the Montjuïc area that is known as Barcelona's "City of Theatre". This is the same part of town that contains Barcelona's drama school and the **Teatre Lliure**, perhaps Barcelona's best-loved independent theatre.

Modern dance has always been popular in Barcelona and performances can often be caught at the city's main theatres. The **Teatre Victòria** on Avinguda del Paral.lel is good for ballet and more classical dance productions, as is the **Liceu** opera house.

OPERA AND CLASSICAL MUSIC

Opera and classical music are loved by Catalans who lap it up with near-religious reverence. Indeed, many

of the great artists of the 20th century were locals, including the celebrated cellist Pablo Casals and opera singers José Carreras and Montserrat Caballé.

The city of Barcelona is also home to some of the most spectacular venues in the world, including the glamorous, gilded **Gran Teatre del Liceu**, which first opened its doors in 1847. The opera house has been a continuing beacon of Catalan arts for more than 150 years, with a rich and dramatic history of fire and bomb attacks. It burned down for the third time in 1994, but careful renovations have restored it to its former glory. Despite its misfortunes, it has sustained a stellar line-up of the greatest composers in the world. Among them are Puccini and Tchaikovsky, as well as Catalan composers such as Felip Pedrell, Vives and Enric Granados. Sergei Diaghilev's Russian ballets were also staged here.

The whimsical fancy of the **Palau de la Música Catalana** is another of Barcelona's architectural triumphs (*see p152*). A jewel-bright vision by the Modernista master Lluís Domènech i Montaner, this sublime concert hall has a dedicated audience, and performers who vie to play here. This is also the main venue for the city's jazz and guitar festivals, as well as national and international symphony orchestras.

Both venues, the Gran Teatre del Liceu and Palau de la Música Catalana, can be visited on daytime guided tours, but booking tickets

for a production is the best way to experience the ambience.

Modern, but no less important as a shrine to the Catalan arts scene, **L'Auditori de Barcelona** was built to accommodate growing demands for better facilities and to attract ever greater numbers of world-class musicians. It began primarily as a place for classical concerts and orchestral recitals, but has since begun to embrace giants of jazz, pop and rock.

It is also worth keeping abreast of regular choral music that is performed at the city's churches and cathedrals. Most notable among these are the **Església Santa Maria del Pi**, the main cathedral on Plaça del Pi, and the **Basílica Santa Maria del Mar**, particularly around Christmas time.

Packed house at the gigantic Nou Camp stadium

SPORTS

The undoubted kings of sport in Catalonia are **FC Barcelona**, known locally as Barça. They have the largest football stadium in Europe, Camp Nou (*see p176*), and a fanatical following.

Tickets for Barça home matches in the national league (*La Liga*), the King's Cup (*Copa del Rey*) and Champions League can be purchased at the FC Barcelona ticket offices (in person or by telephone), at ServiCaixa machines, or perhaps most conveniently, they can be bought online. Barcelona also has a high-ranking basketball team.

AMUSEMENT PARK

In summer, Barcelona's giant amusement park on the summit of **Tibidabo** (*see p178*) is extremely busy and is usually open till the early hours on weekends. Getting there by tram, funicular or cable car is even more fun.

FILM

In recent years, directors such as Alejandro Amenábar (*The Others*), Catalan writer and director Isabel Coixet (*My Life Without You*) and, of course, Spain's bad boy of film, Pedro Almodóvar (*All About My Mother* and *Bad Education*) have revitalized Spanish cinema. Today, Barcelona itself has become the venue for many independent film festivals. The biggest event of the year is the International Film Festival in Sitges, which is held in December.

Most cinemas dub films in Spanish or Catalan, but there are an increasing number of VO (original version) venues that screen Hollywood block-busters as well as independent art-house movies.

The **Icària Yelmo Cineplex** is the town's biggest multi-screen VO complex, built around an American-style mall, with a variety of fast-food eateries and shops. The **Renoir Floridablanca**, a relatively new cinema on the edge of El Raval and the Eixample, screens a range of European and international movies, usually with Spanish or Catalan subtitles. In Gràcia, **Verdi I** and **Verdi II** feature good independent movies, with an interesting selection of foreign films. During summer, both the Castell de Montjuïc and the Piscina Bernat Picornell, the Olympic swimming pool in Montjuïc, host a number of open-air cinema screenings.

The two-screen **Méliès** is a gem showcasing art-house movies, Hollywood classics, B&W horrors and anything by Fellini or Alfred Hitchcock. For children, there is the **IMAX Port Vell**, which shows the usual 3-D roller coaster knuckle-biters,

Everest expeditions and squid entangled journeys to the bottom of the sea.

It's worth knowing that the prices for movie tickets are lower on Monday nights and for weekend matinées. Some cinemas offer midnight and early-hour screenings.

LIVE MUSIC: ROCK, JAZZ AND BLUES

In terms of popular music, Barcelona may not compare to London, whose endless clubs, pubs, stadiums and music emporiums make it one of the best places for live music. However, it doesn't do too badly, given its size. The city attracts a star-studded cast that ranges from pop stars such as Kylie Minogue and Madonna to contemporary jazz musicians such as the Brad Mehldau Quartet, hip-hoppers, rappers and world groove mixers, country singers and good old-fashioned rock and rollers.

In 2004, two of the city's most iconic jazz venues – La Boite and La Cova del Drac – closed down, much to the disbelief of residents. What will fill the gap remains to be seen, but for now Barcelona still has a clutch of tiny, intimate venues. The cellar-like **Jamboree** attracts a number of jazz heavyweights as well as more experimental outfits and solo artists such as the saxophonist Billy McHenry.

Another good bet is the **Jazz Sí Club**, a more obscure destination but much beloved by aficionados of the genre. It doubles up as a jam session space for students from the nearby music school. The narrow, crowded and smoky **Harlem Jazz Club** is one of the city's longest surviving clubs for alternative and lesser-known jazz troupes.

One of the two major venues for pop and rock maestros is **Bikini**, Barcelona's very own Studio 54. It opened in 1953, preceding the New York icon by a year. This veteran of the scene, which is open from midnight onwards, is still going strong with a robust line-up of big-name bands and a cocktail of

different club nights. The other, **Razzmatazz**, arguably the city's most important live music venue, has played host to big-name pop bands Blur and Pulp, and more recently, Welsh rappers Goldie Lookin Chain. Club sessions go on until dawn in Razz Club and The Loft, next door. This trendy club also holds rock and jazz concerts several nights a week.

For a touch of unbeatable glam, **Luz de Gas** is a glitzy ballroom that oozes old-fashioned atmosphere with its lamp-lit tables, chandeliers and a features lists of bands and shows that enjoyed their heyday here in the 1970s and 80s. It's not quite cabaret, but gets close, though not as close as the infamous **El Cangrejo**. This club features outrageous drag cabaret, with shockingly attired queens in full make-up and sequins miming along to numbers by Sara Montiel (the Spanish sex symbol) and back-chatting with the crowd. If your taste is for the small and subtle, the **Bar Pastis** is a miniscule bar, decorated with dusty bottles and yellowing posters from French musicals. French love ballads are performed live here most nights of the week.

FLAMENCO

One of the best places to catch a Flamenco show is **El Tablao de Carmen**, a stylish restaurant serving both Catalan and Andalucian dishes. The venue is named after Carmen Amaya, a famous dancer who performed for King Alfonso XIII in 1929, in the very spot where it now stands. Various dinner and show packages are available.

For a less formal ambience, **Los Tarantos** is an atmospheric nightspot with live flamenco and Latin music every night of the week.

Those who would like to try their hand at this sultry, passionate dance can visit **Soniquete**, a popular bar that encourages spontaneous dancing from the audience with great flamenco sounds. It is open from Thursday to Sunday.

DIRECTORY

FESTIVALS

Classics als Parcs
Tel 010.
www.bcn.es/parcsijardins

Festa de la Mercè
See p157.

Festival del Grec
Tel 010.
Contact any tourist office.

Festival del Sónar
Palau de la Virreina.
Tel 902 88 89 02.
www.sonar.es

TICKETS

Palau de la Virreina
Las Ramblas, 99.
Map 5 A1.
Tel 933 16 10 00.

Serviticket
Tel 902 33 22 11.
www.serviticket.com

TelEntrada
Tel 902 10 12 12.
www.telentrada.com

Tourist Office
Plaça de Catalunya.
Map 5 A1.
Tel 807 11 72 22.

THEATRE AND DANCE

L'Antic Teatre
C/ Verdaguer i Callís 12.
Map 5 A1.
Tel 933 15 23 54.

Llantiol Teatre
C/ Riereta 7.
Map 2 E2.
Tel 933 29 90 09.

Teatre Lliure
Plaça Margarida Xirgu 1.
Tel 932 28 97 48.
www.teatrelliure.com

Mercat de les Flors
C/ de Lleida 59.
Map 1 B2.
Tel 934 26 18 75.

Teatre Apolo
Av del Paral.lel 57.
Map 1 B1.
Tel 934 41 90 07.

Teatre Nacional de Catalunya (TNC)
Plaça de les Arts 1.
Tel 933 06 57 06.

Teatre Poliorama
Las Ramblas 115.
Map 5 A1.
Tel 933 17 75 99.
www.teatrepoliorama.com

Teatre Tívoli
C/ Casp 10–12.
Map 3 B5.
Tel 934 12 20 63.

Teatre Victòria
Av del Paral.lel 67–9.
Map 1 B1.
Tel 934 43 29 29.

OPERA AND CLASSICAL MUSIC

L'Auditori de Barcelona
C/ de Lepant 150.
Map 4 E1.
Tel 932 47 93 00.
www.auditori.org

Gran Teatre del Liceu
Las Ramblas 51–9.
Map 2 F3.
Tel 934 85 99 00.
www.liceubarcelona.com

Església Santa Maria del Pi
Plaça del Pi.
Map 5 A2.
Tel 349 33 18 743.

Basílica Santa Maria del Mar
Plaça de Santa Maria.
Map 5 B3.
Tel 349 331 02 390.

Palau de la Música Catalana
C/ Sant Francesc de Paula 2.
Map 5 B1.
Tel 932 95 72 00.
www.palaumusica.org

SPORTS

FC Barcelona
Camp Nou,
Avda Aristides Maillol.
Tel 934 96 36 00.
www.fcbarcelona.com

AMUSEMENT PARK

Tibidabo
Plaça del Tibidabo, 3.
Tel 932 11 79 42.

FILM

Icària Yelmo Cineplex
C/ Salvador Espriu 61.
Map 6 E4.
Tel 932 21 75 85.
www.yelmocineplex.es

IMAX Port Vell
Moll d'Espanya.
Map 5 A4.
Tel 932 25 11 11.

Méliès
C/ Villarroel 102.
Map 2 E1.
Tel 934 51 00 51.

Renoir Floridablanca
C/ Floridablanca 135.
Map 1 C1.
Tel 932 28 93 93.
www.cinesrenoir.es

Verdi I
C/ Verdi 32.
Map 3 B1.
Tel 932 38 79 90.
www.cines-verdi.com

Verdi II
C/ Torrijos 49.
Map 3 C2.
Tel 932 38 79 90.

LIVE MUSIC: ROCK, JAZZ AND BLUES

Bar Pastis
C/ Santa Mònica 4.
Map 2 F4.
Tel 933 18 79 80.

Bikini
Deu I Mata 105.
Tel 933 22 08 00.
www.bikinibcn.com

El Cangrejo
C/ Montserrat 9.
Map 2 F4.
Tel 933 01 29 78.

Harlem Jazz Club
C/ Comtessa de Sobradiel 8.
Tel 933 10 07 55.

Jamboree
Plaça Reial 17.
Map 5 A3.
Tel 933 01 75 64.
www.masimas.com

Jazz Sí Club
C/ Requesens 2.
Tel 933 29 00 20.
www.tallerdemusics.com

Luz de Gas
C/ Muntaner 246.
Map 2 F1.
Tel 932 09 77 11.
www.luzdegas.com

Razzmatazz
C/ Pamplona 88.
Map 4 F5.
Tel 932 72 09 10.
www.theloftclub.com

FLAMENCO

El Tablao de Carmen
Avda Marqués de Comillas s/n.
Map 1 B1.
Tel 933 25 68 95.
www.tablaodecarmen.com

Los Tarantos
Plaça Reial 17.
Map 5 A3.
Tel 933 18 30 67.

Soniquete
Plaza Milans 5.
Map 5 A3.
Tel. 933 5187 57.

Nightlife

If New York is the city that never sleeps, then Barcelona is the one that never goes to bed and those with energy can party around the clock, all week. It has one of the most varied scenes, with something for everybody. Old-fashioned dance halls rub shoulders with underground brass clubs and trashy techno discos, and club-goers are either glammed-up or grunged-out. Each *barrio* (neighbourhood) offers a different flavour.

NIGHTLIFE

In the summer the beaches become party havens when the *chiringuitos* (beach bars) spring back into life. Wander from Platja de Sant Sebastià in Barceloneta, all the way to Bogatell (a few kilometres beyond the Hotel Arts) and you'll find people dancing barefoot on the sand to the tune of Barcelona's innumerable DJs. Way uptown (above the Diagonal), the city's most glamorous terraces morph into social hubs while the Barri Gòtic – lively at the best of times – becomes one massive street party throughout the summer. If you want to hang with the locals, the demolition of some of El Raval's less salubrious streets has meant that the neighbourhood has become much safer and easier to move about. The underground vibe, however, remains steadfastly intact with tiny hole-in-the-wall-style bars where folks drink and boogie till the early hours. Similarly Gràcia has a bohemian, studenty ambience. If it's an alternative scene you seek Poble Sec has a handful of "ring-to-enter" joints and the city's only serious drum and bass club, **Plataforma**. The city also has a thriving and friendly gay scene, most notably within the Eixample Esquerra, also known as the Gay Eixample, boasting numerous late-night drinking holes, discothèques, saunas and cabarets.

BARRI GÒTIC

The Plaça Reial is overrun with tourists banging on tin drums and whooping it up, but if you're looking for more grown-up fun, check out

Café Royal, just off the square. Here you'll find Barcelona's beautiful people draped over battered leather sofas, sipping cocktails or grooving to the mellow beats of funk, soul and acid jazz.

For the more adventurous, **Moog** is more extreme with blaring, heart-pumping techno for aficionados of the genre. The stark industrial interior gives it the character of a New York nightclub in the mid-1990s. Likewise, the state-of-the-art sound system ensures a thumping, ear-bleedingly good night out. The nightclub **New York**, in contrast, has come over all loungey in a recent revamp and these days is inclined towards more commercially gratifying tunes. The vibe here is more disco.

EL RAVAL

Designer clubs proliferate in Barcelona these days, but check out the original at **Club Salsitas**, an achingly cool space decked with giant white pineapples and palm trees. Amazingly, after several years at the top it's still looking good and resident DJ Toni Bass continues to whip the crowd into a frenzy every Thursday, Friday and Saturday night. Next-door, pint-sized **Milk** offers a 1970s style chill-out space for those exhausted from strutting on the dance floor. Going back in time **La Paloma** is the city's most brilliantly gilded ballroom dating back to 1904. It's still going strong offering dance hall classics, including cha-cha-cha, tango, salsa and the waltz, accompanied by a brass band until midnight. Thereafter, DJs and house take over, catering to a younger set.

PORT VELL AND PORT OLÌMPIC

Beach parties aside, this area continues to be a hub for creatures of the night. The Port Olìmpic itself is nothing but bars and boats, while **Maremagnum** has a clutch of *salsatecas* and a rooftop pub. The **Sugar Club** (another *salsitas* offspring) is the newest kid on the block, which offers a splash of sophistication, not to mention society, to the downtown scene. **C.D.L.C.** in front of the Hotel Arts, however, still manages to draw the celebrities staying nearby.

EIXAMPLE

One of the city's best loved discos **City Hall** is a multiple space and terrace, where you can pick and choose your groove according to your mood. It has different themes every night from Saturday night-fever discos to Sunday chill-outs. **Buda Barcelona** is quite literally oozing with glitz and glamour, beloved by models and their entourages. It is a place where anything goes from dancing on the bar tops to dancing with your top off. For a more understated type of glamour, **Astoria** is housed in a converted cinema and therefore bags the title for the best projections in town. Finally, there's **L'Arquer**. Only in Barcelona would you find a bar that dared combine archery lessons with mammoth shots of vodka.

POBLE SEC

The most alternative nightlife has come to roost in the "dry village," though in name only. The bars are wet and the music is happening. **Apolo** is another old-fashioned music hall, similar to La Paloma, though it attracts a more independent breed of DJ and performer. Expect anything from soulful gypsy folk singers from Marseille, to the legendary purveyor of deep funk, Keb Darge.

Further into the village, **Mau Mau** is an alternative club and cultural centre with a firm eye on what's new and happening. This could mean local DJs, Japanese musicians such as the cultish Cinema Dub Monks, alternative cinema, and multimedia art installations. If it's of the here and now, chances are Mau Mau's on it. For the seriously hardcore and lovers of high-speed garage, **Plataforma** is Barcelona's only serious drum and base club hosting DJs from far and wide in a huge concrete warehouse.

GRÀCIA AND TIBIDABO

Tiny and always packed the **Mond Bar** attracts music-lovers from all over wishing to dip into tunes from the past. Resident DJ Mr Stream

delights a 30-something crowd with his swing-back to the 1970s sessions of northern soul and Motown. And high up above the rest, **Danzatoria** offers the best in mansion house clubbing experiences with chill-out lounges and several dance floors, vodka bars and sprawling terraces, and prices to suit the altitude.

OUT OF TOWN

The mega-clubs are located away from the city centre and from anyone trying to sleep. The big boys are based in Poble Espanyol where folks can party until the sunrise. **Discothèque**, a sleek elegant club has it all – disco lights, strobes and top-name DJs from the international circuit. **La Terrazza** is its summer sidekick for rave-like parties

under the stars. It takes its name from the giant terrace it occupies. Nearby on Plaça Espanya, after much bated breath, the Ibiza-style **Space** finally opened in 2004. Don't even think about getting in without an appropriately glamorous outfit, and remember, less is most definitely more.

Further out of town you will find the world's most famous nightclub, **Pacha**. What most people don't realize, however, is that it was born in Barcelona and continues to stage the most sensational nights out. Alternatively, **Liquid** is the only club with a swimming pool in the city. The only drawback is that should you wish to leave before the party's over, finding a taxi can be a big problem.

DIRECTORY

BARRI GÒTIC

Café Royale
C/Nou de Zurbano 3,
Barri Gòtic.
Tel 93 412 14 33.

Moog
C/Arc del Teatre 3,
El Raval.
Map 2 F4.
Tel 93 301 72 82.
www.masimas.com

New York
C/Escudellers 5,
Barri Gòtic.
Map 5 A3.
Tel 93 318 87 30.

EL RAVAL

Club Salsitas
C/Nou de la Rambla 22.
Map 2 D4.
Tel 93 318 08 40.
www.salsitas.
gruposalsitas.com

Milk
C/Nou de la Rambla 24,
El Raval.
Map 2 D4.
Tel 93 301 02 67.

La Paloma
C/Tigre 27,
El Raval.
Map 2 E1.
Tel 93 301 68 97.
www.lapaloma-bcn.com

PORT VELL AND PORT OLÍMPIC

C.D.L.C.
Passeig Marítim 32,
Port Olímpic.
Map 6 E4.
Tel 93 224 04 70.
www.cdlcbarcelona.com

Sugar Club
Moll de Barcelona s/n,
Port Vell.
Tel 93 508 83 25.

EIXAMPLE

Astoria
C/Paris 193,
Eixample.
Tel 93 414 63 62.
www.costaeste.com

L'Arquer
Gran Via de les Corts
Catalanes 454,
Eixample.
Map 1 A1.
Tel 93 423 99 08.

Buda Barcelona
C/Pau Claris 92,
Eixample.
Map 3 B3.
Tel 93 318 42 52.
www.budabarcelona.com

City Hall
Rambla Catalunya 2–4,
Eixample.
Map 3 A3.
Tel 93 317 21 77.
www.ottozutz.com

POBLE SEC

Apolo
C/Nou de la Rambla 113,
Poble Sec.
Map 2 D4.
Tel 93 441 40 01.
www.salaapolo.com

Mau Mau
C/Fontrodona 33,
Poble Sec.
Map 2 D3.
Tel 60 686 06 17.
www.
maumauunderground.com

Plataforma
C/Nou de la Rambla 145,
Poble Sec.
Map 2 D4.
Tel 93 329 00 29.

GRÀCIA AND TIBIDABO

Danzatoria
Av Tibidabo 61,
Tibidabo.
Tel 93 211 62 61.
www.danzatoria.
gruposalsitas.com

Mond Bar
Plaza del Sol 21, Gràcia.
Map 3 B1.

OUT OF TOWN

Discothèque/ La Terrazza
Poble Espanyol, Avda
Marquès de Comillas.
Map 1 B1.
Tel 93 423 12 85.
www.nightsungroup.com

Liquid
Complex Esportiu
Hospitalet Nord,
C/Manuel Azaña.
Tel 65 009 14 79.
www.liquidbcn.com

Pacha
Avda. Gregorio
Marañon 17.
Tel 93 334 32 33.
www.clubpachabcn.com

Space
C/Tarragona 141–147.
Tel 93 426 84 44.

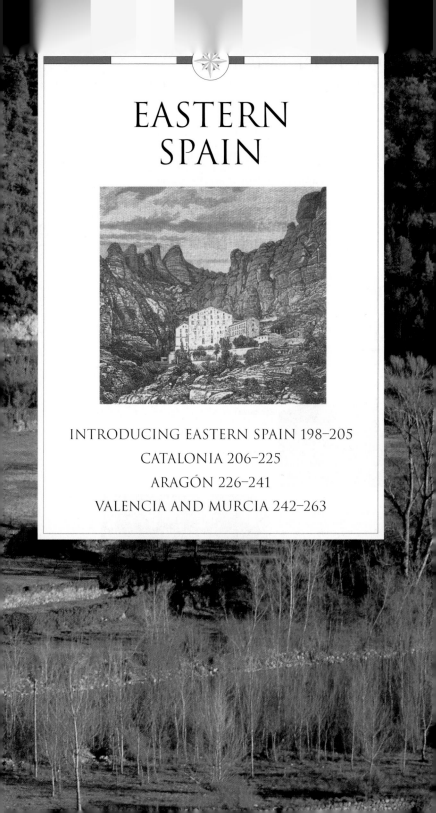

EASTERN
SPAIN

Introducing Eastern Spain

Eastern Spain covers an extraordinary range of climates and landscapes, from the snowbound peaks of the Pyrenees in Aragón to the beaches of the Costa Blanca and Costa Cálida, popular for their winter warmth and sunshine. The region has a wealth of historical sights including ancient monasteries near Barcelona, magnificent Roman ruins in Tarragona, Mudéjar churches and towers in Aragón and the great cathedrals of Valencia and Murcia. Away from the busy coasts, the countryside is often attractive but little visited.

Zaragoza

ARAGON
(see pp226–41)

Teruel

Ordesa National Park (see pp232–3) *in the Pyrenees has some of the most dramatic mountain scenery in Spain. It makes excellent walking country.*

Zaragoza (see pp236–7) *has many striking churches, especially the cathedral, the Basílica de Nuestra Señora del Pilar, and the Mudéjar-style Iglesia de la Magdalena.*

Valencia (see pp250–53) *is Spain's third largest city. It has an old centre of narrow streets overlooked by venerable houses and monuments, such as El Miguelete, the cathedral's conspicuous bell tower. The city hosts a spectacular festival, Las Fallas, in March.*

**VALENC
AND MURC
(see pp242–

Valenc

Alican

Murcia cathedral (see p262), *built in the 14th century, has a Baroque façade and belfry, and two ornate side chapels – one in late-Gothic style and the other Renaissance. In Murcia, you can also visit an elegant 19th-century gentlemen's club, the Casino.*

Murcia

0 kilometres   50

0 miles   50

◁ The 12th-century monastery at Gerri de la Sal in Catalonia

Lleida

uesca

CATALONIA
(see pp206–25)

Girona

Barcelona

Tarragona

istellón

The Costa Brava (see
pp216–7), *stretching
south from the French
border, is a mix of cliffs,
wooded coves and pretty
beaches. Lloret de Mar is
the busiest, most popular
tourist resort on the coast.*

Poblet (see pp222–23),
*enclosed by triple walls, is
one of the most interesting
medieval Cistercian mon-
asteries in Catalonia. It
contains a royal pantheon
with the carved tombs of
six of the kings of Aragón.*

Tarragona (see
pp224–25) *was
one of the most
important cities
in Roman Spain.
Among its
remains are an
amphitheatre and an aqueduct.
A statue of Roger de Llúria, the
great 13th-century Catalan naval
commander, overlooks the beach.*

The Costa Blanca (see pp258–61)
*is an attractive coast, as well as a
popular holiday destination. Calp
is overshadowed by a huge rock,
the Penyal d'Ifach. In La Vila
Joiosa, a line of houses has been
painted in striking colours to
make them visible to sailors at sea.*

The Flavours of Eastern Spain

The current stars of Spain's culinary firmament are Catalans like Ferran Adriá or Carme Ruscalleda, whose creativity and innovation have brought them international acclaim. Fashionable new eateries and traditional country inns alike still place the emphasis firmly on fresh local ingredients. Along with adjoining Murcia and Catalonia, Valencia produces a huge array of fruit, vegetables, seafood, meat and game, all heaped colourfully in local markets. Rice is a key ingredient, in paella and its many local variations. In land-locked Aragón, country cooking is key, with dishes which recall the Arabic occupation more than a thousand years ago.

Valencian rice

Spain's finest chefs create culinary fireworks in their celebrated restaurants, but Catalan cuisine, even at its most experimental, is essentially simple and relies on the wonderful freshness of its produce.

ARAGON

In land-locked, mountainous Aragón, the emphasis is firmly on meat – particularly lamb, but also beef, rabbit and free-range chicken, often served simply grilled or slowly simmered in earthen-ware pots. There is also much excellent charcuterie, including hams and cured sausages, some flavoured with spices, which are are often used to flavour the hearty stews popular in the mountainous north. River trout and eels are regularly found on local menus and,

Fresh octopus lie on the ice of a fish-seller's stall

CATALONIA

The incredible variety of fresh produce in Catalonia is a reflection of the varied landscape – the Mediterranean provides all manner of fish and shellfish, the inland plains offer a wealth of vegetables and fields of golden rice, and the mountains contribute meat, game and wild mushrooms (a Catalan obsession).

Artichokes   Onions   Aubergines (eggplants)

Celery

Tomatoes

Capers   Green beans

A range of fresh vegetables grown in eastern Spain

REGIONAL DISHES AND SPECIALITIES

The lush Mediterranean coastline, backed by fertile plains and cool mountains, offers an extraordinary abundance of fresh produce here. From the sturdy stews of land-locked Aragón and the traditional cured meats of inland Murcia, to the celebrated seafood paellas and other rice dishes of Valencia, this is a region which dazzles with the variety of its cuisine. Spring and summer bring tiny broad beans, asparagus, and all manner of other vegetables and fruits. In autumn and winter, the annual pig slaughter is followed by the preparation of hams and cured meats, mushrooms proliferate on shady hills, and gamey stews keep out the winter cold. Seafood remains a constant, whether in *zarzuela de mariscos* (a rich shellfish stew), or the Murcian favourite of sea bream baked in a salty crust.

Candied fruits

Suquet de peix *A Catalan stew of fresh, firm-fleshed fish, flavoured with tomatoes, garlic and toasted almonds.*

Spectacular harvest of wild autumn mushrooms in a local market

perhaps unusually so far north, the ancient Arabic heritage can still be tasted in exquisite local sweets and desserts, from candied fruits to heavenly *guirlache*, made from almonds and sugar.

VALENCIA

Valencia, the "Orchard of Spain", is magnificently lush and fertile. Most famous for its oranges, it also produces countless other fruits and vegetables, partnered in local recipes with Mediterranean seafood and mountain lamb, rabbit and pork. In spring, hillsides blaze with cherry and almond blossom and, in autumn, the golden rice fields are spectacular. Spain's signature dish, paella, is a Valencian invention – the local plump *bomba* rice is perfect for soaking up juices.

MURCIA

Tiny, arid Murcia is almost a desert in parts but, thanks to irrigation methods introduced by the Arabs more than a thousand years ago, it has become one of the largest

An *embutidos* (cured meats) producer shows off his wares

fruit- and vegetable-growing regions in Europe. The mountainous hinterland is famous for its flavoursome *embutidos* (cured meats), especially *morcilla* (black pudding/blood sausage) and *chorizo* (spicy, paprika-flavoured cured sausage), along with excellent rice which has earned its own DO *(denominación de origen)*. Along the coast, you can enjoy a wide range of fresh Mediterranean seafood, including sea bream baked in a salt crust, or lobster stew from the Mar Menor. The Arabic heritage lingers particularly in the desserts, flavoured with saffron, pine nuts and delicate spices.

ON THE MENU

Arroz Negro A Valencian rice dish; squid ink gives the distinctive dark colour.

Caldero Murciano Fishermen's stew, flavoured with saffron and plenty of garlic.

Dorada a la Sal Sea bream baked in a salty crust to keep the fish moist and succulent.

Fideuá A Catalan paella with shellfish, meat or even snails, and tiny noodles instead of rice.

Guirlache An Aragonese sweet, made of toasted whole almonds and buttery caramel.

Migas con Tropezones Crusty bread fried with garlic, pork and spicy cured sausage.

Paella *In Spain's best-known dish, constants include saffron, round* bomba *rice, and plenty of fish and shellfish.*

Lentejas al estilo del Alto Aragón *Lentils are slowly cooked with garlic, chunks of ham and black sausage.*

Crema Catalana *This hugely popular dessert is an eggy custard topped with a flambéed sugar crust.*

Wines of Eastern Spain

Spain's eastern seaboard offers a wide spread of wines of different styles. Catalonia deserves pride of place, and here the most important region is Penedès, home of *cava* (traditional-method sparkling wine) and some high-quality still wine. In Aragón, Cariñena reds can be good, and Somontano, in the Pyrenees, has fine, international-style varietals. Valencia and Murcia provide large quantities of easy-drinking reds, whites and *rosados* (rosés). Most notable among these are the rosés of Utiel-Requena, the Valencian Moscatels and the strong, full-bodied reds made in Jumilla.

Cabernet Sauvignon vines

Monastery of Poblet and Las Murallas vineyards in Catalonia

Somontano *has had remarkable success because of the COVISA company's cultivation of international grape varieties such as Chardonnay and Pinot Noir.*

```
0 kilometres          100

0 miles          50
```

KEY FACTS ABOUT WINES OF EASTERN SPAIN

Location and Climate
The climate of Eastern Spain varies mainly with altitude – low-lying parts are hot and dry; it also gets hotter the further south you go. The wine regions of Catalonia have a Mediterranean climate along the coast, which becomes drier futher inland. The middle Penedès is a favoured location with a range of climates which suits many grape varieties. Somontano has a cooler, altitude-tempered climate. Valencia and Murcia can be, in contrast, unrelentingly hot.

Grape Varieties
The most common native red grape varieties planted in much of Eastern Spain are Garnacha, Tempranillo – which is called Ull de Llebre in Catalonia – Monastrell and Cariñena. Bobal makes both reds and, to a greater extent, rosés in Utiel-Requena. For whites, Catalonia has Parellada, Macabeo and Xarel·lo (the trio most commonly used for *cava*), while in Valencia, Merseguera and Moscatel predominate. In the regions furthest to the southeast, Airén and Pedro Ximénez are sometimes found. French grape varieties, such as Chardonnay, Merlot, Cabernet Sauvignon and Sauvignon Blanc, flourish in the regions of Penedès, Costers del Segre and Somontano.

Good Producers
Somontano: COVISA (Viñas del Vero), Viñedos del Altoaragón. **Alella:** Marqués de Alella, Parxet. **Penedès:** Codorníu, Conde de Caralt, Freixenet, Juvé y Camps, Masía Bach, Mont-Marçal, René Barbier, Miguel Torres. **Costers del Segre:** Castell del Remei, Raimat. **Priorato:** Cellers Scala Dei, Masía Barril. **Valencia:** Vicente Gandía. **Utiel-Requena:** C. Augusto Egli. **Alicante:** Gutiérrez de la Vega. **Jumilla:** Asensio Carcelén (Sol y Luna), Bodegas Vitivino.

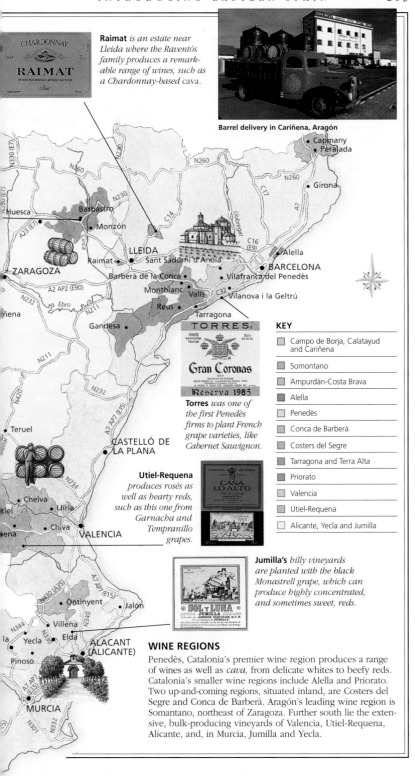

Raimat *is an estate near Lleida where the Raventós family produces a remarkable range of wines, such as a Chardonnay-based cava.*

Barrel delivery in Cariñena, Aragón

KEY

- Campo de Borja, Calatayud and Cariñena
- Somontano
- Ampurdán-Costa Brava
- Alella
- Penedès
- Conca de Barberà
- Costers del Segre
- Tarragona and Terra Alta
- Priorato
- Valencia
- Utiel-Requena
- Alicante, Yecla and Jumilla

Torres *was one of the first Penedès firms to plant French grape varieties, like Cabernet Sauvignon.*

Utiel-Requena *produces rosés as well as hearty reds, such as this one from Garnacha and Tempranillo grapes.*

Jumilla's *hilly vineyards are planted with the black Monastrell grape, which can produce highly concentrated, and sometimes sweet, reds.*

WINE REGIONS

Penedès, Catalonia's premier wine region produces a range of wines as well as *cava*, from delicate whites to beefy reds. Catalonia's smaller wine regions include Alella and Priorato. Two up-and-coming regions, situated inland, are Costers del Segre and Conca de Barberà. Aragón's leading wine region is Somontano, northeast of Zaragoza. Further south lie the extensive, bulk-producing vineyards of Valencia, Utiel-Requena, Alicante, and, in Murcia, Jumilla and Yecla.

Flowers of the Matorral

The Matorral, a scrubland rich in wild flowers, is the distinctive landscape of Spain's eastern Mediterranean coast. It is the result of centuries of woodland clearance, during which the native holm oak was felled for timber and to provide land for grazing and cultivation. Many colourful plants have adapted to the extremes of climate here. Most flower in spring, when hillsides are daubed with pink and white cistuses and yellow broom, and the air is perfumed by aromatic herbs such as rosemary, lavender and thyme. Buzzing insects feed on the abundance of nectar and pollen.

Yellow bee orchid

Spanish broom *is a small bush with yellow flowers on slender branches. The black seed pods split when dry, scattering the seeds on the ground.*

The century plant's flower stalk can reach 10 m (32 ft).

Jerusalem sage, *an attractive shrub which is often grown in gardens, has tall stems surrounded by bunches of showy yellow flowers. Its leaves are greyish-white and woolly.*

Aleppo pine

Rosemary

Rose garlic *has round clusters of violet or pink flowers at the end of a single stalk. It survives the summer as the bulb familiar to all cooks.*

Common thyme *is a low-growing aromatic herb which is widely cultivated for use in the kitchen.*

FOREIGN INVADERS

Several plants from the New World have managed to colonize the bare ground of the *matorral*. The prickly pear, thought to have been brought back by Christopher Columbus, produces a delicious fruit which can be picked only with thickly gloved hands. The rapidly growing century plant, a native of Mexico which has tough spiny leaves, sends up a tall flower shoot only when it is 10–15 years old, after which it dies.

Prickly pear in fruit

Flowering shoots of the century plant

The mirror orchid, *a small plant which grows on grassy sites, is easily distinguished from other orchids by the brilliant metallic blue patch inside the lip, fringed by brown hairs.*

CLIMATE CHART

Most plants found in the *matorral* come into bloom in the warm, moist spring. The plants protect themselves from losing water during the dry summer heat with thick leaves or waxy secretions, or by storing moisture in bulbs or tubers.

WILDLIFE OF THE MATORRAL

The animals which live in the *matorral* are most often seen early in the morning, before the temperature is high. Countless insects fly from flower to flower, providing a source of food for birds. Smaller mammals, such as mice and voles, are active only at night when it is cooler and there are few predators around.

Holm oaks *are very common in Eastern Spain. The leaves are tough and rubbery to prevent water loss.*

The strawberry tree *is an evergreen shrub with glossy serrated leaves. Its edible strawberry-like fruit turns red when ripe.*

Ladder snakes *feed on small mammals, birds and insects. The young are identified by a black pattern like the rungs of a ladder, but adults are marked with two simple stripes.*

Tree heather

Scorpions *hide under rocks or wood by day. When disturbed, the tail is curled quickly over the body in a threatening gesture. The sting, lethal to small animals, can cause some irritation to humans.*

Grey-leaved cistus, *growing on sunny sites, has crumpled petals and bright yellow anthers.*

Narrow-leaved cistus *exudes a sticky aromatic gum used in perfumes.*

The Dartford warbler, *a skulking bird which has dark plumage and a cocked tail, sings melodiously during its mating display. Males are more vividly coloured than females.*

The swallow-tail butterfly *is one of the most conspicuous of the great many insects living in the matorral. Bees, ants and grasshoppers are also extremely common.*

Star clover *is a low-growing annual whose fruit develops into a star-shaped seed head. Its flowers are often pale pink.*

CATALONIA

LLEIDA · ANDORRA · GIRONA
BARCELONA PROVINCE · TARRAGONA

atalonia is a proud nation-within-a-nation which was once, under the count-kings of Barcelona-Aragón, one of the Mediterranean's great sea powers. It has its own semi-autonomous regional government and its own language, Catalan, which has all but replaced Spanish in place names and on road signs throughout the region.

The Romans first set foot on the Iberian Peninsula at Empúries on Catalonia's Costa Brava ("wild coast"). They left behind them great monuments, especially in and around Tarragona, the capital of their vast province of Tarraconensis. Later, Barcelona emerged as the region's capital, economically and culturally important enough to rival Madrid.

In the 1960s the Costa Brava became one of Europe's first mass package-holiday destinations. Although resorts such as Lloret de Mar continue to draw the crowds, former fishing villages such as Cadaqués remain relatively unspoiled on this naturally attractive coast.

Inland, there is a rich artistic heritage to be explored. Catalonia has several spectacular monasteries, especially Montserrat, its spiritual heart, and Poblet. There are also many medieval towns, such as Montblanc, Besalú and Girona – which contain a wealth of monuments and museums.

In the countryside there is a lot to seek out, from the wetland wildlife of the Río Ebro delta to the vineyards of Penedès (where most of Spain's sparkling wine is made). In the high Pyrenees rare butterflies brighten remote mountain valleys, and little hidden villages encircle exquisite Romanesque churches.

Aigüestortes y E. Sant Maurici National Park in the central Pyrenees, in the province of Lleida

◁ **A fisherman inspects his nets in Cadaqués on the Costa Brava**

Exploring Catalonia

Catalonia includes a long stretch of the
Spanish Pyrenees, whose green, flower-
filled valleys hide picturesque villages
with Romanesque churches. The Parc
Nacional d'Aigüestortes and Vall d'Aran are
paradises for naturalists, while Baqueira-
Beret offers skiers reliable snow. Sun-
lovers can choose between the rugged
Costa Brava or the long sandy stretches of
the Costa Daurada. Tarragona is rich in
Roman monuments. Inland are the
monasteries of Poblet and Santes Creus and
the well-known vineyards of Penedès.

**Isolated houses in the countryside
around La Seu d'Urgell**

KEY

▬▬	Motorway (highway)
▬▬	Other highway
▬	Main road
▭	Minor road
▬	Scenic route
▬	Main railway
▬	Minor railway
▬▬	International border
▬▬	Regional border
△	Summit

GETTING AROUND

A tunnel near Puigcerdà has
made the central Catalan
Pyrenees easily accessible.
Buses, more frequent in
summer, connect most towns.
The main north-south railway
hugs the coast from Blanes
southwards. Other lines run
from Barcelona through Vic,
Lleida and Tortosa. Be aware
that Spain has recently
changed its road numbering
system and that some of the
old signs and numbers may
still exist in rural areas, on old
maps and in old road atlases.

SEE ALSO

• *Where to Stay* pp571–4

• *Where to Eat* pp620–24

Church on the seafront of Sitges

Vineyards outside Gandesa, west of Tarragona

SIGHTS AT A GLANCE

The Vall d'Aran, surrounded by the snow-capped mountains of the Pyrenees

BUTTERFLIES OF THE VALL D'ARAN

A huge variety of butterflies and moths is found high in the mountains and valleys of the Pyrenees. In particular, the isolated Vall d'Aran is the home of several unique and rare sub-species. The best time of year to see the butterflies is between May and July.

Grizzled Skipper
(Pyrgus malvae)

Checkered Skipper
(Carterocephalus palaemon)

Clouded Apollo
(Parnassius mnemosyne)

Vall d'Aran **❶**

Lleida N230. 🚌 Vielha. 🛈 Vielha 973 64 01 10. **www**.aran.org

This Valley of Valleys – *aran* means valley – is a beautiful 600-sq km (230-sq mile) haven of forests and flower-filled meadows, surrounded by towering mountain peaks.

The Vall d'Aran was formed by the Riu Garona, which rises in the area and flows out to France as the Garonne. With no proper link to the outside world until 1924, when a road was built over the Bonaigua Pass, the valley was cut off from the rest of Spain for most of the winter. Snow still blocks the narrow pass from November to April, but today access is easy through the Túnel de Vielha from El Pont de Suert.

The fact that the Vall d'Aran faces north means that it has a climate similar to that found on the Atlantic coast. Many rare wild flowers and butter-flies flourish in the perfect conditions created by the damp breezes and shady slopes. It is also a noted habitat for many species of narcissus.

Tiny villages have grown up beside the Riu Garona, often around Romanesque churches, notably at **Bossòst, Salardú, Escunhau** and **Arties**. The valley is also ideal for outdoor sports such as skiing and is popular with walkers.

Vielha **❷**

Lleida. 🏠 2,700. 🚌 🛈 Carrer Sarriulera 10, 973 64 01 10. 🚌 Thu. 🎉 Fiesta de Vielha (8 Sep), Feria de Vielha (8 Oct).

Now a modern ski resort, the capital of the Vall d'Aran preserves relics of its medieval past. The Roman-esque church of **Sant Miquel** has an octagonal bell tower, a tall, pointed roof and a superb wooden 12th-century crucifix, the *Mig Aran Christ*. It once formed part of a larger carving, since lost, which represented the Descent from the Cross. The **Museu de la Vall d'Aran** is a museum devoted to Aranese history and folklore.

🏛 **Museu de la Vall d'Aran**
Carrer Major 26. **Tel** 973 64 18 15.
⬜ daily. ⬛ public hols.

Mig Aran Christ (12th-century), Sant Miquel church, Vielha

Baqueira-Beret ❸

Lleida. 🏔 *100*. 🚌 🏨 *Baqueira-Beret, 973 63 90 00.* 🎭 *Romería de Nuestra Señora de Montgarri (2 Jul).* **www**.baqueira.es

This extensive ski resort, one of the best in Spain, is popular with both the public and the Spanish royal family. There is reliable winter snow cover and a choice of over 40 pistes at altitudes from 1,520 m to 2,470 m (4,987 ft to 8,104 ft).

Baqueira and Beret were separate mountain villages before skiing became popular, but now form a single resort. The Romans took full advantage of the thermal springs located here; nowadays they are appreciated by tired skiers.

Vall de Boí ❹

Lleida N230. 🚌 *La Pobla de Segur.* 🚌 *El Pont de Suert.* 🏨 *Barruera, 973 69 40 00.*

This small valley on the edge of the Parc Nacional d'Aigüestortes is dotted with tiny villages, many of which are built around magnificent Catalan Romanesque churches.

Dating from the 11th and 12th centuries, these churches are distinguished by their tall belfries, such as the **Església de Santa Eulàlia** at Erill-la-Vall, which has six floors.

The two churches at Taüll, **Sant Climent** *(see p24)* and **Santa Maria**, have superb frescoes. Between 1919 and 1923 the originals were taken for safekeeping to the Museu Nacional d'Art de Catalunya in Barcelona *(see p172)* and replicas now stand in their place. You can climb the towers of Sant Climent for superb views of the surrounding countryside.

Other churches in the area worth visiting include those at **Coll**, for its fine ironwork, **Barruera**, and **Durro**, which has another massive bell tower.

At the head of the valley is the hamlet of **Caldes de Boí**, popular for its thermal springs and ski facilities. It is also a good base for exploring the Parc Nacional d'Aigüestortes, the entrance to which is only 5 km (3 miles) from here.

The tall belfry of Sant Climent church at Taüll in the Vall de Boí

Parc Nacional d'Aigüestortes ❺

Lleida. 🚌 *La Pobla de Segur.* 🚌 *El Pont de Suert, La Pobla de Segur.* 🏨 *Barruera, 973 69 61 89.*

The pristine mountain scenery of Catalonia's only national park *(see pp30–1)* is among the most spectacular to be seen in the Pyrenees.

Established in 1955, the park covers an area of 102 sq km (40 sq miles). Its full title is Parc Nacional d'Aigüestortes i Estany de Sant Maurici, named after the lake *(estany)* of Sant Maurici in the east and the Aigüestortes (literally, twisted waters) area in the west. The main village is the mountain settlement of Espot, on the park's eastern edge. Dotted around the park are waterfalls and the sparkling, clear waters of around 150 lakes and tarns which, in an earlier era, were scoured by glaciers to depths of up to 50 m (164 ft).

The finest scenery is around Sant Maurici lake, which lies beneath the twin shards of the Serra dels Encantats, (Mountains of the Enchanted). From here, there is a variety of walks, particularly along the string of lakes that lead north to the towering peaks of Agulles d'Amitges. To the south is the dramatic vista of Estany Negre, the highest and deepest tarn in the park.

Early summer in the lower valleys is marked by a mass of pink and red rhododendrons, while later in the year wild lilies bloom in the forests of fir, beech and silver birch.

The park is also home to a variety of wildlife. Chamois (also known as izards) live on the mountain screes and in the meadows, while beavers and otters can be spotted by the lakes. Golden eagles nest on mountain ledges, and grouse and capercaillie are found in the woods.

During the summer the park is popular with walkers, while in winter, the snow-covered mountains are ideal for cross-country skiing.

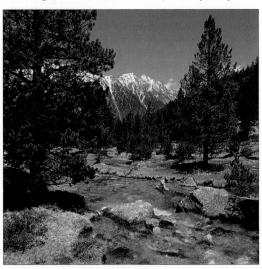

A crystal-clear stream, Parc Nacional d'Aigüestortes

THE CATALAN LANGUAGE

Catalan has now fully recovered from the ban it suffered under Franco's dictatorship and has supplanted Castilian (Spanish) as the language in everyday use all over Catalonia. Spoken by more than eight million people, it is a Romance language akin to the Provençal of France. Previously it was suppressed by Felipe V in 1717 and only officially resurfaced in the 19th century, when the Jocs Florals (medieval poetry contests) were revived during the rebirth of Catalan literature. A leading figure of the movement was the poet Jacint Verdaguer (1845–1902).

Catalonia's national emblem

Andorra ❻

Principality of Andorra. 👥 72,000.
🚌 Andorra la Vella. 🛈 Plaça de la Rotonda, Andorra la Vella, 00 376 82 71 17. www.andorra.ad

Andorra occupies 464 sq km (179 sq miles) of the Pyrenees between France and Spain. In 1993, it became fully independent and held its first ever democratic elections. Since 1278, it had been an autonomous feudal state under the jurisdiction of the Spanish bishop of La Seu d'Urgell and the French Count of Foix (a title adopted by the President of France). These are still the ceremonial joint heads of state.

Andorra's official language is Catalan, though French and Castilian are also spoken. The currency changed from the peseta to the Euro in 2002.

For many years Andorra has been a tax-free paradise for shoppers, reflected in the crowded shops of the capital **Andorra la Vella**. Les Escaldes (near the capital), as well as Sant Julià de Lòria and El Pas de la Casa (near the Spanish and French borders), have also become shopping centres.

Most visitors never see Andorra's rural charms, which match those of other parts of the Pyrenees. The region is excellent for walkers. One of the main routes leads to the **Cercle de Pessons**, a bowl of lakes in the east, and past Romanesque chapels such as **Sant Martí** at La Cortinada. In the north is the picturesque Sorteny valley where traditional farmhouses have been converted into snug restaurants.

La Seu d'Urgell ❼

Lleida. 👥 13,000. 🚌 🛈 Avda Valles de Andorra 33, 973 35 15 11. 🚍 Tue & Sat. 🎊 Fiesta Mayor (Aug).

This ancient Pyrenean town was made a bishopric by the Visigoths in the 6th century. Feuds between the bishops of Urgell and the Counts of Foix over land ownership led to the emergence of Andorra in the 13th century.

The 12th-century **cathedral** has a much venerated Romanesque statue of Santa Maria d'Urgell. The **Museu Diocesà** contains medieval works of art and manuscripts, including a 10th-century copy of St Beatus of Liébana's *Commentary on the Apocalypse* (see p110).

🏛 **Museu Diocesà**
Plaça del Deganat. **Tel** 973 35 32 42.
⬜ daily. ⬛ public hols. 📷 ♿

Carving, La Seu d'Urgell cathedral

Puigcerdà ❽

Girona. 👥 7,000. 🚌 🚍 🛈 Carrer Querol 1, 972 88 05 42. 🚍 Sun. 🎊 Fiesta de l'Estany (third Sun of Aug). www.puigcerda.com

Puig is Catalan for hill. Although Puigcerdà sits on a relatively small hill compared with the encircling mountains, which rise to 2,900 m (9,500

ft), it nevertheless has a fine view right down the beautiful Cerdanya valley, watered by the trout-filled Riu Segre.

Puigcerdà, very close to the French border, was founded in 1177 by Alfonso II as the capital of Cerdanya, which shares a past and its culture with the French Cerdagne. The Spanish enclave of **Llívia**, an attractive little town with a medieval pharmacy, lies 6 km (4 miles) inside France.

Cerdanya is the largest valley in the Pyrenees. At its edge is the nature reserve of **Cadí-Moixeró**, which has a population of alpine choughs.

Portal of Monestir de Santa Maria

Ripoll ❾

Girona. 👥 11,000. 🚌 🚍 🛈 Plaça Abat Oliva, 972 70 23 51. 🚍 Sat. 🎊 Fiesta Mayor (11–12 May). www.elripolles.com

Once a tiny mountain base from which raids against the Moors were made, Ripoll is now best known for the **Monestir de Santa Maria**, built in AD 888. The town has been called "the cradle of Catalonia" as the monastery was both the power base and cultural centre of Guifré el Pélos (Wilfred the Hairy), founder of the 500-year dynasty of the House of Barcelona. He is buried in the monastery.

In the later 12th century, the huge west portal gained a series of intricate carvings, which are perhaps the finest Romanesque carvings in Spain. They depict historical and biblical scenes. The two-storey cloister is the only other part of the original monastery to have survived wars and anticlerical purges. The rest is a 19th-century reconstruction.

The medieval town of Besalú on the banks of the Riu Fluvià

Sant Joan de les Abadesses ❿

Girona. 🏘 3,800. 🚌 🛈 Plaza de Abadia 9, 972 72 05 99. 🚌 Sun. 🎑 Fiesta Mayor (second week of Sep). www.santjoandelesabadesses.com

A fine, 12th-century Gothic bridge arches over the Riu Ter to this unassuming market town, whose main attraction is its **monastery**.

Founded in AD 885, it was a gift from Guifré, first count of Barcelona, to his daughter, the first abbess. The church is unadorned except for a superb wooden calvary, *The Descent from the Cross*. Made in 1150, it looks modern; part of it, a thief, was burnt in the Civil War and replaced with such skill that it is hard to tell which is new. The monastery's museum has Baroque and Renaissance altarpieces.

12th-century calvary, Sant Joan de les Abadesses monastery

Environs
To the north is **Camprodon**, a small town full of grand houses, and shops selling local produce. The region is especially noted for its *llonganisses* (sausages).

Olot ⓫

Girona. 🏘 28,000. 🚌 🛈 Hospici 8, 972 26 01 41. 🚌 Mon. 🎑 Corpus Christi (Jun), Fiesta del Tura (8 Sep). www.olot.org/turisme

This small market town is at the centre of a landscape pockmarked with the conical hills of extinct volcanoes. But it was an earthquake in 1474 which last disturbed the town, destroying its medieval past.

During the 18th century the town's textile industry spawned the "Olot School" of art: finished cotton fabrics were printed with drawings, and in 1783 the Public School of Drawing was founded.

Much of the school's work, which includes sculpted saints and paintings such as Joaquim Vayreda's *Les Falgueres,* is in the **Museu Comarcal de la Garrotxa**, housed in an 18th-century hospice. There are also pieces by Modernista sculptor Miquel Blay, whose damsels support the balcony at No. 38 Passeig Miquel Blay.

🏛 **Museu Comarcal de la Garrotxa**
Calle Hospici 8. **Tel** 972 27 91 30. ⬤ Wed–Mon. ⬤ 1 Jan, 25 Dec. 🎟 🚹

Besalú ⓬

Girona. 🏘 2,000. 🚌 🛈 Plaça de la Llibertat 1, 972 59 12 40. 🚌 Tue. 🎑 Sant Vicenç (22 Jan), Fiesta Mayor (last weekend of Sep). 🎑

A magnificent medieval town, with a striking approach across a fortified bridge over the Riu Fluvià, Besalú has two fine churches. These are the Romanesque **Sant Vicenç** and **Sant Pere**, the sole remnant of Besalú's Benedictine monastery. It was founded in AD 948, but pulled down in 1835 leaving a big, empty square.

In 1964 a **mikvah**, a ritual Jewish bath, was discovered by chance. It was built in 1264 and is one of only three of that period to survive in Europe. The tourist office has the keys to all the town's attractions.

To the south, the sky-blue lake of **Banyoles**, where the 1992 Olympic rowing contests were held, is ideal for picnics.

Sausage shop in the mountain town of Camprodon

GIRONA TOWN CENTRE

Banys Arabs ②
Catedral ④
Centre Bonastruc Ça Porta ⑦
Església de Sant Feliu ③
Església de Sant Pere de
   Galligants ①
Museu d'Art ⑤
Museu d'Història
   de la Ciutat ⑥

0 meters   250
0 yards   250

Key to Symbols *see back flap*

Girona ⓭

Girona. 🏠 *75,000.* ✈ 🚊 🚌 🛈
*Rambla de la Llibertat 1, 972 22 65
75.* 🚌 *Tue, Sat.* 🎭 *El Pedal (last fortnight of Sep), San Narciso (late Oct).*
www.ajuntament.gi/turisme

This handsome town puts on
its best face beside the Riu
Onyar, where tall, pastel-
coloured buildings rise above
the water. Behind them, in
the old town, the Rambla de
la Llibertat is lined with busy
shops and street cafés.

The houses were built in the
19th century to replace sections of the city wall damaged
during a seven-month siege
by French troops in 1809. Most
of the rest of the ramparts, first
raised by the Romans, are still
intact and have been turned
into the **Passeig Arqueològic**
(Archaeological Walk), which
runs right around the city.

The starting point of the
walk is on the north side of
the town, near the **Església de
Sant Pere de Galligants**
(St Peter of the Cock Crows).
The church now houses the
city's archaeological collection.

From here a narrow street
into the old part of town
passes through the north gate,
where huge Roman
foundation stones are still
visible. They mark the route
of the Via Augusta, the road
which originally ran from
Tarragona to Rome. The most
popular place of devotion for
the people of Girona is the
Església de Sant Feliu. The
church, begun in the 14th
century, was built over the
tombs of St Felix and St
Narcissus, both patrons of the
city. Next to the high altar are
eight Roman sarcophagi
embedded in the apse wall.

Despite their name, the
nearby **Banys Arabs** (Arab
Baths), lit by a fine octagonal
lantern, were built in the late
12th century, about 300 years
after the Moors had left.

🏛 Centre Bonastruc Ça Porta
Carrer de la Força 8. *Tel 972 21 67
61.* ◻ *daily.* ◗ *public hols* ⬥ 🖼
⬥ **www**.ajuntament.gi/turisme
Amid the maze of alleyways
and steps in the old town is
the former, partially restored,
Jewish quarter of El Call. The
Centre Bonastruc Ça Porta
gives a history of Girona's
Jews, who were expelled in
the late 15th century.

🛈 Cathedral
◻ *10am–2pm, 4–7pm daily.*
www.lacatedraldegirona.com
The style of Girona Cathedral's
solid west face is pure Catalan
Baroque, but the rest of the
building is Gothic. The single
nave, built in 1416 by Guillem
Bofill, is the widest Gothic
span in Christendom. Behind
the altar is a marble throne

Painted houses crowded along the bank of the Riu Onyar in Girona

For hotels and restaurants in this region see pp571–74 and pp620–24

known as "Charlemagne's Chair" after the Frankish king whose troops took Girona in 785. In the chancel is a 14th-century jewel-encrusted silver and enamel altarpiece. Among the Romanesque paintings and statues in the cathedral's museum are a 10th-century illuminated copy of St Beatus of Liébana's *Commentary on the Apocalypse*, and a 14th-century statue of the Catalan king, Pere the Ceremonious.

The collection's most famous item is a large, well preserved 11th- to 12th-century tapestry, called *The Creation*, decorated with lively figures.

Tapestry of *The Creation*

🏛 Museu d'Art

Pujada de la Catedral 12. *Tel 972 20 95 36.* ☐ *Tue–Sun.* ⏺ *1, 6 Jan, 25–26 Dec.* 🖼 ♿
www.museuart.com
This former episcopal palace is one of Catalonia's best art galleries, with works ranging from the Romanesque period to the 20th century. Items from churches destroyed through war or neglect give an idea of church interiors long ago. Highlights are 10th-century carvings, a silver-clad altar from the church at Sant Pere de Rodes and a 12th-century beam from Cruïlles.

🏛 Museu d'Història de la Ciutat

Carrer de la Força 27. *Tel 972 22 22 29.* ☐ *10am–2pm Sun, 5–7pm Tue–Sat.* ⏺ *1, 6 Jan, 25–26 Dec.* 🖼
The city's history museum is housed in an 18th-century former convent. Parts of the cemetery are preserved, including the recesses where the bodies of members of the Capuchin Order were placed while decomposing. The collection includes old *sardana* (*see p225*) instruments.

Figueres ⓮

Girona. 🏯 *35,000.* 🚉 🚌 ❔ *Plaça del Sol, 972 50 31 55.* 🗓 *Thu.* 🎉 *Santa Cruz (3 May), San Pedro (29 Jun).* **www**.figueresciutat.com

Figueres is in the north of the Empordà (Ampurdán) region, the fertile plain that sweeps inland from the Gulf of Roses. Every Thursday, the market here fills with fruit and vegetables from the area.

The **Museu de Joguets** (Toy Museum) is housed on the top floor of the old Hotel de Paris, on the Rambla, Figueres' main street. Inside are exhibits from all over Catalonia. At the lower end of the Rambla is a statue of Narcís Monturiol i Estarriol (1819–85), claimed to be the inventor of the submarine.

A much better-known son of the town is Salvador Dalí, who founded the **Teatro-Museo Dalí** in 1974. The most visited museum in Spain after the Prado, the galleries occupy Figueras's old main theatre. Its roof has an eye-catching glass dome. Not all the work shown is by Dalí, and none of his best-known works are here.

***Rainy Taxi*, a monument in the garden of the Teatro-Museu Dalí**

But the displays, including *Rainy Taxi* – a black Cadillac being sprayed by a fountain – are a monument to the man who, fittingly, is buried here.

🏛 Museu del Joguet

Calle Sant Pere 1. *Tel 972 50 45 85.* ☐ *daily.* 🖼 ♿

🏛 Teatre-Museu Dalí

Plaça Gala-Salvador Dalí. *Tel 972 67 75 00.* ☐ *Oct–Jun: Tue–Sun; Jul–Sep: daily.* ⏺ *1 Jan, 25 Dec.* 🖼 📷 *by appt.* **www**.salvador-dali.org

---

THE ART OF DALI

Salvador Dalí e Domènech was born in Figueres in 1904 and mounted his first exhibition at the age of 15. After studying at the Escuela de Bellas Artes in Madrid, and dabbling with Cubism, Futurism and Metaphysical painting, the young artist embraced Surrealism in 1929, becoming the movement's best-known painter. Never far from controversy, the self-publicist Dalí became famous for his hallucinatory images – such as *Woman-Animal Symbiosis* – which he described as "hand-painted dream photographs". Dalí's career also included writing and film-making, and established him as one of the 20th century's greatest artists. He died in his home town in 1989.

Ceiling fresco in the Wind Palace Room, Teatro-Museu Dalí

Cadaqués 🟤

Girona. 🏘 *2,000.* 🚉 🛈 *Carrer Cotxe 2 (972 25 83 15).* 🚌 *Mon.* 🎪 *Fiesta major de Verano (first week of Sep), Santa Esperança (18 Dec).*

This pretty resort is overlooked by the Baroque **Església de Santa Maria**. In the 1960s it was dubbed the "St Tropez of Spain", due to the young crowd that sought out Salvador Dalí in nearby Port Lligat. The house where he lived from 1930 until his death in 1989 (made up of fishermen's huts structured in to a labyrinth) is known as the **Casa-Museu Salvador Dalí**. Visitors can see the painter's workshop, the library, private bedrooms and the garden area and swimming pool. Book in advance as group visits are permitted only in small numbers. In summer, a "bustrain" takes visitors there from (but not back to) Cadaqués.

🏛 **Casa-Museu Salvador Dalí**
Port Lligat. *Tel 972 25 10 15. Fax 972 25 10 83.* ☐ *by appointment.* 🖼

Empúries 🟤

Girona. 🚉 *L'Escala. Tel 972 77 02 08.* ☐ *Easter, Jun–Sep: 10am –8pm daily; Oct–May: 10am–6pm daily.* 🖼 *ruins.*

The extensive ruins of this Greco-Roman town *(see p51)* occupy an imposing site beside the sea. Three separate settlements were built between the 7th and 3rd centuries BC: the old town (Palaiapolis); the new town (Neapolis); and the Roman town.

An excavated Roman pillar in the ruins of Empúries

Looking south along the Costa Brava from Tossa de Mar

The **old town** was founded by the Greeks in 600 BC as a trading port. It was built on what was a small island, and is now the site of the tiny hamlet of Sant Martí de Empúries. In 550 BC this was replaced by a larger new town on the shore which the Greeks named Emporion, meaning "trading place". In 218 BC, the Romans landed at Empúries and built a city next to the new town.

A nearby museum exhibits some of the site's finds, but the best are in Barcelona's Museu Arqueològic *(see p172).*

Peratallada 🟤

Girona. 🏘 *150.* 🛈 *C/Unió 3, Ajuntament de Forallac, Vullpellac (972 64 55 22).* 🎪 *Feria Peratallada (last weekend in Apr or first in May), Festa Major (6 & 7 Aug), Medieval Market (first weekend in Oct).*

This tiny village is stunning and only a short inland trip from the Costa Brava. Together with Pals and Palau Sator it forms part of the "Golden Triangle" of medieval villages. Its mountain-top position gives some dramatic views of the area. A labyrinth of cobbled streets wind up to the well-conserved castle and lookout tower, whose written records date from the 11th century. Peratallada's counts and kings made doubly sure of fending off any attackers by constructing a sturdy wall enclosing the entire village that today limits the nucleus from further expansion, ensuring it retains its medieval character.

Tossa de Mar 🟤

Girona. 🏘 *4,000.* 🚉 🛈 *Avinguda Pelegrí 25, 972 34 01 08.* 🚌 *Thu.* 🎪 *Fiesta de Verano (29 Jun–2 Jul), Fiesta de Invierno (22 Jan).* **www**.infotossa.com

At the end of a corniche, the Roman town of Turissa is one of the prettiest along the Costa Brava. Above the new town is the **Vila Vella** (old town), a protected national monument. In the old town, the **Museu Municipal** has a collection of local archaeological finds and modern art including *The Flying Violinist*, by the artist Marc Chagall.

🏛 **Museu Municipal**
Plaça Roig y Soler 1. *Tel 972 34 07 09.* ☐ *Tue–Sun (call to check).* 🖼

Blanes 🟤

Girona. 🏘 *30,000.* 🚉 🚉 🛈 *Passeig de Catalunya 21, 972 33 03 48.* 🚌 *Mon.* 🎪 *El Bilar (6 Apr), Sta Ana (late Jul).* **www**.blanes.net

The working port of Blanes has one of the longest beaches on the Costa Brava, but the highlight of the town is the **Jardí Botànic Mar i Murtra**. These fine gardens, designed by the German Karl Faust in 1928, are spectacularly sited above cliffs. There are 7,000 species of Mediterranean and tropical plants.

🌿 **Jardí Botànic Mar i Murtra**
Passeig Karl Faust 10. *Tel 972 33 08 26.* ☐ *daily.* ● *1 & 6 Jan, 24 & 25 Dec.* 🖼 ♿

The Costa Brava

The Costa Brava ("wild coast") runs for some 200 km (125 miles) from Blanes northwards to the region of Empordà (Ampurdán), which borders France. It is a mix of pine-backed sandy coves, golden beaches and crowded, modern resorts. The busiest resorts – Lloret de Mar, Tossa de Mar and La Platja d'Aro – are to the south. Sant Feliu de Guíxols and Palamós are still working towns behind the summer rush. Just inland there are medieval villages to explore, such as Peralada, Peratallada and Pals. Wine, olives and fishing were the mainstays of the area before the tourists came in the 1960s.

Cadaqués *retains an air of seclusion as it is accessible only by a steep road. It has an arty atmosphere and its small, stony beaches remain unspoiled and less crowded than others.*

L'Estartit *is a good base for the Illes Medes, a former pirates' lair, which now form a marine reserve with clear waters perfect for skin diving.*

Palamós is a working port with modern hotels to the south, and secluded beaches and coves lapped by clear water to the north.

La Platja d'Aro's long and sandy beach is lined with modern hotel blocks. It is one of the most popular resorts on the coast.

Tossa de Mar has a golden beach and a small cove beneath the fortified old town.

Roses lies at the head of a sweeping bay. Its sandy beach, the longest on the Costa Brava, has become a mecca for lovers of water sports.

L'Escala is a small resort, popular mainly with local tourists. It has fine beaches and a small port where fishing nets dry in the sun.

Begur is a hilltop town just inland. It has good views of the coast, and small coves are tucked at its feet.

Llafranc, a whitewashed resort, with a promenade leading to neighbouring Calella, is one of the coast's most pleasant resorts.

Cadaqués
Roses
L'Escala
L'Estartit
Illes Medes
Begur
Llafranc
Calella de Palafrugell
Palamós
Platja d'Aro
S'Agaró
Sant Feliu de Guixols
Tossa de Mar
Lloret de Mar
Blanes

0 kilometres 10

0 miles 5

Lloret de Mar *has more hotels than anywhere else on the coast. But there are unspoiled beaches nearby, such as Santa Cristina.*

Monestir de Montserrat ⑳

The "Serrated Mountain" *(mont serrat)*, its highest peak rising to 1,236 m (4,055 ft), is a magnificent setting for Catalonia's holiest place, the Monastery of Montserrat, which is surrounded by chapels and hermits' caves. The monastery was first mentioned in the 9th century, enlarged in the 11th century, and in 1409 became independent of Rome. In 1811, when the French attacked Catalonia in the War of Independence *(see p63)*, the monastery was destroyed and the monks killed. Rebuilt and repopulated in 1844, it was a beacon of Catalan culture during the Franco years. Today Benedictine monks live here.

A Benedictine monk

Visitors can hear the Escolania singing the *Salve Regina y Virolai* (the Montserrat hymn) at 1pm and 6:45pm every day (Sundays noon only), except in July and during the Christmas period, in the basilica.

Plaça de Santa Maria
The focal points of the square are two wings of the Gothic cloister built in 1477. The modern monastery façade is by Françesc Folguera.

Gothic cloister

Funicular to the holy site of Santa Cova

The Museum has a collection of 19th- and 20th-century Catalan paintings and many Italian and French works. It also displays liturgical items from the Holy Land.

The Way of the Cross
This path passes 14 statues representing the stations of the Cross. It begins near the Plaça de l'Abat Oliba.

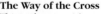

STAR FEATURES

★ Basilica Façade

★ Black Virgin

View of Montserrat
The complex includes cafés and a hotel. A second funicular transports visitors to nature trails above the monastery.

★ Basilica Façade
Agapit and Venanci Vallmitjana sculpted Christ and the apostles on the basilica's Neo-Renaissance façade. It was built in 1900 to replace the Plateresque façade of the original church, consecrated in 1592.

VISITORS' CHECKLIST

Montserrat (Barcelona province).
Tel 93 877 77 75. 🚠 Aeri de Montserrat, then cable car; Monistrol-Enllaç, then rack railway. 🚂 from Barcelona. **Basilica** ⏰ Oct–Jun: 7:30am–7:30pm daily; Jul–Sep: 7:30am–8:15pm daily. 🎵 from 9am Mon–Fri, from 7:30am Sat, from 8am Sun & religious hols. 🛗 **Museum** ⏰ 10am–6pm Mon–Fri, 9:30am–6:30pm Sat–Sun & public hols. 🎫 ♿ 🛗

★ Black Virgin
La Moreneta looks down from behind the altar. Protected behind glass, her wooden orb protrudes for pilgrims to touch.

Basilica Interior
The sanctuary in the domed basilica is adorned by a richly enamelled altar and paintings by Catalan artists.

The rack railway, opened in 2003, follows the course of a historic rail line built in 1880.

Cable car to Aeri de Montserrat station

THE VIRGIN OF MONTSERRAT

The small wooden statue of La Moreneta (the dark one) is the soul of Montserrat. It is said to have been made by St Luke and brought here by St Peter in AD 50. Centuries later, the statue is believed to have been hidden from the Moors in the nearby Santa Cova (Holy Cave). Carbon dating suggests, however, that the statue was carved around the 12th century. In 1881 Montserrat's Black Virgin became patroness of Catalonia.

The blackened Virgin of Montserrat

Inner Courtyard
On one side of the courtyard is the baptistry (1902), with sculptures by Carles Collet. Pilgrims may approach the Virgin through a door to the right.

Vic ㉑

Barcelona. 🏠 *31,000.* 🚌 🚪 ℹ️
Calle Ciutat 4, 93 886 20 91. 🚋 *Tue & Sat.* 🎭 *Mercat del Ram (Sat before Easter), Sant Miquel (5–15 Jul), Música Viva (Sep), Mercat Medieval (6–8 Dec).*
www.victurisme.com

Market days – Tuesdays and Saturdays – are the best time to go to this small country town. This is when the renowned local sausages *(embotits)* are piled high in the large Gothic Plaça Major, along with other produce from the surrounding plains.

In the 3rd century BC Vic was the capital of an ancient Iberian tribe, the Ausetans. The town was then colonized by the Romans – the remains of a Roman temple survive today. Since the 6th century the town has been a bishop's see. In the 11th century, Abbot Oliva commissioned the El Cloquer tower, around which the cathedral was built in the 18th century. The interior of the cathedral is covered with vast murals by Josep Maria Sert (1876–1945). They are painted in reds and golds, and represent scenes from the Bible.

Adjacent to the cathedral is the **Museu Episcopal de Vic**, which has one of the best collections of Romanesque artifacts in Catalonia. Its large display of mainly religious art and relics includes bright, simple murals and wooden sculptures from rural churches. Also on display are 11th- and 12th-century frescoes.

Cardona dominating the surrounding area from its hilltop site

🏛 Museu Episcopal
Plaça Bisbe Oliba. *Tel 93 886 93 60.*
⏰ *daily (except Mon Apr–Sep).* ♿ 🅿️

Cardona ㉒

Barcelona. 🏠 *6,000.* 🚌 ℹ️
Avinguda Rastrillo, 93 869 27 98. 🚋 *Sun.* 🎭 *Fiesta Mayor (2nd Sun of Sep).* **www**.salcardona.com

The 13th-century castle of the Dukes of Cardona, constables to the crown of Aragón, is set on the top of a hill. The castle was rebuilt in the 18th century and is now a parador *(see p558)*. Beside the castle is an early 11th-century church, the **Església de Sant Vicenç**, where the Dukes of Cardona are buried.

The castle gives views of the town below and of the Montanya de Sal (Salt Mountain), a huge salt deposit beside the Riu Cardener which has been mined since Roman times.

Solsona ㉓

Lleida. 🏠 *7,000.* 🚌 ℹ️ *Carrelera de Bassella 1, 973 48 23 10.* 🚋 *Tue & Fri.* 🎭 *Carnival (Feb); Corpus Christi (May/Jun), Fiesta Mayor (8–11 Sep).*
www.elsolsonesinvita.com

Nine towers and three gateways remain of Solsona's fortifications. Inside the walls is an ancient town of noble mansions. The cathedral has a black stone Virgin. The **Museu Diocesà i Comarcal** contains Romanesque paintings and archaeological finds.

🏛 Museu Diocesà i Comarcal
Plaça Palau 1. *Tel 973 48 21 01.* ⏰ *Tue–Sun.* ⏰ *1 Jan & 25, 26 Dec.* ♿

Lleida ㉔

Lleida. 🏠 *120,000.* 🚌 🚪 ℹ️ *Plaça Ramón Berenguer IV, s/n, 973 24 88 40.* 🚋 *Thu & Sat.* 🎭 *Sant Anastasi (11 May), Sant Miquel (29 Sep).*
www.lleidatur.es

Dominating Lleida (Lérida), the capital of Catalonia's only landlocked province, is **La Suda**, a large, ruined fort taken from the Moors in 1149. The old cathedral, **La Seu Vella**, founded in 1203, is situated within the walls of the fort, high above the town. It was transformed into barracks by Felipe V in 1707 but today, sadly, is desolate. It remains imposing, however, with Gothic windows in the cloister.

A lift descends from the Seu Vella to the Plaça de Sant Joan in the town below. This square is at the mid-point of a busy

Twelfth-century altar frontal, Museu Episcopal de Vic

street sweeping round the foot of the hill. The new cathedral is here, as are manorial buildings such as the rebuilt 13th-century town hall, the **Paeria**.

Poblet ㉕

See pp222–3.

Montblanc ㉖

Tarragona. 🏘 *6,000.* 🚉 🚍
ℹ *Antigua Iglesia de Sant Françesc, 977 86 17 33.* 📅 *Tue, Fri.* 🎉 *Fiesta Mayor (8–11 Sep).*

The medieval grandeur of Montblanc lives on within its walls, which are considered to be Catalonia's finest piece of military architecture. At the **Sant Jordi** gate, St George allegedly slew the dragon. The **Museu Comarcal de la Conca de Barberà** has interesting displays on local crafts.

🏛 **Museu Comarcal de la Conca de Barberà**
Carrer Josa 6. **Tel** *977 86 03 49.*
🕐 *Tue–Sun & public hols.* 🎫

Santes Creus ㉗

Tarragona. 🏘 *150.* 🚉 ℹ *Plaça de Sant Bernard 1, 977 63 81 41.* 📅 *Sat & Sun.* 🎉 *Sta Llúcia (13 Dec).*

Home to the the prettiest of the "Cistercian triangle" monasteries is the tiny village of Santes Creus. The other two,

Vallbona de les Monges and Poblet *(see pp222–3)*, are nearby. The **Monestir de Santes Creus** was founded in 1150 by Ramon Berenguer IV *(see p54)* during his reconquest of Catalonia. The Gothic cloisters are decorated with figurative sculptures, a style first permitted by Jaime II, who ruled from 1291 to 1327. His finely carved tomb, along with that of other nobles, is in the 12th-century church, which has a beautiful rose window.

🔒 **Monestir de Santes Creus**
Tel *977 63 83 29.* 🕐 *Tue–Sun.*
🎫 *by appointment* ♿

Vilafranca del Penedès ㉘

Barcelona. 🏘 *35,000.* 🚉 🚍
ℹ *Carrer Cort 14, 93 892 03 58.*
📅 *Sat.* 🎉 *Fiesta Mayor (29–31 Aug).*
www.turismevilafranca.com

This busy market town is set in the heart of Catalonia's main wine-producing region *(see pp202–3)*. The **Museu del Vi** (Wine Museum), in a 14th-century palace, documents the history of the area's wine trade. Local bodegas can be visited for wine tasting.

Eight km (5 miles) to the north is **Sant Sadurní**, the capital of Spain's sparkling wine, *cava (see pp606–7)*.

🏛 **Museu del Vi**
Plaça Jaume I. **Tel** *93 890 05 82.*
🕐 *Tue–Sun & public hols.* 🎫

Anxaneta climbing to the top of a tower of *castellers*

CATALONIA'S FIESTAS

Human Towers *(various dates and locations).* The province of Tarragona is famous for its *castellers* festivals, where teams of men stand on each others' shoulders in an effort to build the highest human tower. Each tower, which can be up to seven people high, is topped by a small boy called the *anxaneta*. *Castellers* can be seen in action in many towns, especially Vilafranca del Penedès and Valls.

Dance of Death *(Maundy Thu)*, Verges (Girona). Men dressed as skeletons perform a macabre dance.

St George's Day *(23 Apr)*. Lovers give each other a rose and a book on the day of Catalonia's patron saint. The book is in memory of Cervantes, who died on this day in 1616.

La Patum *(Corpus Christi, May/Jun)*, Berga (Barcelona province). Giants, devils and bizarre monsters parade through the town.

Midsummer's Eve *(23 Jun)*. Celebrated all over Catalonia with bonfires and fireworks.

Monestir de Santes Creus, surrounded by poplar and hazel trees

Monestir de Poblet ㉕

The Monastery of Santa Maria de Poblet is a haven of tranquillity and a resting place of kings. It was the first and most important of three sister monasteries, known as the "Cistercian triangle" *(see p221)*, that helped to consolidate power in Catalonia after it had been recaptured from the Moors by Ramon Berenguer IV. In 1835, during the Carlist upheavals, it was plundered and seriously damaged by fire. Restoration of the impressive ruins, now largely complete, began in 1930 and monks returned in 1940.

The dormitory is reached by stairs from the church. The vast 87-m (285-ft) gallery dates from the 13th century. Half of it is still in use by the monks.

The 12th-century refectory is a vaulted hall with an octagonal fountain and a pulpit.

View of Poblet
The abbey, its buildings enclosed by fortified walls that have hardly changed since the Middle Ages, is in an isolated valley near the Riu Francolí's source.

Museum

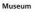
Wine cellar

Library
The Gothic scriptorium was converted into a library in the 17th century, when the Duke of Cardona donated his book collection.

Former kitchen

Royal doorway   Museum

Royal tombs

TIMELINE					
1150 Santes Creus founded – third abbey in Cistercian triangle					
	1175 Founding of sister monastery at Vallbona de les Monges	**14th century** Main cloister finished			
			1479 Juan II, last king of Aragón, buried here		**1940** Monks return
1100	**1300**		**1500**	**1700**	**1900**
	1196 Alfonso II is the first king to be buried here	**1336–87** Reign of Pere the Ceremonious, who designates Poblet a royal pantheon			**1952** Tombs reconstructed. Royal remains returned
	1150 Poblet monastery founded by Ramon Berenguer IV		**1835** Disentailment *(p45)* of monasteries. Poblet ravaged		

Chapterhouse
This perfectly square room, with slender columns, has tiers of benches for the monks. It is paved with the tombstones of 11 abbots who died between 1393 and 1693.

Parlour cloister

San Esteve cloister

New sacristy

The Abbey Church, large and unadorned, with three naves, is a typical Cistercian building.

Baroque church façade

★ Cloisters
The evocative, vaulted cloisters were built in the 12th and 13th centuries and were the centre of monastic life. The capitals are beautifully decorated with carved scrollwork.

VISITORS' CHECKLIST

Off N240, 10 km (6 miles) from Montblanc. **Tel** 977 87 00 89.
L'Espluga de Francolí, then taxi. 9:30am–1pm, 3:30–5:30pm (6pm Mar–Oct) daily. public hols. 8am Mon– Sat; 8am, 10am, 1pm & 6pm Sun & public hols.

★ High Altar Reredos
Behind the stone altar, supported by Romanesque columns, an impressive alabaster reredos fills the apse. It was carved by Damià Forment in 1527.

★ Royal Tombs
The tombs in the pantheon of kings were begun in 1359. In 1950 the sculptures were restored by Frederic Marès.

STAR FEATURES

★ High Altar Reredos

★ Royal Tombs

★ Cloisters

Palm trees lining the waterfront at Sitges

Sitges ㉙

Barcelona. 🏠 20,000. 🚉 🚌
ℹ️ C/ Sínia Morera 1 (93 894 50 04).
🚢 Thu (in summer). 🎭 Festa major
(22–27 Aug).

There are no less than nine
beaches to choose from at
this seaside town. It has a
reputation as a gay resort but
is just as popular with
Barcelonese. Lively bars and
restaurants line its main boulevard, the Passeig Marítim, and
there are many examples of
modernista architecture
amongst the '70s apartment
blocks. Modernista artist
Santiago Rusiñol (1861-1931)
spent much time here and bequeathed his quirky collection
of ceramics, sculptures, painting and ornate iron-work to the
Museu Cau Ferrat. It lies next
to Sitges's landmark, the 17th
century church of **Sant
Bartomeu i Santa Tecla**.

🏛 **Museu Cau Ferrat**
Carrer Fonollar. **Tel** 93 894 03 64.
◯ Tue–Sun. 🔴 public hols. 🎫

Costa Daurada ㉚

Tarragona. 🚉 🚌 Calafell, Sant Vicenç
de Calders, Salou. ℹ️ Tarragona
(977 23 34 15).

The long, sandy beaches of
the Costa Daurada (Golden
Coast) run along the shores of
Tarragona provine. **El Vendrell**
is one of the area's active ports.
The **Museu Pau Casals** in Sant
Salvador (El Vendrell) is dedi-
cated to the famous cellist.

Port Aventura, south of
Tarragona, is one of Europe's
largest theme parks and has
many exotically-themed
attractions, such as Polynesia
and Wild West. **Cambrils and
Salou** to the south are the liveliest resorts – the others are
low-key, family holiday spots.

🏛 **Museu Pau Casals**
Avinguda Palfuriana 59–61.
Tel 977 68 42 76. ◯ Tue–Sun.

🎢 **Port Aventura**
Autovia Salou–Vila-seca. **Tel** 977 77
90 00. ◯ mid-Mar–6 Jan. 🎫 ♿

Tarragona ㉛

Tarragona. 🏠 125,000. ✈️ 🚉 🚌
ℹ️ Carrer Fortuny 4 (977 25 07 95).
🚢 Tue & Thu. 🎭 Sant Magí (19
Aug), Santa Tecla (23 Sep).

Tarragona is now a major
industrial port, but it has
preserved many remnants of its
Roman past. As the capital of

Tarraconensis, the Romans
used it as a base for the conquest of the peninsula in the
3rd century BC *(see pp50-1)*.

The avenue of Rambla
Nova ends abruptly on the
clifftop Balcó de Europa, in
sight of the ruins of the
Amfiteatre Romà and the
ruined 12th-century church
of **Santa Maria del Miracle**.

Nearby is the Praetorium,
a Roman tower that was
converted into a palace in
medieval times. It now
houses the **Museu de la
Romanitat**. This displays
Roman and medieval finds,
and gives access to the cavernous passageways of the
excavated Roman circus, built
in the 1st century AD. Next to
the Praetorium is the **Museu
Nacional Arqueològic**,
containing the most important
collection of Roman artifacts
in Catalonia. It has an
extensive collection of bronze
tools and beautiful mosaics,

The remains of the Roman amphitheatre, Tarragona

including a *Head of Medusa*. Among the most impressive remains are the huge pre-Roman stones on which the Roman wall is built. An archaeological walk stretches 1-km (1,100-yd) along the wall.

Behind the wall lies the 12th-century **cathedral**, built on the site of a Roman temple. This evolved over many centuries, as seen from the blend of styles of the exterior. Inside is an alabaster altarpiece of St Tecla, carved by Pere Joan in 1434. The 13th-century cloister has Gothic vaulting, but the doorway is Romanesque.

In the west of town is a 3rd- to 6th-century Christian cemetery (ask about opening times in the archaeological museum). Some of the sarcophagi were originally used as pagan tombs.

Ruins of the Palaeo-Christian Necropolis

Environs
The **Aqüeducte de les Ferreres** lies just outside the city, next to the A7 motorway. This 2nd-century aqueduct was built to bring water to the city from the Riu Gaià, 30 km (19 miles) to the north. The **Arc de Berà**, a 1st-century triumphal arch on the Via Augusta, is 20 km (12 miles) northeast on the N340.

The bustling, provincial town of **Reus** lies inland from Tarragona. Although its airport serves the Costa Daurada, it is often overlooked by holiday-makers. However there is some fine *modernista* architecture to be seen here, notably some early work by Antoni Gaudí who was born in Reus. The Pere Mata Psychiatric Institute was designed by Domènech i Montaner before his master-piece, the Hospital de la Santa Creu i de Sant Pau *(see p165)*.

🏛 **Museu Nacional Arqueològic de Tarragona**
Plaça del Rei 5. **Tel** 977 23 62 09.
◯ Tue–Sun. 🖼 (senior citizens and under 18s free). ♿ www.mnat.es

🏛 **Museu de la Romanitat**
Plaça del Rei. **Tel** 977 24 19 52.
◯ Tue–Sun. 🖼

Tortosa 🜲

Tarragona. 🏠 30,000. 🚹 Plaça del Binil.lenari, 977 51 08 22. 🚌 Mon. 🎉 Nuestra Señora de la Cinta (late Aug & early Sep).
www.tortosa.altanet.org

A ruined castle and medieval walls are clues to Tortosa's historical importance. Sited at the lowest crossing point on the Riu Ebre (Río Ebro), it has been strategically significant since Iberian times. The Moors held the city from the 8th century until 1148. The old Moorish castle, known as La Zuda, is all that remains of their defences. It has been renovated as a parador *(see p573)*. The Moors also built a mosque in 914. Its foundations were used for the cathedral, on which work began in 1347. Although not completed for 200 years, the style is Gothic.

Tortosa was badly damaged in 1938–39 during one of the fiercest battles of the Civil War *(see pp64–7)*, when the Ebre formed the front line between the opposing forces.

Delta de L'Ebre 🜳

Tarragona. 🚉 Aldea. 🚌 Deltebre, Aldea. 🚹 Deltebre 977 48 96 79. **www**.ebre.com/delta

The delta of the Riu Ebre is a prosperous rice-growing region and wildlife haven. Some 70 sq km (27 sq miles) have been turned into a nature reserve, the **Parc Natural del Delta de L'Ebre**. In Deltebre there is an information centre and an interesting **Eco-Museu**, with an aquarium containing species found in the delta.

The main towns in the area are **Amposta** and **Sant Carles de la Ràpita**, both of which serve as good bases for exploring the reserve.

The best sites for seeing wildlife are along the shore, from the Punta del Fangar in the north to the Punta de la Banya in the south. Everywhere is accessible by car except Illa de Buda. Flamingoes breed on this island and other water birds, such as avocets, can be seen from tourist boats that leave from Riumar and Deltebre.

🏛 **Eco-Museu**
Carrer Martí Buera 22. **Tel** 977 48 96 79. ◯ daily. ● 1 & 6 Jan, 25 & 26 Dec. 🖼 ♿ 🎥

THE SARDANA

Catalonia's national dance is more complicated than it appears. The success of the Sardana depends on all of the dancers accurately counting the complicated short- and long-step skips and jumps, which accounts for their serious faces. Music is provided by a *cobla*, an 11-person band consisting of a leader playing a three-holed flute *(flabiol)* and a little drum *(tabal)*, five woodwind players and five brass players. When the music starts, dancers join hands and form circles. The Sardana is performed during most local fiestas *(see p221)* and at special day-long gatherings called *aplecs*.

A group of Sardana dancers captured in stone

ARAGÓN

HUESCA · ZARAGOZA · TERUEL

*S*tretching almost half the length of Spain, and bisected by the *Ebro, one of the country's longest rivers, Aragón takes in a wide variety of scenery, from the snow-capped summits of Ordesa National Park in the Pyrenees to the dry plains of the Spanish interior. This largely unsung and undervisited region contains magnificent Mudéjar architecture and many unspoiled medieval towns.*

From the 12th–15th centuries Aragón was a powerful kingdom, or, more accurately, a federation of states, including Catalonia. In its heyday, in the 13th century, its dominions stretched across the Mediterranean as far as Sicily. By his marriage to Isabel of Castile and León in 1469, Fernando II of Aragón paved the way for the unification of Spain.

After the Reconquest, Muslim architects and craftsmen were treated more tolerantly here than elsewhere, and they continued their work in the distinctive Mudéjar style, building with elaborate brickwork and patterned ceramic decoration. Their work can be seen in churches all over Aragón and there are outstanding examples in the cities of Teruel and the capital, Zaragoza, Spain's fifth largest city, which stands on the banks of the Ebro.

The highest peaks of the Pyrenees lie in Huesca province. Some of the region's finest sights are in the Pyrenean foothills, which are crossed by the Aragonese variation of the pilgrims' route to Santiago de Compostela. Probably the most spectacular of them is the monastery of San Juan de la Peña – half-concealed beneath a rock overhang – which was founded in the 9th century.

The climate of the region varies as much as the landscape: winters can be long and harsh and summers hot.

A view of the rooftops and medieval walls of Daroca

◁ Torla village church, on the edge of Ordesa National Park

Exploring Aragón

Stone carving, San Juan de la Peña

The landscapes of Aragón range from the high Pyrenees, north of Huesca, through the desiccated terrain around Zaragoza to the forested hills of Teruel province. The cities of Teruel and Zaragoza have some of the most striking Mudéjar monuments in Spain. There are many small, picturesque preserved towns in the region. Ordesa National Park contains stunning mountain scenery, but it can only be visited fully after the snow melts in spring, and even then much of it has to be explored on foot. Pretty Los Valles offers less dramatic but equally enjoyable landscapes and is a popular tourist destination. Other attractive places include the impressively sited Castillo de Loarre and Monasterio de San Juan de la Peña, and the waterfalls of Monasterio de Piedra.

The Puerto de Somport, near Panticosa

SIGHTS AT A GLANCE

Sigüés
N240
Embalse de Yesa
SOS DEL REY CATÓLICO ①
Uncastillo
AG...
Sádaba
Valareña
Ejea de los Caballeros
Burgos
TARAZONA ⑮
Gallur
Tauste
Parque Natural de Moncayo
⑯ MONASTERIO DE VERUELA
N122
N232
Alagón
Tierga
Épila
ZARAGOZ...
Torrelapaja
A2 NII
La Almunia de Doña Godina
CALATAYUD ⑱
FUENDETOL...
Ariza
Ateca
Cariñena
Jalón
Madrid
⑲ MONASTERIO DE PIEDRA
N234
DAROCA ⑳
N330
Jiloca
Calamocha
Segura de los Baño...
Caminreal
N211
Monreal del Campo
Perales del Alfambra
N330
Orihuela del Tremedal
Alfambra
Cella
A420
ALBARRACÍN ㉗
Montes Universales
TERUEL ㉖
La Puebla de Valverd...
N330
RINCÓN D...
㉘ ADEMUZ

Lourdes
**❸ PUERTO DE
SOMPORT**

*Monte Perdido
3355m*

echo
LES
N330
ACA ❼
**❽ ⛪︎ ✝︎
MONASTERIO DE SAN
JUAN DE LA PEÑA**

Sabiñánigo

Torla ○ 🎿🏛️**❹**

*PARQUE NAC.
DE ORDESA*

Boltaña ○

Bielsa ●

Pico de Aneto
3404m △

**❺
BENASQUE**

Castejón
de Sós

N260

N230

❻ AÍNSA

Campo

Roda de
Isábena

**❿ ⛪︎
ASTILLO
LOARRE**

Arguis ○

N330

Sierra de Guara

**SANTUARIO DE
TORRECIUDAD
❸**

❹ GRAUS

N260

disa 🏛️✝︎🕌
HUESCA ⓫

ALQUÉZAR ⓬

N123

dévar

Angüés ○

Benabarre

A23

Grañén ○

Huerto ○

N240

Flumen

Barbastro

❶ Tardienta

Monzón ○

N230

Cinca

era

Alcubierre ○

Sariñena

Binéfar

N240

Tamarite
de Litera

ena

A G Ó N

Ontiñena ○

*Lleida
Barcelona* ⟶

N232 AP2 A2

Fraga

NII

⟵ Pina de Ebro

Bujaraloz ○

Ebro

Quinto ○

*Embalse de
Mequinenza*

Mequinenza ●

Belchite ○

Azaila ○

Escatrón ○

Caspe ○

N211

Fayón ○

Martín

Híjar ○

Maella ○

N232

🏛️✝︎⛪︎
㉒ ALCAÑIZ

hiesa ○

Oliete ○

Andorra ○

Calanda ○

Valjunquera ○

ntalbán ○

N211

VALDERROBRES ㉓ ✝︎⛪︎

Ejulve ○

Castellote ○

Monroyo ○

Guadalope

N232

Aliaga ○

amarillas ○

Mirambel ○

Cantavieja ○

RA DE GUDAR

*Peñarroya
2019m* △

á de
lva

MORA DE RUBIELOS

Rubielos de Mora ○

on

cía

0 kilometres 20

0 miles   20

SEE ALSO

• *Where to Stay* pp574–6

• *Where to Eat* pp624–6

GETTING AROUND

Zaragoza is linked by motorway
to the Basque Country, Navarra,
Madrid and Barcelona. Major roads
link the region's main cities with
each other, and Teruel with
Valencia. Many minor roads have
been improved and may be fast and
uncongested in the flatter, central
areas. The principal railway lines run
from Zaragoza to Madrid (there is a
new high-speed train), Barcelona
and Valencia. Coaches are
infrequent, except between the main
population centres. Zaragoza has a
small international airport. Be aware
that as Spain is in the process of
changing its road numbering system
some of the roads featured here may
differ from new road signs.

KEY

═══	Motorway
═ ═	Motorway under construction
───	Major road
═══	Minor road
───	Scenic route
───	Main railway
───	Minor railway
▬▬▬	International border
───	Regional border
△	Summit

Mudéjar tower of Iglesia de Santa Magdalena, Tarazona

The town hall, Sos del Rey Católico

Sos del Rey Católico ❶

Zaragoza. 🏛 900. 🚗 🛈 *Emilio Alfaro 5, 948 88 82 70 (Mon, Tue); Plaza de la Hispanidad 2, 948 88 85 24 (Wed–Sun).* 🚆 *Fri.* 🎉 *Fiestas mayores (third Wed of Aug).*

Fernando of Aragón – the so-called "Catholic King" who married Isabel of Castile, thereby uniting Spain *(see pp56–7)* – was born in this small town in 1452, hence its distinguished royal name.

The **Palacio de Sada**, the king's reputed birthplace, with a beautiful inner courtyard, is among the town's grandest stone mansions. It stands in a small square amid a maze of narrow cobbled streets. At the top of the town are the remnants of a castle and the **Iglesia de San Esteban**. The church's font and carved capitals are noteworthy, as are the 13th-century frescoes in two of the crypt's apses. From here there are fine views over the surrounding hills.

The Gothic-arched **Lonja** (commodities exchange) and the 16th-century **town hall** *(ayuntamiento)* are located on the adjacent main square.

Environs

The "Cinco Villas" are five towns recognized by Felipe V for their loyalty during the War of the Spanish Succession *(see p62)*. **Sos del Rey Católico** is the most appealing of these. The others are Ejea de los Caballeros, Tauste, Sádaba and **Uncastillo**. This last town, 20 km (12 miles) to the southeast, has a fortress and a Romanesque church, the Iglesia de Santa María.

Los Valles ❷

Huesca. 🚉 *Jaca.* 🚌 *from Jaca to Hecho.* 🛈 *Carretera de Oza, Hecho (ayuntamiento) 974 37 50 02.*

The delightful valleys of Ansó and Hecho, formed by the Veral and Aragón Subordán rivers respectively, were isolated until recently due to poor road links. Their villages have retained traditional customs and a local dialect called *cheso*, passed down the generations. Now the area's crafts and costumes have made it popular with tourists. The Pyrenean foothills and pine forests above the valleys are particularly good for walking, fishing and cross-country skiing.

Ansó lies in the prettiest valley, which becomes a shadowy gorge where the Río Veral and the road next to it squeeze between vertical crags and through rock tunnels. Many of its buildings have stone façades and steep, tiled roofs. In the Gothic church (16th century) there is a museum dedicated to local costume. Pieces of modern sculpture lie scattered around the village of **Hecho**, from an open-air festival previously held in the village. The bucolic village of **Siresa**, which contains the 11th-century church of San Pedro, lies to the north of Hecho.

Puerto de Somport ❸

Huesca. 🚌 *Somport, Astun or Jaca.* 🛈 *Pl Ayuntamiento 1, Canfranc, 974 37 31 41.*

Just inside the border with France, the Somport Pass was for centuries a strategic crossing point for the Romans and Moors, and for medieval pilgrims en route to Santiago de Compostela *(see pp82–3)*. Today the austere scenery is specked with holiday apartments built for skiing. **Astún** is modern and well organized, while **El Formigal**, to the east, is a stylish, purpose-built resort. Non-skiers can enjoy the scenery around the Panticosa gorge. **Sallent de Gállego** is popular for rock-climbing and fishing.

Steep, tiled roofs of Hecho, with a typical pepperpot chimney

Rough and craggy landscape around Benasque

Parque Nacional de Ordesa ❹

See pp232–3.

Benasque ❺

Huesca. 🏠 *1,900.* 🛈 *Calle de San Sebastián 5, 974 55 12 89.* 🚌 *Tue.* 🎉 *San Marcial, San Pedro (29 Jun).*

Tucked away in the northeast corner of Aragón, at the head of the Esera valley, the village of Benasque presides over a ruggedly beautiful stretch of Pyrenean scenery. Although the village has expanded greatly to meet the holiday trade, a sympathetic use of wood and stone has resulted in buildings which complement the existing older houses. A stroll through the old centre filled with aristocratic mansions is a delight.

The most striking buildings in Benasque are the 13th-century **Iglesia de Santa María Mayor**, and the **Palacio de los Condes de Ribagorza**. The latter has a Renaissance façade.

Above the village rises the Maladeta massif. There are magnificent views from its ski slopes and hiking trails. Several local mountain peaks, including **Posets** and **Aneto**, exceed 3,000 m (9,800 ft).

Environs
For walkers, skiers and climbers, the area around Benasque has a great deal to offer, for all levels of ability.

The neighbouring resort of **Cerler** was developed with care from a rustic village into a popular base for skiing and other winter sports.

At Castejón de Sos, 14 km (9 miles) south of Benasque, the road passes through the **Congosto de Ventamillo**, a scenic rocky gorge.

Aínsa ❻

Huesca. 🏠 *1,600.* 🚌 🛈 *Cruce de Carreteras, Avda Pirinaica 1, 974 50 07 67.* 🚌 *Tue.* 🎉 *San Sebastián (20 Jan), Fiestas Mayores (14 Sep).*

The capital of the kingdom of Sobrarbe in medieval times, Ainsa has retained its charm. The Plaza Mayor, a broad cobbled square, is surrounded by neat terraced arcades of brown stone. On one side stands the belfry of the **Iglesia de Santa María** – consecrated in 1181 – and on the other the restored castle.

Jaca ❼

Huesca. 🏠 *30,000.* 🚌 🚌 🛈 *Avda Regimento de Galicia 2, 974 36 00 98.* 🚌 *Fri.* 🎉 *La Victoria (first Fri of May), Santa Orosia San Pedro (25–29 Jun).* **www**.jaca.es

Jaca dates back as far as the 2nd century AD. In the 8th century the town bravely repulsed the Moors – an act which is commemorated in the festival of La Victoria – and in 1035 became the first capital of the kingdom of Aragón. Jaca's 11th-century **cathedral**, one of Spain's oldest, is much altered inside. Traces of its original splendour can be seen on the restored south porch and doorway, where carvings depict biblical scenes. The dim nave and chapels are decorated with ornate vaulting and sculpture. A museum of sacred art, in the cloisters, contains a collection of Romanesque and Gothic frescoes and sculptures from local churches. The streets that surround the cathedral form an attractive quarter.

Jaca's only other significant tourist sight is its 16th-century **citadel**, a fort decorated with corner turrets, on the edge of town. Today the town serves as a principal base for the Aragonese Pyrenees.

Sculpture in Jaca cathedral

The arcaded main square of Ainsa with the Iglesia de Santa María

Parque Nacional de Ordesa ❹

Signpost in Ordesa National Park

Within its borders the Parque Nacional de Ordesa y Monte Perdido combines all the most dramatic elements of Spain's Pyrenean scenery. At the heart of the park are four glacial canyons – the Ordesa, Añisclo, Pineta and Escuain valleys – which carve the great upland limestone massifs into spectacular cliffs and chasms. Most of the park is accessible only on foot: even then, snow during autumn and winter makes it inaccessible to all, except those with specialist climbing equipment. In high summer, however, the crowds testify to the park's well-earned reputation as a paradise for walkers and nature lovers alike.

Valle de Ordesa
The Río Arazas cuts through forested limestone escarpments, providing some of Ordesa's most popular walks.

Torla
This village, at the gateway to the park, huddles beneath the forbidding slopes of Mondarruego. With its core of cobbled streets and slate-roofed houses around the church, Torla is a popular base for visitors to Ordesa.

Brecha de Rolando
El Taillón
3,144 m (10,315 ft)
Gruta de Casteret
Mondarruego
2,848 m (9,344 ft)
VALLE DE ORDE
Cascada Torrombotera
SIERRA DE LAS CUT
Torla
BIESCAS
Broto
Oto
Sarvisé
Jalle
AINSA

0 kilometres   2

0 miles   2

KEY

══	Major road
══	Minor road
– –	Footpath
▬	Spanish/French border
──	National park boundary
🛈	Tourist information
☆	Viewpoint

PYRENEAN WILDLIFE

Ordesa is a spectacle of flora and fauna, with many of its species unique to the region. Trout streams rush along the valley floor, where slopes provide a mantle of various woodland harbouring all kinds of creatures, including otters, marmots and capercaillies (large grouse). On the slopes, flowers burst out before the snow melts, with gentians and orchids sheltering in crevices and edelweiss braving the most hostile crags.

Higher up, the Pyrenean chamois is still fairly common; but the unique Ordesa ibex, or mountain goat, became extinct in 2000. The rocky pinnacles above the valley are the domain of birds of prey, among them the huge bearded vulture, itself now almost extinct.

Spring gentian (*Gentiana verna*)

View from Parador de Bielsa
The parador (see p574), at the foot of Monte Perdido, looks out at stunning sheer rock faces streaked by waterfalls.

Cola de Caballo
The 70-m (230-ft) "Horse's Tail" waterfall makes a scenic stopping point near the northern end of the long hike around the Circo Soaso. It provides a taste of the spectacular scenery found along the route.

(Map labels: Monte Perdido 3,355 m / 11,008 ft, Parador de Bielsa, VALLE DE PINETA, Cinca, BIELSA, Refugio de Góriz, SIERRA DE LAS TUCAS, Cascada Cola de Caballo, las de Soaso, CAÑÓN DE AÑISCLO, GARGANTA DE ESCUAIN, Revilla, Escuaín, BIELSA, Tella, sán, Nerín, Bestué, Puértolas, Vellos)

Hikers in Ordesa National Park

TIPS FOR WALKERS
Several well-marked trails follow the valleys and can be easily tackled by anyone reasonably fit, though walking boots are a must. The mountain routes may require climbing gear so check first with the visitors' centre and get a detailed map. Pyrenean weather changes rapidly – beware of ice and snow early and late in the season. Overnight camping is permitted, but only for a single night above certain altitudes.

Cañon or Garganta de Añisclo
A wide path leads along this beautiful, steep-sided gorge, following the wooded course of the turbulent Río Vellos through dramatic limestone scenery.

Royal pantheon

Lower church

Capilla de San Victorián

Cloister

Residential quarters

Upper church

Capilla de San Voto

Monasterio de San Juan de la Peña ⑧

Huesca. **Tel** *974 35 51 19.*
◯ *mid-Oct–mid-Mar: Tue–Sun; mid-Mar–mid-Oct: daily.* ◉ *1 Jan, 25 Dec.* 🅿 📷 🚻 🛒
www.monasteriosanjuan.com

Set under a bulging rock, this monastery was an early guardian of the Holy Grail *(see p250)*. In the 11th century it underwent reformation in Cluniac style, and was the first monastery to introduce the Latin Mass in Spain. After a fire in the 17th century, the building was abandoned in favour of a newer one further up the hillside. This was later sacked by Napoleon's troops, although the Baroque façade survives.

The church of the old monastery is on two floors. The lower one is a primitive rock-hewn crypt built in the early 10th century. The upper floor contains an 11th-century church with a simple triple apse hollowed out of the side of the cliff. The well-preserved Romanesque pantheon contains the stacked tombs of the early Aragonese kings. The exterior cloister is San Juan de la Peña's *pièce de résistance*, the capitals of its columns carved with biblical scenes.

Agüero ⑨

Huesca. 🏠 *174.* 🚉 *San Jaime 1, 974 38 04 89.* 🎉 *San Roque (15–19 Aug).* **www**.aguero.turincon.com

The picturesque setting of this attractive village, clustered against a dramatic crag of eroded pudding stone, amply rewards a brief detour from the main road. The most important reason for visiting Agüero, however, is to see the 12th-century **Iglesia de Santiago**. This Romanesque church is reached by a long stony track leading uphill just before the village.

The capitals of the columns in this unusual triple-naved building are carved with fantastical beasts as well as scenes from the life of Jesus and the Virgin Mary. The beautiful carvings on the doorway display biblical events, including scenes from the Epiphany and Salome dancing ecstatically. The lively, large-eyed figures are attributed to the mason responsible for the superb carvings in the monastery at San Juan de la Peña.

Castillo de Loarre ⑩

Loarre (Huesca). **Tel** *974 38 26 27.*
🚉 *Ayerbe.* 🚌 *from Huesca.*
◯ *mid-Sep & mid-Oct: Tue–Sun; Jun–Aug: daily; mid-Oct–mid-Mar: Wed–Sun.*

The ramparts of this sturdy fortress stand majestically above the road approaching from Ayerbe. It is so closely moulded around the contours of a rock that at night or in poor visibility it could be mistaken for a natural outcrop. On a clear day, the hilltop setting is stupendous, with views of the surrounding orchards and reservoirs of the

Village of Agüero, situated under a rocky crag

Ebro plain. Inside the curtain walls lies a complex founded in the 11th century on the site of a Roman castle. It was later remodelled under Sancho I (Sancho Ramírez) of Aragón, who established a religious community here, placing the complex under the rule of the Order of St Augustine.

Within the castle walls is a Romanesque church decorated with alabaster windows, a chequered frieze and carved capitals. Its crypt contains the remains of St Demetrius.

Sentry paths, iron ladders and flights of steps ramble precariously around the castle's towers, dungeons and keep.

The formidable Castillo de Loarre looming above the surrounding area

Huesca **⓫**

Huesca. 🏛 *50,000.* 🚌 🚃 **ℹ**
Plaza de la Catedral 1, 974 29 21 70.
📅 *Tue, Thu & Sat.* 🎉 *San Vicente (22 Jan); San Lorenzo (9–15 Aug).*

Altarpiece by Damià Forment, in Huesca cathedral

Founded in the 1st century BC, the independent state of Osca (present-day Huesca) had a senate and an advanced education system. From the 8th century, the area grew into a Moorish stronghold. In 1096 it was captured by Peter of Aragón and was the region's capital until 1118, when the title passed to Zaragoza.

Huesca is now the provincial capital. The pleasant old town has a Gothic **cathedral**. The eroded west front is surmounted by an unusual wooden gallery in Mudéjar style. Above the nave is slender-ribbed star vaulting studded with golden bosses. The cathedral's best feature is an alabaster altarpiece by the master sculptor,

Damià Forment. On the altarpiece, a series of energetic Crucifixion scenes in relief are highlighted by illumination.

Opposite the cathedral is the Renaissance **town hall** *(ayuntamiento)*. Inside hangs *La Campana de Huesca*, a gory 19th-century painting depicting the town's most memorable event: the beheading of a group of troublesome nobles in the 12th century by order of King Ramiro II. The massacre occurred in the former Palacio de los Reyes de Aragón, now the university. This houses the superb **Museo Arqueológico Provincial**, containing archaeological finds and a collection of art.

🏛 **Museo Arqueológico Provincial**
Plaza de la Universidad 1. **Tel** *974 22 05 86.* ⏰ *10am–2pm, 5–8pm Tue–Sat, 10am–2pm Sun & public hols.* ⬛ *1 & 6 Jan, 24, 25, & 31 Dec.* ♿

Alquézar **⓬**

Huesca. 🏛 *310.* **ℹ** *Calle Arrabal, 974 31 82 67.* 🎉 *San Sebastián (20 Jan); San Ipolito (12 Aug).*

This moorish village attracts much attention because of its spectacular setting. Its main monument, the stately 16th-century **collegiate church**, dominates a hill jutting above the strange rock formations of the canyon of the Río Vero. Inside, the church's cloisters have capitals carved with biblical scenes. Next to it is the chapel built after Sancho I recaptured Alquézar from the Moors. Nearby are the ruined walls of the original alcazar, which gives the village its name.

Santuario de Torreciudad **⓭**

Huesca. **Tel** *974 30 40 25.* 🚌 *to El Grado from Barbastro.* ⏰ *daily.* ♿

This shrine was built to honour the devotion of the founder of the Catholic lay order of Opus Dei – San Jose María Escrivá de Balaguer – to the Virgin. It occupies a promontory, with picturesque views over the waters of the **Embalse de El Grado** at Torreciudad. The huge church is made of angular red brick in a stark, modern design.

Inside, the elaborate modern altarpiece of alabaster, sheltering a glittering Romanesque Virgin, is in contrast to the bleak, functional nave.

Environs
The small town of **Barbastro**, which lies 20 km (12 miles) to the south, has an arcaded *plaza mayor* and a 16th-century cathedral with an altar by Damià Forment.

The ruins of Alquézar castle, rising above the village

Houses with frescoed façades on the Plaza de España, Graus

Graus ⓮

Huesca. 🏠 *3,400.* 🚉 🛈 *Calle Fermín Mur i Mur 25, 974 54 61 63.* 🚌 *Mon.* 🎉 *Santo Cristo, San Vicente Ferrer (12–15 Sep); Feria de San Miguel (29 Sep).*

Concealed in the heart of Graus's old town lies the unusual **Plaza de España**, surrounded by brick arcades and brightly frescoed half-timbered houses. One of these was the home of the infamous Tomás de Torquemada, the Inquisitor General *(see p56)*. The old quarter, with its narrow streets, is best explored on foot. At fiesta time, this small town is a good place to see typical Aragonese dancing.

Environs
About 20 km (12 miles) northeast, the hill village of **Roda de Isábena** has the smallest cathedral in Spain. Dating from 1067, this striking building has a 12th-century cloister off which is a chapel with 13th-century frescoes. North of the village is the picturesque Isábena valley.

Tarazona ⓯

Zaragoza. 🏠 *11,000.* 🚉 🛈 *Plaza San Francisco 1, 976 64 00 74.* 🚌 *every other Thu.* 🎉 *San Atilano (27 Aug–1 Sep).* **www**.tarazona.org

Mudejar towers stand high above the earth-coloured, mottled pantiles of this ancient bishopric. On the outskirts of the old town is the **cathedral**, all turreted finials and pierced brickwork with Moorish cloister tracery and Gothic tombs. In the upper town on the

other side of the river, more churches, in typical Mudéjar style, can be found amid the maze of narrow hilly streets. More unusual perhaps are the former bullring, now a circular plaza enclosed by houses, and the splendid Renaissance **town hall** *(ayuntamiento)*. The town hall, built of golden stone, has a façade carved with mythical giants and a frieze showing Carlos V's homage to Tarazona.

Monasterio de Veruela ⓰

Vera de Moncayo (Zaragoza). **Tel** *976 64 90 25.* 🚌 *Vera de Moncayo.* 🕐 *Tue–Sun.* 🎫 ♿

This isolated Cistercian retreat, set in the green Huecha valley near the Sierra de Moncayo, is one of the greatest monasteries in Aragón. Founded in the 12th century by French monks, the huge abbey church has a mixture of Romanesque and Gothic

features. Worn green and blue Aragonese tiles line the floor of its handsomely vaulted triple nave. The well-preserved cloisters sprout exuberantly decorated beasts, heads of human beings and foliage in the Gothic style *(see p24)*. The plain, dignified chambers make a suitable venue for art exhibitions in the summer.

Environs
In the hills to the west the small **Parque Natural de Moncayo** rises to a height of 2,315 m (7,600 ft). Streams race through the woodland of this nature reserve, which throngs with bird life. A tortuous potholed road leads to a chapel at 1,600 m (5,250 ft).

Zaragoza ⓱

Zaragoza. 🏠 *700,000.* ✈ 🚉 🚌 🛈 *Plaza del Pilar, 976 39 35 37.* 🚌 *Wed, Sun.* 🎉 *San Valero (29 Jan), Cincomarzada (5 Mar), San Jorge (23 Apr), Virgen del Pilar (12 Oct).* **www**.turismozaragoza.com

A Celtiberian settlement called Salduba existed on the site of the present city; but it is from the Roman settlement of Cesaraugusta that Zaragoza takes its name. Its location on the fertile banks of the Río Ebro ensured its ascendancy, now Spain's fifth largest city and the capital of Aragón.

Badly damaged during the War of Independence *(see p62)*, the city was largely rebuilt but the old centre retains a number of interesting buildings. Most of the city's main sights are grouped around the vast Plaza del Pilar. The most

Entrance and tower of the Monasterio de Veruela

impresssive of them is the **Basílica de Nuestra Señora del Pilar**, with its huge church sporting 11 brightly tiled cupolas. Inside, the Santa Capilla (Lady Chapel) by Ventura Rodríguez contains a small statue of the Virgin on a pillar amid a blaze of silver and flowers. Her long skirt-like *manta* is changed every day, and devout pilgrims pass behind the chapel to kiss an exposed section of the pillar.

Nearby, on the square, stand the **town hall** *(ayuntamiento)*, the 16th century Renaissance **Lonja** (commodities exchange) and the **Palacio Arzobispal**.

Occupying the east end of the square is Zaragoza's cathedral, **La Seo**, displaying a great mix of styles. Part of the exterior is faced with typical Mudéjar brick and ceramic decoration, and inside are a fine Gothic reredos and splendid Flemish tapestries.

Close by is the flamboyant Mudéjar bell tower of the **Iglesia de la Magdalena**, and remains of the Roman forum. Parts of the **Roman walls** can also be seen at the opposite side of the Plaza del Pilar, near the **Mercado de Lanuza**, a market with sinuous ironwork in Art Nouveau style.

Some of the cupolas of the Basílica de Nuestra Señora del Pilar

The **Museo Camón Aznar** exhibits the eclectic collection of a wealthy local art historian, whose special interest was Goya. The top floor contains a collection of his etchings. Many minor works by artists of other periods can be seen, as well as good contemporary art. The **Museo de Zaragoza** contains a Goya room, as well as archaeological artifacts.

The **Museo Pablo Gargallo** is a showroom for the Aragonese sculptor after whom it is named, who was active at the beginning of the 20th century. One of the most important monuments in Zaragoza lies on the busy road to Bilbao. The **Aljafería** is an enormous Moorish palace built in the 11th century. A courtyard of lacy arches surrounds a sunken garden and a small mosque.

🏛 **Museo Camón Aznar**
Calle Espoz y Mina 23. *Tel 976 39 73 28.* ☐ *Tue–Sun.* ♿ 🖸 *by appt.*

🏛 **Museo de Zaragoza**
Plaza de los Sitios 6. *Tel 976 22 21 81.* ☐ *Tue–Sun.* ♿ 🖸 *free, by appt.*

🏛 **Museo Pablo Gargallo**
Plaza de San Felipe 3. *Tel 976 72 49 23.* ☐ *Tue–Sun.* ♿

ZARAGOZA CITY CENTRE

Basílica de Nuestra Señora del Pilar ④
La Seo (Cathedral) ⑦
Lonja ⑥
Mercado de Lanuza ②
Museo Camón Aznar ⑤
Museo Pablo Gargallo ③
Palacio Arzobispal ⑧
Roman walls ①

0 metres 150
0 yards 150

Key to Symbols see back flap

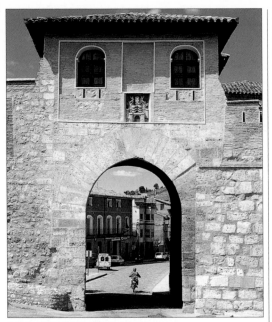

Gateway through the medieval walls of Daroca

Calatayud ⑱

Zaragoza. 🏛 21,000. 🚉 🚌
i Plaza del Fuerte, 976 88 63 22.
🗓 Tue. 🎉 San Roque (14–17 Aug).

The huge Moorish fortress
and minaret-like church
towers are visible from miles
around. Only ruins are left of
the 8th-century Arab castle of
the ruler, Ayub, which gave the
town its name. The church of
Santa María la Mayor has a
Mudéjar tower and an elaborate façade in the Plateresque
style. In the 17th-century
Baroque-style church of **San
Juan Real** there are paintings
from Goya.
    The ruins of the Roman set-
tlement of Bilbilis are east of
Calatayud, near Huérmeda.

Monasterio de Piedra ⑲

3 km (2 miles) south of Nuévalos.
Tel 976 84 90 11. 🚉 Calatayud. 🚌
from Zaragoza. 🕐 daily. 🎫 🅿 ♿

Founded by Alfonso II of
Aragón in 1195, this
Cistercian monastery suffered
damage in the 19th century
and was subsequently rebuilt.

Some of the original buildings
survive, however, including the
chapterhouse, refectory and
hostel – all of which date back
to the 12th century.
    In the damp, blackened cel-
lars, the monks once distilled
strong potions of herbal liqueur in a large alembic. The
kitchen was allegedly the first
place in Europe where drinking
chocolate, from Mexico, was
prepared (see p59).
    The park in which the mon-
astery stands is a picturesque
nature reserve full of grottoes
and waterfalls. A hotel is now
located in the old monastery
buildings.

Daroca ⑳

Zaragoza. 🏛 2,400. **i** Plaza de
España 4, 976 80 01 29. 🗓 Thu.
🎉 Santo Tomás (7 Mar).

An impressive array of battlemented medieval walls
stretches approximately 4 km
(2 miles) around this old Moorish stronghold. Although parts
of the walls have decayed,
some of the 114 towers and
gateways are still a remarkable sight, particularly from
the main road to Zaragoza.
    The **Colegial de Santa
María**, a church in the Plaza
España, houses the Holy Cloths
from the Reconquest (see pp
54–55). After a surprise attack
by the Moors in 1239, priests
celebrating Mass bundled the
consecrated bread into the
linen sheets used for the altar.
Upon being unwrapped, the
cloths were miraculously
stained with blood.

Environs
The agricultural town of
Monreal del Campo, 42 km
(26 miles) south of Daroca,
has a saffron museum. To-
wards Molina de Aragón, 20
km (12 miles) from Daroca, is
the **Laguna de Gallo Canta**, a
lake and wildlife refuge.

Fuendetodos ㉑

Zaragoza. 🏛 170. **i** Cortes de
Aragón 7, 976 14 38 01. 🎉 San
Roque (last Sat of May), San Bartolomé
(24 Aug). www.fuendetodos.org

This small village was the
birthplace of one of Spain's
best-known artists of the late

Interior of Goya's cottage in Fuendetodos

Castle-parador above Alcañiz

18th and early 19th centuries, Francisco de Goya. The **Casa-Museo de Goya** is a neat cottage said to have been the painter's home. It has been restored and furnished in a style appropriate for the period.

Environs
Lying 14 km (9 miles) east of Fuendetodos is **Belchite**, the site of one of the most horrific battles of the Spanish Civil War *(see pp66–7)*, for control of the strategic Ebro valley. Remains of the old, shell-torn town have been left tottering as a monument to the horrors of war.

In **Cariñena**, 25 km (16 miles) west of Fuendetodos, bodegas offer the opportunity to sample and buy the excellent, full-bodied red wine for which the region is justly renowned *(see pp202–3)*.

🏛 **Casa-Museo de Goya**
Calle Zuloaga 3. **Tel** 976 14 38 30.
⬜ 11am–2pm, 4–7pm Tue–Sun. 🎟

Alcañiz ㉒

Teruel. 🏘 15,000. 🚆 🅸 *Calle Mayor 1, 978 83 12 13.* 🚌 *Tue.* 🎭 *Fiestas Patronales (8–13 Sep).*

From a distance, two buildings rise above the town of Alcañiz. One is the **castle**, which was the headquarters of the Order of Calatrava. This historic building has been converted into a parador *(see p574)*. The keep, the Torre del Homenaje, has a collection of 14th-century frescoes depicting the conquest of Valencia by Jaime I.

The other building is the **Colegiata de Santa María**. This church, on the sloping Plaza de España, has a Gothic tower and a Baroque façade.

On the same square are the elegantly galleried **Lonja** (commodities exchange), with its lacy Gothic arches, and the **town hall** *(ayuntamiento)*, with one Mudéjar and one Renaissance façade.

FRANCISCO DE GOYA

Self-portrait by Goya

Born in Fuendetodos in 1746, Francisco de Goya specialized in designing cartoons for the tapestry industry *(see p306)* in his early life, and in decorating churches such as Zaragoza's Basílica del Pilar with vivacious frescoes. In 1799 he became painter to Carlos IV, and depicted the king and his wife María Luisa with unflattering accuracy *(see p33)*. The invasion of Madrid by Napoleon's troops in 1808 *(see pp62–3)* and its attendant horrors had a profound and lasting effect on Goya's temperament, and his later works are imbued with cynical despair and isolation. He died in Bordeaux in 1828.

ARAGON'S FIESTAS

Las Tamboradas
(Maundy Thursday and Good Friday), Teruel province. During Easter Week, brotherhoods of men wearing long black robes beat drums in mourning for Christ. Las Tamboradas begins with "the breaking of the hour" at midnight on Thursday in Híjar. The Tamborada in Calanda begins the following day at midday. The solemn drum rolls continue for several hours. Aching arms and bleeding hands are considered to be signs of religious devotion.

Young drummer in Las Tamboradas, Alcorija

Carnival *(Feb/Mar)*, Bielsa (Huesca). The protagonists of this fiesta, known as *Trangas*, have rams' horns on their heads, blackened faces and teeth made of potatoes. They are said to represent fertility.
Romería de Santa Orosia *(25 Jun)*, Yebra de Basa (Huesca). Pilgrims in folk costume carry St Orosia's skull to her shrine.
Día del Pilar *(12 Oct)*, Zaragoza. Aragón's distinctive folk dance, the *jota*, is performed everywhere during the city's festivities in honour of its patroness, the Virgin of the Pillar *(see p237)*. On the Día del Pilar there is a procession with cardboard giants, and a spectacular display of flowers dedicated to the Virgin.

Alcalá de la Selva castle, overlooking the town

Valderrobres ❷❸

Teruel. 🏘 *2,000.* 🚌 🚉 ℹ *Avda Cortes de Aragón 7, 978 89 08 86.* 🚍 *Sat.* 🎉 *San Roque (mid-Aug).*

Just inside Aragón's border with Catalonia, the town of Valderrobres overlooks the trout-filled Río Matarraña. Dominating the town is the restored **castle**, which was formerly a palace for Aragonese royalty. Below it stands the imposing Gothic **Iglesia de Santa María la Mayor**, with a huge rose window in Catalan Gothic style. The arcaded plaza has a pleasing town hall *(ayuntamiento)* completed in the late 16th century.

Environs
Near Valderrobres is the mountain chain of **La Caixa**. At 14 km (9 miles) are the mountain passes of Beceite.

🏰 **Castillo de Valderrobres**
⬜ *Jul–Sep: Tue–Sun, Oct–Jun: Sat, Sun & public hols.* 🎟

Sierra de Gúdar ❷❹

Teruel. 🚌 *Mora de Rubielos.* 🚌 *Alcalá de la Selva.* ℹ *Plaza de la Iglesia 4, Alcalá, 978 80 10 00.*

This range of hills, northeast of Teruel, is a region of pine woods and jagged limestone outcrops erupting from scrub-covered slopes. At 2,028 m (6,653 ft), **Peñarroya** is the highest point. Nearby Valdelinares, Spain's highest village, is a ski station. From the access roads there are panoramic views of the hills. Especially noteworthy are the views from the towns of **Linares de Mora** and **Alcalá**

de la Selva, which has a castle set against a backdrop of rock faces. Its Gothic-Renaissance church, with shell motifs and twisted columns, shelters the shrine of the Virgen de la Vega.

Mora de Rubielos ❷❺

Teruel. 🏘 *1,500.* ℹ *Diputación 2, 978 80 61 32 (summer); 978 80 00 00 (winter).* 🚍 *Mon & Fri.* 🎉 *San Miguel (28 Sep–1 Oct).*

Dominated by one of the best-preserved castles in Aragón, Mora de Rubielos displays the remains of the old walled city with its bridges and a medieval old town. There is a fine 17th century town hall and the **collegiate church** of Santa María.

Environs
Rubielos de Mora, lying 14 km (9 miles) to the southeast, is worth exploring simply for its well-preserved stone and timber buildings. Among the balconied houses is an Augustinian convent with a Gothic reredos.

Teruel ❷❻

Teruel. 🏘 *30,000.* 🚌 🚉 ℹ *Calle San Francisco 1, 978 64 14 61.* 🚍 *Thu.* 🎉 *Día del Sermón de las Tortillas (Tue of Easter week), La Vaquilla del Ángel (mid-Jul), Feria del Jamón (mid-Sep).* **www**.teruel.org

This industrial town has been the scene of much desperate fighting throughout the centuries. It began with the Romans, the first to capture and civilize Celtiberian Turba.
   During the Reconquest the town became a strategic frontier prize. In 1171 Alfonso II recaptured Teruel for Christian Spain, but many Muslims continued to live peacefully in the city, which they embellished with beautiful Mudéjar towers. The last mosque was closed only at the height of the Inquisition *(see p274)*, in 1502. More recently, during the terrible, freezing winter of 1937, the bitterest battle of the Civil War *(see pp66–7)* was fought here. There were many thousands of casualties.
   The old quarter is home to the wedge-shaped Plaza del Torico, with a monument of a

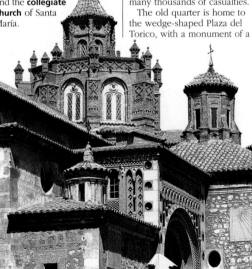
Tiled towers and rooftops of Teruel cathedral

Balconied café above Albarracín's main square

small bull, the city's emblem. Within walking distance lie the five remaining Mudéjar towers. Most striking are those of **San Salvador** and **San Martín**, both dating back to the 12th century. The latter has multi-patterned brickwork studded with blue and green ceramics.

Inside the **Iglesia de San Pedro** are the tombs of the famous Lovers of Teruel. The **cathedral** has more colourful Mudéjar work, including a lantern dome of glazed tiles, and a tower completed in the 17th century. The dazzling coffered ceiling is painted with lively scenes of medieval life.

The **Museo Provincial**, one of Aragón's best museums, is housed in an elegant mansion. It has a large collection of ceramics, testifying to an industry for which Teruel has long been known. North of the centre is the **Acueducto de los Arcos**, a 16th-century aqueduct.

🏛 **Museo Provincial**
Pl Fray Anselmo Polanco 3. **Tel** 978 60 01 50. ◻ Tue–Sun. ♿

Albarracín ㉗

Teruel. 🏘 1,050. 🚌 ℹ Calle Diputación 4, 978 71 02 51. 🚌 Wed. 🎉 Los Mayos (30 Apr–1 May), Fiestas Patronales (13–18 Sep).
www.albarracin.org

It is easy to see why this picturesque town earned an international award for historical preservation. A dramatic cliff above the Río Guadalaviar is the perfect setting for this attractive cluster of mellow

pink buildings. Standing on a ridge behind the town are the defensive walls and towers which date from Muslim times.

There is a good view of the town from below the **Palacio Episcopal** (Bishop's Palace). Inside the neighbouring 16th-century **cathedral**, which is topped by a belfry, there is a Renaissance carved wooden altarpiece depicting scenes from the life of St Peter. The treasury museum contains 16th-century Brussels tapestries and enamelled chalices.

Some of Albarracín's sturdy beamed and galleried houses have an unusual two-tier structure. The ground floor is limestone, and the overhanging upper storey is covered in rough coral-pink plasterwork.

Many have been restored to their medieval form. Just outside the town are the caves of Navazo and Callejón, with their prehistoric rock paintings. Reproductions can be seen in Teruel's Museo Provincial.

Environs
In the surrounding **Montes Universales**, which rise to 1,935 m (6,348 ft), is the source of the Tagus, one of Spain's longest rivers. From fertile cereal plains to crumbling rocks, this area is a colourful mixture of poplars, junipers and thick pine woods, with poppies in spring. At **Cella**, northeast of Albarracín, the Río Jiloca has its source.

Rincón de Ademuz ㉘

Valencia. 🏘 1,200. 🚌 Ademuz. ℹ Plaza del Ayuntamiento 1, 978 78 20 00. 🚌 Wed. 🎉 Fiestas de Agosto (15 Aug), Fiestas de la Virgen del Rosario (early Oct).

This remote enclave south of Teruel belongs to the Comunidad Valenciana (see p243); but is effectively an island of territory, stranded between the borders of Aragón and Castilla-La Mancha. The area has not prospered in recent years, but still has an austere charm and some peaceful tracts of country scattered with red rocks.

THE LOVERS OF TERUEL

According to legend, in 13th-century Teruel two young people, Diego de Marcilla and Isabel de Segura, fell in love and wished to marry. She came from a wealthy family, but he was poor, and her parents forbade the match. Diego was given five years in which to make his fortune and establish a name for himself. At the end of this time he returned to Teruel, laden with wealth, only to find his bride-to-be already married to a local nobleman. Diego died of a broken heart and Isabel, full of despair at his death, died the following day.

Isabel de Segura   Diego de Marcilla

VALENCIA AND MURCIA

CASTELLON · VALENCIA · ALICANTE · MURCIA

oday, the central region of Spain's eastern Mediterranean coast is an important holiday destination – the beaches of the Costa Blanca, the Costa del Azahar and the Costa Cálida draw millions of tourists annually. Centuries ago, Muslim settlers made these regions bloom, and the fertile fields and citrus groves of the coastal plains are still Spain's citrus orchard and market garden.

These productive lands have been occupied for more than 50,000 years. The Greeks, Phoenicians, Carthaginians and Romans all settled here before the Moors arrived, trading the products of land and sea.

The provinces of Castellón, Valencia and Alicante (which make up the Comunidad Valenciana) were reconquered from the Moors by a Catalan army. The language these troops left behind them developed into a dialect, *valenciano*, which is widely spoken and increasingly seen on signposts. Murcia, to the south, is one of Spain's smallest autonomous regions.

The population is concentrated on the coast where the historic towns and cities of Valencia, Alicante and Cartagena have been joined by modern package holiday resorts, such as Benidorm and La Manga del Mar Menor. Inland, where tourism has barely reached, the landscape rises into the chains of mountains that stand between the coast and the plateau of Central Spain. The scenery inland ranges from picturesque valleys and hills in the Maestrat, in the north of Castellón, to the semi-desert terrain around Lorca in southern Murcia.

The warm climate encourages outdoor life and exuberant fiestas. Most famous of these are Las Fallas of Valencia; the mock battles between Moors and Christians staged in Alcoi; and the lavish, costumed Easter processions in Murcia and Lorca.

Hill terraces of olive and almond trees ascending the hillsides near Alcoi

◁ The Penyal d'Ifach, rising directly out of the sea to tower above the Costa Blanca near Calp

Exploring Valencia and Murcia

The coasts of Valencia and Murcia are popular for seaside
holidays and ideal for water sports almost all year round.
Principal resorts include Benidorm, Benicassim and La Manga
del Mar Menor. Some coastal towns such as Peñíscola, Gandía,
Denia, Alicante and Cartagena have charming old quarters,
castles and other monuments well worth visiting. Close to the
sea are several scenic nature reserves: the freshwater lagoon
of L'Albufera, and, on the Costa Blanca, the saltpans of Santa
Pola and the striking limestone crag of the Penyal d'Ifach.

Inland, the region offers excursions to such undiscovered
beauty spots as El Maestrat and the mountains around Alcoi,
as well as the undervisited historic towns of Xàtiva and Lorca.
The two regional capitals, Valencia and Murcia, are both lively
university cities with fine cathedrals and numerous museums.

Fishing nets strung out in the lagoon of L'Albufera

GETTING AROUND

The region's principal roads are the A7 (AP7) motor-way
and the N332 along the coast. Other motorways connect
Valencia with Madrid, A3 (E901), and Alicante with Madrid,
N330 A31. There are main rail lines from Alicante, Valencia
and Murcia to Madrid and Barcelona, but the rest of the rail
network is rather fragmented and buses are often quicker
than trains. A scenic narrow-gauge railway line along the
Costa Blanca connects Denia to Alicante via Benidorm. The
region's international airports are at Alicante and Valencia.
Be aware that as Spain is in the process of changing
its road numbering system some of the roads
featured here may differ from new road signs.

KEY

▬▬	Motorway
▬ ▬	Motorway under construction
▬	Major road
▭	Secondary road
▬	Scenic route
▬▬	Main railway
▬▬	Minor railway
▬	Regional border
△	Summit

(Map of Valencia and Murcia region with place names including: Aras de Alpuente, Alpuente, Chelva, Utiel, Requena, Madrid, N322, N330, Cabriel, Cortes de Pallas, Cofrentes, Ayora, N330, Yecla, Villena, Jumilla, Albacete, N301, A30, Segura, Cieza, Fortuna, Moratalla, Calasparra, Archena, Molina de Segura, ORIHUELA, CARAVACA DE LA CRUZ, Cehegín, C415, Mula, Alcantarilla, MURCIA, El Moral, MURCIA, San Javier, Alhama de Murcia, Corvera, C319, Lucbena, Totana, A7, Guadalentín, San Javier, Torre Pacheco, La, LORCA, CARTAGENA, Granada, A91, Mazarrón, Puerto Lumbreras, Puerto de Mazarrón, Cabo Tiñoso, Almería, Águilas, COSTA CÁLIDA)

La Balma
Forcall
La Poble de
Benifassà
La Sènia
2 MORELLA
Mirambel
Barcelona
ntaviejo
EL MAESTRAT
afranca del Cid
Sant
Mateu
Vinaròs
Ares del
Maestre
Benicarló
Albocàcer
3 PEÑÍSCOLA
Peñ agolosa
1813m
Cabanes
Alcossebre
Torreblanca
VILLAFAMÉS 5
Oropesa
4
goza
Alcora
Benicasim
ONDA 7
CASTELLÓ 6 DE LA PLANA
La Val
d'Uxio
Burriana
8 COVES DE SANT JOSEP
Pucol
10 SAGUNT
11 MONASTERIO DE EL PUIG
Paterna
12 VALENCIA
rente
Catarroja
13 L'ALBUFERA
Alginet
Sueca
Cullera
Alzira
Tavernes de
la Valldigna
14 XÀTIVA
15 GANDÍA
Oliva
Ontinyent
Pego
16 DENIA
Agres
17 XÀBIA
19 GUADALEST
Callosa
d'en Sarrià
Calp
18 PENYAL D'IFACH
Altea
Ibi
Xixona
21 BENIDORM
La Vila Joiosa
El Campello
23 ALICANTE (ALACANT)
Santa Pola
24 ILLA DE TABARCA
Guardamar del Segura
TORREVIEJA
MENOR

COSTA DEL AZAHAR

Costa Blanca

Lemon groves outside Denia

SIGHTS AT A GLANCE

0 kilometres   25

0 miles   20

SEE ALSO

• *Where to Stay* pp576–9

• *Where to Eat* pp626–9

One of the many coves on Xàbia's rugged coast

The unbroken medieval wall surrounding the historic hilltop town of Morella in El Maestrat

El Maestrat ❶

Castellón & Teruel. 🚌 Morella.
ℹ️ Morella, 964 17 30 32.

Crusading warlords of the Knights Templar and the Knights of Montesa – known as *maestres* (masters) – gave their name to this lonely upland region. To rule over this frontier land, which straddles the border between Valencia and Aragón, they built fortified settlements in dramatic defensive positions, often on rocky crags. The best preserved of them is **Morella**, the principal town. **Forcall**, not far from Morella, has two 16th-century mansions on its porticoed

The Torre de la Sacristía, in the restored village of Mirambel

square. To the south, the village of **Ares del Maestre** is spectacularly sited beneath a 1,318-m (4,300-ft) high rock.

Cantavieja is the most important town in the Aragonese part of El Maestrat (where it is known as El Maestrazgo). It has a handsome, arcaded square. The walled village of **Mirambel**, nearby, has been meticulously restored to its medieval condition.

There are several spooky but fascinating shrines to the Virgin in El Maestrat, notably the cave of La Balma at **Zorita**, which is reached via a rocky ledge.

The scenery in most parts is striking: fertile valleys alternate with breathtaking cliffs and bare, flat-topped mountains overflown by eagles and vultures. Tourism is developing very slowly here: there are few places to stay and the roads can be windy and slow.

Morella ❷

Castellón. 🏘️ 2,800. 🚌 ℹ️ Plaza de San Miguel, 964 17 30 32. 🚐 Sun. 🎉 Fiestas patronales (mid–late Aug).

Built on a high, isolated outcrop and crowned by a ruined castle, Morella cuts a dramatic profile. Its unbroken medieval walls retain six gateways, which lead into a fan-shaped maze of streets and

steep, tapering alleys, many of which are shaded by the eaves of ancient houses. The main street is lined with shady porticoes. In the upper part of town is the **Basílica de Santa María la Mayor**. Its unique raised choirloft is reached by a finely carved spiral staircase.

MORELLA'S MIRACLE

A plaque on the wall of Morella's Calle de la Virgen marks the house in which St Vincent Ferrer is said to have performed a bizarre miracle in the early 15th century. A housewife, distraught at having no meat to offer the saint, cut up her son and put him in the cooking pot. When St Vincent discovered this, he reconstituted the boy – except for one of his little fingers, which his mother had eaten to see if the dish was sufficiently salted.

Peñíscola ❸

Castellón. 🏛 6,000. 🚉 ℹ *Paseo Marítimo, 964 48 02 08.* 🚌 *Mon.* 🎉 *Fiestas Patronales (2nd week Sep).*

The fortified old town of Peñíscola clusters around the base of a castle built on a rocky promontory, surrounded on three sides by the sea. This labyrinth of narrow winding streets and white houses is enclosed by massive ramparts. These are entered by either the Fosch Gate – reached by a ramp from the Plaza del Caudillo – or through the San Pedro Gate, from the harbour.

The **Castell del Papa Luna** was built on the foundations of an Arab fortress in the late 13th century by the Knights Templar. Their cross is carved above the door. It later became the residence of the papal pretender Pedro de Luna, cardinal of Aragón. He was elected Pope Benedict XIII during the Great Schism that split the Catholic Church at the end of the 14th century. Although he was deposed by the Council of Constance in 1414, he continued to proclaim his right to the papacy until his death as a nonagenarian in 1423.

The uppermost battlements of the castle are false: they were built for a scene from the 1961 film *El Cid*. Modern Peñíscola is now a thriving holiday resort.

⚑ **Castell del Papa Luna**
Calle Castillo. *Tel 964 48 00 21.*
⬜ *daily.* ⬛ *1 & 6 Jan, 9 Sep, 9 Oct, 25 Dec.* 📷 🎥

Sunset view of the beach and old town of Peñíscola

Costa del Azahar ❹

Castellón. 🚉 *Castelló de la Plana.* 🚌 *Castelló de la Plana.* ℹ *Castelló de la Plana, 964 35 86 88.*

The "Orange Blossom Coast" of Castellón province is named after the dense citrus groves of the coastal plain. The two principal resorts are Benicàssim, where handsome old villas have been supplemented by modern hotels and other tourist amenities, and Peñíscola. Alcossebre and Oropesa also have popular beaches. Vinaròs – the most northerly point – and Benicarló are key fishing ports supplying prawns and date-mussels to local restaurants.

Sculpture in the Casa del Batle

Vilafamés ❺

Castellón. 🏛 1,700. 🚉 ℹ *Plaza del Ayuntamiento 1, 964 32 90 01.* 🚌 *Fri.* 🎉 *San Miguel (late Mar), Patronales (mid-Aug).*

This medieval town climbs from a flat plain along a rocky ridge to the restored round keep of its castle. The older, upper part of the town is a warren of sloping streets filled with sturdy houses.

A 15th-century mansion houses the **Casa del Batle**, a museum of contemporary art. The works on display date from 1959 to the present.

🏛 **Casa del Batle**
Calle Diputación 20. *Tel 964 32 91 52.* ⬜ *Tue–Sun.* 📷

Castelló de la Plana's planetarium, close to the beach

Castelló de la Plana ❻

Castellón. 🏛 166,000. 🚉 🚌 ℹ *Plaza María Agustina 5, 964 35 86 88.* 🚌 *Mon.* 🎉 *Fiesta de la Magdalena (3rd Sun of Lent).*

Originally founded on high ground inland, the capital of Castellón province was relocated nearer to the coast in the 13th century.

The city centre, the Plaza Mayor, is bordered by the market, the cathedral, the town hall and **El Fadrí**, a 58-m (190-ft) high octagonal bell tower begun in 1590 and finished in 1604.

The **Museo Provincial de Bellas Artes** contains a collection of artifacts dating from the middle Palaeolithic era, paintings from the 14th to the 19th centuries and modern ceramics from the region.

The **Convento de las Madres Capuchinas** has an important collection of paintings which are attributed to Francisco de Zurbarán.

In **El Planetario** there are demonstrations of the night sky, the solar system and the nearest stars. It also has a permanent exhibit on holography.

🏛 **Museo Provincial de Bellas Artes**
Avda Hermanos Bou 28.
Tel 964 72 75 00. ⬜ *Tue–Sun.* ♿ 📷 *by appt.*

⛪ **Convento de las Madres Capuchinas**
Calle Núñez de Arce 11. *Tel 964 22 06 41.* ⬜ *4–8pm daily.*

🔭 **El Planetario**
Paseo Marítimo 1, El Grao.
Tel 964 28 29 68. ⬜ *11am–2pm Sat & Sun, 4:30–8pm Tue–Fri.* ⬛ *Sep.* 📷 *(planetarium).* ♿

Onda ❼

Castellón. 🏘 22,000. 🚌 🛈 Calle
Balmes 2, 964 77 64 32.
🚃 Thu. 🎉 Feria del Santísimo
Salvador (6 Aug).

Onda, home to a thriving
ceramics industry, is overlooked by a ruined **castle**,
which was known to its
Moorish founders as the
"Castle of the Three Hundred
Towers". The castle houses a
museum of local history.

However, the main reason
to visit Onda is to take a
look at the **Museo de Ciencias
Naturales El Carmen**, a natural
history museum belonging to
a Carmelite monastery.

The collection was begun in
1952 by the monks for their
own private scientific study.
It was only opened to the
public a decade later. The
clever use of subdued lighting
lends dramatic effect to the
10,000 plant and animal
specimens which are
exhibited over three floors.
Objects include large stuffed
animals placed in naturalistic
settings, butterflies and other
insects, shells, fossils, minerals
and grisly, preserved
anatomical specimens.

🏛 Museo de Ciencias
Naturales El Carmen
Carretera de Tales. **Tel** 964 60 07 30.
⬜ Tue–Sun. ⬤ 20 Dec–6 Jan. 🈺

**Two butterfly exhibits in the Museo
El Carmen**

**Boat ride through the winding
Coves de Sant Josep**

Coves de
Sant Josep ❽

Vall d'Uixó (Castellón). **Tel** 964 69
05 76. 🚌 Vall d'Uixó. ⬜ daily. ⬤
Mon, Dec–Feb 🈺

The caves of St Joseph were
first explored in 1902. The
subterranean river that formed
them, and which still flows
through them, has been chart-
ed for almost 3 km (2 miles).
However, its source has not
yet been discovered and only
part of this distance can be
explored on a visit.

Boats take visitors along the
serpentine course of the river.
You may have to duck to avoid
projections of rock on the way.
Sometimes the narrow caves
open out into large chambers
such as the *Sala de los Murcié-
lagos* (Hall of the Bats – the
bats left when the floodlights
were installed). The water is at
its deepest – 12 m (39 ft) – in
the *Lago Azul* (Blue Lake). You
can explore a further 250 m
(820 ft) along the *Galería
Seca* (Dry Gallery) on foot.
The caves are often closed to
visitors after heavy rain.

Alto Turia ❾

Valencia. 🚌 Chelva. 🛈 CV35
Valencia–Ademúz km 73, 96 163 50 84.

The attractive wooded hills of
the upper reaches of the Río
Turia in Valencia (Alto Turia)
are popular with hikers and
day-trippers. **Chelva**, the main
town, has an unusual clock
on its church which shows

not only the hour but the day
and month as well. The town
is overlooked by the **Pico del
Remedio** (1,054 m/ 3,458 ft),
from the summit of which
there is a fine panoramic view
of the region. In a valley near
Chelva, at the end of an
unsurfaced but drivable track,
are the remains of a Roman
aqueduct, **Peña Cortada**.

The most attractive and interesting village in Alto Turia is
Alpuente, situated above a dry
gorge. Between 1031 and 1089,
when it was captured by El
Cid (*see p370*), Alpuente was
the capital of a small *taifa*, a
Moorish kingdom. In the 14th
century it was still important
enough for the kingdom of
Valencia's parliament to meet
here. The town hall is confined to a small tower over a
14th-century gateway, which
was later extended in the 16th
century by the addition of a
rectangular council chamber.

Requena, to the south is
Valencia's main wine town.
Further south, Valencia's other
principal river, the Xúquer
(Júcar), carves tremendous
gorges near Cortes de Pallas
on its way past the **Muela de
Cortes**. This massive, wild
plateau and nature reserve is
crossed by one small road
and a lonely dirt track.

LA TOMATINA

The highpoint of the annual
fiesta in Buñol (Valencia) is a
sticky food fight on the last
Wednesday of August, which
attracts thousands of visitors
dressed in their worst clothes.
Lorry loads of ripe tomatoes
are provided by the town
council at 11am for
participants to hurl at each
other. No one in range of the
combatants is spared:
foreigners and photographers
are prized targets.

The battle originated in
1944. Some say it began with
a fight between friends.
Others say irreverent locals
pelted civic dignitaries with
tomatoes during a procession.
Increasing national and
international press coverage
means that more people
attend, and more tomatoes are
thrown, every year.

Sagunt's ruined fortifications, added to by successive rulers of the town

Sagunt ❿

Valencia. 🏘 *63,000.* 🚉 🚌 ℹ *Pl Cronista Chabret, 96 266 22 13.* 🛒 *Wed.* 🎉 *Fiestas (mid-Jul).*

Sited near the junction of two Roman roads, Sagunt (Sagunto) played a crucial role in Spain's ancient history.

In 219 BC Hannibal, the Carthaginian commander in southern Spain, stormed and sacked Rome's ally Saguntum. All the inhabitants of the town were said to have died in the assault, the last throwing themselves on to bonfires rather than fall into the hands of Hannibal's troops. The incident sparked off the Second Punic War, a disaster for the Carthaginians, which ended with Rome's occupation of the peninsula *(see pp50–1).*

The town still contains several reminders of the Roman occupation, including the 1st-century AD **Roman theatre**. Built out of limestone in a natural depression on the hillside above the town, it has been controversially restored by the regional government using modern materials. The theatre is now used as a venue for music, plays and Sagunt's annual theatre festival.

The ruins of the **castle**, sprawling along the crest of the hill above the modern-day town, mark the original site of Saguntum. Superimposed on each other are the excavated remains of various civilizations, including the Iberians, the Carthaginians, the Romans and the Moors. The ruins of the castle are divided into seven divisions, the highest being La Ciudadella, and the most important Armas.

⛰ **Castillo de Sagunt**
◯ *Tue–Sun.*

Monasterio de El Puig ⓫

El Puig (Valencia). *Tel 96 147 02 00.* 🚉 🚌 *El Puig.* ◯ *Tue–Sun.* 📷 🎟 *only, 10 & 11am, noon, 4, 5 & 6pm.*

This Mercedarian monastery was founded by King Jaime I of Aragón, who conquered Valencia from the Moors in the 13th century. The monastery is now home to a collection of paintings from between the 16th and 18th centuries and the Museo de la Imprenta y de la Obra Gráfica (Museum of Printing and Graphic Art). The museum commemorates the printing of the first book in Spain – thought to have been in Valencia in 1474 – and illustrates the development of the printing press. Exhibits include printers' blocks and a copy of the smallest printed book in the world.

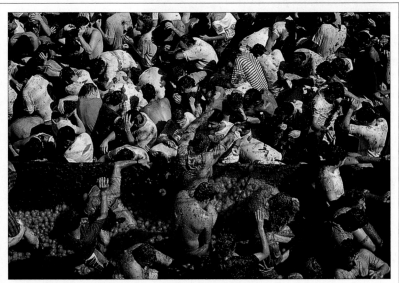

Messy participants throwing tomatoes at each other in the annual fiesta of La Tomatina

Valencia ⑫

Spain's third largest city is sited in the middle of the *huerta*: a fertile plain of orange groves and market gardens, which is one of Europe's most intensively farmed regions. With its warm coastal climate, Valencia is known for its exuberant outdoor living and nightlife. In March the city stages one of Spain's most spectacular fiestas, Las Fallas *(see p255)*, in which giant papier-mâché sculptures are burned in the streets. Modern Valencia is a centre for trade and manufacturing, notably ceramics. A ferry service connects the city with the Balearic Islands.

Flowers in honour of Valencia's patroness, Virgen de los Desamparados

Exploring Valencia

Valencia stands on the course of the Río Turia. The city centre and the crumbling old quarter of El Carmen are on the right bank. Most of the monuments are within walking distance of the Plaza del Ayuntamiento, the triangular main square which is presided over by the town hall.

The city was founded by the Romans in 138 BC and later conquered by the Moors. It was captured by El Cid *(see p370)* in 1096, retaken by the Moors, and finally recaptured by Jaime I, the Conqueror, in 1238, to become absorbed into the kingdom of Aragón.

The three finest buildings in Valencia were built during its economic and cultural heyday in the 14th and 15th centuries: the Torres de Serranos, a gateway that survived the demolition of the medieval walls in the 19th century, La Lonja and the cathedral.

🏛 Palau de la Generalitat
Plaza des Manises. **Tel** 96 386 61 00.
⬜ *by prior appointment only.*
This palace, which is now used by the Valencian regional government, was built in Gothic style between 1482 and 1579 but added to in the 17th and 20th centuries. It surrounds an enclosed stone patio from

which two staircases ascend to splendidly decorated rooms.

The larger of the two Salas Doradas (Golden Chambers), on the mezzanine level, has a multicoloured coffered ceiling and tiled floor. The walls of the parliament chamber are decorated with frescoes.

🏛 Basílica de la Virgen de los Desamparados
Pl de la Virgen. **Tel** 96 391 86 11.
⬜ 7:20am–2pm, 4:20pm–9pm daily.
The ornately dressed statue of Valencia's patroness, the Virgin of the Helpless, stands above an altar in this 17th-century church, lavishly adorned with flowers and candles. She is honoured during Las Fallas by La Ofrenda ("the Offering"), a display of flowers in the square outside the church.

🏛 Cathedral
Pl de la Reina **Tel** 96 391 81 27
Museo ⬜ daily (Sun am). **Miguelete**
⬜ daily. 📷
Built originally in 1262, the cathedral has been added to over the ages, and its three doorways are all in different styles. The oldest is the Romanesque Puerta del Palau but the main entrance is the 18th-century Baroque portal, the Puerta de los Hierros.

A unique court meets on Thursdays at noon in front of the other doorway, the Gothic Puerta de los Apóstoles. For an estimated 1,000 years, the Water Tribunal has settled disputes between farmers over irrigation in the *huerta*.

Inside the cathedral, a chapel holds an agate cup, claimed to be the Holy Grail. According

The Miguelete, the cathedral's bell tower on Plaza de la Reina

to legend it arrived in Valencia from Jerusalem by way of San Juan de la Peña monastery in Aragón *(see p234).*

The cathedral's 68-m (223-ft) high octagonal bell tower, the **Miguelete**, built between 1380 and 1420, is Valencia's main landmark. The cathedral also houses a museum.

🏛 La Lonja
Plaza del Mercado. *Tel 96 352 54 78 ext. 4153.* ○ *Tue–Sun.*
An exquisite Late Gothic hall, built between 1482 and 1498 as a commodities exchange, La Lonja is now used for hosting cultural events. The outside walls are decorated with gargoyles and a variety of other grotesque figures. The high ceiling of the transactions hall is formed by star-patterned vaulting which is supported on graceful spiral columns.

🏛 Mercado Central
Plaza del Mercado 6. *Tel 96 382 91 00.* ○ *8am–2:30pm Mon–Sat.*
This huge iron, glass and tile Art Nouveau building, with its parrot and swordfish weather-

Ornate toilet sign outside Valencia's Mercado Central

vanes, opened in 1928 and is one of the largest and most attractive markets in Europe. Every morning its thousand or so stalls are filled with a bewildering variety of food.

🏛 Museo Nacional de Cerámica Gonzalez Martí
Poeta Querol 2. *Tel 96 351 63 92.* ○ *Tue–Sun.* ● *1 & 22 Jan, 1 May, 24, 25 & 31 Dec.* 🎫 *(free Sat pm & Sun).* ♿
Spain's Ceramics Museum is housed in the mansion of the Marqués de Dos Aguas, an 18th-century fantasy of coloured plasterwork. The

VISITORS' CHECKLIST

Valencia. 🚉 764,000. ✈ 8 km (5 miles) SW. 🚌 C/ Játiva 24, 902 24 02 02. 🚌 Avda Menéndez Pidal 13, 96 346 62 66. 🚢 96 367 43 91. 🛈 Calle de la Paz 48, 96 398 64 22. 🛒 Mon–Sat. 🎭 Las Fallas (15–19 Mar). **www**.comunidadvalenciana.com

doorway is surrounded by a carving by Ignacio Vergara. The 5,000 exhibits include prehistoric, Greek and Roman ceramics, pieces by Picasso and a tiled Valencian kitchen.

🔒 Colegio del Patriarca
Calle Nave 1. *Tel 96 351 41 76.*
This seminary was built in the mid-16th century. The walls and ceiling of the church are covered with frescoes by Bartolomé Matarana. During Friday morning Mass, the painting above the altar, *The Last Supper* by Francisco Ribalta, is lowered to reveal a painting of the crucifixion by an anonymous 15th-century German artist.

VALENCIA CITY CENTRE

0 metres 250

0 yards 250

Key to Symbols *see back flap*

The Palau de la Música, Valencia's prestigious concert hall

Beyond the Centre

The centre of the city is bordered by the Gran Vía Marqués del Turia and the Gran Vía Ramón y Cajal. Beyond these lie the 19th-century suburbs laid out on a grid plan.

The best way to get around beyond the centre is by the metro, one line of which is a tramway to the beaches of El Cabañal and La Malvarrosa.

❧ Jardines del Río Turia

Where once there was a river there is now a 6-km (4-mile) long strip of gardens, sports fields and playgrounds crossed by 19 bridges. In a prominent position above the riverbed stands the Palau de la Música, an international-class concert hall built in the 1980s. The centrepiece of the nearby children's playground is the giant figure of Gulliver pinned to the ground and covered with steps and slides.

The best of Valencia's other public gardens stand near the banks of the river. The largest

Ecce Homo by Juan de Juanes in the Museo de Bellas Artes

of them, the Jardines Reales – known locally as Los Viveros – occupy the site of a royal palace which was torn down during the Peninsular War. Scattered around the gardens are various sculptures and architectural features salvaged from demolished buildings. The intimate Italian-style Monforte Gardens are dotted with marble statues and filled with hibiscus and magnolia. The Jardín Botánico, created in 1802, is planted with 7,000 species of shrubs and trees.

⛿ Museo De Bellas Artes

Museo San Pio V, Calle San Pio V 9. *Tel* 96 360 57 93. ◯ *Tue–Sun.* ◉ *1 Jan, 25 Dec.* ♿ 🖬
An important collection of 2,000 paintings and statues dating from the 14th to the 19th centuries is housed in this former seminary, which was built between 1683 and 1744.

Valencian art dating from the 14th and 15th centuries is represented by a series of golden altarpieces by Alcanyis, Pere Nicolau and Maestro de Bonastre. Velázquez's self-portrait and works by Bosch, El Greco, Murillo, Ribalta, Van Dyck and the local Renaissance painter Juan de Juanes hang on the first floor. On the top floor there are six paintings by Goya and pictures by important Valencian artists from the 19th and 20th centuries: Ignacio Pinazo, Joaquín Sorolla and Antonio Muñoz Degrain. A large collection of the latter's hallucinatory coloured paintings are gathered together in one room, among them the disturbing *Amor de Madre*.

⚓ Torres de Serranos

Plaza de los Fueros. *Tel* 96 391 90 70. ◯ *Tue–Sun.*
Erected in 1391 as a triumphal arch in the city's walls, this gateway combines defensive and decorative features. Its two towers are crowned with battlements and lightened by delicate Gothic tracery.

⛿ Instituto Valenciano de Arte Moderno (IVAM)

Calle Guillem de Castro 118. *Tel* 96 386 30 00. ◯ *10am–8pm Tue–Sun.* 🖼 *(free Sun).* ♿ **www**.ivam.es
The Valencian Institute of Modern Art is one of Spain's most highly respected spaces for displaying contemporary art. The core of its permanent collection is formed by the work of Julio Gonzalez, one of the most important sculptors of the 20th century. All art forms are represented in its programme of temporary exhibitions, with a special emphasis on photography and photomontage. One of the eight galleries, Sala Muralles, incorporates a stretch of the old city walls.

Art Nouveau-style column in the Estación del Norte

🚇 Estación del Norte

Calle Játiva 24. *Tel* 963 52 85 73. ◯ *daily.*
Valencia's mainline railway station was built from 1906–17 in a style inspired by Austrian Art Nouveau. The exterior is decorated with orange and orange blossom flower motifs whilst inside, ceramic murals and stained glass in the foyer and cafeteria depict the life and crops of the *huerta* and L'Albufera *(see p254)*.

The hemispherical IMAX cinema at the Ciutat de les Arts i de les Ciències

🏛 Ciutat de les Arts i de les Ciències

Avenida Autovia del Saler 1–7. **Tel** *90 210 00 31.* ⬤ *daily.* 📷 ♿
www.cac.es

The futuristic complex of the City of Arts and Sciences stands at the seaward end of the Rio Turia gardens. It is made up of five stunning buildings, four of them designed by Valencian architect Santiago Calatrava.

The Palau de les Arts, the final building to be added to the complex, has a concert hall with four performance spaces including an open-air theatre. On the other side of the Puente de Monteolivete is L'Hermisfèric, an architectural pun by Calatrava on the theme of vision, consisting of a blinking eye. The "eyeball" is an auditorium equipped as an IMAX cinema and planetarium. Next to this is the Museu de les Ciències Príncipe Felipe, a science museum contained within a structure of glass and gleaming white steel arches. The displays inside are mainly geared towards visiting school parties. Opposite the museum is L'Umbracle, a giant pergola of parabolic arches covering the complex's car park.

The last part of the "city" is an aquarium, the Oceanografic, designed by architect Felix Candela as a series of lagoons and pavillions linked up by bridges and tunnels.

🏛 Museo de Historia Valencia

Valencia 1, Mislata. **Tel** *963 701 105.* ⬤ *Tue–Sat.* ♿

Valencia's history museum is housed in the 19th-century cistern which used to supply the city with water, now an atmospherically-lit labyrinth of brick, pillars and arches. The displays tell the story of the city's development, as experienced by ordinary inhabitants, from its foundations by the Romans to the restoration of democracy in the late 1970s. In each section there is a "time machine", a full-sized screen on which a typical scene of daily life is reproduced in the language of the visitor's choice.

El Cabañal and La Malvarrosa Beaches

To the east of the city, the beaches of El Cabañal and La Malvarrosa are bordered by a broad and lively esplanade about 2 km (1 mile) long. Although these two former fishermen's districts were carelessly developed in the 1960s and 1970s, they retain some quaint, traditional houses tiled on the outside to keep them cool in summer. The light of La Malvarrosa inspired the Impressionist painter Joaquín Sorolla (*see p305*). The Paseo de Neptuno, near the port, is lined with restaurants, many of which specialize in paella.

Environs

The intensively farmed plain of the *huerta* is a maze of fields planted with artichokes and *chufas*, the raw ingredient of *horchata*.

Manises, near the airport, is renowned for its ceramics, which are sold in shops and factories. There is also a ceramics museum.

VALENCIA'S SUMMER SPECIALITY

In summer, the bars and cafés of Valencia offer a thirst-quenching drink unique to the area. *Horchata*, a sweet, milky drink produced mainly in the nearby town of Alboraia, is made from *chufas* (earth almonds). It is served semi-frozen or in liquid form and usually eaten with *fartons* – soft, sweet bread sticks – or *rosquilletas* – crunchy biscuit sticks. The oldest *horchatería* in the city centre is Santa Catalina, off the Plaza de la Virgen.

Painted tiles showing woman serving *horchata*

Fishing boats on the shore of the freshwater lake, L'Albufera

L'Albufera ⓑ

Valencia. 🚾 🛈 *Carretera del Palmar, Raco de l'Olla, 96 162 73 45.*

A freshwater lake situated on the coast just south of Valencia, L'Albufera is one of the prime wetland habitats for birds in Eastern Spain.

It is cut off from the sea by a wooded sandbar, the Dehesa, and fringed by a network of paddy fields which produce a third of Spain's rice.

L'Albufera is fed by the Río Turia and connected to the sea by three channels, which are fitted with sluice gates to control the water level. The lake reaches a maximum depth of 2.5 m (8 ft), and is gradually shrinking because of natural silting and the reclamation of land. In the Middle Ages the lake encompassed an area over ten times its present size.

Over 250 species of birds – including large numbers of egrets and herons – have been recorded in the lake's reed beds and marshy islands, the *matas*. L'Albufera was declared a nature reserve in 1986 to protect its birdlife. Many birds can be seen with binoculars from the shores of the lake.

A visitors' centre at Raco de l'Olla provides information on the ecology of lake, the paddy fields and the Dehesa.

Xàtiva ⓒ

Valencia. 🚾 *27,000.* 🚾 🚾 🛈 *Alameda de Jaime I 50, 96 227 33 46.* 🚾 *Tue & Fri.* 🚾 *Las Fallas (16– 19 Mar); Fira de agosto (15–20 Aug).*

Along the narrow ridge of Mount Vernissa, above Xàtiva, run the ruins of a once-grand **castle** of 30 towers. It was largely destroyed by Felipe V in the War of the Spanish Succession *(see p62)*. Felipe also set fire to the town, which continues to wreak its revenge in an extraordinary way – by hanging Felipe's full-length portrait upside down in the **Museo Municipal**.

Until the attack, Xàtiva was the second town of the kingdom of Valencia. It is thought

Felipe V's full-length portrait hanging upside down in Xàtiva

to have been founded by the Iberians. Under the Moors it became prosperous, and in the 12th century it was the first European city to make paper.

Among the sights in the streets and squares of the old town are a former hospital with a Gothic–Renaissance façade, and a Gothic fountain in the Plaça de la Trinidad.

The oldest church in Xàtiva is the **Ermita de San Feliú** (Chapel of St Felix) on the road up to the fortress. It dates from around 1262 and is hung with a number of 14th- to 16th-century icons.

⚓ Castillo de Xàtiva
Subida del Castillo. **Tel** *96 227 42 74.* ⏰ *Tue–Sun.* 🖼

🏛 Museo Municipal
Carrer de la Corretgeria 46. **Tel** *96 227 65 97.* ⏰ *Tue–Sun.* 🖼 ♿

Gandía ⓓ

Valencia. 🚾 *74,000.* 🚾 🛈 *Calle Marqués de Campo, 96 287 77 88.* 🚾 *Thu, Sat.* 🚾 *Las Fallas (16–19 Mar).* **www**.*gandiaexcelencia.com*

In 1485, Rodrigo Borja (who became Pope Alexander VI) was granted the title of Duchy of Gandia. He founded the Borgia clan and, together with his children, was later implicated in murder and debauchery.

Rodrigo's great-grandson later redeemed the family name by joining the Jesuit order. He was canonized as St Francis Borja by Pope Clement X in 1671.

The house in which he was born and lived, the **Palacio Ducal** (Duke's Palace), is now owned by the Jesuits. Its simple Gothic courtyard belies the richly decorated chambers within, especially the Baroque Golden Gallery. The small patio has a tiled floor depicting the four elements of earth, air, fire and water.

⚜ Palau Ducal
Duc Alfons el Vell 1. *Tel* 96 287 14 65. ◯ *Tue–Sun.* 📷 ⧉

The ornate and gilded interior of the Palau Ducal, Gandia

Denia ⑯

Alicante. 🏚 *40,000.* 🚌 🚋 ⛴ ⓘ *Plaza Oculista Buigues 9, 96 642 23 67.* 🏛 *Mon.* 🎭 *Fiestas Patronales (early Jul).* **www**.denia.net

This town was founded as a Greek colony. It takes its name from the Roman goddess Diana – a temple in her honour was excavated here. In the 11th century it became the capital of a short-lived Muslim kingdom, whose dominion extended from Andalusia to the Balearic Islands.

It is now a fishing port and holiday resort. The town centre spreads around the base of a low hill. A large **castle**, once an Arab fortress, on its summit overlooks the harbour. The entrance gate, the Portal de la Vila, survives, but it was altered in the 17th century.

The Palacio del Gobernador (Governor's House), within the castle, contains an archaeological museum which shows the development of Denia from 200 BC to the 18th century.

North of the harbour is the sandy beach of Las Marinas. To the south is the rocky and less developed Las Rotas beach, which is good for snorkelling.

⚜ Castillo de Denia
Calle San Francisco. *Tel* 96 642 06 56. ◯ *daily.* ● *1 Jan, 25 Dec.* 📷 ⧉

Xàbia ⑰

Alicante. 🏚 *30,000.* ⓘ ⓘ *Plaza de la Iglesia 6, 96 579 43 56.* 🏛 *Thu.* 🎭 *San Juan (24 Jun), Moros Y Cristianos (third weekend of Jul), Aduanas de Mar (first week of Sep).*

Pirates and smugglers once took advantage of the hiding places afforded by the cliffs, caves, inlets and two rocky islands that make up Xàbia's attractive coastline.

The town centre is perched on a hill a short way inland, on the site of an Iberian walled settlement. Many of the buildings lining its streets are made from the local Tosca sandstone. The 16th-century **Iglesia de San Bartolomé** was fortified to serve its congregation as a refuge in times of invasion. It has openings over the door through which missiles could be dropped on to attackers.

The seafront is overlooked by ruined 17th- and 18th-century windmills, and the beaches are free of the high-rise apartment blocks that spoil many Spanish resorts.

Entrance to the Gothic Iglesia de San Bartolomé in Xàbia

The ceremonial burning of Las Fallas on St Joseph's Day

VALENCIA AND MURCIA'S FIESTAS

Las Fallas *(15–19 Mar).* Huge papier-mâché monuments *(fallas)* are erected in the crossroads and squares of Valencia around 15 March and ceremonially set alight on the night of the 19th, St Joseph's Day. Costing thousands of euros each, the *fallas* depict satirical scenes. During the fiesta, the city echoes to the sound of fire crackers.

Good Friday, Lorca (Murcia). The "blue" and "white" brotherhoods compete to outdo each other in pomp and finery during a grand procession of biblical characters.

Moors and Christians *(21–24 Apr),* Alcoi (Alicante). Two costumed armies march into the city, where they perform ceremonies and fight mock battles in commemoration of the Reconquest.

Bous en la Mar *(early Jul),* Denia (Alicante). People dodge bulls on the quay until one or the other falls into the sea *(see p39).*

Misteri d'Elx *(11–15 Aug),* Elx (Alicante). This choral play, in the Iglesia de Santa María, has spectacular special effects.

La Tomatina *(last Wed of Aug),* Buñol (Valencia). Thousands of participants pelt each other with ripe tomatoes *(see pp248–9).*

The Costa Blanca

Less hectic than the Costa del Sol *(see pp472–3)* and with warmer winters than the Costa Brava *(see p217),* the Costa Blanca occupies a prime stretch of Spain's Mediterranean coastline. Alicante, with its airport and mainline railway station, is the arrival and departure point for most tourists. Between Alicante and Altea there are long stretches of sandy beach which have been heavily built up with apartment blocks and hotels. North of Altea there are more fine beaches, but they are broken by cliffs and coves. South from Alicante, as far as the resort of Torrevieja, the scenery is drier and more barren, relieved only by the wooded sand dunes of Guardamar del Segura.

Gandía marks the southern end of the Costa de Valencia, whose extensive beaches of fine sand and shallow water are popular with the Spanish.

Gandia

Oliva

Denia's Las Marinas beach is a flat, sandy strip lined by hotels. The rocky Les Rotes beach is good for snorkelling.

Denia

Xàbia

Xàbia's busiest beach is El Arenal. Most of the resort's coastline is punctuated by cliffs and coves.

Altea is a resort with an unspoiled, whitewashed old town on a hilltop. Beneath it is a long, shingle beach.

Moraira

Calp

Altea

Benidorm

Benidorm's liveliest beach, Levante, is considered to be one of the ten best beaches in the world. Poniente is further from the town centre.

Santa Pola *is still a working fishing port, but its long, sandy beaches are very popular.*

La Vila Joiosa

El Campello

Platja de Sant Joan

Platja de Sant Joan has a long strip of seamless sand bordered by a road and a narrow-gauge railway, which gives easy access to the beach.

Alacant (Alicante)

Santa Pola

Illa de Tabarca

The Illa de Tabarca attracts daytrippers for its natural beauty and clear waters, good for snorkelling.

Guardamar del Segura

Guardamar del Segura has one of the coast's least busy beaches. It is bordered by windswept sand dunes covered with aromatic pine woods.

Torrevieja

0 kilometres   25

0 miles   25

Torrevieja is a very popular package holiday resort with sweeping, sandy beaches to the south. It has been highly developed in recent years.

Alicante's *city centre is served by the popular Postiguet beach. Nearby are vast, sandy beaches, such as La Albufereta and Sant Joan.*

◁ **Entrance of the Moorish army, part of a festival to commemorate the Reconquest, Ontinyent, Valencia**

Penyal d'Ifach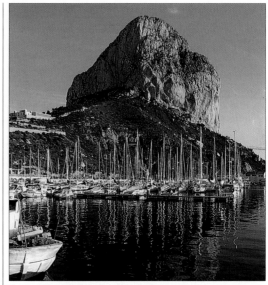

Alicante, Calp. 🚉 Calp. 🚌 Calp.
ℹ️ Avda de los Ejércitos Españoles
44, Calp, 96 583 69 20.

When viewed from afar, the rocky outcrop of the Penyal d'Ifach seems to rise vertically out of the sea. One of the Costa Blanca's most dramatic sights, this 332-m (1,089-ft) tall block of limestone looks virtually unclimbable. However, a short tunnel, built in 1918, allows walkers access to the much gentler slopes on its seaward side.

Allow about two hours for the round trip, which starts at the visitors' centre above Calp harbour. It takes you up gentle slopes covered with juniper and fan palm, with the waves crashing below. As you climb, and at the exposed summit, there are spectacular views of a large stretch of the Costa Blanca. On a clear day you can see the hills of Ibiza (see p510).

The Penyal d'Ifach is also home to 300 types of wild plant, including several rare species. Migrating birds use it as a landmark, and the salt flats below it are an important habitat for them. The rock was privately owned until 1987, when the regional government acquired it and turned it into a nature reserve.

Situated below the rock is the Iberian town of Calp, renowned for its beaches.

Guadalest ⑲

Alicante. 🏘️ 200. ℹ️ Avenida de Alicante, 96 588 52 98. 🎉 Fiestas de los Jóvenes (1st week of Jun), Virgen de la Asunción (14–17 Aug).

Despite drawing coach loads of day-trippers from Benidorm, the pretty mountain village of Castell de Guadalest remains relatively unspoiled. This is largely because its older part is accessible only on foot by a single entrance: a sloping tunnel cut into the rock on which the castle ruins and the church's distinctive belfry are precariously perched.

Guadalest was founded by the Moors, who carved the surrounding hillsides into ter-

The magnificent limestone rock Penyal d'Ifach

races and planted them with crops. These are still irrigated by the original ditches constructed by the Moors. The village was badly damaged by earthquakes in 1644 and 1748.

From the **castle** there are fine views of the surrounding mountains. Access to the castle is through the Casa Orduña.

The **Museo de Micro-Miniaturas**, displays a microscopic version of Goya's *Fusilamiento 3 de Mayo* painted on a grain of rice, his *The Naked Maja (see p293)*, painted on the wing of a fly, and a sculpture of a camel passing through the eye of a needle.

🏛️ Museo de Micro-Miniaturas
Calle de la Iglesia 5. **Tel** 96 588 50 62. ⬜ daily (until 9pm Apr–Sep). 🎫

The belfry of Guadalest, perched on top of a rock

Alcoi ⑳

Alicante. 🏘️ 62,000. 🚉 🚌 ℹ️ San Lorenzo 2, 965 53 71 55. 🛍️ Wed & Sat 🎉 Los Reyes Parade (5 Jan), Moors and Christians (21–24 Apr). **www**.ajualcoi.org

Sited at the confluence of three rivers and surrounded by high mountains, Alcoi is an industrial city. But it is best known for its mock battles between Moors and Christians (see p255) and its *peladillas* – almonds coated in sugar.

On the slopes above it is **Font Roja** (the red spring), a nature reserve and shrine, marked by a towering statue of the Virgin Mary.

Environs
To the north of Alcoi is the **Sierra de Mariola**, a mountain range famed for its herbs. The best point of access is the village of **Agres**. A scenic route runs from here to the summit of Mont Cabrer at 1,390 m (4,560 ft). It passes two ruined *neveras* – pits once used to store ice for preserving fish and meat.

The bullring of **Bocairent**, 10 km (6 miles) west of Agres, was carved out of rock in 1813. A nearby cliff is pockmarked with **Les Covetes dels Moros** ("the Moors' Caves"), but their origin remains a mystery.

Benidorm ㉑

Alicante. 🏠 62,000. 🚌 🚊 🚂
*Avda Martínez Alejos 16, 96 585 13
11.* 🗓 *Wed, Sun.* 🎭 *Virgen del
Carmen (16 Jul), Las Fallas (16–19 Mar),
Fiestas Patronales (second weekend in
Nov), Moros Y Cristianos (late Sep,
early Oct).* www.benidorm.org

With forests of skyscrapers
overshadowing its two long
beaches, Benidorm is more
reminiscent of Manhattan than
the obscure fishing village it
once was in the early 1950s.

Benidorm boasts more ac-
commodation than any other
resort on the Mediterranean,
but its clientele has changed
since the 1980s when its name
was synonymous with "lager
louts". A huge public park and
open-air auditorium used for
cultural events, the **Parque de
l'Aigüera**, is emblematic of
the facelift Benidorm has gone
through in recent years. The
town now attracts more elderly
holidaymakers from the north
of Spain than English youths.
Even so, the top attractions
are still said to be sex, sun,
nightclubs and "English" pubs.

A park on a promontory
between the Levante and
Poniente beaches, the **Balcón
del Mediterráneo**, ends in a
giant waterspout – a single-jet
fountain. From here there is a
panoramic view of the town.
A short way out to sea is the
Illa de Benidorm, a wedge-

**Main staircase with floral lamp in
the Casa Modernista, Novelda**

shaped island served by ferries from the harbour. The
island is being converted into
a nature reserve for sea birds.

Environs
La Vila Joiosa (Villajoyosa), to
the south, is much older than
Benidorm. Its principal sight is
a line of brightly painted houses that overhang the riverbed.
They were painted in such
vivid colours, it is said, so that
their fishermen owners would
be able to identify their homes
when they were out at sea.

The older part of **Altea**, to
the north of Benidorm, stands
on a hill above modern beachfront developments. It is a
delightful jumble of white
houses, narrow streets and
alleys, and long flights of steps
arranged round a prominent,
blue-domed church.

Novelda ㉒

Alicante. 🏠 25,500. 🚌 🚊
🇮 *Calle Mayor 6, 96 560 92 28.* 🗓
Wed, Sat. 🎭 *Santa María Magdalena
(20–25 Jul).* www.novelda.net

The industrial town of
Novelda is dominated by its
many marble factories. But it
is the exquisitely preserved
Art Nouveau house, the **Casa
Modernista**, that is of special
interest. It was built in 1903
and rescued from
demolition in 1970. The
building's three floors are furnished in period style. There
are few straight lines or functional shapes and almost
every inch of wall-space has
some floral or playful motif.

Environs: Villena's town hall
has a collection of Bronze
Age gold objects, the **Tesoro
de Villena** *(see pp48–9).*

🏛 **Casa Modernista**
Calle Mayor 24. **Tel** *965 60 02 37.*
◻ *Mon–Sat.* 🎫 *by appt.*

🏛 **Tesoro de Villena**
Ayuntamiento. **Tel** *965 80 11 50.*
◻ *Tue–Sun.* ♿ 🎫

Alicante ㉓

Alicante. 🏠 290,000. ✈ 🚌
🚊 🚢 🇮 *Calle Portugal 17, 965 92
98 02.* 🗓 *Thu, Sat.* 🎭 *Hogueras
(20–24 Jun).*
www.comunidadvalenciana.com

A port and seaside resort built
around a natural harbour,
Alicante (Alacant) is the principal city of the Costa Blanca.
Both the Greeks and Romans
established settlements here.
In the 8th century the Moors
refounded the city under the
shadow of Mount Benacantil.
The summit of this hill is now
occupied by the **Castillo de
Santa Bárbara**, which dates
mainly from the 16th century.
From its top battlements there
is a view over the whole city.

The focus of the city is the
Explanada de España, a palm-
lined promenade along the
waterfront. The 18th-century
town hall *(ayuntamiento)*, is
worth seeing for the Salón
Azul (Blue Room). A metal
disc on the marble staircase is
used as a reference point in

The old town of Altea, dominated by its domed church

Yachts moored in Alicante harbour, beside the Explanada de España

measuring the sea level all around Spain. A fine collection of 20th-century art can be seen at the small **Casa de la Asegurada**. Local artist Eusebio Sempere (1924–85) assembled works by Dalí, Miró, Picasso *(see pp32–3)*, and others. The museum is currently closed for restoration.

♠ **Castillo de Santa Bárbara**
Playa del Postiguet. *Tel* 965 15 29 69. ⬜ *daily.* 🎫 *(for elevator only).*

🏛 **Ayuntamiento**
Plaza del Ayuntamiento 1. *Tel* 96 514 91 00. ⬜ *9am–2pm Mon–Fri.*

🏛 **Casa de la Asegurada**
Plaza de Santa María 3. *Tel* 96 514 09 59. 🔘 *Closed for restoration.*

Illa de Tabarca ㉔

Alicante. 🚢 *from Santa Pola/Alicante.* 🛈 *Santa Pola, 966 69 22 76.*

The best point of departure for the Illa de Tabarca is Santa Pola. This small, flat island is divided into two parts: a stony, treeless area of level ground known as *el campo* (the countryside), and a walled settlement, which is entered through three gateways. The settlement was laid out on a grid plan in the 18th century, on the orders of Carlos III, to deter pirates.

Tabarca is a popular place to swim or snorkel and it can get crowded in the summer.

Fish and salt have long been important to the economy of Santa Pola. A Roman fish salting works has been excavated here, and outside the town are some modern saltpans.

Elx ㉕

Alicante. 🏘 *210,000.* ⬜ ⬜ 🛈 *Plaza del Parque 3, 96 545 38 31.* 📅 *Mon, Sat.* 🎉 *Virgen de la Asunción (11–15 Aug).*

The forest of over 300,000 palm trees that surrounds Elx (Elche) on three sides is said to have been planted by the Phoenicians around 300 BC. Part of it has been enclosed as a private garden called the **Huerto del Cura**. Some of the palms – one with a trunk which has divided into eight branches – are dedicated to various notable people, such as the Empress Elizabeth of Austria, who visited here in 1894.

The first settlement in the area, around 5000 BC, was at La Alcudia, where a 5th-century BC Iberian stone bust of a priestess, *La Dama de Elche (see p48)*, was discovered in 1897. The original is in Madrid, but there are several replicas scattered around Elx.

The blue-domed Baroque church, the **Basílica de Santa María**, was built in the 17th century to house the **Misteri d'Elx** *(see p41)*. Next to it is **La Calahorra**, a Gothic tower, which is a surviving part of the city's defences.

A clock on the roof next to the town hall has two 16th-century mechanical figures, which strike the hours on bells.

♣ **Huerto del Cura**
Porta de la Morera 49. *Tel* 96 545 19 36. ⬜ *daily.* 🎫 ♿ 📷
www.huertodelcura.com

🏛 **La Calahorra**
Calle Uberna. 🔘 *closed to public.*

Orihuela ㉖

Alicante. 🏘 *80,000.* ⬜ ⬜ 🛈 *Calle Francisco Die 25, 96 530 27 47.* 📅 *Tue.* 🎉 *La Reconquista (17 Jul).*

In the 15th century Orihuela was prosperous enough for Fernando and Isabel to stop and collect men and money on their way to do battle against the Moors at Granada. The Gothic **cathedral** contains Velázquez's *The Temptation of St Thomas Aquinas.* Among the exhibits in the **Museo San Juan de Dios** archaeological museum is a processional float bearing a 17th-century statue of a she-devil, *La Diablesa*.

🏛 **Museo San Juan de Dios**
Calle del Hospital. *Tel* 96 674 31 54. ⬜ *Tue–Sun.* ♿ 📷

La Diablesa, Orihuela

Torrevieja ㉗

Alicante. 🏘 *72,000.* 🛈 *Plaza Ruiz Capdepont, 96 571 59 36.* 📅 *Fri.* 🎉 *Habaneras (22–30 Jul).*

During the 1980s, Torrevieja grew at a prodigious rate as thousands of Europeans purchased homes here. Before tourism, the town's source of income was sea salt. The salt works are the most productive in Europe and the second most important in the world.

Torrevieja stages a festival of *habaneras*, melodic songs originating in Cuba, brought back to Spain by salt exporters.

Capilla del Junterón, Murcia

Murcia ㉘

Murcia. 🏠 350,000. 🚊 🚍
🛈 Plaza Julián Romea 4, 902 10 10
70. 🛒 Thu. 🎭 Semana Santa
(Easter Week).
www.murciaturistica.es

A regional capital and university city on the River
Segura, Murcia was founded in
825 by the Moors, following
successful irrigation of the
surrounding fertile plain.

The centre of the modern
city is the 18th-century square,
La Glorieta. The pedestrianized Calle de la Trapería, linking the cathedral and the former marketplace (now the
Plaza Santo Domingo), is the
city's main street.

On it stands a gentlemen's
club founded in 1847, the
Casino (ask the doorman for
permission to look round). It is
entered through an Arab-style
patio, fashioned on the royal
chambers of the Alhambra. The
huge ballroom has a polished
parquet floor and is illuminated by five crystal chandeliers.
A painting covering the ceiling of the ladies' cloakroom
depicts the goddess Selene.

Work on the **cathedral**
began in 1394 over the foundations of Murcia's central
mosque, and it was finally
consecrated in 1467. The
large tower was added much
later and constructed in
stages from the 16th to the
18th centuries. The architect
Jaime Bort built the main,
Baroque façade between 1739
and 1754.

The cathedral's finest features
are two exquisitely ornate side
chapels. The first, the Capilla

de los Vélez, is in Late Gothic
style and was built between
1490 and 1507. The second,
the Renaissance Capilla del
Junterón, dates from the early
16th century.

The **cathedral museum**
displays grand Gothic altarpieces, a frieze from a Roman
sarcophagus and the third
largest monstrance in Spain.

Francisco Salzillo (1707–83),
one of Spain's greatest sculptors, was born in Murcia, and
a museum in the **Iglesia de
Jesús** (Church of Jesus)
exhibits nine of his *pasos* –
sculptures on platforms. These

Arab-style patio, Murcia Casino

are carried through the streets
of the city on Good Friday
morning. The figures are so
lifelike that a fellow sculptor
is said to have told the men
carrying a *paso*: "Put it down,
it will walk by itself".

The folk museum, the
**Museo Etnológico de la
Huerta de Murcia**, stands
beside a large water wheel –
a 1955 copy in iron of the

original 15th-century wooden
wheel. The three galleries display agricultural and domestic
items, some of them 300 years
old. A traditional, thatched
Murcian farmhouse *(barraca)*
forms part of the museum.

🎰 **Casino**
Calle Trapería 18. **Tel** *968 21 22 55.*
⏰ 10am–9pm daily. 🎟️ ♿

🏛 **Museo Etnológico de la
Huerta de Murcia**
Avda Príncipe. **Tel** *968 89 38 66.* ⏰
Tue–Sun. ⏰ public hols. ♿

Mar Menor ㉙

Murcia. ✈ San Javier. 🚊 to
Cartagena, then bus. 🚍 La Manga.
🛈 La Manga, 968 14 61 36.
www.marmenor.net

The elongated, high-rise
holiday resort of La Manga,
built on a long, thin, sandy
strip, separates the Mediterranean and the Mar Menor,
literally "the Smaller Sea".

Really a large lagoon, the
sheltered Mar Menor can be
5°C (9°F) warmer than the
Mediterranean in summer. Its
high mineral concentrations
first drew rest-cure tourists in
the early 20th century. They
stayed at the older resorts of
Santiago de la Ribera and Los
Alcázares, which still have
pretty wooden jetties.

From either La Manga or
Santiago de la Ribera you can
make a ferry trip to the Isla
Perdiguera, one of the five
islands in the Mar Menor.

The old saltpans at Lo Pagán,
near San Pedro del Pinatar, are
now a nature reserve.

The resort of Los Alcázares on the edge of the Mar Menor

View of the domes and spires of Cartagena's town hall from the seafront

Cartagena

Murcia. 🏠 200,000. ✈ San Javier.
🚉 🚌 ⛴ 🛈 Plaza Almirante Bastar-
reche, 968 50 64 83. 🗓 Wed. 🎭
Semana Santa (Easter Wk), Carthaginians and Romans (last two weeks Sep).

The first settlement founded
in the natural harbour of
Cartagena was constructed in
223 BC by the Carthaginians,
who called it *Quart Hadas*
(New City). After conquering
the city in 209 BC, the Romans
renamed it *Carthago Nova*
(New Carthage). Although the
city declined in importance in
the Middle Ages, its prestige
increased in the 18th century
when it became a naval base.

You can get an overview of
the city from the park which
surrounds the ruins of the
Castillo de la Concepción,
Cartagena's castle. On the
quayside below is a prototype
submarine designed by Isaac
Peral in 1888. The city hall,
opposite, marks the end of
the Calle Mayor, a street overlooked by balconies and lined
with handsome buildings. Excavations in the city include a
Roman street and the **Muralla
Bizantina** (Byzantine Wall),
built between 589 and 590.

The **Museo Nacional de
Arqueología Marítima** has an
interesting collection of ancient
Roman and Greek jars.

🏛 **Muralla Bizantina**
Calle Doctor Tapia Martinez. **Tel**
968 50 79 66. ◯ Tue–Sun.

🏛 **Museo Nacional de
Arqueología Marítima**
Carretera Faro de Navidad. **Tel** 968
12 11 66. ◯ 9:30am–3pm Tue–Sat,
10am–3pm Sun. 🎫 (except Sun).

Costa Cálida

Murcia. 🚉 Murcia. 🚌 Murcia.
🛈 Águilas, 968 49 32 85.
www.murciaturistica.es

The most popular resorts of
Murcia's "Warm Coast" are
around the Mar Menor. Be-
tween Cabo de Palos and Cabo
Tinoso the few small beaches
are dwarfed by cliffs. The
resorts of the southern part of
the coast are relatively quiet.
There are several fine beaches
at Puerto de Mazarrón; and at
nearby Bolnuevo the wind has
eroded soft rocks into strange
shapes. The growing resort of
Águilas marks the southern
limit of the coast, at the border
with Andalusia.

Lorca

Murcia. 🏠 80,000. 🚉 🚌
🛈 Calle Lope Gisbert, 968 46 61 57.
🗓 Thu. 🎭 Semana Santa (Easter
Week), Feria (3rd week of Sep), Día
de San Clemente (23 Nov).

The fertile farmland
around Lorca, Murcia's
third most important town,
is an oasis in one of the
most arid areas of Europe.
Lorca was an important
staging post on the Via
Heraclea, as witnessed
by the Roman milepost
standing in a corner
of the Plaza San
Vicente. During the
wars between Moors
and Christians in the 13th
to 15th centuries, Lorca
became a frontier town
between Al Andalus and
the Castilian territory of

Murcia. Its castle dates from
this era, although only two of
its original 35 towers remain.
After Granada fell the town
lost its importance and, except
for one surviving gateway, its
walls were demolished.

The centre of the town, the
Plaza de España, is lined with
handsome stone buildings.
One side is occupied by the
Colegiata de San Patricio
(Church of St Patrick), built
between 1533 and 1704, the
only church in Spain dedicated
to the Irish saint. At the head
of the square is the town hall.
A former prison, it was built in
two blocks between 1677 and
1739, and later connected by
an arch that spans the street.

Caravaca de la Cruz

Murcia. 🏠 24,000. 🛈 Calle de las
Monjas 17, 968 70 24 24. 🗓 Mon,
3rd Sun of month (crafts). 🎭 Vera Cruz
(1–5 May). **www**.caravaca.org

A town of ancient churches,
Caravaca de la Cruz's fame
lies in its castle which houses
the **Santuario de la Vera Cruz**
(Sanctuary of the True Cross).
This is where a double-armed
cross is said to have appeared
miraculously in 1231 – 12
years before the town was
seized by Christians. The
highlight of the Vera Cruz
fiesta is the Race of the Wine
Horses which commemorates
the lifting of a Moorish siege of
the castle and the appearance
of the cross. The cross was
dipped in wine which the
thirsty defenders then
drank and recovered
their fighting strength.

Environs
Just to the north,
among the foothills on
Murcia's western border,
is the village of
Moratalla, a jumble
of steep streets and
brightly painted houses
lying beneath a 15th-
century castle. **Cehegín**,
east of Caravaca, is a
partially preserved 16th-
and 17th-century town.

**Roman milepost topped by a
statue of St Vincent, Lorca**

MADRID

Introducing Madrid

Spain's capital, a city of over three million people, is situated close to the geographical centre of the country, at the hub of both road and rail networks. Because of its distance from the sea and its altitude – 660 m (2,150 ft) – the city endures cold winters and hot summers, making spring and autumn the best times to visit. Madrid's attractions include three internationally famous art galleries, a royal palace, grand public squares and many museums filled with the treasures of Spain's history. The city is surrounded by its own small province, the Comunidad de Madrid, which takes in the Sierra de Guadarrama and one of Spain's most famous monuments, the palace of El Escorial.

The Palacio Real (see pp276–7), *the royal palace built by Spain's first Bourbon kings, dominates the western part of Old Madrid. Its lavishly decorated chambers include the throne room.*

The Plaza Mayor (see p273), *Old Madrid's great 17th-century square, has been a focal point of the city since the days when it was used as a public arena for bullfights, trials by the Inquisition and executions (see p274). An equestrian statue of Felipe III stands in the middle of the square.*

OLD MADRID
(see pp268–81)

MADRID PROVINCE
(see pp308–9)

0 kilometres   25

0 miles   20

El Escorial (see pp330–31), *the massive, architecturally austere monastery-palace built by Felipe II, has some sumptuous apartments decorated with great works of art. Marble sarcophagi in the octagonal Royal Pantheon contain the mortal remains of most Spanish monarchs.*

◁ Sculpted fountain of the Goddess Cybele in the Plaza de Cibeles, with the main post office behind

The Museo Thyssen-Bornemisza (see pp288–9), *one of the most important privately assembled art collections in the world, was sold to Spain in 1993. The 18th-century palace houses major works by Titian, Rubens, Goya, Van Gogh and Picasso.*

The Plaza de Cibeles
(see p286), *one of the city's most impressive squares, is ringed by distinctive buildings, including the 19th-century Banco de España and Madrid's main post office, with sculptures on its white façade.*

BOURBON MADRID
(see pp282–99)

The Parque del Retiro (see p297) *has leafy paths and avenues, and a boating lake overlooked by a majestic colonnade. It is an ideal place in which to relax between visits to the great art galleries and museums of Bourbon Madrid.*

The Museo del Prado (see pp292–5) *is one of the world's greatest art galleries. It has important collections of paintings by Velázquez and Goya, whose statue stands outside the main entrance.*

0 metres	500
0 yards	500

The Centro de Arte Reina Sofía
(see pp298–9), *an outstanding museum of 20th-century art, is entered by highly original exterior glass lifts. Inside, the star exhibit is* Guernica, *Picasso's famous painting of the horrors of the Civil War.*

OLD MADRID

When Felipe II chose Madrid as his capital in 1561, it was a small Castilian town of little real significance. In the following years, it was to grow into the nerve centre of a mighty empire.

According to tradition, it was the Moorish chieftain Muhammad ben Abd al Rahman who established a fortress above the Río Manzanares. Magerit, as it was called in Arabic, fell to Alfonso VI of Castile between 1083 and 1086. Narrow streets with houses and medieval churches began to grow up on the higher ground behind the old Arab alcazar, which was replaced by a Gothic palace in the 15th century.

Drawer designed for storing herbs, Palacio Real

When this burned down in 1734, it was replaced in turn by the present Bourbon palace, the Palacio Real.

The population had scarcely reached 20,000 when Madrid was chosen as capital, but by the end of the century it had more than trebled. The 16th-century city is known as the "Madrid de los Austrias", after the reigning Habsburg dynasty. During this period royal monasteries were endowed and churches and private palaces were built. In the 17th century, the Plaza Mayor was added and the Puerta del Sol, the "Gate of the Sun", became the spiritual and geographical heart not only of Madrid but of all Spain.

SIGHTS AT A GLANCE

Historic Buildings
Palacio Real pp276–7 **9**

Museums and Galleries
Real Academia de Bellas Artes **14**

Churches and Convents
Catedral de la Almudena **7**
Colegiata de San Isidro **2**
Iglesia de San Nicolás **5**

Monasterio de las Descalzas Reales **13**
Monasterio de la Encarnación **10**

Streets, Squares and Parks
Campo del Moro **8**
Gran Vía **12**
Plaza de España **11**
Plaza Mayor **4**
Plaza de Oriente **6**

Plaza de la Villa **3**
Puerta del Sol **1**

GETTING THERE
The metro is the fastest and easiest way to get to Old Madrid. Take line 1 to Gran Vía or Sol; alternatively, lines 2, 3, 5, and 10 are good for getting to the main sights. Buses 51, 52, 150 and 153 to the Puerta del Sol are useful.

KEY

▨	Street-by-Street map *pp270–71*
Ⓜ	Metro station
🚌	Main bus stop
ℹ	Tourist information

0 metres	500
0 yards	500

◁ **Monument to Cervantes by Lorenzo Coullaut-Valera in the Plaza de España**

Street-by-Street: Old Madrid

Stretching from the charming Plaza de la Villa to the busy Puerta del Sol, the compact heart of Old Madrid is steeped in history and full of interesting sights. Trials by the Inquisition (see p274) and executions were once held in the Plaza Mayor. This porticoed square is Old Madrid's finest piece of architecture, a legacy of the Habsburgs (see pp58–61). Other buildings of note are the Colegiata de San Isidro and the Palacio de Santa Cruz. For a more relaxing way of enjoying Old Madrid, sit in one of the area's numerous cafés or browse among the stalls of the Mercado de San Miguel.

★ **Plaza Mayor**
This beautiful 17th century square competes with the Puerta del Sol as the focus of Old Madrid. The arcades at the base of the three-storey buildings are filled with cafés and craft shops ➍

The Mercado de San Miguel is housed in a 19th-century building with wrought-iron columns. The market sells a variety of food and household goods.

To Palacio Real

Town hall (ayuntamiento)

Casa de Cisneros

Arco de Cuchilleros

0 metres	100
0 yards	100

★ **Plaza de la Villa**
The 15th-century Torre de los Lujanes is the oldest of several historic buildings standing on this square ➌

The Basílica Pontificia de San Miguel is an imposing 18th-century church with a beautiful façade and a graceful interior. It is one of very few churches in Spain inspired by the Italian Baroque style.

STAR SIGHTS

★ Plaza Mayor

★ Plaza de la Villa

★ Puerta del Sol

★ Puerta del Sol
With its shops and cafés, the Puerta del Sol is one of the city's liveliest areas. This sign for Tío Pepe, a brand of sherry, has become synonymous with the square ❶

LOCATOR MAP
See Street Finder map 4

Iglesia de San Ginés

Sol Metro

Casa de Correos

Equestrian statue of Carlos III

To Bourbon Madrid

CALLE DEL ARENAL

PUERTA DEL SOL

CALLE DE ALCALÁ

CALLE MAYOR

CALLE DE POSTAS

CALLE PAZ

CALLE DE CARRETAS

BARCELONA

ESPOZ Y MINA

PLAZA MAYOR

PLAZA PROVINCIA

PLAZA DE JACINTO BENAVENTE

SALVADOR

DUQUE DE RIVAS

CALLE DE LA COLEGIATA

The Palacio de Santa Cruz
was built as the court prison in the 17th century. This Baroque (see p25) palace is now occupied by the Foreign Ministry.

Colegiata de San Isidro
This was Madrid's provisional cathedral until La Almudena was completed (see p275). It is named after the city's patron, St Isidore, a local 12th-century farmer ❷

Tirso de Molina Metro

KEY

--- Suggested route

Kilometre Zero, the centre of Spain's road network, Puerta del Sol

Puerta del Sol ●

Map 4 F2. ● *Sol.*

Noisy with traffic, chatter and policemen's whistles, the Puerta del Sol makes a fitting centre for Madrid. This is one of the city's most popular meeting places, and huge crowds converge here on their way to the shops and sights in the old part of the city.

The square marks the site of the original eastern entrance to the city, once occupied by a gatehouse and castle. These disappeared long ago and in their place came a succession of churches. In the late 19th century the area was turned into a square and became the centre of café society.

Today the "square" is shaped like a half moon. A recent addition is the imposing statue of Carlos III. The southern side of the square is edged by an austere red-brick building, originally the city's post office, built in the 1760s under Carlos III. In 1847 it became the headquarters of the

The bronze bear and strawberry tree of Madrid, Puerta del Sol

Ministry of the Interior. In 1866 the clocktower, which gives the building much of its identity, was added. During the Franco regime (see pp 66–7), the police cells beneath the building were the site of many human rights abuses. In 1963, Julián Grimau, a member of the underground Communist party, allegedly fell from an upstairs window and miraculously survived, only to be executed shortly afterwards.

The building is now home to the regional government and is the focus of many festive events. At midnight on New Year's Eve crowds flock to the square to eat a grape on each stroke of the clock, a tradition supposed to bring good luck for the year. Outside a symbol on the ground marks Kilometre Zero, considered the centre of Spain's huge road network.

The buildings opposite are arranged in a semicircle and contain modern shops and cafés. On the corner of Calle del Carmen is a bronze statue of the symbol of Madrid – a bear reaching for the fruit of a *madroño* (strawberry tree).

The Puerta del Sol has witnessed many important historical events. On 2 May 1808 the uprising against the occupying French forces began here, but the crowd, pitted against the well-armed French troops, was crushed (see p63). In 1912 the liberal prime minister José Canalejas was assassinated in the square and, in 1931, the Second Republic (see p 65) was proclaimed from the balcony of the Ministry of the Interior.

Repair works will be undertaken until 2007 and there may be some disruption.

Colegiata de San Isidro ●

Calle de Toledo 37. **Map** 4 E3. *Tel* 91 369 20 37. ● La Latina. ● 8am–noon, 7–8pm Mon–Sat, 9am–2pm, 6–8pm Sun.

Built in the Baroque style (see p25) for the Jesuits in the mid-17th century, this twin-towered church served as Madrid's cathedral until La Almudena (see p275) was completed in 1993.

After Carlos III expelled the Jesuits from Spain in 1767 (see p62), Ventura Rodríguez was commissioned to redesign the interior of the church. It was then rededicated to Madrid's patron saint, St Isidore, and two years later the saint's remains were moved here from the Iglesia de San Andrés. San Isidro was returned to the Jesuits during the reign of Fernando VII (1814–33).

Altar in the Colegiata de San Isidro

Plaza de la Villa ●

Map 4 D3. ● Ópera, Sol.

The much restored and frequently remodelled Plaza de la Villa is one of the most atmospheric spots in Madrid. Some of the city's most historic secular buildings are situated around this square.

The oldest building is the early 15th-century Torre de los Lujanes, with its Gothic portal and Mudéjar-style horseshoe arches. François I of France was allegedly imprisoned in it following his defeat at the Battle of Pavia in 1525. The Casa de Cisneros was built in 1537 for the nephew

Portal of the Torre de los Lujanes

of Cardinal Cisneros, founder of the historic University of Alcalá *(see pp332–33)*. The main façade, on the Calle de Sacramento, is an excellent example of the Plateresque style *(see p25)*.

Linked to this building, by an enclosed bridge, is the town hall *(ayuntamiento)*. Designed in the 1640s by Juan Gómez de Mora, architect of the Plaza Mayor, it exhibits the same combination of steep roofs with dormer windows, steeple-like towers at the corners and an austere façade of brick and stone. Before construction was finished – more than 30 years later – the building had acquired handsome Baroque doorways. A balcony was later added by Juan de Villanueva, the architect of the Prado *(see pp292–5)*, so that the royal family could watch Corpus Christi processions passing by.

Plaza Mayor ❹

Map 4 E3. Ⓜ *Sol.*

The Plaza Mayor forms a splendid rectangular square, all balconies and pinnacles, dormer windows and steep slate roofs. The square, with its theatrical atmosphere, is very Castilian in character. Much was expected to happen here and a great deal did – bullfights, executions, pageants and trials by the Inquisition *(see p274)* – all watched by crowds, often in the presence of the reigning king and queen.

The first great public scene was the beatification of Madrid's patron, St Isidore, in 1621. In the same year, the execution of Rodrigo Calderón, secretary to Felipe III, was held here. Although hated by the Madrid populace, Calderón bore himself with such dignity on the day of his death that the phrase "proud as Rodrigo on the scaffold" survives to this day. Perhaps the greatest occasion of all, however, was the arrival here – from Italy – of Carlos III in 1760.

The square was started in 1617 and built in just two years, replacing slum houses. Its architect, Juan Gómez de Mora, was successor to Juan de Herrera, designer of Felipe II's austere monastery-palace, El Escorial *(see pp330–31)*. Mora echoed the style of his master, softening it slightly. The fanciest part of the arcaded construction is the Casa de la Panadería (bakery). Its façade, recently and crudely reinvented, is decorated with allegorical paintings.

The equestrian statue in the centre is of Felipe III, who ordered the square's construction. Started by the Italian Giovanni de Bologna and finished by his pupil Pietro Tacca in 1616, the statue was moved here in 1848 from the Casa de Campo *(see p302)*. Nowadays the square is lined with outdoor cafés, and is the venue for a collectors' market on Sundays *(see p317)*. The southern exit of the square leads into the Calle de Toledo towards the streets where the Rastro, Madrid's famous flea-market *(see p302)*, is held. A flight of steps in the south-west corner takes you under the Arco de Cuchilleros to the Calle de Cuchilleros, where there are a number of *mesones*, traditional restaurants.

Allegorical paintings on the Casa de la Panadería, Plaza Mayor

The Spanish Inquisition

The Spanish Inquisition was set up by Fernando and Isabel in 1480 to create a single, monolithic Catholic ideology in Spain. Protestant heretics and alleged "false converts" to Catholicism from the Jewish and Muslim faiths were tried, to ensure the religious unity of the country. Beginning with a papal bull, the Inquisition was run like a court, presided over by the Inquisitor-General. However, the

Inquisition banner

defendants were denied counsel, not told the charges facing them and tortured to obtain confessions. Punishment ranged from imprisonment to beheading, hanging or burning at the stake. A formidable system of control, it gave Spain's Protestant enemies a major propaganda weapon by contributing to the *Leyenda Negra* (Black Legend) which lasted, along with the Inquisition, into the 18th century.

A Protestant heretic appears before the royal family, his last chance to repent and convert.

A convicted defendant, forced to wear a red *sanbenito* robe, is led away to prison.

Those who have refused to confess are sentenced in public by day, and then executed before nightfall.

AUTO-DE-FÉ IN THE PLAZA MAYOR
This painting by Francisco Rizi (1683) depicts a trial, or *auto-de-fé* – literally, show of faith – held in Madrid's main square on 30 June 1680. Unlike papal inquisitions elsewhere in Europe, it was presided over by the reigning monarch, Carlos II, accompanied by his queen.

Torture *was widely used by the Inquisitors and their assistants to extract confessions from their victims. This early 19th-century German engraving shows a man being roasted on a wheel.*

The Procession of the Flagellants *(c.1812) by Goya shows the abiding influence of the Inquisition on the popular imagination. The penitents in the picture are wearing the tall conical hats of heretics tried by the Inquisition. These hats can still be seen in Easter Week processions (see p38) throughout Spain.*

Iglesia de San Nicolás ❺

Plaza de San Nicolás 1. **Map** 3 C2.
Tel *91 559 40 64.* Ópera.
*8:30am–1:30pm, 5:30–8:30pm
Mon, 8–10am, 6:30–8:30pm Tue–
Sat, 10am–2pm, 6:30–8:30pm Sun.*

The first mention of the
church of San Nicolás is in a
document of 1202. Its brick
tower, with horseshoe arches,
is the oldest surviving ecclesiastical structure in Madrid. It
is thought to be 12th-century
Mudéjar in style, and may have
originally been the minaret of
a Moorish mosque.

Plaza de Oriente ❻

Map 3 C2. Ópera.

During his days as king of
Spain, Joseph Bonaparte *(see
p63)* carved out this stirrup-
shaped space from the jumble
of buildings to the east of the
Palacio Real *(see pp276–7)*,
providing the view of the
palace enjoyed today.

The square was once an
important meeting place for
state occasions; kings, queens
and dictators all made public
appearances on the palace
balcony facing the plaza. The
many statues of early kings
which stand here were originally intended for the palace
roofline, but proved too heavy.
The equestrian statue of Felipe
IV in the centre of the square
is by Italian sculptor Pietro

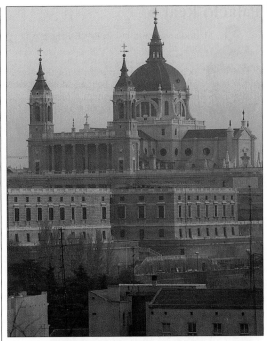

View of the Catedral de la Almudena and the Royal Palace

Tacca, and is based on drawings by Velázquez. Facing the
palace, across the square, is
the imposing Teatro Real, or
Teatro de la Ópera, inaugurated in 1850 by Isabel II.

Catedral de la Almudena ❼

Calle de Bailén 8 –10. **Map** 3 B2.
Tel *91 542 22 00.* Ópera.
9am–8:30pm daily.

Dedicated to the city's
patron, the cathedral of La
Almudena was begun in 1879
and completed over a century
later. The cathedral's Neo-
Gothic grey and white façade
is similar to that of the Palacio
Real, which stands opposite.
The crypt houses a 16th-
century image of the Virgen
de la Almudena.

Further along the Calle
Mayor is the site of archaeological excavations of the
remains of Madrid's Moorish
and medieval city walls.

The first royal wedding
took place in the cathedral
between Prince Felipe and
Letizia Ortíz in May 2004.

Campo del Moro ❽

Map 3 A2. Príncipe Pío.
*Oct–Mar: 10am–6pm Mon–Sat,
9am–6pm Sun & public hols; Apr–
Sep: 10am–8pm Mon–Sat, 9am–8pm
Sun & public hols. 1 & 6 Jan, 1 &
15 May, 12 Oct, 9 Nov, 24–25 & 31
Dec.* **www**.patrimonionacional.es

The Campo del Moro (the
"Field of the Moor") is a
pleasing park, rising steeply
from the Río Manzanares to
offer one of the finest views of
the Palacio Real *(see pp276–7)*.

The park has a varied
history. In 1109 a Moorish
army, led by Ali ben Yusuf
bivouacked here, hence the
name. The park went on to
become a jousting ground for
Christian knights. In the late
19th century it was used as a
lavish playground for royal
children. Around the same
time it was landscaped in what
is described as English style,
with winding paths, grass and
woodland, fountains and
statues. It was reopened to
the public in 1931 under the
Second Republic *(see p65)*,
closed again under Franco, and
not reopened until 1983.

**Equestrian statue of Felipe IV, by
Pietro Tacca, Plaza de Oriente**

Palacio Real ❾

Madrid's vast and lavish Royal Palace was built to impress. The site, on a high bluff over the Río Manzanares, had been occupied for centuries by a royal fortress, but after a fire in 1734, Felipe V commissioned a truly palatial replacement. Construction lasted 26 years, spanning the reign of two Bourbon monarchs, and much of the exuberant decor reflects the tastes of Carlos III and Carlos IV *(see p71)*. The palace was used by the royal family until the abdication of Alfonso XIII in 1931. The present king, Juan Carlos I, lives in the more modest Zarzuela Palace outside Madrid, but the Royal Palace is still used for state occasions.

Statue of Carlos III

★ Dining Room
This gallery was decorated in 1879. With its chandeliers, ceiling paintings and tapestries, it evokes the grandeur of regal Bourbon entertaining.

★ Porcelain Room
The walls and ceiling of this room, built on the orders of Carlos III, are entirely covered in royal porcelain from the Buen Retiro factory. Most of the porcelain is green and white, and depicts cherubs and wreaths.

First floor

The Hall of Columns, once used for royal banquets, is decorated with 16th-century bronzes and Roman imperial busts.

STAR FEATURES

★ Dining Room

★ Porcelain Room

★ Gasparini Room

★ Throne Room

★ Gasparini Room
Named after its Neapolitan designer, the Gasparini Room is decorated with lavish rococo chinoiserie. The adjacent antechamber, with painted ceiling and ornate chandelier, houses Goya's portrait of Carlos IV.

Plaza de Armas
The square in front of the main entrance also gives access to the Royal Armoury. The outstanding collection of weaponry includes the suits of armour belonging to Charles V and Felipe II.

Entrance Hall
A marble staircase by Sabatini, next to the statue of Carlos III as a Roman emperor, leads to the main floor. The painted rococo ceiling by Giaquinto vividly depicts allegorical scenes.

Billiards room

Hall of the Halberdiers

Entrance

Plaza de Armas

Royal Armoury

★ Throne Room
This room maintains the original decor of Carlos III. There are two gold and scarlet thrones and mirrors made in the royal glass factory of La Granja.

VISITORS' CHECKLIST

Calle de Bailén. **Map** 3 C2. *Tel 91 454 88 00.* Plaza de España, Ópera. 3, 25, 33, 39, 148. 9am–6pm Mon–Sat, 9am–3pm Sun (closes 1hr earlier in winter). 1 & 6 Jan, 1 &15 May, 12 Oct, 9 Nov, 24, 25 & 31 Dec. (free Wed for EU citizens). **www.**patrimonionacional.es

Pharmacy
This unique collection includes decorated Talavera pottery storage jars and herb drawers. The Pharmacy Museum has recipe books detailing medications prescribed for the royal family.

KEY TO FLOORPLAN

- ☐ Exhibition rooms
- ☐ Entrance rooms
- ☐ Carlos III rooms
- ☐ Chapel rooms
- ☐ Carlos IV rooms

Visitors' centre

Entrance to the Convento de la Encarnación

Monasterio de la Encarnación ⑩

Plaza de la Encarnación 1. **Map** 3 C3. **Tel** 91 454 88 00. ⓜ *Ópera, Santo Domingo.* ◻ *10:30am–12:45pm, 4–5:45pm Tue–Thu & Sat, 10:30am–12:45pm Fri, 11am–1:45pm Sun & public hols.* ◼ *1 & 6 Jan, 1 & 15 May, 27 Jul, 9 Nov, 24, 25 & 31 Dec.* ▨ *(free Wed for EU residents).* ♿ ▧ www.patrimonionacional.es

Standing in a delightful tree-shaded square, this tranquil Augustinian convent was founded in 1611 for Margaret of Austria, wife of Felipe III. The architect, Juan Gómez de Mora, also built the Plaza Mayor *(see p273)* and the façade clearly reveals his work.

Still inhabited by nuns, the convent has the atmosphere of old Castile, with its blue and white Talavera tiles, wooden doors, exposed beams and portraits of royal benefactors. Inside is a collection of 17th-century art, with paintings by José de Ribera and Vincente Carducho lining the walls. Polychromatic wooden statues include *Cristo Yacente* (*Lying Christ*), by Gregorio Fernández.

The convent's main attraction is the reliquary chamber with a ceiling painted by Carducho. It is used to store the skulls and bones of saints. There is also a phial containing the dried blood of St Pantaleon. According to a popular myth, the blood liquefies each year on 27 July, the anniversary of the

saint's death. Should the blood fail to liquefy, it is said that disaster will befall Madrid. The church was rebuilt by Ventura Rodríguez after a fire in 1767.

Plaza de España ⑪

Map 1 C5. ⓜ *Plaza de España.*

One of Madrid's busiest traffic intersections and most popular meeting places is the Plaza de España, which slopes down towards the Palacio Real *(see pp276–7)* and the Sabatini Gardens. In the 18th and 19th centuries the square was occupied by military barracks, built here because of the square's close proximity to the palace. However, further expansion of Madrid resulted in its being left as a public space.

The square acquired its present appearance during the Franco period *(see pp66–7)*, with the construction, on the northern side, of the massive Edificio España in 1948. Across the square is the Torre de Madrid (1957), known as

La Jirafa (the Giraffe), which, for a while, was the tallest concrete structure in the world. The most attractive part of the square is its centre, occupied by a massive stone obelisk built in 1928. In front of it is a statue of the author Cervantes *(see p333)*. Below him, Don Quixote *(see pp394–5)* rides his horse Rocinante while the plump Sancho Panza trots alongside on his donkey. On the left-hand side is Dulcinea, Don Quixote's sweetheart.

Gran Vía ⑫

Map 2 D5. ⓜ *Plaza de España, Santo Domingo, Callao, Gran Vía.*

A main traffic artery of the modern city, the Gran Vía was inaugurated in 1910. Its construction spanned several decades and required the demolition of large numbers of run-down buildings and small lanes between the Calle de Alcalá and the Plaza de España. This somewhat hap-hazard road-building scheme soon became the subject of a

Stone obelisk with statue of Miguel de Cervantes, Plaza de España

◁ **Night-time traffic on the Gran Vía, seen from the Plaza de España**

One of the many 1930s buildings lining the Gran Vía

zarzuela – a comic opera – that most *Madrileño* of art forms *(see p320)*. Nowadays, the Gran Vía is at the centre of city life and, following a much-needed restoration programme, has become an architectural showpiece.

The most interesting buildings are clustered at the Alcalá end, starting with the Corinthian columns, high-level statuary and tiled dome of the Edificio Metrópolis *(see p284)*.

A temple with Art Nouveau mosaics on its upper levels crowns No. 1 Gran Vía. One striking feature of this end of the street is colonnaded galleries on the upper floors, imitating medieval Aragonese and Catalan architecture. Another is the fine wrought-iron balconies and carved stone details, such as the gargoyle-like caryatids at No. 12. This part of the Gran Vía has a number of old-world Spanish shops.

On the Red de San Luis, an intersection of four major roads, is the Telefónica building. As the first skyscraper to be erected in the capital – in 1929 – it caused a sensation. Beyond here, the Gran Vía becomes much more American in character, with cinemas, tourist shops and many cafés.

Opposite Callao metro station, on the corner of the Calle Jacometrezo, is another of Madrid's well-known buildings, the Art Deco Capitol cinema and bingo hall, which was built in the 1930s.

Monasterio de las Descalzas Reales ⓭

Plaza de las Descalzas 3. **Map** 4 E2.
Tel 91 454 88 00. Ⓜ *Sol, Callao.*
◻ *10:30am–12:45pm, 4–5:45pm Tue–Thu & Sat, 10:30am–12:45pm Fri, 11am–1:45pm Sun & public hols.*
■ *1 & 6 Jan, 1 & 15 May, 9 Nov, 24, 25 & 31 Dec.* ◪ ◪ *(free Wed for EU residents).*
www.patrimonionacional.es

Madrid's most notable religious building has a fine exterior in red brick and granite. This is one of the few surviving examples of 16th-century architecture in the city.

Around 1560 Felipe II's sister, Doña Juana, decided to convert the original medieval palace which stood here into a convent for nuns and women of the royal household. Her high rank, and that of her fellow nuns, accounts for the massive store of art and wealth of the Descalzas Reales (Royal Barefoot Sisters).

The stairway has a fresco of Felipe IV's family looking down, as if from a balcony, and a fine ceiling by Claudio Coello and his pupils. It leads up to a small first-floor cloister, which is ringed with chapels containing works of art relating to the lives of the former nuns. The main chapel houses Doña Juana's tomb. The Sala de

Decorated chapel, Monasterio de las Descalzas Reales

Tapices contains a series of tapestries, one woven in 1627 for Felipe II's daughter, Isabel Clara Eugenia. Another, *The Triumph of the Eucharist*, is based on cartoons by Rubens. Major paintings on show include works by Brueghel the Elder, Titian and Zurbarán.

Fray Pedro Machado **by Zurbarán**

Real Academia de Bellas Artes ⓮

Calle de Alcalá 13. **Map** 7 A2. *Tel* 91 524 08 64. Ⓜ *Sevilla, Sol.* ◻ *9am– 7pm Tue–Fri, 9am–2:30pm Sat–Mon.* ■ *some public hols.* ◪ *(free Wed).* ◪ *by appt.* ♿
www.rabasf.insde.es

Famous former students of this arts academy, housed in an 18th-century building by Churriguera *(see p25)*, include Dalí and Picasso. Its art gallery's collection includes works such as drawings by Raphael and Titian. Among the old masters are paintings by Rubens and Van Dyck. Spanish artists from the 16th to the 19th centuries are well represented, with magnificent works by Ribera, Murillo, El Greco and Velázquez. One of the highlights is Zurbarán's *Fray Pedro Machado*, typical of the artist's paintings of monks.

An entire room is devoted to Goya, a former director of the academy. On show here are his painting of a relaxed Manuel Godoy *(see p62)*, the *Burial of the Sardine (see p39)*, the grim *Madhouse*, and a self-portrait painted in 1815.

BOURBON MADRID

To the east of Old Madrid, there once lay an idyllic district of market gardens known as the Prado, the "Meadow". In the 16th century a monastery was built on this rising ground. The Habsburgs extended it to form a palace (see p297), of which only fragments now remain; the palace gardens are now the popular Parque del Retiro. The Bourbon monarchs,

especially Carlos III, chose this area to expand and embellish the city in the 18th century. Around the Paseo del Prado they built grand squares with fountains, a triumphal gateway, and what was to become the Museo del Prado, one of the world's greatest art galleries. A more recent addition to the area is the Centro de Arte Reina Sofía, a collection of modern Spanish art.

SIGHTS AT A GLANCE

Historic Buildings
Ateneo de Madrid ⑬
Café Gijón ⑮
Casa de Lope de Vega ⑩
Congreso de los Diputados ⑭
Estación de Atocha ㉑
Hotel Ritz ①
Real Academia de la Historia ⑪
Teatro Español ⑫

Museums and Galleries
Centro de Arte Reina Sofía pp298–9 ㉒
Museo Arqueológico Nacional ⑱
Museo del Ejército ⑦
Museo Nacional de Artes Decorativas ⑥
Museo del Prado pp292–5 ⑨
Museo Thyssen-Bornemisza pp288–9 ③

Churches
Iglesia de San Jerónimo el Real ⑧

Monuments
Puerta de Alcalá ⑤

Streets, Squares and Parks
Calle de Serrano ⑰
Parque del Retiro ⑲
Plaza Cánovas del Castillo ②
Plaza de Cibeles ④
Plaza de Colón ⑯
Real Jardín Botánico ⑳

GETTING THERE
The metro is the fastest and easiest way to get to and around Bourbon Madrid. Lines 1, 2 and 4 serve all of the main sights. Useful buses include routes 2, 8, 14, 15, 27, 74, and 146 to the Plaza de Cibeles.

KEY
- Street-by-Street map pp284–5
- Metro station
- Railway station
- Main bus stop
- Tourist information

◁ The expansive Parque del Retiro, which once formed the gardens of a Habsburg palace

Street-by-Street: Paseo del Prado

Façade of Banco de España

In the late 18th century, before the museums and lavish hotels of Bourbon Madrid took shape, the Paseo del Prado was laid out and soon became a fashionable spot for strolling. Today the Paseo's main attraction lies in its museums and art galleries. Most notable are the Museo del Prado (just south of the Plaza Cánovas del Castillo) and the Museo Thyssen-Bornemisza, both displaying world famous collections. Among the grand monuments built under Carlos III are the Puerta de Alcalá, the Fuente de Neptuno and the Fuente de Cibeles, which stand in the middle of busy roundabouts.

The Paseo del Prado, based on the Piazza Navona in Rome, was built by Carlos III as a centre for the arts and sciences in Madrid.

Banco de Espana Metro

The Edificio Metrópolis
(see p281), on the corner of Gran Vía and Calle de Alcalá, was built in 1905. Its façade is distinctively Parisian.

Banco de España

★ **Museo Thyssen-Bornemisza**
This excellent art collection occupies the Neo-Classical Villahermosa Palace, completed in 1806 ❸

STAR SIGHTS

* ★ Museo Thyssen-Bornemisza
---
* ★ Puerta de Alcalá
---
* ★ Plaza de Cibeles

Congreso de los Diputados
Spain's parliament witnessed the transition from dictatorship to democracy (see pp68–9) ⓮

Plaza de Cánovas del Castillo
In the middle of this large square stands a sculpted fountain of the god Neptune in his chariot ❷

PLAZA DE LAS CORTES

PLAZA CÁNOVAS DEL CASTILLO

To Museo del Prado

Hotel Palace

| 0 metres | 100 |
| 0 yards | 100 |

★ Puerta de Alcalá
Sculpted from granite, this former gateway into the city is especially beautiful when floodlit at night ❺

LOCATOR MAP
See Street Finder maps 7–8

★ Plaza de Cibeles
A fountain with a statue of the Roman goddess Cybele stands in this square ❹

The Museo Nacional de Artes Decorativas
This museum, near the Retiro, was founded in 1912 as a showcase for Spanish ceramics and interior design ❻

Palacio de Comunicaciones

Palacio de Linares

Salón de Reinos
The former army museum, this part of the old Retiro Palace will form part of the Prado Museum. ❼

Casón del Buen Retiro
(see p295)

Hotel Ritz
With its Belle Époque interior, the Ritz is one of the most elegant hotels in Spain ❶

The Monumento del Dos de Mayo commemorates the War of Independence against the French *(see p63)*.

KEY

- - - Suggested route

Hotel Ritz ❶

Plaza de la Lealtad 5. **Map** 7 C2.
Tel *91 521 28 57.* ⓜ *Banco de España.* 📷 ⑃ www.ritz.es

A few minutes' walk from the Prado, this hotel is said to be Spain's most extravagant. It was part of the new breed of hotels constructed as luxury accommodation for the wedding guests of Alfonso XIII in 1906.

The opulence of the Ritz *(see p581)* is reflected in its prices. Each of the 158 rooms is beautifully decorated in a different style, with carpets made by hand at the Real Fábrica de Tapices *(see p306)*.

At the start of the Civil War *(see pp66–7)* the hotel was converted into a hospital, and it was here that the Anarchist leader Buenaventura Durruti died of his wounds in 1936.

The Fuente de Neptuno

Plaza Cánovas del Castillo ❷

Map 7 C3. ⓜ *Banco de España.*

This busy roundabout is named after Antonio Cánovas del Castillo, one of the leading statesman of 19th-century Spain *(see p64)*, who was assassinated in 1897.

Dominating the plaza is the Fuente de Neptuno – a fountain with a statue depicting Neptune in his chariot, being pulled by two horses. The statue was designed in 1780 by Ventura Rodríguez as part of Carlos III's scheme to beautify eastern Madrid.

Visitors admiring the works of art in the Museo Thyssen-Bornemisza

Museo Thyssen-Bornemisza ❸

See pp288–9.

Plaza de Cibeles ❹

Map 7 C1. ⓜ *Banco de España.*
Casa de América exhibition room
Tel *91 595 48 00.* ⬜ *11am–2pm, 5–8pm Tue–Sat, 11am–2pm Sun.*

As well as being one of Madrid's best-known landmarks, the Plaza de Cibeles is also one of the most beautiful.

The Fuente de Cibeles stands in the middle of the busy traffic island at the junction of the Paseo del Prado and the Calle de Alcalá. This fine sculpted fountain is named after Cybele, the Graeco-Roman goddess of nature, and shows her sitting in her lion-drawn chariot. Designed in the late 18th century by José Hermosilla and Ventura Rodríguez, it is considered a

symbol of Madrid. Around the square rise four important buildings. The most impressive is the main post office, the Palacio de Comunicaciones, mockingly known as "Our Lady of Communications". Its appearance – white, with high pinnacles – is often likened to a wedding cake. It was built between 1905 and 1917 on the site of former gardens.

On the northeast side of the square is the stone façade of the Palacio de Linares, built by the Marquis of Linares at the time of the second Bourbon restoration of 1875 *(see p64)*. At one time threatened with demolition, the palace was reprieved and converted into the Casa de América, and now displays a collection of paintings by Latin American artists. It is also used as a venue for theatrical performances and lectures.

In the northwest corner of the Plaza de Cibeles, surrounded by attractive gardens, is the heavily guarded Army Headquarters, which is housed in the buildings of the former Palacio de Buenavista. The palace was commissioned by the Duchess of Alba in 1777 as a family residence, though its construction was twice delayed by fires.

Occupying a whole block on the opposite corner is the Banco de España, constructed between 1884 and 1891. Its design was inspired by the Venetian Renaissance style, with delicate ironwork adorning the roof and windows. Much-needed renovation work has returned the bank to its late 19th-century magnificence.

The Fuente de Cibeles, with the Palacio de Linares in the background

View through the central arch of the Puerta de Alcalá

Puerta de Alcalá **5**

Map 8 D1. Ⓜ *Retiro*.

This ceremonial gateway is the grandest of the monuments erected by Carlos III in his attempt to improve the looks of eastern Madrid. It was designed by Francesco Sabatini to replace a smaller Baroque gateway which had been built by Felipe III for the entry into Madrid of his wife, Margarita de Austria.

Construction of the gate began in 1769 and lasted nine years. It was built from granite in Neo-Classical style, with a lofty pediment and sculpted angels. It has five arches – three central and two outer rectangular ones.

Until the mid-19th century the gateway marked the city's easternmost boundary. It now stands in the busy Plaza de la Independencia, and is best seen when floodlit at night.

Museo Nacional de Artes Decorativas **6**

Calle de Montalbán 12. **Map** 8 D2. *Tel* 91 532 64 99. Ⓜ *Retiro, Banco de España*. ◯ 9:30am–3pm Tue–Sat, 10am–3pm, Sun & public hols. ▨ (free Sun). ✆ by app. ♿

Housed in a 19th-century palace overlooking the Parque del Retiro, the National Museum of Decorative Arts contains an interesting collection of furniture and *objets d'art*. The exhibits are mainly from Spain and date back as far as Phoenician times.

One of the finest exhibits on the museum's five floors is a kitchen, moved here from an 18th-century Valencian mansion. Its 1,500 tiles depict a domestic scene from the era. There are also some excellent ceramic pieces from Talavera de la Reina *(see p386)*, and ornaments from the Far East.

Salón de Reinos **7**

Calle Méndez Núñez 1. **Map** 8 D3. *Tel* 91 330 28 00. Ⓜ *Retiro*. ◯ closed for refurbishment from 2006 to 2009.

Built for King Felipe IV as a retreat, the Salón de Reinos (Hall of Kingdoms) is one of the remaining parts of the 17th-century Palacio del Buen Retiro and gets its name from the shields of the 24 kingdoms of the Spanish monarchy, part of the decor supervised by court painter Velázquez.

For many years it was home to the Spain's army museum, the Museo del Ejército, with displays dedicated to the military history of different periods and an array of weapons, from Moorish times to the present day. Among these was the sword of El Cid – *La Tizona*. In 2006 the Museo del Ejército will move to Toledo's Alcázar *(see p390)*, and open in 2007.

Meanwhile the Salón de Reinos will be refurbished to its former glory to become part of the Prado *(see pp292–95)*. Among the exhibits housed in the new gallery will be five equestrian portraits by Velázquez and Zurbarán's series of ten paintings on the life of Hercules, along with other 17th century royal paintings. The sword of El Cid will remain in the Salón de Reinos. It is hoped that the building will be open by 2009.

The sword of El Cid, *La Tizona*, in the Salón de Reinos

Museo Thyssen-Bornemisza ❸

This magnificent museum is based on the collection assembled by Baron Heinrich Thyssen-Bornemisza and his son, Hans Heinrich, the preceding baron. In 1992 it was installed in Madrid's 18th-century Villahermosa Palace, and was sold to the nation the following year. From its beginnings in the 1920s, the collection was intended to illustrate the history of Western art, from Italian and Flemish primitives, through to 20th-century Expressionism and Pop Art. The museum's collection, consisting of more than 1,000 paintings, includes masterpieces by Titian, Goya, Van Gogh and Picasso. Carmen Thyssen's collection of mainly impressionist art is now open to the public. It is regarded by many critics as the most important private art collection in the world.

★ **Our Lady of the Dry Tree** (c.1450)
This tiny painted panel is by Bruges master Petrus Christus. The letter A hanging from the tree stands for "Ave Maria".

★ **Harlequin with a Mirror**
The figure of the harlequin was a frequent subject of Picasso's. The careful composition in this 1923 canvas, which is thought by some to represent the artist himself, is typical of Picasso's "Classical" period.

GALLERY GUIDE

The galleries are arranged around a covered central courtyard, which rises the full height of the building. The top floor starts with early Italian art and goes through to the 17thcentury. The first floor continues the story with 17th-century Dutch works and ends with German Expressionism. The ground floor is dedicated to 20th-century paintings.

STAR PAINTINGS

★ Our Lady of the Dry Tree by Christus

★ Harlequin with a Mirror by Picasso

★ The Toilet of Venus by Rubens

Hotel Room (1931)
Edward Hopper's painting is a study of urban isolation. The solitude is made less static by the suitcases and the train timetable on the woman's knee.

Portrait of Baron Thyssen-Bornemisza
This informal portrait of the previous baron against the background of a Watteau painting, was painted by Lucian Freud.

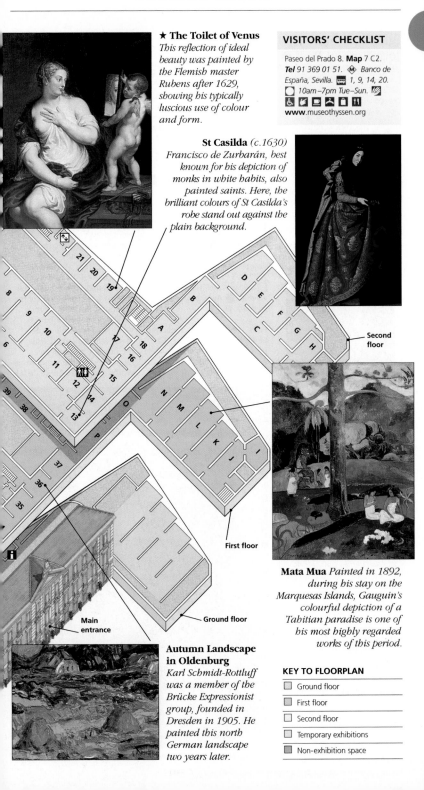

★ **The Toilet of Venus**
This reflection of ideal beauty was painted by the Flemish master Rubens after 1629, showing his typically luscious use of colour and form.

VISITORS' CHECKLIST

Paseo del Prado 8. **Map** 7 C2.
Tel *91 369 01 51.* Ⓜ *Banco de España, Sevilla.* 🚌 *1, 9, 14, 20.*
🕐 *10am–7pm Tue–Sun.* 🎫
♿ 📷 🖥 🛍 🎧 🍴
www.museothyssen.org

St Casilda *(c.1630)*
Francisco de Zurbarán, best known for his depiction of monks in white habits, also painted saints. Here, the brilliant colours of St Casilda's robe stand out against the plain background.

Second floor

First floor

Mata Mua *Painted in 1892, during his stay on the Marquesas Islands, Gauguin's colourful depiction of a Tahitian paradise is one of his most highly regarded works of this period.*

Main entrance

Ground floor

Autumn Landscape in Oldenburg
Karl Schmidt-Rottluff was a member of the Brücke Expressionist group, founded in Dresden in 1905. He painted this north German landscape two years later.

KEY TO FLOORPLAN

☐ Ground floor
☐ First floor
☐ Second floor
☐ Temporary exhibitions
☐ Non-exhibition space

Iglesia de San Jerónimo el Real ❽

Calle del Moreto 4. **Map** 8 D3. **Tel** 91 420 35 78. Ⓜ *Banco de España.* ◯ *Oct–Jun: 10am–1pm, 5:30–8:30pm daily, (6–8:30pm Jul–Sep).* ♿

Built in the 16th century for Queen Isabel, but since remodelled, San Jerónimo is Madrid's royal church. From the 17th century it became virtually a part of the Retiro palace which once stood here *(see p297)*. The church was

Castizos during San Isidro

MADRID'S FIESTAS

San Isidro *(15 May).* Madrid's great party around 15 May is in honour of St Isidore, the humble 12th-century farmworker who became the city's patron. With a *corrida* every day, this is Spain's biggest bullfighting event. Throughout the city there are also art exhibitions, open-air concerts and fire-works. Many people dress in *castizo (see p302)* folk costume for the occasion.

The Passion *(Easter Saturday),* Chinchón. A passion play is performed in the town's atmospheric arcaded Plaza Mayor.

Dos de Mayo *(2 May).* This four-day holiday marks the city's uprising against Napoleon's troops in 1808 *(see p63).*

New Year's Eve. The nation focuses on the Puerta del Sol *(see p272)* at midnight as crowds gather to swallow a grape on each chime of the clock.

originally attached to the Hieronymite monastery. The cloister and part of the atrium form part of a new building at the Prado Museum.

The church was the setting for the marriage of Alfonso XIII and Victoria Eugenia of Battenberg in 1906. King Juan Carlos I's coronation was also held here in 1975.

Museo del Prado ❾

See pp292–5.

Casa de Lope de Vega ❿

Calle de Cervantes 11. **Map** 7 B3. **Tel** 91 429 92 16. Ⓜ *Antón Martin.* ◯ *9:30am–2pm Tue–Fri, 10am–2pm Sat.* ● *Aug & public hols.* 🎟 *(free Sat).* 🚫 📷

Félix Lope de Vega, a leading Golden Age writer *(see p34),* moved into this sombre house in 1610. Here he wrote over two-thirds of his plays,

Félix Lope de Vega

thought to total almost 2,000. Meticulously restored in 1935 using some of Lope de Vega's own furniture, the house gives a great feeling of Castilian life in the early 17th century. A dark chapel with no external windows occupies the centre, separated from the writer's bedroom by only a barred window. The small garden at the rear is planted with the flowers and fruit trees mentioned by the writer in his works. He died here in 1635.

Statue of Goya in front of the Prado

Sunlit balcony of the magnificent Teatro Español

Real Academia de la Historia ⓫

Calle León 21. **Map** 7 A3. **Tel** 91 429 06 11. Ⓜ Antón Martín. ⓟ

The Royal Academy of History is an austere brick building built by Juan de Villanueva in 1788. Its location, in the so-called Barrio de los Literatos (Writers' Quarter), is apt.

In 1898, the great intellectual and bibliophile, Marcelino Menéndez Pelayo, became director of the academy, living here until his death in 1912. The library contains more than 200,000 books and several important manuscripts.

Recently, a museum housing the pictures and antiques of the Academy was constructed; it is due to open in 2007.

Teatro Español ⓬

Calle del Príncipe 25. **Map** 7 A3. **Tel** 91 360 14 80. Ⓜ Sol, Sevilla. ◯ for performances from 7pm Tue–Sun. 🎭 ♿

Dominating the Plaza Santa Ana is the Teatro Español, one of Madrid's oldest and most beautiful theatres. From 1583 many of Spain's finest plays, by leading dramatists of the time such as Lope de Rueda, were first performed in the Corral del Príncipe which originally stood on this site. In 1802 this was replaced by the Teatro Español. The Neo-Classical façade, with pilasters and medallions, is by Juan de Villanueva. Engraved on it are the names of great Spanish dramatists, including that of celebrated writer Federico García Lorca (see p35).

Ateneo de Madrid ⓭

Calle del Prado 21. **Map** 7 B3. **Tel** 91 429 17 50. Ⓜ Antón Martín, Sevilla. ◯ by appt only – apply in writing.

Formally founded in 1835, this learned association has strongly liberal political leanings. It is similar to a gentlemen's club in atmosphere, with a grand stairway and panelled hall hung with the portraits of famous fellows. Closed down during past periods of repression and dictatorship, it is still a mainstay of liberal thought in Spain. Many leading Socialists are members of the Ateneo, along with writers and other Spanish intellectuals.

Carving on the façade of the Ateneo de Madrid

Congreso de los Diputados ⓮

Plaza de las Cortes. **Map** 7 B2. **Tel** 91 390 60 00. Ⓜ Sevilla. ◯ 10:30am–12:30pm Sat, by appt Mon–Fri. ● Aug. ⓟ ♿

This imposing yet attractive building is home to the Spanish parliament, the Cortes. Built in the mid-19th century on the site of a former convent, it is characterized by Classical columns, heavy pediments and guardian bronze lions. It was here, in 1981, that Colonel Tejero of the Civil Guard held the deputies at gunpoint on national television, as he tried to spark off a military coup (see p68). His failure was seen as an indication that democracy was now firmly established in Spain.

Bronze lion guarding the Cortes

Café Gijón ⓯

Paseo de Recoletos 21. **Map** 5 C5. **Tel** 91 521 54 25. Ⓜ Banco de España. ◯ 7:30am–1:30am Sun–Fri, 8am–2am Sat & public hols. ♿

Madrid's café life (see pp320–5) was one of the most attractive features of the city from the turn of the 20th century, right up to outbreak of the Civil War. Of the many intellectuals' cafés which once thrived, only the Gijón survives. Today the café continues to attract a lively crowd of literati. With its cream-painted wrought-iron columns and black and white table tops, it is perhaps better known for its atmosphere than for its appearance.

Museo del Prado ⑨

The Prado Museum contains the world's greatest assembly of Spanish painting – especially works by Velázquez and Goya – ranging from the 12th to 19th centuries. It also houses impressive foreign collections, particularly of Italian and Flemish works. The Neo-Classical building was designed in 1785 by Juan de Villanueva on the orders of Carlos III and it opened as a museum in 1819. The refurbished Casón del Buen Retiro and the new building designed by architect Rafael Moneo over the cloister of Los Jerónimos church are expected to open to the public in 2006.

★ Velázquez Collection
The Triumph of Bacchus *(1629), Velázquez's first portrayal of a mythological subject, shows the god of wine (Bacchus) with a group of drunkards.*

The Three Graces
(c.1635)
This was one of the last paintings by the Flemish master Rubens, and was part of the artist's personal collection. The three women dancing in a ring – the Graces – are the daughters of Zeus, and represent Love, Joy and Revelry.

The Martyrdom of St Philip
(c.1639) José de Ribera moved from his native Valencia to Naples as a young man. There he was influenced by Caravaggio's dramatic use of light and shadow, known as chiaroscuro, as seen in this work.

STAR EXHIBITS

★ Velázquez Collection

★ Goya Collection

The Garden of Delights
(c.1505)
Hieronymus Bosch (El Bosco in Spanish), one of Felipe II's favourite artists, is especially well represented in the Prado. This enigmatic painting depicts paradise and hell.

GALLERY GUIDE

The new link between the Jerónimos Building and the main Villanueva building is expected to open by 2006. Exhibits are arranged in schools, with the oldest works displayed on the lowest floors. The first floor houses 17th century Spanish paintings including works by Goya and Velázquez.

VISITORS' CHECKLIST

Paseo del Prado. **Map** 7 C3. **Tel** 91 330 28 00. Ⓜ Atocha, Banco de España. 🚌 6, 10, 14, 19, 27, 34, 37, 45. ☐ 9am–7pm Tue–Sun. ☐ 1 Jan, Good Fri, 1 May, 25 Dec. 🎟 (free Sun). ♿ 📷 🍴 ☕ 🏊 🛍 📷
Casón del Buen Retiro: Calle de Alfonso XII 28. **Tel** 91 330 28 00. 🔵 Until Spring 2006. **www**.museoprado.mcu.es

Second floor

First floor

★ **Goya Collection**
In The Clothed Maja *and* The Naked Maja *(both c.1800), Goya tackled the taboo subject of nudity, for which he was later accused of being obscene.*

Ground floor

Stairs to lower floor, 💻 🚻 ♿

The Adoration of the Shepherds *(1612–14)*
This dramatic work shows the elongated figures and swirling garments typical of El Greco's style. It was painted during his late Mannerist period for his own funerary chapel.

Main entrance

The Annunciation
Fra Angelico's work of c.1427 is a high point of Italy's Early Renaissance, as illustrated by the detailed architectural setting and deep perspective of the interior.

KEY TO FLOORPLAN

■	Spanish painting
■	Flemish and Dutch painting
■	Italian painting
■	French painting
■	German painting
■	British painting
■	Sculpture
■	Temporary Exhibitions
■	Non-exhibition space

Jerónimos Building

CALLE DE MORETO

Underground link

Villanueva Building

Casón del Buen Retiro

CALLE DE FELIPE IV

Salón de Reinos

PASEO DEL PRADO

CHANGES AT THE PRADO

An underground link in glass and steel will join the Villanueva Building with the Jerónimos Building and house a shop, café, restaurant and cloakroom. In the final phase the Salón de Reinos (*see p285*) will become part of the Prado.

■	Museum Buildings
☐	Due to open in 2007

Exploring the Prado's Collection

The importance of the Prado is founded on its royal collections. The wealth of foreign art, including many of Europe's finest works, reflects the historical power of the Spanish crown (see pp58-63). The Low Countries and parts of Italy were under Spanish domination for centuries. The 18th century was an era of French influence, following the Bourbon accession to the Spanish throne. The Prado is worthy of repeated visits, but if you go only once, see the Spanish works of the 17th century.

St Dominic of Silos Enthroned as Abbot (1474–7) by Bermejo

SPANISH PAINTING

Right up to the 19th century, Spanish painting focused on religious and royal themes. Although the limited subject matter was in some ways a restriction, it also offered a sharp focus that seems to have suited Spanish painters.

Spain's early medieval art is represented somewhat sketchily in the Prado but there are some examples such as the anonymous mural paintings from the Holy Cross hermitage in Maderuelo, which show a Romanesque heaviness of line and forceful characterization.

Spanish Gothic art can be seen in the Prado in the works of Bartolomé Bermejo and Fernando Gallego. The sense of realism in their paintings was borrowed from Flemish masters of the time.

Renaissance features began to emerge in the works of painters such as Pedro de Berruguete, whose *Auto-de-fé* is both chilling and lively. *St Catherine*, by Fernando Yáñez de la Almedina, shows the influence of Leonardo da Vinci, for whom Yáñez probably worked while training in Italy.

What is often considered as a truly Spanish style – with its highly wrought emotion and deepening sombreness – first started to emerge in the 16th century in the paintings of the Mannerists. This is evident in Pedro Machuca's fierce *Descent from the Cross* and in the Madonnas of Luis de Morales, "the Divine". The elongation of the human figure in Morales' work is carried to a greater extreme by Domenikos Theotocopoulos, better known as El Greco (see p32). Although many of his masterpieces remain in his adopted town

Saturn Devouring One of his Sons (1820–23) by Francisco de Goya

of Toledo (see p391), the Prado has an impressive collection, including *The Nobleman with his Hand on his Chest*.

The Golden Age (see pp60–1) was a particularly productive time for Spanish art. José de Ribera, who lived in (Spanish) Naples, followed Caravaggio in combining realism of character with the techniques of chiaroscuro and tenebrism. Another master who used this method was Francisco Ribalta, whose *Christ Embracing St Bernard* is here. Zurbarán, known for his still lifes and portraits of saints and monks, is also a notable presence in the Prado.

This period, however, is best represented by the work of Diego Velázquez. As Spain's leading court painter from his late twenties until his death, he produced scenes of heightened realism, royal portraits, and religious and mythological paintings. Examples of all of these are displayed in the Prado. Perhaps his greatest work is *Las Meninas* (see pp32–3).

Another great Spanish painter, Goya, revived Spanish art in the 18th century. He first specialized in cartoons for tapestries, then became a court painter. His work went on to embrace the horrors of war, as seen here in *The 3rd of May in Madrid* (see pp62–3), and culminated in a sombre series known as *The Black Paintings*.

Still Life with Four Vessels (c.1658–64) by Francisco de Zurbarán

CASÓN DEL BUEN RETIRO

On the hill behind the Prado is its annexe, the Casón del Buen Retiro, once part of the Palacio del Buen Retiro *(see p297)*. Its exhibits have included late 19th-century and early 20th-century works, as well as Neo-Classical and Romantic art, and paintings on historical themes. The Casón del Buen Retiro is expected to re-open to the public in 2006. The exhibits are likely to move to the Prado in about 2009.

Children at the Beach (1910) by Joaquín Sorolla

FLEMISH AND DUTCH PAINTING

Spain's long connection with the Low Countries *(see pp60–1)* led naturally to an intense admiration for the so-called Flemish primitives. Many exceptional works now hang in the Prado. *St Barbara*, by Robert Campin, has a quirky intimacy, and Rogier van der Weyden's *The Deposition* is an unquestioned masterpiece. Most notable of all, however, are Hieronymus Bosch's weird and eloquent inventions, which were collected by Felipe II. The Prado has some of his major paintings, including the *Temptation of St Anthony* and *The Haywain*. Works from the 16th century include the magnificent *Triumph of Death* by Brueghel the Elder. There are nearly 100 canvases by the 17th-century Flemish painter Peter Paul Rubens, of which the greatest is *The Adoration of the Magi*. The two most notable Dutch paintings on display are by Rembrandt: *Artemisia*, and a fine self-portrait.

David Victorious over Goliath (c.1600) by Caravaggio

ITALIAN PAINTING

The Prado is the envy of many museums, not least for its vast collection of Italian paintings. Botticelli's dramatic wooden panels telling *The Story of Nastagio degli Onesti*, a vision of a knight forever condemned to hunt down and kill his own beloved, are a sinister high point. Raphael contributes the superb *Christ Falls on the Way to Calvary* and the sentimental *The Holy Family of the Lamb*.

Christ Washing the Disciples' Feet, by Tintoretto, is a profound masterpiece. Venetian masters Veronese and Titian are also very well represented. Titian served as court painter to Charles V, and few works express the drama of Habsburg rule so deeply as his sombre painting *The Emperor Charles V at Mühlberg*. Also on display are works by Giordano, Caravaggio and Tiepolo, master of Italian rococo.

FRENCH PAINTING

Marriages between French and Spanish royalty in the 17th century, culminating in the Bourbon accession to the throne in the 18th century, brought French art to Spain. The Prado has eight works attributed to Poussin, among them his serene *Parnassus* and *Landscape with St Jerome*. The magnificent *Landscape with the Embarkation of St Paula Romana at Ostia* is the best work here by Claude Lorrain. Among the 18th-century artists featured are Antoine Watteau and Jean Ranc. *Felipe V* is the work of the royal portraitist Louis-Michel van Loo.

GERMAN PAINTING

Although German art is not especially well represented in the Prado, there are several paintings by Albrecht Dürer, such as his lively *Self-Portrait*, painted at the age of 26. Lucas Cranach also figures. Works by the late 18th-century painter Anton Raffael Mengs include portraits of Carlos III.

The Deposition (c.1430) by Rogier van der Weyden

Floor mosaic in the Museo Arqueológico Nacional

Plaza de Colón ⑯

Map 6 D5. Ⓜ Serrano, Colón.

This large square, one of Madrid's focal points, is dedicated to Christopher Columbus (Colón in Spanish).

It is overlooked by huge tower blocks, built in the 1970s to replace the 19th-century mansions which stood here.

On the south side is a palace housing the National Library and Archaeological Museum. The Post-Modernist skyscraper of the Heron Corporation towers over the square from the far side of the Paseo de la Castellana.

The real feature of the square, however, is the pair of monuments dedicated to the discoverer of the Americas. The prettiest, and oldest, is a Neo-Gothic spire made in 1885, with Columbus at its top, pointing west. Carved reliefs on the plinth give highlights of his discoveries. Across the square is the second, more modern – a cluster of four large concrete shapes inscribed with quotations about Columbus's journey to America (see p57).

Constantly busy with traffic, the plaza may seem an unlikely venue for cultural events. Beneath it, however, is an extensive complex, the Centro Cultural de la Villa de Madrid, which includes the city's municipal art centre,

exhibition halls, lecture rooms, a theatre and a café. The terminal for the bus which runs to and from the airport (see p674) is also located underground.

Calle de Serrano ⑰

Map 8 D1. Ⓜ Serrano.

Named after a 19th-century politician, Madrid's smartest shopping street runs north from the Plaza de la Independencia to the Plaza del Ecuador, in the district of Salamanca. The street is lined with shops (p316) – many specializing in luxury items – housed in old-fashioned mansion-blocks. Several of the country's top designers, including Adolfo Domínguez and Purificación García, have boutiques towards the north, near the ABC Serrano (see p317) and the Museo Lázaro Galdiano (see p305). Branches of the Italian shops Versace, Gucci, Escada and Armani, as well as the French Chanel, can be found on the Calle de José Ortega y Gasset.

Lower down the Calle de Serrano, towards Serrano metro station, are two branches of El Corte Inglés. On the Calle de Claudio Coello, which runs parallel with Serrano, there are several lavish antique shops, in keeping with the area's up-market atmosphere.

Statue of Columbus, Plaza de Colón

Museo Arqueológico Nacional ⑱

Calle de Serrano 13. **Map** 6 D5.
Tel 91 577 79 12. Ⓜ Serrano.
◯ 9:30am – 8:30pm Tue – Sat, 9:30am–2:30pm Sun. ● public hols. ⊠ (free Sat pm & Sun). & ☐ 🖼 ☐ www.man.es

With hundreds of exhibits, ranging from prehistoric times to the 19th century, this museum is one of Madrid's best. Founded by Isabel II in 1867, it consists mainly of material uncovered during excavations all over Spain, as well as pieces from Egypt, Ancient Greece and the Etruscan civilization.

The earliest finds – from the prehistoric era – are arranged in chronological order in the basement. Highlights include an exhibition on the ancient civilization of El Argar in Andalusia (see p48), and a display of jewellery uncovered at the Roman settlement of Numantia, near Soria (see p377).

The museum's ground floor is largely devoted to the period between Roman and Mudéjar Spain. Iberian culture is also represented, with two notable sculptures – La Dama de Elche (see p48) and La Dama de Baza. The Roman period is illustrated with some impressive mosaics, including Monks and Seasons, from Hellín (Albacete), and Bacchus and his Train, from Zaragoza.

Outstanding pieces from the Visigothic period include a collection of 7th-century gold votive crowns from Toledo province, known as the Treasure of Guarrazar.

On show from the Islamic era is pottery uncovered from Medina Azahara in Andalusia (see p477), and metal objects. Romanesque exhibits include an ivory crucifix carved in 1063 for Fernando I of Castilla-León and his Queen, Doña Sancha, and the Madonna and Child from Sahagún, considered a masterpiece of Spanish art.

Steps outside the museum's entrance lead underground to an exact replica of the Altamira caves in Cantabria (see p112) – complete with their paintings of the Paleolithic era.

For hotels and restaurants in this region see pp579–82 and pp629–32

Parque del Retiro ⑲

Map 8 E3. **Tel** *91 409 23 36.* Ⓜ *Retiro, Ibiza, Atocha.* 🅿 *at night.* ♿

The Retiro Park, in Madrid's smart Jerónimos district, takes its name from Felipe IV's royal palace complex, which once stood here. Today, all that remains of the palace is the **Casón del Buen Retiro** *(see p295)* and the **Salón de Reinos** *(see p287).*

Used privately by the royal family from 1632, the park became the scene of elaborate pageants, bullfights and mock naval battles. In the 18th century it was partially opened to the public, provided visitors were formally dressed, and in 1869 it was fully opened. Today, the Retiro remains one of the most popular places for relaxing in Madrid.

A short stroll from the park's northern entrance down the tree-lined avenue leads to the pleasure lake, where rowing boats can be hired. On one side of the lake is a half-moon colonnade in front of which an equestrian statue of Alfonso XII rides high on a column. Opposite, portrait painters and fortune-tellers ply their trade.

To the south of the lake are two attractive palaces. The Neo-Classical **Palacio de Velázquez** and the **Palacio de Cristal** (Crystal Palace) were built by Velázquez Bosco in 1887 as venues for exhibitions held in that year.

Statue of Bourbon king Carlos III in the Real Jardín Botánico

Real Jardín Botánico ⑳

Plaza de Murillo 2. **Map** 8 D4. **Tel** *91 420 30 17.* Ⓜ *Atocha.* ⭘ *10am–dusk daily.* 📷 ♿

South of the Prado *(see pp292–5)*, and a suitable place for resting after visiting the gallery, are the Royal Botanical Gardens. Inspired by Carlos III, they were designed in 1781 by botanist Gómez Ortega and Juan de Villanueva, the architect of the Prado.

Interest in the plants of South America and the Philippines took hold during the Spanish Enlightenment *(see p62)*, and the neatly laid out beds offer a huge variety of flora, ranging from trees and shrubs to medicinal plants and herbs.

Estación de Atocha ㉑

Plaza del Emperador Carlos V. **Map** 8 D5. **Tel** *902 240 202.* Ⓜ *Atocha RENFE.* ⭘ *5:30am–midnight daily.* ♿

Madrid's first railway service, from Atocha to Aranjuez, was inaugurated in 1851. Forty years later Atocha station was replaced by a new building, which, in the 1980s, was given a modern extension. The older part of the station, built of glass and wrought iron, now houses an indoor palm garden. Adjoining it is the terminus for the high-speed AVE trains to Seville, Córdoba, Zaragoza and Lleida, extending to Barcelona and France by 2007 *(see p678)*.

The Ministerio de Agricultura, opposite, is a spendid late 19th-century building adorned with tiled corner domes.

Entrance of Madrid's Estación de Atocha, busy with travellers

Monument of Alfonso XII (1901), facing the Retiro's boating lake

Museo Nacional Centro de Arte Reina Sofía **②**

The highlight of this museum of 20th-century art is Picasso's *Guernica*. There are, however, other major works by influential artists, including Miró. The collection is housed in Madrid's former General Hospital, built in the late 18th century. Major extensions to the museum, designed by Jean Nouvel, are due to be completed by 2006, allowing the permanent collection to extend over 3 floors. The new glass buildings will include 2 temporary exhibition rooms, a library, café, art shops and an auditorium.

Portrait II *(1938)*
Joan Miró's huge work shows elements of Surrealism, but was painted more than ten years after his true Surrealist period ended.

New extension

★ **Woman in Blue** *(1901)*
Picasso disowned this work after it won only an honourable mention in a national competition. Decades later it was located and acquired by the Spanish state.

Landscape at Cadaqués
Salvador Dalí was born in Figueres in Catalonia. He became a frequent visitor to the town of Cadaqués, on the Costa Brava (see p217), where he painted this landscape in the summer of 1923.

Accident
Alfonso Ponce de León's disturbing work, painted in 1936, prefigured his death in a car crash later that same year.

STAR EXHIBITS

- ★ Woman in Blue by Picasso
- ★ La Tertulia del Café de Pombo by Solana
- ★ Guernica by Picasso

★ **La Tertulia del Café de Pombo** *(1920)*
José Gutiérrez Solana depicts a gathering of intellectuals (tertulia) *in a famous café in Madrid, which no longer exists.*

Glass lift

Entrance

**Toki-Egin
(Homenaje a San Juan de la Cruz)** *(1952)*
In his abstract sculptures, Eduardo Chillida used a variety of materials, such as wood, iron and steel, to convey strength.

VISITORS' CHECKLIST

Calle Santa Isabel 52. **Map** 7 C5.
Tel *91 467 50 62.* Atocha.
6, 14, 18, 19, 27, 45, 55, 68.
10am–9pm Mon & Wed–Sat,
10am–2:30pm Sun. 1 Jan,
24, 25, 31 Dec & some public
hols. *(free Sat pm & Sun).*
www.museoreinasofia.mcu.es

GALLERY GUIDE

The permanent collection is on the second, third and fourth floors, arranged around an open courtyard. It traces art chronologically through the 20th century, starting on the second floor. The third floor displays works from mid-1930s to 1960s and the fourth floor continues through to present day works. Individual rooms are allocated to significant artists such as Dalí, Miró and Picasso. Two temporary exhibition rooms are located in a new, adjoining building.

KEY TO FLOORPLAN

☐ Exhibition space

☐ Non-exhibition space

Visitors admiring *Guernica*

★ PICASSO'S *GUERNICA*

The most famous single work of the 20th century, this Civil War protest painting *(see pp66–7)* was commissioned by the Spanish Republican government in 1937 for a Paris exhibition. The artist found his inspiration in the mass air attack of the same year on the Basque town of Gernika-Lumo *(see p118)*, by German pilots flying for the Nationalist air force. The painting hung in a New York gallery until 1981, reflecting the artist's wish that it should not return to Spain until democracy was re-established. It was moved here from the Prado in 1992.

FURTHER AFIELD

Several of Madrid's best sights, including some interesting but little-known museums, lie outside the city centre. The axis of modern Madrid is the Paseo de la Castellana, a long, wide avenue lined by skyscraper offices and busy with traffic. A journey along it gives a glimpse of Madrid as Spain's commercial and administrative capital. La Castellana skirts the Barrio de Salamanca, an upmarket district of stylish boutiques, named after the 19th-century aristocrat who built it, the Marquis de Salamanca.

Statue in Plaza de Cascorro

The districts around Old Madrid, especially Malasaña and La Latina, offer a more typically authentic *Madrileño* atmosphere. On Sundays, some of the old streets are crowded with bargain-hunters at the sprawling second-hand market, El Rastro. If you need to escape from the bustle of the city for a while, west of Old Madrid, across the Río Manzanares, is Madrid's vast, green recreation ground, the Casa de Campo, with its pleasant pine woods, boating lake, amusement park and zoo.

SIGHTS AT A GLANCE

Historic Buildings
Palacio de Liria **9**
Real Fábrica de Tapices **16**
Templo de Debod **6**

Churches and Convents
Ermita de San Antonio de la Florida **5**

Museums and Galleries
Museo de América **7**
Museo Cerralbo **8**
Museo Lázaro Galdiano **13**

Museo Municipal **11**
Museo Sorolla **12**

Streets, Squares and Parks
Casa de Campo **4**
La Latina **2**
Malasaña **10**
Paseo de la Castellana **14**
Plaza de la Paja **3**
Plaza de Toros de Las Ventas **15**
El Rastro **1**

| 0 kilometres | | 2 |
| 0 miles | 1 | |

KEY

	Main sightseeing area
	Parks and open spaces
🚊	Railway station
══	Motorway
══	Major road
══	Minor road

SIGHTS OUTSIDE THE CITY CENTRE

◁ **Mudéjar arches and tilework on the exterior of the Plaza de Toros de Las Ventas**

El Rastro ❶

Calle Ribera de Curtidores. **Map** 4
E4. Ⓜ *La Latina, Embajadores.* ☐
10am– 2pm Sun & public hols.

Madrid's celebrated flea
market *(see p317)*, established
in the Middle Ages, has its
hub in the Plaza de Cascorro
and sprawls downhill towards
the Río Manzanares. The
main street is the Calle Ribera
de Curtidores, or "Tanners'
Riverbank", once the centre of
the slaughterhouse and
tanning industry.

Although some people claim
that the Rastro has changed a
great deal since its heyday
during the 19th century, there
are still plenty of *Madrileños*,
as well as tourists, who shop
here. They come in search of
a bargain from the stalls which
sell a huge range of wares –
anything from new furniture
to second-hand clothes. The
wide range of goods and the
lively crowds in the Rastro
make it an ideal way to spend
a Sunday morning.

The Calle de Embajadores is
the market's other main street.
It runs down past the dusty
Baroque façade of the Iglesia
de San Cayetano, designed by
José Churriguera and Pedro
de Ribera. Its interior has been
restored since fire destroyed
it during the Civil War.

Further along the street is the
former Real Fábrica de Tabacos
(the Royal Tobacco Factory),
begun as a state enterprise in
1809 and now an art gallery.
Its female workers had a reputation for taking a hard-line
stance in industrial disputes.

**Shoppers browsing around the
Rastro flea market**

La Latina ❷

Map 4 D4. Ⓜ *La Latina, Lavapiés.*

The district of La Latina,
together with the adjacent
Lavapiés, is considered to be
the heart of *castizo* Madrid.
This term is used to describe
the culture of the traditional
working classes of Madrid –
that of the true *Madrileño*.

La Latina runs along the
city's southern hillside from
the Plaza Puerta de Moros,
southwards through the streets
where the Rastro is held. To
the east it merges with
Lavapiés. La Latina's steep
streets are lined with tall,
narrow houses, renovated to
form an attractive neighbourhood. There are old-fashioned
bars around the Plaza del
Humilladero, although the
streets to the east of La Latina,
in the Lavapiés district, have
sadly become notorious for
petty crime.

**Bottles of wine for sale in an old-
style bar in Lavapiés**

Plaza de la Paja ❸

Map 4 D3. Ⓜ *La Latina.*

Once the focus of medieval
Madrid, the area around the
Plaza de la Paja – literally
Straw Square – is still atmospheric. Despite its location, in
a less than affluent district,
many interesting buildings are
located on the square.

Climbing upwards from the
Calle de Segovia, a glimpse
left along the Calle Príncipe
Anglona yields a view of the
Mudéjar-style brick tower of
the Iglesia de San Pedro, dating

Interior of San Francisco el Grande

from the 14th century. Up
past the fountain, the Plaza
de la Paja ends with the harsh
stone walls of the Capilla del
Obispo, or Bishop's Chapel,
belonging originally to the
adjoining Palacio Vargas. The
superb Plateresque altarpiece
is by Francisco Giralte. Up to
the left, the Baroque, cherub-
covered dome of the Iglesia
de San Andrés stands out.

Nearby is a small cluster of
interlinked squares, ending in
the Plaza Puerta de Moros, a
reminder of the Muslim community which once occupied
the area. From here, a right
turn leads to the domed bulk
of San Francisco el Grande, an
impressive landmark. Inside
the church is a painting by
Goya and his brother-in-law
Francisco Bayeu. The choir-
stalls were moved here from
the monastery of El Paular
(see pp328–9).

Casa de Campo ❹

Avenida de Portugal. **Tel** *91 463
63 34.* Ⓜ *Batán, Lago, Príncipe Pío,
Casa de Campo.*

This former royal hunting
ground, with pines and
scrubland stretching over 1,740
ha (4,300 acres), lies in western Madrid. Its wide range of
amenities make it a popular
daytime recreation area. Attractions include a boating lake, a
zoo, and an amusement park –
the Parque de Atracciones *(see
p321).* Sports enthusiasts can
make use of the swimming
pool and jogging track. In the
summer the park is also used
as a venue for rock concerts.

Egyptian temple of Debod, with two of its original gateways

Ermita de San Antonio de la Florida ❺

Glorieta San Antonio de la Florida 5. **Tel** 91 542 07 22. Príncipe Pío. 10am–2pm, 4 – 8pm Tue – Fri, 10am – 2pm Sat & Sun. public hols. www.munimadrid.es

Goya enthusiasts should not miss a visit to the Neo-Classical Ermita de San Antonio de la Florida, built during the reign of Carlos IV. The present church stands on the site of two previous ones, and is dedicated to St Anthony. It is named after the pasture-land of la Florida, on which the original church was built.

Goya took just four months, in 1798, to paint the cupola with an immense fresco. It depicts the resurrection of a murdered man who rises in order to prove the innocence of the falsely accused father of St Anthony. The characters in it are everyday people of the late 18th century: lurking, low-life types and lively *majas* (see

p293) – shrewd but elegant women. The fresco is considered by many art critics to be among Goya's finest works.

The tomb of the artist is housed in the chapel. His remains were brought here from Bordeaux, where he died in exile in 1828 (*see p239*).

Templo de Debod ❻

Paseo de Pintor Rosales. **Map** 1 B5. **Tel** 91 366 74 15. Ventura Rodríguez, Plaza de España. 10am–2pm Tue–Sun; Apr–Sep: 6–8pm Tue–Fri; Oct– Mar: 4:15–6:15pm Tue–Fri. public hols. www.munimadrid.es

The Egyptian temple of Debod, built in the 2nd century BC, was rescued from the area flooded by the Aswan Dam and given to Spain as a tribute to Spanish engineers involved

in the project. The temple is carved with shallow reliefs, and stands in a line with two of its original three gateways. They are situated on high ground above the Río Manzanares, in the gardens of the Parque del Oeste. From the park there are sweeping views over the Casa de Campo to the Guadarrama mountains.

The park is the site of the former Montaña barracks, which were stormed by the populace at the start of the Civil War in 1936.

Further to the west, below the brow of the hill, there is an attractive rose garden.

Museo de América ❼

Avenida de los Reyes Católicos 6. **Tel** 91 549 26 41. Moncloa. 9:30am–3pm Tue–Sat, 10am–3pm Sun. some public hols. (free Sun). www.museodeamerica.es

This handsome museum houses artifacts related to Spain's colonization of parts of the Americas. Many of the exhibits, which range from prehistoric times to the present, were brought back to Europe by early explorers of the New World (*see pp58–9*).

The collection is arranged on the first and second floors, and individual rooms are given a cultural theme such as society, communication and religion. There is documentation of the Atlantic voyages by the first explorers, and examples of the objects which they found. The highlight of the museum is perhaps the rare Mayan *Códice Trocortesiano* (AD 1250– 1500) from Mexico, a type of parchment illustrated with hieroglyphics of scenes from everyday life. Also worth seeing are the solid gold funereal ornaments from Colombia, the Treasure of the Quimbayas (AD 500–1000), and the collection of contemporary folk art from some of Spain's former American colonies.

Piece of the Treasure of the Quimbayas

Museo Cerralbo 8

Calle Ventura Rodríguez 17. **Map** 1 C5.
Tel *91 547 36 46.* Plaza de España,
Ventura Rodríguez. ☐ Jul & Aug:
9:30am–2pm Tue–Sat; 10am–2pm Sun;
Sep–Jun: 9:30am–3pm Tue–Sat,
10am–3pm Sun. (free Wed &
Sun). **www**.museocerralbo.es

This 19th-century mansion
near the Plaza de España is a
monument to Enrique de
Aguilera y Gamboa, the 17th
Marquis of Cerralbo. A com-
pulsive collector of art and
artifacts, he bequeathed his
lifetime's collection to the
nation in 1922, stipulating that
the exhibits be arranged
exactly as he left them. They
range from Iberian pottery to
18th-century marble busts.

One of the star exhibits is El
Greco's *The Ecstasy of Saint
Francis of Assisi*. There are also
paintings by Ribera, Zurbarán,
Alonso Cano and Goya, which
hang in the Picture Gallery.

The focal point of the main
floor is the ballroom, lavishly
decorated with mirrors. A large
collection of weaponry is on
display on this floor.

Palacio de Liria 9

Calle de la Princesa 20. ***Tel*** *91 547 53
02.* Ventura Rodríguez. ☐ write
a year in advance for permission.

The lavish but much restored
Palacio de Liria was
completed by Ventura
Rodríguez in 1780. Once the
residence of the Alba family,
and still owned by the
Duchess, it can be visited by
appointment only.

The palace houses the Albas'
outstanding collection of art,
and Flemish tapestries. There
are paintings by Titian, Rubens
and Rembrandt. Spanish art is
particularly well represented,
with major works by Goya,
such as his 1795 portrait of the
Duchess of Alba, as well as
examples of work by El Greco,
Zurbarán and Velázquez.

Behind the palace is the
Cuartel del Conde-Duque, the
former barracks of the Count-
Duke Olivares, Felipe IV's
minister. They were built in
1720 by Pedro de Ribera,
who adorned them with a
Baroque façade. The barracks
now house a cultural centre.

Rooftops in the Malasaña district

Malasaña 10

Map 2 F5. Tribunal, Bilbao.

A feeling of the authentic
old Madrid pervades this
district of narrow, sloping
streets and tall houses. For
some years it was the centre
of the *movida*, the frenzied
nightlife which began after
the death of Franco.

A walk along the Calle San
Andrés leads to the Plaza del
Dos de Mayo. In the centre is
a monument to artillery officers
Daoíz and Velarde, who defended the barracks which
stood here at the time of the
uprising against the French in
1808 *(see p63)*.

On Calle de la Puebla is the
Iglesia de San Antonio de los
Alemanes. The church was
founded by Felipe III in the
17th century as a hospital for
Portuguese immigrants, and
was later given over for use by
German émigrés. Inside, the
walls are decorated with 18th-
century frescoes by Giordano.

Museo Municipal 11

Calle de Fuencarral 78. **Map** 5 A4.
Tel *91 588 86 72.* Tribunal. ☐
9:30am–8pm Tue–Fri, 10am–2pm
Sat & Sun (Aug: 9:30am–2:30pm
Tue–Sun). public hols. by
appt. **www**.munimadrid.es

The Municipal Museum is
worth visiting just for its
Baroque doorway *(see p25)*
by Pedro de Ribera, arguably
the finest in Madrid. Housed
in the former hospice of St

Main staircase of the exuberant Museo Cerralbo

Ferdinand, the museum was inaugurated in 1929. The basement is devoted to the city's archaeology, while upstairs is a series of bird's-eye views and maps of Madrid. Among them is Pedro Texeiro's map of 1656, thought to be the oldest of the city. There is also a model of Madrid, made in 1830 by León Gil de Palacio.

Modern exhibits include a reconstruction of the collage-filled study of Ramón Gómez de la Serna, a key figure of the famous literary gatherings in the Café de Pombo *(see p299)*. The museum is undergoing refurbishment until 2007 so parts of the collection may be closed.

Sorolla's former studio in the Museo Sorolla

Baroque façade of the Museo Municipal, by Pedro de Ribera

Museo Sorolla ⓬

Paseo del General Martínez Campos 37. **Tel** *91 310 15 84.* Ⓜ *Rubén Darío, Iglesia, Gregorio Marañón.* ◷ *9:30am–3pm Tue–Sat, 10am–3pm Sun.* ◷ *(free Sun).*

The former studio-mansion of Valencian Impressionist painter Joaquín Sorolla, now a museum housing his paintings, has been left virtually as it was when he died in 1923.

Although Sorolla is perhaps best known for his brilliantly lit Mediterranean beach scenes, the changing styles of his paintings are well represented in the museum, with examples of his gentle portraiture and a series of works representing people from different parts of Spain. Also on display are various objects amassed during the artist's lifetime, including Span-

ish tiles and ceramics. The house, constructed in 1910, has an Andalusian-style garden designed by Sorolla himself.

Museo Lázaro Galdiano ⓭

Calle de Serrano 122. **Tel** *91 561 60 84.* Ⓜ *Núñez de Balboa, Rubén Darío, Gregorio Marañón.* ◷ *10am–4:30pm Wed–Mon* ● *public hols.* ◷ *free on Wed.* **www.flg.es**

This is one of the best art museums in the city. It is housed in the former mansion-home of the editor and financier José Lázaro Galdiano, and consists of his private collection of fine and applied art, bequeathed to the

Charles V's fob watch

nation in 1947. The collection ranges from the 7th to the 19th century and contains items of exceptional quality, ranging from less familiar Goya portraits to a mass of fob watches, including a cross-shaped pocket-watch worn by Charles V when hunting. Among the most beautiful objects are a series of Limoges enamels, miniature sculptures, and *The Saviour*, a portrait attributed to Leonardo da Vinci. The Museo features paintings by English artists Constable, Turner, Gainsborough and Reynolds, as well as 17th-century paintings by the likes of Spanish painters Velázquez, Zurbarán, Ribera, Murillo and El Greco.

LA MOVIDA

With Franco's death in 1975 came a new period of personal and artistic liberty. For the young, this was translated into the freedom to stay out late, drinking and sometimes sampling drugs. The phenomenon was known as *la movida*, "the action", and it was at its most intense in Madrid. Although analysts at the time saw it as having serious intellectual content, *la movida* has had few lasting cultural results, except for the emergence of satirical film director Pedro Almodóvar.

Poster for Almodóvar's *Women on the Verge of a Nervous Breakdown*

Torre de Picasso towering over the Paseo de la Castellana

Paseo de la Castellana 🄸

🚇 Santiago Bernabéu, Cuzco, Plaza de Castilla, Gregorio Marañón, Colón.

The busy traffic artery which cuts through eastern Madrid comprises several parts. Its southernmost portion – the Paseo del Prado (see pp284–5) – starts just north of the Estación de Atocha (see p297). The oldest section of the road, it dates from the reign of Carlos III, who built it as part of his embellishment of eastern Madrid (see p297). At the Plaza de Cibeles, the avenue becomes the handsome Paseo de Recoletos, which boasts fashionable cafés, including the Café Gijón (see p291).

The Plaza de Colón marks the start of the Paseo de la Castellana, whose pavement cafés have become a focal point for young Madrid's social life. This northernmost section has several notable examples of modern architecture, including the huge grey Nuevos Ministerios building, completed under Franco. Further on, before reaching the Plaza de Lima, is the Torre de Picasso (see p25), one of Spain's tallest buildings. East of the square is the Estadio Bernabéu, home of Real Madrid Football Club (see p177). The building that dominates the Paseo, however, is the Puerta de Europa, locally known as "Torres Kio": twin glass blocks on either side of the road, built at an angle as if leaning toward each other.

Plaza de Toros de Las Ventas 🄸

Calle de Alcalá 237. **Tel** 91 356 22 00. 🚇 Ventas. ☐ for bullfights and concerts only. **Museo Taurino Tel** 91 725 18 57. ☐ Mar–Oct: 9:30am–2:30pm Tue–Fri, 10am–1pm Sun; Nov– Feb: 9:30am–2:30pm Mon–Fri. ♿

Whatever your opinion of bullfighting, Las Ventas is undoubtedly one of the most beautiful bullrings in Spain. Built in 1929 in Neo-Mudéjar style, it replaced the city's original bullring which stood near the Puerta de Alcalá. With its horsehoe arches around the outer galleries and the elaborate tilework decoration, it makes an attractive venue for the *corridas* held during the bullfighting season, from May to October. The statues outside the bullring are monuments to two renowned Spanish bullfighters: Antonio Bienvenida and José Cubero.

Adjoining the bullring is the Museo Taurino. The museum contains a varied collection of memorabilia, including portraits and sculptures of famous matadors, as well as the heads of several bulls killed during fights at Las Ventas. Visitors can view close up the tools of the bullfighter's trade: capes and *banderillas* – sharp darts used to wound the bull (see pp36–7). For some people, the gory highlight of the exhibition is the blood-drenched *traje de luces* worn by the legendary Manolete during his fateful bullfight at Linares

in Andalusia in 1947. Also on display is a costume which belonged to Juanita Cruz, a female bullfighter of the 1930s who was forced, in the face of prejudice, to leave Spain. In September and October, the bullring is used as a venue for a season of rock concerts.

Real Fábrica de Tapices 🄸

Calle Fuenterrabía 2. **Tel** 91 434 05 51. 🚇 Menéndez Pelayo. ☐ 10am–2pm Mon–Fri. ● Public hols & Aug. 🖥 www.realfatapices.com

Founded by Felipe V in 1721, the Royal Tapestry Factory is the sole survivor of several factories which were opened by the Bourbons (see pp62–3) during the 18th century. In 1889 the factory was relocated to this building just south of the Parque del Retiro.

Visitors can see the making of the carpets and tapestries by hand, a process which has changed little. Goya and his brother-in-law Francisco Bayeu created drawings, or cartoons, which were the inspiration for tapestries made for the royal family. Some of the cartoons are on display here; others can be seen in the Museo del Prado (see pp292–5). Some of the tapestries can be seen at El Pardo (see p332) and at El Escorial (see pp330–31). Nowadays one of the factory's main tasks is making and repairing the beautiful carpets decorating the Hotel Ritz (see p286).

Plaza de Toros de Las Ventas, Madrid's beautiful bullring

MADRID STREET FINDER

The map references given with the sights, shops and entertainment venues described in the Madrid section of the guide refer to the street maps on the following pages. Map references are also given for Madrid hotels *(see pp579–82),* and for bars and restaurants *(pp629–32).* The schematic map below shows the area of Madrid covered by the *Street Finder.* The symbols used for sights and other features are listed in the key at the foot of the page.

KEY TO STREET FINDER

Major sight	**P** Parking	Railway line
Place of interest	**i** Tourist information	Pedestrianized street
Other building	**+** Hospital with casualty unit	
Railway station	Police station	
Metro station	Church	**SCALE OF MAP PAGES**
Main bus stop	Convent or monastery	0 metres 250
Coach station	Post office	0 yards 250

0 kilometres   1

0 miles   0.5

3

A · B · C

1

Estación del Norte
(Príncipe Pío)

Príncipe Pío

Príncipe Pío

GLORIETA DE
SAN VICENTE

CALLE DE CADARSO

Palacio
del Sena

PASEO DEL REY

C/ ESTANISLAO FIGUERAS

CALLE DE LA ILUSTRACIÓN

CALLE DE ARRIAZA

CALLE DE

CUESTA DE SAN VICENTE

JARDINES DE
SABATINI

Convento de la
Encarnación

C/ DE SAN QUI

JARDINES D
CABO NOVA

AVENIDA DE PORTUGAL

PASEO DE LA VIRGEN DEL PUERTO

JARDINES
DEL PALACIO
REAL

2

CAMPO

DEL

MORO

Palacio
Real

PLAZA DE
ORIENTE

PLAZA DE
ARMAS

CALLE DE REQUE

CALLE DE
REBECO

CALLE DE NOBLEJ/
PLA
RAI

Iglesia de
San Nicolás

C/ DEL
BIOMBO

CALLE DE LA VEGA

Catedral de la
Almudena

C/ DEL FACTOR

CALLE DE LA ALMUDENA

CALLE DE LOS CONSEJOS

C/ DEL RETIL

C/ DE LA V

PASEO DE LA CIUDAD DE PLASENCIA

PARQUE DE ATENAS

CUESTA DE LA VEGA

GTA
AZORÍN

GTA
BOCCHERINI

Muralla
Árabe

CALLE

CALLE DE BAILEN

CALLE DE SEGOVIA

PARQUE EMIR
MOHAMED I

CALLE

DE

SEGOVIA

3

CALLE DE MANZANARES

CALLE DEL MAZARREDO

RONDA DE SEGOVIA

CUESTA DE JAVALQUINTO

JARDINES DE
LAS VISTILLAS

CALLE DE
VALLICIERGO

CALLE DE BEATRIZ GALINDO

CTA DE
RAMÓN

PLAZA DE GABRIEL
MIRÓ

CUESTA DE LOS CIEGOS

PLAZA DEL
ALAMILLO

CAÑOS
VIEJOS

PLAZA DE
LA MORERÍA

C/ DE GRANADO

PLAZA DE
GRANADO

CALLE ANGOSTA DE
LOS MANCEBOS

C/ REDONDILLA

C/ DE LOS MANCE

C/ DEL

C/ DE

CALLE DE LA BAILEN

CALLE DE MORENO NIETO

CALLE DE LINNEO

CALLE DE JUAN

CALLE DEL FOSFORO

CALLE PIZARRA

CALLE JEMENUÑO

CALLE DE LOS MELANCÓLICOS

CALLE DE NIEVA

CALLE DE SANTA MARÍA LA REAL

PASEO DE LA VIRGEN DEL PUERTO

RONDA DE SEGOVIA

PASEO DE SEGOVIA

IMPERIAL

4

CALLE ALGECIRAS

CUESTA DE LAS DESCARGAS

CALLE DE SAN BUENA VENTURA

CALLE DE JERTE

TRAVESÍA DE
LAS VISTILLAS

PLAZA DE
SAN FRANCISCO

San Francisco
el Grande

CARRERA DE SAN ISIDRO LABRADOR

CALLE DE SAN

GRAN VÍA DE SAN FRANCISCO

CALLE DE LAS AGUAS

CALLE DEL ANGEL

CALLE DE CALATRAVA

PLA
LOS E

FRANCISC

PEDRO

DON

CALLE DEL ROSARIO

CALLE DE SAN BERNABÉ

CALLE DE LA VENTOSA

CALLE DE SAN FRANCISCO

CALLE DE LA PALOMA

CALLE DE LA

C/ DE RUY GONZÁLEZ DE CLAVIJO

5

GILMON

TRAVESÍA DE GILMON

CALLE DE LEONOR DE LA VEGA

CALLEJON DEL MERCADO

GLORIE
DE
PUERTA DE T

A · B · C

SHOPPING IN MADRID

Madrid is a shoppers' paradise, where designer stores compete for attention with small, quirky shops. Madrid still has more independent and family-run shops than most European capitals, so it should not be hard to pick up some truly original gifts. There are two main shopping hearts in the city – the

Selection of cakes

crowded and popular streets around the pedestrianized Preciados and the Plaza del Sol, and Calle de la Princesa and adjacent streets. The Salamanca district is host to designer brands as well as up-market antiques, while for the latest streetware visit the Chueca district. The colourful food markets dotted around the city are well worth a visit.

OPENING HOURS

Due to Spanish meal times, shopping hours in Madrid are different from many other European cities. Most shops are open from 10am to 2pm and 5 to 8pm, though larger stores tend to stay open during lunch and close at 10pm. Small shops often close on Saturday afternoon. Shopping centres, department stores and big shops are permitted to open on the first Sunday of the month. Many small shops close for a month (usually August) in the summer.

FOOD AND DRINK

Madrid is a paradise for gourmet food shopping. Strongly scented saffron, matured ewe's cheese or a fruity extra-virgin olive oil all make ideal gifts. Spain has a deep-rooted tradition of pork products, ranging from whole hams to sausages of every shape and size. The best and most expensive ham is Ibérico, from the small, black-hoofed Iberian pig. In Old Madrid, branches of Museo del Jamón have an enormous range of Spanish hams,

cheeses and cured sausages. The department store **El Corte Inglés** has its own department dedicated to gourmet delicacies, as well as a supermarket for more general groceries. There are smaller delicatessens in nearly every district. In the Salamanca area visit **Mantequerías Bravo**, famous for its excellent cheeses, preserves and sweets.

If you are looking for good wine, head to **Reserva y Cata**, an outlet with a long history of selling Spanish and Portuguese wines. It also organizes tasting sessions. **Lavinia**, in the Salamanca district, is said to be Europe's biggest wine shop, with more than 1,500 brands available. For a truly authentic Madrileño souvenir, try **La Violeta**, famous for its fragrant violet sweets.

MARKETS

A favourite local activity is shopping at the street, or flea, markets, where you can spend a pleasant few hours browsing for antiques, second-hand clothes, pottery, handicrafts and furniture. Some markets are focused on only one item, such as the Sunday morning stamp, postcard and coin market under the arches of Plaza Mayor, or the Cuesta de Moyano at the Atocha end of Paseo de Prado, where stalls selling second-hand books are set up daily. The legendary El Rastro Sunday flea market (see p302) is a must for any visitor to Madrid, not only for the variety of goods to be found, from

The enticing frontage of the Museo del Jamón

Inside one of the many antique shops in the streets around El Rastro

antiques to trendy garments, but also for its lively atmosphere. It gets really crowded from 12 noon onwards, with bargain-hunters rubbing shoulders with those out to enjoy a pre-lunch apéritif at the numerous bars of the La Latina area. Be careful, however, as pick-pockets frequent the market.

Visit the handicrafts market in Plaza Comendadoras on Saturday evenings from 6pm for diverse pieces by Madrid's artists. The best place for paintings is the street market near Sol on Sunday mornings, organized by the art association, Taller Abierto.

Among the food markets, it is worth visiting the colourful Mercado de San Miguel in Plaza San Miguel. Set up in an early 20th-century building, it is not the biggest market, but it is certainly one of the nicest. The stallholders offer an array of delicious produce, including traditional cured meats and Spanish cheeses.

ANNUAL FAIRS

The contemporary art fair, ARCO, takes place in February. Whether you want to buy or simply browse, it provides a great opportunity to catch up on the latest trends in the art world.

In the week prior to Madrid's Fiesta de San Isidro (*see p40*) which begins on 15th May, you can buy earthern cookware and wine jugs at the Feria de la Cerámica held in the Plaza de las Comendadores in the colourful district of Malasaña. The Feria del Libro, held at

the end of May, is an impressive outdoor bookfair. Hundreds of stalls are set up in the Parque del Retiro, and publishers and bookshop owners exhibit their wares for two weeks, with the occasional book signing taking place as well.

On the Paseo de Recoletos, the Feria de Artesanos takes place every December, selling all kinds of crafts, making it ideal for Christmas shopping. Throughout December, the Plaza Mayor is the venue for a traditional Christmas fair – the Mercado de Artículos Navideños, where Christmas bric-à-brac can be picked up.

ANTIQUES AND ARTS

The commercial galleries and antiques shops of Madrid are all conveniently located around the Calle Barquillo in the Salamanca district, along the streets of Serrano, Velázquez, Jorge Juán and Claudio Coello. For cutting-edge Spanish art, head to the **Egam** gallery, considered to be one of Madrid's top galleries for contemporary art.

Antique shops can also be found in El Rastro flea market, mainly along Calle de la Ribera de Curtidores. **Hidalgo** is a classic that sells unusual collectors' items, such as keys, metal boxes and corkscrews.

For specialist antique outlets, ranging from 18th-century lacquered furniture, to Spanish paintings from the 16th to 18th centuries, visit **María García Cavestany** and **Theotokopoulos**. On

Calle Lagasca an antique centre, **Centro de Anticuarios**, hosts some of Madrid's top dealers under one roof. There are also opportunities for pricier antique shopping along the streets of the Prado, Santa Catalina and in the Mercado Puerta de Toledo. In Madrid, art and antiques auctions are held by both Spanish and international firms, including Sotheby's and Christie's.

SHOPPING CENTRES AND DEPARTMENT STORES

Among the best shopping centres, or *centros comerciales*, are the tempting and expensive malls of the elegant Salamanca neighbourhood. **El Jardín de Serrano** is a high-quality *galleria*, housed in two restored 19th-century palaces that stocks fashion, jewellery, gifts and accessories. **ABC Serrano** has a range of shops that includes home furniture as well as designer fashions and gifts.

If you want everything under one roof, visit the huge **La Vaguada** on the north side of Madrid, or **El Corte Inglés**, a national institution with branches throughout the city. The latter also has a travel agency and offers services such as photo development and shoe repairs.

The hip **Mitsuoko** multi-space store in Fuencaral stocks designer men's and women's fashions, and also has a large newspaper and magazine section, sushi bar and café.

Sunday morning in the busy Rastro flea market

FASHION

The Spanish chain stores **Zara** and **Mango** have now become an international phenomena, offering easy-to-wear clothes for women at very good prices. Zara also caters to men and children. Both stores have branches all over the city. For up-market fashion there are many well-known Spanish designers, such as **Amaya Arzuaga** and **Antonio Miró**, who have their own shops in Madrid, mainly in the Salamanca district.

Those in favour of a more unusual or original look should try **Ágata Ruiz de la Prada**'s creations (for children and adults), while the minimalist **Antonio Pernas'** shop specializes in more classic styles.

For high-quality designer menswear check out **Roberto Verino**, **Antonio Miró**, **Adolfo Domínguez** or **Caramelo**. These shops also offer women's clothes. Another popular, reasonably-priced Spanish chain store for men is **Springfield**. At the top end of the market is the **Loewe** store for men, where a silk tie with a Spanish art motif makes a stylish gift.

The Chueca district is the best place for the latest in streetwear, with offbeat local designers and second-hand shops on almost every corner. Many outlets also sell international brands at reduced prices.

SHOES AND LEATHER GOODS

Madrid is a haven for those with a shoe fetish. You will find every type of shoe here, from the traditional espadrille sold at **Antigua Casa Crespo** to the popular Majorcan **Camper** shoes. For comfort, try **Yanko** for their soft and snug shoes that feel like slippers, while for sophistication, opt for the elegant **Farrutx**. If you are after trendy flip-flops head to Jocomomola in Callejón de Jorge Juan. For something a little different, visit the avant-garde **Excrupulus Net** in Chueca, or **Bravo** for some of the best national and international labels. For trainers or other budget buys, visit the shops along Calle de Fuencarral, or go to **Los Guerrilleros** in Puerta del Sol.

Spain produces some of the best quality leather in the world. The ultimate in bags and leather goes under the prestigious label of **Loewe**, whose products are sold all over the world. Another impressive (and more budget friendly) national brand is **Salvador Bachiller**, where you will find quality leather and exclusively designed bags, suitcases, wallets and other accessories. For a touch of the more traditional Andalusian style, take a look at the handbags and belts for sale at **El Caballo**.

JEWELLERY

In Calle Serrano and Gran Vía you'll find both small shops, stacked with trays of gold studs, chains and bracelets, and grand jewellers. Man-made "Majorica" pearls, as well as the cultivated variety, can be found all over Madrid, including at the department store El Corte Inglés.

The innovative Catalan **Tous** is popular among the young for its ubiquitous teddy-bear logo. If you are interested in original, simple designs, visit the acclaimed jeweller **Joaquín Berao**. His shop resembles an art gallery devoted to tastefully designed pieces. Museum shops are also a good place to shop for designer jewellery. Look out for original pieces from Verili, sold at the main museums in the city.

CRAFTS AND DESIGN

Traditional crafts such as woven baskets or embroidered linen are hard to find in Madrid and often tend to be Asian imports. However, lovely and inexpensive ceramics are widely available, though sometimes the more colourful pieces are from Morocco. A wide choice of ceramics can be found at **Cántaro**, near the Plaza de España. Well stocked in regional styles, the shop also carries so-called "extinct" ceramics – traditional styles of pottery no longer regularly produced. **El Caballo Rojo** in the Old Town, offers a bewildering array of 17th-and 18th-century ceramic objects, whose uses often can't be imagined today. Many shops around Puerta del Sol stock embroidered tablecloths and shawls, but the authentic ones can be quite pricey.

In the Mercado de Puerta de Toledo, you will find **Artesanos de la Villa**, an association of more than a 100 craft workshops that sell all kind of traditional and modern crafts such as pottery, leather goods, glassware and metalwork.

For contemporary design, head to **Víctimas del Celuloide**, an original shop with a great variety of unusual goods, from Chinese chopsticks to kits to make-your-own silicone lamps. It is the perfect place to find something a little different.

BOOKS AND MUSIC

The giant French-owned **FNAC** book and video store has a good selection of books and magazines in English and other languages, as does **Casa del Libro**. **Booksellers**, a little further afield, stocks English classics, though only a limited selection of new books. The second-hand bookstalls of the Mercado del Libro near the Parque del Retiro are good for cheap paperbacks and, sometimes, rare volumes. Art books can be found at one of the best specialist art bookshops, **Gaudí**, near Chueca.

For all types of music, go to the FNAC or one of the El Corte Inglés branches, either in Calle de Preciados or Paseo de la Castellana.

For flamenco buffs, the specialist **El Flamenco Vive** stocks the widest selection of books, guitars and CDs in the world.

DIRECTORY

FOOD AND DRINK

Lavinia
C/ de José Ortega y
Gasset 16.
Map 6 F3.
Tel 914 26 06 04.

La Violeta
Plaza Canalejas 6.
Map 7 A2.
Tel 915 22 55 22.

Museo del Jamón
Carrera de San
Jeronimo 6. **Map** 5 A1.
Tel 915 21 03 46.

**Mantequerías
Bravo**
C/ de Ayala 24.
Map 6 E4.
Tel 915 76 76 41.

Reserva y Cata
C/ del Conde de
Xiquena 13.
Map 5 C5.
Tel 913 19 04 01.

ANTIQUES AND ARTS

**Centro de
Anticuarios**
C/ de Lagasca 36.
Map 6 E5.

Egam
C/ de Villanueva 29.
Map 6 F5.
Tel 914 35 31 61.

Hidalgo
Galerías Piquer, shop 23.
C/ de la Ribera de
Curtidores 29.
Map 4 E5.
Tel 915 30 56 53.

**María García
Cavestany**
C/ de Jorge Juan 14.
Map 6 E5.
Tel 915 77 76 32.

Theotokopoulos
C/ de Alcalá 97.
Map 8 E1.
Tel 915 75 84 66.

SHOPPING CENTRES AND MALLS

ABC Serrano
C/ de Serrano 61.
Map 4 F2.
Tel 915 77 50 31.
www.abcserrano.com

El Corte Inglés
C/ de Preciados 1–3.
Map 4 F2.
Tel 913 79 80 00.
www.elcorteingles.es
One of several branches.

El Jardín de Serrano
C/ de Goya 6–8.
Map 1 A1.
Tel 915 77 00 12.

La Vaguada
Av Monforte de Lemos 36.
Tel 917 30 10 00.
www.enlavaguada.com

Mitsuoko
C/ de Fuencarral 59.
Map 4 F2.
Tel 917 01 08 35.

FASHION

Adolfo Domínguez
C/ de Serrano 18.
Map 6 E4.
Tel 915 77 82 80.

**Ágata Ruiz de la
Prada**
C/ de Serrano 27.
Map 6 E4.
Tel 913 19 05 01.

Amaya Arzuaga
C/ de Lagasca 60.
Map 6 E5.
Tel 914 26 28 16.

Antonio Miró
C/ de Lagasca 65.
Map 6 E5.
Tel 914 26 02 25.

Antonio Pernas
C/ de Claudio Coello 46.
Map 6 E4.
Tel 915 78 16 76.

Caramelo
C/ de Serrano 19.
Map 6 E4.
Tel 914 35 01 77.

Mango
C/ de la Princesa 68.
Map 1 B2.
Tel 915 44 46 96.
One of several branches.

Roberto Verino
C/ de Serrano 33.
Map 6 E4.
Tel 914 26 04 75.

Springfield
C/ de Fuencarral 107.
Map 2 F3.
Tel 914 47 59 94.
One of several branches.

Zara
C/ de Preciados 18.
Map 4 F2.
Tel 915 21 09 58.
One of several branches.

SHOES AND LEATHER GOODS

**Antigua Casa
Crespo**
C/ del Divino Pastor 29.
Map 2 F4.
Tel 915 21 56 54.

Bravo
C/ de Serrano 42.
Map 6 E4.
Tel 914 35 27 29.
One of several branches.

Camper
C/ de la Princesa 75.
Map 1 B2.
Tel 902 36 45 98.
www.camper.es

El Caballo
C/ de Lagasca 55.
Map 6 E5.
Tel 915 76 40 37.

Excrupulus Net
C/ del Almirante 7.
Map 5 V5.
Tel 915 21 72 44.

Farrutx
C/ de Serrano 7.
Map 8 D1.
Tel 915 76 94 93.

Loewe
C/ de Serrano 26.
Map 6 E4.
Tel 915 77 60 56.

Los Guerrilleros
Plaza de la Puerta del
Sol 5.
Map 4 F2.
Tel 915 21 27 08.

Salvador Bachiller
Gran Vía 65.
Map 2 D5.
Tel 915 59 83 21.

Yanko
C/ de Lagasca 52.
Map 6 F4.
Tel 915 76 16 78.

JEWELLERY

Joaquín Berao
C/ de Claudio
Coello 35.
Map 6 E5.
Tel 915 77 28 28.

Tous
C/ de Serrano 86.
Map 6 E3.
Tel 915 77 48 37.

CRAFTS AND DESIGN

**Artesanos de
la Villa**
Mercado Puerta de Toledo,
Ronda de Toledo 1.
Map 4 D5.
Tel 913 64 05 38.

Cántaro
Calle de la Flor Baja 8.
Map 2 D5.
Tel 915 47 95 14.

El Caballo Rojo
C/ de Segovia 7.
Map 4 D3.
Tel 913 66 43 90.

**Víctimas de
Celuloide**
C/ de Santiago 4.
Map 4 D2.
Tel 915 47 61 35.

BOOKS AND MUSIC

Booksellers
C/ de José Abascal 48.
Tel 914 42 79 59.

Casa del Libro
Gran Vía 29.
Map 4 F1.
Tel 915 21 21 13.
www.casadellibro.com

El Flamenco Vive
C/ del Conde de Lemos 7.
Map 4 D2.
Tel 915 47 39 17.

FNAC
C/ de Preciados 28.
Map 4 E1.
Tel 915 95 61 00.
www.fnac.es

Gaudí
C/ de Argensola 13.
Map 5 C4.
Tel 913 08 18 29.

ENTERTAINMENT IN MADRID

As a major European capital, Madrid takes its arts and entertainment very seriously, hosting the finest and most diverse dance, music and theatre productions from around the world. Vibrant art, music and film festivals are held around the year, supplemented by a pulsating nightlife, raucous street parties and lively

Flamenco guitarist in Parque del Retiro

cafés. Even traditional art forms, such as flamenco, bullfighting and Madrid's version of the operetta, *zarzuela*, are characterized by flamboyance and spectacle. Football is also a major draw, and Real Madrid is a hugely celebrated team. Between fiestas, flamenco, football and much more, the revelry never stops in Madrid.

Madrid's Teatro Real (*see p322*)

ENTERTAINMENT GUIDES

Madrid's entertainment guides are mostly in Spanish. *Guía del Ocio*, a handy weekly guide to what's on in the city, comes out every Friday and can be bought from kiosks. Three daily newspapers have entertainment supplements on Friday as well: *El Mundo, ABC* and *El País*.

The English-language monthly, *InMadrid*, publishes cultural listings and reviews of the latest bars and clubs. It is available in bookshops, record stores and **Barajas Airport** information office.

Information on forthcoming events can also be obtained from one of the tourist information offices in the city, where English will be spoken. The tourist board also publishes *What's On*, a free, bilingual brochure.

SEASONS AND TICKETS

There is always something going on in Madrid's theatres and stadiums, but the cultural season is at its peak from

September to June. May's Fiesta de San Isidro, Madrid's patron saint festival, and the Festival de Otoño, a music, theatre and dance festival held from October to November, attract many big Spanish and international names. Tickets can be bought in advance from **Caja de Madrid**.

In July and August, Madrid hosts Veranos de la Villa (book through tourist offices), a special programme that includes art exhibitions, jazz, opera, flamenco, cinema and drama at various venues.

Tickets for a number of events can be bought at **FNAC** and **El Corte Inglés** stores and websites. Many other reliable internet sites also sell tickets. Check the websites of venues too, since many of them offer online booking services.

CAFÉS, BARS AND TERRACES

Madrid's social life revolves around an endless array of cafés, bars and summer terraces. These venues are

perfect places to relax and people-watch. Especially popular areas for *terraceo* (doing the rounds of various terraces) are Plaza de Santa Ana, Paja Chueca and Dos de Mayo. The glamorous crowd often spend evenings strolling down avenues, such as Paseo de la Castellana and Rosales, stopping now and then to nip into a terrace bar or café.

Madrid has retained many of its old grand cafés. **Café Comercial**, a city landmark, is an excellent meeting place with its wonderful early 20th-century ambience. Recently opened to the public, **Café del Círculo de Bellas Artes** is housed in a theatre, and is a cultural institution in itself. It is ideal for coffee or lunch after spending a day pursuing cultural interests. Of the literary cafés, the famous **Café Gijón** (*see p291*) should not be missed.

In the evening, it is almost essential to head to a *taberna*, where you can order a *ración*, the more

Dancing the night away at the Joy Eslava Discoteque (*see p324*)

Exterior of the historic Café Gijón

substantial version of tapas, and accompany it with a good local wine. Go for a *taberna* crawl and visit the the older and most interesting establishments such as **Taberna Antonio Sánchez**, which is well known for its history and the quality of its tapas. **La Bola** is popular with both tourists and locals, and **Taberna Maceiras** is favoured for its Galician wines and other specialities.

BULLFIGHTING

Although bullfighting *(see pp36–7)* is not as popular as it used to be in many other parts of Spain, it continues to thrive in Madrid. The **Plaza de Toros de las Ventas** is the most important ring in the world, holding *corridas* every Sunday from March to October. In May, during the Fiesta de San Isidro, there are *corridas* every day, with some of the biggest names participating in the spectacle.

The Las Ventas box office is open from 10am to 2pm and from 5pm to 8pm. You can also purchase tickets from abroad through the **Taquilla Toros** website, and collect them at the box office up to two hours before the fight.

FOOTBALL

Madrid is very proud of its team, **Real Madrid** *(see p177),* and the players are no less than celebrities in Spain. With a capacity of 80,000, their home stadium Santiago Bernabéu is one of the greatest theatres of the game. Tickets can be bought on the phone, or through the stadium's internet site.

For those who wish to visit the stadium, guided tours are conducted everyday between 10:30am and 6:30pm, except

on 25 December, 1 January and on days when there are matches. Tickets can be bought at the box office with no need to book in advance.

Real Madrid's rivals, **Atlético de Madrid**, are based at the Vicente Calderón stadium.

DANCE

Madrid's dance scene has come a long way over recent years, with international companies and local talent performing regularly around the city. Madrid is the home of Spain's prestigious Ballet Nacional de España and the more contemporary Compañía Nacional de Danza, directed by the world famous dancer and choreographer Nacho Duarte. Víctor Ullate's Ballet de la Comunidad de Madrid presents a more avantegarde mix of classical and contemporary dance.

A good time to experience Madrid's rich dance tradition is around April, when the annual En Danza festival takes place. Both Spanish and international dancers perform at this time.

The **Teatro Albéniz** is the main venue for ballet. The two other major venues are the **Teatro Madrid** and the Teatro Real where opera is usually performed. Smaller venues such as **Cuarta Pared** occasionally present alternative dance performances.

Details can usually be found in the entertainment listings or on the individual venues' website.

FLAMENCO

Although flamenco originated in Andalucia *(see pp424–5)*, Madrid is often seen as its spiritual home and some of the best flamenco dancers and musicians regularly perform here. The scene is sparklingly vibrant, and interpretations of the art range from the traditional to the daringly innovative, inspired by dancers such as Joaquín Cortés.

Most *tablaos* (flamenco venues) offer drinks and dinner with the show. Do note, however, that the show may sometimes feature only singing and not the familar rhythmic dancing.

Café de Chinitas and **Casa Patas** are among the older and better *tablaos* in town, but are somewhat touristy. Also well worth a visit are **Arco de Cuchilleros** and **Corral de la Morería**.

Flamenco bars such as **Cardamomo** are full of boisterous young people, but are a fun way of experiencing the sound and feel of flamenco. Two bars that feature regular, spontaneous performances are the atmospheric **Candela** and **La Soleá**. Note that as these places are frequented by local flamenco aficionados, visitors should be respectful of the art.

Take into account that although bars are fun and a good introduction to the art of flamenco, some of the best dance troupes, singers and players usually perform at the city's theatres.

Las Ventas bullring on the day of a bullfight

CLASSICAL MUSIC, OPERA AND ZARZUELA

Madrid's **Auditorio Nacional de Música** is home to Spain's national orchestra, Orquesta Nacional, as well as its national choir, Coro Nacional de España. With two concert halls, the auditorium also hosts many high-profile performances.

The illustrious and recently renovated **Teatro Real** is best known as the home of the city's opera company. It also houses Orquesta Sinfónica de Madrid, Spain's oldest orchestra with a rich history dating back to more than a century. The magnificent Real is the best place to watch top-class international and national opera performances. Tickets for a show can be bought at a maximum of two weeks in advance by phone or from the website and can be collected at the box office up to half an hour before the show begins.

The **Teatro Monumental** is the main venue for the excellent Orquesta Sinfónica y Coro de RTVE, the orchestra and choir of Spain's state television and radio company. The **Auditorio Conde Duque** hosts classical concerts among many other art events.

The **Teatro Calderón** is also a good venue, hosting some outstanding classical and modern opera productions.

Those who want to experience a Spanish, especially a *Madrileño*, take on the operetta, should definitely make time to see a *zarzuela* being performed. The origins of this lively form of musical drama-cum-social satire can be traced back to early 17th-century Madrid, and the tradition is still going strong. With both spoken and sung parts as well as dancing, the *zarzuela* can be comic, ribald and even romantic. It is always enjoyable to watch.

The best productions are usually staged at the **Teatro de la Zarzuela**. Other theatres also host *zarzuela* performances occasionally. Check listings for details.

ROCK, JAZZ AND WORLD MUSIC

Madrid's music scene is eclectic and energetic, mixing top international pop stars with independent local bands performing at a variety of venues. Madrid's increasingly multicultural mix has ensured an explosion of Latin American and African sounds recently, as well as intersting fusions of both with more familiar Spanish sounds. In the 1980s, the heady days of *la movida* (*see p305*) gave birth to Spanish pop and the momentum continues to this day with Madrid remaining the centre of the country's music scene.

For rock music, **Sala la Riviera** has an excellent and well-deserved reputation. It has hosted major international stars such as Bob Dylan, the Cranberries and guitarist Joe Satriani among countless others. **Honky Tonk**, located next to the Manzanares river, holds some of the city's best rock'n'roll concerts, so keep an eye out for posters advertising events. Needless to say, this partially covered venue is at its best during the summer months.

Siroco has devoted itself to discovering new alternative and indie bands, and also doubles as a club with live music performances.

One of Europe's best jazz clubs, **Café Central**, with its Art Deco elegance, is one place that should not be missed. Also popular is the lively **Populart** jazz and blues venue.

Musicians from all over the world representing a range of musical genres can be heard at **Suristán**. One of the most trendy and interesting clubs in Madrid, it is also a venue for painting and photography exhibitions.

There are plenty of other well-reputed venues in the city that feature live music daily. The best way to keep abreast of the latest events is to check out weekly listings and to keep an eye out for adverts on the street.

THEATRE

Madrid has a theatrical tradition that stretches back to the Golden Age of the 17th century, with writers such as Lope de Vega and Calderón de la Barca creating a canon of work that is still performed today.

One of the most prestigious theatres in the city, the **Teatro de la Comedia** is traditionally home to the Compañía Nacional de Teatro Clásico, which stages classic works by Spanish playwrights. However, since the Comedia is under renovation, the company is now performing at the **Teatro Pavón** (until the year 2008).

Another one of the most highly regarded theatres is the **Teatro María Guerrero**, which presents Spanish modern drama, as well as foreign plays.

For contemporary and alternative theatre, Madrid has a thriving network of fringe venues such as **Cuarta Pared** and **Círculo de Bellas Artes**.

For musicals, try **Teatro Nuevo Apolo**. Other venues such as **La Latina** and **Teatro Muñoz Seca** specialize in comedy productions.

A wide range of Spanish and international theatrical talent take part in the annual Festival de Otoño in October and November.

CINEMA

Spanish cinema (*see p192*) has earned great international acclaim in recent years. For those with a grasp of the language, Spanish film is a rewarding experience, especially enjoyed at one of the grand film theatres along Gran Vía, such as **Capitol**, which has screened films since the early 1900s.

Non-Spanish movies can be seen in their original-language versions at **Luna**, **Ideal**, **Alphaville** and **Renoir**. Screenings will be found listed in newspapers and listings magazines. Note that tickets cost less on the *día del espectador*, which is usually on Monday or Wednesday.

DIRECTORY

TOURIST OFFICES

Barajas Airport (Terminal 1)
C/ Duque de Medinacelli 2. **Map** 7 B3.
Tel 913 05 86 56.

Madrid Information
Pl Mayor 3. **Map** 4 E3.
Tel 915 88 16 36.

TICKETS

Caja de Madrid
Tel 902 48 84 88.

El Corte Inglés
Tel 902 40 02 22.
www.elcorteingles.com

FNAC
Tel 902 10 06 32.
www.fnac.es

Tel Entrada
Tel 902 10 12 12.
www.telentrada.com

CAFÉS, BARS AND TERRACES

Café Comercial
Glorieta de Bilbao 7.
Map 4 F2.
Tel 915 21 56 55.

Café del Circulo de Bellas Artes
C/ Alcalá 42. **Map** 4 E3.
Tel 915 21 69 42.

Café Gijón
Paseo de Recoletos 21.
Map 7 C1.
Tel 915 21 54 25.

La Bola
C/ de la Bola 5. **Map** 4 D1.
Tel 915 47 69 30.

Taberna Maceiras
C/ de Jesús 7.
Map 7 B3.
Tel 914 29 15 89.

Taberna Antonio Sánchez
C/ de Mesón de Paredes 13.
Map 4 F5.
Tel 915 39 78 26.

BULLFIGHTING

Las Ventas
C/ Alcalá 237.
Tel 913 56 22 00.
www.las-ventas.com

Taquilla Toros
www.taquillatoros.com

FOOTBALL

Atlético de Madrid
Estadio Vicente Calderón,
Paseo de la Virgen del
Puerto 67.
Tel 913 66 47 07.
www.clubateletico
madrid.com

Real Madrid
Estadio Santiago
Bernabéu, C/ de Concha
Espina 1.
Tel 913 98 43 00.
www.realmadrid.es

DANCE

Cuarta Pared
C/ del Ercilla 17.
Tel 915 32 44 37.

Teatro Albéniz
C/ de la Paz 11.
Map 4 F2.
Tel 915 31 83 11.

Teatro Madrid
Avda de la Ilustración s/n.
Map 3 B1.
Tel 915 47 69 30.
www.teatromadrid.es

FLAMENCO

Arco de Cuchilleros
C/ de los Cuchilleros 7.
Map 4 E3.
Tel 913 64 02 63.

Café de Chinitas
C/ de Torija 7. **Map** 4 D1.
Tel 915 59 51 35.

Candela
C/ del Olmo 2.
Map 7 A4.
Tel 914 67 33 82.

Cardamomo
C/ de Echegaray 15.
Map 7 A2.
Tel 913 69 07 57.

Casa Patas
C/ de Caòazares 10.
Map 7 A3.
Tel 913 69 04 96.

Corral de la Morería
C/ de la Morería 17.
Map 3 C3.
Tel 913 65 84 46.

La Soleá
C/ de Cava Baja 34.
Map 4 D4.
Tel 913 66 05 34.

CLASSICAL MUSIC OPERA AND ZARZUELA

Auditorio Conde Duque
C/ del Conde Duque 9.
Map 2 D4.
Tel 915 88 58 34.

Auditorio Nacional de Música
C/ del Príncipe de Vergara
146. *Tel 913 37 01 00.*
www.auditorionacional.m
cu.es

Teatro Calderón
C/ de Atocha 18.
Map 4 F3.
Tel 915 23 76 35.

Teatro Monumental
C/ de Atocha 65.
Map 7 A3.
Tel 914 29 12 81.

Teatro Real
Pl de Oriente.
Map 4 D2.
Tel 915 16 06 60.
www.teatro-real.com

Teatro de la Zarzuela
C/ de los Jovellanos 4.
Map 7 B2.
Tel 915 24 54 00. www.
teatrodelazarzuela.mcu.es

ROCK, JAZZ AND WORLD MUSIC

Café Central
Pl del Ángel 10.
Map 7 A3.
Tel 913 69 41 43.

Honky Tonk
C/ de Covarrubias 24.
Map 5 B3.
Tel 914 45 68 86.

Populart
Huertas 22. **Map** 7 A3.
Tel 914 29 84 07.

Sala La Riviera
Paseo Virgen del Puerto
s/n. *Tel 913 65 24 15.*

Siroco
C/ de San Dimas 3.
Map 2 E4.
Tel 915 93 30 70.

Suristán
C/ de la Cruz 7.
Map 7 A2.
Tel 915 32 39 09.

THEATRE

Círculo de Bellas Artes
Marqués de Casa Riera 2.
Map 7 B2.
Tel 915 32 44 37.

La Latina
Pl de la Cebada 2.
Map 4 D4.
Tel 913 65 28 35.

Lope de Vega
Gran Vía 57. **Map** 4 E1.
Tel 915 47 20 11.

Teatro de la Comedia
C/ del Príncipe 14.
Map 7 A2.
Tel 915 21 49 31.

Teatro María Guerrero
C/ de Tamayo y Baus 4.
Map 5 C5.
Tel 913 10 15 00.

Teatro Muñoz Seca
Pl del Carmen 1.
Map 4 F1.
Tel 915 23 21 28.

Teatro Nuevo Apolo
Pl Tirso de Molina 1. **Map**
4 F3.
Tel 913 69 06 37.

Teatro Pavón
C/ de Embajadores 9.
Map 4 E4.
Tel 915 28 28 19.

CINEMA

Alphaville
C/ de Martín de los Heros
14. **Map** 1 A1.
Tel 915 59 38 36.

Capitol
Gran Vía 41. **Map** 4 E1.
Tel 902 33 32 31.

Ideal
C/ del Doctor Cortezo 6.
Map 4 F3.
Tel 913 69 25 18.

Luna
C/ de la Luna 2.
Map 2 E5.
Tel 915 22 47 52.

Renoir
C/ de Martín de los Heros
12. **Map** 1 C5.
Tel 915 41 41 00.

Nightlife

Madrid's reputation as the city that never sleeps persists, despite recent political measures for earlier closing times. In fact, partygoers in Madrid are known as *gatos* (cats) around Spain because of their nocturnal habits. The best nightlife is concentrated around specific districts, each with its own unique atmosphere and a wealth of places for people to get down to one of Madrid's best talents: *la marcha* (partying). Things hot up first in the Huertas area, moving on to Malasaña, Bilbao, Lavapiés and Chueca into the early hours of the morning. You don't need to go to a club for dancing as *Madrileños* also dance to DJs and live music in smaller clubs, called *pubs* – all sorts of musical tastes are catered to more than amply *(see p322)*. Expect to find places crowded from Thursday to Sunday. Also prepare for late nights because things don't get going for *gatos* until midnight.

SANTA ANA AND HUERTAS

With many tapas bars, cafés and terraces, the Huertas area is the perfect place to begin preparing for the wild night ahead. The atmosphere is made by the crowd, which is a heady amalgam of ages, looks and origins. If you want to stay in one area, this is a good choice.

There are several little bars overlooking the lively Plaza de Santa Ana. Pop into any one of them to begin the night. **Viva Madrid** attracts a vivacious crowd of locals and foreigners. **Los Gabrieles**, a famous *taberna*, is known for its painted ceramic tiles, and is a mandatory stop for any bar crawl. There is live flamenco at least once a week.

For late-night dancing, try the house DJs at **Joy Eslava Discoteque** or the extravagant 19th-century **Palacio Gaviria** near Sol, resplendent in its Baroque decor. Also close by, you will find the spectacular seven-floor **Kapital**, which features every kind of music, and a rooftop bar that allows drinkers to gaze at the starlit sky. **Popullart**, also a hugely popular club, features live jazz and occasional shows by Latin and world music bands. Weekends can get crowded.

It is a local tradition to end the night with hot chocolate and *churros* (doughnuts) in one of the cafés around Plaza del Sol. The **Chocolatería San Ginés** is open all night.

ALONSO MARTÍNEZ AND BILBAO

This is one of the city's most animated areas. You will find hundreds of great haunts that play music ranging from R&B to Spanish pop.

To begin with, try some of the local bars around Plaza de Santa Bárbara, such as the **Cervecería Santa Bárbara**, the perfect place to start the night with a *caña* (beer). Later on (if you can get past the queues), try the glamorous club **Chantilly** with its Baroque decor and pop music, where you can dance until late with the beautiful people. Close by, you will find **Pachá**, one of Madrid's most famous discotheques. There are also plenty of live-music venues around, such as **Clamores**, one of Madrid's many temples of jazz music. However, note that areas such as Huertas are more active during weekdays.

ARGÜELLES AND MONCLOA

This area is a favourite haunt of students, thanks to its proximity to the halls of residence of one of Madrid's major universities. The celebrated "basements of Argüelles" are huge double-storeyed patios with several bars and discotheques. The atmosphere is fresh and young.

Another popular district is Moncloa, which has a more mature crowd, as well as several places where you can listen to local Spanish pop and dance tunes. Still, it is mainly an area for techno music clubs.

CHUECA

The Chueca district dominates Madrid's gay scene. As well as having a large resident gay community, there are plenty of trendy late-night bars and clubs where gays and non-gays party together. In fact, what sets Chueca apart from other gay neighbourhoods in the world is the *mezcla*, the tolerant gay/straight mix.

The heart of the area is the Plaza de Chueca, packed with crowds visiting the terraces in the summer. Close by are mixed bars such as **Liqüid** and **Acuarela**, with its camp, religious artefact decor. The Gay Pride Week in late June, focuses around this area, though there are also plenty of well-established gay bars elsewhere in the city.

MALASAÑA

Malasaña was the centre of *la movida* in the Madrid of the 1980's *(see p305)*, and still has an alternative flavour that attracts many young bohemian types. The hub of this cosmopolitan district is the Dos de Mayo square. However, the characteristic atmosphere of the area is changing rapidly into a more design driven space. An example is the **La Ida** bar which has cultivated a revolutionary, arty atmosphere. **Bar & Co** is a typical Malasaña venue, where local bands play weekly. You can relax there after 3am if you don't feel like clubbing.

Tupperware, a fusion of past and present, is a rock bar with an ultra pop decor, where you can also listen to garage, indie and pop music.

LAVAPIÉS

Once the Jewish quarter of Madrid, the narrow streets of Lavapiés are rich with an eclectic mix of races and cultures. One of the most fascinating and diverse districts in town, the locals' old habit of sitting outside their doors on summer nights continues as does the the multiracial crowd on the terraces of Calle de Argumosa. Lavapiés offers a culturally vibrant fusion of artists, immigrants, hipsters and squatters. The result is some of the most brilliant music, art, food, alternative theatre and nightlife in the city.

Taqué has funky electronica playing every night except on Monday. The endearingly eccentric bar, **La Colonia de San Lorenzo**, hosts Verbena de San Lorenzo, a street party with live bands, dancing, stalls and freely flowing drink.

LA LATINA

Still the best district in town for cosy little hideaways and tapas bars, La Latina is an especially good place to go on Sundays after wandering around the Rastro flea market.

For an excellent cocktail, head to **Delic**, and for a cultural experience try **Anti Café**, where you can listen to unique DJs, poetry, drama and jazz on Sundays. For a taste of the best Spanish wines, visit **La Carpanta**, where top quality wines are available at reasonable prices. Another worthwhile bar is **Taberna de Tempranillo**, which also serves a variety of Spanish wines, cheeses and ham. In the exquisite **María Pandora** bar, you can try a selection of champagnes and *cavas*, surrounded by books and antiques. Afterwards, you can dance until late at **Berlín Cabaret**, a modern nightclub that runs a 1930s cabaret from Monday to Thursday.

AZCA

With a skyline punctuated by the highest buildings, this is one of the most modern areas

in town. Near the Paseo de la Castellana and the Santiago Bernabéu stadium, this financial district has a multitude of clubs and bars doing brisk business in basements.

If you feel the urge to dance to the sensuous rhythms of salsa, Calle Orense is the place for you. The **Caché Cubano** nightclub is a partygoer's delight and its Mojitos are excellent. Avenida de Brasil is also full of large clubs that tend to be a little overcrowded.

Around the Chamartín train station nearby, you will find the hardcore clubbing scene unfolding late at night. Of the many clubs in the area, **Macumba** is known to have the most cutting-edge sound and lighting equipment in Europe. It is famous for its "Space of Sound" sessions on Sunday mornings and for hosting the Ministry of Sound on Saturday nights.

DIRECTORY

BARS, CLUBS AND CAFÉS

Acuarela
C/ de Gravina 10.
Map 5 B5.
Tel 915 22 21 43.

Anti Café
Unión 2.
Map 4 E2.
Tel 915 59 41 63.

Bar & Co
C/ de Barco 34.
Map 2 F5.

Berlín Cabaret
Costanilla de San Pedro 11. **Tel** 913 66 20 34.

Caché Cubano
C/ Orense 24.
Tel 915 55 96 32.

Chantilly
C/ de Lagasca 31.
Map 6 F4.
Tel 915 76 97 15.

Cervecería Santa Bárbara
Pl Santa Bárbara 8.
Tel 913 19 04 49.

Chocolatería San Ginés
Pasadizo de San Ginés, C/ de Arenal 11.
Map 4 E2.
Tel 913 65 65 46.

Clamores
C/ de Alburquerque 14.
Map 4 E2.
Tel 914 45 79 38.

Delic
Pl De La Paja s/n.
Map 4 D3.
Tel 913 64 54 50.

Joy Eslava Discoteques
C/ de Arenal 11.
Map 4 E2.
Tel 913 66 37 33.

Kapital
C/ de Atocha 125.
Map 7 C4.
Tel 914 20 29 06.

La Carpanta
C/ de Almendro 22.
Map 4 D3.
Tel 913 66 57 83.

La Colonia de San Lorenzo
C/ de Salitre 38.
Map 7 A5.

La Ida
C/ de Colón 11.
Map 5 A5.
Tel 915 22 91 07.

Liqüid
C/ de Barquillo 8.
Map 7 B1.
Tel 915 32 74 28.

Los Gabrieles
C/ De Echegaray 17.
Map 7 A3.
Tel 914 29 62 61.

Macumba
Agustín de Foxá s/n, Estación de Charmartín.
Tel 902 49 99 94.

María Pandora
Pl Gabriel Miró 1.
Map 3 B3.
Tel 913 66 45 67.

Pachá
C/ de Barceló 11.
Map 5 A4.
Tel 914 47 01 28.

Palacio Gavira
C/ de Arenal 9.
Map 4 E2.
Tel 915 26 60 69.

Populart
Huertas 22.
Map 7 A3.
Tel 914 29 84 07.

Taberna de Tempranillo
C/ de la Cava Baja 38.
Tel 913 64 15 32.

Taqué
C/ de Lavapiés 11.
Map 4 F4.

Tupperware
C/ Corredera Alta de San Pablo 26.
Tel 914 48 50 16.

Viva Madrid
C/ Manuel Fernández González 7.
Tel 914 29 36 40.

MADRID PROVINCE

Madrid province (the Comunidad de Madrid) sits high on Spain's central plateau. There is plenty of superb scenery and good walking country in the sierras to the north, which are a refuge for city dwellers who go there to ski in winter or cool down during the torrid summers. In the western foothills of these mountains stands El Escorial, the royal palace-cum-monastery built by Felipe II, from which he ruled his empire. Close by is the Valle de los Caídos, the war monument erected by Franco. The smaller royal palace of El Pardo is on the outskirts of Madrid, and south of the city is the 18th-century summer palace of Aranjuez, set in lush parkland. Historic towns include Alcalá de Henares, which has a Renaissance university building, and Chinchón, where taverns cluster around a picturesque arcaded market square.

SIGHTS AT A GLANCE

Towns and Cities
Alcalá de Henares ❾
Buitrago del Lozoya ❷
Chinchón ❿
Manzanares el Real ❼

Historic Buildings
El Escorial pp330–31 ❻
Monasterio de Santa María de
  El Paular ❸
Palacio de El Pardo ❽

Palacio Real de Aranjuez ⓫
Santa Cruz del Valle de los
  Caídos ❺

Mountain Ranges
Sierra Centro de Guadarrama ❹
Sierra Norte ❶

KEY

	Madrid city
	Madrid province
✈	Barajas Airport
—	Motorway
—	Major road
—	Minor road
– – –	Province boundary

0 kilometres   25

0 miles   20

SIGHTS IN MADRID PROVINCE

◁ Celebration of Mass in the church of the Monasterio de Santa María de El Paular

The village of Montejo de la Sierra in the Sierra Norte

Sierra Norte ❶

Madrid. 🚉 *Montejo.* 🛈 *Calle Real 64, Montejo, 91 869 70 58.*

The black slate hamlets of the Sierra Norte, which were once known as the Sierra Pobre (Poor Sierra), are located in the most attractively rural part of Madrid province.

At **Montejo de la Sierra**, the largest village in the area, an information centre organizes riding, the rental of traditional houses (*see p555*), and visits to the nearby nature reserve of the **Hayedo de Montejo de la Sierra**. This is one of the most southern beech woods (*see p80*) in Europe, and a relic of a previous era, when climatic conditions here were more suitable for the beech. From Montejo, you can drive on to picturesque hamlets such as **La Hiruela** or **Puebla de la Sierra**, both of which are set in lovely walking country.

The drier southern hills slope down to the **Embalse de Puentes Viejas**, a reservoir where summer chalets cluster around artificial beaches. On the eastern edge of the sierra is the village of **Patones**, which is thought to have escaped invasion by the Moors and Napoleon's troops because of its isolated location.

Buitrago del Lozoya ❷

Madrid. 👥 *1,700.* 🛈 *Calle Tahona 11, 91 868 16 15.* 🚌 *Sat.* 🎉 *La Asunción and San Roque (15 Aug), Cristo de los Esclavos (15 Sep).*

Picturesquely sited above a meander in the Río Lozoya is the walled town of Buitrago del Lozoya. Founded by the Romans, it was fortified by the Arabs, and became an important market town in medieval times. The 14th-century Gothic-Mudéjar castle is in ruins, although the gatehouse, arches and stretches of the original Arab wall have survived. To-day, the castle is used as a venue for bullfights and hosts a festival of ancient theatre and music in the summer.

The old quarter, within the walls, retains its charming atmosphere. The church of **Santa María del Castillo**, dating from the 15th century, has a Mudéjar tower and ceilings which were moved here from the old hospital. The **town hall** *(ayuntamiento)*, in the newer part of Buitrago, preserves a 16th-century processional cross. In the basement is the **Museo Picasso**. The prints, drawings and ceramics were collected by the artist's friend, Eugenio Arias.

🏛 **Museo Picasso**
Plaza de Picasso 1. *Tel* 91 868 16 15. ⬤ *Mon, Wed & Sun pm.*

Altarpiece in the Monasterio de Santa María de El Paular

Monasterio de Santa María de El Paular ❸

Southwest of Rascafría on M604. *Tel* 91 869 14 25. 🚉 *Rascafría.* ⬤ *noon–5pm Mon–Wed & Fri–Sat, noon–1pm Thu, 1–6pm Sun.* 📷

Founded in 1390 as Castile's first Carthusian monastery, Santa María de El Paular stands on the site of a medieval royal hunting lodge. Although it is mainly Gothic in style, Plater-esque and Renaissance features were added later. The monastery was abandoned in 1836 when government minister Mendizábal ordered the sale of church goods (*see p63*). It fell into disrepair until its restoration in the 1950s. Today the complex comprises a working Benedictine monastery, church and private hotel (*see p582*).

The church's delicate alabaster altarpiece, attributed to

Buitrago del Lozoya, standing next to the river

Flemish craftsmen, dates from the 15th century. Its panels depict scenes from the life of Jesus. The lavish Baroque *camarín* (chamber), behind the altar, was designed by Francisco de Hurtado in 1718.

Every Sunday, the monks sing an hour-long Gregorian chant in the church. If they are not busy, they will show you the cloister's Mudéjar brick vaulting and double sun-clock.

The monastery is a good starting point for exploring the country towns of **Rascafría** and **Lozoya** in the surrounding Lozoya valley. To the south-west is the nature reserve of **Lagunas de Peñalara**.

Sierra Centro de Guadarrama ❹

Madrid. 🚉 *Puerto de Navacerrada, Cercedilla.* 🚌 *Navacerrada, Cercedilla.* 🛈 *Navacerrada, 91 856 00 06.*

The central section of the Sierra de Guadarrama was little visited until the 1920s, when the area was first linked by train to Madrid. Today, the granite slopes are planted with pines and specked by holiday chalets. Villages such as **Navacerrada** and **Cercedilla** have grown into popular resorts for skiing, mountain-biking, rock-climbing and horse riding. Walkers wanting to enjoy the pure mountain air can follow marked routes from Navacerrada.

The **Valle de Fuenfría**, a nature reserve of wild forests, is best reached via Cercedilla. It has a well-preserved stretch of the original Roman road, as well as several picnic spots and marked walking routes.

The gigantic cross at Valle de los Caídos

Santa Cruz del Valle de los Caídos ❺

North of El Escorial on M600. **Tel** *91 890 56 11.* 🚌 *from El Escorial.* 🕐 *Tue–Sun.* ⬤ *some public hols.* 🎫 *(free Wed for EU residents).* 📷 **www**.patrimonionacional.es

General Franco had the Holy Cross of the Valley of the Fallen built as a memorial to those who died in the Civil War *(see pp66–7)*. The vast cross is located some 13 km (8 miles) north of El Escorial *(see pp330–31)*, and dominates the surrounding countryside. Some Spanish people find it too chilling a symbol of the dictatorship to be enjoyable, while for others its sheer size is rewarding.

The cross is 150 m (490 ft) high and rises above a basilica carved 250 m (820 ft) deep into the rock by prisoners. A number of them are said to have died in the 20-year-plus project.

Next to the basilica's high altar is the plain white tomb-stone of Franco, and, opposite, that of José Antonio Primo de Rivera, founder of the Falange Española party. A further 40,000 coffins of soldiers from both sides in the Civil War lie here out of sight, including those of two unidentified victims.

From the arms of the cross, there are magnificent views over the pine forests.

Navacerrada pass in the Sierra de Guadarrama

El Escorial **6**

Felipe II's imposing grey palace of San Lorenzo de El Escorial stands out against the foothills of the Sierra de Guadarrama to the northwest of Madrid. It was built between 1563 and 1584 in honour of St Lawrence, and its unornamented severity set a new architectural style which became one of the most influential in Spain. The interior was conceived as a mausoleum and contemplative retreat rather than a splendid residence. Its artistic wealth, which includes some of the most important works of art of the royal Habsburg collections, is concentrated in the museums, chapterhouses, church, royal pantheon and library. In contrast, the royal apartments are remarkably humble.

Fresco by Luca Giordano

★ **Royal Pantheon**
The funerary urns of Spanish monarchs line the marble mausoleum.

Main entrance

Bourbon Palace

Architectural Museum

Sala de Batallas

Basílica
The highlight of this huge decorated church, is the lavish altarpiece. The chapel houses a superb marble sculpture of the cruci-fiction by Cellini.

The Alfonso XII College
was founded by monks in 1875 as a boarding school.

Patio de los Reyes

Entrance to Basilica only

★ **Library**
This impressive array of 40,000 books incorporates Felipe II's personal collection. On display are precious manuscripts, including a poem by Alfonso X the Learned. The 16th-century ceiling frescoes are by Tibaldi.

STAR FEATURES

★ Royal Pantheon

★ Library

★ Museum of Art

The royal apartments, on the second floor of the palace, consist of Felipe II's modestly decorated living quarters. His bedroom opens directly on to the high altar of the basilica.

★ **Museum of Art**
Flemish, Italian and Spanish paintings hang in the museum, located on the first floor. One of the highlights is The Calvary, by 15th-century Flemish artist Rogier van der Weyden.

The Patio de los Evangelistas is a temple by Herrera. The Jardín de los Frailes makes a nice walk.

Chapterhouses
On display here is Charles V's portable altar. The ceiling frescoes depict monarchs and angels.

The monastery was founded in 1567, and has been run by Augustinian monks since 1885.

The Glory of the Spanish Monarchy by Luca Giordano
This beautiful fresco, above the main staircase, depicts Charles V and Felipe II, and scenes of the building of the monastery.

The Building of El Escorial
When chief architect Juan Bautista de Toledo died in 1567 he was replaced by Juan de Herrera, royal inspector of monuments. The plain architectural style of El Escorial is called desornamentado, *literally, "unadorned".*

Climber resting on a rock face of La Pedriza, near Manzanares el Real

Manzanares el Real ❼

Madrid. 🏛 5,180. 🚌 🛈 *Plaza del Pueblo 1, 91 853 00 09.* 🚗 *Tue & Fri.* 🎉 *Fiesta de Verano (early Aug), Cristo de la Nave (14 Sep).*

The skyline of Manzanares el Real is dominated by its restored 15th-century castle. Although the castle has some traditionally military features, such as double machicolations and turrets, it was used mainly as a residence by the Dukes of Infantado. Below the castle is a 16th-century church, a Renaissance portico and fine

capitals. Behind the town, bordering the foothills of the Sierra de Guadarrama, is **La Pedriza**, a mass of granite screes and ravines, very popular with climbers. It now forms part of an attractive nature reserve.

Environs
Colmenar Viejo, 12 km (7.5 miles) to the southeast of Manzanares, has a superb Gothic-Mudéjar church.

Palacio de El Pardo ❽

El Pardo, northwest of Madrid on N605. **Tel** *91 376 15 00.* 🚌 *from Moncloa.* 🗓 *daily.* ⬤ *during royal visits.* 🎟 *(free Wed for EU residents).* **www**.patrimonionacional.es

This royal hunting lodge and palace, set in parkland just outside Madrid's city limits, boasts General Franco among its former residents. A guided tour takes visitors round the moated palace's Habsburg wing and the identical 18th-century extension, designed by Francesco Sabatini.

The ornamental Bourbon interior is heavy with frescoes, gilt mouldings and tapestries, many of which were woven to designs by Goya *(see p306)*. Today the palace lodges visiting heads of state and

entertains royal guests. Surrounding the palace and the elegant 18th-century village of El Pardo is an enormous forest of holm oak. The area is popular for picnicking, and some game animals still run free.

Façade of Colegio de San Ildefonso in Alcalá de Henares

Alcalá de Henares ❾

Madrid. 🏛 188,500. 🚌 🚃 🛈 *Callejón Santa María, 91 889 26 94.* 🚗 *Mon, Wed.* 🎉 *Feria de Alcalá (late Aug).*

At the heart of a modern industrial town is one of Spain's most renowned university quarters. Founded in 1499 by Cardinal Cisneros, Alcalá's

Lavish 18th-century tapestry inside the Palacio de El Pardo

For hotels and restaurants in this region see p582 and pp632–3

university became one of the foremost places of learning in 16th-century Europe. The most historic college, **San Ildefonso**, survives. Former students include Golden Age playwright Lope de Vega *(see p290)*. In 1517 the university produced Europe's first polyglot bible, with text in Latin, Greek, Hebrew and Chaldean.

Alcalá's other sights are the cathedral and the **Casa-Museo de Cervantes**, birthplace of the Golden Age author. The newly restored 19th-century neo-Moorish palace, **Palacio de Laredo** has splendid decorations.

🏛 **Casa-Museo de Cervantes**
Calle Mayor. **Tel** *91 889 96 54.*
◐ *Tue–Sun.* ● *1 & 6 Jan.*

Chinchón ⓾

Madrid. 🏠 *4,576.* 🚉 ℹ *Plaza Mayor 3, 91 894 00 84.* 🚌 *Sat.* 🎭 *Semana Santa (Easter Week), San Roque (12–18 Aug).* **www**.*ciudadchinchon.com*

Chinchon is arguably Madrid province's most picturesque town. The 16th-century, typically Castilian, porticoed **Plaza Mayor** has a splendidly theatrical air. It comes alive for the Easter passion play, acted out by the townspeople *(see p290)*, and during the August bullfights. The 16th-century church, perched above the square, has an altar painting by Goya, whose brother was a priest here. Just off the square is the 18th-century Augustinian monastery, which has been converted into a **parador** with

Chinchón's unique porticoed Plaza Mayor

a peaceful patio garden *(see p582)*. A ruined 15th-century castle is on a hill to the west of town. Although it is closed to the public, there are views of Chinchón and the countryside from outside it.

Chinchón is a popular weekend destination for *Madrileños*, who come here to sample the excellent chorizo and locally produced *anís (see p607)* in the town's many taverns.

Palacio Real de Aranjuez ⓫

Plaza de Parejas, Aranjuez. **Tel** *91 891 13 44.* 🚉 🚌 ◐ *10am– 6:15pm Tue–Sun, gardens until 8:30pm (Oct–Mar: until 5:15pm, gardens until 6:30pm).* ● *some public hols.* 🎟 *(free Wed for EU residents).* ♿ 🅿

The Royal Summer Palace and Gardens of Aranjuez grew up around a medieval hunting lodge standing beside a natural weir, the meeting point of the Tagus and Jarama rivers.

Today's palace of brick and white stone was built in the 18th century by the Habsburgs and redecorated by the Bourbons. A guided tour takes you

through numerous Baroque rooms, among them the Chinese Porcelain Room, the Hall of Mirrors and the Smoking Room, modelled on the Alhambra in Granada. It is worth visiting Aranjuez to walk in the 300 hectares (740 acres) of shady royal gardens which inspired Joaquín Rodrigo's *Concierto de Aranjuez*. The Parterre Garden and the Island Garden, between the rivers, survive from the original 16th-century palace.

Between the palace and the River Tagus is the 18th-century Prince's Garden, decorated with sculptures, fountains and lofty trees from the Americas. In the garden is the Casa de Marinos (Sailors' House), a museum housing the launches once used by the royal family for trips along the river. At the far end of the garden is the Casa del Labrador (Labourer's Cottage), a decorative royal pavilion built by Carlos IV.

The town's restaurants are popular for the exceptional quality of their asparagus and strawberries. In summer, a 19th-century steam train, built to carry strawberries, runs between here and the capital.

MIGUEL DE CERVANTES

Miguel de Cervantes Saavedra, Spain's greatest literary figure *(see p34)*, was born in Alcalá de Henares in 1547. After fighting in the naval Battle of Lepanto (1571), he was held captive by the Turks for more than five years. In 1605, when he was almost 60 years old, the first of two parts of his comic masterpiece *Don Quixote (see p395)* was published to popular acclaim. He continued writing novels and plays until his death in Madrid on 23 April 1616, the same day that Shakespeare died.

Gardens surrounding the Royal Palace at Aranjuez

CENTRAL SPAIN

Introducing Central Spain

Much of Spain's vast central plateau, the *meseta*, is covered with wheat fields or dry, dusty plains, but there are many attractive places to explore. Central Spain's mountains, gorges, forests and lakes are filled with wildlife. A deep sense of history permeates the towns and cities of the tableland, reflected in some stunning architecture: the Roman ruins of Mérida, the medieval mansions of Cáceres, the Gothic cathedrals of Burgos, León and Toledo, the Renaissance grandeur of Salamanca, and castles almost everywhere.

León Cathedral (see p354–5), *an outstanding Gothic building, was completed during the 14th century. As well as many glorious windows of medieval glass, it has superb carved choir stalls depicting biblical scenes and everyday life.*

DAVID·REX·

León

CASTILLA Y LEÓN
(see pp346–77)

Zamora

Vallado

Salamanca (see pp358–61) *is the site of some of the finest Renaissance and Plateresque architecture in Spain. Among the city's most notable buildings are the university, its façade a mass of carved detail; the old and new cathedrals (built side by side); and the handsome Plaza Mayor, built in warm golden sandstone.*

Salamanca

Ávila

Cáceres

EXTREMADURA
(see pp400–13)

Tol

The Museo Nacional de Arte Romano *in Mérida (see p410) houses Roman treasures. The city has a well-preserved Roman theatre.*

Badajoz

0 kilometres 50

0 miles 50

◁ **Roofs and walls in the old part of Toledo**

Burgos Cathedral (see pp372–3) *is the work of some of the great medieval architects and artists, and it is full of treasures from all periods. This Baroque fresco of the coronation of the Virgin covers the domed ceiling of the sacristy.*

Segovia (see p364) *extends along a rocky spur that divides two rivers. The city's landmarks are the Alcázar (see pp344–5) – a castle with distinctive fairy-tale towers – and the Roman aqueduct, built in the 1st century AD, which towers 29 m (95 ft) above a busy urban square.*

Cuenca's *old town (see pp384–5) was built on a ridge high above two gorges. One of the picturesque but precariously sited "Hanging Houses" is now home to a museum of abstract art.*

CASTILLA-LA MANCHA
(see pp370–99)

Toledo Cathedral *(see pp392–3), with its exuberant sculptured decoration, is a great medieval building in a city of monuments. Toledo's architectural wealth stems from a fusion of Jewish, Christian and Muslim cultures.*

Burgos

Soria

Guadalajara

Madrid

Cuenca

Albacete

The Flavours of Central Spain

Madrid is famous for its extremes of temperature – a climate that has given rise to the rueful local saying "nine months of winter and three months of hell". The surrounding regions suffer the same extremes, and their traditional cuisines reflect both the wintry cold and the dusty, scorched terrain. Meat predominates as roasts and stews and in warming soups, thickened with beans and pulses, which thrive despite the weather. Cured hams, spicy sausages and pungent cheeses are excellent accompaniments to the strong local wine. The finest ham is from Extremadura, where black-footed *(pata negra)* pigs forage freely among the oaks.

Manchego cheese

A chef preparing *gambas ajillo*, a popular tapas dish

MADRID

Restaurants in Madrid, as befits the Spanish capital, offer cuisine from every corner of the country. Curiously, considering its distance from the ocean, the capital is famed for its seafood, flown in freshly every day. Madrileños

appreciate every part of an animal: a local saying goes "if it runs, walks or flies – into the pot". Madrid menus regularly feature brains, ears, pigs' trotters, and *callos a la Madrileña* (tripe) is a classic local dish. Sturdy stews, such as the celebrated *cocido Madrileño*, keep out the bitter winter cold. The *tapeo* – a bar crawl between tapas bars – is an institution in the city, and each bar has its own speciality dish.

CASTILLA Y LEON

Spread out high on a plain, searingly hot in summer, and bitingly cold in winter, Castilla y León is famous for its roasted meats, served in *asadores* (grillhouses). The most celebrated local dish is *cochinillo*, but pork, chicken, game in season and lamb are also popular. These are often combined with local pulses and lentils in hearty soups and stews, which are given

Pinto beans　White (butter) beans　Red (kidney) beans

Castillian garbanzos (chickpeas)

Black beans

Armuña lentils

Beans and pulses, key ingredients in the cooking of central Spain

REGIONAL DISHES AND SPECIALITIES

The cuisine of Spain's often wild and remote interior is characterized by warming soups and stews; traditionally made hams, cured meats and cheeses; plenty of filling beans and pulses; and flavourful fruit and vegetables. On the high plains of Castilla y León, locals keep out the winter cold with succulent roasted meats, and Extremaduran ham is the best you'll taste. In Don Quijote country, a glass of robust local wine and a chunk of Manchegan cheese is sheer delight. Fancy restaurants with fashionable food are few and far between, but welcoming, old-fashioned inns offer simple and tasty home-cooking. Madrid, of course, is the exception: here you'll find every possible cuisine, along with excellent seafood, which is hard to find anywhere else in this landlocked region.

Fresh figs

Cocido Madrileño *This rich stew is traditionally eaten in two stages: first the broth, and then the meat.*

Plucking the stamens from crocus flowers to make saffron

extra flavour with local *embutidos* (cured meats). The region also produces delicious cheeses such as soft white Burgos, often served with honey, *membrillo* (quince jelly) or nuts for dessert. Local wines are robust and simple, a good accompaniment to the strong flavours of the regional cuisine of Castilla y León.

CASTILLA LA MANCHA

This is Don Quijote country: empty, flat, dusty and scattered with windmills. Local inns and taverns serve traditional country cooking, with plenty of hearty soups, substantial casseroles and simply grilled local meat, poultry and seasonal game. Manchegan *gazpacho*, unlike its cold, vegetable soup, Andaluz namesake, is a hefty stew made with whatever meat is available. A common accompaniment to it is *pisto*, a ratatouille-like dish made with a range of tasty, fresh local vegetables. The Arabs brought with them saffron, which is still grown around Consuegra, and their influence also lingers on in Toledo's famous marzipan sweets and the fragrant Alajú almond soup from Cuenca.

Cured hams hanging in an *embutidos* shop

EXTREMADURA

Wild, beautiful Extremadura sees few visitors and, in many places, life continues virtually untouched by the 21st century. Endless rolling fields dotted with holm oak shelter the acorn-fed, black-footed pigs that make Spain's most highly prized hams (*jamón Ibérico*). Thanks to the deeply rooted hunting tradition, partridge, hare and wild boar regularly feature on local menus along with river fish such as tench and trout. There are some delicious cheeses, as well as perfumed local honey and wonderful fruit, particularly cherries, peaches and figs.

ON THE MENU

Chocolate con Churros The typical Spanish breakfast – thick hot chocolate with sugary strips of fried batter for dipping, originated in Madrid.

Cochinillo The speciality of Segovia: 21-day-old suckling pig, roasted until so tender it can be cut with a plate.

Gazpacho Manchego Sometimes called a galiano, this is a rich stew traditionally made with hare and partridge.

Macarraca Extremaduran salad of chopped ripe tomatoes with peppers, onion and garlic.

Tortilla de Patata A simple potato omelette, now a staple in restaurants all over Spain.

Albóndigas de la Abuela *"Grandmother's meatballs": sturdy country fare from the high plain of Castilla y León,*

Migas Extremeñas *Chunks of country bread are fried up with peppers, pork and chorizo or cured sausage.*

Yemas *A delicious treat from Ávila, these lemony, custardy cakes are made with egg yolks and sugar.*

Wines of Central Spain

The wines of Central Spain originate in either the small, high-quality regions of northwest Castilla y León or in the vast wine-producing plains of La Mancha and Valdepeñas. Ribera del Duero has become Spain's most fashionable red wine region, with its aromatic, rich yet fine reds made from Tinto Fino grapes (the local name for Tempranillo) and, more recently, lighter, fruity wines. Rueda makes a good white wine, made from the Verdejo grape. La Mancha and Valdepeñas both produce lots of simple white wine, and reds which can be mellow and fruity.

Harvesting Viura grapes at Rueda

Artesian well for irrigating vines in La Mancha

Toro *makes the most powerful and fiery of all red wines from the ubiquitous Tempranillo grape.*

Villafranca del Bierzo
Ponferrada • Cacábelos
ZAMORA
Duero
SALAMANCA

KEY FACTS ABOUT WINES OF CENTRAL SPAIN

Location and Climate
Ribera del Duero, Rueda and Toro are all high-lying areas with extreme climates – very hot summer days combined with cool nights, and cold winters. The marked difference of temperature between day and night helps to preserve the acidity in the grapes. Both La Mancha and Valdepeñas are extremely hot and dry areas. In recent years, droughts have caused a severe shortage of grapes.

Grape Varieties
The Tempranillo grape – also known as Tinto Fino, Tinto del Toro and Cencibel – produces nearly all the best red wines of Central Spain. Cabernet Sauvignon is permitted in some regions; it is used in some Ribera del Duero wines and occasionally

surfaces as a single varietal, as at the estate of the Marquis of Griñón in Méntrida. Verdejo, Viura and Sauvignon Blanc are used for white Rueda. The white Airén grape predominates in the vineyards of Valdepeñas and La Mancha.

Good Producers
Toro: Fariña (Gran Colegiata). **Rueda:** Álvarez y Diez, Los Curros, Marqués de Riscal, Sanz. **Ribera del Duero:** Alejandro Fernández (Pesquera), Boada, Hermanos Pérez Pascuas (Viña Pedrosa), Ismael Arroyo (Valsotillo), Vega Sicilia, Victor Balbás. **Méntrida:** Marqués de Griñón. **La Mancha:** Fermín Ayuso Roig (Estola), Vinícola de Castilla (Castillo de Alhambra). **Valdepeñas:** Casa de la Viña, Félix Solís, Luis Megía (Marqués de Gastañaga), Los Llanos.

Traditional earthenware *tinaja,* still used for fermenting wine

0 kilometres   100
0 miles   50

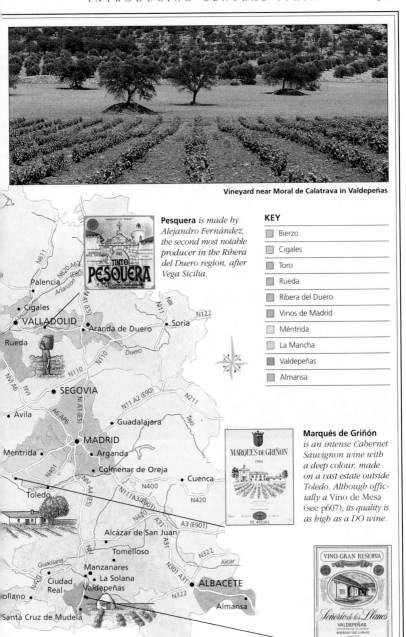

Vineyard near Moral de Calatrava in Valdepeñas

Pesquera *is made by Alejandro Fernández, the second most notable producer in the Ribera del Duero region, after Vega Sicilia.*

KEY

- Bierzo
- Cigales
- Toro
- Rueda
- Ribera del Duero
- Vinos de Madrid
- Méntrida
- La Mancha
- Valdepeñas
- Almansa

Marqués de Griñón *is an intense Cabernet Sauvignon wine with a deep colour, made on a vast estate outside Toledo. Although officially a Vino de Mesa (see p607), its quality is as high as a DO wine.*

Señorío de los Llanos *is produced in Valdepeñas. Its fine reds – made from Cencibel (Tempranillo) and aged in oak – are of excellent value.*

WINE REGIONS

The wine regions of Ribera del Duero, Toro and Rueda, are situated on remote, high plateaus, straddling the Río Duero. To the northwest lies the isolated region of Bierzo, whose wines have more in common with neighbouring Valdeorras in Galicia. Some wine is produced around Madrid, and southwest of the capital is the largely undistinguished region of Méntrida. Most of Central Spain's wine is produced in La Mancha – the world's largest single wine region – and in the smaller enclave of Valdepeñas, which produces a great deal of "vino de mesa".

Birds of Central Spain

The vast and varied wild habitats of Central Spain are home to the richest avifauna in the peninsula. White storks' nests are a common sight on the church towers and chimneypots of towns. Grebes, herons and shovelers can be seen in the marshlands; the distinctive hoopoe is often spotted in woods; and grasslands are the nesting grounds of bustards and cranes. The mountains and high plains are the domain of birds of prey such as the imperial eagle, peregrine falcon and vultures. Deforestation, changing agricultural practices and hunting have all taken their toll in recent decades. Today, almost 160 bird species are the subject of conservation initiatives.

Bee-eater

MIGRATION ROUTES

— Cranes
— Storks
— Raptors
— Wildfowl

MARSHLAND AND WET MEADOW

Wetlands, such as Lagunas de Ruidera (see p397), on the edge of the plains of La Mancha, are vital feeding grounds for a wide range of waterfowl, some of which may remain in Spain throughout the year. Other migratory species use such sites as stopover points to feed, rest and build up enough energy to enable them to complete their journeys.

Little egrets *are recognized by their snow white plumage and graceful slow flight. They feed largely on frogs, snails and small fish.*

Shovelers *feed on the water surface with a characteristic shovelling motion. The male has brightly coloured plumage but the female is a dull brown.*

WOODLAND AND SCRUB

Habitats in areas of woodland, such as the Parque Nacional de Cabañeros (see p387), and scrub support many species, such as rollers and woodpeckers, throughout the year. Food is plentiful and there are many places to roost and nest. Early in the morning is the best time for spotting some of the rarer species, such as the bluethroat.

Rollers *are commonly found in woodland, often nesting in tree stumps or holes left by woodpeckers. Their food includes grasshoppers, crickets and beetles.*

Hoopoes *can be easily identified by their striking plumage and by the crest which can be raised if the bird is alarmed. They feed on ground insects.*

STORKS

Both the white and the (much rarer) black stork breed in Spain. They can be recognized in flight by their slow, steady wingbeats and may occasionally be seen soaring on thermals, usually during migrations. During the breeding season they put on elaborate courtship displays, which involve "dancing", wing-beating and bill-clapping. Their large nests, made of branches and twigs and lined with grasses, are constructed on roofs, towers, spires and chimneypots, where they are easy to watch. They feed on insects, fish and amphibians. Stork populations are threatened by wetland reclamation and the use of pesticides.

The endangered black stork

Nesting on a monastery roof

GRASSLAND AND FIELD

Many of Spain's natural grasslands have been ploughed over to plant cereals and other crops. Remaining vestiges are rich in wild grasses and flowers and are vital habitats for species such as bustards and larks.

Cranes *perform elegant courtship dances and are also stately birds in flight, their long necks extended to the limit. They are omnivores, feeding on amphibians, crustaceans, plants and insects.*

Great bustards *nest in shallow depressions formed in open grassland and cultivated fields. Spain is home to half of the world's population.*

MOUNTAIN AND HIGH PLAIN

Some of Spain's most spectacular birds of prey live in mountain ranges, such as the Sierra de Gredos *(see p362)*, and the high plains of Central Spain. The broad wingspans of eagles and vultures allow them to soar on currents of warm air as they scan the ground below for prey and carrion.

Imperial eagles, *with their vast wingspan of 2.25 m (7 ft), are extremely rare – only around 100 pairs are left in the whole of Spain.*

Griffon vultures, *a gregarious species, nest in trees and on rocky crags, often using the same place from year to year. Their broad wingspans can exceed 2 m (6 ft).*

The Castles of Castile

The greatest concentration of Spain's 2,000 castles is in Castile (now part of Castilla y León), which derived its name from the word *castillo*, or castle. In the 10th and 11th centuries this region was the battleground between Moors and Christians. Villages and towns were fortified as protection against one side or the other. Most of the surviving castles in Castile, however, were built as noble residences after the area had been reconquered and there was no longer a military purpose for them. Fernando and Isabel *(see pp56–7)* banned the building of new castles at the end of the 15th century; many existing ones were converted to domestic use.

13th-century fresco of the siege of a castle

Coca Castle *(see p365)*, a classic Mudéjar design in brick

Patio de armas (courtyard)

Bartizan turrets

The Torre de Juan II contained the dungeons.

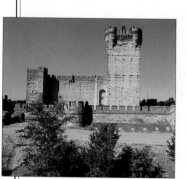

La Mota Castle (see p366), *at Medina del Campo, near Valladolid, was originally a Moorish castle but was rebuilt after 1440 and later became the property of Fernando and Isabel. The square-shaped Torre del Homenaje has twin bartizan turrets at its corners and machiolations beneath its battlements. Great curtain walls surround the castle.*

The barbican, with the coat of arms of the Catholic Monarchs carved over the gate, contains the portcullis and guards' watchrooms.

Belmonte Castle (see p394) *was built in the 15th century as the stronghold of the quarrelsome Marquis of Villena, Juan Pacheco. Late-Gothic in style, it has a sophisticated, hexagonal ground plan, with a triangular bailey.*

THE ALCAZAR, SEGOVIA

The plan of the royal castle of Segovia (*see p364*) is determined by the contours of the rocky outcrop on which it stands. Begun in the 12th century, the Alcázar was mostly built between 1410 and 1455. It had to be largely rebuilt following a fire in 1862. The fortress's formidable walls conceal several sumptuous apartments.

Torre del Homenaje has pointed turrets, atypical of Spanish castles.

Curtain wall

The King's Room, the most important room in the castle, is Gothic in style.

The Pine Cone Room gets its name from the golden pine cones on the ceiling.

The Galley Room

The Throne Room has ornate plasterwork and a Mudéjar ceiling.

TERMS USED IN THIS GUIDE

Alcazar: Castle or palace used as a royal residence.

Bartizan: A small turret which projects from the battlements of a tower above attackers.

Cross and orb loophole: Narrow slit, shaped to allow archers to shoot at various angles.

Curtain wall: Outer, windowless wall, often low enough for archers to fire over it from the keep and other towers.

Machicolation: A projection overhanging the wall beneath a battlement to allow boiling oil, missiles or human waste to be dropped on to the enemy.

Torre del Homenaje: The fortified tower or keep at the heart of a castle, often built to a square plan, in which the nobleman's family lived.

Peñafiel Castle (see p367) *has been compared to a battleship because of its long, narrow shape. The site above the Duero valley has been defended since the 10th century, but the present castle is 15th-century.*

THE CASTLES OF CASTILLA Y LEÓN

Some of Central Spain's finest surviving castles can be visited today. A few, such as Ciudad Rodrigo (*see p357*), have been turned into luxurious paradors (*see pp558–9*).

CASTILLA Y LEÓN

LEÓN · ZAMORA · SALAMANCA · ÁVILA · SEGOVIA
VALLADOLID · PALENCIA · BURGOS · SORIA

*A*wesome expanses of ochre plains stretch to hills crowned
with the castles that cover this vast region. Through Spain's
history, these central provinces have had a major influence
on its language, religion and culture. Their many historic cities
preserve some of the country's most magnificent architectural sights.

The territories of the two rival medieval kingdoms of Castile and León, occupying the northern half of the great plateau in the centre of Spain, now form the country's largest region, or *comunidad autónoma*.

Castile and León were first brought together under one crown in 1037 by Fernando I; but the union was not consolidated until the early 13th century. The kingdom of Castile and León was one of the driving forces of the Reconquest. El Cid, the legendary hero, was born near Burgos.

Wealth pouring in from the wool trade and the New World, reaching a peak in the 16th century, financed the many great artistic and architectural treasures that can be seen today in the cities of Castilla y León. Burgos has an exuberantly decorated Gothic cathedral. León cathedral is famous for its wonderful stained glass. At the heart of the monumental city of Salamanca is the oldest university in the peninsula. Segovia's aqueduct is the largest Roman structure in Spain and its Alcázar is the country's most photographed castle. Ávila is surrounded by an unbroken wall, built by Christian forces against the Moors. In Valladolid, the regional capital, a superb collection of multicoloured sculpture is displayed in a magnificent 15th-century building.

Beyond the cities, in Castilla y León's varied countryside, there are many attractive small towns which preserve outstanding examples of the region's vernacular architecture.

Cereal fields and vineyards covering the fertile Tierra de Campos in Palencia province

◁ The battle-scarred castle of Calatañazor (Soria), site of a Christian victory against the Moors in 1002

Exploring Castilla y León

Covering the northern part of Central Spain's vast tableland, Castilla y León has a huge variety of sights. Many – the university of Salamanca, the Alcázar and aqueduct of Segovia, the medieval walls of Ávila, the monastery at Santo Domingo de Silos, and the great cathedrals of Burgos and León – are well known. Other historic towns and villages worthy of a detour include Ciudad Rodrigo, Covarrubias, Pedraza de la Sierra and Zamora. This region also has beautiful mountainous countryside in the Sierra de Francia, Sierra de Bejar and Sierra de Gredos.

0 kilometres 50

0 miles 30

SIGHTS AT A GLANCE

SEE ALSO

GETTING AROUND

Madrid makes a convenient springboard for touring in Castilla y León. The major cities of the region are connected by rail but the coach is often a quicker alternative. If you intend exploring rural areas or visiting small towns it is advisable to hire a car. Be aware that as Spain is in the process of changing its road numbering system some of the roads featured here may differ from new road signs.

Sunflowers growing in Burgos province

KEY

═══	Motorway
═ ═	Motorway under construction
───	Major road
═══	Secondary road
───	Scenic route
───	Main railway
───	Minor railway
▬▬	International border
───	Regional border
△	Summit

Peñaranda de Duero castle

El Bierzo ❶

León. 🚉 Ponferrada. 🚌
Ponferrada. 🛈 Ponferrada, 987 42
35 51. **www**.bierzonet.es

This northwestern region of
León province was at one
time the bed of an ancient
lake. Sheltered by hills from
the worst extremes of Central
Spain's climate, its sun-soaked,
alluvial soils make for fertile
orchards and vineyards. Over
the centuries, the area has also
yielded rich mineral pickings
including coal, iron and gold.
Many hiking routes and picnic spots are within reach of
the main towns of Ponferrada
and Villafranca del Bierzo.

In the eastern section, you
can trace the course of the old
Road to Santiago (see pp82–3)
through the **Montes de León**,
past the pilgrim church and
medieval bridge of Molinaseca.
Turning off the road at the remote village of Acebo you pass
through a deep valley where
there are signs pointing to the
Herrería de Compludo, a
fascinating water-powered 7th-
century ironworks. The equipment is still in working order
and is demonstrated regularly.

The **Lago de Carucedo**, to
the southwest of Ponferrada,
is an ancient artificial lake. It
acted as a reservoir in Roman
times, a by-product of a vast
gold-mining operation. Using
slave labour, millions of tonnes
of alluvium were washed from

A *palloza* in the Sierra de Ancares

the hills of Las Médulas by a
complex system of canals and
sluice gates. The ore was then
panned, and the gold dust collected on sheep's wool. It has
been estimated that more than
500 tonnes of precious metal
were extracted from the hills
between the 1st and 4th centuries AD. These ancient workings lie within a memorable
landscape of wind-eroded
crags, and hills pierced by tunnels and colonized by gnarled
chestnut trees. You can best
appreciate the area from a
viewpoint at Orellán, which is
reached via a rough, steep
track. **Las Médulas**, a village
south of Carucedo, is another
place to go for a fine view.

To the north of the NVI highway lies the Sierra de Ancares,
a wild region of rounded, slate
mountains marking the borders

of Galicia and Asturias. Part
of it now forms the **Reserva
Nacional de los Ancares
Leoneses**, an attractive nature
reserve. The heathland dotted
with oak and birch copses is
home to deer, wolves, brown
bears and capercaillies.

Several isolated villages high
in the hills contain *pallozas* –
primitive, pre-Roman stone
dwellings thatched with rye.
One of the most striking collections of these huts can be
found in the isolated village of
Campo del Agua, in the west.

🏛 **Herrería de Compludo**
Compludo. **Tel** 987 69 54 21.
☐ Tue–Sun. 📷

Villafranca del Bierzo ❷

León. 👥 3,900. 🚌 🛈 C/ Diez Ovelar
10, 987 54 00 28. 🚌 Tue & Fri. 📷
Winter Fiesta (28 Jan), Spring Fiesta
(1 May), Fiesta del Cristo (14 Sep).

Emblazoned mansions line the
ancient streets of this delightful
town on the Road to Santiago.
The solid, early 16th- century,
drum-towered castle is still
inhabited. Near the Plaza Mayor
a number of imposing churches
and convents compete for
attention. Particularly worth
seeing are the fine sculptures
adorning the north portal of
the simple, Romanesque **Iglesia
de Santiago**. At the church's
Puerta del Perdón (Door of

Craggy, tree-clad hills around the ancient gold workings near the village of Las Médulas

For hotels and restaurants in this region see pp582–5 and pp633–6

Mercy), pilgrims who were too weak to make the final gruelling hike across the hills of Galicia could obtain dispensation. Visitors to the town can also sample the local speciality, cherries marinated in *aguardiente*, a spirit.

Environs

One of the finest views over El Bierzo is from **Corullón,** to the south. This pretty village with grey stone houses is set in a sunny location above the broad, fertile basin of the Río Burbia where the vines of the Bierzo wine region flourish (*see pp78–9*). Two churches, the late 11th-century San Miguel and the restored, Romanesque San Esteban, are worth a visit. Down in the valley, the Benedictine monastery at **Carracedo del Monasterio** stands in splendour. Founded in 990, it was once the most powerful religious community in El Bierzo.

Puerta del Perdón of Villafranca's Iglesia de Santiago

Ponferrada ❸

León. 🏠 70,000. 🚉 🚌 ℹ️ *C/ Gil y Carrasco 4, 987 42 42 36.* 🗓️ *Wed & Sat.* 🎉 *Virgen de la Encina (8 Sep).*

A medieval bridge reinforced with iron (*pons ferrata*), erected for the benefit of pilgrims on their way to Santiago de Compostela, gave this town its name. Today, prosperous from both iron and coal deposits, Ponferrada has expanded into a sizeable town.

Most of its attractions are confined to the small old quarter. Ponferrada's majestic **castle** was constructed between the

The imposing Templar castle of Ponferrada

12th and 14th centuries by the Knights Templar to protect pilgrims. During the Middle Ages it was one of the largest fortresses in northwest Spain.

Standing on the main square is the Baroque **town hall** (*ayuntamiento*). One entrance to the square is straddled by a tall clock tower which sits above one of the gateways of the medieval wall. Nearby is the Renaissance **Basílica de la Virgen de la Encina**. The older **Iglesia de Santo Tomás de las Ollas** is hidden away in the town's village-like northern suburbs. Mozarabic, Romanesque and Baroque elements combine in the architecture of this simple church. The 10th-century apse has beautiful horseshoe arches. Ask at the nearest house for the key.

Environs

A drive through the idyllic **Valle de Silencio** (Valley of Silence), south of Ponferrada, follows a poplar-lined stream past several bucolic villages. The last and most beautiful of these is **Peñalba de Santiago**, just beneath an attractive ring of mountains. The 10th-century Mozarabic church of Santiago de Peñalba has horseshoe arches above its double portal.

Puebla de Sanabria ❹

Zamora. 🏠 1,700. 🚌 ℹ️ *Calle Rua 13, 980 62 07 34.* 🗓️ *Fri.* 🎉 *Candelas (last weekend in Jan), Las Victorias (8 & 9 Sep).*

This attractive old village lies beyond the undulating broom and oak scrub of the Sierra de la Culebra. A steep cobbled street leads past stone and slate houses with huge, overhanging eaves and walls bearing coats of arms, to a hilltop church and castle.

The village has become the centre of a popular inland holiday resort based around the largest glacial lake in Spain, the **Lago de Sanabria**, now a nature park. Among the many activities available are fishing, walking and water sports.

Local touring routes beckon visitors to Ribadelago on the lakeshore, though the road to the quaint hill village of **San Martín de Castañeda** gives better views. There's a small visitors' centre for the nature reserve in San Martín's restored monastery. The village is very traditional – you may see cattle yoked to carts, and women dressed completely in black.

The 12th-century church and 15th-century castle of Puebla de Sanabria

The nave of Astorga cathedral

Astorga 5

León. 🏛 12,400. 🚉 🚌 ℹ️ *Plaza Eduardo de Castro 5.* **Tel** *987 61 82 22.* 🛒 *Tue.* 🎉 *Santa Marta (late Aug).*

The Roman town of Asturica Augusta was a strategic halt on the Vía de la Plata (Silver Road), a Roman road linking Andalusia and northwest Spain. Later it came to form a stage on the pilgrimage route to Santiago *(see pp82–3).*

Soaring above the ramparts in the upper town are Astorga's two principal monuments, the cathedral and the Palacio Episcopal. The **cathedral** was built between the 15th and the 18th centuries and displays a variety of architectural styles ranging from its Gothic apse to the effusive Baroque of its two towers, which are carved with various biblical scenes. The gilt altarpiece by Gaspar Becerra is a masterpiece of the Spanish Renaissance. Among the many fine exhibits found in the cathedral's museum are the 10th-century carved casket of Alfonso III the Great, the jewelled Reliquary of the True Cross and a lavish silver monstrance which is studded with enormous emeralds.

Opposite the cathedral is a fairy-tale building of multiple turrets and quasi-Gothic windows. The unconventional **Palacio Episcopal** (Bishop's Palace) was designed at the end of the 19th century by Antoni Gaudí, the highly original Modernista architect *(see p164),* for the incumbent bishop, a fellow Catalan, after a fire in 1887 had destroyed the previous building. Its bizarre appearance as well as its phenomenal cost so horrified the diocese that no subsequent bishops ever lived in it. Today it houses an assembly of medieval religious art devoted to the history of Astorga and the pilgrimage to Santiago. Roman relics, including coins unearthed in the Plaza Romana, are evidence of Astorga's importance as a Roman settlement. The palace's interior is decorated with Gaudí's ceramic tiles and stained glass.

Reliquary of the True Cross

🏛 **Palacio Episcopal**
Pl Eduardo de Castro. **Tel** *987 61 68 82.* ⬜ *Tue–Sun.* ⬛ *Mon, Sun pm, public hols.* 📷

Cueva de Valporquero 6

Valporquero. **Tel** *987 57 64 08.* 🚌 *from León.* ⬜ *Apr–May: Fri–Sun; Jun–Sep: daily; Oct: Fri–Sun.* 📷

This complex of limestone caves – technically a single cave with three separate entrances – is directly beneath the village of Valporquero de Torío in the northern part of León province. The caves were formed in the Miocene period between 5 and 25 million years ago. Severe weather conditions in the surrounding mountains make the water-sculpted caverns inaccessible between December and Easter. Less than half of the huge system, which stretches 3,100 m (10,200 ft) under the ground, is open to the public.

Guided tours take parties through an impressive series of galleries in which lighting picks out the beautiful limestone concretions. Iron and sulphur oxides have tinted the rocks many subtle shades of red, grey and black. The massive Gran Rotonda, covering an area of 5,600 sq m (18,350 sq ft) and reaching a height of 20 m (65 ft), is the most stunning cave in the complex.

As the interior is cold, and the surface often slippery to walk on, it is advisable to wear warm clothes and sturdy shoes.

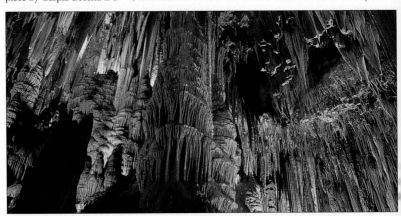

Illuminated stalactites hanging from the roof of one of the chambers in the Cuevas de Valporquero

León ❼

León. 147,000. 🚉 🚌 ℹ️ *Plaza de la Regla 4, 987 23 70 82.* 🗓️ *Wed & Sat.* 🎉 *San Juan and San Pedro (21–29 Jun).* www.castillayleon.com

Founded as a camp for the Romans' Seventh Legion, León became the capital of a kingdom in the Middle Ages. As such it played a central role in the early years of the Reconquest *(see pp52–3)*.

The city's most important building – apart from its great **cathedral** *(see pp354–5)* – is the **Colegiata de San Isidoro**, built into the Roman walls which encircle the city. A separate entrance leads through to the Romanesque **Panteón Real** (Royal Pantheon), the last resting place of more than 20 monarchs. It is superbly decorated with carved capitals and 12th-century frescoes illustrating a variety of biblical and mythical subjects, as well as scenes of medieval life.

The alleyways in the picturesque old quarter around the Plaza Mayor are interspersed with bars and cafés, decrepit mansions and churches. Two well-preserved palaces stand near to the Plaza de Santo Domingo: the **Casa de los Guzmanes**, with its elegantly arcaded Renaissance patio, and Antoni Gaudí's unusually restrained **Casa de Botines** (which is now a bank).

The **Hostal de San Marcos**, down beside the river, is a prime example of Spanish

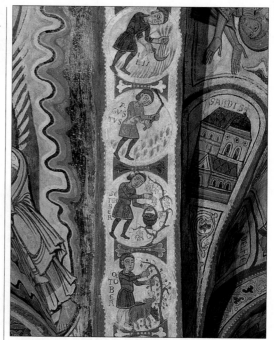

Frescoes in Basílica de San Isidoro showing medieval seasonal tasks

Renaissance architecture *(see p25)*. It was founded during the 12th century as a monastery to lodge travellers en route to Santiago. The present building was begun in 1513 as the headquarters of the Knights of Santiago. The incredibly elaborate project continued into the 18th century, when a Baroque pediment added a final flourish to the beautiful Plateresque façade studded with scallop

shells. The main hall has a fine 16th-century coffered ceiling. A parador *(see p558)* now occupies the main part of the Hostal de San Marcos. In the vaulted galleries off the church and cloister is the **Museo de León**, whose many treasures include a haunting little ivory crucifix, the *Cristo de Carrizo*.

Environs

Around 30 km (20 miles) east of León is the **Iglesia de San Miguel de Escalada**. Dating from the 10th century, it is one of the finest surviving churches built by the Mozarabs – Christians influenced by the Moors. Notice the Visigothic panels and the exterior gallery of stately horseshoe arches resting on carved capitals. At **Sahagún**, 70 km (40 miles) southeast of León, are the Mudéjar churches of San Tirso and San Lorenzo, with triple apses and belfries. A colossal ruined castle overlooks the Río Esla beside **Valencia de Don Juan**, 40 km (25 miles) south of León.

🏛️ **Museo de León**
Plaza de San Marcos. **Tel** 987 24 50 61. ◯ Tue–Sun. 🎫 *(free Sat & Sun).*

THE MARAGATOS

Astorga is the principal town of the Maragatos, an ethnic group of unknown origin, thought to be descended from 8th-century Berber invaders. By marrying only among themselves, they managed to preserve their customs through the centuries and keep themselves apart from the rest of society. Although the demise of their traditional trade of mule-driving has changed their way of life, the Maragatos still keep to their communities. Their costumes can be seen during fiestas.

Maragatos dressed in traditional costume

León Cathedral

Carved detail from the choir

The master builders of this Spanish Gothic cathedral *par excellence (see p24)* were inspired by French techniques of vaulting and buttressing. The present structure of golden sandstone, built on the site of King Ordoño II's 10th-century palace, was begun in the mid-13th century and completed less than 100 years later.

It combines a slender but very high nave with the huge panels of stained glass which are the cathedral's most magnificent feature. Although it has survived for 700 years, today there is concern about air pollution attacking the soft stone.

West Rose Window
This largely 14th century window depicts the Virgin and Child, surrounded by twelve trumpet blowing angels.

The 13th- to 14th-century cloister galleries are decorated with Gothic frescoes by Nicolás Francés.

The silver reliquary is an ornate chest dating from the 16th century.

Cathedral Museum
Pedro de Campaña's panel, The Adoration of the Magi, *is one of the many magnificent treasures displayed in the museum.*

Entrance

★ West Front
The three portals are decorated with 13th-century carvings. Those above the Portada del Juicio *depict a scene from the Last Judgment, where the Blessed pass into paradise.*

Inside the Cathedral
*The plan of the building is a
Latin cross. The tall nave is
slender but long, measuring
90 m (295 ft) by 40 m (130 ft)
at its widest. To appreciate
the dazzling colours of the
stained glass it is best to visit
on a sunny day.*

VISITORS' CHECKLIST

Plaza de Regla. **Tel** 987 87 57
70. ☐ Jul–Sep: 8:30am–
1:30pm & 4–8pm; Oct–Jun:
8:30am–1:30pm & 4–7pm daily.
✝ 9am, noon, 1pm & 6pm daily,
plus 11am & 2pm Sun. ☒ ♿
Museum ☐ 9:30am–1pm,
4–6:30pm (7pm Jul–Sep)
Mon–Sat. ☒

The altarpiece
includes five original
panels created by
Gothic master
Nicolás Francés.

The Virgen Blanca
*is a Gothic sculp-
ture of a smiling
Virgin. The ori-
ginal is kept in
this chapel. A
copy stands by
the west door.*

The choir has
two tiers of 15th-
century stalls. Behind it is
the carved and gilded retrochoir,
in the shape of a triumphal arch.

★ Stained Glass
*The windows, covering
an area of 1,800 sq
metres (19,350 sq ft),
are the outstanding
feature of the cathedral.*

LEÓN'S STAINED GLASS

León cathedral's great glory is its magnificent
glasswork. The 125 large windows and 57
smaller, round ones date from every century
from the 13th to the 20th.
They cover an enormous
range of subjects, from
fantastical beasts to
plants. Many depict
saints and characters
from biblical stories.

**Window with
plant motif**

Some of the windows reveal fascinating details about medieval
life: *La Cacería*, in the north wall,
depicts a typical hunting scene,
while the rose window in the
Capilla del Nacimiento shows
pilgrims worshipping at the tomb
of St James in Santiago de Compostela in Galicia (*see pp92–3*).

A large window in the south wall

STAR FEATURES

★ West Front

★ Stained Glass

Zamora ⑧

Zamora. 🏘 65,000. 🚃 🚌 🛈
Calle de Santa Clara 20, 980 53 18 45.
🗓 Tue. 🎭 Semana Santa (Easter
Week), San Pedro (29 Jun).
www.turismocastillayleon.com

Little remains of Zamora's
past as an important strategic
frontier town. In Roman times,
it was on the Vía de la Plata
(see p352), and during the
Reconquest was fought over
fiercely. The city has now
expanded far beyond its
original boundaries, but the
old quarter contains a wealth
of Romanesque churches.

The ruins of the **city walls**,
built by Alfonso III in 893, are
pierced by the Portillo de la
Traición (Traitor's Gate),
through which the murderer
of Sancho II passed in 1072.
The 16th-century **parador** *(see
p585)* is in an old palace with
a Renaissance courtyard
adorned with coats of arms.

Two other palaces, the **Casa
de los Momos** and the **Casa
del Cordón**, have ornately
carved façades and windows.
Zamora's most important
monument is its unique
cathedral, a 12th-century
structure built in Romanesque
style but with a number of
later Gothic additions. The
building's most eyecatching
feature is its striking, scaly,
hemispherical dome. Inside,
there are superb iron grilles
and Mudéjar pulpits surround

Peaceful gardens of the Colegiata
de Santa María in Toro

Juan de Bruselas' 15th-century
choir stalls. The allegorical
carvings of nuns and monks
on the misericords and arm-
rests were once considered
risqué. The museum, off the
sober cloisters, has a collection
of 15th- and 16th-century
Flemish tapestries. These
illustrate biblical passages and
classical and military scenes.

Nearby, several churches exhibit features characteristic of
Zamora's architectural style,
notably multi-lobed arches and
heavily carved portals. The best
are the 12th-century **Iglesia de
San Ildefonso** and the **Iglesia
de la Magdalena**.

Another reason for visiting
Zamora is for its lively Easter
Week celebrations, when elaborate *pasos* (sculpted floats) are
paraded in the streets. Otherwise they can be admired in
the **Museo de Semana Santa**.

Environs
The 7th-century Visigothic
church of **San Pedro de la
Nave**, 23 km (14 miles)
northwest of Zamora, has

Sierra de Francia and Sierra de Bejar ⑩

These attractive schist hills buttress the
western edges of the Sierra de Gredos
(see p362). Narrow roads wind their way
through picturesque chestnut, olive and
almond groves, and quaint rural villages
of wood and stone. The highest point of
the range is La Peña de Francia, which,
at 1,732 m (5,700 ft), is easily recognizable
from miles around. The views from the
peak, and from the roads leading up to
it, offer a breathtaking panorama of the
surrounding empty plains and rolling hills.

La Peña de Francia ①
Crowning the peak is a
windswept Dominican
monastery sheltering a
blackened, Byzantine-
style statue of the
Virgin and Child.

La Alberca ②
This pretty and much-
visited village sells local
honey, hams and handi-
crafts. On 15 August each
year it celebrates the
Assumption with a
traditional mystery
play performed
in costume.

CIUDAD RODRIGO
SA 202
Aga
SA 201
EX 204
CORIA

0 kilometres   5
0 miles   5

KEY

▬▬ Tour route
══ Other roads
🔆 Viewpoint

Las Batuecas ③
The road from La
Alberca careers down
into a green valley, p
the monastery where
Luis Buñuel made his
film *Tierra sin Pan
(Land without Bread*

The unmistakable peak of La Peña de Francia

Fish-scale tiling on dome of Zamora cathedral

carvings adorning its capitals and friezes. **Toro**, 33 km (21 miles) east of Zamora, is at the heart of a wine region *(see pp 340–1)*. The highlights of its **Colegiata de Santa María** are the Gothic west portal and a fine 16th-century Hispano-Flemish painting, *La Virgen de la Mosca*. In 1476, the forces of Isabel I *(see pp56–7)* secured a victory over the Portuguese at Toro, confirming her succession to the Castile throne.

Ciudad Rodrigo ⑨

Salamanca. 🏘 *14,000.* 🚉 🚌 🅸
Plaza de Amayuelas 5, 923 46 05 61.
🛒 *Tue.* 🎉 *San Sebastián (20 Jan),*
Carnaval del Toro (before Lent).
www.ciudadrodrigo.net

Despite its lonely setting – stranded on the country's western marches miles from anywhere – this lovely old town is well worth a detour. Its frontier location inevitably

gave rise to fortification, and its robust 14th-century castle is now an atmospheric **parador** *(see p583)* with good views over the Río Agueda. The prosperous 15th and 16th centuries were Ciudad Rodrigo's heyday. During the War of Independence *(see pp62–3)*, the city, then occupied by the French, was besieged for for two years before falling to the Duke of Wellington's forces.

The golden stone buildings within the ramparts are delightful. The main monument is the **cathedral**, whose belfry still bears the marks of shellfire from the siege. The exterior has a shapely curved balustrade and accomplished portal carvings. Inside, it is worth seeing the cloisters and the choir stalls, carved with lively scenes by Rodrigo Alemán. The main attraction of the adjacent **Capilla de Cerralbo** (Cerralbo Chapel) is a 17th century altarpiece. Off the chapel's south side is the quiet, arcaded Plaza del Buen Alcalde.

Miranda del Castañar ④
The narrow streets of this pretty, fortified village are lined with ancient houses with wide eaves.

SALAMANCA
Santibáñez de la Sierra
Cristóbal
Cepeda
adronal
Sotoserrano
La Calzada
Sangusín

Béjar ⑤
This textile town is strung out along a ridge at the foot of the Sierra de Béjar. From the approach road, 19th-century factories and mills can be seen.

SALAMANCA

TIPS FOR DRIVERS

Tour length: *72 km (45 miles).*
Stopping-off points:
Candelario, Miranda del Castañar and La Alberca all have good eating places, and are renowned for their hams and sausages. In summer, refreshments are available from the hospedería (inn) in La Peña's monastery.

Candelario ⑥
The steep, cobbled streets are lined with deep channels and stormgates to cope with the spring melt-water from the surrounding mountains and flash floods.

Street-by-Street: Salamanca ⓫

Shell detail, façade of the Casa de las Conchas

The great university city of Salamanca is Spain's finest showcase of Renaissance and Plateresque architecture. Founded as an Iberian settlement in pre-Roman times, the city fell to Hannibal in 217 BC. Preeminent among its artists and master craftsmen of later years were the Churriguera brothers *(see p25)*. Their work can be seen in many of Salamanca's golden stone buildings, notably in the Plaza Mayor. Other major sights are the two cathedrals and the 13th-century university, one of Europe's oldest and most distinguished.

The Casa de las Conchas is easily identifiable from the stone scallop shells that stud its walls. It is now a library.

The Palacio de Monterrey is a Renaissance mansion.

★ Universidad
In the centre of the university's elaborate façade is this medallion, carved in relief, which depicts the Catholic Monarchs.

★ Catedral Vieja and Catedral Nueva
Despite being in different architectural styles, the adjoining old and new cathedrals blend well together. This richly coloured altarpiece painted in 1445 is in the old cathedral.

Puente Romano
The Roman bridge across the Río Tormes, built in the 1st century AD, retains 15 of its original 26 arches. It provides an excellent view of the city.

CALLE DE LA COMPAÑÍA

CALLE DE SERRANOS

CALLE DE LOS LIBREROS

CALLE VERACRUZ

PASEO D

STAR SIGHTS

★ Universidad

★ Catedral Vieja and Catedral Nueva

★ Plaza Mayor

0 metres   100

0 yards   100

Museo Art Nouveau y Art Deco

KEY

– – – Suggested route

★ Plaza Mayor
This 18th-century square is one of Spain's largest and grandest. On the east side is the Royal Pavilion, decorated with a bust of Felipe V, who built the square.

VISITORS' CHECKLIST

Salamanca. 🏠 165,000. ✈ 15 km (9 miles) east. 🚉 Paseo de la Estación, 902 24 02 02. 🚌 Avda de Filiberto Villalobos 71, 923 23 67 17. 🛈 Plaza Mayor 32, 923 21 83 42. 🗓 Sun. 🎉 San Juan de Sahagún (12 Jun), Virgen de la Vega (8 Sep).

Iglesia de San Martín

The **Palacio de Fonseca** was built in 1538 by Archbishop Alonso de Fonseca.

Torre del Clavero
This 15th-century tower still has its original turrets. They are adorned with the coats of arms of its founders, and Mudéjar trelliswork.

Iglesia-Convento de San Esteban
The Plateresque façade of the church is carved with delicate relief. Above the door is a frieze decorated with medallions and coats of arms.

Convento de las Dueñas
Sculptures on the capitals of the beautiful two-storey cloister show demons, skulls and tormented faces, which contrast with serene carvings of the Virgin.

PLAZA MAYOR

AZA RRILLO

CALLE DE SAN PABLO

CALLE DEL CONSUELO

PLAZA DEL CONCILIO DE TRENTO

ARROYO SANTO DOMINGO

OR ESPERABÉ

Exploring Salamanca

The majority of Salamanca's monuments are located inside the city centre, which is compact enough to explore on foot. The university, the Plaza Mayor, and the old and new cathedrals are all unmissable.

🔒 Catedral Vieja and Catedral Nueva

Unusually, the 16th-century new cathedral did not replace the old, but was constructed beside it. It is in a mix of architectural styles, being mainly Gothic, with Renaissance and Baroque additions. The west front has elaborate Late Gothic stonework, and a central panel carved with religious scenes.

The 12th- to 13th-century Romanesque old cathedral is entered through the new one. The highlight is a wonderful altarpiece of 53 panels, painted in lustrous colours by Nicolás Florentino. It frames a statue of Salamanca's patron saint, the 12th-century Virgen de la Vega, which was crafted in Limoges enamel. In the vault above it is a fresco depicting scenes from the Last Judgment, which is also by Florentino.

The 15th-century Capilla de Anaya (Anaya Chapel) contains the superb 15th-century alabaster tomb of Diego de Anaya, an archbishop of Salamanca.

Façade of Salamanca University, on the Patio de las Escuelas

🏛 Universidad

Patio de las Escuelas 1. *Tel* 923 29 44 00. ◯ daily. ● 25 Dec. ✍ (free Mon am).

Salamanca's historic university was founded by Alfonso IX of León in 1218. The 16th-century façade of the Patio de las Escuelas (Schools Square) is a perfect example of the Plateresque style *(see p25)*. Opposite is a statue of Fray Luis de León, who taught theology here. Inside, his former lecture room is preserved in its original style. Off the Patio de las Escuelas is the Escuelas Menores building, which houses a huge zodiac fresco, *The Salamanca Sky*.

🏛 Plaza Mayor

This magnificent square was built by Felipe V to thank the city for its support during the War of the Spanish Succession *(see p62)*. Designed by the Churriguera brothers *(see p25)* in 1729 and completed in 1755, it was once used for bullfights, but nowadays is a delightful place to stroll or shop. Within the harmonious blend of arcaded buildings and cafés are the Baroque town hall and, opposite, the Royal Pavilion, from where the royal family used to watch events in the square. The Plaza Mayor is built of warm golden sandstone, and is especially resplendent at dusk.

Royal Pavilion in Salamanca's beautiful Plaza Mayor

🔒 Iglesia-Convento de San Esteban

The 16th-century church of this Dominican monastery is particularly interesting for its superb ornamented façade. The relief on the central panel, completed by Juan Antonio Ceroni in 1610, depicts the stoning of St Stephen, to whom the monastery is dedicated. Above this is a frieze, delicately carved with figures of children and horses.

The interior of the large single-nave church is equally stunning. The ornate altarpiece, of twisted gilt columns decorated with vines, is the work of José Churriguera and dates from 1693. Below it is one of Claudio Coello's last paintings, another representation of the martyrdom of St Stephen.

The double-galleried Claustro de los Reyes, completed in Plateresque style in 1591, has capitals which are carved with the heads of the prophets.

Salamanca's double cathedral, towering over the city

For hotels and restaurants in this region see pp582–5 and pp633–6

Sculpted shells on the walls of the Casa de las Conchas

🏛 Casa de las Conchas

Calle de la Compañia 2. *Tel* 923 26 93 17. ◻ daily. **Library** ◻ Mon–Sat am.
The name of this mansion – House of the Shells – derives from the golden stone scallop shells that cover most of its walls. The shells are a symbol of the Order of Santiago, one of whose knights, Rodrigo Maldonado, built the mansion at the beginning of the 16th century. He also adorned the building with his family's coat of arms. It is now a library.

🔒 Convento de las Dueñas

Plaza del Concilio de Trento. *Tel* 923 21 54 42. ◻ 11:30am–12:45pm, 4:30–5:30pm daily. 🔲
The main feature of this Dominican convent, near San Esteban, is its Renaissance double cloister, whose tranquil gardens seem strangely at odds with the grotesques carved on the capitals. The cloister also preserves tiled Moorish arches.

🏛 Museo Art Nouveau y Art Deco

Calle Gibraltar 14. *Tel* 923 12 14 25. ◻ Tue–Sun. 🔲
This important art collection, housed in a 19th-century building, includes paintings, jewellery and furniture from all over Europe. Individual rooms are devoted to porcelain and Limoges enamel, and stained-glass work by Lalique.

🏛 Colegio de los Irlandeses

Calle de Fonseca 4. *Tel* 923 29 45 70. ◻ daily. 🔲
The Archbishop of Toledo, Alfonso de Fonseca, built this Renaissance palace in 1519 and the coat of arms of the Fonseca family appears over the main entrance. Its name arises from the fact that it became a seminary for Irish priests at the end of the 16th century. The interior Italianate courtyard has a first-floor gallery and a chapel. Today the building is used as council and university offices.

🔒 Convento de las Úrsulas

Calle de las Úrsulas 2. *Tel* 923 21 98 77. ◻ daily. 🔲
In the church of this convent is the superbly carved tomb of its founder, Alonso de Fonseca, the powerful 16th-century Archbishop of Santiago. The museum includes fine paintings by Luis de Morales.

🏛 Casa de las Muertes

Calle Bordadores. ● to public.
The House of the Dead takes its name from the small skulls that embellish its façade. Grotesques and other figures also feature, and there is a cornice

Skull carving on the façade of the Casa de las Muertes

decorated with cherubs. The façade is a wonderfully accomplished example of the early Plateresque style.
The adjacent house is where author and philosopher Miguel de Unamuno died in 1936. The Casa-Museo de Unamuno, next door to the university, contains information about his life.

🏛 Torre del Clavero

Plaza de Colón.
The tower is the last vestige of a palace that once stood here. It was built around 1480 and is named after a former resident, the key warden (*clavero*) of the Order of Alcántara.

Tower opposite Casa de las Muertes

Environs

Northwest of the city, the Río Tormes leads through the fortified old town of **Ledesma**, across lonely countryside to the Arribas del Duero, a series of massive reservoirs near to the Portuguese border.
Dominating the town of **Alba de Tormes**, 20 km (12 miles) east of Salamanca, is the Torre de la Armería, the only remaining part of the castle of the Dukes of Alba. The Iglesia de San Juan was built in the 12th century in Romanesque style. The Iglesia-Convento de las Madres Carmelitas was founded by St Teresa of Ávila in 1571, and is where her remains are now kept.
The castle of **Buen Amor**, 26 km (16 miles) to the north, was founded in 1227. Later, it was converted into a palace and used by the Catholic Monarchs while fighting Juana la Beltraneja (*see p56*).

Sierra de Gredos **⑫**

Ávila. ▣ *Navarrendonda.*
🔲 *Navarrendonda C/Del Rio, s/n,*
920 34 52 52.

This great mountain range,
west of Madrid, has abundant
wildlife, especially ibex and
birds of prey. Some parts
have been developed to cater
for weekenders who come skiing, fishing, hunting or hiking.
Tourism here isn't a recent
phenomenon – Spain's first
parador opened in Gredos in
1928 *(see p584)*. Despite this,
there are many traditional villages off the beaten track.

The slopes on the south side
of the range, extending into
Extremadura, are fertile and
sheltered, with pinewoods, and
apple and olive trees. The
northern slopes, in contrast,
have a covering of scrub and
a scattering of granite boulders.

A single main road, the
N502, crosses the centre of the
range via the Puerto del Pico, a
pass at 1,352 m (4,435 ft), leading to Arenas de San Pedro, the
largest town of the Sierra
de Gredos. On this road is the
castle of **Mombeltrán**, built at
the end of the 14th century.

Near Ramacastañas, south of
the town of Arenas de San
Pedro, are the limestone caverns of the **Cuevas del Águila**.

The sierra's highest summit,
the Pico Almanzor (2,592 m,
8,500 ft) dominates the west.
Around it lies the **Reserva
Nacional de Gredos**, pro-
tecting the mountain's wildlife.

The Toros de Guisando near El Tiemblo in the Sierra de Gredos

Near El Tiemblo, in the east,
stand the **Toros de Guisando**,
four stone statues resembling
bulls, believed to be of Celtiberian origin *(see pp48–9)*.

Ávila **⑬**

Ávila. 🏠 *50,000.* 🚌 🚉 🔲 *Plaza de
la Catedral 4, 920 21 13 87.* **Walls**
🕐 *Tue–Sun (daily in summer).*
📅 *Fri.* 🎉 *San Segundo (2 May);
Santa Teresa (15 Oct).*
www.castillayleon.com

At 1,131 m (3,710 ft)
above sea level, Ávila de
los Caballeros ("of the
Knights") is the highest
provincial capital in
Spain. In winter access
roads can be blocked
with snow, and at night
the temperature plummets.
The centre of the city is
encircled by the finest-
preserved **medieval
walls** in Europe. The
walls are open to visitors.
One of the best views of the
walls is from Los Cuatro Postes

Tuna in Ávila

(Four Posts) on the road to
Salamanca. Built in the 12th
century, the walls are over
2 km (1 mile) long. They are
punctuated by 88 sturdy
turrets, on which storks can be
seen nesting in season. The
ground falls away very steeply
from the walls on three sides,
making the city practically
impregnable. The east side,
however, is
relatively flat,
and therefore
had to be fortified
more heavily. The
oldest sections of
the wall are here.
They are guarded by
the most impressive
of the city's nine gate-
ways, the **Puerta de
San Vicente**. The apse
of the **cathedral** also
forms part of the walls.
The cathedral's warlike
(and unfinished) ex-
terior, decorated with
beasts and scaly wild
men, is an unusual design.
The interior is a mixture of
Romanesque and Gothic styles

The superbly preserved 11th-century walls, punctuated with 88 cylindrical towers, which encircle Ávila

using an unusual mottled red and white stone. Finer points to note are the carvings on the retrochoir and, in the apse, the tomb of a 15th-century bishop known as El Tostado, "the Tanned One", because of his dark complexion.

Many churches and convents in Ávila are linked to St Teresa, who was born in the city. The **Convento de Santa Teresa** was built on the site of her home within the walls and she also lived for more than 20 years in the **Monasterio de la Encarnación** outside the walls. There is even a local sweetmeat, *yemas de Santa Teresa*, named after the saint.

The **Basílica de San Vicente**, also located just outside the eastern walls, is Ávila's most important Romanesque church, distinguished by its ornamented belfry. It was begun in the 11th century but has some Gothic features which were added later. The west door-

Beautiful gardens and palace of San Ildefonso

way is often compared to the Pórtico da Gloria of Santiago cathedral (*see p92*). Inside, the carved tomb of St Vincent and his sisters depicts their hideous martyrdom in detail. Another Romanesque-Gothic church worth seeing is the **Iglesia de San Pedro**.

Some way from the centre is the **Real Monasterio de Santo Tomás**, with three cloisters. The middle one, carved with the yoke and arrow emblem of the Catholic Monarchs, is the most beautiful. The last cloister leads to a museum displaying chalices and processional crosses. The church contains the tomb of Prince Juan, the only son of Fernando and Isabel. In the sacristy lies another historic figure: Tomás de Torquemada, head of the Inquisition (*see p56*).

In Ávila, you may see groups of *tunas* – students dressed in traditional costume walking the town's streets while singing songs and playing guitars.

Cloisters of the Real Monasterio de Santo Tomás in Ávila

La Granja de San Ildefonso ⓮

Segovia. **Tel** 921 47 00 19. 🚌 from Madrid or Segovia. ◯ 1 Oct–31 Mar: 10am–1:30pm, 3–5pm Tue–Sat, 10am–2pm Sun; 1 Apr–30 Sep: 10am–6pm Tue–Sun. ● 1, 6 & 23 Jan, 1 May, 25 Aug, 24, 25 & 31 Dec. 🎫 (free Wed for EU residents). 🔲

This sumptuous royal pleasure palace is set against the backdrop of the Sierra de Guadarrama mountains, standing on the site of the old Convento de Jerónimos.

In 1720, Felipe V embarked on a project to create a fine palace. A succession of different artists and architects contributed to the rich furnishings inside and the splendid gardens without.

A guided tour meanders through countless impressive salons decorated with ornate *objets d'art* and Classical frescoes against settings of marble, gilt and velvet. Huge glittering chandeliers, produced in the local crystal factory, hang from the ceiling. In the private apartments there are superb court tapestries. The church is fittingly adorned in lavish high Baroque style, and the Royal Mausoleum contains the tomb of Felipe V and his queen.

In the gardens, stately chestnut trees, clipped hedges and statues frame a complex series of pools. On 30 May, 25 July and 25 August each year all of the spectacular fountains are set in motion. Four fountains run every Wednesday, Saturday and Sunday at 5:30 pm.

ST TERESA OF JESUS

Teresa de Cepeda y Ahumada (1515–82) was one of the Catholic Church's greatest mystics and reformers. When aged just seven, she ran away from home in the hope of achieving martyrdom at the hands of the Moors, only to be recaptured by her uncle on the outskirts of the city. She became a nun at 19 but rebelled against her order. From 1562, when she founded her first convent, she travelled around Spain with her disciple, St John of the Cross, founding more convents for the followers of her order, the Barefoot Carmelites. Her remains are in Alba de Tormes near Salamanca (*see p361*).

Statue of St Teresa in the cathedral museum

SEGOVIA CITY CENTRE

Alcázar ⑦
Aqueduct ②
Casa de los Picos ③
Cathedral ⑥

Iglesia de San Esteban ⑤
Iglesia de San Juan
de los Caballeros ①
Iglesia de San Martín ④

0 metres   250
0 yards   250

Key to Symbols see back flap

Segovia ⑮

Segovia. 🏠 55,000. 🚉 🚌 ℹ️
Plaza Mayor 10, 921 46 03 34. 🛒
Tue, Thu & Sat. 🎉 San Pedro (29
Jun), San Fru-tos (25 Oct).
www.infosegovia.com

Segovia is the most spectacularly sited city in Spain. The
old town is set high on a rocky
spur and surrounded by the
Río Eresma and Río Clamores.
It is often compared to a ship –
the Alcázar on its sharp crag
forming the prow, the pinnacles of the cathedral rising
like masts, and the aqueduct
trailing behind like a rudder.
The view of it from the valley
below at sunset is magical.

The **aqueduct**, in use until
the late 19th century, was
built at the end of the 1st century AD by the Romans, who
turned the ancient town into
an important military base.

The **cathedral**, dating from
1525 and consecrated in 1678,
is the last great Gothic church
in Spain. It was built to replace
the old cathedral, which was
destroyed in 1520 during the
revolt of the Castilian towns
(see p58). The cloister, however, survived and was rebuilt
on the new site. The pinnacles,
flying buttresses, tower and
dome form an impressive sil-

houette, while the interior is
light and elegantly vaulted.
Graceful ironwork grilles enclose the side chapels. The
chapterhouse museum, with a
coffered ceiling, houses 17th-
century Brussels tapestries.

At the city's western end is
the **Alcázar** (see pp344–5).
Rising sheer above crags with
a multitude of gabled roofs,
turrets and crenellations, it
appears like the archetypal
fairy-tale castle. The present
building is mostly a fanciful
reconstruction following a fire
in 1862. It contains a museum
of weaponry and a series of

elaborately decorated rooms.
Notable churches include the
Romanesque **San Juan de los
Caballeros Templarios**, which
has an outstanding sculptured
portico, **San Martín** with its
beautiful arcades and capitals,
and **San Miguel**, where Isable
the Catholic was crowned
Queen of Castille. Just inside
the city walls is the **Casa de
los Picos**, a mansion whose
unique façade is adorned
with diamond-shaped stones.

Environs

The vast palace of **Riofrío**, 11
km (7 miles) to the southwest,

The imposing Gothic cathedral of Segovia

SEGOVIA'S AQUEDUCT

Water channel

Slots used to support blocks of ashlar

Arches reach a maximum height of 29 m (95 ft).

Water from the Río Frío flowed into the city, filtered through a series of tanks along the way.

Two tiers of arches – a total of 728 m (2,400 ft) in length – were needed to cope with the ground's gradient.

In this niche a statue of the Virgin Mary replaces an earlier inscription relating to the founding of the aqueduct.

Segovia's distinctive Alcázar, towering over the city

is set in a deer park. It was built as a hunting lodge in 1752, and has richly decorated rooms.It also houses a hunting museum.

♠ Alcázar de Segovia
Plaza de la Reina Victoria Eugenia.
Tel 921 46 07 59. ◯ *daily.* ● *1 &
6 Jan, 25 Dec.* 🏛 *(free Tue.)* & 📷

⊞ Palacio de Riofrío
Tel 921 47 00 19. ◯ *Tue–Sun.*
🏛 *(free Wed EU residents).*

Pedraza de la Sierra 🌀

Segovia. 🎎 *500.* 🛈 *C/ Real 3, 921
50 86 66.* 🎭 *Nuestra Señora la
Virgen del Carrascal (8 Sep).*

The aristocratic little town of Pedraza de la Sierra is perched high over rolling countryside. Within its medieval walls, old streets lead past mansions to the porticoed **Plaza Mayor** *(see p27).* The huge, austere **castle**, standing on a rocky outcrop, was owned by Basque artist Ignacio Zuloaga (1870–1945). The castle

museum shows some of his works. On July evenings, torchlit classical music concerts are held in the Plaza Mayor.

Environs
The main sight at **Turégano**, 30 km (19 miles) west, is a large hilltop castle which incorporates the 15th-century Iglesia de San Miguel.

Sepúlveda 🌀

Segovia. 🎎 *1,350.* 🛈 *Plaza del
Trigo 6, 921 54 02 37.* 🎭 *Wed.*
🎭 *Los Toros (last week of Aug).*

Spectacularly sited on a slope above the Río Duratón, this picturesque town offers views of the Sierra de Guadarrama. Parts of its medieval walls and castle survive. Of its several Romanesque churches, the **Iglesia del Salvador**, behind the main square, is notable for possessing one of the oldest atria in Spain (1093).

Environs
Winding through a canyon haunted by griffon vultures is the Río Duratón, 7 km (4 miles) west of Sepúlveda. This area of striking beauty has been designated a natural park, the **Parque Natural de las Hoces del Duratón.**
Ayllón, 45 km (28 miles) northeast of Sepúlveda, has an arcaded main square and the Plateresque *(see p25)* Palacio de Juan de Contreras of 1497.
The Iberian and Roman ruins at **Tiermes**, 28 km (17 miles) further southeast, have been partially excavated, and finds can be seen in Soria's Museo Numantino *(see p377).*

Castillo de Coca 🌀

Coca (Segovia). **Tel** *617 57 35 54.*
🚌 *from Segovia.* ◯ *daily.* ● *1st
Tue of mth.* 🏛 📷

Built in the late 15th century for the influential Fonseca family, Coca castle *(see p344)* is one of Castilla y León's most memorable fortresses. It was used more as a residential palace than a defensive castle, although its turrets and battlements are a fine example of Mudéjar military architecture. The complex moated structure comprises three concentric walls around a massive keep. It is now a forestry school, with a display of Romanesque woodcarvings.

Environs
The 14th-century castle of **Arévalo** in Avila, 26 km (16 miles) southwest, is where Isabel I spent her childhood. The porticoed Plaza de la Villa is surrounded by some attractive half-timbered houses.

Massive keep of the 15th-century Castillo de Coca

Medina del Campo ⑲

Valladolid. 🏠 20,500. 🚉 🚌
ℹ️ *Plaza Mayor 48, 983 81 13 57.*
🎭 *Sun.* 🎉 *San Antolín (2–8 Sep).*

Medina became wealthy in medieval times on the proceeds of huge sheep fairs and is still an important agricultural centre today. The vast brick Gothic-Mudéjar **Castillo de la Mota** *(see p344)*, on its outskirts, was built in 1440 by the powerful Fonseca family. However, the town transferred the castle's ownership to the Crown in 1475. Isabel I and her daughter Juana "la Loca" ("the Mad") both stayed here. Later, it served as a prison – Cesare Borja, one of its more celebrated inmates, was incarcerated here from 1506–08. In a corner of the Plaza Mayor stands the modest house (built over an arch) where Isabel died in 1504.

Castillo de la Mota at Medina del Campo

Environs
Towering over the plains, some 25 km (16 miles) to the south of Medina del Campo, are the walls of **Madrigal de las Altas Torres**, which owes its name to the hundreds of bastions that marked the old wall; only 23 still remain. In 1451 Isabel was born here in a palace that later became the Monasterio de las Agustinas in 1527.

🏰 **Castillo de la Mota**
Tel 983 80 10 24. 🕐 daily.
🚫 public hols.

Tordesillas ⑳

Valladolid. 🏠 8,000. 🚉 ℹ️ *Casas del Tratado, 983 77 10 67.* 🎭 *Tue.* 🎉 *Fiestas de la Peña (16–22 Sep).*

This pleasant town is where the historic treaty between Spain and Portugal was signed in 1494, dividing the lands of the New World *(see p57)*. A fateful oversight by the Spanish map makers left the immense prize of Brazil to Portugal.

The town's main place to visit is the **Convento de Santa Clara**. It was constructed by Alfonso XI around 1340 and then converted by his son Pedro the Cruel into a stunning residence for his mistress, María de Padilla. Pining for her native Andalusia, she had the convent decorated with fine Moorish arches, baths and tiles. Most impressive are the beautiful patio and the main chapel. There is a fantastic display of royal musical instruments, including the portable organ of Juana "la Loca".

In the old quarter, the **Iglesia de San Antolín** now houses a fascinating religious art museum, which displays paintings as well as liturgical objects.

🏛️ **Convento de Santa Clara**
Tel 983 77 00 71. 🕐 Tue–Sun. 📷
Free Wed for EU citizens.

🏛️ **Iglesia de San Antolín**
Calle Postigo. *Tel* 983 79 69 03.
🕐 Tue–Sun. 📷

Moorish patio in the Convento de Santa Clara, Tordesillas

Valladolid ㉑

Valladolid. 🏠 333,000. 🚉 🚌
ℹ️ *Acera de Recoletos, 983 35 18 01.* 🎭 *Sun.* 🎉 *San Pedro Regalado (13 May); Virgin de San Lorenzo (8 Sep).* **www**.valladolidturismo.com

The Arabic city of Belad-Walid (meaning "Land of the Governor") is located at the confluence of the Río Esgueva and Río Pisuerga. Although it has become sprawling and industrialized, Valladolid has some of Spain's best Renaissance art and architecture.

Fernando and Isabel *(see pp56–7)* were married in the Palacio Vivero in 1469 and, following the completion of the Reconquest in 1492, they made Valladolid their capital. Less spectacularly, Columbus died here, alone and forgotten, in 1506. In 1527 Felipe II was born in the Palacio de los Pimentel. José Zorrilla, who popularized the legendary Don Juan in his 1844 play *(see p35)*, was also born in the city.

The city's **university** dates from the 15th century. The Baroque façade *(see p25)* was begun in 1715 by Narciso Tomé, who later created the remarkable Transparente of Toledo cathedral *(see p393)*.

The **Iglesia de San Pablo** has a spectacular façade, embellished with angels and coats of arms in Plateresque style. Among the other noteworthy churches are **Santa María la Antigua**, with its Romanesque belfry, and the **Iglesia de Las Angustias**, where Juan de Juni's fine sculpture of the Virgen de los Cuchillos (Virgin of the Knives) is on display.

🏛 Casa de Cervantes
Calle Rastro. **Tel** 983 30 88 10.
◯ *Tue–Sun.* ● *public hols.*
🔲 *(free Sun am)* 🔲
The author of *Don Quixote (see p35)* lived in this simple house with white-washed walls from 1603 to 1606. The rooms have been restored and contain some of Cervantes' original furnishings.

🔓 Cathedral
Calle Arribas 1. **Tel** 983 30 43 62.
● *Mon.* 🔲
Work started on the unfinished cathedral in 1580 by Felipe II's favourite architect, Juan de Herrera, but gradually lost momentum over the centuries. Churrigueresque *(see p25)* flourishes on the façade are in contrast to the sombre, square-pillared interior, whose only redeeming flamboyance is a Juan de Juni altarpiece. The Museo Diocesano inside, however, contains some fine pieces of religious art and sculpture.

🏛 Museo Nacional de Escultura
Cadenas de S Gregorio 1–2. **Tel** 983 25 03 75. ◯ *Tue–Sun.* ● *public hols.* 🔲 *(free Sat pm & Sun am).* 🔲 **www**.mne.es
This art collection, usually in the Colegio de San Gregorio, has moved to the nearby Palacio de Villena until renovations finish. The display consists mainly of wooden

Façade of Colegio de San Gregorio, Valladolid

Berruguete's *Natividad*, in Museo Nacional de Escultura, Valladolid

religious sculptures from the 13th–18th centuries. They include Juan de Juni's emotive depiction of the burial of Christ and *Recumbent Christ* by Gregorio Fernández. An Alonso Berruguete altarpiece, and walnut choir stalls by Diego de Siloé and other artists, are among the other fine works to be found here.

The building itself is worthy of attention, particularly the Plateresque staircase, the chapel by Juan Güas, and the patio of twisted columns and delicate basket arches. The façade is an fine example of Isabelline *(see p24)* sculpture, portraying a mêlée of naked children scrambling about in thorn trees, hairy wild men, and strange birds and beasts.

🏛 Museo de Arte Contemporáneo Español
Convento de San Benito, Calle Jorge Guillén 6. **Tel** 983 36 29 08. ◯ *daily.* 🔲
This private collection of contemporary Spanish art opened in 2002, housed in the former Monastery of San Benito with its fine cloisters. More than 1,000 works by 200 Spanish artists are displayed, including work by Joan Miró, Eduardo Chillida, Antoni Tàpies and Miquel Barceló.

Environs
The moated grey castle that dominates the village of **Simancas**, 11 km (7 miles) southwest of Valladolid, was converted by Charles V into Spain's national archive. The

Visigothic church in the village of Wamba, 15 km (9 miles) to the west, contains the tomb of King Recceswinth.

An unusual long, narrow 15th-century castle on a ridge overlooks the wine town of Peñafiel, 60 km (40 miles) east of Valladolid *(see p345)*.

Medina de Ríoseco 22

Valladolid. 🔣 *5,000.* 🔲 🔲 *Canal de Castilla, 983 72 50 43.* 🔲 *Wed.* 🔲 *San Juan (24 Jun), Virgen del Castillviejo (8 Sep).*

During the Middle Ages this town grew wealthy from the profitable wool trade, enabling it to commission leading artists, mainly of the Valladolid school, to decorate its churches. The dazzling star vaulting and superb woodwork of the **Iglesia de Santa María de Mediavilla**, near the centre of town, are evidence of this. Inside, the Los Benavente Chapel is a *tour de force*, with a colourful stucco ceiling by Jerónimo del Corral (1554), and an altarpiece by Juan de Juni. The enormous monstrance (1585) in the treasury is by Antonio de Arfe.

The interior of the **Iglesia de Santiago** is stunning, with a triple altarpiece designed by the Churriguera brothers of Salamanca *(see p25)*.

The ancient buildings on Medina de Rioseco's main street, the Calle de la Rúa, are supported on wooden pillars, forming shady porticoes.

Altarpiece by Juan de Juni, Iglesia de Santa María de Mediavilla

CASTILLA Y LEON'S FIESTAS

El Colacho *(Sun after Corpus Christi, May/Jun)*, Castrillo de Murcia (Burgos). Babies born during the previous 12 months are dressed in their best Sunday clothes and laid on mattresses in the streets. Crowds of people, including the anxious parents, watch as *El Colacho* – a man dressed in a bright red and yellow costume – jumps over the babies in order to free them from illnesses, especially hernias. He is said to represent the devil fleeing from the sight of the Eucharist. This ritual is thought to have originated in 1621.

El Colacho **jumping over babies in Castrillo de Murcia**

St Agatha's Day *(Sun closest to 5 Feb)*, Zamarramala (Segovia). Every year two women are elected as mayoresses to run the village on the day of St Agatha, patron saint of married women. They ceremonially burn a stuffed figure representing a man.
Good Friday, Valladolid. The procession of 28 multicoloured sculptures which depict various scenes of the Passion is one of the most spectacular in Spain.
Fire-walking *(23 Jun)*, San Pedro Manrique (Soria). Men, some carrying people on their backs, walk barefoot over burning embers. It is said that only local people can do this without being burned.

The beautiful carved retrochoir of Palencia cathedral

Palencia ㉓

Palencia. 🏛 80,000. 🚊 🚌 🛈 Calle Mayor 105, 979 74 00 84. 🖪 Tue, Wed. 🎉 Virgen de la Calle (2 Feb). **www.**turismocastillayleon.com

In medieval times, Palencia was a royal residence and the site of Spain's first university, founded in 1208. The city gradually diminished in importance following its involvement in the failed revolt of the Castilian towns of 1520 *(see p58)*.

Although Palencia has since expanded considerably on profits from coal and wheat, its centre, by the old stone bridge over the Río Carrión, remains almost village-like.

The city's main sight is the **cathedral**, known as *La Bella Desconocida* (the Unknown Beauty). It is especially worth a visit for its superb works of art, many the result of Bishop Fonseca's generous patronage. The retrochoir, exquisitely sculpted by Gil de Siloé and Simon of Cologne, and the two altarpieces, are also noteworthy. The altarpiece above the high altar was carved by Philippe de Bigarny early in the 16th century. The inset panels are by Juan de Flandes, Isabel I's court painter. Behind the high altar is the Chapel of the Holy Sacrament, with an altarpiece dating from 1529 by Valmaseda. In this chapel, high on a ledge to the left, is the colourful tomb of Doña Urraca of Navarra. Below the retrochoir, a Plateresque *(see p25)* staircase leads down to the fine Visigothic crypt.

Environs
Baños de Cerrato, 12 km (7 miles) to the south, boasts the tiny Visigothic Iglesia de San Juan Bautista, founded in 661. It is alleged to be the oldest intact church in Spain. Carved capitals and horseshoe arches decorate the interior.

Frómista ㉔

Palencia. 🏛 1,000. 🛈 Paseo Central, 979 81 01 80. 🖪 Fri. 🎉 Patrón de Frómista (week after Easter). **www.**fromista.com

This town on the Road to Santiago de Compostela *(see pp82–3)* is the site of one of Spain's purest Romanesque churches. The **Iglesia de San Martín** is the highlight of the town, partly due to a restoration in 1904, leaving the church, dating from 1066, entirely Romanesque in style. The presence of Pagan and Roman motifs suggest it may have pre-Christian origins.

Environs
Carrión de los Condes, 20 km (12 miles) to the northwest, is also on the Road to Santiago. The frieze on the door of the Iglesia de Santiago depicts not religious figures but local artisans. There are carvings of bulls on the façade of the 12th-century Iglesia de Santa María del Camino. The Convento de San Zoilo has a Gothic cloister and offers simple accommodation.

Located at **Gañinas**, 20 km (12 miles) to the northwest (just south of Saldaña), is the well-preserved Roman villa,

Interior of the Iglesia de San Juan Bautista at Baños de Cerrato

Posada of the Monasterio de Santa María la Real, Aguilar de Campoo

La Olmeda. It has a number of impressive mosaics, including a hunting scene with lions and tigers. Finds from the villa are displayed in the archaeological museum located in the Iglesia de San Pedro in Saldaña.

Villa Romana La Olmeda
Pedrosa de la Vega. ☐ *Tue–Sun.* ⬤ *23 Dec–31 Jan.* ticket includes archaeological museum.

Aguilar de Campoo ㉕

Palencia. 7,340. *Plaza España 30, 979 12 36 41.* *Tue.* *San Pedro (29 Jun); Romería de la Virgen del Llano (1st Sun in Sep).* www.aguilardecampoo.com

Situated between the parched plains of Central Spain and the lush green foothills of the Cantabrian Mountains is the old fortified town of Aguilar de Campoo. In the centre of its ancient porticoed main square is the impressive bell tower of the **Colegiata de San Miguel**. In this church is a mausoleum containing the tomb of the Marquises of Aguilar.

Among the other places of interest are the **Ermita de Santa Cecilia**, and the restored Romanesque-Gothic **Monasterio de Santa María la Real**, which has a small, friendly *posada* (inn), ideal for a night's stay.

Environs
Six km (4 miles) south, at **Olleros de Pisuerga**, is a church built in a cave. From the parador at **Cervera de Pisuerga**, 25 km (15 miles) northwest of Aguilar, there are stunning views, and tours of the **Reserva Nacional de Fuentes Carrionas**. This is a rugged region overlooked by Curavacas, a 2,540-m (8,333-ft) peak.

Briviesca ㉖

Burgos. 6,600. *Calle Santa María Encimera 1, 947 59 39 39.* *Sat.* *Feria de San José (19 Mar), Santa Casilda (late Apr/early May).*

This little walled town, in the northeast of Burgos province, has an arcaded main square and several dignified mansions. The best known of its churches is the **Convento de Santa Clara**, with its 16th-century walnut reredos carved with religious scenes. In 1387 Juan I of Aragón created the title Príncipe de Asturias for his son, Enrique, in the town. The Santuario de Santa Casilda, situated outside Briviesca, has a collection of votive objects.

Environs
Oña, 25 km (15 miles) north, is an attractive town. A Benedictine monastery was founded here in 1011.

Overlooking a fertile valley, 20 km (12 miles) further northeast, is the little hilltop town of **Frías**. Its castle overlooks cobbled streets and pretty old houses. Crossing the Río Ebro is a fortified medieval bridge, still with its central gate tower.

At **Medina de Pomar**, 30 km (20 miles) north of Oña, there is a 15th-century castle, once the seat of the Velasco family. Inside are the ruins of a palace with fine Mudéjar stucco decoration and Arabic inscriptions.

The medieval bridge over the Río Ebro at Frías, with its central gate tower

Flemish triptych inside the collegiate church in Covarrubias

Covarrubias ⓗ

Burgos. ▨ 650. ▣ ▤ ▦ *Calle Monseñor Vargas, 947 40 64 61 (Mar–Nov).* ▣ *Tue.* ▨ *San Cosme and San Damián (26–27 Sep).*

Named after the reddish caves on its outskirts, Covarrubias stands on the banks of the Río Arlanza. Medieval walls surround the charming old centre with its arcaded half-timbered houses *(see p26)*. The distinguished **collegiate church** shows the historical importance of Covarrubias: here is the tomb of Fernán González, first independent Count of Castile, and one of the great figures in Castilian history. By uniting several fiefs against the Moors in the 10th century, he started the rise in Castilian power that ensured the resulting kingdom of Castile would play a leading role in the unification of Spain. The church museum contains treasures, notably a Flemish triptych of the Adoration of the Magi, attributed to the school of Gil de Siloé, and a 17th-century organ.

Environs

A short distance east along the Río Arlanza lies the ruins of the 11th-century Romanesque monastery of San Pedro de Arlanza. At Quintanilla de las Viñas, 24 km (15 miles) north of Covarrubias, is a ruined 7thcentury Visigothic church. The reliefs on the columns of the triumphal arch are remarkable, depicting sun and moon symbols that may be pagan.

Burgos ⓤ

Burgos. ▨ 168,000. ▣ ▤ ▦ *Plaza de Alonso Martínez 7, 947 20 31 25.* ▣ *Tue, Wed, Sun.* ▨ *San Lesmes (30 Jan); Pedro and San Pablo (29 Jun).* **www**.aytoburgos.es

Founded in 884, Burgos has played a significant political and military role in Spanish history. It was the capital of the united kingdoms of Castile and León from 1073 until losing that honour to Valladolid after the fall of Granada in 1492 *(see pp56–7)*. During the 15th and 16th centuries Burgos grew rich from the wool trade and used its riches to finance most of the great art and architecture which can be seen in the city today. Less auspiciously, Franco chose Burgos as his headquarters during the Civil War *(see pp66–7)*.

The city's strategic location on the main Madrid–France highway and on the route to Santiago *(see pp82–3)* ensure many visitors; but even without this Burgos would justify a long detour. Despite its size and extremes of climate, it is one of most agreeable provincial capitals in Castilla y León.

Approach via the bridge of Santa María, which leads into the old quarter through the **Arco de Santa María**, a gateway carved with statues of various local worthies. The main bridge into the city, however, is the Puente de San Pablo, where a statue commemorates the city's hero, El Cid. Not far

from the bridge stands the **Casa del Cordón**, a 15th-century palace (now a bank) which has a Franciscan cord motif carved over the portal. A plaque declares that this is the spot where the Catholic Monarchs welcomed Columbus on his return, in 1497, from the second of his famous voyages to the Americas.

The lacy, steel-grey spires of the **cathedral** *(see pp372–3)* are a prominent landmark from almost anywhere in the city. On the rising ground behind it stands the **Iglesia de San Nicolás**, whose main feature is a superb altarpiece by Simon of Cologne (1505). The crowded carvings vividly depict a number of scenes from the life of St Nicholas. Other churches worth visiting are the **Iglesia de San Lorenzo**, with its superb Baroque ceiling, and the **Iglesia de San Esteban**, which has a museum of altarpieces. The **Iglesia de Santa Águeda**, is the place where El Cid made King Alfonso VI swear that he

The Arco de Santa María in Burgos, adorned with statues and turrets

EL CID (1043–99)

Rodrigo Díaz de Vivar was born into a noble family in Vivar del Cid, north of Burgos, in 1043. He served Fernando I, but was banished from Castile after becoming embroiled in the fratricidal squabbles of the king's sons, Sancho II and Alfonso VI. He switched allegiance to fight for the Moors, then changed side again, capturing Valencia for the Christians in 1094, ruling the city until his death. For his heroism he was named El Cid, from the Arabic *Sidi* (Lord). He was a charismatic man of great courage, but it was an anonymous poem, *El Cantar del Mío Cid*, in 1180, that immortalized him as a romantic hero of the Reconquest *(see pp54–5)*. The tombs of El Cid and his wife, Jimena, are in Burgos cathedral.

Statue of El Cid in Vivar del Cid

BURGOS CITY CENTRE

Arco de Santa María ⑥
Casa del Cordón ⑦
Cathedral ④
Iglesia de San Esteban ①
Iglesia de San Lorenzo ⑤
Iglesia de San Nicolás ②
Iglesia de Santa Águeda ③
Museo de Burgos ⑧

0 metres   150
0 yards   150

Key to Symbols *see back flap*

played no part in the murder of his elder brother, King Sancho II *(see p356)*.

Across the river, the palace of the Casa de Miranda houses the archaeological section of the **Museo de Burgos**, with finds from the Roman city of Clunia. Nearby, the **Casa de Angulo** contains the Fine Arts section, whose prize exhibits are Juan de Padilla's tomb by Gil de Siloé, and a Moorish casket in enamelled ivory.

Two religious houses, on the outskirts of Burgos, are worth visiting. Just west of the city is the **Real Monasterio de**

Sculpted tomb of Juan de Padilla by Gil de Siloé, in Museo de Burgos

Huelgas, a late 12th-century Cistercian convent founded by Alfonso VIII. It was lavishly endowed and soon achieved great prestige. One of the most interesting parts is the **Museo de Ricas Telas**, a textile museum containing ancient fabrics from the convent's many royal tombs. Other highlights include a Romanesque cloister dating from the late 12th century, and the Gothic cloister of San Fernando, decorated with Moorish designs. In the Capilla de Santiago is a curious wooden figure of St James holding a sword, with which, according to tradition, royal princes were dubbed Knights of Santiago.

To the east of Burgos is the **Cartuja de Miraflores**, a Carthusian monastery founded during the 15th century. The church includes two of Spain's most notable tombs, attributed to Gil de Siloé. One holds the bodies of Juan II and Isabel of Portugal (the parents of Isabel the Catholic); the other contains that of her brother, Prince Alfonso. Equally spectacular is the multicoloured altarpiece by Gil de Siloé, allegedly gilded with the first consignment of gold brought back to Spain from the New World.

Polychrome altarpiece by Gil de Siloé, in Cartuja de Miraflores

🏛 **Museo de Burgos**
Calle Calera 25. **Tel** 947 26 58 75.
🕐 *Tue–Sun.* 🎫 *(free Sat & Sun).* ♿
🔒 **Real Monasterio de Huelgas**
Calle de las Huelgas. **Tel** 947 20 16 30.
🕐 *Tue–Sun.* 🎫 ♿ 📷 *free on Wed.*
🔒 **Cartuja de Miraflores**
Ctra Burgos-Cardeña, km 3. 🕐 *daily.*

Environs
Ten km (6 miles) southeast of Burgos is the **Monasterio de San Pedro de Cardeña**. El Cid led his family to safety here while he rode into exile after King Alfonso VI had banished him from the territory of Castile.

Burgos Cathedral

Christ at the Column, by Diego de Siloé

Spain's third-largest cathedral was founded in 1221 by Bishop Don Mauricio under Fernando III. The groundplan – a Latin cross – measures 84 m (92 yds) by 59 m (65 yds). Its construction was carried out in stages over three centuries and involved many of the greatest artists and architects in Europe. The style is almost entirely Gothic, and shows influences from Germany, France, and the Low Countries. First to be built were the nave and cloisters, while the intricate, crocketed spires and the richly decorated side chapels are mostly later work. The architects cleverly adapted the cathedral to its sloping site, incorporating stairways inside and out.

West Front
The lacy, steel-grey spires soar above a sculpted balustrade depicting Castile's early kings.

★ Golden Staircase
This elegant Renaissance staircase by Diego de Siloé (1523) links the nave with a tall door (kept locked) at street level.

Lantern

Tomb of El Cid

STAR FEATURES

★ Golden Staircase

★ Constable's Chapel

★ The Crossing

Capilla de Santa Tecla

Puerta de Santa María (main entrance)

Capilla de Santa Ana
The altarpiece (1490) in this chapel is by the sculptor Gil de Siloé. The central panel shows Saint Anne with St Joachim.

Capilla de la Presentación (1519–24) is a funerary chapel with a star-shaped, traceried vault.

Retrochoir

Several of the reliefs around the chancel were carved by Philippe de Bigarny. This expressive scene, which was completed in 1499, depicts the road to Calvary.

Capilla de San Juan Bautista and museum

★ Constables' Chapel

The tomb of the High Constable of Castile and his wife lies beneath the openwork vault of this chapel of 1496.

Sacristy *(1765)*

The sacristy was rebuilt in Baroque style, with an exuberant plasterwork vault and Rococo altars.

Puerta Del Sarmental

The tympanum of this portal of 1240 shows Christ flanked by the Evangelists. Statues of the apostles sit below.

Capilla de la Visitación

★ The Crossing

The magnificent star-ribbed central dome, begun in 1539, rises on four huge pillars. It is decorated with effigies of prophets and saints. Beneath it is the tomb of El Cid and his wife.

Capilla del Santísimo Cristo

Lerma ㉙

Burgos. 🏛 *2,600*. 🚉 🚌
ℹ *Calle Audiencia 6, 947 17 70
02*. 🗓 *Wed*. 🎉 *Nuestra Señora
de la Natvidad (8 Sep)*.
www.citlerma.com

The grandiose appearance of
this town is largely due to the
ambition of the notorious first
Duke of Lerma *(see p60)*,
Felipe III's corrupt favourite
and minister from 1598–1618.
He misused vast quantities of
Spain's new-found wealth on
new buildings in his home
town – all strictly Classical in
style, in accordance with prevailing fashion. At the top of
the town, the **Palacio Ducal**,
built in 1605 as his residence,
has been transformed into
a parador.

There are good views over
the Río Arlanza from the arch-
ways near to the **Convento de
Santa Clara** and also from the
Colegiata de San Pedro
church, which has a bronze
statue of the Duke's uncle.

The narrow, sloping streets of the
old town of Lerma

Cloisters of the Monasterio de
Santo Domingo de Silos

Monasterio de
Santo Domingo
de Silos ㉚

Santo Domingo de Silos (Burgos).
Tel *947 39 00 49*. 🚌 *from Burgos*.
◻ *Tue–Sat, Sun pm*. 📷 🕐 *9am
Mon–Fri, 1pm Sat, noon Sun*.

St Dominic gave his name to
the monastery that he rebuilt
in 1041 over the ruins of an
old abbey destroyed by the
Moors. It is a place of spiritual
and artistic pilgrimage, and its
tranquil setting has inspired
countless poets.

Others come to admire the
beautiful Romanesque cloisters,
whose capitals are sculpted in
a great variety of designs, both
symbolistic and realistic. The
carvings on the corner piers
depict various scenes from the
Bible and the ceilings are coffered in Moorish style. The
body of St Dominic rests in a
silver urn, supported by three

Romanesque lions, in a chapel
in the north gallery. The old
pharmacy, just off the cloister,
has a display of jars from
Talavera de la Reina *(see p386)*.

The Benedictine community
holds regular services in Gregorian chant in the Neo-Classical
church by Ventura Rodríguez.
The monastery offers accommodation for male guests.

Environs
To the southwest lies the
Garganta de la Yecla (Yecla
Gorge), where a path leads to
a narrow fissure cut by the
river. To the northeast, the
peaks and wildlife reserve
of the **Sierra de la Demanda**
extend over into La Rioja.

The 15th-century castle of
Peñaranda de Duero

Peñaranda de
Duero ㉛

Burgos. 🏛 *600*. 🚌 ℹ *Calle
Trinquete 7*, **Tel** *947 55 20 63*. 🗓 *Fri*.
🎉 *Santiago (25 Jul); Santa Ana (26
Jul); Virgen de los Remedios (8 Sep)*.

The castle of Peñaranda was
built during the Reconquest
(see pp54–5) by the Castilians,
who had driven the Moors
back south of the Río Duero.
From its hilltop site, there are
views down to one of the
most charming villages in old
Castile, where pantiled
houses cluster around a huge
church. The main square is
lined with porticoed, timber-
framed buildings and the
superb Renaissance **Palacio de
Avellaneda**. Framing its main
doorway are various heraldic
devices, and inside is a patio

GREGORIAN PLAINCHANT
At regular intervals throughout the
day, the monks of Santo Domingo
de Silos sing services in plainchant,
an unaccompanied singing of Latin
texts in unison. The origins of
chant date back to the beginnings
of Christianity, but it was Pope
Gregory I (590–604) who codified
this manner of worship. It is an
ancient and austere form of music
which has found a new appeal
with modern audiences. In 1994 a
recording of the monks became a
surprise hit all over the world.

Manuscript for an 11th-
century Gregorian chant

Curtain walls and drum towers of Berlanga de Duero castle

which has double galleries and fine decorated ceilings. On Calle de la Botica is a 17th-century **pharmacy** with antique apothecary jars.

Environs
In the old quarter of **Aranda de Duero**, 20 km (12 miles) to the west, the **Iglesia de Santa María**, has an Isabelline façade (see p24).

🏛 **Palacio de Avellaneda**
Plaza Condes de Miranda 1. *Tel* 947 55 20 13. ⬚ Tue–Sun.

El Burgo de Osma ㉜

Soria. 🏘 5,000. 🚏 Plaza Mayor 9, 975 36 01 16. 🚌 Sat. 🎉 Virgen del Espino and San Roque (14–19 Aug).

The most interesting sight in this attractive village is the **cathedral**. Although it is mostly Gothic (dating from 1232), with Renaissance additions, the tall tower is Baroque (1739). Its treasures include a Juan de Juni altarpiece, a white marble pulpit and the tomb of the founder, San Pedro de Osma. The museum contains a valuable collection of illuminated manuscripts and codices.

Porticoed buildings line the streets and the Plaza Mayor, and storks nest on the Baroque Hospital de San Agustín.

Environs
Overlooking the Río Duero at **Gormaz**, 12 km (7 miles) south, is a massive castle with 28 towers. There are also medieval fortresses at **Berlanga de Duero**, 20 km (12

miles) further southeast, and at **Calatañazor**, 25 km (16 miles) northeast of El Burgo de Osma, near to where the Moorish leader al Mansur was killed in 1002 (see p53).

Soria ㉝

Soria. 🏘 35,000. 🚏 C/Medinaceli 2, 975 21 20 52. 🚌 Thu. 🎉 San Juan (24 Jun).

Castilla y León's smallest provincial capital stands on the banks of the Río Duero. Soria's stylish, modern parador (see p557) is named after the poet Antonio Machado (1875–1939, see p35), who wrote in praise of the town and the surrounding plains. Many of the older buildings are gone, but notable among those remaining are the imposing russet **Palacio de los Condes de Gómara**, and the handsome **Concatedral de San Pedro**, both built in the 16th century.

The **Museo Numantino**, opposite the municipal gardens, displays a variety of finds from the nearby Roman ruins of Numantia and Tiermes (see

p365). Across the Duero is the ruined monastery of **San Juan de Duero**, with a 13th-century cloister of interlacing arches.

Environs
North of Soria are the ruins of **Numantia**. The Celtiberian inhabitants endured a year-long Roman siege in 133 BC before defiantly burning the town and themselves (see p50). To the northwest is the Sierra de Urbión, a range of pine-clad hills with a lake, the **Laguna Negra de Urbión**.

🏛 **Museo Numantino**
Paseo de Espolón. *Tel* 975 22 14 28. ⬚ Tue–Sun. 🎫 (free Sat, am Sun). ♿

Medinaceli ㉞

Soria. 🏘 800. 🚉 🚏 Campo de San Nicolás, 689 73 41 76. 🎉 Beato Julián de San Agustín (28 Aug); Cuerpos Santos (13 Nov).

Only a triumphal arch remains of Roman Ocilis, perched on a high ridge over the Río Jalón. Built in the 1st century AD, it is the only one in Spain with three arches. It has been adopted as the symbol for ancient monuments on Spanish road signs.

Environs
Lying just to the east are the red cliffs of the Jalón gorges. On the Madrid–Zaragoza road is the Cistercian monastery of **Santa María de Huerta**, founded in 1179. Its glories include a 13th-century Gothic cloister and the superb, crypt-like Monks' Refectory.

🏛 **Monasterio de Santa María de Huerta**
Tel 975 32 70 02. ⬚ daily. 🎫 ♿

Decorative arches in the cloister of the monastery of San Juan de Duero

CASTILLA–LA MANCHA

GUADALAJARA · CUENCA · TOLEDO · ALBACETE · CIUDAD REAL

*L**a Mancha's empty beauty, its windmills and medieval castles, silhouetted above the sienna plains, was immortalized by Cervantes in Don Quixote's epic adventures. Its brilliantly sunlit, wide horizons are one of the classic images of Spain. This scarcely visited region has great, scenic mountain ranges, dramatic gorges and the two monument-filled cities of Toledo and Cuenca.*

You will always find a castle nearby in this region – as the name Castilla suggests. Most were built in the 9th–12th centuries, when the region was a battleground between Christians and Moors. Others mark the 14th- and 15th-century frontiers between the kingdoms of Aragón and Castile. Sigüenza, Belmonte, Alarcón Molina de Aragón and Calatrava La Nueva are among the most impressive.

Toledo, which was the capital of Visigothic Spain, is an outstanding museum city. Its rich architectural and artistic heritage derives from a coalescence of Muslim, Christian and Jewish cultures with medieval and Renaissance ideas and influences.

Cuenca is another attractive city. Its old town is perched above converging gorges; on two sides it spills down steep hillsides. Villanueva de los Infantes, Chinchilla, Alcaraz and Almagro are towns of character built between the 16th and 18th centuries. Ocaña and Tembleque each has a splendid *plaza mayor* (main square).

La Mancha's plains are brightened by natural features of great beauty in its two national parks – the Tablas de Daimiel, and Cabañeros, within the Montes de Toledo. Rimming the plains are beautiful upland areas: the olive groves of the Alcarria; Cuenca's limestone mountains; and the peaks of the Sierra de Alcaraz. The wine region of La Mancha is the world's largest expanse of vineyards. Around Consuegra and Albacete fields turn mauve in autumn as the valuable saffron crocus blooms.

Windmills above Campo de Criptana on the plains of La Mancha

◁ Old houses in Cuenca, a city dramatically located over two gorges

Exploring Castilla-La Mancha

The historic city of Toledo is Castilla-La Mancha's major tourist destination. Less crowded towns with historical charm include Almagro, Oropesa, Alcaraz and Guadalajara. At Sigüenza, Calatrava, Belmonte and Alarcón there are medieval castles, reminders of the region's eventful past. Some towns on the plains of La Mancha, such as El Toboso and Campo de Criptana, are associated with the adventures of Don Quixote (see p395). The wooded uplands of the Serranía de Cuenca, the Alcarria and the Sierra de Alcaraz provide picturesque scenic routes. A haven for bird lovers is the wetland nature reserve of the Tablas de Daimiel.

The village of Alcalá del Júcar

SIGHTS AT A GLANCE

SEE ALSO

Cattle grazing on the isolated plains of La Mancha

GETTING AROUND

Castilla-La Mancha is best explored by car as it is well-endowed with a network of motorways radiating outwards from Madrid. The region is also served by the high-speed AVE train which runs between Madrid and Seville, stopping at Ciudad Real. Otherwise, public transport is infrequent and slow. Be aware that as Spain is in the process of changing its road numbering system some of the roads featured here may differ from new road signs.

KEY

Motorway

Motorway under construction

Major road

Secondary road

Scenic route

Main railway

Minor railway

Regional border

△ Summit

pisábalos

ENZA 1

SIGÜENZA 2

ogolludo

Alcolea del Pinar

Zaragoza

Maranchón

Embid

N211

Cifuentes

Tajuña

Virgen de la Hoz

3 MOLINA DE ARAGÓN

N211

A2

rihuega

N204

Tajo

Parque Natural del Alto Tajo

JADALAJARA

Lupiana

LA ALCARRIA 4

Alcocer

Villanueva de Alcorón

Betera

Priego

SERRANÍA DE CUENCA

Sacedón

rana

Tajo

Embalse de Buendía

Buendía

Cañaveras

Tragacete

6

Villalba

N320

Ciudad Encantada

Huete

Carrascosa del Campo

N400

7 CUENCA

Cañete

Teruel

Moya

N420

A3 9 UCLÉS

BRIGA 8

Saelices

N320

Guadazaón

Carboneras de Guadazaón

Santa Cruz de Moya

N330

San Lorenzo de la Parrilla

Cardenete

ral de Almaguer

Villaescusa de Haro

N420

Embalse de Alarcón

Honrubia

Mira

OBOSO

18

BELMONTE 19

Mota del Cuervo

NIII

20 ALARCÓN

Minglanilla

A3

Valencia

CAMPO DE CRIPTANA

zar de uan

San Clemente

A31

N310

Iniesta

Cabriel

Socuéllamos

N301

Júcar

N320

Alborea

A MANCHA

Mahora

21 ALCALÁ DEL JÚCAR

Tomelloso

La Gineta

Jorquera

25 LAGUNAS DE RUIDERA

Munera

N322

Casas de Juan Núñez

ana

N430

Cueva de Montesinos

El Bonillo

ALBACETE 22

N330

arlos alle

Balazote

Chinchilla de Monte Aragón

N430

A31

Valencia

26

Viveros

Robledo

Pozo Cañada

Bonete

Almansa

Caudete

Alicante (Alacant)

NUEVA DE IFANTES

24 ALCARAZ

Guadalmena

A30

N301

Ontur

Ubeda

N332

Mundo

Ayna

Liétor

Hellín

SIERRA DE ALCARAZ

Yeste

Elche de la Sierra

Murcia

Arguellite

Férez

Letur

23

Nerpio

0 kilometres   50

0 miles   30

The tranquil Montes de Toledo

Atienza ❶

Guadalajara. 🏛 *500.* ℹ *Plaza de España 11, 949 39 90 01.* 🚌 *Fri.* 🎭 *La Caballada (Pentecost Sun).*

Rising high above the valley it once protected, Atienza contains vestiges of its medieval past. Crowning the hill are a ruined 12th-century castle. The arcaded Plaza Mayor and the Plaza del Trigo are joined by an original gateway. The **Museo de San Gil**, a religious art museum, is in the church of the same name. The **Iglesia de Santa María del Rey**, at the foot of the hill, displays a Baroque altarpiece.

Environs
Campisábalos, to the west, has an outstanding 12th-century Romanesque church. The **Hayedo de Tejera Negra**, further west, is a nature reserve of beech woods.

> 🏛 **Museo de San Gil**
> Bruno Pascual Arilopez 6.
> **Tel** *949 39 90 41.* ◯ *Sep–Jun: Sat & Sun; Jul–Aug: daily; by appt weekdays.* 📷

Sigüenza ❷

Guadalajara. 🏛 *5,000.* 🚉 ℹ *Calle Serrano Sanz, 949 34 70 07.* 🚌 *Sat.* 🎭 *San Vicente (22 Jan), San Juan (24 Jun), Fiestas Patronales (mid-Aug).* **www**.sigüenza.com

Dominating the hillside town of Sigüenza is its impressive castle-parador *(see p587)*. The **cathedral**, is Romanesque, with later additions, such as the Gothic-Plateresque cloisters. In one of the chapels is the Tomb of El Doncel, built

Semi-recumbent figure of El Doncel on his tomb in Sigüenza cathedral

for Martín Vázquez de Arce, Isabel of Castile's page *(see p56)*. He was killed in battle against the Moors in 1486. The sacristy has a ceiling carved with flowers and cherubs.

Molina de Aragón ❸

Guadalajara. 🏛 *3,900.* ℹ *C/ Carmen 1, 949 83 20 98.* 🚌 *Thu.* 🎭 *Día del Carmen (16 Jul), Ferias (30 Aug–5 Sep).*

Molina's attractive medieval quarter is at the foot of a hill next to the Río Gallo. The town was disputed during the Reconquest and captured from the Moors by Alfonso I of Aragón in 1129. Many monuments were destroyed during the War of Independence *(see p63)*, but the 11th-century hilltop castle preserves six original towers. It is possible to visit the Romanesque-Gothic **Iglesia de Santa Clara**.

Environs
West of Molina is the **Virgen de la Hoz** chapel, set in a rust-red ravine. Further southwest is a nature reserve, the **Parque Natural del Alto Tajo**.

Arab ramparts above Molina de Aragón's old town

La Alcarria ❹

Guadalajara. 🚉 *Guadalajara.* ℹ *Pastrana, 949 37 06 72 (closed Mon).* **www**.pastrana.org

This vast stretch of undulating olive groves and fields east of Guadalajara is still evocative of Camilo José Cela's *(see p35)* classic book *Journey to the Alcarria.* Driving through the rolling hills, it seems that little has changed since this account of the hardship of Spanish rural life was written in the 1940s.

Towards the centre of the Alcarria are three immense, adjoining reservoirs called the **Mar de Castilla** (Sea of

Olive groves in La Alcarria in the province of Guadalajara

Castile). The first reservoir was built in 1946, and holiday homes have subsequently sprung up close to the shores and on the outskirts of villages.

Historic **Pastrana**, 45 km (28 miles) southeast of Guadalajara, is one of the prettiest towns in the Alcarria. The town developed alongside the **Palacio Mendoza**, and by the 17th century was larger and more affluent than Guadalajara. The **Iglesia de la Asunción** contains four 15th-century Flemish tapestries and paintings from El Greco's school.

Brihuega, 30 km (19 miles) northeast of Guadalajara, has a pleasant old centre.

Guadalajara ❺

Guadalajara. 🏘 *75,000.* 🚌 🚍 ℹ️ *Plaza de los Caidos 6, 949 21 16 26.* 📅 *Tue, Sat.* 🎉 *Virgen de la Antigua (Sep).* **www**.jccm.es

Guadalajara's history is largely lost within the modern city, although traces of its Renaissance splendour survive. The **Palacio de los Duques del Infantado**, built between the 14th and 17th centuries by the powerful Mendoza dynasty, is an out-standing example of Gothic-Mudéjar architecture *(see p24)*. The main façade and patio are adorned with carving. The restored palace now houses the Museo Provincial. Among the churches in the town is the **Iglesia de Santiago**, with a Gothic-Plateresque chapel by

Detail of the façade of the Palacio de los Duques del Infantado

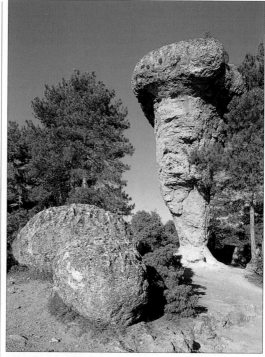
Sculpted rock figures in Ciudad Encantada

Alonso de Covarrubias. The 15th-century **Iglesia de San Francisco** is home to the mausoleum of the Mendoza family; it cannot, however, be visited. The cathedral is built on the site of a mosque.

Environs
At **Lupiana**, 11 km (7 miles) east of Guadalajara, is the two-storey Monasterio de San Bartolomé, which was founded in the 14th century.

> 🏛 **Palacio de los Duques del Infantado**
> Avenida del Ejército. **Tel** 949 21 33 01. ☐ *daily.*

Serranía de Cuenca ❻

Cuenca. 🚌 *Cuenca.* ℹ️ *Cuenca, 969 23 21 19.* **www**.cuenca.es

To the north and east of Cuenca stretches the vast *serranía*, a mountainous area of forests and pastures dissected by deep gorges. Its two most popular beauty spots are the

Ciudad Encantada (Enchanted City), where the limestone has been eroded into spectacular shapes, and the moss-clad waterfalls and rock pools of the **Nacimiento del Río Cuervo** (Source of the River Cuervo).

The main river flowing through the area, the Júcar, carves a gorge near Villalba de la Sierra. The viewpoint of the **Ventano del Diablo** gives the best view of the gorge.

Between Beteta and Priego (known for its pottery and canework), to the north, is an-other spectacular river canyon, the **Hoz de Beteta**, where the Río Guadiela has cut its way through the surrounding cliffs. There are good views from the convent of **San Miguel de las Victorias**. A small road leads to the 18th-century royal spa of **Solán de Cabras**

In the emptier eastern and southern tracts is **Cañete**, a pretty fortified old town with a parish church displaying 16th-century paintings. To the southeast of Cañete are the eerie ridgetop ruins of the abandoned town of **Moya**.

Street-by-Street: Cuenca ❼

Cuenca's picturesque old town sits astride a steeply sided spur which drops precipitously on either side to the deep gorges of the Júcar and Huécar rivers. Around the Moorish town's narrow, winding streets grew the Gothic and Renaissance city, its monuments built with with the profits of the wool and textile trade. The main sight is the cathedral, one of the most original works of Spanish Gothic, with Anglo-Norman influences. One of the picturesque Hanging Houses, which jut out over the Huécar ravine, has been converted into the excellent Museum of Abstract Art.

The Plaza de la Merced buildings contrast with the modern Museo de las Ciencias (Science Museum).

Museo de las Ciencias

CALLE DE SANTA MARÍA

CALLE DE ALFONSO VIII

CALLE MOSEN DIEGO DE VALERA

Torre Mangana
This ruined lookout tower at the top of the town is all that remains of an Arab fortress. There are wonderful panoramic views from the top.

| 0 metres | 50 |
| 0 yards | 50 |

Ayuntamiento

Museo Arqueológico
The collection, covering prehistory up to the 17th century, includes an excellent exhibition on Roman Cuenca.

KEY

– – – Suggested route

★ **Museo de Arte Abstracto**
Spain's abstract art museum is inside one of the Hanging Houses. It contains works by the movement's leading artists, including Antoni Tàpies and Eduardo Chillida.

Plaza Mayor
This café-lined, arcaded square is in the heart of the old town. The 18th-century Baroque town hall (ayuntamiento), built with arches, stands at the south end.

VISITORS' CHECKLIST

Cuenca. 50,000. Calle Mariano Catalina, 902 24 02 02. Calle Fermín Caballero 20, 969 22 70 87. Plaza Mayor 1, 969 23 21 19. Tue. **Museo Diocesano** Tue–Sun. **Museo de Arte Abstracto** Tue–Sun. **Museo de las Ciencias** Tue–Sun. **Museo Arqueológico** Tue–Sun. www.cuenca.es

The Iglesia de San Miguel, perched over the Júcar gorge, was built in the Romanic style.

SEVERO CATALINA

PLAZA MAYOR

CALLE DE SAN PEDRO

CALLE DE JULIÁN ROMERO

OBISPO VALERO

To Parador de Cuenca

Museo Diocesano
The cathedral's treasures, which are housed in the Palacio Episcopal, include paintings by El Greco.

★ Cathedral
Highlights of the 12th- to 18th-century building are the decorated altar, chapter-house and the side chapels.

STAR SIGHTS

★ Museo de Arte Abstracto

★ Hanging Houses

★ Cathedral

★ Hanging Houses
The 14th-century beamed Casas Colgadas were once used as a summer residence for the royal family.

Remains of a Roman building in Segóbriga

Segóbriga **8**

Saelices (Cuenca). *Tel* 969 13 20 64.
⬤ *Tue–Sun.* **Museum** ⬤ *public hols, 24, 25 & 31 Dec.* 📷

The small ruined Roman city of Segóbriga, near the town of Saelices, is located in open, unspoiled countryside close to the Madrid–Valencia motorway. The Romans who lived here exploited the surrounding area, growing cereals, felling timber and mining minerals.

Many parts of the city can be explored. The 1st-century theatre – which has a capacity of 2,000 people – is sometimes used for dramatic performances today. Segóbriga also had a necropolis, an amphitheatre, a temple to Diana and public baths. The quarries which supplied the stone to build the city can also be seen.

Nearby, there is a small museum containing some of the site's finds, although the best statues are in Cuenca's Museo Arqueológico *(see p384)*.

Monasterio de Uclés **9**

Uclés (Cuenca). *Tel* 969 13 50 58.
⬤ *9am – dusk daily.* 📷

The small village of Uclés, to the south of the Alcarria, is dominated by its impressive castle-monastery, nicknamed "El Escorial de La Mancha" for the similarity of its church's profile to that of El Escorial *(see pp330–31)*. Originally an impregnable medieval fortress, Uclés became the monastery seat of the Order of Santiago from 1174, because of its cen-

tral geographical location. The austere building you see today, used as a seminary school, is mainly Renaissance, but overlaid with ornamental Baroque detail. Among its attractive features are a magnificent carved wooden ceiling and staircase.

Illescas **10**

Toledo. 🏠 15,000. 🚉 **ℹ** *Plaza Mayor 1, 925 51 10 51.* 🚍 *Thu.* 📷 *Fiesta de Milagro (11 Mar); Fiesta Patronal (31 Aug).*

Just off the Madrid–Toledo motorway, Illescas was the summer location for Felipe II's court. While there is little to see of its old town, the 16th-century **Hospital de la Caridad**, near the Iglesia de Santa María (built in the 12th and 13th centuries and renovated in the 15th), is important for its art collection. The hospital has five outstanding late El Grecos *(see p373)*. The subjects of three of these are the Nativity, the Annunciation and the Coronation of the Virgin.

🔒 **Hospital de la Caridad**
Calle Cardenal Cisneros 2. *Tel* 925 54 00 35. ⬤ *daily.* 📷 ♿

Talavera de la Reina **11**

Toledo. 🏠 80,000. 🚉 🚌 **ℹ** *C/ Palenque 2, 925 82 63 22.* 🚍 *Wed & 1st Sat of month.* 📷 *Feria de San Isidoro (15–18 May), Virgen del Prado (8 Sep), Feria de San Mateo (20–23 Sep), Las Mondas (Sat after Easter).*

A ruined 15th-century bridge across the Tagus marks the entrance to the old part of this busy market town. From the bridge you can walk past the surviving section of the Roman and medieval wall to the 12th-century **collegiate church**. It has a small but beautiful Gothic cloister, and the belfry is from the 18th century.

Talavera's ceramic workshops still produce the blue and yellow *azulejos* (tiles) which have been a trademark of the town since the 16th century; but nowadays they also make domestic and decorative objects. A good selection of *azulejos* can be seen in the large **Ermita del Virgen del Prado** by the river. Many of the interior walls have superb 16th- to 20th-century tile friezes of religious scenes.

Ceramics in Talavera workshop

Part of a frieze of tiles in Talavera's Ermita del Virgen del Prado

Traditional embroidery work in Lagartera, near Oropesa

Oropesa **⑫**

Toledo. 🏠 2,871. 🚉 ℹ️ Plaza del Navarro 9, 925 43 00 02. 🅿️ Mon & Thu. 🎉 Virgen de Peñitas (8–10 Sep), Beato Alonso de Orozco (19 Sep).

Oropesa's medieval and Renaissance splendour as one of Toledo's satellite communities has left a charming old quarter at the centre of today's small farming town. A circular Ruta Monumental starts from the massive, mainly 15th-century **castle** on the top of the hill. A Renaissance extension – thought to be the work of Juan de Herrera, co-architect of El Escorial (see pp330–31) – was added to the castle in the 16th century by the wealthy and influential Álvarez family. A large part of the castle has been converted into a parador (see p587).

The Ruta Monumental continues around the town, taking in a number of churches, convents, a small ceramics museum and the town hall which presides over the main square.

Environs
The area around Oropesa is excellent for buying handicrafts. **Lagartera**, just to the west of the town, is famous for the embroidery and lacework by the women in the village and **El Puente del Arzobispo**, 12 km (7 miles) south of Oropesa, is a good source of painted ceramics and *esparto* (grass-weaving) work. **Ciudad de Vascos**, further southeast, is a ruined 10th-century Arab city in splendid countryside around Azután.

Montes de Toledo **⑬**

Toledo. 🚉 San Martín de Montalbán. ℹ️ Toledo, 925 22 08 43.

To the southwest of Toledo a range of low mountains sweeps towards Extremadura. In medieval times the Montes de Toledo were owned by bishops and the kings. They cover an area of approximately 1,000 sq km (386 sq miles).

The attractive new nature reserve of the **Parque Nacional de Cabañeros** (see pp30–1) encloses a sizeable area of woodland and pastures used for grazing sheep. The easiest access to the park is from **Pueblo Nuevo del Bullaque**. From here it is possible to make four-hour guided trips in Land Rovers, during which you may spot wild boar, deer and imperial eagles. In the pasturelands stand *chozos*, conical refuges for shepherds and their families.

In the eastern foothills of the Montes de Toledo is **Orgaz**, with a parish church which contains works by El Greco. Nearby villages, such as **Los Yébenes** and **Ventas con Peña Aguilera**, are known for their leather goods and restaurants serving game.

On the plains stands the small church of **Santa María de Melque**, believed to date back to the 8th century. Close by is the Templar castle of **Montalbán**, a vast but ruined 12th-century fortress. Nearer to Toledo, at **Guadamur**, there is another handsome castle.

A *chozo* (shepherd's cabin) in the Parque Nacional de Cabañeros

CASTILLA-LA MANCHA'S FIESTAS

La Endiablada (2–3 Feb) Almonacid del Marquesado (Cuenca). At the start of the two-day-long "Fiesta of the Bewitched", men and boys, gaudily dressed as "devils", with cowbells strapped to their backs, gather in the house of their leader, the *Diablo Mayor*. They accompany the images of the Virgen de la Candelaria (Virgin of Candlemas) and St Blaise in procession. As the devils dance alongside the floats bearing the saints' images, they ring their bells loudly and incessantly.

One of the so-called "devils" in La Endiablada fiesta

Romería del Cristo del Sahúco (Pentecost, May/ Jun), Peñas de San Pedro (Albacete). A cross-shaped coffin bearing a figure of Christ is carried 15 km (9 miles) here from its shrine by men dressed in white. **La Caballada** (early Jun), Atienza (Guadalajara). Horsemen follow the route across country taken by the 12th-century muleteers of Atienza, who are said to have saved the boy King Alfonso VIII of Castile from his uncle, Fernando II. **Corpus Christi** (May/ Jun), Toledo. One of Spain's most dramatic Corpus Christi (see p38) processions. The cathedral monstrance (see p392) is paraded in the streets.

Street-by-Street: Toledo ⑭

Damascene work, typical of Toledo

Picturesquely sited on a hill above the River Tagus is the historic centre of Toledo. Behind the old walls lies much evidence of the city's rich history. The Romans built a fortress on the site of the present-day Alcázar. The Visigoths made Toledo their capital in the 6th century AD, and left behind several churches. In the Middle Ages, Toledo was a melting pot of Christian, Muslim and Jewish cultures, and it was during this period that the city's most outstanding monument – its cathedral – was built. In the 16th century the painter El Greco came to live in Toledo, and today the city is home to many of his works.

Puerta de Valmardón

The Iglesia de San Román, of Visigothic origin, now contains a museum relating the city's past under the Visigoths.

| 0 metres | 100 |
| 0 yards | 100 |

★ **Iglesia de Santo Tomé**
This church, with a beautiful Mudéjar tower, houses El Greco's masterpiece, The Burial of the Count of Orgaz *(see p32).*

To Sinagoga de Santa María la Blanca and Monasterio de San Juan de los Reyes

To Sinagoga del Tránsito and Casa-Museo de El Greco

CARDENAL LORENZANA

CALLE DE SAN ROMÁN

CALLE DE ALFONSO X

CALLE DE ALFONSO XII

CALLE DE LA TRINIDAD

Archbishop's Palace

Taller del Moro
This Mudéjar palace houses a museum of Mudéjar ceramics and tiles. It is, however, currently closed for renovation.

STAR SIGHTS

★ Iglesia de Santo Tomé

★ Museo de Santa Cruz

★ Cathedral

The Puerta del ... has a double ...rish arch and ... two towers.

Mezquita del Cristo de la Luz

This mosque, one of the city's two remaining Muslim buildings, dates from around AD 1000.

To tourist information, Estación de Autobuses, and Estación de RENFE

The Plaza de Zocodover is named after the market which was held here in Moorish times. It is still the city's main square, with many cafés and shops.

PLAZA DE ZOCODOVER

CALLE DEL COMERCIO

COSTA DE CARLOS V

LFILERITOS

★ **Museo de Santa Cruz**

The city's main fine arts collection includes several tapestries from Flanders. Among them is this 15th-century zodiac tapestry, with well-preserved rich colours.

SIXTO RAMÓN PARRO

NAL CISNEROS

KEY

– – – Suggested route

★ **Cathedral**

Built on the site of a Visigothic cathedral and a mosque, this impressive structure is one of the largest cathedrals in Christendom (see pp392–3). The Flamboyant Gothic high altar reredos (1504) is the work of several artists.

Alcázar

In the central patio of the fortress is a replica of the statue Carlos V y el Furor: the original is housed in the Prado Museum.

Toledo cathedral rising above the rooftops of the medieval part of the city

Exploring Toledo

Toledo is easily reached from Madrid by rail, bus or car, and is then best explored on foot. To visit all the main sights you need at least two days, but it is possible to walk around the medieval and Jewish quarters in a long morning. To avoid the heavy crowds, go midweek and stay for a night, when the city is at its most atmospheric.

♟ Alcázar

Cuesta de Carlos V. **Tel** 925 22 30 38. ● for expansion until 2007.
Charles V's fortified palace stands on the site of former Roman, Visigothic and Muslim fortresses. Its severe square profile suffered damage by fire three times before being almost completely destroyed in 1936 when the Nationalists survived a 70-day siege by the Republicans. Restoration followed the original plans and the siege headquarters have been preserved as a monument to Nationalist heroism. The building houses an army museum which is currently closed pending the arrival of the Museo del Ejército (see p287) from Madrid in 2005, making this the main army museum in Spain.

The Borbón-Lorenzana Library (not open to the public) contains 100,000 books and manuscripts from the 16th to 19th centuries.

🏛 Museo de Santa Cruz

Calle Miguel de Cervantes 3. **Tel** 925 22 14 02. ○ daily. ● some collections, because of renovation.
This museum is housed in a 16th-century hospital founded by Cardinal Mendoza. The building has some outstanding Renaissance architectural features, including the main doorway, staircase and cloister. The four main wings, laid out in the shape of a Greek cross, are dedicated to the fine arts. The collection is especially strong in medieval and Renaissance tapestries, paintings and sculptures. There are also works by El Greco, including one of his last paintings, *The Assumption* (1613), still in its

The Assumption by El Greco (1613) in the Museo de Santa Cruz

original altarpiece. Decorative arts on display include two typically Toledan crafts: armour and damascened swords, made by inlaying blackened steel with gold wire. Damascene work, such as plates and jewellery (as well as swords), is still produced in the city.

🔒 Iglesia de Santo Tomé

Plaza del Conde 4. **Tel** 925 25 60 98. ○ daily. 🎫 (free Wed pm for EU residents).
Visitors come to Santo Tomé mainly to admire El Greco's masterpiece, *The Burial of the Count of Orgaz (see p32).* The Count paid for much of the 14th-century building that stands today. The painting, commissioned in his memory by a parish priest, depicts the miraculous appearance of St Augustine and St Stephen at his burial, to raise his body to heaven. It has never been moved from the setting for which it was painted, nor restored. Nevertheless, it is remarkable for its contrast of glowing and sombre colours. In the foreground, allegedly, are the artist and his son (both looking out) as well as Cervantes. The church is thought to date back to the 11th century, and its tower is a fine example of Mudéjar architecture.

Nearby is the **Pastelería Santo Tomé**, a good place to buy locally made marzipan.

🕎 Sinagoga de Santa María la Blanca

Calle de los Reyes Católicos 4. *Tel* 925 22 72 57. ☐ *daily.* ● *24 (pm), 25, 31 (pm) Dec & 1 Jan.*

The oldest and largest of the city's original synagogues, this monument dates back to the 12th century. In 1405 it was taken over as a church by San Vincente Ferrer after expulsion of the Jews. Restoration has returned it to its original beauty – carved stone capitals and wall panels stand out against white horseshoe arches and plasterwork. In the main chapel is a Plateresque altarpiece. In 1391 a massacre of Jews took place on this site, a turning point after years of religious tolerance in the city.

Mudéjar arches in the Sinagoga de Santa María la Blanca

🕎 Sinagoga del Tránsito

Calle Samuel Leví. *Tel* 925 22 36 65. ☐ *Tue–Sun (Sun am only).* 🎫 *(free Sat pm & Sun am).*

The most elaborate Mudéjar interior in the city is hidden behind the deceptively humble façade of this former synagogue, built in the 14th century by Samuel Ha-Leví, the Jewish treasurer to Pedro the Cruel. The interlaced frieze of the lofty prayer hall harmoniously fuses Islamic, Gothic and Hebrew geometric motifs below a wonderful coffered ceiling.

Inside the synagogue is a museum dedicated to Sephardi (Spanish Jewish) culture. The manuscripts, costumes and sacred objects of worship date from both before and after the Jews' expulsion from Spain at the end of the 15th century *(see p57).*

Ornate ceiling in the Monasterio de San Juan de los Reyes

🔒 Monasterio de San Juan de los Reyes

Calle de los Reyes Católicos 17. *Tel* 925 22 38 02. ☐ *daily.* 🎫 *(free Wed pm, for EU members).*

A wonderful mixture of architectural styles, this monastery was commissioned by the Catholic Monarchs in honour of their victory over the Portuguese at the battle of Toro in 1476 *(see p357).* Originally, it was intended to be their burial place, but they were actually laid to rest in Granada *(see p486).* Largely the work of Juan Guas, the church's main Isabelline structure was completed in 1504. Although it was badly damaged by Napoleon's troops in 1808 *(see p63),* it has been restored to its original splendour with features such as a Gothic cloister (1510) which has a multicoloured Mudéjar ceiling. Near to the church is a stretch of the Jewish quarter's original wall.

🏛 Casa-Museo de El Greco

Calle Samuel Leví. *Tel* 925 22 40 46. ☐ *Tue–Sun.* 🎫 *(free Sat pm, Sun).*

It is not clear whether El Greco actually lived in or simply near to this house in the heart of the Jewish quarter, now a museum housing a collection of his works. Canvases on display include *View of Toledo*, a detailed depiction of the city at the time, and the superb series *Christ and the Apostles*. Underneath the museum, on the ground floor, is a domestic chapel with a fine Mudéjar ceiling and a collection of art by painters of the Toledan School, such as Luis Tristán, a student of El Greco.

🔒 Iglesia de Santiago del Arrabal

Calle Arrabal

This is one of Toledo's most beautiful Mudéjar monuments. It can be easily identified by its tower, which dates from the 12th-century Reconquest *(see pp54–5).* The church, which was built slightly later, has a beautiful woodwork ceiling. The ornate Mudéjar pulpit and Plateresque altarpiece stand out against the otherwise plain Mudéjar interior.

🕎 Puerta Antigua de Bisagra

When Alfonso VI conquered Toledo in 1085, he entered it through this gateway, alongside El Cid. It is the only gateway in the city to have kept its original 10th-century military architecture. The huge towers are topped by a 12th-century Arab gatehouse.

EL GRECO

Born in Crete in 1541, El Greco ("the Greek") came to Toledo in 1577 to paint the altarpiece in the convent of Santo Domingo el Antiguo. Enchanted by the city, he stayed here, painting religious portraits and altarpieces for other churches. Although El Greco was trained in Italy and influenced by masters such as Tintoretto, his works are closely identified with the city where he settled. He died in Toledo in 1614.

Domenikos Theotocopoulos, better known as El Greco

Toledo Cathedral

The splendour of Toledo's massive cathedral reflects its history as the spiritual heart of the Church in Spain and the seat of the Primate of all Spain. The Mozarabic Mass, which dates back to Visigothic times, is still said here today. The present cathedral was built on the site of a 7th-century church. Work began in 1226 and spanned three centuries, until the completion of the last vaults in 1493. This long period of construction explains the cathedral's mixture of styles: pure French Gothic – complete with flying buttresses – on the exterior; with Spanish decorative styles, such as Mudéjar and Plateresque work, used in the interior.

★ Sacristy
El Greco's The Denuding of Christ, above the marble altar, was painted especially for the cathedral. Also here are works by Titian, Van Dyck and Goya.

The Cloister, on two floors, was built in the 14th century on the site of the old Jewish market.

View of Toledo Cathedral
Dominating the city skyline is the Gothic tower at the west end of the nave. The best view of the cathedral, and the city, is from the parador (see p588).

The belfry in the tower contains a heavy bell known as *La Gorda* ("the Fat One").

The Puerta del Mollete, on the west façade, is the main entrance to the cathedral. From this door, *mollete,* or soft bread, was distributed to the poor.

Monstrance
In the Treasury is the 16th-century Gothic silver and gold monstrance. It is carried through the streets of Toledo during the Corpus Christi celebrations (see p387).

STAR FEATURES

★ Sacristy

★ Transparente

★ High Altar Reredos

★ Choir

★ **Transparente**
This Baroque altarpiece of marble, jasper and bronze, by Narciso Tomé, is illuminated by an ornate sky-light. It stands out from the mainly Gothic interior.

VISITORS' CHECKLIST

Calle Cardenal Cisneros 1. **Tel** 925 22 22 41. ☐ 8am–6:30pm daily, 8am–1pm, 5:30–6:30pm Sun. ☐ 8am, 8:30am (Ecumenical), 9:30 am (Mozarabic Mass – every half hour until 11am), 5:30pm, 6:30pm daily (noon & 1pm Sun). **Choir, Treasury, Sacristy and Chapterhouse** ☐ 10:30am–6:30pm Mon–Sat, 2pm–6:30pm Sun (last admission 6pm).

Capilla de Santiago

The Capilla de San Ildefonso contains the superb Plateresque tomb of Cardinal Alonso Carrillo de Albornoz.

Chapterhouse
Above 16th-century frescoes by Juan de Borgoña is this multicoloured Mudéjar ceiling, unique in the city.

Puerta de los Leones

Puerta Llana

The Puerta del Perdón, or Door of Mercy, has a tympanum decorated with religious characters.

The Capilla Mozárabe has a beautiful Renaissance ironwork grille, carved by Juan Francés in 1524.

★ **High Altar Reredos**
The polychrome reredos, one of the most beautiful in Spain, depicts scenes from Christ's life.

★ **Choir**
The carvings on the wooden lower stalls depict scenes of the fall of Granada. The alabaster upper ones show figures from the Old Testament.

Windmills on the ridge above Consuegra, overlooking the plains of La Mancha

Tembleque **⓯**

Toledo. 🏛 *2,200.* ℹ *Plaza Mayor 1, 925 14 52 61.* 🚍 *Wed.* 🎉 *Jesús de Nazareno (24 Aug).*

The well-preserved stone Plaza Mayor *(see p27)* at Tembleque dates from the 17th century. It is decorated with the red cross of the Knights Hospitallers, the military order which once ruled the town.

Environs
Ocaña, 30 km (20 miles) north of Tembleque, centres on the huge yet elegant, late 18th-century *plaza mayor*, the third largest town square in Spain, after Madrid and Salamanca.

Consuegra **⓰**

Toledo. 🏛 *10,500.* 🚉 ℹ *Cerro Calderico, 925 47 57 31.* 🚍 *Sat.* 🎉 *Medieval Consuegra (mid Aug), La Rosa de Azafrán (last weekend Oct).*

Consuegra's 11 windmills *(see p27)* and restored castle stand on a ridge, overlooking the plains of La Mancha. One windmill which has working macinery is set in motion every year during the town's festival to celebrate the autumn harvest of saffron *(see p338)*. During the fiesta, pickers compete to see who can strip petals from the saffron crocus the fastest.

Environs
About 4 km (2 miles) on the road to **Urda** is a Roman dam. An old restaurant *(see p638)* at **Puerto Lápice**, off the NIV 20 km (13 miles) south of Consuegra, claims to be the inn in which Don Quixote was "knighted" by the indulgent landlord.

Campo de Criptana **⓱**

Ciudad Real. 🏛 *13,000.* 🚉 ℹ *Calle Barbero 1, 926 56 22 31.* 🚍 *Tue.* 🎉 *Virgen de Criptana (17 Apr), Cristos de Villejos (25 Aug).*

The remaining ten windmills of what was originally La Mancha's largest collection – 32 – stand on a hillcrest in the town. Three date back to the 16th century and have their original machinery intact. One is the tourist information office, and three others are museums.

Environs
More windmills stand nearby above **Alcázar de San Juan** and **Mota del Cuervo**, a good place to buy *queso Manchego*, local sheep's cheese *(see p339)*.

El Toboso **⓲**

Toledo. 🏛 *2,100.* ℹ *C/ Daoiz y Velarde 3, 925 56 82 26.* 🚍 *Wed.* 🎉 *Carnival (17–20 Jan), Cervantes Days (23 Apr), San Agustin (27–30 Aug).*

Of all the villages of La Mancha claiming links to Don Quixote, El Toboso has the clearest ties. It was chosen by Cervantes as the birthplace of Dulcinea, Don Quixote's sweetheart. The **Casa de Dulcinea**, the home of Doña Ana Martínez Zarco, on whom Dulcinea was allegedly based, has been refurbished in its original 16th-century style.

Considered of such cultural importance, the French army allegedly refused to attack the village during the War of Independence *(see pp62–3)*.

🏛 **Casa de Dulcinea**
***Tel** 925 19 72 88.* ⏰ *Tue–Sun.* 🎫 *(free pm Sat & am Sun).* ♿

Belmonte **⓳**

Cuenca. 🏛 *2,500.* 🚉 ℹ *Castillo de Belmonte, 967 17 07 41.* 🚍 *Mon.* 🎉 *San Bartolomé (late Aug); Virgen de Gracia (second weekend of Sep).*

Belmonte's magnificent 15th-century **castle** *(see p344)* is one of the best preserved in the region. It was built by Juan Pacheco, Marquis of Villena, after Enrique IV gave him the town in 1456. Inside it has decorative carved coffered ceilings, and Mudéjar plasterwork. The **collegiate church** is especially remarkable for its

Belmonte's splendid 15th-century castle

richly decorated chapels and Gothic choir stalls, which were brought here from Cuenca cathedral (*see p385*). There is also outstanding ironwork, a Renaissance reredos and the font at which the Golden Age poet Fray Luis de León (1527–91), was baptized.

Environs
Two villages near Belmonte also flourished under the Marquis of Villena. The church at **Villaescusa de Haro**, 6 km (4 miles) to the northeast, has an outstanding 16th-century reredos. **San Clemente**, some 40 km (25 miles) further southeast, clusters around two near-perfect Renaissance squares. There is a Gothic alabaster cross in the Iglesia de Santiago Apóstol.

🏰 **Castillo de Belmonte**
Tel 627 40 66 80. ◯ *Tue–Sun*. 🖼️

The chalk cliffs of Alcalá del Júcar, honeycombed with tunnels

The castle of Alarcón, which has been converted into a parador

Alarcón 🌀

Cuenca. 🏘️ *200.* 🚪 *Calle Posadas 1, 969 33 03 01.* 🎉 *Cristo de la Fé (14 Sep), San Sebastián (20 Jan), Fiesta del Emigrante (2nd weekend in Aug).*

Perfectly preserved, the fortified village of Alarcón guards a narrow loop of the Río Júcar from on top of a rock. As you drive through its defences, you may have the impression of entering a film-set for a medieval epic.

The village dates back to the 8th century. It became a key military base for the Reconquest (*see pp54–5*) and was recaptured from the Moors by Alfonso VIII in 1184 following a nine-month siege. It was later acquired by the Marquis of Villena. Alarcón has dramatic walls and three defensive precincts. The small, triangular **castle**, high above the river, has been turned into a parador (*see p586*), preserving much of its medieval atmosphere.

The **Iglesia de Santa María** is a lovely Renaissance church, with a fine portico and an altarpiece attributed to the Berruguete school. The nearby **Iglesia de Santísima Trinidad** is in Gothic-Plateresque style (*see p25*).

Alcalá del Júcar 🌀

Albacete. 🏘️ *1,500.* 🚪 *Avenida de los Robles 1, 967 47 30 90.* 🚌 *Sun* 🎉 *San Lorenzo (7–15 Aug).*

Where the Rio Júcar runs through the chalk hills to the northeast of Albacete, it cuts a deep, winding gorge, the Hoz de Júcar, along which you can drive for a stretch of 40 km (25 miles). Alcalá del Júcar is dramatically sited on the side of a spur of rock jutting out into the gorge. The town is a warren of steep alleys and flights of steps. At the top of the town, below the castle, houses have been extended by digging caves into the soft rock. Some of these have been transformed into tunnels cut from one side of the spur to the other.

Environs: To the west, the gorge runs past fertile orchards to the Baroque **Ermita de San Lorenzo**. Further on is the picturesque village of **Jorquera**, which was an independent state for a brief period during the Middle Ages, refusing to be ruled by the crown. It retains its Arab walls. A collection of shields is on display in the Casa del Corregidor.

DON QUIXOTE'S LA MANCHA

Cervantes (*see p333*) doesn't specify where his hero was born but several places are mentioned in the novel. Don Quixote is knighted in an inn in Puerto Lápice, believing it to be a castle. His sweetheart, Dulcinea, lives in El Toboso. The windmills he tilts at, imagining them to be giants, are thought to be those at Campo de Criptana. Another adventure takes place in the Cueva de Montesinos (*see p397*).

Illustration from a 19th-century edition of *Don Quixote*

Albacete ②

Albacete. 🚗 150,000. 🚉 🚌 ℹ️
Calle del Tinte 2, 967 58 05 22. ⊖
Tue. 🎪 Virgen de los Llanos (8 Sep).

Despite being labelled one of Spain's least interesting cities, this provincial capital is not without its attractions. The main one is the excellent **Museo Provincial**, which has exhibits ranging from Iberian sculptures and unique Roman amber and ivory dolls to 20th-century paintings. The city's **cathedral**, begun in 1515, has Renaissance altarpieces.

Albacete is also known for its daggers and jackknives, crafted here since Muslim times, and the agricultural fair, held each September.

🏛 **Museo Provincial**
Parque Abelardo Sánchez.
Tel 967 22 83 07. ☐ Tue–Sun. 🎟
Sun am. ♿

Environs
Chinchilla de Monte Aragón, 12 km (7 miles) to the southeast, has a well-preserved old quarter around a main square. Above the town is the picturesque shell of its 15th-century castle.

Almansa, 70 km (43 miles) further east, is dominated by another imposing castle, which is of Moorish origin.

Alcaraz ④

Albacete. 🚗 1,700. ℹ️ Calle Mayor 1, 967 38 08 27. ⊖ Wed. 🎪 Canto de Los Mayos (30 Apr–1 May), Feria (4–9 Sep), La Romería de la Virgen (4–9 Sep).

An important Arab and Christian stronghold, Alcaraz's military power waned after the Reconquest but its economy flourished around its (now defunct) carpet-making industry.

Standing in the attractive Renaissance Plaza Mayor are the "twin towers" of **Tardón** and **Trinidad**, and an 18th-

The castle of Chinchilla de Monte Aragón, overlooking the town

Sierra de Alcaraz ③

Where the Sierras of Segura and Alcaraz push northwards into the southeastern plains of La Mancha, they form spectacular mountains, broken up by dramatic gorges and fertile valleys. The source of the Río Mundo is a favourite beauty spot. Nearby Riópar, perched on the side of the mountain, has a 15th-century parish church. Among the less-explored villages, Letur, Ayna, Yeste and Liétor are especially picturesque. Their narrow, winding streets and craft traditions clearly reflect their Muslim origins.

Source of the Río Mundo ⑤
The river begins as a waterfall, inside the Cueva de Los Chorros, and tumbles down a dramatic cliff face into a bubbling spring at the bottom.

0 kilometres 5

0 miles 5

KEY
▦ Tour route
═ Other roads
🌼 Viewpoint

Yeste ④
The village of Yeste, which stands at the foot of the Sierra de Ardal, is crowned by a hilltop Arab castle. It was reconquered under Fernando III, and was later ruled by the Order of Santiago.

ALBACETE
N322
Peñascosa
JAÉN
Alcaraz
Cortes
CM3216
SIERRA DE ALCARAZ
CM3216
CM3204
CM412
Mundo
El Par
⑤
CALAR DEL MUNDO

century commodity exchange, the **Lonja del Corregidor**, with Plateresque decoration. The square is surrounded by lively, narrow streets with traditional houses. On the outskirts of the town are the castle ruins and surviving arch of a Gothic aqueduct. Alcaraz makes a good base for touring the sierras of Alcaraz and Segura.

The twin towers of Tardón and Trinidad on Alcaraz's main square

Lagunas de Ruidera 25

Cuidad Real. 🚌 Ossa de Montiel. 🏠 Ruidera (Wed–Sun), 926 52 81 16. **www**.lagunaruidera.com

Once nicknamed "The Mirrors of La Mancha", the 15 interconnected lakes which make up the Parque Natural de las Lagunas de Ruidera stretch for 39 km (24 miles) through a valley. They allegedly take their name from a story in *Don Quixote (see p395)* in which a certain Mistress Ruidera, her daughters and her nieces are said to have been turned into lakes by a magician.

Although La Mancha's falling water table has led to a decline in the amount of water in the lakes, they are still worth visiting for their wealth of wildlife, which includes great and little bustards, herons and many types of duck. The wildlife has recently come under threat due to the increasing number of

One of the lakes in the Parque Natural de las Lagunas de Ruidera

tourists, and the development of holiday chalets on the lakes' shores. Near one of the lakes, the Laguna de San Pedro, is the **Cueva de Montesinos**, a deep, explorable cave which was also used as the setting for an episode in *Don Quixote*.

To the northwest, the lakes link up with the Embalse de Peñarroya reservoir, which is overlooked by a castle.

Ayna ①
The village of Ayna is set deep in a gorge of the Río Mundo. There are spectacular views over the countryside from the Mirador del Diablo.

Foothills of the Sierra de Alcaraz

Liétor ②
Worth visiting in this small hillside village are the Gothic Ermita de Belén and the Iglesia de Santiago, with a *trompe l'oeil* altarpiece.

TIPS FOR DRIVERS

Tour length: 280 km (175 miles).
Stopping-off points: All of these villages have bars and restaurants. Alternatively, there are numerous places along the way to stop for a picnic.

Letur ③
With its pretty whitewashed Jewish quarter, this is perhaps the most picturesque village in the area.

Villanueva de los Infantes 26

Ciudad Real. 🏘 6,000. 🚌 🛈 *Plaza Mayor 3, 926 36 13 21.* 🗓 *Fri.* 🎉 *Cruz de Mayo (2–3 May), Ferias (late Aug), Virgen de Antigua (8 Sep), Santo Tomás (18 Sep).* **www**.infantes.org

Villanueva's old town, which centres on the graceful Neo-Classical Plaza Mayor, is one of the most attractive in La Mancha. Many buildings on the square have wooden balconies and arcades. Also on the square is the **Iglesia de San Andrés**, which has a Renaissance façade. Inside are a Baroque altarpiece and organ, as well as the now empty tomb of the Golden Age author Francisco de Quevedo. He lived and died in the **Convento de los Dominicos**.

Environs
The village of **San Carlos del Valle**, 25 km (15 miles) to the northwest, has an 18th-century square and galleried houses of rust-red stone.

Valdepeñas 27

Ciudad Real. 🏘 27,000. 🚌 🚉 🛈 *Pl de España, 926 31 25 52.* 🗓 *Thu.* 🎉 *Grape Harvest (first week of Sep).*

Valdepeñas is the capital of La Mancha's vast wine region, the world's largest expanse of vineyards, producing vast quantities of red wine *(see pp202–3)*. This largely modern town comes alive for its September wine festival. In the network of older streets around the café-lined Plaza de España are the **Iglesia de la Asunción** and the municipal museum.

Valdepeñas has over 30 bodegas which can be visited. One of them, **Bodega Museo**, has some of the few remaining traditional cellars, with huge earthenware jars, *tinajas*.

🍷 Bodega Museo
Calle Torrecillas 116. **Tel** 926 31 28 49. 🕐 *daily.* 📷 ♿

Courtyard of the Palacio del Viso in Viso del Marqués

Viso del Marqués 28

Ciudad Real. 🏘 3,000. 🚌 🛈 *Plaza de la Oretania 8, 926 33 60 01.* 🗓 *Tue.* 🎉 *San Andrés (second Sun of May), Feria (24 – 8 Jul).*

The small village of Viso del Marqués in La Mancha is the unlikely setting of the **Palacio del Viso**, a grand Renaissance building. This mansion was commissioned in 1564 by the Marquis of Santa Cruz, the admiral of the fleet which defeated the Turks at Lepanto in 1571 *(see p59)*. One of the main features of the house is a Classical patio. Inside, the principal rooms have been decorated with Italian frescoes.

Environs
About 25 km (16 miles) to the northeast of Viso del Marqués is Spain's oldest bullring at **Las Virtudes**. Square and galleried, it was built in 1641 next to a 14th-century church, which has a Churrigueresque altarpiece.

🏛 Palacio del Viso
Plaza del Pradillo 12. **Tel** 926 33 60 08. 🕐 *Tue–Sun.*

Calatrava la Nueva 29

Cuidad Real. Aldea de Rey. **Tel** 926 22 13 37. 🕐 *Tue–Sun.* **www**.elquijote.com

Magnificent in its isolated hilltop setting, the ruined castle-monastery of Calatrava la Nueva is reached by a stretch of original medieval road.

It was founded in 1217 by the Knights of Calatrava, Spain's first military-religious order *(see p54)*, to be their headquarters. The complex is of huge proportions, with a double patio and a church with a triple nave. The church has been restored and is illuminated by a beautiful rose window above the entrance.

Expanse of vineyards near Valdepeñas

Calatrava la Nueva castle-monastery, dominating the plains of La Mancha

After the Reconquest, the building continued to be used as a monastery until it was abandoned in 1802 following fire damage.

Opposite the castle are the ruins of a Muslim frontier fortress, **Salvatierra**, which was captured from the Moors by the Order of Calatrava in the 12th century.

Almagro ⑳

Ciudad Real. 🏘 *8,600.* 🚌 🚗
🛈 *Plaza Mayor 1, 926 86 07 17.* 🛍
Wed. 🎉 *Virgen de las Nieves (5 Aug), San Bartolomé (23–28 Aug).*
www.ciudad-almagro.com

Almagro was disputed during the Reconquest, until the Order of Calatrava captured it and built the castle of Calatrava la Nueva to the southwest of the town. The rich architectural heritage of the atmospheric old town is partly the legacy of the Fugger brothers, the Habsburgs' bankers who settled in nearby Almadén during the 16th century.

The town's main attraction is its colonnaded stone plaza, with characteristic enclosed, green balconies. On one side is a 17th-century courtyard-theatre – the **Corral de Comedias** – where a drama festival is held for the Festival de Teatro Clásico.

Other monuments worth seeing include the Fuggers' Renaissance warehouse and former university, and also the parador *(see p586)*.

Environs
To the northwest is **Ciudad Real**, founded by Alfonso X the Learned in 1255. Its sights include the Iglesia de San Pedro and the Mudéjar gateway, the Puerta de Toledo.

Raised walkway in the Parque Nacional de Las Tablas de Daimiel

Tablas de Daimiel ㉛

Ciudad Real. 🚗 *Daimiel.* 🛈 *Daimiel, Santa Teresa, s/n 1.*

The marshy wetlands of the Tablas de Daimiel, northeast of Ciudad Real, are the feeding and nesting grounds of a huge range of aquatic and migratory birds. Despite being national parkland since 1973, they have become an ecological *cause célèbre* due to the growing threat from the area's lowering water table. This has affected the area's wildlife in recent years.

One corner of the park is open to the public, with walking routes to islets and observation towers. Breeding birds here include great crested grebes and mallards. Otters and red foxes are among the mammals which have traditionally inhabited the park.

Valle de Alcudia ㉜

Ciudad Real. 🚗 *Fuencaliente.* 🛈 *Ciudad Real, Calle Alarcos 21, 926 20 00 37.* **www**.castillalamancha.es

Alcudia's lush lowlands, which border the Sierra Morena foothills to the south, are among central Spain's most unspoiled countryside. The area is used largely as pasture land. In late autumn it is filled with sheep, whose milk makes the farmhouse cheese for which the valley is known.

The mountain village of **Fuencaliente** has thermal baths that open in the summer. Further north, **Almadén** is the site of a large mercury mine. **Chillón**, to the northwest, has a late Gothic church.

Small isolated farmhouse in the fertile Valle de Alcudia

EXTREMADURA

CÁCERES · BADAJOZ

O f all the Spanish regions, far-flung Extremadura – "the land beyond the River Douro" – is the most remote from the modern world. Green sierras run southwards through rolling hills strewn with boulders. Forests and reservoirs shelter rare wildlife. The towns, with their atmospheric old quarters, have a romantic, slow-paced charm. In winter, storks nest on their spires and chimneys.

The finest monuments in Extremadura are the ruins of ancient settlements scattered across the region. Many are exceptionally well preserved. Some of Spain's finest Roman architecture is to be seen in Mérida, capital of the Roman province of Lusitania, which has an aqueduct and a magnificent theatre. Other Classical remains dot the countryside – notably a Tartessan temple at Cancho Roano and a Roman bridge at Alcántara. Smaller finds are displayed in Badajoz museum.

Modern development has bypassed the old town of Cáceres, whose ancient walls, winding streets and nobles' mansions are still marvellously intact. Trujillo, Zafra and Jerez de los Caballeros have medieval and Renaissance quarters; and there are small, splendidly decorated cathedrals in Plasencia, Coria and Badajoz. The castles and stout walls of Alburquerque and Olivenza mark frontiers embattled through history. Many cathedrals and monasteries were built in the troubled times during and after the Reconquest by the large military-religious orders which then governed the region for the crown.

Extremadura was the birthplace of many conquistadors and emigrants to the New World; the riches they found there financed a surge of building. Guadalupe monastery, in the eastern hills, is the most splendid monument to the region's New World ties.

View over the rooftops of the historic town of Cáceres

◁ An old stone cross in the woods near Yuste, a Hieronymite monastery founded in 1404

Exploring Extremadura

Extremadura is ideal for nature lovers and those who want to get off the beaten track to discover the old Spain. It offers beautiful driving and walking country in its northern sierras and valleys, and exceptional wildlife in Monfragüe Natural Park. Some of the best Roman ruins in Spain can be found throughout Extremadura, especially in the regional capital, Mérida. The walled old town of Cáceres, with its well-preserved Jewish quarter, and the monasteries of Guadalupe and Yuste, are other historic sights not to be missed. To the south, the Templar towns in the Sierra Morena, such as Jerez de los Caballeros, have fine old buildings, while the small, historic towns of Coria, Zafra and Llerena all make charming bases for excursions.

SIGHTS AT A GLANCE

Orchards near Hervás in the Valle del Ambroz

nca

Ávila

años de Montemayor

ERVÁS

MONASTERIO DE YUSTE
6

Cuacos de Yuste

Jaraiz de la Vera

Talayuela

Navalmoral de la Mata *Madrid*
NV = A5

atejada

ARQUE NATURAL
E MONFRAGÜE

Embalse de Valdecañas

Tajo

Jaraicejo

Castañar de Ibor

Almonte

Sierra de Villuercas

RUJILLO

GUADALUPE
8

Madroñera

Alía

N502

Sierra de Guadalupe

Logrosán

Zorita

Embalse de García de Sola

Castilblanco

Embalse de Cijara

D U R A

Herrera del Duque

das

Navalvillar de Pela

N430

Guadiana

Embalse de Orellana

Ciudad Real

Villanueva de la Serena

Puebla de Alcocer

n Benito

Campanario

Embalse de Zújar

Embalse de La Serena

Cabeza del Buey

Castuera

NCHO ANO **17**

Zalamea de la Serena

Helechal

Zújar

Peraleda del Zaucejo

nga N432

Azuaga

Córdoba

Cattle grazing in the fields near Cáceres

KEY

═══	Motorway
= =	Motorway under construction
──	Major road
═══	Secondary road
──	Scenic route
──	Main railway
──	Minor railway
▬▬	International border
──	Regional border
△	Summit

GETTING AROUND

Extremadura is not very well connected by air or rail services. Badajoz has the only (domestic) airport in the region, while the region's main rail link is the line from Madrid to Cáceres, Mérida and Badajoz. Coach services are infrequent, and in many areas, such as the northern sierras, they are non-existent. It is generally much more convenient to travel by car. Be aware that as Spain is in the process of changing its road numbering system some of the roads featured here may differ from new road signs.

0 kilometres   25

0 miles   15

Roman bridge crossing the Río Guadiana at Mérida

Beehives, a common sight in Las Hurdes

Las Hurdes ❶

Cáceres. 🚌 *Pinofranqueado, Caminomorisco, Nuñomoral.* 🛈 *Pinofranqueado, 927 67 41 33.*

Las Hurdes' slate mountains, goats and beehives were memorably caught in the 1932 Luis Buñuel film, *Tierra sin Pan (Land without Bread)*. The area's legendary poverty disappeared with the arrival of roads in the 1950s, but the black slopes, riverbeds and hill terraces remain.

From Pinofranqueado or Vegas de Coria, roads climb past picturesque "black" villages like Batuequilla, Fragosa, and El Gasco, which sits under an extinct volcano. The more developed **Lower Hurdes** area, crossed by the Río Hurdano and the main access route (C512), is dotted with camp sites and restaurants serving traditional cuisine.

Sierra de Gata ❷

Cáceres. 🚌 *Cáceres.* 🛈 *Moraleja, 927 14 70 88.* **www**.sierradegata.com

There are 40 hamlets in the Sierra de Gata, scattered between olive groves, orchards and fields. The area has retained its old-fashioned rural charm by conserving hunters' paths for woodland walking, and its local crafts, most notably lace-making. In the lowland towns of **Valverde de Fresno** and **Acebo**, the local dialect, *chapurriau*, is still spoken. On the higher slopes, **Eljas**, **Gata** and **Villamiel** have ruins of medieval fortresses. The old granite houses have carved family crests on the front and distinctive outside staircases.

Coat of arms on a house front in Acebo

Hervás ❸

Cáceres. 🚶 *4,000.* 🛈 *C/ Braulio Navas 6, 927 47 36 18.* 🗓 *Sat.* 🎉 *Nuestra Señora de la Asunción (14–17 Aug).* **www**.valleambroz.org

Sitting at the top of the wide Valle del Ambroz, Hervás is known for its medieval Jewish quarter, with its whitewashed houses. The tiny streets, dotted with taverns and craft workshops, slope down towards the Río Ambroz. Just off the main plaza is the **Museo Pérez Comendador-Leroux**, named after the town's noted 20th-century sculptor and his wife, whose work is exhibited here.

The next town up towards the Béjar pass is **Baños de Montemayor**, whose name comes from its sulphurous baths, which date back to Roman times. These were revived in the early 1900s and are open to the public. At **Cáparra**, southwest of Hervás, four triumphal arches stand on the Roman road, the Vía de la Plata *(see p352).*

🏛 **Museo Pérez Comendador-Leroux**
C/ Asensio Neila 5. **Tel** 927 48 16 55. ⏰ *pm Tue–Sun.* ⛔ *public hols.* 🎫

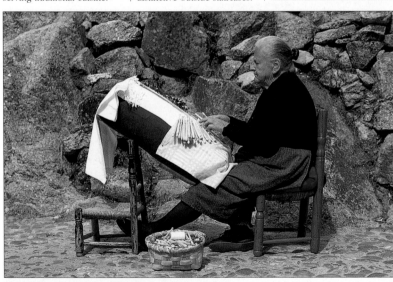

Traditional lace-making in one of the villages of the Sierra de Gata

Ancient wall and olive groves in the Valle del Ambroz

Coria ❹

Cáceres. 🏘 *13,000*. ▯ ᵢ *Avenida de Extremadura 39, 927 50 13 51.* 🚌 *Thu.* 🎉 *Día de la Virgen (2nd Mon in May), San Juan (24 Jun).*

Coria's walled old town, perched above the Río Alagón, boasts a Gothic-Renaissance **cathedral** with rich Plateresque carving, and the 16th-century **Convento de la Madre de Dios**, which has a fine Renaissance cloister.

Forming part of the town walls, which are a Muslim and medieval patchwork, are an impressive castle tower, and four gates, two of which date back to Roman times. The gates are closed during the fiesta of San Juan in June for night-time bull-running. Situated below the old town is the **Puente Seco**, a Roman bridge over the river.

Plasencia ❺

Cáceres. 🏘 *40,500*. ▯ ▯ ᵢ *Santa Clara 2, 927 42 38 43.* 🚌 *Tue.* 🎉 *Ferias (6–8 Jun).*

Plasencia's golden-grey walls, rising above a curve in the banks of the Río Jerte, tell of the town's past as a military bastion. Nowadays Plasencia is best known for its Tuesday market, dating back to the 12th century, which is held in the main square.

A short walk away are the town's two cathedrals, which are built back-to-back. The 16th-century **Catedral Nueva**

has a Baroque organ and carved wooden choir stalls. The Romanesque **Catedral Vieja**, next to it, has a museum with works by Ribera, and a late 14th-century Bible.

The nearby **Museo Etnográfico y Textil**, housed in a 14th-century hospital, has displays of crafts and costumes.

The rest of the Jerte valley has pockets of outstanding beauty, such as the **Garganta de los Infiernos**, a nature reserve with dramatic, rushing waterfalls.

🏛 **Museo Etnográfico y Textil**
Plaza del Marqués de la Puebla. **Tel** *927 42 18 43*. ◯ *Wed–Sun.*

Monasterio de Yuste ❻

Cuacos de Yuste (Cáceres). **Tel** *927 17 21 30*. ◯ *daily.* 🎟

The Hieronymite monastery of Yuste, where Charles V *(see p59)* retired from public life in 1556 and died two years later, is remarkable for its simplicity and its lovely setting in the wooded valley of La Vera.

The church's Gothic and Plateresque cloisters and the austere palace are open to visitors. Just below it is **Cuacos de Yuste**, the most unspoiled of La Vera's old villages, where peppers, for making paprika, hang outside the houses.

Paprika peppers hanging up around a door in Cuacos de Yuste

A *Carantoña*, during the fiesta of St Sebastian, Acehuche

EXTREMADURA'S FIESTAS

Carantoñas *(20–21 Jan)*, Aceúche (Cáceres). During the fiesta of St Sebastian, the *Carantoñas* take to the streets of the town dressed up in animal skins, with their faces covered by grotesque masks designed to make them look terrifying. They represent the wild beasts which are said to have left the saint unharmed.
Pero Palo *(Carnival Feb/Mar)*, Villanueva de la Vera (Cáceres). In this ancient ritual a wooden figure dressed in a suit and representing the devil is paraded around the streets and then destroyed – except for the head, which is reused the year after.
Los Empalaos *(Maundy Thursday)*, Valverde de la Vera (Cáceres). Men do penance by walking in procession through the town with their arms outstretched and bound to small tree trunks.
La Encamisá *(7–8 Dec)*, Torrejoncillo (Cáceres). Riders on horseback parade around town, where bonfires are set alight for the occasion.
Los Escobazos *(7 Dec)*, Jarandilla de la Vera (Cáceres). At night, the town is illuminated by bonfires in the streets, and torches are made from burning brooms

Parque Natural de Monfragüe ❼

Cáceres. 🚉 *Villareal de San Carlos.* ℹ️ *Villareal de San Carlos, 927 19 91 34.*

To the south of Plasencia, rolling hills drop from scrubby peaks through wild olive, cork and holm oak woods to the dammed Tagus and Tiétar river valleys. In 1979, some 500 sq km (200 sq miles) of these hills were granted natural park status in order to safeguard the area's outstandingly varied wildlife species, which includes a large proportion of Spain's protected bird species *(see pp342–3)*.

The many species of bird which breed here include the black-winged kite, black vulture and, most notably, the black stork, as well as more

Birdwatchers in the Parque Natural de Monfragüe

common aquatic species on and near the water. Mammals living here include the lynx, red deer and wild boar. At **Villareal de San Carlos**, a hamlet founded in the 18th

century, there is parking and an information centre which gives out maps of walks. An ideal time to visit the park is September, when many migrating birds stop off here.

Guadalupe ❽

Cáceres. 🏘 *2,500.* 🚉 ℹ️ *Plaza Mayor, 927 15 41 28.* **Monasterio** ⬜ *daily.* 📷 *guided tour only.* 🚉 *Wed.* 🎉 *Cruz de Mayo (3 May), La Virgen Y Dia de la Comunidad (8 May).* **www**.monasterioguadalupe.com

This village grew around the magnificent Hieronymite **Monasterio de Guadalupe**, founded in 1340. In the main square there are shops that sell handmade ceramics and beaten copper cauldrons, both traditional monastic crafts, now made as souvenirs.

The turreted towers of the monastery, which is set in a deep wooded valley, help give it a fairy-tale air. According to legend, a shepherd found a wooden image of the Virgin Mary here in the early 14th century. The monastery grew

to splendour under royal patronage, acquiring schools of grammar and medicine, three hospitals, an important pharmacy and one of the largest libraries in Spain.

The 16th-century *hospedería* where royalty once stayed was destroyed by fire; the 20th-century reconstruction is now a hotel run by the monks *(see p589)*. The old hospital has been converted into a parador. In the car park is a plaque commemorating Spain's first human dissection, which took place here in 1402.

By the time the New World was discovered, the monastery was very important and in 1496 was the site of the baptism of some of the first native Caribbeans brought to Europe by Columbus *(see pp56–7)*.

The monastery was sacked by Napoleon in 1808 but was

refounded by Franciscans a century later. It is a major centre of Catholicism, visited by thousands of pilgrims.

Guided tours (in Spanish only) begin in the museums of illuminated manuscripts, embroidered vestments and fine art. They continue to the choir and the magnificent Baroque sacristy, nicknamed "the Spanish Sistine Chapel", because of Zurbarán's portraits of monks hanging on the highly decorated walls. For many, the chance to touch or kiss the tiny Virgin's dress in the *camarín* (chamber) behind the altar is the highlight of the tour. The 16th-century Gothic cloister has two tiers of horseshoe arches around an ornate central pavilion. The church, with a magnificent 16th-century iron grille partly forged from the chains of freed slaves, may be visited separately.

Environs
The surrounding **Sierra de Villauercas** and **Los Ibores** sierras, where herbs were once picked for the monastery pharmacy, have good woodland walks. The road south also gives access to the pasture lands of **La Serena**, a vital breeding ground for birds of the steppe *(see pp342–3)*, and the huge reservoir of **Cíjara**, surrounded by a game reserve.

Monasterio de Guadalupe, overlooking the town

For hotels and restaurants in this region see pp588–90 and pp638–40

Trujillo ❾

Cáceres. 🏚 *10,000.* 🚌 ❓ *Plaza Mayor, 927 65 90 39.* 🚉 *Thu.* 🎭 *Chiviri (Easter Sun), Feria del Queso (weekend of 1 May).*

When the Plaza Mayor of the medieval hilltop town of Trujillo is floodlit at night, it is one of the most beautiful squares in Spain. By day, there is much to visit, including the **Iglesia de Santa María la Mayor**, on one of the town's winding streets, which contains various sarcophagi.

At the top of the hill there is an Islamic fortress, which defended the town against the Christian advance during the Reconquest *(see pp54–5)*; but in 1232 it was retaken by the forces of Fernando III. Trujillo was the birthplace of

Statue of Francisco Pizarro in Trujillo's main square

several conquistadors, most notably Francisco Pizarro, who conquered Peru *(see p58)*, of whom there is a statue in the main square. His brother, Hernando Pizarro, founded

the **Palacio del Marqués de la Conquista**, one of several palaces and convents built with New World wealth. It has an elaborate corner window with carved stone heads of the Pizarro brothers and their Inca wives. The beautiful 16th-century **Palacio de Pizarro-Orellana** was built by descendants of Francisco de Orellana, the explorer of Ecuador and the Amazon. It has a fine Plateresque patio.

In late April or early May, gourmets flock here for the week-long cheese fair.

🏛 **Palacio del Marqués de la Conquista**
Plaza Mayor. ⬤ *to the public.*

🏛 **Palacio de Pizarro-Orellana**
Plaza de Don Juan Tena. *Tel 927 32 11 58.* ☐ *daily.*

The Virgin of Guadalupe, *her face blackened by smoke from smouldering lamps, is worshipped by pilgrims from around the world. She is kept in the* camarín, *and dressed up for feast days. On her lap sits the infant Jesus.*

Gothic cloister

Embroidery museum

Painting and sculpture museum

Church

The chapterhouse *has 87 illuminated manuscripts by the monks of Guadalupe.*

The sacristy *contains Zurbarán's* Father Gonzalo de Illescas at Work.

Street-by-Street: Cáceres ⑩

After Alfonso IX of Leon conquered Cáceres in 1227, its growing prosperity as a free trade town attracted merchants, and later aristocracy, to settle here. They rivalled each other with stately homes and palaces fortified by watchtowers, most of which Isabel and Fernando, the reigning monarchs *(see pp56–7)*, ordered to be demolished in 1476 to halt the continual jostling for power. Today's serene Renaissance town dates from the late 15th and 16th centuries, after which economic decline set in. Untouched by the wars of the 19th and 20th centuries, Cáceres became Spain's first listed heritage city in 1949.

★ Casa de los Golfines de Abajo
The ornamental façade of this 16th-century mansion displays the shield of one of the town's leading families, the Golfines.

Casa y Torre de Carvajal
This typical Renaissance mansion has a 13th-century round Arab tower and a peaceful garden with a patio.

PLAZA DE SANTA MARÍA

★ Iglesia de Santa María
Facing the Palacio Episcopal, this Gothic-Renaissance church has a beautiful cedarwood reredos and a 15th-century crucifix – the Cristo Negro (Black Christ).

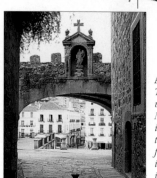

Arco de la Estrella
This low-arched gateway was built by Manuel Churriguera in 1726. It leads through the city walls from the Plaza Mayor into the old town and is flanked by a 15th-century watchtower.

| 0 metres | 50 |
| 0 yards | 50 |

KEY

— — — Suggested route

Barrio de San Antonio

This quaint old Jewish quarter, with narrow streets of whitewashed houses restored to their original condition, takes its name from the nearby hermitage of St Anthony.

VISITORS' CHECKLIST

Cáceres. ⬛ 82,000. ⬛ Avenida de Alemania, 927 23 50 61. ⬛ Avenida de Alemania, 927 23 25 50. ⬛ Plaza Mayor 40, 927 01 08 34. ⬛ Wed. ⬛ Las Candelas (Feb), San Jorge (23 Apr). **Museo Provincial** ⬛ Tue–Sun.

★ Museo Provincial

Housed in the Casa de las Veletas, this museum has contemporary art and archaeology from the region.

The Convento de San Pablo sells delicious *yemas* (candied egg yolks) made by the nuns.

Casa y Torre de la Cigüeña

The slender, battlemented tower of the House of the Stork was allowed to remain after 1476 because of the owner's loyalty to Isabel. It is now owned by the army.

The Iglesia de San Mateo, built between the 14th and 17th centuries, is one of Cáceres' earliest churches.

Casa del Sol (Casa de los Solis)

The façade of this elegant Renaissance building, once home of the Solis family, is emblazoned with a sun (sol) motif.

STAR SIGHTS

- ★ Casa de los Golfines de Abajo
- ★ Iglesia de Santa María
- ★ Museo Provincial

Arroyo de la Luz ⓫

Cáceres. 🏘 6,650. � 🛈 Travesía Regajal 12, 927 27 16 23. 🌅 Thu. 🎑 Día de la Patrona (Easter Mon), Fiestas (15 Aug).

The small town of Arroyo de la Luz is home to one of the artistic masterpieces of Extremadura. Its **Iglesia de la Asunción**, completed in 1565, contains a spectacular altar-piece which incorporates 20 paintings by the mystical religious painter Luis de Morales.

Environs
The area has a large population of white storks *(see p343)*. Nearby **Malpartida** is home to the largest colony, whose nests adorn the church roof. There are some good picnic spots in the surrounding countryside.

Alterpiece in the Iglesia de la Asunción, Arroyo de la Luz

Alcántara ⓬

Cáceres. 🏘 1,720. 🚍 🛈 Avenida de Mérida 21, 927 39 08 63. 🌅 Tue. 🎑 Feria (15–17 Apr); Classic Drama Festival (1st week Aug); San Pedro (19 Oct).

Alcántara has two important sights. One is the drystone **Roman bridge**, above the Tagus river, with its honorary arch and a temple. The other the restored **Convento de San Benito**. This was built as the headquarters of the Knights of the Order of Alcántara during the 16th century and was sacked by Napoleon. Its surviving treasures are in the **Iglesia de Santa María de Almocovar**.

Walls of the 16th-century Convento de San Benito, Alcántara

Valencia de Alcántara ⓭

Cáceres. 🏘 7,500. 🚍 🚍 🛈 Calle de Hernán Cortés, 927 58 21 84. 🌅 Mon. 🎑 Día de los Mayos (1 May).

The Gothic quarter of this hilltop frontier town is given an elegant air by its fountains and shady orange trees. The **Castillo de Piedra Buena** was built by the Knights of the Order of Alcántara and on the outskirts of the town there are more than 40 dolmens, or megalithic burial sites.

Environs
Alburquerque, to the southeast, is sited on a rocky outcrop with a magnificent panoramic view from the ramparts and keep of its castle. Below is the old town and the 15th-century Iglesia de Santa María del Mercado.

Mérida ⓮

Badajoz. 🏘 52,058. 🚍 🚍 🛈 Avenida José Álvarez Saez de Buruaga, 924 00 97 30. 🌅 Tue. 🎑 Classic Drama Festival (Jul–Aug), Fiestas Patronales (10 Dec).

Founded by Augustus in 25 BC, Augusta Emerita grew into the cultural and economic capital of Rome's westernmost province, Lusitania, but lost its eminence under the Moors. Though a small city, Mérida, the capital of Extremadura, has many fine Roman monuments.

The best approach is from the west of town, via the modern suspension bridge over the Río Guadiana, bringing you to the original entrance of the Roman city and Arab fortress.

The city's centrepiece is the **Roman theatre** *(see pp50–1)*. One of the best-preserved Roman theatres anywhere, it is still used in summer for the city's drama festival and is part of a larger site with an **amphitheatre** *(anfiteatro)* and gardens. Nearby are the remains of a Roman house, the **Casa del Anfiteatro**, where there are underground galleries and large areas of well-preserved mosaics.

Opposite stands Rafael Moneo's stunning red-brick **Museo Nacional de Arte Romano**. The semicircular arches of its main hall are built to the same height as the city's Los Milagros aqueduct. Off this hall, which features sculptures from the Roman theatre, there are three galleries exhibiting ceramics, mosaics, coins and statuary. There is also an ex-

Megalithic tomb on the outskirts of Valencia de Alcántara

For hotels and restaurants in this region see pp588–90 and pp638–40

Mérida's well-preserved Roman theatre, still used as a venue for classical drama

cavated Roman street. Near the museum are several other monuments, namely two villas with fine mosaics, and a racecourse.

A chapel in front of the 3rd-century **Iglesia de Santa Eulalia** is dedicated to the child saint who was martyred on this site in Roman times. Towards the centre of the town are the **Templo de Diana** (1st century AD), with tall, fluted

Sculpture of Emperor Augustus

columns, and the **Arco de Trajano**. The **Museo de Arte Visigodo** (Museum of Visigothic Art) is in the Convento de Santa Clara, which is situated off the main square. From the huge **Puente de Guadiana** there is a good view of the massive walls of the **Alcazaba**, one of Spain's oldest Moorish buildings (AD 835), whose precinct includes towers, a cistern and

Roman ruins. To the east stands the **Casa del Mithraeo**, with its Pompeiian-style frescoes and fine mosaics.

The magnificent, ruined Los Milagros aqueduct, with its granite and brick arches, are off the N630 towards Cáceres.

🏛 **Museo de Arte Visigodo**
Calle Santa Julia. **Tel** 924 30 01 06.
◯ Tue–Sun. ● 1 May, 25 Dec.

🏛 **Museo Nacional de Arte Romano**
Calle José Ramón Mélida. **Tel** 924 31 16 90. ◯ Tue–Sun. 🎫 (free Sat pm & Sun). ♿ www.mnar.es

MERIDA TOWN CENTRE

Alcazaba ⑦
Amphitheatre ④
Arco de Trajano ⑩
Casa del Anfiteatro ③
Casa del Mithraeo ⑥
Iglesia de Santa Eulalia ①
Museo de Arte Visigodo ⑨
Museo Nacional de Arte Romano ②
Puente de Guadiana ⑧
Roman theatre ⑤
Templo de Diana ⑪

Estación de RENFE

Iglesia de Santa Eulalia ①

CÁCERES, MADRID

AVENIDA DE EXTREMADURA

MARQUESA DE PINARES

STA. LUCÍA

CABO VERDE

Casa del Anfiteatro ③

Obelisco de Sta. Eulalia

PLAZA DE LA VILLA

Museo Nacional de Arte Romano ②

J. RAMÓN MÉLIDA

Amphitheatre ④

PLAZA DE CONSTITUCIÓN

Arco de Trajano ⑩

Templo de Diana ⑪

Roman Theatre ⑤

Museo de Arte Visigodo ⑨

PLAZA DE ESPAÑA

Santa María la Mayor

GUARDIA CIVIL

Alcazaba ⑦

CALDERÓN DE LA BARCA

Puente de Lusitania

BADAJOZ, SEVILLA

Puente de Guadiana ⑧

OVIEDO

Plaza de Toros

Casa del Mithraeo ⑥

ATARAZANAS

Río Guadiana

0 metres   250
0 yards   250

Key to Symbols see back flap

Badajoz ⑮

Badajoz. 🏙 150,000. ✈ 🚆 🚌
ℹ *Pasaje de San Juan, 924 22 49 81.*
🚌 *Tue & Sun.* 🎉 *Feria (24 Jun).*

Badajoz is a plain, modern
city, though it retains traces of
its former importance. It was a
major city under the Moors
but centuries of conflict robbed
Badajoz of its former glories.

The Alcazaba now houses
the **Museo Arqueológico**,
which has over 15,000 pieces
from around the province, as
far back as Paleolithic times.
Nearby is the cathedral,
dating from the 13th–18th
centuries, with a stunning
tiled cloister. A museum of
contemporary art has opened
on Calle Museo and is open
every day except Sunday
evening and Monday .

🏛 **Museo Arqueológico**
Pl José Álvarez Saez de Buruaga.
Tel *924 00 19 08.* ⭘ *Tue–Sun.* ♿

Olivenza ⑯

Badajoz. 🏙 10,800. 🚌 ℹ *Plaza de
España, 924 49 01 51.* 🚌 *Sat.*
🎉 *Muñecas de San Juan (23 Jun).*

A Portuguese enclave until
1801, Olivenza has a
colourful character. Within
the walled town are the
medieval castle, housing the
**Museo Etnográfico Gonzalez
Santana**, a museum of rural
life, and three churches.
Santa María del Castillo has
a naive family tree of the
Virgin Mary. **Santa María
Magdalena**, is a fine example
of the 16th-century Portuguese

Interior of Santa María Magdalena
church, Olivenza

Manueline style. The 16th-
century **Santa Casa de
Misericordia** has blue and
white tiled friezes. In one, God
is shown offering Adam and
Eve 18th-century coats to cover
their nakedness.

Off the main square is the
Pastelería Fuentes, which sells
Pécula Mécula cake.

🏛 **Museo Etnogràfic
Gonzalez Santana**
Plaza de Santa María. **Tel** *924 49 02
22.* ⭘ *Tue–Sun am.* 📷 ♿

Cancho Roano ⑰

Zalamea de la Serena. **Tel** *924 78 01
53.* ⭘ *Tue–Sun.*

This sanctuary-palace, which
is thought to have been built
under the civilization of Tartessus *(see p49)*, was discovered in 1978. Excavations on
this small but unique site
have revealed a moated temple
that was rebuilt three times –

many of the walls and slate
floors are still intact. Each
temple was constructed on a
grander scale than the previous one and then burned in
the face of invasion during
the 6th century BC.

Most of the artifacts unearthed, including jewellery, ceramics and furniture, are on
display in the archaeological
museum at Badajoz.

Environs
A Roman funereal monument
stands next to the church in
nearby **Zalamea de la Serena**.
The town comes alive during
the August fiestas, when the
townsfolk act out the classic
17th-century play, *The Mayor
of Zalamea*, by Calderón de
la Barca *(see p34)*, which was
supposedly based on a local
character. Shops in the town
also sell *torta de la Serena*, a
cheese made of sheep's milk.

Remains of the Tartessan sanctuary
at Cancho Ruano

Zafra ⑱

Badajoz. 🏙 15,000. 🚆 🚌
ℹ *Plaza de España 8, 924 55 10 36.*
🚌 *Sun.* 🎉 *San Miguel (30 Sep–6
Oct).* **www**.*zafraturismo.com*

At the heart of this graceful
town, nicknamed "little
Seville" because of its similarity
to the capital of Andalusia,
are two arcaded squares. The
Plaza Grande, the larger of the
two, is near the **Iglesia de la
Candelaria**, which has a " on
it is the older, 15th-century
Plaza Chica, which used to be
the marketplace. On Calle
Sevilla is the 15th-century

The colourful tiled cloister in the cathedral of Badajoz

Altarpiece by Zurbarán in the Iglesia de la Candelaria at Zafra

Convento de Santa Clara. Nearby is the **Alcázar de los Duques de Feria**, now a parador *(see p590)* with a patio of Herriano style.

Environs
Some 25 km (16 miles) to the south, in **Fuente de Cantos**, is the house in which the painter Francisco de Zurbarán was born in 1598.

Jerez de los Caballeros ⑲

Badajoz. 🚶 *9,600.* 🚉 🚌 🚶 *Plaza Constitución 1, 924 73 03 72.* 🚌 *Wed.* 🎪 *Feria del Jamón (early May and Easter).* www.dip-badajoz.es

The hillside profile of Jerez, which is broken by three Baroque church towers, is one of the most picturesque in Extremadura. This small town is also historically important – Vasco Núñez de Balboa, who discovered the Pacific, was born here. In the **castle**, now

laid out as gardens, knights of the Order of Knights Templar were beheaded in the Torre Sangrienta (Bloody Tower) in 1312. The old quarters of the town grew up around three churches: **San Bartolomé**, its façade studded with glazed ceramics; **San Miguel**, whose brick tower dominates the Plaza de España; and **Santa María de la Encarnación**.

Environs
Fregenal de la Sierra, 25 km (16 miles) to the south, is an attractive old town with a bullring.

Llerena ⑳

Badajoz. 🚶 *5,700.* 🚉 🚌 🚶 *Calle Aurora 2, 924 87 05 51.* 🚌 *Thu.* 🎪 *Nuestra Señora de la Granada (1–15 Aug).* www.llerena.org

Extremadura's southeastern gateway to Andalusia, the town of Llerena, is a mixture of Mudéjar and Baroque buildings. In the pretty square,

lined with palm trees, stands the arcaded, whitewash-and-stone church of **Nuestra Señora de la Granada**, its sumptuous interior reflecting its former importance as a seat of the Inquisition *(see p274)*. At one end of the square is a fountain designed by Zurbarán, who lived here for 15 years. Also worth seeing is the 16th-century **Convento de Santa Clara**, on a street leading out of the main square.

Environs
At **Azuaga**, 30 km (20 miles) to the east, is the Iglesia de la Consolación, containing Renaissance and Mudéjar tiles.

Tentudía ㉑

Badajoz. 🚉 *Calera de León.* 🚶 *Calera de León, 924 584 101* **Monasterio** ◻ *Tue–Sun.* ◪ www.tentudia.org

Where the Sierra Morena runs into Andalusia, fortified towns and churches founded by the medieval military orders stand among the wooded hills of Tentudía. Here, on a hilltop, stands the tiny **Monasterio de Tentudía**. Founded in the 13th century by the Order of Santiago, the monastery contains a superb Mudéjar cloister, and reredos with Seville *azulejos* (tiles).

At **Calera de León**, just 6 km (4 miles) north of Tentudía, there is a Renaissance convent, which was also founded by the Order of Santiago. The convent has a Gothic church and a cloister on two floors.

Bullring at Fregenal de la Sierra

Laujar de Andarax ㊱

Almería. 👥 1,900. 🚗 ℹ️
Carretera Laujar–Berja km 1, 950 51
35 48. 🗓 3 & 17 of each month.
🎉 San Vicente (22 Jan), San Marcos
(25 Apr), Virgen de la Salud (19 Sep).

Laujar, in the arid foothills
of the Sierra Nevada
looks southwards
across the Andarax
valley towards the
Sierra de
Gádor.
  Andarax
was founded
by one of the
grandsons of
Noah. In the
16th century, Abén
Humeya, leader of
the greatest Morisco
rebellion (see p59),
made his base here.
The revolt was
crushed by Christian troops
and Abén Humeya was killed
by his own followers. Inside

Painting, Iglesia de
la Encarnación

Laujar's 17th-century church,
La Encarnación, is a statue of
the Virgin by Alonso Cano.
Next to the Baroque **town hall**
(ayuntamiento) is a fountain
inscribed with some lines
written by Francisco
Villespesa, a dramatist and
poet who was born in Laujar
in 1877: *"Six fountains has
my pueblo/He who drinks
their waters/ will never
forget them/so heav-
enly is their taste."*
  El Nacimiento,
a park to the
east of Laujar,
is a suitable
place to have
a picnic. You
can accompa-
ny it with one of
the area's hearty
red wines. **Ohanes**,
above the Andarax
valley further to the
east, is an attractive
hill town of steep streets and
whitewashed houses known
for its crops of table grapes.

Sierra Nevada ㊲

Granada. 🚗 from Granada.
ℹ️ Plaza de Andalucía, Cetursa
Sierra Nevada, 958 24 91 19.

Fourteen peaks more than
3,000 m (9,800 ft) high crown
the heights of the Sierra
Nevada. The snow lingers
until July and begins falling
again in late autumn. One of
Europe's highest roads, the
GR411, runs past **Solynieve**,
an expanding ski resort at
2,100 m (6,890 ft), and skirts
the two highest peaks, **Pico
Veleta** at 3,398 m (11,149 ft)
and **Mulhacén** at 3,482 m
(11,420 ft).
  The Sierra's closeness to the
Mediterranean and its altitude
account for the great diversity
of the indigenous flora and
fauna found on its slopes – the
latter including golden eagles
and some rare butterflies.
  There are several mountain
refuges for the use of serious
hikers and climbers.

Yegen ⑥
A plaque marks the
house where Gerald
Brenan, the author of
South from Granada,
lived in the 1920s.

↑ *LACALAHORRA*

Puerto de la Ragua ⑧
This pass, which leads across the
mountains to Guadix, is nearly
2,000 m (6,560 ft) high and is often
snowbound in winter.

Válor ⑦
Abén Humeya, leader of a rebellion
by Moriscos in the 16th century, was
born here. A commemorative battle
between Moors and Christians is
staged each year in mid-September.

Cádiar ⑤
Free wine is traditionally
on tap during the village's
October fiesta.

E V A D A

Maitena

A337

Alcolea

Al-4401

GR431

⑥ ⑦

• *Yátor* *Ugíjar*

Cherín

A348

Ugíjar

A348

O N T R A V I E S A

0 kilometres   5

0 miles   5

KEY

🚌 Tour route

== Other roads

▲ Mountain peak

TIPS FOR DRIVERS

Tour length: 85 km (56 miles).
Stopping-off points: There are
bars and restaurants in Orgiva,
Capileira, Bubión (see p643) and
Trevélez. Orgiva, Bubión and
Trevélez have good hotels (see
pp592–96). Orgiva is the last
petrol stop before Cádiar.

Granada ❸

Stone relief, Museo Arqueológico

The guitarist Andrés Segovia (1893–1987) described Granada as a "place of dreams, where the Lord put the seed of music in my soul". It was first occupied by the Moors in the 8th century, and its golden period came during the rule of the Nasrid dynasty *(see p55)* from 1238 to 1492, when artisans, merchants, scholars and scientists all contributed to the city's international reputation as a centre for culture. Under Christian rule, following its fall to the Catholic Monarchs in 1492 and the expulsion of the Moors *(see pp56–7)*, the city blossomed in Renaissance splendour. There was a period of decline in the 19th century, but Granada has recently been the subject of renewed interest and efforts are being made to restore parts of it to their past glory.

Entrance to the Moorish *mihrab* in the Palacio de la Madraza

Façade of Granada cathedral

Exploring Granada

The old city centre around the cathedral is a maze of narrow one-way streets. It contains the Alcaicería – a reconstruction of a Moorish bazaar that burned down in 1843. Granada's two main squares are the Plaza Bib-Rambla, near the cathedral, and the Plaza Nueva. From the latter, Cuesta de Gomérez leads up to the city's two principal monuments: the Alhambra and the Generalife. On a hill opposite is the Albaicín district.

Churches well worth a visit are the Iglesia de San Juan de Dios, almost overwhelming in its wealth of Baroque decoration, and the Renaissance Iglesia de San Jerónimo.

⛪ Cathedral

On the orders of the Catholic Monarchs, work on the cathedral began in 1523 to plans in a Gothic style by Enrique de Egas. It continued under the Renaissance maestro, Diego

de Siloé, who also designed the façade and the magnificent, circular Capilla Mayor. Under its dome, windows of 16th-century glass depict Juan del Campo's *The Passion*. The west front was designed by the Baroque artist Alonso Cano, who was born in the city. His grave and many of his works can be seen in the cathedral.

⛪ Capilla Real

The Royal Chapel was built for the Catholic Monarchs between 1506 and 1521 by Enrique de Egas. A magnificent *reja* (grille) by Maestro Bartolomé de Jaén encloses the high altar and the Carrara marble figures of Fernando and Isabel, their daughter Juana la Loca (the Mad) and her husband Felipe el Hermoso (the Fair). Their coffins are in the crypt. In the sacristy there are art treasures, including paintings by Botticelli and Van der Weyden, as well as Isabel's crown, Fernando's sword and their army banners.

♛ Palacio de la Madraza

Calle Oficios 14. **Tel** *958 24 34 84.* 🔘 *for refurbishment.*

Originally an Arab university, this building later became the city hall. The façade dates from the 18th century. Inside is a Moorish hall with a finely decorated *mihrab* (prayer niche).

♛ Corral del Carbón

Calle Mariana Pineda. **Tel** *958 22 59 90.* 🔘 *for refurbishment.*

This galleried courtyard, formerly a storehouse and inn for merchants, is a unique relic of the Moorish era. In Christian times it was a theatrical venue, and later a coal exchange. Today it houses craft shops and the main tourist office.

♛ Casa de los Tiros

Calle Pavaneras. **Tel** *958 22 10 72.* 🔘 *2:30pm-8.30pm Tue, 9am-8:30pm Wed-Sat, 9am-2.30pm Sun.*

This palace was built in Mudéjar style in the 1500s. It originally belonged to the family that was awarded the Generalife after the fall of

Grille by Maestro Bartolomé de Jaén enclosing the altar of the Capilla Real

Cupola in the sanctuary of the Monasterio de la Cartuja

VISITORS' CHECKLIST

Granada. 🏙 241,000. ✈ 12 km
(7 miles) southwest of city. 🚉
Avenida Andaluces, 902 24 02
02. 🚌 Carretera de Jaen, 958
18 54 80. 🛈 Plaza Mariana
Pineda 10, 958 24 71 28 🛆 Sat
& Sun. 🎭 Semana Santa (Easter
Week), Día de la Cruz (3 May),
Corpus Christi (May/Jun).

Granada. Among their pos-
sessions was a sword that had
belonged to Boabdil. This is
carved on the façade, along
with statues of Mercury, Hercules, and Jason. The building
owes its name to the muskets
projecting from its battlements: *tiro*, meaning shot.

♟ Alhambra and Generalife
See pp490–92.

♟ El Bañuelo
Carrera del Darro 31. **Tel** 958 22 23
39. ◻ 10am–2pm Tue–Sat. ◉
public hols.
These Arab baths were built in
the 11th century. The columns
are topped by Visigothic,
Roman and Arab capitals.

🏛 Museo Arqueológico
Carrera del Darro 43. **Tel** 958 22 56
40. ◻ Tue–Sun. ◉ public hols.

This museum occupies the
Casa de Castril, a Renaissance
mansion with a Plateresque
(see p25) portal. It displays
Iberian, Phoenician and Roman
finds from Granada province.

🏛 Monasterio de la Cartuja
A Christian warrior called El
Gran Capitán founded this
monastery outside Granada
in 1516. There is a dazzling
cupo-la by Antonio Palomino,
and an extravagant Churrigueresque *(see p25)* sacristy by Luis
de Arévalo and Luis Caballo.

GRANADA CITY CENTRE

Alhambra ⑥
El Bañuelo ⑦
Capilla Real ②
Casa de los Tiros ⑤

Cathedral ①
Corral del Carbón ④
Museo Arqueológico ⑧
Palacio de la Madraza ③

0 metres 250
0 yards 250

Key to Symbols see back flap

Street-by-Street: the Albaicín

Ornate plaque on a house in the Albaicín

This corner of the city, clinging to the hillside opposite the Alhambra, is where one feels closest to Granada's Moorish ancestry. A fortress was first built here in the 13th century and there were once over 30 mosques. Most of the city's churches were built over their sites. Along the cobbled alleys stand *cármenes*, villas with Moorish decoration and gardens, secluded from the world by their high walls. In the jasmine-scented air of evening, take a walk up to the Mirador de San Nicolás. The view over the maze of rooftops of the Alhambra glowing in the sunset is magical.

Street in the Albaicín
Steep and sinuous, the Albaicín's streets are truly labyrinthine. Many street names start with Cuesta, *meaning slope.*

Real Chancillería
Built in 1530 by the Catholic Monarchs, the Royal Chancery has a beautiful Renaissance façade.

0 metres   50
0 yards   50

Casa de los Pisa, belonging to the Knights Hospitallers, displays works of art – some depicting St John of God, who died here in 1550.

STAR SIGHTS

★ Iglesia de Santa Ana

★ Museo Arqueológico

★ El Bañuelo

★ Iglesia de Santa Ana
At the end of the Plaza Nueva stands this 16th-century brick church in Mudéjar style. It has an elegant Plateresque portal and, inside, a coffered ceiling.

Carrera del Darro
The road along the Río Darro leads past crumbling bridges and the fine façades of ancient buildings, now all restored.

★ **Museo Arqueológico**
The ornate Plateresque carvings on the museum's façade include this relief of two shields. They show heraldic devices of the Nasrid kings of Granada, who were defeated by the Catholic Monarchs in 1492 (see pp56–7).

KEY

‒ ‒ ‒ Suggested route

To Mirador de San Nicolás

PLAZA CONCEPCIÓN

DE LOS REYES

CARNERO

BAÑUELO

CONCEPCIÓN

CALLE ZAFRA

CALLE GLORIA

CARRETERA DEL SANTÍSIMO

CARRERA DEL DARRO

→ **To Sacromonte**

RÍO DARRO

The **Convento de Santa Catalina** was founded in 1521.

★ **El Bañuelo**
Star-shaped openings in the vaults let light into these well-preserved Moorish baths, which were built in the 11th century.

SACROMONTE

Granada's gypsies formerly lived in the caves honey-combing this hillside. In the past, travellers would go there to enjoy spontaneous outbursts of flamenco. Today, virtually all the gypsies have moved away, but touristy flamenco shows of variable quality are still performed here in the evenings *(see pp424–5).* Sitting at the very top of the hill is the Abadía del Sacromonte, a Benedictine monastery. The ashes of St Cecilio, Granada's patron saint, are kept inside.

Gypsies dancing flamenco, 19th century

The Alhambra

A magical use of space, light, water and decoration characterizes this most sensual piece of architecture. It was built under Ismail I, Yusuf I and Muhammad V, caliphs when the Nasrid dynasty *(see pp54–5)* ruled Granada. Seeking to belie an image of waning power, they created their idea of paradise on Earth. Modest materials were used (plaster, timber and tiles), but they were superbly worked. Although the Alhambra suffered pillage and decay, including an attempt by Napoleon's troops to blow it up, in recent times it has undergone extensive restoration and its delicate craftsmanship still dazzles the eye.

Sala de la Barca

★ Salón de Embajadores

The ceiling of this sumptuous throne room, built from 1334 to 1354, represents the seven heavens of the Muslim cosmos.

★ Patio de Arrayanes

This pool, set amid myrtle hedges and graceful arcades, reflects light into the surrounding halls.

Patio de Machuca

Entrance

Patio del Mexuar
This council chamber, completed in 1365, was where the reigning sultan listened to the petitions of his subjects and held meetings with his ministers.

PLAN OF THE ALHAMBRA

To the Generalife

Main gate

The Alhambra complex includes the Casas Reales, the 13th-century Alcazaba, the 16th-century Palace of Charles V, and the Generalife *(see p492)*, which is located just off the map.

KEY

- Casas Reales (shown above)
- Palace of Charles V
- Alcazaba
- Park
- Other buildings

Palacio del Partal

A pavilion with an arched portico and a tower is all that remains of this palace, the oldest building in the Alhambra.

Washington Irving's apartments

Baños Reales

Jardín de Lindaraja

Sala de las Dos Hermanas, with its honeycomb dome, is regarded as the ultimate example of Spanish Islamic architecture.

Sala de los Reyes

This great banqueting hall was used to hold extravagant parties and feasts. Beautiful ceiling paintings on leather, from the 14th century, depict tales of hunting and chivalry.

Puerta de la Rawda

★ Sala de los Abencerrajes

This hall takes its name from a noble family, who were rivals of Boabdil (see pp56–7). According to legend, he had them massacred while they attended a banquet here. The geometrical ceiling pattern was inspired by Pythagoras' theorem.

The Palace of Charles V (1526) houses a collection of Spanish-Islamic art, whose highlight is the Alhambra vase (see p52).

★ Patio de los Leones

Built by Muhammad V, this patio is lined with arcades supported by 124 slender marble columns. At its centre, a fountain rests on 12 stocky, marble lions.

STAR FEATURES

★ Salón de Embajadores

★ Patio de Arrayanes

★ Sala de los Abencerrajes

★ Patio de los Leones

Granada: Generalife

From the Alhambra's northern side, a footpath leads
to the Generalife, the country estate of the Nasrid
kings. Here, they could escape from palace intrigues
and enjoy tranquillity high above the city, a little closer
to heaven. The name Generalife, or Yannat al Arif, has
various interpretations, perhaps the most pleasing
being "the garden of lofty paradise". The gardens,
begun in the 13th century, have been modified over
the years. They originally contained orchards and
pastures. The Generalife provides a magical setting for
Granada's annual music and dance festival *(see p41).*

The Patio de la Acequia *is an
enclosed oriental garden built
round a long central pool. Rows
of water jets on either side make
graceful arches above it.*

Sala Regia

**Jardines Altos
(Upper Gardens)**

**The Escalera del
Agua** is a staircase with
water flowing gently down it.

The Patio de los Cipreses,
otherwise known as the Patio de
la Sultana, was the secret meeting
place for Zoraya, wife of the
Sultan Abu-l-Hasan, and her lover,
the chief of the Abencerrajes.

Entrance

The Patio de Polo
was the courtyard
where palace visitors,
arriving on horse-
back, would tether
their steeds.

The Patio del Generalife *lies just
before the entrance to the Generalife.
The walk from the Alhambra to the
Generalife gardens passes first through
the Jardines Bajos (lower gardens),
before crossing this Moorish patio with
its characteristic geometric pool.*

The forbidding exterior of the castle above Lacalahorra

Castillo de Lacalahorra ❸❾

Lacalahorra (Granada). **Tel** 958 67 70 98. 🚌 Guadix. ⬜ 10am–1pm, 4–6pm Wed.

Grim, immensely thick walls and stout, cylindrical corner towers protect the castle on a hill above the village of Lacalahorra. Rodrigo de Mendoza, son of Cardinal Mendoza, had the castle built for his bride: the work was carried out between 1509 and 1512 by Italian architects and craftsmen. Inside is an ornate, arcaded Renaissance courtyard over two floors with pillars and a Carrara marble staircase.

Guadix ❹⓿

Granada. 🏠 20,100. 🚍 🚌 🛈 Avenida Mariana Pineda, 958 66 26 65. 🗓 Sat. 🎪 Fiesta & Feria (31 Aug – 5 Sep). **www**.guadixymarquesado.org

The troglodyte quarter, with 2,000 caves that have been inhabited for centuries, is the town's most remarkable sight. The **Cueva-Museo Al Fareria** and **Cueva-Museo Costumbres Populares** shows how people live underground.

The **cathedral** was begun in 1594 and finished between 1701 and 1796. Relics of San Torcuato, who founded Spain's first Christian bishopric, are kept in the cathedral museum.

Near the Moorish **Alcazaba** is the Mudéjar-style **Iglesia de Santiago**, a church with a fine coffered ceiling.

🏛 **Cueva-Museo Al Fareria**
C/ San Miguel. ⬜ Mon–Sun. 📷

🏛 **Cueva-Museo Costumbres Populares**
Plaza de Ermita Nueva. ⬜ daily. 📷

Jaén ❹❶

🏯 115,000. 🚍 🚌 🛈 Calle Maestra 13, 953 24 26 24. 🚌 Thu. 🎪 Nuestra Señora de la Capilla (11 Jun), San Lucas (18 Oct), Romería de Santa Catalina (25 Nov).

The Moors called Jaén *Geen* – meaning "way station of caravans" – because of its strategic site on the road beween Andalusia and Castile. Their hilltop fortress was rebuilt as the **Castillo de Santa Catalina** after it was captured by King Fernando III in 1246. Part of it is now a parador *(see p594)*.

Andrés de Vandelvira, who was responsible for many of Úbeda's fine buildings *(see pp496– 7)*, designed Jaén's **cathedral** in the 16th century. Later additions include the two 17th-century towers that now flank the west front.

An old mansion, the **Palacio Villardompardo**, houses a museum of arts and crafts, and also gives access to the **Baños Árabes**, the 11th-century baths of Ali, a Moorish chieftain. These have horseshoe arches, ceilings with small, star-shaped windows and two ceramic vats in which bathers once immersed themselves. Tucked away in an alley is the **Capilla de**

San Andrés, a Mudéjar chapel founded in the 16th century by Gutiérrez González who, as treasurer to Pope Leo X, was endowed with extensive privileges. A gilded iron screen by Maestro Bartolomé de Jaén is the highlight of the chapel.

The **Real Monasterio de Santa Clara** was founded in the 13th century and has a lovely cloister dating from the late 16th century. Its church, which has a coffered ceiling, contains a bamboo image of Christ made in Ecuador.

The **Museo Provincial** displays Roman mosaics and sculptures, and Iberian, Greek and Roman ceramics.

Horseshoe arches supporting the dome at the Baños Árabes, Jaén

⛪ **Castillo de Santa Catalina**
Carretera al Castillo.
Tel 953 12 07 33. 🔴 Mon.

🏛 **Palacio Villardompardo**
Plaza Santa Luisa de Marillac. **Tel** 953 24 80 68. ⬜ Tue – Sun. 🔴 public hols. **www**.promojaen.es

🏛 **Museo Provincial**
Paseo de la Estación 29. **Tel** 953 25 06 00. ⬜ Tue – Sun. 🔴 public hols.

Whitewashed cave dwellings in the troglodyte quarter of Guadix

Roman bridge spanning the Guadalquivir at Andújar

Andújar ❷

Jaén. 40,000. 🚉 🚌 🅸 Pl Santa María. Torre del Reloj, 953 50 49 59. 🛒 Tue. 🎉 Romería (last Sun of Apr).

Andújar is known for its olive oil and its pottery. It stands on the site of an Iberian town, Iliturgi, which was destroyed in the Punic Wars (*see p50*) by Scipio. The Roman conquerors built the 15-arched bridge spanning the Río Guadalquivir.

In the central square is the Gothic **Iglesia de San Miguel**, with paintings by Alonso Cano. The **Iglesia de Santa María** la Mayor has a Renaissance façade and a Mudéjar tower. Inside it is El Greco's *Christ in the Garden of Olives* (c.1605). A pilgrimage to the nearby **Santuario de la Virgen de la Cabeza** takes place in April.

Environs
The mighty fortress of **Baños de la Encina** has 15 towers and ramparts built by Caliph Al Hakam II in AD 967. Further north, the road and railway between Madrid and Andalusia squeeze through a spectacular gorge in the eastern reaches of the Sierra Morena, the **Desfiladero de Despeñaperros.**

Baeza ❸

See pp498–9.

Úbeda ❹

Jaén. 35,000. 🚌 🅸 Palacio Marqués de Contadero, C/ Baja del Marqués 4, 953 75 08 97. 🛒 Fri. 🎉 San Miguel (28 Sep).

Úbeda is a showcase of Renaissance magnificence, thanks to the patronage of some of Spain's most influential men of the 16th century. These included such dignitaries as Francisco de los Cobos, secretary of state, and his greatnephew, Juan Vázquez de Molina, who gave his name to Úbeda's most historic square. Surrounded by elegant palaces and churches, it is undoubtedly the jewel in Úbeda's crown. The old town is contained within city walls that were first raised by the Moors in 852.

Created on the orders of the Bishop of Jaén around 1562, the colossal former **Hospital de Santiago** was designed by Andrés de Vandelvira, who refined the Spanish Renaissance style into its more austere characteristics. The façade is flanked by square towers, one topped with a blue-and-white-tiled spire. Today the building is a conference centre.

ÚBEDA CITY CENTRE

Capilla del Salvador ④
Hospital de Santiago ①
Iglesia de San Pablo ③
Museo Arqueológico ②
Palacio de las Cadenas ⑥
Parador de Úbeda ⑤
Santa María de los
   Reales Alcázares ⑦

| 0 metres | 250 |
| 0 yards | 250 |

Key to Symbols *see back flap*

◁ **Fields of poppies and olive groves south of Andújar in the province of Jáen**

Laguna de Valdeazores in the Parque Nacional de Cazorla

Parque Natural de Cazorla ⑮

Jaén. 🚌 *Cazorla*. 🛈 *Calle Martinez Falero 41, 953 72 01 15.*

First-time visitors are amazed by the spectacular scenery of this 214,336-ha (529,409-acre) nature reserve with thickly wooded mountains rising to peaks of 2,000 m (6,500 ft) and varied, abundant wildlife.

Access to the Parque Natural de Cazorla, Segura y Las Villas is via the town of Cazorla. Its imposing Moorish **Castillo de la Yedra** houses a folklore museum. From Cazorla, the road winds upwards beneath the ruins of the clifftop castle at **La Iruela**. After crossing a pass it drops down to a crossroads (El Empalme del Valle) in the valley of the Río Guadalquivir. Roads lead to the source of the river and to the peaceful modern parador (*see p593*).

The main road through the park follows the river. The information centre at Torre del Vinagre is 17 km (11 miles) from the crossroads.

Sited in the 15th-century Casa Mudéjar, the **Museo Arqueológico** exhibits artifacts from Neolithic to Moorish times.

The **Iglesia de San Pablo** has a 13th-century apse and a beautiful 16th-century chapel by Vandelvira. It is surmounted by a Plateresque tower that was completed in 1537.

A monument to the poet and mystic St John of the Cross (1549–91) stands in the **Plaza de Vázquez de Molina**. The **Capilla del Salvador**, on the square, was designed by three 16th-century architects – Diego de Siloé, Andrés de Vandelvira and Esteban Jamete – as the personal chapel of Francisco de los Cobos. Behind it stand Cobos' palace, with a Renaissance façade, and the Hospital de los Honrados Viejos (Hospital of the Honoured Elders), looking on to the Plaza de Santa Lucía. From here, the Redonda de Miradores follows the line of the city walls and offers views of the countryside.

Plaza Vázquez de Molina also holds Úbeda's **parador** (*see p596*). Built in the 16th century, but much altered in the 17th, it was the residence of Fernando Ortega Salido, dean of Málaga and chaplain of the Capilla del Salvador.

Úbeda's town hall and tourist office occupy the **Palacio de las Cadenas**, a mansion built for Vázquez de Molina by Vandelvira. It gets its name from the iron chains (*cadenas*) once attached to the columns supporting the main doorway.

Also on the square are the church of **Santa María de los Reales Alcázares**, which dates mainly from the 13th century, and the **Cárcel del Obispo** (Bishop's Jail), where nuns who had been punished by the bishop were confined.

🏛 **Museo Arqueológico**
Casa Mudéjar, Calle Cervantes 6. **Tel** *953 75 37 02*. ⬜ *Tue–Sun.* ♿

🏥 **Hospital de Santiago**
Calle Obispo Cobos. **Tel** *953 75 08 42*. ⬜ *daily.*

Capilla del Salvador, Úbeda, one of Spain's finest Renaissance churches

Environs
There is a well-restored Moorish castle at **Segura de la Sierra**, 30 km (19 miles) from the reserve's northern edge. Below it is an unusual rockhewn bullring.

⛪ **Castillo de la Yedra**
Tel *953 71 00 39*. ⬜ *Tue–Sun.* 🔴 *17 Sep, 24, 25, 31 Dec & 1 Jan.* 💶 *(free for EU citizens).*

CAZORLA'S WILDLIFE
More than 100 bird species live in this nature reserve, some very rare, such as the golden eagle and the griffon vulture. Cazorla is the only habitat in Spain, apart from the Pyrenees, where the lammergeier lives. Mammals in the park include the otter – active at dawn and dusk – mouflon and wild boar, and a small remaining population of Spanish ibex. The red deer was reintroduced in 1952. Among the flora supported by the limestone geology is the indigenous *Viola cazorlensis*.

Wild boar foraging for roots, insects and small mammals

For hotels and restaurants in this region see pp591–7 and pp642–8

Street-by-Street: Baeza 🅭

Coat of arms, Casa del Pópulo

Nestling amid the olive groves that characterize much of Jaén province, beautiful Baeza is a small town, unusually rich in Renaissance architecture. Called Beatia by the Romans and later the capital of a Moorish fiefdom, Baeza is portrayed as a "royal nest of hawks" on its coat of arms. It was conquered by Fernando III in 1226 – the first town in Andalusia to be definitively won back from the Moors – and was then settled by Castilian knights. An era of medieval splendour followed, reaching a climax in the 16th century, when Andrés de Vandelvira's splendid buildings were erected. In the early 20th century, Antonio Machado, one of his generation's greatest poets, lived here.

★ Palacio de Jabalquinto
An Isabelline-style (see p24) façade, flanked by elaborate, rounded buttresses, fronts this splendid Gothic palace.

Antigua Universidad
From 1542 until 1825, this Renaissance and Baroque building was one of Spain's first universities.

Torre de los Aliatares is a 1,000-year-old tower built by the Moors.

Ayuntamiento
Formerly a jail and a courthouse, the town hall is a dignified Plateresque structure (see p25). The coats of arms of Felipe II, Juan de Borja and of the town of Baeza adorn its upper façade.

To ↑ Úbeda

PLAZA DE ESPAÑA

COMPAÑÍA

PLAZA SANTA CRUZ

SAN FELIPE

BEATO AVILA

ROMANO

BARBACANA

MERCADERÍAS

PASEO DE LA CONSTITUCIÓN

PASEO DE TUNDIDORES

O. NARVAEZ

GASPAR BECERRA

Casas Consistoriales Bajas

La Alhóndiga, the old corn exchange, has impressive triple-tier arches running along its front.

VISITORS' CHECKLIST

Jaén. 19,000. Linares-
Baeza, 902 24 02 02.
Avenida Alcalde Puche Pardo,
953 74 04 68. Plaza del
Pópulo, 953 74 04 44. Tue.
Semana Santa (Easter), Feria
(mid-Aug), Romería de la Yedra
(early Sep). www.andalucia.org

★ **Cathedral**
*The impressive
cathedral was
rebuilt by Andrés de
Vandelvira in 1567.
The Capilla
Sagrario has a
choir screen by
Bartolomé de Jaén.*

Fuente de Santa María
*Architect-sculptor Ginés
Martínez of Baeza designed
this fountain in the form of
a triumphal arch. It was
completed in 1564.*

**Antigua
Carnicería** is the
16th-century former
slaughterhouse.

**Puerta de Jaén y
Arco de Villalar**
*This gateway in the city
ramparts is adjoined by
an arch erected in 1521
to appease Carlos I (see
p58) after a rebellion.*

0 metres 75

0 yards 75

KEY

Tourist information

— — — Suggested route

STAR SIGHTS

★ Palacio de Jabalquinto

★ Cathedral

★ Plaza del Pópulo

★ **Plaza del Pópulo**
*The Casa del Pópulo, a fine Plateresque palace,
now the tourist office, overlooks this square. In
its centre is the Fuente de los Leones, a fountain
with an Ibero-Roman statue flanked by lions.*

Renaissance castle overlooking the village of Vélez Blanco

Vélez Blanco ⑯

Almería. 🏠 2,200. 🚌 Vélez Rubio.
🛈 Avenida Marqués de los Vélez,
950 41 53 54. 🗓 Wed. 🎉 Cristo
de la Yedra (second Sun of Aug).

Dominating this pleasant village is the mighty **Castillo de Vélez Blanco**. It was built between 1506–13 by the first Marquis of Los Vélez. The Renaissance interiors are now displayed in the Metropolitan Museum in New York, but there is a reconstruction of one of the patios.

Just outside Vélez Blanco, the **Cueva de los Letreros** contains paintings from c.4000 BC. One depicts the Indalo, a figure holding a rainbow and believed to be a deity with magical powers, now adopted as the symbol of Almería.

🐾 **Cueva de los Letreros**
Camino de la Cueva de los Letreros.
Tel 617 88 28 08. 🔲 daily. 🎟

Mojácar ㊼

Almería. 🏠 6,000. 🚌 🛈 Calle
Glorieta 1, 950 61 50 25. 🗓 Wed,
Sun. 🎉 Moors and Christians (second
weekend of Jun), San Agustín (28 Aug).

From a distance, Mojácar shimmers like the mirage of a Moorish citadel, its white houses cascading over a lofty ridge, 2 km (1 mile) inland from long, sandy beaches.

Following the Civil War (see pp66–7), the village fell into ruin as most of its inhabitants emigrated, but in the 1960s it was discovered by tourists, which gave rise to a new era of prosperity. The old gateway in the walls still remains, but otherwise the village has been completely rebuilt and holiday complexes have grown up along the nearby beaches. The coast south from Mojácar is among the least built up in Spain, with only small resorts and villages along its length.

Tabernas ㊽

Almería. 🏠 3,000. 🚌 🛈
Carretera Nacional 340 km 364, 950
52 50 30. 🗓 Wed. 🎉 Virgen de
las Angustias (11–15 Aug).

Tabernas is set in Europe's only desert. The town's Moorish fortress dominates the harsh surrounding scenery of cactus-dotted, rugged, eroded hills and dried-out riverbeds, which has provided the setting for many classic spaghetti westerns, such as *A Fistful of Dollars*. Two film sets can be visited: **Mini-Hollywood** and

Texas Hollywood, 1 km (1 mile) and 4 km (2 miles) from Tabernas respectively.

Not far from town is a solar energy research centre, where heliostats follow the course of Andalusia's powerful sun.

Environs
Sorbas sits on the edge of the chasm of the Río de Aguas. It has two notable buildings: the 16th-century Iglesia de Santa María and a 17th-century mansion said to have been a summer retreat for the Duke of Alba.

Nearby is the karst scenery, honeycombed with hundreds of cave systems, of the **Yesos de Sorbas** nature reserve. Permission to explore them is required from Andalusia's environmental department.

🎬 **Mini-Hollywood**
Carretera N340. **Tel** 950 36 52 36.
🔲 daily. ● Mon in winter. 🎟

🎬 **Texas Hollywood**
Carretera N340, Tabernas. **Tel** 950
16 54 58. 🔲 daily. 🎟

Desert landscape around Tabernas, reminiscent of the Wild West

Still from *For a Few Dollars More* by Sergio Leone

SPAGHETTI WESTERNS

Two Wild West towns lie off the N340 highway west of Tabernas. Here, visitors can re-enact classic film scenes or watch stunt men performing bank hold-ups and saloon brawls. The *poblados del oeste* were built during the 1960s and early 1970s when low costs and eternal sunshine made Almería the ideal location for spaghetti westerns. Sergio Leone, director of *The Good, the Bad and the Ugly*, built a ranch here and film-sets sprang up in the desert. Local gypsies played Indians and Mexicans. The deserts and Arizona-style badlands are still used for television commercials and series, and by film directors such as Steven Spielberg.

The 10th-century Alcazaba, which dominates Almería's old town

Almería ⑲

Almería. 🏛 170,000. 🚉 ✈ Estación Intermodal 🛈 Parque Nicolás Salmerón, 950 27 43 55. 🚢 Tue, Fri & Sat. 🎪 Feria (last week of Aug). **www**.andalucia.org

Almería's colossal **Alcazaba**, dating from AD 995, is the largest fortress built by the Moors in Spain. The huge structure bears witness to the city's golden age, when it was an important port under the Caliphate of Córdoba *(see pp52–3)*. The Moorish city, known as Al Mariyat (Mirror of the Sea), exported mainly brocade, silk and cotton.

During the Reconquest, the Alcazaba withstood two major sieges before eventually falling to the armies of the Catholic Monarchs *(see pp56–7)* in 1489. The royal coat of arms can be seen on the Torre del Homenaje, built during their reign. The Alcazaba also has a Mudéjar chapel and gardens.

Adjacent to the Alcazaba is the old fishermen's and gypsy quarter of **La Chanca**, where some families live in caves with brightly painted façades and modern interiors. On Mondays a lively street market is held. Although this district is picturesque, it is also desperately poor and it is unwise to walk around here alone or at night with valuables.

Berber pirates from North Africa often raided Almería. Consequently, the **cathedral** looks almost more like a castle than a place of worship, with its four towers, thick walls and small windows. The site was originally a mosque. This was converted into a church, but in 1522 it was destroyed in an earthquake. Work on the present building began in 1524 under the direction of Diego de Siloé, who designed the nave and high altar in Gothic style. The Renaissance façade and the carved walnut choir stalls are by Juan de Orea.

Brightly coloured entrance to a gypsy cave in La Chanca district

Traces of Moorish Almería's most important mosque can be seen in the **Templo San Juan.** The **Plaza Vieja** is an attractive 17th-century arcaded square. On one side is the **town hall** *(ayuntamiento)*, with a cream and pink façade (1899).

Environs

One of Europe's most important examples of a Copper Age settlement lies at **Los Millares**, near Gádor, 17 km (11 miles) north of Almería. As many as 2,000 people may have occupied the site around 2500 BC.

♠ Alcazaba
Calle Almanzor. **Tel** 950 27 16 17.
⏱ Tue–Sun. ⬤ 1 Jan, 25 Dec.
🎟 (free for EU citizens).

⋒ Los Millares
Santa Fé de Mondújar. **Tel** 677 90 34 04. ⏱ Wed–Sun. ⬤ public hols.

Parque Natural de Cabo de Gata ⑳

Almería. 🚉 San José. 🛈 Centro de Visitantes de las Amoladeras, Carretera–Cabo de Gata km 6, 950 16 04 35. ⏱ daily.

Towering cliffs of volcanic rock, sand dunes, salt flats and secluded coves characterize the 29,000-ha (71,700-acre) Parque Natural de Cabo de Gata. Within its confines are a few fishing villages, and the small resort of San José. A lighthouse stands at the end of the *cabo* (cape), which can be reached by road from the village of Cabo de Gata. The park includes a stretch of seabed 2 km (1 mile) wide and the marine flora and fauna protected within it attract scuba-divers and snorkellers.

The dunes and saltpans between the cape and the Playa de San Miguel are a habitat for thorny jujube trees. Many migrating birds stop here, and among the 170 or so bird species recorded are flamingoes, avocets, griffon vultures and Dupont's larks.

Environs

Set amid citrus trees on the edge of the Sierra de Alhamilla, **Níjar's** fame stems from the pottery and the hand-woven *jarapas* – blankets and rugs – that are made here. The barren plain between Níjar and the sea has been brought under cultivation using vast plastic greenhouses to conserve the scarce water.

The dramatic, dark volcanic rocks at Cabo de Gata, east of Almería

SPAIN'S ISLANDS

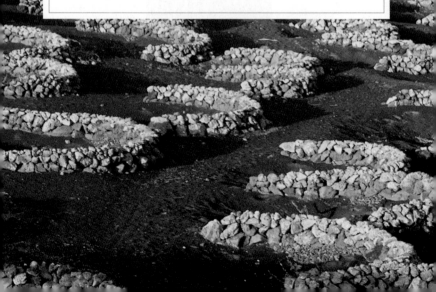

Introducing Spain's Islands

Spain's two groups of islands lie in separate seas –
the Balearics in the Mediterranean and the Canaries in
the Atlantic, off the African coast. Both are popular
package-tour destinations blessed with warm climates,
good beaches and clear waters. But each has more to
offer than high-rise hotels, fast-food restaurants and
discos. The Balearics have white villages, wooded
hills, caves and prehistoric monuments, while the
extraordinary volcanic landscapes of the Canaries are
unlike any other part of Spain. Four of Spain's national
parks *(see pp30–1)* are in the Canary Islands.

Ibiza (see pp510–12) *is the liveliest
of the Balearic Islands. Ibiza town
and Sant Antoni are the main tourist
centres, offering good nightlife and
excellent beaches.*

Eivissa
(Ibiza)

Formentera

CANARY ISLANDS
(See pp528–51)

Tenerife (see pp534–
9), *the largest of the
Canary Islands, is fertile
in the north but arid in
the south. The volcanic
summit of Mount Teide
dominates the island.
Tenerife's beaches are
black but many have
been improved with
white sand imported
from the Sahara Desert.*

La Palma

Tenerife

La Gomera

El Hierro

0 kilometres   50

0 miles   25

◁ Vines growing in the volcanic soil of Lanzarote, protected by drystone walls

In Menorca (see pp522–7) *tourism has developed more slowly than in Mallorca and Ibiza, and the island has largely avoided being over-commercialized. Scattered across the countryside are the ruins of unique Bronze Age buildings.*

BALEARIC ISLANDS
(See pp506–27)

Menorca

Mallorca

0 kilometres _____ 50

0 miles _____ 25

Mallorca (see pp514–21), *best known for its beaches, has caves and other natural features to explore. The most spectacular of the island's historic sights is the great Gothic cathedral in Palma, which rises above the boats moored in the old harbour.*

Lanzarote (see pp548–50) *is the most attractive of the Canary Islands, even though the landscape is strikingly bare. White houses contrast starkly with black volcanic fields. The most dramatic attraction is Timanfaya National Park, including the Montañas del Fuego.*

Lanzarote

Fuerteventura

ran Canaria

Gran Canaria (see p542–5) *centres on a symmetrical volcanic cone. The capital city of Las Palmas has some interesting museums and monuments. In contrast, the sprawling Maspalomas, on the south coast, is the biggest holiday resort in Spain.*

THE BALEARIC ISLANDS

IBIZA · FORMENTERA · MALLORCA · MENORCA

*C*hic resorts and attractive coves and beaches, combined with a
climate which is hot but never uncomfortably so, have made
tourism the mainstay of life along the coasts of the Balearic
Islands. Inland, there is peace and quiet in abundance, and a great
variety of sights to seek out: wooded hills, pretty white villages,
monasteries, country churches, caves and prehistoric monuments.

Standing at a crossroads in the Mediterranean, the Balearic Islands have been plundered or colonized in turn by Phoenicians, Greeks, Carthaginians, Romans, Moors and Turks. In the 13th century Catalan settlers brought their language, a dialect of which is widely spoken today.

The islands can justifiably claim to cater for all tastes: from sun-seekers on package holidays, for whom the larger resorts serve as brash fun factories, to jet-setters and film stars, who head for luxurious but discreet hideaways in the hills. The largest island, where tourism has been established the longest, is Mallorca. A massive Gothic cathedral stands near the waterfront of Palma, the capital.

The green countryside of Menorca is dotted with prehistoric monuments and its towns full of noble, historic mansions. The coast of Ibiza is notched by innumerable rocky coves. The island's hilly interior is characterized by brilliant white farmhouses and robust churches. On Formentera, small and relatively undeveloped, the pace of life is slow. The islets surrounding the four principal islands are mainly uninhabited; one of them, Cabrera (off Mallorca), is a national park.

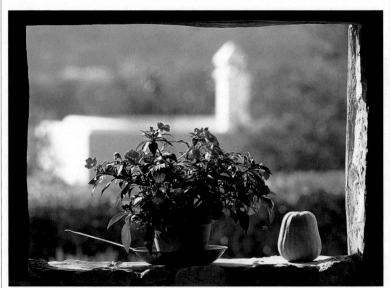

View through the window of one of Ibiza's traditional, whitewashed farmhouses

◁ The massive, heavily buttressed cathedral overlooking Palma de Mallorca's harbour

Exploring the Balearics

Though the Balearic islands are often associated
with high-density, inexpensive package tourism,
they offer enough variety to satisfy everyone's
tastes. For those unattracted by the bustle of the
coastal resorts and their beautiful beaches, the
countryside and the old towns of Palma, Ibiza,
Maó and Ciutadella are relatively undisturbed.
Mallorca is by far the most culturally rich of the
Balearics, with its distinguished collection of
modern and traditional galleries, and interesting
museums. Menorca is strong on Neolithic remains
and neo-colonial architecture, while Ibiza is for
lovers of clear, painterly light and rustic peasant
houses; it also has some of the wildest nightclubs
in Europe. Formentera – for many, the most
alluring island – has crystal water, white sand, a
pure, parched landscape and total tranquillity.

**Poblat des Pescadors in the tourist
village of Binibeca**

Early-morning mist on the waters of Port de Pollença in Mallorca

```
0 kilometres        25
0 miles          15
```

GETTING AROUND

Nearly all foreign visitors to the Balearics
arrive by plane – the no-frills airlines
making it all the more popular. Mallorca,
Menorca and Ibiza have connections to
major European cities as well as Madrid,
Barcelona and Valencia. Several airlines
fly to most other Spanish cities out of Son
Sant Joan airport in Palma. Another way
of arriving is by boat from Barcelona,
Valencia, Alicante or Dénia. Between the
islands there are regular ferry services, run
by Transmediterránea and Flebasa. Mallorca is the only island with rail services,
which run between Palma and Inca, and
between Palma and Sóller, which is now
extended to Sa Pobla and Manacor. Roads
vary from excellent to poor. The best
way to get around is by car, except on
Formentera, where cycling is best.

For additional map symbols *see back flap*

SIGHTS AT A GLANCE

A peaceful stroll on the sands of
Ibiza's Sant Miquel beach

MENORCA

Cap de Cavalleria · Fornells

CIUTADELLA ⓴ 🏛🏺 C721 FERRERIES ㉑ ㉒ ES MERCADAL

Cala Sta Galdana · Alaior

Cap d' Artrutx

CALES COVES ㉔ 🏛🏺 MAÓ ㉓

Binibeca · Sant Lluís

ra
Cap de Formentor
Port de Pollença
⓭ POLLENÇA 🏛🛉
⓬ SANTUARIO DE LLUC · Alcúdia
lutx
BIA C713 · Sa Pobla
Badia d'Alcúdia
Inca C712 Capdepera · Cala Rajada
37 Sineu Santa Margalida · Artà · Coves d'Artà
Petra C715 Son Servera
Montuïri Manacor
Coves dels Hams · Portocristo
⓯ PUIG DE RANDA ⓳ COVES DEL DRAC
nal C714
Llucmajor ⓲ FELANITX
Campos
❻ C717 Castell de Santueri
APOCORB 'ELL Santanyí · Portopetro
Colònia o · Cala Figuera
Sant Jordi
Cap de ses Salines

⓱ CABRERA

SEE ALSO

• *Where to Stay* pp597–9

• *Where to Eat* pp648–51

KEY

━━ Motorway

── Major road

══ Secondary road

── Scenic route

── Minor railway

△ Summit

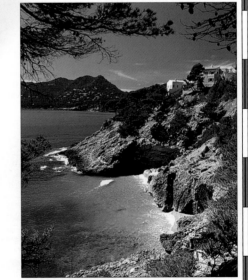

The rocky coast around the Coves d'Artà in Mallorca

Ibiza

This small island, the nearest of the Balearics to the coast of Spain, was unknown and untouched by tourism until the 1960s, when it suddenly appeared in Europe's holiday brochures along with Benidorm and Torremolinos. There is still a curious, indefinable magic about Ibiza (Eivissa) and the island has not entirely lost its character. The countryside, particularly in the north, is a rural patchwork of groves of almonds, olives and figs, and wooded hills. Ibiza town retains the air of a 1950s Spanish provincial borough. At once package-tour paradise, hippie hideout and glamour hot spot, this is one of the Mediterranean's mythical destinations.

An Ibizan shepherdess

The bustling harbour of the resort of Sant Antoni

Sant Antoni ❶

Baleares. 🏠 16,500. 🚌 🛳
ℹ️ Passeig de Ses Fonts, 971 34
33 63. 🎉 Sant Antoni (17 Jan),
Sant Bartolomé (24 Aug).
www.santantoni.net

Ibiza's second town, Sant Antoni was known by the Romans as Portus Magnus because of its large natural harbour. Formerly a tiny fishing village, it has turned into a sprawling and exuberant resort. Although it was once notoriously over-commercialized, the town has recently undergone a dramatic facelift. Nevertheless, the 14th-century parish church of Sant Antoni is practically marooned in a sea of modern high-rise hotels.

To the north of Sant Antoni, on the road to Cala Salada, is the chapel of **Santa Agnès**, an unusual early Christian temple (not to be confused with the village of the same name). When this catacomb-like chapel was discovered, in 1907, it contained Moorish weapons and fragments of pottery.

Sant Josep ❷

Baleares. 🏠 15,000. ℹ️ Carrer
Pedro Escanellas 33-39, 971 34 33
63. 🎉 Sant Josep (19 Mar).

The village of Sant Josep, the administrative centre of southwest Ibiza, lies in the shadow of Ibiza's highest mountain. At 475 m (1,560 ft) Sa Talaiassa offers a panorama of all Ibiza, including the islet of **Es Vedrá**, rising from the sea like a rough-

The salt lakes of Ses Salines, a haven for many bird species

cut pyramid. For the most accessible view of this enormous rock, take the coastal road to the sandy cove of Cala d'Hort where there are a number of good restaurants and a quiet beach.

Environs
Before tourism, salt was Ibiza's main industry, most of it coming from the salt flats at **Ses Salines** in the southeast corner of the island. Mainland Spain is the chief consumer of this salt, but much goes to the Faroe Islands and Scandinavia for salting fish. It is loaded on to ships at Ibiza's southernmost port, La Canal. Ses Salines is also an important refuge for birds, including the flamingo. **Es Cavallet,** 3 km (2 miles) east, is an unspoiled stretch of soft, white sand.

Ibiza ❸

Baleares. 🏠 35,000. ✈️ 🚌 🛳
ℹ️ Calle Antonio Riquer 2, Andenes
del Puerto, 971 30 19 00. 🚌 Mon–
Sat. 🎉 Fiestas Patronales (1–8
Aug), San Juan Bautista (24 Jun).
www.visitbalears.com

The old quarter of Ibiza (Eivissa), known also as Dalt Vila, or upper town, is a miniature citadel guarding the mouth of the almost circular bay. The **Portal de ses Taules,** a magnificent gateway in the north wall of the 16th-century fortifications, carries the finely carved coat of arms of the kingdom of Aragón, to which the Balearic Islands belonged in the Middle Ages (see p227). Inside the walls is the 16th-century **Església de Santo**

Domingo with its three red-tiled domes. The Baroque interior, with its barrel-vaulted ceiling and frescoed walls, has been restored to its former glory. Works of art by Erwin Bechtold, Barry Flanagan and other artists connected with Ibiza are on display in the **Museu d'Art Contemporani**, just inside the Portal de ses Taules. Crowning the whole Dalt Vila is the **cathedral**, a 13th-century Catalan Gothic building with 18th-century additions. The cathedral's Museo de la Sacristia houses assorted works of art.

Under the Carthaginians, the soil of Ibiza was considered holy. The citizens of Carthage deemed it an honour to be buried in the **Necròpolis Púnica de Puig des Molins**, thought to contain over 4,000 graves. The museum is currently closed for restoration.

The crossroads village of **Jesús**, 3 km (2 miles) north, is

A backstreet in the Sa Penya district of Ibiza town

well worth a visit for its pretty 16th-century church. Originally built as part of a Franciscan monastery, it has a 16th-century altarpiece by Rodrigo de Osona the Younger.

🏛 Museu d'Art Contemporani
Ronda Narcís Puget Viñas. **Tel** 971 302 723. ⬜ daily. ⬤ public hols. 📷 ♿

⋔ Necropolis de Puig d'es Molins
Via Romana 31. **Tel** 971 30 16 71. ⬜ Tue–Sun. ⬤ public hols.

A view across the port towards Ibiza's upper town

Els Amunts ❹

Baleares. 🚌 Sant Miquel. ℹ Santa Eulària d'es Riu, 971 33 07 28.

Els amunts is the local name for the uplands of northern Ibiza, which stretch from Sant Antoni on the west coast to Sant Vicenç in the northeast. Though hardly a mountain range – Es Fornás is the highest point, at a mere 450 m

(1,480 ft) – the area's inaccessibility has kept it unspoiled. There are few special sights here, apart from the landscape: pine-clad hills sheltering fertile valleys whose rich red soil is planted with olive, almond and fig trees, and the occasional vineyard. Tourist enclaves are also scarce – except for a handful of small resorts, such as Port de Sant Miquel, Portinatx and Sant Vicenç. Inland, villages like Sant Joan and Santa Agnès offer an insight into Ibiza's quiet, rural past.

The architectural highpoints of northern Ibiza are several beautiful white churches, like the one in **Sant Miquel** which, on Thursdays in summer, is host to a display of Ibizan folk dancing. Outside Sant Llorenç is the tranquil, fortified hamlet of **Balàfia**, with flat-roofed houses, tiny whitewashed alleys, and a watchtower that was used as a fortress during raids by the Turks.

IBIZA'S HOTTEST SPOTS

Ibiza's reputation for extraordinary summer nightlife is largely justified. The main action takes place in two areas: the Calle de la Virgen in the old harbour district, with its bars, fashion boutiques and restaurants; and the mega-discos out of town – Privilege, Pachá, Amnesia and Es Paradis. When the last of these is closing, at about 7am, the wildest club of them all, Space, is only just opening its doors. Ibiza has long been a magnet for the rich and famous. Celebrities seem to have become more elusive of late, but a few well-known faces can often be glimpsed dining in the restaurant Las Dos Lunas, and taking the rays the next day on the beach at Ses Salines.

Nightclubbers enjoying a bubble bath at Amnesia

One of the many beautiful beaches along the unspoiled shores of the island of Formentera

Santa Eulària **5**

Baleares. 🚶 24,000. 🚗 🚢 🛈
Carrer Mariano Riquer Wallis 4, 971
33 07 28. 🚢 Wed & Sat. 🎭 Fiesta
(12 Feb), Es Cana (15 Aug).

Despite catering for tourism, the town of Santa Eulària d'es Riu (Santa Eulalia del Río), situated on the island's only river, has managed to hold on to its character far more than many other Spanish resorts.

The 16th-century church, with its pretty covered courtyard, and the surrounding old town, were built on the top of a little hill, the **Puig de Missa**, because this site was more easily defended in times of war than the shore below.

Ajdacent to the church is the **Museu Etnològic**, a folk museum, which is housed in an ancient but tastefully adapted Ibizan farmhouse. Included in the exhibits (labelled in Catalan only) are traditional costumes,

The domed roof of Santa Eulària's 16th-century church

farming implements, toys and an olive press. A collection of old photographs reveals the irreversible changes Ibiza has suffered over the last 50 years.

🏛 **Museu Etnològic**
Can Ros, Puig de Missa. **Tel** 971 33 28
45. ⭕ Tue–Sat. 🎟 📷 (by appt).

Formentera **6**

Baleares. 🚶 7,000. 🚢 from Ibiza. 🛈
Calle Calpe, La Savina, 971 32 20 57.
🚢 Sun. 🎭 Fiesta Sant Jaume (25 Jul).

An hour's boat ride from Ibiza harbour will bring you to this largely unspoiled island where the waters are blue and the way of life slow.

From the small port of La Savina, where the boat docks, there are buses to other parts of the island, or you can hire a car, moped or bicycle from one of the shops nearby. **Sant Francesc Xavier**, Formentera's tiny capital, is situated 3 km (2 miles) from La Savina. Most of the island's amenities are in this town, plus a pretty 18th-century church in the main square, and a folk museum.

From Sant Francesc, a bumpy minor road leads for 9 km (6 miles) southwards, ending at Cap de Barbaria, the site of an 18th-century defensive tower and a lighthouse. Formentera is entirely flat, apart from the small plateau of **La Mola**, which takes up the whole eastern end of the island. From the fishing port of Es Caló the road winds up-

wards past the Restaurante Es Mirador, with its panoramic view of western Formentera, to the village of Nostra Senyora del Pilar de la Mola on top of the plateau. About 3 km (2 miles) to the east is a lighthouse, Far de la Mola, sited on the highest point of the island. Nearby stands a monument to Jules Verne (1828–1905), who used Formentera for the setting of one of his novels, *Hector Servadac*.

Although there are many purple road signs indicating places of cultural interest on Formentera, most lead only to disappointment. But one sight well worth seeking out is the megalithic sepulchre of **Ca Na Costa** (2000 BC) near Sant Francesc, the only one of its kind in the Balearics. This monument, a circle of upright stone slabs, pre-dates the Carthaginians *(see pp49–50)*.

However, the island's great strength is not its history and culture, but its landscape, which has a spare and delicate beauty and some of the Mediterranean's last unspoiled shorelines. More than 60% of the island's landscape is protected by law. The finest beaches are, arguably, Migjorn and Cala Sahona, both southwest of Sant Francesc.

Illetes and Llevant are two beautiful beaches on either side of a long sandy spit in the far north of the island. To the north, between Formentera and Ibiza, is the island of **Espalmador**, with its natural springs, beaches and lighthouse.

The Flavours of the Balearics

This quartet of beautiful islands, strategically positioned on ancient trading routes, has been fought over for thousands of years. Each occupying force – Arabs, Catalans, French and British among them – has left its mark and the local cuisine reflects this. Mediterranean seafood, particularly spectacular lobster and crayfish, remains the most prominent local ingredient, but the islands are also known for their delicious pastries and desserts, like the feather-light *ensaimada* from Mallorca and the typical Ibizan *flaó*. Cured meats *(embutits)* and traditionally made cheeses are also local specialities.

Locally grown oranges

Seafood from the Mediterranean in a Mallorcan fish market

MALLORCA AND MENORCA

Seafood predominates in the Balearic islands. Menorca is renowned for *caldereta de langosta* (spiny lobster stew), once a simple fishermen's dish but now an expensive delicacy. The classic Mallorcan dish is *pa amb oli*, a slice of toasted country bread rubbed with garlic and drizzled with local olive oil. Menorca's creamy garlic sauce *all i oli* is a delicious accompaniment to meat and seafood dishes, and the island also produces fine cheese, *formatge de Maó*.

IBIZA AND FORMENTERA

Seafood also reigns supreme on Ibiza and its quieter little sister, Formentera, especially in *calders* (stews) such as *borrida de rajada* (skate with potatoes, eggs and pastis), and *guisat de peix*. Pork is the staple meat. For a picnic, try *cocarrois*, pastries filled with meat, fish or vegetables and *formatjades*, soft-cheese-filled pastries flavoured with cinnamon. Delicious local desserts include *gató* (almond cake served with ice-cream) and Ibizan *flaó*, made with creamy cheese and eggs, and flavoured with mint.

Cuscussó Menorquin (bread pudding)
Ensaimadas
Flaó Ibicenco
Galletas de Alaior (aniseed biscuits
Formatjades
El Gató (almond tart)

Appetizing selection of delicious Balearic pastries

REGIONAL DISHES AND SPECIALITIES

All i oli

Fish and shellfish (particularly the revered local lobster) are omnipresent in the Balearics, particularly along the coast. Try them simply grilled to fully appreciate their freshness (many seaside restaurants have their own fishing boats), but you'll also find wonderful, slow-cooked stews which are bursting with flavour. The rugged inland regions provide mountain lamb and kid, along with pork, which is also used to make *embutits* including spicy Mallorcan *sobrassada* which is delicious with *pa amb oli*. The tourist industry hasn't killed off the long-standing farming tradition on the Balearics, which produce plentiful fruit and vegetables. Mallorca makes its own robust wines, particularly around the village of Binissalem, while Menorca, thanks to the long British occupation of the island, makes its own piquant gin.

Tumbet de peix *A fish pie, made with layers of firm white fish, peppers, aubergine (eggplant) and sliced boiled egg.*

Mallorca

Mallorca is often likened to a continent rather than simply an island. Its varied nature never fails to astonish, whether you are looking for landscape, culture or just entertainment. No other European island has a wider range of scenery, from the fertile plains of central Mallorca to the almost alpine peaks of the Tramuntana. The island's mild climate and lovely beaches have made it one of Spain's foremost package tour destinations but there is a wealth of culture, too, evident in sights like Palma Cathedral (*see pp520–1*). Mallorca's appeal lies also in its charm as a living, working island: the cereal and fruit crops of the central plains, and the vineyards around Binissalem are vital to the island's economy.

Terraced orange grove in the Sierra Tramuntana

Andratx **7**

Baleares. 🏠 9,000. 🚍 🔁 ℹ️
Avinguda de Curia 1, 971 75 20 51.
🕒 *Wed.* 🎉 *San Pedro (29 Jun).*
www balearweb.com

This small town lies amid a valley of almond groves in the shadow of Puig de Galatzó, which rises to 1,026 m (3,366 ft). With its ochre and white shuttered houses and the old watchtowers perched high on a hill above the town, Andratx is a very pretty place.

The road southwest leads down to **Port d'Andratx** 5 km (3 miles) away. Here, in an almost totally enclosed bay, expensive yachts are moored in rows along the harbour and luxury holiday homes pepper the surrounding hillsides. In the past, Port d'Andratx's main role was as the fishing port and harbour for Andratx, but since the early 1960s it has gradually been transformed into an exclusive holiday resort for the rich and famous. When visiting Port d'Andratx, it is a good

idea to leave all thoughts of the real Mallorca behind and simply enjoy it for what it is – a chic and affluent resort.

La Granja **8**

Carretera de Esporlas-Bañabufar.
Tel 971 61 00 32. 🚍 ⭕ *daily.* 🎟
🔁 **www**.lagranja.net

La Granja is a private estate, or *possessió*, near the little country town of Esporles. Formerly a Cistercian convent, it is now the property of the Seguí family, who have opened their largely unspoiled 18th-century house to the public as a kind of living museum. Peacocks roam the gardens, salt cod and hams hang in the kitchen, *The Marriage of Figaro* plays in the ballroom, and the slight air of chaos just adds to the charm of the place.

Bust of Frédéric Chopin at Valldemossa

Valldemossa **9**

Baleares. 🏠 1,800. 🚍 🔁 ℹ️ *Avenida Palma 7, 971 61 20 19.* 🕒 *Sun.*
🎉 *Santa Catalina Thomás (28 Jul), San Bartolomé (24 Aug).*
www.valldemossa.com

This pleasant mountain town will forever be linked with the name of George Sand, the French novelist who stayed here during the winter of 1838–9 and later wrote unflatteringly of the island in *Un Hiver à Majorque*. Dearer to Mallorcans is the Polish composer Frédéric Chopin (1810–49) who stayed with Sand at the **Real Cartuja de Jesús de Nazaret**. "Chopin's cell", off the monastery's main courtyard, is where a few of his works were written, and still houses the piano on which he composed.

Nearby is a 17th-century pharmacy displaying outlandish medicinal preparations such as "powdered nails of the beast". In the cloisters is an art museum with works by Tàpies, Miró and the Mallorcan artist Juli Ramis (1909–90), and a series of Picasso illustrations, *The Burial of the Count of Orgaz*, inspired by the El Greco painting of the same name (*see p32*).

🔒 **Real Cartuja de Jesús de Nazaret**
Plaça de la Cartuja de Valldemossa.
Tel 971 61 21 06. ⭕ *daily.* 🎟 🔁

A view across the harbour of Port d'Andratx

Alfàbia ⑩

Carretera de Sóller km 17. **Tel** 971
61 31 23. 🚌 tour bus from Palma.
⬤ Sat pm & Sun. 🈺

Very few possessións in
Mallorca are open to the
public, which makes Alfàbia
worth visiting. The house and
garden are an excellent example of a typical Mallorcan
aristocratic estate and exude a
Moorish atmosphere. Very little
remains of the original 14th-
century architecture, so it is
well worth looking out for the
Mudéjar inscription on the ceiling of the entrance hall and the
Hispano-Arabic fountains and
pergola. The garden is a sumptuous 19th-century creation,
making imaginative use of
shade and the play of water.

Sóller ⑪

Baleares. 🏘 11,500. 🚉 🚌 ℹ
Plaza España, 971 63 02 00. 🚪 Sat.
🎉 Sofia (2nd Sun of May), Sa Fira &
Es Firó (11 May). **www**.a-soller.es

Soller is a little town grown
fat on the produce of its olive
groves and orchards, which
climb up the slopes of the
Sierra Tramuntana. In the
19th century Sóller traded its
oranges and wine for French
goods, and the town retains a
faintly Gallic, bourgeois feel.
  One of Sóller's best-known
features is its delightfully old-
fashioned narrow-gauge railway, complete with quaint
wooden carriages. The town,
whose station is in the Plaça
d'Espanya, lies on a scenic
route between Palma and the
fishing village of Port de Sóller
5 km (3 miles) to the west.

Environs
From Sóller a road winds southwards along the spectacular
west coast to **Deià** (Deyá). This
village was once the home of
Robert Graves (1895–1985), the
English poet and novelist,
who came to live here in 1929.
His simple tombstone can be
seen in the small cemetery.
The **Museu Arqueològic**, curat-
ed by the archaeologist William
Waldren, offers a glimpse into
prehistoric Mallorca. Outside
the village is **Son Marroig**, the

Houses and trees crowded together on the hillside of Deià

estate of Austrian Archduke
Ludwig Salvator (1847–1915),
who documented the Balearics
in a series of books included in
a display of his possessions.

🏛 **Museu Arqueològic**
Calle Teix 4, Es Clot Deià. **Tel** 971
63 90 01. ⬤ Fri–Sun. 🈺

**Statue of La Moreneta at the
Santuario de Lluc**

Santuario de Lluc ⑫

Lluc. 🚌 from Palma. **Tel** 971 87 15
25. ⬤ daily. 🈺 museum only.
www.lluc.net

High in the mountains of the
Sierra Tramuntana, in the
remote village of Lluc, is an
institution regarded by many
as the spiritual heart of
Mallorca. The Santuario de
Lluc was built mainly in the
17th and 18th centuries on the
site of an ancient shrine. The
monastery's Baroque church,

with its imposing façade,
contains the stone image of
La Moreneta, the Black Virgin
of Lluc, supposedly found by
a young shepherd boy on a
nearby hilltop in the 13th
century. The altar and sanctuary of one chapel are by
Catalan architect and designer
Antoni Gaudí (see pp140–1).
Along the Camí dels Misteris,
the paved walkway up to this
hilltop, there are some bronze
bas-reliefs by Pere Llimona.
Just off the main Plaça dels
Pelegrins are a café and bar, a
pharmacy and a shop. The
museum, situated on the first
floor, includes Mallorcan paintings and medieval manuscripts.
The monastery incorporates a
guest house (see p598).
  From Lluc, 13 km (8 miles)
of tortuous road winds through
the hills and descends towards
the coast, ending at the beautiful rocky bay of **Sa Calobra.**
From here, it is just 5 minutes'
walk up the coast to the deep
gorge of the Torrent de Pareis.

**Sheer cliff face rising out of the
sea at Sa Calobra**

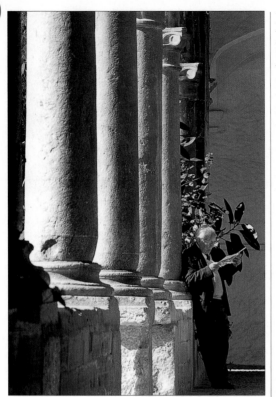
The cloisters of the Convent de Santo Domingo in Pollença

Pollença ⑬

Baleares. 👥 15,000. 🚍 ℹ️ Calle Guillem Cife de Colonya, 971 53 50 77. 🛍️ Sun. 🎉 Sant Antoni (17 Jan), Patron Saint (2 Aug).
www.ajpollenca.net

Although Pollença has become one of Mallorca's most popular tourist spots, it still appears unspoiled. The town, with its ochre-coloured stone houses and winding lanes, is picturesquely sited on the edge of fertile farmland. The Plaça Major, with its bars frequented mainly by locals, has an old-world atmosphere.

Pollença has fine churches, including the 18th-century **Parròquia de Nostra Senyora dels Angels** and the Convent de Santo Domingo, containing the **Museu Municipal,** with its displays of archaeology and art. It also holds Pollença's Classical Music Festival in July and August. A chapel on the hilltop, **El**

Calvari, is reached either by road or a long climb of 365 steps. On the altar there is a Gothic Christ, carved in wood.

Environs
Alcúdia, 10 km (6 miles) to the east, is surrounded by 14th-century walls with two huge gateways. Near the town centre is the **Museu Monografico de Pollentia**, exhibiting statues, jewellery and other remains found in the Roman settlement of Pollentia, 2km (1 mile) south of Alcúdia.

🏛 **Museu Municipal**
Calle Guillem Cife de Colonya 33.
Tel 971 53 11 66. ☐ Mon–Sat. 🎫

🏛 **Museu Monografico de Pollentia**
Calle San Jaume 30, Alcúdia.
Tel 971 54 70 04. ☐ Tue–Sun. 🎫

Palma de Mallorca ⑭

See pp518–21.

Puig de Randa ⑮

8 km (5 miles) northeast of Llucmajor. 🚍 to Llucmajor, then taxi. ℹ️ El Arenal, 971 44 04 14.

In the middle of a fertile plain called the *pla* rises a mini-mountain 543 m (1,780 ft) high, the Puig de Randa. It is said that Mallorca's greatest son, the 14th-century theologian and mystic Ramon Llull, came to a hermitage on this mountain to meditate and write his religious treatise, *Ars Magna*. On the way up Puig de Randa there are two small monasteries, the 14th-century Santuari de Sant Honorat and the Santuari de Nostra Senyora de Gràcia. The latter, built on a ledge under an overhanging cliff, contains a 13th-century chapel with fine Valencian tiles inside, and offers an open view of the *pla*.

On the mountain top is the **Santuari de Cura**, built to commemorate Llull's time on the *puig*, and largely devoted to the study of his work. Its central courtyard is built in the typical beige stone of Mallorca. A small museum, housed in a 16th-century former school off the courtyard, contains some of Llull's manuscripts.

The philosopher Ramon Llull

Capocorb Vell ⑯

14 km (9 miles) south of Llucmajor. **Tel** 971 18 01 55. 🚍 El Arenal. ☐ Fri–Wed. 🎫 **www**.mytoragus.com

Mallorca is not as rich in megalithic remains as Menorca, but this *talaiotic* village *(see p527)* in the stony flatlands of the southern coast is worth seeing – particularly on a quiet day when you can wander among the stones in peace. The settlement, which dates back to around 1000 BC, originally consisted of five *talaiots* (stone tower-like structures with timbered roofs) and 28 smaller dwellings. Little is known about its inhabitants and the uses for some of the rooms inside the buildings, such as the tiny underground gallery. Too small for living in, this room may have been used to perform magic rituals.

Part of the charm of this place lies in its surroundings among fields of fruit trees and dry stone walls, a setting that somehow complements the ruins. Apart from a snack bar nearby, the site remains mercifully undeveloped.

One of the *talaiots* of Capocorb Vell

Cabrera ⑰

Baleares. 🚢 from Colònia Sant Jordi. 🏠 Carrer Doctor Barraquer 5, Colònia Sant Jordi, 971 64 90 34.

From the beaches of Es Trenc and Sa Ràpita, on the south coast of Mallorca, Cabrera looms on the horizon. The largest island in an archipelago of the same name, it lies 18 km (11 miles) from the most southerly point of Mallorca. Cabrera is home to several rare plants, reptiles and seabirds, such as Eleonora's falcon. The waters are important for marine life. All this has resulted in it being declared a national park *(see pp30–1)*. For centuries Cabrera was used as a military base and it has a small population. On it stands a 14th-century castle.

A street in Felanitx

Felanitx ⑱

Baleares. 🚶 16,000. 🚌 🏠 Avenida Cala Marsas 15, 971 82 60 84. 🏠 Sun. 🎉 Sant Joan Pelós (24 Jun).

This bustling agricultural town is the birthplace of Renaissance architect Guillem Sagrera (1380–1456) and the 20th-century painter Miquel Barceló. Felanitx is visited mainly for three reasons: the imposing façade of the 13th-century church, the **Esglesia de Sant Miquel**; its *sobrassada de porc negre* (a spiced raw sausage made from the meat of the local black pig) and its lively religious fiestas including Sant Joan Pelós *(see p523)*.

About 5 km (3 miles) southeast is the **Castell de Santueri**, founded by the Moors but rebuilt in the 14th century by the kings of Aragón, who ruled Mallorca. Though a ruin, it is worth the detour for the views to the east and south from its vantage point, 400 m (1,300 ft) above the plain.

Coves del Drac ⑲

1 km (1 mile) south of Porto Cristo. 🚌 from Porto Cristo. **Tel** 971 82 07 53. 🕐 daily. 🌑 1 Jan, 25 Dec. 🎫

Mallorca has innumerable caves, ranging from mere holes in the ground to cathedral-like halls. The four vast chambers of the **Coves del Drac** are reached by a steep flight of steps, at the bottom of which is the beautifully lit cave known as "Diana's Bath". Another chamber holds the large underground lake, Martel, which is 29 m (95 ft) below ground level and is 177 m (580 ft) long. Music fills the air of the cave, played from boats plying the lake. Equally dramatic are the two remaining caves, charmingly named "The Theatre of the Fairies" and "The Enchanted City".

Environs

The **Coves dels Hams** is so called because some of its stalactites are shaped like hooks – *hams* in Mallorcan. The caves are 500 m (1,640 ft) long and contain the "Sea of Venice", an underground lake on which musicians sail in a small boat.

The entrance to the **Coves d'Artá**, near Capdepera, is 40 m (130 ft) above sea level and affords a wonderful view. The caves' main attraction is a stalagmite 22 m (72 ft) high.

🕳 **Coves dels Hams**
11 km (7 miles) from Manacor towards Porto Cristo. **Tel** 971 82 09 88. 🕐 daily. 🌑 1 Jan, 25 Dec. 🎫

🕳 **Coves d'Artá**
Carretera Canyamel. **Tel** 971 84 12 93. 🕐 daily. 🌑 1 Jan, 25 Dec. 🎫

The dramatically lit stalactites of the Coves d'Artá

Street-by-Street: Palma ⑭

On an island whose name has become synonymous with mass tourism, Palma surprises by its cultural richness. Under the Moors it was already a prosperous town of fountains and cool courtyards. After he had conquered it in 1229, Jaime I wrote, "It seemed to me the most beautiful city we had ever seen". Signs of Palma's past wealth are still evident in the sumptuous churches,

Forn des Teatre pastry shop

grand public buildings and fine private mansions that crowd the old town. The hub of the city is the old-fashioned Passeig des Born, whose cafés invite you to try one of Mallorca's specialities, the ensaimada, a spiral of pastry dusted with icing sugar.

The Forn des Teatre is an old pastry shop noted for its *ensaimadas* and *gató* (almond cake).

The Fundació la Caixa, once the Gran Hotel, is now a cultural centre.

Palau Reial de l'Almudaina
This palace belongs to the Spanish royal family and houses a museum, whose highlights include the chapel of Santa Ana, with its Romanesque portal, and the Gothic tinell or salon.

STAR SIGHTS

★ Cathedral

★ Basílica de Sant Francesc

La Llotja is a beautiful 15th-century exchange with tall windows and delicate tracery.

To Castell de Bellver and Fundació Pilar i Joan Miró

★ Cathedral
Built of golden limestone quarried from Santanyi, Palma's huge Gothic cathedral stands in a dramatic location near the waterfront.

Parc de la Mar

KEY

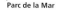 Suggested route

To Plaça Espanya,
bus and train stations

Plaça del Marqués
de Palmer

0 metres   100

0 yards   100

A view along the circular walls of
the Castell de Bellver

★ **Basílica de Sant
Francesc**
*The church and
cloister of St Francis are
in a refined Gothic style
with a Baroque altarpiece
and rose window.*

The **Museu
Diocesà**,
housed in the
Bishop's Palace,
has a collection of
religious treasures.

Museu de Mallorca
*The museum has displays on
local history, art and
architecture, including this
statue of an ancient warrior.*

Banys Àrabs
*The 10th-century baths,
with their well-preserved
arches, are a remnant of
the Balearic Islands'
Moorish culture.*

♣ **Castell de Bellver**
West side of Palma Bay. **Tel** 971 73
06 57. Mon–Sat.
About 5 km (3 miles) from
the city centre, standing 113 m
(370 ft) above sea level, is
Palma's Gothic castle. It was
commissioned by Jaime II
during the short-lived Kingdom of Mallorca (1276–1349)
as a summer residence, but
soon after became a prison,
and remained as such until
1915. The castle, situated on
a wooded hill overlooking
the bay of Palma, is of an
unusual circular design.
   Three of its towers are set
into the main castle wall; the
other is set apart from it, but
linked by a high walkway.
From some angles the castle
looks more decorative than
defensive: witness the cloister
of delicate arches that rings
the central courtyard.

🏛 **Fundació Pilar
i Joan Miró**
Carrer Joan de Saridakis 29. **Tel** 971
70 14 20. Tue–Sun.
When Joan Miró died in 1983,
his wife took on the task of
converting his former studio
and gardens into an art centre.
The building – christened
"the Alabaster Fortress" by
the Spanish press – is a
stunning example of modern
architecture designed by
Navarrese architect Rafael
Moneo. It incorporates Miró's
original studio (complete with
unfinished paintings), a
permanent collection of the
painter's work, a shop, a
library and an auditorium.

Palma Cathedral

According to legend, when Jaime I of Aragón was caught in a storm on his way to conquer Mallorca in 1229, he vowed that if God led him to safety he would build a great church in his honour. In the following years the old mosque of Medina Mayurqa was torn down and architect Guillem Sagrera (1380–1456) drew up plans for a new cathedral. The last stone was added in 1587, and in subsequent years the cathedral has been rebuilt, notably early last century when parts of the interior were remodelled by Antoni Gaudí *(see pp140–1)*. Today Palma Cathedral, or Sa Seu, as Mallorcans call it, is one of the most breathtaking buildings in Spain, combining vast scale with typically Gothic elegance *(see p24)*.

Bell Tower
This robust tower was built in 1389 and houses nine bells, the largest of which is known as N'Eloi, mean-ing "praise".

Palma Cathedral
One of the best-sited cathedrals anywhere, it is spectacularly poised high on the sea wall, above what was once Palma's harbour.

STAR FEATURES

★ Great Rose Window

★ Baldachino

Cathedral Museum
One of the highlights of the beautifully displayed collection in the Old Chapterhouse is a 15th-century reliquary of the True Cross which is encrusted with jewels and precious metals.

19th-century tower

Entrance to cathedral museum

Portal Major

Flying buttresses

★ Great Rose Window
The largest of seven rose windows looks down from above the High Altar like a gigantic eye. Built in 1370 with stained glass added in the 16th century, the window has a diameter of over 11 m (36 ft).

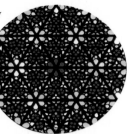

VISITORS' CHECKLIST

Plaça Almonia. **Tel** 971 72 31 30.
◯ Apr–Oct: 10am–6pm Mon–Fri; Nov–Mar: 10am–3pm Mon–Fri, (10am–2pm Sat all year).
public hols. ✦ 9am, 7pm Mon–Sat, 9am, 10:30am, noon, 1pm, 7pm Sun. ♿

The Great Organ was built with a Neo-Gothic case in 1795, and restored in 1993 by Gabriel Blancafort.

Capella de la Trinitat
This tiny chapel was built in 1329 as the mausoleum of Jaime II and III of Aragón. It contains their alabaster tombs.

The Capella Reial, or Royal Chapel, was redesigned by Antoni Gaudí between 1904 and 1914.

Bishop's Throne
Built in 1269 and made of Carrara marble, the chair is embedded in a Gothic vaulted niche.

Choir stalls

Portal del Mirador

Nave
The magnificent ceiling, 44 m (144 ft) high, is held up by 14 slender pillars. At over 19 m (62 ft) wide, it is one of the broadest naves in the world.

★ Baldachino
Gaudí's bizarre wrought-iron canopy above the altar incorporates lamps, tapestries and a multicoloured crucifix.

Menorca

Menorca is the Balearic island furthest from the mainland and it is set apart from the rest of the country in many other ways. The coastline of Menorca is, arguably, more unspoiled than in any other part of Spain. Its countryside remains largely green and pleasant with cows roaming the meadows. The old towns of Maó – the island's capital – and Ciutadella are filled with noble, historic buildings and beautiful squares. Menorca also has abundant reminders of its more distant history: the island boasts a spectacular hoard of Bronze Age stone structures, which provide an invaluable insight into its prehistoric past. The Menorcans are often more inclined to drink the locally brewed gin *(ginebra)* than the wine which is favoured elsewhere in Spain.

Fishermen mending their nets in Ciutadella's harbour

The peaceful seafront of Ciutadella at twilight

Ciutadella **⑳**

Baleares. 🏔 *24,000.* 🚍 🚢 🛈 *Plaça de la Catedral 5, 971 38 26 93.* 🚌 *Fri & Sat.* 🎏 *Sant Joan (23–24 Jun).* **www**.ciutadella.org

The key date in the history of Ciutadella is 1558. In that year the Turks, under Barbarossa, entered and decimated the city, consigning 3,495 of its citizens to the slave markets of Constantinople. Of Ciutadella's main public buildings, only the fine Catalan Gothic **Església Catedral de Menorca** managed to survive this fearsome onslaught in more or less its original condition, only later to be stripped of all its paintings, ornaments and other treasures by Republican extremists during the Civil War.

The nearby **Plaça d'es Born** was built as a parade ground for Moorish troops and from 1558 was gradually rebuilt in

Renaissance style. Today it is one of Spain's most impressive squares, containing pleasant cafés and bordered by shady palm trees. At the centre of the Plaça d'es Born is an obelisk which commemorates the "Any de sa Desgràcia" (Year

The historic Plaça d'es Born in the centre of Ciutadella

of Misfortune), when the Turks invaded the city. Around the square are the Gothic-style **town hall** *(ajuntament)*, the late 19th-century **Teatre Municipal d'es Born**, and a series of aristocratic mansions with Italianesque façades, the grandest of which is the early 19th-century **Palau de Torre-Saura.** From the northern end of the square there is a fine view over the small harbour.

If you walk up the Carrer Major d'es Born past the cathedral, you come to **Ses Voltes**, an alley lined on both sides by whitewashed arches. Turn right along the Carrer des Seminari for the Baroque **Església dels Socors** and the **Museu Diocesà** with its displays of ecclesiastical paraphernalia. In the narrow streets of the old town there are many impressive palaces, but only the early 19th-century **Palau Salort**, on the Carrer Major d'es Born, is open to the public. The Art Nouveau **market** (1895), its ironwork painted in smart municipal dark green, stands nearby.

The peace of Ciutadella is disturbed every June by the Festa de Sant Joan, a spectacular ritual of horsemanship. During the festival the local gin *(ginebra)* is drunk copiously and the city grinds to a halt.

🏛 **Museu Diocesiano**
Seminari 5. **Tel** 971 48 12 97.
⭘ *Tue–Sat.* 🈂 ♿ 🈂 *(by appt).*
🏛 **Palau Salort**
Carrer Major d'es Born 9. **Tel** 971 38 00 56. ⭘ *May–Oct: 10am–2pm Mon–Sat.* 🈂

Ferreries ㉑

Baleares. 👥 *4,000.* 🚌 ℹ️ *Carrer Sant Bartomeu 55, 971 37 30 03.* 🚉 *Tue, Fri, Sat.* 🎉 *Sant Bartomeu (23–5 Aug).*

Ferreries lies in between Mercadal and Ciutadella and sprang up when a road was built to connect the two towns. Today Ferreries is an attractive village of white houses, built against the slope of a hill. The simple church, Sant Bartomeu, dates from 1770.

The bay of **Santa Galdana**, 10 km (6 miles) to the south, is even prettier. You can take a pleasant walk from the beach inland through the fertile riverbed of Barranc d'Algendar.

Courtyard in the Santuari del Toro

Es Mercadal ㉒

Baleares. 👥 *4,000.* 🚌 ℹ️ *Carrer Major 16, 971 37 50 02.* 🚉 *Sun.* 🎉 *Sant Martí (third Sun of Jul).*

Es Mercadal is a small country town – one of the three, with Alaior and Ferreries, that are strung out along the main road from Maó to Ciutadella.

The town is unremarkable in itself, but within reach of it are three places of interest. **El Toro**, 3 km (2 miles) to the east, is Menorca's highest mountain, at 350 m (1,150 ft). It is also the spiritual heart of the island and at its summit is the Santuari del Toro, built in 1670, which is run by nuns.

About 10 km (6 miles) north of Es Mercadal, the fishing village of **Fornells** transforms itself every summer into an outpost of St Tropez. In the harbour, smart yachts jostle with fishing boats, and the local jet-set crowd into the Bar Palma. Fornells' main culinary speciality is the *caldereta de llagosta* (lobster casserole), but the quality varies and prices can be high.

The road-cum-dirt track to the **Cap de Cavalleria**, 13 km (8 miles) north of Es Mercadal, passes through one of the Balearics' finest landscapes. Cavalleria is a rocky promontory, whipped by the tramontana wind from the north. It juts out into a choppy sea which, in winter, looks more like the North Atlantic than the Mediterranean. At the western edge of the peninsula are the remains of Sanisera, a Phoenician village mentioned by Pliny in the 1st century AD. The road leads to a headland, with a lighthouse and cliffs 90 m (295 ft) high, where peregrine falcons, sea eagles and kites ride the wind.

Further west along the coast is a string of fine, unspoiled beaches, though with difficult access: Cala Pregonda, Cala del Pilar and La Vall d'Algaiarens are three of the most beautiful.

Horse rearing in the fiesta of Sant Lluís

THE BALEARIC ISLANDS' FIESTAS

Sant Antoni Abat *(16– 17 Jan)*, Mallorca. This fiesta is celebrated with parades and the blessing of animals all over Mallorca and in Sant Antoni in Ibiza.

Sant Joan *(24 Jun)*, Ciutadella (Menorca). The horse plays a major part in Menorca's festivals. In the streets and squares of Ciutadella on 24 June, the Day of St John the Baptist, elegantly dressed riders put their horses through ritualized medieval manoeuvres. The fiesta reaches a climax when the horses rear up on their hind legs and the jubilant crowds swarm around them trying to hold them up with their hands. Similarly, the annual fiesta in Sant Lluís, which takes place at the end of August, sees many of the locals taking to the streets on horseback.

Sant Joan Pelós *(24 Jun)*, Felanitx (Mallorca). As part of this fiesta, a man is dressed in sheepskins to represent John the Baptist.

Romeria de Sant Marçal *(30 Jun)*, Sa Cabeneta (Mallorca). A feature of this fiesta is a market selling *siurells*, primitive Mallorcan whistles.

Our Lady of the Sea *(16 Jul)*, Formentera. The island's main fiesta honours the Virgen del Carmen, patroness of fishermen, with a flotilla of fishing boats.

A quiet stretch of beach at Santa Galdana

The steep hillside of Maó running up from the harbour

Maó ㉓

Baleares. 🏠 24,000. ✈ 🚌 🛥 ℹ
Sa Rovellada de Dalt 24, 971 36 37 90.
🛒 Tue, Sat. 🎉 Fiestas de Gracia (7–8
Sep), Fiesta de Sant Antoni (17 Jan).

The quietly elegant town of
Maó has lent its Spanish
name, Mahón, to mayonnaise
(see p513). It was occupied
by the British three times during the 18th century. The legacy of past colonial rule can be
seen in sober Georgian town
houses, with their dark green
shutters and sash windows.

Maó's harbour is one of the
finest in the Mediterranean.
Taking the street leading from
the port to the upper town,
the S-shaped Costa de Ses
Voltes, you come to the 18th-
century **Església del Carme**, a
former Carmelite church
whose cool white cloister now
houses an attractive fruit and
vegetable market. Behind the
market is Maó's only museum,
the **Col·lecció Hernández**

Sanzy Hernández Mora,
which houses Menorcan art
and antiques. The nearby Plaça
Constitució is overlooked by
the church of Santa Maria,
which has a huge organ.
Next door is the **town hall**
(ajuntament) with its Neo-
Classical façade, into which is
mounted the famous clock
donated by Sir Richard Kane
(1660–1736), the first British
governor of Menorca.

Located at the end of the
Carrer Isabel II is the **Església
de Sant Francesc**, with an
intriguing Romanesque doorway and Baroque façade. The
church houses the newly
refurbished Museu de
Menorca. Two minutes' walk
south of here will take you to
Maó's main square, the Plaça
de S'Esplanada, behind which
is the **Ateneu Cientific Lliterat
Artistic**, a centre of Menorca-
related culture and learning.
Inside are collections of local
ceramics and maps, and a
library. It is advisable to

obtain permission before
looking around. On the north
side of the harbour is a mansion known as **Sant Antoni** or
the Golden Farm. As Maó's
finest example of Palladian
architecture, it has an arched
façade, painted plum red, with
white arches, in the traditional
Menorcan style. The British
admiral, Nelson, is thought to
have stayed here. The house
has a collection of Nelson
memorabilia and a fine library
but is closed to the public.

🏛 **Col·lecció Hernández
Sanzy Hernández Mora**
Claustre del Carme 5. **Tel** 971 35
05 97. ⬜ 10am–3pm Mon–Sat.

🏛 **Ateneu Científic Literari i
Artistic**
C/ Rovellada de Dalt 25. **Tel** 971 36
05 53. ⬛ Sun, public hols.

Cales Coves ㉔

Baleares. 🚌 Sant Climent, then
25 mins walk. **Tel** Maó, 971 36 37 90.

On either side of a pretty
bay can be found Cales Coves
– the site of Neolithic
dwellings of up to 9 m (30 ft)
in length, hollowed out of the
rock face. The caves, thought
to have been inhabited since
prehistoric times, are today
occupied by a community of
people seeking an alternative
lifestyle. Some of the caves
have front doors, chimneys
and even butane cookers.

About 8 km (5 miles) west,
along the coast, lies Binibeca,
a tourist village built in a style
sympathetic to old Menorca.
The jumble of white houses
and tiny streets of the Poblat
de Pescadors, an imitation
fishing village, have the look
of the genuine article.

Modern sculpture outside one of
the dwellings at Cales Coves

◁ The clear blue waters of Cala Turqueta in Menorca

Ancient Menorca

Menorca is exceptionally rich in prehistoric remains – the island has been described as an immense open-air museum. The majority of the sites are the work of the "talayot" people who lived between 2000–1000 BC and are named after the *talaiots* or huge stone towers that characterize the Menorcan landscape. There are hundreds of these Bronze Age villages and structures dotted around the island. Usually open to the public and free of charge, these sites provide an invaluable insight into the ancient inhabitants of the Balearics.

Huge *talaiot* amid the settlement of Trepucó

DIFFERENT STRUCTURES

The ancient stone structures scattered around the countryside of Menorca and, to a lesser extent, Mallorca can be placed into three main categories: *taulas, talaiots* and *navetas*.

 Taulas *are two slabs of rock, one placed on top of the other, in a "T" formation. Suggestions as to their possible function range from a sacrificial altar to a roof support.*

 Talayots *are circular or square buildings that may have been used as meeting places and dwellings.*

 Navetas *are shaped like upturned boats and apparently had a dual role as dwellings and burial quarters. At least ten of these remain in Menorca.*

Spectacular *taula* at Talatí de Dalt, standing 3 m (10 ft) high

Menorca *has an estimated 1,600 megalithic sites, and the most interesting of these are shown here. Talayot remains are found all over the island, usually in rural settings, though most are in the flatter and more fertile south.*

Cala Morell
Fornells
Ciutadella
Naveta d'es Tudons
Torrellafuda
Ferreries
Es Mercadal
Torretrencada
Alaior
Torralba d'en Salord
Torre d'en Gaumés
Talatí de Dalt
Maó
Trepucó
Sant Lluís

0 kilometres   10

0 miles   5

THE CANARY ISLANDS

LA PALMA · EL HIERRO · LA GOMERA · TENERIFE
GRAN CANARIA · FUERTEVENTURA · LANZAROTE

*P*oised on the edge of the tropics west of Morocco, the Canaries enjoy a generous supply of sunshine, pleasantly tempered by the trade winds. Their scenery ranges from lava desert to primeval forest and from sand dunes to volcanic peaks. The old towns on the main islands have colonial centres, full of character.

Seven islands and half a dozen islets make up the Canary archipelago. They are the tips of hundreds of volcanoes that first erupted from the sea bed 14 million years ago. Teneguía on La Palma last erupted in 1971.

In the 14th and 15th centuries, when navigators discovered the islands and claimed them for Spain, they were inhabited by the Guanches, who practised a stone culture. Sadly, little evidence of them remains.

Today the islands are divided into two provinces. The four western isles, making up the province of Santa Cruz de Tenerife, are all mountainous; Tenerife's colossal dormant volcano, Mount Teide, casts the world's biggest sea-shadow. La Palma, El Hierro and La Gomera, where Columbus stayed on his voyages, are all small, unspoiled islands, not yet developed for mass tourism.

The eastern islands belong to the province of Las Palmas. Forested Gran Canaria is the biggest and its capital, Las Palmas de Gran Canaria, is a colonial town. Lanzarote, by contrast, is flat, with lunar landscapes, while Fuerteventura has long, virgin beaches.

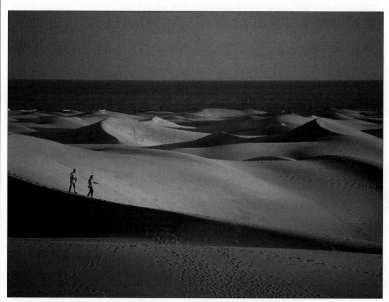

Protected area of sand dunes at Maspalomas, next to the busy Playa del Inglés, Gran Canaria

◁ La Rambla banana plantation on the north coast of the island of Tenerife

Exploring the Western Islands

Tenerife has the widest range of holiday attractions of any of the Canary Islands. The province of Santa Cruz de Tenerife also includes the three tiny westerly islands of La Palma, La Gomera and El Hierro, which are scarcely developed for tourism and have no large resorts. Gradually, more visitors are discovering these peaceful, green havens. If you enjoy walking, wildlife and mountain scenery, visit one of these hideaways. All three islands have comfortable hotels, including paradors. But compared with Gran Canaria and the eastern islands, there are fewer sandy beaches here, and little organized entertainment or sightseeing.

Las Teresitas artificial beach, Santa Cruz de Tenerife

LA PALMA

Los Sauces
Puntagorda
Caldera de Taburiente
C830
C832
Santa Cruz de la Palma
Breña Alta
Los Llanos de Aridane
Tazacorte
El Paso
LA PALMA
①
C832
Fuencaliente

SIGHTS AT A GLANCE

Candelaria ⑧
Los Cristianos ④
La Gomera ③
El Hierro ②
La Laguna ⑨
Montes de Anaga ⑩
La Orotava ⑦
La Palma ①
Parque Nacional del Teide
pp538–9 ⑤
Puerto de la Cruz ⑥
Santa Cruz de Tenerife ⑪

LA GOMERA

Villahermoso
Parque de Gara
Valle Gran Rey
③
LA GOMERA
Allajero
Sar

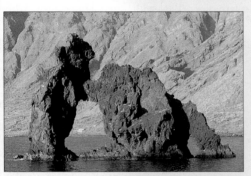

Roque Bonanza on the rocky east coast of El Hierro

EL HIERRO

Valverde
Ermita de los Reyes
Frontera
Puerto de la Estaca
②
EL HIERRO
La Restinga

KEY

═══ Motorway
─── Major road
═══ Secondary road
─── Scenic route
▲ Summit

For additional map symbols *see back flap*

Terraced hillside, maximizing cultivation in the lush green Valle Gran Rey, in western La Gomera

GETTING AROUND

From mainland Spain there are flights *(see p676)* and ferries *(see p677)* to the Canary Islands. Transport to the small islands is mainly from Tenerife. La Gomera is easily reached by ferry or hydrofoil from Los Cristianos, or by plane from Gran Canaria or Tenerife. Airports on La Palma and El Hierro are served by regular flights from Tenerife's northern airport of Los Rodeos. Unless you take an organized coach trip, a car is essential to see the island scenery. Roads are improving, but great care is needed for mountain driving.

MONTES DE ANAGA

LA LAGUNA ⑩

Playa de Las Teresitas

Tacoronte ○

TENERIFE

⑨

TF5

⑪ SANTA CRUZ DE TENERIFE

PUERTO DE LA CRUZ

El Rosario

⑥

Buenavista del Norte ○ Garahico ○

LA OROTAVA ⑦

Punta de Teno

C820

C824

TF1

⑧ CANDELARIA

C821

Güimar ○

Pico del Teide
3718m △

PARQUE NACIONAL DEL TEIDE

⑤

Guia ○

C823

Parador de
Cañades del Teide

C822

Vilaflor ○

Adeje ○

C821

Granadilla de Abona ○

Punta de Abona

Arona ○

ebastián

Playa de las Américas ○

LOS CRISTIANOS ④

○ El Medano

Punta de la Rasca

TF1

Punta Roja

Costa del
Silencio

0 kilometres — 25

0 miles — 10

SEE ALSO

• *Where to Stay* pp591–601

• *Where to Eat* pp651–3

The wild landscape of Punta de Teno in western Tenerife

La Palma ❶

Santa Cruz de Tenerife. 🏘 85,000.
✈ 🚢 Santa Cruz de la Palma.
ℹ Calle O'Daly 22, Santa Cruz de la Palma, 922 41 21 06.
www.lapalmaturismo.com

Reaching an altitude of 2,426 m (7,959 ft) on a land base of less than 706 sq km (280 sq miles), La Palma is the world's steepest island. It lies on the northwestern tip of the archipelago and has a cool, moist climate and lush vegetation. The mountainous interior is covered with forests of pine, laurel and giant fern.

The centre of the island is dominated by **La Caldera de Taburiente**, a volcano's massive crater, more than 8 km (5 miles) wide. National park status *(see pp30–1)* is an indication of its botanical and geological importance. The International Astrophysics Observatory crowns the summit. A couple of roads traverse

The Parque Nacional de la Caldera de Taburiente, La Palma

Pastel façades and delicate wooden balconies in Santa Cruz, La Palma

La Palma's dizzy heights, offering spectacular views of the craters of La Cumbrecita and Roque de los Muchachos.

Santa Cruz de la Palma, the island's main town and port, is an elegant place of old houses with balconies, some fine churches and several 16th-century buildings. In the cobbled street behind the seafront, Calle O'Daly (named after an Irish banana trader), are the Iglesia El Salvador, boasting a Mudéjar coffered ceiling, and the town hall *(ayuntamiento)*, which is housed in a cardinal's palace. A full-sized cement replica of the *Santa María*, Columbus's flagship, stands at the end of the Plaza Alameda.

The tortuous mountain road southwest of Santa Cruz winds over Las Cumbres mountains via Breña Alta to **El Paso** in the centre of the island. A relatively sizeable community, the village is known for its silk production and hand-rolled cigars.

Among the almond terraces and vineyards of southern La Palma, solidified lava from the Teneguia volcano is a reminder of its recent activity *(see p551).*

Craters on El Hierro, Spain's most western territory

El Hierro ❷

Santa Cruz de Tenerife. 🏘 10,000.
✈ 🚢 Puerto de la Estaca. ℹ Calle Doctor Quintero Magdaleno 4, Valverde, 922 55 03 02.
www.el-hierro.org

Due to a dearth of sandy beaches, El Hierro has escaped tourist invasions. Instead it has caught the attentions of naturalists. Its hilly landscape and unusual fauna and flora are part of its appeal. El Hierro is the smallest of the Canaries, and the furthest west; consequently it is the last place in Spain where the sun sets.

Valverde, the island's capital; stands inland at 600 m (2,000 ft) above sea level. Canary pines and peculiarly twisted

---

LA GOMERA'S WHISTLE LANGUAGE

The problems of communication posed by La Gomera's rugged terrain produced an unusual language, known as El Silbo. This system of piercing whistles probably developed because its sounds carry across the great distances from one valley to the next. Its origins are mysterious, but it was allegedly invented by the Guanches *(see p547).* Few young Gomerans have any use for El Silbo today, and the language would probably be dead if it were not for the demonstrations that it still held for interested visitors at the parador, and in the restaurant at Las Rosas.

El Silbo practised on La Gomera

---

juniper trees cover El Hierro's mountainous interior, best seen from the many footpaths and scenic viewpoints along the roads. A ridge of woodland, curving east-west across the island, marks the edge of a volcano. The crater forms a fertile depression known as El Golfo.

In the far west is the **Ermita de los Reyes**, a place of pilgrimage and the starting point of the island's biggest fiesta, held in July every four years.

The turquoise seas off the south coast are popular with skin-divers, who base themselves in the small fishing village of **La Restinga**.

La Gomera ❸

Santa Cruz de Tenerife. 🏠 *19,000.* ✈ ⛴ ℹ *Calle Real 4, San Sebastián de la Gomera, 922 14 15 12.* **www**.gomera-island.com

La Gomera is the most accessible of the smaller western islands, only 40 minutes by hydrofoil from Los Cristianos on Tenerife (90 minutes by ferry), or by plane from Tenerife or Gran Canaria. Many come to La Gomera for a day only, taking a coach trip. Others hire a car and explore on their own: a scenic but exhausting drive for a single day as the terrain is intensely buckled, and the central plateau is deeply scored by dramatic ravines. Driving across these gorges involves negotiating countless dizzying hairpin bends.

The best way to enjoy the island is to stay awhile and

Terraced hillsides in the fertile Valle Gran Rey, La Gomera

explore it at leisure, preferably doing some walking. On a fine day, La Gomera's scenery is glorious. Rock pinnacles jut above steep slopes studded with ferns while terraced hillsides glow with palms and flowering creepers. The best section, the **Parque Nacional de Garajonay**, is a UNESCO World Heritage Site.

San Sebastián, La Gomera's main town and ferry terminal, is situated on the east coast, a scattering of white buildings around a small beach. Among its sights are some places associated with Columbus (*see pp58–9*), who topped up

his water supplies here before setting out on his adventurous voyages. A well in the customs house bears the grand words "With this water America was baptized". According to legend he also prayed in the Iglesia de la Asunción, and stayed at a local house.

Beyond the arid hills to the south lies **Playa de Santiago**, the island's only real resort, which has a grey pebble beach. **Valle Gran Rey**, in the far west, is a fertile valley of palms and staircase terraces. These days it is colonized by foreigners attempting alternative lifestyles. In the north, tiny roads weave a tortuous course around several pretty villages, plunging at intervals to small, stony beaches. **Las Rosas** is a popular stop-off for coach parties, who can enjoy the visitors' centre and a restaurant with a panoramic view.

The road towards the coast from Las Rosas leads through the town of **Vallehermoso**, dwarfed by the huge **Roque de Cano**, which is an impressive mass of solidified lava. Just off the north coast stands **Los Órganos**, a fascinating rock formation of crystallized basalt columns resembling the pipes of an organ.

Juniper trees on El Hierro, twisted and bent by the wind

Tenerife

In the language of its aboriginal Guanche inhabitants
Tenerife means "Snowy Mountain", a tribute to its most
striking geographical feature, the dormant volcano of
Mount Teide, Spain's highest peak. The largest of the
Canary Islands, Tenerife is a roughly triangular landmass
rising steeply on all sides towards the cloud-capped
summit that divides it into two distinct climatic zones:
damp and lushly vegetated in the north, sunny and arid
in the south. Tenerife offers a more varied range of
attractions than any of the other Canary Islands, including
its spectacular volcanic scenery, water sports and a
vibrant atmosphere after dark. Its beaches, however, have
unenticing black sand and are rather poor for swimming.
The main resorts are crowded with high-rise hotels and
apartments, offering nightlife but little peace and quiet.

Bananas in northern Tenerife

Los Cristianos ❹

Santa Cruz de Tenerife. 🔼 60,000.
🚌 🚢 🛈 Plaza del Pescador 1, 922
75 71 37. 🚌 Sun. 🎭 Fiesta del
Carmen (first Sun of Sep).
www.arona.org

The old fishing village of Los
Cristianos, on Tenerife's south
coast, has grown into a town
spreading out along the foot
of barren hills. Ferries and
hydrofoils make regular trips
from its little port to La Gomera
and El Hierro *(see pp532–3)*.
To the north lies the modern
expanse of **Playa de las
Américas**, Tenerife's largest
development. It offers visitors
a cheerful, relaxed, undemand-
ing cocktail of sun and fun.
A brief sortie inland leads to
the much older town of **Adeje**
and to the **Barranco del
Infierno**, a wild gorge with an
attractive waterfall (two hours'
round walk from Adeje).
Along the coast to the east,
the **Costa del Silencio** is a
pleasant contrast to most of

the other large resorts, with
its bungalow developments
surrounding fishing villages.
Los Abrigos has lively fish restaurants lining its harbour.
Further east, **El Médano**
shelters below an ancient
volcanic cone. Its two beaches
are popular with windsurfers.

Parque Nacional del Teide ❺

See pp538–39.

Puerto de la Cruz ❻

Santa Cruz de Tenerife. 🔼 21,500.
🚌 🛈 Plaza Europa, 922 38 60 00.
🚌 Sat. 🎭 Carnival (Feb–Mar),
Fiesta del Carmen (second Sun of Jul).

Puerto de la Cruz, the oldest
resort in the Canaries, first
sprang to prominence in 1706,
when a volcanic eruption
obliterated Tenerife's principal
port of Garachico. Puerto de

la Cruz took its place, later
becoming popular with genteel
English convalescents. The
town's older buildings give it
much of its present character.
The beautiful Lago Martiánez
lido, designed by the Lanzarote
architect César Manrique *(see
p548)*, compensates for a lack
of good beaches with its sea
water pools, palms and fountains. Other attractions include
the tropical gardens of **Loro
Parque**, where visitors can
also see parrots and dolphins.
Outside town, the **Bananera
El Guanche** plantation has an
exhibition on bananas and
other tropical crops. **Icod de
los Vinos**, a short drive west,
attracts crowds for its spectacular ancient dragon tree.

🌴 **Loro Parque**
Avenida Loro Parque
Tel 922 37 38 41. ⬜ daily. 🎟️ ⬜
🌴 **Bananera El Guanche**
Carretera Botánico, La Orotava.
Tel 922 33 18 53. ⬜ daily. 🎟️ ⬜

The landscaped Lago Martiánez
lido, Puerto de la Cruz

THE DRAGON TREE

The Canary Islands have many
unusual plants, but the dragon
tree *(Dracaena draco)* is one of
the strangest. This primitive creature
looks a little like a giant cactus, with
swollen branches that sprout multiple tufts of
spiky leaves. When cut, the trunk exudes a
reddish sap once believed to have magical and
medicinal properties. Dragon trees form no
annual rings, so their age is a mystery. Some
are thought to be hundreds of years old. The
most venerable surviving specimen can be
seen at Icod de los Vinos.

La Orotava 🟡

Santa Cruz de Tenerife. 🏙 *40,000.*
🚌 🛈 *Carrera del Escultor Estevez
2, 922 32 30 41.* 🎭 *Carnival
(Feb/Mar), Corpus Christi (May/Jun),
Romeria San Isidoro Labrador (Jun).*

A short distance from Puerto
de la Cruz, in the fertile hills
above the Orotava valley, La
Orotava makes a popular
excursion. The old part of this
historic town clusters around
the large **Iglesia de Nuestra
Señora de la Concepción**. This
domed Baroque building with
twin towers was built in the
late 18th century to replace an
earlier church that was destroyed in earthquakes at the
beginning of that century.

In the surrounding streets
and squares are many old
churches, convents and grand
houses with elaborate wooden
balconies. The **Casas de los
Balcones** and **Casa del Turista**
have interior courtyards that
are open to the public.

**Nuestra Señora de la Candelaria,
patron saint of the Canary Islands**

Candelaria 🟤

Santa Cruz de Tenerife. 🏙 *13,000.*
🚢 🛈 *Plaza del Cit, 922 50 04 15.*
🛒 *Sat, Sun.* 🎭 *Nuestra Señora de
la Candelaria (14–15 Aug).*

This coastal town is famous
for its shrine to Nuestra
Señora de la Candelaria, the
Canary Islands' patron saint,
whose image is surrounded
by flowers and candles in a
modern church in the main
square. This gaudy Virgin,
supposedly washed ashore in

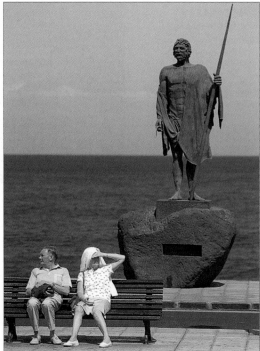

Statue of a Guanche chief on the seafront of Candelaria

pagan times, was venerated
before Christianity reached
the island. In 1826 a tidal wave
returned her to the sea, but a
replica draws pilgrims to worship here every August. Outside, stone effigies of Guanche
chiefs line the sea wall.

La Laguna 🟢

Santa Cruz de Tenerife. 🏙 *130,000.*
🚌 🛈 *C/ Obispo Rey Redondo 1, 922
63 11 94.* 🛒 *daily.* 🎭 *San Benito
(15 Jul), Santismo Cristo de la Laguna
(14 Sep).* **www**.historiaviva.org

A bustling university town
and former island capital, La
Laguna is the second largest
settlement on Tenerife.

In its old quarter, best explored on foot, there are many
atmospheric squares, historic
buildings and good museums.
Most of the sights lie between
the bell-towered **Iglesia de
Nuestra Señora de la Concepción** (1502), and the Plaza del
Adelantado, on which stand
the town hall, a convent and
the **Palacio de Nava.**

Montes de Anaga 🔟

Santa Cruz de Tenerife. 🚌 *Santa
Cruz de Tenerife, La Laguna.*

The rugged mountains north
of Santa Cruz are kept green
and lush by a cool, wet
climate. They abound with a
wide variety of interesting
birds and plants, including
cacti, laurels and tree heathers.
Walking the mountain trails is
very popular, and maps showing many of the best paths
are readily available from the
tourist office. A steep road
with marker posts climbs up
from the village of San Andrés
by the beautiful but artificial
beach of Las Teresitas. On
clear days there are marvellous
vistas along the paths, especially from the viewpoints of
Pico del Inglés and Bailadero.

Winding down through the
laurel forests of Monte de las
Mercedes and the colourful
valley of Tejina you reach
Tacoronte with its interesting
churches, an ethnographic
museum and a bodega, where
you can sample local wines.

THE CANARY ISLANDS' FIESTAS

Carnival *(Feb/Mar)*, Santa Cruz de Tenerife. One of Europe's biggest carnivals, this grand street party is a lavish spectacle of extravagant costumes and Latin American dance music to rival that of Rio de Janeiro. For years under the Franco regime, Carnival was suppressed for its irreverent frivolity. It begins with the election of a queen of the festivities and builds up to a climax on Shrove Tuesday when there is a large procession. The "funeral" of an enormous mock sardine takes place on Ash Wednesday. Carnival is also celebrated on the islands of Lanzarote and Gran Canaria.

Revellers in Carnival outfits on Tenerife

Corpus Christi *(May/Jun)*, La Orotava (Tenerife). The streets of the town are filled with flower carpets in striking patterns, while the Plaza del Ayuntamiento is covered in copies of works of art, formed from coloured volcanic sands.
Descent of the Virgin of the Snows *(Jul, every five years: 2005, 2010)* Santa Cruz de La Palma.
Romería de la Virgen de la Candelaria *(15 Aug)*, Candelaria (Tenerife). Pilgrims come here in their thousands to venerate the Canary Islands' patroness.
Fiesta del Charco *(7–11 Sep)*, San Nicolás de Tolentino (Gran Canaria). People leap into a large saltwater pond to catch mullet.

Large ships moored at the busy port of Santa Cruz de Tenerife

Santa Cruz de Tenerife ⓫

Santa Cruz de Tenerife. 🏙 *213,000.*
🚉 🚌 🛈 *Plaza de España 1, 922 23 95 92.* 🚢 *Sun.* 🎭 *Carnival (Feb/Mar), Día de la Cruz (3 May).* **www**.cabtfe.es

Tenerife's capital city is an important regional port, with a deep-water harbour suitable for large ships. Its most attractive beach, **Las Teresitas**, lies 7 km (4 miles) to the north. Completely artificial, it was created by importing millions of tonnes of golden Saharan sand and building a protective reef just offshore. Shaded by palms, backed by mountains and so far devoid of concrete hotel developments, the result improves on anything nature has bestowed on Tenerife.

Santa Cruz can boast many handsome historic buildings. The hub of the town is around the **Plaza de España**, situated near the harbour. Just off it is the Calle de Castillo, the main shopping street. Its two most noteworthy churches are the **Iglesia de Nuestra Señora de la Concepción**, with parts dating from 1500, and Baroque **Iglesia de San Francisco**.

Particularly interesting is the **Museo de la Naturaleza y el Hombre**, in the Palacio Insular, where Guanche mummies grin in glass cases. Inside the museum you can also see the cannon which is alleged to have removed the arm of the British admiral Nelson

during an unsuccessful raid on the city in the late 18th century.

Other attractions include the **Museo de Bellas Artes** which features old masters as well as modern works. Many of its paintings focus on local events and landscapes. Contemporary sculptures adorn the **Parque Municipal García Sanabria,** a pleasant park with shady paths, laid out in 1926.

In the morning, visit the **Mercado de Nuestra Señora de África**, which combines a bazaar with a food market. Outside stalls sell domestic goods; those inside offer an eclectic mix of live chickens, spices and cut flowers. Santa Cruz is especially worth a visit during its flamboyant carnival.

🏛 **Museo de la Naturaleza y el Hombre**
Calle Fuentes Morales. *Tel 922 53 58 16.* ⬜ *Tue–Sun.* 🎟 🛇
🏛 **Museo de Bellas Artes**
Calle José Murphy 12. *Tel 922 24 43 58.* ⬜ *Tue–Fri.*

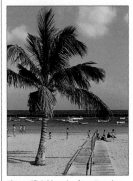

The artificial beach of Las Teresitas in Santa Cruz

The Flavours of the Canary Islands

The exotic fruits and vegetables which grow in the sub-tropical Canaries climate, and the unusual fish which are caught in local waters, have led to a cuisine very different from that of the Iberian peninsula. From the original inhabitants, the Guanche, culinary traditions survive in local staples like *gofio* (maize meal). Over the centuries, Spanish, Portuguese and North African influences have been incorporated into the local cuisine, but the underlying theme is always one of simplicity and a reliance on ultra-fresh local produce. All kinds of unusual delicacies are available, from sweet-fleshed parrot-fish to succulent tropical fruits.

Maize (corn)

Fish straight from the ocean, being dried in the sun to preserve them

SEAFOOD AND MEAT

The Canaries offer an incredible array of seafood, with varieties unknown on the Spanish mainland. Delicacies like *lapas* (limpets) are around only for a few months during the summer, and are usually served simply grilled (*a la plancha*). Other unusual varieties include wreckfish, damselfish, dentex and parrot-fish. These, along with more common varieties, are usually fried, baked in a salt crust, or dried in the sun.

Meats include standard Iberian favourites like pork, kid and beef, but they are often prepared according to ancient Guanche traditions.

FRUIT AND VEGETABLES

The mild, stable Canarian climate is perfect for growing luscious tropical fruits (the most famous crop of the islands being bananas). Exotic vegetables thrive, too, as well as potatoes and tomatoes, which were introduced here 500 years ago from the newly discovered Americas. The islands boast varieties of potato unknown elsewhere, and these feature in the local favourite *papas arrugadas* ("wrinkly potatoes"), which are made by boiling potatoes in their skins in very salty water – sometimes seawater.

Dates Bananas Pineapple Papayas (paw paw)

Mangoes Guavas

Mouthwatering fresh fruits from the Canary Islands

CANARIAN DISHES AND SPECIALITIES

The Greeks named the Canaries "the fortunate islands", and they are certainly blessed in terms of the freshness and abundance of the local produce. What ever you choose to eat, you can be sure of encountering a bowl of the ubiquitous *mojo* sauce. This aromatic Canarian creation accompanies almost every dish, and appears in countless versions: the main ones are red *picón*, which is spiced up with pepper and paprika, and green *verde*, with parsley and coriander. The Canarian staple, *gofio* (roasted maize meal), is served for breakfast and used in local dishes such as *gofio de almendras*, a rich almond dessert. The islands are also known for delicious pastries like the honey-drizzled *bienmesabes* (meaning "tastes good to me") and traditional cheeses.

Almonds

Sopa de pescados tinerfeña
This Tenerife fish soup of sea bass and potatoes is scented with saffron and cumin.

Parque Nacional del Teide ❺

Towering over Tenerife, Mount Teide, surrounded by a wild volcanic landscape, is an awesome sight. 180,000 years ago a much larger adjacent cone collapsed leaving behind the devastation of Las Cañadas, a 16-km (10-mile) wide caldera, and the smaller volcano, Teide, on its northern edge. Today volcanic material forms a wilderness of weathered, mineral-tinted rocks, ash beds and lava streams. A single road crosses the plateau of Las Cañadas, passing a parador, cable car station, and visitors' centre. Follow the marked paths for unforgettable views of this unique, protected area.

Volcanic Landscapes
The eight-minute cable car ride leaves you 160 m (525 ft) short of Teide's summit. Authorisation must be given to climb up to the summit.

Pico del Teide, which is still volcanically active, is Spain's highest summit.

PICO DEL TE

3,718 m

Pico Viejo, a volcanic cone also known as Montaña Chahorra, last erupted in the 18th century.

PICO VIEJO

3,414 m

CHÍO

Mirador de Chío

ROQUES DE GARCÍA

Mirador de La Ruleta

TF-36

LLANO DE UCANCA

Mirador de Boca Tauce

TF21

VILAFLOR

Mir de L

0 kilometres 2
0 miles 1

KEY

▭▭ Road
━━ Track
- - Footpath

Los Roques de García
These flamboyantly shaped lava rocks near the parador are some of the most photographed in the whole park. The rocks of Los Azulejos, nearby, glitter blue-green because of the copper deposits within them.

WILD FLOWERS

The inhospitable badlands of Las Cañadas are inhabited by some rare and beautiful plants. Many of these are unique to the Canary Islands. Most striking is the tall *Echium wildprettii*, a kind of viper's bugloss, whose red flowers reach 3 m (9 ft) in early summer. Other common plants include Teide broom, the Teide daisy, and a unique species of violet. The best time of year for flower-spotting is May to June. Displays housed in the visitors' centre will help identify them. Don't take any plants away with you: all vegetation within the park is strictly protected and must not be uprooted or picked.

La Caldera de Las Cañadas
A rim of fractured crags forms a pie-crust edge to the sides of this enormous caldera – a wide volcanic crater (see p551). Now collapsed and intensely eroded, the perimeter of the caldera measures 45 km (28 miles).

VISITORS' CHECKLIST

Tel 922 29 01 29. 🚌 342 & 348 from Puerto de la Cruz. *El Portillo Visitors' Centre & cable car (to NE of park on C821).* ⬜ 9:15am–4:15pm daily. ♿ 🍴 🎞

At El Portillo Visitors' Centre,
a video film and exhibition chart the origins of the park.

SANTA CRUZ
DE TENERIFE

🅿 ℹ El Portillo

efugio de Altavista

Mirador
de San José

Mirador del
Tabonal Negro

LAS CAÑADAS

Las Cañadas
The flat expanses of the seven cañadas (small sandy plateaux) were created by the collapse of ancient craters. Several colourful plants have managed to colonize this dusty, barren wasteland.

rador de
ñadas del
de

Parador
The recently refurbished visitor centre and Parador de Cañadas del Teide (see p601) is set in the surreal scenery, and makes an excellent base for those who want to explore the park thoroughly.

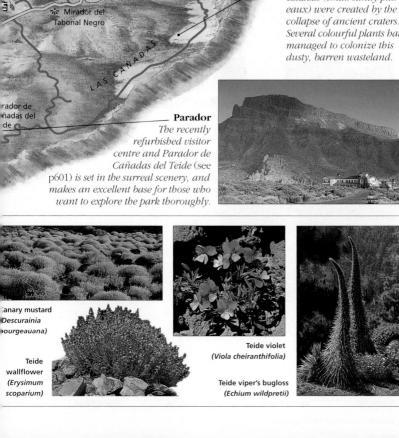

Canary mustard
(Descurainia bourgeauana)

Teide
wallflower
(Erysimum scoparium)

Teide violet
(Viola cheiranthifolia)

Teide viper's bugloss
(Echium wildpretii)

Exploring the Eastern Islands

The Eastern Province of the Canary Islands – Las Palmas – comprises the islands of Gran Canaria, Lanzarote and Fuerteventura. All feature unusual and spectacular scenery, plenty of sunshine and excellent sandy beaches, but each has a very different atmosphere. Gran Canaria boasts the only really large town, Las Palmas de Gran Canaria, which is also the administrative centre for the eastern islands. It also offers the biggest resort, Maspalomas, with its Playa del Inglés, which has a package holiday feel. As a contrast, the white beaches of Fuerteventura have been left fairly undeveloped and it is still possible to find privacy among their sand dunes. Lanzarote has fine beaches, too, while its interior is dominated by a volcanic landscape which makes for great excursions.

Corralejo's beach, in the north of Fuerteventura

The marina at Puerto Rico, in southern Gran Canaria

GETTING AROUND

Most people travel from mainland Spain to the eastern islands by air (see p676). The alternative is a long sea crossing from Cádiz (see p677). There are flights between all the islands, mainly from Gran Canaria. There are also regular inter-island ferries. Taxis and public transport are fine within resorts, but expensive over long distances. Cars can be hired on all the islands, usually at airports or ferry terminals. The main roads are well-surfaced and fast on the flatter sections, though traffic in Gran Canaria can be heavy in places. A four-wheel drive Jeep is advisable to reach some remoter beaches.

Cenobio de Valerón
Gáldar
Arucas
AGAETE **15** Firgas
Teror
17 LAS PALMAS DE GRAN CANARIA
16 TARIFA
San Nicolás de Tolentino
CRUZ DE TEJEDA **18**
San Mateo
Telde
Roque Nublo
Pico de las Nieves 1949m
Mogán
Santa Lucía
PUETRO DE MOGÁN **12**
Agüimes
13 PUERTO RICO
14 MASPALOMAS

GRAN CANARIA

KEY

▬▬	Motorway
▬	Major road
═══	Secondary road
▬	Scenic route
△	Summit

0 kilometres   25

0 miles   10

SIGHTS AT A GLANCE

Agaete **15**
Arrecife **27**
Betancuria **20**
Caleta de Fustes **21**
Corralejo **23**
Costa Teguise **28**
Haría **30**
Jameos del Agua **31**
Maspalomas **14**
Las Palmas de
  Gran Canaria **17**
Parque Nacional de
  Timanfaya **25**
Península de Jandía **19**

Playa Blanca **24**
Puerto del Carmen **26**
Puerto de Mogán **12**
Puerto del Rosario **22**
Puerto Rico **13**
Tafira **16**
Teguise **29**

Tour
Cruz de Tejeda **18**

Alegranza

Montaña Clara

La Graciosa

Orzola

JAMEOS DEL AGUA **31**

HARÍA **30**

Tinajo

PARQUE NATIONAL
DE TIMANFAYA **25**

Mozaga

29 TEGUISE

San
Bartolomé

COSTA
TEGUISE **28**

Yaiza

Tias

27 ARRECIFE

Salinas de Janubio

26

PUERTO
DEL CARMEN

PLAYA BLANCA **24**

*Playa del
Papagayo*

LANZAROTE

*Isla de
los Lobos*

CORRALEJO **23**

La Oliva

Tindaya

22 PUERTO DEL ROSARIO

BETANCURIA **20**

Antigua

21 CALETA DE FUSTES

Pájara

Tuineje

Gran Tarajal

Tarajalejo

PENÍNSULA DE JANDÍA

FUERTEVENTURA

19

Morro Jable

SEE ALSO

• **Where to Stay** pp599–601

• **Where to Eat** pp651–3

Volcanoes of Montañas de Fuego in Parque Nacional de Timanfaya, Lanzarote

Gran Canaria

Gran Canaria is the most popular of the Canary Islands, with over 3 million holiday-makers visiting it each year. The island offers a surprising range of scenery, climate, resorts and attractions within its compact bounds. Winding roads follow the steep, ruggedly beautiful terrain which rises to a symmetrical cone at the centre of the island. Las Palmas, Gran Canaria's capital and port, is the largest city in the Canaries, and Maspalomas/Playa del Inglés, in the south, is one of the biggest resorts in Spain.

Farmer and donkey

Both tourist meccas are packed with high-rise hotels and villa complexes, but not far away there is some marvellous scenery to discover.

Holiday-makers on the golden sands of Puerto Rico beach

Puerto de Mogán ⑫

Las Palmas. 🏠 1,500. 🛈 Avenida Tomás Roca Bosch, 928 56 00 29. 🚢 Fri. 🎭 Virgen del Carmen (Jul).

Situated at the end of the verdant valley of Mogán,this is one of Gran Canaria's most appealing and successful developments – an idyll to many visitors after the brash concrete of Playa del Inglés. Based around a small fishing port, it consists of a village-like complex of pretty, white, creeper-covered houses and a similarly designed hotel built around a marina. Boutiques, bars and restaurants add an ambience without any of the accompanying rowdiness.

The sandy beach, sheltered between the cliffs, is scarcely big enough for all visitors; a car is recommended to reach more facilities at Maspalomas. Ferries provide a leisurely way to get to nearby resorts.

Sun worshippers in Puerto Rico

Puerto Rico ⑬

Las Palmas. 🏠 1,800. 🛈 Avenida de Mogán, 928 56 00 29. 🎭 Maria de Auxiliadora (May), San Antonio (13 Jun), Carmen (16 Jul).

The barren cliffs west of Maspalomas now sprout apartment complexes at every turn. Puerto Rico is an over-developed resort, but has one of the more attractive beaches on the island, a firm crescent of imported sand supplemented by lidos and excellent water sports facilities. It is a great place to learn sailing, diving and windsurfing, or just to soak up the ultraviolet – Puerto Rico enjoys the best sunshine record in the whole of Spain.

Maspalomas ⑭

Las Palmas. 🏠 38,700. 🚢 🛈 Avda de España, 928 76 25 91. 🚢 Wed & Sat. 🎭 Santiago (25 Jul), San Bartolomé (24 Aug).

When the fast motorway from Las Palmas airport first tips you into this bewildering mega-resort, it seems like a homogeneous blur, but gradually three separate communities emerge. **San Agustín**, the furthest east, is sedate compared with the others. It has a series of beaches of dark sand, attractively sheltered by low cliffs and landscaped prom-enades, and a casino.

The next exit off the coastal highway leads to **Playa del Inglés**, the largest and liveliest resort, a triangle of land jutting into a huge belt of golden sand. Developed from the end of the 1950s, the area is built up with giant blocks of flats linked by a maze of roads. Many hotels lack sea views, though most have spacious grounds with swimming pools.

Floral arches decorating a street of apartments in Puerto de Mogán

For hotels and restaurants in this region see pp599–601 and pp651–3

At night the area pulsates with bright disco lights and flashing neon. There are more than 300 restaurants and over 50 discos in this resort alone.

West of Playa del Inglés the beach undulates into the **Dunas de Maspalomas**. A relieving contrast to the hectic surrounding resorts, these dunes form a nature reserve protected from further development. The western edge of the dunes (marked by a lighthouse) is occupied by a cluster of luxury hotels. Just behind the dunes lies a golf course encircled by bungalow estates.

Everything is laid on for the package holiday: water sports, excursions, fast food, as well as go-karts, camel safaris and funfairs. Best of these include **Palmitos Park,** with exotic birds in subtropical gardens; and **Sioux City**, a fun-packed Western theme park.

Palmitos Park
Barranco de los Palmitos. *Tel* 928 14 02 76. ☐ daily. 🖼 ♿

Sioux City
Cañón del Águila. *Tel* 928 76 25 73. ☐ Tue–Sun. 🖼 ♿

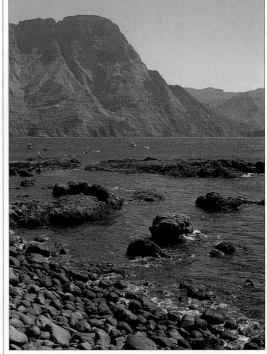

The rocky shore and steep cliffs of the northeast coast near Agaete

Agaete ⑮

Las Palmas. 🏠 5,600. ℹ️ Avenida Senura de las Nieves 1, 928 55 43 82. 🎉 Fiesta de la Rama (4 Aug).

The cloudier northern side of the island is far greener and lusher than the arid south, and banana plantations take up most of the coastal slopes. Agaete, on the northwest coast, a pretty scatter of white houses around a striking rocky bay, is growing into a small resort.

Every August, Agaete holds the Fiesta de la Rama, a Guanche *(see p547)* rain-making ritual which dates from long before the arrival of the Spanish. An animated procession of villagers bearing green branches heads from the hills above the town down to the coast and into the sea. The villagers beat the water to summon the rain.

Sights in Agaete include the little **Ermita de las Nieves**, containing a fine 16th-century Flemish triptych and model

sailing ships, and the **Huerto de las Flores**. This botanical garden is being extended. Until completion, access is by key, held at the town hall.

Environs
A brief detour inland up along the Barranco de Agaete takes you through a fertile valley of papaya, mango and citrus trees. North of Agaete are the towns of Guía and Gáldar. Though there is little to see here, both parish churches do contain examples of the religious statuary of the celebrated 18th-century sculptor, José Luján Pérez.

Nearby, towards the north coast, lies the **Cenobio de Valerón**. One of the most dramatic of the local Guanche sights, this cliff-face is pock-marked with nearly 300 caves beneath a basalt arch. These are believed to have been hideaways for Guanche priestesses, communal grainstores and refuges from attack.

Huerto de las Flores
Calle Huertas. ☐ Mon–Fri. ♿ ✏️

Miles of wind-sculptured sand: the dunes at Maspalomas

Tafira ⑯

Las Palmas. 🏠 *23,000.* 🚌 ℹ️ *Calle León y Castillo 322, 928 44 66 02.* 🎉 *San Francisco (Oct).*

The hills southwest of Las Palmas have long been desirable residential locations. A colonial air still wafts around Tafira's patrician villas. The **Jardín Canario**, a botanical garden founded in 1952, is the main reason for a visit. Plants from all of the Canary Islands can be studied in their own, re-created habitats.

Near La Atalaya lies one of Gran Canaria's most impressive natural sights – the **Caldera de la Bandama**. This is a volcanic crater 1,000 m (3,300 ft) wide, best seen from the Mirador de Bandama where you gaze down into the green depression about 200 m (660 ft) deep. Some of the inhabited caves in the **Barranco de Guayadeque**, a valley of red rocks to the south, were dug in the late 15th century. A few of them have electricity.

♣ **Jardín Canario**
Carretera de Dragonal, Tafira. **Tel** *928 35 36 04.* ⬜ *daily.* ⬤ *Good Fri & 1 Jan* www.jardincanario.org

Las Palmas de Gran Canaria ⑰

Las Palmas. 🏠 *355,000.* 🚌 ⛴ ℹ️ *Calle León y Castillo 322, 928 44 66 02.* 🎉 *Carnival (Feb/Mar).*

Las Palmas is the largest city in the Canary Islands. A bustling seaport and industrial city, it sees 1,000 ships docking

Palm trees in a natural setting in the Jardín Canario, Tafira

each month. Las Palmas has faded somewhat from the days when wealthy convalescents flocked here in winter and glamorous liners called in on transatlantic voyages. But it remains a vibrant place to visit.

Las Palmas is a sprawling city built around an isthmus and its layout can be confusing. The modern commercial shipping area, Puerto de la Luz, takes up the eastern side of the isthmus, which leads to the former island of La Isleta, a sailors' and military quarter. On the other side of the isthmus is the crowded **Playa de las Canteras**, a 3-km (2-mile) long stretch of golden beach. The promenade behind has been built up with bars, restaurants and hotels.

The town centre stretches along the coast from the isthmus. For a pleasant scenic tour, begin in the **Parque Santa Catalina**, near the port. This is a popular, shady square of

Bronze dog at Plaza Santa Ana

cafés and newspaper kiosks. In the leafy residential quarter of Ciudad Jardín are the Parque Doramas and the traditional casino hotel of Santa Catalina.

The **Pueblo Canario** is a tourist enclave where visitors can watch folk dancing, and browse in the craft shops and the small art gallery. All this can be viewed from above by walking uphill towards the Altavista district and the Paseo Cornisa.

At the end of town is the Barrio Vegueta, an atmospheric quarter which dates back to the Spanish conquest. At its heart stands the **Catedral de Santa Ana**, begun in 1500. The adjacent **Museo Diocesano de Arte Sacro** contains works of religious art. The square in front is guarded by Canarian dogs in bronze.

Nearby, the **Casa de Colón** is a 15th-century governor's residence where Columbus stayed. A museum dedicated to his voyages displays charts, models and diary extracts.

Early history can be seen in the **Museo Canario**, which contains Guanche mummies, skulls, pottery and jewellery.

🏛 **Museo Diocesano de Arte Sacro**
Calle Espíritu Santo 20. **Tel** *928 31 49 89.* ⬜ *Mon–Sat.* ⬤ *until Jul.* 📷

⛪ **Casa de Colón**
Calle Colón 1. **Tel** *928 31 23 84.* ⬜ *daily.* 📷 *(by appointment for groups).*

E **Museo Canario**
Calle Doctor Verneau 2. **Tel** *928 33 68 00.* ⬜ *daily.* 📷 📷

The Casa de Colón museum, Las Palmas, dedicated to Columbus

For hotels and restaurants in this region see pp599–601 and pp651–3

Tour of Cruz de Tejeda ⑱

Gran Canaria's mountainous interior makes for an ideal day tour, from any part of the island. Choose a fine day or the views may be obscured. The route from Maspalomas leads through dry ravines of bare rock and cacti, becoming more fertile with altitude. Roads near the central highlands snake steeply through shattered, tawny crags, past caves and pretty villages to panoramic viewpoints from which you can see Mount Teide (*see pp538–9*) on Tenerife. On the north side, the slopes are much lusher, growing citrus fruits and eucalyptus trees.

White farmhouses en route to Teror

Artenara ②
One of the inhabited caves in this town houses a little church. Another has been converted into an unusual restaurant, the Mesón de la Silla.

Teror ①
This charming old town has many well-preserved, typical Canary Islands houses. Its church, Nuestra Señora del Pino, is dedicated to Gran Canaria's patron saint.

Pico de las Nieves ④
A meteorological station crowns Gran Canaria's highest peak. At 1,949 m (6,395 ft), it is often chilly up here and it sometimes snows, so take extra clothing.

KEY

▬ Tour route
═ Other roads
☆ Viewpoint

0 kilometres   2
0 miles   1

LAS PALMAS
GC21
① GC21
Valleseco
Lanzarote
GC21
Cuevas Corcho
PINAR DE TAMADABA
GC21
②
Tejeda
GC15
GC150
GC60
GC600
③
GC130
TELDE
④
Ayacata
GC60
MASPALOMAS

Roque Nublo ③
This 60-m (195-ft) high jagged spike of basalt tops a 1,700-m (5,578-ft) peak. Together with nearby Roque Bentayga, it was sacred to the Guanches. It's a stiff climb to the summit.

TIPS FOR DRIVERS

Length: 35–45 km (22–28 miles).
Stopping-off points: the Mesón de la Silla cave-restaurant in Artenara is a popular lunch spot.
Note: roads can be narrow with few passing places; sudden patches of cloud or mist may loom without warning.

Fuerteventura

Lying just 100 km (60 miles) off the Atlantic coast of
Morocco, leaf-shaped Fuerteventura is continually
battered by coastal winds. It is the second largest of the
Canary Islands after Tenerife, and the most sparsely
populated: its 69,500 inhabitants are outnumbered by
goats. The island used to be densely wooded, but
European settlers cut down the timber for shipbuilding;
the dry climate and the goats have since reduced the
vegetation to parched scrub. It is so dry that water has to
be shipped over from the mainland. The only significant
revenue is tourism, but the tourist industry is still in its
infancy compared with the other main islands. However,
visitors are increasing in number as thousands of sun-
worshippers flock to more than 150 splendid beaches.
The island is popular with water sports fans and naturists.

**A herd of goats near the airport
on Fuerteventura**

Península de Jandía ⓳

Las Palmas. 🚌 *Costa Calma, Morro
Jable.* ⛴ *(jetfoil) from Gran Canaria.*
ℹ️ *Centro Comercial Cosmo, Jandía
Beach Local 88, 928 54 07 76.*

Excellent beaches of pale
sand fringe the elongated
Jandía peninsula in the south
of Fuerteventura. A string of
urbanizaciones (apartment
complexes) now takes up
much of the peninsula's sheltered east coast (Sotavento).

Costa Calma, a burgeoning
cluster of modern complexes,
offers the most interesting
beaches with long stretches of
fine sand interrupted by low
cliffs and coves. **Morro Jable**,
a fishing village now swamped
by new developments, lies at
the southern end of a vast,
glittering strand. Beyond Morro
Jable, the access road dwindles
away into a potholed track
leading towards the lonely
lighthouse at Punta de Jandía.

Expanses of deserted sand,
accessible only by four-wheel
drive vehicle, line the westerly,
windward coast (Barlovento)
– too exposed for all but the
hardiest beach lovers. Some
of the island's best subtropical
marine life can be found in
this area, however, making it
popular with skin divers.

From 1938 to the early
1960s, Jandía belonged to a
German entrepreneur and
was out of bounds to locals.
Even today, rumours of spies,
submarines and secret Nazi
bases still circulate.

Betancuria ⓴

Las Palmas. 🏠 *850.* 🚌 ℹ️ *Calle
Amador Rodríguez 6, 928 87 80 92.*
🎉 *San Buenaventura (14 Jul),
Romería de La Pena (3rd Sat of Sep).*

Inland, rugged peaks of extinct
volcanoes, separated by wide
plains, present a scene of
austere grandeur. Scattered,
stark villages and obsolete
windmills occupy the lowlands
which are occasionally fertile
enough to nurture a few crops
or palm trees. Beyond, devoid
of vegetation, the hills form
stark outlines. From a distance
they appear brown and grey,
but close up the rocks glow
with an astonishing range of
mauves, pinks and ochres. The
richness of colour in this

**The gilded interior of the Iglesia
Santa María in Betancuria**

interior wilderness is at its most
striking at sunset, when a
leisurely drive can reveal some
breathtaking scenes.

Betancuria, built in a valley
surrounded by mountains in
the centre of the island, is
named after Jean de Béthen-
court, Fuerteventura's 15th-
century conqueror, who moved
his capital inland to thwart
pirates. Nestling in the mountains, this peaceful oasis is now
the island's prettiest village.
The **Iglesia de Santa María**
contains gilded altars, decorated beams and sacred relics.
The **Museo Arqueológico**
houses many local artifacts.

Environs
To the south, the village of
Pájara boasts a 17th-century
church with a curiously
decorated doorway. Its design
of serpents and strange beasts
is believed to be of Aztec influence. Inside, the twin aisles
both contain statues: one of a
radiant Madonna and Child in
white and silver, the other a
Virgen de los Dolores in black.

La Oliva, to the north, was the
site of the Spanish military
headquarters until the 19th century. The Casa de los Coroneles
(House of the Colonels) is a
faded yellow mansion with a
grand façade and hundreds of
windows. Inside it has coffered
ceilings. The fortified church
and the arts centre displaying
works of Canary Islands artists
are also worth a visit.

🏛 **Museo Arqueológico**
Calle Roberto Roldán. ***Tel*** *928 87
82 41.* 🕐 *Tue–Sun.* 📷 ♿

For hotels and restaurants in this region see pp599–601 and pp651–3

Caleta de Fustes 🌀

Las Palmas. 🕍 1,600. 🚗 ℹ️ *Calle Juan Ramón Soto Morales 10, El Castillo, 928 16 32 86.* 🚌 *Sat.* 🎉 *Día del Carmen (16 Jul), Nuestra Senora de Antigua (8 Sep).*

South of Puerto del Rosario about halfway down the eastern coast, lies Caleta de Fustes. The attractive low-rise, self-catering holiday centres surround a horseshoe bay of soft, gently shelving sand. The largest complex, El Castillo, takes its name from an 18th-century watchtower situated by the harbour.

There are many water sports facilities, including diving and windsurfing schools, as well as the Pueblo Majorero, an attractive "village" of shops and restaurants around a central plaza near the beach. These features make Caleta de Fustes one of Fuerteventura's most relaxed and pleasant resorts.

Fishing boats on a beach on the Isla de Lobos, near Corralejo

Puerto del Rosario 🌀

Las Palmas. 🕍 25,000. ✈️ 🚗 🚢 ℹ️ *Avenida de la Constitución 5, 928 53 08 44.* 🎉 *El Rosario (7 Oct).*

Fuerteventura's commercial and administrative capital was founded in 1797. It was originally known as Puerto de Cabras (Goats' Harbour), after a nearby gorge that was once used for watering goats, but was rechristened to smarten up its image in 1957. As Puerto del Rosario is the only large port on Fuerteventura, it is the base for inter-island ferries and a busy fishing industry. The town is also enlivened by the presence of the Spanish Foreign Legion, which occupies large barracks here.

Corralejo 🌀

Las Palmas. 🕍 6,000. 🚢 ℹ️ *Plaza de Patricio Calero, 928 86 62 35.* 🚌 *Mon & Fri.* 🎉 *Día del Carmen (16 Jul).*

This much-expanded fishing village is now (together with the Jandía peninsula) one of the island's two most important resorts. Its main attraction is a belt of glorious sand dunes stretching to the south, resembling the Sahara in places, and protected as a nature reserve. This designation arrived too late, however, to prevent the construction of two obtrusive hotels right on the beach.

The rest of the resort, mostly consisting of apartments and hotels, spills out from the town centre. The port area is lively, with busy fish restaurants and an efficient 40 minute ferry service to Lanzarote.

Offshore is the tiny Isla de los Lobos, named after the once abundant monk seals *(lobos marinos)*. Today, scuba divers, snorkellers, sport fishers and surfers claim the clear waters. Glass-bottomed cruise boats take less adventurous excursionists to the island for barbecues and swimming trips.

THE GUANCHES

When Europeans first arrived in the Canary Islands in the late 14th century, they discovered a tall, white-skinned race, who lived in caves and later in small settlements around the edges of barren lava fields. Guanche was the name of one tribe on Tenerife, but it came to be used as the European name for all the indigenous tribes on the islands, and it is the one that has remained. The origins of the Guanches are still unclear, but it is probable that they arrived on the islands in the 1st or 2nd century BC from Berber North Africa. Within 100 years of European arrival the Guanches had been subdued and virtually exterminated by the ruthless conquistadors. Very few traces of their culture remain today.

Reminders *of the Guanches can be seen in many places in the Canaries. Specimens of their mummified dead, as well as baskets and stone and bone artifacts, are on display in several museums and there are statues of chiefs in Candelaria (see p535) on Tenerife.*

Guanche bowl for preparing gofio (see p537)

A Guanche basket

Lanzarote

The easternmost and fourth largest of the Canary Islands is virtually treeless and relies on desalination plants for some of its water. Yet many visitors consider Lanzarote the most attractive of all the islands for the vivid shapes and contrasting colours of its volcanic landscapes. Despite low rainfall, carefully tended crops flourish in its black volcanic soil. Locals pride themselves on the way their island has been preserved from the worst effects of tourism; there are no garish billboards, overhead cables or high-rise buildings. Its present-day image owes much to the artist César Manrique. Touring the spectacular volcanic Timanfaya National Park is a favourite trip.

Wind turbines harnessing Lanzarote's winds for power

Playa Blanca ㉔

Las Palmas. 🏠 *4,000.* 🚌 🛥
ℹ️ *Calle El Varadero 2, 928 51 90
18.* 🎭 *Nuestra Señora del Carmen
(16 Jul).*

The fishing village origins of this resort are readily apparent around its harbour. Although it has expanded in recent years, Playa Blanca

**Las Coloradas beach near Playa
Blanca in southern Lanzarote**

remains an agreeably family-oriented place with some character. It has plenty of cafés and restaurants, shops and bars, and several large hotels. However, the buildings are well dispersed and the resort is rarely noisy at night. Visitors converge here not for nightlife or contrived entertainment, but for relaxing beach holidays. There are one or two good stretches of sand near to the town, but the most enticing lie hidden around the rocky

headlands to the east, where the clear, warm sea laps into rocky coves, and clothes seem superfluous. **Playa Papagayo** is the best known of these, but a diligent search will probably gain you one all to yourself. A four-wheel drive vehicle is advisable to negotiate the narrow, unsurfaced roads which lead to these beaches.

Parque Nacional de Timanfaya ㉕

Las Palmas Yaiza. �

 *Icona, 928 84
02 38.* 🕐 *daily.* 🖥 **www**.mma.es

From 1730–36, a series of volcanic eruptions took place on Lanzarote. Eleven villages were buried in lava, which eventually spread over 200 sq km (77 sq miles) of Lanzarote's most fertile land. Miraculously, no one was killed, though many islanders subsequently emigrated.

Today, the volcanoes that once devastated Lanzarote provide one of its most lucrative and enigmatic attractions, aptly known as the **Montañas del Fuego** (Fire Mountains). They are part of the Parque Nacional de Timanfaya, established in 1974 to protect a fascinating and important geological record. The entrance to the park lies just north of the small village of Yaiza. Here you can pause and take a 15-minute camel ride up the volcanic slopes for wonderful views across the park. Afterwards, you pay the entrance fee and drive through haunting scenery of dark, barren lava cinders topped by brooding red-black

CÉSAR MANRIQUE (1920–92)

Local hero César Manrique trained as a painter, and spent time in mainland Spain and New York before returning to Lanzarote in 1968. He campaigned for traditional and environmentally friendly development on the island for the remaining part of his life, setting strict building height limits and colour requirements. Dozens of tourist sites throughout the Canaries benefited from his talents and enthusiasm.

César Manrique in 1992

For hotels and restaurants in this region see pp599–601 and pp651–3

Camel rides from Yaiza across the Montañas de Fuego

volcano cones. Finally, you will reach **Islote de Hilario**. You can park at El Diablo panoramic restaurant. From here, buses take visitors for exhilarating 30 minute tours of the desolate, lunar-like landscapes.

Afterwards, back at Islote de Hilario, guides will provide graphic demonstrations that this volcano is not extinct but only dormant: brushwood pushed into a crevice bursts instantly into a ball of flame, while water poured into a sunken pipe shoots out in a scorching jet of steam.

The road from Yaiza to the coast leads to the **Salinas de Janubio** where salt is extracted from the sea. At **Los Hervideros** the rough coast can create spectacular seas and further north, at **El Golfo**, is an eerie emerald-coloured lagoon.

Puerto del Carmen ❷⓺

Las Palmas. 🏚 *13,700.* 🚌 🚢 ℹ️
Avenida de la Playa, 928 51 53 37.
🎊 *Nuestra Señora del Carmen (Jul).*
www.turismolanzarote.com

More than 60 per cent of Lanzarote's tourists stay in this resort, which stretches several kilometres along the seafront. The coastal road carves its way through a solid slab of holiday infrastructure: car hire offices, banks, bureaux de change, shops, bars, restaurants and discos. Behind the roadside arcades lie countless villas, apartments and hotels.

Though dense, the buildings are pleasantly designed and unoppressive. All have easy access to a long golden beach, Playa Blanca, which in places is very wide. Another beach nearby is Playa de los Pocillos. The original village lies west of the port, away from the hustle and bustle of the resort.

Fishing boat in Arrecife port

Arrecife ❷⓻

Las Palmas. 🏚 *42,200.* ✈️ 🚌 ℹ️
Blas Cabrera Felipe, 928 81 17 62.
🎊 *San Ginés (25 Aug).*

Arrecife, with its modern buildings and lively streets, is the commercial and administrative centre of the island.

Despite its modern trappings, the capital retains much of its old charm, with palm-lined promenades, a fine beach and two small forts. Only the 18th-century **Castillo de San José**, now a museum of contemporary art, is open to the public. The fort was renovated by César Manrique, and one of his paintings is on display here. An historic house, **La casa de los Arroyo**, is noted for its scientific library and is open to the public.

⚓ **La Casa de los Arroyo**
Avda Coll 3, Arrecife. *Tel 928 80 17 29.* ◻ *Mon–Fri.*

⚓ **Castillo de San José**
Puerto de Naos. *Tel 928 81 23 21.*
◻ *daily.* ● *1 Jan, 25 Dec.*

Costa Teguise ❷⓼

10 km (6 miles) north of Arrecife. 🚌
ℹ️ *Avda Islas Canarias, Centro Comercial los Charcos, local 13, 928 82 72 92.*

This resort, largely financed by a mining conglomerate, has transformed the arid, low-lying terrain north of Arrecife into an extensive cluster of timeshare accommodation, leisure clubs and luxury hotels. The contrast between old town Teguise, Lanzarote's former capital, and the exclusive, new Costa Teguise is striking. Fake greenery and suburban lamps line boulevards amid barren ashlands. White villas line a series of small sandy beaches. The high level of investment has succeeded in attracting jet-set clientele. King Juan Carlos also has a villa here.

Umbrellas on the beach, Puerto del Carmen

Iglesia de San Miguel on the main square in Teguise

Teguise ㉙

Las Palmas. 👥 11,500. 🚌 ℹ️ Plaza General Franco 1, 928 84 50 72. 🚌 Sun. 🎉 Día del Carmen (16 Jul), Las Nieves (5 Aug).

Teguise, the island's capital until 1852, is a well-kept, old-fashioned town with wide, cobbled streets and patrician houses grouped around the **Iglesia de San Miguel**. The best time to visit is on a Sunday, when there is a lively handicrafts market and folk dancing. Just outside Teguise, the castle of Santa Bárbara contains the **Museo del Emigrante Canario**, which tells the story of Canarian emigrants to South America.

Environs
To see more of inland Lanzarote, follow the central road south of Teguise, through the strange farmland of **La Geria**. Black volcanic ash has been scooped into protective, crescent-shaped pits which trap moisture to enable vines and other crops to flourish. **Mozaga**,

one of the main villages in the area, is a major centre of wine production. On the roadside near Mozaga is the *Monumento al Campesino*, Manrique's *(see p548)* striking modern sculpture dedicated to Lanzarote's farmers.

Halfway between Teguise and Arrecife is the **Fundación César Manrique**. The fascinating former home of the artist incorporates five lava caves. It contains some of his own work and his collection of contemporary art.

🏛 **Museo del Emigrante Canario**
Montaña de Guanapay. *Tel* 686 47 03 76. 🕐 Mon–Fri. 🎫

🏛 **Fundación César Manrique**
Taro de Tahíche. *Tel* 928 84 31 38. 🕐 daily. 🎫

Haría ㉚

Las Palmas. 👥 5,000. 🚌 ℹ️ Plaza de la Constitución 1, 928 83 52 51. 🚌 Sat. 🎉 San Juan (24 Jun).

Palm trees and white, cube-shaped houses distinguish this picturesque village. It acts as a gateway to excursions round the northern tip of the island. The road to the north gives memorable views over exposed cliffs, and the 609-m (2,000-ft) high Monte Corona.

Environs
From Manrique's **Mirador del Río** you can see La Graciosa, and the northernmost of the Canary Islands, Alegranza. **Orzola** is a delightful fishing village providing fish lunches as well as boat trips to La Graciosa. To the south are the Mala prickly pear plantations, where cochineal (crimson dye)

is extracted from the insects which feed on the plants. Nearby is the **Jardín de Cactus**, a well-stocked cactus garden, which has a smart restaurant, again designed by Manrique.

📷 **Mirador del Río**
Haría. *Tel* 928 17 35 36. 🕐 daily. 🎫

🌵 **Jardín de Cactus**
Guatiza. *Tel* 928 52 93 97. 🕐 daily. 🎫

Landscaped pool on top of the caves of Jameos del Agua

Jameos del Agua ㉛

Las Palmas. *Tel* 928 84 80 20. 🕐 daily. 🎫

An eruption of the Monte Corona volcano formed the Jameos del Agua lava caves on Lanzarote's northeast coast. In 1965–8, these were landscaped by César Manrique into an imaginative subterranean complex containing a restaurant, nightclub, a swimming pool edged by palm trees, and gardens of oleander and cacti. Steps lead to a shallow seawater lagoon where a rare species of blind white crab, unique to Lanzarote, glows softly in the dim light. An exhibition on volcanology and Canarian flora and fauna also deserves a look. Folk-dancing evenings are regularly held in this unusual setting.

Environs
Another popular attraction is the nearby **Cueva de los Verdes**, a tube of solidifed lava stretching 6 km (4 miles) underground. Guided tours of the caves are available.

📷 **Cueva de los Verdes**
Haría. *Tel* 928 17 32 20. 🕐 daily. 🎫

Volcanic ash swept into crescent-shaped pits for farming, La Geria

For hotels and restaurants in this region see pp599–601 and pp651–3

Volcanic Islands

The volcanic activity which formed the Canary Islands has created a variety of scenery, from distinctive lava formations to enormous volcanoes crowned by huge, gaping craters. The islands are all at different stages in their evolution. Tenerife, Lanzarote, El Hierro and La Palma are still volcanically active; dramatic displays of flames and steam can be seen in Lanzarote's Montañas de Fuego *(see p548)*. The last eruption was on La Palma in 1971.

Origin of the Islands
The Canaries are situated above faults in the earth's crust, which is always thinner under the oceans than under the continents. When magma (molten rock) rises through these cracks volcanoes are formed.

Atlantic Ocean · Transform fault · Atlas Fault · Canary Islands · Thin oceanic crust · Upper mantle · Africa · Dense lower mantle · Thick continental crust · Continental mantle between crust and earth's core

EVOLUTION OF THE CANARY ISLANDS

Fissures · Feeder dikes · Basalt lava flows · Crust · Mantle · Magma chamber

1 Lanzarote, El Hierro and La Palma *are wide, gently sloping shield volcanoes standing on the sea floor. All of them are composed of basalt formed by a hot, dense magma. The flexible crust is pressed down by the weight of the islands.*

Caldera · Shallow magma chamber

2 An explosive eruption *can empty the magma chamber, leaving the roof unsupported. This collapses under the weight of the volcano above to form a depression, or caldera, such as Las Cañadas on Tenerife. There are thick lava flows during this stage of the island's evolution.*

Sea level · Exposed solidified magma chamber

3 If eruptions cease *a volcano will be eroded by the action of the sea, and by wind and rain. Gran Canaria's main volcano is in the early stages of erosion, while the volcano on Fuerteventura has already been deeply eroded, exposing chambers of solidified magma.*

Rope lava near La Restinga, El Hierro

Pico Viejo crater, next to Mount Teide, Tenerife *(see p538)*

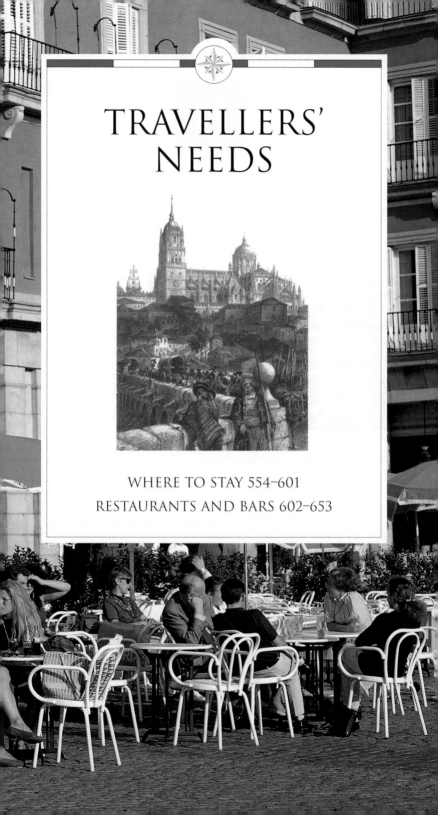

TRAVELLERS' NEEDS

WHERE TO STAY

Medieval castles turned into luxury hotels and mansions converted into youth hostels typify the variety of places to stay in Spain. The tourists who sustain Spain's economy have almost 10,000 establishments to choose from, offering around one million beds. Suites in once-royal palaces are at the top of the scale. Then there are luxury beach hotels on the

Logo for a luxury five-star hotel

Costa del Sol and in the Balearic and the Canary Islands. Visitors can also stay on remote farms, or in villas and old houses let for self-catering. For budget travel there are pensions, family-run *casas rurales* and guest houses, camp sites, and refuges with stunning views for mountaineers. Some of the best hotels in all these categories and in every style and price range are listed on pages 560–601.

Hotel de la Reconquista, Oviedo, an 18th-century mansion *(see p563)*

HOTEL GRADING AND FACILITIES

All of Spain's hotels are classified into categories and awarded stars by the country's regional tourist authorities. Hotels (indicated by an H on a blue plaque near the hotel door) are awarded from one to five stars. Hostals (Hs) and pensions (P) offer fewer comforts but are correspondingly cheaper than hotels.

Spain's star-rating system reflects the number and range of facilities available – whether the hotel has air conditioning, for instance, or a lift – rather than the quality of service.

Most hotels have restaurants that are open to non-residents. Although hotel-residencias (HR) and hostal-residencias (HsR) do not have dining rooms, some serve breakfast. Among Spain's largest hotel chains are **Grupo Sol Meliá, Grupo Riu** and **NH**. Many large tour operators book rooms in Spain's best hotels.

PARADORS

Paradors are government-run hotels, classified from three to five stars. Spain's first parador opened in the Sierra de Gredos in 1928 *(see p584)*; there is now a wide network of them on the mainland and the islands. They are located close together so that there is never more than a day's drive to the nearest one. The best are in former royal hunting lodges, monasteries, castles and other monuments; some modern paradors have been purpose-built, often in spectacular scenery or in towns of historic interest *(see pp558–9)*.

A parador is not necessarily the best hotel in town, but it can be counted on to

deliver a predictably high level of comfort. The bedrooms are usually spacious and comfortable, and are furnished in a way that varies little from parador to parador.

If you plan to tour in high season or to stay in the smaller paradors, it is wise to reserve a room. The paradors may be booked through the **Central de Reservas** in Madrid or through their London agent, **Keytel International**.

PRICES

Spanish law requires all hotel managements to display their prices behind reception and in every room. As a rule, the higher a hotel's star-rating, the more you pay. Rates for a double room can be as little as 20–25 euros a night for a cheap one-star hostal; a five-star hotel will cost more than 180 euros a night, but a room price higher than 240 euros a night is exceptional.

Prices usually vary according to room, region and season. A suite or a very spacious room, or one with a view, a balcony or other special feature, may cost more than average. Rural and suburban hotels are generally less expensive than those in the city centre.

All the prices given on pages 560–601 are based on midseason or highseason rates.

Jaén's parador, a modern extension of the medieval castle *(see p594)*

◁ *Madrileños* enjoying afternoon sunshine, drinks and conversation in the Plaza Mayor

High season covers July and August, but in some areas it runs from April to October and in the Canary Islands the winter is high season.

Many of Spain's city hotels charge especially inflated rates for their rooms during major fiestas, such as the April Fair in Seville *(see p431)*, Los Sanfermines in Pamplona *(see p132)*, Carnival in Santa Cruz de Tenerife and Easter Week *(see p38)* in many places.

Most hotels quote prices per room and meal prices per person without including VAT *(IVA)*, which is 7 per cent in most of Spain, but 5 per cent in the Canary Islands.

The glass-domed foyer of the Palace Hotel, Madrid *(see p581)*

BOOKING AND CHECK-IN

Off-season in rural or small towns you are unlikely to need to book ahead; but if you plan to travel in high season or want to stay in a particular hotel, you should reserve a room by phone, e-mail or through a travel agent. You will need to reserve if you want a special room: one with a double bed (twin beds are the norm); on the ground floor; away from a noisy main road; or a room with a view.

The resort hotels often close from autumn to spring. Before you travel, it is always advisable to check that your preferred hotels will be open at that time of year.

You will not normally be asked for a deposit when you book a hotel room. However, a deposit of 20–25 per cent

may be requested if you book during a peak period or for a stay of more than a few nights. Send it by credit card or giro in Spain and by credit card or banker's draft from outside the country. If you have to cancel, do so at least a week before the booking date or you may lose all or some of the deposit.

Most hotels will honour a booking only until 8pm unless business is poor. If you are delayed, call the hotel to assure them you are coming and to tell them when to expect you.

When you check in you will be asked for your passport or identity card to comply with Spanish police regulations. It will normally be returned to you promptly as soon as your details have been copied.

You are expected to check out of your room by noon on the last day of your stay, or to pay for another night.

PAYING

The listings on pages 560–601 indicate which hotels accept credit cards. In some large, busy hotels you may be asked to sign a blank credit card pay slip on arrival. Under Spanish law it is illegal to ask this; you should refuse.

Eurocheques are accepted in some hotels, but personal cheques are not accepted in Spanish hotels, even if backed by a cheque guarantee card or drawn on a Spanish bank. Many people pay cash in and some cheap hotels this may be the only payment accepted.

Around 1.5–2 euros is the usual tip for all hotel staff.

The pretty beach of Meliá Salinas Hotel, Lanzarote *(see p601)*

CASAS RURALES

The owners of some country houses *(casas rurales)* accept a few visitors, usually in high season. They are most numerous in Asturias, Navarra, Aragón and Catalonia (where they are called *cases de pagès*). They are becoming common in Galicia and Cantabria (where they are called *casonas*), and in Andalusia.

Casas rurales range in style from stately manor houses to small, isolated farms. Some offer bed and breakfast; some an evening meal or full board. Most are self-catering. Do not expect hotel service or a long list of facilities. You may, however, be given a friendly welcome and good home cooking, all at a very affordable price. You can book *casas rurales* directly or through regional associations, such as **RAAR** in Andalusia, **Ruralia** in Asturias, **TVR (Turismo Verde y Rural)** in Huesca, Aragón, and **Turisverd** in Catalonia.

El Nacimiento, Turre, a charming Andalusian *casa rural (see p596)*

SELF-CATERING

Villas and holiday flats let by the week are plentiful along the Spanish coasts. In scenic areas of the countryside there are many *casas rurales* (farm and village houses) for rent by the day. To obtain information about the *casas rurales*, contact their regional organizations *(see p555)*. They also take bookings. **The Individual Traveller's Spain** is a UK organization that acts as an agent for owners of holiday houses and flats in Spain, as does **Hometours International Inc.** in the US. Other organizations and owners of holiday homes advertise in the travel sections of UK Sunday newspapers. Tour operators offer a range of self-catering accommodation.

The prices for self-catering accommodation vary according to the location, the property and the season. A four-person villa with a pool can cost under 240 euros for a week if it is inland and 960 euros a week or more if it is on the coast.

An apartment hotel is a new type of accommodation; in Andalusia it is called a *villa turística*. Half hotel, half holiday flats, it gives guests a choice between self-catering (all rooms have a kitchen) or eating in the hotel restaurant. Holiday villages are similar, often catering for specialist interests. One example is the village of Ainsa in the mountain sports region of Aragón *(see p574)*, which offers a mix of camping and hostel accommodation, with restaurants and bars.

Typical holiday villas in Lanzarote's Puerto del Carmen, the Canary Islands

YOUTH HOSTELS AND MOUNTAIN REFUGES

To use the network of *albergues juveniles* (youth hostels) in Spain you need to show a YHA (Youth Hostel Association) card from your country or an international card, which you can buy from any hostel. Prices per person for bed and breakfast are lower than hotel prices.

Youth hostels can be booked directly or via the **Red Española de Albergues Juveniles** (Spanish Network of Youth Hostels). Despite the name, there is no age limit.

Mountaineers heading for the more remote areas may use the *refugios* (refuges). These are shelters with a dormitory, cooking facilities and heating. Some are huts with about six bunks; others are mountain houses with up to 50 beds.

The *refugios* are marked on large-scale maps of mountain areas and national parks and administered by the regional mountaineering associations.

The **Federación Española de Deportes de Montaña y Escalada (FEDME)** and the local tourist offices will supply their addresses.

La Oliva monastery, Navarra *(see p130)*, welcomes paying guests

MONASTERIES AND CONVENTS

If you have a taste for peace and austerity you may enjoy a night in one of Spain's 150 religious houses where guests are welcome. Most belong to the Benedictine and the Cistercian orders. Room prices are inexpensive. They are not hotels, however; you have to book ahead by writing or by phone; and few have private telephones or television. The guests may be asked to tidy their rooms, observe the same strict mealtimes as the monks or nuns and to help with the washing up. Some convents admit only women and some monasteries only men.

Youth hostel in rustic style on the edge of Cazorla nature reserve, Jaén

CAMP SITES

There are nearly 1,200 camp sites scattered across Spain. Most of them are on the coasts, but there are also some outside the major cities and in the most popular areas of countryside. Most sites have electricity and running water; some also have launderettes, playgrounds, restaurants, shops, a swimming pool and other amenities.

It is sensible to carry a camping carnet with you. This can be used instead of a passport to check in at sites and it covers you for third-party insurance. Carnets are issued in the UK by the AA, RAC and **The Camping and Caravanning Club**.

Every year, the *Guía Oficial de Campings* is published by Turespaña. Information about camp sites is available from the **Federación Española de Empresarios de Campings y Ciudades de Vacaciones**

(Spanish Camp Site and Holiday Camp Federation). In Spain, camping is only permitted on official sites.

DISABLED TRAVELLERS

Hotel managers will advise on access for people in wheelchairs, and the staff will help, but few hotels are well equipped for disabled guests, although some of the youth hostels are. **Servi-COCEMFE** (the Confederación Coordinadora Estatal de Minusválidos Físicos de España) runs a hotel in Madrid for disabled people's groups. Servi-COCEMFE and Viajes 2000 *(see p665)* advise on hotels for guests with special needs. A UK charity, Holiday Care Service, produces a fact sheet on Spain. **IHD** (International Help for the Disabled), which is based in France, will arrange transport, hotels and other help for visitors to the Costa del Sol and Mallorca.

Sign for a camp site

View from the Cabina Verónica mountain refuge, Picos de Europa

FURTHER INFORMATION

Every spring, Turespaña publishes the *Guía Oficial de Hoteles*, which is sold in Spanish bookshops and newsstands and can be consulted in Spanish tourist offices. It lists every pension, hostal and hotel in Spain and gives their star-rating, their prices and a resumé of their facilities.

Each *comunidad autónoma* distributes a list of the hotels and other accommodation in its area via the tourist offices.

DIRECTORY

HOTEL CHAINS

Grupo Riu
Tel 971 49 08 21.
Fax 971 74 38 98.
www.riuhotels.com

Grupo Sol-Meliá
Tel 902 14 44 44.
Fax 91 579 13 92.
www.solmelia.com

NH-Hoteles
Tel 91 451 97 18.
Fax 91 442 44 02.
www.nh-hotels.com

PARADORS

Central de Reservas
Calle Requena 3,
28013 Madrid.
Tel 91 516 66 66.
Fax 91 516 66 57.
www.parador.es

Keytel International
402 Edgware Road,
London W2 1ED.
Tel 020 7616 0300
in UK.
www.keytel.co.uk

SELF-CATERING AND BED AND BREAKFAST

Asociación Gallega de Turismo Rural
Recinto Ferial, Apdo 26,
Silleda 36540 Pontevedra.
Tel 986 58 00 50.
Fax 986 58 01 62.

Hometours International Inc.
1108 Scottie Lane,
Knoxville, TN 37919, USA.
@ hometours@aol.com

The Individual Traveller's Spain
Bignor, Pulborough,
West Sussex RH20 1QD.
Tel 01798 869485 in UK.

RAAR
Apartado (de Correos)
2035, 04080 Almería.
Tel 950 26 50 18.
Fax 950 27 04 31.
www.raar.es

Ruralia
C/ Marques de Canillejas
12, Bajo, 33500 Llanes
(Asturias).
Tel 902 10 70 70.
www.ruralia.com

Turisverd
Plaça Sant Josep Oriol 4,
08002 Barcelona.
Tel 93 412 69 84.
Fax 93 412 50 16.

TVR
C/ Miguel Servet 12,
22002 Huesca.
Tel 902 29 41 41.
Fax 974 24 20 61.

YOUTH HOSTELS

Red Española de Albergues Juveniles
Calle Barquillo 15A, 1° G,
28004 Madrid.
Tel 915 22 70 07.
Fax 915 22 80 67.

MOUNTAIN REFUGES

FEDME
C/ Floridablanca 84,
08015 Barcelona.
Tel 93 426 42 67.
www.fedme.es

CAMPING

The Camping and Caravanning Club
Tel 02476 694995 in UK.

Federación de Empresarios de Campings
C/ San Bernardo 97–99,
28015 Madrid.
Tel 91 448 12 34.
www.fedcamping.com

DISABLED TRAVELLERS

SATH
347 Fifth Ave, Suite 610,
New York, NY 10016
Tel 212 447 7284.
www.sath.org

Servi-COCEMFE
C/ Luis Cabrera 63,
28002 Madrid.
Tel 91 744 36 00.
Fax 91 413 19 96.

FURTHER INFORMATION

Spanish Tourist Office
Tel 020 7486 8077 in UK.
www.tourspain.co.uk

Tel 212 265-8822 in US.
www.okspain.org

Spain's Best: Paradors

Parador is an old Spanish word for a lodging place for travellers of respectable rank. In the late 1920s a national network of state-run hotels called paradors was established. Many of the nearly 90 paradors are converted castles, palaces or monasteries, although some have been purpose-built in strategic tourist locations. They are generally well signposted and the prices are comparable with other luxury hotels. All offer a high degree of comfort and service, and have restaurants which offer regional cuisine.

Hotel de los Reyes Católicos, *one of the sights of Santiago de Compostela (see p90), may be the world's oldest hotel. It was founded as a hospital in 1499 (see p562).*

Hotel de los Reyes Católicos

Parador de León *is housed in the Hostal San Marcos, one of Spain's finest Renaissance buildings (see p25). The main hall has a magnificent coffered ceiling (see p584).*

Parador de León

Parador de Guadalupe is a 16th-century former hospice for pilgrims. It stands beside a famous monastery in Extremadura *(see p589).*

Parador de Guadalupe

Parador de Arcos de la Frontera *is situated in one of the* archetypal *pueblos* blancos *(white towns). Its wide, semicircular terrace offers panoramic views of the Moorish castle, the Guadalete river and the rolling farmland beyond (see p592).*

Parador de Arcos de la Frontera

Parador de Granada

Parador de Granada *is a captivating 15th-century convent built in the beautiful gardens of the Alhambra at the instruction of the Catholic Monarchs. Antique Spanish furniture fills the halls and rooms of this atmospheric parador, and an old roofless chapel forms a patio. Advance booking is essential (see p594).*

Parador de Sigüenza, *a massive hilltop castle enclosing a large courtyard, was formerly a Visigothic, then a Moorish, fortress. It is approached from the historic town below by a steep cobbled street* (see p587).

Parador de Viella is set in the spectacular Vall d'Arán and surrounded by high peaks. There is ample opportunity for outdoor activity, from skiing to hunting and fishing *(see p574)*.

Parador de Viella

Parador de Alcañiz *is located in a castle-monastery built by the Knights of Calatrava in the 12th century. Despite its imposing size, the parador has only 12 rooms. The cloister is now a peaceful garden* (see p574).

Parador de Sigüenza

Parador de Alcañiz

| 0 kilometres | 200 |
| 0 miles | 100 |

Parador de Cuenca is housed in the converted 16th-century convent of San Pablo. It enjoys magnificent views of the attractive old town *(see p586)*.

Parador de Cuenca

Parador de Cañadas del Teide *is a recently refurbished parador situated in the Mount Teide National Park (see pp538–9) on Tenerife. From its terraces there are views of the volcanic landscape* (see p601).

THE CANARY ISLANDS

Choosing a Hotel

The hotels in this guide have been selected across a wide price range for excellent facilities and location. Many also have a highly recommended restaurant. The chart lists hotels by region, starting in the north and moving to the south. For more details on restaurants see pages 608–653.

PRICE CATEGORIES
Standard double room per night, with tax and service charge included.

€ under 75 euros
€€ 75–125 euros
€€€ 125–175 euros
€€€€ 175–225 euros
€€€€€ over 225 euros

GALICIA

A CORUÑA Ciudad de la Coruña
€€€
Juan Sebastián El Cano 13, 15002 **Tel** *981 21 21 00* **Fax** *981 22 46 10* **Rooms** *131*

Situated in the residential district of Adormideras, close to San Amaro beach, this hotel offers views of A Coruña bay. It has spacious bedrooms, meeting rooms, a gym and Jacuzzi. It also provides indoor and outdoor parking. The Torremar restaurant specializes in lobster and seafood. **www.eurostarciudaddelacoruna.com**

A ESTRADA Fonteclara
€
Sta Marina de Ribeira 6, 36685 (Pontevedra) **Tel** *986 57 32 09* **Fax** *981 36 49 99* **Rooms** *8*

A 17th-century Galician country house, peacefully located in the valley of the Río Ulla, close to both Santiago de Compostela and the Rías Baixas. This hotel offers reasonably priced bed and breakfast and the use of a sitting room with an open fireplace. The house is surrounded by an extensive garden. **www.fonteclara.rural.tripod.com**

A GUARDA Convento San Benito
€
Plaza de San Benito, 36780 (Pontevedra) **Tel** *986 61 11 66* **Fax** *986 61 15 17* **Rooms** *24*

A converted 16th-century convent, where the nuns' cells, surrounding a small cloister with a palm tree and a stone fountain, have been transformed into bedrooms for the guests. Two rooms have their own sitting rooms and two their own terraces; there is also a suite. All rooms have Internet access. **www.conventosanbenito.com**

BAIONA Pazo de Mendoza
€€
C/ Elduayen 1, 36300 (Pontevedra) **Tel** *986 38 50 14* **Fax** *986 38 59 88* **Rooms** *11*

This 18th-century town house on the seafront is close to the beach and Baiona's shops. The former residence of the dean of Santiago de Compostela, it was converted into a hotel in 1998. The restaurant serves "New Galician" cuisine. Its cafeteria, with a variety of imported coffees, has tables set out on the Paseo Maritimo. **www.pazodemendoza.es**

BAIONA Parador de Baiona
€€€
C/ Castillo Monterreal, 36300 (Pontevedra) **Tel** *986 35 50 00* **Fax** *986 35 50 76* **Rooms** *122*

This parador, built in an old Galician *pazo* (manor house) style, is located within the walls of Monterreal castle *(see p96)*. The restaurant serves seafood accompanied by the local Ribeiro wine. Some rooms have four-poster beds and offer sea views, while others look out onto the gardens. **www.parador.es**

BARREIROS Casa do Merlo
€€
C/ Sargendez 4, 27793 (Lugo) **Tel** *982 13 49 06* **Fax** *982 13 49 07* **Rooms** *10*

A walled 17th-century country *pazo* in a small coastal village. The decoration is reminiscent of English colonial style and the rooms are bright; some have sea views. Breakfast is served in a winter garden with tropical plants. There is also an inner patio and several public rooms, including a library and a games room. **www.casadomerlo.com**

BENTRACES Pazo Bentraces
€€€
Ctra 540, Celanobas km 7/ Bentraces Bardabás, 32890 (Ourense) **Tel** *988 38 33 81* **Fax** *988 38 30 35* **Rooms** *7*

This 15th-century *pazo*, a short way southwest of Ourense city, was transformed into a palace by an aristocratic Portuguese family. It has since been totally refurbished keeping the original features of wood and marble and part of the family's furniture. Its restaurant has received a one-star Michelin rating. **www.pazodebentraces.com**

BRIÓN Casa Rosalía
€
Soixgrexa 19 Os Anxeles Brion, 15280 (A Coruña) **Tel** *981 88 75 80* **Fax** *981 88 75 57* **Rooms** *30*

A country house hotel, stone-built and surrounding a cloister, and named after the "national" poetess of Galicia. It offers simple accommodation 25 km (16 miles) from the coast and Santiago de Compostela. Has a restaurant which offers special "gourmet days". A fire is lit in the sitting room in winter. **www.hotelcasarosalia.com**

CAMBADOS Parador de Cambados
€€€
Paseo de la Calzada, 36630 (Pontevedra) **Tel** *986 54 22 50* **Fax** *986 54 20 68* **Rooms** *58*

Sited in the middle of the Rías Baixas coast, this parador occupies a handsome *pazo* built around a large courtyard garden, surrounding a fountain where drinks are served. Within easy reach of beaches and pleasant places to walk. Galician specialities and local wines (Cambados is a production centre) are served in the restaurant. **www.parador.es**

Key to Symbols *see back cover flap*

CERVO Pousada O'Almacen

Ctra de Sargadelos 2, 27891 (Lugo) **Tel** *982 55 78 36* **Fax** *982 55 78 94* **Rooms** *7*

A restored 18th-century building on the north coast of Galicia. Once an *almacén* (food store) for neighbouring hamlets, it is now run by a family as a homely rural hotel. O'Almacen makes a good base for walking or horse riding, or from which to discover the lesser known parts of Galicia. The best bedrooms look on to the Río Xunco.

CORNIDE Casa Grande de Cornide

Calo, Teo, 15886 (A Coruña) **Tel** *981 80 55 99* **Fax** *981 80 57 51* **Rooms** *10*

A welcoming small bed-and-breakfast hotel in a renovated house, 10 minutes by car from Santiago de Compostela. It is beautifully decorated with antiques and has a library and a garden with two traditional *hórreos* (granaries), a grand old magnolia and an 18th-century dovecote. Selection of international wines. **www.casagrandedecornide.com**

MIÑO Casa Grande Fontao

C/ Fontao 1A, 15639 (A Coruña) **Tel** *981 78 27 72* **Fax** *981 78 27 17* **Rooms** *7*

A traditional Galician stone and whitewashed country house built in the 17th century with a bay window that overlooks the garden and fields. The interior is welcoming and warm and has a well-equipped library. The bedrooms are decorated in white with traditional furniture and have comfortable beds. **www.casagrandefontao.com**

NOIA Pesqueria del Tambre

Central del Tambre, Santa Maria Roo, 15211 (A Coruña) **Tel** *981 05 16 20* **Fax** *981 05 16 29* **Rooms** *16*

On the bank of Río Tambre, and surrounded by a wonderful forest, this is a place to get lost in nature. The main building was a hydroelectric plant built in the early 20th century. The bedrooms, elegantly restored and decorated using traditional fabrics, are in a group of houses near the river. **www.pesqueriadeltambre.com**

O GROVE Gran Hotel de la Toja

Isla de la Toja, 36991 (Pontevedra) **Tel** *986 73 00 25* **Fax** *986 73 00 26* **Rooms** *199*

This majestic hotel, built at the turn of the 19th century, stands on its own small island planted with palm and pine trees, and is reached from the mainland by a bridge. It has an old-fashioned feel to it with a ballroom and a piano bar. Offers lovely sea views, and has good beaches nearby. It also has a spa. **www.latojagranhotel.com**

O SAVIÑAO Torre Vilariño

C/ Fión 47, 27548 (Lugo) **Tel** *982 45 22 60* **Fax** *982 45 22 60* **Rooms** *9*

A 17th-century inn converted into a hotel offering bed and breakfast, mainly to tourists following Galicia's "Romanesque Route". The owners serve home-made food and wine. In the large garden populated by peacocks, pheasants and geese, is a box tree over 700 years old. Bicycles are available for touring. **www.torrevilarino.com**

POBRA DE TRIVES Casa Grande de Trives

C/ Marqués de Trives 17, 32780 (Ourense) **Tel** *988 33 20 66* **Fax** *988 33 20 66* **Rooms** *9*

A *posada* (small hotel) in an 18th-century stone manor, with a coat of arms on its central tower, in the hills of eastern Galicia. Antiques and old paintings decorate the cosy interior. There is a chapel with a magnificent reredos. Also has three sitting rooms and a garden in which to relax. Serves breakfast only. **www.casagrandetrives.com**

POBRA DE TRIVES Pazo A Freiría

C/ A Freiría, 32780 (Ourense) **Tel** *988 33 70 86* **Fax** *988 33 70 86* **Rooms** *7*

Beautifully located in hills and surrounded by chestnut forests, this old stone *pazo* was originally a 12th-century monastery. It has been restored respecting the unique structure which incorporates exposed stone, ancient chestnut timbers and wrought iron details. One of the rooms is a suite with magnificent views. **www.pazoafreiria.com**

PONTEVEDRA Parador de Pontevedra

Rua del Barón 19, 36002 **Tel** *986 85 58 00* **Fax** *986 85 21 95* **Rooms** *47*

A parador in a 16–18th-century Renaissance palace, which was once a school, granary, masonic lodge and an aristocratic residence. The decor incorporates antiques, gilt mirrors, chandeliers and tapestries. Some rooms are in a new wing. The restaurant specializes in seafood of the Rías Baixas. **www.parador.es**

RIBADEO Casa de Doñano

Vilela (Cubelas), 27714 (Lugo) **Tel** *982 13 74 29* **Fax** *982 13 48 00* **Rooms** *9*

This country house, built in 1907, has since been converted into a homely hotel surrounded by its own land. There is a large public area downstairs, and the library, which offers fine views from its windows, has telescopes for star gazing. Two rooms have double beds. One room is suitable for disabled guests. Breakfast included. **www.casadonano.com**

RIBADUMIA Pazo Carrasqueira

C/ Carrasqueira, 36638 (Pontevedra) **Tel** *986 71 00 32* **Fax** *986 71 00 32* **Rooms** *9*

A thick-walled 18th-century country mansion, with a stone staircase outside and a coat of arms set into its façade. Some of the bedrooms are cosy and have heating, TV and Internet. Seafood and Albariño wine (produced on the estate) are served in the dining room. Also has a laundry service and a library. **www.pazocarrasqueira.com**

SAN PEDRO DE VIANA Pazo As Casas

Chantada, 27513 (Lugo) **Tel** *982 17 15 12* **Fax** *982 44 05 53* **Rooms** *12*

A restored 17th-century house north of Ourense, eclectically decorated with original heavy furniture of dark wood and exposed stone. It has a pleasant terrace for relaxing in the summer. All the bedrooms are distinctly styled with brilliant white and have baths, TV and heating. The salon doubles as a library. **www.pazoascasas.com**

SANTIAGO DE COMPOSTELA As Artes €€

Trav de Dos Puertas 2, 15707 (A Coruña) **Tel** *981 555 254* **Fax** *981 577 823* **Rooms** *7*

Each room in this comfortable small hotel, close to the cathedral, is dedicated to one of the arts: theatre, sculpture, dance, architecture, painting, music or cinema. The place is decorated with flair, incorporating parquet floors and wrought-iron beds. A small cafeteria offers breakfast. Hospitable and friendly owners. **www.asartes.com**

SANTIAGO DE COMPOSTELA Pazo Cibrán €€

San Xulian de Sales, Vedra, 15885 (A Coruña) **Tel** *981 51 15 15* **Fax** *981 81 47 66* **Rooms** *11*

This noble house, with its own chapel, is situated in a very peaceful hamlet a short way from Santiago de Compostela. It has belonged to the same family since the 18th century and has been lovingly restored, keeping original antiques and furniture. It also has a library. Lunch is not served but the breakfast is particularly good.

SANTIAGO DE COMPOSTELA Hesperia Compostela €€€

C/ Horreo 1, 15702 (A Coruña) **Tel** *981 58 57 00* **Fax** *981 58 52 90* **Rooms** *99*

A hotel in an imposing renovated historic building on the Plaza de Galicia sporting a crest of arms on the corner of its tower. The interior decoration is modern, and some rooms have four-poster beds. There is a bar and a restaurant, TV, heating and laundry service. Internet and meeting rooms are available as well. **www.hesperia-compostela.com**

SANTIAGO DE COMPOSTELA Parador Hostal Dos Reis Catolicos €€€€

Praza do Obradoiro 1, 15705 (A Coruña) **Tel** *981 58 22 00* **Fax** *981 56 30 94* **Rooms** *137*

Built under the Catholic monarchs as a hostel for poor pilgrims, this luxurious 16th-century parador, on the same square as Santiago de Compostela's famous cathedral, is one of the world's grandest hotels. It is built around four arcaded courtyards with fountains. The public rooms have regal touches such as hanging tapestries. **www.parador.es**

TUI Parador de Tui €€€

Av de Portugal, 36700 (Pontevedra) **Tel** *986 60 03 09* **Fax** *986 60 21 63* **Rooms** *32*

This pretty parador is a perfect replica of a traditional Galician *pazo* combining granite with chestnut beams. The public and guest rooms have superb views of the town of Tui and across the Río Miño, which forms the frontier with Portugal. It has a lovely garden. Dishes on the menu include baby eels and scallops. **www.parador.es**

VILAGARCIA DE AROUSA Pazo O'Rial €€

C/ El Rial 1, 36600 (Pontevedra) **Tel** *986 50 70 11* **Fax** *986 50 16 76* **Rooms** *60*

A beautiful 17th-century manor with a tower, tiled floors, stone walls and arches, just outside Vilagarcía de Arousa and a walk away from the seashore. It is stylishly decorated with fine furnishings and comfortable armchairs, and has its own chapel. There are four lounges-cum-reception-rooms, one with a massive old fireplace. **www.pazorial.com**

VILALBA Parador de Vilalba €€

Valeriano Valdesuso, 27800 (Lugo) **Tel** *982 51 00 11* **Fax** *982 51 00 90* **Rooms** *48*

Six rooms of this hotel are found in a medieval octagonal tower which was built between the 11th and 13th centuries and restored in the 15th century. Other rooms as well as the bar and restaurant are in a modern stone building beside it. The castle preserves its moat and portcullis. Facilities include a gym, sauna and Turkish bath. **www.parador.es**

ASTURIAS AND CANTABRIA

CALAMEÑO El Jisu €

Ctra Potes–Camaleño, 39587 (Cantabria) **Tel** *942 73 30 38* **Fax** *942 73 03 15* **Rooms** *8*

A modern, purpose-built chalet hotel in the heart of the Picos de Europa *(see p108–9)*. It stands in its own grounds in the Liébana Valley, on the road up to Fuente Dé, close to Liébana monastery. El Jisu enjoys great views of the mountains and makes a good base for walking or exploring the Picos by car. The sitting rooms are decorated with antiques.

CANGAS DE ONIS Aultre Naray €€

Peruyes, 33547 (Asturias) **Tel** *985 84 08 08* **Fax** *985 84 08 48* **Rooms** *10*

This country hotel, in a renovated 19th-century Asturian house, has superb views of the mountains of the Sierra de Escapa and the Picos de Europa from the first floor bedrooms. The second floor has cosy attic rooms. The sitting room has a warm atmosphere and big windows. Also has a library with a fireplace and a bar. **www.aultrenaray.com**

CANGAS DE ONIS Parador de Cangas de Onis €€€

Villanueva (km 2 from Cangas), 33550 (Asturias) **Tel** *985 84 94 02* **Fax** *985 84 95 20* **Rooms** *64*

A restored 12th-century Benedictine monastery with magnificent cloisters, located on the bank of the Río Sellar just outside the town of Cangas de Onis. The rooms are spacious and comfortable, and the restaurant serves regional dishes. Includes facilities such as meeting rooms, gym, sauna and a swimming pool. **www.parador.es**

CARAVIA El Babú €€

Carrales, 33343 (Asturias) **Tel** *985 85 32 72* **Fax** *985 85 32 73* **Rooms** *7*

A small and intimate hotel in an 19th-century country house, which has been renovated and decorated in modern style using muted, neutral colours. The rooms have mountain or garden views: the cosiest ones are in the attic. A filling breakfast is served. The hotel has ample grounds to walk around. Also has a library and a bar. **www.elbabu.com**

Key to Price Guide *see p560* **Key to Symbols** *see back cover flap*

CASTROPOL Palacete Peñalba

C/ Granda, Figueras del Mar, 33794 (Asturias) **Tel** *985 63 61 25* **Fax** *985 63 62 47* **Rooms** *23*

Made up of two beautiful Art Nouveau mansions, the Palacete Cotalerelo and the Palacete Granada, this hotel is near the Ria de Eo. The Granada is a magnificent fantasy, with a façade of oval windows and two curved staircases to the front door. Inside it has much of its original furniture. **www.hotelpalacetepenalba.com**

COLOMBRES La Casona de Villanueva

La Casona, 33590 (Asturias) **Tel** *985 41 25 90* **Fax** *985 41 25 14* **Rooms** *8*

An 18th-century village house restored in traditional style and dotted with antiques and works of art. It is well located for visits either to the Picos de Europa or to the beaches of the Asturian coast. They serve home-made jams at breakfast, and have a wine celler and private parking. **www.lacasonadevillanueva.com**

COMILLAS Casal del Castro

C/ San Jerónimo, 39520 (Cantabria) **Tel** *942 72 00 36* **Fax** *942 72 00 61* **Rooms** *43*

Casal del Castro is a large, 17th-century house furnished with antiques. On a hill on the edge of the town, it is known for its charmingly mixed collection of early 20th-century aristocratic architecture. There is a restaurant, cafeteria and a garden. It is not far from Comillas' excellent beaches which have fine sand and clear water.

ESCALANTE (CANTABRIA) San Román de Escalante

Ctra Escalante–Castillo km 2, 39795 (Cantabria) **Tel** *942 67 77 45* **Fax** *942 67 76 43* **Rooms** *16*

A Relais et Châteaux hotel in an exquisitely decorated 17th-century manor house overlooking trees and meadows. All the rooms are different, and one of them has a terrace. An indoor swimming pool, horse riding, water-skiing and golf are also available. The restaurant has an impressive wine list. **www.sanromandeescalante.com**

FUENTE DE (CANTABRIA) Parador de Fuente Dé

Ctra Fuente Dé, a 3.5 km de Espinama, 39588 (Cantabria) **Tel** *942 73 66 51* **Fax** *942 73 66 54* **Rooms** *78*

This modern parador stands in an unbeatably dramatic location in the rock amphitheatre of Fuente Dé, at the foot of the Picos de Europa cable car. It has pleasant bedrooms and long galleries with huge windows. There is only one road in and out, so it is peaceful at night. This hotel makes an ideal base for walking. **www.parador.es**

GIJÓN La Casona de Jovellanos

Plazuela de Jovellanos 1, 33201 (Asturias) **Tel** *985 34 20 24* **Fax** *985 35 61 51* **Rooms** *13*

A small hotel in an 18th-century building overlooking a little square in the old part of the city, near San Lorenzo beach. One of its two dining rooms incorporates the remains of the old city wall which was discovered during restoration work. A five person aparthotel is also available. **www.lacasonadejovellanos.com**

GIJÓN Parador de Gijón

Parque de Isabel la Católica, 33203 (Asturias) **Tel** *985 37 05 11* **Fax** *985 37 02 33* **Rooms** *40*

A parador in a converted 18th-century watermill, located in a corner of what has been described as one of Spain's prettiest parks. The old watercourse in the grounds has been preserved. The speciality of the restaurant is the regional stew, *fabada Asturiana*, but choice seafood is also served. **www.parador.es**

LIÉRGANES Balneario de Liérganes

C/ J.A. Primo de Rivera, 39722 (Cantabria) **Tel/Fax** *942 52 80 11* **Rooms** *50*

This 20th-century mountain house, now a spa hotel near the Río Miera, still has many of its original features. It has a covered heated swimming pool and offers various beauty treatments at extra cost. The restaurant serves regional Cantabrian cuisine. Liérganes is also close to Santillana del Mar *(see p112)*. **www.relaistermal.com**

LLANES La Posada de Babel

La Pereda, 33509 (Asturias) **Tel** *985 40 25 25* **Fax** *985 40 26 22* **Rooms** *12*

The spectacular Picos de Europa peaks lie behind this small, family-run hotel. It is partly modern, but has huge, traditional fireplaces and one bedroom is a converted *hórreo* (granary). It has a modern suite, recently built, in the garden. Also has a small library and a bar. Tango lessons are available. **www.laposadadebabel.com**

MOLLEDA, VAL DE SAN VICENTE Casona de Molleda

Barrio la Fuente 7, 39569 (Cantabria) **Tel** *942 71 95 67* **Fax** *942 71 95 79* **Rooms** *11*

A renovated village house decorated in warm colours and using lots of textiles. The bedrooms are spacious and some have sitting areas with relaxing views of the Río Deva and the mountains. The hotel is suitably located close to the Picos de Europa. Most rooms have a lounge separate from the bedroom.

OVIEDO Hotel de la Reconquista

C/ Gil de Jaz 16, 33004 (Asturias) **Tel** *985 24 11 00* **Fax** *985 24 11 66* **Rooms** *142*

A luxury hotel in a magnificent 18th-century building, originally an orphanage, with a massive stone coat of arms above the main entrance. Its name commemorates the Reconquest of Spain which was launched from Asturias. The public rooms are arranged around several courtyards. **www.hoteldelareconquista.com**

PECHÓN Don Pablo

C/ El Cruce, 39594 (Cantabria) **Tel** *942 71 95 00* **Fax** *942 71 95 23* **Rooms** *34*

Three houses joined together make up this family-run rural hotel along the coast from San Vicente de la Barquera, which is close to the sea and the Picos de Europa. The rooms are cosy, with old beams of oak and chestnut, and have marble bathrooms. The hotel also has large sitting rooms and pretty terraces. **www.donpablohotel.com**

PRAVIA Casa del Busto   🍴   €€

Plaza del Rey Don Silo 1, 33120 (Asturias) **Tel** *985 82 27 71* **Fax** *985 82 27 72* **Rooms** *30*

In a town 10 km (6 miles) from the beaches of the Asturian coast, is this hotel in a 16th-century house which has the feel of a South American hacienda. The bedrooms overlook a central patio. The hotel is decorated with period pieces and the owners run courses on furniture restoration. An Asturian breakfast buffet is served. **www.hotelbusto.com**

QUIJAS Casona Torre de Quijas   🍴   €€

Barrio Vinueva 76, 39590 (Cantabria) **Tel** *942 82 06 45* **Fax** *942 83 82 55* **Rooms** *22*

This hotel is in a restored, 19th-century stone house near Santillana del Mar. It has wood-framed bay windows and a large garden, and is decorated with Art Nouveau furniture. There are some attic rooms, a sitting room with a library and two rooms have disabled access. The restaurant offers only light dinners. **www.casonatorredequijas.com**

QUIJAS Hostería de Quijas   🍴🛏   €€

Barrio Vinueva, 39590 (Cantabria) **Tel** *942 82 08 33* **Fax** *942 83 80 50* **Rooms** *19*

A family-run hotel in an 18th-century stone-built mansion on the Santander–Oviedo road, close to Santillana del Mar and the Altamira caves. It has bay windows, timbered ceilings and a garden. Six of the rooms are suites. The menu is strong on seafood, and breakfast can be served outdoors. Closed 20 Dec–15 Jan. **www.hosteriadequijas.com**

RIBADEDEVA Mirador de la Franca   🍴🎿   €€

Playa de la Franca, 33590 (Asturias) **Tel** *985 41 21 45* **Fax** *985 41 21 53* **Rooms** *61*

A beach hotel, popular with families, with spacious sitting areas, a tennis court and great views from the lounge and restaurant. The waters of the bay are safe for water sports and underwater fishing. It has a three-nights' minimum stay policy in the spring and five-nights in July and August. Close to the Picos de Europa. **www.hotelmirador.com**

RIBADESELLA Gran Hotel del Sella   🛏🍴🛏   €€€

Ricardo Cangas 17, 33560 (Asturias) **Tel** *985 86 01 50* **Fax** *985 85 74 49* **Rooms** *89*

The former summer palace of the Marquis of Argüelles is dwarfed by the new hotel wing, but it still lends this family-run beach hotel some class. It is sited at the mouth of the Río Sella, on Santa Marina beach. It has a pool, tennis courts and vast gardens. Four of the rooms are suites. The restaurant specializes in seafood. **www.granhoteldelsella.com**

SAN VICENTE DE TORANZO Posada del Pas   🍴🛏   €

Ctra N623 Burgos–Santander, 39699 (Cantabria) **Tel** *942 59 44 11* **Fax** *942 59 43 86* **Rooms** *32*

An 18th-century stone mountain house standing in a green valley beside the Santander–Burgos road, which is used as a stopover by travellers arriving or departing on the ferry between Plymouth and Santander. The restaurant specializes in regional Cantabrian dishes. **www.hotelposadadelpas.com**

SANTANDER Las Brisas   €€

La Braña 14, El Sardinero, 39005 (Cantabria) **Tel** *942 27 50 11* **Fax** *942 28 11 73* **Rooms** *13*

A recently-refurbished homely hotel in an early 20th-century white turret-shaped villa, close to the popular Sardinero beach. Each room is different with floral fabrics predominating. Breakfast, included in the price, can be served on a seaside terrace. The hotel also has five self-catering apartments. **www.hotellasbrisas.net**

SANTANDER Hotel Real   🛏🍴📺🛏   €€€€€

Paseo Pérez Galdós 28, 39005 (Cantabria) **Tel** *942 27 25 50* **Fax** *942 27 45 73* **Rooms** *123*

An elegant, formal hotel visible on the city's highest hill. It was built in the early 20th century for nobility accompanying the royal family on holiday. Its chandeliers and moulded plaster still testify to its status. The balconies offer spectacular views of the bay, especially those on the top floor. The hotel has its own spa. **www.hotelreal.es**

SANTILLANA DEL MAR Los Infantes   🍴   €

Avda Le Dorat 1, 39330 (Cantabria) **Tel** *942 81 81 00* **Fax** *942 84 01 03* **Rooms** *88*

The 18th-century country mansion, comprising three buildings, houses this hotel that was formerly the residence of the Calderons family. It is just outside the town centre, set slightly back from the road. The massive beams, stone floors, carved chests and leather armchairs in the lobby give it an old-fashioned feel. **www.grupolosonfantes.com**

SANTILLANA DEL MAR Altamira   🍴   €€

C/ Cantón 1, 39330 (Cantabria) **Tel** *942 81 80 25* **Fax** *942 84 01 36* **Rooms** *32*

A town-centre hotel in a restored 16th-century palace very close to the Romanesque church of La Colegiata. The old wooden staircase leads to bedrooms with beams and polished floors, two of them with private sitting rooms. Also well located for the visitor centre of the famous caves after which the hotel is named. **www.hotelaltamira.com**

SANTILLANA DEL MAR Parador Gil Blas   🛏🍴🛏   €€€

Plaza Ramón Pelayo 11, 39330 (Cantabria) **Tel** *942 02 80 28* **Fax** *942 81 83 91* **Rooms** *28*

This stone mansion, begun in the 15th century, blends perfectly into the unspoiled medieval town, which is busy with tourists during the day but quiet at night. The building has a pretty patio. Inside bare walls and tiled floors enhance the medieval atmosphere. Rooms are spacious and tastefully decorated. **www.parador.es**

SOLARES Hosteria Palacio de los Marqueses de Valbuena   🍴   €€

General Mola 6, 39710 **Tel** *942 52 28 66* **Fax** *942 52 21 76* **Rooms** *27*

A late 17th-century Baroque mansion with imposing façade and its own chapel, built by the Inquisitor General of Spain. It is conveniently located for an overnight stop, just off the Bilbao–Santander motorway. The public rooms are spacious and the bedrooms comfortable. It has a cafeteria and a restaurant. **www.marquesesdevalbuena.com**

Key to Price Guide *see p560* **Key to Symbols** *see back cover flap*

TARAMUNDI La Rectoral ⬛ €€€

Taramundi, 33775 (Asturias) **Tel** *985 64 67 60* **Fax** *985 64 67 77* **Rooms** *18*

An 18th-century former priest's house, built of stone and timber with a slate roof, deep in the Asturian countryside. It has been tastefully converted into a quiet and atmospheric hotel. All the bedrooms have views of the surrounding mountains. An alternative to the main house are some cottages with room service. **www.larectoral.com**

VILLACARRIEDO Palacio Soñanes 🔲⬛🏊 €€€

Barrio del Quintanal 1, 39640 (Cantabria) **Tel** *942 59 06 00* **Fax** *942 59 06 14* **Rooms** *30*

An imposing 18th-century Baroque palace of beautiful golden stone that dominates this quiet rural town. Inside, it has a superb Renaissance main staircase. The bedrooms are very comfortable, all different, and decorated in a rich variety of colours. The verdant Valle de la Pas is a good area for gentle walking. **www.palaciodevillacarriedo.com**

THE BASQUE COUNTRY, NAVARRA AND LA RIOJA

ANGUIANO Abadía de Valvanera ⬛ €

Monasterio de Valvanera, 26323 (La Rioja) **Tel** *941 37 70 44* **Fax** *941 37 71 94* **Rooms** *27*

This old Benedictine abbey with simple rooms offers no-frills accommodation, good food and lots of history. Queen Isabel I stayed in the cells here in 1482. It is located in the beautiful surroundings of one of Spain's least-known range of hills, the Sierra de la Demanda, in a town which holds a stilt-dancing festival. **www.abadiavalvanera.com**

ARGOMÁNIZ Parador de Argomániz 🔲⬛ €€

Ctra Nal Madrid-Irún km 363, 01192 (Alava) **Tel** *945 29 32 00* **Fax** *945 29 32 87* **Rooms** *53*

Sited in a splendid 17th-century Renaisance stone palace, complete with coat of arms, this parador is located on the slopes of Mount Zabalgaña, just outside Vitoria. It is a peaceful spot with good views. The common areas are spacious and rooms tastefully decorated. Basque cuisine is served in the dining room. **www.parador.es**

ARNEDILLO Hospedería Las Pedrolas 🔲▤ €

Plaza Felix Merino 16, 26589 (Arnedillo) **Tel** *941 39 44 01* **Fax** *941 39 44 04* **Rooms** *7*

A 16th-century whitewashed Gothic town house with a coat of arms set into the façade. It has been restored and decorated simply but elegantly in clear tones. There is an inner patio with a fountain and flowers. The bedrooms are spacious and comfortable. The only noise to disturb you will be the bells of the church next door. **www.rusticae.es**

AXPE-ATXONDO Mendi Goikoa ⬛ €€

Barrio de San Juan 33, 48292 (Vizcaya) **Tel** *946 82 08 33* **Fax** *946 82 11 36* **Rooms** *12*

Ancient twin stone-built Basque farmhouses, lovingly converted into a pleasant rural hotel and restaurant, in the peaceful heart of the Valle de Atxondo in the hills southeast of Durango. The hotel's slogan is "where you can hear the silence". Ideal for relaxing or taking gentle strolls. One of the rooms has a balcony. **www.mendigoikoa.com**

BAKIO Hostería del Señorío de Bizkaia ⬛ €

José María Cirarda 4, 48130 (Vizcaya) **Tel** *946 19 47 25* **Fax** *946 19 47 25* **Rooms** *16*

A stone building with wooden balconies houses this hotel in the resort of Bakio on the Basque coast not far from Bilbao. In summer, concerts are held in the garden. Guests can play the local racket game of pelota, take a guided tour or visit the nearby beach. The restaurant serves typical Basque cuisine. **www.hosteriasreales.com**

BERUETE Peruskenea ⬛▤ €€

Diseminado, Beruete (Basaburua Mayor), 31866 (Navarra) **Tel** *948 50 33 70* **Fax** *948 50 32 84* **Rooms** *9*

An "enchanted house" in which all the bedrooms are named after local fairies or nature spirits. Peruskenea is located in the heart of the Beruete forest between Pamplona and San Sebastián, where there are walking trails to dolmens and craft workshops. The restaurant prepares deliciously creative dishes. **www.peruskenea.com**

BILBAO Iturrienea Ostatua €

Santa Maria 14, 48005 (Vicaya) **Tel** *944 16 15 00* **Fax** *944 15 89 29* **Rooms** *21*

A small hotel occupying the first and second floors of an old house in the lively old quarter of the city centre, the Casco Viejo – ideal for bar hopping. It is clean and welcoming, combining rustic decorations with some modern flourishes in its large bedrooms. Street-facing rooms, however, catch the noise from below.

BILBAO Ercilla 🔲⬛🏊📺▤ €€€

Ercilla 37–9, 48011 (Vicaya) **Tel** *944 70 57 00* **Fax** *944 43 93 35* **Rooms** *354*

Bilbao's largest hotel, a modern tower block in the main business district, is close to the Plaza Moyúa. It is comfortable and bustling with life, and has a well-known restaurant, the Bermeo. There is also a bar, a coffee shop and a nightclub. Secretarial and baby-sitting services available. All rooms have wireless Internet. **www.hotelercilla.es**

BILBAO Carlton 🔲⬛📺▤ €€€€

Plaza Federico Moyúa 2, 48009 (Vicaya) **Tel** *944 16 22 00* **Fax** *944 16 46 28* **Rooms** *144*

This luxury hotel, with a domed stained-glass ceiling, is one of the landmarks of Bilbao. Built in 1919, it was formerly the seat of the Basque government. Kings, opera singers, poets and celebrities (including Einstein and Pierce Brosnan) have stayed here. Bedrooms are decorated in classical style. Disabled access **www.aranzazu-hoteles.com**

BILBAO Mirohotel
Alameda Mazarredo 77, 48009 (Vicaya) **Tel** *946 61 18 80* **Fax** *944 25 51 82* **Rooms** *50*

This glass-fronted boutique hotel designed by Antonio Miró, located between the Guggenheim and Fine Arts Museums, also has its own art collection. Facilities include a library, a gym and a spa. The bar, which hosts jazz or other live music some evenings, acts as a meeting point for art lovers. **www.mirohotelbilbao.com**

BRIÑAS Hospedería Señorío de Briñas
Travesia de la Calle Real 3, 26290 (La Rioja) **Tel** *941 30 42 24* **Fax** *941 30 43 45* **Rooms** *14*

Beautifully restored 18th-century palace just outside the wine town of Haro, which was used during the Spanish Civil War as barracks for Italian troops. It is decorated with antiques, frescoes and works of art by a Polish artist. The bedrooms are spacious and colourful. Close to La Rioja, the Basque Country and Burgos. **www.hotelesconencanto.org**

CASALARREINA Hospedería Señorío de Casalarreina
Plaza Sto Domingo de Guzmán 6, 26230 (La Rioja) **Tel** *941 32 47 30* **Fax** *941 32 47 31* **Rooms** *15*

This austere but welcoming 16th-century Plateresque monastery has been refurbished, retaining old architectural elements. Some innovative touches have been added to create a warm, elegant and cosy atmosphere. Bedrooms are big and well equipped, and all the bathrooms have hydromassage baths. **www.hotelesconencanto.org**

DONAMARIA Donamaria'ko Benta
Barrio Ventas 4, 31750 (Navarra) **Tel** *948 45 07 08* **Fax** *948 45 07 08* **Rooms** *5*

This is a small, family-run hotel in a stone-built Pyrenean mountain house north of Pamplona. Close to the Señorío de Bertiz, this is a good base for walking. The proprietors create a pleasant atmosphere in both the restaurant and the antique-furnished rooms, which are in an annexe. Cookery courses are also held. **www.donamariako.com**

FITERO Gustavo Adolfo Bécquer
Baños de Fitero, Extramuros, 31593 (Navarra) **Tel** *948 77 61 00* **Fax** *948 77 62 25* **Rooms** *205*

One of two hotels on the site of the Roman baths south of Navarra, the hotel is named after the Spanish poet who supposedly recovered from ill health here in the 19th century and was inspired to write two poems. It has a thermal spring in the basement providing spa bathing, massage and a range of other treatments. **www.fitero.com/balneario**

HARO Los Agustinos
C/ San Agustín 2, 26200 (La Rioja) **Tel** *941 31 15 62* **Fax** *941 30 31 48* **Rooms** *62*

A lounge in a vast, arched chamber hung with tapestries is one of the highlights of this hotel in a former Augustinian monastery. Another is the grand central patio in the old cloister. In the middle of La Rioja's main wine town, the in-house restaurant, El Campanario, serves good Basque and Riojan dishes. **www.aranzazu-hoteles.com**

HONDARRIBIA Pampinot
Kalea Nagusia 5, 20280 (Guipúzcoa) **Tel** *943 64 06 00* **Fax** *943 64 51 28* **Rooms** *8*

An atmosphere of warmth and elegance is achieved by the team of women who run this hotel in a 16th-century palace, which has been declared a historic national monument. It is located in the heart of old Hondarribia. The ceilings of the bedrooms are hand painted with images of angels, birds and clouds. **www.hotelpampinot.com**

HONDARRIBIA Parador de Hondarribia
Plaza de Armas 14, 20280 (Guipúzcoa) **Tel** *943 64 55 00* **Fax** *943 64 21 53* **Rooms** *36*

An elegant parador in a 10th-century restored fortress that occupies the highest point of this historic town. It has a beautiful inner patio incorporating a ruined part of the castle and a terrace overlooking the Bidasoa estuary. Weapons and other memorabilia of its colourful history adorn the walls of the public rooms. **www.parador.es**

LAGUARDIA Castillo El Collado
Paseo El Collado 1, 01300 (Alava) **Tel** *945 62 12 00* **Fax** *945 60 08 78* **Rooms** *8*

In an unusual building with a Gothic tower reminiscent of a folly, the bedrooms of this small hotel offers views of the Sierra de Cantabria and the vineyards surrounding the atmospheric wine town of Laguardia. Bodega visiting is the biggest attraction, but it is handily located also for visiting Estella and other sights in southern Navarra.

LAGUARDIA Posada Mayor de Migueloa
C/ Mayor 20, 01300 (Alava) **Tel** *945 62 11 75* **Fax** *945 62 10 22* **Rooms** *8*

Occupying the beautiful 17th-century Baroque Palacio de Viana, this hotel is in the pedestrianized old wine-making town of Laguardia. It has been refurbished keeping many of its original features. It has its own bodega and one of the best restaurants of Northen Spain, offering both Basque and La Rioja cuisine. **www.mayordemigueloa.com**

LOGROÑO Herencia Rioja
Marqués de Murrieta 14, 26005 (La Rioja) **Tel** *941 21 02 22* **Fax** *941 21 02 06* **Rooms** *83*

A modern chain hotel close to the Paseo del Espolon and near Logroño's historic quarter. It has comfortable bedrooms and a restaurant serving *haute cuisine*. Rooms have wireless Internet and guests are supplied with pay-per-view films and video games. Other services include a gym, dry cleaning and car rental. **www.nh-hotels.com**

MUNDAKA El Puerto
Portu Kalea 1, 48360 (Vizcaya) **Tel** *946 87 67 25* **Fax** *946 87 67 26* **Rooms** *12*

A fisherman's house in one of the prettiest towns on the Basque coast. Located at the mouth of the Genika estuary, which is renowned for its surfing beaches, the windows offer great views of the sea. Converted into a simple, cosy hotel it is decorated in contemporary style. It has a cafeteria and a bar. Close to Bilbao. **www.hotelelpuerto.com**

Key to Price Guide *see p560* **Key to Symbols** *see back cover flap*

MUNDAKA Atalaya 🛏️🍴 €€
Itxaropen Kalea 1, 48360 (Vizcaya) **Tel** *946 17 70 00* **Fax** *946 87 68 99* **Rooms** *11*

This hotel, in a pretty early 20th-century English-inspired villa next to the fishing port, has small but pleasant bedrooms, large window galleries with views of the sea and a terrace. A good area for strolling on the beach, surfing or lingering over lunch. Has a small cafeteria-restaurant only for guests. **www.hotel-atalaya-mundaka.com**

OLITE Parador de Olite 🛏️🍴▤ €€
Plaza de los Teobaldos 2, 31390 (Navarra) **Tel** *948 74 00 00* **Fax** *948 74 02 01* **Rooms** *43*

Occupying a wing of the 15th-century castle and palace of Carlos III, king of Navarra, this parador is decorated on a medieval theme with armour, tapestries, stained glass and wrought-iron lamp brackets. The most atmospheric (and pricey) rooms are in the old part of the castle; there are also some modern bedrooms. **www.parador.es**

PAMPLONA Ciudad de Pamplona 🛏️🍴📺▤ €€€
Iturrama 21, 31007 (Navarra) **Tel** *948 26 60 11* **Fax** *948 17 36 26* **Rooms** *117*

An ultra-modern luxury hotel, decorated in warm tones and scattered with avant-garde furniture. It has four sitting rooms and ample facilities for business people. The hotel is at some distance from the old part of Pamplona, in one of the streets behind the Ciudadela fortress. The restaurant serves classic Navarran dishes. **www.ac-hotels.com**

RONCESVALLES La Posada 🍴 €
Ctra de Francia, 31650 (Navarra) **Tel** *948 76 02 25* **Fax** *948 76 02 66* **Rooms** *19*

This historic inn opened in 1612 to cater for pilgrims to Santiago de Compostela – Roncesvalles being one of the principal crossing points from France. It has been renovated but its austere bedrooms with tiled floors are simply furnished and still cheap. The restaurant serves Basque cuisine and game. **www.laposadaderoncesvalles.com**

SAN MILLAN DE LA COGOLLA Hostería del Monasterio de San Millán 🛏️🍴 €€
Monasterio de Yuso, 26326 (La Rioja) **Tel** *941 37 32 77* **Fax** *941 37 32 66* **Rooms** *25*

A hotel occupying a wing of the Monasterio de Yuso, which is inhabited by Agustinian friars. Two long corridors give access to the bedrooms, which are soberly decorated and have thick walls to guarantee complete peace. Three of the rooms are suites. Best of all is the Royal Room, which has a balcony over the inner patio. **www.sanmillan.com**

SAN SEBASTIÁN La Galería 🛏️▤ €€
Infanta Cristina 1–3, 20008 (Guipúzcoa) **Tel** *943 31 75 59* **Fax** *943 21 12 98* **Rooms** *23*

This late 19th-century French-style building is situated on Ondarreta beach and offers views of La Concha bay. The bedrooms are dedicated to famous painters such as Renoir, Picasso, Dali, Miró and Regoyos, and contain replicas of their works. It has two charming attic rooms. Internet and bicycles are available. **www.hotellagaleria.com**

SAN SEBASTIÁN Niza 🛏️🍴▤ €€
C/ Zubieta 56, 20007 (Guipúzcoa) **Tel** *943 42 66 63* **Fax** *943 44 12 51* **Rooms** *40*

Niza is a beautiful seafront hotel in *belle époque* style in the middle of La Concha beach, not far from the city centre. The bedrooms are warm and airy and 18 of them have sweeping views of the bay. All have wireless Internet. The hotel has a bar and an Italian restaurant, La Pasta Gansa, on the beachfront. **www.hotelniza.com**

SAN SEBASTIÁN Mercure Monte Igueldo 🛏️🍴♒▤ €€€
Paseo del Faro 134, 20008 (Guipúzcoa) **Tel** *943 21 02 11* **Fax** *943 21 50 28* **Rooms** *125*

Superbly located on Monte Igueldo, one of the hills marking the end of La Concha bay, this Mercure chain hotel has panoramic views across the city and the bay. The restaurant, enjoying the same views, serves Basque *haute cuisine*. It also has a rooftop swimming pool. Next door is San Sebastian's amusement park. **www.monteigueldo.com**

SAN SEBASTIÁN Abba de Londres y de Inglaterra 🛏️🍴▤ €€€€
C/ Zubieta 2, 20007 (Guipúzcoa) **Tel** *943 44 07 70* **Fax** *943 44 04 91* **Rooms** *148*

This classical-style luxury hotel with grand public spaces within occupies a 19th-century palace on La Concha beach. It was transformed into a hotel in 1902. Twelve of the rooms are suites. The Mari Galant brasserie in the hotel serves buffet meals and offers a children's menu. Five salons double as meeting rooms. **www.hlondres.com**

SAN SEBASTIAN María Cristina 🛏️🍴🧒▤ €€€€€
C/ Oquendo 1, 20004 (Guipúzcoa) **Tel** *943 43 76 00* **Fax** *943 43 76 76* **Rooms** *136*

Built in 1912 and named after Queen Maria Cristina, this is a landmark of the city and one of the most historic hotels in Spain. It was designed by the architect of the London and Paris Ritz hotels and is decorated in *belle époque* style. The restaurant serves both Basque and international dishes. It is also the venue of the San Sebastián film festival.

SANTO DOMINGO DE LA CALZADA Parador de Santo Domingo 🛏️🍴📺▤ €€€
Plaza del Santo 3, 26250 (La Rioja) **Tel** *941 34 03 00* **Fax** *941 34 03 25* **Rooms** *61*

A hospital founded in the 12th century for pilgrims on the road to Santiago de Compostela, now converted into a parador. Next to Santo Domingo's cathedral, it has an imposing lounge divided by Gothic arches and a carved timber ceiling. The restaurant serves stuffed Piquillo peppers and has a good list of wines from La Rioja. **www.parador.es**

UDABE Venta Udabe 🍴♒ €
Udabe-Basaburua, 31869 (Navarra) **Tel** *948 50 31 05* **Fax** *948 50 34 00* **Rooms** *9*

Decorated with dried flowers and rural implements, this small hotel in a typical old Basque farmhouse stands in a unique natural setting at the heart of the Basaburua Valley, just off the Pamplona to San Sebastián motorway. The owners are hospitable and can organize "an infinity of activities" for their guests. **www.hotelventaudabe.com**

VERA DE BIDASOA Churrut

Plaza de los Fueros 2, 31780 (Navarra) **Tel** *948 62 55 40* **Fax** *948 62 55 41* **Rooms** *17*

A beautifully renovated family-run hotel in an 18th-century house. Downstairs there is a gallery with wicker armchairs and plants arranged beside a glass wall with relaxing views of the garden. The bedrooms are comfortable and homey. Churrut has a good restaurant and a small gym in the attic. The rooms include two suites. **www.hotelchurrut.com**

VITORIA General Álava

Av Gasteiz 79, 01009 (Alava) **Tel** *945 21 50 00* **Fax** *945 24 83 95* **Rooms** *114*

A modern hotel with comfortable bedrooms in a spectacular spot in the new town, near the Palacio de Congresos, making it suitable for business travellers. The restaurant serves regional dishes and avant-garde cuisine, with a daily changing menu. The buffet breakfast includes fruit salads and home marinaded salmon. **www.hga.info**

YESA Hospedería de Leyre

Monasterio de Leyre, 31410 (Navarra) **Tel** *948 88 41 00* **Fax** *948 88 41 37* **Rooms** *30*

This hotel occupies part of an 11th-century Benedictine monastery, spectacularly located beneath crags. The rooms are plain and clean, some looking onto the garden. The monastery can be busy by day but is quiet at night. The restaurant serves typical Navarran cuisine. Men can stay in the monastery by written request. **www.monasteriodeleyre.com**

ZARATUZ Karlos Arguiñano

C/ Mendilauta 13, 20800 (Guipúzcoa) **Tel** *943 13 00 00* **Fax** *943 13 34 50* **Rooms** *12*

A stone tower-cum-mansion on the beach of Zarautz, this is a restaurant-with-rooms owned by a celebrated TV chef. The bedrooms are decorated with antiques and traditional furniture; some have terraces and sea views. The tower has a rooftop terrace. There are two restaurants: one traditional, one *haute cuisine*. **www.hotelka.com**

BARCELONA

OLD TOWN Fontanella

Via Laietana 71, 08002 **Tel** *933 17 59 43* **Fax** *933 17 59 43* **Rooms** *11*   **Map** *5 B1*

Fontanella is a simple, family-run hostal where the owners do their best to make visitors feel at home. There is a wonderful antique lift, which creaks up to a knick-knack filled lobby. The basic rooms are made cosy and welcoming with flowery prints and lots of goodies in the bathrooms. **www.hostalfontanella.com**

OLD TOWN Peninsular

Carrer de Sant Pau 34, 08001 **Tel** *933 02 31 38* **Fax** *934 12 36 99* **Rooms** *59*   **Map** *2 F3*

Rooms are truly basic, but of good value in this former Carmelite convent. Just off La Rambla behind the Liceu opera house, this hotel's charms lie in its luminous, plant-filled inner courtyard and friendly staff. Breakfast is served in an old-fashioned dining room with a high ceiling, but there is no restaurant. **www.hpeninsular.com**

OLD TOWN Rembrandt

Carrer de Portaferrissa 23, 08002 **Tel** *933 18 10 11* **Fax** *933 18 10 11* **Rooms** *28*   **Map** *5 A2*

A simple, clean hotel in the Barri Gòtic, popular with students. The rooms have old-fashioned wicker furniture, but are all spotlessly clean and the best have wrought-iron balconies overlooking the shopping street below. It is quiet, considering the city centre location. Some bedrooms share bathrooms. **www.hostalrembrandt.com**

OLD TOWN Hotel Urquinaona

Ronda de Sant Pere 24, 08010 **Tel** *932 68 13 36* **Fax** *932 95 41 37* **Rooms** *18*   **Map** *5 B1*

This has a perfect city centre location, close to the Plaça de Catalunya. A modest hotel, Hotel Urquinaona has been recently renovated and offers bright, well-equipped rooms with modern furnishings. There is also a good restaurant and free Internet access for guests. Triple and quadruple rooms are also available. **www.hotelurquinaona.com**

OLD TOWN Jardí

Plaça Sant Josep Oriol 1, 08002 **Tel** *933 01 59 00* **Fax** *933 42 57 33* **Rooms** *40*   **Map** *5 A2*

A popular hostal overlooking a pretty leafy square in the heart of the Barri Gòtic quarter. Some bedrooms have been renovated and have good views of the square and the handsome Gothic church of Santa María del Pi; others are cheaper but not as atmospheric. Because of its location, this is the best place for nightowls.

OLD TOWN Monegal

Carrer Pelai 60, 08001 **Tel** *933 02 65 66* **Fax** *934 12 24 88* **Rooms** *23*   **Map** *2 F1*

Right in the middle of the city centre, just off the Plaça de Catalunya, Monegal is a comfortable modern hotel. Rooms are simple but spacious, and some have wrought-iron balconies overlooking the bustling shopping street below. Geared towards business travellers, it offers good deals on its website. **www.mediumhoteles.com**

OLD TOWN Montecarlo

La Rambla 124, 08002 **Tel** *934 12 04 04* **Fax** *933 18 73 23* **Rooms** *76*   **Map** *5 A2*

This beautiful hotel right on La Rambla in the centre of Barcelona occupies a former 19th-century palace. The lobby is a gorgeous whirl of gilt and marble, while the rooms are smart and modern. Staff are particularly helpful here, and there are fantastic deals available on the website. **www.montecarlobcn.com**

Key to Price Guide *see p560* **Key to Symbols** *see back cover flap*

OLD TOWN Nouvel   €€
Carrer de Santa Anna 18–20, 08002 **Tel** *933 01 82 74* **Fax** *933 01 83 70* **Rooms** *54*   **Map** *5 A1*

In a pretty little shopping street off La Rambla, near the Plaça Catalunya, this well-managed old-style hotel is tastefully decorated and furnished. The best rooms have curving Modernista-style balconies, and there is a charming lobby and lounge area with 1920s style chandeliers. **www.hotelnouvel.com**

OLD TOWN Park Hotel   €€
Carrer de Marquès de l'Argentera 11, 08003 **Tel** *933 19 60 00* **Fax** *933 19 45 19* **Rooms** *91*   **Map** *5 C3*

A rare gem of 1950s architecture, designed by Antonio Moragas in 1951 and well preserved by his son's award-winning renovations in 1990. The slim wraparound staircase is a highlight. Rooms are small but smartly furnished and the best have balconies. The restaurant, Abac, is outstanding. **www.parkhotelbarcelona.com**

OLD TOWN Jazz Hotel   €€€
Carrer Pelai 3, 08001 **Tel** *935 52 96 96* **Fax** *935 52 96 97* **Rooms** *108*   **Map** *5 A1*

A glassy ultra-modern hotel, close to the Plaça de Catalunya, Jazz offers better facilities than its three-star rating would suggest. There is a rooftop pool with sun deck, and the rooms (all soundproofed) are stylishly decorated with contemporary furniture and fabrics. **www.hoteljazzbarcelona.com**

OLD TOWN Arts   €€€€€
Carrer de Marina 19–21, 08005 **Tel** *932 21 10 00* **Fax** *932 21 10 70* **Rooms** *455*   **Map** *6 E4*

Set in a soaring tower overlooking the Port Olímpic, Arts is one of the most luxurious and glamorous hotels in Europe. Huge rooms boast spectacular views along with every imaginable modern convenience. There are stunning suites on the upper floors for those with very deep pockets. **www.hotelartsbarcelona.com**

OLD TOWN Colón   €€€€€
Avda de la Catedral 7, 08002 **Tel** *933 01 14 04* **Fax** *933 17 29 15* **Rooms** *145*   **Map** *5 B2*

A classic in Barcelona, this traditional, rather formal hotel has a fabulous location opposite the Gothic cathedral. The best rooms have terraces overlooking the square, where guests can watch the *Sardana*, the traditional Catalan folk dance, performed in the Plaça de Catedral on Sunday mornings. **www.hotelcolon.es**

OLD TOWN Neri   €€€€€
Carrer de Sant Server 5, 08002 **Tel** *933 04 06 55* **Fax** *933 04 03 37* **Rooms** *22*   **Map** *5 A2*

An enchanting hotel which stunningly combines the architectural features of the original 18th-century palace with sleek contemporary fittings. Airy, stylish rooms are draped in sensuous fabrics, and there is a magnificent rooftop terrace with views of the Gothic cathedral. Fabulous restaurant too. **www.hotelneri.com**

EIXAMPLE Hotel Paseo de Gracia   €
Passeig de Gràcia 102, 08008 **Tel** *932 15 58 24* **Fax** *932 15 37 24* **Rooms** *33*   **Map** *3 B3*

There are few budget choices in the chichi Eixample district, but this modest little hotel is a good option. It has a fabulous location on the city's most desirable boulevard, close to the finest Gaudi buildings. Some of the simple rooms have views over the Plaça de Catalunya. **www.hotelpaseodegracia.com**

EIXAMPLE Windsor   €
Rambla Catalunya 84, 08007 **Tel** *932 15 11 98* **Rooms** *15*   **Map** *3 A4*

A rickety old-fashioned hostal on an elegant tree-lined boulevard, this has pretty streetside rooms with balconies. Interior rooms are quieter but lack charm and can be stuffy in summer. All are decorated in plain, traditional style. The Windsor is a stone's throw from the Gaudí buildings on the Passeig de Gràcia.

EIXAMPLE Felipe II   €€
Carrer de Mallorca 329, 08037 **Tel** *934 58 77 58* **Fax** *932 07 21 04* **Rooms** *11*   **Map** *3 C4*

A basic, clean hotel in an old apartment block in the Eixample, with a particularly fine antique elevator. You will get a good welcome from the friendly owners, and all the rooms come complete with TV and choice of plumbing (shared or *en suite* facilities). Breakfast is not available.

EIXAMPLE Gran Vía   €€
Gran Vía de les Corts Catalanes 642, 08010 **Tel** *933 18 19 00* **Fax** *933 18 99 97* **Rooms** *53*   **Map** *3 B5*

A hotel in a late 19th-century building with an ageing grandeur, north of the Plaça de Catalunya adjoining the Passeig de Gràcia. The rooms are spacious and all have polished wooden floors and antique-style furnishings. Best of all is the terrace and garden, a delightful oasis in the heart of the city. Breakfast included. **www.nnhotels.com**

EIXAMPLE Hostal Palacios   €€
Rambla Catalunya 27, 08007 **Tel** *933 01 3079* **Fax** *933 01 3792* **Rooms** *11*   **Map** *3 A3*

This friendly hostal is housed in a magnificent Modernista building. Many of the original fittings, including the huge carved doors and colourful tiles, have been retained, and are stylishly complemented by modern fabrics and contemporary bathrooms. Guests can use the piano in the comfortable lounge. **www.hostalpalacios.com**

EIXAMPLE Alexandra   €€€
Carrer de Mallorca 251, 08008 **Tel** *934 67 71 66* **Fax** *934 88 02 58* **Rooms** *109*   **Map** *3 A4*

A stylish, modern interior behind a 19th-century façade sets the tone at this hotel, which is well equipped for business meetings. It offers rooms and suites, all comfortably and tastefully furnished. There is a good restaurant, and the website offers excellent weekend packages. **www.hotel-alexandra.com**

EIXAMPLE Actual

€€€€

Carrer Rosselló 238, 08008 **Tel** *935 52 05 50* **Fax** *935 52 05 55* **Rooms** *29* **Map** *3 B3*

This modern hotel is fashionably decorated in sleek minimalist style. It has a superb location on the same block as Gaudí's La Pedrera, and the upmarket boutiques of the Passeig de Gràcia are on the doorstep. Like many hotels in this area, it is geared towards business travellers, which means good weekend deals. **www.hotelactual.com**

EIXAMPLE Axel

€€€€

Carrer Aribau 33, 08011 **Tel** *933 23 93 93* **Fax** *933 23 93 94* **Rooms** *66* **Map** *2 F1*

Axel is Barcelona's best gay hotel, a chic four-star establishment with a wealth of excellent facilities. The rooms are sleek and modern, there is a fabulous rooftop bar, and business facilities are available in the small library. There is also a dipping pool, and a good restaurant (with drag shows). **www.hotelaxel.com**

EIXAMPLE Condes de Barcelona

€€€€

Passeig de Gràcia 73–75, 08008 **Tel** *934 67 47 80* **Fax** *933 17 34 42* **Rooms** *183* **Map** *3 A4*

This hotel is located in two handsomely renovated Modernista palaces, with marble lobbies and creamy façades. The rooms in both locations are cool and contemporary, and some have Jacuzzis. Choose a room with a terrace to admire Gaudí's "La Pedrera" building directly across the street. **www.condesdebarcelona.com**

EIXAMPLE NH Calderón

€€€€

Rambla de Catalunya 26, 08007 **Tel** *933 01 00 00* **Fax** *934 12 41 93* **Rooms** *253* **Map** *3 A5*

Calderón is a modern hotel from the reliable NH chain, near the Plaça de Catalunya, offering spacious, comfortable rooms and suites. The excellent facilites include indoor and rooftop pools (with panoramic views), and a good restaurant. **www.nh-hoteles.es**

EIXAMPLE Claris

€€€€€

Carrer Pau Claris 150, 08009 **Tel** *934 87 62 62* **Fax** *932 15 79 70* **Rooms** *124* **Map** *3 B4*

Antique kilims and elegant English and French furniture ornament this hotel off the Passieg de Gràcia. Claris occupies the converted Vedruna Palace, and is scattered with fabulous artworks from around the world. There's a panoramic rooftop pool and sun deck, and guests may use the hotel's Smart cars. **www.derbyhotels.es**

EIXAMPLE Gallery

€€€€€

Carrer Rosselló 249, 08008 **Tel** *934 15 99 11* **Fax** *934 15 91 84* **Rooms** *110* **Map** *3 A3*

A modern, efficient and comfortable hotel that is well situated and retains the personal atmosphere of a family-run business. Soundproofed rooms are smartly furnished with contemporary black and white decor and have large, marble bathrooms. An attractive garden restaurant leads into a public garden. **www.galleryhotel.com**

EIXAMPLE Majèstic

€€€€€

Passeig de Gràcia 68, 08007 **Tel** *934 88 17 17* **Fax** *934 88 18 80* **Rooms** *303* **Map** *3 A4*

A grand, traditional hotel in Neo-Classical style in a chic street (adjoining Carrer de València). The stylish bedrooms are decorated with plush drapes and elegant prints, and are all equipped with five-star amenities. There are also some very luxurious suites, and a superb rooftop pool with spectacular views. **www.hotelmajestic.es**

EIXAMPLE Omm

€€€€€

Carrer Rosselló 265, 08008 **Tel** *934 45 40 00* **Fax** *934 45 40 04* **Rooms** *59* **Map** *3 B3*

From the glistening ultra-modern façade with its peeled-back balconies, to the fluid, glassy public spaces, Omm is the epitome of sleek Barcelona design. The fashionably minimalist rooms are very comfortable, and the slick bar and club make it popular with fashionistas. Also has spa facilities. **www.hotelomm.es**

EIXAMPLE Prestige Paseo de Gracia

€€€€€

Passeig de Gracia 62, 08007 **Tel** *932 72 41 80* **Fax** *932 72 41 81* **Rooms** *45* **Map** *3 A4*

Zen meets Modernism in this luxury hotel near Gaudí's most important buildings. Rooms are filled with light and have up-to-the-minute amenities including Bang and Olufsen TVs and music systems. In the Zeroom, you can browse through art and design books. There's also an Oriental garden. Breakfast included. **www.prestigehotels.com**

EIXAMPLE Ritz

€€€€€

Gran Via de les Corts Catalanes 668, 08010 **Tel** *933 18 52 00* **Fax** *933 18 01 48* **Rooms** *133* **Map** *3 B5*

Ritz has recently been refurbished and is the most elegant of Barcelona's grand hotels. The large luxurious bedrooms are decorated in classical style and boast huge marble bathrooms inspired by Roman spas. Contains a health club and a beauty parlour. Famous guests have included the Spanish royal family and Frank Sinatra. **www.ritzbcn.com**

FURTHER AFIELD (POBLE NOU) Hostel Poble Nou

€

Carrer Taulat 30, 08005 **Tel** *932 21 26 01* **Fax** *932 21 26 01* **Rooms** *5*

This charming little hostal is located in a colourful 1930s town house in the traditional neighbourhood of Poble Nou. It's close to the city's best beaches and well connected by metro and tram to the city centre. The *en suite* rooms are simple, and there is a pretty breakfast terrace as well. Breakfast is included in the price. **www.hostalpoblenou.com**

FURTHER AFIELD (VALLVIDRERA) Gran Hotel La Florida

€€€€€

Carretera Vallvidrera al Tibidabo 83–93, 08035 **Tel** *932 59 30 00* **Fax** *932 59 30 01* **Rooms** *74*

In a luxurious palace in the hills above Barcelona, this outstanding hotel is set in beautiful gardens offering great views of the whole city. The suites are all equipped with every imaginable facility, and there is a wonderful spa and a restaurant. A shuttle service takes you to the heart of the city in minutes. **www.hotellaflorida.com**

Key to Price Guide *see p560* **Key to Symbols** *see back cover flap*

CATALONIA

ANDORRA LA VELLA Andorra Park Hotel   €€€
Les Canals 24 **Tel** *376 87 77 77* **Fax** *376 82 09 83* **Rooms** *40*

One of Andorra's most luxurious hotels, this modern structure is built into a steep, wooded hillside. There is a library, a swimming pool hewn out of rock, and a pleasant bar-restaurant. Rooms come with satellite TV and a mini-bar, and the hotel also provides a laundry and ironing service. **www.hotansa.com**

ARTIES Parador Don Gaspar de Portolà   €€€
Ctra Bequeira-Beret, 25999 (Lleida) **Tel** *973 64 08 01* **Fax** *973 64 10 01* **Rooms** *57*

A modern, comfortable parador, Don Gaspar de Portolà is built in the local traditional stone and slate. It is located in one of the prettiest villages of the Vall d'Aran, with attractive narrow streets dotted with medieval chapels. The parador is handy for local ski resorts, and makes a good base for mountain walkers. **www.parador.es**

AVINYONET DE PUIGVENTÓS Mas Pau   €€
Ctra Figueres-Besalú, 17742 (Girona) **Tel** *972 54 61 54* **Fax** *972 54 63 26* **Rooms** *20*

A beautiful hotel in a 16th-century house, surrounded by gardens and wooded farmland. Many of the luxurious bedrooms and suites are located in the 25-m (82-ft) high tower, and have splendid views. There is a spectacular restaurant, secluded terraces and a separate swimming pool and games area for children. **www.maspau.com**

BANYOLES Mirallac   €€
Passeig Darder 50, 17820 (Girona) **Tel** *972 571 045* **Fax** *972 580 887* **Rooms** *27*

Mirallac is a cheerful, old-style hotel overlooking the vast lake at Banyoles, offering traditionally decorated rooms with their own balcony/terrace, a huge swimming pool and lots of lakeside activities. Also houses a good restaurant serving tasty, local specialities. Guests also have use of a bar and a reading room.

BEGUR Aigua Blava   €€€€€
Platja de Fornells, 17255 (Girona) **Tel** *972 62 20 58* **Fax** *972 62 45 62* **Rooms** *86*

This charming whitewashed Mediterranean-style hotel overlooks Fornells Bay, one of the prettiest spots on the Costa Brava. Surrounded by pine trees and gardens, the arched windows of the hotel frame beautiful sea views. The rooms are light and airy. Aigua Blava also offers 10 fully-equipped apartments. **www.aiguablava.com**

BEQUEIRA-BERET Royal Tanau   €€€€€
Ctra de Beret, 25598 (Lleida) **Tel** *973 64 44 46* **Fax** *973 64 43 44* **Rooms** *30*

A luxurious boutique hotel in the Tanau skiing area that has all kinds of amenities, including indoor and outdoor Jacuzzis and a spa. In winter, a private ski lift whisks guests directly to the pistes. There are full après-ski facilities are available. Elegant, fully-equipped suites as well as rooms. **www.solmelia.com**

BOLVIR DE CERDANYA Torre del Remei   €€€€
Camí Reial s/n, 17539 (Girona) **Tel** *972 14 01 82* **Fax** *972 14 04 49* **Rooms** *21*

One of the most deluxe hotels in the region, this opulent Modernista mansion is set in magnificent gardens with a stunning mountain backdrop. The classically decorated rooms are perfectly equipped with up-to-the-minute gadgetry, and the extensive facilities include a new spa and a gym. **www.torredelremei.com**

CADAQUÈS Hotel Llane Petit   €€
Platja Llane Petit, 17488 (Girona) **Tel** *972 25 10 20* **Fax** *972 25 87 78* **Rooms** *37*

Llane Petit is a delightful seaside hotel with a peaceful and welcoming ambience, set right on the beach in the whitewashed village of Cadaquès. Simple, friendly and family-run, the best rooms boast terraces where you can relax in a hammock and soak up the sun. The restaurant is open in summer only. **www.llanepetit.com**

CARDONA Parador de Cardona   €€€
Carrer de Castell s/n, 08261 (Barcelona) **Tel** *938 69 12 75* **Fax** *938 69 16 36* **Rooms** *54*

One of the most striking paradors in Spain, this luxuriously converted medieval castle dominates Cardona and offers spectacular views of the countryside. Many of the elegant rooms boast four-poster beds. The parador has a fine Catalan restaurant as well. **www.parador.es**

CASTELLÓ D'EMPURIES Allioli   €€
Urbanització Castell Nou, 17486 (Girona) **Tel** *972 25 03 00* **Fax** *972 25 03 00* **Rooms** *40*

A 17th-century Catalan farmhouse, just off the main Roses-Figueres road, with simple rooms, some suitable for families. The restaurant, open all year round, is popular for Sunday lunch among locals. The swimming pool is only open in the summer, and the hotel is closed from mid-December until the end of February. **www.hotelallioli.com**

FIGUERES Hotel Durán   €€
Carrer de Lasauca 5, 17600 (Girona) **Tel** *972 50 12 50* **Fax** *972 50 26 09* **Rooms** *65*

Established in 1855, this ochre-and-pink hotel is set above one of the finest restaurants in the region. It is still owned by the same family, who are warm and friendly. Rooms are attractively, if simply, furnished, and many have pretty wrought-iron balconies overlooking the street below. **www.hotelduran.com**

GIRONA Pensión Bellmirall

Carrer de Bellmirall 3, 17004 (Girona) **Tel** *972 20 40 09* **Rooms** *7*

Pensión Bellmirall is a rickety, old-fashioned charmer tucked away in the ancient heart of Girona. The old house has preserved its massive stone walls, and bedrooms are individually decorated with traditional furniture and original art. A huge breakfast is served in a pretty garden area.

GRANOLLERS Fonda Europa

Carrer Anselm Clavé 1, 08400 (Barcelona) **Tel** *938 70 03 12* **Fax** *938 70 79 01* **Rooms** *7*

This small hotel has been an inn for travellers since 1714, and is still owned by the same family. The bedrooms, on the second floor, have been completely modernized and are simply decorated. The restaurant is the big draw here, with its hearty Catalan specialities prepared using traditional recipes. **www.casafonda.net**

LA SEU D'URGELL El Castell

Ctra N260 km 229, 25700 (Lleida) **Tel** *973 35 00 00* **Fax** *973 35 15 74* **Rooms** *38*

This extravagant hotel is a low, modern building beneath the medieval castle of Seu d'Urgell. It has plenty of facilties, including an outdoor Jacuzzi and an immense covered pool. There are impressive views across the mountains of El Cadí and the ski slopes of Andorra are nearby. **www.hotelelcastell.com**

LA SEU D'URGELL Parador de La Seu d'Urgell

Carrer Sant Domènec 6, 25700 (Lleida) **Tel** *973 35 20 00* **Fax** *973 35 23 09* **Rooms** *73*

Only the Renaissance cloister, now used as the lounge, remains of a convent that occupied this site close to the 12th-century cathedral of La Seu. The modern parador has good facilities, including a covered pool, and there are excellent opportunities for hiking and skiing on the doorstep. **www.parador.es**

L'ESCALA El Roser

Plaça L'Església 7, 17130 (Girona) **Tel** *972 77 02 19* **Fax** *972 77 45 29* **Rooms** *22*

El Roser is a charming, old-fashioned seaside hotel right on the beach, in the heart of the historic centre of L'Escala. The restaurant is smart and elegant, with old wood and stone walls, and is one of the best in the area. Rooms are immaculate and brightly furnished, if somewhat basic. Closed in November. **www.elroserhostal.com**

L'ESPLUGA DEL FRANCOLÍ Hostal del Senglar

Plaça de Montserrat Canals 1, 43440 (Tarragona) **Tel** *977 87 01 21* **Fax** *977 87 01 27* **Rooms** *38*

A three-storey, whitewashed hotel with simply furnished, traditional rooms including family rooms. There is a delightful shady garden where barbecues are held in summer. A menu of delicious dishes, traditional to the area, is served in the restaurant. **www.hostaldesenglar.com**

LLORET DE MAR Santa Marta

Platja Santa Cristina, 17310 (Girona) **Tel** *972 36 49 04* **Fax** *972 36 92 80* **Rooms** *78*

This low, white-painted modern hotel overlooks a beautiful cove on the fringes of the frenetic resort of Lloret de Mar. Rooms vary from rustic to contemporary decor with up-to-the-minute amenities. Tranquil pine woods and gardens extend to the shore, and there are tennis courts and other sporting facilities. **www.hstamarta.com**

MONTSENY Sant Bernat

Finca El Clot, Ctra Sant Maria de Palautordera a Seva, km 20.7, 08460 (Barcelona) **Tel** *938 47 30 11* **Rooms** *23*

A gorgeous country house in the Serra de Montseny, the old stone walls of which are cloaked in greenery. The rooms and suites are stylishly decorated with traditional prints and rustic furniture. The house is surrounded by extensive gardens with lawns and a pond. All kinds of outdoor activities can be arranged. **www.santbernat.com**

MONTSERRAT Abat Cisneros

Plaça del Monestir, 08199 (Barcelona) **Tel** *938 77 7 01* **Fax** *938 7 77 24* **Rooms** *86*

Part of the celebrated monastery complex at Montserrat, Abat Cisneros is where Catalan newly-weds come to ensure that they have the blessing of La Moreneta, the miraculous figure of the Virgin. Rooms are modest but more comfortable than the ascetic setting would suggest. **www.montserratvisita.com**

PERAMOLA Can Boix de Peramola

Carrer Afores s/n, 25790 (Lleida) **Tel** *973 47 02 66* **Fax** *973 47 02 81* **Rooms** *41*

This good value, traditional mountain hotel has been in the same family for 10 generations. It has charming rooms and apartments with breathtaking views, a quiet garden and a swimming pool. Can Boix de Peramola is very convenient for walking in the Pyrenean foothills. **www.canboix.com**

REGENCÓS Hotel del Teatre

Plaça Major s/n, 17214 (Girona) **Tel** *972 30 62 70* **Fax** *972 30 62 73* **Rooms** *7*

In the heart of a rambling, medieval village, this boutique-style hotel is located in a pair of handsomely restored 18th-century mansions. Sleek minimalism and charming original features are stylishly combined in the bedrooms. Has a lovely semi-shaded pool in the garden. **www.hoteldelteatre.com**

SA TUNA (BEGUR) Hotel Sa Tuna

Platja Sa Tuna, 17255 (Girona) **Tel** *972 62 21 98* **Fax** *972 62 21 98* **Rooms** *5*

Sa Tuna is a simple, whitewashed small hotel on one of the Costa Brava's prettiest coves. Recent improvements by the grandson of the original owner have added to its charms. Some rooms have their own terrace overlooking the bay. The restaurant is well known in the area. Open from April to September only. **www.hostalsatuna.com**

SADURNI D'ANOIA Sol i Vi
Ctra San Sadurni–Vilafranca km 4, Lavern, 08739 (barcelona) **Tel** *938 99 32 04* **Fax** *938 99 33 26* **Rooms** *25*

A cheery, traditional hotel set amid a sea of vines, thus making this a good base for exploring the wine and *cava*-producing region southwest of Barcelona. It offers comfortable, simple rooms and boasts a superb restaurant which specializes in traditional Catalan cuisine. **www.solivi.com**

S'AGARÓ Hostal de la Gavina
Plaça de la Rosaleda, 17248 (Girona) **Tel** *972 32 11 00* **Fax** *972 32 15 73* **Rooms** *74*

This elegant Mediterranean-style beach mansion is set in its own exclusive estate with beautiful gardens and a sea water pool. Bedrooms are splendidly decorated with silk-lined walls and burnished antiques. The many facilities include a luxurious spa and a fine restaurant. **www.lagavina.com**

SANTA CRISTINA D'ARO Mas Torrellas
Ctra Santa Cristina-Platja d'Aro, 17246 (Girona) **Tel** *972 83 75 26* **Fax** *972 83 75 27* **Rooms** *17*

An attractive 18th-century country house hotel, with ancient stone walls and flower-filled gardens. Its most comfortable bedroom is in the distinctive yellow tower, built at a later date. There is a pool and tennis courts and horse riding can be arranged. The restaurant is excellent. Closed from October to March.

SITGES Romàntic
Carrer Sant Isidre 33, 08870 (Barcelona) **Tel** *938 94 83 75* **Fax** *938 94 81 67* **Rooms** *58*

Well known in Sitges, this memorable hotel lives up to its name. Bedrooms are simple, but attractively decorated with antiques and paintings. There is a gloriously shady garden with tinkling fountains that is perfect for breakfast and evening cocktails. **www.hotelromantic.com**

SITGES San Sebastián Playa
Carrer de Port Alegre 53, 08870 (Barcelona) **Tel** *938 94 86 76* **Fax** *938 94 04 30* **Rooms** *51*

This modern hotel on the beach near the old part of the town has attentive staff and comfortable bedrooms, many directly overlooking the sea. There is also a decent restaurant and good facilities for business travellers, including meeting rooms. **www.hotelsansebastian.com**

SOLDEU (ANDORRA) Sport Hotel Village
Ctra General s/n **Tel** *376 87 05 00* **Fax** *376 87 05 33* **Rooms** *165*

Sport Hotel Village is the best-equipped hotel in the popular ski resort of Soldeu, and many of the comfortable rooms overlook the slopes. The four-star facilities include a pool and Jacuzzi, and – best of all – the lift to the top of the slopes leaves directly from the hotel. **www.sporthotels.ad**

TARRAGONA Lauria
Rambla Nova 20, 43004 (Tarragona) **Tel** *977 23 67 12* **Fax** *977 23 67 00* **Rooms** *72*

A modern, functional hotel in the town centre and close to the sea, with an elegant entrance under balustraded stone stairs. Although the decor is dated, the rooms are large and the hotel offers good amenities, including a pool and facilities for business travellers for the price. **www.hlauria.es**

TARRAGONA Imperial Tarraco
Passeig Les Palmeres s/n, 43004 (Tarragona) **Tel** *977 23 30 40* **Fax** *977 21 65 66* **Rooms** *170*

The plushest option in Tarragona, this large, modern hotel has a panoramic location right on the *balcón del Mediterrani* (the balcony of the Mediterranean). Many of the spacious, elegant rooms and suites have large terraces. The hotel is conveniently close to the historic centre of the city. **www.husa.es**

TAVERTET El Jufré
Tavertet, 08511 (Barcelona) **Tel** *938 56 51 67* **Fax** *938 56 51 67* **Rooms** *8*

This converted farmhouse is now a delightful *casa rural* with stunning mountain views. It has been in the same family for over 800 years, and warm comfortable rooms have replaced what were previously animal quarters. A perfect base for walking and exploring nearby Osona. Price includes dinner, bed and breakfast.

TORRENT Mas de Torrent
Afueras, 17123 (Girona) **Tel** *972 30 32 92* **Fax** *972 30 32 93* **Rooms** *39*

A superbly converted 18th-century country house, Mas de Torrent offers handsome accommodation in one of the 10 beautiful rooms in the main house, or in elegant bungalows scattered around the extensive gardens. There are also deluxe suites with private pools available. **www.mastorrent.com**

TORTOSA Parador Castillo de la Zuda
Castillo de la Zuda, 43500 (Tarragona) **Tel** *977 44 44 50* **Fax** *977 44 44 58* **Rooms** *72*

A medieval Moorish castle makes a superb hilltop parador with views of the town and valley of the Riu Ebre. The fine restaurant offers al fresco dining on the terrace, and there are plenty of luxurious extras including a swimming pool – in summer only, however. **www.parador.es**

TOSSA DE MAR Diana
Plaça d'Espanya 6, 17320 (Girona) **Tel** *972 34 11 16* **Fax** *972 34 11 03* **Rooms** *21*

A fine Modernista mansion is the gorgeous setting for this delightful hotel. There are nice views of the castle from the terrace and the best of the modest rooms have private balconies. The elegant lobby is full of original details and has been converted into a comfortable lounge area.

TREDÒS Hotel de Tredòs

Ctra a Baqueira-Beret km 177.5, 25598 (Lleida) **Tel** *973 64 40 14* **Fax** *973 64 43 00* **Rooms** *43*

Skiers and mountain walkers find the Hotel de Tredòs in the Val d'Aran good value. It is built of stone and slate in the local style, and offers attractive rooms with wooden beams. The cosy lounge has a fireplace in winter, and a heart-shaped outdoor pool to cool off in summer. **www.hoteldetredos.com**

VIC Parador de Turismo de Vic-Sau

Paratge Bac de Sau, 08500 (Barcelona) **Tel** *938 12 23 23* **Fax** *938 12 23 68* **Rooms** *36*

This recently refurbished and comfortable stone-built parador, 14 km (9 miles) from Vic, has magnificent views of the Sau reservoir. It is a peaceful retreat amid pine forests and dramatic rock formations. Facilities include a tennis court and an outdoor pool (in summers only). **www.parador.es**

VIELHA (VIELLA) Parador Valle de Arán

Ctra de Túnel s/n, 25530 (Lleida) **Tel** *973 64 01 00* **Fax** *973 64 11 00* **Rooms** *118*

Valle de Arán is a modern parador that has a panoramic circular lounge dominated by a large window from which there are magnificent mountain views. There is a wonderful spa and a fine restaurant, and the rooms are bright, spacious and well appointed. **www.parador.es**

ARAGÓN

AÍNSA Casa Cambra

Morillo de Tou s/n, 22395 (Huesca) **Tel** *974 50 07 93* **Fax** *974 50 07 93* **Rooms** *17*

Casa Cambra is a modest farmhouse located in the picturesque medieval village of Morillo de Tou. A perfect location for visiting historical sites as well as natural wonders. The rooms are spacious and many feature the original exposed brick arches. More basic accommodation can be had in the adjoining bungalows. **www.morillodetou.com**

ALBARRACÍN Casa de Santiago

C/ Subida a las Torres 11, 44100 (Teruel) **Tel** *978 70 03 16* **Fax** *978 71 01 41* **Rooms** *9*

Close to the city's main square, the Plaza Mayor, this small hotel was once a residence of the Knights of Santiago, who used to protect the pilgrims from roaming bandits. The rooms are modest (only the suite possesses a TV), but the owners are friendly and the home-cooked breakfasts and dinners are good. **www.casadesantiago.net**

ALBARRACÍN Posada del Adarve

Portal de Molina 23, 44100 (Teruel) **Tel** *978 70 03 04* **Fax** *978 70 03 04* **Rooms** *5*

In the heart of the Albarracín, Teruel's one-time Moorish stronghold, this hotel used to be a nobleman's home. Each room has its own character and decoration. Try the "Fogon" suite, which used to be the house's kitchen, or the "La Alcoba" suite, with its countless stars painted on the deep blue ceiling. **www.hotelposadadeladarve.com**

ALBARRACÍN La Casona del Ajimez

C/ San Juan 2, 44100 (Teruel) **Tel** *978 71 03 21* **Fax** *978 70 03 26* **Rooms** *6*

This 16/17th-century residence has been decorated in the style of the three religions that once resided in Teruel's old town – Judaism, Islam and Christianity. The pretty pink and red façade houses rooms with king-size beds, eclectic antiques and period knick-knacks. The garden has fabulous views of the cathedral. **www.casonadelajimez.com**

ALCAÑIZ Parador de Alcañiz

Castillo Calatravos s/n, 44600 (Teruel) **Tel** *978 83 04 00* **Fax** *987 83 03 66* **Rooms** *37*

This used to be the castle of the 12th-century Knights of Calatrava, a particularly violent and independent order who ruled the area with an iron fist. Now, it is a luxurious parador, with many atmospheric corners, including a keep, a bell tower and a chapel; just be careful you do not end up in the dungeon while exploring. **www.parador.es**

ALQUÉZAR Santa María

Arrabal s/n, 22145 (Huesca) **Tel** *974 31 84 36* **Fax** *974 31 84 35* **Rooms** *21*

A simple hotel set inside a heavily altered and extended medieval palace offering comfortable accommodation with wonderful views of the Colegiata and Vero rivers. The hotel's lounge has an open, cosy fireplace around which to spend your evenings, and the staff can also organize "adventure sports". **www.hotel-santamaria.com**

BENASQUE Hotel Hospital de Benasque

Plan del Hospital s/n, 22440 (Huesca) **Tel** *974 55 20 12* **Fax** *974 55 10 52* **Rooms** *56*

A huge old hospital and pilgrims' shelter has been converted into a hotel with various types of lodging available, from duplexes to suites to apartments or cheaper hostel-type rooms. Nestled in a gorgeous valley (and prime cross-country skiing territory), the in-house restaurant is also well known. **www.llanosdelhospital.com**

BIELSA Parador de Bielsa

Valle de Pineta s/n, 22350 (Huesca) **Tel** *974 50 10 11* **Fax** *974 50 11 88* **Rooms** *39*

The name of the mountain which rises above this parador – Monte Perdido (Lost Mountain) – gives an idea of its isolated location in one of the most beautiful spots of Northern Spain. The modern building has been tastefully constructed with wooden beams and offers great views of the Ordesa National Park. **www.parador.es**

Key to Price Guide *see p560* **Key to Symbols** *see back cover flap*

DAROCA Posada del Almudí

🈺 🍴 ⓔ

C/ Grajera 5–7–9, 50360 (Zaragoza) **Tel** *976 80 06 06* **Fax** *976 80 11 41* **Rooms** *13*

The rooms in this converted 16th-century palace are situated around a stunning Renaissance patio. After a grand entrance, the rooms themselves lack a bit in character, but are comfortable enough for the price. There is a lovely garden terrace, library and a decent restaurant serving local cuisine.

FUENTESPALDA La Torre del Visco

🍴 🗏 ⓔⓔⓔ

Fuentespalda, 44587 (Teruel) **Tel** *978 76 90 15* **Fax** *978 76 90 16* **Rooms** *15*

The King of Spain, Juan Carlos I, has been known to use this beautiful, solitary and labyrinthine 15th-century estate house, overlooking 220 acres of rose gardens, olive and almond trees. This hotel prides itself on offering a relaxing and quiet environment for its guests with no TVs or phones in the rooms. **www.torredelvisco.com**

HUESCA Pedro I de Aragón

🈺 🍴 🏊 🗏 ⓔⓔ

Avda del Parque 34, 22003 **Tel** *974 22 03 00* **Fax** *974 22 00 94* **Rooms** *130*

This comfortable, if slightly soulless, hotel is conveniently located in the centre of the city and is a good bet for those who want to spend some time exploring Huesca. The rooms are large and pleasant and some have terraces. The hotel's restaurant is justifiably popular for its hearty Aragonese stews. **www.gargallo-hotels.com**

JACA Conde Aznar

🍴 ⓔⓔ

Paseo Constitución 3, 22700 (Huesca) **Tel** *974 36 10 50* **Fax** *974 36 07 97* **Rooms** *24*

Conde Aznar is a traditional, double-story residence that was renovated in 2004; each room has pretty ceramic tiled bathrooms, lace curtains and embroidered bedspreads. Exposed beams and polished floors complete the rustic look. Perfect for taking advantage of Jaca's excellent access to all the Aragonese ski resorts. **www.condeaznar.com**

JACA Hotel Canfranc

🈺 ⓔⓔ

Avda Oroel 23, 22700 (Huesca) **Tel** *974 36 31 32* **Fax** *974 36 49 79* **Rooms** *20*

Located on Jaca's main boulevard, this hotel has rooms which can accommodate up to five people, some with terraces. Hotel Canfranc is a no-frills, family-type lodging with spectacular views of the dramatic, stony peak of the Peña de Oroel. It also offers guests a free private parking space. **www.hotelcanfranc.com**

LANUZA-SALLENT DE GALLEGO La Casueña

🍴 ⓔⓔ

El Troniecho (Lanuza) 11, 22640 (Huesca) **Tel** *974 10 60 01* **Fax** *974 33 78 49* **Rooms** *10*

The literary inclinations of the owners of La Casueña are evident by the dedication of each of the rooms to a Spanish writer. The austere stone walls of this country house give way to a luxuriously decorated interior, with dramatic murals on the slanted roofs. The rooms have comfy king-size beds and a huge bath. **www.lacasuena.com**

PANTICOSA Gran Hotel de Panticosa

🈺 🍴 🏊 🗏 ⓔⓔⓔⓔ

Ctra del Balneario km 10, 22650 (Huesca) **Tel** *902 25 25 22* **Fax** *902 25 25 32* **Rooms** *42*

Situated next to a lake and surrounded by the stunning mountain scenery of the Panticosa resort, this old spa was converted in 2004 into a five-star hotel by the renowned architect Rafael Moneo. Its luxurious facilities include a hairdresser, a spa and a private skiing piste, which takes you right up to the front door. **www.panticosa.com**

SALLENT DE GÁLLEGO Almud

🍴 ⓔⓔ

C/ Espadilla 3, 22460 (Huesca) **Tel** *974 48 83 66* **Fax** *974 48 81 43* **Rooms** *11*

Conveniently placed in a pretty village near the Formigal and Panticosa ski resorts, this family-run hotel occupies an old building which used to be the village stables. Visitors will find welcoming staff, comfortable rooms furnished with rustic furniture and the atmosphere of a typical Aragonese mountain retreat. **www.hotelalmud.com**

SOS DEL REY CATOLICO Parador Sos del Rey Católico

🈺 🍴 🗏 ⓔⓔⓔ

Arquitecto Sainz de Vicuña s/n, 50680 (Zaragoza) **Tel** *948 88 80 11* **Fax** *948 88 81 00* **Rooms** *57*

This reconstructed Aragonese home offers modern accommodation. All rooms have large windows and are decorated in a somewhat heavy, faux-Castillian style. The in-room facilities are abundant and include Internet. The restaurant is a good place to sample the non-diet friendly local cuisine. **www.parador.es**

TARAZONA Condes de Visconti

🍴 🗏 ⓔⓔ

C/ Visconti 15, 50500 (Zaragoza) **Tel** *976 64 49 08* **Fax** *976 64 18 58* **Rooms** *15*

A rather grand hotel which borders on being overdone with its Provençal decorative touches; frescoes, stucco and enough throws to bury yourself in. Facilities include in-room hydro-massage tubs, Internet and satellite TV. Extras include the super-friendly staff and a great in-house restaurant. **www.condesdevisconti.com**

TERUEL Parador de Teruel

🈺 🍴 🏊 ⓔⓔ

Ctra Sagunto–Burgos N234, 44080 **Tel** *978 60 18 00* **Fax** *978 60 86 12* **Rooms** *60*

On the outskirts of the city in an Arabesque palace inspired by the culture of the Mudéjars, this highly impressive parador offers spacious rooms, an excellent restaurant, a landscaped garden and a pool. With its fanciful tilework, swathes of marble and arches, staying here is like taking a trip into the Arabian Nights. **www.parador.es**

TERUEL Torico Plaza

🈺 🗏 ⓔⓔ

Yagüe de Salas 5, 44001 **Tel** *978 60 86 55* **Fax** *978 60 86 55* **Rooms** *31*

An attractive, functional and central hotel offering plenty of natural light, cheery decor in earthy tones and family-size rooms. The hotel terrace has a stunning view of the Albarracín and is an impressive place to enjoy a candlelight dinner looking out over the city walls. **www.bacohoteles.com**

TORRE DEL COMPTE Parada del Compte   €€€

Finca la Antigua Estación del Ferrocarril, 44597 (Teruel) **Tel** *978 76 90 72* **Fax** *978 76 90 74* **Rooms** *9*

Parada del Compte is a quirky hotel located in a disused railway station and is ideal for those looking for something a little different. Each room is named after a famous international city train station with supposedly "matching" decor, ranging from a minimalist "loft" treatment in the New York suite to a lush Oriental Istanbul suite.

UNCASTILLO Posada La Pastora   €

Roncesvalles 1, 50678 (Zaragoza) **Tel** *976 67 94 99* **Fax** *976 67 92 11* **Rooms** *8*

This charmingly renovated 18th-century country retreat offers just eight rooms with exposed brick walls contrasted with bright furnishings. Breakfast features fresh produce from local farmers. Fishing, golfing, rafting and horse riding facilities are also available close by. **www.lapastora.net**

ZARAGOZA Hotel Avenida   €

Avda César Augusto 55, 50003 **Tel** *976 43 93 00* **Fax** *976 43 93 64* **Rooms** *85*

What this hotel may lack in character it more than makes up for in comfort and in its location in the historical and commercial centre of Zaragoza. The rooms are well equipped with Internet and satellite TV and some have a terrace. Well placed for those who want to visit all of Zaragoza's major sites on foot. **www.hotelavenida-zaragoza.com**

ZARAGOZA Palafox   €€€€

Casa Jimenez s/n, 50004 **Tel** *976 23 77 00* **Fax** *976 23 47 05* **Rooms** *179*

The Spanish architect Pascual Ortega went to town on his design for this luxurious hotel. The grand entrance is flanked by full-scale representations of the old gates to the city. The rooms, on the other hand, are tasteful and minimalist. In terms of location and facilities this is one of the best places in the city. **www.palafoxhoteles.com**

VALENCIA AND MURCIA

ÁGUILAS Carlos III   €

C/ Rey Carlos III 22, 30880 (Murcia) **Tel** *968 41 16 50* **Fax** *968 41 16 58* **Rooms** *32*

This modern, town-centre hotel is located close to the beach, and offers spectacular views of a beautiful bay, dramatic volcanic cliffs and nearby islands. Rooms are comfortably, if simply, furnished. The hotel's restaurant is a good place to try the local seafood dishes. **www.hotelcarlosiii.com**

ALICANTE Les Monges Palace   €

San Augustin 4, 03002 (Alicante) **Tel** *965 21 50 46* **Fax** *965 14 71 89* **Rooms** *18*

Ideal for budget travellers, this hotel is often fully booked well in advance. Situated in the heart of Alicante's old town, it features original Modernista details, including colourfully tiled floors, and rooms with antique furnishings. Two slightly more expensive rooms with a sauna and Jacuzzi are also available. **www.lesmonges.net**

ALICANTE Amerigo   €€€

C/ Rafael Altamira 7, 03002 (Alicante) **Tel** *965 14 65 70* **Fax** *965 14 65 71* **Rooms** *59*

What was once a Dominican convent has now been spectacularly converted into Alicante's smartest and most stylish hotel. A striking fusion of ancient and ultra-modern, it offers minimalist rooms, an excellent restaurant, a fashionable bar and a health centre. The rooftop pool has great views of the old city. **www.hospes.es**

ALICANTE Sidi San Juan   €€€€

La Doblada 8, Playa San Juan, 03540 (Alicante) **Tel** *965 16 13 00* **Fax** *965 16 33 46* **Rooms** *176*

A gleaming, modern luxury hotel overlooking the lively and popular San Juan beach on the outskirts of the city centre. Surrounded by beautiful gardens, the hotel hosts a spa, health centre and various sports facilities, as well as a play area and paddling pool for kids. **www.hotelessidi.es**

ARCHENA Termas   €€

Ctra Balneario, 30600 (Murcia) **Tel** *968 68 80 22* **Fax** *968 67 10 02* **Rooms** *66*

This spa hotel boasts an elegant and charming complex set amid flower-filled gardens and palm trees. The spa treatment areas are decorated in a glorious Mudéjar style and feature ornate plasterwork, domes and Moorish arches. The outdoor pool has massaging jets. **www.balneariodearchena.com**

BENISSA Casa del Maco   €€

Pou Roig s/n, 03720 (Alicante) **Tel** *965 73 28 42* **Fax** *965 73 01 03* **Rooms** *4*

An exquisite rural retreat, this hotel is located on a beautifully restored, 18th-century *finca* (farm estate). Surrounded by groves of olives, almonds and oranges, each of the rooms is stylishly decorated. The terrace and pool provide splendid views of the mountains. Also has a romantic French restaurant. **www.casadelmaco.com**

CALABARDINA Al Sur   €€

Torre de Cope 24, 30889 (Near Águilas, Murcia) **Tel** *968 41 94 66* **Rooms** *9*

Situated in a tiny village, this cosy, whitewashed hotel overlooks one of the wildest and most beautiful stretches of the Murcian coast. The rooms are painted in soothing shades of blue and green. Ideal for those looking for an intimate and relaxing getaway. They also have bikes for rent. Breakfast included in rate. **www.halsur.com**

Key to Price Guide *see p560* **Key to Symbols** *see back cover flap*

CALP Venta La Chata

Ctra Nacional 332 km 172, 03710 (Alicante) **Tel** *965 83 03 08* **Fax** *965 83 03 08* **Rooms** *17*

An old coaching inn on the main road between Alicante and Valencia now houses this slightly battered, yet appealing, small hotel. The bedrooms are simple, mixing old and new furniture, and some have terraces looking out on a pretty garden. Guests can play tennis or head down to the beach nearby.

CARTAGENA Los Habaneros

C/ San Diego 60, 30202 (Murcia) **Tel** *968 50 52 50* **Fax** *968 50 91 04* **Rooms** *87*

At the entrance to Cartagena's old quarter, this long-established hotel offers modern and well-equipped rooms at affordable prices. Has a great restaurant and tapas bar. The town's famous Roman and Carthagenian antiquities are located close by. **www.hotelhabaneros.com**

CASTELL DE CASTELLS Pensión Castells

C/ San Vicente 18, 03793 (Alicante) **Tel** *965 51 82 54* **Rooms** *4*

A 200-year-old house in an inland village not far from the Costa Blanca. The stone walls keep the rooms cool even in the height of summer. The charming British owners offer bed and breakfast and can prepare packed lunches and dinners for patrons. Guests are also taken for walks in the surrounding hills. **www.mountainholidays-spain.com**

CHULILLA Balneario de Chulilla

Afueras s/n, 46167 (Valencia) **Tel** *961 65 70 13* **Fax** *961 65 70 31* **Rooms** *97*

This spa hotel, surrounded by gardens and set in a tranquil location on the banks of the Río Túria, is an inexpensive place to stop while exploring the woods and hills of inland Valencia. It has all the facilities for a rest-cure, including massage and vapour baths, a gym and a beauty centre. **www.balneariodechulilla.com**

DENIA Rosa

C/ Congre 3, Las Marinas, 03700 (Alicante) **Tel** *965 78 15 73* **Fax** *966 42 47 74* **Rooms** *40*

A modern, white villa with a perfect location close to the beach. It was built and is run by a hospitable Parisian expat who has several repeat customers. Comfortable rooms have sun-trapping, Florentine-style balconies. Guests can also opt for one of the garden bungalows. The family-friendly pool has a section for toddlers. **www.hotelrosadenia.com**

EL SALER Parador de El Saler

Avda de los Pinares 151, 46012 (Valencia) **Tel** *961 61 11 86* **Fax** *961 62 70 16* **Rooms** *58*

A contemporary parador, situated beside the sea near L'Albufera and surrounded by a renowned golf course. It overlooks one of Valencia's loveliest and least crowded beaches. The rooms are light and modern. Features tennis courts and a football pitch. The restaurant serves Valencian cuisine, specializing in *paella*. **www.parador.es**

ELX (ELCHE) Huerto del Cura

Porta de la Morera 14, 03203 (Alicante) **Tel** *966 61 20 50* **Fax** *966 61 60 60* **Rooms** *95*

A secluded hotel in Europe's largest palm tree forest, surrounded by landscaped grounds. The bedrooms are located in Mediterranean-style bungalows. Furnishings and fittings are somewhat dated, but the hotel's reputation rests on its extraordinary array of sports facilities, which remain top-notch. **www.huertodelcura.com**

FORCALL Hotel GHI Palau dels Osset-Miro

Plaza Major 16, 12310 (Castellón) **Tel** *964 17 75 48* **Fax** *964 17 75 56* **Rooms** *20*

A tastefully renovated, 16th-century mansion in a quiet village at the heart of the mountainous region of El Maestrat. Old wooden beams and tile floors decorate the public areas. The rooms are charmingly old-fashioned yet equipped with modern amenities. The restaurant serves regional specialities. **www.ghihoteles.com/palau**

FORTUNA Balneario Leana

C/ Balneario, 30630 (Murcia) **Tel** *968 68 50 11* **Fax** *968 68 50 87* **Rooms** *58*

This is the oldest hotel in Murcia and has the ambience of a former grand hotel. Many of the original Modernista details, including swirling woodwork and original doors, have been retained. Also boasts a splendid staircase. An array of spa and health treatments, as well as a series of thermal pools are available. **www.leana.es**

JÁTIVA (XATIVA) Hostería Mont Sant

Ctra de Castillo, 46800 (Valencia) **Tel** *962 27 50 81* **Fax** *962 28 19 05* **Rooms** *17*

A country hotel in a magnificently restored mansion. There are just six elegant rooms in the main building, and the remaining are located in charming wooden bungalows scattered throughout the beautiful gardens. It offers all kinds of amenities, including a spa and gym, and the restaurant is superb. **www.mont-sant.com**

JÁVEA (XABIA) Hotel Jávea

Calle Pio X 5, 03730 (Alicante) **Tel** *965 79 54 61* **Fax** *965 79 54 63* **Rooms** *24*

A cheerful, simple, typically Spanish seaside hotel. This good-value option is just a stone's throw from the pebbly beach in Jávea's picturesque port. The restaurant serves local specialities and offers wonderful views over the bay from its large picture windows. **www.hotel-javea.com**

JÁVEA (XABIA) Parador de Jávea

Avda Mediterráneo 7, 03730 (Alicante) **Tel** *965 79 02 00* **Fax** *965 79 03 08* **Rooms** *70*

A large, modern parador surrounded by lush Mediterranean gardens right on the beach. The rooms are bright and spacious and almost all have balconies overlooking the sea. Offers a wide range of sports facilities, including horse riding, diving and sailing. The restaurant serves regional cuisine. **www.parador.es**

LA MANGA DEL MAR MENOR Regency Hyatt La Manga

La Manga Club, 30385 (Murcia) **Tel** *968 33 12 34* **Fax** *968 33 12 35* **Rooms** *189*

A luxurious hotel, part of an exclusive resort complex built in the style of a Spanish village. Frequented by several celebrities, the hotel is surrounded by palm and olive groves, and has three golf courses, 28 tennis courts and four swimming pools. Also boasts a Centre for Professional Football among other amenities. **www.lamanga.hyatt.com**

LA VILA JOIOSA El Montiboli

Partida El Montiboli, 03570 (Alicante) **Tel** *965 89 02 50* **Fax** *965 89 38 57* **Rooms** *89*

This beautiful, cliff-side luxury hotel overlooks a secluded beach. The rooms are decorated in warm Mediterranean colours, and most have spacious terraces offering glorious sea views. There are a handful of plush suites as well, and guests can also stay in one of the romantic bungalows scattered around the gardens. **www.servigroup.es**

MORAIRA Hotel Albahia

Solnaciente 6, 03016 (Alicante) **Tel** *965 15 59 79* **Fax** *965 15 53 73* **Rooms** *93*

This modern hotel, five minutes from the city centre, has a beachfront location and offers numerous luxuries and comforts, including both indoor and outdoor pools, a gym, business centre and babysitting facilities. They also have a Mediterranean restaurant specializing in regional rice dishes. Access for disabled guests. **www.sercotel.es**

MORATELLA Barceló Cenajo

Embalse del Cenajo, 30440 (Murcia) **Tel** *968 72 10 11* **Fax** *968 72 06 45* **Rooms** *42*

At night, silence descends on this creamy-yellow hotel beside the Cenajo dam. Few tourists stray into this lovely, remote corner of Murcia, but the surrounding hills and wealth of animal and bird life attract many hikers and nature enthusiasts. The hotel offers several activities, including horse riding. **www.hotelcenajo.com**

MORELLA Cardenal Ram

Cuesta Suñer 1, 12300 (Castellón) **Tel** *964 17 30 85* **Fax** *964 17 32 18* **Rooms** *19*

This country hotel, housed in a 16th-century mansion with stone arches and beamed ceilings, overlooks the main porticoed street. Rooms have sturdy wooden furniture and colourful local prints, and there is an excellent restaurant. Newly renovated bathrooms include hydromassage baths or showers. **www.cardenalram.com**

MÚRCIA Arco de San Juan

Plaza de Ceballos 10, 30003 (Murcia) **Tel** *968 21 04 55* **Fax** *968 22 08 09* **Rooms** *115*

The award-winning restoration of this old palace combines contemporary materials with antique furnishings. This luxury hotel is often chosen for wedding dinners and other celebrations by local Murcians. Rooms are large and comfortable, although they lack character. Also has a popular restaurant and bar. **www.arcosanjuan.com**

MÚRCIA Conde de Floridablanca

C/ Princesa 18, 30002 (Murcia) **Tel** *968 21 46 26* **Fax** *968 21 32 15* **Rooms** *82*

A comfortable, good-value hotel, situated across the river from the old city centre and overlooking the manicured Floridablanca gardens. The rooms were renovated in 2002 and are well furnished. A wide range of services makes it popular among business travellers. Offers excellent deals on their website. **www.hoteles-catalonia.es**

OLIVA Pensión Oliva

C/ San Luis 35, 46780 (Near Gandia, Valencia) **Tel** *962 85 53 04* **Rooms** *5*

A delightful, British-run guesthouse, located in a restored, stone-built cottage close to the coast. The rooms are comfortable with modern amenities such as a TV, minibar and tea and coffeemakers. Also has two family rooms and one especially adapted for disabled guests. Serves a daily breakfast buffet. **www.hotelitooliva.com**

ONTINYENT Pou Clar

Mayans 67, 46870 (Valencia) **Tel** *962 38 12 00* **Fax** *962 38 70 34* **Rooms** *47*

Situated in a quiet part of the old city, near the town hall, this modest hotel is popular with business travellers. The bedrooms are simple and furnished in a classic style. It has little in the way of charm, but is clean, quiet and friendly. The hotel's restaurant serves local cuisine.

ORIHUELA (ORIOLA) Hotel Palacio Tudemir

C/ Alfonso XIII, 03300 (Alicante) **Tel** *966 73 80 10* **Rooms** *51*

This hotel is housed in a superbly restored, 18th-century palace. The coat-of-arms of the original owner still sits proudly over the main door, and the interior is palatial. The latest modern conveniences have been added, but many original details have been retained. Also has a good restaurant. Disabled access. **www.sh-hoteles.com**

PENÁGUILA Mas de Pau

Ctra Alcoi-Penáguila km 9, 03815 (Alicante) **Tel** *965 51 31 11* **Fax** *965 51 31 09* **Rooms** *18*

A 19th-century house set amid a remote and striking landscape of almond and olive trees, and located halfway between Guadalest and Alcoi. The rooms are a little small, but most offer splendid views of the beautiful Sierra de Penáguila. The hotel is popular with families. The restaurant serves regional cuisine.

PENÍSCOLA Benedicto XII

C/ Dinamarca 2, Urbanización Las Atalayas, 12598 (Castellón) **Tel** *964 48 08 01* **Fax** *964 48 95 23* **Rooms** *30*

A white villa in a quiet private estate on a hillside near Peñíscola. The rooms are plain and functional, but spotlessly clean and equipped with modern conveniences and large bathrooms. Most have spacious terraces. Features two tennis courts, and the beach is just a 10-minute walk away. **www.hotelbenedicto.com**

Key to Price Guide *see p560* **Key to Symbols** *see back cover flap*

PENÍSCOLA Hostería del Mar
Av Papa Luna 18, 12598 (Castellón) **Tel** *964 48 06 00* **Fax** *964 48 13 63* **Rooms** *86*

A contemporary, beachfront hotel. The rooms and suites are equipped with modern amenities, including Internet facilities and a minibar. The restaurant is famous for its animated medieval banquets. Note that the half-board, which includes dinner, is obligatory for all stays between end-June and mid-September. **www.hosteriadelmar.net**

VALENCIA Hotel Venecia
C/ En Llop 5, 46002 (Valencia) **Tel** *963 52 42 67* **Fax** *963 52 44 21* **Rooms** *54*

An excellent, modestly priced hotel in the centre of the city. Although set in a historic building, the hotel's interior is modern. The rooms are functionally decorated and provide basic amenities such as a TV, telephone and electronic safe. Several eateries can be found within walking distance. A breakfast buffet is served. **www.hotelvenecia.com**

VALENCIA Ad Hoc
C/ Boix 4, 46003 (Valencia) **Tel** *963 91 91 40* **Fax** *963 91 36 67* **Rooms** *28*

This chic hotel is housed in a renovated, soundproofed, 19th-century building near the Río Turia gardens. The bedrooms are furnished in a mixture of old and new styles, with brick walls, antiques and modern fabrics. Book early for one with a terrace. The restaurant offers an excellent, fixed-price lunch. **www.adhochoteles.com**

VALENCIA Inglés
C/ Marqués de Dos Aguas 6, 46002 (Valencia) **Tel** *963 51 64 26* **Fax** *963 94 02 51* **Rooms** *65*

This convenient and stylish city-centre hotel is in the old palace of the Dukes of Cardona, next to the National Ceramics Museum. The rooms and suites overlook the street, and are equipped with amenities such as Internet access, a TV, a minibar and a safe. The restaurant serves regional specialties. **www.solmelia.com**

VALENCIA Reina Victoria
C/ Barcas 4, 46002 (Valencia) **Tel** *963 52 04 87* **Fax** *963 52 27 21* **Rooms** *97*

The grande dame of Valencia's hotels retains its splendid 19th-century decor in the public salons, which are a dazzling whirl of gilt and marble. Rooms are disappointingly bland in comparison, but all are reasonably spacious and comfortably equipped. They were renovated in 2004 and offer Internet facilities. Disabled access. **www.husa.es**

MADRID

OLD MADRID Hostal Buenos Aires
Gran Vía 61, 28013 **Tel** *915 42 22 50* **Fax** *915 42 28 69* **Rooms** *30* **Map** *2 D5*

A simple, economical hotel, conveniently located on the busy Gran Vía. The public rooms are pleasantly decorated, and almost all the bedrooms have their own balcony or small terrace. Moreover, the rooms are soundproofed against the capital's noisy nightlife. A buffet breakfast is also available. **www.hoteleshn.com**

OLD MADRID Hostal Madrid
C/ Esparteros 6–2°, 28012 **Tel** *915 22 00 60* **Fax** *915 32 35 10* **Rooms** *12* **Map** *4 F2*

One of the best budget options in Madrid, this hotel is set in the heart of the old city. Offers both rooms and apartments decorated in a mixture of traditional and modern styles, with amenities such as Wi-Fi. The staff is friendly, and the city's sights, restaurants, bars and nightlife are right on the doorstep. **www.hostal-madrid.com**

OLD MADRID HH Campomanes
C/ Campomanes 4, 28004 **Tel** *915 48 85 48* **Fax** *915 59 12 88* **Rooms** *30* **Map** *4 D2*

Hotel Campomanes is situated close to many major sights, as well as great shopping and dining. The rooms are small, but slickly decorated in black-and-white minimalist style with splashes of colour and high-tech gadgets. A self-service buffet breakfast is also available. **www.hhcampomanes.com**

OLD MADRID Hotel Moderno
C/ Arenal 2, 28013 **Tel** *915 31 09 00* **Fax** *915 31 35 50* **Rooms** *97* **Map** *4 E2*

A comfortable, modern hotel in a central location. The rooms are decorated with chintzy prints and traditional furniture; some have terraces with a view of the city's skyline. Offers free Wi-Fi access, and is popular with both business travellers and tourists. A range of restaurants can be found nearby. **www.hotel-moderno.com**

OLD MADRID Inglés
C/ de Echegaray 8, 28014 **Tel** *914 29 65 51* **Fax** *914 20 24 23* **Rooms** *58* **Map** *7 A2*

A good-value, family-run hotel with its own garage (for which there is a fee). Situated in the city's literary and theatre district, the hotel is a little rundown, but remains a bargain thanks to its location. The bedrooms facing the street are sunny but the rooms at the back are quieter. **www.ingleshotel.com**

OLD MADRID Reyes Católicos
C/ del Ángel 18, 28005 **Tel** *913 65 86 00* **Fax** *913 65 98 67* **Rooms** *38* **Map** *3 C4*

Set in the heart of the city, this modern hotel is very popular and always busy. Children are made welcome, and there are board games to keep them amused. The bedroom windows are double-glazed for soundproofing, and five of the rooms have their own terraces. **www.hreyescatolicos.com**

OLD MADRID Carlos V

C/ Maestro Victoria 5, 28013 **Tel** *915 31 41 00* **Fax** *915 31 37 61* **Rooms** *67*   **Map** *4 E2*

A city-centre hotel in a pedestrian street beside the Puerta del Sol. This family-run hotel has interconnecting bedrooms as well as family rooms. Some of the rooms also have balconies and sun terraces. A generous buffet breakfast is served in the café bar, and the staff are friendly and helpful. **www.hotelcarlosv.com**

OLD MADRID Tryp Gran Vía

Gran Vía 25, 28013 **Tel** *915 22 11 21* **Fax** *915 21 24 24* **Rooms** *175*   **Map** *2 D5*

A large, chain hotel on one of the city's busiest streets, close to main sightseeing and shopping areas. The service is brisk and efficient, and the rooms, although blandly decorated, are reasonably comfortable. Some are better than others, and are worth checking in advance. The hotel's website offers good discounts. **www.solmelia.com**

OLD MADRID Tryp Rex

Gran Vía 43, 28013 **Tel** *915 47 48 00* **Fax** *915 47 12 38* **Rooms** *145*   **Map** *2 D5*

This expansive hotel, renovated in 2004, is situated in an old building between the Plaza del Callao and the Plaza de España, close to a large public car park. It has spacious public rooms and well-equipped bedrooms, each with its own safe. Offers good value for money considering the central location and reasonable amenities. **www.solmelia.com**

OLD MADRID Casa de Madrid

C/ Arrieta 2, 28013 **Tel** *915 59 57 91* **Fax** *915 40 11 00* **Rooms** *7*   **Map** *4 D1*

Housed in an 18th-century palace, this stylish little hotel is ideal for a romantic getaway. The seven rooms – two of which are suites – are exquisitely decorated with antiques. The breakfast includes freshly squeezed juice and home-made marmalade. Highly recommended. **www.casademadrid.com**

BOURBON MADRID Hostal Cervelo

C/ Atocha 43, 28012 **Tel** *914 29 95 94* **Fax** *914 29 09 64* **Rooms** *24*   **Map** *7 A3*

A simple pension with a friendly atmosphere, close to three museums and the lively bars and cafés of the Santa Ana neighbourhood. The rooms are clean, decorated with flowery prints and well equipped – all have free Internet connections and *en suite* facilities. **www.hostalcervelo.com**

BOURBON MADRID Hostal Gonzalo

C/ Cervantes 34, 28014 **Tel** *914 29 27 14* **Fax** *914 20 20 07* **Rooms** *15*   **Map** *7 B3*

A family-run hostal, which often fills up well in advance. Provides good facilities, immaculate bedrooms and excellent value for money. The multi-lingual owners are hospitable and offer helpful information regarding nearby attractions and entertainments. Several restaurants can be found within walking distance. **www.hostalgonzalo.com**

BOURBON MADRID Hotel Plaza Mayor

C/ Atocha 2, 28012 **Tel** *913 60 06 06* **Fax** *913 60 06 10* **Rooms** *31*   **Map** *7 A3*

Just around the corner of Madrid's central square, this popular hotel fills up fast, so book well in advance. Rooms vary in size and decor, but are spotless and brightly painted. The attic suite is more expensive, but offers fine views from its private terrace. Also has a reading room. Free wireless Internet in cafeteria. **www.h-plazamayor.com**

BOURBON MADRID Hotel Miau

C/ Príncipe 26, 28012 **Tel** *913 69 71 20* **Fax** *914 29 74 60* **Rooms** *20*   **Map** *7 A2*

This modest hotel, housed in a handsome 19th-century building, is located in the famous Plaza Santa Ana Square at the heart of Madrid's literary quarter. The rooms are simply, but comfortably decorated, with basic amenities. In addition, all the rooms are soundproofed. A car park is also available. **www.hotelmiau.com**

BOURBON MADRID Mora

Paseo del Prado 32, 28014 **Tel** *914 20 15 69* **Fax** *914 20 05 64* **Rooms** *62*   **Map** *7 C2*

A 1930s hotel with an attractive entrance and a lobby with an original glass skylight. The recently renovated rooms are modern, functional and brightly furnished. Located near the Prado, the hotel offers very good value for money. Families can request an extra bed in the room for a small surcharge. **www.hotelmora.com**

BOURBON MADRID Santander

C/ de Echegaray 1, 28014 **Tel** *914 29 66 44* **Fax** *913 69 10 78* **Rooms** *35*   **Map** *7 A2*

This small, popular, family-run hotel is situated in Madrid's literary quarter, which is filled with lively tapas bars and cafés. Opened in the 1920s, the hotel has neat, comfortable rooms, decorated in a traditional Spanish style. The staff are very helpful, and are happy to arrange theatre and flamenco tickets. **www.hotelsantandermadrid.com**

BOURBON MADRID Hotel Liabeny

C/ Salud 3, 28013 **Tel** *915 31 90 00* **Rooms** *222*   **Map** *4 F2*

An elegant, modern hotel, located just a short walk from the main sights, yet away from the hubbub of the city centre. The extensively renovated hotel features traditionally decorated rooms and suites with every modern amenity, a good restaurant and excellent service. The private parking and disabled access is a plus. **www.liabeny.es**

BOURBON MADRID Suite Prado

Manuel Fernández y González 10, 28014 **Tel** *914 20 23 18* **Fax** *914 20 05 59* **Rooms** *18*   **Map** *7 A3*

A stylish apartment-hotel of luxurious suites, all fully equipped with a kitchen, dining room, telephone lines and marble bathrooms. The hotel is very popular with business travellers, but its proximity to attractions such as the Prado and the Museo Thyssen-Bornemisza makes it a good choice for tourists as well. **www.suiteprado.com**

Key to Price Guide *see p560* **Key to Symbols** *see back cover flap*

BOURBON MADRID Hotel Petit Palace Londres

🔲🔢📧 €€€€

C/ Galdo 2, 28013 **Tel** *915 31 41 05* **Fax** *915 31 41 01* **Rooms** *76* **Map** *4 F2*

Behind the façade of this turn-of-the-20th-century mansion is a modern hotel with many rooms and suites. The four High Tech rooms offer everything the business traveller could require, including a personal computer, an excercise bike and a business centre. Two specially-adapted rooms are also available for disabled travellers. **www.hthoteles.com**

BOURBON MADRID Suecia

🔲🔢📧 €€€€

C/ Marqués de Casa Riera 4, 28014 **Tel** *915 31 69 00* **Fax** *915 21 71 41* **Rooms** *128* **Map** *7 B2*

Centrally situated near the Puerta del Sol, this hotel does a good job of living up to its motto – "we just want to be the nicest". The public spaces and bedrooms are decorated in warm colours and scattered with objets d'art, while the extra services include everything from Wi-Fi to feng shui consultations. **www.hotelsuecia.com**

BOURBON MADRID Ritz

🔲🔢📷📧 €€€€€

Plaza de la Lealtad 5, 28014 **Tel** *917 01 67 67* **Fax** *917 01 67 76* **Rooms** *167* **Map** *7 C2*

Inaugurated in 1910 as a hotel for aristocrats, the Ritz is still one of Spain's most elegant hotels. Close to the Prado, the hotel has an ornate, circular foyer and a terraced garden, and serves tea and brunch along with live music. Rooms are luxurious and offer every imaginable comfort. **www.ritzmadrid.com**

BOURBON MADRID Villa Real

🔲🔢📧 €€€€€

Plaza de las Cortes 10, 28014 **Tel** *914 20 37 67* **Fax** *914 20 25 47* **Rooms** *113* **Map** *7 B2*

Close to the Prado and the Retiro gardens, this stylish hotel is based in an opulent, early 19th-century building. One of Madrid's smartest hotels, the spacious rooms and suites are decorated in a tasteful mixture of traditional and contemporary styles, and scattered with ancient Roman art. Some suites even have a Jacuzzi. **www.derbyhotels.es**

BOURBON MADRID Westin Palace

🔲🔢📷📧 €€€€€

Plaza de las Cortes 7, 28014 **Tel** *913 60 80 00* **Fax** *913 60 81 00* **Rooms** *465* **Map** *7 B2*

This *belle époque* hotel with a glass dome and a colonnade has accommodated statesmen, as well as Mata Hari, the spy. The decor features marble columns, chandeliers and huge oil paintings and statues. Rooms are nicely decorated, and the service is charmingly old-fashioned and efficient. They also have a wine cellar. **www.palacemadrid.com**

FURTHER AFIELD (NORTH) Hostal Bianco II

📧 €

C/ Echegaray 5, 1° D, 28014 **Tel** *913 69 13 32* **Fax** *913 69 13 32* **Rooms** *15* **Map** *7 A2*

A well-kept hostal with a convenient location right off Gran Vía – all the museums and other attractions are close by. The rooms are simply decorated with all the basic amenities including TVs and a safety box. The friendly staff can speak some English. **www.hostalbianco.com**

FURTHER AFIELD (NORTH) Hostal San Lorenzo

🔳🔲📧 €

C/ Clavel 8, 28004 **Tel** *915 21 30 57* **Fax** *915 32 79 78* **Rooms** *17* **Map** *7 A1*

A smart, well-kept hostal conveniently located on the Gran Vía, within walking distance of several sightseeing attractions and shopping areas. The crisply decorated rooms have attached bathrooms; some of the rooms feature balconies as well. Also offers a family room with two interconnected bedrooms. **http://hotel-sanlorenzo.com**

FURTHER AFIELD (NORTH) Hostal Sil

🔲📧 €

C/ Fuencarral 95, 28004 **Tel** *914 48 89 72* **Fax** *914 47 48 29* **Rooms** *20* **Map** *2 F3*

This comfortable hostal is situated in one of the city's liveliest nightlife districts, which is also a prominent gay neighbourhood. Offers simple, but adequate bedrooms, with *en suite* facilities at a reasonable price. There are plenty of fashionable bars, cafés, shops and restaurants nearby. **www.hostalsilserranos.com**

FURTHER AFIELD (NORTH) NH Alcalá

🔲🔢📧 €€€

C/ de Alcalá 66, 28009 **Tel** *914 35 10 60* **Fax** *914 35 11 05* **Rooms** *146* **Map** *4 F2*

A large, chain hotel close to the lovely Retiro gardens. Features spacious, well-equipped rooms with amenities that include Wi-Fi and Internet access. This reasonably priced hotel also has a café, bar and private car park. It is within walking distance to the up-market shopping district in Salamanca, and three museums. **www.nh-hotels.com**

FURTHER AFIELD (NORTH) Castellana Intercontinental

🔲🔢📷📧 €€€€€

Paseo de la Castellana 49, 28046 **Tel** *917 00 73 00* **Fax** *913 19 58 53* **Rooms** *307* **Map** *6 D1*

This glossy, modern chain hotel in Madrid's business and financial district centre is a favourite with business travellers. The rooms and suites offer several amenities. The hotel also hosts a well-equipped business centre, as well as a cocktail lounge for relaxing after work. **www.interconti.com**

FURTHER AFIELD (NORTH) Miguel Ángel

🔲🔢🏊📷📧 €€€€€

C/ Miguel Ángel 31, 28010 **Tel** *914 42 00 22* **Fax** *914 42 53 20* **Rooms** *263* **Map** *6 D2*

Located beside the Paseo de la Castellana, this large hotel combines modern comfort with classic style. It is popular with both business travellers, who appreciate the business centre and related amenities, as well as tourists, who enjoy the central location and luxurious extras. **www.occidentalmiguelangel.com**

FURTHER AFIELD (NORTH) Santo Mauro

🔲🔢🏊📷📧 €€€€€

C/ Zurbano 36, 28010 **Tel** *913 19 69 00* **Fax** *913 08 54 77* **Rooms** *51* **Map** *5 C2*

This palace, built in 1894 on one of Madrid's most elegant streets, is surrounded by beautiful wooded gardens. The rooms and suites are stylishly decorated, and the two fine restaurants offer romantic outdoor dining in summer. Also houses a swimming pool in the vaulted cellars. **www.achotelsantomauro.com**

FURTHER AFIELD (NORTH) Villamagna Park Hyatt   🖥️🍴🛗   €€€€€

Paseo de la Castellana 22, 28046 **Tel** *915 87 12 34* **Fax** *914 31 22 86* **Rooms** *182*   **Map** *6 D1*

Set in attractive, tree-filled gardens, the luxurious Villamagna combines 18th-century decor with 21st-century amenities. Features spacious and comfortable rooms, decorated with antiques and contemporary furnishings. It also offers an excellent business centre, a health club and a choice of restaurants and bars. **www.madrid.hyatt.com**

FURTHER AFIELD (NORTHEAST) Hotel Galiano   🖥️🛗   €€

C/ Alcalá Galiano 6, 28010 **Tel** *913 19 20 00* **Fax** *913 19 99 14* **Rooms** *29*   **Map** *5 C2*

A charming hotel in the city's quiet embassy district, close to the Paseo Castellana and the Prado. The hotel was once a convent and then a palace – part of it is still a private mansion – and is scattered with fine antiques. The decor is flowery and flouncy, and rooms are spacious. Offers good value for money. **www.hotelgaliano.com**

FURTHER AFIELD (NORTHEAST) NH Príncipe de Vergara   🖥️🍴🏊🛗   €€€€€

C/ Príncipe de Vergara 92, 28006 **Tel** *915 63 26 95* **Fax** *915 63 72 53* **Rooms** *173*   **Map** *4 D2*

Part of a chain of well-appointed hotels, this large, modern property is extremely popular with business travellers. Offers a range of luxuries, including a sauna and massage service and baby-sitting facilities. The hotel's website offers excellent weekend deals. **www.nh-hotels.com**

MADRID PROVINCE

ALAMEDA DEL VALLE Hotel Rural Luces del Poniente   🖥️🍴🏇🛗   €€

C/ Lina de Avila 4, Cercedilla, Madrid, 28470 **Tel** *918 52 55 87* **Fax** *918 52 32 47* **Rooms** *10*

Sited in a picturesque chalet town on the fringes of the Sierra de Guadarrama, this place provides respite from the summer heat. The rooms are chic and stylish in their decor, yet provide a warm inviting ambience. It is an ideal base for nearby ski resorts and additionals include mountain bikes and horseback riding. **www.lucesdelponiente.com**

ARANJUEZ El Cocherón 1919   🖥️🍴🛗   €€

C/ Montesinos 22, 28300 **Tel** *918 75 43 50* **Fax** *918 75 43 47* **Rooms** *18*

This small, charming family-run hotel is set around a historic *corrala* (central courtyard), but has been decorated in a fine mixture of contemporary and traditional styles. The bedrooms look out onto the ochre-painted courtyard. Perfectly located in the city centre, it has a small café for guests. Serves breakfast only.

CHINCHÓN Parador de Chinchón   🍴🏊🛗   €€€

Av del Generalísimo 1, 28370 **Tel** *918 94 08 36* **Fax** *918 94 09 08* **Rooms** *38*

Housed in a 17th-century monastery, this stunning parador is set around a tree-filled courtyard, and adorned with frescoes, *azulejos* (tiles) and antiques. The handsome bedrooms have immensely thick stone walls, and the restaurant serves traditional Castillian fare, including garlic soup and roast suckling pig. **www.parador.es**

RASCAFRÍA Santa María de El Paular   🖥️🍴🏊🏇🛗   €

Ctra M–604, km 26.5, 28741 **Tel** *918 69 10 11* **Fax** *918 69 10 06* **Rooms** *56*

A relaxing retreat in the beautiful Sierra de Guadarrama, this hotel occupies a section of a 15th-century Benedictine monastery. Part of the Sheraton chain of hotels, it offers several facilities, from tennis courts and an outdoor pool to an elegant restaurant and an informal tavern. **www.hotelsantamariapaular.com**

SAN LORENZO DEL ESCORIAL El Botánico   🖥️🍴🛗   €€

C/ Timoteo Prados 16, 28200 **Tel** *918 90 70 79* **Fax** *918 90 81 58* **Rooms** *20*

An appealing hotel, housed in a handsome, whitewashed country mansion. A stone's throw from the vast El Escorial monastery, it is surrounded by beautiful gardens and is situated opposite the golf course. The bedrooms are decorated with modern furnishings, and offer a great view of the mountains. **www.valdesimonte.com**

TORREJÓN DE ARDOZ La Casa Grande   🍴🛗   €€€

C/ Madrid 2, 28850 **Tel** *916 75 39 00* **Fax** *916 75 06 91* **Rooms** *8*

This luxurious hotel is located in a 16th-century former convent. The ornate suites are decorated with antiques which once belonged to the Russian royal family – Catherine the Great is said to have slept in the bed now in the main suite. The hotel also houses two art museums and a gourmet grocery shop. **www.lacasagrande.es**

CASTILLA Y LEÓN

ASTORGA Asturplaza   🖥️🍴🛗   €

Plaza España 2–3, 24700 **Tel** *987 61 89 00* **Fax** *987 61 89 49* **Rooms** *37*

A popular hotel with striking views of some of Astorga's best sites, including the cathedral, the city wall and the Episcopal palace. The rooms are comfortably furnished. Those overlooking the Plaza España can get noisy at nights during the holiday season, but offer guests the chance to soak up the town's atmosphere. **www.asturplaza.com**

Key to Price Guide *see p560* **Key to Symbols** *see back cover flap*

ÁVILA Rey Niño

Plaza José Tomé 1, 05001 **Tel** *920 25 52 10* **Fax** *920 22 62 80* **Rooms** *24*

Located within the city's medieval walls, in a tranquil pedestrian street, this hotel proves the old adage – "Ávila, the city where one hears the silence". The building was completely renovated in 2001 and offers spacious and comfortable rooms. **www.hotelreynino.com**

ÁVILA Hospedería la Sinagoga

Reyes Católicos 22, 05001 **Tel** *920 35 23 21* **Fax** *920 35 34 74* **Rooms** *22*

This 15th-century building, situated in the centre of the old town, was formerly a synagogue serving Ávila's thriving Jewish commmunity. Some decorative elements from the original structure remain, lending an atmospheric touch to this well-equipped and comfortable hotel. **www.lasinagoga.com**

ÁVILA Parador de Ávila

C/ Marqués Canales de Chozas 2, 05001 **Tel** *920 21 13 40* **Fax** *920 22 61 66* **Rooms** *61*

Ideal for history lovers, this hotel is set in a 16th-century palace, next to the walls that surround Ávila's old town. Refurbished with stone and adobe, the hotel is furnished with many antiques. It also boasts a covered interior patio and a garden replete with archaeological remains. **www.parador.es**

BURGOS La Puebla

La puebla 20, 09004 **Tel** *947 20 00 11* **Fax** *947 20 47 08* **Rooms** *15*

A grand 19th-century building houses this good-value hotel, equipped with comfortable but no-frills rooms. With its excellent location near the Teatro Principal, La Puebla offers its guests a great all-round package. The old-fashioned atmosphere and friendly staff give this place a timeless feel. **www.hotellapuebla.com**

BURGOS Landa Palace

Ctra N.I (E-5) de Madrid a Irún km 235, 09001 **Tel** *947 25 77 77* **Fax** *947 26 46 76* **Rooms** *39*

Considered one of the best hotels in the region, this family-run establishment offers guests a taste of luxurious living with large, elegant and comfortable rooms equipped with Jacuzzis, DVD players and other creature comforts. The highlight, however, is the magnificent swimming pool covered by Gothic arches. **www.landapalace.es**

BURGOS NH Palacio de la Merced

C/ de la Merced 13, 09002 **Tel** *947 47 99 00* **Fax** *947 26 04 26* **Rooms** *110*

Part of the NH chain, this spectacular hotel is set in a 17th-century palace. Tastefully renovated, it comes complete with its own Gothic cloister. Modern amenities and luxuries, such as saunas, massage services and baby-sitting facilities are also available. **www.nh-hotels.com**

CARRIÓN DE LOS CONDES Hotel Monasterio de San Zoilo

Obispo Souto Vizoso s/n, 34120 **Tel** *979 88 00 49* **Fax** *979 88 10 90* **Rooms** *50*

Situated along the Santiago pilgrimage route, this former Benedictine monastery has been welcoming travellers for centuries. It provides a perfect place to relax after a long day exploring the stunning surroundings. The restaurant serves food grown in the hotel's own vegetable patch. **www.sanzoilo.com**

CIUDAD RODRIGO Parador de Ciudad Rodrigo

Plaza Castillo 1, 37500 (Salamanca) **Tel** *923 46 01 50* **Fax** *923 46 04 04* **Rooms** *35*

Located in a castle on a hill overlooking the river, this comfortable parador is famous for the medieval Homenaje tower, which provides great views of the local scenery. The rooms are decorated with traditional Castillian furniture, and the garden and patio offer guests an ideal spot to spend some quiet time. **www.parador.es**

COVARRUBIAS Arlanza

Plaza Mayor 11, 09346 (Burgos) **Tel** *947 40 64 41* **Fax** *947 40 05 02* **Rooms** *40*

Set in a beautiful, historical building in the centre of town, this small, family-run hotel offers excellent value for money. The bedrooms are simple, yet well equipped, and feature an austere, Castillian-style decor. Try to book one of the attic rooms with double beds and wooden beams. **www.hotelarlanza.com**

EL BURGO DE OSMA Virrey II

Mayor 2, 42300 (Soria) **Tel** *975 34 13 11* **Fax** *975 34 08 55* **Rooms** *52*

Housed in a section of an ancient hospital for ailing pilgrims, this hotel has been luxuriously refurbished. The decor features classical busts, a grand piano, chandeliers, a grandfather clock and a range of other lavish flourishes. The staff are friendly, and the rooms are comfortable and clean. **www.virreypalafox.com**

HOYOS DEL ESPINO El Milano Real

C/ Toleo s/n, 05634 (Ávila) **Tel** *920 34 91 08* **Fax** *920 34 91 56* **Rooms** *21*

This recently-renovated hotel has managed to maintain its rustic charm and is ideal for those in search of a relaxing and tranquil retreat. Guests can explore the scenic beauty of the surrounding Gredos mountains by foot or on horseback. Spectacular views are available from most of the rooms. **www.elmilanoreal.com**

LA ALBERCA Hotel Antiguas Eras

Av Batuecas 29 bajo, 37624 (Salamanca) **Tel** *923 41 51 13* **Fax** *923 41 51 13* **Rooms** *34*

This unique building is a mishmash of different and somewhat clashing architectural styles. The rooms are large, comfortable and functional. Some of them offer views of the Béjar mountain range, while others have a terrace and a Jacuzzi. **www.antiguaseras.com**

LEON Paris
C/ Ancha18, 24003 **Tel** *987 23 86 00* **Fax** *987 27 15 72* **Rooms** *55*

Most Spanish towns seem to have a hotel called "Paris" and, generally, they are as different from the Parisian style as can be imagined. Léon's version is very Spanish, with simple, unsophisticated decor and an efficient, if not overly-enthusiastic, staff. **www.hotelparisleon.com**

LEÓN Alfonso V
Padre Isla 1, 24002 **Tel** *987 22 09 00* **Fax** *987 22 12 44* **Rooms** *62*

This hotel, built in the 1920s to accommodate tourists passing through, has managed to maintain much of its "golden age" charm. The lobby has an impressive glass dome that floods the entrance with natural light. The rooms are large and comfortable, if a little old-fashioned. The walls showcase works by local artists. **www.iova-sa.com**

LEÓN Parador de San Marcos
Plaza de San Marcos 7, 24001 **Tel** *987 23 73 00* **Fax** *987 23 34 58* **Rooms** *226*

The dramatic Renaissance façade of this former San Marcos monastery gives way to an interior full of stone work and wooden masterpieces by medieval maestros. The rooms are comfortable and luxurious. A stay at this museum-like hotel is an experience in itself. **www.parador.es**

MOLINASECA La Posada de Muriel
Plaza Santo Cristo s/n, 24413 **Tel** *987 45 32 01* **Fax** *987 45 31 35* **Rooms** *8*

A small and welcoming country inn on the Santiago pilgrimage route. This renovated farmhouse offers simple and well-equipped rooms with traditional furnishings. The two rooms on the upper floor are smaller, but have a beautiful view through the skylight windows. **www.laposadademuriel.com**

NAVARREDONDA DE GREDOS Parador de Gredos
Ctra Barraco-Béjar km 42, 05635 (Ávila) **Tel** *920 34 80 48* **Fax** *920 34 82 05* **Rooms** *74*

Built in 1928, this is considered by many as one of Spain's best paradors. The hotel is decorated in a sober, no-frills Castillian style, and offers excellent views over the Tormes valley and the nearby peaks of the Gredos mountains. Some of the rooms have their own terrace. The restaurant serves local cuisine. **www.parador.es**

PALENCIA AC Palencia
Av de Cuba 25, 34004 **Tel** *979 16 57 01* **Fax** *979 16 57 02* **Rooms** *65*

This modern hotel is located near the town centre, and is very popular with both business travellers and weekend tourists. The hotel offers guests the chance to unwind in its sauna, and enjoy the buffet at its restaurant. The rooms are equipped with high-speed Internet and cable TV. **www.ac-hoteles.com**

PEDRAZA Hospedería de Santo Domingo
Matadero 3, 40172 (Segovia) **Tel** *921 50 99 71* **Fax** *921 50 86 83* **Rooms** *17*

The coat of arms on the façade of this converted 18th-century manor reads "Jesus and Mary's slaves. Year 1703". What was once an austere establishment is now a comfortable, modern hotel, which tastefully incorporates the numerous remaining historical elements with contemporary touches. **www.hospederiadesantodomingo.com**

PONFERRADA AC Ponferrada
Avda de Astorga 2, 24400 **Tel** *987 40 99 73* **Fax** *987 40 99 74* **Rooms** *60*

A steep climb up paved alleys takes guests to the entrance of this recently refurbished hotel, situated near the city's castle. Offers comfortable, well-equipped rooms and adequate service at a good price. Also has parking facilities for those who find the walk too challenging. **www.ac-hotels.com**

POZAL DE GALLINAS La Posada del Pinar
Finca Pinar de San Rafael s/n, 47450 (Valladolid) **Tel** *983 48 10 04* **Fax** *983 48 10 04* **Rooms** *19*

Very close to Valladolid and less than an hour from Ávila, Salamanca and Segovia, this country house comes with a beautiful, expansive garden. The cosy living room, library and dining room give this hotel a homely touch. Bikes are available for guests to explore the surrounding area. **www.laposadadelpinar.com**

SALAMANCA Hostería Casa Vallejo
San Juan de la Cruz 3, 37001 **Tel** *923 28 04 21* **Fax** *923 21 31 12* **Rooms** *14*

This comfortable hotel near the Plaza Mayor is one of town's oldest hotels. The staff are friendly and willing to help guests make the most of their stay by pointing them in the right direction and suggesting some hidden corners off the well-beaten tourist track. **www.hosteriacasavallejo.com**

SALAMANCA Rector
Paseo Rector Esperabé 10, 37008 **Tel** *923 21 84 82* **Fax** *923 21 40 08* **Rooms** *13*

This hotel is set in an elegant building with a beautiful, wide entrance hall with stained-glass windows in an Art Nouveau style. Tastefully designed rooms with mahogany furniture and white marble bathrooms make this one of the town's best-looking places to stay. **www.hotelrector.com**

SALAMANCA AC Palacio de San Esteban
Arroyo de Santo Domingo 3, 37001 **Tel** *923 26 22 96* **Fax** *923 26 88 72* **Rooms** *51*

The AC hotel chain took over this old convent in 2002 and converted it into one of the city's finest hotels. The original character of the building has been kept alive within the context of a modern hotel. The vaulted ceilings and stone walls breathe history, while the comfortable rooms do not lack any amenities. **www.ac-hotels.com**

Key to Price Guide *see p560* **Key to Symbols** *see back cover flap*

SAN ROMÁN DE LOS INFANTES Posada Dehesa Congosta

Finca la Congosta, 49281 (Zamora) **Tel** *615 21 76 42* **Fax** *980 98 05 04* **Rooms** *10*

Welcoming and friendly inn located in a natural environment. Offers cosy and beautifully decorated rooms, each priced individually. One of the rooms is in an adjacent building, separate from the main hotel. Activities such as trekking, mountain biking, canoeing and horse riding are also available. **www.dehesacongosta.com**

SANTA MARÍA DE MAVE EL Convento

Monasterio de Santa María de Mave s/n, 34402 (Palencia) **Tel** *979 12 36 11* **Fax** *979 12 54 92* **Rooms** *25*

Located in the Montaña Palentina Natural Park, close to Aguilar de Campoo. The rooms are comfortable, even if they do occasionally resemble a nun's cell, and are well equipped with amenities such as minibars, TVs and hairdryers. The restaurant serves up some satisfying Castilian stews. **www.hosteriaelconvento.com**

SANTO DOMINGO DE SILOS Santo Domingo de Silos

Santo Domingo de Silos 18–20, 09610 (Burgos) **Tel** *947 39 00 53* **Fax** *947 39 00 52* **Rooms** *40*

A modest and functional hotel, located in front of the Santo Domingo de Silos monastery. The rooms evoke the seriousness and austerity of Castilian monastic life with forged-iron bedsteads and solid wooden furniture. The hotel's restaurant serves some good, hearty local fare. **www.hotelsantodomingodesilos.com**

SEGOVIA Parador de Segovia

Ctra de Valladolid s/n, 40003 **Tel** *921 44 37 37* **Fax** *921 43 73 62* **Rooms** *113*

This country house is just a short distance from the aqueduct and offers magnificent views of Segovia. The abstract art in the large lobby forms a nice contrast to the sober lines of the classical interior. The restaurant is one of the best places to sample the city's favourite dish, *cochinillo* (suckling pig). **www.parador.es**

SORIA Hostería Solar de Tejada

Claustrilla 1, 42002 **Tel** *975 23 00 54* **Fax** *975 23 00 54* **Rooms** *18*

Situated in the heart of the city, this hotel is equipped with comfortable and modern facilities. The bright and somewhat chintzy rooms have a special charm and offer amenities such as TVs, hairdryers and iron-forged headboards by Luis Saénz, a local artist. **www.hosteriasolardetejada.com**

SORIA Parador de Soria

Parque del Castillo s/n, 42005 **Tel** *975 24 08 00* **Fax** *975 24 08 03* **Rooms** *63*

The highlight of this parador is, without doubt, its privileged location on a hill overlooking Soria and the Duero valley. The hotel itself is surrounded by ancient oaks and green pastures. Many of the rooms are decorated with photos and poems by the city's most famous poet, Antonio Machado. **www.parador.es**

TORDESILLAS Parador de Tordesillas

Ctra de Salamanca 5, 47100 (Valladolid) **Tel** *983 77 00 51* **Fax** *983 77 10 13* **Rooms** *68*

An ancestral home located in a beautiful pine forest. The hotel's spectacular location is complemented by its numerous facilities, including sauna, gym, winter and summer swimming pools, golf course and conference room. The large and comfortable rooms are luxuriously furnished with Castilian antiques. **www.parador.es**

VALLADOLID Hostal París

Especería 2, 47001 **Tel** *983 37 06 25* **Fax** *983 35 83 01* **Rooms** *33*

A simple, four-story building conveniently set in the heart of the city, near the Plaza Mayor. This friendly, family-run hotel has comfortable bedrooms with all modern facilities, and offers good value for those travelling on a budget. The service here is impeccable. **www.hostalparis.com**

VALLADOLID Tryp Recoletos

Acera de Recoletos 13, 47001 **Tel** *983 21 62 00* **Fax** *983 21 62 10* **Rooms** *80*

This recently opened hotel is situated in Valladolid's beautiful historical city centre, and offers great views of the Campo Grande park. The hotel is well equipped with all modern conveniences. What it lacks in character, it makes up with its excellent location close to the town's main train station. **www.solmelia.com**

VILLAFRANCA DEL BIERZO Parador del Bierzo

Avda Calvo Sotelo 28, 24500 (León) **Tel** *987 54 01 75* **Fax** *987 54 00 10* **Rooms** *39*

An unassuming and welcoming hotel near the entrance to the town. The surrounding landscapes of the Ancares mountain range create a tranquil atmosphere. Large and comfortable rooms with traditional Castilian decor and a good restaurant make this one of the best-value paradors around. **www.parador.es**

ZAMORA NH Palacio del Duero

Plaza de la Horta1, 49002 **Tel** *980 50 82 62* **Fax** *980 53 37 22* **Rooms** *49*

The Duero Palace used to house one of the city's first distilleries, and remains a good place to indulge in a tipple at the hotel's restaurant. Like all NH chain properties, the decor here follows a modern, minimalist style that contrasts nicely with the ancient stone walls. Modern amenities and good value for money. **www.nh-hoteles.com**

ZAMORA Parador de Zamora

Plaza del Viriato 5, 49001 **Tel** *980 51 44 97* **Fax** *980 53 00 63* **Rooms** *52*

Located in a 15th-century palace, this hotel's medieval decor features aristocratic tapestries, armour and beds with canopies. The Renaissance patio, embellished with heraldic motifs, is a perfect place to sample some of the restaurant's star dishes, including a mouthwatering almond custard. **www.parador.es**

CASTILLA-LA MANCHA

ALARCÓN Parador de Alarcón   €€€

Avda Amigos de los Castillos s/n, 16214 (Cuenca) **Tel** *969 33 03 15* **Fax** *969 33 03 03* **Rooms** *14*

A medieval fortress stunningly located above the Júcar valley. The lounge and dining rooms are vaulted chambers with thick walls. However, modern artworks by some of Spain's most renowned artists create a contemporary look. The large suites are all spectacular; the one in the lookout tower is the best. **www.parador.es**

ALBACETE Parador de Albacete   €€

Ctra N301 km 251, 02000 (Albacete) **Tel** *967 24 53 21* **Fax** *967 24 32 71* **Rooms** *68*

This parador is set in expansive gardens, with shady terraces and a large outdoor pool. Provides a perfect setting for activities such as walking, fishing and horse riding. The public spaces are decorated with ox yokes and other rural implements, and the fine restaurant serves local cuisine. **www.parador.es**

ALMAGRO Posada del Almagro   €

C/ Gran Maestre 5, 13270 (Ciudad Real) **Tel** *926 26 12 01* **Fax** *926 26 12 01* **Rooms** *9*

This lovely, 16th-century *posada* has been prettily renovated into a simple and charming guesthouse. Features a timbered gallery and cool, rustically-decorated rooms, overlooking a delightful courtyard. Also has a typical tavern serving regional specialities. **www.laposadadealmagro.com**

ALMAGRO Parador de Almagro   €€€

Ronda de San Franciso 31, 13270 (Ciudad Real) **Tel** *926 86 01 00* **Fax** *926 86 01 50* **Rooms** *54*

An exquisite parador, housed in a 16th-century convent, and set around a series of courtyards and cloisters. The former cells have been converted into bedrooms, though their austerity has been replaced by modern comforts. A lace-maker works in one of the courtyards, keeping the town's tradition alive. **www.parador.es**

AYNA Felipe II   €

Ctra Albacete-Elche, 02125 (Albacete) **Tel** *967 29 50 83* **Fax** *967 29 50 83* **Rooms** *39*

This modern hotel is set in a charming village in the mountains of Alabacete. Its semi-circular layout allows a panoramic view of the town and the valley from every bedroom. The staff are friendly and can arrange various outdoor activities, including rafting, horse riding and even stargazing. **www.hotelfelipeiiayna.com**

BALLESTEROS DE CALATRAVA Palacio de la Serna   €€

C/ Cervantes 18, 13432 (Ciudad Real) **Tel** *926 84 22 08* **Fax** *926 84 22 24* **Rooms** *19*

An 18th-century farmhouse in the plains of La Mancha, decorated in a mix of Castilian and modern styles. The rooms are large and painted in bold, contemporary colours. The staff can arrange horseback and mountain bike excursions into the surrounding hills. Also has art galleries and a sculpture garden. **www.palaciodelaserna.com**

BELMONTE Palacio Buenavista   €

C/ La Iglesia 2, 16640 (Cuenca) **Tel** *967 18 75 80* **Fax** *967 18 75 88* **Rooms** *22*

A charming country hotel in a renovated 16th-century palace. Features spacious rooms, decorated in a traditional style, wooden galleries and a delightful garden. Some of the rooms have views of Belmonte's magnificent castle. A primrose-yellow dining room serves delicious oven-roasted lamb and steak. **www.hotelpalaciobuenavista.com**

CUENCA Posada de San José   €

C/ Julián Romero 4, 16001 (Cuenca) **Tel** *969 21 13 00* **Fax** *969 23 03 65* **Rooms** *29*

Run by a Canadian-Spanish couple, this hotel is set in a 17th-century convent. Perched vertiginously above the gorge, it is one of Cuenca's famous hanging houses *(see pp384–5)*. The rooms are stylishly decorated with white fabrics, and offer splendid views. Curiously labyrinthine, it showcases many antiques and frescoes. **www.posadasanjose.com**

CUENCA La Cueva del Fraile   €€

Ctra Cuenca-Buenache km 7, 16001 (Cuenca) **Tel** *969 21 15 71* **Fax** *969 21 15 72* **Rooms** *76*

Set in a green valley outside Cuenca, this 16th-century hotel is built around a white patio and surrounded by vast gardens. The rooms are elegantly furnished with all modern comforts. The special duplex apartments are ideal for families. Also has tennis courts, and guests can rent bicycles to explore the countryside. **www.hotelcuevadelfraile.com**

CUENCA Leonor de Aquitania   €€

C/ San Pedro 58–60, 16001 (Cuenca) **Tel** *969 23 10 00* **Fax** *969 23 10 04* **Rooms** *46*

Named after a medieval princess, this hotel is located in a historic building in the heart of old Cuenca. The spacious bedrooms and suites are decorated in a traditional style, and the public areas are adorned with tapestries and hunting trophies. The restaurant offers panoramic views from its terrace. **www.hotelleonordeaquitania.com**

CUENCA Parador de Cuenca   €€€

Subida de San Pablo s/n, 16001 (Cuenca) **Tel** *969 23 23 20* **Fax** *969 23 25 34* **Rooms** *63*

The 16th-century convent of San Pablo has been transformed into an elegant parador. The town's famous old hanging houses, draped vertiginously over the gorge, can be seen from the bedrooms. Offers a range of modern facilities, including a fine regional restaurant. **www.parador.es**

Key to Price Guide *see p560* **Key to Symbols** *see back cover flap*

EL TOBOSO Casa de la Torre

C/ Antonio Machado 16, 45820 **Tel** *925 56 80 06* **Fax** *925 56 80 06* **Rooms** *14*

A rural inn in the heart of Don Quixote country, El Toboso was once home to Dulcinea, the object of the knight's affections. The hotel is set in a 17th-century mansion, built around a typical Manchegan galleried courtyard. The rooms and suites are attractively decorated. Three dining areas serve regional specialities. **www.casadelatorre.com**

GUADALAJARA España

C/ Teniente Figueroa 3, 19001 (Guadalajara) **Tel** *949 21 13 03* **Fax** *949 21 13 05* **Rooms** *40*

A family-run hotel in a modernized, 19th-century mansion located in the centre of the city. Offers excellent amenities, including a small sauna. The simple, spotlessly clean rooms are decorated in a traditional style. The restaurant serves local specialities, and the staff can advise on nearby attractions.

MANZANARES Parador de Manzanares

Ctra Madrid-Cádiz km 174, 13200 (Ciudad Real) **Tel** *926 61 04 00* **Fax** *926 61 09 35* **Rooms** *50*

Set in the heart of the city's principal wine region, this parador is a good base for exploring Don Quixote country. With three natural parks just a short distance away, it is also perfect for nature enthusiasts. The hotel is modern, but built in traditional Manchegan style, and is surrounded by extensive gardens. **www.parador.es**

OROPESA Parador de Oropesa

Plaza de Palacio 1, 45560 (Toledo) **Tel** *925 43 00 00* **Fax** *925 43 07 77* **Rooms** *48*

The Sierra de Gredos forms a scenic backdrop to this medieval fortress rising above a plain of olive groves and vineyards. The bedrooms are spacious; some of them have Jacuzzis. The parador also arranges activities such as pheasant hunting and horse riding excursions. The romantic restaurant serves regional cuisine. **www.parador.es**

OSSA DE MONTIEL Albamanjón

Laguna de San Pedro 16, 02611 (Albacete) **Tel** *926 69 90 48* **Fax** *926 69 91 20* **Rooms** *8*

A tranquil retreat by the Lagunas de Ruidera, La Mancha's attractive string of turquoise lakes. This modern complex has been built in a traditional style, and is beautifully decorated with colourful tiles and climbing plants. The bedrooms are elegant and comfortable, and present far-reaching views of the countryside. **www.albamanjon.net**

PASTRANA Hospedería Real de Pastrana

Convento del Carmen, Ctra Pastrana-Zorita km 1, 19100 (Guadalajara) **Tel** *949 37 10 60* **Rooms** *27*

This hotel occupies a wing of the Monasterio del Carmen, founded by St Teresa of Ávila. Located near the picturesque town of Pastrana, it overlooks the Río Tajo, and offers simple rooms. Trips to sights associated with the famous saint, as well as hunting, fishing and sailing can also be arranged. **www.hosteriasreales.com**

SAN CLEMENTE Casa de los Acacio

C/ Cruz Cerrada 10, 16600 (Cuenca) **Tel** *969 30 03 60* **Fax** *969 30 00 67* **Rooms** *8*

Located in a historic Manchegan village, this rural hotel is housed in a carefully restored, 17th-century stone mansion. The rooms and suites are set around a graceful patio, and decorated with traditional Castillian furniture. Also has a garden, games room and barbecue area.

SIGÜENZA El Molino de Alcuneza

Ctra de Alboreca km 0.5, 19264 (Guadalajara) **Tel** *949 39 15 01* **Fax** *949 34 70 04* **Rooms** *11*

A restored mill in the Alcarria now contains this intimate country hotel. Each room has been stylishly decorated with traditional furnishings and pretty prints, and many feature the original beams and cool stone walls. A stream burbles beneath the public lounge. Dinner includes fresh produce from the kitchen garden. **www.molinodealcuneza.com**

SIGÜENZA Parador de Sigüenza

Plaza del Castillo, 19250 (Guadalajara) **Tel** *949 39 01 00* **Fax** *949 39 13 64* **Rooms** *81*

Sigüenza's massive castle overlooks the city from a hilltop – its crenellated towers and battlements are a stirring sight. Former VIP guests here include the Catholic Monarchs *(see pp56–7)*. Bedrooms are handsomely furnished with every modern amenity and overlook a striking courtyard. **www.parador.es**

TOLEDO La Almazara

Ctra Toledo-Argés km 3.4, 45080 (Toledo) **Tel** *925 22 38 66* **Fax** *925 25 05 62* **Rooms** *24*

This 16th-century country-house hotel is set high on a wooded hilltop oustide Toledo, and has a magnificent view. Renowned artist, El Greco, was reputedly a frequent guest here, and painted from this vantage point. The hotel is surrounded by olive trees, oaks and junipers, and has simple rooms; some with a terrace. **www.hotelalmazara.com**

TOLEDO Hostal del Cardenal

Paseo de Recaredo 24, 45004 (Toledo) **Tel** *925 22 49 00* **Fax** *925 22 29 91* **Rooms** *27*

Now a historic hotel near the city walls, this 18th-century mansion was once the residence of Toledo's archbishop. It has sculpted ceilings and brick courtyards, and the bedrooms and suites are traditionally decorated with plush fabrics and every modern comfort. Some overlook the lovely, jasmine-scented gardens. **www.hostaldelcardenal.com**

TOLEDO Pintor El Greco

C/ Alamillos del Tránsito 13, 45002 (Toledo) **Tel** *925 28 51 91* **Fax** *925 21 58 19* **Rooms** *33*

A 17th-century bakery in Toledo's former Jewish quarter has been discreetly extended behind the original façade and patio. Wrought iron, traditional ceramics and lots of flowering plants add character to the hotel. The bedrooms are modern, yet in keeping with the historic surroundings. **www.hotelpintorelgreco.com**

TOLEDO Parador de Toledo 🖼️🔢🏊📋 €€€

Cerro del Emperador s/n, 45002 (Toledo) **Tel** 925 22 18 50 **Fax** 925 22 51 66 **Rooms** 77

The terrace of this graceful, stone-built parador, which is located on the brow of a hill overlooking the city, offers a spectacular view of Toledo. The bedrooms are large and have beamed ceilings. Many have terraces as well. The hotel is popular with sightseers and photographers, so book well in advance. **www.parador.es**

TRAGACETE Hotel El Gamo 🖼️🔢 €

Plaza de los Caídos 2, 16150 (Cuenca) **Tel** 969 28 90 08 **Fax** 969 28 92 28 **Rooms** 39

A good-value hostal in a peaceful village, among the hills and woods in the Serranía de Cuenca, near the Río Cuervo's source. The bedrooms are simply furnished, but more than adequate. The hotel is ideally located for hiking, mountain biking and other active pursuits. The restaurant serves generous portions of local cuisine.

UCLÉS Casa Palacio Fernández Contreras 🔢🏊📋 €€

C/ Angustias 2, 16450 (Cuenca) **Tel** 969 13 50 65 **Fax** 969 13 50 11 **Rooms** 7

This historic mansion, built in 1546 in the centre of the beautiful town of Uclés, has been transformed into an intimate and stylish hotel. Great care has been taken with the decor, which presents a perfect blend of original details and contemporary furnishings. **www.lacasapalacio.com**

VALDEPEÑAS Hotel Central 🖼️🔢📋 €

C/ Capitán Fillol 4, 13300 (Ciudad Real) **Tel** 926 31 33 88 **Fax** 926 31 35 09 **Rooms** 25

A modest but reliable hotel in the centre of Castilla-La Mancha's largest wine-producing town. This modern establishment is tucked behind a historic façade, and makes a good base for touring the local bodegas. The rooms are simply yet comfortably decorated, with amenities such as 24-hour room service. **www.hotelcentralval.com**

VALVERDE DE LOS ARROYOS El Nido de Valverde 📋 €€€€€

C/ Escuelas 1, 19224 (Guadalajara) **Tel** 949 85 42 21 **Fax** 949 30 74 48 **Rooms** 2

This exceptional little hotel is set in a storybook village of black slate-roofed houses in the northernmost tip of Guadalajara, and has just two rooms. The owners of this stone-built cottage offer creative, home-cooked meals – dinner and breakfast are included. A magical and unforgettable spot. **www.nidodevalverde.com**

VILLANUEVA DE LOS INFANTES Hospederia Real El Buscón de Quevedo 🔢📋 €€

C/ Frailes 1, 13320 (Ciudad Real) **Tel** 926 36 17 88 **Fax** 926 36 17 88 **Rooms** 24

Originally a 16th-century Dominican convent, this appealing country inn has traditional bedrooms decorated with local wrought-iron furniture and a fine patio in the former cloister. The hotel is named after Francisco de Quevedo, author of the satirical and amusing *The Swindler*, who died here in 1645. **www.hospederiasreales.com**

EXTREMADURA

ALMENDRAL Monasterio de Rocamador 🔢🏊📋 €€€

Ctra Badajoz-Huelva, 06171 (Badajoz) **Tel** 924 48 90 00 **Fax** 924 48 90 01 **Rooms** 30

An enchanting country hotel, in a restored former monastery, built in honey-coloured stone. The rooms at this stylish, romantic retreat retain many of their original details, and are beautifully furnished in a mixture of contemporary and traditional styles. Most have their own fireplaces, and all enjoy breathtaking views. **www.rocamador.com**

BADAJOZ Río 🖼️🔢🏊📋 €€

Av Adolfo Díaz Ambrona 13, 06006 (Badajoz) **Tel** 924 27 26 00 **Fax** 924 27 38 74 **Rooms** 101

A large, comfortable modern hotel in the city centre, with spacious, spotlessly clean rooms decorated in bland chain-hotel style. It is geared towards business travellers, which means that rates drop impressively at weekends. The facilities include a café, airy public lounges and even a bingo hall. **www.hotelrio.net**

CÁCERES Meliá Cáceres 🖼️🔢📋 €€€

Plaza de San Juan 11, 10003 (Cáceres) **Tel** 927 21 58 00 **Fax** 927 21 40 70 **Rooms** 86

This 16th-century mansion beside the city walls has been renovated by a hotel chain, though it retains the feel of a chic boutique hotel. Rooms are decorated with light, modern furnishings, and some have vaulted stone ceilings. Also showcases many antique hunting implements. Several outdoor activities can be arranged. **www.solmelia.com**

CÁCERES Parador de Cáceres 🖼️🔢📋 €€€

C/ Ancha 6, 10003 (Cáceres) **Tel** 927 21 17 59 **Fax** 927 21 17 29 **Rooms** 31

A small parador in the converted 14th-century Palace of Torreorgaz. Inside a labyrinth of stairs, doors, patios and corridors unfolds. The rooms are elegantly decorated in creamy fabrics and understated floral prints. Some boast coffered ceilings. Also has extensive, well-maintained gardens. **www.parador.es**

CUACOS DE YUSTE El Relojero 🔢🏊 €€

Paraje de las Majadillas, 10430 (Badajoz) **Tel** 927 17 23 60 **Fax** 915 12 31 37 **Rooms** 11

On a quiet hillside next to the Monasterio de Yuste, this country hotel features antique furnishings and exquisite art from around the world. Each of the cool, stone rooms has a fireplace, and offers breathtaking views of the countryside. Dinner is available only for guests. **www.elrelojerodeyuste.com**

Key to Price Guide *see p560* **Key to Symbols** *see back cover flap*

GUADALUPE Hospedería del Real Monasterio

Plaza de Juan Carlos I, 10140 (Cáceres) **Tel** *927 36 70 00* **Fax** *927 36 71 77* **Rooms** *47*

This hotel is part of the 16th-century Franciscan monastery which dominates Guadalupe. Many of the rooms, which surround the Gothic stone courtyard, were originally pharmacies, and are simply decorated with traditional, carved wooden furnishings. Also has several public lounges, with board games or TVs. **www.monasterioguadalupe.com**

GUADALUPE Parador de Guadalupe

C/ Marqués de la Romana 12, 10140 (Cáceres) **Tel** *927 36 70 75* **Fax** *927 36 70 76* **Rooms** *39*

Located in a 16th-century hospital and convent, this beautiful parador is set in flower-filled gardens very close to the monastery. The elegant bedrooms overlook whitewashed patios full of citrus trees. The rooms in the annexe are larger, but those in the original building have much more character. **www.parador.es**

JARANDILLA DE LA VERA Parador de Jarandilla

Av de García Prieto 1, 10450 (Cáceres) **Tel** *927 56 01 17* **Fax** *927 56 00 88* **Rooms** *53*

This imposing 15th-century castle, where Emperor Carlos V stayed for a year, has been modernized without losing its medieval feel. The swimming pool is surrounded by olive trees and rose gardens, and there is a tennis court and children's play area. It boasts one of the region's best restaurants, along with a café-bar. **www.parador.es**

JEREZ DE LOS CABALLEROS Los Templarios

Ctra de Villanueva, 06380 (Badajoz) **Tel** *924 73 16 36* **Fax** *924 75 03 38* **Rooms** *49*

A modern hotel named after the Knights Templar, who played an important part in the history of the area. All the bedrooms have views over the valley and are decorated with contemporary furnishings. A wide terrace surrounds the pool and there is a children's play area. The friendly staff can arrange biking and horse riding excursions.

LOSAR DE LA VERA Antigua Casa del Heno

Finca Valdepimienta, 10460 (Cáceres) **Tel** *927 19 80 77* **Fax** *927 19 80 77* **Rooms** *7*

A farmhouse surrounded by oak trees and meadows in a beautiful setting near the Sierra de Gredos. Offers B&B, and is popular during spring when the cherry trees bloom. The bedrooms are simply decorated, and the old stone walls and wooden beams add a rustic charm. Dinner is provided on request. **www.antiguacasadelheno.com**

LOSAR DE LA VERA Hostería Fontivieja

C/ Mártires 11, 10460 (Cáceres) **Tel** *927 57 01 08* **Fax** *927 57 01 08* **Rooms** *20*

A small, family-run hotel in a peaceful olive grove outside the town. Built in the traditional style, it offers rooms in the main building, as well as luxurious suites in the bungalows scattered in the gardens. All are comfortable and decorated with locally made furniture. The amenities are excellent. **www.hosteriafontivieja.com/**

MALPARTIDA DE PLASENCIA Cañada Real

Ctra Ex-108 km 42, 10680 (Cáceres) **Tel** *927 45 94 07* **Fax** *927 45 94 34* **Rooms** *61*

This modern hotel is located within easy distance of Plasencia and nearby nature reserves. The bedrooms are comfortable and spacious, and there are three suites with Jacuzzis. All are decorated with floral prints and traditional furniture. A children's play area and board games are also available. **www.hotelcreal.es**

MÉRIDA Velada Mérida

Av Princesa Sofía, 06800 (Badajoz) **Tel** *924 31 51 10* **Fax** *924 31 15 52* **Rooms** *99*

Conveniently located near the cultural centre of Mérida, this hotel has good transport links to the rest of the city. Its modern design draws inspiration from classical temples. The rooms are large, traditionally decorated and have every modern convenience. The restaurant offers regional cuisine. **www.veladahoteles.com**

MÉRIDA Meliá Mérida Boutique Hotel

Plaza España 19, 06800 (Badajoz) **Tel** *924 38 38 00* **Rooms** *76*

One of the newest hotels in the Meliá chain, this charming retreat is housed in a pair of elegant historic palaces. Illustrious former guests include three Spanish monarchs. The hotel maintains a regal atmosphere with a profusion of antiques and original architectural details. All modern conveniences are available. **www.meliamerida.solmelia.com**

MÉRIDA Parador de Mérida

Plaza de la Constitución 3, 06800 (Badajoz) **Tel** *924 31 38 00* **Fax** *924 31 92 08* **Rooms** *82*

A converted, 17th-century Baroque convent, which was built on the ruins of an ancient Roman temple. Roman columns, inscriptions in Arabic and Visigothic capitals have been preserved and incorporated into the wonderful "Garden of Antiquities". Also arranges activities such as hunting, golf, fishing and tennis. **www.parador.es**

PLASENCIA Alfonso VIII

Av Alfonso VIII 32, 10600 (Cáceres) **Tel** *927 41 02 50* **Fax** *927 41 80 42* **Rooms** *55*

A modern hotel, centrally located near the Parque de la Isla. Offers all the expected four-star facilities. The rooms are large and bright, with contemporary furnishings, and the staff are attentive. The hotel itself is ideally situated for exploring this beautiful, rural region. **www.hotelalfonsoviii.com**

TRUJILLO Mesón La Cadena

Plaza Mayor 8, 10200 (Cáceres) **Tel** *927 32 14 63* **Fax** *927 32 31 16* **Rooms** *8*

This restaurant-with-rooms, in an attractive granite house on the main square, is a good budget option. The bedrooms, decorated with locally-made textiles, are on the third floor, and the best offer spectacular views over Trujillo's beautiful Plaza Mayor. The eatery on the ground floor is a classic in the city, serving regional specialities.

TRUJILLO Parador de Trujillo
€€

C/ Santa Beatriz de Silva 1, 10200 (Cáceres) **Tel** *927 32 13 50* **Fax** *927 32 13 66* **Rooms** *43*

This charming parador and former chapel, where breakfast is now served, incorporates parts of a 16th-century convent. The hotel is within the spellbinding old city of Trujillo, but located on a quiet street away from the noise. The elegant rooms look out onto a series of lovely patios, filled with orange trees. **www.parador.es**

ZAFRA Parador de Zafra
€€

Pl del Corazón de María 7, 06300 (Badajoz) **Tel** *924 55 45 40* **Fax** *924 55 10 18* **Rooms** *45*

This fairytale castle, with its round towers, was built in the 15th century on the ruins of a Moorish fortress. A beautiful staircase leads from the courtyard, with an arcaded gallery, to the bedrooms. These are regally furnished with traditional furnishings which evoke the ducal palace of former times. It is set in elegant gardens. **www.parador.es**

ZAFRA Huerta Honda
€€€

Av López Asme 30, 06300 (Badajoz) **Tel** *924 55 41 00* **Fax** *924 55 25 04* **Rooms** *48*

Many regular guests feel that the accommodation at this hotel is as good as that at the parador next door. Set around patios with fountains and flowers, the hotel's construction is stylish, yet traditional. The chic bedrooms are decorated in a contemporary style and are extremely comfortable. **www.hotelhuertahonda.com**

SEVILLE

EL ARENAL NH Plaza de Armas
€€

C/ Marqués de Paradas, 41001 **Tel** *954 69 19 92* **Fax** *954 90 18 32* **Rooms** *262*   **Map** *1 B5*

A reliable, modern chain hotel built in 1992 and refurbished in 1999 in a functional, minimalist style. Offers excellent facilities for business travellers, and tourists can benefit from the hotel's hefty weekend discounts. This city-centre hotel is handily located for sightseeing. **www.nh-hotels.com**

EL ARENAL Simón
€€

C/ García de Vinuesa 19, 41001 **Tel** *954 22 66 60* **Fax** *954 56 22 41* **Rooms** *29*   **Map** *3 B2*

A central hotel in an 18th-century mansion built around a pretty patio planted with ferns and covered with local *azulejos* (tiles). The public areas are tiled and hung with chandeliers, but the bedrooms are simpler and vary in size and quality. A buffet breakfast is available. The hotel is very popular, so book early. **www.hotelsimonsevilla.com**

EL ARENAL Taberna del Alabardero
€€€

C/ Zaragoza 20, 41001 **Tel** *954 50 27 21* **Fax** *954 56 36 66* **Rooms** *7*   **Map** *3 B1*

The former home of Sevillano poet J. Antonio Castevany, this little hotel occupies a mansion, and is set above one of the city's finest restaurants. Each of the individually decorated bedrooms is furnished with antiques and stylish fabrics. The central courtyard is illumintated through a stained-glass roof. **www.tabernadelalabardero.com**

EL ARENAL Vincci la Rabida
€€€

C/ Casterlar 24, 41001 **Tel** *954 50 12 80* **Fax** *954 21 66 00* **Rooms** *81*   **Map** *3 B1*

Located in El Arenal district, close to shops, restaurants and a bullring, this 18th-century palace was restored and opened as a four-star hotel in 2003. The guestrooms combine warm, earthy tones with dark furnishings and wrought-iron beds. Some rooms have views of the central courtyard. **www.vincci-hotels.com**

EL ARENAL Los Seises
€€€€

C/ Segovia 6, 41004 **Tel** *954 22 94 95* **Fax** *954 22 43 34* **Rooms** *42*   **Map** *6 D4*

Perfectly situated in Barrio Santa Cruz, this 16th-century palace was restored in the early 1990s, when an eccentric mix of Roman mosaics, Renaissance panelling and Arabic tiles was discovered – most are on display now. This well-appointed hotel has charming architecture, although the decor in the rooms could be improved. **www.husa.es**

SANTA CRUZ Murillo
€

C/ Lope de Rueda 7 & 9, 41004 **Tel** *954 21 60 95* **Fax** *954 21 96 16* **Rooms** *57*   **Map** *4 D2*

A pleasant, reasonably-priced hotel in an ochre-and-white building off Plaza Alfaro, a short walk from the cathedral. The public areas are decorated with antiques, hand-carved furniture, coffered ceilings and even suits of armour. The bedrooms are plain and functional, and are located on a quiet pedestrian street. **www.hotelmurillo.com**

SANTA CRUZ Alcántara
€€

C/ Ximenez de Encisco 28, 41004 **Tel** *954 50 05 95* **Fax** *954 50 06 04* **Rooms** *21*   **Map** *6 E4*

This 18th-century mansion can be accessed through the old coach entrance, which takes guests into a modern, welcoming hotel. The rooms are simple, with stripped pine floors and painted headboards, but comfortable and clean. They vary in size and some are suitable for families. **www.hotelalcantara.net**

SANTA CRUZ La Casa del Maestro
€€€

C/ Almudena 5, 41002 **Tel** *954 50 00 07* **Fax** *954 50 00 06* **Rooms** *11*   **Map** *6 E2*

Once the home of celebrated flamenco guitarist Niño Ricardo, this charming yellow-and-ochre painted town house is built around a patio bursting with plants and flowers. Rooms are on the small side, but full of thoughtful touches such as a jug of iced water and chocolates placed by the bed. Has a lovely roof terrace. **www.lacasadelmaestro.com**

Key to Price Guide *see p560* **Key to Symbols** *see back cover flap*

SANTA CRUZ Casa Numero Siete

€€€€

C/ Virgenes 7, 41004 **Tel** *954 22 15 81* **Fax** *954 21 45 27* **Rooms** *7* **Map** *6 E3*

One of the loveliest and most romantic hotels in Seville. This elegant guesthouse occupies a mansion and features just a handful of rooms. The decor includes a range of antiques and family heirlooms. Also has an opulent sitting room with a bar. The breakfasts here are delicious. **www.casanumero7.com**

SANTA CRUZ Las Casas del Rey de Baeza

€€€€

Plaza Jesus de la Redencion 2, 41003 **Tel** *954 56 14 96* **Fax** *954 56 14 41* **Rooms** *41* **Map** *4 D1*

Located in a beautiful unique setting, this hotel expertly fuses the past and present. Bright, whitewashed walls blend with the ochres and reds of the courtyard, shaded by arched walkways. Indoors, cool stone flooring and natural tones lead to the rooms, where chic interiors pay tribute to modernity. **www.hospes.es**

SANTA CRUZ Alfonso XIII

€€€€€

C/ San Fernando 2, 41004 **Tel** *954 91 70 00* **Fax** *954 91 70 99* **Rooms** *147* **Map** *3 C2*

Seville's legendary grand hotel, built in Neo-Mudéjar style as a royal guesthouse, is still fit for kings. Elegance and formal service are assured, and bedrooms are decorated with opulent furnishings. Crystal chandeliers, marble columns and palm trees adorn the public spaces. Also has a posh cocktail bar. **www.westin-alfonsoxiii.com**

FURTHER AFIELD (LA MACARENA) Baco

€€

Plaza Ponce de León 15, 41003 **Tel** *954 56 50 00* **Fax** *954 56 36 54* **Rooms** *25* **Map** *2 E5*

A historic mansion in the centre of the old city has been transformed into a modern hotel in Sevillian style. A spiral staircase ascends from reception. The quieter back bedrooms overlook patios with tiles and potted palms. All rooms are simply but comfortably decorated in traditional style. **www.baco.es**

FURTHER AFIELD (LA MACARENA) Patio de la Cartuja

€€

C/ Lumbreras 8 & 10, 41002 **Tel** *954 90 02 00* **Fax** *954 90 20 56* **Rooms** *56* **Map** *1 C4*

A group of old mansions with large patios have been converted into this unusual apartment-hotel. Situated in the bohemian neighbourhood of La Macarena, the apartments are simple, but well equipped. The hotel is just a short walk from the cathedral and the Barrio Santa Cruz. Also has a paid car park. **www.patiosdesevilla.com**

FURTHER AFIELD (LA MACARENA) Alcoba del Rey de Sevilla

€€€

C/ Bécquer 9, 41002 **Tel** *954 915 800* **Fax** *95 491 56 75* **Rooms** *15* **Map** *2 D3*

This is a stylish little hotel, full of small details which create a romantic atmosphere. Furnishings include lovely glasswork, tiles, silk cushions, objets d'art and beds – all of which are for sale. Each of the rooms is named after a personality from the Moorish period and are elegantly decorated. **www.alcobadelrey.com**

FURTHER AFIELD (LA MACARENA) Casa Romana Hotel Boutique

€€€

C/ Trajano 15Parras 28, 41003 **Tel** *954 91 51 70* **Fax** *954 37 31 91* **Rooms** *26*

Rooms are distributed around the picturesque central courtyard, with all the comforts you would expect of a four-star hotel. All the rooms are tastefully decorated in subdued elegance while some have Jacuzzis. Website offers specials including flamenco tickets with reservations. **www.hotelcasaromana.com**

FURTHER AFIELD (SOUTH) Ciudad de Sevilla

€€

Av Manuel Siurot 25, 41003 **Tel** *954 23 85 39* **Rooms** *94* **Map** *4 D5*

Located in a residential neighbourhood on the outskirts of the city, this luxurious chain hotel occupies a mansion. Behind the old façade is a contemporary hotel with all modern conveniences, including business facilities, a small rooftop pool and a sun terrace. The hotel's website offers some good deals. **www.ac-hoteles.com**

ANDALUSIA

ALCALÁ DE GUADAIRA Hotel Oromana

€€

Av de Portugal, 41500 (Sevilla) **Tel** *955 68 64 00* **Fax** *955 686 424* **Rooms** *31*

On the fringes of the historic town of Alacala, just 15 km (9 miles) from Seville, this country hotel is located in a handsome mansion built in the 1920s. It is surrounded by huge gardens with an outdoor pool. Welcoming, helpful staff, and a good restaurant serving local specialities. Disabled access. **www.hoteloromana.com**

ALMERÍA AM Torreluz IV

€€

Plaza Flores 5, 04001 (Almería) **Tel** *950 23 49 99* **Fax** *950 23 47 09* **Rooms** *109*

Smart and modern, this is the grandest of the Torreluz group of hotels, all sited in the centre of Almería. A grand spiral staircase sweeps up to bedrooms with every imaginable amenity, including interactive TVs. There is also a rooftop pool and a little sun terrace with loungers. The nearby sister hotels are cheaper. **www.amtorreluz.com**

ARACENA Sierra de Aracena

€

Gran Via 21, 21200 (Huelva) **Tel** *959 12 61 75* **Fax** *959 12 62 18* **Rooms** *43*

This quiet hotel is in the centre of the attractive town of Aracena. Although it is a modern building, the design integrates pretty Arabic-style details. The rooms are simply furnished, and some have views of the town's castle. Staff can arrange outdoor activities such as hiking, rafting, mountain biking and horse riding.

ARACENA Finca Buen Vino　　　🔳🔳🔳　　€€€
Los Marines, 21293 (Huelva) **Tel** *959 12 40 34* **Fax** *959 50 10 29* **Rooms** *4*

A wonderful guesthouse located in an elegant villa on a hilltop surrounded by olive and citrus groves. The owners grow their own organic produce – used for breakfasts, afternoon teas and cordon bleu cuisine served at dinner (guests only). Stay in one of the villas, or rent a cottage in the grounds. **www.fincabuenvino.com**

ARCOS DE LA FRONTERA Casa Grande　　　🔳🔳　　€
C/ Maldonado 10, 11630 (Cádiz) **Tel** *956 70 39 30* **Fax** *956 71 70 95* **Rooms** *7*

A charming little hotel set in a whitewashed 18th-century mansion, which still bears the escutcheon of its original owner. Each of the originally decorated rooms is full of character. Family-run, it is warm, intimate and full of details such as home-made marmalade for breakfast. Offers splendid views from the roof terrace. **www.lacasagrande.net**

ARCOS DE LA FRONTERA Parador de Arcos de Frontera　　　🔳🔳🔳　　€€
Plaza del Cabildo s/n, 11630 (Cádiz) **Tel** *956 70 05 00* **Fax** *956 70 11 16* **Rooms** *24*

Formerly a magistrate's house, this mansion perched on a cliff above the old city is now a smart parador. A huge terrace offers great views of ancient spires and rooftops below, and the rooms are set around a series of beautifully tiled patios with wells and fountains. Rooms are plush and comfortable and some have Jacuzzis. **www.parador.es**

AYAMONTE Riu Canela　　　🔳🔳🔳🔳🔳🔳　　€€€€
Playa de Isla Canela, 21470 (Huelva) **Tel** *959 47 71 24* **Fax** *959 47 71 70* **Rooms** *349*

The beachside Riu Canela is located in Isla Canela, near the Portuguese border. This modern complex, built in an Andalusian-style village surrounded by palm-filled gardens, is actually more of a summer holiday centre than a hotel. One of its three pools is especially for children. Room prices include breakfast and dinner. **www.riu.com**

BAEZA Hotel Fuentenueva　　　🔳🔳🔳　　€
Calle del Carmen 15, 23440 (Jaén) **Tel** *953 74 31 00* **Fax** *953 74 32 00* **Rooms** *13*

Relocated in to a 19th-century house from a converted women's prison, this hotel offers all the mod-con facilities. These include a library, cafeteria, conference hall, a Japanese Garden and wireless Internet. Rooms boast hydromassage baths and sleek modern decor. **www.fuentenueva.com**

BUBIÓN Villa Turística del Bubión　　　🔳🔳🔳　　€€
C/ Barrio Alto s/n, 18412 (Granada) **Tel** *958 76 39 09* **Fax** *958 76 39 05* **Rooms** *43*

This mini-village is in the distinct building style of the Alpujarras, and each bungalow has the typical flat roofs and tall chimneys of the region. Set within Sierra Nevada's natural park, staff can arrange outdoor activities such as horse riding, hikes or paragliding. Good regional restaurant. Special offers on the website. **www.villabubion.com**

CAÑOS DE MECA La Breña　　　🔳🔳　　€€
Av Trafalgar 4, 11160 (Cádiz) **Tel** *956 43 73 68* **Fax** *956 43 73 68* **Rooms** *7*

The beaches of the Costa de la Luz are some of the most beautiful and unspoilt in Spain. This charming beachside hotel is painted a crisp blue and white, and the rooms and suites are simple and spacious. Most offer fine sea views. It has an excellent restaurant with a modern Andalusian menu, and a shady terrace. **www.hotelbrena.com**

CARMONA Parador de Carmona　　　🔳🔳🔳🔳　　€€€
C/ Alcázar, 41410 (Sevilla) **Tel** *954 14 10 10* **Fax** *954 14 17 12* **Rooms** *63*

This magnificent clifftop parador was built as a fortress by the Moors and became the palace of the Christian king, Pedro the Cruel. It is hung with tapestries and scattered with antiques, and the plush rooms have superb views of the countryside. There is a huge outdoor pool, and one of the best parador restaurants. **www.parador.es**

CARMONA Casa de Carmona　　　🔳🔳🔳🔳🔳　　€€€€
Plaza de Lasso 1, 41410 (Sevilla) **Tel** *954 19 20 00* **Fax** *954 19 01 89* **Rooms** *34*

A 16th-century palace, decorated in a blend of contemporary and period styles, has been converted into a hotel which has featured in numerous fashion magazines. The luxurious rooms and suites are filled with art and opulent furniture, and there is a superb restaurant. A good base for exploring Seville province. **www.casadecarmona.com**

CASTELLAR DE LA FRONTERA Casa Convento La Almoraima　　　🔳🔳🔳🔳　　€€
Finca La Almoraima, 11350 (Cádiz) **Tel** *956 69 30 02* **Fax** *956 69 32 14* **Rooms** *23*

Surrounded by a protected forest of Mediterranean cork trees, this stunning mansion and former convent is now a tranquil rural hotel. The cloisters are now a flower-filled patio, and the public areas are decorated with antiques. The rooms are simple, and the hotel can arrange tours of the estate and the region. **www.la-almoraima.com**

CASTILLEJA DE LA CUESTA Hacienda de San Ygnacio　　　🔳🔳🔳　　€€€
C/ Real 190, 41950 (Sevilla) **Tel** *954 16 92 90* **Fax** *954 16 14 37* **Rooms** *13*

Once a Jesuit monastery, then an Andalusian hacienda, this is now a relaxed hotel and estate set in whitewashed walls. Huge palms tower above the graceful central patio, and the fine restaurant is in the former olive oil mill. The rooms are functional, with few comforts, but the public areas are beautiful. **www.haciendasanignacio.com**

CAZALLA DE LA SIERRA Las Navezuelas　　　🔳🔳　　€
Ctra Cazalla-Ed Pedroso, 41370 (Sevilla) **Tel** *954 88 47 64* **Fax** *954 48 45 94* **Rooms** *10*

The spacious rooms in this family-run farmhouse are furnished with handworked fabrics. Staying here gives visitors a rare opportunity to experience living in an authentic Andalusian *cortijo* (farmstead). The rooms look out over vast orchards of olive trees and cork oaks, and home-cooked meals are served. **www.lasnavezuelas.com**

Key to Price Guide *see p560* **Key to Symbols** *see back cover flap*

CAZALLA DE LA SIERRA Hospedería La Cartuja

Ctra Cazalla-Constantina km 2.5, 41370 (Sevilla) **Tel** *954 88 45 16* **Fax** *954 88 47 07* **Rooms** *12*

An old monastery has been converted into a charming refuge for artists by its crusading owner. Painters, sculptors and musicians sometimes offer their art in exchange for their stay, and there is a gallery exhibiting work by resident artists, which can be purchased. Choose from rooms , suites or a cottage. **www.cartujadecazalla.com**

CAZORLA Molino de la Farraga

Camino de la Hoz s/n, 23470 (Jaén) **Tel** *953 72 12 49* **Fax** *953 72 12 49* **Rooms** *9*

A recently-renovated, 200-year-old mill on the fringes of the lovely rural village of Cazorla, this is perfect for anyone seeking tranquility. Shrouded by abundant greenery, the whitewashed mill is surrounded by rambling gardens, and the rooms are simple but very pretty. They also have an annexe. **www.molinolafarraga.com**

CAZORLA Parador de Cazorla

Sierra de Cazorla, 23470 (Jaén) **Tel** *953 72 70 75* **Fax** *953 72 70 77* **Rooms** *34*

The forests and mountains of the Sierra de Cazorla, a major Andalusian nature reserve, are the superb setting for this parador. It is modern, but has been designed with the rural setting in mind. Nestled into the side of the hill, it offers fine views from the well-equipped bedrooms. The restaurant serves local game in season. **www.parador.es**

COLMENAR Cortijo La Reina

Ctra Málaga-Colmenar km 549.5, 29013 (Málaga) **Tel** *951 01 40 00* **Fax** *951 01 40 49* **Rooms** *32*

A relaxed, country hotel with gardens filled with huge trees. The mansion contains elegant bedrooms and public lounges, all traditionally decorated with floral prints and paintings. The suites are in an annexe, each with a private terrace. Sports facilities, a large pool and a children's playground are also available. **www.hotelcortijolareina.com**

CÓRDOBA Maestre

C/ Romero Barros 4–6, 14003 (Córdoba) **Tel** *957 47 24 10* **Fax** *957 47 53 95* **Rooms** *26*

Near the Mezquita in the centre of Córdoba, this is a simple hotel with basic amenities. It is set around a series of pretty Andalusian patios with colourful tiles, fountains and trailing plants, and is perfectly placed for sightseeing. They offer both rooms and self-catering apartments. Private underground parking. **www.hotelmaestre.com**

CÓRDOBA Casa de los Azulejos

C/ Fernando Colón 5, 14002 (Córdoba) **Tel** *957 47 00 00* **Fax** *957 47 54 96* **Rooms** *8*

The "House of the Tiles" is an enchanting 17th-century mansion set around a typical patio with exquisite local tiles, pretty wrought iron and lush greenery. The pretty rooms are cool and modern, with extras such as Internet. A terrific restaurant offers a fusion of Andalusian and South American cuisine. **www.casadelosazulejos.com**

CÓRDOBA Maciá Alfaros

C/ Alfaros 18, 14001 (Córdoba) **Tel** *957 49 19 20* **Fax** *957 49 22 10* **Rooms** *133*

In a busy street, but soundproofed against traffic noise, the Alfaros is a sleek contemporary hotel built around three courtyards in Neo-Mudéjar style. One of the marble courtyards contains an elegant swimming pool. Geared towards business travellers, it offers good facilities including Wi-Fi. Rooms and suites are comfortable. **www.maciahoteles.com**

CÓRDOBA Occidental

C/ Poeta Alonso Bonilla 3, 14012 (Córdoba) **Tel** *957 76 74 76* **Fax** *957 40 04 39* **Rooms** *153*

A modern hotel in the north of the city, surrounded by its own extensive gardens. It is lavishly decorated with marble floors, coffered ceilings and smart brass lanterns. The bedrooms are tastefully decorated, with wooden furnishings and crisp fabrics. The restaurants overlook the gardens or the large swimming pool. **www.occidental-hoteles.com**

EL PUERTO DE SANTA MARÍA Monasterio de San Miguel

C/ Larga 27, 11500 (Cádiz) **Tel** *956 54 04 40* **Fax** *956 54 05 25* **Rooms** *150*

An elegant and luxurious hotel in a magnificent 18th-century Baroque monastery, which is well placed for visits to Cádiz, the bodegas of Jerez de la Frontera and the typical tapas bars and nightlife of Puerta de Santa María. The rooms sadly don't match up to the opulent public areas, but there are extensive gardens, and excellent facilities.

EL ROCÍO Hotel Toruño

Plaza Acebuchal 22, 21750 (Huelva) **Tel** *959 44 23 23* **Fax** *959 44 23 38* **Rooms** *30*

A charming whitewashed villa just a short distance from the hermitage containing the image of the virgin of El Rocío. It is set on the fringes of the Doñana National Park *(see pp464–5)*, one of the important wetlands and wildlife refuges in Europe. Popular with bird-watchers. Prices double during the El Rocío pilgrimage. **www.toruno.com**

GIBRALTAR The Rock

3 Europa Road, **Tel** *956 77 30 00* **Fax** *956 77 35 13* **Rooms** *104*

Built in 1932 by the Marquess of Bute, Gibraltar's first five-star hotel still trades on its old-fashioned colonial style and service. Perched on the cliff-side, high above the town and harbour, it offers all imaginable amenities from a hair and beauty centre to a casino. Popular with both business travellers and tourists. **www.rockhotelgibraltar.com**

GRANADA Pensión Landázuri

Cuesta de Gomérez 24, 18009 (Granada) **Tel** *958 22 14 06* **Rooms** *15*

Perhaps the nicest budget option in Granada, this tiled little pension has two terraces offering great city views. All the rooms are simple, but surprisingly spacious, and those on the top floor (book in advance) enjoy magical views of the Alhambra. Not all rooms have *en suite* facilities, but those without are extremely cheap. **www.pensionlandazuri.com**

GRANADA Hotel Los Tilos

Plaza Bib Rambla 4, 18001 (Granada) **Tel** *958 26 67 12* **Fax** *958 26 68 01* **Rooms** *30*

Conveniently located in the picturesque Plaza Bib Rambla, Los Tilos is close to shops, restaurants and the cathedral. Recently refurbished, it is tastefully decorated offering good value options and well-appointed rooms. Makes a good base for sightseeing. **www.hotellostilos.com**

GRANADA Alhambra Palace

C/ Arquitecto Garcia de Paredes 1, 18009 (Granada) **Tel** *958 22 14 68* **Fax** *958 22 64 04* **Rooms** *136*

A gloriously kitsch mock-Moorish building on the same hill as the Alhambra, with a terrace offering fine views of old Granada. The rooms and suites are decorated with carved wooden furnishings and the lobbies and lounges are filled with Moorish-style horseshoe arches and stucco detailing. Excellent business facilities. **www.h-alhambrapalace.es**

GRANADA Parador de Granada

C/ Real de la Alhambra, 18009 (Granada) **Tel** *958 22 14 40* **Fax** *958 22 22 64* **Rooms** *36*

This elegant parador in the jasmine-scented gardens of the Alhambra was once a convent, and the cloister has been transformed into a tree-filled oasis filled with flowers. From the elegant bedrooms, you can hear the fountains of the Generalife and enjoy blissful views of the city and the ancient palace. Book well in advance. **www.parador.es**

JAÉN Parador de Jaén

Ctra Sta Catalina, 23001 (Jaén) **Tel** *953 23 00 00* **Fax** *953 23 09 30* **Rooms** *45*

Looming massively from the hills above Jaén, this medieval castle is now a pretty parador which evokes the Middle Ages with its sturdy walls and crenellated battlements. There are great views across the Sierra Morena. Dine on local fare in the restaurant, which retains its Arabic detailing. An excellent base for hiking. **www.parador.es**

LAS CABEZAS Hotel Cortijo Soto Real

Ctra Las Cabezas-Villamartin km 13, 41730 (Sevilla) **Tel** *955 86 92 00* **Fax** *955 86 92 02* **Rooms** *25*

A luxury retreat, this exquisite country mansion is one of the finest hotels in Andalusia. You can explore the extensive grounds in a horse and carriage, indulge in outdoor activities, including hunting or bike excursions, or simply laze by the pool. The elegant rooms and suites are ultra-stylish, and there is a fine restaurant. **www.hotelcortijosotoreal.com**

LOJA La Bobadilla

Finca La Bobadilla, 18300 (Granada) **Tel** *958 32 18 61* **Fax** *958 32 18 10* **Rooms** *62*

Looking rather like a labyrinthine Andalusian village surrounded by its own vast estate, this is one of the most luxurious hotels in Europe. Each of the rooms and suites is different, but all are fitted with every imaginable amenity. There is a lake-size pool, and guests can take part in a wide range of sports and activities. **www.la-bobadilla.com**

MÁLAGA Don Curro

C/ Sancha de Lara 7, 29015 (Málaga) **Tel** *952 22 72 00* **Fax** *952 21 59 46* **Rooms** *118*

The exterior may not be attractive, but this hotel's interior is charming and comfortable, with a welcoming ambience. Rooms are tastefully furnished with dark wood and marble, and they offer some thoughtful extras, including a valet parking service. Houses a simple bar-restaurant and is popular with business travellers.**www.hoteldoncurro.com**

MARBELLA El Fuerte

Av El Fuerte, 29600 (Málaga) **Tel** *952 86 15 00* **Fax** *952 82 44 11* **Rooms** *263*

El Fuerte was the first purpose-built hotel in Marbella and is still one of the best. It is unmissable – a big pink building surrounded by tropical gardens. Some rooms have mountain views but the best look out to sea. Next to the beach-front, it has a heated, glassed-in pool, an outdoor pool and a health and beauty centre. **www.fuertehoteles.com**

MARBELLA Marbella Club Hotel

Blvr Príncipe von Hohenlohe, 29600 (Málaga) **Tel** *952 82 22 11* **Fax** *952 82 98 84* **Rooms** *137*

Built for a prince in the 1950s, this is now an ultra-luxurious beachside complex with two pools (one indoors) and extensive subtropical gardens. Located in the Golden Mile (between Marbella and Puerto Banus), it includes a world-class golf course and a spa. The rooms, suites and villas have private heated pools. **www.marbellaclub.com**

MAZAGÓN Parador de Mazagón

Ctra San Juan del pto, A Matalascañas km 30, 21130 (Huelva) **Tel** *959 53 63 00* **Fax** *959 53 62 28* **Rooms** *63*

A modern parador on the Huelva coast with a perfect location right on the seafront. Draped in ivy and surrounded by gardens, it has bright, modern rooms and is well-located for visiting the wildlife reserve of Doñana National Park. Offers outdoor sports and activities such as cycling, horse riding, golf, and windsurfing. **www.parador.es**

MIJAS Club Puerta del Sol

Ctra Fuengirola-Mijas km 4, 29650 (Málaga) **Tel** *952 48 64 00* **Fax** *952 48 51 75* **Rooms** *130*

A whitewashed modern hotel complex in the foothills of the Sierra de Mijas offering spacious rooms. There are impressive views of Fuengirola and the coast. Facilities include tennis courts, a gym, indoor and outdoor pools and a host of other sports amenities. It is child friendly, and the beaches are nearby. **www.hotelclubpuertadelsol.com**

MOJÁCAR Mamabel's

C/ Embajadores 5, 04638 (Almeria) **Tel** *950 47 24 48* **Fax** *950 47 24 48* **Rooms** *9*

Mamabel's restaurant has long been an institution in Mojácar, and the addition of guestrooms (and a suite) has given it an added bonus. The rooms are simple and small, but they are decorated with traditional furnishings and Moorish-style arches. The best rooms have sea views, and the suite contains a Jacuzzi. **www.mamabels.com**

Key to Price Guide *see p560* **Key to Symbols** *see back cover flap*

MOJÁCAR Parador de Mojácar €€

Playa de Mojácar s/n, 04638 (Almería) **Tel** *950 47 82 50* **Fax** *950 47 81 83* **Rooms** *98*

The architecture of this purpose-built parador on the dry sunny coast of Almería echoes that of the dazzling white cube houses in nearby Mojácar. It has excellent facilities for all manner of water sports. The light, airy bedrooms have terraces with wonderful sea views, and the restaurant offers local specialities. **www.parador.es**

MONACHIL La Almunia del Valle €€

Camino de la Umbria s/n, 18193 (Granada) **Tel** *958 30 80 10* **Fax** *958 30 80 10* **Rooms** *11*

High in the Sierra Nevada mountains, this is a stylish rural retreat surrounded by extensive gardens. In winter, it is just 20 minutes by car from the ski slopes and the hotel offers all-inclusive packages. In summer, guests can lounge by the pool, enjoy the mountain views, or take a stroll through the shady gardens. **www.laalmuniadelvalle.com**

MOTRIL Casa de los Bates €€€

Ctra Nacional km 329.5, 18600 (Granada) **Tel** *958 34 94 95* **Fax** *958 83 41 31* **Rooms** *4*

A country villa set in its own gardens, with stunning views of the sea, the mountains and the castle of Salobreña. It is a chic retreat with an aristocratic ambience – antiques, family portraits and even a grand piano. The rooms are furnished in soothing pastel tones, and for breakfast you can enjoy fresh tropical juices. **www.casadelosbates.com**

NÉRJA Hostal Miguel €

C/ Almirante Ferrándiz 31, 29780 (Malaga) **Tel** *952 52 15 23* **Fax** *661 22 82 50* **Rooms** *9*

Recently refurbished in 2004, this friendly, eclectic hostal with Moroccan touches first opened in the 1960s. The rooms are decorated in subdued styles and all have ceiling fans, mini-fridges and airy balconies. Breakfast can be taken on the rooftop terrace, and the lounge has a selection of books and magazines. **www.hostalmiguel.com**

NÉRJA La Solanilla €€

C/ Larga 36, Niguelas, 18657 **Tel** *958 78 05 75* **Fax** *958 78 05 75* **Rooms** *4*

Recently-renovated La Solanilla is located in this quiet, scenic village in the Sierra Nevada Valley. It offers accommodation in two tastefully designed guesthouses, each of which has two bedrooms, one bath, a living room, a fireplace and a kitchen. There is also a swimming pool. **www.cortijolasolana.com**

ORGIVA Taray €

Ctra Tablate-Albuñol km 18, 18400 (Granada) **Tel** *958 78 45 25* **Fax** *958 78 45 31* **Rooms** *15*

A whitewashed rural hotel set in lovely gardens, with olive groves and orange trees. The bedrooms are large enough to be small apartments, but they have even larger suites. A good base for walking or pursuing outdoor activities such as horse riding. The hotel is also equipped for disabled visitors, with specially adapted rooms.

PALMA DEL RÍO Hospedería de San Francisco €€

Av de Pio XII 35, 14700 (Córdoba) **Tel** *957 71 01 83* **Fax** *957 71 02 36* **Rooms** *35*

Built in the 15th century as a Franciscan monastery and located in the centre of the pretty country town of Palma del Ríoy. This hotel has some bedrooms in former monks' cells, furnished with hand-painted basins and bedcovers woven by nuns. The kitchen uses organic produce from their own gardens and meals are served in the old refectory.

PECHINA Balneario de Sierra Alhamilla €

Pechina, 04359 (Almería) **Tel** *950 31 74 13* **Fax** *950 31 75 51* **Rooms** *19*

This spa hotel in the peaceful hills of the Sierra de Alhamilla has been beautifully restored to its 18th-century glory. The thermal waters have long been known for their healing properties – the Romans and then the Arabs built spas on this spot. Treatments include soaking in an outdoor thermal pool with underwater jets, mudpacks and massages.

PRADO DEL REY Cortijo Huerta Dorotea €

Ctra Vilamartín-Ubrique km 12, 11660 (Cádiz) **Tel** *956 72 42 91* **Fax** *956 72 42 89* **Rooms** *25*

On a hill surrounded by olive trees, near the white town of Prado del Rey, sits this tranquil rural hotel. Guests can choose from simply decorated rooms to cosy log cabins. There are large gardens with lakes, paths and swimming pools, and plenty of outdoor activities are available. Good regional restaurant. **www.huertadorotea.com**

RINCÓN DE LA VICTORIA Molino de Santillán €€

Ctra de Macharaviaya km 3, 29730 (Málaga) **Tel** *952 40 09 49* **Rooms** *22*

Perched on a wooded hilltop, this is a charming hotel set in a traditional Andalusian *finca*. Rooms are painted in warm colours, and all offer memorable views. The hotel offers a wide range of outdoor activities and is close to the beaches. Their own organic produce is served in the restaurant. **www.hotel-msantillan.net**

RONDA Husa Reina Victoria €€€

C/ Jérez 25, 29400 (Málaga) **Tel** *952 87 12 40* **Fax** *952 87 10 75* **Rooms** *89*

The Reina Victoria, perched on the edge of the famous gorge which divides Ronda, was built in 1906. It remains the grand dame of Ronda's hotels, although its facilities have been eclipsed by modern upstarts. Rooms are traditionally decorated, and the restaurant offers more panoramic views. **www.husa.es**

RONDA Parador de Ronda €€€

Plaza España, 29400 (Málaga) **Tel** *952 87 75 00* **Fax** *952 87 81 88* **Rooms** *78*

Edging up to Ronda's famous cliff, yet close to the town centre, this modern, purpose-built parador has stunning views over the gorge, especially from the top-floor suites. The bedrooms are full of light and stylishly decorated. The parador is surrounded by huge gardens with an outdoor pool right on the cliff edge. **www.parador.es**

SAN JOSÉ Cortijo El Sotillo   €€€

Ctra San Jose s/n, 04118 (Almería) **Tel** *950 61 11 00* **Fax** *950 61 11 05* **Rooms** *20*

An elegant 18th-century farmhouse set in the beautiful countryside of the natural parks of Cabo de Gata and Níjar. The perfect place for a walking holiday, with hikes into the volcanic hills, with the beaches of this stunning stretch of coastline just a short drive away. The restaurant uses produce from the estate. Disabled access. **www.elsotillo.org**

SANLÚCAR DE BARRAMEDA Los Helechos   €

Plaza Madre de Dios 9, 11540 (Cádiz) **Tel** *956 36 13 49* **Fax** *956 36 96 50* **Rooms** *54*

Decorated with tiles and potted plants, Los Helechos is a delightful, relaxing seaside hotel. Rooms are light, spacious and prettily, if simply, decorated, and are set around a plant-filled courtyard. The friendly staff are very informative and can arrange visits to the nearby Doñana National Park. **www.hotelloshelechos.com**

SANLÚCAR LA MAYOR Hacienda de Benazuza   €€€€€

Virgen de las Nieves, 41800 (Sevilla) **Tel** *955 70 33 44* **Fax** *955 70 34 10* **Rooms** *44*

This ultra-luxurious hotel is part of the El Bullí empire, and contains an exceptional restaurant *(see p647)* among other five-star comforts. Set in an ancient Moorish farmhouse, the opulent rooms and suites contain original vaulted ceilings. The hotel offers myriad excursions, from river cruises to tours of the sherry bodegas. **www.hbenazuza.com**

SIERRA NEVADA Santa Cruz   €

Ctra Sierra Nevada, 18160 (Granada) **Tel** *958 48 48 00* **Fax** *958 48 48 06* **Rooms** *66, 25 bungalows*

From this high-altitude hotel guests can contemplate the snowy peaks of the lovely Sierra Nevada. Open fires make this modern building cosy in winter, and in summer it is popular with hikers. You can also rent one of their 25 bungalows, each with their own fireplace, and most with Jacuzzis. A good family option with lots of sports facilities.

TARIFA Hurricane   €€€

Ctra N340 km 77, 11380 (Cádiz) **Tel** *956 68 49 19* **Fax** *956 68 03 29* **Rooms** *33*

Tarifa is a mecca for windsurfers and the Hurricane is a temple to the sport. It is an imaginative, open-plan building set in subtropical gardens, which lead out onto the beach. Rooms are decorated in Andalusian style. It is one of the least crowded corners of the Spanish coast, with fine views across the sea to Africa. **www.hotelhurricane.com**

TOLOX Cerro de Hijar   €€

Cerro de Hijar s/n, 29019 (Málaga) **Tel** *952 11 21 11* **Fax** *952 11 97 45* **Rooms** *18*

This hotel offers stunning views of the surrounding natural beauty and the pretty white village of Tolox. The estate is Andalusian in style with a central patio and spacious rooms. All kinds of outdoor pursuits can be arranged, including horse riding and excursions. The restaurant serves local specialities and their own wines. **www.cerrodehijar.com**

TORREMOLINOS Hotel Miami   €

C/ Aladino 14, 29620 (Málaga) **Tel** *952 38 52 55* **Rooms** *26*

The Miami offers welcome respite from the Costa del Sol's modern growth. It has whitewashed walls, tiles, iron grilles, balconies and potted plants. Rooms are simple, and vary in terms of size and amenities, but they are all comfortable and the staff are friendly and helpful. The pool is an added bonus. **www.residencia-miami.com**

TREVÉLEZ Hotel La Fragua   €

C/ San Antonio 4, 18417 (Granada) **Tel** *958 85 86 26* **Fax** *958 85 86 14* **Rooms** *24*

This simple whitewashed *mesón* (inn) is in what claims to be the highest village in Spain. There are great views from the rooftop terrace. The rooms vary considerably in size and character, but most have lovely beamed ceilings, terracotta tiled floors and simple decor. There is a wonderful open fire in winter. **www.hotellafragua.com**

TURRE El Nacimiento   €

Cortijo El Nacimiento, 04639 (Almería) **Tel** *950 52 80 90* **Rooms** *5*

A friendly couple runs this remote and lovely old farmhouse set in unspoilt rolling countryside. They offer bed and breakfast and home-cooked vegetarian dinners (on request) using organic produce from their farm. Rooms are cosy and pretty, and there are fabulous views from the terrace. Best of all is the natural swimming pool in the grounds.

TURRE Finca Listonero   €€

Cortijo Grande, 04639 (Almería) **Tel** *950 47 90 94* **Rooms** *4*

This beautifully restored farmhouse, run by two Australian restaurateurs, is in the hills behind Mojácar. The room are individually and stylishly decorated, and all open out onto terraces overlooking the mountains or the pool and gardens. The breakfasts are generous, and home-grown vegetables are served at meals. **www.fincalistonero.com**

ÚBEDA María de Molina   €€

Plaza del Ayuntamiento s/n, 23400 (Jaén) **Tel** *953 79 53 56* **Fax** *953 79 36 94* **Rooms** *27*

Located in the heart of the historic centre of Úbeda, next to the City Hall, this hotel is housed in a 16th-century palace. Rooms, clustered around the central courtyard with a marble fountain, are decorated in Renaissance style with all the modern amenities. Enjoy local cuisine in the cafeteria. **www.hotel-maria-de-molina.com**

ÚBEDA Parador de Úbeda   €€€

Plaza Vázquez de Molina 1, 23400 (Jaén) **Tel** *953 75 03 45* **Fax** *953 75 12 59* **Rooms** *36*

Presiding over Úbeda's monumental central square, this parador is in a former 16th-century aristocratic palace. Blue and white tiles adorn the façade and the house surrounds a Renaissance two-storied patio. The spacious, high-ceilinged rooms are decorated with traditional furniture, and the restaurant serves regional cuisine. **www.parador.es**

Key to Price Guide *see p560* **Key to Symbols** *see back cover flap*

VEJER DE LA FRONTERA Casa Cinco   ⊞▤   €€
C/ Sancho IV el Bravo 5, 11150 (Cádiz) **Tel** *956 45 50 29* **Fax** *956 45 11 25* **Rooms** *4*

This beautiful little hostal on the town's hilltop aims to stimulate all five senses. All the rooms are decorated individually with a mixture of contemporary and traditional furnishings from around the world. Thoughtful details such as CD players add to its charm. Bookings are for a minimum of two nights. **www.hotelcasacinco.com**

ZUHEROS Zuhayra   ⊞▤   €
C/ Mirador 10, 14870 (Córdoba) **Tel** *957 69 46 93* **Fax** *957 69 47 02* **Rooms** *19*

The principal charm of this simple rural hotel is its location in a white town on the edge of a range of high hills. The building is modern, but imitates the style of the noble mansion it replaced. It is a perfect base for hiking in the Sierra Subbética, and the hotel rents mountain bikes. The restaurant serves local specialities. **www.zercahoteles.com**

THE BALEARIC ISLANDS

FORMENTERA Hotel Cala Saona   ▦⊞▩★▥▤   €€€
Cala Saona, 07860 (Formentera) **Tel** *971 32 20 30* **Fax** *971 32 25 09* **Rooms** *116*

A modern hotel, this is the only accommodation option in the secluded Playa Cala Saona, one of the prettiest of Formentera's wild and unspoilt beaches. The interior is classic Spanish beach-hotel style with chintzy fabrics and TVs. Also has a pool with a sun terrace and good facilities for children including a play area. **www.hotelcalasaona.com**

FORMENTERA, ES PUJOLS Sa Volta   ▦⊞▩▤   €€€
C/ Miramar 94, 07871 (Formentera) **Tel** *971 32 81 25* **Fax** *971 32 81 43* **Rooms** *25*

A family-run hotel in a modern block close to the beach in one of Formentera's main resorts. The standard rooms are simple, but comfortable. It is worth splashing out on one of the three semi-suites, which have plush modern decor, including canopied beds and spacious private terraces. Charming staff. Open Mar–Dec. **www.savolta.com**

IBIZA (EIVISSA), IBIZA TOWN Hostal La Marina   ⊞▤   €€
C/ Barcelona 7, 07800 (Formentera) **Tel** *971 31 01 72* **Fax** *971 31 48 94* **Rooms** *25*

A classic on the seafront, Hostal La Marina is located in a modernized 19th-century building, which retains some charming original details. Rooms are brightly painted in Mediterranean colours and the best have lovely sea views. In high season, it is a little overpriced, but a good deal otherwise. **www.hostal-lamarina.com**

IBIZA (EIVISSA), IBIZA TOWN El Palacio   ▤   €€€€€
C/ de la Conquista 2, 07800 (Ibiza) **Tel** *971 30 14 78* **Fax** *971 39 15 81* **Rooms** *7*

The beautiful building that houses this quirky hotel dates back 1,000 years, and is tucked away in Ibiza's old town. It calls itself the "Hotel of the Movie Stars", and each room has been dedicated to a silver screen icon – you can stay in the Marilyn Monroe penthouse. Film star memorabilia and posters are hung throughout. **www.elpalacio.com**

IBIZA (EIVISSA), SANTA EULÀRIA D'ES RIU Les Terrasses   ⊞▩▤   €€€€€
Apto 1235 Ctra Santa Eulalia km 1, 07600 (Ibiza) **Tel** *971 33 26 43* **Fax** *971 33 89 78* **Rooms** *10*

A country house decorated simply but beautifully in Ibizan style, painted white, blue and sunshine yellow. Each room is individually styled with a perfect mixture of traditional and contemporary influences. It is a tranquil place with flower-filled gardens. Dinner is prepared with organic produce from the kitchen garden. **www.lesterrasses.net**

IBIZA, BAHÍA DE SANT ANTONI Osiris Ibiza   ▦⊞▩★▥   €€
Playa Es Puet s/n, 07820 (Ibiza) **Tel** *971 34 16 88* **Fax** *971 34 16 85* **Rooms** *97*

A family-run modern hotel in the popular resort of Sant Antoni, this is a great place for families on a budget. Osiri Ibiza is not only close to the beach and all kinds of water sports facilities, but it has its own pool with a section for young children. The rooms are large and bright and offer views of the sea or the gardens. **www.hotelosiris.com**

IBIZA, CALA MOLÍ Hostel Cala Molí   ⊞▩   €€
Cala Molí, 07830 (Ibiza) **Tel** *971 80 60 02* **Fax** *971 80 61 50* **Rooms** *8*

This is a simple, family-friendly little hostal overlooking a lovely bay. All the rooms face a pretty, tree-shaded terrace, and there is a swimming pool if you cannot make the walk to the nearby beach. The rooms are whitewashed and simply furnished with private terraces. The cheerful staff will give you tips on what to see. **www.calamoli.com**

IBIZA, IBIZA TOWN Casa de Huéspedes Vara de Rey   ▤   €
C/ Vara de Rey 7, 07800 (Ibiza) **Tel** *971 30 13 76* **Rooms** *15*

In the heart of the whitewashed maze of Ibiza's old town, this is an intimate little pension with quirkily decorated rooms painted by young artists from the island. None have private facilities, but this means bargain prices, making it ideal for those travellers on a budget. All the rooms enjoy fine views. Friendly staff. **www.hibiza.com**

MALLORCA, ALCÚDIA Es Convent   ⊞▤   €€
C/ Progrés 6, 07400 (Mallorca) **Tel** *971 54 87 16* **Fax** *971 89 70 42* **Rooms** *4*

The most charming option in Alcúdia, this is a delightful restaurant with just four individually decorated rooms. Each has wooden beams, pared down wooden furnishings and pale cream fabrics – tasteful, elegant and stylish. The charming restaurant, with a leafy terrace, serves Mediterranean cuisine. Breakfast is included. **www.esconvent.com**

MALLORCA, BANYALBUFAR Sa Baronía

C/ Sa Baronía 16, 07191 (Mallorca) **Tel** *971 61 81 46* **Fax** *971 14 87 38* **Rooms** *39*

Situated in a small village on the island's unspoilt, northwest coast, this simple family-run hotel was built as a modern extension onto a 17th-century baronial tower. The extension itself is unattractive, but the warm welcome and the tranquility of the area makes up for it. The simple bedrooms have terraces with sea views. **www.hbaronia.com**

MALLORCA, BINISSALEM Scott's Hotel

Plaza de la Iglesia 12, 07350 (Mallorca) **Tel** *971 87 01 00* **Fax** *971 87 02 67* **Rooms** *17*

This restored and elegantly decorated 18th-century town house in the wine-producing town of Binissalem has won countless awards – every one richly deserved. The charming owners have given thought to every detail, right down to the handmade beds. Try their excellent bistro for dinner. Also has an indoor pool. **www.scottshotel.com**

MALLORCA, DEIÀ La Residencia

Finca Son Canals, 07179 (Mallorca) **Tel** *971 63 90 11* **Fax** *971 63 93 70* **Rooms** *64*

Two magnificently restored 16th- and 18th-century manors have been combined into a legendary hotel, which has long been a favourite hideaway of celebrities. The rooms and suites (some with private pools) are beautifully done with traditional Mallorcan furniture and pale linen. It also has a spa and a restaurant. **www.hotel-laresidencia.com**

MALLORCA, LLUC Santuari de Lluc

Santuari de Lluc, 07315 (Mallorca) **Tel** *971 87 15 25* **Fax** *971 51 70 96* **Rooms** *129*

The spectacular Santuari de Lluc in the Tramuntana mountains is Mallorca's most important place of pilgrimage, and home to a much-venerated statue of the Madonna, the island's patron saint. If you are seeking spiritual calm then book yourself into one of the austere former monks' cells. They also offer simple apartments. **www.lluc.net**

MALLORCA, PALMA DE MALLORCA Born

C/ Sant Jaume 3, 07012 (Mallorca) **Tel** *971 71 29 42* **Fax** *971 71 86 18* **Rooms** *30*

The Marquis of Ferrandell's town mansion, built in the 16th century and restored in the 18th, makes a splendid little hotel. The simple but comfortable bedrooms are set around a typical Mallorcan courtyard with palms and a grand staircase. A few have tiny balconies overlooking the courtyard. One of the best budget options. **www.hotelborn.com**

MALLORCA, PORT D'ANDRATX Villa Italia

Camino Sant Carles 13, 07157 (Mallorca) **Tel** *971 67 40 11* **Fax** *971 67 33 50* **Rooms** *16*

A pink, Florentine-style villa, built in the 1920s by an Italian millionaire, has been lovingly restored to house this ultra-luxurious hotel. Inside there are stucco ceilings and marble floors, and the huge gardens – with fountains, tiles and Italianate balustrades – offer great sea views. Has a fine restaurant and a spa. **www.hotelvillaitalia.com**

MALLORCA, PUERTO DE POLLENÇA Formentor

Playa de Formentor, 07470 (Mallorca) **Tel** *971 89 91 00* **Fax** *971 86 51 55* **Rooms** *127*

Writers, opera singers, film stars and the Dalai Lama have signed the visitors' book of this luxury hotel on the island's northwest tip. No longer quite the celebrity haunt that it was, it still remains an elegant retreat. The rooms are traditionally decorated. Superb sports facilities available and the beach is on the doorstep. **www.hotelformentor.net**

MALLORCA, PUERTO DE SÓLLER Hostal Brisas

Camino sw Muleta 15, 07108 (Mallorca) **Tel** *971 63 13 52* **Rooms** *47*

A simple seaside hostal, built in the 1960s in traditional style. Rooms are basic, but more than adequate, and the best have views of the sea from private terraces. It is perfectly located for a relaxed beach holiday, just metres from the sands, and has a simple café-bar that serves local dishes. **www.mallorcahotelguide.com**

MALLORCA, RANDA Es Recó de Randa

C/ Font 21, 07629 (Mallorca) **Tel** *971 66 09 97* **Fax** *971 66 25 58* **Rooms** *16*

A restaurant-with-rooms in an old stone house in a quiet village at the foot of the Puig de Randa mountain. The rustically decorated rooms have wooden beams and traditional furnishings, and many offer breathtaking views of the mountains and citrus groves. There is a lovely outdoor pool and a terrace. **www.esrecoderanda.com**

MALLORCA, SES SALINES Es Turó

Camí Casperets, 07640 (Mallorca) **Tel** *971 64 95 31* **Fax** *971 64 95 48* **Rooms** *10*

Rural calm, tasteful comfort and timeless Mallorcan life are combined in this romantic stone-built hotel. Converted from an old farmhouse, it is surrounded by almond and olive groves and is just a short distance from Es Trenc beach. All the suites are spacious and nicely decorated in traditional style. Has a fine restaurant. **www.esturo.com**

MALLORCA, SÓLLER Ca N'Aí

Camí de Son Sales, 07100 (Mallorca) **Tel** *971 63 24 94* **Fax** *971 63 18 99* **Rooms** *17*

This enchanting hotel has been converted from an old Mallorcan mansion, built into the side of the Sóller valley and surrounded by orange and palm groves. Inside, the decor is a refined mixture of local and contemporary styles. Also has a garden and a pool. The service has a personal touch and the cooking is excellent. **www.canai.com**

MALLORCA, VALLDEMOSSA Cases de C'as Garriguer

Ctra de Valldemossa-Andratx km 2-5, 07170 (Mallorca) **Tel** *971 61 23 00* **Fax** *971 61 25 83* **Rooms** *10*

A peaceful rural hotel located in a series of stone-built country houses, erected early in the 20th century. The spacious bedrooms are furnished with antiques and have wooden-beamed ceilings. Most have private terraces, with spellbinding views of the hills. A perfect destination for walkers. **www.vistamarhotel.es**

Key to Price Guide *see p560* **Key to Symbols** *see back cover flap*

MENORCA, CIUTADELLA Hostal Sa Prensa

Plaça de Madrid s/n, 07760 (Menorca) **Tel** *971 38 26 98* **Rooms** *7*

Probably the best of the cheaper hotels in Ciutadella, which has a shortage of good budget accommodation. Book early to get one of the four bedrooms which have terraces with fabulous views of the port; the other three bedrooms are plain and overlook nondescript apartments. A simple café-bar downstairs serves breakfast.

MENORCA, CIUTADELLA Hostal Ciutadella

C/ San Eloi 10, 07760 (Menorca) **Tel** *971 38 34 62* **Fax** *971 38 34 62* **Rooms** *17*

Just around the corner from the Plaça de Alfons III, this simple, modern hotel offers good-value, no-frills lodging. Renovated in 2005, the rooms are plainly furnished and spotless, and are cooled with ceiling fans in summer. Simple meals are served in the family-friendly café-bar on the ground floor. Friendly staff. **www.menorcaok.com**

MENORCA, CIUTADELLA Patricia

Paseo San Nicolás 90–92, 07760 (Menorca) **Tel** *971 38 55 11* **Fax** *978 48 11 20* **Rooms** *44*

A modern, cream-coloured chain hotel with white bay windows near the harbour. Rooms are spacious and blandly furnished. Geared towards business travellers, it has conference facilities and a business centre. The convenient location and efficient staff make it a good bet for tourists. Offers weekend discounts. **www.hesperia-patricia.com**

MENORCA, MAÓ Hostal Jumé

C/ Concepció 6, 07701 (Menorca) **Tel** *971 36 32 66* **Fax** *971 36 48 78* **Rooms** *35*

A very basic pension, run by a charming elderly couple, offering functional rooms (all *en suite*) with no frills at low prices. It is conveniently central (close to the port and the market) and the owners go out of their way to make guests comfortable. There is a simple, old-fashioned café-bar serving breakfast and local dishes.

MENORCA, MAÓ Del Almirante

Ctra de Es Castell, 07720 (Menorca) **Tel** *971 36 27 00* **Fax** *971 36 27 04* **Rooms** *39*

Built in the 18th century in classic Georgian style, this fine mansion house became the home of Admiral Lord Collingwood, a friend of Lord Nelson. Some bedrooms are in a modern annexe overlooking the swimming pool and a pretty terrace has views of Port Mahón. Disabled access. **www.hoteldelalmirante.net**

MENORCA, MAÓ Capri

C/ San Esteban 8, 07703 (Menorca) **Tel** *971 36 14 00* **Fax** *971 35 08 53* **Rooms** *75 & 7 apartments*

This is a central hotel in a modern block, five floors high, close to shops, the harbour and the beach. Although the exterior is unappealing, the interior is light and modern. The hotel offers exceptionally good facilities, including a fully equipped spa, a health centre and a swimming pool. Some rooms have Jacuzzis. **www.rtmhotels.com**

MENORCA, MAÓ Casa Alberti

C/ Isabel II 9, 07701 (Menorca) **Tel** *971 35 42 10* **Fax** *971 35 42 10* **Rooms** *6*

Located in a handsome 18th-century mansion, this is perhaps the most charming hotel in Maó. All the rooms are beautifully and individually decorated in chic, modern style. The winding, whitewashed staircase leads to a glorious roof terrace with good views of the sea. The charismatic owner is full of local information. **www.casalberti.com**

MENORCA, MAÓ Port Mahón

C/ Fort de l'Eau 13, 07701 (Menorca) **Tel** *971 36 26 00* **Fax** *971 35 10 50* **Rooms** *82*

Housed in an attractive red and white colonial-style building, this hotel – probably the most luxurious in the city – overlooks Maó harbour. Its grounds include wide terraces and a curving swimming pool surrounded by lawns. The best rooms, comfortably furnished in chain-hotel style, have private terraces. **www.sethotels.com**

THE CANARY ISLANDS

EL HIERRO, FRONTERA Ida Inés

Camino del Hoyo Belgara Alta 2, 38911 **Tel** *922 55 94 45* **Fax** *922 55 60 88* **Rooms** *12*

Located in the valley of El Golfo, roughly in the middle of the island, this small and cosy hotel looks onto the Atlantic Ocean and the bedrooms have superb views of either the sea or the hills inland. The small swimming pool has a solarium and guests have Internet access. A good base for walking or mountain biking. **www.hotelitoidaines.com**

EL HIERRO, VALVERDE Parador de El Hierro

Las Playas 15, 38910 **Tel** *922 55 80 36* **Fax** *922 55 80 86* **Rooms** *47*

Black cliffs are the backdrop for this modern, pantiled parador which stands in a peaceful spot on an isolated beach facing the Roque de Bonanza. It has an elegant colonial decor with white walls, and wooden balconies with sea views. An ideal option for walking or relaxing. El Hierro specialities served in the restaurant. **www.parador.es**

FUERTEVENTURA, ANTIGUA Era de la Corte

La Corte 1, 35630 **Tel** *928 87 87 05* **Fax** *928 87 87 10* **Rooms** *11*

A low-lying 19th-century house in a residential area of Antigua village, mostly painted in gleaming white, with exposed stone walls inside, but with some touches of striking colour here and there. All the rooms are individually decorated and two have four-poster beds. It has two sitting areas. **www.eradelacorte.com**

FUERTEVENTURA, PÁJARA Casa Isaitas   🔢 €€

Pàjara, 35626 **Tel** *928 16 14 02* **Fax** *928 16 14 82* **Rooms** *4*

This tiny rural B&B in a 200-year old Canarian house is located in a village in the middle of the island. Offering simple lodging and home-made food, Casa Isaitas has only four bedrooms and an inner patio. A room which was formerly used as a corn mill now houses a lounge-library and bar where snacks are available. **www.casaisaitas.com**

FUERTEVENTURA, VILLAVERDE Mahoh   🔢 📶 €

Sitio de Juan Bello, 35660 **Tel** *928 86 80 50* **Fax** *928 86 86 12* **Rooms** *9*

Mahoh (a Guanche word meaning "my land, my country") is an early 19th-century traditional rural house in the north of Fuerteventura, built of the island's volcanic stone and local timber. The bedrooms are simply decorated, often with bare stone walls. Some of them have four-poster beds. The hotel has horses for hire. **www.mahoh.com**

GRAN CANARIA, AGAETE Finca Las Longueras Hotel Rural   🔢 📶 €

Finca Las Longueras, 35480 **Tel** *928 89 81 45* **Fax** *928 89 87 52* **Rooms** *10*

This 19th-century colonial manor in the Agaete Valley, also known as the "Red House", is located in a plantation of bananas, oranges, papayas and avocados. It is tastefully decorated, with its own gardens and a chapel. In the grounds a self-catering house for rent sleeps four. Close to the ferry terminal of Tenerife. **www.laslongueras.com**

GRAN CANARIA, AGAETE Princesa Guayarmina   📶 €

Los Berrazales, Valle de Agaete, 35489 **Tel** *928 89 80 09* **Fax** *928 89 85 25* **Rooms** *25*

A small and peaceful former spa hotel in the Agaete Valley run by friendly staff. The simply furnished rooms overlook subtropical countryside. It is a good base for walking, relaxing or for visiting the beach nearby. It offers various health treatments including acupuncture and holistic health techniques. Also has a bar. **hotelprincesaguayarmina.net**

GRAN CANARIA, ARUCAS Hacienda del Buen Suceso   🔢 📶 €€€

Finca del Buen Suceso, Ctra de Arucas a Bañaderos km 1, 35400 **Tel** *928 62 29 45* **Fax** *928 62 29 42* **Rooms** *18*

An elegant hotel occupying an 18th-century colonial farmhouse, once the residence of the Marquis of Arucas. Located on the way up to Arucas town from the coast, it is surrounded by a banana plantation and is very quiet at night. There are various outdoor spaces, and a heated swimming pool. **www.haciendabuensuceso.com**

GRAN CANARIA, CRUZ DE TEJEDA El Refugio   🔢 📶 🔢 €

Cruz de Tejeda, 35328 **Tel** *928 66 65 13* **Fax** *928 66 65 20* **Rooms** *10*

This hotel stands on the remote Cruz de Tejeda crossroads at a high point in the middle of the island. It can be busy with trippers during the day but is peaceful at night. Offers sauna, mini golf, sundeck, and bikes. A long way from the coast and the nearest nightlife, but a great area for walking or horse riding. **www.hotelruralelrefugio.com**

GRAN CANARIA, LAS PALMAS Las Tirajanas   🔢 🔢 📶 🔢 🔢 €

Oficial Mayor José Rubio, San Bartolomé de Tirajana, 35290 **Tel** *928 12 30 00* **Fax** *928 12 30 23* **Rooms** *60*

High above the brash and noisy resorts on Gran Canaria's southern coast, this spa hotel is raised on the edge of an ancient caldera and enjoys breathtaking mountain scenery. A suitable place to unwind or use as base for walking. It also has a restaurant serving Canarian cuisine, a covered swimming pool and a gym. **www.hotel-lastirajanas.com**

GRAN CANARIA, LAS PALMAS Santa Catalina   🔢 🔢 📶 🔢 🔢 €€€€

C/ León y Castillo 227, 35005 **Tel** *928 24 30 40* **Fax** *928 24 27 64* **Rooms** *202*

This traditional Canarian building with its wooden balconies and Colonial atmosphere has been a classic hotel since it opened in 1890. Many of the rooms have either a park or sea view. Among them are 14 junior suites and 2 senior suites. Facilities include an opulent casino and a well-equipped spa centre. **www.hotelsantacatalina.com**

GRAN CANARIA, MASPALOMAS Riu Grand Palace Maspalomas Oasis 🔢🔢📶🔢🔢🔢 €€€€

Plaza de las Palmeras, 35106 **Tel** *928 14 14 48* **Fax** *928 14 11 92* **Rooms** *332*

In a prime, palm-shaded spot by Maspalomas' renowned (and unspoilt) sand dunes is this secluded, modern, grand hotel, surrounded by subtropical gardens. The guests are stylishly accommodated in split-level suites with spacious bedrooms. The staff are efficient and pleasant. The restaurant has a no smoking section. **www.riu.com**

GRAN CANARIA, VEGA DE SAN MATEO Las Calas   🔢 €€

El Arenal 36, La Lechuza, 35320 **Tel** *928 66 14 36* **Fax** *928 66 07 53* **Rooms** *9*

This small, friendly, countryside hotel is in a 17th-century Canarian building, located down a winding lane at La Lechuza. It has been tastefully decorated with traditional furniture, while keeping some unusual features of the house, such as a bread oven in one of the rooms. There are good walks up and down the hills. **www.hotelrurallascalas.com**

LA GOMERA, PLAYA DE SANTIAGO Jardín Tecina   🔢 🔢 📶 🔢 🔢 🔢 €€€€

Lomada de Tecina, 38811 **Tel** *922 14 58 50* **Fax** *922 14 58 51* **Rooms** *434*

The main reason to stay at this attractive hotel is to go walking around the island of La Gomera. Its many facilities and entertainments make the complex, which is in the hills behind the Playa de Santiago, virtually a self-contained resort. It is surrounded by gardens. A cliff-side lift takes guests down to the beach club. **www.jardin-tecina.com**

LA GOMERA, SAN SEBASTIAN Parador de la Gomera   🔢 🔢 📶 🔢 €€€

San Sebastián de La Gomera, 38800 **Tel** *922 87 11 00* **Fax** *922 87 11 16* **Rooms** *60*

On a clifftop above La Gomera's main town and port, this traditional parador is decorated with a variety of maritime paraphernalia. The bedrooms have dark wood fittings and tiled bathrooms. From the hotel and its luxuriant subtropical gardens there are impressive views across the sea to Mt Teide on Tenerife. **www.parador.es**

Key to Price Guide *see p560* **Key to Symbols** *see back cover flap*

LA PALMA, BARLOVENTO La Palma Romántica

Topo de Las Llanadas, 38726 **Tel** *922 18 62 21* **Fax** *922 18 64 00* **Rooms** *41*

Nestling into a hillside in the northeast tip of the island, high above the sea, is this airy hotel with spacious rooms. Apart from double and single rooms there are some suites and rooms in bungalows. It has both indoor and outdoor swimming pools, a sauna, a solarium and a fitness centre. Pets are allowed. **www.hotellapalmaromantica.com**

LA PALMA, SANTA CRUZ DE LA PALMA Parador de la Palma

Ctra de el Zumacal, Breña Baja, 38720 **Tel** *922 43 58 28* **Fax** *922 43 59 99* **Rooms** *78*

This new, purpose-built parador, in the traditional Canarian style, looks out on to the sea and is surrounded by a lovely garden. It is located near the island's main town and the airport. Various excursions and activities are available. The restaurant excels in fish and other Canarian specialities and wine made on the island. **www.parador.es**

LANZAROTE, ARRECIFE Lancelot

Av Mancomunidad 9, 35500 **Tel** *928 80 50 99* **Fax** *928 80 50 39* **Rooms** *112*

This modern hotel stands on Arrecife's Reducto beach, a tempting stretch of soft, pale sand with coral reefs lying just offshore. The hotel has all the standard services including a reception desk open 24 hours. The restaurant has sea views and is also close to other good restaurants in the town. The piano bar has live music once a week.

LANZAROTE, COSTA TEGUISE Gran Melia Salinas

Av Islas Canarias, Urbanización Costa Teguise, 35509 **Tel** *928 59 03 40* **Fax** *928 59 03 90* **Rooms** *319*

A vast atrium with central water gardens and ornamental plants is the focus of this modern luxury hotel in the northern area of Costa Teguise. It has two bars and five restaurants offering a wide choice of food and drink. A swimming pool, three tennis courts, a gym, mini-golf and a newsagent are add-ons. **www.solmelia.com**

LANZAROTE, PLAYA BLANCA H10 Lanzarote Princess

C/ Maciot Urb Playa Blanca, 35570 **Tel** *928 51 71 08* **Fax** *928 51 70 11* **Rooms** *407*

A resort hotel popular with families in the south of Lanzarote facing Fuerteventura. It is cool and light, with split-level areas ornamented with water gardens. There is a large swimming pool. Tennis and golf are available and there are bikes for hire. They also have evening entertainments and a "miniclub" for children. **www.h10.es**

LANZAROTE, PUERTO DEL CARMEN Los Fariones

C/ Roque del Este 1, 35510 **Tel** *928 51 01 75* **Fax** *928 51 02 02* **Rooms** *248*

This seven-storey hotel has direct access to an attractive beach. All the rooms are spacious and have sea views. The hotel has a good range of facilities including a dive centre and two swimming pools. Outside is a large tropical garden. Two bars offer a range of snacks and live music most evenings. **www.grupofariones.com**

TENERIFE, GARACHICO Hotel San Roque

Esteban de Ponte 32, 38450 **Tel** *922 13 34 35* **Fax** *922 13 34 06* **Rooms** *20*

This charming hotel decorated with avant-garde art occupies an 18th-century house built around two pretty patios, in a historic north coast town away from the island's tourist resorts. All rooms have Jacuzzi, flat-screen TVs and video and DVD players. Dinner and breakfast are served at tables set by the poolside. **www.hotelsanroque.com**

TENERIFE, LA LAGUNA Costa Salada

Camino La Costa, Finca Oasis Valle de Guerra, 38270 **Tel** *922 69 00 00* **Fax** *922 54 10 55* **Rooms** *13*

A pretty rural hotel standing on a series of terraces over the rocky northern coast of Tenerife, at the end of a subtropical nursery for plants. The hotel has cosy bedrooms, mostly with terraces and sea views. It also has a wine cellar in a natural cave. Located off the coast road between Tejina and Valle de Guerra. **www.costasalada.com**

TENERIFE, LA OROTAVA Hotel Rural La Orotava

C/ Carrera 17, 38300 **Tel** *922 32 27 93* **Fax** *922 32 27 25* **Rooms** *8*

This 16th-century house, with cosy bedrooms around an attractive Canarian patio, was formerly the home of the Marquis of La Florida. Now transformed into a hotel, it is one of the historic buildings that forms the compact, harmonious centre of La Orotava. It also has a wine cellar. Breakfast included in price. **www.saborcanario.net**

TENERIFE, LA OROTAVA Parador de Cañadas del Teide

Las Cañadas del Teide, 38300 **Tel** *922 37 48 11* **Fax** *922 38 23 52* **Rooms** *37*

This modern parador, which looks like an Alpine chalet, is the only place to stay inside the national park. It stands in an otherwise uninhabited volcanic landscape looking out at the Roques de Garcia and towards Mt Teide. In the daytime its cafeteria caters for day-trippers but at night the guests have the park to themselves. **www.parador.es**

TENERIFE, SANTA CRUZ DE TENERIFE Pelinor

Bethencourt Alfonso 8, 38002 **Tel** *922 24 68 75* **Fax** *922 24 08 33* **Rooms** *73*

Pelinor is a comfortable and recently renovated modern hotel, mainly frequented by business people. Well located in a pedestrian street in the centre of Santa Cruz and close to the Teresitas beach. It only offers a cafeteria and a snack bar. There is a public car park a very short distance away. **www.hotelpelinor.com**

TENERIFE, SANTA CRUZ DE TENERIFE Taburiente

Dr José Navieras 24A, 38001 **Tel** *922 27 60 00* **Fax** *922 27 05 62* **Rooms** *116*

An elegant hotel in the city centre facing the beautiful Parque Garcia Sanabria. The bedrooms are well equipped and the hotel has its own boutique, a shop and a restaurant offering international cuisine. They also have a swimming pool, Jacuzzi, sauna and a solarium. A few rooms are available for business meetings. **www.hoteltaburiente.com**

RESTAURANTS AND BARS

One of the joys of eating out in Spain is the sheer sociability of the Spanish. Family and friends, often with children in tow, can be seen eating out from early in the day until after midnight.

Spanish food has a regional bias. Traditional restaurants originated as taverns and tapas bars serving dishes based on local produce. Spain also has

Wall tile advertising a Barcelona restaurant

its fair share of top-quality gourmet restaurants, notably in the Basque Country.

The restaurants listed on pages 608–53 have been selected for their food and conviviality. Pages 604–7 illustrate some of the best tapas and drinks; and each of the book's five regional sections includes features on the area's unique food and wines.

Bodegas are bars that specialize in wines and do not serve food

RESTAURANTS AND BARS

The cheapest and quickest places to eat are the bars and cafés that serve tapas. Some bars, however, especially pubs (late-opening bars for socializing) serve no food.

Family-run bar-restaurantes, ventas, posadas, mesones and fondas – all old words for the different types of inn – serve inexpensive, sit-down meals. Chiringuitos are beachside bars. They open only during the summer season.

Spain's top restaurants tend to be clustered in the Basque Country, Galicia, Barcelona, Catalonia and Madrid.

Most restaurants close one day a week, some for lunch or dinner only, and most for an annual holiday. They also close on some public holidays. The main closing times of the restaurants on pages 608–53 are listed at the end of each entry. Always check these opening times, however, when phoning to book a table.

EATING HOURS IN SPAIN

The spanish often have two breakfasts (*desayunos*). The first is a light meal of biscuits or toast with olive oil or butter and jam and café con leche (milky coffee). A more substantial breakfast may follow between 10 and 11am, perhaps in a café. This may consist of a savoury snack, such as a *bocadillo* (sandwich) with sausage, ham or cheese, or a thick slice of *tortilla de patatas* (potato omelette). Fruit juice, coffee or beer are the usual accompaniments.

From about 1pm people will stop in the bars for a beer or a *copa* (glass) of wine with tapas. By 2pm those who can will have arrived home from work for *la comida* (lunch), which is the main meal of the day. Others will choose to have lunch in a restaurant.

The cafés, *salones de té* (tea rooms) and *pastelerías* (pastry shops) fill up by about 5:30 or

Decoration, Barcelona bar

6pm for *la merienda* (tea) of sandwiches, pastries or cakes, with coffee, tea or juice. Snacks like *churros* (fried batter sticks) can also be bought from stalls.

By 7pm bars are crowded with people having tapas with sherry, wine or beer. In Spain *la cena* (dinner or supper), begins at about 10pm. Restaurants sometimes begin their evening service earlier for tourists. In summer, however, Spanish families and groups of friends often do not sit down to eat until as late as midnight. At weekend lunch times, especially in summer, you may find that restaurants are filled by large and noisy family gatherings.

HOW TO DRESS

A jacket and tie are rarely required, but the Spanish dress smartly, especially for city restaurants. Day dress is casual in beach resorts, but shorts are frowned on in the evenings.

The elegant Egaña Oriza restaurant in Seville (*see p641*)

Pavement tables outside a cafeteria, in Cadaqués on the Costa Brava

READING THE MENU

Aside from tapas, perhaps the cheapest eating options in Spanish restaurants are the fixed-price *platos combinados* (meat or fish with vegetables and, usually, chips) and the *menú del día*. A *plato combinado* is only offered by cheaper establishments. Most restaurants – but not all – offer an inexpensive, fixed-price *menú del día*, normally of three courses, but with little choice. Some gourmet restaurants offer a *menú de degustación* consisting of a choice of six or seven of the head chef's special dishes.

The Spanish word for menu is *la carta*. It starts with *sopas* (soups), *ensaladas* (salads), *entremeses* (hors d'oeuvres), *huevos y tortillas* (eggs and omelettes) and *verduras y legumbres* (vegetable dishes).

Main courses are *pescados y mariscos* (fish and shellfish) and *carnes y aves* (meat and poultry). Daily specials are chalked on a board or clipped to menus. Paella and other rice dishes may be served as the first course. A useful rule is to follow rice with meat, or start with serrano ham or salad and then follow with a paella.

Desserts are called *postres* in Spanish. All restaurants offer fresh fruit (the usual dessert in Spain) but otherwise the range of *postres* is generally poor. The better restaurants offer a limited choice, perhaps *natillas* (custard) and *flan* (crème caramel). Gourmet restaurants have more creative choices.

Vegetarians are rather poorly catered for in Spain, but in big cities such as Madrid there are a handful of vegetarian restaurants. Most menus have a vegetable or egg dish.

All eating places welcome children and will serve small portions if requested.

Las Torres de Ávila (see p191), a distinctive Barcelona bar

WINE CHOICES

Dry fino wines are perfect with shellfish, serrano ham, olives, soups and most first courses. Main courses are commonly accompanied by wines originating from Ribera del Duero, Rioja, Navarra or Penedès. A typical bar might serve wines from Valdepeñas or the local vineyards. Oloroso wines (see p607) are often ordered as a digestif.

SMOKING

In fine restaurants customers are offered puros (cigars) with their coffee and brandy. Many people in Spain smoke and very few restaurants have non-smoking areas or tables.

PRICES AND PAYING

If you order from la carta in a restaurant, your bill can soar way above the price of the menú del día, especially if you order pricey items, such as fresh seafood, fish or ibérico ham (see p462). If there is an expensive fish such as sole or swordfish on the menu at a bargain price, it may be frozen. Sea bass and other popular fish and shellfish, such as large prawns, lobster and crab, are priced by weight as a rule.

La cuenta (the bill) includes service charges and perhaps a small cover charge. Prices on menus do not include 7 per cent VAT (IVA), which is usually added when the bill is totalled. The Spanish hardly ever tip restaurant waiters more than 5 per cent, often just rounding up the bill.

Cheques are rarely used in Spain. Traveller's cheques are usually accepted but you may be given a poor rate of exchange. The major credit cards and international direct debit cards are now accepted in most restaurants. However, do not expect to pay by credit card in smaller eating or drinking places like tapasbars, cafés, village *mesones*, road-side *ventas*, pubs or *bodegas*.

WHEELCHAIR ACCESS

Since restaurants are rarely designed for wheelchairs, phone in advance (or ask the hotel staff to call) to check on access to tables and toilets.

Early 20th-century decor in a Madrid bar

Choosing Tapas

Tapas, sometimes called *pinchos*, are small snacks that
originated in Andalusia in the 19th century to accompany sherry. Stemming from a bartender's practice of
covering a glass with a saucer or *tapa* (cover) to
keep out flies, the custom progressed to a chunk of
cheese or bread being used, and then to a few olives
being placed on a platter to accompany a drink. Once free
of charge, tapas are usually paid for nowadays, and a selection makes a delicious light meal. Choose from a range of
appetizing varieties, from cold meats to elaborately prepared
hot dishes of meat, seafood or vegetables.

Mixed green olives

Patatas bravas *is a
piquant dish of
fried potatoes
spiced with
chilli and
paprika.*

Albondigas *(meatballs)
are a hearty tapa, often
served with a spicy
tomato sauce.*

**Almendras
fritas** *are
fried, salted
almonds.*

Banderillas *are
canapes
skewered on
toothpicks.
The entire
canape should
be eaten at once.*

Calamares fritos *are
squid rings and tentacles
which have been dusted with
flour before being deep fried in
olive oil. They are usually served
garnished with a piece of lemon.*

Jamón serrano *is salt-
cured ham dried in
mountain (serrano) air.*

ON THE TAPAS BAR

Alitas de pollo Chicken wings

Almejas Clams

Berenjenas horneadas Roasted
aubergines (eggplants)

Boquerones Anchovies

Boquerones al natural Fresh
anchovies in garlic and olive oil

Bunyols de bacalao Salt cod
fritters

Butifarra Catalonian sausage

Calamares a la romana Fried
squid rings

Callos Tripe

Carbassó arrebossat Battered
courgettes (zucchini)

Chistorra Spicy sausage

Chopitos Cuttlefish fried in batter

Chorizo al vino Chorizo sausage
cooked in red wine

Chorizo diablo Chorizo served
flamed with brandy

Cogoles fritos Lettuce fried in
oil with garlic

Costillas Spare ribs

Criandillas Bulls' testicles

Croquetas Croquettes

Diablitos picantes Spicy mini
hamburgers

Escopinyes Cockles

Figatell Pork and liver meatballs
from Valencia

Gambas pil pil Spicy, garlicky
fried king prawns (shrimp)

Garotes Raw sea urchins,
usually served with bread and
garlic or onions

Huevas de codorniz Hard-boiled
quails' eggs

Judias blancas Butterbeans and
whole garlic cloves in white
wine vinegar

TAPAS BARS

Even a small village will have at least one bar where the locals go to enjoy drinks, tapas and conversation with friends. On Sundays and holidays, favourite places are packed with whole families enjoying the fare. In larger towns it is customary to move from bar to bar, sampling the specialities of each. A tapa is a single serving, whereas a *ración* is two or three. Tapas are usually eaten standing or perching on a stool at the bar rather that sitting at a table, for which a surcharge is usually made.

Diners make their choice at a busy tapas bar

Chorizo, *a popular sausage flavoured with paprika and garlic, may be eaten cold or fried and served hot.*

Salpicón de mariscos *is a luxurious cold salad of assorted fresh seafood in a zesty vinaigrette.*

Gambas a la plancha *is a simple but flavourful dish of grilled prawns (shrimp).*

Tortilla española *is the ubiquitous Spanish omelette of onion and potato bound with egg.*

Queso manchego *is a sheep's-milk cheese from La Mancha.*

Pollo al ajillo *consists of small pieces of chicken (often wings) sautéd and then simmered with a garlic-flavoured sauce.*

Longaniza roja Spicy red pork sausage from Aragón (Longaniza blanca is paler and less spicy.)

Magro Pork in a paprika and tomato sauce

Manitas de cerdo Pig's trotters

Mejillones Mussels

Merluza a la romana Hake fried in a light batter

Morcilla Black (blood) pudding

Muslitos del mar Crab-meat croquette, skewered onto a crab claw

Orejas de cerdo Pig's ear

Pa de fetge Liver pâté

Paella Rice dish made with meat, fish and/or vegetables

Pan de ajo Garlic bread

Panadons d'espinacs Small spinach pasties or pies

Patatas a lo pobre Potato chunks sautéd with onions and red and green peppers

Patatas alioli Potato chunks in a garlic mayonnaise

Pernil Ham made from leg of pork, seasoned and air-dried

Pescaditos small fried fish

Pimientos rellenos Stuffed peppers

Pinchito Kebab on a skewer

Popets Baby octopus

Rabo de toro Oxtail

Sepia Cuttlefish

Sesas Brains, usually lamb or calf

Tortilla riojana Ham, sausage and red pepper omelette

Truita de patates Another name for tortilla española

Xató Salt cod and tuna salad with romesco sauce

What to Drink in Spain

Spain is one of the world's largest wine-producing countries and many fine wines are made here, particularly reds in La Rioja and sherry in Andalusia. Many other beverages – alcoholic and non-alcoholic – are served in bars and cafés, which provide an important focus for life in Spain. The Spanish are also great coffee drinkers. In the summer, a tempting range of cooling drinks is on offer, in addition to beer, which is always available. Brandy and a variety of liqueurs, such as *anís*, are drunk as apéritifs and *digestifs*, as is chilled pale gold fino sherry.

Customers enjoying a drink at a terrace café in Seville

Hot chocolate

A plate of *churros* (batter sticks)

Café con leche

Camomile   Lime flower

HOT DRINKS

Café con leche is a large half-and-half measure of milk and coffee; *café cortado* is an espresso with a splash of milk; *café solo* is a black coffee. Hot chocolate is also popular and is often served with *churros* (batter sticks). Herbal teas include *manzanilla* (camomile) and *tila* (lime flower).

COLD DRINKS

In most Spanish towns and cities it is safe to drink the tap water, but people generally prefer to buy bottled mineral water, either still (*sin gas*) or sparkling (*con gas*). Besides soft drinks, a variety of other thirst-quenching summer beverages is available, including *horchata (see p253)*, a sweet, milky drink made from ground *chufas* (earth almonds). Another popular refreshing drink is *leche merengada* (lemon and cinnamon flavoured milk ice cream). *Gaseosa*, fizzy lemonade, can be drunk either on its own or as a mixer, usually with wine. *Zumo de naranja natural* (freshly squeezed orange juice) is an excellent thirst quencher.

Sparkling and still mineral water

Horchata*, made from *chufas

SPANISH WINE

Wine has been produced in Spain since pre-Roman times and there is a great variety on offer today, including famous types such as Rioja. The key standard for the industry is the *Denominación de Origen* (DO) classi-fication, a guarantee of a wine's origin and quality. *Vino de la Tierra* is a classification of wines below that of DO in which over 60 per cent of the grapes come from a specified region. *Vino de Mesa*, the lowest category, covers basic unclassified wines. For more detailed information on Spain's principal wine-producing regions, refer to the following pages: Northern Spain (*see pp78–9*), Eastern Spain (*see pp202–3*), Central Spain (*see pp340–1*), and Southern Spain (*see pp420–1*).

Penedès white wine   **Rioja red wine**   **Sparkling wine (*cava*)**

SPIRITS AND LIQUEURS

Spanish brandy, which comes mainly from the sherry bodegas in Jerez, is known as *coñac*. Most bodegas produce at least three different labels and price ranges. Magno is a good middle-shelf brandy; top-shelf labels are Cardenal Mendoza and Duque de Alba. *Anís*, which is flavoured with aniseed, is popular. *Pacharán*, made from sloes, is sweet and also tastes of aniseed. Licor 43 is a vanilla liqueur. Ponche is brandy that has been aged and flavoured with herbs.

Anís   *Pacharán*   *Licor 43*   *Ponche*

BEER

Most Spanish beer *(cerveza)* is bottled lager, although you can almost always find it on draught. Popular brands include San Miguel, Cruzcampo Mahou and Águila. To order a glass of beer in a bar ask for *una caña*. Alcohol-free lager *(cerveza sin alcohol)* is also available in most bars in Spain.

Bottled beers

SHERRY

Sherry is produced in bodegas in Jerez de la Frontera (Andalusia) and in nearby towns Sanlúcar de Barrameda and El Puerto de Santa María *(see pp420–1)*. Although not officially called sherry, similar kinds of wine are produced in Montilla near Córdoba. Pale fino is dry and light and excellent as an apéritif. Amber amontillado (aged fino) has a strong, earthy taste while oloroso is full-bodied and ruddy.

Two brands of fino sherry

MIXED DRINKS

Red wine and lemonade

Sangria is a refreshing mixture of red wine, *gaseosa* (lemonade) and other ingredients including chopped fruit and sugar. Wine diluted with lemonade is called *vino con gaseosa*. Another favourite drink is *Agua de Valencia*, a refreshing blend of *cava* (sparkling wine) and orange juice. Young people will often order the popular *cubalibres*, cola with rum.

Sangria   **Cubalibre**   **Vino con gaseosa**

HOW TO READ A WINE LABEL

If you know what to look for, the label will provide a key to the wine's flavour and quality. It will bear the name of the wine and its producer or bodega, its vintage if there is one, and show its *Denominación de Origen* (DO) if applicable. Wines labelled *cosecha* are recent vintages and the least expensive, while *crianza* and *reserva* wines are aged a minimum of two or three years – part of that time in oak casks – and therefore more expensive. Table wine *(Vino de Mesa)* may be *tinto* (red), *blanco* (white) or *rosado* (rosé). *Cava* is a sparkling wine made by the *méthode champenoise* in specified areas of origin.

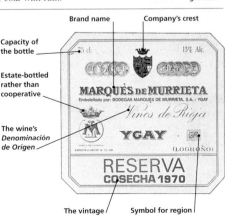

Brand name   Company's crest

Capacity of the bottle

Estate-bottled rather than cooperative

The wine's *Denominación de Origen*

The vintage   Symbol for region

Choosing a Restaurant

The restaurants in this guide have been selected across a wide range of price categories for their good value, exceptional food and interesting location. This chart lists the restaurants by region. Within each town or city, entries are listed by price category, from the least expensive to the most expensive.

PRICE CATEGORIES
For a three-course evening meal for one including a half bottle of house wine, service and taxes:

€ under 25 euros
€€ 25–35 euros
€€€ 35–45 euros
€€€€ over 45 euros

GALICIA

A CORUÑA La Penela   €

Plaza de María Pita 12, 15001 **Tel** *981 20 92 00*

In the square dedicated to a Galician heroine, and very close to the harbour, is this simple, unpretentious but very popular restaurant which serves traditional Galician fare. The roast veal, tripe with *garbanzos* (chickpeas), Spanish omelette and Galician-style monkfish are specialities. Closed Sun & 10–25 Jan.

A CORUÑA Taberna Pil-Pil   *Tapas*   €

C/ Pelamios 7, 15001 **Tel** *981 21 27 12*

Located in front of the Escuela de Artes Picasso, this pleasant, though rather small, taberna restaurant uses traditional produce to create dishes such as marinated salmon, bonito with peppers, and *codillo de jamón braseado* (braised knuckle of ham). For dessert, try apple pudding. Closed Sun & 15–31 Oct.

A CORUÑA Casa Pardo   €€€€

C/ Novoa Santos 15, 15006 **Tel** *981 28 00 21*

High-quality cooking and an extensive menu of Galician dishes are the characteristics of this restaurant by the fishing port. It is renowned for its monkfish, *caldeirada de rape*, a dish which does not always get mentioned on the menu but is always available. The blackberry crème caramel is also popular. Closed Sun & 15–31 Mar.

A GUARDA Anduriña   €€

C/ Paseo Do Porto 58, 36780 (Pontevedra) **Tel** *986 61 11 08*

Watch the fishing boats bring in their catch as you enjoy fresh hake, turbot or a fish casserole from the covered terrace of this port-side restaurant. It also serves traditional *empanada gallega* (a pie stuffed with cod, tuna or shellfish), a good stew with monkfish and clams, and a fair variety of desserts. Closed Nov.

ALLARIZ Casa Tito Fandiño   *Tapas*   €€

C/ Rúa do Carcere 7, 32660 (Ourense) **Tel** *988 44 22 16*

A famous restaurant, specializing in traditional Galician cooking with modern touches. It is a good place to try *pulpo* (octopus) or *empanada* (pie). For something more elaborate try the *lubina* (sea bass) with mushroom sauce or the Galician steak with potatoes and mushrooms. Closed Sun evenings & Mon in winter & 15–31 Oct.

BAIONA Moscón   *Tapas*   €€

C/ Alférez Barreiro 2, 36300 (Pontevedra) **Tel** *986 35 50 08*

This restaurant in Baiona serves mainly Galician cuisine with fish stews predominating on the menu. These include a tasty fish *caldeirada* (casserole) spiced with paprika. There is also seafood from the estuary; all complemented by a good selection of Galician wines. The harbour view makes for a pleasant dining experience.

BETANZOS La Casilla   *Tapas*   €€

Ctra de Castilla 90, 15300 (A Coruña) **Tel** *981 77 01 61*

Located in an old-stone house, this restaurant is famous throughout Spain for its omelettes, especially the potato variety – *tortilla de patata* – but it also serves traditional Galician food. It is very busy during the summer and at weekends. Closed Sun evenings except in summer, Mon & 15 days in Nov.

BUEU A Centoleira   *Tapas*   €€

Playa de Beluso 27, 36937 (Pontevedra) **Tel** *986 32 08 96*

What started as an old fishermen's inn 120 years ago is now a popular restaurant run by the same family, serving Galician food such as *guisotes marineros* (fish stews), *empanada de maiz* (sweetcorn pie) and cheese mousse over tomato compote. Closed Mon (except summer) & 15 Oct–15 Nov.

CAMBADOS Ribadomar   €€

C/ Terra Santa 17, 36630 (Pontevedra) **Tel** *986 54 36 79*

A welcoming family-run restaurant offering mainly seafood and traditional dishes, although there are a few innovations as well, such as the *Perdiz O Arco* (partridge). Try the *vieiras al horno* (oven-baked scallops) and sole with cockles; and for dessert the home-made almond pie. Closed Sun evenings, Mon & 15–31 Oct.

Key to Symbols *see back cover flap*

CAMBADOS María José   🗒🍷   €€€

C/ San Gregorio 2– 1º, 36630 (Pontevedra) **Tel** *986 54 22 81*

Situated on the first floor of the building opposite the Parador de Cambados, this restaurant offers experimental cooking, combining traditional dishes with modern creations. It has a good selection of Albariño wines. Try the *langostino* (king prawn) salad wrapped in bacon. Closed Sun evenings & Mon (except in summer) & 1–15 Nov.

COMBARRO Taberna de Alvariñas   🗒🍴🍷   €€€

C/ Mar 63, 36993 (Pontevedra) **Tel** *986 77 20 33*

Located in a picturesque fishing village, famous for its *hórreos* (granaries) on the seafront, this restaurant has a lovely terrace to dine out on. Try the *ragu de langostinos* (scallops with prawns) with Alvariño wine, the *lomos de merluza* (hake) and the crêpes filled with cream and toffee. Closed Mon except in summer & 1 Dec–31 Jan.

LUGO Verruga   *Tapas* 🗒♿🍷   €€€

C/ Cruz 12, 27001 **Tel** *982 22 95 72*

This restaurant, in the heart of the old town, has been serving good classic and uncomplicated Galician fare for more than 50 years. It also offers a wide variety of seafood from its own hatchery. Try the red peppers stuffed with crab meat and the delicious home-made *filloas rellenas fritas* (Galician crêpes). Closed Sun evenings & Mon.

LUGO Mesón de Alberto   *Tapas* 🗒♿🍷   €€€€

C/ Cruz 4, 27001 **Tel** *982 22 83 10*

An institution of Galician cooking, located in a stone house in the monumental area of town. Award-winning chef Alberto García offers a selection of traditional delicacies and more modern creations. The fish and shellfish are excellent, including small squid and sea bass with baby eels. Wide selection of Galician cheeses and wines. Closed Sun.

O GROVE El Crisol   🗒   €€€€

C/ Hospital 10–12, 36980 (Pontevedra) **Tel** *986 73 00 29*

A restaurant renowned for its traditional Galician cooking as well as creative dishes. It serves mainly fish and seafood and is a good place to discover new species of fish such as sargo, dentón or pinto, or sample traditional ones such as sea bass and turbot. The dining room overlooks the sea. Closed Mon, for lunch in Jul–Aug, 15–31 Jan & 15–30 Nov.

OURENSE San Miguel   *Tapas* 🗒🍴🍷   €€€

C/ San Miguel 12–14, 32005 **Tel** *988 22 07 95*

One of the best restaurants in Ourense, run by the same family for more than half a century. Soberly decorated, it has a wide choice of fish and seafood dishes. Its meats are also excellent, notably the veal medallions with truffles and foie gras. Try the chocolate cream with pineapple juice and mint for dessert. Closed Jan.

OURENSE A Reixdora   🗒♿🍴🍷   €€€€

Ctra N540 Bentraces-Celanova, km 6, Bentraces, 32890 **Tel** *988 38 31 47*

An award-winning restaurant in an old building in Bentraces offering modern Galician cuisine prepared in a personal and adventurous way. It is worth having the *empanada con masa de castañas* (chestnut pie), the sea bass or the wild boar with leeks and pumpkin. Closed Sun evenings, Mon, 10 days in Feb & 10 days in Oct.

PADRÓN Casa Ramallo   🗒   €

C/ Castro 5, Rois, 15900 (A Coruña) **Tel** *981 80 41 80*

A short way from Padrón, this pleasant *casa de comidas* has been serving good value traditional Galician fare for more than 100 years. Especially good are its *guisos marineros*, shellfish and seasonal dishes including lamprey. Casa Ramallo also has a good selection of meats and home-made pie for dessert. Closed Mon.

PADRÓN Chef Rivera   *Tapas* 🗒🍷   €€€

C/ Enlace Parque 7, 15900 (A Coruña) **Tel** *981 81 04 13*

In this restaurant, chef Jose Antonio Rivera's varied menu offers fish, seafood, game specialities and traditional Galician cooking with a French touch. Particularly good are his seasonal dishes, among them lamprey, a freshwater fish from the Río Ulla. Wide variety of port wine and cigars. Closed Sun evenings & Mon (except Aug).

PONTEVEDRA Casa Román   🗒♿   €€

C/ Augusto García Sánchez 12, 36003 **Tel** *986 84 5 60*

A busy restaurant with fast and efficient service serving traditional cuisine prepared with the best quality produce. It specializes in rice dishes, and in eels from the Río Miño, when in season. Favourites are the lobster pie, monkfish in green sauce and *lubina a la sal* (sea bass baked in salt). Closed Sun evenings & Mon (except Aug).

PONTEVEDRA Alameda 10   🗒🍷   €€€

C/ Alameda 10, 36001 **Tel** *986 85 35 12*

An efficient restaurant preparing good traditional seafood and excellent fish, including seasonal varieties such as lamprey and eels from the Río Miño. Try the *croquetas de marisco* (fish balls), the famous *bacalao* (cod) Alameda or the *solomillo de cerdo ibérico* (pork steak). Try *tarta del abuelo con frutos secos* for dessert. Closed Sun.

PONTEVEDRA Alameda de Doña Antonia   🗒🍷   €€€

C/ Soportales de la Herrería 4–1º, 36002 **Tel** *986 84 72 74*

Regional cuisine in a refined and beautiful setting overlooking the lovely Plaza de la Herrería. The monkfish salad, the marinated sea bass salad, the oven-cooked lamb with honey, and the *mero al vapor* (grouper) with vegetables and olive oil are favourites. Also worth trying is the nougat ice cream with hazelnuts and candied fruits. Closed Sun.

SAN SALVADOR DE POIO Casa Solla
Av Sineiro 5, 36163 (Pontevedra) **Tel** *986 87 28 84*

Housed in a lovely old *pazo* (manor house) outside Pontevedra, this restaurant is worth the journey. It serves "designer" Galician cuisine based on traditional recipes with a modern touch. Try the *bacalao confitado con pisto* (confit of cod) or the *costilla de cerdo deshuesada y confitada* (confit of boned pork rib). Closed Sun, Mon & Thu evenings.

SANTIAGO DE COMPOSTELA Vilas
Tapas
C/ Rosalía de Castro 88, 15706 (A Coruña) **Tel** *981 59 10 00*

This family-run, and somewhat old-fashioned, restaurant specializes in Galician cooking. Some favourites in its extensive menu are the *guiso de pulpo* (octopus stew), Galician-style tripe and *grelos con jamón* (local vegetables with ham). Try *filloas con miel y nata* (crêpes with honey and cream) for dessert. Closed Sun & Sat evenings.

SANTIAGO DE COMPOSTELA Moncho Vilas
Tapas
Av de Villagarcía 21, 15706 (A Coruña) **Tel** *981 59 83 87*

Exemplary Galician dishes are served at this long-standing restaurant, which was one of the best in Santiago de Compostela and has picked up again after a rather downish period. The fish and seafood, such as clams, scallops and spiny lobster, are ultra-fresh, and the meat and *empanadas* excellent. Closed Sun evenings and Mon.

SANTIAGO DE COMPOSTELA La Tacita D'Juan
C/ Hórreo 31, 15702 (A Coruña) **Tel** *981 56 20 41*

The service is careful and professional in this busy restaurant serving classical Galician meat, fish and seafood dishes. They prepare a famous seasonal *cocido* (stew), but otherwise try the *lenguado* (filet of sole) or the *entrecot de buey* (ox steak). End with the *filloas rellenas de crema pastelera* (custard cream filled crêpes). Closed Sun and Aug.

SANTIAGO DE COMPOSTELA Toñi Vicente
C/ Rosalia de Castro 24, 15706 (A Coruña) **Tel** *981 59 41 00*

Worshippers of Galician *haute cuisine* flock faithfully to Toñi Vicente's culinary temple, in an elegant and pretty venue. Among her creations are the marinated sea bass salad, the duck liver sautéed with apple, the red tuna fish in pickle and the carpaccio of venison with truffle oil, salad and parmesan. Closed Sun & 15–31 May.

SANXENXO Pepe Vieira
Plaza de la Constitución 2, 36960 (Pontevedra) **Tel** *986 69 17 49*

A small restaurant run by the award-winning Torres Cannas brothers, who offer creative cooking combining unusual tastes and textures, with surprisingly good results. These include the *pulpo en su sangre* (octopus in its own blood) or *rape en emulsión de almendras* (monkfish in almond sauce). Closed Sun–Thu dinner (winter) & Mon lunch (summer).

SANXENXO La Taberna de Rotilio
Av del Puerto 7–9, 36960 (Pontevedra) **Tel** *986 72 02 00*

Located in the cellar of the Hotel Rotilio, this restaurant is famous for its innovative approach to Galician cuisine. The chef's creations include monkfish *caldeirada*, an interesting oyster omelette and an unusual original rice dish. Wonderful pies. There is also a cheaper menu. Closed Sun evenings (except summer), Mon & mid-Dec–mid-Jan.

VEDRA Roberto
San Julián de Sales-Vedra, 15880 (A Coruña) **Tel** *981 51 17 69*

Housed in a magnificent *pazo*, 7 km (4.5 miles) from Santiago de Compostela, the emphasis of this restaurant is fish and vegetables. Owner Roberto Crespo uses home-grown produce to create dishes such as sea bass with tomato compote and mushroom stew or scallops over potato purée with balsamic vinegar. Closed Sun evenings, Mon & Jan.

VIGO La Oca
C/ Purificación Saavedra 8, 36207 (Pontevedra) **Tel** *986 37 12 55*

A cosy restaurant specializing in modern Galician cuisine, using fresh ingredients from the nearby Teis market. *Erizo de mar revuelto con huevos de la casa* (sea urchin omelette), lamprey salad and oven-baked suckling pig are the delicacies here. Booking essential. Closed Sat, Sun; Mon & Tue evenings, Easter week & Aug.

VIGO Casa Alfredo
C/ Tameiga 87–88, Mos, 36415 (Pontevedra) **Tel** *986 33 85 40*

This restaurant is in Mos, 10 km (6 miles) from Vigo (take exit 660 from the Vigo-Portugal motorway). It specializes in game dishes and organizes game days. Try the partridge cooked differently in summer or winter. It also has excellent *lubina* and a good selection of breads and desserts. Closed Sun, Mon & Tue evenings & 15–31 Aug.

VILAGARCÍA DE AROUSA Casa Bóveda
C/ La Marina 2, Carril, 36600 (Pontevedra) **Tel** *986 51 12 04*

It is better to book in advance to eat in this busy restaurant situated on Carril harbour, a short way from Vilagarcía de Arousa. It specializes in fish and shellfish from the Rias Baixas and also prepares excellent *guisos* and rice dishes. Favourites are clams in an onion, garlic and parsley sauce and stewed hake. Closed Sun evenings & Mon (except Aug).

VILANOVA DE AROUSA O'Paspallas
C/ A Cerca 46, 36620 (Pontevedra) **Tel** *986 55 52 21*

Sited in the Ria de Arousa, near Vilagarcía de Arousa, a popular resort with a pretty promenade and water sports facilities, this small restaurant is so popular that advanced booking is advised. Sit on the terrace to try the *milhojas* (millefeuille) or the *solomillo con trufas* (steak with truffles). Closed Sun evenings & Mon (Oct–May).

Key to Price Guide *see p608* **Key to Symbols** *see back cover flap*

ASTURIAS AND CANTABRIA

AJO La Casona de la Peña 🔲🔲 €€€€
Barrio de la Peña, Ajo, 39195 (Cantabria) **Tel** *942 67 05 67*

Located in the highest part of Ajo, a village east of Santander, this restaurant and hotel has an extraordinary dining room which doubles as a permanent exhibition of paintings and antiques. La Casona serves fairly modern cuisine with traditional sauces such as prawns with curry sauce and mango ravioli. Closed Sun evenings & Mon.

AVILÉS La Cofradia del Puerto *Tapas* 🔲 €€
Av Los Telares 11, 33400 (Asturias) **Tel** *985 56 12 30*

This is a typical no-frills, no-fuss *sidreria* (cider bar), where you can sample Asturias' famous beverage and eat excellent fish and seafood fresh from the Cantabrian sea. If you are more inclined to meat, they offer a selection of red meats cooked over embers, as well as *frixuelos* (crêpes typical of the region). Closed Sun, 23 Jun–9 Jul & 2–18 Nov.

CANGAS DE NARCEA Blanco 🔲 €
C/ Mayor 11, 33800 (Asturias) **Tel** *985 81 03 16*

Despite its unprepossessing appearance, the food here is of a very good quality. There are various fish dishes on the menu such as sardines marinated with vegetables and vinagrette and *bacalao confitado* with risotto. As for meat, the deboned shoulder of lamb is delicious. Closed Sun evenings, Mon in winter & Sun in summer.

CANGAS DE ONIS El Molín de la Pedrera *Tapas* 🔲🔲🔲 €€
C/ Bernabé Pendás 1, 33550 (Asturias) **Tel** *985 84 91 09*

A stylish *sidreria*, decorated with traditional objects and implements which give it a rustic air. It serves original combinations such as *crujiente de cabrales con avellanas* (Cabrales cheese from the Picos de Europa with hazelnuts) and more traditional dishes such as *bonito* and *frixuelos* (grapes). Closed Wed except in summer & Feb.

CASTAÑEDA Hostería de Castañeda 🔲🔲🔲🔲 €
C/ Barrio Villabañez, 39660 (Cantabria) **Tel** *942 59 81 13*

After seeing the nearby caves at Puente Viesgo, which are very close to Castañeda, relax in the converted stables of this 17th-century mansion with its own chapel and terrace. Tuck into the hake with green asparagus or the sirloin steak with mushrooms. Or try the white beans with wild boar. Orange jelly for dessert is a must.

CASTRO URDIALES El Ruso 🔲🔲 €€€
C/ Allendelagua 2, 39700 (Cantabria) **Tel** *942 87 06 18*

A modest restaurant in Allendelagua, a village outside Castro Urdiales, serving quality cooking. There is no written menu; you will need to ask the waiter to reel off what is available and the prices. Dishes include traditional stews, seafood and grilled fish, all in sizeable portions. Home-made desserts. Closed Sun evenings & Oct.

CASTRO URDIALES Mesón del Marinero *Tapas* 🔲🔲🔲 €€€
C/ Correria 23, 39700 (Cantabria) **Tel** *942 86 00 05*

This listed historic building, decorated as its name suggests in a maritime theme, houses a stylish seafood restaurant. The portions are generous and its proximity to the fishing port is evident in the freshness of the produce. It also serves excellent *ternera* (veal) and other local meats. The traditional *leche frita* is a sweet ending to the meal.

COMILLAS La Rabia *Tapas* 🔲🔲🔲 €€
C/ Barrio de la Rabia 8, 39520 (Cantabria) **Tel** *942 72 02 75*

The terrace of this restaurant enjoys views of the estuary in the Oyambre nature reserve making it a popular place for a pre-lunch apéritif. The menu is focused on fish, including *almejas a la marinera* (clams), *rape al ajillo* (monkfish with garlic). Choice of classic desserts. Lunch-time menu for 12 euros. Closed Mon except in summer & Jan.

COMILLAS El Capricho de Gaudí 🔲🔲🔲🔲 €€€€
C/ Barrio de Sobrellano, 39520 (Cantabria) **Tel** *942 72 03 65*

Antoni Gaudí's architectural wonder *(see p111)*, clad in green tiles and sunflowers, provides a unique setting for this sophisticated restaurant. Recommended are the salmon in mustard cream and the turbot with garlic sprouts. End with *canutillos de castaña con helado de caramelo* (chestnuts with caramel ice cream). Closed Sun evenings & Mon.

COSGAYA Mesón del Oso 🔲🔲 €€€
Ctra C621 Potes-Fuente Dé, km 14, 39539 (Cantabria) **Tel** *942 73 30 18*

Delightful country hotel and restaurant by the Río Deva in the peaceful Liebana Valley, with dramatic views of the Picos de Europa. The veal steaks and *cocido lebaniego* (a rich stew with chickpeas and pork) are local specialities. The *arroz con leche* (rice pudding) makes a traditional dessert. Closed 7 Jan–15 Feb.

CUDILLERO La Casona de Pio 🔲 €€
C/ Riofrío 3, 33150 (Asturias) **Tel** *985 59 15 12*

This small hotel and restaurant occupies a renovated old fish-salting factory in the heart of Cudillero, a resort on the Asturian coast with lovely beaches and impressive cliffs. It serves traditional Asturian food, based mainly on fish and seafood. Choices for dessert include grandmother's home-made pie. Closed 7 Jan–7 Feb.

CUDILLERO Mariño   *Tapas* 🅰🎵🚻   €€

C/ Concha de Artedo, 33155 (Asturias) **Tel** *985 59 11 88*

Located west of the lively seaside resort of Cudillero, with views of the beach, this restaurant-with-rooms serves fish casseroles, delicious *almejas a nuestro modo* (clams "cooked our way") and *curadillo*, a typical dish made with a fish from the shark family. Try the apple *frixuelos* (crepes). Closed Sun evenings & Mon (except Jul & Aug).

ESCALANTE San Román de Escalante   *Tapas* ▤🅿   €€€€€

Ctra Escalante–Castillo, km 2, 39795 (Cantabria) **Tel** *942 67 77 28*

This lovely old mountain house is set in gardens and woodland with its own 12th-century chapel. The dining room, decorated with paintings, is the setting for modern seasonal cuisine inspired by traditional recipes. Dishes include fried clams with spinach and pine kernels and hake with clam ravioli. Home-made desserts. Closed 20 Dec–20 Jan.

GIJÓN Casa Victor   ▤🅿   €€€

C/ Carmen 11, 33206 (Asturias) **Tel** *985 34 83 10*

This restaurant is an institution in Gijón. It specializes in dishes based on fish caught in the Cantabrian sea. Try the *lomos de salmonete rellenos de marisco* (red mullet filled with seafood). For dessert there is chocolate covered with *turrón* (nougat) sauce. It offers various menus at cheaper prices. Closed Sun & 20 Dec–20 Jan.

LAREDO Casa Felipe   *Tapas* ▤   €€

C/ Travesía José Antonio 5, 39770 (Cantabria) **Tel** *942 60 32 12*

A simple restaurant in Laredo, one of Cantabria's most popular holiday resorts with a long sandy beach and an attractive old town. It serves simple traditional food, emphasizing good fresh fish and seafood. It also specializes in local cheeses, mainly made from cow's milk, both fresh and semi-mature. Closed Mon & 20 Dec–15 Jan

LAREDO El Camarote   *Tapas* ▤🅰🚻🅿   €€

Av de la Victoria 105, 39770 (Cantabria) **Tel** *942 60 67 07*

This restaurant, decorated with marine paraphernalia, offers simple cooking based on seasonal market produce. There is a wide range of fish and seafood, cooked in an uncomplicated way. Try the home-style clams, scallops with cheese and for dessert millefeuille with strawberries and cream. Closed Sun evenings except Jul & Aug.

LUGONES La Máquina   *Tapas* ▤🅰   €€

Av Conde de Santa Bárbara 59, 33420 (Asturias) **Tel** *985 26 36 36*

Although La Máquina is about 6 km (4 miles) from the Asturian capital, it is a good place for an excellent *fabada* Asturiana, the region's typical hearty stew made with white beans and chorizo. For dessert try the delicious home-made *crema de arroz con leche* (rice pudding). Open only for lunch. Closed Sun & mid-Jun–mid-Jul.

OVIEDO Casa Fermín   ▤🅰🅿   €€€

C/ San Francisco 8, 33003 (Asturias) **Tel** *985 21 64 52*

The cosy Casa Fermín is one of Oviedo's most classic restaurants offering a combination of traditional and modern cuisine. Try the *salmón ahumado* (smoked salmon) with yoghurt and vanilla oil or the *salmonetes* (red mullet) with black rice. For dessert, try mascarpone with ice cream or bizcocho with ice cream and chocolate. Closed Sun.

POTES El Cenador del Capitán   🅿   €

C/ Cervantes 3, 39570 (Cantabria) **Tel** *942 73 21 61*

On the top floor of a big stone house in the centre of Potes is this restaurant with a beamed ceiling and decorated in a simple rustic fashion. It specializes in local food, especially *cocido lebaniego* and game dishes. It offers a cheap *Menú del Peregrino* ("pilgrim's" menu). Closed Mon–Thu in winter.

POTES Paco Wences   ▤🅰🚻   €€

C/ Roscabao 5, 39570 (Cantabria) **Tel** *942 73 00 25*

The restaurant of the Picos de Valdecoro hotel, in the Picos de Europa, offers simple traditional food from the Liebana Valley, with filling *cocidos* made from quality locally-grown ingredients. Try the *cocido lebaniego* or the *solomillo al queso de Tresviso* (steak cooked with a local cheese). Typical Cantabrian desserts. Closed Jan.

PRAVIA Casa Juan de la Tuca   ▤🅰   €€

Ctra Grado–Pravia km 14, Beifar, 33120 (Asturias) **Tel** *985 82 06 94*

Located in Beifar, not far from Pravia, this simple restaurant offers magnificent home cooking by the Temprano sisters. Their cuisine is primarily Basque-Navarrese in inspiration with Asturian touches. Try the *cardo con almejas* (a type of thistle with clams), the *rape* (monkfish) or the *merluza frita* (fried hake). Closed Thu & Jan.

PRENDES Casa Gerardo   *Tapas* ▤🅰🅿   €€€€

Ctra AS–19 km 9, 33430 (Asturias) **Tel** *985 88 77 97*

This delightful restaurant, run by the fifth generation of the same family since its opening, is one of the landmarks of Asturian cooking. It reputedly serves the best *fabada* Asturiana and also offers other delights such as king prawn with fresh pasta and Asturian cabbage, and a good rice pudding. Closed Sun–Thu evenings & 20 days in Jan.

RAMALES DE LA VICTORIA Río Asón   ▤🅿   €€€€

C/ Barón de Adzaneta 17, 39800 (Cantabria) **Tel** *942 64 61 57*

Hidden off the beaten track is one of Cantabria's best restaurants. The salmon is caught in the nearby Río Asón, and the seasonal menu will delight even the most sophisticated palates. Try the sea bass tartar with Iranian caviar or the *rape* stuffed with anchovies. Reasonable price fixed menu. Closed Sun evenings, Mon & 22 Dec–1 Feb.

Key to Price Guide *see p608* **Key to Symbols** *see back cover flap*

SALINAS Real Balneario de Salinas
Tapas 目 🚻 🚻 🚻 €€€€

Av Juan Sitges 3, 33400 (Asturias) **Tel** *985 51 86 13*

This lovely restaurant in the seaside resort of Salinas is owned by a family of restaurateurs who work together in the kitchen and the dining room. They offer a combination of classical and modern cuisine using high-quality ingredients. Try the oven-baked grouper with tomatoes, artichokes and fennel oil. Closed Sun evenings & 7 Jan–7 Feb.

SAN VICENTE DE LA BARQUERA Augusto
Tapas 目 🚻 🚻 🚻 €€€

C/ Mercado 1, 39540 (Cantabria) **Tel** *942 71 20 40*

Located in the porticoed part of town, this renovated tavern specializes in fresh fish, seafood and rice. You can also eat in a lovely shaded terrace in summer. Try the *ensalada de mariscos* (seafood salad), *almejas con arroz* (clams with rice), *calamares en su tinta* (squid cooked in its own ink) and other delicacies. Closed Mon (except Jun–Sep).

SAN VICENTE DE TORANZO Casona de Toranzo
Tapas 目 🚻 🚻 €€

Ctra N623, Burgos-Santander km 115, 39699 **Tel** *942 59 44 11*

The restaurant of the hotel Posada del Pas *(see p564)* has a separate entrance for non-residents beside the main road between Santander and Burgos. The menu is strong on Cantabrian food and includes an excellent *cocido montañés* (mountain stew), as well as entrecôte with Tresviso cheese sauce and lovely sorbet. Closed 15 Oct–1 Jan.

SANTANDER Hostería de Adarzo
目 🚻 €

C/ Adarzo 68, 39011 (Cantabria) **Tel** *942 33 23 11*

A restaurant and hotel serving traditional cooking using fresh, seasonal market produce, with special emphasis on red meats and daily caught fish. Adarzo serves dishes such as octopus salad with vegetables, cod loin with tomatoes, trotters and veal chinstraps. Has its own parking which is an advantange in the capital. Closed Mon.

SANTANDER Bodega del Riojano
Tapas 🚻 €€

C/ Río de la Pila 5, 39003 (Cantabria) **Tel** *942 21 67 50*

This colourful bodega (wine cellar) is as famous for its decorative wine barrels, painted by Spanish artists, as it is for its delicious food. The red peppers stuffed with anchovies and other ingredients are renowned. It also serves a tasty leek salad and oxtail stew. Closed Sun evenings & Mon except in summer.

SANTANDER El Nuevo Molino
目 🚻 🚻 🚻 €€€€

Ctra N611 Santander Torrelavega km 13, Barrio Monseñor 18, Puente Arce, 39478 (Cantabria) **Tel** *942 57 50 55*

Sited in Puente Arce, this ancient mill belongs to El Serbal in Santander. It offers creative cooking with dishes such as cod salad with mushrooms and *pil pil* (a creamy parsley sauce) and monkfish ravioli filled with king prawn and cream. There is a divine ice cream with sultanas and brandy over toffee cream. Closed Sun evenings & Tue.

SANTANDER El Serbal
目 🚻 🚻 €€€€

C/ Andrés del Río 7 (Puerto Chico), 39004 (Cantabria) **Tel** *942 22 25 15*

A nice restaurant that is becoming very popular for its innovative cuisine, created by adding personal touches to traditional dishes. It also offers some originals such as oven-baked ray in mushroom *pil pil* and creamy rice and a distinctive chicken curry. For dessert, strawberries with apple jelly and basil. Closed Sun evenings & Mon.

SANTILLANA DEL MAR La Joraca
🚻 🚻 €€

Los Hornos 20, 39330 (Cantabria) **Tel** *942 84 01 37*

The restaurant of the Hotel Colegiata may be uninspiringly furnished and decorated, and lacking the beautiful views of the hotel, but it is still a good place to eat excellent food made with local produce. Choice dishes are grilled monkfish with salad onions *pil pil* and ham. For dessert, order cream of smoked cheese. Closed Sun evenings & Mon.

SOLARES Casa Enrique
Tapas 目 🚻 🚻 🚻 €€

Paseo de la Estación 18, 39710 (Cantabria) **Tel** *942 52 00 73*

Casa Enrique hotel's restaurant is popular with locals and tourists alike. It is a decent place to sample traditional home cooking, which results in tasty stews and dishes such as *albóndigas de ternera* (veal meatballs) or *ventresca de bonito con cebolla y pimiento* (tuna fish with onions and peppers). Closed Sun evenings & 20 Sep–10 Oct.

THE BASQUE COUNTRY, NAVARRA & LA RIOJA

AMOREBIETA Juantxu
目 🚻 🚻 🚻 €€€

C/ Barrio Enartze 2, 48340 (Vizcaya) **Tel** *946 73 26 50*

Housed in a traditional Basque rural house on the road between Amorebieta and Gernika, this restaurant with a garden specializes in both fish (particularly cod) and meats including roast lamb. Good choice of salads and vegetarian options. The dessert menu includes a selection of home-made ice creams. Closed Sun–Thu evenings, Tue & Nov.

AOIZ Beti Jai
Tapas 目 🚻 🚻 €€€

C/ Santa Agueda 2, 31430 (Navarra) **Tel** *948 33 60 52*

A well-known restaurant in an old house on the main square of the town, with views of the river. Beti Jai serves high-quality Navarrese cuisine and some modern and creative dishes based on seasonal market produce. Try the *menudicos* (tripe) and any of the excellent home-made desserts. Closed Sun evenings & 15–31 Aug.

AZPEITIA Kiruri
Tapas 🍽️♿🖼️🍷 €€€

C/ Loiola Hiribidea 24, 20730 (Guipúzcoa) **Tel** *943 81 56 08*

Located in front of the shrine of Loyola, this family-run restaurant offers simple cooking and traditional Basque dishes such as *txangurro* (spider crab baked and served in the shell) and *menestra de verduras* (vegetable stew) and a choice of pies for dessert. The car park is convenient for visiting the shrine. Closed Mon evenings & 24 Dec–7 Jan.

BERMEO Jokin
Tapas 🍽️♿🖼️🍷 €€€

C/ Eupeme Deuna 14, 48370 (Vizcaya) **Tel** *946 88 40 89*

Jokin, with pretty views of Bermeo's fishing port, specializes in seasonal fish dishes such as *habitas frescas con bacalao fresco* (small broad beans with fresh cod) or *rollitos de merluza confitados en aceite de oliva* (hake in olive oil). Meat-eaters can try the crispy trotters in sauce. Closed Sun evenings.

BILBAO Café Iruña
Tapas €

C/ Berastegi 5, 48001 (Vizcaya) **Tel** *944 23 70 21*

The classic café opened in 1903 opposite the Jardines de Albia. It has a marvellous, ornately decorated mock-Mudéjar interior of ceramic tiles evocative of the age of Islamic Spain. The *menú del día* is good and surprisingly inexpensive for such a charming place. A place worth dipping into even if you only feel like drinking coffee.

BILBAO Café La Granja
Tapas €

Plaza Circular, 40001 (Vizcaya) **Tel** *944 230 813*

An old-fashioned café created in "the French style" of the 1920s. It stands in the centre of Bilbao, amidst office blocks, facing the statue of the city's founder. A full and inexpensive *menú del día* is served, but the café also does a good breakfast. Snacks and sandwiches are available throughout the day. Closed evenings.

BILBAO Ein Prosit
🍷 €

Plaza Ensanche 7, 48009 (Vizcaya) **Tel** *944 24 13 11*

An authentic German restaurant run by the descendants of a renowned Saxon *charcutier* (butcher) who settled in Bilbao in the early 20th century. The specialities are all meaty except for salmon marinaded in vodka. Draught German beer is the accompanying drink of choice and there is also a selection of different types of schnapps.

BILBAO Xukela
Tapas €

C/ Perro 2, 48005 (Vizcaya) **Tel** *944 15 97 72*

A refreshingly informal place to eat snacks or a light meal in the Casco Viejo. Choice morsels include fine Spanish ham, crab meat, cheeses, peppers with anchovies and caviar and mushrooms topped with smoked cod and a dollop of apple purée. The name Xukela means "dog" in Basque.

BILBAO Víctor
🍽️🖼️🍷 €€€

Plaza Nueva 2, 48005 (Vizcaya) **Tel** *944 15 16 78*

A classic restaurant located in the historic square of the old quarter. Specialities are cod dishes, *chipirones* (Cantrabrian squid), green peppers filled with spider crab, *lenguado a la plancha*, ostrich in mushroom sauce and, for dessert, *tarta capuchina*. Closed Sun, second week in Jan, Easter week & 1–15 Sep.

BILBAO Zortziko
🍽️🍴🍷 €€€€

C/ Alameda Mazarredo 17, 48001 (Vizcaya) **Tel** *944 23 97 43*

Contemporary *haute cuisine* served in a beautiful building, not far from the Guggenheim Museum. The menu is seasonal with creative Basque touches. Among the specialities are *pintada a baja temperatura* (guinea fowl cooked at a low temperature), foie gras, turbot and a delicious tiramisu. Closed Sun, Mon & 15 Aug–15 Sep.

CINTRUÉNIGO Maher
🍽️🖼️🍷 €€€€

La Ribera 19, 31592 (Navarra) **Tel** *948 81 11 50*

Innovative cuisine is impeccably presented in the Hotel Maher restaurant, although the service can be variable. Salad with different kinds of lettuces, asparagus pudding, rice with hare and suckling lamb in mushroom sauce, are all house specialities. Order bitter chocolate soufflé with caramel ice cream. Closed Sun evenings, Mon & 20 Dec–20 Jan.

ESTELLA Navarra
Tapas 🍽️♿🖼️ €€

C/ Gustavo de Maeztu 16, 31200 (Navarra) **Tel** *948 55 00 40*

Traditional regional cuisine is served in this grand house, with tiles depicting Navarra's former kings. The *Blanca de Navarra* (a lemon and honey ice cream, served with fresh cream and nuts) is superb. Other specialities are *espárragos rellenos* (stuffed asparagus), roast piglet and lamb, and *crema tostada* for dessert. Closed Sun evenings & Mon.

EZCARAY El Rincón del Vino
🍽️♿🖼️🍷 €€

C/ Jesús Nazareno 2, 26280 (La Rioja) **Tel** *941 35 43 75*

Vino also has a shop selling local wines and other delicacies typical of La Rioja region. They serve traditional Riojan cuisine with an emphasis on seasonal produce including vegetables, mushrooms and truffles. During the hunting season, it offers good game dishes. Closed Mon–Thu evenings in winter & Wed except in Jun & Aug.

EZCARAY Echaurren
🍽️♿🖼️🍷 €€€

Héroes del Alcázar 2, 26280 (La Rioja) **Tel** *941 35 40 47*

One of La Rioja's emblematic restaurants, run by the Paniego family who also have a small hotel. The vegetables are cooked to perfection and there is a great variety of Rioja and Albariño wines. Special dishes include *solomillos de rape negro sobre purrusalda* (monkfish with leaks). Closed Sun evenings (winter), two weeks in Jun & 9–28 Dec.

Key to Price Guide *see p608* **Key to Symbols** *see back cover flap*

GETARIA Elkano 📋🔲🔳 €€€€

C/ Herrerieta 2, 20808 (Guipúzcoa) **Tel** *943 14 06 14*

This restaurant is famous for its grilled fish dishes and seafood. The baby squid and the turbot are excellent. Also good are the local grilled hake cheeks and small squid Pelayo style. The best Basque brand of Txacoli wine, Txomín Echaniz, is available. Closed Sun evenings in winter, two weeks in Feb & two weeks in Nov.

GUERNIKA Zallo Barri 📋🔲🔳 €€€

C/ Juan Calzada 79, 48300 (Vizcaya) **Tel** *946 25 18 00*

Barri offers both traditional Basque cuisine and innovative dishes. Specialities are *atún marinado con lentejas salteadas* (marinated tuna with lentils), *cordero a la parilla con patata y foie gras a la plancha* (grilled lamb with foie gras) and *bizcocho de almendra* (almond sponge cake). Closed Sun, Mon, Tue & Wed evenings.

HARO Beethoven 📋 €€

C/ Santo Tomás 8–10, 26200 (La Rioja) **Tel** *941 31 11 81*

The Fresno family owns the two restaurants Beethoven I and Beethoven II in the same street at Haro. Both use local Riojan products to prepare traditional fare, with emphasis on local seasonal vegetables and *chuletillas de cordero* (lamb chops). *Torrijas* (slices of bread soaked in milk and egg and then fried) make a popular dessert.

HARO Terete 📋🔲 €€

C/ Lucrecia Arana 17, 26200 (La Rioja) **Tel** *941 31 00 23*

An ancient wood-burning oven has been roasting lamb here since 1877. Sit at the long wooden tables and savour the Riojan specialities, accompanied by a bottle of house wine. You can start with asparagus, and end the meal with traditional *cuajada* that is served with walnuts and honey. Closed Sun evenings, Mon, 1–15 Jul & 15–31 Oct.

HONDARRIBIA Sebastián 📋🔲🔳 €€€€

C/ Mayor 11, 20280 (Guipúzcoa) **Tel** *943 64 01 67*

A 16th-century house in the historic part of town. Andalucian chef Sebastián Arance serves Basque-French cuisine, with the obvious touch of his homeland in the delicious *ajo blanco* (a cold soup made with garlic and almonds), perfect for summer, and his olive oil ice cream. Game dishes are available in season. Closed Sun evenings, Mon & Nov.

LAGUARDIA Posada Mayor de Migueloa *Tapas* 📋🔲🍴🔳 €€€

C/ Mayor de Migueloa 20, 01300 (Alava) **Tel** *945 62 11 75*

The restored 17th-century palace of Viana now houses a small hotel and one of northern Spain's best restaurants. The cuisine is a Basque-La Rioja fusion, strong on fish and seafood (try the baked hake), meat (roast lamb or venison) and vegetables. Excellent choice of home-made desserts, one made with sweet peppers. Closed 21 Dec–14 Jan.

LASARTE Martin Berasategui 📋🔲🍴🔳 €€€€

C/ Loidi 4, 20160 (Guipúzcoa) **Tel** *943 36 64 71*

One of the top restaurants of Spain is located in a converted farmhouse, 7 km (4.5 miles) from San Sebastián. The specialities change with the season but Martín Berasategui, a trendsetter among chefs, always surprises with his creations. Reservations essential especially for terrace tables. Closed Sun evenings, Mon, Tue & mid-Dec–mid-Jan.

LEITZA Basa Kabi *Tapas* 📋 €€

C/ Alto de Leiza, 31880 (Navarra) **Tel** *948 51 01 25*

In the middle of lovely woodland and mountain scenery, Basa Kabi serves traditional food with modern touches. Try the sautéed broad beans and peas with grilled bacon and cauliflower cream, grilled tuna with mushroom sauce or, for dessert, vanilla rice pudding with cherries and chocolate cream. Open only in summer, Jul–Aug.

LOGROÑO Asador de Emilio 📋🔲🔳 €€

Av República Argentina 8, 26000 (La Rioja) **Tel** *941 25 88 44*

A good-value restaurant in the heart of the city specializing in high-quality roasted red meats, grilled fish and oven-baked kid. Particular specialities are *ensalada de perdiz* (partridge salad) and *taco de rape con crema suave de ajos confitados* (creamed monkfish) and venison served with grape and plum sauce. Closed Sun except in May & Aug.

LOGROÑO Cachetero 📋🔲🔳 €€€

C/ Laurel 3, 26001 (La Rioja) **Tel** *941 22 84 63*

Tasty home cooking is served in this cosy restaurant, well known in the city for its basic dishes capturing the best of each season. Standards include *morcilla* (black pudding) and stuffed peppers. Desserts include *helado de queso de roquefort con nueces* (Roquefort cheese ice cream with walnuts). Closed Sun, Wed evenings & 25–31 Aug.

OIARTZUN Zuberoa Jatetxea *Tapas* 📋🔲🍴🔳 €€€€

C/ Iturriotz Auzoa 8, Plaza Bekosoro 1, 20180 (Guipúzcoa) **Tel** *943 49 12 28*

The celebrated restaurant of the Arbelaitz brothers is in a 600-year-old farmhouse. Among the dishes are Cantabrian squid cooked in a traditional sauce and roast piglet with ginger and potato purée. Exquisite desserts to follow. They also have a sampler menu. Closed Sun, Wed, 1–15 Jan, 15–30 Apr & 15–31 Oct.

OLITE Casa Zanito 📋🔳 €€€

C/ Rúa Mayor 16, 31390 (Navarra) **Tel** *948 74 00 02*

Probably the best option for a lunch of traditional Navarrese cuisine with a few modern touches. One speciality is a salad of fried artichokes with prawns. Desserts include apple pie with cinnamon ice cream. They also have a reasonable fixed lunch and dinner menu. The service is good. Closed Mon, Tue (in winter) & 15 Dec–15 Jan.

PAMPLONA Alhambra   🍴♿🔒🍷   €€€€
C/ Francisco Bergamín 7, 31003 (Navarra) **Tel** *948 24 50 07*

Typical Navarrese cooking as well as some unusual combinations are the hallmark of this welcoming and elegant restaurant. The artichokes, the truffle and vegetable purée and the mushroom risotto are all delicious appetizers. Dessert could be the hot chocolate soufflé with saffron ice cream and pumpkin seeds. Closed Sun & Easter week.

PAMPLONA Europa   🍴🍷   €€€€
C/ Espoz y Mina 11, 31002 (Navarra) **Tel** *948 22 18 00*

Located in the Hotel Europa, in the old part of the city near the cathedral, is one of Pamplona's best places to eat. It offers a range of traditional Navarrese dishes such as *menestra de verduras* (vegetable stew), *sopa de castañas* (chestnut soup) and *chateaubriand de lomo de ciervo con mango a la parrilla* (grilled pork with mango). Closed Sun.

PASAI DONIBANE Casa Camara   ♿🔒🍷   €€
C/ San Juan 79, 20110 (Guipúzcoa) **Tel** *943 52 36 99*

A restaurant with wonderful views of Pasai Donibane port (just outside San Sebastián), where you can dine watching the boats and choose your own live lobster from the aquarium. Try the baked mushrooms with crunchy vegetables or the Basque speciality of *txangurro al horno*. Alternatively, there are steaks. Closed Sun evenings & Mon.

PUENTE LA REINA Mesón del Peregrino   🍴🔒🍷   €€€€
Irumbidea, Ctra N111 Pamplona-Logroño km 23, 31100 (Navarra) **Tel** *948 34 00 75*

The restaurant-cum-hotel of a well-known chef is sited on the pilgrimage route to Santiago de Compostela. The cuisine combines Mediterranean and Navarrese influences. A main course to go for is the *cochinillo en salsa de trufas* (suckling pig in a truffle sauce). On the dessert menu is white chocolate mousse. Closed Sun evenings & Mon.

SAN SEBASTIÁN Bar Sport   ***Tapas*** 📋   €
C/ Fermín Calbetón 10, 20001 (Guipúzcoa) **Tel** *943 42 68 88*

One of several bars lining the streets of the old part of San Sebastián, which have counters stacked with *pinchos* (tapas). For an informal meal, point to what you want and keep going until you are full, then settle the bill. It is an enjoyable way of having your meal but beware that the price can add up to more than you expect.

SAN SEBASTIÁN Akelarre   🍴♿🔒🍷   €€€€
Paseo Padre Orkolaga 56, Barrio de Igueldo, 20008 (Guipúzcoa) **Tel** *943 21 40 86*

One of the famous restaurants of Spain, a gourmet temple with great views of rolling hills which plunge into the sea. The safest option, if you have room for it, is to choose the seven-course *menú de degustación* (a sampler menu). Spectacular desserts. Closed Sun evenings, Mon–Tue (Jan–Jun); Sun evenings & Mon (Jul–Dec); Feb & 1–15 Oct.

SAN SEBASTIÁN Arzak   🍴♿🔒🍷   €€€€
Av Alcalde José Elósegui 273, 20015 (Guipúzcoa) **Tel** *943 27 84 65*

Celebrity chef Juan Mari Arzak has earned a reputation beyond Spain for his perfectly presented, creative dishes. His daughter Elena works here as well. They even run a "laboratory" where a team of cooks experiment with new tastes and textures. Closed Sun evenings Mon, & Tue (Jan–Jun); Sun evenings & Mon (Jul–Dec); 15–30 Jun–Nov.

SAN VICENTE DE LA SONSIERRA Casa Toni   🍴🍷   €
C/ Zumalacárregui 27, 26338 (La Rioja) **Tel** *941 33 40 01*

Book in advance for this restaurant serving modern Riojan cuisine based on traditional dishes. Its best-known speciality is the *crema de patatas a la riojana con espuma de piquillos y láminas de chorizo* (Riojan cream of potatoes with peppers and chorizo). Closed Sun–Thu evenings (winters), Mon (except in summer), 15–30 Jun & 15–30 Sep.

SANTO DOMINGO DE LA CALZADA El Rincón de Emilio   🍴🔒🍷   €€
Plaza Bonifacio Gil 7, 26250 (La Rioja) **Tel** *941 34 09 90*

This classic restaurant offers both traditional and contemporary Riojan cuisine. Specialities are *ensalada templada de jamáon de pato y foie gras con frutos secos a la miel* (duck salad with foie gras, nuts and honey) and *arroz con leche con helado de caramelo* (rice pudding with caramel ice cream). Closed Tue evenings & three weeks in Feb.

SORAUREN Txarrantxena   🍴🍷   €€
C/ del Medio 3, 31194 (Navarra) **Tel** *948 33 18 05*

Located in the village of Sorauren, 7 km (4.5 miles) from Pamplona, in a beautiful 18th-century house, this restaurant offers modern and well-presented Navarrese cuisine. Specialities include eggs filled with foie gras, sea bass and for dessert, yoghurt mousse with tomato jam. Closed Sun evenings; two weeks in Feb; Mon & all evenings (Oct–Jun).

TAFALLA Túbal   🍴♿🔒🍷   €€€€
Plaza de Navarra 14, 31300 (Navarra) **Tel** *948 70 08 52*

Túbal, one of the best in Navarra, is housed in a historic building with 18 balconies overlooking the square. If you are not sure what to have they will prepare a personalized *menú de degustación* for you. Its forté is regional cuisine with an accent on vegetables of the season. Closed Sun evenings, Mon, 21 Aug–5 Sep & Christmas.

TUDELA Restaurante 33   🍴♿🍷   €€€
C/ Capuchinos 7, 31500 (Navarra) **Tel** *948 82 76 06*

A busy restaurant in the largest town of the Ribera region, where the menu reflects the local skill of growing vegetables. In spring, try the *menú de degustación*, which includes the choice of the season's crop. One speciality is *lomo de lubina salvaje asado con verduritas* (roasted wild sea bass with vegetables). Closed Sun & Aug.

Key to Price Guide *see p608* **Key to Symbols** *see back cover flap*

VIANA Borgia   ♿   €€€

C/ Serapio Urra, 31230 (Navarra) **Tel** *948 64 57 81*

Located in the centre of Viana, this family-run restaurant only opens for lunch, except on Fridays and Saturdays when it is open all day. Borgia offers varied and refreshingly eclectic dishes. Try the *espárragos frescos con crema de remolacha* (fresh asparagus with creamed beetroot) and *bonito asado* (roast tuna). Closed Sun & Aug.

VINIEGRA DE ABAJO Venta de Goyo   ▤♿🚼   €

Ctra de Lerma km 98, 26325 (La Rioja) **Tel** *941 37 80 07*

Part of an old *venta* (inn), also a hotel, in the Sierra de la Demanda, about 40 km (25 miles) southwest of Nájera, this simple restaurant offers good value. The menu is based on the culinary heritage of the Sierra with good game dishes. Try the red beans, the *cordero a la cazuela* (lamb casserole) and the *tarta de manzana* (apple pie). Closed Christmas.

VITORIA Casa Felipe   *Tapas* ▤♿   €€€

C/ Fueros 28, 01005 (Alava) **Tel** *945 13 45 54*

This bar-restaurant is a traditional, no-nonsense *casa de comidas* and a classic in Vitoria. It serves mainly Basque fare, with some standards such as *merluza rebozada* (batter hake) and *menestra de cordero* (lamb stew). Other specialities are grilled mushrooms and clams. For dessert try *tarta de la casa* (home-made pie). Closed Mon & 22 Jun–22 Jul.

VITORIA Dos Hermanas   ▤🎌   €€€

C/ Madre Vedruna 10, 01008 (Alava) **Tel** *945 13 29 34*

A pleasant and cosy restaurant serving classic regional cooking with a seasonally-changing menu. The tuna served on a bed of peppers and the oxtail stew are both delicious. Other specialities include venison and *almejas a la plancha* (grilled clams). Ask for the *surtido de la casa* (selection) to try the different home-made desserts. Closed Sun evenings.

BARCELONA

OLD TOWN Bar Pinotxo   *Tapas* 📋   €

C/ Mercat de la Boqueria (La Rambla 89), 08002 **Tel** *933 17 17 31*   **Map** *5 A2*

The most famous of all the bars in the Boqueria. Steel buckets hold chilled bottles of *cava* (Catalan champagne-style wine), and fresh ingredients from neighbouring market stalls are cooked and served hot on the spot. Try the squid cooked in diverse styles and the fresh oysters. The bar is closed on Sundays and in the evenings after 8pm.

OLD TOWN Dim Sum House   *Tapas*   €

C/ Bergara 7, 08007 **Tel** *932 70 12 93*   **Map** *5 A1*

Not the typical kitsch Chinese restaurant that you usually find in Spain. Clean and modern, this popular establishment offers good value set lunches and a decent range of dim sum. The shrimps are definitely worth a try; other specialities include steamed prawns and meat dumplings. Closed Sun.

OLD TOWN Elisabets   *Tapas* 📋▤   €

C/ Elisabets 2, 08001 **Tel** *933 17 58 26*   **Map** *2 F2*

A local institution, this homely bustling restaurant specializes in traditional Catalan cuisine. It is a favourite for diners in search of hearty, home-cooked mid-day meals and Friday night tapas. Dishes include rabbit stew, chicken cooked in beer and a variety of *bocadillos* (sandwiches). Closed Sun & three weeks in Aug.

OLD TOWN Mosquito   *Tapas* ▤   €

C/ Carders 46, 08003 **Tel** *932 68 75 69*   **Map** *5 C2*

A laid-back bar, frequented by a healthy mix of Catalans and resident expats. Trendy music, friendly staff, cheap drinks and a solid array of Asian favourites such as chicken tikka brochettes, Singapore noodles and *gyoza* dumplings. Try the exotic tapas that can change in the middle of the evening from Indian to Japanese. Closed Mon.

OLD TOWN Organic   📋▤♿🎵   €

C/ Junta de Comerç 11, 08001 **Tel** *933 01 09 02*   **Map** *2 F3*

Spacious, clean and pleasantly lit, this good-value vegetarian restaurant offers an imaginative menu of Asian dishes, lasagnes, stews and an all-you-can-eat salad buffet. The home-made bread with nuts is a must. Occasionally, they have live music. They also have a small shop selling organic products. Has an excellent lunch menu.

OLD TOWN El Salón   ▤🎌   €€

C/ Hostal d'en Sol 6–8, 08002 **Tel** *933 15 21 59*   **Map** *5 B3*

The Baroque-style interior gives this establishment the feel of an 18th-century boudoir. The menu changes constantly but promises sumptuous ingredients and inventive dishes, often featuring French and Catalan specialities. Closed Sun & two weeks in Aug.

OLD TOWN Euskal Etxea   *Tapas* ▤♿🎌   €€

C/ Placeta Montcada 1–3, 08003 **Tel** *933 10 21 85*   **Map** *5 B3*

Home to the Basque Cultural Institute, the Euskal Etxea is one of the best places in town for Basque *pintxos* (small rounds of bread with a myriad of toppings). Other specialities include fish and meat stews, roasted meat and fresh seafood dishes. It also serves exceptionally good à la carte meals. Closed Sun evenings & one week in Aug.

OLD TOWN Mam i Teca
Tapas 🖥️🍷 €€

C/ Lluna 4, 08001 **Tel** *934 41 33 35*

Map 2 F2

Tiny, sunflower-yellow bar that plays well-known jazz, blues and rock tunes. The tapas is superb, and includes locally sourced cheeses, organic sausages and country dishes such as ham and broad beans. They also have an excellent wine list and a good range of Scottish single malts. Closed Tue & Sat lunch.

OLD TOWN 7 Portes
🖥️♿🍷 €€€

Passeig Isabel II 14, 08003 **Tel** *933 19 30 33*

Map 5 B3

A long-standing Barcelona institution since 1836, with a who's who of past guests, including Winston Churchill and Che Guevara. It is famed for its classic marble tiles and wood-panelled dining room, and most of all for paella, which comes in 10 different varieties. They serve a different paella everyday of the week.

OLD TOWN Agua
🖥️♿🌐🍷 €€€

Passeig Marítim de la Barceloneta 30, 08003 **Tel** *932 25 12 72*

Map 6 D4

Classy seafront restaurant with floor-to-ceiling windows and abstract fish sculptures. It is popular with a young crowd and serves excellent fish and rice dishes. Specials include steamed mussels, butan potatoes, Norway lobsters au gratin and grilled fish. Agua is also known for cooking rice over coal. There is an appealing terrace too.

OLD TOWN Biblioteca
🖥️♿🍷 €€€

C/ Junta de Comerç 28, 08001 **Tel** *934 12 62 21*

Map 2 F3

Elegant restaurant-cum-cookbook shop with Modernista tiles and an open kitchen. The cooking focuses on seasonal ingredients and comforting flavours. Specialities include rice with pigeon and black pudding, black spaghetti with *calçots* (leek-sized green onions) and poached egg. Service can be erratic. Closed Sun, Mon & two weeks in Aug.

OLD TOWN Café de l'Academia
🖥️🌐🍷 €€€

C/ Lledó 1, Plaça Sant Just, 08002 **Tel** *933 19 82 53*

Map 5 B3

An intimate, candle-lit restaurant with exposed brick walls and a pretty terrace in the lovely Plaça Sant, in the centre of Barri Gòtic. The menu offers superb Catalan fare, interesting salads and home-made pasta. The cod dishes, from raw to baked, are excellent. The desserts are top-notch. Closed Sun & Sat.

OLD TOWN Cal Pep
Tapas 🖥️🍷 €€€

Plaça de les Olles 8, 08003 **Tel** *933 10 79 61*

Map 5 B3

Arguably the best bar in town for fresh fish and seafood, right off the boats. Cal Pep has an excellent selection of tapas as well. The long, narrow, standing bar means it gets crowded at peak times. Arrive early for one of five tables out back. Closed Sun, Mon lunch & Aug.

OLD TOWN Can Majó
🖥️🌐🍷 €€€

C/ Almirall Aixada 23, 08003 **Tel** *932 21 54 55*

Map 5 B5

As places for paella go, this is one of the best, especially when eaten on a warm summer's day on the terrace with sea views. If you start getting into the shellfish, prices hike right up, but it is worth it for freshness and quality of produce, cooked to perfection. Closed Sun evenings and Mon.

OLD TOWN Pla de la Garsa
🖥️🍷 €€€

C/ Assaonadors 13, 08003 **Tel** *933 15 24 13*

Map 5 B2

Situated in the stables of a 17th-century palace, the cosy atmosphere of this pretty, split-level restaurant makes it a good place for romantic evenings. Lunch is excellent value and for cheese-lovers the 40-strong list is a winner. There is also an interesting selection of red wines.

OLD TOWN Taxidermista
🖥️♿🌐🍷 €€€

Plaça Reial 8, 08002 **Tel** *934 12 45 36*

Map 5 A3

Soft colour schemes and high ceilings give this trendy restaurant an edge over the touristy competition on the bustling Plaça Reial. Inventive market cooking offers a wide range of dishes from around the Mediterranean Rim, including *baba ghanoush* (Lebanese eggplant purée), sardine tarts and duck confit. Closed Mon.

OLD TOWN Carballeira
🖥️♿🍷 €€€€

C/ Reina Cristina 3, 08003 **Tel** *933 10 10 06*

Map 5 B3

The first Galician seafood restaurant in Barcelona, Carballeira is well known for its simply grilled fish and seafood, perfect paellas and the house special – Galician-style tender octopus sprinkled with paprika. The *vieiras* (escallops) are a popular dish. Lobsters and sea crabs are brought live from the Galician coasts. Closed Sun evenings & Mon.

OLD TOWN Comerç 24
Tapas 🖥️♿🍷 €€€€

C/ Comerç 24, 08003 **Tel** *933 19 21 02*

Map 5 C3

Designer tapas bar with charcoal grey walls and primary colour accents, serving some of the most inventive tapas in town. A "festival" of tapas is served for groups of six or more. Try the *arròs a banda* (rice with fish) or the *tortilla de patatas* (potato omelette). Reservations necessary. Closed Sun & Mon.

OLD TOWN Hofmann
🖥️🍴🍷 €€€€

C/ Argenteria 74–78, 08003 **Tel** *933 19 58 89*

Map 5 B2

The recent recipient of a Michelin star, this restaurant-cum-cookery school produces high-quality cuisine in a sophisticated locale with attentive service. Daily specials are always a good bet. Do not miss the desserts as they are highly elaborated and artistic. Closed Sat & Sun.

Key to Price Guide *see p608* **Key to Symbols** *see back cover flap*

EIXAMPLE Cata 1.81
Tapas 目📖 €€

C/ València 181, 08011 **Tel** *933 23 68 18*

Map *3 A4*

Long, slim and blindingly white, this modern tapas bar was one of the pioneers of Post-Modernist *pinchos*, turning classics such as Russian salad into state-of-the-art taste explosions. The excellent wine list is on offer by the glass. A top choice for those interested in the wonders of New Catalan cuisine. Closed daily for lunch & Sun.

EIXAMPLE Madrid-Barcelona
Tapas 目👍📖 €€

C/ Aragó 282, 08007 **Tel** *932 15 70 27*

Map *3 A4*

This smart, split-level restaurant with its cast-iron balustrades and polished wood looks more expensive than it is. It is hugely popular, often with long queues coming out the door, for Málaga-style *pescaditos fritos* (fried fish) and other good value tapas.

EIXAMPLE Thai Lounge
目 €€

C/ València 205, 08007 **Tel** *934 54 90 32*

Map *3 A4*

Typical of a Thai restaurant with lots of Buddhas and teakwood furniture, Thai Lounge succeeds where others have failed in bringing the flavour of the country to Barcelona. The curries are the house speciality, but there are also a good range of less obvious dishes. The reasonably priced evening menu special is a bargain.

EIXAMPLE Cinc Sentits
目📖 €€€

C/ Aribau 58, 08011 **Tel** *933 23 94 90*

Map *2 F1*

This warm yet minimal restaurant offers impeccable service, while preparing dishes such as duck and pear salad and "6-hour" tender suckling pig. Meticulously sourced products are cooked with flair and creativity. The Omakase (chef's choice) tasting menu is recommended. Kids are welcome during the week and at lunch. Closed Mon evenings & Sun.

EIXAMPLE Shibui
目👍 €€€

C/ Comte d'Urgell 272–274, 08036 **Tel** *933 21 90 04*

Map *2 E1*

With its sleek blonde wood fittings, Japanese cardboard-brick walls and trim waiting staff, this excellent sushi bar has Tokyo written all over it. The basement dining room also has custom-made tatami mat areas and sliding screens, making them a brilliant choice for parties. Closed Sun.

EIXAMPLE Alkimia
目👍🚭📖 €€€€

C/ Indústria 79, 08025 **Tel** *932 07 61 15*

Map *3 C2*

One of the rising stars of Barcelona's gastronomic scene, this small designer restaurant revitalizes traditional Catalan dishes with new techniques and foreign flavours. Signature dishes include creamy rice with crayfish and nyora peppers, sticky, slow roasted bull tail and mandarin essence with *hortchata* (tiger nut) foam. Closed Sat lunch & Sun.

EIXAMPLE Casa Calvet
目👍🚭📖 €€€€

C/ Casp 48, 08010 **Tel** *934 12 40 12*

Map *3 B5*

A beautiful restaurant that was originally designed by Gaudí as a private home and offices for a wealthy textile merchant. The cosy seating booths, formal table settings and old-school service set the ambience. Try the lamb meatballs with creamy risotto and pine nut tart with foamed *crema catalana*. Closed Sun.

EIXAMPLE El Prinicipal del Tragaluz
目👍🚭📖 €€€€

C/ Provença 286–288, 08008 **Tel** *932 72 08 45*

Map *3 A3*

The smartest of the Tragaluz restaurants, the sleek, cream-toned interior with floor-to-ceiling windows and a romantic plant-filled terrace is perfect for special occasions. The menu offers scallops, foie gras, truffles, lobster and other luxury goodies. Service, however, can be a touch frosty. Closed Sun (Jul–Aug).

EIXAMPLE Moo
Tapas 目👍🚭📖 €€€€

C/ Rosselló 265, 08008 **Tel** *934 45 40 00*

Map *3 A3*

In the short time that Moo has been open it has walked away with a string of accolades, thanks to the inspired cooking of the Roca brothers, who manage the restaurant. The tasting menu with matching wines is magical: Dublin bay prawns with rose and licorice, sea bass with lemon thyme, as well as desserts inspired by perfumes.

FURTHER AFIELD (GRÀCIA) Chido One
目 €

C/ Torrijos 30, 08012 **Tel** *932 85 03 35*

Map *3 C2*

Lined floor to ceiling with Mexican Day of the Dead artifacts and trophies, as well as retro jalapeño chilli cans, this trendy eatery serves excellent regional fare including steaming bowls of heart-warming *posole* (soup made with pork and hominy), soft fat enchiladas slathered with chilli sauce, *tacos* and lethal margaritas. Live music once a week.

FURTHER AFIELD (GRÀCIA) Envalira
目 €€

Plaça del Sol 13, 08012 **Tel** *932 18 58 13*

Map *3 B1*

A real neighbourhood joint in the spirited Plaça del Sol, Envalira is noisy, raucous and fun with a laid-back, anything-goes ambience. Intimate it is not, but it is a great place for hearty, no-nonsense fare with rice dishes topping the bill. Specialities include the black squid rice and the Milanese rice. Closed Sun evenings & Mon.

FURTHER AFIELD (GRÀCIA) La Rosa del Desierto
目👍 €€

Plaça Narcís Oller 7, 08006 **Tel** *932 37 45 90*

Map *3 A2*

This was Barcelona's first ever Moroccan restaurant and is still widely regarded to be the best. With its atmospheric decor it is a fun place for couscous and delicious *tagines*. They have interesting meat dishes, soups and salads on their menu. Also try one of their typical Arab teas. Closed Sun evenings.

FURTHER AFIELD (GRÀCIA) Botafumeiro   *Tapas* 🍴♿🎵🍴🍷   €€€€

C/ Gran de Gràcia 81, 08012 **Tel** *932 18 42 30*   **Map** *3 A2*

A legendary seafood restaurant with ice-banks piled high with boat-fresh fish and seafood at the entrance. A-listers from Woody Allen to Madonna have all made this a favourite haunt while in town, thanks to discreet management and luxury surroundings. Try the tender *pulpo Gallego* (Galician octopus). Reservations essential.

FURTHER AFIELD (GRÀCIA) Ot   🍴🍴🍷   €€€€

C/ Torres 25, 08012 **Tel** *932 84 77 52*   **Map** *3 B2*

Small, intimate and painted in sunset tones, this eatery arrived on the scene with a bang. It has just one tasting menu, boasting dishes such as wild garlic foam with smoked salt, wild boar and violet potatoes, or tuna stew with grape gratin, that changes daily depending on what is in season at the local Mercat de la Llibertat. Closed Sat lunch & Sun.

FURTHER AFIELD (GRÀCIA) Roig Robí   🍴🏠🍴🍷   €€€€

C/ Sèneca 20, 08006 **Tel** *932 18 92 22*   **Map** *3 A2*

This little and friendly restaurant, with a pretty interior courtyard for summer dining, is a classic for genuine Catalan cuisine. The menu boasts a good selection of *bacalao* dishes as well as typical vegetable preparations of broad beans and artichokes. Closed Sat lunch & Sun.

FURTHER AFIELD (HORTA) Can Travi Nou   ♿🏠🍷   €€€

C/ Jorge Manrique, 08035 **Tel** *934 28 03 01*

Few people venture so far from the centre for their supper, but this 14th-century farmhouse is well worth the trek to soak up the atmosphere of yesteryear, and the rolling terraces are wonderful for al fresco dining. Roast meats, rice dishes and fresh fish are on the menu. Closed Sun evenings.

FURTHER AFIELD (POBLENOU) Els Pescadors   🍴♿🏠🍷   €€€€

Plaça Prim 1, 08005 **Tel** *932 25 20 18*

The multiple-spaced restaurant – terrace, formal dining room and old-fahioned tiled cafeteria – is named after the fishermen that used to frequent it. It is an excellent place for a catch of the day special, zingy-fresh mussels and other fishy delights. Also try the anchovies. Closed Easter & Christmas.

FURTHER AFIELD (SANT GERVASI) La Balsa   🏠🍴🍷   €€€€

C/ Infanta Isabel 4, 08060 (Barcelona) **Tel** *932 11 50 48*

Much-loved by Barcelona's glitterati; sportspersons, artists, actors and politicians are all in attendance at this uptown eatery. Service is discreet, the decor tasteful and the terraces among the best in town for enjoying Basque, Catalan and Mediterranean food at its finest. Closed Sun, Mon lunch & Easter.

FURTHER AFIELD (TIBIDABO) L'Orangerie   🍴♿🎵🏠🍴🍷   €€€€

La Florida Hotel, Ctra de Vallvidrera 83–93, 08035 (Barcelona) **Tel** *932 59 30 00*

Perched high on the mountain above Barcelona and the sea, this beautiful restaurant has wonderful views and is well worth the 30-minute taxi ride. Try the lobster *carpaccio* with tomato bread or grilled sea-bream in a clam and potato *caldereta* stew. Live music on special days.

CATALONIA

ALCANAR Taller de Cuina Carmen Guillemot   🍴   €€€

C/ Colón 26, 43530 (Tarragona) **Tel** *977 73 03 23*

A series of elegant dining rooms spread over three floors, each individually but classically decorated, is the setting for this restaurant. The cuisine is Mediterranean, with French influences, and what you'll find on the menu depends on what is freshest at the market. Among several fixed-price menus, they also offer a vegetarian option. Closed Tue.

ALELLA El Niu   🍴   €€€

Rambla Ángel Guimerá 16, 08238 (Barcelona) **Tel** *935 55 17 00*

A mother-and-daughter team are in charge of the kitchen at this elegant and stylish restaurant. The exquisite, creative Catalan cuisine is prepared with the freshest regional produce and beautifully presented. Try the oven-baked lamb with local pears and finish with spectacular flambéed bananas. Closed Sun evenings, Mon & two weeks in Aug.

ALTAFULLA Faristol   🏠🍷   €€

C/ Sant Martí 5, 43893 (Tarragona) **Tel** *977 65 00 77*

Experience traditional Catalan fare at this charming 18th-century farmhouse. The English-Catalan couple that run it are welcoming and it makes for a romantic getaway from the bustle of Barcelona. Rooms are also available. They usually have music on Friday and Saturday nights. Open Fri–Sun (Oct–May) & for dinner only in summer.

ANDORRA LA VELLA Borda Estevet   🍴🏠🍷   €€€

Ctra de la Comella 2, 23500 **Tel** *376 86 40 26*

This old-country manor is still used for the traditional practice of drying tobacco that is grown nearby, and oozes an old-world atmosphere. Extensive menu of Andorran-Catalan and French fare. The meat dishes are exceptional, particularly *carns a la llosa* (lamb or beef) which arrive sizzling on a hot slate.

Key to Price Guide *see p608* **Key to Symbols** *see back cover flap*

ARENYS DE MAR Hispania 🟦♿🏠   €€€€
C/ Real 54, Ctra NII, 08350 (Barcelona) **Tel** *937 91 04 57*

A famous bistro that has earned numerous awards for the quality of its cooking. People travel from far and wide for its *clam suquet* (fish stew) and home-made *crema catalana* (traditional vanilla custard with a burnt, caramel crust). Closed Sun evenings, Tue, Easter & Oct.

BERGA Sala   *Tapas* 🟦🏠   €€€€
Passeig de la Pau 27, 08600 (Barcelona) **Tel** *938 21 11 85*

A good choice for hearty winter dishes that feature freshly picked mushrooms from the nearby forests; wild game is available in season. Sala offers extremely innovative cuisine, and they also have a set tasting menu. Try partridge in vinegar sauce or the roasted young goat. Closed Sun evenings & Mon.

BOLVIR DE CERDANYA Torre del Remei 🟦♿🏠🏠🏠   €€€€
C/ Camí Reial, 17539 (Girona) **Tel** *972 14 01 82*

One of the region's finest hotels *(see p571)* and restaurants, set in a summer palace and surrounded by verdant countryside. The chef de cuisine uses regional products to create meals such as melting veal cheeks with sweet and sour berries, fresh scallops in Priorato sauce, desserts and local cheeses.

CADAQUÉS Casa Nun 🏠🏠   €€
Plaça Port Ditxos 6, 17488 (Girona) **Tel** *972 25 88 56*

In an old town house, this prettily decorated seafood restaurant overlooks one of the most charming towns of the Catalan coast. The fish couldn't be fresher as the restaurant has its own fishing boat. Book a table on the balcony for perfect views of the harbour. Closed Tue–Thu lunch (Jun–Oct except Aug); & Tue–Wed & Thu lunch (Nov–May).

CAMBRILS Can Bosch 🟦🏠   €€€€
Rambla Jaume I 19, 43850 (Tarragona) **Tel** *977 36 00 19*

A classic and highly-respected restaurant serving superb fish, seafood and rice dishes. Their *arroz negro* (rice cooked in squid ink) is justly famous; also try sole with crayfish and black rice with lobster. Patrons rave about their wine list almost as much as the food. Closed Sun evening, Mon, one week in Jun & 22 Dec–22 Jan.

CERCS Estany Clar 🟦🏠🏠   €€€€
Ctra C 16 km 99.4, 08698 (Barcelona) **Tel** *938 22 08 79*

A little off the beaten track, this much-praised restaurant is set in a restored Catalan farmhouse near Berga. The contemporary Catalan cuisine includes dishes such as rice with lobster and foie gras, snails with local ham, roasted Iberian suckling pig and for dessert order *cuajada*. Exquisite service. Closed Mon & Christmas.

COLLSUSPINA Can Xarina 🟦🏠   €
C/ Mayor 30, 08178 (Barcelona) **Tel** *938 30 05 77*

A friendly welcome awaits at this lovely old-village house, now a cosy little restaurant and guesthouse. In the vaulted dining room, you can enjoy rustic mountain cuisine, charcuterie and cheeses, grilled local lamb and rabbit, as well as fresh fish. Features classic wines from around Spain. Closed Sun evenings, Mon, 24–30 Jun, 1–7 July, 15–30 Nov.

ESPONELLÀ Can Roca 🟦♿🏠   €€
Avda Carles de Fortuny 1, 17832 (Girona) **Tel** *972 59 70 12*

A miniature village, 10 km (6 miles) from Banyoles, hosts this family-run restaurant. This remote inland region is known for its *embutits* (Catalan charcuterie), and the menu features delicious locally made cured hams and sausages along with other Catalan staples. Excellent fixed-price lunch menu. Closed Tue, 15–30 Sep & 1–15 Mar.

FIGUERES Hotel Empordà 🟦🏠🏠🏠   €€€€
Hotel Empordà, Ctra Antigua de Francia, 17600 (Girona) **Tel** *972 50 05 62*

A legendary restaurant that played a great part in putting Catalan cuisine on the map for travelling gourmets. Established in 1961, folks still gather here to enjoy the legacy of chef Jaime Subirós's cuisine including classic dishes such as *mar y muntaña* (produce of sea and mountain).

GIRONA El Celler de Can Roca 🟦♿🏠🏠   €€€€
Ctra Taialá 40, 17007 (Girona) **Tel** *972 22 21 57*

Celler de Can Roca offers a fusion of Catalan and French *nouvelle cuisine* cooking. A must on the list of dedicated food enthusiasts, the Roca brothers turn out innovative, technically brilliant dishes at terrifying speed. This is place to wow and be wowed. Closed Sun, Mon, 1–15 July & Christmas.

GOMBREN Fonda Xesc 🟦♿🏠   €€€€
Plaça del Roser 1, 17531 (Girona) **Tel** *972 73 04 04*

Picasso drew inspiration from this lovely mountain village near Berga. Fonda Xesc is a charming, low-key restaurant-with-rooms, serving good Catalan food. Everything is fresh and locally sourced, from the tender lamb to the artisanal cheeses. In season, you can try a dizzying variety of wild mushrooms. Closed Mon & Sun, Tue & Wed evenings.

GRANOLLERS El Trabuc 🟦♿🏠🏠   €€
Ctra de Masnou s/n, 08400 (Barcelona) **Tel** *938 708 657*

A restored *masia* (farmhouse) on the outskirts of Granollers, El Trabuc offers an extensive menu of classic Catalan dishes. The sautéed wild mushrooms make a wonderful starter, and there is a fine wine selection. You might spot the odd Formula One driver during the annual Catalan Grand Prix. Closed Sun evenings & three weeks in Aug.

GRATALLOPS Cellers de Gratallops   *Tapas* 🍽️♿🍷   €€€€
C/ Piró 32 (Priorat), 43737 (Tarragona) Tel 977 83 90 36

This smart village restaurant is owned by the bodega's Clos l'Obac, one of the pioneers of new Priorato wines and serves their entire range, along with local olive oils and an excellent Moroccan influenced menu. They serve delicious duck confits and foie gras. Well worth seeking out during a trip to wine country. Closed Mon & all evenings.

LA SEU D'URGELL El Castell – Tàpies   🍽️🛏️🍷   €€€€
Ctra N260 km 229, 25700 (Lleida) Tel 973 35 07 04

Situated at the foot of La Seu d'Urgell castle, lies this idyllic one-star Michelin hotel-restaurant. El Castell serves top-flight modern Catalan cuisine and superlative wines. Many of the dishes include a variety of wild local mushrooms from the Pyrenean mountains and meat from the region. A different menu is served to outside tables.

LA VALL DE BIANYA Ca L'Enric   🍽️♿🛏️🍷   €€€€
Ctra de Camprodón s/n, 17813 (Girona) Tel 972 29 00 15

This restaurant serves some of the finest cuisine in the region and has won numerous accolades. It has justly become a place of pilgrimage during the hunting season, when you can try authentic Catalan specialities from wild boar to venison, all finely prepared by chef Maria Isabel Juncá. Booking advisable. Closed Mon & two weeks in Jul & Dec.

LLAGOSTERA Els Tinars   🍽️♿🛏️🍷   €€€€
Ctra Sant Feliú-Girona km 7.2, 17240 (Girona) Tel 972 83 06 26

A classic, Els Tinars offers exceptionally fresh modern Catalan cuisine, including the house speciality of trotter salad served with calamari and prawns. Less adventurous diners can try grilled fish, but the charm of this place is in the details: home-baked bread, served warm and crusty and great desserts. Closed Sun evenings, Mon & 8 Jan–8 Feb.

LLEIDA Lo Punt del Gourmet   🍽️♿   €
C/ Salmerón 10, 25004 (Lleida) Tel 973 23 45 10

Excellent regional cooking including chargrilled red peppers and aubergines (eggplants) and snails *à la llauna*. Specialities include *xatonada* with beans, mushrooms and cod and a Basque salad of smoked fish, tomatoes and olives with cod and elvers. It has a fixed-price menu Monday to Friday. Closed Sun evenings & Mon.

LLORET DE MAR El Trull   🍽️♿🎵🛏️🍷   €€€€
Ronda Europa 1, Cala Canyelles, 17310 (Girona) Tel 972 36 49 28

Should your travels take you through the uninspiring Lloret de Mar, this characterful rustic dining room is handy at a pinch. It serves good grilled lobster, fresh fish, *fideuá* (Catalan noodle) and paella. They also have a wide range of wines and sparkling wines. Live music in summer only.

MANRESA Sibar   🍽️♿🛏️🍷   €€€
C/ Carrasco i Formiguera 18, 08242 (Barcelona) Tel 938 74 81 71

This modern establishment has a cafeteria on the ground floor for coffee and cakes, and a sleek elegant restaurant in the basement for formal dining. The *chuletón* (T-bone steak), for a minimum of two people, is exquisite, as are the unlikely sounding fried eggs and potatoes. Regional wines are a must.

MARTINET Boix   🍽️♿🛏️🍷   €€
Ctra N260 Lleida-Puigcerdá km 204.5, 25724 (Lleida) Tel 973 51 50 50

A famous Catalan restaurant located on the banks of the Río Segre. Boix serves a slow-roasted leg of lamb so tender you could eat it with a spoon, complemented perfectly by a bottle of soft luscious local wine from the Costers del Segre. The meat stews are also very popular. Closed Sun evenings & Mon.

MONT-RAS La Cuina de Can Pipes   🍽️♿🛏️🍴🍷   €€€€
Barri Canyelles, 17253 (Girona) Tel 972 30 66 77

This elegant, 18th-century farmhouse serves excellent regional dishes. Scallops with seaweed gratin, salmon caviar on roasted red peppers, baby squid with velvety rich trotters and turbot with wild mushroom rice are good. The desserts are heavenly, and the wine menu boasts more than 200 vintages. Bookings recommended. Check timings.

MONTSENY Can Barrina   🍽️♿🛏️🍷   €€
Ctra Palautordera–Montseny km 12.6, 08560 (Barcelona) Tel 938 47 30 65

In the hills of the Montseny natural park, this restored 17th-century *masia* is now a fine country hotel and restaurant. Dine in the stone-walled dining room or out on the garden terrace on delicious Catalan specialities, including wild mushrooms and game in season, kid with honey and aniseed and home-made desserts. Closed Sun evenings.

PALS Sa Punta   🍽️♿🛏️🍷   €€€€
C/ des Forns 65, 17256 (Girona) Tel 972 63 64 10

The cuisine of the Empordà region in Catalonia is known for its mixture of seafood and meat – known here as *mar y muntaña*. This elegant hotel-restaurant is a good place to try classic Empordan dishes such as chicken with local prawns. The dessert selection will have you drooling, and the service is impeccable. Excellent wine list too.

PERALADA Castell de Peralada   🍽️🍴🍷   €€€€
Hotel Castell de Peralada, C/ Sant Joan, 17491 (Girona) Tel 972 53 81 25

The setting of this medieval castle makes for a truly special lunch or dinner. It specializes in traditional Empordan cuisine, while the castle's own bodegas provide the wine. As the restaurant is inside a casino, under-18s are not allowed. Kids are allowed in July and August when a buffet is served on outside tables. Closed Mon & Tue (Sep–Jun).

Key to Price Guide *see p608* **Key to Symbols** *see back cover flap*

ROSES El Bulli

Cala Montjoi Ap 30, 17480 (Girona) **Tel** *972 15 04 57*

Critics and foodies alike widely believe this bistro to be, not only the best in Spain, but one of the best in the world. Super-chef Ferran Adrià produces state-of-the-art dishes in one of Spain's prettiest beachside settings. They have a fixed tasting menu. Reservations required one year in advance! Closed Oct–Mar.

S'AGARÓ La Taverna del Mar

Platja de Sant Pol s/n, 17248 (Girona) **Tel** *972 32 38 00*

This century-old tavern serves a dazzling array of spectacularly cooked fresh fish. Recipes include Mediterranean classics such as spiny lobster stew and fish baked in a salt crust. Comfortable wicker armchairs and whitewashed arches frame perfect sea views. Bookings essential. Closed Mon evenings & Tue (except Jul–Aug) & last week of Nov–Dec.

SANT CELONI El Racó de Can Fabes

C/ de Sant Joan 6, 08470 (Barcelona) **Tel** *938 67 28 51*

Santi Santamaría is one of Spain's most emblematic chefs and this country restaurant, in the house where he was born, is a gastronomic wonderland. The seasonal menu is full of delights including fennel cream with crab, sweetbreads with mashed potato and wild duck in cocoa bean sauce. Reservations essential. Closed Sun evenings & Mon.

SANT POL DE MAR Sant Pau

C/ Nou 10, 08395 (Barcelona) **Tel** *937 60 06 62*

This restaurant is an hour-long train ride from Barcelona and makes a good lunch excursion. The bounty of earth and sea make for some wonderful dishes created from courgette (zucchini) flowers, sea cucumbers and wild boar. Only apéritif and coffee is served at the outside tables. Closed Sun evenings, Mon, Thu lunch & three weeks in May & Nov.

SANTES CREUS Grau

Tapas

C/ Pere el Gran 3, 43815 (Tarragona) **Tel** *977 63 83 11*

The honey-coloured stone monastery of Santes Creus is one of the most beautiful places in Catalonia, and is part of the great Cistercian monastery route. This simple hostel and restaurant offers great home cooking, which you can enjoy in the garden terrace. Try the wonderful roasted *calçots* in season. Closed 15 Oct–1 Jul (except Easter).

SITGES El Velero

Passeig de la Ribera 38, 08870 (Barcelona) **Tel** *938 94 20 51*

A seaside restaurant whose imaginative creations are a cut above more standard offerings of paella and grilled fish. Here sole comes on a bed of wild mushrooms and is drizzled with unctuous crab sauce, lobster comes with chickpea cream and boat-fresh razor clams are the best starters. Closed Mon, Tue lunch, Sun evenings in winter & 22 Dec–22 Jan.

TARRAGONA El Merlot

C/ Cavallers 6, 43003 (Tarragona) **Tel** *977 22 06 52*

Situated in the old part of town, this restaurant serves classical Mediterranean dishes. House specials include game in season, fresh fish and addictive home-made desserts. Specialities include flower salad with vinaigrette of seeds and apples, tartar with foie gras and anise ice cream. They also serve good wines. Closed Sun & Mon lunch.

TORRENT (PALAFRUGELL) Mas de Torrent

C/ Afores s/n, 17123 (Girona) **Tel** *972 30 32 92*

An elegant country hotel, the Mas de Torrent has a wonderful restaurant under the direction of renowned chef Joan Piqué. The 18th-century mansion and gardens provide the perfect backdrop for a romantic dinner on the terrace. Go for the spectacular *menú de degustación*, a showcase for Piqué's dazzling talents. Closed 7 Jan–7 Feb.

TORROELLA DE MONTGRÍ Palau Lo Mirador

Passeig l'Esglesia 1, 17257 (Girona) **Tel** *972 75 80 63*

For royal treatment head to this hotel, the residence of Catalonia's most powerful King Jaume I. The dining rooms, with their stone walls, vaulted ceilings and chandeliers are truly palatial. Fine regional cuisine with international touches – Indian spices and Oriental flavours appear on the menu alongside classic Catalan dishes. Check timings.

TORTOSA Rosa Pinyol

C/ Hernán Cortés 17, 43500 (Tarragona) **Tel** *977 50 20 01*

One of the most creative restaurants in the area, Rosa Pinyol serves deftly prepared Catalan cuisine with Italian and Mediterranean influences. The sautéed baby squid with wild mushrooms melt in the mouth, and the desserts, particularly anything made with chocolate, are heavenly. Outstanding service. Closed Sun, Mon evenings & 15–30 Sep.

TOSSA DE MAR La Cuina de Can Simón

C/ Portal 24, 17320 (Girona) **Tel** *972 34 12 69*

A delightful family-run restaurant, serving very good contemporary Mediterranean cuisine. In summer, you can dine al fresco on the terrace. Try the rice cooked in squid ink with a mouthwatering *romesco* sauce (made with crushed almonds, peppers and garlic). Closed Tue (except Aug), 15–30 Nov & 15–30 Jan.

VALLS Masia Bou

Ctra Lleida km 21.5, 43800 (Tarragona) **Tel** *977 60 04 27*

A large and noisy country house with room for more than 600 people. The specialities here are game, wild mushrooms and *calçots*, chargrilled over hot vines and served with a scrumptious almond, hazelnut and red pepper dipping sauce. Closed Mon evenings & Tue in summers.

VIC Floriac

Ctra Manresa-Vic N141 km 39.5, Collsuspina, 08500 (Barcelona) **Tel** *937 43 02 25*

This 16th-century *masia* serves huge platters of regional fare along with excellent game dishes in season. They also serve all kinds of meats cooked in a coal grill. Home-made desserts are just delicious. Floriac opens only for Friday dinners, Saturdays and Sundays.

VIELHA Era Lucana

Avda Calbetó Barra 16, 25530 (Lleida) **Tel** *973 64 17 98*

Era Lucana has long been a classic in Vielha. With its warm wood panelling, locally made lace tablecloths and roaring fires, it is a cosy and welcoming place to rest after a day on the slopes. The menu offers creative renditions of classic Catalan fare, including succulent meats grilled over charcoal, served with wild mushroom sauce. Closed Mon.

VILAFRANCA DEL PENEDÉS Cal Ton

C/ Casal 8, 08720 (Barcelona) **Tel** *938 90 37 41*

Capital of Catalonia's main wine-producing region, Vilafranca del Penedès is a tranquil little town. Cal Ton is an old-fashioned favourite in the centre, with rustically furnished dining rooms serving sturdy Catalan classics such as *butifarra amb mongetes* (a classic bean and sausage dish) and tender local lamb. Closed Sun & Tue evenings & Mon.

ARAGÓN

ALBARRACÍN El Bodegón

C/ Azagra 2, 44100 (Teruel) **Tel** *978 70 03 55*

El Bodegón is located in one of the typical "hanging houses". Apart from the fine views, traditional Aragonese fare such as trout stuffed with *jámon*, roast lamb and bull's tail stew is offered. Finish off with a *cuajada*, a bitter yoghurt sweetened with honey and cinnamon, known for its digestive properties. Excellent value. Closed first week in Jun.

ALCAÑIZ (TERUEL) La Oficina

Avda de Aragón 12, 44600 (Teruel) **Tel** *978 87 08 01*

Situated in the historic town of Alcañiz, renowned for its Easter celebrations, this small, excellent value *mesón* (inn) specializes in traditional, home-made food using local produce, including the area's famed olive oil. Seafood is the star feature but they will also appease carnivores with the succulent steak with Roquefort sauce. Closed Sun.

BARBASTRO El Portal del Somontano

Ctra N 240 Tarragona-San Sebastian km 162, 22300 (Huesca) **Tel** *974 31 53 68*

Restaurant, cellar and delicatessen shop in a renovated building with a fireplace in the dining room. It offers fixed-price and children's menus, with simple dishes based on lentils, free-range chicken, home-made *morcilla*, local lamb, artichokes with foie gras and grilled fish. It also offers an extensive list of *cavas*, champagne and cigars.

BIESCAS Casa Ruba

Tapas

C/ Esperanza 18–20, 22630 (Huesca) **Tel** *974 48 50 01*

This simple dining room, founded in 1884, is the best choice for traditional cuisine. Try the cod wrapped in pastry and served with artichokes or the tender local steaks cooked to perfection. Desserts include the caramelized custard served with ice cream and hot chocolate sauce. The lunchtime fixed menu is good value. Closed Sun evenings & Nov.

BORJA La Bóveda del Mercado

Plaza del Mercado 4, 50540 (Zaragoza) **Tel** *976 86 82 51*

In a 17th-century cellar, in the historic centre of Borja, you will find this magnificently decorated little gem, serving traditional dishes perfectly cooked, at prices that belong to yesteryear. Try the *morcilla* crêpe, eel with saffron or preserved plums with anise. Closed Sun evenings, Mon & Jan.

CARIÑENA La Rebotica

C/ San José 3, 50400 (Zaragoza) **Tel** *976 62 05 56*

This lovely eatery retains vestiges of its old life as a pharmacy. Salads, vegetable and pasta dishes are the order of the day. Favourites include rice with beetroot and prawns, *morcilla* lasagne, salad with goat's cheese and pine nuts with apricot mousse. The atmosphere is friendly. Le Rebotica is open for lunch only (except Saturdays). Closed Mon.

ESQUEDAS Venta del Sotón

Ctra A132 Huesca a Puente la Reina km 14, 22810 (Huesca) **Tel** *974 27 02 41*

Very pleasant, homespun restaurant located 14 kms (8.6 miles) from Huesca in a typical Pyrenean chalet. The cuisine is traditional and includes such local treats as cod *pil pil*, baby lamb with potatoes or beef baked in rock salt. They also have a good fixed-price menu. Closed Sun evenings, Mon & 18 Jan–17 Feb.

HUESCA Bodegasde Sobrarbe

Plaza Mayor 2, Aínsa, 22330 (Huesca) **Tel** *974 50 02 37*

Located in medieval cellars under the Plaza Mayor of Aínsa town, with a beautiful courtyard. They serve regional cuisine based on game, wild mushrooms and the Aragónese veal, cooked over a wood fire, accompanied by wine. The home-made desserts are not to be missed, especially the apple pastry with strawberry sauce. Closed Jan & Feb.

Key to Price Guide *see p608* **Key to Symbols** *see back cover flap*

HUESCA Lillas Pastia   目点品里   €€€€

Plaza de Navarra 4, 22004 **Tel** *974 21 16 91*

Located in the salon of the casino, this is one of the most popular restaurants in Huesca. A highly creative "market" cuisine is on offer, using the freshest seasonal produce. Try the honey-baked cod served with milk foam or new potatoes with wild mushrooms. For dessert, order "chocolate passion". Closed Sun, Mon evenings & 15–30 Nov.

JACA Lilium   目点品里   €€

Avda Primer Viernes de Mayo 8, 22700 (Huesca) **Tel** *974 35 53 56*

This split level eatery has a split personality; contemporary upstairs and reassuringly rustic in the basement. The cuisine is typical of Aragón's high country and features dishes such as chargrilled lamb chops with wild mushrooms and lettuce hearts filled with goat's cheese. Rich home-made desserts. Closed Mon, 1, 15–30 May & 15–30 Oct.

LA IGLESUELA DEL CID Casa Amada   目点   €

C/ Fuente Nueva 10, 44142 (Teruel) **Tel** *964 44 33 73*

This simple, quality restaurant offers a good fixed menu from Monday to Friday and a more varied à la carte on the weekends. Its specialities include stuffed potatoes, bean stew, garlic chickpeas, partridge and grilled meats and trout. The home-made desserts are excellent. There are a few rooms available. Closed Sun evenings (except Jul–Aug).

NUÉVALOS Reyes de Aragón   目点品   €€

Ctra Monasterio de Piedra, 50210 (Zaragoza) **Tel** *976 84 90 11*

Located in a 12th-century monastery complex inside Monasterio de Piedra, and surrounded by cascades and grottos, the setting is perfect for enjoying Aragónese specialities such as local trout stuffed with *jamón* (ham) and roasted veal and much more. Leave room for the tasty desserts; baked apples or chocolate and almond mousse.

PANTICOSA Restaurante del Lago   目点品里   €€€€

Ctra del Balneario km 10, 22650 (Huesca) **Tel** *974 48 71 61*

Part of the Panticosa Resort and designed by the Spanish architect Rafael Moneo, Restaurante del Lago is top class. Chef Pedro Subijana fuses Basque and Navarran cuisines with dishes such as baby lobster *iguales pero diferentes*, eggs with caviar over a cauliflower mousse and gin and tonic jelly served with lemon sorbet.

RUBIELOS DE MORA Portal del Carmen   目点品里   €€€

C/ Glorieta 2, 44415 (Teruel) **Tel** *978 80 41 53*

Sited in an old 17th-century monastery, this restaurant offers summer al fresco dining and an interior dining room for winters. The Aragónese menu is imaginative, preparing dishes such as baby broad beans with ham and prawns, chicken with pepper and tomatoes and a walnut parfait with hot chocolate sauce. Closed Thu (except Aug) & 5–25 May.

SENEGÜE Casbas   *Tapas* 目点品里   €

Ctra N260 Biescas s/n, 22666 (Teruel) **Tel** *974 48 01 49*

Casbas specializes in cod, which can be combined with imaginative starters such as warm salad with goat's cheese, walnuts and a honey vinaigrette, all washed down with a well-sourced selection of local wines. Skiers gather here in the mornings for a hearty cooked breakfast and there are also rooms for rent on the upper floors. Closed Sep.

TERUEL La Menta   目点里   €€

C/ Bartolomé Esteban 10, 44001 **Tel** *978 60 75 32*

One of the most charming restaurants with paintings from celebrated local artists adorning the walls. The seasonal cuisine includes warm prawn salad, white beans and clams, partridge *escabechada* and a caramelized cheese cake with pine nuts. Attentive table service. Reservations recommended. Closed Sun, 7–27 Jan & 15 days in July.

UNCASTILLO Un-Castello   目点里   €

Plaza de la Villa 24, 50678 (Zaragoza) **Tel** *976 67 91 05*

Located next to the city hall in a typically rustic building, Un-Castello offers surprisingly innovative Basque and Aragónese cuisine. Try the aubergines with mushrooms wrapped in pastry, stuffed leg of lamb or good old roast beef with mustard sauce. Great selection of local wines. Closed Sun evenings.

ZARAGOZA Casa Juanico   *Tapas* 目   €

Plaza de Santa Cruz 21, 50003 **Tel** *976 39 72 52*

In Zaragoza's old town, close to the famous Pilar Cathedral, this perpetually crowded, classic bar offers the best tapas in town. Grilled meats, a great selection of *pinchos* and cold cod salad are the highlights. There is also a rear dining room for more formal eating, for which reservations are recommended. Closed Sun.

ZARAGOZA Espejo   品   €€

C/ Santiago 30–32, 50003 **Tel** *976 29 34 32*

Near to the soaring Pilar Cathedral and frequented by artists, politicians and Zaragoza's intelligentsia. The speciality of the house is foie gras sautéed in vinegar – particularly memorable when eaten on the lovely outside terrace. Closed Sat lunch, Sun two weeks in Aug & public holidays.

ZARAGOZA Las Lanzas   目点里   €€

Melia Hotel, Avda César Augusto 13, 50004 **Tel** *976 28 55 22*

This award-winning restaurant has large dining rooms and a refined, Provençal atmosphere. It features an avant-garde creative cuisine with attention to every detail. Highlights include the watercress and oyster soup with liquid bomb of red pearls and the chef's home-made foie gras. Excellent wine list. Closed Sun evenings.

ZARAGOZA Don Pascual

C/ Residencial Paraíso 48, 50008 **Tel** *976 21 87 14*

Inside this romantic, intimate space, creative cooking wows the regulars. The promise of using only the freshest market ingredients is reflected in the concise menu of daily specials which revolve around a theme; Monday is vegetables, Tuesday is lentils, Wednesdays sees pasta dishes and so on. Closed Sun, Easter & 1–15 Aug.

ZARAGOZA La Rinconada de Lorenzo

C/ La Salle 3, 50006 **Tel** *976 55 51 08*

This emblematic restaurant, decorated in the colourful tiles typical of the area, offers excellent home-style cooking. Specialities include chickpeas with lobster, ham and grapes and other hearty meat and fish dishes. There is a distinctly fun and family-friendly atmosphere here. Closed Sun evenings & Mon in summer & Easter week.

VALENCIA AND MURCIA

ALICANTE Mesón de Labradores

C/ Labradores 19, 03001 (Alacant) **Tel** *965 20 48 46*

Decorated with colourful tiles and huge wine barrels, Mesón de Labradores is one of the best and most authentic of Alicante's many tapas bars. Cheerful waiters breeze between the crowded tables, with platters of deliciously fresh snacks held aloft. Try the *croquetas* (meat-stuffed rolls), a speciality of the house.

ALICANTE Dársena

Marina Deportiva, Muelle Levante 6, Puerto, 03001 (Alacant) **Tel** *965 20 75 89*

A classic restaurant overlooking the port, Dársena has an elegant interior, with crisp white linen. The nautical-style brass lamps give it the feel of a luxurious ocean liner. Gaze out at the sea of yachts through the enormous picture windows, and choose from around 200 delicious rice dishes. Do not miss the *arròs a banda* (rice with fish).

ALICANTE Nou Manolín

C/ Villegas 3, 03001 (Alacant) **Tel** *965 20 03 68*

An Alicantino favourite, this attractive restaurant is tucked away in the old quarter in the former home of local author Gabriel Miró. There is an excellent tapas bar downstairs, while upstairs you can dine in an elegant brick-lined salon on classic Valencian seafood, rice dishes, accompanied by an extensive wine list.

ALTEA Racó de Toni

C/ de la Mar 127, 03590 (Alicante) **Tel** *965 84 17 63*

An old-fashioned charmer, this cosy, traditional *mesón* serves good regional specialities including excellent rice dishes and locally caught fish. Specialities include rice with salt cod and vegetables and peppers stuffed with anchovies. There's a good-value *menú del día*, or you can join the lively crowd of locals in the tapas bar.

BENIDORM Ulía

C/ Vicente Llorca Alós 15, 03502 (Alicante) **Tel** *965 85 68 28*

This old-fashioned seaside restaurant is one of the best places in Benidorm to try an authentic paella, with the subtle aroma of saffron and a light, crisp crust. The good food, made with the freshest local produce, makes it popular with families that flock from the beach on Sundays for long lunches on the lovely, breezy terrace. Closed Mon.

BENIDORM La Palmera-Casa Paco Nadal

Av Severo Ochoa, Rincón de Loix, 03501 (Alicante) **Tel** *965 85 32 82*

La Palmera is one of the best places to try the huge range of rice dishes for which Valencia is famous. A large, typically Spanish seaside restaurant with a flower-filled terrace, it's a popular place for long Sunday lunches with the family. If you find it hard to make a selection, go for the reasonably priced *menú de degustación*.

BENIMANTELL L'Obrer

Ctra de Alcoi 27, 03516 (Alicante) **Tel** *965 88 50 88*

L'Obrer's popularity rests on its great food, bargain prices and welcoming ambience. A rustic-style restaurant, decorated with locally made ceramics, it serves traditional, home-cooked country dishes such as oven-baked lamb or roasted rabbit. Tasty home-made desserts include almond tart with chocolate.

BENIMANTELL Venta la Montaña

Ctra de Alcoi 9, 03516 (Alicante) **Tel** *965 88 51 41*

This mountain inn, decorated with antique farming implements, serves wholesome dishes such as the typical *olleta de trigo* (a broth made with pork, vegetables and wheat). Accompany it with a sturdy local wine and finish up with a delectable caramel soufflé. If you do not want a big meal, tuck into the tapas at the bar. Check timings.

BENISSANO Levante

C/ Virgen del Fundamento 27, 46181 (Valencia) **Tel** *962 78 07 21*

You cannot leave Valencia without trying Levante's excellent paellas, cooked to perfection over a wood fire. Other house recommendations include the delicious *croquetas de atún* (home-made tuna croquettes). The restaurant boasts one of the region's largest and best wine cellars. Open for lunch only. Closed Tue.

Key to Price Guide *see p608* **Key to Symbols** *see back cover flap*

BUÑOL Venta L'Home
Tapas 🍴♿🎵🚗🍷 €€€

Autovía A3 Madrid-Valencia km 306, 46360 (Valencia) **Tel** *962 50 35 15*

A whitewashed 18th-century staging post is the setting for this attractive country restaurant. You can dine on great regional cuisine, such as rabbit with honey, or artichokes with baby squid, in a rustically decorated dining room. There is a good wine list, which features an interesting selection of regional wines.

CABO DE PALOS Miramar
🍴🚗🍷 €

Paseo del Puerto 14, 30370 (Murcia) **Tel** *968 56 30 33*

Every seaside resort in Spain has a Miramar restaurant, and the lively town of Cabo de Palos is no exception. It is a family-friendly seafood restaurant with huge picture windows overlooking the port and the bay. Specialities include local rice dishes, and fish baked in salt. Try the local desserts, particularly the *pan de Calatrava*. Closed Tue in winter.

CARAVACA DE LA CRUZ Los Viñales
Tapas 🍴♿🎵🚗🍷 €

Av Juan Carlos I 41, 30400 (Murcia) **Tel** *968 70 84 58*

An old-fashioned, down-to-earth inn, Los Viñales is justly famous for its fine *guisos* (mountain stews), prepared with locally-reared lamb or pork and the delicious vegetables for which Murcia is famous. These stews are perfect for the cool nights in this enchanting hill-top town. The tapas bar draws a lively crowd of locals. Closed Tue & 25–31 Jan

CARTAGENA Los Sauces
🍴♿🚗🍷 €€€

Ctra La Palma km 4.5, 30300 (Murcia) **Tel** *968 53 07 58*

Stylish and intimate, Los Sauces is set in a pretty chalet-style building on the outskirts of Cartagena. The menu features regional and international cuisine with Basque and French influences, all prepared with a creative twist. The hake, baked in a salt crust and accompanied by baby squid, is outstanding. Closed Sun evenings.

CASTELLÓ DE LA PLANA Rafael
🍴🔞🍷 €€€€

C/ Churruca 28, 12100 (Castellón) **Tel** *964 28 21 85*

Rafael has long been a fixture on Castellón's port, El Grao, close to the main city centre. Welcoming and unfussy, the restaurant has always focused on the quality of its ingredients, particularly the incredibly fresh fish. Service is excellent and the wine list offers a good range of regional labels. Closed Sun, 1–15 Sep, bank holidays & Christmas.

COCENTAINA L'Escaleta
🍴♿🚗🔞🍷 €€€

Subida Estación Norte 205, 03824 (Alicante) **Tel** *965 59 21 00*

One of the best restaurants in the Cocentaina region, L'Escaleta is tucked away in an elegant brick-vaulted cellar, decorated with old photographs and dried flowers. On the menu are creative interpretations of classic dishes: try the turbot with mushrooms and hazelnut butter. The wine list has both Spanish and international wines.

CULLERA Casa Salvador
🍴♿🚗🍷 €€

L'Estany de Cullera, 46400 (Valencia) **Tel** *961 72 01 36*

Sitting pretty on the edge of the *estany* (lake) of Cullera, this family-run restaurant has a beautiful wooden terrace overlooking the lake. Choose from a wide variety of traditional rice dishes, locally-caught seafood, and vegetables grown in their own orchard. Paella with duck is a speciality. The wine cellar has more than 4,000 bottles of wine.

DENIA El Poblet
🍴♿🚗🍷 €€€€

Ctra Las Marinas km 2.5, 03600 (Alicante) **Tel** *965 78 41 79*

El Poblet offers exceptional and highly creative Spanish cuisine, created by Enrique Dacosta, one of the most exciting chefs in Spain. This is one of the best places to try Dénia's famous prawns. There is a wonderful *menú de degustación*. Parking facilities are available. Closed Mon (except Aug), one week in Oct & two weeks in Mar.

ELCHE (ELX) Asador Ilicitano
🍴♿🍷 €€€

C/ Maestro Giner 9, 03201 (Alicante) **Tel** *965 43 58 64*

A fine old *mesón*, with handsome traditional decor and ancient wooden beams, Asador Ilicitano serves succulent roasted meats prepared over charcoal to give them a delicate smoky flavour. Specialities include roast kid and lamb, but they also serve some delicious seafood dishes such as cod in Basque style. Closed Sun & 16–31 Aug.

FORCALL Mesón de la Vila
Tapas 🍴♿ €

Plaza Mayor 8, 12310 (Castellón) **Tel** *964 17 11 25*

Right on Forcall's expansive main square, this handsome *mesón* is located in the 16th-century cellars of the Ayuntamiento (Town Hall). In the elegant vaulted dining rooms, you can try affordable regional dishes such as the *sopa forcallana* (broth with vegetables, boiled eggs, ham and meatballs). Closed Mon except Jul & Aug.

GANDIA Gamba
🍴♿🚗 €€€€

Ctra Nazaret-Oliva, Gandia-Playa, 46730 (Valencia) **Tel** *962 84 13 10*

Although you cannot see the sea from here, the fish and shellfish are straight from the fishermen's nets. There are three airy dining areas, where you can enjoy grilled shrimps, home-style aubergines or squids cooked in diverse ways. In summer, they occasionally host live music. Open lunch (winter); lunch & Fri–Sat dinner (summer). Closed Mon.

JÁTIVA (XÀTIVA) Casa La Abuela
🍴 €€

C/ Reina 17, 46800 (Valencia) **Tel** *962 27 05 25*

Tucked away in the higgledy-piggledy maze in the centre of Játiva, this pretty turn-of-the-19th-century house is now a delightful restaurant set around a plant-filled interior patio. The cuisine is refined and creative: try the magret of duck with red fruits, or the lamb with rosemary mousse. A *menú del día* is available.

LORCA El Teatro   📭🔊🎵   €€
Plaza de Colón 12, 30800 (Murcia) **Tel** *968 46 99 09*

El Teatro is a simple little restaurant with a good range of Murcian dishes, many featuring delicious local vegetables as well as variations of the classic rice dishes for which Eastern Spain is famous. Seafood is freshly caught in the nearby bay of Águilas. Try the aubergine gratin with a tasty meaty sauce. Closed Sun evenings, Mon & Aug.

MORAIRA Girasol   📭🔊🔳🎵   €€€€
Ctra Moraira-Calpe km 1.5, 03724 (Alicante) **Tel** *965 74 43 73*

Joachim Koerper's innovative Mediterranean cuisine, which has won over gourmets throughout Europe, is perfectly complemented by the refined decoration of this seaside villa. One of the best restaurants in Spain, it always keeps its promise of a memorable dining experience. Book early for a table on the terrace. Closed Nov; check timings.

MORELLA Casa Roque   📭   €€
C/ Cuesta de San Juan 1, 12300 (Castellón) **Tel** *964 16 03 36*

An old stone mansion houses this classic in mountainous Maestrat. Diners come from near and far to savour Roque Guttiérez's lamb with truffles in puff pastry, or the rabbit terrine with pistachios and olive oil. Fixed-price menu includes an excellent *menú de degustación*. Closed Sun evenings, Mon, 1–15 Feb, 24–5 Dec, & 1 Jan.

MURCIA Comedor de Casino   €
C/ Trapería 18, 30001 (Murcia) **Tel** *968 22 06 58*

Murcia's spectacular Casino – a cultural centre, not a gambling den – is the setting for this popular restaurant where you can dine on simple Mediterranean and Murcian cuisine. They serve a daily set-price lunch menu, which includes dessert and wine. Sunday lunch is a local institution. It is also a good spot for a coffee. Open daily 10am–5pm.

MURCIA La Tapa   *Tapas* 🔊🔳   €
Plaza de las Flores 13, 30004 (Murcia) **Tel** *968 21 13 17*

Upbeat and brightly lit, with a terrace out on one of Murcia's liveliest squares, La Tapa is a classic on the Murciano tapas route. There is an excellent range of tasty snacks, especially fried prawns, usually washed down with an ice-cold beer or a glass of crisp local wine. It may be wise to arrive early to grab a table on the square. Closed Mon.

MURCIA Hispano   *Tapas* 📭🔊🎵   €€
C/ Radio Murcia 3, 30001 (Murcia) **Tel** *968 21 61 52*

A long-established restaurant in the centre of old Murcia, Hispano is known for its delicious regional cooking, with specialities such as *caldero marinero del Mar Menor* (a typical seafood casserole), and dorado baked in salt. A stalwart on Murcia's lively tapas scene, it has a bustling bar. Closed Sun evenings (winter) & Sat evenings & Sun (summer).

MURCIA Acuario   📭🔊🎵   €€€€
Plaza Puxmarina 3, 30004 (Murcia) **Tel** *968 21 99 55*

Warmly painted in ochres and rosy tones, this enchanting restaurant is the perfect place for a romantic dinner. The cuisine is contemporary, highly original and based on the extraordinary range of local produce available in Murcia – delicious vegetables, fresh seafood and succulent meat. Unusually, they also offer a vegetarian menu.

MURCIA Hostería Palacete Rural La Seda   📭🔊🔳🎵   €€€€
Vereda del Catalan s/n, km 8 from Murcia City, 30162 (Murcia) **Tel** *968 87 08 48*

Housed in an 18th-century mansion, this restaurant is one of Murcia's most prestigious. Dine on elegant contemporary cuisine such as game salad with caramalized onions and partridge or wild mushrooms and partridge soup, and save room for the spectacular desserts. The wine list was recently voted the finest in all of Spain.

ORIHUELA Cabo Roig   *Tapas* 📭🔊🎵🔳🎵   €€€
Urbanización Cabo Roig, Playas de Orihuela, 03189 (Alicante) **Tel** *966 76 02 90*

Perched on top of the cliff with magnificent views of the Costa Blanca, Cabo Roig offers a great variety of seafood and rice dishes. Some of the best are the simplest, particularly the wonderfully fresh fish of the day which is served grilled to perfection. The ancient watchtower houses a historic wine collection of more than 20,000 bottles.

PEÑÍSCOLA Casa Jaime   📭🔊🔳🎵   €€€€
Av Papa Luna 5, 12598 (Castellón) **Tel** *964 48 00 30*

With spectacular views of the castle of Papa Luna, Casa Jaime is a reliable seafood restaurant right on the seafront. Freshly-caught fish is served either simply grilled or in one of the many paellas and rice dishes available here. Try the prawn carpaccio, or *arroz de la huerta* (rice flavoured with local vegetables). Closed Sun evenings & Wed (winter).

POLOP DE LA MARINA Ca l'Ángeles   📭🔊🔳🎵   €€€
C/ Gabriel Miró 12, 03520 (Alicante) **Tel** *965 87 02 26*

Run by the same family for three generations, Ca l'Ángeles is a charming country restaurant with dining rooms that have ancient beams and lovely, rustic decoration. The menu offers sophisticated regional fare, including kid baked with roasted garlic, or oven-baked locally-caught fish. Closed Tue & 15 Jun–15 Jul.

SAGUNTO L'Armeler   📭🔊🔳🎵   €€
C/ Subida al Castillo 44, 46500 (Valencia) **Tel** *962 66 43 82*

In the labyrinthine old Jewish quarter of Sagunt, a historic house contains this chic restaurant. There are two dining areas, with wooden beams and colourful painted tiles. The menu fuses Mediterranean and French cuisine, with signature dishes such as duck with figs and aniseed sauce and a wild mushroom salad. Closed Sun & Mon (evenings).

Key to Price Guide *see p608* **Key to Symbols** *see back cover flap*

SANTA POLA El Faro
Tapas 目 & 🔲 🔲   €€€

Ctra N-332 Alicante-Cartagena km 89,7, 03130 (Alicante) **Tel** *965 41 21 36*

El Faro is a typical Spanish seaside restaurant with a good range of delicious regional rice dishes and wonderful fresh fish caught locally. Located on the edge of town, near the hill of Santa Pola, it is a lovely walk to the tip of the headland, with beautiful views. The wine list has a fine selection from all around Spain. Good value fixed-price menu.

VALENCIA Bar Pilar
Tapas 目 🔲   €

C/ Moro Zeit 13, 46002 (Valencia) **Tel** *963 91 04 97*

Although Valencia has been shooting up in the style stakes in recent years, wonderful El Pilar has remained untouched by the whims of fashion. A cheerful, noisy tapas bar where customers shout their orders to the waiters, who shout them to the kitchen, it is justly famous for mussels. Chuck the shells in the buckets lined up under the bar.

VALENCIA Corretgeria 33
目 🔲 🔲   €

C/ Corretgeria 33, 46001 (Valencia) **Tel** *963 92 41 61*

A stylish little restaurant painted in bright colours, Corretgeria 33 serves sandwiches, salads, tapas and a good-value *menú del día* for lunch. There is an elaborate menu of creative versions of local dishes in the evenings. The handful of tables, out on the pavement terrace, are great people-watching spots and highly sought-after. Check timings.

VALENCIA Ca Sento
目 & 🔲   €€€€

C/ Méndez Núñez 17, 45024 (Valencia) **Tel** *963 30 17 75*

Probably the finest restaurant in Valencia, Ca Sento is renowned for its exquisite regional and international cuisine. The decor is sleek and subtle. The food, imaginatively cooked by a mother-and-son team, uses spectacularly fresh produce and is immaculately presented. The *menú de degustación* for 85 euros is excellent. Closed Sun & Aug.

VILLENA Warynessy
Tapas 目 🔲 🔲   €€

C/ Isabel la Católica 13, 03400 (Alicante) **Tel** *965 80 10 47*

This chic restaurant-bar comes as a pleasant surprise in the otherwise sleepy mountain town of Villena. The decor is elegant with contemporary furnishings and clean lines. The menu offers creative, yet unfussy, local dishes prepared with flair and imagination. The bar is a lively spot for a pre-dinner cocktail.

VINARÒS El Faro
目 & 🔲 🔲   €€€

Port de Vinaròs s/n, 12500 (Castellón) **Tel** *964 45 63 62*

Overlooking the port, this smart restaurant is housed in a 19th-century primrose-yellow villa with a pretty garden. Dine in the classy salons with sea views, or out on the less formal summer terrace. The menu changes regularly and offers sophisticated and highly creative Spanish and international cuisine, which leans towards seafood.

MADRID

OLD MADRID Casa Patas
Tapas 目 & 🎵   €

C/ Cañizares 10, 28012 **Tel** *913 69 04 96*   **Map** *7 A3*

Casa Patas is primarily known for its flamenco shows in the evenings, which are among the best and most authentic in the city. It is also an original place to eat in the heart of Old Madrid, with a well-stocked tapas bar and an unbeatable fixed-price lunch menu. Wheelchair-users must call in advance for assistance. Closed Sun.

OLD MADRID El Estragón
目 &   €

Plaza de la Paja 10, 28005 **Tel** *913 65 89 82*   **Map** *4 D3*

El Estragón is located in a pretty spot, overlooking one of Madrid's loveliest and most fashionable squares. *Madrileño* cuisine is decidedly meaty, but this long-standing vegetarian restaurant provides a welcome break for veggies. The menu features a variety of delectable vegetable- and soy-based dishes. Note that there are two sittings for dinner.

OLD MADRID Malacatín
Tapas 目 🔲 🔲   €

C/ de la Ruda 5, 28005 **Tel** *913 65 52 41*   **Map** *4 D4*

This bar is full of bullfighting memorabilia, such as paintings, photographs and even bulls' heads, reflecting the owner's former occupation as a bullfighter. To try their star dish *cocido Madrileño* (meat and vegetable stew), you will need to order the day before. Other favourites include tripe cooked Madrid-style. Closed Sat evenings, Sun & Aug.

OLD MADRID Taberna Bilbao
Tapas 目 & 🔲   €

C/ Costanilla de San Andrés 8, 28005 **Tel** *913 65 61 25*   **Map** *3 C3*

A hugely popular Basque tavern, Taberna Bilbao serves home-made specialities such as *bacalao* cooked in a range of styles. The *chipirones* (baby squid), prepared in their own ink, are excellent. Definitely worth trying is the typical Basque wine, *txakoli*, which is light, tart and very refreshing. Reservations are highly recomended. Closed Mon.

OLD MADRID Taberna Los Cuatro Robles
Tapas 目   €

Plaza de Celenque 1, 28013 **Tel** *915 23 08 09*   **Map** *4 E2*

A simple, brightly-lit tapas bar, lined with colourful tiles, this tavern brings a taste of Andalusia to the capital. Although it is in the heart of the city, it isn't on the well-trodden tourist route. You can try the delicious croquettes and all kinds of seafood specialities in the company of *Madrileño* workers. Closed Sun.

OLD MADRID Al Norte
🍽 ♿ 🍴 🍷   €€

C/ San Nicolás 8, 28012 **Tel** *915 47 22 22*   **Map** *3 C2*

Al Norte is a modern, glassy designer restaurant, with slick minimalist furnishings and an excellent menu featuring cuisine from Spain's Atlantic coast. Fish is served predominantly, but there are plenty of meat specialities too. Try the hake stuffed with shellfish or the meaty seared tuna. A short but interesting wine list. Closed Sun evenings.

OLD MADRID Cornucopia
🍽 🍴 🍷   €€

C/ Navas de Tolosa 9, 28013 **Tel** *915 21 38 96*   **Map** *4 E1*

Charming and intimate, Cornucopia has an interesting cuisine that blends European and American flavours. Ultra-fresh ingredients are used in the cooking, with a plenty of choice for vegetarians. Do not miss the wonderful desserts, especially the strawberry mousse. There is a reasonable lunch menu and a well-considered wine list.

OLD MADRID Botín
🍽 ♿ 🍷   €€€

C/ de Cuchilleros 17, 28011 **Tel** *913 66 42 17*   **Map** *4 E3*

Dating back to 1725, Botín is reputedly the oldest restaurant in the world. With its brick-lined vaults and heavy wooden beams, it has changed little since. Even the original wood-burning oven is still used to cook the traditional roast lamb and suckling pig. There is a reasonable fixed-price lunch menu. Book well in advance.

OLD MADRID Casa Ciriaco
Tapas 🍽 ♿ 🍴 🍷   €€€

C/ Mayor 84, 28013 **Tel** *915 48 06 20*   **Map** *3 C3*

A traditional Castilian-style tavern near the Royal Palace, Casa Ciriaco is renowned for its *gallina en pepitoria* (a chicken stew with egg and saffron), which it has been making for more than a century. Other home-made delights include game in season, and *cocido Madrileño*. Book in advance. Closed Wed.

OLD MADRID Casa Lucio
Tapas 🍽 ♿ 🍷   €€€€

C/ Cava Baja 35, 28005 **Tel** *913 65 32 52*   **Map** *4 D4*

Casa Lucio is a historic tavern serving Castillian specialities. The *huevos estrellados* (fried eggs with potatoes) are so exquisite that they have even made it into a celebrated Spanish poem. The typical *Madrileño* tripe and rice pudding are equally renowned. The wine list has some fine wines from around Spain. Closed Sat lunch & Aug.

OLD MADRID Lhardy
Tapas 🍽 🍴 🍷   €€€€

Carrera de San Jerónimo 8, 28014 **Tel** *915 21 33 85*   **Map** *4 F2*

Established in 1839 and preserving its true character with chandeliers, mirrors and dark wood-panelled walls, this restaurant serves what is arguably the most classic *cocido Madrileño*. Legend has it that Isabel II once entertained her lovers in the upstairs dining rooms. Downstairs is a celebrated shop and tapas area. Closed Sun evenings & Aug.

BOURBON MADRID Arrocería Gala
Tapas 🍷 🍽 ♿   €

C/ Moratín 22, 28014 **Tel** *914 29 25 62*   **Map** *7 B3*

Admire the indoor patio and chandeliers and enjoy a generous set menu with Catalan specialities, such as paellas and other rice dishes, at an unbelievably reasonable price. Accompany them with one of the excellent range of Catalan wines or *cavas*. They also serve tapas, including snails and grilled prawns.

BOURBON MADRID Casa Labra
Tapas 🍽   €

C/ Tetuán 12, 28013 **Tel** *915 32 14 05*   **Map** *4 F2*

Founded in 1860, Casa Labra is one of Madrid's most atmospheric tapas bars. It is tucked away on a small street close to the Puerta del Sol, and retains its gleaming wood panels and pretty tiles. In the same family since 1947, the restaurant has since been known for its *bacalao*. The *croquetas de bacalao* (cod croquettes) are fabulous.

BOURBON MADRID El Txoco
Tapas 🍷 🍽 🍷   €

C/ Jovellanes 3, 28014 **Tel** *915 32 34 43*   **Map** *7 B2*

There is no better place to try delicious Basque delicacies than the Eusko-Etxea (a Basque club). The restaurant is simple but appealing, and offers a good fixed-price lunch menu, which is so popular with local workers that it is sometimes hard to get a seat. Try the stuffed peppers and baby squid. Closed Aug.

BOURBON MADRID La Fábrica
Tapas 🍷 🍽 🍷   €

C/ Jesús 2, 28014 **Tel** *913 69 06 71*   **Map** *7 B3*

A down-to-earth tapas bar, which is always crammed with customers, La Fábrica has long counters groaning with a bewildering array of fresh tapas. The octopus, which sits steaming on the bar-top, is particularly good, as are the freshly made *montaditos* (crusty bread with delicious toppings). Try them with the Cabrales, pungent Asturian cheese.

BOURBON MADRID Las Bravas
Tapas 🍷 🍽 ♿   €

C/ Álvarez Gato 5, 28012 **Tel** *915 32 26 20*   **Map** *4 F3*

Patatas bravas (chunks of fried potato doused in a lurid pink sauce) are now found everywhere in Spain, but they were created at Las Bravas. There are four locations, all within a stone's throw of each other, and they are always packed. The generous portions and low prices particularly attract local students.

BOURBON MADRID Terra Mundi
Tapas 🍽 ♿   €

C/ Lope de Vega 32, 28014 **Tel** *914 29 52 80*   **Map** *7 B3*

A friendly restaurant with rustic decor, Terra Mundi serves specialities from Glacia. The *pulpo* is a favourite, along with home-made *empanadas* (pies filled with tuna, meat or vegetables). They serve tapas from Sunday to Thursday, with restaurant service only on other days. There's a good *menú del dia*. Closed Mon evenings.

BOURBON MADRID Café Gijón
Tapas 🖥️ ♿ 🎵 �Y
€€

Paseo Recoletos 21, 28007 **Tel** *915 21 54 25*
Map *7 C1*

A legendary café, established in 1888 and still decorated with original Art Nouveau style furnishings, Café Gijón is perfect for breakfast, a fixed-price lunch or afternoon tea with cakes. Specialities include hake with cider and seafood paella. There is an elegant terrace, frequented by the well-heeled.

BOURBON MADRID Teatriz
Tapas 🖥️ ♿
€€€

C/ Hermosilla 15, 28001 **Tel** *915 77 53 79*
Map *6 D4*

Formerly a theatre, Teatriz was completely transformed by French designer Philippe Starck in 1989 and now houses a chic restaurant and a stylish tapas bar. In the restaurant, you can dine on fresh Mediterranean cuisine with Italian influences, while the tapas bar offers gourmet tapas. Prices reflect the glamorous setting.

BOURBON MADRID Thai Gardens
🖥️ 🎵
€€€

C/ Jorge Juan 5, 28001 **Tel** *915 77 88 84*
Map *6 D5*

Spain's first-ever Thai restaurant, Thai Gardens is beautifully decorated with wicker furniture, exquisite orchids and spectacular Thai artwork. The award-winning food has been toned down to suit Spanish palates, but the delicate authentic spices are deftly handled. It is a romantic spot, ideal for an intimate dinner.

BOURBON MADRID El Amparo
🖥️ 🍴 Y
€€€€

Callejón de Puigcerdá 8, 28001 **Tel** *914 31 64 56*
Map *6 E5*

Enjoy new Basque cuisine in what many consider to be Madrid's nicest setting, with a skylight that lets you gaze up at the stars. The dining rooms are spread out over three levels, and the cuisine is assured and highly creative, such as tuna mousse with lobster and parsley oil. The hot chocolate soufflé should not be missed. Closed Sat & Sun lunch.

BOURBON MADRID Paradis
🖥️ ♿ Y
€€€€

C/ Marques de Cubas 14, 28014 **Tel** *914 29 73 03*
Map *7 B2*

Part of a successful Catalan chain, Paradis offers high-quality Mediterranean cuisine. The grilled vegetables and the rice dishes make delicious starters, followed by any of the fresh fish available. The restaurant has two other branches in the Casa de los Americas (Paseo Recoletos 2) and the Thyssen museum. Closed Sat lunch, Sun & bank holidays.

BOURBON MADRID Viridiana
🖥️ 🍴 Y
€€€€

C/ Juan de Mena 14, 28014 **Tel** *915 23 44 78*
Map *7 C2*

Innovative Spanish cuisine, complemented by an encyclopedic wine list, is offered in this restaurant decorated with stills from Luís Buñuel's film, *Viridiana*. The creative menu changes frequently, and features elaborate creations prepared with the best seasonal produce. The wine list was recently voted one of the best in the world. Closed Sun.

FURTHER AFIELD (EAST) La Taberna de la Daniela
Tapas 🖥️ ♿ Y
€€

C/ General Pardiñas 21, 28001 **Tel** *915 75 23 29*

In the heart of the smart Salamanca district, this authentic Castillian tavern is famous for its excellent tapas. It also serves an excellent *cocido* (the typical Madrid stew) at lunch and has a short menu of other traditional *Madrileño* dishes, including *callos* (tripe) and lamb chops. Make your reservation a day in advance.

FURTHER AFIELD (EAST) Los Timbales
Tapas 🖥️ 🚇 Y
€€

C/ Alcalá 227, 28028 **Tel** *917 25 07 68*

Conveniently located to the Las Ventas bullring, Los Timbales is the classic meeting place for bullfighting aficionados. Posters, photographs and bulls' heads deck the walls. Tuck into tapas, including good hams, or enjoy the substantial fixed-price lunch menu. The wine list features some excellent Riojas.

FURTHER AFIELD (NORTH) Bluefish
Tapas 🖥️
€

C/ San Andrés 26, 28004 **Tel** *914 48 67 65*
Map *2 F4*

A stylish café-bar, run by young American expats, Bluefish lies in the heart of the Malasaña district. The menu features light meals and snacks, including excellent salads, asparagus wrapped in ham and grilled goat's cheese, and an amazing artichoke dip. The US-style Sunday brunch is exceptionally good. Closed Sun evenings, Mon & Aug.

FURTHER AFIELD (NORTH) Casa Ricardo
🖥️ ♿
€

C/ Fernando el Católico 31, 28015 **Tel** *914 47 61 19*
Map *2 D1*

Inaugurated in 1935, this delightful *Madrileño* restaurant has changed little since. It is crammed with bullfighting memorabilia and is popular with an arty crowd as well as local politicians. Try typical dishes such as *callos a la Madrileña* (tripe in a spicy white wine sauce). Disabled access is limited to the downstairs salon. Closed Sun evenings.

FURTHER AFIELD (NORTH) Chantarella
🖥️ 🎵 Y
€€€€

C/ Doctor Fleming 7, 28036 **Tel** *913 44 10 04*

A little way out of the centre in the Chamartín district, this small and chic restaurant is well worth the trek. Its sleek, minimalist decor is the perfect showcase for the excellent contemporary Spanish cuisine, prepared with the freshest seasonal produce available. Impeccable service and an interesting wine list add the finishing touches. Closed Sun.

FURTHER AFIELD (NORTH) Goizeko Kabi
🖥️ ♿ 🍴 Y
€€€€

C/ Comandante Zorita 37, 28020 **Tel** *915 33 01 85*

At Goizeko Kabi, traditional Basque cuisine is served in a refined setting. Excellent fresh produce and seafood are the basis of the chef's creations, winning plaudits from gourmets across Europe. The spider crab is outstanding, and the *chipirones encebollados* (baby squid) remains a signature dish. There is an excellent wine list. Closed Sun.

FURTHER AFIELD (NORTH) Jockey   🔲♿🎩🍷 €€€€
C/ Amador de los Ríos 6, 28010 **Tel** *913 19 10 03*   **Map** 6 D4

Among Madrid's top five restaurants, frequented by gourmets and celebrities, Jockey offers a seasonal menu which specializes in top-of-the-range Castillian cuisine. There are excellent poultry and game dishes. The place has the air of a sophisticated gentleman's club, complete with equestrian paintings. Closed Sun, Aug & bank holidays.

FURTHER AFIELD (NORTH) La Castafiore   *Tapas* 🔲♿🎩🍷 €€€€
C/ Marqués de Monasterio 5, 28004 **Tel** *915 32 21 00*   **Map** 5 C5

A charming Italian restaurant, this unique dining spot features singing waiters. All trained opera singers, they burst into magnificent arias as they serve fine Italian cuisine. The food may play second fiddle to the service, but it remains consistently good. Booking is recommended. Closed Sun & Sat lunch.

FURTHER AFIELD (NORTH) Santceloni   🔲♿🍷 €€€€
Hotel, Hesperia, Paseo de la Castellana 57, 28046 **Tel** *912 10 88 40* **Map** 6 D1

Sister to the famous Santi Santamaría in Catalonia, Santceloni is one of the best places in Madrid to appreciate Spain's culinary revolution over the last few years. The menu is short, but exquisite: try the fabulous *menú gastrónimco* which features their finest dishes. Outstanding wine list. Closed Sat evenings, Sun & Aug.

FURTHER AFIELD (NORTH) Zalacaín   🔲♿🎩🍷 €€€€
C/ Álvarez de Baena 4, 28006 **Tel** *915 61 48 40*

Considered Madrid's finest restaurant, Zalacaín has a splendidly formal setting, attentive service and superb Basque-oriented cuisine. The menu changes four times a year and features the finest seasonal produce. The *menú de degustación* features house specialities. Closed Sat lunch, Sun, Easter, Aug & bank holidays.

FURTHER AFIELD (NORTHEAST) Sacha   🔲♿🎴🍷 €€€
C/ Juan Hurtado de Mendoza, 11 Entrada Posterior, 28036 **Tel** *913 45 59 52*

Decorated like a cosy bistro, this charming and much-lauded restaurant serves sensational, creative cuisine including specialities such as partridge with rice and mushrooms and marinated oysters. Book early to get a table out on the lovely terrace, shaded with pines and cypress trees. Excellent wines and unmissable desserts. Closed Sun.

FURTHER AFIELD (NORTHEAST) Asador Aguinaga   🔲🎩🍷 €€€€
C/ Velázquez 102, 28036 **Tel** *915 77 15 91*

A rather formal restaurant in the chichi Salamanca district, this restaurant offers delicious Basque specialities, including *angulas* (eels) from Aguinaga, a sought-after Basque delicacy, and salads made with spider crab or prawns. Although seafood features prominently, the meat dishes are also excellent. Closed Sat lunch, Sun & Aug.

FURTHER AFIELD (NORTHEAST) El Olivo   🔲🍷 €€€€
C/ General Gallegos 1, 28036 **Tel** *913 59 15 35*

El Olivo is popular for its top-of-the-line Mediterranean cuisine using excellent-quality seasonal produce. Olive oil is the underlying culinary theme, and there's even an olive oil and honey ice cream on the menu. The wine list includes a range of sherries. They also own a shop with a range of olive oils across the street. Closed Mon & 15–30 Aug.

FURTHER AFIELD (SOUTH) Delic   *Tapas* 🔲♿🎴🎩 €
Plaza de la Paja s/n, 28005 **Tel** *913 64 54 50*   **Map** 4 D3

Stylish Delic is a popular café-bar, doubling as a hip local drinking hole. It serves everything from delicious breakfasts, to light snacks and more substantial cuisine with an exotic touch. With a perfect location on the trendy Plaza de la Paja, the terrace is a good place to watch a smart crowd of locals hang out on hot summer nights.

FURTHER AFIELD (SOUTH) Naôa   *Tapas* 🔲🎴🍷 €€
Plaza de la Paja 3, 28005 **Tel** *913 66 27 83*   **Map** 4 D3

The newest arrival on the ultra-trendy Plaza de la Paja, this glassy modern restaurant is currently a favourite with Madrid's fashionistas. Dine on deftly prepared Mediterranean cuisine out on the terrace – a perfect vantage point to admire the beautiful old square. There is also a reasonably priced *menú del día*. Closed Sun evenings & Mon.

MADRID PROVINCE

ALCALÁ DE HENARES Gran Mesón La Casa Vieja   *Tapas* 🔲🎴 €
C/ San Felipe Neri 7, 28302 **Tel** *918 83 62 81*

A wonderful old inn in the heart of the beautiful and historic town of Alcalá de Henares, La Casa Vieja has wooden-beamed dining areas spread over three floors, and a charming summer terrace out on the patio. Juicy grilled meats, *migas* (breadcrumbs fried with chunks of pork) and other hearty Castillian favourites are on the menu.

ARANJUEZ Casa Pablo   *Tapas* 🔲♿🍷 €€€
C/ Almíbar 42, 28300 **Tel** *918 91 14 51*

A centrally located tavern, Casa Pablo has been offering solid home cooking for more than 60 years. You can dine on typical dishes such as pheasant with grapes, taste the asparagus and strawberries for which Aranjuez is famous, or pile into the tapas area with everyone else for generous *raciones* (large portions) of Castillian favourites. Closed Aug.

Key to Price Guide *see p608* **Key to Symbols** *see back cover flap*

CHINCHÓN Mesón de la Virreina
Tapas 🖥️♿🚇 €€

Plaza Mayor 28, 28370 **Tel** *918 94 00 15*

Under the porticoes of Chinchón's celebrated Plaza Mayor, this classic *mesón* serves traditional fare such as *sopa castellana* (a garlic soup with chickpeas). Located in a handsome 16th-century building, it also has a terrace on the square, which has appeared in countless films. Wheelchair access is limited to the lower level.

MORALZARZAL El Cenador de Salvador
🖥️♿🎵🚇🅿️ €€€€

Av de España 30, 28411 **Tel** *918 57 77 22*

Many gourmets make the trek from Madrid to Moralzarzal just for the pleasure of dining in this lovely chalet. The exquisite seasonal cooking has won several prestigious international awards. Try the house speciality: hake in the style of grandmother Salvadora. A pianist entertains diners in summer. Closed Sun evenings; Mon; Tue lunch.

NAVACERRADA La Fonda Real
Tapas 🖥️♿🎵 €€

Ctra N-601 km 52.5, 28491 **Tel** *918 56 03 05*

This 18th-century country house was once a staging post on the royal route from Madrid to the palace at La Granja. With sturdy furnishings and a welcoming fireplace, it's the perfect setting for Castillian country cooking. The house speciality is suckling pig, roasted in an old brick oven, along with game in season. Closed Sun evenings & Mon.

PATONES DE ARRIBA El Poleo
🖥️🅿️ €€€€

Travesía del Arroyo 2–3, 28189 **Tel** *918 43 21 01*

Set in a picturesque town with slate-roofed houses, El Poleo is a wonderful restaurant serving Navarrese-style dishes. Try the crab-stuffed crêpes with a wild mushroom sauce. The same owner runs El Jardín del Poleo on the same street, which is cheaper and offers a simpler menu of grilled meat and seafood. Closed 15 Jul–5 Aug & 25–21 Dec.

RASCAFRÍA Barondillo
Tapas ♿ €€

Cuesta del Chorro 4, 28740 **Tel** *918 69 18 19*

Brick walls, wooden beams, and hefty iron chandeliers decorate this country restaurant in a mountain town. The menu features whatever is in season, from wild mushrooms in spring to game in autumn. Home-made bread and desserts are also available. If you are too full to make it home, they also have rooms. Closed Tue & two weeks in Jul.

SAN LORENZO DE EL ESCORIAL Taberna La Cueva
Tapas 🚇🅿️ €€

C/ San Antón 4, 28200 **Tel** *918 90 15 16*

Juan de Villanueva, architect of the Prado, designed this 18th-century inn whose specialities include the *heuvos a la cueva* (fried eggs and ham served in a nest of straw potatoes). A cool stone house, it is cosy in winter and cool in summer, when you can also tuck into tapas out on the terrace. A good range of local wines. Closed Mon.

SAN LORENZO DE EL ESCORIAL Charolés
🖥️♿🚇🅿️ €€€€

C/ Floridablanca 24, 28200 **Tel** *918 90 59 75*

A well-established classic in San Lorenzo de el Escorial, this elegant restaurant serves polished Castillian cuisine with creative touches. Nonetheless, the trademark dish here is the authentic *cocido Madrileño*, served on Wednesdays and Fridays when you would be well advised to book. The thoughtfully chosen wine list has around 300 labels.

CASTILLA Y LEÓN

AMPUDIA Restaurante Arambol-Casa del Abad
🖥️🚇🅿️ €€€

Plaza Francisco Martín Gromaz 12, 34160 (Palencia) **Tel** *979 76 80 08*

Located in the wine cellar of the old residence of the Colegiata of San Miguel's Abbot, this spectacular setting offers design and decorative elements dating back to the 17th century. Exquisite cuisine from the Michelin-starred chef, Joachim Koerper, is based on local vegetables, game, spring lamb as well as fresh fish and various rice dishes.

ARANDA DE DUERO Mesón de la Villa
Tapas 🖥️🅿️ €€€

Plaza Mayor, 09400 (Burgos) **Tel** *947 50 10 25*

Mesón de la Villa is renowned throughout the province, and serves up typical Castillian cuisine. Amongst the favourites are the famous roasted baby lamb and the creative pork, lentil, bean and chickpea combinations. A great selection of wines is stocked in their underground cellar. Closed Mon & two weeks in Aug.

ARÉVALO Asador Las Cubas
🖥️🅿️ €

Figones 11, 05200 (Avila) **Tel** *920 30 01 25*

Complete with period furniture and fittings, Asador las Cubas is a popular carvery serving roast meats at reasonable prices. Veal is the star here. The dining room is tiny, so reservations are recommended. If you do not get a table, you could always try their Figón de Arévalo restaurant, located just next door. Closed evenings except Sat.

ASTORGA La Peseta
Tapas 🖥️♿🅿️ €

Plaza de San Bartolomé 3, 24700 (León) **Tel** *987 61 72 75*

This 100-year-old restaurant is a classic in Astorga for its high-quality traditional cooking. Among its specialities are *maragato* stew (a heavy dish of nine different meats, chickpeas and vegetables), local beans with chorizo and conger. There is a decent wine list. Closed Sun & Tue (evenings), 15–31 Jan & 15–31 Oct.

ÁVILA El Almacén

Crta Salamanca 6, 05002 **Tel** *920 25 44 55*

This restaurant, located in an old warehouse, is generally regarded as one of the best in all of Castilla, and is particularly noted for its wine cellar. It offers creative cooking with prime-quality local produce, all cooked to perfection. There are views of Ávila's famous wall from the dining room. Closed Sun evenings, Mon & Sep.

BENAVENTE El Ermitaño

Ctra de Benavente-León km 1.2, 49600 (Zamora) **Tel** *980 63 22 13*

This 18th-century house is a great family option with plenty of outdoor space. There are various rooms to explore as well as an attic for coffee. The menu is typical of the area's rural cooking with some hints of modernity in the salads and desserts. Closed Sun evenings, Mon & 1–15 Nov.

BURGOS Mesón del Cid

Plaza Santa María 8, 09003 **Tel** *947 20 87 15*

In a 15th-century edifice located in front of the cathedral, this rustic place is named after Spain's most notorious conqueror. A favourite among locals, it is celebrated for its home-style cooking. The menu features traditional fare such as roast lamb, garlic soup and cod cooked with garlic. There is an excellent house wine. Closed Sun evenings.

CANEDO Prada a Tope-Palacio de Canedo

La Iglesia s/n, 24546 (León) **Tel** *902 40 01 01*

Prada a Tope is a popular restaurant located in a grand 17th-century palace. The food, however, is more down to earth. Some of the best dishes to try are *chorizo* with potatoes, pastries filled with meat, tuna or vegetables and preserves. The house wine is made on the premises. Closed Mon.

COVARRUBIAS Casa Galín

Tapas

Plaza Doña Urraca 4, 09346 (Burgos) **Tel** *947 40 65 52*

This modest little eatery, in the medieval village of Covarrubias, is an ideal place to sample Castillian home-cooked fare such as organic chicken with peppers, thick and hearty bean-based soups and the ominous sounding *olla podrida*, a slow-cooked stew of pigs ears and feet, black sausage and assorted vegetables. Closed Sun evenings & Tue.

EL BURGO DE OSMA Virrey Palafox

Universidad 7, 42300 (Soria) **Tel** *975 34 02 22*

The most popular time to dine at Virrey Palafox is January to March, the months when suckling pig is in season. For wine buffs interested in trying the local wines from the Ribera del Duero region, this is the best place to start, with over 500 varieties to choose from. Closed Sun evenings.

FRÓMISTA Hostería de los Palmeros

Tapas

Plaza San Telmo 4, 34440 (Palencia) **Tel** *979 81 00 67*

An excellent restaurant, Hostería de los Palmeros is housed in an ancient building, which formerly served as a pilgrims' hospital and is now a rural hostal. Travellers can enjoy hearty cooking based on fresh products, such as *morcilla*, *chorizo* and peppers, in a lovely garden setting if weather permits. Closed Tue, Easter & 25–26 Dec.

LEÓN Vivaldi

Platerías 4, 24003 **Tel** *987 26 07 60*

In the historic Húmedo district, Vivaldi is one of the better-known restaurants in León. Original creations include fresh pasta with fungi and foie gras, sautéed vegetables with octopus and chickpeas with garlic prawns. On the ground floor is a tavern-like wine bar for pre-dinner drinks. Closed Sun evenings and Mon; Sun (Jul–Aug).

MOLINASECA Casa Ramón

Tapas

Jardines Ángeles de Balboa 2, 24413 (León) **Tel** *987 45 31 53*

Casa Ramón is a popular rural restaurant in a beautiful village near Ponferrada, surrounded by a river which is also a popular swimming spot. The varied menu includes Cantabrian fish dishes, lentils *a la Marinara*, king prawns with clams and entrecôte with Bierzo peppers. Closed Mon & 24–30 Sep.

MORALES DEL TORO Chivo

Av Comuneros s/n, 49810 (Zamora) **Tel** *980 69 82 19*

Located 8 km (5 miles) from the village of Toro on the vineyard belt, El Chivo is regularly frequented by workers in the area, who come here for the satisfying meat and fish creations, washed down with local wine. The focus is on Basque and Castillian-style cooking. Closed Sun evenings.

NAVALENO El Maño

Tapas

Calleja del Barrio 5, 42149 (Soria) **Tel** *975 37 42 01*

Set in an old, rambling country home, El Maño has a large and lively dinning room. They churn out regional cooking based on local game, wild mushrooms and river fish, and truffles. The attentive staff will make you feel more than welcome. A popular and busy restaurant. Closed Mon evenings.

NAVALONGUILLA El Remanso de Gredos

Iglesia s/n, 05668 **Tel** *920 34 38 98*

In the Sierra de Gredos park, this small, welcoming hotel offers a restaurant open to non-guests. Try the satisfying local bean dishes or fresh and succulent steaks from the region's famed livestock. Afterwards, take a stroll through the surrounding peaceful natural parkland.

Key to Price Guide *see p608* **Key to Symbols** *see back cover flap*

PALENCIA Casa Lucio 🗏🍴 €€

Don Sancho 2, 34001 **Tel** *979 74 81 90*

Traditional cooking is at its best in this classic restaurant in the centre of Palencia. At lunch time businessmen flock here for the meats roasted in a firewood oven. Fish is also on offer and specialities include chickpeas with crab and wild turbot *a la gallega*. Closed Sun & three weeks in Jul.

PEDRAZA DE LA SIERRA La Olma de Pedraza 🗏🍴 €€

Plaza del Ganado 1, 40172 (Segovia) **Tel** *921 50 99 81*

If it is suckling pig you are after, this 16th-century mansion in a pretty square is definitely the place to visit, although ordering it in advance is required. Fish dishes, such as baby squid cooked in its own ink, and peppers stuffed with hake, also feature. There is a pleasant covered terrace looking out onto the square for outdoor dining.

PONFERRADA Menta y Canela 🗏🍴 €€

Alonso Cano 10, 24400 (León) **Tel** *987 40 32 89*

This carvery offers succulent dishes from local livestock, with the best grilled meats in the province. The menu varies according to availability and prices. Other ingredients are celebrated in their "thematic weeks". In March, there's a special menu of rice dishes. Welcoming atmosphere and friendly staff. Closed Sun evenings.

SALAMANCA Momo *Tapas* 🗏🍴 €€

San Pablo 15, 37002 **Tel** *923 28 07 98*

Momo is a retro-modern eatery complete with furniture from the mid-20th century. Tapas are served downstairs, while on the first floor, you can indulge in beautifully prepared dishes such as the imaginative salads, *solomillo* with Arbequina olive oil, tuna chunks with caramelized onions and cheesecake with wild berries. Closed Sun (Jul) & Aug.

SALAMANCA El Río de la Plata *Tapas* 🗏🍴 €€€

Plaza del Peso 1, 37001 **Tel** *923 21 90 05*

Located in the heart of the old town, this traditional restaurant, run by the locally celebrated Andrés brothers, serves slow-cooked lamb, pork and veal stews and suckling pig for hearty appetites. Lighter eaters may wish to stick to the excellent selection of tapas. Amongst the tasty desserts is apple baked in a secret sauce! Closed Mon & Jul.

SALAMANCA Víctor Gutiérrez 🗏🍴 €€€€

San Pablo 66–88, 37008 **Tel** *923 26 29 73*

This romantic and cosy restaurant in Salamanca's old town, with views over the San Esteban church, offers creative and modern cooking using seasonal products. The restaurant is particularly noted for its perfectly cooked game dishes, interesting vegetable combinations and excellent wine list. Closed Sun evenings.

SANTA MARÍA DE MAVE Hostería el Convento 🗏🍴 €€

Santa María de Mave, 34492 (Palencia) **Tel** *979 12 36 11*

Once a Benedictine convent in the Montaña Palentina Natural Park, this Romanesque jewel is the setting for a charming restaurant that combines traditional dishes with modern influences. Try their scrambled eggs with wild mushrooms and foie gras or game loin with oatmeal cream and wild fruits. Particularly good is the vegetable stew.

SARDÓN DE DUERO Sardón *Tapas* 🗏🍴 €

Ctra Valladolid-Soria km 335, 47340 (Valladolid) **Tel** *983 68 03 07*

A pleasant restaurant in the heart of the Ribera del Duero wine-growing area, Sardón is located very close to some of the most famed bodegas. The extensive, high-quality menu features local products with original touches. As is to be expected, the wine list is top-notch and you can purchase some to take home from their adjoining shop.

SEGOVIA Mesón de Cándido 🗏🍴 €€€

Azoguejo 5, 40001 **Tel** *921 42 59 11*

One of the region's better-known restaurants, Mesón de Candido is located in a 15th-century home, close to a Roman aqueduct. The restaurant is famed for its roast suckling pig (so tender they carve it for you with the side of a plate) and hearty Castillian soups. A favourite amongst locals, it is always busy, so reservations are recommended.

SEPÚLVEDA Cristóbal *Tapas* 🗏🍴 €€

Conde de Sepúlveda 9, 40300 (Segovia) **Tel** *921 54 01 00*

Renovated in 2005 and located just near the famous theatrical school Hoces del Río Duratón, Cristóbal is the best restaurant in the village. The extensive menu features regional dishes that can be savoured in the fittingly rustic setting of an underground cave. Closed Mon–Fri evenings, Tue, 1–15 Sep & 1–15 Dec.

SORIA Casa Augusto 🗏🍴 €€

Plaza Mayor 5, 42002 **Tel** *975 21 30 41*

This emblematic restaurant in the centre of Soria is tastefully decorated with period furniture and offers a fusion of traditional and original dishes. Specialities include spring lamb's breast, stuffed Piquillo peppers, and aubergines with wild mushrooms. The staff are more than happy to recommend an accompaniment from the list of local wines.

TORDESILLAS El Torreón 🗏🍴 €€€

Dimas Rodriguez 11, 47100 (Valladolid) **Tel** *983 77 01 23*

This restaurant, founded in 1981, has a reputation for excellent meats grilled in an open kitchen. The highlights are the grilled ox steaks, deliciously succulent lamb chops, fresh duck liver, anchovies with leeks and tasty, original salads. There is also an excellent selection of wines. Closed Sun & 8–19 Sep.

VALLADOLID Vinotinto   *Tapas* 🍽🍷   €

Campanas 4, 47001 **Tel** *983 34 22 91*

In a neighbourhood famous for its bars and bodegas, this modest eatery serves well-portioned tapas on the ground floor, while the cellar is reserved for slightly more formal sit-down dining. Satisfying dishes, such as steaks, spring lamb and duck breast, are used in simple, traditional recipes that are cooked to perfection. Closed 15–30 Aug.

VALLADOLID Fátima   🍽🍷   €€€

Pasión 3, 1° izq, 47001 **Tel** *983 34 28 39*

Elegant, contemporary Fátima is located in a century-old building, a stone's throw from the Plaza Mayor. The imaginative cuisine includes wild mushrooms, cooked in a variety of ways, and cod served with foie gras. Wine buffs must let the knowledgeable sommelier guide them through their excellent list. Closed Sun evenings & Mon.

VILLAFRANCA DEL BIERZO Casa Méndez   🍽   €

Plaza de la Concepción s/n, 24500 (León) **Tel** *987 54 24 08*

This welcoming family-run restaurant is located 20 km (12.4 miles) from Ponferrada, a village on the famous Santiago Route. Among its homespun specialities are stuffed Bierzo peppers and roasted veal. For dessert, try the delicious *tarta de Santiago*, a cake made of almond flour bearing the cross of St James, or Santiago.

ZAMORA Serafín   *Tapas* 🍽♿🔲🍷   €€

Plaza del Maestro Haedo 10, 49003 (Zamora) **Tel** *980 53 14 22*

Located in the centre of the city, Serafín has an exhaustive menu offering all that the regional cuisine is famous for. Especially good are the fish and rice dishes, and the eggs and chicken come straight from the restaurant's own farm. Tapas are also available and there is a lovely terrace for al fresco dining.

CASTILLA-LA MANCHA

ALBACETE Nuestro Bar   *Tapas* 🍽♿🔲🍷   €€

C/ Alcalde Conangla 102, 02002 (Albacete) **Tel** *967 24 33 73*

Decorated with local handicrafts, this welcoming local restaurant has three dining areas serving regional dishes, one from each of the villages in the province. The *menú de degustación* includes specialities of La Mancha such as *gazpacho manchego* (a rich game stew thickened with biscuits). Closed Sun evenings & July.

ALCÁZAR DE SAN JUAN Casa Paco   *Tapas* 🍽🔲   €

Av Álvarez Guerra 5, 13600 (Ciudad Real) **Tel** *926 54 10 15*

Casa Paco, a comfortable, traditional restaurant, has been going for more than 80 years. On the menu are delicious local dishes such as scrambled eggs with wild mushrooms and ham, lamb baked in a brick oven, and traditional regional desserts. There is a bargain lunch menu which can be enjoyed out on the terrace.

ALMAGRO El Corregidor   *Tapas* 🍽♿🔲🍷   €

C/ Fray Fernando Fernández de Córdoba 2, 13270 (Ciudad Real) **Tel** *926 86 06 48*

This delightful old house, with many dining rooms and a central patio, is one of Castilla-La Mancha's prettiest restaurants. Menu features creative, regional cuisine, including the town's speciality, pickled aubergines. Try the Manchego menu (26 euros) or the more elaborate *menú de degustación* (45 euros). Closed Mon.

ALMANSA Mesón de Pincelín   *Tapas* 🍽♿🍷   €€

C/ Las Norias 10, 02640 (Albacete) **Tel** *967 34 00 07*

Mesón de Pincelín is considered by many to be one of the region's best restaurants, with traditional Castilian decor. You can try authentic regional dishes prepared with a dash of creativity, including their famous *gazpacho manchego*. Home-made desserts are excellent and the wine list is very good. Closed Sun evenings & Mon.

ATIENZA Restaurante El Mirador   🍽♿🍷🍷   €€€

C/ Barruelo s/n, 19270 (Guadalajara) **Tel** *949 39 90 38*

Restaurante El Mirador is a sophisticated restaurant specializing in *ollas* and *pucheros*, the hearty stews and casseroles which are typical of this mountainous region. Fresh seasonal vegetables and excellent local meats are prominently used in the cooking. The cosy dining room is decorated with antlers, brass knickknacks and paintings.

BELMONTE Palacio Buenavista Hospedería   🍽♿   €

C/ José Antonio González 2, 16640 (Cuenca) **Tel** *967 18 75 80*

The elegant restaurant at this stylish and graceful hotel, in a beautifully restored 16th-century palace, has ochre walls and wooden beams. The subtle decor complements the refined regional cuisine, which includes oven-baked lamb and steaks and a wonderful array of Manchegan cheeses and country pâtés.

BRIHUEGA Asador El Tolmo   🍽♿🎵   €€

Av de la Constitución 26, 19400 (Guadalajara) **Tel** *949 28 11 30*

A restaurant-bar popular with locals, Asador El Tolmo is located in a pretty, walled Alcarrian village. The traditional Castillian decor is in keeping with the cuisine, which includes roast kid, beans with partridge and other regional favourites. There's a good *menú del día*, and delicious home-made desserts. Also offers a fixed-price lunch menu.

Key to Price Guide *see p608* **Key to Symbols** *see back cover flap*

CHINCHILLA DE MONTE ARAGÓN Montearagón *Tapas* 🖥️♿🎴 €

C/ Arenal 35 (7 km from Albacete), 02520 (Albacete) **Tel** *967 26 05 97*

In a historic town, praised for its loyalty by the Catholic Monarchs and dominated by a ruined castle, this is a very popular local café-bar. An easy jaunt from Alabacete, it is an ideal stopover for lunch. Serves a wide range of tapas along with some sturdy local dishes and a cheap and filling fixed lunch menu.

CIUDAD REAL Gran Mesón 🖥️♿🍷 €€€

Ronda de Ciruela 34, 13004 (Ciudad Real) **Tel** *926 22 72 39*

Friendly, charming and recommended by locals, Gran Mesón offers an ample set menu with regional specialities such as *gachas* (gruel), *pisto* (a kind of ratatouille), suckling pig and local cheese and wines. The seasonal meat and game are roasted over charcoal and the wine list has more than 200 hundred varieties. Closed Sun evenings.

CUENCA Mesón Casas Colgadas *Tapas* 🖥️ €€

C/ Canonigos s/n, 16001 **Tel** *969 22 35 09*

Dine in one of Cuenca's famous hanging houses, an upside-down medieval skyscraper that clings to the gorge. There are unbeatable views to go with great regional cuisine. There is a tapas bar downstairs, and a dining room up a narrow medieval staircase. Staff are utterly delightful. Closed Mon evenings & Tue.

CUENCA Marlo *Tapas* 🖥️♿🎴🍷 €€€

C/ Colón 41, 16002 **Tel** *969 21 11 73*

Fish and shellfish feature predominantly on Marlo's modern menu, created by adventurous young chef, Maripaz Martínez. Recommended dishes include confit of lamb with wild mushroom sauce, or the stuffed partridge in season. Service is impeccable and there is an interesting choice of reasonably priced wines as well. Closed Sun evenings.

DAIMIEL Mesón Bodegón *Tapas* 🖥️♿🎵🍷 €

C/ Luchana 20, 13250 (Ciudad Real) **Tel** *926 85 26 52*

An atmospheric 18th-century cellar and olive oil press is the setting for this charming restaurant, on the fringes of the lakes of Daimiel, a natural park. Dine on typical Manchego cuisine, accompanied by a spectacular wine list. Theatrical performances and flamenco take place regularly. Check in advance for more details. Closed Tue evenings.

GUADALAJARA Minaya *Tapas* 🖥️♿ €

C/ Mayor 23, 19001 (Guadalajara) **Tel** *949 21 22 53*

Minaya is a reasonably priced, elegant restaurant housed in a romantic 16th-century mansion. There is a dining area upstairs, with several fixed-price menus, while downstairs houses a tapas bar. The house speciality is *carnes a la brasa* (meat grilled over charcoal). The home-made desserts are excellent. Service, sadly, is patchy.

GUADALAJARA Amparito Roca 🖥️♿🎴🍷 €€€€

C/ Toledo 19, 19002 (Guadalajara) **Tel** *949 21 46 39*

The chefs of Amparito Roca, the finest restaurant in the region, reinvent classic Spanish recipes with flair. Traditional Castillian suckling pig is served boned and caramelized. Other highlights are fresh broad beans and clams delicately scented with bergamot. The desserts are outstanding and the service impeccable. Closed Sun, Easter & 15–30 Aug.

ILLESCAS El Bohío 🖥️♿🍷 €€€€

Av Castilla La Mancha 81, 45200 (Toledo) **Tel** *925 51 11 26*

Two brothers have taken over this once-traditional restaurant, and transformed it into a place of pilgrimage for local gastronomes. Sophisticated and creative versions of Manchegan recipes include pigeon with wild rice. The magnificent *menú de degustación* is a real treat. Closed Sun, Mon evenings & Aug.

JADRAQUE El Castillo *Tapas* 🖥️🎴 €€

Ctra de Soria km 46, 19240 (Guadalajara) **Tel** *949 89 02 54*

After visiting the 10th-century castle, stop here for delicious roast kid or any of the other classic Castillian dishes prepared in this typical *mesón*. The traditional, delightfully old-fashioned decor matches the menu, which features typical dishes such as kid roasted in a brick oven (the house speciality). Finish up with home-made desserts.

LAS PEDROÑERAS Las Rejas 🖥️♿🍷 €€€€

C/ General Borreros 49, 16660 (Cuenca) **Tel** *967 16 10 89*

This chic restaurant has won countless international gourmet awards. Manuel de la Osa's superb, highly creative cuisine is prepared with the finest and freshest local produce. Do not miss the fresh Manchego cheese salad. A *menú de degustación* and a day menu is available. Closed Sun evenings, Mon & two weeks in Jul.

MANZANARES Mesón Sancho *Tapas* 🖥️ €

C/ Jesús del Perdón 26, 13200 (Ciudad Real) **Tel** *926 61 10 16*

This simple, down-to-earth restaurant serves typical robust dishes such as garlic soup, *duelos y quebrantos* (scrambled eggs with pork) and rabbit *a la Manchega* (in a sauce), washed down with local wine. There is a good-value *menú del día*, and a more elaborate *menú de degustación*.

OROPESA La Hostería *Tapas* 🖥️♿🎴🍷 €

Paseo Escolar 5, 45560 (Toledo) **Tel** *925 43 08 75*

A charming stone-built inn nudged up against the castle walls, La Hostería is a typical, traditional restaurant. Try the *revuelto de morcilla* (scrambled eggs flavoured with pungent blood sausage) or the *rabo de toro* (braised bull's tail). Choose from a good range of local and national wines, and finish up with a home-made dessert. Closed 24–5 Dec.

PUERTO LÁPICE Venta del Quijote
Tapas 🞖 🞖 🞖 €

C/ El Molino 4, 13650 (Ciudad Real) **Tel** *926 57 61 10*

Set in the heart of Don Quixote country, this legendary inn evokes Cervantes' masterpiece, and the episode is recreated in a colourful tile. Sit around the pebbled courtyard and enjoy any of the Manchegan specialities, or try some of the tasty tapas and a glass of the robust local wine.

SIGÜENZA El Motor
🞖 🞖 🞖 🞖 €€

Av Juan Carlos I 2, 19250 (Guadalajara) **Tel** *949 39 08 27*

A hostal-restaurant in a classic, stone-built house, El Motor specializes in elegant versions of regional dishes including roast suckling pig and lamb, *migas* (breadcrumbs fried with pork) or *sopa castellana* (garlic soup). The menu also features seafood, prepared to traditional Basque recipes. The extensive wine list has some excellent local wines.

TALAVERA DE LA REINA Antonio
Tapas 🞖 🞖 €

Av de Portugal 8, 45600 (Toledo) **Tel** *925 80 40 17*

A simple hostal with a popular local bar, Antonio serves good-quality tapas at reasonable prices. It is well-known for its chickpeas and vegetable stews. A separate dining room offers typical regional fare. Fill up on the hearty lunchtime *menú del día*, after exploring the old-fashioned, ceramic-producing town. Closed two weeks in Jul.

TOLEDO Hostal del Cardenal
🞖 🞖 €€

Paseo de Recadero 24, 04504 (Toledo) **Tel** *925 22 08 62*

Once the summer residence of Cardinal Lorenzana, this 18th-century palace retains its beautiful Arabic-style gardens, enclosed by the city walls. It serves suckling pig, traditionally roasted in a brick oven, along with game (particulalry pheasant) in season. Desserts often feature the famous Toledo *mazapán*.

TOLEDO Locum
🞖 🞖 🞖 €€€

C/ Locum 6, 45001 (Toledo) **Tel** *925 22 32 35*

An elegant fusion of old and new, both in the cuisine and decor, this relative newcomer to Toledo's culinary scene is located in a beautifully restored 17th-century mansion. Classic Castillian recipes, such as roast suckling pig, are superbly reinvented. The desserts are splendid: try the pear tart with hazelnut caramel. Closed Mon evenings & Tue.

TOLEDO Adolfo
🞖 🞖 🞖 €€€€

C/ de la Granada 6 and at C/ Hombre de Palo 7, 45001 (Toledo) **Tel** *925 22 73 21*

Set in the heart of Toledo's Jewish quarter, the Adolfo, with its tiles, columns, antiques and a wonderful 15th-century coffered Mudehar ceiling, serves game in winter and fresh trout from the Río Tajo. The wine list is exceptional. There is a fine *menú de degustación*. Closed Sun evenings & 15–30 Jul.

TRAGACETE El Gamo
🞖 🞖 🞖 €

Plaza de los Caídos 2, 16150 (Cuenca) **Tel** *969 28 90 08*

This mountain inn in the heart of the attractive town of Tragacete enjoys superb views over the countryside. It has a simple family-run restaurant where you can try home-style cooking, such as venison stew and *migas ruleras* (a local version of Castilian breadcrumbs fried with pork). There is a good-value lunch menu.

VALDEPEÑAS Venta la Quinteria
Tapas 🞖 🞖 🞖 🞖 €€

A4 197 Madrid-Cadiz, 13300 (Ciudad Real) **Tel** *926 33 82 93*

Set in a pretty garden and cobbled courtyard, this old country inn has a rustic decor. The menu offers tasty specialities from the La Mancha region, including hearty stews, and home-made desserts such as pears poached in local wine. Located in the heart of wine country, it boasts an excellent selection on the wine list.

EXTREMADURA

ALMENDRALEJO Nando
Tapas 🞖 🞖 €

C/ Ricardo Romero 12, 06200 (Badajoz) **Tel** *924 66 12 71*

A comfortable country inn, with wooden beams and a rustic interior, Nando serves generous portions of rice with rabbit – the house speciality, *judiones* (locally-grown beans prepared with pig's knuckle or partridge) and fresh fish. There is also a good tapas bar for trying local dishes.

BADAJOZ Aldebarán
🞖 🞖 🞖 🞖 🞖 €€€€

Av de Elvas, Urbanización Guadiana, 06006 (Badajoz) **Tel** *924 27 42 61*

Deep red walls, crisp white linen, chandeliers and antiques adorn the dining rooms of this formal, elegant restaurant. The menu offers superb contemporary Spanish and Extremaduran cuisine. The *menú de degustación* (53 euros) features highlights from the chef's repertoire. An impressive wine and cigar list. Closed Sun & two weeks in Aug.

CÁCERES El Pato
Tapas 🞖 🞖 🞖 🞖 🞖 €

Plaza Mayor s/n, 10003 (Cáceres) **Tel** *927 24 87 36*

An atmospheric, classic inn right on the main square with all kinds of tasty local tapas, including *migas* and unusual partridge croquettes at the bar. Relish the home-cooked Extremaduran specialities in the old-fashioned dining room with whitewashed, brick-lined walls.

Key to Price Guide *see p608* **Key to Symbols** *see back cover flap*

CÁCERES El Figón de Eustaquio   *Tapas* 🍴♿   €€
*Plaza de San Juan 14, 10003 (Cáceres) **Tel** 927 24 81 94*

In the heart of Cáceres' beautiful old centre, this long-standing and resolutely old-fashioned restaurant has been preparing genuine Extremaduran food since 1947. Try traditional dishes like trout *a la extremeña* (stuffed with ham) and the house speciality, *sopa 'el Figón* (tomato soup with poached egg).

CÁCERES Atrio   🍴♿🎩🍷   €€€€
*Avl de España 30, Bloque 4, 10002 (Cáceres) **Tel** 927 24 29 28*

One of the finest restaurants in Spain, with countless international gourmet awards to prove it, Atrio serves innovative, contemporary cuisine. Try tender kid with rosemary or bream with wild mushrooms. Stylish, modern decor and perfect service make this restaurant a memorable gourmet experience. Closed Sun evenings & 1–15 Sep.

GUADALUPE Hospedería del Real Monasterio   🍴🖼   €
*Plaza de Juan Carlos I, 10140 (Cáceres) **Tel** 927 36 70 00*

Owned by the Franciscan order, this restaurant (linked to a simple *hospederia*) offers simple regional cooking in the unforgettable surroundings of the magnificent monastery of Guadalupe. The tomato soup, the roast kid and the *migas extremeñas* are all recommended. There is also a simple café-bar. Closed 15 Jan–15 Feb.

GUADALUPE Posada del Rincón   *Tapas* 🍴♿🖼   €€
*Plaza Santa María de Guadalupe 11, 10140 (Cáceres) **Tel** 927 36 71 14*

Part of a charming rural hotel, Posada del Rincón is a delightful restaurant and café-bar. Inside, there are brick-lined walls, wooden beams and wrought-iron furniture out on the plant-filled patio. Fine regional cuisine, prepared with the freshest seasonal produce, has touches of creativity. Try the partridge with honey. Good fixed-price menu.

JARANDILLA DE LA VERA Puta Parió   *Tapas* 🍴   €€
*C/ Francisco Pizarro 8, 10450 (Cáceres) **Tel** 927 56 03 92*

This old stone house was once home to Don Luis de Quijada, major domo to Emperor Charles V (Carlos I). It is now a lively and popular tavern with good regional dishes, including tomato soup and lamb casserole, and locally-produced house wine. There is a good value fixed-price lunch menu.

JEREZ DE LOS CABALLEROS La Ermita   *Tapas* 🍴🖼   €
*C/ Doctor Benítez 9, 06380 (Badajoz) **Tel** 924 73 14 76*

Housed in a 17th-century chapel converted into a wine cellar, La Ermita serves authentic local dishes. Sample the partridge stew or the typical *revuelto de espárragos*, made with scrambled eggs and asparagus tips. They also have fabulous tapas, including the delectable Iberian hams, made from pigs raised on acorns. Closed Wed.

LOSAR DE LA VERA Carlos V   *Tapas* 🍴♿   €
*Av de Extremadura 45, 10460 (Cáceres) **Tel** 927 57 06 36*

Home cooking and lovely views of the mountains are the fare at this charming rural inn, which is decorated with antlers and hunting trophies. Specialities include scrambled eggs with white truffles, roast kid and steaks. There is a good-value lunch menu. Finish up with *flan de almendras* (almond crème caramel). Closed Mon & 15–30 Oct.

MÉRIDA Nicolás   🍴🖼🍷   €€
*C/ Félix Valverde Lillo 13, 06800 (Badajoz) **Tel** 924 31 96 10*

Nicolás is a long-standing restaurant in a handsome historic mansion in the heart of Mérida. You might want to visit the brick wine cellar for an apéritif before tucking into the regional specialities such as the delicious lamb with plums or the pork sirloin with pepper. There is also a pretty garden terrace. Closed Sun evenings.

MÉRIDA Rufino   *Tapas* 🍴🖼   €€
*Plaza Santa Clara 2, 06800 (Badajoz) **Tel** 924 31 20 01*

With a terrace out on a delightful pedestrianized square, this much-loved local institution is the perfect place to start the *tapeo* (a pub crawl from tapas bar to tapas bar). Try the delicious local hams. It also serves typical Extremaduran cuisine, including *revuelto con criadillas de tierra* (roast kid).

MÉRIDA Altair   🍴♿🖼🍷   €€€
*Av José Fernández López s/n, 06800 (Badajoz) **Tel** 924 30 45 12*

Sleekly mimimalist in design, this fashionable, glassy restaurant overlooks Santiago Calatrava's gleaming modern bridge, also echoed in the crisp white furnishings. Altair is linked to the spectacular Atrio in Cáceres, and offers fine contemporary cuisine, best appreciated in the good-value *menú de degustación*. Closed Sun.

OLIVENZA Alcañices   *Tapas* 🍴♿🖼   €€
*C/ Colón 3, 06100 (Badajoz) **Tel** 924 49 15 70*

Elegant, yet informal, Alcañices is a charming restaurant in the attractive border town of Olivenza. The light and creative cuisine uses fresh local produce: try the wonderful black pudding spiced with red peppers, or the succulent game in season. Offers a good *menú de degustación*. Closed two weeks in Oct; check timings.

PLASENCIA Alfonso VIII   *Tapas* 🍴♿🍷   €€
*Avenida Alfonso XIII 32–34, 10700 (Cáceres) **Tel** 927 41 02 50*

This smart hotel-restaurant offers creative cuisine that relies heavily on local produce and updated traditional recipes. Try the kid stew, or the cod with courgette (zucchini) ratatouille and finish up with a delicious flan made with pine nuts and chestnuts. A relaxed tapas bar serves wonderful Iberian hams. Fixed-price menu available.

PLASENCIA Puerta Talavera
Tapas 目占♫¶   €€

C/Talavera 30, 10600 (Cáceres) **Tel** *927 42 42 69*

A stylish, modern restaurant with a wide-ranging menu, Puerta Talavera offers several fixed-price options to suit all pockets. The cuisine is based on fresh local ingredients, and includes delicacies, such as local trout and game, as well as a range of tapas at the informal bar. The wine list has plenty of regional wines to choose from.

PUEBLA DE LA REINA Mesón La Jara-Casa Andrés
Tapas 目占⊞¶   €

Calle Luis Chamizo 14, 06228 (Badajoz) **Tel** *924 36 00 05*

This charming *mesón* has become a sanctuary of authentic regional food, often prepared using ancient recipes. The classic dish here is rabbit in "La Jara" sauce – flavoured with chestnuts and bay leaf, though the partridge is also good. There is a cheap lunch menu and a more complete *menú de degustación*. Closed 15–30 Sep.

TRUJILLO Mesón La Troya
Tapas 目占⊞   €

Plaza Mayor 10, 10200 (Cáceres) **Tel** *927 32 13 64*

A typical 16th-century *mesón*, on the main square of the magnificent Renaissance town, La Troya serves regional food in hearty portions in a pair of old-fashioned dining rooms with lacy curtains and ceramics. The *migas* with pork are recommended. The tapas bar, with photographs lining the wall, is worth visiting.

TRUJILLO Pizarro
目   €

Plaza Mayor 13, 10200 (Cáceres) **Tel** *927 32 02 55*

On Trujillo's beautiful central square, this restaurant has retained much of its decor since it opened before the Civil War. Enjoy traditional dishes such as tomato soup with figs and grapes; chicken stuffed with truffles; and potatoes cooked in Extremaduran style. Family run, it is friendly and welcoming. Closed two weeks in Feb & Jun.

TRUJILLO Corral del Rey
目占⊞¶   €€

Plaza Corral del Rey (Plaza Mayor), 10200 (Cáceres) **Tel** *927 32 17 80*

One of the best in the city, Corral del Rey is a classic *asador* specializing in roasted meat and fish. Traditional decor consists of brick walls and wooden beams. Recommended delicacies include wild sea bass baked in salt and beef seared on the grill. They also have a cigar list and a good liqueur menu. Closed Sun, 1–15 Jul & 15–30 Jan.

ZAFRA Josefina
目   €€

Av López Asme 1, 06300 (Badajoz) **Tel** *924 55 17 01*

A warm welcome awaits in this delightful family-run restaurant, which serves typical Extremeño cuisine with a dash of creativity. The adventurous can try trotters au gratin, a local delicacy, or stick with a platter of Iberian ham, produced from free-range, acorn-fed pigs. A good-value lunch menu on weekdays. Closed Sun evenings & Mon.

ZAFRA La Rebotica
目占¶   €€

C/ Boticas 12, 06300 (Badajoz) **Tel** *924 55 42 89*

In the heart of lovely, whitewashed Zafra, chic little La Rebotica has a series of intimate dining areas linked by arches. The deftly prepared local dishes include a wonderful partridge soup, and codfish served with baby squid. They also do fabulous home-made desserts, including a refreshing orange and fig ice cream. Closed Sun evenings & Mon.

SEVILLE

EL ARENAL El Cabildo
目   €€

Plaza del Cabildo, 41001 (Seville) **Tel** *954 22 79 70*   **Map** *3 C2 (5 C4)*

Part of the ancient Arabic walls have been conserved in this classic and delightfully old-fashioned restaurant. All the traditional Andalusian favourites are on the menu, excellently cooked with fresh local ingredients. Try a platter of fresh fried fish, *Sevillian revueltos* (scrambled eggs with different fillings) accompanied by sturdy local wine.

EL ARENAL La Eslava
Tapas 目   €€

C/ Eslava 3, 41002 **Tel** *954 90 65 68*   **Map** *1 C4*

La Eslava is a favourite local haunt with no cutesy decor geared towards tourists. Instead, the emphasis is firmly on assured Andalusian cuisine with touches of creativity. The dining area has a full menu of seafood dishes and some excellent salads, while the bar serves up tasty, fresh tapas. Go early for a table. Closed Sun evenings & Mon.

EL ARENAL Enrique Becerra
Tapas 目占¶   €€€

C/ Gamazo 2, 41001 **Tel** *954 21 30 49*   **Map** *3 B1 (5 C4)*

Housed in a beautifully renovated 19th-century mansion, this plush restaurant-bar offers a fine selection of fish and meat dishes. The daily specials feature Andalusian home-style cooking. The classic apéritif is a wonderful ice-cold Manzanilla sherry, which you can follow with tapas or specialities like roast lamb with pine nuts. Closed Sun.

EL ARENAL El Burladero
Tapas 目占⊤¶   €€€€

Hotel Colón, C/ Canalejas 1, 41001 **Tel** *954 50 55 99*   **Map** *3 B1 (5 B3)*

A smart hotel-restaurant in a grand 19th-century building, El Burladero is decorated with bullfighting memorabilia. You can enjoy caviar and filet mignon as well as local dishes such as *puchero* (meat-in-a-pot) and, of course, a very fine version of the Andalusian classic, *rabo de toro* (braised bull's tail). Also houses a great upmarket tapas bar.

EL ARENAL La Isla
Tapas 目 🖥 🍷   €€€€

C/ Arfe 25, 41001 **Tel** 954 21 26 31   Map 3 B2 (5 C4)

This attractive, centrally located restaurant features superb seafood specialities from Galicia, including turbot, bream and delicacies such as *percebes* (sea barnacles). Some Andalusian dishes, such as a meaty beef stew, also feature. There is a small tapas bar where you can enjoy fabulous prawns, oysters and a wide range of local hams.

SANTA CRUZ Ajoblanco
Tapas 🍽 目   €

C/ Alhóndiga 19, 41004 **Tel** 954 22 93 20   Map 2 D5 (6 E2)

Tucked away down a narrow street, this relaxed, boho-chic café-bar is fully covered with jazz posters. Good for a coffee, it also serves great tapas – everything from standards such as *patatas bravas*, to more unusual offerings such as fried Camembert with raspberry sauce, and even spicy burritos and *tacos*. Closed Mon evenings.

SANTA CRUZ El Rincón de Anita
Tapas 目 ♿ 🖥 🍷   €

Plaza del Cristo de Burgos 23, 41004 **Tel** 954 21 74 61   Map 6 E2

This delightful little restaurant is decorated with colourful tiles, polished wood, images of the Semana Santa processions, and lots of plants. This is the perfect place to tuck into tasty Andalusian specialities. Try the *cola de toro* (bull's tail), kidneys cooked in sherry, and home-made desserts. Classic tapas can be enjoyed at the bar.

SANTA CRUZ Mesón de la Infanta
Tapas 目   €

C/ Dos de Mayo 26, 41002 **Tel** 954 22 19 09   Map 3 B2 (5 C5)

Set in a restored historic building in the heart of the lively Arenal district, Mesón de la Infanta offers an excellent choice of traditional dishes, including delicious *guisos*. The tapas bar is a classic on the Sevillano tapas route, with a bewildering array of fine local hams and *embutidos* (charcuterie), along with all the usual favourites.

SANTA CRUZ Corral del Agua
目 🖥   €€

Callejón del Agua 6, 41004 **Tel** 954 22 48 41   Map 3 C2 (6 D/E5)

Dine on the cool patio in a lee of the Reales Alcázares gardens, with plants trailing romantically around wrought-iron grilles and a marble fountain burbling quietly. Antique furniture and paintings adorn the dining room, and the menu emphasizes seasonal specialities, traditionally prepared. Closed Sun.

SANTA CRUZ Becerrita
Tapas 目 ♿ 🍷   €€€

C/ Recaredo 9, 41004 **Tel** 954 41 20 57   Map 2 E5 (6 F3)

Becerrita is a beautiful restaurant, warmly decorated in modern Andalusian style. Delicious Andaluz specialities include outstanding croquettes made with bull's tail, or kid flavoured with thyme. At the bar, you can choose from a superb range of tapas that changes daily, depending on the season. Closed Sun evenings & Aug.

SANTA CRUZ La Albahaca
目 🖥 🍷   €€€

Plaza de Santa Cruz 12, 41004 **Tel** 954 22 07 14   Map 4 D2 (6 E4)

Overlooking a charming, verdant square dominated by a wrought-iron cross, La Albahaca is one of the most authentic restaurants in the Barrio Santa Cruz. Its fine setting in a 1920s mansion furnished with 17th-century antiques, makes it a perfect place to enjoy Basque-influenced food, along with excellent local dishes. Closed Sun.

SANTA CRUZ Casa Robles
目 ♿ 🖥   €€€€

C/ Álvarez Quintero 58, 41001 **Tel** 954 56 32 72   Map 3 C1 (6 D3)

Right in the heart of Seville, close to the cathedral, this elegant restaurant is decorated with oil paintings, statuary and pretty tiles. Although the menu leans towards seafood, there are also plenty of local meat dishes to choose from, all exquisitely presented. The desserts, in particular, are miniature works of art.

SANTA CRUZ Egaña Oriza
目 ♿ 🖥 🍷   €€€€

C/ San Fernando 41, 41004 **Tel** 954 22 72 11   Map 3 C2 (6 D5)

Tucked against the walls of the Alcázar gardens, Egaña Oriza is located in a beautiful early 20th-century mansion. The dining room is in an elegant light-filled conservatory, and the sophisticated modern Basque cuisine leans heavily towards fish. Meat dishes and desserts are equally delicious. The wine list is superb. Closed Sat lunch & Sun.

SANTA CRUZ Taberna del Alabardero
Tapas 目 ♿ 🖥 🍷   €€€€

C/ Zaragoza 20, 41001 **Tel** 954 50 27 21   Map 3 B3 (5 C3)

Housed in a beautiful tile-lined mansion, Taberna del Alabardero is one of the finest and loveliest restaurants in Seville. The menu offers spectacular contemporary Spanish cuisine, prepared with the freshest seasonal ingredients. There is also an inexpensive bistro for a lighter fare, and a vaulted snack bar.

FURTHER AFIELD (SOUTH) Salvador Rojo
目 ♿ 🖥 🍷   €€€€

C/San Fernando 23, 41004 **Tel** 954 22 97 25   Map 3 C2 (6 D5)

A stylish, modern little restaurant opposite the old Fábrica de Tabaco, Salvador Rojo offers contemporary Spanish cuisine. The freshest local produce is used with innovation: try the stir-fried prawns with Thai rice. Leave room for the fabulous desserts. Classic Spanish wines feature along with some excellent but lesser-known labels. Closed Sun.

FURTHER AFIELD (WEST) Kiosko de las Flores
Tapas ♿ 🖥   €

C/ Betis (Triana), 41010 **Tel** 954 27 45 76   Map 3 A2 (5 A5)

A long-standing institution on the banks of the Guadalquivir, with sublime views of the old city from the terrace. This old-fashioned ochre building, tucked into the side of the emblematic Triana bridge, is a historic *freiduría*, where heaped platters of fried fish have been the classic dish for more than 70 years. Closed Mon.

FURTHER AFIELD (WEST) Sol y Sombra
Tapas 🍽️🍷   €

C/ Castilla 149 (Triana), 41010 **Tel** *954 33 39 35*   **Map** *3 A1*

A sea of hams suspended from the ceiling and peeling bullfighting posters adorn the walls of this historic tavern. Though tucked away in Triana, the restaurant is well worth seeking out for the authentic Sevillano ambience. Visit the tapas bar for freshly prepared large portions of tapas, or dine more substantially at the adoining restaurant.

FURTHER AFIELD (WEST) Río Grande
Tapas 🍽️♿🍴🍷   €€

C/ Betis s/n, 41010 **Tel** *954 27 39 56*   **Map** *3 A2 (5 A5)*

Río Grande has a terrific location on the liveliest steet in the old sailor's barrio of Triana. Enjoy the *rabo de toro* on a terrace overlooking the Guadalquivir with views of the Torre del Oro. There is a formal, English-style dining area and an ever-lively tapas bar, where shellfish is the speciality. Good range of wines.

ANDALUSIA

ALARAQUE Las Candelas
🍽️♿🍷   €€€

Av de Huelva 3, 21110 (Huelva) **Tel** *959 31 84 33*

A long-established classic in a village 6 km (3.7 miles) from Huelva, this restaurant is decorated with maritime motifs. Seafood, unsurprisingly, dominates the Mediterranean menu, with delicacies such as monkfish in almond sauce, but there is a range of good local meat dishes as well. Traditional Spanish wines. Closed Sun & 24–5, 31 Dec.

ALMERÍA Rincón de Juan Pedro
Tapas 🍽️   €

C/ Federico Castro 2, 04130 (Almería) **Tel** *950 23 58 19*

A much-loved stalwart on Almería's busy tapas scene, this Andalusian bar serves a wonderful range of tapas – still included in the price of a drink. You can dine more substantially on *raciones*, as well as meat and seafood specialities, and local dishes, such as *trigo a la cortijera* (a stew with wheat berries, meat and sausage). Closed Sun & Mon evenings.

ALMERÍA Bodega Bellavista
🍽️♿🍴🍷   €€

Urbanización Bellavista, Llanos del Alquián, 04130 (Almería) **Tel** *950 29 71 56*

In an unlikely location in a housing complex near the airport, this charmingly old-fashioned restaurant offers a range of classic and innovative Andalusian dishes prepared with top-quality local products. Fish and shellfish predominate, but you can also try good beef and kid. A huge range of wines from all around Spain. Closed Sun evenings & Mon.

ALMERÍA Club de Mar
🍽️♿🍴   €€

Playa de la Almadrabillas 1, 04007 (Almería) **Tel** *950 23 50 48*

Enjoy fresh fish and shellfish right on the seafront at the Almerían yacht club, where well-heeled locals and sailors mingle on the breezy terrace. The fresh seafood complements the views over the port, and the *bullabesa* (Spanish bouillabaisse) and *fritura* (mixed fried fish) are specialities. Also offers a good-value lunch menu.

ANTEQUERA La Espuela
Tapas 🍽️♿🍴   €€

C/ San Agustin 1, 29200 (Málaga) **Tel** *952 70 30 31*

Uniquely situated in a bullring, this restaurant prepares Andalusian dishes including the town speciality, *porra* (a thick gazpacho). With its brightly coloured tiles, brick walls and perpetually busy tapas bar, it offers a taste of authentic Andalusia. It is enormously popular with tourists and locals alike, so be sure to book ahead.

ARCOS DE LA FRONTERA El Convento
🍽️♿🍷   €€

C/ Marqués de Torresoto 7, 11630 (Cádiz) **Tel** *956 70 32 22*

A charming restaurant located in a lovely 17th-century palace, with an interior patio. They serve unusual local specialities, including the wonderfully named "pheasant in paradise" (stewed in sherry), and a delicious local soup, *abajao*, made with wild asparagus and eggs. It is linked to a delightful hotel. Closed 1–7 Nov, 7–21 Jan & 1–7 Jul.

BAEZA Juanito
🍽️   €€

Plaza Arca del Agua s/n, 23440 (Jaén) **Tel** *953 74 00 40*

A comfortable family-run hotel and restaurant in the heart of the olive belt. The good home cooking is based on traditional regional recipes which feature plenty of olive oil. Try the artichokes or the *patatas a lo pobre*, a tasty potato dish flavoured with ham. The home-made desserts are scrumptious. Closed Sun evenings & Mon.

BAEZA Vandelvira
🍽️♿🍴🍷   €€€

C/ San Francisco 14, 23440 (Jaén) **Tel** *953 74 81 72*

Located in a 16th-century monastery built by Andrés de Vandelvira, Jáen's Renaissance architect, this beautiful, classically decorated restaurant serves typical regional food: *cardos* (cardoons, a type of artichoke) in a cream sauce, partridge salad and a mouthwatering pine-nut ice cream.

BAILÉN Zodíaco
Tapas 🍽️♿🍴🍷   €€

Antigua Ctra Madrid-Cádiz km 294, 23710 (Jaén) **Tel** *953 67 10 58*

A modern hotel with a large and popular restaurant. Cold soups are on the menu in summer, such as *ajo blanco* (white garlic) with almonds. Other specialities include the scrambled eggs with ham, asparagus, prawn/shrimp and elves and partridge. Has a lovely, tree-shaded garden terrace in summer.

Key to Price Guide *see p608* **Key to Symbols** *see back cover flap*

BENAHAVIS Los Abanicos   🖼️♿🛗🍷   €€
C/ Málaga 15, 29679 (Málaga) **Tel** *952 85 51 31*

A well known and consistently good restaurant decorated with pretty painted *abanicos* (fans) in the heart of the lovely village of Benahavís. Dine on tasty regional dishes. The house speciality, *paletilla de cordero* (shoulder of lamb) is particularly good. It is a favourite for Sunday lunch, so book early. Closed Tue except Jul & Aug.

BUBIÓN Teide   ***Tapas*** 🛗   €
C/ Carretera s/n, 18412 (Granada) **Tel** *958 76 30 84*

Lost in the beautiful wilderness of the Alpujarras, this is a simple, stone-built restaurant surrounded by a charming, informal garden with pots of flowers and shady trees. They serve traditional dishes such as roast kid and generous salads of local vegetables. It also serves free tapas with a drink in the time-honoured Andalusian tradition.

CÁDIZ Balandro   🖼️♿🛗   €
C/ Alameda Apodaca 22, 11004 (Cádiz) **Tel** *956 22 09 92*

The Balandro is a modest local restaurant, but the cuisine is creative and sophisticated. The house speciality is seafood from the Bay of Cádiz, fresh and prepared with imagination, but there are plenty of local meat (especially beef) dishes too. Try octopus salad or the beef medallions with port. Closed Sun evenings & Mon except Jul & Aug.

CÁDIZ Freiduria Cerveceria Las Flores   ***Tapas*** 🖼️🖼️♿🛗   €
Plaza Topete 4, 11009 (Cádiz) **Tel** *956 22 61 12*

The classic Andalusian dish is *pescaíto frito*, and every town has several *freiduría*.(fried-fish shops) This is the best in Cádiz. Order your fish (anything from shark to squid), which is fried on the spot and wrapped up to takeaway for a picnic. You can also eat it out on the terrace near the square. Non-fish snacks include croquettes and *empanadas*.

CÁDIZ El Faro   ***Tapas*** 🖼️♿🍷   €€
C/ San Félix 15, 11011 (Cádiz) **Tel** *902 21 10 68*

El Faro restaurant has a warm atmosphere in the old fishermen's barrio of Cádiz. The menu, a wonderful blend of modern and traditional, changes daily but always features local seafood, such as the *tortillitas de camarones* (fritters of tiny shrimps), or the rice dishes flavoured with shellfish from the bay. There is a popular tapas bar too.

CÁDIZ Ventorillo del Chato   🖼️♿🛗🍷   €€€
Vía Augusta Julia s/n, 11011 (Cádiz) **Tel** *956 25 00 25*

A picturesque inn, in an 18th-century staging post next to the sea, this place offers Andalusian cuisine. Recipes use superbly fresh fish from the bay, local meat and fresh vegetables, often combined in one of the restaurant's *guisos*. A very popular spot for Sunday lunch, when families pile off the glorious beach for a huge feast. Closed Sun.

CARMONA Ancla   ***Tapas*** 🖼️♿🛗🍷   €€
C/ Bonifacio IV 8, 41410 (Sevilla) **Tel** *954 14 38 04*

Sturdy home cooking is served at this friendly family-run restaurant, which takes pride in choosing the freshest local ingredients. There is an excellent lunch menu which you can enjoy on the terrace, and specialities include prawns in garlic sauce, roast lamb, *pescaíto frito* (fried fish platter) and home-made desserts. Closed Wed.

CARMONA San Fernando   🖼️🍷   €€
C/ Sacramento 3, 41410 (Sevilla) **Tel** *954 14 35 56*

An exquisite mansion, built in 1700, houses this elegant restaurant, which offers fresh seasonal cuisine from the region. The *salmorejo*, a thick tomato soup garnished with boiled egg and ham, is particularly good, and the *bacalao* is prepared in myriad ways, including with a delectable squid ink and garlic sauce. Closed evenings & Mon.

CÓRDOBA Caballo Rojo   ***Tapas*** 🖼️🛗🍷   €€
C/ Cardenal Herrero 28, 14003 (Córdoba) **Tel** *957 47 53 75*

Right next to the Mezquita, this lovely restaurant has a central patio with wrought-iron balconies thickly hung with brightly coloured flowers. The dishes are based on ancient recipes, many adapted from Moorish and Sephardic recipes. Enjoy lamb with honey or Sephardi salad of wild mushrooms, asparagus, roasted peppers and salt cod.

CÓRDOBA Federación de Peñas   ***Tapas*** 🖼️   €€
C/ Conde y Luque, 14003 (Córdoba) **Tel** *957 47 54 27*

Located right next to the Mezquita, Peñas offers simple but excellent local food. Try the *rabo de toro*, a house speciality or the *cardos* with clams. There's always a good variety of seafood and prices are exceptionally reasonable. The city has awarded it a gold medal in recognition of its high standards.

CÓRDOBA Taberna Pepe de la Judería   ***Tapas*** 🖼️♿🛗   €€
C/ Romero 1, 14003 (Córdoba) **Tel** *957 20 07 44*

This has been one of Córdoba's most appealing restaurants since it opened in 1928. Dine on a lovely Córdoban patio blazing with flowers, or sit in the dining rooms festooned with photos of notable customers. Try the *flamenquín* (fried rolls of veal and ham), or the unusual cherry gazpacho flavoured with mint.

CÓRDOBA Almudaina   🖼️♿   €€€
Jardines de los Santos Mártires 1, 14004 (Córdoba) **Tel** *957 47 43 42*

Once the palace of Bishop Leopold of Austria, this mansion serves typical local dishes which draw on the cuisines from the distinct cultures that have shaped Córdoba. The Córdoban *salmorejo* is excellent here, also try angler fish with stewed tomatoes. Closed Sun evenings.

CÓRDOBA El Blasón
Tapas 🍽️📶   €€€

C/ José Zorrila 11, 14008 (Córdoba) **Tel** *957 48 06 25*

A typical Andalusian mansion, set around a magical tiled patio, this is a perfect place to try a wide range of Córdoban specialities, including seafood, sturdy meat stews and wonderful home-made desserts. It is also a lively and very popular tapas bar and café – and has a handy location close to the main shopping district.

CÓRDOBA El Churrasco
Tapas 🍽️♿📶🍷   €€€

C/ Romero 16, 14003 (Córdoba) **Tel** *957 29 08 19*

A traditional Andalusian mansion, the speciality here is charcoal-grilled meat, but vegetable dishes and soups such as *salmorejo* are also good. The dining rooms are set around two patios: in the lovely Patio del Limonera you can eat under a fragrant lemon tree. Sip an apéritif in the nearby wine cellars. Closed Easter, Aug & Christmas.

EL PUERTO DE SANTA MARÍA Casa Flores
Tapas 🍽️♿📶   €€

C/ Ribera del Río 9, 11500 (Cádiz) **Tel** *956 54 35 12*

A family-run traditional restaurant, with a series of intimate dining rooms decorated with pretty tiles, paintings and a smattering of bullfighting memorabilia. Seafood and shellfish are the house specialities, with a spectacular array, which includes everything from the local sweet striped prawns to unusual delicacies such as sea urchins.

EL PUERTO DE SANTA MARÍA El Faro del Puerto
🍽️♿📶🍷   €€€

Ctra de Fuentebravía km 0.5, 11500 (Cádiz) **Tel** *956 87 09 52*

Part of a small group which includes the El Faro and the Ventorrilo del Chato in Cádiz, this is the most refined restaurant of a remarkable trio. Set in an elegant, low-built villa surrounded by gardens, the menu here offers sophisticated interpretations of modern dishes. Do not miss the desserts, especially the Oloroso sherry ice cream.

ESTEPONA La Alborada
🍽️♿📶   €€

Puerto Deportivo de Estepona, 29680 (Málaga) **Tel** *952 80 20 47*

This quayside eatery serves excellent paella and other rice dishes, such as *arroz a la banda* (a kind of fish risotto). It also serves delicious *pescaíto frito* and has tasty home-made desserts such as the *pudín de almendras* (creamy almond pudding). There are lovely views of the yacht-filled harbour from the terrace. Closed Mon.

ESTEPONA Lido
🍽️♿📶🍴🍷   €€€€

Hotel Las Dunas, Urb La Boladilla Baja, 29680 (Málaga) **Tel** *952 79 43 45*

In the opulent surroundings of the luxurious Las Dunas Hotel, this is a stylish restaurant serving contemporary international cuisine. It has magnificent outdoor seating on a balustraded terrace overlooking gardens, or in an elegant conservatory. Signature dishes include a foie gras mousse and seafood cannelloni. Closed Mon & Tue.

FUENGIROLA Portofino
🍽️♿📶🍷   €€

Edificio Perla 1, Paseo Marítimo 29, 29640 (Málaga) **Tel** *952 47 06 43*

This seafront restaurant is popular for its friendly service and good Italian food, such as the fish and shellfish brochette or delicious pastas with rich sauces. It also prepares traditional Andalusian dishes, all served in generous portions. The terrace has views over the glossy, yacht-filled port. Closed Mon & Jul.

GRANADA Bodegas Castañeda
Tapas 🍽️♿   €

C/ Almireceros 1–3, 18010 (Granada) **Tel** *958 215 464*

With its time-worn tiles, huge wooden barrels and battered air, Castañeda is one of the most delightful and authentic of Granada's tapas bars. Try the melt-in-the-mouth Trevélez ham (which has its own *denominación de origen*) or the wide variety of seafood conserves. A glass of ice-cold sherry is the perfect way to begin the evening.

GRANADA Mirador de Morayma
🍽️🎵📶   €€

C/ Pianista Garcia Carrillo 2, 18010 (Granada) **Tel** *958 22 82 90*

Situated in the Albaícin with views of the Alhambra, this charming patio-restaurant specializes in typical dishes of Granada, such as *remojón* (a salad of oranges and codfish) and kid fried with garlic. The wine list includes organic wines produced on the restaurant's own estate. Flamenco on Tuesdays, call to confirm times. Closed Sun evenings.

GRANADA Chikito
Tapas 🍽️📶🍷   €€€

Plaza del Campillo 9, 18009 (Granada) **Tel** *958 22 33 64*

Built on the site of a café where Lorca and his contemporaries used to meet, Chikito serves broad beans with ham and Sacromonte omelette (prepared with brains, but tastier than you might think) as specialities. Try the *piononos* (aniseed-scented cake). At the brick bar, inset with painted tiled scenes, you can enjoy the tapas. Closed Wed.

GRANADA Velázquez
Tapas 🍽️♿🍷   €€€

C/ Profesor Emilio Orozco 1, 18010 (Granada) **Tel** *958 28 01 09*

The ambience here is warm and the food imaginative, with modern interpretations of such Moorish dishes as *bstella*, a pigeon pastry with pine nuts and almonds and savoury almond cream soup. Velázquez has an old-fashioned lively tapas bar where you can enjoy tapas along with good local wines and Andalusian sherries. Closed Sun & Aug.

GRANADA Carmen de San Miguel
🍽️♿📶   €€€€

Plaza Torres Bermejas 3, 18009 (Granada) **Tel** *958 22 67 23*

The Andalusian specialities at this pretty restaurant with Moorish-style decor include the seafood salad and a dessert made with almonds and strawberries. Everything is fresh and prepared with imagination by a talented young chef. There are wonderful views of the whitewashed maze of the Albaícin from the terrace.

Key to Price Guide *see p608* **Key to Symbols** *see back cover flap*

GRANADA Ruta del Veleta   🅰️🏠🍴   €€€€

Ctra Sierra Nevada 136, km 5,400 Cenes de la Vega, 18190 (Granada) **Tel** *958 48 61 34*

Out on the winding old road to the Sierra Nevada, on the fringes of Granada, this traditional restaurant has an excellent reputation for its hearty regional cuisine. The decoration, with typical Alpujarran textiles and ceramic jugs, goes well with dishes such as roast baby kid and good seafood. Be sure to try the game in season. Closed Sun evenings.

HUELVA Farqueo   *Tapas* 📋🅰️🎵🏠🍴   €€

Glorieta de las Canoas, Muelle de Levante s/n, 21003 (Huelva) **Tel** *959 25 26 90*

With the best views in the city, Farqueo sits right on the port and has an admirable restaurant upstairs, preparing delectable modern Andalusian cuisine including cod with a mixed shellfish sauce. There is a hugely popular bar downstairs where you can snack on tapas and enjoy the Thursday night jazz sessions. Closed Sun 15–30 Jul.

HUELVA Las Meigas   📋🅰️🍴   €€

Avda Guatemala 44, 21003 (Huelva) **Tel** *959 27 19 58*

Some of the freshest seafood can be found at this crisply decorated Galician restaurant. The Gallegos are famed throughout the country for their skill with seafood, and here it is simply prepared – grilled, baked in a salt crust or served Gallego style – in order to appreciate its exquisite freshness. Fabulous home-made desserts. Closed Sun.

HUELVA El Portichuelo   *Tapas* 📋🅰️🍴   €€€

Avda Vázquet López 15, 21110 (Huelva) **Tel** *959 24 57 68*

A simple spot in the centre of the city, serving traditional Andalusian cuisine in the dining room and at the bar, where there is a range of tapas. The excellent local hams feature prominently, as does seafood and shellfish. There are no culinary surprises, just well-cooked food made with fresh regional products. Staff are cheerful. Closed Sun.

ISLA CRISTINA Casa Rufino   *Tapas* 📋🏠🍴   €€

Av de la Playa, 21410 (Huelva) **Tel** *959 33 08 10*

A popular beachside place whose *el tonteo* (for four) menu comprises eight different fish in eight different sauces, including angler fish in raisin sauce. It has a well-deserved reputation for outstandingly fresh seafood and shellfish, and excellent wines including all the classics. Closed 22 Dec–2 Feb & evenings except Jul–Oct & Easter.

JABUGO Mesón 5 Jotas   *Tapas* 📋🅰️🏠   €€

Ctra San Juan del Puerto s/n, 21290 (Huelva) **Tel** *959 12 10 71*

Fine Jabugo hams are made here and the adjoining bar-restaurant is a good place to sample them. This is the original and best of a Spanish chain of tapas bars, which have mushroomed across the country. Besides ham and sausage dishes, you can also try the fresh Iberian pork dishes, such as *presa de paletilla al mesón*.

JAÉN Casa Antonio   📋🅰️🍴   €€€

C/ Fermín Palma 3, 23008 (Jaén) **Tel** *953 270 262*

An elegant restaurant with bold contemporary art and blonde wood panelling serving excellent contemporary Andalusian cuisine. Traditional recipes are reinvented with style and creativity: try the *carpaccios* (Huelva prawns or tuna). They have an excellent *menú de degustación*. Closed Sun evenings & Mon.

JAÉN Casa Vicente   *Tapas* 📋🅰️🏠   €€€

C/ Francisco Martín Mora 1, 23002 (Jaén) **Tel** *953 23 22 22*

A classic restaurant with a bullfighting theme in an Andalusian mansion, Vicente serves typical dishes from Jaén. A good *menú de degustación* features local specialities such as lamb stew or artichokes in a delicate sauce. Have an apéritif at the bar, which has just a few simple tapas.

JEREZ DE LA FRONTERA Bar Juanito   *Tapas* 📋🅰️🏠   €€

C/ Pescadería Vieja 8, 11403 (Cádiz) **Tel** *956 33 48 38*

This atmospheric tapas bar and restaurant has a heady reputation for its exceptionally large portions of tapas. A fabulous array is offered, of which the local artichokes remain the star dish. You can also dine more substantially on traditional stews and casseroles and a fine *pescaíto frito* from the Bay. Closed Sun evenings & Mon.

JEREZ DE LA FRONTERA La Mesa Redonda   📋   €€

C/ Manuel de la Quintana 3, 11402 (Cádiz) **Tel** *956 34 00 69*

A charming, family-run restaurant, which remains a favourite with locals for the quality and excellence of its cuisine. The creative menu changes with the seasons offering seafood, meat dishes and game. Try the *mojama* (cured tuna) as a starter, and do not miss the spectacular beef *salteado* (sautéed with black sausage). Closed 15 Jul–16 Aug.

LOJA La Finca   📋🅰️🏠🍴   €€€€

Hotel La Bobadilla, Autovía Granada-Sevilla, 18300 (Granada) **Tel** *958 32 18 61*

Worth a detour off the Autovía, this exceptional restaurant in a luxury hotel is a place for fine dining. The chef makes creative use of farm-fresh vegetables, capon and pork, game (in season) and seafood. Splash out on the wonderful *menú de degustación*, and soak up the romance of the garden terrace. Opens daily for dinner only.

LOS BARRIOS Mesón El Copo   📋🅰️🏠🍴   €€€€

Autovía Cádiz-Málaga km 111 Palmones, 11370 (Cádiz) **Tel** *956 67 77 10*

In the village of Palmones, 9 km (5.6 miles) from Los Barrios, Mesón El Copo is one of the most reliable restaurants on this stretch of coastline. Dine on superb seafood, from fried anchovies to lobster and sea bass. Order a few shellfish dishes to share as a starter, and follow with the *dorada al horno* (bream casserole with potatoes). Closed Sun.

MÁLAGA Antigua Casa de Guardia
Tapas 🗇🗏   €

C/ Alameda 18, 29015 (Málaga) **Tel** *952 21 46 80*

This is Málaga's oldest bar, housed in the fomer guard post which gives it its name. The speciality is sherry, poured straight from one of the vast barrels stacked behind the bar. Accompany it with a few simple tapas – a plate of prawns or mussels, or silvery *boquerones* (anchovies) which bear no resemblance to their salty cousins. Closed Sun.

MÁLAGA Mesón Astorga
Tapas 🗏🗏🗏   €

C/ Gerona 11, 29006 (Málaga) **Tel** *952 34 25 63*

Using Málaga's superb local produce with flair, makes this classically decorated and typically Andalusian restaurant popular. Try the fried aubergine (eggplant) drizzled with molasses or the salad of fresh tuna with sherry vinegar dressing. At the lively tapas bar, you can join the locals tucking into generous *raciones*. Closed Sun.

MÁLAGA Café de Paris
🗏🗏🗏🗏   €€€€

C/ Vélez Málaga 8, 29016 (Málaga) **Tel** *952 22 50 43*

An unprepossessing exterior conceals this elegant, classically decorated restaurant, which serves sublime, contemporary Spanish and Mediterranean cuisine. Creative dishes are exquisitely presented, particularly in the exceptional *menú de degustación*. Excellent wine list and immaculate service. Closed Sun.

MANILVA Macues
🗏🗏🗏   €€

Puerto Deportivo de la Duquesa Local 13, 26961 (Málaga) **Tel** *952 89 03 95*

At this upmarket restaurant at the very tip of the Costa del Sol, you can dine on good international and Spanish cuisine on a shaded terrace, overlooking the sea of masts in the impressive yacht harbour below. House specialities include all kinds of fish baked in salt and juicy local meat grilled over charcoal. Opens for dinner only. Closed Mon.

MARBELLA Altamirano
🗏🗏   €

Plaza Altamirano 3, 29600 (Málaga) **Tel** *952 82 49 32*

In the heart of Marbella's lovely, whitewashed old town, this is a welcoming, family-run restaurant with a pretty terrace. Tasty home-cooked dishes include plenty of local seafood such as a platter of freshly fried fish, typical of the area. Staff are charming. This is one of the best-value options in the old town. Closed Wed & 8 Jan–15 Feb.

MARBELLA El Portalón
Tapas 🗏🗏🗏🗏🗏   €€€€

Ctra Cádiz-Málaga (N340) km 178, 29600 (Málaga) **Tel** *952 86 10 75*

Elegantly decorated dining rooms overlooking flower-filled gardens is the setting of this classic Andalusian restaurant. The highlight here is the meat and seafood cooked in a traditional brick oven, and you can also enjoy tapas and a glass of local wine in the attractive adjoining Vinoteca. Closed Sun except Aug.

MARBELLA La Meridiana
🗏🗏🗏🗏🗏   €€€€

C/ Camino de la Cruz s/n km 3,5, 29600 (Málaga) **Tel** *952 77 61 90*

Situated in Marbella's rarified heights, La Meridiana is a magnificent restaurant with a canopied garden room and an adjoining patio bar. This is creative Mediterranean cuisine at its finest: recommendations include the succulent lamb, the prawns delicately flavoured with curry spices or the wild mushroom ravioli with truffles. Opens daily for dinner only.

MARBELLA Santiago
Tapas 🗏🗏🗏🗏   €€€€

C/ Paseo Marítimo 5, 29600 (Málaga) **Tel** *952 77 00 78*

This is probably the best place for seafood on the Costa del Sol. On any day, there might be 40 or 50 fish and shellfish dishes, all very fresh. Famous for more than 50 years, it's essential to book your table well in advance. Tapas are served at the bar, but there is a huge variety (more than 500) on offer at the adjoining Tabernita de Santiago.

MARBELLA Toni Dalli
🗏🗏🎵🗏🗏   €€€€

El Oasis, Ctra de Cádiz km 176, 29600 (Málaga) **Tel** *952 77 00 35*

This handsome white palace flanked by palms makes for a great night out. It has been a classic on Marbella's Golden Mile since 1981. The Italian-influenced food includes home-made pastas, meat and fish. Live music is sometimes provided by Tony – formerly a popular singer with his own show in California – himself. Opens for dinner only.

MIJAS El Castillo
🗏🗏🗏   €

Plaza de la Constitución, Pasaje de los Pescadores 2, 29650 (Málaga) **Tel** *952 48 53 48*

This rustic-style restaurant is right on the main square of the enchanting white village. It serves both typically Andalusian and international dishes, which you can enjoy out on the breezy terrace. There is a flamenco show on certain nights of the week (usually Tuesdays, Thursdays and Sundays, but call to confirm). Closed Fri.

MOTRIL Tropical
🗏   €€

Av Rodríguez Acosta 23, 18600 (Granada) **Tel** *958 60 04 50*

A simple hostal with a good restaurant, serving a wide choice of typical Andalusian dishes in a classic Spanish seaside setting. Both seafood, such as bass with *ajo verde* (green garlic), and meat, such as *choto a la brasa* (roast baby kid) are specialities. For dessert try the sorbet made with *chirimoya* (custard apple). Closed Sun & Jun.

OSUNA Casa del Marqués
🗏🗏🗏🗏   €€

C/ San Pedro 20, 41640 (Sevilla) **Tel** *954 81 22 23*

A luxurious hotel in the heart of historic Osuna, Casa del Marqués is located in a flamboyant Baroque mansion set in gardens. The restaurant offers superb, highly creative Andalusian cuisine which reinvents traditional recipes. The scallops sautéed with tiny broad beans and ham and the cod fillet cooked with baby squid are signature dishes.

Key to Price Guide *see p608* **Key to Symbols** *see back cover flap*

PALMA DEL RÍO El Refectorio (Hospedería de San Francisco)

Av Pío XII 35, 14700 (Córdoba) **Tel** *957 71 01 83*

Dine in the 15th-century refectory of this out-of-the-way former monastery, now an elegant hotel. The restaurant has an ever-changing menu which features Andalusian cuisine, with lots of typically Córdoban dishes. In autumn and winter, game features prominently, and in summer dinner is served on an enchanting candle-lit patio.

PALOS DE LA FRONTERA El Bodegón
Tapas

C/ Rábida 46, 21810 (Huelva) **Tel** *959 531 105*

An atmospheric former wine cellar now houses this cosy, informal restaurant, where the menu features local culinary stalwarts such as fish baked in a salt crust and meat grilled traditionally over holm oak firewood. The menu is short, but care is taken over selecting fresh local ingredients, and the result is always delicious. Closed Tue & 16–30 Sep.

RONDA Del Escudero

Paseo de Blás Infante 1, 29400 (Málaga) **Tel** *952 87 13 67*

With an incomparable garden setting near Ronda's famous bullring, this elegant restaurant offers spectacular views over the valley to go with its traditional Andalusian cuisine. Go for the good-value fixed-price lunch menu which you can enjoy on the panoramic garden terrace. Closed Sun evenings.

RONDA Pedro Romero

C/ Virgen de la Paz 18, 29400 (Málaga) **Tel** *952 87 11 10*

Facing Ronda's graceful bullring, this restaurant is filled with paintings and photographs of famous *toreros*, historic costumes and mounted bulls' heads. It serves well-prepared country food, including (of course) braised bull's tail, as well as rabbit with thyme and traditional stews and casseroles. There is a good range of Spanish wines.

RONDA Tragabuches

C/ José Aparicio 1, 29400 (Málaga) **Tel** *952 19 02 91*

A stylish fusion of contemporary and traditional, the dining room at this fabulous restaurant has red-brick walls and chunky industrial-chic fittings. The Andalusian cuisine is simply superb, and the *menú de degustación* (70 euros) allows diners to appreciate the chef's skillful handling of textures and flavours. Closed Sun evenings & Mon.

SAN FERNANDO Venta de Vargas
Tapas

Plaza de San Juan Vargas s/n, 11100 (Cádiz) **Tel** *956 88 16 22*

This popular small-town eatery has lots of flamenco atmosphere, and was immortalized by the mythical Camarón de la Isla. Order *raciones* of classics such as *aliñadas* (potato salad), or tuck into typical local stews and fresh fish from the bay. Finish up with creamy *tocino de cielo* ("heavenly bacon") for dessert. Closed Mon.

SAN ROQUE Villa Victoria (Los Remos Rest)

Ctra San Roque-La Línea 351 km 2.8, Campamento, 11314 (Cádiz) **Tel** *956 69 84 12*

Housed in a restored Victorian mansion with Mediterranean decor, this restaurant serves exquisite dishes. The focus is on first-rate seafood and a *menú de degustación* includes shrimp fritters and sea nettles. There is always a good list of seasonal specialities, including wild mushrooms. Closed Sun evenings & Mon.

SANLÚCAR DE BARRAMEDA Casa Bigote
Tapas

C/ Bajo de Guía 10, 11540 (Cádiz) **Tel** *956 36 26 96*

At the mouth of the Río Guadalquivir, this typical sailor's tavern is legendary throughout Andalusia. The tapas bar, hung with hams and lit up with wooden barrels, offers fabulous seafood tapas, or you can dine in the wooden-beamed *comedor* on *langostinos de Sanlúcar* (large, sweet striped prawns) and fresh fish. Closed Sun & Nov.

SANLÚCAR LA MAYOR La Alquería
Tapas

Hacienda de Benazuza, C/ Virgen de las Nieves s/n, 41800 (Sevilla) **Tel** *955 70 33 44*

A luxurious hotel (part of the El Bullí empire) with a spectacular restaurant, where the cuisine is modelled on the culinary fireworks of celebrity chef, Ferran Adriá. Expect the unexpected and prepare to be dazzled: go for the *menú de degustación*, a series of miniature marvels. Closed Sun, Mon; check days for summer & winter.

TARIFA (CÁDIZ) Mesón de Sancho
Tapas

Ctra Cádiz-Málaga km 94, 11380 (Cádiz) **Tel** *956 68 49 00*

A classic inn, just outside Cádiz on the road to Algeciras. Warm and friendly, it is decorated in typical *mesón* style, and offers set menus featuring sturdy Andalusian meats such as beef with mushrooms. It also serves a range of generous *raciones* in the bar. Sancho is a popular spot for family outings, particularly Sunday lunch.

TARIFA (CÁDIZ) Arte-Vida

Ctra Nacional 340 km 79.3, 11380 (Cádiz) **Tel** *956 68 52 46*

This is a fabulous hotel, set in dunes right on Tarifa's endless beach. Its pretty restaurant-café with a stylishly simple blue-and-white decor serves fresh salads, pizzas and grilled seafood, along with a few more exotic dishes such as Thai coconut soup. They also do cakes, delicious brownies and coffee. The views reach all the way to Africa.

TORREMOLINOS Bar Restaurante Casa Juán
Tapas

C/ Mar 14, 29620 (Málaga) **Tel** *952 38 41 06*

A popular beachfront restaurant with an expansive terrace offering home-cooked favourites such as fish baked in salt and *fritura Malagueña*, which are based on old family recipes (provided by Juan's mother and grandmother). It has been going since the tourist boom first transformed this former fishing village.

TORREMOLINOS Frutos   *Tapas* 🍽️🔲🔳🍷   €€€€
Av de la Riviera 80, 29620 (Málaga) **Tel** *952 38 14 50*

The grande dame of Costa del Sol restaurants, serving superb meat and fish. There is a terrace, and two glassy dining areas where you can enjoy suckling pig, followed by *arroz con leche*. The remarkable wine cellar in the basement can be visited. An informal tapas bar at the entrance serves lighter meals. Closed Sun evenings.

ÚBEDA El Seco   *Tapas* 🍽️🔲   €
C/ Corazon de Jesús 8, 23400 (Jaén) **Tel** *953 79 14 52*

A delightful find in the heart of the lovely Renaissance town of Úbeda. A charming, family-run restaurant, with a modest, but spick and span dining room, El Seco serves fresh and tasty home cooking, including delicious croquettes, game in season and country soups and stews. Opens daily for lunch and also for dinner on Fri & Sat. Closed July.

VÉJER DE LA FRONTERA Venta Pinto   *Tapas* 🍽️🔲🔳🍷   €€€
La Barca de Véjer s/n, 11150 (Cádiz) **Tel** *956 45 08 77*

Véjer de la Frontera is a magical, hill-top town on the Costa de la Luz with a shadowy maze of narrow alleys which evoke its Moorish past. This pretty restaurant, in a former staging post 3 km (1.8 miles) from the town centre, serves creative versions of local dishes, and has a popular tapas bar where you can also buy local specialities.

VERA Terraza Carmona   *Tapas* 🍽️🔲🔳🍷   €€
C/ Manuel Giménez 1, 04620 (Almería) **Tel** *950 39 07 60*

A simple roadside hotel, with a fine restaurant which has won several local awards. The specialities here are excellent seafood, and unusual regional dishes such as *gurullos con conejo* (pasta with rabbit). In season, game dishes feature prominently, including wild boar with olives and almonds. Houses a pretty tapas bar. Closed Mon & 8–21 Jan.

ZAHARA DE LOS ATUNES Casa Juanito   *Tapas* 🍽️🔳🍷   €€
C/ Alcalde Ruiz Cana 7, 11393 (Cádiz) **Tel** *956 43 92 11*

In a pretty fishing village and low-key seaside resort, this is a charming, typically Andalusian restaurant with an airy, expansive terrace just steps from the beach. Seafood is the house speciality, particularly the tuna which gives the town its name. It also has a dining area with tapas bar. Closed Wed (except Aug), Nov, Dec & Jan.

THE BALEARIC ISLANDS

FORMENTERA Restaurante Pascual   🍽️🔲🔳🍷   €€
C/ Es Caló, 07872 (Formentera) **Tel** *971 32 70 14*

A friendly, family-run restaurant in the pretty little bay of Es Caló, this is one of the most popular seafood restaurants on Formentera. Tucked behind a grove of pines only steps from the beach, it is enjoyably chaotic and informal, but the seafood dishes, particularly the stews and rice are exceptionally good. Closed Oct–Apr.

FORMENTERA Juan y Andrea   🍽️🔳🍷   €€€€
Playa de Illetas s/n, 07860 (Formentera) **Tel** *971 18 71 30*

Dine on beautifully fresh fish and shellfish, including lobster, caught by the restaurant's own fishing boat, in this wonderful beach restaurant. It overlooks the Playa de Illetas, one of the wildest and most beautiful beaches in the Mediterranean. Local rice dishes are a speciality here. Opens daily 1–8pm & closed 15 Oct–1 Apr.

FORMENTERA, ES PUJOLS Sa Palmera   🍽️🔲🔳🍷   €€
Playa Es Pujols, C/Aguadulce 15–31, 07871 (Ibiza) **Tel** *971 32 83 56*

Freshly caught seafood is served at this classic seafront restaurant, which specializes in traditionally prepared regional cuisine. Try the mixed fish paella or the *zarzuela de mariscos* (shellfish casserole), although you will also find a few meat dishes on the menu. You can eat out on the breezy terrace and enjoy great sea views. Closed Nov–Apr.

IBIZA (EIVISSA), SANT ANTONI Sa Capella   🍽️🔲🔳   €€
Ctra de Cala Salada km 1, 07820 (Ibiza) **Tel** *971 34 00 57*

Exquisitely housed in a former chapel, this elegant restaurant offers a wide range of fresh Mediterranean cuisine. There are lots of good fish dishes, including grilled sea bream, sea bass baked in a salt crust as well as juicy steaks cooked over charcoal. For dessert, try the delicious *tarte tatín*. Opens for dinner only from Easter to Oct.

IBIZA (EIVISSA), SANT JOSEP Ca Na Joana   🍽️🔳🍷   €€€
Ctra Ibiza-Sant Josep km 10, 07380 (Ibiza) **Tel** *971 80 01 58*

One of the island's most interesting gastronomic offers, this is housed in an ancient farmhouse set in beautiful countryside. The seasonal menu, with Catalan and Mediterranean influences, includes dishes such as potatoes served with truffles or a sea urchin sauce. The dining room offers lovely garden views. Closed Nov–15 Jan; check timings.

IBIZA (EIVISSA), SANTA GERTRUDIS Ca'n Pau   🍽️🔲🔳🍷   €€€€
Ctra de Sant Miquel km 2.9, 07814 (Ibiza) **Tel** *971 19 70 07*

A beautifully restored Ibizan *masia* surrounded by gardens, Ca'n Pau serves fine Catalan and Mediterranean cuisine. The house specialitiy is *bacalao* prepared in several different ways, but tender roast kid, quail with cabbage and rabbit are also on the menu. A good selection of Catalan wines and *cavas*. Closed 1 Jan–10 Feb; check timings.

Key to Price Guide *see p608* **Key to Symbols** *see back cover flap*

IBIZA, CALA BENIRRÀS Roca y Mar 　　　　　　　　　　　🍽️🚬　　€

Cala Benirràs, 07815 (Ibiza) **Tel** *971 33 35 32*

This restaurant is located on one of Ibiza's loveliest coves, with a small curving beach of golden sand. You can watch sunsets from the palm-shaded terrace, where simple snacks and more substantial Mediterranean cuisine, often featuring local seafood, is offered. The beach is hidden between Sant Miquel and Sant Joan. Closed Nov–mid-Apr.

IBIZA, IBIZA TOWN La Masía d'en Sort 　　　　　　　　🍽️♿🚬　€€€

Ctra San Miguel km 1, 07814 (Ibiza) **Tel** *971 31 02 28*

A sturdy Ibizan *masía* set in orange groves is home to this elegant restaurant, with stylish dining rooms which double as art galleries for local artists. The food is no less artistic, and features dynamic reinventions of classic Balearic cuisine prepared with fresh local ingredients. Try the refreshing *langoustine* salad. Closed Sun evenings.

IBIZA, IBIZA TOWN La Oliva 　　　　　　　　　　　　🍽️🚬　€€€

C/ Santa Cruz 2–4, 07800 (Ibiza) **Tel** *971 30 57 52*

An intimate restaurant tucked away in Ibiza town's labyrinthine old quarter, serving Mediterranean, French and Balearic cuisine. Try the sea bream baked in a salt crust, a flaky pie filled with goat's cheese, and finish up with the creamy chocolate Charlotte for dessert. Opens only for dinner. Closed 15 Oct to Easter.

IBIZA, SAN RAFEL DE FORCA Clodenis 　　　　　　　🍽️🚬🍷　€€€

Plaza de la Iglesia s/n, 07816 (Ibiza) **Tel** *971 19 85 45*

A lovely country house, surrounded by shady gardens, Clodenis serves elegant Provençal and Mediterranean cuisine and offers lots of vegetarian specialities. Dine out on the romantic terrace under tendrils of trailing greenery, on tender marinated chicken or a fragrant au gratin of local vegetables. Closed Sun in winter & Nov.

IBIZA, SANT GERTRUDIS DE FRUITERA Ama Lur 　🍽️🚬🍷　€€€€

Ctra San Miguel km 2.3, 07815 (Ibiza) **Tel** *971 31 45 54*

One of the best restaurants on the island, it is housed in a villa with Mediterranean decor. The menu features refined Basque cuisine, with the emphasis on fresh seafood, although Balearic meat dishes appear too. Try the sea bream with almonds and pistachios or local spring lamb with honey. Opens only for dinner. Closed Wed except Jul & Aug.

MALLORCA, ALCÚDIA Mesón Los Patos 　　　　　🍽️♿🚬🍷　€

C/ Camí Can Blau 42, 07400 (Mallorca) **Tel** *971 89 02 65*

An agreeably decorated family restaurant with a garden and children's playground, close to the Parque Natural de la Albufera. It offers simple and traditional Mallorcan dishes, including *arroz brut* (a soupy rice served with meat), or roast shoulder of lamb. There is a good-value lunch menu. Closed Tue & 7 Jan–1 Mar.

MALLORCA, CALA RATJADA Ses Rotges 　　　　　　🍽️🚬　€€€€

C/ Rafael Blanes 21, 07590 (Mallorca) **Tel** *971 56 31 08*

An enchanting family-run rural hotel, this lovely stone mansion is an ideal setting for dining on Mediterranean cuisine prepared with prime local produce. They offer a range of fixed-price menus, including a Medieval Menu which features ancient Balearic recipes. Booking essential. Opens Mon, Wed, Fri & Sat evenings only. Closed 15 Oct–Easter.

MALLORCA, DEIÀ Ca'n Costa 　　　　　　　　　　🍽️♿🚬🍷　€€

Ctra Valldemossa-Deià km 2.5, 07170 (Mallorca) **Tel** *971 61 22 63*

An attractive, rural restaurant located in a prettily restored olive oil mill, Ca'n Coasta serves honest Mallorcan cuisine at reasonable prices. Traditional *sopas Mallorquinas* (thick broths) and barbecued meats are the specialities here. You can also enjoy glorious mountain views from the terrace, and there is a playground for kids. Closed Tue in winters.

MALLORCA, DEIÀ El Olivo 　　　　　　　　🍽️♿🚬🛏️🍷　€€€€

Hotel la Residencia, Finca Son Canals, 08179 (Mallorca) **Tel** *971 63 93 92*

A magnificent hotel set in a fine 16th-century mansion houses this excellent restaurant, where you can dine on cool stone patios with breathtaking views of the mountains and sea. The delicious *nouvelle cuisine* incorporates Mediterranean influences, with dishes such as lamb baked with mustard croustade. Excellent wine list.

MALLORCA, DEIÀ / PORT DE SÓLLER Bens d'Avall 　🍽️♿🚬🍷　€€€

Urbanización CostaDeià, Ctra Sóller-Deià s/n, 07100 (Mallorca) **Tel** *971 63 23 81*

This cliff-top restaurant offers wonderful views of the magnificent stretch of coastline, pocketed with turquoise-blue bays. The superb, contemporary cuisine reinvents traditional Mediterranean recipes with style and originality, and uses the finest regional produce. Go for the *menú de degustación*. Closed Sun evenings & Mon.

MALLORCA, INCA Celler Ca'n Amer 　　　　　　　　　🍽️🍷　€

C/ Pau 39, 07300 (Mallorca) **Tel** *971 50 12 61*

This wonderful old wine cellar, lined with battered wine barrels, is now home of one of the island's most authentic regional dishes, *sopes Mallorquinas*, made with bread and braised vegetables. They also have delicious local lamb, prepared with aubergine and *sobrasada* (Mallorcan sausage). Closed Sun evenings & Jun–Oct (Sat–Sun).

MALLORCA, PALMA La Bóveda 　　　　　　*Tapas* 🍽️🚬🍷　€

C/ Botería 3, 07012 (Mallorca) **Tel** *971 71 48 63*

The most popular and characterful tapas bar in Palma, this has lazy paddle fans, multi-coloured tiles and huge wooden barrels. The menu ranges from simple *pa amb olí*, country bread rubbed with garlic and tomato and drizzled with olive oil, to fresh seafood like the *bacalao al pil pil* (cod in a Basque sauce) and succulent grilled prawns. Closed Sun.

MALLORCA, PALMA DE MALLORCA Ca'n Carlos 🍴🍷 €€
*C/ del Agua 5, 07011 (Mallorca) **Tel** 971 71 38 69*

Old Balearic recipes have been revived, providing diners with an authentic version of the island's food, with a new touch of creativity from the original owner's son. This is a much-loved local favourite, and bookings are essential. The oven-roasted suckling lamb and the hake with cabbage are particularly good. Great local wines.

MALLORCA, PALMA DE MALLORCA Porto Pí 🍴♿🏧🍴🍷 €€€€
*C/ Garita 25, 07015 (Mallorca) **Tel** 971 40 00 87*

This elegant old house, surrounded by gardens, is an ideal spot to savour creative Mediterranean and international cuisine using first-class ingredients. Try the sea bream cooked in wine or the duck with lime and curry spices. They also offer a range of elaborate dishes using foie gras. Delicious desserts. Closed Sat lunch & Sun.

MALLORCA, PEGUERA La Gran Tortuga 🍴🏧 €€€
*Urb Aldea Cala Fornells I, 07160 (Mallorca) **Tel** 971 68 60 23*

The spellbinding sea views from the terrace stretch all the way to the Magrat islands at this seaside restaurant overlooking a lovely bay. Try home-made foie gras, hake stuffed with salmon in a spinach sauce or lamb, all creatively prepared with fresh local ingredients. The set-price lunch and tasting menus are good value. Closed Dec & Jan.

MALLORCA, PORT D'ANDRATX Layn 🍴♿🏧🍷 €€€
*C/ Almirante Riera Alemany 20, 07157 (Mallorca) **Tel** 971 67 18 55*

This charming seaside villa is home to a delightful, simple restaurant, where the fish arrives straight from local fishing boats. The fabulous views of the sea from the terrace are the perfect accompaniment to the wonderfully fresh fish, but there are also meat specialities including roast suckling pig and beef with cabbage. Closed Mon.

MALLORCA, PORT DE POLLENÇA Stay 🍴♿🏧🍷 €€€
*C/ Muelle Nuevo s/n, 07470 (Mallorca) **Tel** 971 86 40 13*

With tables right on the bay, this popular local restaurant serves tasty regional cuisine with emphasis on fish and seafood. Try the *salsa de eneldo*, filets of white fish grilled with vegetables and served with a dill sauce. They also have a cheap and cheerful snack bar (for sandwiches and burgers), good for families coming off the beaches.

MALLORCA, PORTOCOLOM Celler Sa Sinia 🍴🏧 €€€
*C/ Pescadores 5, 07670 (Mallorca) **Tel** 971 82 43 23*

Exceptional Mallorcan cuisine at modest prices. With a perfect location overlooking the port, it specializes in fresh seafood such as the wonderful salmon and prawn brochettes. It also serves delicious local meats. Try the duck with orange. Desserts include tiramisu made with *ensaimada*, Mallorca's famous pastry. Closed Mon, Nov, Dec & Jan.

MALLORCA, SÓLLER Sa Cova Tapas 🍴♿🏧 €
*Plaça de la Constitució 7, 07100 (Mallorca) **Tel** 971 63 32 22*

On Sóller's main square, shaded by vast plane trees, this is a simple, welcoming restaurant serving honest home cooking. The menu of classic Mallorcan dishes changes every three months, according to what is in season, and they also offer delicious home-made desserts. There is a good fixed-price lunch menu.

MALLORCA, SÓLLER El Guía 🍴🏧🍷 €€
*C/ Castanyer 2, 07100 (Mallorca) **Tel** 971 63 02 27*

A pretty, old-fashioned hotel with a delightful flower-filled garden, El Guía's dining room is a popular local favourite. The charming dining rooms retain some of its original Modernista details, and the good, home-cooked food includes tasty dishes such as locally grown artichokes stuffed with spinach. Reasonably priced. Closed Mon in winters.

MENORCA, CIUTADELLA Café Balear Tapas 🍴♿🏧 €€€
*C/ Plá de Sant Joan 15, 07760 (Menorca) **Tel** 971 38 00 05*

A legendary restaurant right on the port, Café Balear specializes in fish and seafood including *caldera de langosta* (lobster casserole) and *fritada de gambas* (fried prawns). The fish arrives on the restaurant's own boat, and is prepared with the minimum of fuss to better appreciate its freshness. Reservations essential. Closed Sun.

MENORCA, CIUTADELLA Cas Ferrer de Sa Font 🍴♿🏧 €€€
*C/ Portal de Sa Font 16, 07760 (Menorca) **Tel** 971 48 07 84*

A rustically decorated 18th-century mansion set around a patio, Cas Ferrer de Sa Font offers a range of set menus, including a special children's one. The focus is on Menorcan and Mediterranean cuisine, with local ingredients prepared with touches of creativity. Try the stuffed courgettes (zucchinis) with prawns. Closed Sun & Mon lunch.

MENORCA, ES MERCADEL Ca'n Olga 🍴♿🏧🍷 €€
*C/ Pont de na Macarrana, 07740 (Menorca) **Tel** 971 37 54 59*

A pretty country cottage, which doubles as an exhibition space for local artists, is the attractive setting for this charming restaurant. Delicious, sophisticated Menorcan and Mediterranean cuisine is on offer, accompanied by some sturdy local wines. In summer, dine in the garden terrace at the back. Closed Nov–Mar & Tue except Jun–Sep.

MENORCA, ES MIGJORN GRAN 58 S'Engolidor 🍴🏧 €€
*C/ Major 3, 07749 (Menorca) **Tel** 971 37 01 93*

An old country house, now a small rural inn, is home to this restaurant which serves home-cooked Menorcan specialities at very reasonable prices. The menu features refreshing salads and simple but delicious local meat and fish. The garden terrace overlooks the gorge of S'Engolidor which gives the restaurant its name. Closed Nov–Easter.

Key to Price Guide *see p608* **Key to Symbols** *see back cover flap*

MENORCA, FORNELLS Es Cranc 🔳♿ €€€

C/ Escoles 31, 07748 (Menorca) **Tel** 971 37 64 42

Fornells has long been associated with the typically Menorcan dish of lobster *caldereta* (spiny lobster stew), once a poor fishermen's dish and now a pricey delicacy. No other place does it better than this traditional bar-restaurant. It also offers a good-value lunch menu. Closed Wed (except Aug), Dec, Jan & Feb.

MENORCA, MAÓ Cap Roig 🔳♿🔲 €€

Urb Cala Mesquida 14, 07700 (Menorca) **Tel** 971 18 83 83

A classic, informal seafood restaurant right on the beach, which has an imaginative set menu at lunch time and tasty specialities with fresh fish and lobster. The *pescaíto frito* is outstandingly good, and they also do a wonderful version of the *caldereta de langostinos*, Menorca's famous stew of spiny lobsters. Closed Mon.

MENORCA, MAÓ Andaira 🔳🔲♟ €€€

C/ des Forn 61, 07700 (Menorca) **Tel** 971 36 68 17

This beautiful restaurant is perfect for a romantic dinner. The dining room is a stylish fusion of old and new where outstanding Mediterranean cuisine is served: fresh, inventive and exquisitely presented. Try their sea bass stew with red peppers or puff pastry of fried local sausage. Jul–Aug (dinner only); closed Sun (winter).

MENORCA, SANT CLIMENT Es Molí de Foc 🔳♿🎵🔲♟ €€€

C/ Sant Llorenç 65, Sant Climent, 07712 (Menorca) **Tel** 971 15 32 22

A country-house restaurant located in a tiny village a few kilometres southeast of Maó. Delicious creative Menorcan and international cuisine makes excellent use of varied local produce, and includes rice and seafood dishes. There is an attractive garden terrace, where traditional sea shanties are sung in summer. Closed Sun evenings & Mon in winters.

THE CANARY ISLANDS

EL HIERRO, VALVERDE El Mirador de la Peña 🔳🔲♟ €

Ctra General Norte 40, Guarazoca, 38900 **Tel** 922 55 03 00

This house hanging from a rock on the north coast of the island with spectacular views of the Valle del Golfo was designed by celebrated Canarian architect César Manrique. It serves typical El Hierro food such as *ensalada templada de ventresca de bonito* (warm tuna salad) and *mousse de gofio*, made with the typical Guanche cereal. Closed Mon.

EL HIERRO, VALVERDE La Higuera de la Abuela *Tapas* ♿🎵🔲 €€

C/ Tajaniscaba 10, Echedo, 38900 **Tel** 922 55 10 26

A low-lying building with colourful walls and a courtyard planted with cactuses, this restaurant is 10 km (6 miles) to the north of Valverde. It serves no-frills traditional, home-made island cooking, notably *cordero herreño a la herreña* (El Hierro lamb in El Hierro style) and a variety of local fish. Also try bass with mojo sauce. Closed Tue in winters.

FUERTEVENTURA, BETANCURIA Casa Santa María *Tapas* ♿🔲♟ €

Plaza de la Concepcion, 35510 **Tel** 928 87 82 82

Situated on the same square as the 15th-century Iglesia de Santa María (now Fuerteventura's cathedral), this restaurant-cum-museum, in a 16th-century house, is worth a visit. It has its own bodega and a garden. A good place to try the traditional *puchero canario* (Canarian stew) and, for dessert, the *crema Canaria*. Opens daily for lunch only.

FUERTEVENTURA, PUERTO DEL ROSARIO Fabiola 🔲 €€

C/ Caserio de Ampuyenta 43, 35510 **Tel** 928 17 46 05

An old country house, decorated with antiques, and with an atmosphere somewhat evocative of the Belle Epoque. It is run by two Belgian men who offer creative cuisine based on market produce. Try the warm salad of endives with bacon and goat's cheese or the John Dory fillets. For dessert there is cheese cake. Open for lunch only, Mon–Fri.

FUERTEVENTURA, PUERTO DEL ROSARIO La Barca del Pescador 🔳♿🔲♟ €€

Franchi Roca, El Castillo, Caleta de Fuste, 35510 **Tel** 928 16 35 00

Built on two levels and decorated with maritime paraphernalia, this restaurant offers traditional cuisine based mainly on fish and seafood brought directly from Galicia. They do a good salt-crusted sea bass. For starters try the *crema de berros* (watercress soup) and for dessert *tocino de cielo*. Pescador serves classic Spanish wines as well.

GRAN CANARIA, AGÜIMES La Farola 🔳♿ €€

C/ Alcalá Galiano 3, 35260 **Tel** 928 18 04 10

On Arinaga beach, down the coast from the airport, is this restaurant with a sea-inspired decor, which appropriately specializes in fish and seafood. Worth trying, in particular, is the oven-baked salted fish or the *paella* made with fish or shellfish. Desserts are home made, including a pleasing *tarta de turrón*. Open lunchtime only except Fri–Sat.

GRAN CANARIA, ARUCAS Casa Brito 🔳♿♟ €€

Pasaje Teror 17, Ctra Arucas-Teror km 1.3, 35400 **Tel** 928 62 23 23

Meats are the main specialities of this rustic restaurant in Visvice, just outside Arucas, but the fish dishes are just as good. Both are cooked in a wood-fired oven. Start with *potaje de berros* (watercress broth) and finish with the *millefeuille of turrón* (flaky pastry made with almonds and honey). Closed Mon, Tue, Easter week & 1–15 Sep.

GRAN CANARIA, ARUCAS El Mesón de la Montaña   🗐 ♿ 🖼   €€

*C/ Montaña de Arucas, 35400 **Tel** 928 60 08 44*

A spiralling road leads to this restaurant perched on the top of a mountain outside the town of Arucas offering great views of the northern part of the island. It serves a selection of international and Canarian dishes – some of the latter need to be ordered in advance. Good fish and seafood, including cod and prawns. Also has a playground.

GRAN CANARIA, LAS PALMAS Kamakura   ***Tapas*** 🗐   €

*C/ Galileo Galieli 4, 35010 **Tel** 928 22 26 70*

A small Japanese restaurant (seats only 40 people) near the Playa de las Canteras, with Oriental decor. Choose between the sushi bar or one of the tables. The specialities include tempura (lightly battered vegetables and prawns), fish tartar with aromatic herbs and sushimi (a plate of slices of raw fish), all served with an attention to detail.

GRAN CANARIA, LAS PALMAS Amaiur   🗐 ♿ 🖼 🍷   €€

*C/ Perez Galdós 2, 35002 **Tel** 928 37 07 17*

Housed in a 19th-century colonial home in the Barrio de Tirana, this restaurant is run by two brothers who offer traditional Basque cooking with innovations, depending upon the fresh market produce available. Among the tempting items on the menu are foie gras with grape sauce and Armagnac and hake with seafood. Closed Sun & Aug.

GRAN CANARIA, LAS PALMAS La Hacienda   🗐 ♿ 🍷   €€

*Edificio Venegas, Profesor Agustín Millares Carló 9, 35003 **Tel** 928 37 31 97*

The serious approach to food is accentuated by a minimalist decor. It offers creative cuisine of Mediterranean origin. On the menu is duck with ginger and moschatel and cod with fried green tomatoes. Do not miss the souffle *cremoso* made with Tanzanian chocolate. *Menú de degustación* at lunchtime. Closed Sun & Mon–Wed evenings.

GRAN CANARIA, SANTA BRIGIDA Las Grutas de Artiles   ♿ 🖼   €

*Las Meleguinas, Valle de la Angostura, 35300 **Tel** 928 64 05 75*

More a leisure complex built around two natural caves and various outdoor spaces, including terraces and a pool, than a mere restaurant. The food is Canarian, with specialities including *pescado al mojo verde* (fish with a spicy green sauce) and *buñuelos de plátano al vino tinto* (banana dumplings in red wine). Also has pool-side tables.

LA GOMERA, SAN SEBASTIÁN El Palmarejo   €

*Ctra General de Arure, El Palmarejo, Valle del Gran Rey, 38800 **Tel** 922 80 58 68*

A restaurant located at the Mirador, a lookout at 780 m (2,559 ft) above sea level with magnificent views of the Valle del Gran Rey. This is a good place to try traditional Canarian fare such as the black sausage with sweet Canarian tomatoes. The best choice of dessert is *leche asada con miel de palma* (a milk pudding made with palm honey).

LA GOMERA, SAN SEBASTIÁN El Silbo   ***Tapas*** 🖼   €

*Ctra General 102, Hermigua, 38800 **Tel** 922 88 03 04*

This restaurant on the Hermigua beach offers no-frills dining. Instead, it serves simple food and a small selection of mainstream wines. For a typical lunchtime meal, you can start with the *croquetas de pescado* (fish croquettes), followed by *filetes de atun en adobo* (tuna fish in sauce) and finish with bananas covered with the local palm honey.

LA GOMERA, SAN SEBASTIÁN Marqués de Oristano   ***Tapas*** ♿ 🍷   €€

*C/ del Medio 24, 38800 **Tel** 922 87 29 09*

On the second floor of a beautiful old house, this restaurant offers modern Canarian food using traditional products both from the land and the sea. It has a grill and a bar on the ground floor. If you like rabbit, try the *conejo con verduras y plátanos verdes*. For dessert order the *cilindro de chocolate blanco con almendras*. Closed Sun & Mon lunch.

LA PALMA, LOS LLANOS DE ARIDANE El Bernegal   €

*Diaz y Suarez 5, Santo Domingo, Garafia, 38760 **Tel** 922 40 04 85*

This restaurant, sited in an old house with an inner patio on the west coast of the island, serves traditional Canary Islands cuisine and vegetarian dishes, notably *potaje de berros* and, if you like kid, *cabrito palmero*. For dessert there is *delicias con naranja* (a kind of biscuit with orange). Open only at lunchtime. Closed Mon & mid-May–early Jul.

LA PALMA, LOS LLANOS DE ARIDANE La Casona de Argual   ♿ 🖼   €

*Plaza Sotomayor 6, 38760 **Tel** 922 40 18 16*

A restaurant-with-rooms in a noble house built in 1732 with a romantic garden. It serves international cuisine with a creative touch such as the cream of pumpkin soup and the chicken with tropical fruits. Another good bet is a selection of pâtés with home-made delicacies. For dessert try tiramisu. Closed Sun lunch, Thu & 15 May–15 Jun.

LA PALMA, SANTA CRUZ Chipi Chipi   ♿ 🖼 🍷   €

*C/ Velhoco 42, 38700 **Tel** 922 41 10 24*

Around 6 km (4 miles) out of the island capital, this good-value restaurant with a pretty patio adorned with tropical plants, specializes in grilled meats and local dishes such as chickpea soup, roasted cheese with *mojo verde* and kid. Good selection of wines from the island. Private room available. Closed Sun, Wed & Oct–mid-Nov.

LA PALMA, SANTA CRUZ La Ola   ♿ 🖼   €

*Aparthotel Las Olas, Los Cancajos, Breña Baja, 38700 **Tel** 922 41 52 66*

In a small tourist resort 4 km (2.5 miles) down the coast from Santa Cruz, this restaurant has good sea views. It serves international food using fresh market products such as *tosta de anchoas y pimientos* (toasted bread with anchovies and peppers). For dessert try the local *bienmesabe* (an almond sweet) with vanilla ice cream. Closed Sun.

Key to Price Guide *see p608* **Key to Symbols** *see back cover flap*

LANZAROTE, ARRECIFE Castillo de San José *Tapas* 🍽 €

Castillo de San José, Ctra de Puerto Nao, 35340 Tel 928 81 23 21

Puerto Nao's converted fortress was built in 1779 by King Carlos III and restored by the Lanzarote architect César Manrique. It now houses a contemporary art gallery and a restaurant. Enjoy international and regional specialities as you admire the art and views of the harbour. Ironically the castle has always been known locally as the "Hungry Fort".

LANZAROTE, COSTA TEGUISE Mesón La Jordana *Tapas* 🍽🔊🔲🍴 €

Centro Comercial de Lanzarote Bay, Av de los Geranios, 35509 Tel 928 59 03 28

A popular restaurant in one of Costa Teguise's shopping centres, King Hussein of Jordan was once a customer here, where local fare is given a French touch. For starters there are Burgundy snails. Main course includes stewed partridge, braised duck and sole with almonds. Desserts include papaya sorbet and crêpe suzette. Closed Sun & Sep.

LANZAROTE, COSTA TEGUISE Neptuno *Tapas* 🍽🔊🔲🍴 €€

Av del Jabillo, Centro Comercial Neptuno, local 6, 35509 Tel 928 59 03 78

This airy restaurant in a shopping centre serves traditional Canary Islands cooking. The menu is strong on all types of meat but there are also some excellent fresh fish dishes such as *atun adobado al horno* (oven-cooked tuna fish) and *salmón ahumado de Uga* (smoked salmon). Wines and cheeses from the island. Closed Sun and 20 Jun–22 Jul.

LANZAROTE, YAIZA La Era 🍽🔊 €€

C/ El Barranco 3, 35340 Tel 928 83 00 16

La Era occupies one of the few old houses to survive the island's volcanic eruptions of 1730–36. It was built in the 17th century and restored as a restaurant by César Manrique, who created murals for it. Enjoy a salad of octopus and Canary-style potatoes, stew and fish caught fresh at Playa Blanca and cooked to the customer's orders. Closed Mon.

TENERIFE, ADEJE El Patio 🍽🔊🎵🔲🎫🍴 €€€€

Hotel Jardín Tropical, Urbanización San Eugenio, Gran Bretaña s/n, 38670 Tel 922 74 60 00

The restaurant of the luxurious Hotel Jardín Tropical, provides an enchanting setting for a special evening. Imaginative, modern dishes are created using local produce. Try the lobster on a pyramid of fresh pasta or the roasted young pigeon with walnut cream and wild mushroom sauce. Arguably overpriced. Open for dinner only. Reservation recommended.

TENERIFE, EL SAUZAL Casa del Vino La Baranda 🔲🍴 €€

Autopista general del Norte km 21 (Enlace de El Sauzal, La Baranda), 38360 Tel 922 57 25 35

Tenerife's wine industry is explained by this museum in an old house on the northwest coast near Tacoronte. The restaurant serves modern Canary Islands cuisine based on fresh local market produce though, of course, the wine is the centre of focus here. There are sometimes concerts in summer on the central patio. Closed May.

TENERIFE, GRANADILLA DE ABONA Bodeja El Jable 🍽🔊🍴 €€

C/ Bentenjui 9, San Isidro, 38611 Tel 922 39 06 98

A Canary Islands' *casa de comidas* serving both traditional and creative cooking, particularly fish. The menu includes *potaje de berros*, warm fish salad with thyme, roasted cheese with *mojo verde* and bass with tomato vinagrette and lentils.Try the *tarta de millo* for dessert. Only local wines served. Closed Sun, Mon lunch & 1–15 July.

TENERIFE, PUERTO DE LA CRUZ Regulo 🍽🔊 €€

Plaza Perez Zamora 16, 38400 Tel 922 38 45 06

An old house dating from the 18th century, with an agreeable inner patio which attempts to recreate a traditional decor. It is close to the Plaza del Charco in the centre of town. The menu is noted for its locally caught grilled fish and Argentinian roast lamb. Try the fig mousse for dessert. Closed Sun, Mon lunch & Jul.

TENERIFE, SANTA CRUZ El Rincón de Elis 🍽🍴 €

Angel Guimerá 38 (Puerta Canseco), 38003 Tel 922 27 58 93

Creative Lebanese and Mediterranean cuisine is served in El Rincón de Elis, which is run by a French chef from Marseilles, who also adds exotic touches from his travels. The staff are charming and helpful. Reservation recommended. Closed Sun, Mon & Sep.

TENERIFE, SANTA CRUZ El Bacalao de la Cazuela 🍽🍴 €€

C/ General Goded 11, 38006 Tel 922 29 32 49

A union of Basque cuisine, with emphasis on multiple ways of cooking cod, and Canarian ideas. Try the toast served with home-made foie gras and onion marmalade and, instead of fish, order the *cerdo iberico en salsa de vino tinto* (pork in red wine sauce). End with *tarta de queso fresco y mango* (cheesecake with mango). Closed Sun & Sat lunch.

TENERIFE, SANTA CRUZ El Coto de Antonio 🍽🔊🍴 €€€

C/ General Goded 13, 38006 Tel 922 27 21 05

One of Tenerife's most celebrated restaurants where you can expect excellent food and good service but, of course, there is a price to match. A serious place which welcomes business people and VIPs. The black potato salad with salt cod, peppers and olive oil and the bass in a coriander sauce are favourites. Closed Sun evenings & Sep.

TENERIFE, TEGUESTE Mesón El Drago 🔊🔲 €€

Marqués de Celada 2, Urbanización San Gonzalo, El Socorro, 38280 Tel 922 54 30 01

An 18th-century farmhouse provides a rustic setting for creative Canary Islands cooking including watercress soup, stew, fish casserole and *conejo frito con papas arrugadas* (rabbit with Canarian-style potatoes). There is a gourmet tasting menu and a selection of Canarian cheeses. Vegetarian menu available. Reservation only . Closed Mon & Tue.

SHOPPING IN SPAIN

Spain has a thriving shopping culture, with many unique, family-run boutiques as well as a few reliable chain stores and big department stores. Good buys include leather, fashion, wine and ceramics, though these days it is possible to find anything you are looking for, from traditional gifts to designer clothes. Spain has its own rules

A traditional fan

of etiquette when it comes to shopping. In small shops, most merchandise is behind the counter, and the clerk will retrieve whatever you need, making for a time-consuming, but friendly way to shop. It is considered polite to greet the shop owner and fellow shoppers with a "*buenos días*" as you enter, and to call out "*adiós*" as you leave.

Fresh produce in a market in Pollença (Mallorca)

OPENING HOURS

Most shops in Spain, barring some supermarkets or department stores, close at midday. Small shops are open Monday to Saturday (10am–2pm and 5–8pm). Service-related shops such as dry cleaners usually open an hour earlier and close an hour later. Nearly all shops are closed on Sunday and holidays, except during the Christmas season and sales.

PAYMENT METHODS

Cash is still the payment of choice in Spain. Cheques are rarely accepted, and credit cards may not be accepted in small shops or markets. Even in large stores, there may be a minimum purchase required for credit card users.

ATMs are widely available throughout the country, even in small towns, so getting cash should not be a problem.

VAT & VAT EXEMPTION

Value added tax (VAT), known as *IVA* in Spanish, is included in the price of nearly everything in Spain. However, non-EU residents are eligible for a VAT refund. Before leaving a shop, request a VAT refund form, detailing your transactions. If you buy goods worth a total of €90.15 or more, you can get the form stamped at a Spanish customs office. Present the stamped form at a Spanish bank for a same-day refund, or mail it for the refund to be credited to your credit card.

SALES

Spain's twice-annual *rebajas* (sales) are a fantastic opportunity to find good deals on everything from shoes and clothes to linens, electronics and household goods. Some stores offer a reduction of 50% or more.

The first *rebajas* of the year begin on 7 January (the day after Three Kings Day) and last until mid-February.

Summer *rebajas* start in early July and last until early August.

MARKETS

A visit to a Spanish market is a great lesson in local culture. Every town, large or small, has at least one fresh market, where you can buy local produce, Spanish cheeses and sausages and other foods.

Markets in the cities follow regular store opening hours, but in smaller towns, they may only be open in the morning, or on certain days of the week.

Speciality markets for antiques, arts and crafts are popular in Spain, as are the *mercadillos* (flea markets). These are usually open only on Saturday mornings, though the times vary across markets and towns.

The country's most celebrated market is El Rastro *(see p302)*, a massive flea market in Madrid, which has been running for many generations. It is frequented by locals and tourists alike.

Display of hand-painted ceramics in Toledo

Shopping in Barcelona pp186–9; Madrid pp316–9; in Seville pp454–5

REGIONAL PRODUCTS

Spain has a strong artisan heritage, and the best places to buy authentic traditional items are the artisan markets and speciality shops. All over Spain, you'll find great pottery and ceramics. Spain's pottery is sturdy and colourful and each region puts its own spin on the traditional forms. Andalusia, El Bisbal in Catalonia, Paterna and Manises near Valencia and Talavera de la Reina in Castilla-La Mancha are the main centres for ceramic production.

Leather goods are another traditional craft. Reasonably-priced shoes, wallets and accessories are available almost everywhere.

In Toledo, filigree metalwork and swords are sold on almost every street corner. Other sought-after products include guitars, traditional fans, Lladró porcelain figures and Majorica pearls.

FOOD & DRINK

Spain is second only to Italy in wine production, and Spanish wine is rated to be of the best value in Europe. Major wine regions are Penedès (reds, whites and *cava*), Priorat (reds), Rias Baixas (whites), Ribera del Duero (reds), Rioja (reds) and Toro (whites). Sherry from Jerez is another popular Spanish drink.

A gourmet's paradise, Spain is great for food shopping. Olives and olive oil are always a good buy. Prominent olive-growing areas include Andalusia and southern Catalonia. You can also buy Spain's famous *Jamón Ibérico* (Iberian cured ham), or one of the many region-specific sausages such as Catalan *butifarra* and Castillian *morcilla*.

Gourmet chocolate shops are becoming popular now, especially in the cities. Escribà in Barcelona has a good reputation for producing exquisite confectionery.

A Madrid branch of the fashionable Camper shoe store

ONE-STOP SHOPPING

Small family-run shops are quaint, but when you're in a hurry department stores and one-stop shops are more convenient. Spain's most famous department store, El Corte Inglés, is found in every major city in Spain, sometimes with multiple branches. This mega store sells everything from clothes and sports goods, to furniture and food. Other one-stop shops include hypermarkets such as Carrefour (the Walmart of Europe) and Hipercor. American-style malls, called *centros comerciales* in Spain, are gaining popularity and can be found on the outskirts of most large cities.

Basketware, sold in all parts of Spain

FASHION

Spain has a long textile history, so it's no surprise to find good quality clothing here. In large cities such as Madrid and Barcelona, you'll find boutiques of major Spanish labels, including Antonio Miro, Lydia Delgado, Josep Font, Adolfo Dominguez and Loewe. Spanish fashion may not be on par with Paris or Milan yet, but designers here are increasingly gaining a reputation for quality and originality.

For something trendy and a bit easier on the wallet, Spanish-owned chains such as Zara, Mango and Massimo Dutti are great places to shop.

Mallorca is a good place to buy shoes, home to Spain's most famous shoe company, Camper. Along with branded shoes, *Espadrilles* (traditional Spanish rope-soled shoes) are a good informal option.

SIZE CHART

Women's dresses, coats and skirts

European	36	38	40	42	44	46	48
British	10	12	14	16	18	20	22
American	8	10	12	14	16	18	20

Women's shoes

European	36	37	38	39	40	41
British	3	4	5	6	7	8
American	5	6	7	8	9	10

Men's suits

European	44	46	48	50	52	54	56	58 (size)
British	34	36	38	40	42	44	46	48 (inches)
American	34	36	38	40	42	44	46	48 (inches)

Men's shirts (collar size)

European	36	38	39	41	42	43	44	45 (cm)
British	14	15	15½	16	16½	17	17½	18 (inches)
American	14	15	15½	16	16½	17	17½	18 (inches)

Men's shoes

European	39	40	41	42	43	44	45	46
British	6	7	7½	8	9	10	11	12
American	7	7½	8	8½	9½	10½	11	11½

ENTERTAINMENT IN SPAIN

Spain has always been known for its vibrant, colourful culture – wherever you are, there is usually a fiesta going on somewhere nearby, or some impromptu celebration taking place in the street. So while there's usually no need to seek out formal entertainment, those who do want to plan a day or night out will find plenty of choice, ranging from

Traditional singers in Santa Cruz, Seville

raucous cabarets to live flamenco and high-brow cultural events. Although Madrid, Barcelona and, to a lesser extent, Seville have the widest selection of programmes, the other regional capitals are not far behind. The coastal resorts also witness a lot of action in the summer months. Regular annual events in various parts of Spain are detailed on pages 38–9.

Preparing for a dressage display at the equestrian school in Jerez

TRADITIONAL MUSIC AND DANCE

Spain's rich musical heritage is marked by typical regional instruments, musical styles and dance forms. The *txistu*, a small wind instrument is typical to the Basque Country, Galicia and Asturias lilt to the notes of the *gaita* (bagpipes), while Valencia is proud of its countless brass bands.

Andalusia is the home of flamenco, while Aragón's rhythm comes from the hopstep of its folk dance, *jota*. In Catalonia, the famous *sardana* (see p205) is accompanied by a *flabiol* (flute), *tabal* (drum) and *gralla* (a type of oboe).

JAZZ, ROCK AND POP

Television talent shows tend to dominate the Spanish pop industry, but many creative bands fail to get international recognition only because they sing in Spanish. At the cultural crossroads of southern Europe,

the Spanish music scene is also enriched by influences from South America and Africa.

The Benicassim festival in August is fast becoming the preferred live event for those in search of new music. Keep an eye out for show posters as big international jazz artists can surprisingly turn up in small town stadiums and bullrings.

The Spanish music channel RNE 3 broadcasts an eclectic selection of Spanish as well as international music.

FLAMENCO

Flamenco *(see pp424–5)* is a traditional art form that combines song, music and dance. Infused with sensuality and emotion, it originated in Andalusia but is performed all over Spain. It is a highly varied musical form, and acts can range from spontaneous performances in gypsy patios to international spectacles in major concert halls.

However, note that shows are often adapted to tourists'

tastes. To see and hear flamenco that even purists admire, try the smaller venues or catch a performance during an Andalusian fiesta, particularly in the provinces of Seville and Jerez.

Córdoba hosts the National Flamenco Competition in May every third year. The next one will be held in 2007.

CLASSICAL MUSIC, OPERA AND BALLET

Opera, classical music and ballet are performed in all the major cities in imposing concert halls. The best-known venues include the Auditorio Nacional de Música in Madrid *(see p322)*, Palau de la Musica in Valencia *(se p242)*, Teatro de la Maestranza *(see p456)* and Gran Teatre del Liceu *(see p191)* in Barcelona.

For a more unusual concert setting, look out for performances in Spain's spectacular caves such as those found in Nerja *(see p483)* Drac *(see p517)* and the Cuevas de

Palau de la Musica, Valencia

A performance at the beautifully preserved Roman theatre in Mérida, Extremadura

Canelobre near Alicante. Sacred music can still be heard in some of Spain's many functioning monasteries. Monserrat *(see p219)* is famous for its all-boy choir. In Leyre monastery *(see p135)*, the Gregorian plainchant is performed during mass.

THEATRE

Spain has a great repertoire of classical theatre and although most performances are in Spanish, it may be worth going to a show for the venue alone.

Corral de Comedias in Almagro *(see p417)* is a perfectly preserved 17th-century Golden Age theatre. Mérida's stunning Roman theatre *(see pp54–5 and pp428–9)* serves as the splendid backdrop for an annual summer festival of classical theatre.

CINEMA

Spain's thriving film scene has gained international exposure in recent years. The country makes around 100 feature films a year with directors such as Pedro Almodóvar.

Most foreign-language films are dubbed in Spanish, but select cinemas in university cities and areas with a large number of foreign residents show films in their original language. San Sebastián hosts an acclaimed international film festival *(see p127)* in summer and the Sitges Film

Festival which takes place in November and December.

The open-air summer cinemas in some coastal resorts are an experience in themselves, but do remember to carry a mosquito repellant with you.

NIGHTLIFE

Spain's prodigious nightlife starts later than in most other countries, with 11pm considered an early start for most revellers. The idea is to spend the first part of the evening in pubs or *bares de copa*: sparsely decorated drinking dens, usually with loud music blaring. Then move on to the clubs and discos, often located out of town, where the noise will not bother anyone.

You can enjoy a floorshow while dining out at coastal package-holiday resorts such as Lloret del Mar on the Costa Brava, Maspalomas on Gran Canaria, Torremolinos on the Costa del Sol and Benidorm on the Costa Blanca.

SPECTATOR SPORTS

Football is Spain's favourite sport and is centred on the battle between the two top teams, Real Madrid and Barcelona. Other teams with large followings include Real Betis from Seville, Deportivo La Coruña, Valencia and Real Zaragoza. Tennis, basketball and golf are also popular.

BULLFIGHTING

For an authentic spectacle of Spain's most recognized traditional sport *(see pp36–7)*, watch a bullfight in a large arena – Madrid *(see p306)*, Seville *(see p430)*, Valencia, Bilbao and Zaragoza have the best bullrings. All bullfights start in the early evening at around 5pm. Tickets should be bought directly at the venue to avoid the mark up of touts and ticket agencies.

ENTERTAINMENT FOR CHILDREN

Spain's big theme parks are Port Aventura on the Costa Daurada *(see p224)* and Terra Mitica outside Benidorm *(see p260)*. Other amusements suitable for kids include the cowboys of Mini-Hollywood *(see p500)* and the dancing horses of Jerez *(see p466)*.

Rollercoaster ride at Port Aventura on the Costa Daurada

OUTDOOR ACTIVITIES & SPECIALIST HOLIDAYS

Spain is one of Europe's most geographically varied countries, with mountain ranges, woodlands and river deltas suitable for scenic tours and sports holidays. The options are endless and include sailing on the Mediterranean or surfing in the Atlantic, mountain climbing in the Pyrenees or rambling though the plains of Castille, snow skiing in the Sierra Nevada or water skiing off the coast of Mallorca. To focus on just one activity, sign up for a specialist holiday. Weekend or week-long holidays, featuring everything from yoga to horseback riding, are gaining popularity in Spain. Local tourist offices can provide information on outdoor activities.

Golfer preparing to tee off

WALKING AND TREKKING

Spain offers exciting choices for a challenging week-long trek through the Pyrenees, or a gentle walk along the coast. Look out for the wide, well-marked GR (*Grandes Recorridos* meaning long-distance) trails, that criss-cross Spain. Though most people usually choose to walk only a small portion of each GR trail, long-distance trekkers use them to traverse all the way across the country.

Nearly 8 per cent of Spain's total terrain is protected parkland, and the countless natural parks and 13 large national parks are the most popular and attractive hiking options. Some of the best parks for walking include Aragón's Parque Nacional de Ordesa y Monte Perdido, Catalunya's Parque Nacional d'Aigüestortes i Estany de Sant Maurici and Asturias' Parque Nacional de los Picos de Europa. For details about

trails in the parks, contact the **Environment Ministry of Spain**. For information on other trails, contact the **Federación Española de Deportes de Montaña y Escalada**.

AIR SPORTS

The best way to take in Spain's landscape is to view it from above. Options for thrilling aerial views include hot-air ballooning, skydiving, paragliding and hang-gliding. Some of the well-known hot-air balloon companies include **Kon-Tiki**, which flies throughout the Costa Brava and the rest of Catalonia. **Andalucía Balloons** operates in southern Spain. Standard rides cost €120–€300, depending on the trip's length. For details contact the **Real Federación Aeronáutica Española**.

For those who have forever been fascinated by the birds' ability to fly, paragliding and hang-gliding are two excellent options. The Real

Federación Aeronáutica Española can provide information on schools and outfitters across Spain.

When it comes to a real thrill, nothing surpasses skydiving. Reputable companies offering skydiving courses or tandem jumps include **Skydive Lillo** in Madrid and **Skydive Spain** near Seville. Expect a single tandem jump (a jump made while attached to a qualified instructor) to cost between €150 and €200.

WATER SPORTS

Spain is virtually surrounded by water, so it is little surprise that sailing is popular here. The country's most celebrated yacht ports are those of upscale resorts including La Palma de Mallorca and Marbella, whose Puerto Banús is Spain's most luxurious marina. Mooring a private yacht or sailboat in one of these top-notch marinas is expensive and often impossible. A much easier alternative is to rent a sailboat by the day or week, or to sign up for a half- or full-day sailing excursion. Most other seaside towns also have small recreational ports offering sailboats and yacht charters which can be rented by providing a sailing licence. For details, contact the **Real Federación Española de Vela**.

Scuba diving is available up and down the coast of Spain and on nearly all the islands. However, the best places for underwater exploration are around the Canary Islands.

Paragliding above the Vall d'Aran in the eastern Pyrenees

Whitewater rafting in the Spanish Pyrenees

Just off the island of El Hierro are the warm, calm waters of the Mar de las Calmas, which is full of colourful coral and dozens of marine species. In the Mediterranean, head to the Balearic Islands or to the Illes Medes, seven tiny islets off the Costa Brava that are home to some of the most diverse marine life in all the Mediterranean. The local Illes Medes information office, **Estació Nàutica**, will provide detailed information about area outfitters.

Surfing and windsurfing are other popular sports. On mainland Spain the best places for either kind of surfing are the Basque coast (especially towns such as Zarautz and Mundaka) and Tarifa, on the Costa de la Luz. In the Canary islands, try Lanzarote or Fuerteventura for surfing and El Médano (Tenerife) for windsurfing. El

Windsurfing off Fuerteventura in the Canary Islands

Médano's **Surf Center Playa Sur** is a useful place to look for rentals and information.

Sea kayaking is becoming very popular and kayak rental is now available in many Mediterranean resort towns. Since rentals are cheap and little prior experience is necessary, kayaking is a great option for boating novices who might want to spend some time out on the water.

ADVENTURE SPORTS

Since Spain is Europe's second-most mountainous country after Switzerland, mountain climbing is a natural sport here. Head to the Aragon Pyrenees or the Catalan Pyrenees for a wide range of challenging rock faces. Other popular spots include the mountain of Montserrat in Catalonia, the Parque Natural de los Cañones y Sierra de Guara in Aragón, the Sierra Nevada in Andalusia and the Picos de Europa in Asturias. For more information, contact the Federación Española de Deportes de Montaña y Escalada.

If mere mountain climbing doesn't sound interesting enough, go for *barranquismo* (canyoning), a thrilling adventure sport that lets you explore canyons, cliffs and rivers with a combination of hiking, climbing, rappelling and swimming.

The undisputed capital of canyoning is Parque Natural de la Sierra y los Cañones de Guara, a park and natural area in central Aragón that is

home to dozens of "wet" and "dry" canyons. Outfitters such as **Camping Lecina** provide wetsuits and experienced guides – a must for novices – for €40 per person. Most services and lodging are in, or near, the pretty town of Alquezar.

Another fun way to explore rivers is whitewater rafting. Although Spain is not known for its raging rivers, there are a few places where some white water can be found. Head for the rivers: Noguera Pallaresa in Catalunya, the Carasa in Asturias, or the Miño in Galicia. Late spring and early summer are the best times for rafting, since run-off from melted snow ensures a good deal of water and big rapids.

Fly-fishing in the rivers of Castilla y León, famous for their trout

FISHING

Deep-sea fishing excursions are offered all along Spain's coasts. Fishing in the Mediterranean or the Atlantic is unregulated except for marine reserves and some parks. Trout fishing in lakes and streams is possible; some of the best trout rivers are in Asturias, Rioja and Castilla y León. It is challenging to fish in the narrow, tree-lined streams of the Pyrenees.

It is essential to acquire a seasonal or a daily permit specifying if the fishing area is *sin muerte* (catch and release). Bring your own equipment, as only a few companies offer guided trips. For details on fishing sites and regulations, contact **Real Federación Española de Pesca y Casting**.

CYCLING

Road biking and mountain biking are both popular in Spain. Helmets are recommended while cycling, especially on highways where extreme caution should be exercised. Drivers here are not accustomed to sharing the road and accidents on highways are not uncommon. The **Real Federación Española de Ciclismo** will provide useful information as well as advice on how to plan a safe cycling excursion.

Mountain bikers will find plenty of trails to keep them busy pedalling in Spain. Several walking paths are also suitable for mountain biking, which are referred to as "BTT" (Bici Todo Terreno or all-terrain bikes). Throughout Catalunya, Centros BTT are set up to inform bikers about trails and conditions. In other regions, where this service is not available, trail information and maps can be found at tourist offices.

For young or inexperienced cyclers, *vias verdes* (rail trails) are a fantastic option. These flat, long-distance trails follow the paths of discontinued rail lines, ideal for those who want lovely views without making an effort. Many *vias verdes* cut through historic towns, making interesting pit stops along the way. The **Fundación de los Ferrocariles Españoles** has detailed information about routes.

GOLF

Golf is popular throughout Spain, though most courses can be found near the coasts and coastal resort areas. There are too many important golfing areas to highlight just one; the **Real Federación Española de Golf** has detailed information on all the courses. Some of the golf courses offer activities for non-golfers as well. For year-round golf head to the island of Tenerife, where nearly a dozen courses, including the beautifully situated **Golf Las Américas**, are huddled in the southern corner of the island.

SNOW SKIING AND WINTER SPORTS

Spain's mountainous terrain makes it an excellent place for skiing, and resorts here are often cheaper than those in the Alps or other places in Europe. The top ski resorts are the Sierra Nevada in Granada, and the Spanish royal family's favourite skiing spot, Baqueria-Beret, in the Pyrenean Val d'Aran. It is also possible to ski in the Sierra de Guadarrama, just north of Madrid, and in a handful of other high-altitude areas. Details are available through the **Real Federación Española de Deportes de Invierno**.

BIRD-WATCHING

Spain's mild climate attracts a huge variety of fowl year-round. In winter, one can observe birds native to northern Europe; in spring, native Mediterranean species come to nest. There are numerous natural parks working to conserve Spain's diverse bird population. The top bird-watching site is Extremadura's Parque Natural Monfragüe, where big birds of prey can be seen swooping and hunting. Other excellent places to observe birds in their natural habitat are Andalusia's Parque Nacional de Doñana, Guadalquivir Delta and Laguna de Fuente de Piedra, and Delta de l'Ebre in southern Catalonia.

SPAS

Health and wellness spas, or *balnearios*, are nothing new in Spain. As far back as Roman times residents here were enjoying the healthy benefits of mineral-rich waters along the Mediterranean or in the interior. Day spas offering a range of beauty and therepeutic treatments are popular as well, especially in cities and resorts. The **Asociación Nacional de Estaciones Termales** website (National Association of Thermal Resorts) has details on reputable spas throughout the country.

NATURISM

Specially designated nudist, or naturist, beaches are not hard to find in Spain. Contact the **Asociación Naturista de Almeria y Murcia**, or coastal tourist offices for nudist beaches. Alternatively, log on to the official website of Federación Española de Naturismo (www.naturismo.com), which has a comprehensive list.

SPECIALIST HOLIDAYS

A weekend or week-long specialist holiday provides the luxury of practising a favourite hobby, or probably learning a new one.

Food and wine holidays are more popular than ever in Spain with its varied cuisine and excellent wines. A growing number of companies – many of them owned by expat British – have opened in recent years, offering everything from tours of well-known wine regions to the chance to harvest grapes or olives. For upscale, made-to-order tours of wine regions all over Spain, contact the Madrid-based company **Cellar Tours**. For daily cooking classes and an in-depth look at local Spanish cuisines and customs, try a cooking holiday like those offered by the Priorat-based **Catacurian** or the Granada-based **Alhambra Travel**.

The scenic landscapes of Spain are a wonderful inspiration to indulge the artistic temperament. A painting holiday offers the chance to escape to the quiet countryside and paint. Companies including **Andalucian Adventures** offer multi-day holidays for artists of all levels. Holidays include instruction with an experienced painter as well as practising independently. Sculpture or drawing classes are often available too.

Activity-focused holidays are a great option as well. Spain's pleasant weather is particularly favourable for walking, biking, water skiing or horseback riding. The holiday company **On Foot in Spain** offers a variety of walking holidays in northern Spain, while **Mountain Biking España** has cycling holidays for all levels in Andalusia. For water sports enthusiasts, **Xtreme Gene** specializes in water skiing holidays. Those interested in dance can try **Club Dance**, a London-based company offering dancing holidays. **Fantasia Adventure Holidays** specializes in horseback riding holidays in southern Spain.

To relax, a yoga holiday may be ideal. There are some great alternatives for getting away from the stress of daily life, such as **Kaliyoga** that offers yoga instruction in a pristine setting. A healthy menu and ample free time for hiking or meditating add to the general feel-good factor of a yoga holiday.

A specialist holiday is also a great opportunity to learn Spanish. Language holidays are available in many parts of Spain, where the Spanish language can be learnt in the best way possible – by immersing oneself completely in the country's culture. Language holidays provide the chance to observe the Spanish way of life from close quarters, for an extended period of time. The **Instituto Cervantes** has information on schools and classes across Spain.

DIRECTORY

WALKING AND TREKKING

Environment Ministry of Spain
Pl San Juan de la Cruz, Madrid. **Tel** 915 97 60 00.
www.mma.es

Federación Española de Deportes de Montaña y Escalada
C/ Floridablanca 75, Barcelona.
Tel 934 26 42 67.
www.fedme.es

AIR SPORTS

Andalucía Balloons
C/ San Francisco 3, Villamartín, Cadiz.
Tel 952 16 63 58. www. andaluciaballoons.com

Kon-Tiki
Alt Empordà, Girona.
Tel 639 20 64 54.
www.globuskontiki.com

Real Federación Aeronáutica Española
Carretera de la Fortuna, Madrid. **Tel** 915 08 29 50.
www.rfae.org

Skydive Lillo
C/ Antequera 2, Portal 1. Madrid. **Tel** 916 34 57 63.
www.skydivelillo.com

Skydive Spain
Bullullos de la Mitación, Seville. **Tel** 687 72 63 03.
www.skydivespain.com

WATER SPORTS

Estació Nàutica
C/ de la Platja 10–12, L'Estartit. **Tel** 972 75 06 99. www. enestartit.org

Real Federación Española de Vela
C/ Luis de Salazar 9, Madrid. **Tel** 915 10 20 69.
www.rfev.es

Surf Center Playa Sur
El Médano, Tenerife.
Tel 922 176 688.
www.surfcenter.info

ADVENTURE SPORTS

Camping Lecina
Lecina, Sierra de Guara.
Tel 974 318 386.
www.campinglecina.com

FISHING

Real Federación Española de Pesca y Casting
C/ Navas de Tolosa 3, Madrid.
Tel 915 32 83 52.

CYCLING

Fundación de los Ferrocariles Españoles
C/ Santa Isabel 44, Madrid. **Tel** 911 51 10 64.
www.ffe.es.

Real Federación Española de Ciclismo
C/ Ferraz 16, 5º, Madrid.
Tel 915 40 08 41.
www.rfec.es

GOLF

Golf Las Américas
Playa de las Américas, Tenerife.
Tel 922 75 20 05.
www.golf-tenerife.com

Real Federación Española de Golf
C/ Capitán Haya 9, 5º, Madrid. **Tel** 915 55 26 82.
www.golfspain.com

SNOW SKIING AND WINTER SPORTS

Real Federación Española de Deportes de Invierno
C/ Madroños 36, Madrid.
Tel 913 769 930.

SPAS

Asociación Nacional de Estaciones Termales
C/ Rodriguez San Pedro 56, Madrid.
Tel 915 490 300.
www.balnearios.org

NATURISM

Asociación Naturista de Almeria y Murcia
Apartado 301, Almeria.
Tel 950 25 40 44.
www.naturismo.com

SPECIALIST HOLIDAYS

Alhambra Travel
C/ San Luis 23, Upper Albaycin, Granada.
Tel 958 20 15 57.
www.alhambratravel.com

Andalucian Adventures
Washpool, Gloucestershire (UK). **Tel** 1453 834 137.
www.andalucian-adventures.co.uk

Catacurian
C/ Progrés 2, El Masroig, Tarragona. **Tel** 977 82 53 41. www.catacurian.com

Cellar Tours
C/ Infantas 27, 3º derecha, Madrid. **Tel** 915 21 39 39.
www.cellartours.com

Club Dance Holidays
24–32 Stephenson Way, London (UK). **Tel** 00 44 (0) 870 386 6000.
www.danceholidays.co.uk

Fantasia Adventure Holidays
C/ Martin Machuca P7–3A, Barbate, Cadiz.
Tel 956 43 16 09. www. fantasiaadventureholidays. com

Instituto Cervantes
Palacio de la Trinidad, C/ Francisco Silvela 82, Madrid. **Tel** 914 36 76 00.
www.cervantes.es

Kaliyoga
Las Alpujarras, Granada.
Tel 958 78 44 96.
www.kaliyoga.com

Mountain Biking España
La Chicharra 77, Alhaurin El Grande, Málaga.
Tel 952 49 11 37.
www.mountbik-espana.co.uk

On Foot in Spain
Rosalia de Castro 29, Teo, A Coruña.
Tel 981 819 357.

Xtreme Gene
C/ Rosario 5, Almodovar del Rio, Córdoba.
Tel 957 635 437.
www.xtreme-gene.com

SURVIVAL
GUIDE

PRACTICAL INFORMATION

Spain has finally begun to market itself beyond the attractions of its coastline, and now has a solid tourist information infrastructure. There are national tourist offices in every large city, and regional offices in the smaller towns. All offer help with finding accommodation, restaurants and activities in their area. August is Spain's main holiday month.

Old street signs

Many businesses close for the whole month and roads are very busy at the beginning and end of this period. At any time of year, try to find out in advance if your visit coincides with local fiestas, because although these are attractions, they often entail widespread closures. It is a good idea to plan leisurely lunches, as most of Spain stops from 2pm to 5pm.

ERRESERBATUA

BIZKAIKO FORU ALDUNDIA

RESERVADO

DIPUTACION FORAL

DE BIZKAIA

A bilingual Basque/Castilian reserved parking sign

LANGUAGE

The main language of Spain, *Castellano* (Castilian), is spoken by almost everyone. There are three main regional languages: Catalan, spoken in Catalonia, *Gallego* (Galician) in Galicia and *Euskera* (Basque) in the Basque Country. Variants of Catalan are spoken in the Valencia region and also in the Balearic Islands.

People who speak English are often employed in places that deal with tourists.

MANNERS

The Spanish greet and say goodbye to strangers at bus stops and in lifts, shops and other public places. They often talk to people they do not know. Men shake hands when introduced and whenever they meet. Women usually kiss on both cheeks when they meet, and friends and family members may kiss or embrace briefly.

VISAS AND PASSPORTS

Visas are not required for citizens of EU countries, Iceland or Norway.

A list of entry requirements, which is available from Spanish embassies, specifies 35 other countries, including New Zealand, Canada, the USA and Australia, whose nationals do not need to apply for a visa if visiting Spain for less than 90 days. Thereafter they may apply to the *Gobierno Civil* (a local government office) for an extension. You need proof of employment or of sufficient funds to support yourself during a long stay. Visitors from other countries must obtain a visa before travelling.

If you intend to stay for a long time in Spain, you should contact your nearest Spanish embassy several months in advance about your needs.

British visitors should note that a Visitor's Passport is no longer available. A full passport must be obtained.

TAX-FREE GOODS AND CUSTOMS INFORMATION

Non-EU residents can reclaim *IVA* (VAT) on single items worth over 90 euros bought in shops displaying a "Tax-free for Tourists" sign. (Food, drink, tobacco, cars, motorbikes and medicines are exempt.) You pay the full price and ask the sales assistant for a *formulario* (tax exemption form). On leaving Spain, you

ask customs to stamp your *formulario* (this must be within six months of the purchase). You receive the refund by mail or on your credit card account.

Banco Exterior branches at Barcelona, Madrid, Málaga, Mallorca, Oviedo, Santander and Seville airports will give refunds on *formularios* stamped by customs.

TOURIST INFORMATION

All major cities and towns have *oficinas de turismo*. They will provide town plans, lists of hotels and restaurants, information about the locality and details of activities and events for tourists.

There is a **Spanish National Tourist Office** in several large cities abroad.

OPENING HOURS

Most monuments and museums close on Mondays. On other days they generally open from 10am to 2pm, close from 2pm to 5pm, and in some cases, reopen from 5pm to 8pm. Churches may follow these hours or only be opened for services. Admission is charged for most museums and monuments. Public museums are free on Sundays. In smaller towns it is common for churches, castles and other sights to be kept locked. The key, available to visitors on request, will be lodged with a caretaker in a neighbouring house, in the town hall, or perhaps at the local bar.

 OFICINA DE TURISMO

Spanish tourist office sign with distinctive "i" logo

◁ **The old town of Ibiza enclosed by its 16th-century walls, seen from the harbour**

Students enjoy reduced admission fees to many museums and galleries

FACILITIES FOR THE DISABLED

Spain's national association for the disabled, the Confederación Coordinadora Estatal de Minusválidos Físicos de España (COCEMFE), has a tour company, Servi-COCEMFE *(see p557)*, which publishes guides to facilities in Spain and will help plan a holiday to individual requirements.

COCEMFE sign for disabled access

Tourist offices and the social services departments of town halls can provide information on local conditions and facilities. A travel agency, **Viajes 2000**, specializes in holidays for disabled people. RADAR and Holiday Care Service in the UK *(see p557)* offer limited information on facilities for the disabled in Spanish resorts.

SPANISH TIME

In winter, Spain is one hour ahead of Greenwich Mean Time (GMT) and in summer an hour ahead of British Summer Time (BST). The Canary Islands are on GMT in winter and an hour ahead in summer. Spain uses the 24-hour clock, so 1pm = 13:00.
La madrugada is the small hours. *Mañana* (morning) lasts until the late Spanish lunch time at about 2pm and *mediodía* (midday) from about 1–4pm. *La tarde* is the afternoon and *la noche* evening.

STUDENT INFORMATION

Holders of the International Student Identity Card (ISIC) are entitled to benefits, such as discounts on travel and reduced entrance charges to museums and galleries. Information is available from all national student organizations and, in Spain, from the local government-run **Centros de Información Juvenil (CIJ)** in large towns. **Turismo y Viajes Educativos (TIVE)** specializes in student travel.

ELECTRICAL ADAPTORS

Spain's electricity supply is 220 volts, but the 125-volt system still operates in some old buildings. Plugs for both have two round pins. A three-tier standard travel converter enables you to use appliances from abroad on both supplies. Heating appliances should be used only on 220 volts.

CONVERSION CHART

Imperial to metric
1 inch = 2.54 centimetres
1 foot = 30 centimetres
1 mile = 1.6 kilometres
1 ounce = 28 grams
1 pound = 454 grams
1 pint = 0.6 litre
1 gallon = 4.6 litres

Metric to imperial
1 millimetre = 0.04 inch
1 centimetre = 0.4 inch
1 metre = 3 feet 3 inches
1 kilometre = 0.6 mile
1 gram = 0.04 ounce
1 kilogram = 2.2 pounds
1 litre = 1.8 pints

Personal Security and Health

In Spain, as in most European countries, rural areas are generally safe, but certain parts of cities are subject to petty crime. Carry cards and money in a belt and never leave anything visible in your car when you park it.

Taking out medical insurance cover is advisable, but for minor health problems pharmacists are a good source of assistance. Emergency phone numbers vary – the most important ones are on the opposite page. If you lose your documents, contact your consulate or the local police.

Spanish pharmacy sign

IN AN EMERGENCY

Only the *Policía Nacional* operate a nationwide emergency phone number. Call it even if you need some other service and they will assist you in getting help. Telephone directories list local emergency numbers under *Servicios de Urgencia,* and they appear on tourist maps and leaflets.

For emergency medical treatment call the Cruz Roja (Red Cross), look under *Ambulancias* in the phone book, or go to a hospital casualty department *(Urgencias)*.

Sign identifying a Cruz Roja (Red Cross) emergency treatment centre

MEDICAL TREATMENT

All EU nationals are entitled to Spanish social security cover. To claim, you must obtain the European Health Insurance Card from the UK Department of Health or from a post office before you travel. You give this card to anyone who treats you and it comes with a booklet, *Health Advice for Travellers,* which explains

exactly what health care you are entitled to and where and how to claim. You may find you have to pay and reclaim the money later.

Not all treatments are covered by the card and some are costly, so arrange for medical cover before travelling.

If you want private medical care in Spain, ask at a tourist office, or at your embassy or hotel for the name and number of a doctor. If necessary, ask for one who speaks English.

PHARMACIES

Spanish pharmacists have wide responsibilities. They can advise and, in some cases, prescribe without consulting a doctor. In a non-emergency a *farmacéutico* is a good

person to see first. It is easy to find one who speaks English.

The *farmacia* sign is a green illuminated cross. Those open at night in a town are listed in the windows of all the local pharmacies. Do not confuse them with *perfumerías*, which sell toiletries only.

PERSONAL SECURITY

Violent crime is rare in Spain but visitors should avoid walking alone in poorly lit areas. Wear a bag or camera across your body, not on your shoulder. Men occasionally make complimentary remarks *(piropos)* to women in public, particularly in the street. This is an old custom and not intended to be intimidating.

SPANISH POLICE

There are essentially three types of police in Spain. The *Guardia Civil* (National Guard) mainly police rural areas. Their uniform is olive green but there are local and regional variations. They impose fines for traffic offences.

The *Policía Nacional,* who wear a blue uniform, operate in towns with a population of more than 30,000. The *Policía Nacional* have been replaced with a regional force, the *Ertzaintza,* in the Basque country, and with the *Mossos d'Esquadra* in Catalonia. These can be distinguished by their respective red and blue berets.

The *Policía Local,* also called *Policía Municipal* or *Guardia Urbana,* dress in blue. They operate independently in each town and also have a separate branch for city traffic control.

All three services will direct you to the relevant authority in the event of an incident requiring police help.

Guardia Civil   **Policía Nacional**   **Policía Local**

Patrol car of the Policía Nacional, Spain's main urban police force

DIRECTORY

EMERGENCY NUMBERS

Emergency: all services
Tel 112 *(in most important cities).*

Policía
Tel 091 *Nacional (nationwide).*

**Fire Brigade
(Bomberos)**
Tel 080 *(in most major cities).*

**Ambulance:
(Red Cross, Cruz Roja)**
Tel 112 *or* 91 522 22 22. *(This
Madrid number is now the nat-
ional number for the Red Cross.)*

*For other cities' emergency services,
consult the local phone directory.*

Policía Local patrol car, mainly seen in small towns

LEGAL ASSISTANCE

Some insurance policies
cover legal costs, for instance
after an accident. If you are
not covered, telephone your
nearest consulate.

You can also contact the
Colegio de Abogados (lawyers'
association) of the nearest
town or city, which can advise
you where to obtain legal advice or representation locally.

If you need an interpreter,
consult the *Páginas Amarillas
(Yellow Pages)* telephone directory for the region under
Traductores or *Intérpretes.*
Both *Traductores Oficiales*
and *Traductores Jurados* are
qualified to translate legal or
official documents.

Cruz Roja (Red Cross) ambulance

The emergency number on the side of fire engines varies regionally

PERSONAL PROPERTY

Holiday insurance is there
to protect you financially
from the loss or theft of your
property, but it is always best
to take obvious precautions
against loss and theft.

If you have to carry large
sums of money with you, take
traveller's cheques and, if you
have two credit cards, do not
carry them together. Never
leave a bag or handbag un-
attended anywhere and do
not put down a purse or handbag on the tabletop in a café.

The moment you discover a
loss or theft, report it to the
local police station. To claim
insurance you must do this
immediately, as many com-
panies give you 24 hours only.
Ask the police for a *denuncia*

(written statement), which you
need to make a claim. If your
passport was one of the items
stolen, or if you lose it, report
it to your consulate.

PUBLIC CONVENIENCES

Public pay-toilets are rare in
Spain. Department stores are
often good places to try, as
are bars and restaurants
where you are a customer. On
motorways, there are toilets
at service stations. You may
have to ask for a key *(la
llave)*, not only at the service
stations but also in some bars
in country areas. It is best to
bring your own tissues, too.
The term generally used for
toilets in Spain is *los servicios.*

OUTDOOR HAZARDS

Spain is prey every summer
to forest fires fanned by
winds and fuelled by bone-
dry vegetation. Be sensitive to
fire hazards and use car ashtrays. Broken glass can start a
fire so be careful to take your
empty bottles away with you.

The sign *coto de caza* in
woodland areas identifies a
hunting reserve where you
must follow the country codes.
Toro bravo means "fighting
bull" – do not approach. A
camino particular sign indicates a private driveway.

If you are climbing or hill-
walking go properly equipped
and let someone know when
you expect to return.

Banking and Local Currency

You may enter Spain with any amount of money, but if you intend to export more than 6,000 euros, you should declare it. Traveller's cheques may be exchanged at banks, *cajas de cambio* (foreign currency exchanges), some hotels and some shops. Banks generally offer the best exchange rates. The cheapest exchange may be offered on your credit or direct debit card, which you can use in cash dispensers (automated teller machines, ATMs) displaying the appropriate sign.

24-hour cash dispenser

BANKING HOURS

Spanish banks are beginning to extend their opening hours, but expect extended hours only at large central branches in the big cities.

Generally, banks are open from 8am to 2pm during the week. Some open until 1pm on Saturdays. Most close on Saturdays in August; in some areas they also close on Saturdays from May to September.

Bureau de change

CHANGING MONEY

Most banks have a foreign exchange desk with the sign *Cambio* or *Extranjero*. Always take your passport as ID to effect any transaction.

You can draw up to €300 on major credit cards at a bank. If you bank with **Barclays** or **Lloyds TSB**, it is possible to cash a cheque in the usual way at one of their branches in Spain.

Bureaux de change, with the sign *Caja de Cambio* or "Change", invariably charge higher rates of commission than banks, but they are often open after hours. They are commonly found in the tourist areas of Spanish towns and cities.

Cajas de Ahorro (savings banks) also exchange money. They open from 8:30am to 2pm on weekdays and also on Thursday afternoons from 4:30pm to 7:45pm.

CHEQUES AND CARDS

Traveller's cheques can be purchased at **American Express** (AmEx), **Travelex** or your bank. All are accepted in Spain. If you exchange AmEx cheques at an AmEx office, commission is not charged.

Banks require 24 hours' notice to cash cheques larger than €3,000. If you draw more than €600 on traveller's cheques, you may be asked to show the purchase certificate as proof.

The most widely accepted card in Spain is the **VISA** card, although **MasterCard** (Access)/Eurocard and American Express are also useful currency. The major banks will allow cash withdrawals on credit cards. All cash dispensers accept most foreign cards, although the level of commission charged on your withdrawal will depend on your own bank.

When you pay with a card, cashiers will usually pass it through a card reading machine. In shops you will always be asked for additional photo ID. As leaving your passport in the hotel safe is preferable, make sure you have an alternative original document on hand (photocopies will rarely do) such as a driver's license.

As is common throughout Europe, cards are not always accepted in some smaller bars and restaurants. Checking first will avoid unnecessary embarrassment.

CASH DISPENSERS

If your card is linked to your home bank account, you can use it with your PIN to withdraw money from cash dispensers. Nearly all take VISA or Mastercard (Access).

When you enter your PIN, instructions are displayed in English, French, German and Spanish. These days, many dispensers are inside buildings and to gain access you will have to run your card through a door-entry system.

Cards with Cirrus and Maestro logos can also be widely used to withdraw money from cash machines.

DIRECTORY

FOREIGN BANKS

Barclays Bank
Plaza de Colón 1, 28046 Madrid.
Tel 91 336 10 00.

Citibank
C/ Velazquez 31, 28001 Madrid.
Tel 91 426 07 82.

LOST CARDS AND TRAVELLER'S CHEQUES

American Express
Pl de Las Cortes 2, 28014 Madrid.
Tel 902 37 56 37.

Diners Club
Tel 91 701 59 00.

MasterCard
Tel 900 97 12 31 (toll free).

Travelex
Tel 900 94 89 71 (toll free).

VISA
Tel 900 99 11 24 (toll free).

THE EURO

Introduction of the single European currency, the euro, has taken place in 12 of the 25 member states of the EU. Austria, Belgium, Finland, France, Germany, Greece, Ireland, Italy, Luxembourg, The Netherlands, Portugal and Spain chose to join the new currency; the UK, Denmark and Sweden stayed out, with an option to review the decision. The euro was introduced on 1 January 1999, but only for banking purposes. Notes and coins came into circulation on 1 January 2002. After a transition period allowing the use of both national currencies and the euro, Spain's own currency, the peseta, was completely phased out by March 2002. All euro notes and coins can be used anywhere within the participating member states.

Bank Notes

Euro bank notes have seven denominations. The 5-euro note (grey in colour) is the smallest, followed by the 10-euro note (pink), 20-euro note (blue), 50-euro note (orange), 100-euro note (green), 200-euro note (yellow) and 500-euro note (purple). All notes show the 12 stars of the European Union.

5 euros

10 euros

20 euros

50 euros

100 euros

200 euros

500 euros

2 euros

1 euro

50 cents

20 cents

10 cents

Coins

The euro has eight coin denominations: 2 euros and 1 euro (silver and gold); 50 cents, 20 cents and 10 cents (gold); and 5 cents, 2 cents and 1 cent (bronze). The reverse (number) side of euros are the same in all euro-zone countries, but the front is different in each state.

5 cents

2 cents

1 cent

Communications

Telefonica, the Spanish telecommunications company, has improved its service since it was digitized in 1995, and the state monopoly was removed in 1998. Public telephones are easy to find and most operate with a card or coins, but international calls have a high charge.

The postal service, Correos, is identified by a crown insignia in red or white on a yellow background. Registered post and telegrams can be sent from all Correos offices *(see pp672–3)*. They sell stamps as well, but most people buy them from state-run *estancos* (tobacconists). There are no public phones in Correos offices.

Logo of the Spanish telecom system

USING A COIN AND CARD TELEPHONE

1 Lift the receiver, and wait for the dialling tone and for the display to show *Inserte monedas o tarjeta*.

2 Insert either coins *(monedas)*, using the button on the top right if there is one, or a card *(tarjeta)*.

3 Key in the number firmly, but not too fast – Spanish phones require a pause between each digit.

4 As you press the digits, the number you are dialling will appear on the display. You will also be able to see how much money or how many units are left. The display will indicate when you need to deposit more coins.

5 When your call is finished, replace the receiver. The phonecard will then re-emerge automatically or any excess coins will be returned.

Spanish phonecard

TELEPHONING IN SPAIN

As well as public telephone boxes (cabinas), there are nearly always payphones in Spanish bars. Both types take coins. Generally, there will be a high minimum connection charge, especially for international calls, so make sure that you have plenty of change at the ready.

Phonecards are far more convenient and can be bought at newsstands and *estancos*. Some phones are equipped with multilingual electronic instruction displays.

There are public telephone offices called *locutorios* where you can make a call and pay for it afterwards. They are usually quieter than phone booths and you do not need coins. Telefónica run the official ones, which are the cheapest type; private ones, often located in shops, are pricier.

There are four charge bands for international calls: European Union countries; non-European Union countries and Northwest Africa; North and South America; and the rest of the world. With the exception of local calls, using the telephone system can be expensive, especially from a hotel, which may add a

USEFUL SPANISH DIALLING CODES

- Whether you are making a call from within a province or a city, or making a call from one province to another, it is necessary to include the area code. Area codes are listed in the A-K phone book or obtained from directory enquiries.
- To make an international call, dial 00, then dial the country code, the area code and the number.
- Country codes are: UK 44; Eire 353; France 33; USA and Canada 1; Australia 61; New Zealand 64. It may be necessary to omit the initial digit of the destination's area code.

- For operator/directory service, dial 11818.
- For international directories, dial 11825.
- To make a reversed-charge (collect) call within the EU, dial 900 99 00 followed by the country code; to the USA or Canada, dial 900 99 00 followed by 11 or 15 respectively. Numbers for other countries can be found in the front of the A-K telephone directory under *Modalidades del Servicio Internacional*.
- To report technical faults, dial 1002.
- For the speaking clock dial 093, for the weather 094, for a wake-up call 096.

surcharge. A call from a *cabina* or a *locutorio* costs 35 per cent more than one made from a private phone in someone's home. Reversed-charge (collect) calls made to European Union countries may be dialled directly, but most other reversed-charge calls must be made through the operator.

The Spanish dialling code system works on a provincial basis, with each area code prefixed by the number 9. For example, Barcelona is 93. Since 1998, this code always has to be included, even if you are phoning within a city or province.

When calling Spain from abroad, first dial the international code for Spain (34) followed by the area code. So, to call Barcelona, you dial 34 93.

Public payphone booth, easily visible in a city street

TELEVISION AND RADIO

Television Española, Spain's state television company, broadcasts two channels which are called TVE1 and TVE2.

Several of the *comunidades* *(see pp672–3)* have their own publicly owned television channels which broadcast in the language of the region.

There are three national independent television stations: Antena 3, Tele-5 (Telecinco) and Canal+ (Canal Plus). Some Canal+ programmes are only

Spanish daily papers

available on payment of a subscription for a station decoder.

Most foreign films shown on Spanish television (and in cinemas) are dubbed and subtitled films are listed as *V.O. (versión original).*

Several satellite channels, such as CNN, Eurosport and Cinemanía, can be received throughout Spain.

The state radio station, Radio Nacional de España has four stations plus the World Service. News programmes are on R1, classical music on R2, pop music on R3 and news on R5. Local stations also rebroadcast the BBC World Service. They are: Onda Cero Radio in Marbella and Tenerife; Radio Maspalomas in Gran Canaria; and Sunshine Capital Radio in Palma de Mallorca.

NEWSPAPERS AND MAGAZINES

Newsagents and kiosks in town centres often stock periodicals in English. The newspapers available on publication day are the *International Herald Tribune,* the *Financial Times* and the *Guardian International.* Other English-language and European titles are on sale, but usually not until a day after they have been published.

The European newspaper and popular weekly news magazines such as *Time, Newsweek* and *The Economist* are readily available throughout the country. The most

Spanish magazines

Logo of Radio Nacional de España

widely read of the Spanish newspapers, in descending number of sales, are *El País, El Mundo, ABC, La Razon,* and *La Vanguardia* (in Catalonia). *El Mundo* is feature led and aimed at a younger market than the other three, which cover international news in more depth. Weekly listings magazines for arts and events are published in Barcelona *(see p190),* Madrid *(see p320)* and Seville. They are the *Guía del Ocio* in Barcelona and Madrid, and *El Giraldillo* in Seville. Several other cities also have listings magazines.

Local newspapers in Spanish, such as *Levante* in Valencia and *La Gaceta de Canarias* in the Canary Islands, are a useful source of information on local and regional events.

Foreign-language periodicals are published by expatriates in Madrid and in the country's main tourist areas. Examples in English include *Sur* on the Costa del Sol, the *Costa Blanca News* and the *Mallorca Daily Bulletin.* One of the longest-running magazines is *Lookout.* Published in Fuengirola, it features in-depth reports covering all aspects of life in Spain.

A *prensa* (press) sign identifies a newsstand

POSTAL SERVICE

Correos is the name of Spain's postal service. Mail sent to an address in the city where it is posted usually takes a day to arrive. Deliveries

Shops with this sign sell stamps

between cities take between two to three days. Urgent or important post can be sent by *urgente* (express) or *certificado*

(registered) mail. To be sure of fast delivery it is wise to use the Correos Postal Express Service or a private courier.

Post can be registered and telegrams sent from all Correos offices. However, it is much easier to buy stamps for letters and postcards from an *estanco* (tobacconist). Postal rates fall into four price bands: the EU; the rest of Europe; the US; and the rest of the world. Parcels have to be weighed and stamped at Correos offices and must be securely tied with string.

The main Correos offices open 8am– 9pm from Monday to Friday and 9am–7pm on Saturday. Branches in the suburbs and small towns and villages open 9am–2pm from Monday to Friday and 9am–1pm on Saturday.

Spanish postbox

SPAIN'S LOTTERIES

Lottery fever is greater in Spain than in any other European country. The Lotería Nacional runs prize draws most Saturdays, plus a few special ones, the *extraordinarios*, of which the biggest is El Gordo ("the Fat One") at Christmas *(see p43)*. It is common to buy a *décimo* (one-tenth of a number), rather than a full ticket. Punters can also try their luck with the ONCE lottery, which has draws daily, the twice-weekly Lotería Primitiva, and the Bono-loto, with four draws a week.

ONCE lottery booth

LETTERS AND FAXES

Letters posted at a central post office usually arrive more quickly than if posted in a postbox *(buzón)*.

Postboxes in cities are yellow pillar boxes; in towns and villages they are small, wall-mounted postboxes. Poste restante letters should be addressed care of the *Lista de Correos* and the town. You can collect them from main offices. To send and receive money by post ask for a *giro internacional*.

When dealing with businesses in Spain, it is best to phone or fax. The post tends to be used only as a last resort. There are fax facilities in some *locutorios (see p670)* and in hotels and many private shops. Look for a *telefax* sign.

LOCAL GOVERNMENT

Spain is one of Europe's most decentralized states. Many powers have been devolved to the 17 regions, *comunidades autónomas*, which have their own elected parliaments. These regions have varying degrees of independence from Madrid, with the Basques and Catalans enjoying the most autonomy. The *comunidades* provide some services – such as the promotion of tourism – which were once carried out by central government.

The country is subdivided into 50 provinces, each with its *diputación* (council). The affairs of each of the Balearic and Canary islands are run by an island council.

Every town, or group of villages, is administered by an *ayuntamiento* (town council – the word also means town hall) which is supervised by an elected *alcalde* (mayor) and a team of councillors.

Spanish stamps

ADDRESSES

In Spanish addresses the house number follows the name of the street. The floor of a block of flats comes after a hyphen. Therefore 4-2° means a flat on the second floor of number four. All postcodes have five digits, the first two being the province number.

Murcia's town hall *(ayuntamiento or casa consistorial)*

The Provinces of Spain
These are grouped into 17 comunidades autónomas *and 2* ciudades autónomas *(autonomous cities): Ceuta and Melilla in North Africa. A province's number is used as the first two digits of its postcode.*

THE CANARY ISLANDS

THE COMUNIDADES OF SPAIN AND THEIR PROVINCES

NORTHERN SPAIN

Galicia
15 A Coruña
27 Lugo
32 Ourense
36 Pontevedra

Asturias   **Cantabria**
33 Asturias
39 Cantabria

Basque Country   **Navarra**   **La Rioja**
Basque Country (Euskadi)
01 Álava
20 Guipúzcoa
48 Vizcaya
Comunidad Foral de Navarra
31 Navarra
La Rioja
26 La Rioja

EASTERN SPAIN

Catalonia
08 Barcelona
17 Girona
25 Lleida
43 Tarragona

Aragón
22 Huesca
44 Teruel
50 Zaragoza

Valencia   **Murcia**
Comunidad Valenciana
03 Alicante
12 Castellón
46 Valencia
Murcia
30 Murcia

CENTRAL SPAIN

Madrid
28 Comunidad de Madrid

Castilla-La Mancha
02 Albacete
13 Ciudad Real
16 Cuenca
19 Guadalajara
45 Toledo

Extremadura
06 Badajoz
10 Cáceres

Castilla y León
05 Ávila
09 Burgos
24 León
34 Palencia
37 Salamanca
40 Segovia
42 Soria
47 Valladolid
49 Zamora

SOUTHERN SPAIN

Andalusia
04 Almería
11 Cádiz
14 Córdoba
18 Granada
21 Huelva
23 Jaén
29 Málaga
41 Sevilla

SPAIN'S ISLANDS

The Balearic Islands (Islas Baleares)
07 Baleares

The Canary Islands (Islas Canarias)
35 Las Palmas
38 Santa Cruz de Tenerife

TRAVEL INFORMATION

Spain has an increasingly efficient transport system. All the major cities have airports and flights from all over the globe arrive at those of Madrid and Barcelona. Both the road and rail networks were greatly improved during the 1980s and in the run-up to Expo and the Olympics in 1992 *(see p69)*. Intercity rail services are efficient, but coaches are a faster and more frequent option between smaller towns. In much of rural Spain, however, public transport is limited and a car is the most practical solution for getting about. Ferries connect mainland Spain with the UK, North Africa and the Balearic and Canary islands.

→ aeropuerto

Sign for an airport

Shopping at Barcelona's El Prat airport

ARRIVING BY AIR

Spain is served by most international airlines. **Iberia**, the national airline, has scheduled flights daily into Madrid and Barcelona from all west European capitals, and once or twice weekly from most east European capitals.

British Airways offers scheduled flights to Madrid and Barcelona daily from London Heathrow and London Gatwick; and Madrid from Manchester, and Barcelona from Birmingham. Three budget airlines, **Easyjet**, **Bmibaby** and **Ryanair**, fly to mainland and island Spain from regional airports throughout the UK.

Of the US airlines serving Spain, **Delta Airlines** flies to both Madrid and Barcelona, **American Airlines** flies to Madrid. Iberia has a comprehensive service from the USA, as well as direct flights to many destinations in Spain from Toronto and Montreal.

BARAJAS AIRPORT, MADRID

Madrid's airport is 13 km (8 miles) from the city centre. The international terminal is Terminal 1. Iberia flights to the EU countries of Germany, Austria, Belgium, France, Holland, Italy, Luxembourg and Portugal use Terminal 2. Domestic flights are served from Terminals 2 and 3. It takes only 12 minutes by metro to reach the central station of Nuevos Ministerios, where numerous airlines have set up check-in facilites. Taxis are also available and a shuttle bus runs every 10 minutes to the city centre.

TERMINAL ONE   **TERMINAL TWO**   **TERMINAL THREE**

Second floor

To further gates

Meeting point

First aid

To parking

First floor

Ground floor

KEY

- Departures
- Arrivals
- Check-in
- Passport control/Customs
- Public access
- Ticket sales
- No public access
- Restricted access

INTERNATIONAL AIRPORTS

The most regular international services operate from Madrid and Barcelona. The busiest international airports for scheduled and charter flights in Spain are marked on the map on pages 14–15.

Palma de Mallorca, Tenerife Sur, Las Palmas de Gran Canaria, Málaga, Lanzarote, Ibiza, Alicante, Fuerteventura and Menorca handle large amounts of holiday traffic. The first four are especially busy – Palma topped 19 million passengers in 2001. Most is seasonal traffic, mainly from north European countries, and at peak summer holiday time these airports can get crowded. Details of public transport to and from Spain's most important airports are given on page 676.

All the Balearic and Canary islands have international air ports, except Hierro and La Gomera which have domestic

Iberia plane on the tarmac of Seville airport

ones. Melilla and Ceuta are also served by domestic flights only.

AIR FARES

Air fares for flights to Spain vary through the year, depending on demand. They are generally highest during the summer months. Special deals, particularly for weekend city breaks, are often offered in the winter and may include a number of nights at a hotel. Look out for Iberia's reduced

air fares, and for **Easyjet**, **Bmibaby** and **Ryanair** for competitive deals. Christmas and Easter flights are often booked up well in advance.

Charter flights from the UK serve airports such as Alicante, Málaga and Girona near beach resorts. These can be very cheap, but less reliable, and often fly at unsociable hours. Make sure your agent is ABTA bonded before booking. Local car hire companies may offer good deals at resort airports, but read rental terms carefully.

EL PRAT AIRPORT, BARCELONA

Barcelona's airport is 12 km (7 miles) from the city centre. Terminal A handles international arrivals and foreign airlines' departures. Terminals B and C are for departures on Spanish airlines and arrivals from European Union countries. Trains to the Plaça de Catalunya in the city centre leave every 30 minutes. For intercity rail services get off at Sants mainline station. There is also a shuttle bus, the Aerobús, running every 15 minutes, which will also leave you in Plaça de Catalunya.

FIRST FLOOR — Terminal C

Terminal B

Terminal A

GROUND FLOOR

Bank

Car hire

KEY

- ☐ Departures
- ☐ Arrivals
- ☐ Public access
- ☐ Check-in
- ☐ Customs
- ☐ Passport control
- ☐ Passengers only
- ☐ Restricted access

Bank

Car hire

Meeting point

Bank

Car hire

Bank

Insignia of Spain's national airline

DOMESTIC FLIGHTS

Most of Spain's domestic flights have traditionally been operated by **Iberia**. In recent years, however, this monopoly has been broken to encourage competition. The two main alternative carriers are **Air Europa** and **Spanair**.

The most frequent shuttle service is the Puente Aéreo, run between Barcelona and Madrid by Iberia. It flies every 15 minutes at peak business times, hourly at other times. A self-ticketing machine allows passengers to buy tickets up to 15 minutes before a flight departs. When a flight is full, waiting passengers are always offered a seat on the next available shuttle. The flight usually takes 50 minutes.

Air-Nostrum, Air Europa and Spanair services between Madrid and the regional capitals are not as frequent as the Puente Aéreo, but their prices are usually slightly lower. They operate in a similar way to Apex tickets:

the earlier the booking is made, the greater the discount. The cheapest ticket, which must be booked a week in advance, can save up to one-third of the full price. Flights to the provincial cities usually operate in the morning and evening. They can be expensive, costing as much as €120 for a one-way trip. Pressure from the intercity rail services may eventually result in lower air fares.

Self-ticketing machine

Flights to the Balearic and Canary islands, and island-hopping flights between them, are operated by an Iberia-affiliated company: **Binter**. Travel agencies often offer a variety of special deals on internal flights, which may include one night or more in a hotel. It is worth shopping around. These deals are advertised in the Spanish press.

Some flights from domestic airports are billed as international flights but they do not go directly to foreign destinations. Instead, they stop en route at major cities like Madrid or Barcelona.

The departures concourse in Seville Airport

AIRPORT	INFORMATION	DISTANCE TO CITY CENTRE	TAXI FARE TO CITY CENTRE	PUBLIC TRANSPORT TIME TO CITY CENTRE
Alicante	96 691 91 00	10 km (6 miles)	12–14 *euros*	Bus: 20 mins
Barcelona	93 298 38 38	14 km (9 miles)	20 *euros*	Rail: 20 mins Bus: 25 mins
Bilbao	94 486 96 64	12 km (7 miles)	20 *euros*	Bus: 30 mins
Madrid	90 235 35 70	16 km (10 miles)	11 *euros*	Bus: 20 mins Metro: 30–40 mins
Málaga	95 204 88 38	8 km (5 miles)	15 *euros*	Rail: 15 mins Bus: 20 mins
Palma de Mallorca	971 78 90 99	9 km (6 miles)	15–20 *euros*	Bus: 30 mins
Las Palmas de Gran Canaria	928 57 91 30	24 km (14 miles)	24 *euros*	Bus: 60 mins
Santiago de Compostela	981 54 75 01	12 km (7 miles)	15 *euros*	Bus: 20–30 mins
Seville	95 444 90 00	10 km (6 miles)	17–20 *euros*	Bus: 25–30 mins
Tenerife Sur – Reina Sofía	922 75 95 10	64 km (40 miles) to Santa Cruz	50 *euros*	Bus: 60 mins
Valencia	96 159 85 15	9 km (5 miles)	15–20 *euros*	Bus: 60 mins

ARRIVING BY SEA

Ferries connect the Spanish mainland to the Balearic and Canary islands, to North Africa and to the UK. All the important routes are served by car ferries. It is always wise to make an advance booking, especially in summer.

Two routes link Spain with the UK. **Brittany Ferries** sails between Plymouth in the UK and Santander in Cantabria; and **P&O European Ferries** sails from Portsmouth into Santurce harbour, near Bilbao in the Basque Country. The crossings take over 24 hours. Each ship has cabins, chairs to sleep on, a restaurant, cafés and a cinema. Discos are sometimes held on board.

FERRIES TO THE ISLANDS

Frequent crossings run from Barcelona and Valencia to the three main Balearic islands. On **Trasmediterránea** ferries the crossings take from three-and-a-half hours (using the fast ferry from Barcelona) to eight hours. The same company also operates frequent inter-island services; and small operators take day-trippers (passengers only) from Ibiza to Formentera. Storms are rare in summer and crossings are usually calm and comfortable.

Trasmediterránea operates a weekly service from Cádiz in Andalusia to the main ports of the Canary Islands – Las Palmas de Gran Canaria and Santa Cruz de Tenerife.

Ferry in port at Los Cristianos (Tenerife) in the Canary Islands

Crossings normally take 39 hours. Car ferries link the islands with each other. Trasmediterránea also runs passengers-only services between the islands of Gran Canaria, Tenerife and Fuerteventura, and between Tenerife and La Gomera.

The ferries to Spain's islands have cabins, cafés, restaurants, bars, shops, cinemas, pools and sunbathing decks. They are also fitted with lifts and other facilities for people with special needs, and even have kennels. Entertainment is provided on crossings from the mainland to the Canary Islands.

Trasmediterránea Ferries logo

FERRIES TO AFRICA

Trasmediterránea operates ferries daily to the Spanish territories in North Africa: from Málaga and Almería to Melilla, and from Algeciras to Ceuta. Ferries also cross to Tangier in Morocco from Algeciras.

DIRECTORY

AIRLINES

Air Europa
www.aireuropa.com

American Airlines
Tel 1 800 633 3711 in USA.
www.americanair.com

Bmibaby
Tel 902 100 737 in Malaga.
Tel 0870 264 2229 in UK.
www.bmibaby.com

British Airways
Tel 902 111 333 in Spain.
Tel 08708 509 850 in UK.
www.british-airways.com

Delta Air Lines
Tel 91 749 66 30 in Madrid.
Tel 800 241 41 41 in USA.
www.delta.com

Easyjet
Tel 902 29 99 92 in Spain.
Tel 0905 821 0905 in UK.
www.easyjet.com

Iberia
Tel 902 400 500 in Madrid.
Tel 08456 012 854 in UK.
www.iberia.com

Ryanair
Tel 0871 246 0000 in UK.
www.ryanair.com

Spanair
Tel 902 13 14 15 in Spain.
Tel 8701 266 710 in UK.
www.spanair.com

FERRIES

Trasmediterránea
Tel 902 454 645.
www.trasmediterranea.es

OTHER FERRIES

Brittany Ferries
Tel 08705 360 360 in UK.
Tel 942 36 06 11 in Spain.
www.brittany-ferries.com

P&O European Ferries
Tel 0870 520 2020 in UK.
Tel 91 270 23 32 in Spain.
www.poferries.com

Trasmediterránea car ferry to the Balearic Islands in Barcelona harbour

Travelling by Train

The Spanish state railway, **RENFE** *(Red Nacional de Ferrocarriles Españoles),* operates a service that is continually improving, particularly between cities. The fastest intercity services are called the TALGO and the AVE – their names are acronyms for the high-speed, luxury trains that run on these routes. *Largo recorrido* (long-distance) and *regionales y cer-*

Logo of the Spanish national railways

canías (regional and local) trains are notoriously slow, many stopping at every station. They are much cheaper than the high-speed trains but can take hours longer.

ARRIVING BY TRAIN

There are several routes to Spain from France. The main western route runs from Paris through Hendaye in the Pyrenees to San Sebastián. The eastern route from Paris runs via Cerbère and Port Bou to Barcelona. The trains from London, Brussels, Amsterdam, Geneva, Zurich and Milan all reach Barcelona via Cerbère. At Cerbère there are connections with the TALGO and the *largo recorrido* (long-distance) services to Valencia, Málaga, Seville and Madrid, and other major destinations. If you book a sleeper on the TALGO from Paris, you travel to your destination without having to change trains.

EXPLORING BY TRAIN

Spain offers many options for train travellers. In the last ten years, the TALGO high-speed services have belied Spain's reputation for inefficiency and it is now possible to travel the long distances between the main cities extremely quickly. Ticket prices compare very favourably with the cost of high-speed train fares in many other countries in Europe. Efficient high-speed AVE rail services currently link Madrid with Seville in two and a half hours and with Lleida in two hours 40 minutes.

The *largo recorrido* (long-distance) trains are so much slower you usually need to travel overnight. You can

AVE high-speed trains at Estación de Santa Justa in Seville

choose between a *cochecama* (compartment with two *camas* or beds) or a *litera*, one of six seats in a compartment which converts into a bunk bed. You reserve these when booking and pay a supplement. You should book at least a month in advance, but bear in mind that it is difficult to change a ticket you have paid for.

Regionales y cercanías (the regional and local services) are frequent and very cheap. You buy the tickets from machines on the station.

Some cities have more than one station. In Madrid the major stations for regional and long-distance trains are Atocha, Chamartín and Norte. The AVE runs from Atocha, the TALGO from all three. Sants and Francia are Barcelona's two principal stations. In Seville Santa Justa is the only station for regional and international services.

Logo for a high-speed rail service

DIRECTORY

NATIONAL ENQUIRIES AND RESERVATIONS

RENFE
Tel 902 24 02 02.
www.renfe.es

REGIONAL RAILWAYS

ET
Tel 944 16 19 50.
www.euskotren.es

FEVE
Tel 902 100 818.
www.feve.es

FGC
Tel 93 205 15 15.
www.fgc.net

FGV
Tel 96 526 27 31.
www.fgv.es

FARES

Spanish railways offer a 10 per cent discount on specified days to encourage people to travel. They are called *días azules* (blue days) and are indicated in the timetables in blue.

Fares for rail travel in Spain are structured according to the speed and quality of the service. Tickets for the TALGO and AVE are most expensive.

Interrail tickets for people under 26, and Eurodomino tickets for people over 26, are available from major travel agencies in Europe and from RENFE ticket offices in Spain. Always take proof of your identity when booking.

Holidays on Spain's two luxury trains (see p679) are expensive but offer high standards of comfort.

REGIONAL RAILWAYS

Three of the *comunidades autónomas* have regional rail companies. Catalonia and Valencia each has its own *Ferrocarrils de la Generalitat:* respectively the

SPAIN'S PRINCIPAL RENFE NETWORK

Spain's Rail Network operates a wide variety of services. Study a RENFE brochure or train timetable before you buy your ticket.

KEY

- Main station
- — Major rail route
- — High-speed AVE route
- - - AVE route under construction

FGC and the **FGV**; and the Basque Country has the **ET** (*Eusko Trenbideak*).

Tickets for two special trains, similar to the Orient Express, can be obtained from travel agents. Tickets for *Al Andalus Expres*, which tours Andalusia, including Seville and Granada, can also be bought through RENFE. While **FEVE** (*Ferro-carriles de Vía Estrecha*) run *El Transcantábrico*, which travels Spain's north coast between San Sebastián and Santiago de Compostela. Passengers travel in style in 14 period carriages built between 1900–30 and since restored.

The regional tourist offices publicize unusual rail services, such as the narrow-gauge lines to Inca and Sóller in Mallorca.

BOOKING TICKETS

TALGO, AVE and any other tickets for *largo recorrido* travel by train may be booked and bought at any of the major railway stations from the *taquilla* (ticket office). They are also sold by all travel agents in Spain, who will charge a commission. RENFE tickets are sometimes sold by travel agents in other countries. Telephone reservations may be made directly to all RENFE

Ticket machine for local and regional lines

ticket offices using a credit card number. Tickets can also be purchased via the RENFE internet site. Tickets must be collected in person. Tickets for local and regional services are purchased from the station *taquilla*. In larger stations they can be bought from ticket machines but these only accept coins. Tickets for *cercanías* (local services) cannot be reserved. For a one-way journey ask for *ida* and for a return ask for *ida y vuelta*.

TIMETABLES

RENFE timetables change in May and October each year. Your travel agent will be able to provide the correct times of trains for your journey. Timetables can also be accessed in English via the RENFE internet site. In Spain timetables are available from RENFE offices. Most come as leaflets and are broken down into the various types of journey: intercity, *largo recorrido* and *regionales*. *Cercanías* timetables are posted on boards at local railway stations.

Atocha, one of Madrid's largest mainline railway stations

Travelling by Road

Spain's fastest roads are its *autopistas*. They are normally dual carriageways and are subsidized by *peajes* (tolls). *Autovías* are similar but have no tolls. The *carretera nacional* is the countrywide network of main roads or highways with the prefix N. Smaller minor roads are generally less well kept but are often a more leisurely and enjoyable way to see rural areas of Spain. These

Sign for national highway N110

pages tell you how to use the roads, tolls and parking meters, how to buy petrol, and explain important driving regulations.

Cambio de sentido (slip road)
300 m (330 yd) ahead

ARRIVING BY CAR

Many people drive to Spain via the French motorways. The most direct routes across the Pyrenees, using the motorways, pass through Hendaye on the western flank and Port Bou in the east. Other, rather more tortuous routes may be used, from Toulouse through the Vall d'Aran, for instance. From the UK there are car ferries from Plymouth to Santander and from Portsmouth to Bilbao in northern Spain *(see p677)*.

WHAT TO TAKE

A Green Card and a bail bond from a motor insurance company are needed in order to extend your comprehensive cover to Spain. The RAC, the AA and Europ Assistance have sound rescue and recovery policies with European cover.

Spanish law requires you to carry with you at all times your vehicle's registration document, a valid insurance certificate and your driving licence. You must always be able to show a passport or a national identity card as ID. You must also display a sticker with the car's country of registration on the rear of the vehicle.

The headlights of right-hand drive vehicles will have to be adjusted or deflected. This is done with stickers that can be bought at ferry ports and on ferries. You risk on-the-spot fines if you do not carry a red warning triangle, spare light bulbs and a first-aid kit.

In winter you should carry chains if you intend to drive in

mountain areas. In summer, it is a good idea to take drinking water with you if you are travelling in a remote area.

BUYING PETROL

In Spain *gasolina* (petrol) and *gasóleo* (diesel) are priced by the litre. *Gasolina sin plomo* (unleaded petrol) is available everywhere. All cost more at the *autopista* service stations. Self-service stations, where you fill up yourself, are common. You must wait for service if there are attendants. They will ask *¿cuánto?* (how much?); you should reply *lleno* (fill the tank) or specify an amount in euros: *dos euros por favor*. Small stations do not all accept credit cards. If you use your credit card to pay at a motorway service station you will be asked to show your passport or ID. Modern pumps sometimes operate by credit card. You run your card through the machine, press the buttons to indicate the amount of petrol you want in euros, and then serve yourself.

50

Speed limit 50 km/h (31 mph)

Pedestrian crossing sign

RULES OF THE ROAD

Most traffic regulations and warnings to motorists are represented on signs by easily recognized symbols. But Spain has a few road rules and signs that may be unfamiliar to some drivers from other countries.

To turn left at a busy junction or across oncoming traffic you may have to turn right first and cross a main road, often by way of traffic lights, a bridge or an underpass. If you are going the wrong way on a motorway or a main road with a solid white line, you are allowed to turn round where you see a sign for a *cambio de sentido*.

At any crossing you must give way to the right unless a sign indicates otherwise. It is compulsory always to wear seat belts if they are fitted in front and rear seats. Oncoming drivers may flash their headlights at you to mean "you go"; "danger"; "your lights are on unnecessarily"; or (most often) "speed trap ahead".

A filling station run by a leading chain with branches throughout Spain

SPEED LIMITS AND FINES

Speed limits on the roads
in Spain for cars without
trailers are as follows:
• 120 km/h (75 mph) on
autopistas (toll motorways).
• 100 km/h (62 mph) on
autovías (non-toll motorways).
• 90 km/h (56 mph) on
carreteras nacionales (main
roads) and *carreteras
comarcales* (secondary roads).
• 50 km/h (31 mph) in built-
up areas.

Speeding fines are imposed
on the spot at the rate of six
euros for every kilometre per
hour over the limit. Fines for
other traffic offences (such as
turning the wrong way into a
one-way street) depend on
the severity of the offence and
the whim of a police officer.

Tests for drink-driving and
fines for drivers over the
blood alcohol legal limit,
which is 30 mg per millilitre,
are now imposed frequently
throughout the country.

MOTORWAYS

Spain has more than 2,000 km
(1,240 miles) of *autopistas*,
and many more are planned.
They are generally toll roads
and can be expensive to use.

Be aware that Spain is in the
process of changing its road
numbering system so some of
the roads featured here may
differ from new road signs.
However, you can establish
whether a motorway is toll or
toll-free by the letters that
prefix the number of the road:
A = free motorway, AP = toll
motorway.

The long-distance tolls are
calculated per kilometre and
the rate varies from region to
region. Among the busiest
and most expensive are the
A7 along the south coast to
Alicante and the A68 Bilbao-
Zaragoza *autopista*.

There are service stations
every 40 km (25 miles) or so
along the *autopistas,* marked
by a blue and white parking
sign (P) or a sign indicating
the services available. About
1 km (550 yd) from a service
station, a sign indicates the
distance to the next one and
lists its services. Most have
fuel, toilets, a shop for maps,

Driving through the Sierra Nevada along one of Europe's highest roads

coffee and snacks, and a café
which serves full meals.

Emergency telephones occur
every 2 km (2 miles) along
the *autopistas.*

USING AUTOPISTA TOLLS

If you are travelling a long
distance on the *autopista* you
pick up a ticket from a toll
booth *(peaje)* as you drive on
to it and give it up at a booth
as you exit. Your toll will be
calculated according to
the distance you have
covered. Over some
short stretches of
motorways near to
cities a fixed price is
charged. Tolls can be
paid either in cash or
by credit card.

PEAJE
TOLL

Autopista toll
booths ahead

You must join one
of three channels at
the *peaje* leading to different
booths. Do not drive into
telepago, a credit system for
which you need a chip on
your windscreen. *Automático*
has machines for you to pay
by credit card or with exactly
the right coins. In *manual* an
attendant in the booth takes
your ticket and your money.

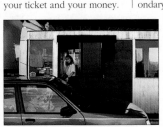

The *peaje manual* channel, with attendant

OTHER ROADS

Carreteras nacionales, Spain's
main roads, have black and
white signs and are
designated N *(Nacional)* plus
a number. Those with Roman
numerals (NIII) start at the
Puerta del Sol, Madrid. The distance from the Kilometre Zero
mark in the Puerta del Sol *(see
p272)* appears on kilometre
markers. Those with ordinary
numbers (N6) have kilometre
markers giving the dis-
tance from the provin-
cial capital. Some
carreteras nacionales
are dual carriage-
ways, but most are
single-lane roads and
can be slow. They
tend to be least busy
at lunch time, from
2–5pm, when many
lorry drivers stop for lunch.

Autovías are new roads built
in recent years to motorway
standard to replace N roads.
They have blue signs similar
to *autopista* signs. Because
they have no tolls they are
busier than *autopistas.*

Carreteras comarcales, secondary roads, have a number
preceded by a letter C.
Other minor roads have
numbers preceded by
letters representing the
name of the province
such as the LE 1313 in
Lleida. On any road in
winter, watch out for
signs indicating wheth-
er a mountain pass
ahead is open *(abierto)*
or closed *(cerrado).*

CAR HIRE

As well as the international car hire companies, a few Spanish companies, such as **Atesa**, operate nationwide. You can probably negotiate the best deal with an international company from home. There are also fly-drive and other package deals, including car hire. Fly-drive, an option for two or more travellers, can be arranged by travel agents.

There are car hire desks at airports and offices in the large towns. Alternatively, if you wish to hire a car locally for, say, a week or less, you can arrange it with a local travel agent. A car for hire is called a *coche de alquiler*.

For chauffeur-driven cars in Spain, **Avis** offer deals from major cities. Car-hire prices and conditions vary according to the region and locality.

Some of the leading car-hire companies operating in Spain

MAPS

Fold-out road maps can be obtained at airports, on the ferries and from tourist offices. The Spanish Ministry of Transport publishes a comprehensive road map in book form, the *Mapa Oficial de Carreteras*. Campsa, the oil company, publishes the *Guía Campsa*, a road map and restaurant guide in one book. Michelin publishes a useful series of maps (440–448, with orange covers) at a scale of 1:400,000 (1 cm:4 km), which covers Spain in eight sections, including the islands. They are sold at bookshops and petrol stations all over Spain.

A series of more detailed maps at 1:200,000 for cycling, walking and other specialist uses is published by Plaza y Janés. Military maps at scales of 1:50,000 and 1:100,000 are available from **Stanfords Travel Bookshop** in London and from specialist bookshops

City taxis with their logo and official numbers

and some local bookshops in Spain. Tourist offices in towns and cities usually have a give-away street map of the town showing the principal sights.

There are detailed street maps of central Barcelona on pages 180–85, of Madrid on pages 308–15 and of Seville on pages 448–53 of this guide.

PARKING

The hours for which drivers have to pay for parking in Spain are 8am until 2pm and 4pm until 8pm on Mondays to Saturdays.

As a rule, you may not park where the pavement edge is painted yellow or where a no parking sign is displayed. Occasionally there is a no parking sign on both sides of a city street, one saying "1–15" and the other "16–30". This means that you can park on one side of the street only for the fortnight indicated on the sign.

In the cities, non-metered, on-street parking is generally hard to find, but there are blue pay and display parking spaces. To use them you buy a ticket from the machine and display it on the inside of your windscreen. The cost varies, but averages about 1–2 euros per hour. You can usually park at the same spot for up to two hours. The penalties for infringements vary from town to town.

Major cities have many large underground car parks. You collect a ticket when you enter, retain it, and pay the attendant as you drive out.

A parking ticket machine

No parking at any time of day

TAXIS

There is no central system for taxis in Spain. Every city and/or region has its own design and tariffs for its taxis. All will display a green light if they are free. Most taxis are metered and at the start of the journey a minimum fee will be shown on the meter. In smaller villages the taxi service may well be run by a resident driving an unmetered private car. Ask at the hotel reception or in a nearby shop for the name and number of a local driver. It is best to negotiate a price for the trip before you set off.

In the cities there are taxi ranks at the airports, the railway and bus stations and usually in the main shopping areas. Tips of about 1 euro will be acceptable.

ROAD CONDITIONS AND WEATHER FORECASTS

To hear recorded road and traffic information call the national toll-free number for **Información de Tráfico de Carreteras**. This service is in Spanish only. Ask your hotel receptionist to call for you if you need a translation. The RAC offers route-planning services tailored to individual requirements, which may include current road conditions. The weather information service, **Teletiempo**, gives forecasts for the regions and provinces, as well as the national and international weather. It also gives information on maritime and mountain conditions.

ARRIVING BY COACH

Often the cheapest way to reach and travel around Spain is by coach. **Eurolines** operates routes throughout Europe and runs daily services to Madrid and Barcelona.

Coaches from the UK depart from London Victoria Coach Station. Tickets may be bought from National Express offices or travel agents, or a credit card booking may be made by phone. The journey to both cities takes about 24 hours.

TRAVELLING AROUND SPAIN BY COACH

There is no Spanish national coach company, but private regional companies operate routes around the country. The largest coach tour company, **Autocares Juliá**, which acts as an agent for Eurolines in Spain, offers itineraries, coach holidays and sightseeing trips nationwide. Other coach companies operate in particular regions – Alsina Graells, for instance, covers most of the south and east of Spain. Tickets and information for long-distance travel are available at all main coach stations and

CYCLING

Cycling is popular in Spain and there are bicycles for hire in most tourist spots but there are few cycle lanes, even in towns. Bicycles may be carried on *cercanías* trains after 2pm on Fridays until the last train on Sunday night, on any *regional* train

Cycle touring, a popular holiday activity

with a goods compartment, and on all long-distance overnight trains. If you need to take your bicycle long-distance at other times, you should check it in an hour before the train departs. You may have to send it as luggage and pay a baggage charge based on its weight. It might not travel with you so you will have to collect it when it arrives.

Alsina Graells, a regional coach service

from travel agents but they cannot always be booked in advance. In Madrid the biggest coach stations are **Estación Sur**, which serves the whole of Spain; **Intercambiador des Autobuses**, for terminals in the north; and **Terminal Auto Res**, serving Valencia, Extremadura and parts of Castilla-León.

LOCAL BUSES

Local bus routes and timetables are posted at bus terminuses and stops. You pay on the bus or buy strips of ten tickets called *billetes bonobus* from *estancos* (tobacconists).

Indicators for Seville's circular bus routes

DIRECTORY

CAR HIRE

Atesa
Tel 902 10 01 01.
www.atesa.es

Avis
Tel 08706 060 100 in UK.
Tel 902 13 55 31 in Spain.
www.avisworld.com
www.avis.es

Europcar
Tel 08457 222 525 in UK.
Tel 902 10 50 30 in Spain.
www.europcar.com
www.europcar.es

Hertz
Tel 0870 844 8844 in UK.
Tel 901 10 10 01 toll-free in Spain.
www.hertz.co.uk
www.hertz.es

COACH OPERATORS

Autocares Juliá
Tel 93 402 69 00 in Barcelona.
www.autocaresjulia.net

Eurolines
Tel 0158 240 4511 in UK.
Tel 93 490 40 00 in Barcelona.
Tel 91 506 33 60 in Madrid.
www.eurolines.es

COACH STATIONS

Madrid
Estación Sur, Calle Méndez Álvaro, 83. *Tel 91 468 42 00.* www.estacionauto busesmadrid.com

Intercambiador de Autobuses, Avenida de América, 9. *Tel 91 745 63 00.75*

Terminal Auto Res
Calle Fernández Shaw 1.

Tel 902 02 09 99.
www.auto-res.net

Barcelona
Estació del Nord, Calle Ali Bei 80. *Tel 902 26 06 06.*
www.barcelonanord.com

Estació de Sants
Calle Viriato.

Seville
Estación Plaza de Armas, Calle Cristo de la Expiración. *Tel 95 490 80 40.*

MAPS

Altair S.A.
Gran Via 616, 08007 Barcelona. *Tel 93 342 71 71.*

Instituto Geográfico Nacional
C/ General Ibáñez Ibero 3, 28003 Madrid.
Tel 91 597 50 00.
www.cnig.ign.es

Stanfords
12–14 Long Acre, London WC2E 9LP.
Tel 020 7836 1321.

WEATHER FORECASTS

Teletiempo Nacional
Tel 807 170 365.

Teletiempo Provincial
Tel 807 17 03 + first two digits of provincial postcode.

TRAFFIC AND ROAD CONDITIONS

Información de Tráfico de Carreteras
Tel 900 12 35 05 toll-free.

General Index

Acknowledgments

Dorling Kindersley would like to thank the following people whose contributions and assistance made preparation of this book possible.

Main Contributors
John Ardagh is a journalist and writer, and the author of several books on modern Europe.

David Baird, resident in Andalusia from 1971 to 1995, is the author of *Inside Andalusia*.

Vicky Hayward, a writer, journalist and editor, lives in Madrid, and has travelled extensively in Spain.

Adam Hopkins is an indefatigable travel writer and author of *Spanish Journeys: A Portrait of Spain*.

Lindsay Hunt has travelled widely and has contributed to several Eyewitness Travel Guides.

Nick Inman writes regularly on Spain for books and magazines.

Paul Richardson is the author of *Not Part of the Package*, a book on Ibiza, where he lives.

Martin Symington is a regular contributor to the *Daily Telegraph*. He also worked on the *Eyewitness Travel Guide to Great Britain*.

Nigel Tisdall, contributor to the *Eyewitness Travel Guide to France*, is the author of the *Insight Pocket Guide to Seville*.

Roger Williams has contributed to Insight Guides on Barcelona and Catalonia, and was the main contributor to the *Eyewitness Travel Guide to Provence*.

Additional Contributors
Mary Jane Aladren, Sarah Andrews, Pepita Aris, Emma Dent Coad, Rebecca Doulton, Harry Eyres, Josefina Fernández, Anne Hersh, Nick Rider, Mercedes Ruiz Ochoa, David Stone, Clara Villanueva, Christopher Woodward, Patricia Wright.

Additional Illustrations
Arcana Studio, Richard Bonson, Louise Boulton, Martine Collings, Brian Craker, Jared Gilbey (Kevin Jones Associates), Paul Guest, Steven Gyapay, Claire Littlejohn.

Additional Photography
David Cannon, Tina Chambers, Geoff Dann, Phillip Dowell, Mike Dunning, Neil Fletcher, Steve Gorton, Frank Greenaway, Derek Hall, Colin Keates, Alan Keohane, Dave King, Ella Milroy, D Murray, Cyril Laubsouer, Ian O'Leary, Stephen Oliver, J Selves, Mathew Ward, P. Wojcik.

Cartography
Lovell Johns Ltd (Oxford), ERA-Maptec Ltd.

Design And Editorial Assistance
Sam Atkinson, Pilar Ayerbe, Rosemary Bailey, Vicky Barber, Teresa Barea, Cristina Barrallo, Jill Benjamin, Vandana Bhagra, Sonal Bhatt, Chris Branfield, Gretta Britton, Daniel Campi, Lola Carbonell, Peter Casterton, Elspeth Collier, Carey Combe, Jonathan Cox, Martin Cropper, Linda Doyle, Aruna Ghose, Elena González, Des Hemsley, Tim Hollis, Michael Lake, Erika Lang, Rebecca Lister, Sarah Martin, Jane Oliver, Simon Oon, Mike Osborn, Malcolm Parchment, Anna Pirie, Tom Prentice, Mani Ramaswamy, Sadie Smith, Anna Streiffert, Leah Tether, Helen Townsend, Andy Wilkinson, Suzanne Wales, Robert Zonenblick.

Proofreader Stewart J Wild.

Indexer Hilary Bird.

Special Assistance
DORLING KINDERSLEY would like to thank the regional and local tourist offices, *ayuntamientos*, shops, hotels, restaurants and other organizations in Spain for their invaluable help. Particular thanks also to Dr Giray Ablay (University of Bristol); María Eugenia Alonso and María Dolores Delgado Peña (Museo Thyssen-Bornemisza); Ramón Álvarez (Consejería de Educación y Cultura, Castilla y León); Señor Ballesteros (Santiago de Compostela Tourist Office); Carmen Brieva, Javier Campos and Luis Esteruelas (Spanish Embassy, London); Javier Caballero Arranz; Fernando Cañada López; The Club Taurino of London; Consejería de Turismo, Castilla-La Mancha; Consejería de Turismo and Consejería de Cultura, Junta de Extremadura; Mònica Colomer and Montse Planas (Barcelona Tourist Office); María José Docal and Carmen Cardona (Patronato de Turismo, Lanzarote); Edilesa; Klaus Ehrlich; Juan Fernández, Lola Moreno and others at El País-Aguilar; Belén Galán (Centro de Arte Reina Sofía); Amparo Garrido; Adolfo Díaz Gómez (Albacete Tourist Office); Professor Nigel Glendinning (Queen Mary and Westfield College, University of London); Pedro Hernández; Insituto de Cervantes, London; Victor Jolín (SOTUR); Joaquim Juan Cabanilles (Servicio de Investigación Prehistórica, Valencia); Richard Kelly; Mark Little (*Lookout* Magazine); Carmen López de Tejada and Inma Felipe (Spanish National Tourist Office, London); Caterine López and Ana Roig Mundi (ITVA); Julia López de la Torre (Patrimonio Nacional, Madrid); Lovell Johns Ltd (Oxford); Josefina Maestre (Ministerio de Agricultura, Pesca y Alimentación); Juan Malavia García and Antonio Abarca (Cuenca Tourist Office); Mario (Promoción Turismo, Tenerife); Janet Mendel; Javier Morata (Acanto Arquitectura y Urbanismo. Madrid); Juan Carlos Murillo; Sonia Ortega and Bettina Krücken (Spain Gourmetour); Royal Society for the Protection of Birds (UK); Alícia Ribas Sos; Katusa Salazar-Sandoval (Fomento de Turismo, Ibiza); María Ángeles Sánchez and Marcos; Ana Sarrieri (Departamento de Comercio, Consumo y Turismo, Gobierno Vasco); Klaas Schenk; María José Sevilla (Foods From Spain); The Sherry Institute of Spain (London); Anna Skidmore (Fomento de Turismo, Mallorca); Philip Sweeney; Rupert Thomas; Mercedes Trujillo and Antonio Cruz Caballero (Patronato de Turismo, Gran Canaria); Gerardo Uarte (Gobierno de Navarra); Fermín Unzue (Dirección General de Turismo, Cantabria); Puri Villanueva.

Artwork Reference

Sr Joan Bassegoda, Catedral Gaudí (Barcelona);
José Luis Mosquera Muller (Mérida); Jorge Palazón,
Paisajes Españoles (Madrid).

Photography Permissions

THE PUBLISHER would like to thank the following for
their kind assistance and permission to photograph at
their establishments:© Patrimonio Nacional, Madrid;
Palacio de la Almudaina, Palma de Mallorca; El
Escorial, Madrid; La Granja de San Ildefonso;
Convento de Santa Clara, Tordesillas; Las Huelgas
Reales, Burgos; Palacio Real, Madrid; Monasterio de
las Descalzas; Bananera "El Guanche S.L."; Museo
Arqueológico de Tenerife-OACIMC del Excmo,
Cavildo Insular de Tenerife; Asociación de Encajeras
de Acebo-Cáceres; Museo de Arte Abstracto Español,
Cuenca; Fundación Juan March; Pepita Alia Lagartera;
Museo Naval de Madrid; © Catedral de Zamora;
Museo de Burgos; Claustro San Juan de Duero,
Museo Numantino, Soria; San Telmo Museoa
Donostia-San Sebastián; Hotel de la Reconquista,
Oviedo; Catedral de Jaca; Museo de Cera, Barcelona;
Museu D'Història de la Ciutat, Barcelona; © Capitol
Catedral de Lleida; Jardí Botànic Marimurtra, Estació
Internacional de Biologia Mediterrània, Girona;
Museo Arqueológico Sagunto (Teatro Romano-
Castillo); Museo Municipal y Ermita de San Antonio
de la Florida, Madrid. Also all the other churches,
museums, hotels, restaurants, shops, galleries and
sights too numerous to thank individually.

Picture Credits

Key: t=top; tl=top left; tlc=top left centre; tc=top
centre; trc=top right centre; tr=top right; cla=centre left
above; ca=centre above; cra=centre right above;
cl=centre left; c=centre; cr=centre right; clb=centre left
below; crb=centre right below; cb=centre below;
bl=bottom left; br=bottom right; b=bottom;
bc=bottom centre; bcl=bottom centre left; bcr=bottom
centre right; (d)=detail.

Every effort has been made to trace the copyright
holders. Dorling Kindersley apologizes for any
unintentional omissions and would be pleased,
in such cases, to add an acknowledgment in
future editions.

Works of art have been published with the
permission of the following copyright holders: *Dona
i Ocell* Joan Miró © ADAGP, Paris & DACS, London
176tl; *Guernica* Pablo Ruiz Picasso 1937 © DACS
1996 299cb; *Morning* George Kolbe © DACS 1996;
Peine de los Vientos Eduardo Chillida 122b; Various
works by Joaquín Sorolla © DACS 1996 305t; *Rainy
Taxi* Salvador Dalí © DEMART PRO ARTE BV/DACS
1996 215tr; *Tapestry of the Foundation* Joan Miró 1975
© ADAGP, Paris & DACS, London; *Three Gypsy Boys*
© Joan Rebull 1976 144bl.

The publisher would like to thank the following
individuals, companies and picture libraries for their
kind permission to reproduce their photographs:
ACE PHOTO AGENCY: Bob Masters 26b; Mauritius 23t; Bill
Wassman 320b; AISA ARCHIVO ICONOGRÁFICO,
BARCELONA: 22t, 36bl, 46l, 48ca, 48cb, 49bl, 49br,

50cra, 50cb, 51tl, 52cla, 52bl(d), 54bl, 54br, 54cla,
54–55, 55cl, 55cra, 55bl, 56bl, 61br, 65tr, 67tl, 67b,
274t, 303b, 355bl, 423bl, 423br, 424cl, 489br;
Biblioteca Nacional, Madrid *Felipe V* Luis Meléndez
71bl; Catedral de Sevilla *Ignacio de Loyola* Alonso
Vázquez 124bl(d); *Camilo José Cela* Álvaro Delgado
1916 © DACS 1996 35br (d); *La Tertulia del Pombo*
José Gutiérrez Solana 1920 © DACS 1996 299t; Museo
de América, Madrid *Vista de Sevilla* Alonso Sánchez
Coello 58cb; Museo de Bellas Artes, Seville *Sancho
Panza y El Rucio* Moreno Carbonero 60ca; Museo de
Bellas Artes, Valencia *Ecce Homo* Juan de Juanes
252br; Museo Frankfurt *La Armada* 59tl; Museo de
Historia de México *Hernán Cortés* S.E. Colane
58bl(d); Museo Histórico Militar, San Sebastián
Guerra Carlista 63br(d); Museo Lázaro Galdiano,
Madrid *Lope de Vega* Caxes 290tr; Museo Nacional del
Teatro *Poster for "Yerma"* (FG Lorca) Juan Antonio
Morales y José Caballero © DACS 1996 35tr; Museo
del Prado, Madrid *La Rendición de Breda* Diego
Velázquez 61cb, *El Tres de Mayo de 1808 en Madrid*
Francisco de Goya y Lucientes 62-63(d), La Reina
María Luisa María Francisco de Goya 62cla, *Carlos IV*
Francisco de Goya 71bc, *Los Borrachos* Diego de
Velázquez 292t, *Saturno devorando a un hijo*
Francisco de Goya 294tr, *El Descendimiento* Van der
Weyden 295b; Real Academia de Bellas Artes de San
Fernando, Madrid *El Sueño del Caballero* Antonio de
Pereda 60–61(d); AKG, London: 67cr; ALLSPORT:
Stephen Munday 42cr; AQUILA: Adrian Hoskins 210cla,
210clb; Mike Lane 343clb; James Pearce 205bl;
ARCAID: Paul Raftery 120bl; ARXIU MAS: 36br, 37bl,
51crb, 54tl, 57cl, 53br(d); Museo del Prado, Madrid
Felipe II Sánchez Coello 70br(d); Patrimonio Nacional
59cl, 59b(d); ALAMY IMAGES: Paul Hardy Carter 200cla;
Michelle Chaplow 456b; Ian Dagnall 11br;
Expuesto/Nicholas Randall 656b; Robert Harding
Picture Library 419cr, 656cla; paulbourdice 513cla;
Photo3 76l; Profimedia.CZ s.r.o. 537cl; Alex Segre 77t,
605tr; Peter Titmuss 201t; Renaud Visage 418cla.

JAUME BALANYA: 167crb; BIOFOTOS: Heather Angel
80cla, 80bl; BRIDGEMAN ART LIBRARY: *St Dominic
enthroned as Abbot* Bartolomé Bermejo 294tl; Index/
Museo del Prado, Madrid *Auto-da-fé in the Plaza
Mayor* Francisco Rizi 274c; Musée des Beaux Artes,
Berne *Colossus of Rhodes* Salvador Dalí 1954 DEMART
PRO ARTE BV/DACS 1996 33tr; Museo del Prado,
Madrid *Charles IV and his Family* Francisco de Goya
y Lucientes 33cb, *The Adoration of the Shepherds* El
Greco 293br, *The Annunciation* Fra Angelico 293bc,
The Clothed Maja Francisco de Goya y Lucientes
293t, *The Naked Maja* Francisco de Goya y Lucientes
293ca, *The Three Graces* Peter Paul Rubens 292ca,
The Martydom of St Philip José de Ribera 292cb;
Museo Picasso, Barcelona *Las Meninas, Infanta
Margarita* Pablo Ruiz Picasso 1957 © DACS 1996
32tl; *Children On the Beach* Joaquin y Bastida Sorolla
© DACS 1996 295t; Phoenix Galleries, London
Rooftops, Fortna Luxt, Majorca Frederick Gore 8-9;
MICHAEL BUSSELLE: 207r, 209b, 210t.

CAMPER STORE: Madrid 655tr; CENTRO DE ARTE REINA
SOFÍA: *Bertsolaris* Zubiaurre © DACS 1996 125cb,
Paisaje de Cadaqués Salvador Dalí 1923 © DEMART
PRO ARTE BV/DACS 1996 298cb, *Accidente* Ponce
de León 298b, *Toki-Egin (Homenaje a San Juan de la*

Cruz) Eduardo Chillida 1952 © DACS 2002 299bl; CEPHAS: Mick Rock 29bl, 42t, 78t, 202tr, 202cl, 203tr, 340tr, 420tr, 421br, 421cr; Roy Stedall 421tr; CIUDAD DE LAS ARTES Y LAS CIENCES (CACSA): Javier Yaya Tur 253t; COCOMFE: 665b; BRUCE COLEMAN: Eric Crichton 204tr; José Luis González Grande 205tr; Werner Layer 343tl; Andy Purcell 31ca; Hans Reinhard 80crb; Norbert Schwirtz 205tl; Colin Varndell 205crb; DEE CONWAY: 425cl, 425cr; CORBIS: Peter Aprahmanian 154b; Ric Ergenbright 456t; Owen Franken 77c, 201c, 338cl, 339c, 419t; Carloine Penn 339t; Jose Fuste Raga 10cr; Reuters/Marcelo del Pozo 12br; SYLVIA CORDAIY PHOTO LIBRARY: Chris North 40tl; JOE CORNISH: 28ca, 346, 364b, 372tr; GIANCARLO COSTA: 37bc; COVER: Genin Andrada 40b, 43b; Austin Catalan 70bl; Juan Echeverria 31cra, 41br, 545bl; Pepe Franco 185c; Quim Llenas 125ca, 317tl; Matías Nieto 43c; F J Rodríguez 125bl.

J D DALLET: 70tr, 464tl, 605br. EDEX: 51bl, 405b; EDILESA: 352b; EL DESEO: Pedro Almodóvar 305b; EGANA ORIZA RESTAURANT: Seville: Manolo Manosalbas 602b; PACO ELVIRA: 30crb; EMI: Hispavox 376b; EQUIPO 28: 425t; ET ARCHIVE: 52br; EUROPA PRESS: 23c, 68tl, 69ca; MARY EVANS PICTURE LIBRARY: 9t, 56cla, 63bl, 73t, 137r, 197t, 265r, 274bl, 335, 415r, 471b, 503, 553t, 663r; Explorer 424t; EYE UBIQUITOUS: James Davis Travel Photography 21t, 218br.

FIRO FOTO: 157c; 533t; FLAMENCOCOOL: Seville, 455tr; FUNDACIÓN CÉSAR MANRIQUE: 548br; FUNDACIÓN COLECCIÓN THYSSEN-BORNEMISZA: *Madonna of Humility* Fra Angelico 177t, *La Virgen del Árbol* Petrus Christus 288tr, *Mata Mua* Paul Gauguin 1892 289crb, *Harlequin with a mirror* Pablo Ruiz Picasso 1923 © DACS 1996 288cl, *Hotel Room* © Edward Hopper 1931 288bl, *Portrait of Baron HH Thyssen-Bornemisza* © Lucian Freud 1981–82 288br, *Venus y Cupido* Peter Paul Rubens (after 1629) 289tl, *Santa Casilda* Francisco de Zurbarán 1640–1645 289cra, *Autumn Landscape in Oldenburg* Karl Schmidt-Rottluff 1907 © DACS 1996 289b; FUNDACIÓ JOAN MIRÓ, BARCELONA: *Flama en L'espai i dona nua* Joan Miró 1932 © ADAGP, Paris and DACS, London 1996 172t.

GODO FOTO: 220b, 221t, 225t, 249b, 255t, 333bl; RONALD GRANT ARCHIVE: *For a Few Dollars More* © United Artists 500b. © FMBG GUGGENHEIM BILBAO MUSEOA: London 1999. Erica Barahona Ede. All rights reserved. Partial or total reproduction is prohibited 120t, 120br, 121t, 121b.

ROBERT HARDING PICTURE LIBRARY: 19t, 141tr, 160ca, 172b, 173b, 249t, 303t, 511br; Julia Bayne 196–197; Nigel Blythe 19b, 149c; Bob Cousins 26clb; Robert Frerck 439tr; James Strachan 270tl; MARÍA VICTORIA HERNÁNDEZ: 533b; HULTON DEUTSCH COLLECTION: 66b, 391br.

IBERDIAPO: Triangle 524–525; THE IMAGE BANK, London: Andra Pistolesi 174; Mark Romanelli 140bl; Mathew Weinreb 161b; IMAGES COLOUR LIBRARY: 677b; A.G.E Fotostock 28tr, 29tr, 30cra, 30ca, 30br, 36tr, 37ca, 40c, 42cl, 122b, 168, 187t, 187c, 211br, 233ca, 233br, 316t, 335c, 343cla, 349 tr, 421cl, 424br, 466b, 497t, 531t, 557tr, 659c, 659b; Horizon International 36-37, 140cb; INCAFO: J A Fernández & C De Noriega 75bl, 125br;

Juan Carlos Muñoz 396b, 497b; A Ortega 30bl; INDEX: 34tl, 48c, 48b, 49c, 49cb, 50tl, 50b, 54cra, 56br (d), 59tr, *Los Moriscos suplicando al rey Felipe III* 61c, 64–65, 65b, 67 cl, *Carlos I* 70tc, 70bl, 71br, 491ca; Bridgeman, London 58cra; CCJ 23b; X Correa 48tl; *Garrote Vil* José Gutiérrez Solana 1931 © DACS 1996 65clb(d); Galería del Ateneo, Madrid *Lucio Anneo Seneca* Villodas 50cla (d); Galeria Illustres Catalonia, Barcelona *Joan Prim I Prats* J Cusachs 63ca(d); Image *José Zorilla* 35bl; Instituto Valencia de Don Juan, Madrid *Carlos V* Simón Bening 59crb; Iranzo 56cra; Mithra 52clb, 58br (d), 64tl; Museo de América, Madrid *Indio Yumbo y Frutas Tropicales* 59cra; Museo Lázaro Galdiano, Madrid *Lope de Vega* Anonymous 34c, *Félix Lope de Vega* Francisco Pacheco 60br(d); Museo Municipal, Madrid *Fiesta en la Plaza Mayor de Madrid* Juan de la Corte 61tl; Museo del Prado, Madrid *Ascensión de un globo Montgolfier en Madrid* Antonio Carnicero 62cra(d), *José Moreño Conde de Floridablanca* Francisco de Goya 62br(d), *Flota del Rey Carlos III de España* A Joli 63tr(d); National Maritime Museum, Greenwich *Batalla de Trafalgar* Chalmers 62cb; A Noé 56cb; Palacio del Senado, Madrid *Alfonso X "El Sabio"* Matías Moreno 34b(d), *Rendición de Granada* Francisco Pradilla 56–57(d); Patrimonio Nacional 51br; Private Collection, Madrid *Pedro Calderón de la Barca* Antonio de Pereda 61bl(d); Real Academia de Bellas Artes de San Fernando, Madrid *San Diego de Alcalá dando de comer a los pobres* Bartolomé Esteban Murillo 61ca(d), *Fernando VII* Francisco de Goya 71tl(d), *Isabel* II 71tc, *Self-Portrait* Francisco de Goya 239b; A Tovy 69cb; NICK INMAN: 204bc, 253tr, 664t, 667cb, 672tr, 679b; INSTITUT TURÍSTIC VALENCIÀ: 245br.

CÉSAR JUSTEL: 353b.

ANTHONY KING: 291t.

L'ESTARTIT TOURIST BOARD: 217c; LIFE FILE PHOTOGRAPHIC: 217c; Tony Abbott 342cla; Xavier Catalan 141cb; Emma Lee 141cra, 420tl, 683tr; NEIL LUKAS: 464cb, 464b.

MAGNUM: S Franklin 68cb; Jean Gaumy 68br, 69tl; MARKA MILAN: Sergio Pitamitz 154t; IMAGEN MAS, LEON: 355tr; JOHN MILLER: 206l, 502–503, 505cb, 529r, 538b, 543b, 548t, 549b; MUSEO ARQUEOLÓGICO DE VILLENA: 48–49; MUSEO NACIONAL DEL PRADO: *El Jardín de las Delicias* 292b; MUSEU ARQUEOLÓGIC DE BARCELONA: 171c; MUSEU PICASSO BARCELONA: *Auto Retrato* Pablo Ruiz Picasso 1899–1900 © DACS 1996 153b.

NATURPRESS: Oriol Alamany 31bl; J L Calvo & J R Montero 343crb; José Luis Grande 465b; Walter Kwaternik 30clb, 81bc, 342cra, 343cra; Francisco Márquez 465cb, 416bl; Aurelio Martín 31br, Sebastián Martín 343br; José A Martínez 80tr, 207b, 342clb, 342crb; © NATIONAL MARITIME MUSEUM: 58–59; Network: Bilderberg/W Kunz 421tl; NHPA: Laurie Campbell 80cra; Stephen Dalton 81cl; Vicente García Canseco 31cla, 465ca; Manfred Daneggar 80br, 81br; NATURAL SCIENCE PHOTOS: Nigel Charles 108tl; C Dani & I Jeske 104b, 343br; Richard Revels 342br; Brian Sutton 342bl; W Tarboton 342tl; P & S Ward 232br.

OMEGA FOTO: 110tl, Manuel Pinilla 42b, 123b; ORONOZ: 4,

33br, 36cl, 37br, 47b, 49t, 50b, 53t, 53clb, 53crb, 54tl, 54cb, 55t, 55br, 59tl, 58cla, 60cb, 65tl, 68ca, 69c, 82tl, 112t, 305cr, 355br, 363br, 370b, 434bl, 441bl, 467tl, 479t, 480l, 489bl,, 657t; Biblioteca Nacional, Madrid *Isabel la Católica* Luis Madrazo 70tl(d); Iglesia Santo Tomé, Toledo *El Entierro del Conde de Orgaz* El Greco 32ca; *Portrait II* Joan Miró 1938 © ADAGP, Paris and DACS, London 1996 298t; Monasterio Santa Maria, Barcelona *Virgen con Niño* Ferrer Bassa 32clb(d); Museo de Bellas Artes, Cádiz *San Bruno en Éxtasis* Zurbarán 467tr; Museo Casa Gredo, Toledo *Carlos II* Miranda Correño 70tr(d); Museo del Ejército, Madrid *Isabel II* Madrazo 62tl; Museo Municipal de Bellas Artes, Tenerife *Retrato de Boabdil o Abu Abdala* 57tr(d); Museo Nacional de Escultura, Valladolid *Natividad* Berruguete 367tr; Museo Naval, Madrid *Desembarco de Colón* José Garnelo 57tl; Museo Naval Laminas, Madrid *Carabelas de Colón* Monleón 57bl(d); Museo del Prado, Madrid *El Salvador* José de Ribera 32crb, *Las Meninas o Familia de Felipe V* Diego Velázquez 32–33, *Felipe III* Pedro A Vidal 60bl, *Felipe V* 62bl, Guernica Pablo Ruiz Picasso 1937 © DACS 1996, 66–67, *Felipe IV* Diego Velázquez 66bc(d), *Bodegón* Zurbarán 294b, *David Vencedor de Goliat* Caravaggio 295c; Palacio Moncloa *Interior de la Catedral de Santiago* Villaamil Pérez 82–83; *Mujer en Azul* Pablo Ruiz Picasso 1901 © DACS 1996 298ca; Private Colection, Palma *Oleo Sobre Lienzo* Joan Miró 1932 © ADAGP, Paris and DACS, London 33ca; Real Academia de Bellas Artes de San Fernando *Fray Pedro Machado* Zurbarán 281tr.

Panos Pictures: Adrian Evans 68–69; José M Pérez De Ayala: 30cr, 464tr, 464ca, 465t, 465ca; The Photographers Library: 523tr; Pictures Colour Library: 22b, 30tr, 162-163, 258b, 416cl; Prisma 64ca, 65crb, 66ca, 66cb, 67tr, 97t, 140br, 239c, 250t, 321t, 475tl, 459, 516br, 532cl, 539clb, 539cb, 539crb, 539bl, 543t, 551bl, 551br; *Franco* Aguiar 71tr; *El ingenioso hidalgo Don Quixote de la Mancha* 1605 Ricardo Balaca 395br; Diputación de Madrid *Francisco Bahamonde Franco* Enrique Segura 66tl; Domènech & Azpiliqueta 118t; Albert Heras 186b; Marcel Jaquet 531b, 541b; Hans Lohr 483b; *Los Niños de la Concha* Bartolomé Esteban Murillo 33bl(d); Museo de Arte Moderno, Barcelona *Pío Baroja* Ramón Casas 64cb(d); Museo de Bellas Artes, Bilbao *Condesa Mathieu de Noailles* Ignacio Zuloaga y Zubaleta © DACS 1996 118b; Museo de Bellas Artes, Zaragoza *Príncipe de Viana* José Moreno Carbonero 130b (d); Mateu 191c; Palacio del Senado, Madrid *Alfonso XIII*

Aquino © DACS 1996 71cr; Patrimonio Nacional Palacio de Riofrío, Segovia: 64br; *Auto Retrato* Pablo Ruiz Picasso 1907 © Succession Picasso DACS 1996 65ca; Marta Povo 674t; Real Academia de Bellas Artes de San Fernando, Madrid *Las Bodas de Camacho* José Moreno Carbonero 35tl(d), *Procession of the Flagellants* Francisco de Goya 274br(d); *Emilio Castelar* Joaquin Sorolla © DACS 1996 64bl; Pure Espana: Port Aventura 657br.

Rex Features: Sipa Press 215cb; © Royal Musuem Of Scotland: Michel Zabé 47t; Jose Lucas Ruiz: 456cl. María Ángeles Sánchez: 38tr, 39b, 43t, 79t, 98cl, 18l, 290tl, 304b, 387c, 405tr, 532t, 532cr, 532b, 536c, 547t; Science Photo Library: Geospace 14l; 6 Toros 6: 37cb; Spanish Tourist Board: 255c; Spectrum Colour Library: 136–137, 140tr, 552–553; Stockphotos, Madrid: Marcelo Brodsky 40t; Campillo 659t; Heinz Hebeisen 41bl; Mikael Helsing 658b, 332tl; David Hornback 21b; Javier Sánchez 332tl; Werner Otto Reisefotografie 663t; James Strachan: 291b, 302t, 302c, 304t; Tony Stone Worldwide: Doug Armand 20b; Jon Bradley 316bl; Robert Everts 440ca.

Visions of Andalucía: Michelle Chaplow 424–425; J D Dallet 397tr; Vu: Christina García Rodero 2–3, 20c, 38b, 39c, 39t, 132cl, 256–257, 368l, 431cr.

Charlie Waite: 494–495; Werner Forman Archive: Museo de Arte Hispanomusulmán 52t; Museum of Catalan Art, Barcelona 344tl; National Maritime Museum, Greenwich 52cr; Alan Williams: 78b; Peter Wilson: 264–265, 282, 468b, 469c, 475t, 481t; World Pictures: 317b, 512t. Zefa: 1.

Front endpaper: All special photography except Joe Cornish cbl; John Miller tr; Spectrum Colour Library ca; Peter Wilson cbr.

JACKET
Front - Mary Evans Picture Library: Explorer/Courau bl; Getty Images: Taxi/Peter Adams main image. Back - Argence Vu: Cristina Garcia Roberto tl; DK Images: Max Alexander clb; Neil Lukas cla; John Miller: bl. Spine - DK Images: Max Alexander b; Getty Images: Taxi/Peter Adams t.

All other images © Dorling Kindersley.
For further information see www.DKimages.com

SPECIAL EDITIONS OF DK TRAVEL GUIDES

Phrase Book

In an Emergency

Help!	¡Socorro!	soh-**koh**-roh
Stop!	¡Pare!	pah-reh
Call a doctor!	¡Llame a un médico!	yah-meh ah oon meh-dee-koh
Call an ambulance!	¡Llame a una ambulancia!	yah-meh ah oonah ahm-boo-**lahn**-thee-ah
Call the police!	¡Llame a la policía!	yah-meh ah lah poh-lee-**thee**-ah
Call the fire brigade!	¡Llame a los bomberos!	yah-meh ah lohs bohm-**beh**-rohs
Where is the nearest telephone?	¿Dónde está el teléfono más próximo?	dohn-deh ehs-**tah** ehl teh-**leh**-foh-noh mahs prohx-ee-moh
Where is the nearest hospital?	¿Dónde está el hospital más próximo?	dohn-deh ehs-**tah** ehl ohs-pee-**tahl** mahs prohx-ee-moh

Communication Essentials

Yes	Sí	see
No	No	noh
Please	Por favor	pohr fah-**vohr**
Thank you	Gracias	**grah**-thee-ahs
Excuse me	Perdone	pehr-**doh**-neh
Hello	Hola	**oh**-lah
Goodbye	Adiós	ah-dee-**ohs**
Goodnight	Buenas noches	**bweh**-nahs noh-chehs
Morning	La mañana	lah mah-**nyah**-nah
Afternoon	La tarde	lah **tahr**-deh
Evening	La tarde	lah **tahr**-deh
Yesterday	Ayer	ah-**yehr**
Today	Hoy	oy
Tomorrow	Mañana	mah-**nya**-nah
Here	Aquí	ah-**kee**
There	Allí	ah-**yee**
What?	¿Qué?	keh
When?	¿Cuándo?	**kwahn**-doh
Why?	¿Por qué?	pohr-**keh**
Where?	¿Dónde?	**dohn**-deh

Useful Phrases

How are you?	¿Cómo está usted?	**koh**-moh ehs-**tah** oos-**tehd**
Very well, thank you.	Muy bien, gracias.	mwee bee-**ehn grah**-thee-ahs
Pleased to meet you.	Encantado de conocerle.	ehn-kahn-**tah**-doh deh koh-noh-**thehr**-leh
See you soon.	Hasta pronto.	ahs-tah **prohn**-toh
That's fine.	Está bien.	ehs-**tah** bee-**ehn**
Where is/are …?	¿Dónde está/están …?	dohn-deh ehs-**tah**/ehs-**tahn**
How far is it to …?	¿Cuántos metros/ kilómetros hay de aquí a …?	**kwahn**-tohs meh-trohs/kee-**loh**-meh-trohs **eye** deh ah-**kee** ah
Which way to …?	¿Por dónde se va a …?	pohr dohn-**deh** seh **bah** ah
Do you speak English?	¿Habla inglés?	**ah**-blah een-**glehs**
I don't understand	No comprendo	noh kohm-**prehn**-doh
Could you speak more slowly please?	¿Puede hablar más despacio por favor?	pweh-deh ah-**blahr** mahs dehs-pah-thee-oh pohr fah-**vohr**
I'm sorry.	Lo siento.	loh see-**ehn**-toh

Useful Words

big	grande	**grahn**-deh
small	pequeño	peh-**keh**-nyoh
hot	caliente	kah-lee-**ehn**-teh
cold	frío	**free**-oh
good	bueno	**bweh**-noh
bad	malo	**mah**-loh
enough	bastante	bahs-**tahn**-teh
well	bien	bee-**ehn**
open	abierto	ah-bee-**ehr**-toh
closed	cerrado	thehr-**rah**-doh
left	izquierda	eeth-kee-**ehr**-dah
right	derecha	deh-**reh**-chah
straight on	todo recto	toh-doh **rehk**-toh
near	cerca	**thehr**-kah
far	lejos	**leh**-hohs
up	arriba	ah-**ree**-bah
down	abajo	ah-**bah**-hoh
early	temprano	tehm-**prah**-noh
late	tarde	**tahr**-deh
entrance	entrada	ehn-**trah**-dah
exit	salida	sah-**lee**-dah
toilet	lavabos, servicios	lah-**vah**-bohs sehr-**bee**-thee-ohs
more	más	mahs
less	menos	**meh**-nohs

Shopping

How much does this cost?	¿Cuánto cuesta esto?	**kwahn**-toh **kwehs**-tah **ehs**-toh
I would like …	Me gustaría …	meh goos-ta-**ree**-ah
Do you have?	¿Tienen?	tee-**yeh**-nehn
I'm just looking, thank you.	Sólo estoy mirando, gracias.	**soh**-loh ehs-**toy** mee-**rahn**-doh **grah**-thee-ahs
Do you take credit cards?	¿Aceptan tarjetas de crédito?	ah-**thehp**-tahn tahr-**heh**-tahs deh **kreh**-dee-toh
What time do you open?	¿A qué hora abren?	ah **keh** oh-rah **ah**-brehn
What time do you close?	¿A qué hora cierran?	ah keh oh-rah thee-**ehr**-rahn
This one.	Éste	**ehs**-teh
That one.	Ése	**eh**-seh
expensive	caro	**kahr**-oh
cheap	barato	bah-**rah**-toh
size, clothes	talla	**tah**-yah
size, shoes	número	**noo**-mehr-oh
white	blanco	**blahn**-koh
black	negro	**neh**-groh
red	rojo	**roh**-hoh
yellow	amarillo	ah-mah-**ree**-yoh
green	verde	**behr**-deh
blue	azul	ah-**thool**
antiques shop	la tienda de antigüedades	lah tee-**ehn**-dah deh ahn-tee-gweh-**dah**-dehs
bakery	la panadería	lah pah-nah-deh-**ree**-ah
bank	el banco	ehl **bahn**-koh
book shop	la librería	lah lee-breh-**ree**-ah
butcher's	la carnicería	lah kahr-nee-theh-**ree**-ah
cake shop	la pastelería	lah pahs-teh-leh-**ree**-ah
chemist's	la farmacia	lah fahr-**mah**-thee-ah
fishmonger's	la pescadería	lah pehs-kah-deh-**ree**-ah
greengrocer's	la frutería	lah froo-teh-**ree**-ah
grocer's	la tienda de comestibles	lah tee-**yehn**-dah deh koh-mehs-**tee**-blehs
hairdresser's	la peluquería	lah peh-loo-keh-**ree**-ah
market	el mercado	ehl mehr-**kah**-doh
newsagent's	el kiosko de prensa	ehl kee-**ohs**-koh deh **prehn**-sah
post office	la oficina de correos	lah oh-fee-**thee**-nah deh kohr-**reh**-ohs
shoe shop	la zapatería	lah thah-pah-teh-**ree**-ah
supermarket	el supermercado	ehl soo-pehr-mehr-**kah**-doh
tobacconist	el estanco	ehl ehs-**tahn**-koh
travel agency	la agencia de viajes	lah ah-**hehn**-thee-ah deh bee-**ah**-hehs

Sightseeing

art gallery	el museo de arte	ehl moo-**seh**-oh deh **ahr**-teh
cathedral	la catedral	lah kah-teh-**drahl**
church	la iglesia la basílica	lah ee-**gleh**-see-ah lah bah-**see**-lee-kah
garden	el jardín	ehl hahr-**deen**
library	la biblioteca	lah bee-blee-oh-**teh**-kah
museum	el museo	ehl moo-**seh**-oh
tourist information office	la oficina de turismo	lah oh-fee-**thee**-nah deh too-**rees**-moh
town hall	el ayuntamiento	ehl ah-yoon-tah-mee-**ehn**-toh
closed for holiday	cerrado por vacaciones	thehr-**rah**-doh pohr bah-kah-thee-**oh**-nehs
bus station	la estación de autobuses	lah ehs-tah-thee-**ohn** deh owtoh-**boo**-sehs
railway station	la estación de trenes	lah ehs-tah-thee-**ohn** deh **treh**-nehs

Staying in a Hotel

Do you have a vacant room?	¿Tienen una habitación libre?	tee-**eh**-nehn **oo**-nah ah-bee-tah-thee-**ohn** lee-breh
double room	habitación doble	ah-bee-tah-thee-**ohn doh**-bleh
with double bed	con cama de matrimonio	kohn **kah**-mah deh mah-tree-**moh**-nee-oh
twin room	habitación con dos camas	ah-bee-tah-thee-**ohn** kohn dohs **kah**-mahs
single room	habitación individual	ah-bee-tah-thee-**ohn** een-dee-vee-doo-**ahl**
room with a bath	habitación con baño	ah-bee-tah-thee-**ohn** kohn **bah**-nyoh
shower	ducha	**doo**-chah
porter	el botones	ehl boh-**toh**-nehs
key	la llave	lah **yah**-veh
I have a reservation.	Tengo una habitación reservada.	tehn-goh **oo**-na ah-bee-tah-thee-**ohn** reh-sehr-**bah**-dah

Eating Out

Have you got a table for . . .?	¿Tienen mesa para . . .?	tee-**eh**-nehn meh-sah pah-**rah**
I want to reserve a table.	Quiero reservar una mesa.	kee-**eh**-roh reh-sehr-**bahr oo**-nah **meh**-sah
The bill please.	La cuenta por favor.	lah **kwehn**-tah pohr fah-**vohr**
I am a vegetarian	Soy vegetariano/a	soy beh-heh-tah-ree-**ah**-no/na
waitress/ waiter	camarera/ camarero	kah-mah-**reh**-rah kah-mah-**reh**-roh
menu	la carta	lah **kahr**-tah
fixed-price menu	menú del día	meh-**noo** dehl **dee**-ah
wine list	la carta de vinos	lah **kahr**-tah deh **bee**-nohs
glass	un vaso	oon **bah**-soh
bottle	una botella	oo-nah boh-**teh**-yah
knife	un cuchillo	oon koo-**chee**-yoh
fork	un tenedor	oon teh-neh-**dohr**
spoon	una cuchara	oo-nah koo-**chah**-rah
breakfast	el desayuno	ehl deh-sah-**yoo**-noh
lunch	la comida/ el almuerzo	lah koh-**mee**-dah/ ehl ahl-**mwehr**-thoh
dinner	la cena	lah **theh**-nah
main course	el primer plato	ehl pree-**mehr plah**-toh
starters	los entremeses	lohs ehn-treh-**meh**-sehs
dish of the day	el plato del día	ehl **plah**-toh dehl **dee**-ah
coffee	el café	ehl kah-**feh**
rare	poco hecho	**poh**-koh **eh**-choh
medium	medio hecho	**meh**-dee-oh **eh**-choh
well done	muy hecho	mwee **eh**-choh

Menu Decoder

al horno	ahl **ohr**-noh	baked
asado	ah-**sah**-doh	roast
el aceite	ah-**thee-eh**-teh	oil
las aceitunas	ah-theh-**toon**-ahs	olives
el agua mineral	**ah**-gwa mee-neh-**rahl**	mineral water
sin gas/con gas	seen gas/kohn gas	still/sparkling
el ajo	**ah**-hoh	garlic
el arroz	ahr-**rohth**	rice
el azúcar	ah-**thoo**-kahr	sugar
la carne	**kahr**-neh	meat
la cebolla	theh-**boh**-yah	onion
la cerveza	thehr-**beh**-thah	beer
el cerdo	**therh**-doh	pork
el chocolate	choh-koh-**lah**-teh	chocolate
el chorizo	choh-**ree**-thoh	red sausage
el cordero	kohr-**deh**-roh	lamb
el fiambre	fee-**ahm**-breh	cold meat
frito	**free**-toh	fried
la fruta	**froo**-tah	fruit
los frutos secos	**froo**-tohs **seh**-kohs	nuts
las gambas	**gahm**-bahs	prawns
el helado	eh-**lah**-doh	ice cream
el huevo	oo-**eh**-voh	egg
el jamón serrano	hah-**mohn** sehr-**rah**-noh	cured ham

el jerez	heh-**rehz**	sherry
la langosta	lahn-**gohs**-tah	lobster
la leche	**leh**-cheh	milk
el limón	lee-**mohn**	lemon
la limonada	lee-moh-**nah**-dah	lemonade
la mantequilla	mahn-teh-**kee**-yah	butter
la manzana	mahn-**thah**-nah	apple
los mariscos	mah-**rees**-kohs	seafood
la menestra	meh-**nehs**-trah	vegetable stew
la naranja	nah-**rahn**-hah	orange
el pan	**pahn**	bread
el pastel	pahs-**tehl**	cake
las patatas	pah-**tah**-tahs	potatoes
el pescado	pehs-**kah**-doh	fish
la pimienta	pee-mee-**yehn**-tah	pepper
el plátano	**plah**-tah-noh	banana
el pollo	**poh**-yoh	chicken
el postre	**pohs**-treh	dessert
el queso	**keh**-soh	cheese
la sal	sahl	salt
las salchichas	sahl-**chee**-chahs	sausages
la salsa	**sahl**-sah	sauce
seco	**seh**-koh	dry
el solomillo	soh-loh-**mee**-yoh	sirloin
la sopa	**soh**-pah	soup
la tarta	**tahr**-tah	pie/cake
el té	teh	tea
la ternera	tehr-**neh**-rah	beef
las tostadas	tohs-**tah**-dahs	toast
el vinagre	bee-**nah**-greh	vinegar
el vino blanco	**bee**-noh **blahn**-koh	white wine
el vino rosado	**bee**-noh roh-**sah**-doh	rosé wine
el vino tinto	**bee**-noh **teen**-toh	red wine

Numbers

0	cero	**theh**-roh
1	uno	**oo**-noh
2	dos	dohs
3	tres	trehs
4	cuatro	**kwa**-troh
5	cinco	**theen**-koh
6	seis	says
7	siete	**see**-eh-teh
8	ocho	**oh**-choh
9	nueve	**nweh**-veh
10	diez	dee-**ehth**
11	once	**ohn**-theh
12	doce	**doh**-theh
13	trece	**treh**-theh
14	catorce	kah-**tohr**-theh
15	quince	**keen**-theh
16	dieciséis	dee-eh-thee-**seh-ees**
17	diecisiete	dee-eh-thee-see-**eh**-teh
18	dieciocho	dee-eh-thee-**oh**-choh
19	diecinueve	dee-eh-thee-**nweh**-veh
20	veinte	**beh**-een-teh
21	veintiuno	beh-een-tee-**oo**-noh
22	veintidós	beh-een-tee-**dohs**
30	treinta	**treh**-een-tah
31	treinta y uno	treh-een-tah ee **oo**-noh
40	cuarenta	kwah-**rehn**-tah
50	cincuenta	theen-**kwehn**-tah
60	sesenta	seh-**sehn**-tah
70	setenta	seh-**tehn**-tah
80	ochenta	oh-**chehn**-tah
90	noventa	noh-**vehn**-tah
100	cien	thee-**ehn**
101	ciento uno	thee-**ehn**-toh **oo**-noh
102	ciento dos	thee-**ehn**-toh dohs
200	doscientos	dohs-thee-**ehn**-tohs
500	quinientos	khee-nee-**ehn**-tohs
700	setecientos	seh-teh-thee-**ehn**-tohs
900	novecientos	noh-veh-thee-**ehn**-tohs
1,000	mil	meel
1,001	mil uno	meel **oo**-noh

Time

one minute	un minuto	oon mee-**noo**-toh
one hour	una hora	**oo**-na oh-**rah**
half an hour	media hora	**meh**-dee-a oh-**rah**
Monday	lunes	**loo**-nehs
Tuesday	martes	**mahr**-tehs
Wednesday	miércoles	mee-**ehr**-koh-lehs
Thursday	jueves	hoo-**weh**-vehs
Friday	viernes	bee-**ehr**-nehs
Saturday	sábado	**sah**-bah-doh
Sunday	domingo	doh-**meen**-goh

BARCELONA TRANSPORT MAP

Barcelona's metro runs from 5am–11pm Mon–Thu; 5am–1am Fri and Sat; and 6:30am–12pm Sun. In the stations the lines are identified by number and colour; platform signs display the name of the last station on the line. A multi-journey (for example a T-10) card allows the traveller to interchange between different modes of transport. The tourist Barcelona Card, available in one-day to five-day values, offers unlimited travel on metro and bus. Tickets for the interconnecting FF CC suburban rail network, which runs from the city centre out to the airport and to Barcelona's environs, and for the funiculars, must be purchased separately.

KEY

- Metro line 1
- Metro line 2
- Metro line 3
- Metro line 4
- Metro line 5
- Metro line 11
- FF CC train line (Ferrocarrils de la Generalitat de Catalunya)
- RENFE airport train line
- Funicular railway
- Tramvia Blau (Blue Tram)
- ○ Interchange station
- ⧸ RENFE main line rail station